D0845822

THE ART OF
M&A

FIFTH EDITION

THE ART OF M&A

A Merger, Acquisition, and Buyout Guide

Alexandra Reed Lajoux

with

Capital Expert Services, LLC

NEW YORK CHICAGO SAN FRANCISCO ATHENS LONDON MADRID
MEXICO CITY MILAN NEW DELHI SINGAPORE SYDNEY TORONTO

2 3 4 5 6 7 8 9 LCR 24 23 22 21 20

ISBN: 978-1-260-12178-0
MHID: 1-260-12178-X

e-ISBN: 978-1-260-12179-7
e-MHID: 1-260-12179-8

Library of Congress Cataloging-in-Publication Data

Name: Lajoux, Alexandra Reed. The art of M & A.
Title: The art of M & A : a merger, acquisition, and buyout guide / by Alexandra Reed Lajoux ; with Capital Expert Services, LLC.
Other titles: Art of M and A
Description: Fifth Edition. | New York : McGraw-Hill Education, [2019] | Revised edition of The art of M & A, c2007.
Identifiers: LCCN 2019001228 (print) | LCCN 2019004531 (ebook) | ISBN 9781260121797 (ebook) | ISBN 1260121798 (ebook) | ISBN 9781260121780 (adhesive-hard : alk. paper) | ISBN 126012178X (adhesive-hard : alk. paper)
Subjects: LCSH: Consolidation and merger of corporations.
Classification: LCC HD2746.5 (ebook) | LCC HD2746.5 .R44 2019 (print) | DDC 658.1/62—dc23
LC record available at https://lccn.loc.gov/2019001228

Dedicated to the members of the Strategic Advisory Board of Capital Expert Services, LLC:

Hon. Carlos C. Campbell, Former US Assistant Secretary of Commerce
Prof. Charles M. Elson, Edgar S. Woolard Chair in Corporate Governance, University of Delaware
Dr. Reatha Clark King, Former Chair, General Mills Foundation
Gregory E. Lau, Managing Director, RSR Partners
John F. Olson, Esq., Chair, American College of Governance Counsel
Hon. E. Norman Veasey, Retired Chief Justice of the Delaware Supreme Court

In Memory of Stanley Foster Reed (1917–2007)

CONTENTS

FOREWORD TO THE FIFTH EDITION OF *THE ART OF M&A*

It was nearly 20 years ago that I had the honor of meeting Alexandra Reed Lajoux at a small restaurant in Reston, Virginia. I had just founded a small start-up consulting firm specializing in M&A integration, when a friend told me about *The Art of M&A Integration* recently published by McGraw-Hill. He was a friend of the author and encouraged me to schedule a lunch to meet with her. Alex, as she is known by her friends, and I talked for two hours—not so much about mergers and acquisitions, financial matters, or even general business. We discussed music, theater, education, and even politics. I was mesmerized by this animated lady who had become one of the most prominent and influential businesspeople on the planet yet had knowledge and opinions on so many other topics.

Alex told me she hadn't grown up dreaming of a career in business. The performing arts and language (French in particular) were the subjects of her focus—but not for long. In 1965, Alex's father, Stanley Foster Reed, founded the original *Mergers & Acquisitions* journal and leveraged his teenage daughter as a summer intern. Alex quickly became interested in the complex content she was reading and was driven to research the topics discussed in her father's magazine. Before long, she was editor of the magazine and hobnobbing with some of the great names in M&A and business in general. She and her father were in the same XMBA class at

Loyola University—each for different reasons. She had plenty of degrees but wanted business knowledge; he had plenty of business knowledge but, as a child of the Depression denied college, needed a degree. They received both and went on to produce many books together.

The book you are about to read was first published 30 years ago when Reed joined forces with the law firm of Lane & Edson, PC, to author the first edition. Alex became the project manager, and her efforts on this historic work launched her into notoriety for M&A research and writing. She would go on to coauthor the next four editions of *The Art of M&A*, known by some as the "big book," due to its 1,000-page heft. H. Peter Nesvold joined her for the fourth edition in 2007 for a three-way authorship that included her father, who passed away the year of publication.

This edition, published more than a decade later, comes full circle. Like her father, who teamed up with a law firm for the first edition, Alex joins forces with the many business specialists affiliated with Capital Expert Services, LLC, or "CapEx," a litigation support consulting firm founded in Delaware, with affiliations around the globe. (Full disclosure: Alex is one of the owners of CapEx, and I am one of the experts available for assignments.)

This "big book" draws upon a vast community of experts that predates CapEx by many years. This M&A expert community began two decades ago when, in 1998, Alex began to produce a series of books focused on the various segments of the M&A life cycle, from strategy through integration, spinning off each of the chapters in the original "big book" with the help of a series of coauthors she had come to know through her work at the National Association of Corporate Directors, where she covered national legal and accounting issues for decades, eventually being named chief knowledge officer.

Alexandra's coauthors in series books deserve credit here. They include strategy consultant Ken Smith on strategy, the late great finance professor J. Fred Weston on deal financing, governance professor Charles Elson on due diligence, and investment banker Dennis Roberts on bank M&A. H. Peter Nesvold also coauthored the fourth edition of this book and collaborated with Lajoux to produce books on valuation (with Elizabeth Bloomer Nesvold and Lajoux), structuring (with Lajoux), and distressed M&A (with Anapolsky and Lajoux).

With the help of these and many other coauthors and expert reviewers, the series has garnered impressive results:

- Nine different titles, several of which have been translated into foreign languages
- Fifteen books in all, including updated editions
- More than 50,000 copies of this original "big book" title sold in the marketplace, and countless readers at the more than 1,000 libraries with this book on their shelves
- Well over 30,000 copies of the spin-off titles in the hands of practitioners, through both purchase and library use

During the time *The Art of M&A* readership was building, McGraw-Hill itself was experiencing M&A vicissitudes. In 2013, Apollo Global Management, LLC, bought the educational division of McGraw-Hill for $2.5 billion, forming McGraw-Hill Education. In 2019, the company announced an intent to merge with Cengage, a leader in professional education.

On a personal note, Alex Lajoux has been an inspiration to me since our first meeting. As my business career unfolded in the M&A arena, Alex cheered me on when I founded the M&A Leadership Council as a way to give back to the M&A community by creating and delivering executive training seminars and workshops around the country. Some of the best professional services firms like BDO, Willis Towers Watson, and M&A Partners give of their time, talent, and expertise to help the council improve M&A outcomes for our corporate alumni, who now number over 3,000 as of this writing.

In 2015, Alex became a founding member of another organization that is a critical addition to the M&A community. The Board of M&A Standards oversees the Certified M&A Specialist program for corporate and consulting professionals, and the Lajoux book series has become an integral part of this certification program. Alex continues her association as Board Member Emerita and has featured members of the Board of M&A Standards in this book.

I am honored to write the foreword to my friend's magnum opus. Whenever I can, I try to emulate the "give back" spirit of Alexandra Reed

Lajoux. We all thank her for her unselfish devotion to her interests and contributions to society, many of which are beyond mergers and acquisitions. But today we recognize and applaud the culmination of a great career introducing us all to the art—and, I daresay, science—of M&A. Enjoy.

Jim Jeffries, Co-Founder
M&A Leadership Council and Board of M&A Standards
May 2019

PREFACE AND ACKNOWLEDGMENTS

> There are no foolish questions, and no man becomes a fool until he has stopped asking questions.
>
> —*Charles Proteus Steinmetz (1865–1923)*

The past decade has been a virtual roller coaster for mergers and acquisitions (M&A). After soaring into the pre-Crisis peak of 2007, global deal activity slumped—particularly when measured in dollar terms—for the next several years, even as the US equity markets rallied back from their Crisis lows. Deal appetites improved toward the middle of the current decade, as CEO confidence firmed and the economic rebound gradually spread to other parts of the world, with 2018 bringing in a strong year for M&A, especially for mega-deals. The year saw only 48,000 announced transactions (down 7 percent from the previous year) but raked in deal value of more than $4 trillion (up 19 percent from the previous year).

But while M&A volumes and values will ebb and flow from year to year, Exhibit A-1 underscores that the overall trend during the past 30 years has been an ever-higher march forward—reflecting the economic reality that M&A is here to stay as a permanent fixture in the corporate finance landscape.*

What's driving this recent resurgence in consolidation activity? How has dealmaking changed in the past decade? For example, how have innovations in financial technology (fintech) affected the M&A process?

* For a detailed report on trends, see Thomson Reuters "League Table" reports at https://financial.thomsonreuters.com/en/products/data-analytics/company-data/investment-banking-league-tables.html. Or see https://www.refinitiv.com.

Exhibit A-1 Global M&A Activity

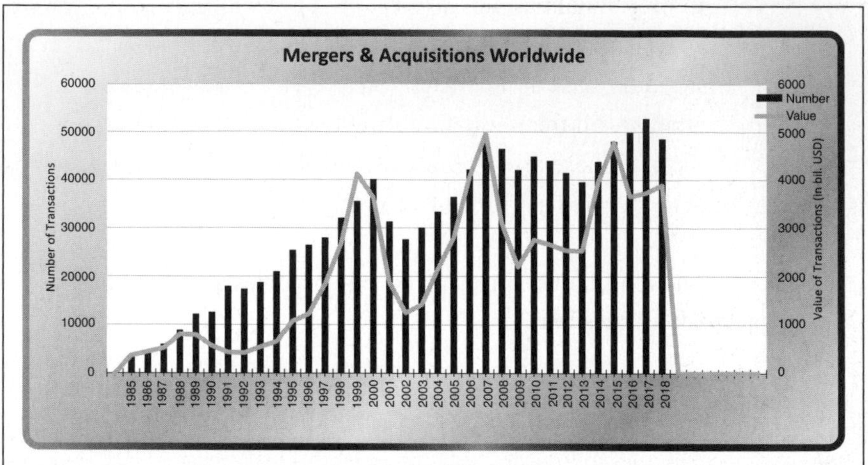

Source: Institute of Mergers, Acquisitions & Alliances (IMAA), 2019

The Art of M&A: A Merger, Acquisition, and Buyout Guide, Fifth Edition, attempts to provide accurate, practical, and up-to-date answers to these and another 1,000 questions that dealmakers—spanning investment bankers, lawyers, accountants, consultants, boards of directors, and business managers and owners, among other constituents in the M&A process—may have in this new environment. Like its four predecessors, the fifth edition is organized in its trademark question-and-answer format, moving from general to specific questions in each topic area. Feedback from more than 30 years of readers overwhelmingly supports this unique format as a user-friendly way to convey material to beginners without sacrificing the in-depth research valued by learned industry professionals. That *The Art of M&A*'s unique question-and-answer format is still so widely celebrated after 30 years is a testament to the foresight and vision of our founding author, Stanley Foster Reed.

What is your burning question of the moment? It may be as basic as "What is a merger?" or it may be as arcane as "After a Section 338 acquisition, must the purchaser retain the acquired company as a subsidiary?" Whatever you want to know, you are likely to find the answers here—or at least a useful source reference.

Building upon its Socratic roots, and reflecting inevitable changes in how industry professionals and business constituents approach research, the fifth edition also takes a step in a new direction—the 2019 edition includes more diagrams, case studies, and references to web-based and other electronic resources—all the while honoring the wisdom embedded in our introductory quote: "There are no foolish questions, and no man becomes a fool until he has stopped asking questions."

ACKNOWLEDGMENTS

The Art of M&A first saw the light of day some three decades ago as the joint effort of founding author and serial entrepreneur Stanley Foster Reed and a law firm, Lane & Edson. This new edition still retains much of the timeless expertise of Lane & Edson attorneys and many other experts cited in the earlier editions. The following acknowledgments emphasize contributions to this fifth edition.

Capital Expert Services, LLC

This think tank and consultancy, founded in 2016, is dedicated to helping law firms and other professional services firms find the most qualified expert witnesses or consulting experts in areas outside the ordinary. CapEx is jointly owned by John Hotta, special advisor to this edition, and Alexandra Lajoux, lead author. Most of the experts consulted for this fifth edition and named below are part of this network of specialists. This book is dedicated to the CapEx Strategic Advisory Board. For more information visit capitalexpertservices.com.

Board of M&A Standards

In addition, it is an honor to include expertise of the members of the Board of M&A Standards (BMAS), a group of executives and advisors developing standards for M&A education. For additional information, see www.mastandards.com. Alexandra Reed Lajoux recently retired from the board and now holds *emerita* status. Current members of the board, whose specific contributions to this edition will be noted in endnotes, are as follows:

Jim Jeffries, Founder, BMAS. Jim is co-founder of the M&A Leadership Council, a global organization delivering best-practice training to the M&A community for the past decade. He spent 25 years leading consulting companies in performance improvement, private equity, and M&A, providing advice to Fortune 1000 C-level executives on valuations for M&A transactions that spanned values from niche players to $20 billion-plus multinationals.

Bill Blandford, Manager of M&A, Retired, Nokia. Bill has participated in over 50 transactions including the de-merger of Motorola, which led to the creation of two separate companies within Motorola. He successfully integrated more than 25 acquisitions and led the divestiture of 15 businesses. Bill also has extensive experience in divestitures, spin-offs, and internal reorganizations across the globe, with a primary focus on information technology (IT).

John Christman, Vice President of Corporate Development & Global Head of M&A Integration, Cognizant. John has 25 years of experience leading business transformation, including executive-level positions at Dell Inc., where he built and led global cross-functional programs and post-merger integration management teams as well as finance organizations. He has led a variety of teams focused on integration issues, from strategy to postacquisition integration planning and cross-functional integration.

Anthony Enlow, Partner, Transaction Advisory Services, BDO. Tony has over 15 years of experience providing financial due diligence and transaction advisory services. He has worked on over 300 transactions ranging in size from $5 million to $40 billion and has assisted buyers and sellers that include private equity, public, and private companies focused on transactional quality of earnings, cash flows, and working capital.

Dr. Bruce Fleming, Executive Vice President of Strategy & Growth, Calumet Specialty Products. A noted business executive and competitive strategist, Bruce directs internal and external growth initiatives including alliances, acquisitions, and targeted divestitures for Calumet. He has held senior business development and planning roles with Amoco Oil, Orient Refining, and Tesoro Corporation, where he directed acquisition of BP's Carson (CA) refinery, including Federal Trade Commission (FTC) approval of this transaction, which *Barron's* noted as "Acquisition of the Year" for 2012.

Len Gray, Global Head of M&A, Retired, Mercer Consulting. Len spent 30 years at Mercer in a variety of leadership roles in the United States and the Asia-Pacific region, including serving as the head of Mercer's international M&A practice. Len provided talent management, human capital strategy, cultural integration, and leadership development consulting services to Mercer's clients during mergers, acquisitions, divestitures, and new business initiatives.

Jennifer Lee, Vice President, McKesson Corporation. Jennifer established McKesson's Corporate Integration Office, which has been engaged in over $25 billion in acquisitions since inception—including direct oversight of the IT workstream for a major healthcare transaction. She has led integration and divestiture/carveout teams and served as program/project manager and relationship manager.

Ellen Owens Karcsay, Director of Business Transformation, Avnet. Ellen directs business change at Avnet, a global technology company with abilities that can support the customer from concept through creation and design to distribution. In her current role, Ellen leads highly collaborative global business transformation initiatives that result in growth opportunities, cost savings, and process efficiencies. Most notably, Ellen served as the global lead for the divestiture of a significant portion of the Avnet business in 2016–17.

Dan Menge, former Director of M&A Integration & Corporate Development, Cisco; currently Head of M&A Integration and Corporate Development at Xilinx. Cisco as a company is widely recognized as being both highly acquisitive and successful in driving growth and transformation via inorganic activity. As leader of the M&A Integration Lead team and integration management office at Cisco, Dan led and engaged in over 60 transactions, ranging from multi-billion-dollar acquisitions to point product and talent deals to strategic divestitures. He also contributed to building Cisco's scalable, industry-leading, workstream-based Acquisition Integration methodology. Today Dan is Head of M&A Integration at Xilinx, a leading "fabless" semiconductor company—one that designs and sells devices while outsourcing fabrication to a trusted foundry.

Wendy Parkes, Managing Director of Human Resources, Global Acquisitions and Divestitures, BMO Financial Group, Retired. Serving in London, Wendy led Global Acquisitions and Divestitures (A&D) for BMO Financial and created a new center of expertise (COE) for all M&A, A&D, and human resources (HR) related activities. She created the strategy, vision, principles, standards, operating model, and practices that are now used in all deals for BMO, including acquisitions, divestitures, and outsourcings.

Sue Rider, Vice President of Global M&A Integration, World Fuel Services. Sue is an HR leader with over 30 years' experience in more than 35 M&A transactions spanning Europe, Asia, and the Americas. She led due diligence and integration for 23 strategic acquisitions, with a particular focus on organization design, talent retention, communications, change management, and compliance.

In addition, chapter by chapter, the following sources are notable:

Chapter 1, Getting Started in Mergers and Acquisitions, still contains wisdom from the many experts cited in previous editions. ***Chapter 2, Strategy***, also draws from the legacy editions, but is primarily informed by Dr. Ken Smith, Managing Partner, Dundee Associates Limited, and lead author of *The Art of M&A Strategy*, a title in the Art of M&A series. Dr. Christopher Kummer, President, Institute for Mergers, Acquisitions, and Alliances, generously provided permission to include IMAA graphics depicting M&A activity. Charles Re Corr and Clark Abrahams, authors with the National Association of Corporate Directors, provided a model for decision making. Michael Nall, President, Alliance of M&A Advisors (AMAA), Chicago, Illinois, and Diane Niederman, AMAA Vice President of Alliances, advised us on the ever-important role of brokers and finders, especially for emerging growth companies. Also instrumental in reviewing the chapter was Dan Menge, Senior Director and Head of M&A Integration at Xilinx, and past Director of M&A Integration & Corporate Development, Cisco. Adam Epstein, Principal, Third Creek Advisors, provided insights on small-cap issues. Rob Baker, Founder, TeqAcq, advised on broker issues. Dr. Bruce Fleming, Executive Vice President of Strategy & Growth, Calumet Specialty Products, provided a case in antitrust approval as well as a discussion of predeal antitrust issues. H. Peter Nesvold, past managing director of Silver Lane Advisors, now part of Raymond James Financial, Inc., provided helpful comments on this chapter. As noted earlier, Peter was a coauthor of the fourth edition of this book.

Chapter 3, Valuation and Modeling, still benefits from the expertise of Al Rappaport, Principal, The LEK/Alcar Consulting Group, La Jolla (CA), and other experts cited in previous editions. In this edition, special thanks go to Nitin Kumar, Chairman, CyberSky Holdings, and Past Senior Managing Director, FTI Consulting, for reviewing the section on valuation of artificial intelligence; to Mike Adhikari, founder of ValueXpress, for conversations over the years; to Vladimir Antikarov, Principal, Vera Group, LLC, for his writings on real option value; to BDO's Tony Enlow for comments on quality of earnings; and to Paul Chan, founder Malaysian Alliance of Corporate Directors, for the discussion of International Valuation Standards. Ken Hoganson, founder of the Private Directors Association and past President of the Chicago Chapter of the Association for Corporate Growth, offered insightful comments on the importance of negotiation as an aspect of valuation. A major source for this chapter was *The Art of M&A Valuation and Modeling* (McGraw-Hill Education, 2016), by H. Peter Nesvold, Elizabeth Bloomer Nesvold, and Alexandra R. Lajoux. This chapter also draws from a book Lajoux coauthored with Robert A. G. Monks, *Corporate Valuation for Portfolio Investment* (Wiley, 2011). The philosophy and writings of Bob Monks have had a profound impact on these pages.

Chapter 4, Financing and Refinancing, owes its greatest debt to the wisdom of the late J. Fred Weston, Cordner Professor of Money and

Financial Markets at the University of California, Los Angeles. With Alexandra R. Lajoux, he coauthored another book in this series, *The Art of M&A Financing and Refinancing: Sources and Instruments for Growth* (McGraw-Hill, 1999). Also instrumental in creating this chapter was Dennis Roberts, coauthor with Lajoux of *The Art of Bank M&A* (McGraw-Hill Education, 2012). Dr. Heath P. Tarbert, currently Assistant Secretary of the Treasury, deserves credit for the early contributions he made to the financing material contained in that book. Francis Byrd, Managing Partner, Alchemy Strategies Partners, LLC, advised on the role of institutional investors in financing.

Chapter 5, Structuring Transactions: General, Tax, and Accounting Considerations, owes its greatest debt to Michael J. Kliegman, who provided the original answers to most of the questions here when he was an attorney at Lane & Edson, and who reviewed and improved this entire chapter. He is currently Senior Counsel at Akin Gump Strauss Hauer & Feld LLP in New York. Another key reviewer of this chapter was Dr. Solange Charas, founder, Charas Consulting. Dr. Charas provided detailed commentary on all compensation material in the chapter. This edition also remains indebted to experts cited in previous editions of this book, including Jack S. Levin, a longtime coauthor with the late Martin Ginsberg of the multivolume book *Mergers, Acquisitions, & Buyouts: A Transactional Analysis of the Governing Tax, Legal & Accounting Considerations* (Wolters Kluwer Law & Business, 2009). Professor Levin is both a Lecturer at the University of Chicago Law School and a Senior Partner with Kirkland & Ellis.

Chapter 6, The Due Diligence Inquiry, benefits greatly from the expertise of Charles M. Elson, Corporate Director and Director of the John L. Weinberg Center for Corporate Governance at the University of Delaware, coauthor with Alexandra Lajoux of *The Art of M&A Due Diligence* (McGraw-Hill Education, 2000, 2010). This chapter has a checklist that includes elements suggested by Dan L. Goldwasser, of Vedder Price Kaufman & Kammholz. Dialogue with Dr. Sri Ramamoorti, Partner, Grant Thornton, was also instructive. Professor Dana Kamenstein of the University of Pennsylvania's School of Education provided insights on diagnosing corporate culture. ***Chapter 7, Negotiating the Letter of Intent and Acquisition Agreement***, and ***Chapter 8, Closing***, build upon the basic wisdom of the original edition, but include updates from the author and guidance from attorney Michael Kliegman, mentioned earlier as a reviewer of Chapter 5. Our discussion of smart contracts in the introduction to Chapter 7 builds on conversations with Marti Tirinnanzi, President, Financial Standards, Inc., and author Peet van Biljon, CEO and Founder, BMNP Strategies, LLC.

Chapter 9, Postmerger Integration and Divestitures, is adapted from Alexandra Lajoux, *The Art of M&A Integration* (McGraw-Hill, 2006), and subsequent updates of that material in other publications of the author. As such, the chapter owes a debt to the experts quoted in that book. Of special note is the author of the foreword to this book, Jim Jeffries, as well as all his colleagues at the M&A Leadership Counsel, especially John Bender, Larry Dell, Mark Herndon, and Jack Prouty. This chapter also draws from the work of Dr. Sanjai Bhagat, a thought leader with valuable perspectives on postmerger performance. Insights into "deals from hell" are inspired by the M&A guru Robert Bruner, Dean Emeritus, Darden School of Business, University of Virginia. The following corporate directors and board advisors, all prominently affiliated with the National Association of Corporate Directors (NACD), were influential in informing the board-related material in this chapter: Dr. Urmi Ashar; Thomas Bakewell, CPA; Dennis Beresford; Marty Coyne; Dr. Nina Dixon; Fay Feeney; Michele Hooper; James Lam; Shep Pryor; Charles Re Corr; Hal Shear; Dr. Ernie Smith; John Stout, Esq.; Dr. Larry Taylor; and Craig W. White, Esq. Ken Daly, past CEO of NACD, and Peter R. Gleason, current CEO, in addition to past NACD leaders Dr. Roger Raber and John Nash, brought governance insights to this section of the book. This chapter also benefits greatly from the expertise of John Hotta, a corporate director and retired Microsoft executive now serving as Cofounder and Board Member of Capital Expert Services, who read the entire chapter for its technological relevance. Thanks also go to Jennifer Lee, Vice President, McKesson, and to Ellen Owens Karcsay, Director of Business Transformation at Avnet, for the section on change management. Professor Antonio Nieto-Rodriguez offered wisdom on M&A project management. Also contributing were Sue Rider, Vice President of Global M&A Integration, World Fuel Services, on global HR; and Wendy Parkes, Managing Director of Human Resources, Global Acquisitions and Divestitures, BMO Financial Group,

Retired. Last but not least, Bill Blandford, Manager of M&A, Retired, Nokia, provided experienced commentary on divestitures. Ethical guidance informing this book came from Dr. Jacques Cory of Haifa University in Israel; Stephen Jordan, Co-CEO, IO Sustainability; Dr. Lester A. Myers, Professorial Lecturer, Georgetown University; and Stephen R. Young, Esq., Executive Director, the Caux Round Table for Moral Capitalism.

Chapter 10, Special Issues for M&A in Public Companies, as well as ***Chapter 11, Workouts, Bankruptcies, and Liquidations***, owe a general debt to the many major law firms that keep the author and expert reviewers educated on trends in securities law, bankruptcy law, and legal trends in general. Their legal briefs are cited throughout this book. Chapter 10 features the knowledge of Robert D. Ferris, Corporate and Investor Relations Counsel, who has shaped best practices for the investor relations community through volunteer leadership positions at the National Investor Relations Institute. This chapter also benefits from the expertise of Francis G. X. Pileggi, Partner and Vice Chair of the Litigation Group at Eckert Seamans Cherin & Mellott, LLC, in Delaware, who has graciously allowed the author to cite his material extensively in this chapter and throughout the book.

Chapter 11 benefits from the expertise of Jeff Anapolsky, who joined the author and H. Peter Nesvold to write *The Art of Distressed M&A* (McGraw-Hill Education, 2011). Thanks also go to Deborah Hicks Midanek Bailey, a veteran in turnarounds, who reviewed this entire chapter for relevancy and accuracy; John Collard, Chairman and CEO, Strategic Management Partners, Inc., whose writings have been influential; and Howard Brod Brownstein, Founder, The Brownstein Corporation, who advised on certain terminology. ***Chapter 12, Global Deals: Structuring for Success***, owes its greatest debt to the two Lane and Edson attorneys who helped shape the original book. For tax review, we credit Michael Kliegman, Senior Advisor, Akin Gump. For other topics, we sincerely thank Ken August, Owner, August Law Group, PC, who was involved in the original edition. Also of assistance here: Paul Chan, Cofounder, Malaysian Alliance of Corporate Directors; Lew Lederman, QC, CEO, Knowledge E*Volutions, Inc.; Raoul Schuddeboom, Director, Corporate Advisory Services, Eurasia Group; Ka-Yin Li, Advisor, Hong Kong Institute of Directors; Anthony Riha, Partner at Advanced Technology Solutions (Asia); Rocky Lee, King & Wood Mallesons, Beijing China; Van Kirk Reeves, Reeves & Porter, an international law firm based in Paris, France; and Riccardo Trigona, an attorney in Milan, Italy.

In addition to the names listed earlier, the following individuals are acknowledged for their impact on M&A and corporate governance: Gerald Adolph, author of *Merge Ahead: The Five Enduring Trends of Artful M&A* (McGraw-Hill Education, 2009); Roger Aguinaldo, Founder, The M&A Advisor; Dr. David Anderson, founder and CEO, the Anderson Governance Group; Howard Bailen, veteran publicist; Hank Boerner, Chairman and CEO, Governance and Accountability Institute; David Brown, Executive Director, KPMG Board Leadership Center; Douglas Chia, Fellow, Center for Corporate Law and Governance, Rutgers Law School; Dr. John Coughlan, Founder and Director, CPA School of Washington; April Thurmond Dumas and Melissa Foster Follis, M&A Leadership Council; Allan Grafman, CEO, All Media Ventures; Holly Gregory, Esq., Partner, Sidley Austin, LLP; Pamela S. Harper, CEO, Business Advancement, Inc.; James Hatch, President, Oleum Technology, LLC; Debra Santini Hennelly, Founder, Resiliti; Gary Lutin, Chairman, The Shareholder Forum; Edith Orenstein, Manager, PricewaterhouseCoopers; Mike Lovdal, Emeritus Partner, Oliver Wyman; Jon Lukomnik, Managing Partner, Sinclair Capital; Jon J. Masters, Member, Private Sector Advisory Group, Global Corporate Governance Forum, International Finance Corporation; Ira M. Millstein, Esq., Senior Partner, Weil Gotshal & Manges, LLP; Cary Nicholson, Bank Examiner, Office of the Comptroller of the Currency; Gene Panasenko, Financial Advisor, Moloney Securities Co., Inc.; Michael Pocalyko, CEO, SI; Jeffrey Possinger, Managing Member, Possinger Law Group, PLLC; James Reda, Managing Director, Executive Compensation, Arthur J. Gallagher & Co.; Matthew Scott, Past Editor, *Corporate Secretary Magazine*; Dean Shaw, Managing Director, Shaw & Sullivan, PC; Brendan Sheehan, Vice President, Moody's Investors Service; and Gabe Shawn Varges, Partner, HCM International.

The ***legal case summaries*** at the end of this book come from previous editions, but include updates based on the writings of Francis G. X. Pileggi, cited earlier.

In closing, the author extends sincere thanks to the top-notch professional editorial and production team at McGraw-Hill Education that made this book possible, including Noah Schwartzberg, Senior Editor, Business; Ami Li, Editorial Assistant; Donya Dickerson, Editorial Director; and Christopher Brown, Publisher. Working with the team, Ginny Carroll of North Market Street Graphics (NMSG), provided excellent copyediting and project management services. Thanks also go to the other key players on the NMSG team: painstaking compositor Mark Righter, and eagle-eyed proofreaders Mike Dunnick and Stewart Smith. Our careful indexer was Erika Millen. Also deserving thanks is Chris Smith of Quarternative.com, who provided many of the exhibits in this book. Finally, we thank Cal Hunter, Manager, Business Development and Business Department, Barnes & Noble, 555 Fifth Avenue, New York, for his belief in this book.

CHAPTER 1

Getting Started in Mergers and Acquisitions

A little learning is a dangerous thing;
Drink deep, or taste not the Pierian spring;
There shallow draughts intoxicate the brain,
And drinking largely sobers us again.

Alexander Pope
"An Essay on Criticism"

INTRODUCTION

Perhaps nowhere else does Pope's maxim prove truer than in the area of mergers, acquisitions, and buyouts. The purchase or sale of a business enterprise is one of the most challenging transactions—indeed, journeys—one can undertake. And the wise traveler should set off on this journey for the right reasons—for the most common catalysts to doing a deal can also be the most ill-fated. Consider the business owners who want to revolutionize their technology without realizing that they are in the wrong business to begin with—or are going about it the wrong way.

And beyond the boardroom debate about *whether* to do an acquisition of some type is the issue of *how* the potential transaction is actually structured. Not only does an M&A deal cut across countless securities and tax laws, accounting rules, and regulatory requirements, but it also has the potential to either reinforce, or disrupt, the cultural underpinnings of the buyer or seller. Key intangibles—such as the cultural alignment and logistical integration of two previously disparate organizations—win or lose deals. They can be the determining factor in whether an otherwise well-structured merger or acquisition ultimately harvests its intended benefits and builds long-term value. As such, M&A can be a make-or-break decision for many executives of major corporations; likewise, the sale of a business can be a once-in-a-lifetime realization event for many small business owners. In both cases, the players *must* know what they are doing.

More than 50 years ago, in the fall of 1965, Stanley Foster Reed, the original author of this book, launched the first issue of *Mergers & Acquisitions* magazine. He prefaced the magazine, which continues to this day via the SourceMedia platform,[1] as follows:

Dedicated to the Ever-Renewing Corporate Society

As we take part in this third great wave of merger and acquisition activity in America, we are struck by the rate of economic growth, and by the speed with which corporations are merging and being formed. Research indicates that at present rates, one out of every three corporations will either merge or be acquired during the next ten years. This makes change the condition by which we grow and develop.

Each day here in the United States one thousand new businesses are born. Some drive for the heights like a great Fourth of July rocket and end in a burst of color—a hasty life, beautiful but short. . . . A few, carried on a quick tide of youthful energy and special knowledge, will grow great and strong and eventually wise and will become a shelter for the less strong and the less wise.

This is the ever-renewing corporate society.[2]

As Reed's prologue shows, *Mergers & Acquisitions* magazine was founded with one clear goal in mind: to show buyers and sellers of companies how to create strategies—and shelter—for continual growth in a world of constant change.

Reed had this same purpose in mind when he teamed up with the law firm of Lane & Edson, PC, to produce the first edition of this guidebook in 1988, the height of the LBO movement, as romanticized by the character Gordon Gekko in Oliver Stone's unforgettable movie *Wall Street.* The L&E attorneys shaping the first edition of this book were really there on the front lines of M&A change, advising buyout kings like former Treasury secretary William E. Simon and Ray Chambers, founders of Wesray. The first edition of the "big book" featured Reed as coauthor and Alexandra Reed Lajoux, his daughter, initially as project manager.

The 1988 text was an instant classic, but as deal structures shifted under the weight of hundreds of legal precedents, temperamental financing markets, and constantly changing accounting and tax rules, a major revision in the original text proved necessary. Subsequent editions by Reed and Lajoux followed in 1995 and 1999, as did a series of spin-off titles, exploring each of the major topics in greater depth. H. Peter Nesvold joined the series in 2001, serving as coauthor of not only three special titles in the series but also most notably as coauthor of the fourth edition with Reed and Lajoux. That edition was published in 2007—shortly before Reed passed away at age 90, his mission accomplished. As detailed in the front matter to this book, the current edition contains the wisdom of countless professionals dedicated to M&A—including experts associated with Capital Expert Services, LLC, coproducer of this edition.

To state the obvious, much has changed over the past decade. This fifth edition continues the legacy of the original book and the broader Art of M&A series, capturing key trends and technical changes that have occurred over the 10-plus years as the M&A arena suffered through a global financial crisis and emerged with new, sometimes painful, lessons learned. Yet Reed's vision from 50 years ago of M&A as central to an ever-renewing corporate society remains as true today as it did in 1965.

Every year trillions of M&A dollars change hands globally—not only in the purchase of huge companies or of major interests in them, but in the tens of thousands of smaller companies that are bought and sold from Peoria to Paris. As we go to press, M&A remains very much a part of the global economy. As illustrated in Exhibit A-1 in the Preface to this book, dealmakers closed M&A transactions worth more than $4 trillion globally in 2018. Aggregate global M&A transaction values have recently more than doubled off their Crisis lows of 2009; what's more, recent annual values have increased nearly fourfold from 2002's cyclical lull and have soared more than 13 times over since 1985. Even considering the multiplier effect of inflation,[3] the growth is still obvious. (See Exhibit 1-1.)

Exhibit 1-1 Global M&A Transaction Value (1988 vs. 2018)

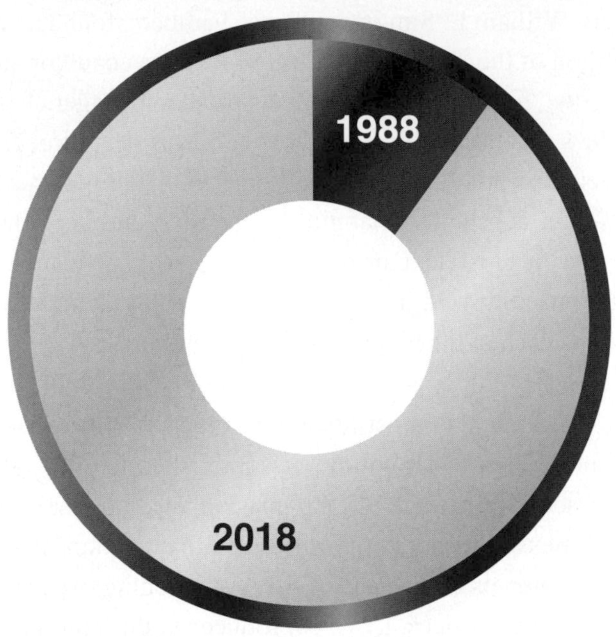

Source: Institute of Mergers, Acquisitions & Alliances (IMAA), 2019.

To be sure, this decade's resurgence in M&A activity will eventually come to a pause; there will always be cyclical highs and lows in deal volume, driven by myriad forces explored throughout this book. But just as that pause is inevitable, so too will it prove temporary. M&A clearly is here to stay: the buying and selling of companies remains a key option for many companies seeking to enhance growth or to harvest value created. Yet we can't emphasize enough how complex and dangerous the merger process can be. A great deal of hard-earned value is at stake in any transaction, and while there are success stories, there are also "deals from hell," in the words of Robert Bruner, dean emeritus of the Darden School of Business.[4] Often divestiture is the cure.

To strike lasting deals, acquirers and sellers—both large and small—must drink from the ever-renewing spring of M&A knowledge. To drink deep, they must recognize first that there is something called an *acquisition process,* with many crucial stages and many key players. To carry out any one stage well requires solid grounding in the entire process, which typically unfolds in the following phases (see Exhibit 1-2):

Exhibit 1-2 The M&A Process

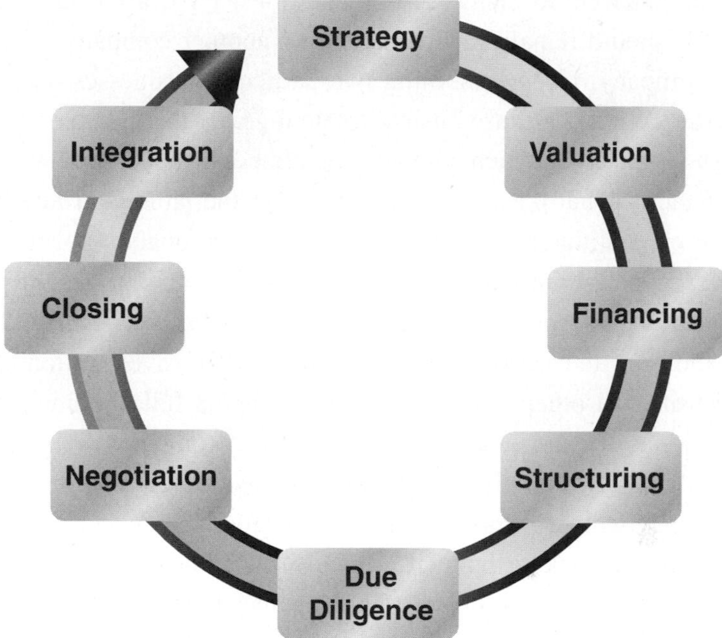

- Strategy Phase—Deciding whether, and if so how, to buy or sell whether as a strategic buyer or a financial buyer
- Valuation Phase—Determining the value of the company to be bought or sold
- Financing Phase—Obtaining the funds, internal or external, to make the deal happen
- Structuring Phase—Making the proper accounting, financial, legal, and tax designations for the transaction
- Due Diligence Phase—Verifying that the company is what it claims to be and discovering risk exposures material to the transaction
- Negotiation Phase—Convincing the other party to agree to your terms without jeopardizing the deal
- Closing Phase—Consummating the transaction, thereby making it official
- Integration Phase—Managing postmerger operations through stand-alones, integration, and/or divestiture

As these eight key chapters show, the M&A journey involves exploring the answers to many serious questions. First, an acquirer needs to ask if it should remain independent, buy another company, or sell to another company. Does combining two particular businesses make strategic sense? What can those businesses do together that neither could accomplish separately? Which company should be the buyer, and which the seller? Exactly what does each party bring to the table, and how much are those capabilities really worth? What is a reasonable closing price, and how will post-transaction risk be distributed among buyer and seller? How should the deal be financed, and what are the tax, financial, and legal ramifications of the various options? What sort of investigation should we make of each other? How can we encourage a full alignment of interests among all constituents in the go-forward company? What should the obligations of the parties be under the acquisition agreement? How do we avoid the "winner's curse" and "seller's remorse"? And all along the process, let us be asking how (if at all) we will integrate the resources, processes, and responsibilities of the companies being combined—while bearing in mind the option of divestiture.

The next eight chapters will explore each of these phases in detail, before covering public companies, distressed transactions, and the global scene. Landmark legal cases will conclude our book.

GOAL

The objective of this book is to acquaint the specialist and the nonspecialist alike with the basics of the friendly negotiated acquisition, including the financial, legal, accounting, and business practices and rules that govern deals done today. It is also intended to give the reader some feel for the way that today's deals are being negotiated.

As mentioned earlier, the chapters of this book follow the basic sequence of the acquisition process, from strategy and valuation to financing, structuring, investigating, and negotiating deals—right up to, and including, closing and postmerger integration. Much of the content of these chapters is advanced and sophisticated; it would not be particularly useful if it were not. Yet the hope is to explain such material as plainly as possible. Each chapter starts with the relevant fundamentals of each topic. Through the Socratic question and answer process, each point builds organically on the one preceding it—a dialogue, if you will, that leads a novice to the point of asking advanced questions, while still serving as a technical reference to the sophisticated dealmaker. It is an ambitious goal, to be sure, but one which we are hopeful that this book has refined over the past 30 years.

For example, since the subtitle of this book is *A Merger, Acquisition, and Buyout Guide,* it makes sense to differentiate among these key terms. Let's begin by exploring each of them.

KEY TERMS

What's the difference between a merger and an acquisition?

The answer to this question is not as simple as it may seem. The term *merger* suggests two companies of similar size and market value coming together, whereas the word *acquisition* implies a large company purchasing a smaller business. Colloquially, these descriptions do reflect conventional, everyday use in most circumstances—at least as such terms might be used in the business media such as CNBC or *The Wall Street Journal.* For instance, it would not be surprising to witness two equally sized businesses announcing their consolidation to the public as a *merger of equals.*[5]

But "merger" talk is really more about public posturing and boardroom politics than it is about the legal structure of the transaction. Indeed, the terms *merger* and *acquisition* really have nothing to do with the relative sizes of the constituent companies; a large company by all means can merge with a small company, just as a purchasing company can acquire a like-sized target. Rather, the terms *merger* and *acquisition* actually allude to the legal structure of a particular deal. *Acquisition* is the generic term used to describe a transfer of ownership. Merger is a narrow, technical term for a particular legal procedure that may or may not follow an acquisition. Chapter 5, "Structuring Transactions," explains how that works.

What then, exactly, is an acquisition?

A corporate *acquisition* is the process by which the stock or assets of a corporation come to be owned by a buyer. The transaction may take the form of a purchase of stock or a purchase of assets. In this book, we often refer to the acquired corporation as the *company* or the *target.*

And what is the technical definition of a merger?

The word *merger* has a strictly legal meaning and has nothing to do with how the combined companies are to be operated in the future, or which side's management team is ultimately in control of the post-transaction business.

Simply stated, a merger occurs when one corporation is combined with and disappears into another corporation. For instance, the Missouri Corporation, just like the river, merges and disappears *legally* into the Mississippi Corporation. Missouri Corporation stock certificates are surrendered and exchanged for Mississippi stock certificates. Missouri Corporation has ceased to exist. Missouri is the *nonsurvivor,* while Mississippi Corporation is the *survivor.*

All mergers are *statutory* mergers, since all mergers occur as specific formal transactions in accordance with the laws, or *statutes,* of the states where they are incorporated. However, there are rarely major differences between states. (Outside the United States, of course, there are differences from country to country.)

The postdeal manner of operating or controlling a company has no bearing on whether a merger has occurred. It is misleading for a prospective acquirer to state to a prospective seller, "We don't do acquisitions; we only do mergers," implying that the two groups will be equal partners in enterprise, when in fact, and by statute law, one corporation is owned and, without an agreement by the stockholders to the contrary, is *controlled* by another.

In a merger, who gets to be the survivor? Is it always the larger company?

Not necessarily. For tax and other reasons, sometimes big Mississippi Corporation might be merged into little Missouri Corporation, with Missouri the survivor. Size of operations, net worth, number of employees, who winds up as chairperson, even the name selected, have nothing to do with which company is the corporate survivor.

What is a buyout–and in particular, what is a leveraged buyout?

The term *buyout* is used to describe a transaction in which an acquirer such as a private equity firm takes all or part of a public company private by purchasing all of its equity and/or assets.

The most common form of buyout is a *leveraged buyout* (LBO), in which all or part of a company's capital stock or its assets are purchased with borrowed money, with the assets of the target serving as the primary collateral for the loan, resulting in an above-average percentage of the company's new capital structure to be in the form of this acquisition debt. The cash flows of the acquired business are then harvested over time and used to repay this debt.

For many readers who are new to LBOs, the most tangible analogy might be the process of purchasing a house. Many homeowners might put, say, 20 percent of the purchase price down in the form of equity toward the acquisition of the house and borrow the remaining 80 percent from a bank, using the house as collateral for the home. To more closely tailor this home-buying example to an LBO, we might further assume that the house will be a rental property investment of the buyer. Accordingly, the buyer will use the rental income from the investment property to subsequently pay down a portion of the acquisition debt. Over time, and assuming the investment is successful, the amount of debt decreases and the value of the buyer's equity interest in the property increases. In the same way, the buyer-borrower in a leveraged buyout hopes that future income will more than offset the debt payments that must be made.

There are several types of leveraged buyouts, including:

- *Management buyouts* (*MBOs*), in which a key ingredient is bringing in the existing management team as shareholders
- *Employee buyouts* (*EBOs*), in which the employees, using funds from an employee stock ownership plan (ESOP), most of which will have been borrowed, buy out the company's owners
- *Restructurings,* in which a major part of the acquired assets is subsequently sold off to retire the debt that financed the transaction

What is a hostile acquisition or takeover?

A hostile acquisition or takeover is one in which the would-be buyer bypasses the board and management and directs its overtures directly to the target's shareholders. These types of transactions are rare; the vast majority of acquisitions are "friendly" or "negotiated" transactions—largely because it can be unusually difficult to force someone to sell his or her business if the owners are unwilling to entertain negotiations. Nevertheless, hostile acquisitions can, and do, occur when the target is publicly traded, because although the public company's board and management might be unwilling to engage with a potential buyer, that buyer has the option of bidding for the target's shares directly from the investing public. This book addresses some issues relating to hostile takeovers in Chapter 10, on public company acquisitions. In general, however, this book focuses on friendly transactions—negotiated deals struck voluntarily by both buyers and sellers. They are based on mutual accommodation of the interests of two or more parties that believe they will be better off together than apart if they can just work things out through the deal process.

ABOUT OUR QUESTION-AND-ANSWER FORMAT

All along the M&A journey questions arise. This book attempts to anticipate them on your behalf, no matter where you are in the process. If you are involved in a transaction, you will find yourself using this book's extensive index to find answers to your specific, timely questions. If you have a term for a specific point—if you want to know about *fraudulent conveyance* or the *Herfindahl-Hirschman Index,* for example—look it up directly in the index. If the point has a number but not a name—for example, *Section 338* or *Rule 10b-5*—look it up under *Section* or *Rule* in the index. If you want to review a broad area of the acquisition process—for example, *financing*—look that up in the index and there you will find the book's entire coverage of that area, organized alphabetically by each aspect of financing that appears in the book. Run your eye down the headings until you see where to start reading.

Throughout the book, where legal cases contribute important precedent, we have provided brief descriptions in the text. The most important cases in the merger/acquisition/buyout area are fully described in the landmark case summaries, also found in "Landmark and Recent M&A Legal Cases," at the end of this book.

CONCLUDING COMMENTS

We cannot claim comprehensiveness in all areas. After all, there are not that many universalities or even commonalities to the merger process—especially those that involve the growing and constantly changing field of transnational agreements and financings.

What we *have* delivered, however, is a sourcebook in readable form where the entrepreneur and the professional alike can find not only the *answers* to a myriad of M&A-related questions, but also the *questions* that must (or at least should) be asked about the M&A process. Such thirsting for knowledge is good.

Drink deep!

NOTES

1. See https://www.sourcemedia.com/about.
2. Stanley Foster Reed, "Dedicated to the Ever-Renewing Corporate Society," Mergers & Acquisitions, vol. 1, no. 1 (Fall 1965).
3. $1 from January 1985 was worth $2.30 in January 2017. See https://www.bls.gov/data/inflation_calculator.htm.
4. Robert F. Bruner, *Deals from Hell: M&A Lessons That Rise Above the Ashes* (New York: John Wiley & Sons, 2005). Dean Bruner cites the merger of AOL and Time Warner, which led to $100 billion in losses reported in 2003, and the acquisition program of Tyco International, among other bad deals.
5. "Harris Corporation and L3 Technologies to Combine in Merger of Equals," press release, November 5, 2018, https://www.marketwatch.com/press-release/united-states-harris-corporation-and-l3-technologies-to-combine-in-merger-of-equals-2018-11-05.

CHAPTER 2

Strategy

INTRODUCTION

This chapter addresses the first stage in the merger/acquisition/buyout process: *strategy.*[1] In this crucial phase, company leaders chart the future of the business with a plan that may include a future merger, acquisition, or divestiture.[2]

When thinking about M&A strategy and the rationale behind a particular transaction, it is helpful as a starting point to consider whether the buyer is a strategic acquirer or a financial acquirer—particularly as the two types of acquirers will typically have different motivations and objectives when evaluating an opportunity.

A *strategic acquirer,* sometimes referred to as a corporate buyer,[3] is generally an operating company with at least one, and perhaps several, business lines that is considering whether to transact with another operating company to either grow or more narrowly focus the acquirer's business. There are many reasons why a strategic buyer might pursue acquisition efforts; such objectives might include strengthening the acquirer's existing enterprise by purchasing one or more companies to build a portfolio of business lines; reducing costs, perhaps by spreading fixed costs over a larger number of sales units; increasing market share and therefore pricing power; and/or enhancing long-term value by securing one or more strategic "options" for the future. The pages that follow in this chapter are focused primarily on the needs and alternatives of strategic buyers, and these four main M&A strategies will be detailed in the first section of this chapter.

The other kind of buyer is known as a *financial acquirer*—usually an investor group such as a private equity fund making an investment in a company with the specific intent of reselling later at a profit. Such a purchaser will focus principally on whether the company will either generate enough cash flow to handle the debt service requirements of the transaction or perhaps have sufficient severable assets that can be sold off piecemeal, while still representing an attractive whole-company sale candidate looking ahead three to seven years. Indeed, the eventual divestiture of the target—whether in part or in whole—is an integral part of a financial buyer's plans from the outset, whereas most strategic buyers evaluate deals from the perspective of potentially managing the asset "forever."[4]

One might say, then, that a financial buyer is an "opportunity taker," whereas a strategic buyer is an "opportunity maker." Although this chapter emphasizes the motivations of strategic acquirers over financial acquirers, it is worth noting that financial buyers have never been a bigger part of the corporate M&A market than they are today.[5] Moreover, financial acquirers can benefit from studying this chapter as well—for instance, if the financial buyer is embarking on a *consolidation play* or a *roll-up* in which the financial sponsor intends to make multiple acquisitions in a particular market segment with the intent of wringing out cost savings—although not all sections will apply.

The corporate acquirer reading this chapter will receive guidance for *M&A strategic planning*—be it to diversify, save, grow, or hedge. Nevertheless, this planning is only the beginning because any decision to acquire means finding a willing seller, and any decision to sell means finding a willing buyer. Thus, strategy naturally influences the *search process*—that is, the would-be buyer's acquisition criteria and means for screening the market, as described in the second section of this chapter—whether that process is managed internally or with help from business brokers in the small and midsized market[6] or, at the higher end of the market, investment bankers. Finally, all strategic planning requires attention to *legal and regulatory constraints.* The third and final section of this chapter will address those necessary limits.

With this introduction in mind, then, let us now begin at the beginning, by getting acquainted with that somewhat mysterious activity known as strategy—or, more dynamically, strategic planning.

STRATEGIC PLANNING

What is strategic planning?

Perhaps you have heard the old saw "Failing to plan is planning to fail." Goals—whether personal or corporate—do not magically arrive on one's doorstep like a parcel delivered from Amazon. Strategic planning involves thinking ahead about the specific, desired outcomes one wishes to accomplish and how best to achieve those goals. To say that a plan is "strategic" means that the plan is linked to a targeted outcome that is simultaneously broad, long term, and core to the central mission of the organization. Strategic plans are the kind set by leaders. (In fact, the Greek root, *strategein*, means the general of an army.)

A strategic plan for a company—sometimes referred to as a corporate strategy or enterprise strategy—will typically be led by individuals with a high degree of responsibility for the enterprise's overall strategy—the board and senior management—and then used as a road map to guide the direction of countless individual decisions by the broader organization.

Most strategic plans (again harkening to the word's root meaning) are based on the idea of competition, showing awareness of an opposing force such as a competitor who wants the same thing the planner does—for example, more customers. A thoughtful and effective strategic plan may chart a path for upending a rival firm, whether by lowering production costs, developing a better product or service, or delivering the product or service in a competitively superior way. These are the three generic strategies identified by Michael Porter of Harvard University in his classic book *Competitive Strategy.*[7]

For the outline of a strategic plan, see Exhibit 2-1.

Exhibit 2-1 Outline for a Typical Strategic Plan

Our Strategy
- Our goals
- Our plans for achieving them*

Our Market
Our Competitors
SWOT Analysis
Timetable
Milestones
Contingencies

*May include growth through M&A.

What are some typical strategic planning approaches?

For many years, under the banner of diversification, strategic planning systems abounded. Some prepackaged solutions segmented a company's operations into market-share/market-growth categories and yielded such classifications as *star* for high-growth/high-share, *dog* for low-growth/low-share, *cash cow* for high-share/low-growth, and *wildcat* (or *question mark*) for low-share/high growth. The basic point of this strategy—originally developed and successfully promulgated worldwide by the Boston Consulting Group (BCG) more than half a century ago—was to redeploy revenues from cash cows to wildcats. Many other such matrix approaches to diversification were also popular, especially General Electric's nine-element construct. Such concepts have been widely taught and used. Why? Because they were certainly better than the random processes that had gone on in previous decades, during which many deals were made for noneconomic reasons—fads, friendship, or family ties.

But now, in the age of big data, these simple four-element and nine-element matrixes have been supplanted by multivariate analyses. Rather than four or nine, there are literally hundreds of variables that may be considered when contemplating a growth-by-acquisition strategy. These more systematic approaches to planning will isolate the key variables, and use those variables to develop strategic plans that will work.

In addition, some companies have begun supplementing their systematic approaches with adaptive adjustments to respond to changes in the environment.[8]

How does strategy relate to vision and mission?

Building a successful business is like constructing a stable building. Start with a firm foundation and work your way upward. Before pursuing any strategy, decision makers should recognize an organization's mission (why it exists) and vision (what it is striving to become). Strategy is the path to fulfill the mission and reach a vision. Merger, acquisition, and/or divestiture plans are vehicles for moving down the path.

THE ROLE OF M&A IN STRATEGIC PLANNING

How does M&A fit into strategic planning?

First and foremost, M&A is a decision that occurs along a path of decisions. A typical decision "tree" would proceed as shown in Exhibit 2-2.

Can M&A be called a kind of strategy?

No. M&A is not a corporate strategy in and of itself, although such transactions can play a pivotal role in implementing a strategic plan. As Porter notes, "[A] merger can instantaneously propel a weak competitor into prominence or strengthen an already formidable one."[9]

Before deciding to enter a new area of business, strategic thinkers will make industry forecasts and study the fit of the proposed acquisi-

Exhibit 2-2 M&A in a Strategic Decision Tree

If Keep, Integrate or Ignore?
If Buy, Keep or Sell?
If Grow, Buy or Build?
Start: Grow or Shrink?

Source: Alexandra Reed Lajoux, 2019.

tion with their present operations. Furthermore, because strategic planning requires choices, any opportunity, no matter how hot, should always be forced to stand trial against other potential entries. This means taking a formal inventory of opportunities and then methodically comparing them.

The plan resulting from strategic thinking, once installed, acts as a disciplining force on everyone at the decision-making level. Any proposed transaction can simply be matched against pre-agreed-upon criteria that describe the company's strategy. If the proposed transaction doesn't meet most of these strategic criteria, the opportunity is rejected, saving executive time and resources.

Strategic planning can also help in the divestiture process. In any multi-profit-center operation, strategic planning that does not automatically produce candidates for sell-off or shutoff is probably not truly strategic. It is necessary in any strategy to weigh what a business is doing against what the business could be doing with its resources. If the potential is greater in new areas of opportunity, the old lines of business should be converted to cash by selling them off, possibly at a premium to a firm where they fit, and the cash should be redeployed to new lines through internal or external development. Controlling this continuous redeployment process is an important aspect of strategic planning.[10]

The best M&A strategies are based on an analysis of an organization's strengths and weaknesses, as well as its opportunities and threats—a SWOT model that holds true today, after half a century.[11]

Overall, why does M&A activity rise and fall? For example, what is driving the current M&A resurgence?

An FTC panel report (based on a focus group with 10 executives) once counted 31 motives, ranging from expanding product lines to increasing managerial strength.[12] At the other extreme, legendary investor Warren Buffett has philosophized that there is only *one* reason for M&A activity: to move investment out of cash and into assets. For many companies, there are usually a variety of motives. Scholars generally agree on the following 10 most common reasons why companies make acquisitions:[13]

- Achieve economies of scale by buying a customer, supplier, or competitor (operating synergy)
- Accomplish strategic goals more quickly and more successfully (strategic planning)
- Realize a return on investment by buying a company with less efficient managers and making them more efficient (differential efficiency)
- Realize a return by buying a company with inefficient managers and replacing them (inefficient management)
- Increase market share (market power)
- Lower cost of capital by smoothing cash flow and increasing debt capacity (financial synergy)
- Take advantage of a price that is low in comparison to past stock prices and/or estimated future prices, or in relation to the cost the buyer would incur if it built the company from scratch (undervaluation)[14]
- Assert control at the board of directors level in an underperforming company with dispersed ownership (agency problems)
- Obtain a more favorable tax status (tax efficiency)[15]
- Increase the revenues or size of a company and therefore increase the pay and/or power of managers (managerialism—never a stated goal, but an explanation offered in many academic studies)

ALTERNATIVES TO M&A

Is M&A the primary type of corporate transaction that businesses use to fulfill strategy, mission, and vision?

Not necessarily. When two organizations wish to collaborate in some way to accomplish similar objectives, there is a wide range of corporate transaction structures that management might consider—M&A is just one option. The precise structure that might work best in any given situation may depend on a wide variety of factors. The initial question to ask oneself is whether some degree of shared ownership between the respective parties is necessary to accomplish the intended goals or whether the parties might be able to achieve those goals though contractual or even less formal relationship. Among the factors to consider include the following: How much influence does one party want over the other's corporate decision making, and how receptive is the other side to that request? How much capital does each party have, does each party need, and is each party willing to commit to maximize the results of the collaboration? How closely integrated should the collaboration be, and must that integration be permanent?

Exhibit 2-3 illustrates a range of structures for business collaboration.

As illustrated in Exhibit 2-3, these structures might be as informal as a trading relationship, in which the buyer and seller periodically enter into one-off purchase-and-sale transactions of goods or services. In some circumstances, the parties might be capable of achieving their strategic objectives merely through a contractual relationship. Examples include a supply agreement that outlines the basis upon which the buyer and seller

Exhibit 2-3 Range of Structures for Business Collaboration

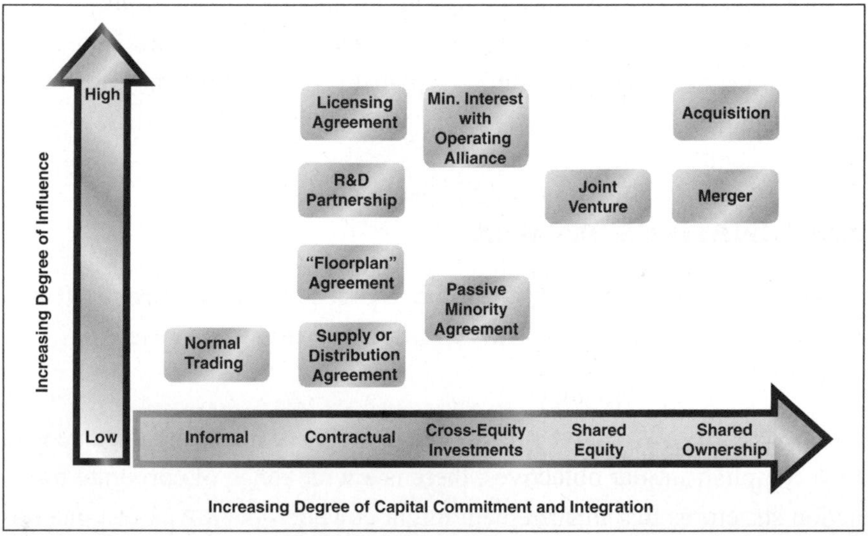

Source: Silver Lane Advisors, 2018.

will operate over time; a *floorplan agreement,* which is common between original equipment manufacturers (OEMs) and distributors to provide short-term inventory financing from the OEM to the distributor to take inventory and offer it for resale (e.g., GM and its auto dealership partner); or some form of licensing agreement, which dictates precisely how the licensee can and cannot use the rights granted by the licensor. Alternatively, the contemplated business collaboration might be optimized if the parties were to somehow integrate equity ownership into the structure—whether in the form of a passive minority stake, a minority stake with a formal operating alliance, or a joint venture of some kind. A full-out merger or acquisition involving the constituent companies might be thought of as the most extreme form of business collaboration—reserved for scenarios in which the buyer seeks a high degree of influence over the other party and is prepared to commit meaningful capital to the operation. A merger or acquisition is also a logical transaction structure in the event the acquirer wants to fully integrate the target into the acquirer's business. However, integration is not a *requirement* of M&A. There are plenty of examples in which an acquirer wished to operate the target as a stand-alone but, for strategic reasons, wanted to own 100 percent of its equity.

Research shows that a significant percentage of acquisitions "fail" in some way. Are they worth the risk?

This is a question of facts and circumstances. Sometimes an acquisition is the right strategic choice, and other times this would be the wrong move. Chapter 9 of this book, on postmerger integration, discusses postmerger returns, based on the latest research.

To begin with, let's consider the clearly positive case of one small company buying another in an emerging industry. Few would criticize Coinbase's decision to take over other start-ups in its fields through a series of "acqhires," buying companies to engage the talents of their founders. This is a new twist on the roll-up strategy mentioned earlier.[16]

This said, it is notable that acquisitions are particularly risky for small-cap firms in public markets because of the chain of events that may occur if shareholders do not agree with the deal. Whereas companies with a vast number of holders can weather a shareholder revolt, a small-cap company cannot.[17]

- First, if investors sell the company's stock, short it, or simply don't trade it at all, stock price and/or volume might suffer, making any attempts to access the equity capital markets more dilutive. In the worst-case scenario, it could all but foreclose access to the equity markets.
- Second, if trading volume dries up, the company also won't be able to use its stock as acquisition currency; that is, high-quality companies won't want illiquid stock as purchase consideration.
- Third, high-quality, sell-side research firms have seen the same small-cap M&A "movies" that fund managers have, so the chance of getting impactful research is going to be diminished.
- And, fourth, but certainly not least important, many small-cap officers and directors—in my experience—underestimate how much a pressured/languishing stock can impact employee recruitment, retention, and morale.

Do you mean to say that small-cap, buy-side folks are intuitively against *all acquisitions*? Even "one-offs"?

The short answer is that organic growth is nearly always going to be valued more highly than corporate acquisitions in the small-cap realm. That said, there is a "flavor" of small-cap M&A that can be quite successful: "tuck-in" technology/IP asset purchases—an art perfected by Cisco. In other words, unique situations, where it's faster, easier, and cheaper to buy technology, intellectual property, or physical property rights from a third party, can be quite accretive. The reason they can work well is that you're buying a "widget," and perhaps a small team of technical people, and that's it. You're not acquiring liabilities, business models, corporate cultures, and the rest.

SWOT ANALYSIS

What exactly is SWOT analysis and how is it used in the strategic planning process?

SWOT analysis is a useful framework often used at the kickoff of a strategy formulation that is intended to help management develop a sustainable niche in the company's target market. Some people attribute the original development of the tool to Albert S. Humphrey, a management consultant for the Stanford Research Institute (now known as SRI International) in the 1960s, although that attribution has been debated over the years. Ultimately, SWOT analysis is intended to identify the internal and external factors that either support or hinder an organization's ability to achieve its stated mission. Factors that are internal to the organization are its strengths and weaknesses, while factors that are external are the opportunities and threats presented by the outside operating environment. Exhibit 2-4 summarizes sample questions that can help to guide an organization's SWOT analysis.

Exhibit 2-4 Sample SWOT Analysis Questions

Strengths

- What advantages does your organization have?
- What do you do better than anyone else?
- What unique or lowest-cost resources can you draw upon that others can't?
- What do people in your market see as your strengths?
- What factors mean that you "get the sale"?
- What is your organization's unique selling proposition?

Weaknesses

- What could you improve?
- What should you avoid?
- What are people in your market likely to see as weaknesses?
- What factors lose you sales?

Exhibit 2-4 *(Continued)*

Opportunities

- What good opportunities can you spot?
- What interesting trends are you aware of?
- What changes in technology or government policy are shaping your market?
- What changes in social patterns, population profiles, lifestyle changes, etc., are influencing your field?

Threats

- What obstacles do you face?
- What are your competitors doing?
- Are quality standards or specifications for your job, products, or services changing?
- Is changing technology threatening your position?
- Do you have bad debt or cash flow problems?
- Could any of your weaknesses seriously threaten your business?

Source: https://www.mindtools.com/pages/article/newTMC_05.htm.

The SWOT approach implies that the ideal M&A process will target industries and companies where an acquisition will both exploit strengths and shore up weaknesses. In the process, the M&A staff truly becomes an opportunity maker, pursing only those opportunities that will fit with its chosen strategy. The original senior author of this work, Stanley Foster Reed, developed a proprietary methodology for determining strategic direction and target fit called the Wheel of Opportunity and Fit Chart (WOFC) approach, which allows decision makers to generate and prioritize target criteria. Planning of this sort greatly reduces the cost of analyzing randomly submitted opportunities. Do they fit at all? If so, how well do they fit? A truly sophisticated strategic plan will measure quantitatively how well or how poorly potential opportunities fit into it, and, given several competing opportunities, it will rank them against each other by degree of desirability to a team of senior managers and trusted advisors. (See Exhibits 2-5 and 2-6 for sample checklists.)

Exhibit 2-5 Sample Checklist of Assets for Use in Complement/Supplement Analysis

An asset checklist can help companies see what they may need in an acquisition, whether complementary (to correct an asset weakness) or supplementary (to reinforce an asset strength).

PHYSICAL ASSETS

What equipment, inventory, materials, land, or buildings does our company have?

- Are any of these a source of weakness? Can we correct it through a complementary acquisition? For example, if our equipment is outmoded, can we buy a company with more modern equipment?
- Are any of these areas a source of strength? Can we build on it through a supplementary acquisition? For example, if we have had success buying and developing farmland, can we buy a company that has land in need of development?

FINANCIAL ASSETS

What are our financial assets?

- Are our financial ratios weak? Can we correct these via a complementary acquisition? For example, if our debt-equity ratio is too high, can we buy a company in our industry that has a low debt-equity ratio to compensate?
- Are our financial ratios strong? Can we build on this via a supplementary acquisition? For example, if our interest coverage (earnings before interest and taxes minus interest charges) is high, can we buy a company that can benefit from this strength (because it is overleveraged but otherwise desirable)?

INTELLECTUAL ASSETS

- Do we have a notable weakness in our nonfinancial assets? For example, do we lack adequate patents in our core technology? If so, can we buy a company with the kind of patents we need?
- Do we have a notable strength in our nonfinancial assets? For example, do we have strong brands? If so, can we buy a company with good products that need brand recognition?

EXHIBIT 2-5 *(Continued)*

HUMAN ASSETS (PEOPLE)

- Do we have a notable weakness in our human assets? For example, do our workers lack the technological skills we need in our industry? If so, can we buy a company that has experience training and employing such workers?
- Do we have a notable strength in our human assets? For example, is our sales and distribution team successful? If so, can we buy a company with products they can sell and distribute?

ORGANIZATIONAL ASSETS (SYSTEMS/ACTIVITIES)

- Do we have a notable weakness in our organizational systems or activities? For example, are our distribution channels insufficient? If so, can we buy a company with the channels we need?
- Do we have a notable strength in our organizational systems or activities? For example, do we have superior systems for design and production? If so, is there a product line we could buy that can benefit from those systems?

EXTERNAL RELATIONSHIP ASSETS

- Do we have notable weaknesses in our external relationships? For example, are our labor relations poor? If so, can we merge with a competitor that has strong relations with the appropriate unions?
- Do we have notable strengths in our external relationships? For example, do we have an excellent reputation for customer service? If so, can we buy a company and enhance its value by training its employees in our service culture or transferring our customer-oriented employees to its workforce?

Exhibit 2-6 lists risks a company might face. Not surprisingly, the risk-based list is almost identical to the lists regulators require—namely, the categories required in the Management Discussion and Analysis (MD&A) section of the annual report.[18] Such a list can be useful in generating a list of desirable acquisition candidates. In the end, the lists should make sense to management.

Exhibit 2-6 Sample Checklist of Risks for Use in Seeking Complementary Acquisitions

RISK: VULNERABILITY TO BUSINESS CYCLES

- Seasonal or annual factors (buy company with summer products to offset winter products)
- Long-term economic factors (buy company with boom products to offset bust products)
- Product life cycles (buy company with slow-growth products to offset fast-growth products)
- Random factors (buy company with diverse range of products to offset variety of risks)

RISK: HIGH TURNOVER

- Disruption caused by short employee tenure (buy company with stable workforce)
- Intellectual capital drain from retirement, poaching of stars (buy company with star talent)

RISK: TECHNOLOGY CHANGE/MALFUNCTION

- Core products are prone to technology change (buy technology-rich company)
- Information systems prone to cyberattack (buy firm with capability in IT security)

RISK: COMPETITIVE DISADVANTAGE

- Open entry (buy competitor to reduce chances of new competition)
- Closed exit (buy company outside industry to enable industry exit)

RISK: STAGNATION/GROWTH

- Low growth in sales (buy to increase sales)
- Low growth in profits (buy to increase profits)

RISK: POOR INVESTOR RELATIONS

- Excessive leverage (buy debt-free firm to lower debt-equity ratio)
- Volatile earnings (buy company with countertrend)

EXHIBIT 2-6 *(Continued)*

- Poor lender relations (buy company with strong lender ties to offset weak lender relations)
- No access to equity markets (buy company that is listed or has a more prestigious or secure listing)
- Poor financial image (buy high-prestige company to counteract low or no reputation)

RISK: POOR MARKET/MARKETING

- Low market share (buy company to offset low market share)
- Low price (buy competitor with higher prices to offset low prices)
- Single customer type (e.g., if a defense supplier, buy nondefense company)
- Weak marketing approach (buy company with superior marketing)
- Inadequate shelf space (buy company that gives more shelf space)
- Incomplete product line (buy company that completes, bundles with, or competes internally with a product line)
- Low customer appeal (buy a company with good service reputation to offset a negative one)

RISK: REGULATORY/LEGAL PROBLEMS

- Regulatory burden (buy company in nonregulated industry to offset necessary but burdensome issues of compliance)
- Poor union relations (buy company in nonunion industry to offset exposure to strikes)
- High market concentration (buy company in nonconcentrated industry to offset any problems of antitrust)
- High tax bracket (buy company offering legitimate tax advantages)
- Weak patent/trademark/copyright protection (buy company with patent protection processes)
- Insufficient technology (buy company to offset lack of technology)

DISCLOSURE OF STRATEGY

Should a company disclose its strategy (including M&A aspects) to the public, or keep it confidential?

An enterprise's management and board should not necessarily keep its strategic priorities a secret, as a well-crafted mission can be a key factor in motivating shareholders to buy or hold stock and can form a meaningful connection with employees. For this reason, a company's management generally should be prepared to disclose its strategic priorities. Indeed, one recent study on strategy disclosures suggests that disclosure of growth strategy through M&A can have a positive effect on stock price, hence market value. The researchers scrutinized nearly 900 disclosures for nearly 500 transactions and concluded that "increasing the transparency of M&A strategy to investors through voluntary communications can bring share-price related benefits."[19]

But while disclosure about strategy—including one's M&A strategy—can help to set expectations and influence behaviors among a company's various constituencies, it is not necessary—or even advisable—to disclose the detailed plan or plans that support the strategy. For sample strategy statements, see Exhibit 2-7. As this exhibit shows, most strategy statements are general, but some mention M&A.

As a general strategy, Cisco seeks a leadership position in digital. What is Cisco's approach to M&A?

Cisco has long recognized that acquisitions provide an opportunity to both enter new markets and accelerate growth in existing ones. Since the early 1990s, Cisco has announced acquisitions at the rate of nearly one every six weeks. With the breadth of customers across industries that it serves—and coupled with the incredible pace of innovation and change in technology generally—augmenting in-house development efforts through inorganic activity makes sense, and is critical to evolution as a company.

Many of Cisco's acquisitions over the years have been relatively small "Tech & Talent" deals, enabling the rapid onboarding of skilled and innovative teams, and the associated IP and technology; these can often be readily folded into existing business units, and they allow for faster

Exhibit 2-7 Sample Strategy Statements

GENERAL STRATEGY STATEMENTS

Apple

Business Strategy: The Company is committed to bringing the best user experience to its customers through its innovative hardware, software and services. The Company's business strategy leverages its unique ability to design and develop its own operating systems, hardware, application software and services to provide its customers products and solutions with innovative design, superior ease-of-use and seamless integration. . . . The Company believes a high-quality buying experience with knowledgeable salespersons who can convey the value of the Company's products and services greatly enhances its ability to attract and retain customers. Therefore, the Company's strategy also includes building and expanding its own retail and online stores and its third-party distribution network to effectively reach more customers and provide them with a high-quality sales and post-sales support experience. The Company believes ongoing investment in research and development ("R&D"), marketing and advertising is critical to the development and sale of innovative products, services and technologies.
Apple Annual Report 2018*

BP

Our industry is changing at a pace not seen in decades. . . . Our strategy allows us to be competitive at a time when prices, policy, technology and customer preferences are evolving. We believe having a balanced portfolio with advantaged oil and gas, competitive downstream and low carbon activities, as well as a dynamic investment strategy give us resilience. With the experience we have, the portfolio we have created and the flexibility of our strategy, we can embrace the ***energy*** transition in a way that enhances our investor proposition, while meeting the need for energy today.
BP Annual Report 2018

Cisco

Our vision is to deliver a highly secure, intelligent platform for digital business. Our strategic priorities include accelerating our pace of innovation, increasing the value of the network, and delivering technology the way our customers want to consume it.
Cisco Annual Report 2017

PWC U.K.

Our strategy is built around five priorities: be technology enabled; deliver exceptional value to our clients; empower our people; lead by example and invest in sustainable, profitable growth.
PWC U.K. Annual Report 2017

Nestle

Our strategy focuses on delivering distinct benefits to people through the food and beverages, products and services we provide.
Nestle Annual Report 2016

Tesla

Tesla's mission is "to accelerate the world's transition to sustainable energy."
Tesla website: https://www.tesla.com/about

M&A-SPECIFIC STRATEGY STATEMENTS

General Electric

In recent years, we have been making our $125 billion company simpler by focusing on core industrial businesses and deeper by means of building new capabilities. We create value through technology, delivering essential systems like engines, scanners, and turbines. We have a diversified model: product and service, multiple geographies, industry balance, creating demand through data, and financing. It is important that all our businesses achieve a competitive cost position and superior organic growth. . . .

Over time, we have been our own "portfolio activist," buying and selling more than $100 billion worth of businesses. This was necessary, but difficult. It meant that every leader juggled strategic and operational tasks, while financial reporting was often complex as we move in and out of businesses. But today, the GE portfolio is pretty well set.
GE Annual Report 2016

Schaeffler Group

Following the successful realignment of its capital structure and its renewed financial flexibility resulting from the reduced level of debt, the Schaeffler Group will no longer rely only on purely organic growth. The company will generally focus on acquisitions related to the future-oriented fields of E-Mobility, Industry 4.0, and digitalization. Smaller acquisitions will serve to expand and strengthen our expertise.
Schaeffler Management Report 2016[†]

EXHIBIT 2-7 *(Continued)*

Proactis

The Group's M&A strategy is to acquire businesses that fit strict selection criteria based around the following principles:

Consolidation of complementary customer bases and solutions—the procurement space is sufficiently fragmented to offer significant scope for this;

Organisations with long term customer relationships, ideally contracted with a proven track record of retention and renewal;

Technology led solutions and service offerings that are complementary to the Group's existing offering; and

Technology that is compatible with the Group's existing technology.

Proactis Annual Report and Accounts 2016[‡]

* http://files.shareholder.com/downloads/AAPL/6259110456x0xS320193-17-70/320193/filing.pdf

† https://www.schaeffler.com/remotemedien/media/_shared_media_rwd/08_investor_relations/reports/2016_ar/2016_schaeffler_ar_mr_01_3_group_strategy_and_management_en.pdf

‡ http://www.proactis.com/Proactis/media/Proactis/Documents/UK/Reports%20and%20Announcements/PROACTIS_Report_and_Accounts_2016.pdf

time to market for subsequent offers than could be realized organically. Of course, Cisco has not focused solely on small acquisitions and tuck-ins; larger-scale, "platform"-level M&A has also long been a component of the strategy and has delivered some of the greatest shareholder returns. This type of activity has allowed the company to move into new product areas and even entire new lines of business, while meeting market transitions (e.g., to Cloud and SaaS).

M&A—with the talent, technology, new business models, and so forth, that come with it—thus not only drives growth for Cisco, but infuses and changes the greater company through new innovative ideas, capabilities, practices, and leadership.

Not all companies include a general statement about the company's "strategy." Tesla for example, emphasizes it larger social mission: "to accelerate the world's transition to sustainable energy."[20]

LEVELS OF STRATEGY

What are the typical strategic planning levels for large, complex companies?

It depends on whether an organization is organized by division, product, or function. (See Appendix 2A.) Larger, more mature companies are organized by divisions. Such companies can have as many as six levels for planning.

Enterprise strategy generally is developed at the board-of-director level. Thus, a strategy might develop at the enterprise level to *expand* the enterprise by making a major horizontal acquisition—acquiring a major competitor of about the same size or bigger. Alternatively, the board may opt to temporarily *contract* the enterprise by selling off major lines and later reallocating cash flows into entirely new and higher-yielding lines unrelated to historic lines.

Corporate strategy calls for putting together under common management several groups of strategic business units (SBUs) that have some common operating elements—technology, marketing, geographic location, and so on. These megagroups are formed via the group strategy described in the following. Cash flows from the group members are reallocated internally to maximize long-term return. The group is also constantly seeking new investment opportunities that fit with the group's commonalities. In some decentralized companies, the group may administer its own M&A activity independent of headquarters.

Sector or group strategy calls for assembling, under one corporate or operating group, SBUs that share some commonality. Then, as in the corporate strategy, cash flows are allocated and reallocated back to the individual business units or into new internal or external investments.

Business unit strategy deals with assembling under common management those product lines that have some commonalities—most often manufacturing or marketing. Cash flows are reinvested back into the most promising of the units after comparing the potential return that could be realized from the acquisition of new product lines or start-ups.

Product-line strategy deals with product life cycles—supplementing or replacing mature or aging products with new products.

Functional strategy deals with alternative methods of manufacture—for instance, changing from aluminum die casting to plastic injection molding, or switching from wood to fiberglass or aluminum for a line of boats. It should also include plant relocation—looking for lower labor rates, cheaper rents, more employee amenities, proximity to raw materials, and so forth.

Who is responsible for strategy and any resulting transactions in larger companies?

Planning begins with the board of directors, which sets the tone. Directors should ensure that managers make M&A decisions only in accordance with a plan, and should impose discipline on the implementation of that plan. The greater the percentage of company assets involved in a transaction, be it a purchase or a sale, the more imperative it is for the board to be involved. Indeed, by state law, the board alone can authorize the sale of a company.

What, precisely, is the board's role in strategy generally, and in M&A specifically?

Boards have a vital role in strategy. As stated in the *Report of the NACD Blue Ribbon Commission on Strategy Development,* published by the National Association of Corporate Directors, every board should "[e]ngage with management on strategy issues on an ongoing basis, including early involvement to improve strategy development, adjustment, and monitoring."[21] Ideally, an acquirer's board will be constructively engaged with management to ensure the appropriate development, execution, and modification of the company's strategy, including any parts of the strategy that involve growth through acquisition or shrinkage via divestiture.

More recently, the Board of Directors of the Federal Reserve Banking System published standards for "board effectiveness" (BE) that insist on board involvement in strategy. The proposed BE guidance describes "effective boards" as boards that, among other actions, "[s]et clear, aligned, and consistent direction regarding the firm's strategy and risk tolerance."[22]The nature and extent of the board's involvement in strategy will depend on the particular circumstances of the company and the industry in which it is operating. While the board can—and, in some cases, should—use a committee of the board or an advisory board to analyze specific aspects of a proposed strategy, the full board should be engaged in the development of the strategy for the enterprise. This strategy may be supported by one or more specific M&A strategies developed by management to support the overall enterprise strategy. There are different kinds of M&A strategy.

FOUR TYPES OF M&A STRATEGY

What are the main kinds of M&A strategy?

As mentioned earlier when introducing the concept of the strategic acquirer, the main kinds of M&A strategy are portfolio-building, cost cutting, revenue boosting, and hedging via strategic options.

What is a portfolio strategy for M&A?

A *portfolio strategy* for M&A is the path a company chooses to diversify its products and markets. The portfolio company is an enterprise composed of multiple independent companies obtained through acquisition. Portfolio companies have varying investment philosophies and varying governance structures.[23] A good example of a portfolio company is Alphabet, the parent of Google. (See Exhibit 2-8.)

A portfolio builder may make investments for a variety of reasons.[24] (For a longer list of reasons, see Appendix 2-A.)

- To reduce risk by diversifying into a new sector. This is the classic capital asset pricing model for portfolio management
- To improve returns on investment by buying a better-performing stock
- To gain tax credits by buying a business that offers these
- To complement an existing investment for strategic reasons
- To create a kind of franchise through a roll-up

Exhibit 2-8 What Is Alphabet?

What is Alphabet? Alphabet is mostly a collection of companies. The largest of which, of course, is Google. This newer Google is a bit slimmed down, with the companies that are pretty far afield of our main Internet products contained in Alphabet instead. What do we mean by far afield? Good examples are our health efforts: Life Sciences (that works on the glucose-sensing contact lens), and Calico (focused on longevity). Fundamentally, we believe this allows us more management scale, as we can run things independently that aren't very related. Alphabet is about businesses prospering through strong leaders and independence. In general, our model is to have a strong CEO who runs each business, with Sergey and me in service to them as needed. We will rigorously handle capital allocation and work to make sure each business is executing well. We'll also make sure we have a great CEO for each business, and we'll determine their compensation. In addition, with this new structure we plan to implement segment reporting for our Q4 results, where Google financials will be provided separately than those for the rest of Alphabet businesses as a whole.

Larry Page
Blog of August 10, 2015, announcing Alphabet
https://googleblog.blogspot.com/2015/08/google-alphabet.html

Source: Larry Page, blog post announcing Alphabet, August 10, 2015, https://googleblog.blogspot.com/2015/08/google-alphabet.html.

A typology of business portfolio companies can be defined by the differing roles of the entity that leads them—often called the parent company or corporate center.[25] In a portfolio of businesses, the parent can add value by making changes to the portfolio and/or by improving the performance of the units.

The first approach is clearly the role of M&A—that is, the portfolio can be changed by selling units or buying new units. However, the second approach also has a bearing on M&A strategy. Unit performance can be improved by changes in strategy, management disciplines, staff, or access to skills or resources—all of which can be influenced by what else is in the portfolio and/or how the portfolio is managed.

The roles of a parent can vary widely. Strategists John C. Naman and Bruce McKern have defined six parental roles for the corporate center based on the degree of business integration and the type of parent company intervention. The roles are controller, coach, orchestrator, surgeon, and architect.[26] Each role implies a strategy to create value, and each strategy can involve M&A in some form.

What is an example of a cost-cutting strategy using M&A?

Many industries undergo periods of consolidation, triggered by companies' needs for greater scale or scope. They need larger scale to compete in a changed market and/or broader scope to achieve superior competitive position. When companies buy others for scale or scope reasons, revenues get an automatic boost while cost-per-sale declines. Simply put, sales volume for two companies is higher than sales volume for one, and it usually takes less than twice the costs to run a company twice the size. The availability of such economies of scale has been the principal motivation of many corporate combinations, particularly mergers of equals. (We use the term *corporate combinations* to include mergers or acquisitions that result in a new, larger *integrated* entity. This is distinct from acquisitions made by holding companies, after which the target remains a separate company held as a subsidiary or holding.)

Consolidation opportunities can be classified based on the part of the value chain that offers the consolidation benefit or "synergy." Examples include:

- In *research and product development,* the synergies usually relate to the ability to better diversify risks and optimize the development process across a broader research and development portfolio.
- *In operations,* the major cost savings are usually found in operations—larger purchasing scale, the elimination of manufacturing and distribution redundancies, reduction of data centers by moving to public and private clouds, and the consolidation of corporate headquarters.
- *In sales and marketing,* the cost savings potential is usually less important than the revenue potential afforded by brand and marketing scale and scope.

- *In technology,* cost cuts come from reducing the number of information systems and the number of IT people who support those systems. As noted in Chapter 9, on postmerger integration, reducing the number of IT systems and people must be handled carefully and may take longer than planned originally.

What is an example of a revenue-growth strategy using M&A?

There are four main ways to use acquisitions in profitable growth:

1. Growth within a current market with current product offerings
2. Growth within a current market with new products
3. Growth into a new market with current products
4. Growth into a new market with new products

In each case, there could be a buy-versus-build decision. That is, if there is growth potential available, is it best achieved via acquisition or organically? While most acquisitions cover more than one of these four vectors, the categorization listed here can provide a convenient framework for examining the unique issues associated with each.

In addition to building a portfolio, cutting costs, or increasing in size, is there any other basic M&A strategy?

Yes. When it comes to buying companies, some of the highest value strategies may not create value directly, but rather will position the company for possible subsequent steps that could create value depending on future circumstances. These possible subsequent steps can be considered as options—that is, *real options* to distinguish from stock options.

Real options[27] are like stock options, but instead of deriving from stock they derive from real capital assets. A stock option is a right that allows the holder to acquire a certain number of shares of a certain stock during a future period of time called the *exercise period,* at a predetermined price called the *exercise price.* If the value of the stock goes higher than the exercise price during that period, then the holder is in the money and can choose to exercise the option. However, if the value of the stock is lower than the exercise price during the exercise period, the holder is under water, and the holder can then choose not to exercise. In this case, the option expires worthless but at least the holder's loss may be less than the decline in the underlying shares.

The situation with a real option is parallel. As mentioned, a real option is not a stock, but rather a physical asset or a company. Like the stock option holder, the holder of the real option is in a position to make further investments in the future that could pay off under favorable circumstances. If the future circumstances are unfavorable, the subsequent investments need not be made. However, the value of the original real asset may diminish in value—and even become totally worthless, like the stock option—if the future is such that the further investments will not pay off.

Like the chess player, the acquirer of real options is thinking several steps ahead. The early moves create favorable positioning for future stages of the game. Whether or not these early moves pay off depends on subsequent actions and reactions of each player.

As an example, let us consider a gold mine that will only be economic to develop at all if the price of gold goes up by 30 percent. The mine (as a real option) is worth something today because there is some probability (i.e., greater than zero) that the price of gold will go up by at least 30 percent. It will require further investment to develop the mine, but the cost of development, or exercise price, depends on the sequence and pace of development and need only be paid if and when the mine will be in the money.

Stock options have value because circumstances *may* be favorable in the future for exercise. Similarly, real options have value because they *may* provide a basis for additional value creation depending upon future circumstances.

Many acquisitions can incorporate real options. In fact, some of the most successful acquisition strategies create real options—options to take subsequent steps in future that are of uncertain value at the time of the deal, but that would not be possible at all without the deal.

In the best case, strategic value refers to specific steps the company could take in the future that would not be possible without this acquisition or that could have higher value with this acquisition. Such value is the value of the real options inherent in the deal.

Are real options quantifiable?

It is difficult to properly quantify the value of real options because of the combination of uncertainties. The standard method is to identify a security with parallel characteristics and to extrapolate the market's valuation of that security to a valuation of the real option.[28]

For most purposes, it suffices to identify and estimate the key variables—for example, the exercise price/cost, the probability of a favorable outcome, and the return under a range of plausible future scenarios. This will often be enough information to put a range on the value, which may in turn be all the information needed to show that the value is sufficient to justify the price or not.

What types of real options can be found in acquisitions?

The options that can be provided through an acquisition generally fall into one of three categories:

- *Growth options,* which provide the potential to pursue alternate markets in the future
- *Flexibility options,* which allow for different ways to exploit acquired assets in alternative future scenarios
- *Divestiture options,* which mitigate risk by enabling a company to dispose of all or part of an acquisition in the future

Exhibit 2-9 provides examples of options embedded in various strategic acquisitions.

Whether an M&A strategy focuses on building a portfolio, cutting costs, growing revenues, and/or securing a potential strategic option, a company must move forward along some path. These opportunities are commonly referred to as horizontal, vertical, or diversifying (diagonal).

Exhibit 2-9 Examples of Options Embedded in Strategic Acquisitions

Growth Options

- A computer firm purchases a software start-up company for its development capabilities in a target market rather than its existing products.
- An overseas airline acquires a US airline to break into the US market and increase traffic on potential future routes.
- A large publishing firm buys a smaller, niche periodical firm, enabling launches of related periodicals in the future.

Flexibility Options

- A firm in the aggregates business buys undeveloped quarry sites that have future potential for municipal waste disposal.
- A retailer diversifies to facilitate switching formats among its leased spaces in shopping malls as market conditions for its retail formats vary over time.
- A newsprint maker with virgin fiber mills acquires a mill capable of using recycled fiber to have the ability to swing production as demand favors one or the other type.

Divestiture Options

- A company purchases a holding company whose real estate may in the future have a valuable alternative use.
- An airline purchases another airline recognizing that some routes or gates can be sold if they do not prove to be needed in the business.
- A company can sell acquisitions that do not meet growth targets, thereby truncating downside risk.

Horizontal opportunities are those that involve direct competitors or companies in the same business in another market. A horizontal play can be accomplished by merging with a single competitor of similar size (a merger of equals), or by buying up many smaller companies in the same industry (a roll-up).

Horizontal ploys can work well in mature industries that are experiencing decelerating growth—whether from commoditization of products, cyclicality of demand, or some other factor. Industries prone to roll-ups in more recent times include craft breweries,[29] industrial distribution,[30] and various healthcare practices (physician practices, emergency clinics, and eye-care centers).[31]

In industries such as these, there are often pressures to increase market share so as to gain economies of scale to either increase margins or support price cuts. Accordingly, a horizontal opportunity is often followed by cost cutting, as further described later in this chapter.

On the other hand, a company need not be mature to experience roll-ups. The new field of artificial intelligence (AI) has been prone to intensive roll-ups, as CB Insights.com reports.[32] (See Exhibit 2-10.)

Exhibit 2-10 The AI Acquisition Race

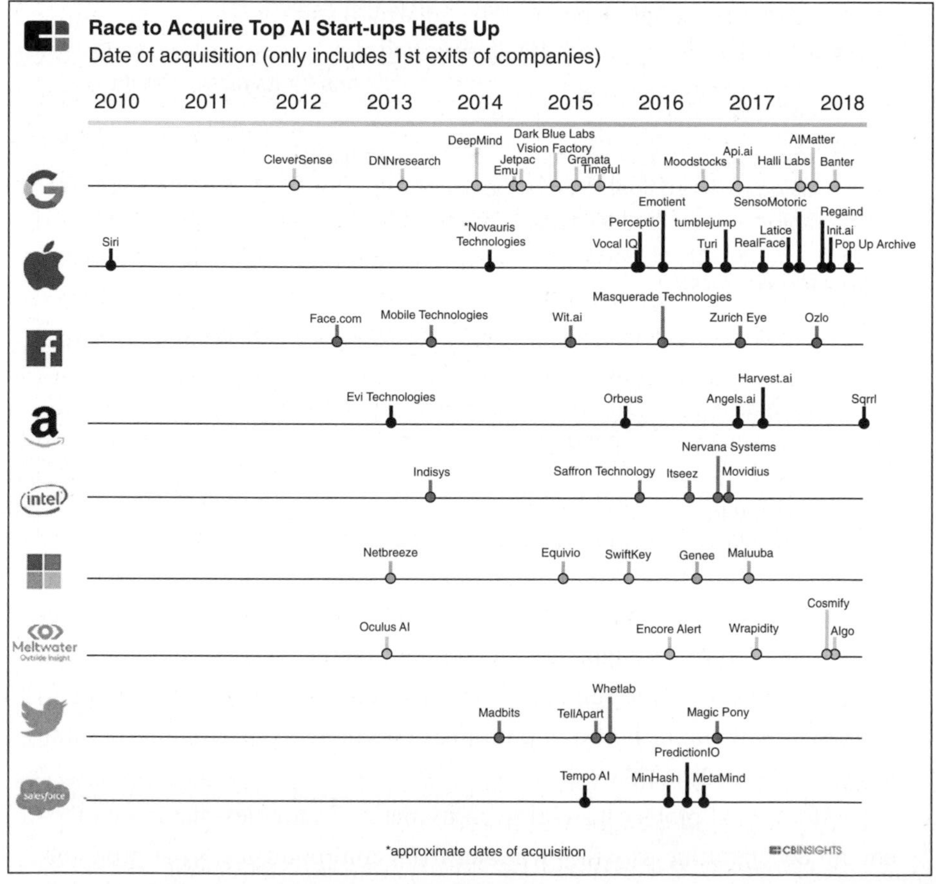

Source: cbinsights.com. Based on data provided by CBINSIGHTS.

Mergers and acquisitions that involve horizontal opportunities are more likely to be scrutinized by regulators than vertical plays, although both are perceived as potentially anticompetitive.[33]

Vertical opportunities are those that involve companies that operate in the same supply chain. The constituent companies are not competitors, but rather involve some type of vendor or customer relationship. Vertical opportunities occur when a company buys a supplier (vertical backward integration) or customer (vertical forward integration). Like any merger, a vertical merger increases revenues, but it may not improve profits unless it reduces costs; much depends on the acquirer's postdeal transfer pricing and the limits that regulators may put on it.[34] Quality control is one of the prime advantages of a vertical integration strategy, whether buying up or down the supply line. Where there is a high level of technology, vertical integration can pay off in an increasingly better product produced at increasingly lower cost because parts and materials can be produced to exact tolerances—neither overengineered, which cuts into profit margins, nor underengineered, which creates assembly and service problems. Product planning, research and development, product engineering, and in some cases distribution and service functions are all aided by vertical integration. Inventory control in times of tight money, just-in-time (JIT) deliveries, and reduction in sales costs are other positive results of vertical integration. And in times of shortages, owning a supplier has saved many a company from failure. Sherwin-Williams offers a good example of a company that used vertical integration to achieve strength. This in turn enabled it to pursue a horizontal merger at a later time. See Exhibit 2-11. Antitrust regulators tend to focus more on horizontal deals than on vertical deals, but they still scrutinize verticals for their market impact.[35]

Diagonal opportunities include product and market extensions—that is, new products for existing markets or new markets for existing products. These deals are generally oriented toward revenue growth—or it may be a matter of survival. For example, a company may plan to move out of a legacy industry and into a new one by 2023. Divestitures and acquisitions will typically play a major role in such a plan.

Some strategies combine horizontal, vertical, and/or diagonal opportunities. (See Exhibit 2-11).

Exhibit 2-11 Sherwin-Williams-Vertical Strategy Leads to Horizontal Move

At the time of its 100th anniversary a half century ago, Sherwin-Williams—producer of Dutch Boy, Kem-Tone, and so on—was having trouble making money manufacturing paint. But its customers—distributors and retailers—were doing well.

In the house paint industry, there are five levels of activity: raw material extracting, processing, manufacturing, distributing, and retailing. Sherwin-Williams made profits in the extraction stage—mining titanium dioxide—and at the distribution and retail level, but because competitive conditions in the industry forced it to make intensified investment in plant and facilities, it received little return at the manufacturing level. In response to these findings, 30 years ago Sherwin-Williams converted itself from a manufacturer of paint to a manufacturer, distributor, and retailer of household paints and the equipment to apply it. Today as it celebrates 150 years of continuous existence, the company has more than 4,000 retail paint stores with sales of nearly $16 billion following the 2017 merger with competitor Valspar in a major horizontal move.*

* "Sherwin-Williams Completes Acquisition of Valspar—Creates Global Leader in Paint and Coatings," press release of June 1, 2017. https://investors.sherwin-williams.com/press/2017/601_VALclosing/index.jsp. See also https://investors.sherwin-williams.com/press/2017/601_VALclosing/index.jsp.

Who should make M&A decisions, and how should these decisions be made?

Under normal circumstances, boards of directors should make the final decision on M&A transactions. This is especially true when it comes to the sale of a company or merger into another company. In the United States, by state corporation law, directors alone can make such decisions; they may not delegate the decision to management. In some cases, stockholders must then ratify the board's decision.

When courts evaluate director M&A decisions for legitimacy, standards of review vary.[36] According to governance experts writing for the National Association of Corporate Directors, sound decision making involves two steps: defining the decision to be made and then making the decision. See Exhibit 2-12.

Beyond this common-sense approach there are a number of facilitated techniques that have been developed, such as the Delphi method for

Exhibit 2-12 A Guide to M&A Decisions

I. Defining the Decision

Reason for the Decision

1. *What problem is the board facing that its decision will solve?*
2. *Is doing nothing an option?*

Analysis of the Problem

3. *What key assumptions is the board making about the problem?*
4. *How accurate are the assumptions?*

Importance of the Decision

5. *If this decision results in an unqualified success, what would the impact be on the company?*
6. *If this decision went catastrophically wrong what would be the impact on the company?*

Timing of the Decision

7. *What is the deadline for this decision; by what date must it be made?*
8. *How much time is needed to spend in making a good decision?*

Agents of the Decision

9. *Who (besides the board) should be making this decision?*
10. *Who are the stakeholders and how should the board consider and/or involve them in the decision?*

II. *Making the Decision*

Information for the Decision

11. *What does the board need to find out about the problem before making this decision?*
12. *Does the board have enough information to make a reasonable decision about the problem? If not, how can the board get the information it needs?*

Director Decision Making: A Sensible Approach

Formality of the Decision

13. *How formal does the board need to be about the decision?*
14. *How detailed a record should the board keep about its process for this decision?*

Range of Possible Solutions to the Decision

15. *What solutions will be considered vs. off the table/prohibited?*
16. *What is the likely probability of each solution's success?*

EXHIBIT 2-12 *(Continued)*

Desired Outcome of the Decision

17. How would the board describe success?

18. How would the board describe failure?

Monitoring the Decision

19. After the board makes the decision, how will it be monitored?

20. What will be the milestones or stumbling blocks of achievement—signals that things are going right or wrong?

Source: Adapted with permission from Charles ReCorr and Clark Abraham, *Director Decision Making: A Common-Sense Approach* (NACD, 2013).

anonymous voting, discussed at length in earlier editions of this book in connection with the WOFC approach mentioned earlier.[37]

THE SEARCH PROCESS

When does the M&A search process begin?

The search-and-screen program begins once the acquiring company has completed its strategic self-evaluation and has developed its acquisition strategy. It is now ready to start some search activity. The first step is to identify the target industry and isolate specific acquisition candidates that might meet the fit chart criteria.

How should a search be organized?

Search is one of the few M&A activities that can be delegated to subsidiaries or advisors. While strategy, pricing, legal, and negotiation must be closely controlled by corporate headquarters, the search process can be conducted in the field.

How long does a search-and-screen program last?

For strategic acquisitions, it depends on the scope of the program and how much in-house data is available on the subject. Normally, to produce a few viable candidates to fit specific criteria, a search-and-screen program can require several months. In changing industries, however, the search can and should often be continuous.

What are the primary steps in completing a full search-and-screen program?

The following steps can be performed by the search leaders or support staff, as appropriate.

1. Define target industries.
2. Find publications, websites, and associations that are dedicated to the target industries, especially those that report on M&A activity in those specific industries.
3. Develop an industry situation analysis. This analysis determines an industry's pricing and current profitability structure, growth, maturity, cyclicality, seasonality, and other economic indicators.
4. Compile a list of industry players. These are the companies that are moving and shaking in the field.
5. Join the trade associations in the industries and get active in their chapters and trade shows.
6. Assemble a list of industry gurus. These are the people who know almost everything worth knowing about an industry sector. In addition to search engines, communities such as LinkedIn or Twitter can be useful.
7. Use online resources to identify companies for sale. (Note: It is not necessary to limit the search to companies that are for sale, but it does make negotiations easier.) Numerous lists of varying and changing quality exist, and the best way to proceed is to start fresh. Go to an online search engine and type in "companies for sale." Immediately, you will see page after page of resources, some new, some established. For example, check bizbuysell.com, businessesforsale.com, dealstream.com, and mergerplace.com.
8. Start building specific company target profiles.
9. Contact principals.

10. Begin developing preliminary postacquisition integration plans.
11. Obtain a price expression from any potential sellers.
12. Get Dun & Bradstreet (D&B) and credit reports if targets are stand-alones.
13. Begin the negotiation process. Get expressions of preliminary price and terms.
14. Engage in the due diligence process and make a business integration plan for the targets.
15. Move toward closing your chosen transactions, while remaining open to alternatives.

How can candidates be narrowed down?

The best way is to look at candidates in stages, with cuts at each stage. For the first stage, basic information is assembled on the company's products, markets, revenues, profitability, ownership structure, executives, and directors. Then the corporate development team can select 10 to 15 candidates for stage-two analysis. The second-stage analysis uses secondary research and analysis of all available data to further prioritize candidates to select up to five. The third stage then conducts more detailed research (i.e., preliminary due diligence) and prepares for a possible approach to the target. (See Exhibit 2-13.)

In gathering and weighing information, two types of criteria are considered: those that determine target attractiveness and those that determine the likelihood of a deal. Candidates that are not subject to detailed analysis are not rejected, but merely set aside in favor of candidates that appear more attractive or more likely to become interested. If the candidates selected for detailed analysis or approach prove unattractive or impossible, then those candidates that were left behind can be reconsidered in priority order.

What is an example of desirable target characteristics and how they might be analyzed?

Obviously, different buyers could be looking for companies with quite different characteristics. For example, companies like Berkshire Hatha-

Exhibit 2-13 Opportunity Prioritization

Opportunity Prioritization

Highest
Access to / Interest of Decision Makers
Lowest
Lowest Need to Deal Highest

Highest
Probability of Making a Deal
Lowest
Lowest Target Attractiveness Highest

Highest
Target Characteristics
Lowest
Lowest Value Creation Potential Highest

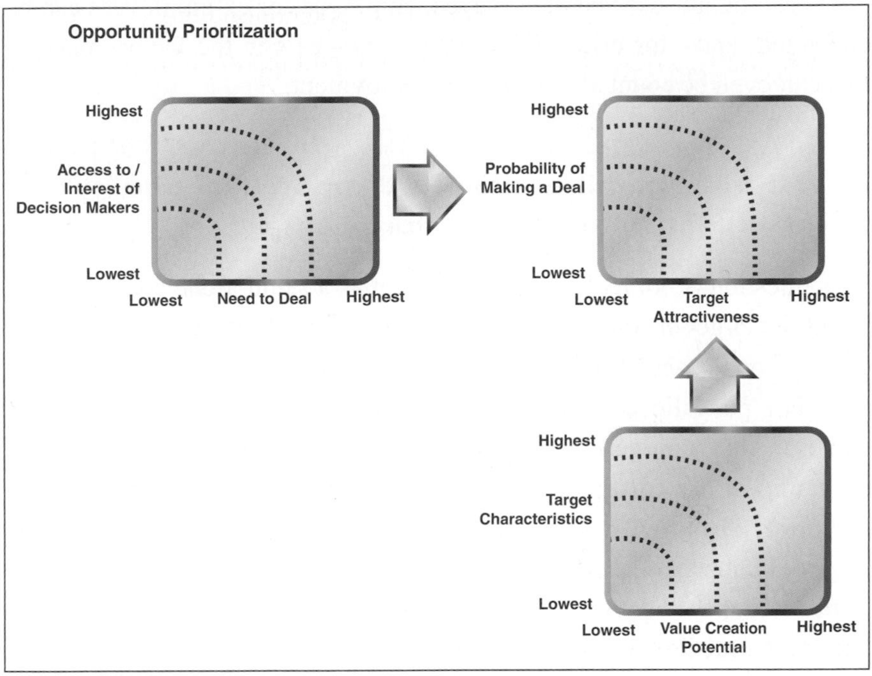

Source: Concept by Silver Lane Advisors, 2018; art by Chris Smith of Quarternative.com.

way may be looking for companies with good management and strong performance based in a sound business plan, whereas a buyer looking for turnaround or raider opportunities may be attracted to companies with weak performance that would respond to new management and/or a new strategy.

However, in any case, the basic analysis of the target includes an understanding of all the business basics, including the company's products and markets, market share and competitive position in each business line, capital structure and financial performance, ownership and governance structure, organizational structure, and management team. At the second level of analysis, these same dimensions would be examined at the more detailed level of a stock analyst's report—including ratios, industry comparisons, and assessment of strategies and potential.

At the third level, the analysis can go deeper as required. For example, executive search firms can be employed to assess management. Customers can be surveyed (blindly) to assess competitive position of products and market share. If the relative cost position is important, suppliers can be interviewed or surveyed, employees or ex-employees can be contacted, and—for brick-and-mortar firms—cars in the factory parking lots can even be counted to estimate employment.

How can an acquirer assess the potential of a given target company to create future value?

This question is not really about the target as a stand-alone company; it's about the target in combination with the acquiring company, so its answer depends on the acquirer's strategy and capabilities.

For portfolio company acquirers, the question is: Can the parent add value to the target? In other words, is the target financially better off operating in the portfolio than independently? In the case of Berkshire Hathaway, the answer is yes, according to a survey of the CEOs running acquired subsidiaries of the company, who cited the company's "long-term investment horizon" as the key to its success.[38] Or, for another example, if a media holding company bought the target, the question would be whether the access to content or the technology platform of the media holding company improves the success of a target media company.

For consolidation or revenue growth companies, the analysis involves the identification of cost or revenue synergy opportunities and successively more detailed estimates of the value of each opportunity at the three levels. For a proposition to merge two courier companies, for example, the third-level analysis included an extensive disguised survey of customers to determine with whom they would ship under various merger scenarios, including the one under study. The cost synergies in this case could only be determined accurately by designing the new route plan for the combined company—a painstaking analysis that also provided a detailed postmerger operations plan.

For consolidation deals in particular, as an acquirer you should highlight the value-adding opportunities unique to your company versus other buyers/partners. This will make you more attractive to the seller, and will make the transaction more interesting to stakeholders such as shareholders. Remember that common opportunities will usually be negotiated into the price, so the real value-creation potential of any transaction relies on unique opportunities or distinctive implementation ability.

What would motivate a target to be acquired?

The answer will vary by company. You need to see the world from the target's perspective. The best way to do this is to use the information you have or can gather on the company and the industry to develop the target's strategic options. At the first and second levels, this may be available in analyst reports. This is usually sufficient on this dimension.

If a more detailed assessment is required, then the same techniques already noted to detail the target's cost and market position can be used here to understand problems and opportunities from the target's perspective. Once sufficient data is gathered, competitive simulations can be used to develop strategy. Consultants, advisors, and/or internal resources can be assigned to play the roles of each key competitor in the industry. With sufficient data, the role play will usually determine the key elements of the strategy. If the strategy calls for merger, then at the most detailed level of analysis the role play can even estimate acceptable terms with reasonable accuracy. This kind of scenario analysis can be especially useful for companies in industries undergoing transformation.

What industry resources can be used to define the universe of companies and inform screening?

For high-level analysis, there are many possible public sources of information. Start by looking for publications/websites/associations that are dedicated to the target industries, especially those that report on M&A activity in those specific industries.

In the United States, public companies are classified by SIC (Standard Industrial Classification) code (required by the SEC) and are easily identified.[39]

Globally, companies are classified by the Global Industry Classification Standard (GICS), developed by Standard & Poor's and MSCI/Barra. This service categorizes companies into sectors and industries.[40] Many acquirers globally use the GICS methodology as an industry analysis framework for investment research, portfolio management, and asset allocation. The GICS classification system currently consists of 11 sectors:

- Consumer Discretionary
- Consumer Staples
- Energy
- Financials
- Health Care
- Industrials
- Information Technology
- Materials
- Real Estate
- Telecommunication Services
- Utilities

Within each of those there are further industry groups (24 of them), industries (68), and subindustries (157).

A basic overview of industry trends is often available in security analyst reports. Sources are listed annually in Lipper Marketplace (formerly *Nelson's Directory of Investment Managers*). Consulting firms may also have an analysis of an industry that they may share at a cost or for marketing purposes, or they can be engaged to create an industry analysis, but this will only be worthwhile if the screen has taken you to a level where the cost of the assistance is warranted.

If necessary, a high-level industry analysis can be developed from scratch using a framework like Porter's five forces.[41] An industry analysis should include such elements as:

- Market size and structure
- Key industry players and market share of each
- Level of market concentration
- Supply chain and key players in the supply chain, both upstream and downstream of the industry

- External forces that may be affecting the industry (e.g., market, technology, or regulatory changes)
- The nature of competition in the industry, for example, aggressive price-based competition, capital investments, and so forth

Find and get to know the industry gurus—those who write about the industry and/or sell industry reports. These people can often share a quick understanding of the industry dynamic and may also have data on employees, pricing, market shares, product reputation, and key player contacts.

Industry associations may have data available only to members. If the search gets serious about an industry it can be worthwhile to join the association to get access to available data and to attend conferences and meetings organized by the association.

Also, the US government (as well as other national governments) has an abundance of free or low-cost data about industries and even about specific companies. Trade magazines and websites are another good source. Consider also M&A publications and databases, such as *Mergers & Acquisitions: The Dealmakers Journal* and its website.[42] There are a number of sites that identify companies that are "for sale," although a search need not be limited to companies that are overtly "selling."

Once an acquirer finds companies of interest within a particular sector or industry, how should it organize the information?

Company profiles should be assembled as the layers of analysis are completed. Initially they may be sketchy, but for those companies that survive the initial screens, detailed profiles can be developed, including:

- Financial information in annual reports, 10-Ks, and D&B credit reports
- Company fact books and product catalogs
- Press releases, print advertisements, published articles, and executive speeches
- Director and officer profiles

Take advantage of the free information available because of securities disclosure rules affecting public companies. In addition to annual reports, look at the company's SEC filings (10-Ks, 10-Qs, prospectuses, and proxy statements at www.sec.gov), press releases, product literature, catalogs, company case studies, and executive speeches. The US Treasury also has good data based on tax filings (www.irs.gov/taxstats/index).

Other current sources for public companies include:

- *Corporate Affiliations*—in eight volumes or on CD-ROM (https://www.lexisnexis.com/en-us/products/corporate-affiliations.page)[43]
- Frost & Sullivan (www.frost.com)
- Moody's publications (www.moodys.com)
- Proquest Dialog (www.proquest.com/products-services/ProQuest-Dialog.html)[44]
- Standard & Poor's publications (www.standardandpoors.com)
- *Thomas Register* (www.thomasnet.com)
- *Value Line Investment Survey* (www.valueline.com)

How can a buyer find information on private companies?

Most companies today, including private companies, have websites as well as pages on social media (Facebook, LinkedIn), and these reveal some basic information about the companies.

This said, however, private companies rarely give out financial information such as balance sheet and profit and loss numbers. Even when they have done it for credit purposes, many do not keep it up to date. However, some states compile the information through their chambers of commerce or their economic development programs.

A good starting place is Dun & Bradstreet's *Million Dollar Directory,* which lists both public and private companies. (Two other companies that offer similar products—Harris InfoSource and Hoovers—now operate under the D&B brand.) The *Million Dollar Directory* and related services are all available through Mergent, Inc.[45] Many libraries subscribe to the *Million Dollar Directory,* providing a no-cost alternative for companies not prepared to make the investment in a subscription.

If D&B does not have financial information on a particular private company, it is extremely difficult to obtain the information without getting it directly from the company itself. However, many states, especially those with extractive activity, require both public and private businesses, whether incorporated or not, to file annually various types of information, including year of establishment, names of principal owners, key personnel, number of employees, annual sales, principal lines of business, plant size, and import/export activity. Sometimes asset, liability, and profit information must also be submitted.

D&B Hoovers (to cite just one product of this nature) enables an acquirer to create "targeted lists to identify more prospects . . . with direct phone numbers on-hand for more than 16 million contacts."[46] Such an approach would not be appropriate for an important and sensitive inquiry, but it could prepare the way through information gathering. An acquirer looking at hundreds of companies in a specific sector who wants to know if they do or do not sell a particular product might send out a personalized e-mail asking about availability. While this can hardly be called "approaching the company," it may turn out to be the key that opens the door, so it should be done in the most professional way possible.

When contacting prospects, what means of communication should be used?

One approach that has become a classic in recent decades is to combine an email and a phone call, in either order:

- An opportunity hunter can email a prospect, promising a phone call, and then follow up with the phone call "following up on my email."
- Conversely, the first contact can be with a phone call followed by an email saying "Good talking with you" or "Sorry I missed you."

To be sure, it is not always easy to find direct phone numbers and emails for prospects, and even then, seekers must get around gatekeepers—be they human (executive assistants) or electronic (spam filters). Moreover, any e-mail or voicemail is vulnerable to the delete key.

How can social media help?

Fortunately for opportunity seekers, social media are making inroads into the communications market. Even when colleagues know each other's email addresses, they may choose to communicate through LinkedIn. The basic free subscription allows communications between individuals who have accepted each other as contacts. A "premium" subscription enables a seeker to send a communication to a complete stranger, who can opt to open or delete the message. A compelling subject line from a person of substance is just as likely to be opened and read as a traditional email. Even Facebook, Twitter, and other social venues can be avenues for contact.

Given the dominance of social media contacts, are telephone calls still viable?

Telephone calls from live (human) cold callers are still viable, but barriers to contact success are increasing in this legacy technology. The increasing use of telemarketing, most of it robo-calling,[47] has led to an increase in protective screens by call recipients, including not only the traditional live gatekeepers such as executive assistants but, beyond them, the use of voicemail. It is extremely rare for executives to answer their own phones unless they know (through caller ID) the identity of the caller.

If a telephone call is appropriate and possible, who should be contacted at the target company?

Callers should start at the top. The principals contacted may include the CEO, the CFO, and the COO. In a wide-ranging search, the target's directors, outside counsel, accountants, and bankers—both commercial and investment—can also be contacted. Contacting a target's outside counsel is usually unproductive. First, attorneys, because of attorney-client confidentiality, are not supposed to give out any information; and second, they have their own agendas. They may want to initiate the deal so that they will continue to be retained, and will try to discourage you. The same thing, to a lesser extent, applies to the target's accounting firm.

Try to structure any conversation with a principal officer or owner so as to avoid a direct turndown. One technique that has been honed to a fine art by executive headhunters is to call target executives and ask if they know of an executive who might be available. They might then offer themselves. It works the same way in an acquisition search. Tell a prospective target that you are considering making an entry in the industry either by a de novo entry (a start-up) *or* an acquisition, and ask if they know of any for sale. That is sure to get their attention; their response might just be, "Well, if the price were right, *we* might be for sale."

If the acquisition proposal involves a relatively small subsidiary of any relatively large company, the contact person should be the senior vice president of corporate planning or corporate development—but don't call the division head unless it's public knowledge that the unit is on the block. Even then, it's best to deal with planning at either the corporate, sector, or business unit level rather than with the executives who might be intimately affected by a sale, and may, in fact, be trying to buy the operation themselves in a management buyout.

What should the caller say–and not say?

The person answering the phone at a target company will be impressed with any expertise demonstrated by the caller. The target profile will give the buyer more information leverage because the target will often know very little about the buyer. To set the management more at ease, the buyer or its agent should provide some useful information about itself or the target's management.

The ultimate goal of the initial conversation is to set up a meeting to discuss working together or teaming up through a possible business combination. The business combination could be a merger, acquisition, or joint venture. The more broadly you define it, the better. Price discussions would not be appropriate at this stage; there are far too many unknowns and neither side should want to be boxed into a set valuation range so soon in the process.

Where should buyer and target representatives meet at this early stage?

The parties will need to agree on a mutually satisfactory meeting place. Visiting the target may start the rumor mill, and that can hurt a deal. On the other hand, the buyer can get a better feel for the target's operations and personnel if it is at least eyeballed. But the usual practice of a large group of suits visiting a target should be discouraged.

An alternative would be meeting at the offices of an investment banker or law firm, or in neutral territory, such as a conference room at a hotel. Try not to meet in airline clubs, hotel lobbies, restaurants, or other public places—it starts the rumor mill and can create competition for the target.

A good cover for meetings is the prospect of a joint venture or a supplier or customer relationship. This plays very well where a company is not on the block, but be careful of any out-and-out misrepresentation.

Having agreed on a meeting place, it will benefit the buyer to have obtained the target's financials prior to the meeting. (We assume you already have all of the sales literature, D&B reports, and, if it's a public company, the 10-Ks.) The target may ask you to sign a confidentiality agreement at this point. By all means do so, but make sure you are protected. (See Chapter 7 on acquisition agreements.)

With such information in hand, an agenda for the meeting can be easily set. (And it's important to have a written agenda at least for your side so that all of the important subjects will be covered.)

What can be accomplished at the first meeting with a target?

The meeting should give the buyer a sense of the company and its operations, whether there are any skeletons in the seller's closets that may preclude a deal, and whether the chemistry is right if there are to be any continuing management relationships. The meeting should give the target management a sense of the buyer and its management and the benefits to target managers if they are to stay and to owners if they are to continue to own.

There must be *reasons* for combining companies corporately and operationally. In most cases these are discussed in the early meetings, unless the buyer wants to keep plans confidential. However, if the target is a public company, this is a sensitive area; whether and how a company discloses or conceals future plans can trigger legal exposure. (See, for example, *Basic v. Levinson* in the last chapter of this book, "Landmark M&A Legal Cases.") In many circumstances, it is better to say "no comment" than to disclose what could be later interpreted as misleading. As one legal expert has noted, it is not always clear what statements can be considered misleading under securities fraud law and "little upside" for the company itself from disclosing more than what is required.[48] For public companies, it is good to have copies of any financial analysis performed by investment bankers, even if issued by a regional house. Also ask the sellers if they ever used a management consultant to run a survey. If they did, ask to see the report, no matter how old it might be. Ask to see the outside auditors' management letters or reports. Find out if the company has changed auditors within the past five years, and if so, get permission to talk to the old auditors.

It is important in this meeting for the seller to avoid making exaggerated claims. When representations are made that later prove untrue, buyers can sue, citing fraudulent conveyance, also called fraudulent transfer.[49] (For more on fraudulent conveyance, see Chapter 4.)

BROKERS AND FINDERS

How can brokers help in the search process?

Much of the preceding material describes in-house search processes, but many companies seeking to expand by the M&A route—especially the opportunity makers—use brokers.[50] A broker can help a seller find a buyer, or vice versa.

How can I locate and contact a business broker?

Most brokers have websites and can be found via Internet search using the word *broker* and the location desired. In addition, a number of websites can assist, for example:

- www.bizbuysell.com/business-brokers
- www.ibba.org
- www.bizbrokerdirectorpy.com

What's the difference between a broker and a finder?

A *broker* is an agent and a legal fiduciary with all the responsibilities and restrictions that those terms imply in law. Among brokers there are business brokers (local Main Street), M&A brokers (lower middle market), and investment bankers (registered as broker-dealers with the Financial Industry Regulatory Authority [FINRA], and typically serving the upper middle market and public companies). Brokers may represent only one side in a transaction. The rules governing their behavior have been established over the past five centuries by the common law. In the United States, anyone using exchange facilities to effect transactions is required to register with the Securities and Exchange Commission, but the SEC has indicated that it will not take action against unregistered brokers if they are brokering small transactions. A congressional bill, H.R. 609, pending in 2019, would codify that assurance as an outright exemption. The bill would amend securities law exempting brokers in transactions with small companies, defined as those with earnings of less than $25 million and revenues of less than $250 million. Generally, brokers represent sellers and as fiduciaries must try to get a top price for a company. There can be civil or even criminal lawsuits if the broker favors buyers over sellers in a transaction or secretly takes money from a buyer to knock down the price.

Finders, as opposed to brokers, are not agents of or for anyone. They are not fiduciaries. Unlike brokers, they represent the deal rather than one of the parties. Finders can be paid by both parties or by either party, even without the knowledge of the other. Finders, however, must be careful not to negotiate, for it is the act of negotiation that takes them out of the finder class, creates an act of agency, places them squarely in the broker category, creating fiduciary responsibilities and putting them under regulatory supervision. Depending on the locale, a business opportunity or business chance broker's license may be required. Payments to a finder, if that person is deemed an unlicensed broker, can cause an entire transaction to violate securities laws, giving investors a right to undo the deal.[51]

How is negotiation defined?

Generally, if the finder merely introduces the prospective purchasers and otherwise acts only to maintain contact between the parties to make the introduction effective, no negotiation will be deemed to have taken place. If, however, the finder gets involved in determining the purchase price and stands in the place of the buyer or seller, a court may decide that the finder negotiated. In a few states, the courts have stated that they cannot see how a finder can operate *without* negotiating, and automatically lump finders in the brokers category.

What is an intermediary?

People who are foggy about the distinction between brokers and finders try to solve their dilemma by billing themselves as *intermediaries*. This straddling category can be risky because intermediaries are supposed to negotiate, and a *negotiating intermediary* is an agent of one party or the other in a contemplated transaction unless both sides have agreed—usually in writing—that the negotiation is in their common interest. Clients of brokers who turn into intermediaries should be cautious; the intermediary, depending on the language of the agreement, may be relieved of the fiduciary duties of a broker.

Are business brokers and finders regulated, and if so, by whom?

In general, the act of the brokering and finding of businesses is not regulated. The fact that some investment bankers or stockbrokers have passed exams run by the Financial Industry Regulatory Authority (FINRA) or that they must register with the SEC, although an onerous requirement for some, does not directly affect their actual work in finding and brokering the sale and purchase of businesses—even very large businesses.

What does matter is regulation by state and local authorities, including local real estate boards, of acts of business brokerage. This includes the licensing and regulation of business opportunity and business chance brokers. Generally, such brokers deal with independent retail service businesses, such as bars, car washes, dry cleaning shops, gas stations, and taxi licenses.

Many states have passed laws regulating the activity of such brokers, or allow cities and counties to enact local ordinances to regulate their activity. Often state regulation is combined with the regulation of real estate brokerage activity, usually through the acts of examination, licensing, inspection of the broker's premises, and so on. Lawyers, contrary to popular belief, are seldom exempted from the requirement to be licensed as business opportunity brokers if they negotiate the sale of a business and collect a success fee as a result.

No state has yet regulated the activity of the nonnegotiating finder, with the possible exception of New York. In a long series of tortured court decisions and supporting legislation, New York law has said, in effect, that no finder can perform the act of finding without negotiating. Finders are, therefore, ipso facto agents and brokers involved in the transfer of property, and, in order to comply with a specific provision of New York's statute of frauds, anyone (except attorneys) dealing in the transfer of property must have an agreement in writing to collect a finder's or a broker's fee.

Other states have similar statutes of fraud, but do not bar collection under general concepts of contract law. They rely on concepts such as *quantum meruit,* in which the services of the finder, even in the absence of a written contract, must be valued and paid for so as not to unjustly enrich a buyer or seller from the services provided. In New York State, however, *quantum meruit* recovery not supported by a written contract is strictly barred. As a result, many frauds have been perpetrated on unknowing finders and brokers. Even major investment banking houses have been cheated out of legitimately earned fees for failure to have a verbal fee agreement reduced to writing.

Many states try to regulate finders and brokers if real estate is involved in the transaction—even if the real assets, which include leases, are only a tiny fraction of the assets transferred. Prodded by real estate brokers, many suits result. Most are lost by the state and the brokers, but once in a while one slips through, especially when an out-of-state finder or broker does deals across a state line. In this case it is extremely important that the finder or broker not perform any act that a court could consider to be negotiation, and make sure that the principals do all of the negotiating and acknowledge it in writing.

What about fees?

Fees are not regulated by anyone. They are what the traffic will bear. In the 1920s, the investment bankers were happy to get straight commissions for the shares exchanged. But when the conglomerate merger boom began in the 1950s, Lehman Brothers—long before it fell victim to the 2008 global financial panic—dreamed up the Lehman scale, also known as the M&A formula, or the Wall Street rule. This is a sliding scale—generally the 5-4-3-2-1 formula: 5 percent of the first $1 million of the price of the transaction, 4 percent of the second, 3 percent of the third, 2 percent of the fourth, and 1 percent of the balance. Another typical variation of this is 6-3-2.[52] In recent years, some finders have been charging 10 percent, or asking for a retainer. Alternatively, some use a fee scale that is based on Lehman, but with some difference. Variations include the double Lehman of 10-8-6-4-2 and the stuttering Lehman of 55-44-33. Commission amounts for a $5 million transaction would be $300,000 (overall percentage 6 percent) under the double Lehman; $201,000 (overall percentage 4.2 percent) under the stuttering Lehman; and $150,000 (overall percentage 3 percent) under the traditional Lehman.

A 2018 survey of more than 400 investment bankers found that 18 percent used some version of the Lehman formula, described earlier. But 42 percent of respondents to this survey used a *scaled percent formula* to determine success fees, and 40 percent used a *simple percentage.* For a scaled percentage structure, a valuation target is set and a base-level success fee for this valuation is determined, with increments above this target valuation earning successively higher fees. So, for example, a $50 million dollar target valuation could earn a 2 percent fee, the next $10 million might earn 3 percent, and the next $10 million perhaps 3.5 percent. A scaling percentage fee structure more closely aligns banker interests with sellers' than the Lehman formula fee structure, wherein both parties are rewarded for a higher total deal value.

Many finders who bill themselves as investment bankers, though they have only a website and a phone number, try to get Lehman scale for their services, but usually are forced to settle for a flat fee or forced to sue. Some have successfully sued and collected very large fees using the Lehman scale.

Fees are sometimes modified by the type of deal. If it is a hostile deal, the bankers might be involved for many months or even years. Hostile deals carry much larger fees than friendly deals, especially when they are successful. If the deal is complicated, fees can be even higher. In hostile deals, many a tendering corporation has failed to reach a final fee agreement with the bankers, lawyers, consultants, accountants, and others that may be involved until after the deal is closed, and then there are problems, which sometimes wind up in court, with a judge or jury making the fee decisions. Juries are particularly tough on finder's and broker's fees that are legally due; they find it hard to believe that the simple act of introducing a potential seller to a potential buyer is worth a large sum.

The fee payment often depends on the final price paid in the deal. But determining the final price in a complicated, highly leveraged deal with equity kickers such as detachable warrants and rights, simultaneous spin-offs or spinouts, or sales of subsidiaries can be very difficult and can lead to disagreements about the price of the transaction. As a result, more and more fees are negotiated ahead of time in round numbers. "If we do the deal you get $3 million" might be the language that one hears today for a prospective $400 million deal. That works out to 0.75 percent. In such an arrangement, whether the buyer pays $300 million or $500 million, the finder or broker gets a $3 million fee for initiating the transaction.

Do investment banking firms pay fees to finders for bringing them prospective deals?

Yes. Most investment banking firms will pay a finder's fee to someone who brings them a deal. Some successful firms are happy to pay in the area of 10 percent of their fees for a successful lead.

What is a mere volunteer?

Volunteers usually cannot collect finder's or broker's fees. For instance, if a person decides to suggest to two companies that they merge and they decide to do so, this initiator is considered a *mere volunteer* and cannot collect a fee when a transaction takes place. Some degree or sign of invitation or consent is necessary to establish a compensable finder or broker relationship.

As a buyer, how can you protect yourself against claims for payment of unwarranted broker's or finder's fees?

There are several ways:

- Keep a log of inquiries and correspondence.
- Keep your contacts up to date. Finder A refers your company to a business, then you drop the deal for six months, until Finder B revives your interest and you acquire. You may owe fees to both Finder A and Finder B.
- Find out whether your state regulates business opportunity brokers. If the broker is not licensed, you can defeat an illegitimate claim for a fee if the broker negotiates. But you must prove that he or she negotiated, and that is often hard to do.
- Research whether the state you're in has a statute of frauds. If so, the broker or finder may need a written agreement to collect a fee. On the other hand, brokers or finders may be able to obtain punitive damages if you conspire to defraud them of a legitimate fee.

As broker or finder, how can I ensure that I will be paid if I do a deal?

You can take action in a number of ways:

- Get some early writings on the record that you expect to be paid, that you are not a mere volunteer or are doing it out of friendship. A retired president of Joy Manufacturing worked for a year and a half to bring about the sale of his best friend's coal-mining business for $275 million. He had ample proof of correspondence in support of his efforts. But the "best friend" testified that the finder had never told him he expected to be paid and there was nothing in all those filing cabinets that stated he expected to be paid. Always get a written agreement that includes specific language on the fee schedule.
- Keep a log of conversations and correspondence. Such message logs can be powerful evidence in some courts.
- Get the other side to agree that it won't close unless you get paid. A mutually signed written agreement is best, but at least get your expectations in writing by mailing or emailing your request.
- Insist on participating in all meetings of the principals. If you are acting as a finder, be sure to clearly state in writing (via email or mail) that you are there as a facilitator and not a negotiator. If possible, get a letter from the other side that you did not negotiate.
- Get some paper on the record. The more the better. Be sure to save your telephone bills, travel and lodging expenses, and so on.
- Sue the second you're not paid—and be sure to get a lawyer with some experience in finder's and broker's cases.

If a broker advises a buyer about an opportunity that another broker closes, which broker should be paid?

Such contingencies should be spelled out in the broker or finder agreement. If they are not so defined, however, the fee award depends on the circumstances. If the second deal succeeds because it is restructured, then the second, successful, intermediary, not the first, should be paid. If the second one merely presents the same transaction, then the first one is entitled to the fee—or the buyer can arrange for the fee to be split.

How can investment bankers help in the search process?

First, let's start with definitions. An *investment bank* is neither an investor nor a bank. That is, it does not invest its own money and it does not act as a repository for other people's funds. Rather, an investment bank is an intermediary between saving and investing. It is a financial institution that helps operating companies raise debt and equity capital in securities markets.

Investment banks often raise capital on behalf of a company, or issuer, through underwriting—the purchase and resale of a new offering of equity securities. Investment banks also help market the new stock, distributing it to retail stockbrokers, often through a retail brokerage unit affiliated directly with the bank. These brokerage units in turn may have securities analysts who make, buy, sell, or hold recommendations on specific issues.

Also, some investment bankers get retained to locate entire businesses to buy, and so act as finders or brokers. They may also represent stockholder groups wanting to sell a company or one or more of its divisions, generally by a practice known as an auction. But it is nothing like the usual auction; it usually winds up in an extensive negotiation as to price and terms. As a result, they might get a series of fees—finder's, broker's, consulting, origination, and underwriting fees, and, if the securities are exchanged through their offices, a security broker's fee. Finally, investment bankers may render a fairness opinion on a transaction, if they are not the ones getting a commission from it.

Together, all these fees are called investment banking fees. In times of heavy merger activity, these fees bring in as much revenue as their retail stock brokerage and in some years considerably more.

Investment banking firms typically have research departments that issue reports on equities. Prior to 2002, those firms would often include reports on client companies, including positive reports on companies whose stock the firm was bringing to market. Since passage of the Sarbanes-Oxley Act, such potential conflicts of interest have come under heavy regulation.[53]

BANKERS

What is the difference between the M&A services offered by an investment bank and those offered by a commercial bank?

In today's increasingly competitive market for financial services, the differences in M&A services offered by investment banks, and at least some commercial banks, have narrowed considerably. As commercial banks' lending margins have shrunk in recent years, they have sought other sources of income. Many added M&A advisory services to their work in financing highly leveraged transactions (HLTs). In the process, many banks developed capabilities that rivaled those of the most prestigious investment banking houses.

The commercial banks' capabilities include developing strategies for their clients with respect to acquisitions, recapitalizations, and leveraged buyouts, and acting as dealer-manager in tender offers, as well as rendering fairness opinions (as long as they are not the ones receiving a fee on a transaction).

Investment banks, meanwhile, began to invade some of the commercial banks' traditional territories by offering to commit their capital in the form of bridge loans to their M&A clients to underwrite at least a portion of the cost of an acquisition, something that commercial banks may not do.

Although they compete against each other, commercial and investment banks often need each other. It is not unusual for them to share clients. For example, a Wall Street investment banker might act as an advisor to a company doing an acquisition. The Wall Street firm might then take its deal to a commercial bank to obtain an acquisition bridge loan plus the long-term senior bank debt needed to refinance existing senior debt, later refinancing some or all of the bank debt with a private placement and/or an underwriting of senior or subordinated public debt. (See Chapter 4.) Because commercial banks have not been that involved with stock market operations, they have been spared the temptations faced by investment bankers to engage in illegal activity. Virtually every big name on Wall Street has been tainted with one scandal or another. Several big-name firms were dragged into the Enron scandal for analyst conflicts of interest.

Is it illegal for a bank to fund one offeror for a company and to advise another, competing, offeror?

No, it is not illegal. But many commercial and investment banks avoid such situations for fear of offending one or the other client or creating the impression of a conflict of interest. However, it is more common for commercial banks to offer financing for more than one offeror if an advisory role is involved. In this case a commercial bank will attempt to erect firewalls between the different areas of the bank involved to avoid the possibility of a breach of confidence with respect to confidential information. Tie-in deals, where a client is given a loan only if the client also buys the bank's advisory services, are illegal. However, some clients prefer a bank as an advisor if it is also willing to commit its capital in the form of a loan to facilitate the acquisition.

What is merchant banking?

Merchant banks are essentially the same as investment banks, but the term *merchant* is often associated with first-round financing, particularly in international markets. These banks deal mostly in international finance, long-term loans for companies, and underwriting. They do not provide regular banking services to the general public. (See Chapter 4.)

Are US commercial banks involved in merchant banking?

Yes, but still in only a limited way. Many commercial banks have subsidiary venture capital groups that invest in both the equity and mezzanine securities in promising ventures, including start-up companies and leveraged buyouts. Commercial banks, in their role as investment bankers, are also increasingly becoming partners with their clients by purchasing both the equity and mezzanine securities of companies to which they also provide senior debt.

INITIAL REGULATORY AND LEGAL CONSIDERATIONS

What sorts of legal issues can be raised by an acquisition?

Review of any potential restrictions on acquisition decision making, particularly those relating to antitrust, should be performed as a part of the initial planning process. It is also an important part of due diligence, discussed in Chapter 6. It makes no sense for either a plan-driven or a deal-driven buyer to evaluate and search out a candidate unless it can legally acquire that company and operate it afterward without regulatory hassles or lawsuits.

Depending on the facts and nature of the transaction, an acquisition may require compliance with federal, state, or local statutes or regulations in a variety of areas. The most common areas triggered by the transaction itself include laws with respect to antitrust, securities, employee benefits, bulk sales, foreign ownership, and the transfer of title to stock or assets. Some of these laws require only routine acts to achieve compliance, which can be attended to relatively late in the acquisition process. Other laws pose potential regulatory barriers that must be considered before proceeding with a given acquisition plan.

Furthermore, in acquiring any company, the acquirer may inherit the acquired company's legal liabilities. This kind of legal exposure is not just legal exposure arising from the transaction, but from the simple fact of doing business in a risky and litigious world. For an overview of the more general kind of liability exposure, see Chapter 6, on due diligence.

How does the purchaser determine what regulatory barriers may exist for a proposed transaction?

Unless the purchaser is a veteran in the relevant field of business it plans to enter, the purchaser must engage legal counsel familiar with the field or skilled in the legal complexities of acquisitions.

Can the failure to identify and satisfy all regulatory requirements in a timely manner delay or kill a deal?

Yes. In some cases, one or both parties must obtain the consent or approval of the responsible agency or agencies before the transaction can be consummated. Failure to do so can result in penalties or even rescission of the contract covering the transaction. This "out" is discussed in Chapter 7, at Sections 9.1 and 9.2 of Appendix 7D.

What regulatory hurdles must be surmounted in consummating an acquisition?

Each industry has its own regulatory maze, but some general areas can be identified:

- *Antitrust.* Certain business combinations require filings and clearances with the Federal Trade Commission (FTC) or Department of Justice (DOJ) under the Hart-Scott-Rodino Act.[54] Only a small number of these filings trigger a review for antitrust law violation, and most of these are horizontal mergers.[55]
- *Disclosure to shareholders.* Companies that sell securities to the general public (called public companies) have a myriad of rules to consider, including filings to the SEC. These rules are discussed in Chapter 10.

- *Environmental concerns.* Corporate acquisitions can trigger state law requirements relating to cleanup of sites contaminated by hazardous wastes. A buyer can also be hit under both federal and state law with cleanup costs even if it had no involvement in or knowledge of the pollution. In *United States v. Bestfoods,* the Supreme Court ruled that a parent corporation may be held derivatively liable under the Comprehensive Environmental Response, Compensation, and Liability Act (CERCLA) for the polluting activities of its subsidiary, if the corporate veil is misused to accomplish fraud or other wrongful purposes on the shareholders' behalf.[56] Regulators obtained orders requiring responsible parties to spend nearly $230 million to clean up contaminated sites and to reimburse the Superfund more than $300 million for federal cleanup costs. Commercial banks acting as trustees are also exposed. (See Chapter 6, on due diligence.) Also, certain federal or state laws preclude the transfer by one party to another of environmental operating permits issued in the name of the first party.
- *Foreign (non-US) ownership of US assets.* Federal law prohibits or requires reporting of ownership of certain industrial or commercial assets by non-US citizens or entities, including US flag–registered vessels and aircraft, telecommunications facilities, newspapers, nuclear power plants, and certain defense industries. (See Chapter 12, on international transactions.)
- *US ownership of foreign assets.* Many non-US governments closely regulate the ownership by noncitizens of domestic corporations or assets and reserve the right to refuse transfer of any such property to a noncitizen.
- *European Commission approval of non-EU transactions.* Any merger affecting the economy of Europe may be subject to approval by the European Union (EU) even if it involves non-EC companies.
- *Industry concerns.* The transfer of title to certain types of industrial or commercial assets may be subject to approval by one or more regulating agencies, as in the following US examples:

—Airlines (the Department of Transportation)
—Banks and other financial services institutions have five main regulators[57] (Office of the Comptroller of the Currency, which now includes an office of thrift supervision; the Federal Reserve Board;[58] the Federal Deposit Insurance Corporation [FDIC]; the National Credit Union Administration; and various state agencies)
—Insurance companies (state regulatory agencies)
—Public utilities (the Federal Energy Regulatory Commission, the Nuclear Regulatory Commission, and state public utilities commissions)
—Shipping (Federal Maritime Commission)
—Telecommunications facilities (Federal Communications Commission [FCC])

Some transactions require approval from multiple authorities. A good example is the merger of Bayer and Monsanto, which was reviewed by the European Commission, in cooperation with the US Department of Justice as well as authorities in Australia, Brazil, Canada, China, India, and South African authorities.[59]

How can the parties assess the significance of regulatory barriers at the planning stage of an acquisition?

Interested parties should determine early on how likely it is that they will obtain the necessary consents, how long this will take, and how difficult and expensive it will be. When the procedures and the criteria for obtaining consents are well defined, this regulatory audit can be performed relatively quickly and reliably. Avoid flexible or discretionary procedures and criteria for approvals, as these can extend the time and increase the uncertainty of obtaining approvals in a timely fashion.

Remain informed about major regulatory and deregulatory developments in your industry and in target industries of interest to you as a potential acquirer. Regulatory and deregulatory developments can change the business climate dramatically.

In general, and especially where third-party financing is involved, it may be not only imprudent but impossible to proceed with the affected part of the transaction prior to obtaining the necessary approval. Therefore, potential buyers and sellers should be sure at the initial planning stages to provide adequate time and resources for the regulatory compliance effort.

What general antitrust considerations should acquisition planners consider when contemplating an acquisition?

Antitrust practitioners divide corporate acquisitions into three types:

- *Vertical acquisitions*—acquisition of suppliers or customers, which may foreclose markets to competitors
- *Horizontal acquisitions*—between competitors, which may give monopoly power or cause overconcentration
- *Other acquisitions*—or example, between firms in different industries, which might remove potential competition or discourage competition by others because of the financial or marketing strength of the resulting firm

Section 7 of the Clayton Act prohibits a corporation from acquiring stock or assets of another corporation if the acquisition might "substantially lessen competition or tend to create a monopoly" in any line of commerce in any section of the country. A violation of Section 7 may give rise to a court-ordered injunction against the acquisition, an order compelling divestiture of the property or other interests, or other remedies. Section 7 is enforced by the Antitrust Division of the DOJ and FTC. Thresholds are set annually.

Another federal law that can affect mergers today is the Interlocking Directorate Act passed nearly three decades ago (1990). This law amended Section 8 of the Clayton Act to state that "no person shall, at any time, serve as a director or officer in any two corporations (other than banks, banking associations, and trust companies) that are: A) engaged in whole or in part in commerce; and B) by virtue of their business and location of operation competitors." The provision does not apply if both companies are small (with capital and surplus and undivided profits under a threshold amount subject to annual adjustments, currently at $22.761 million) or if the competitive sales involved are low (if either one has competitive sales of less than $2.2761 million).

In conjunction with the federal laws, there are state laws that can restrict mergers. Under federal law—the McCarran-Ferguson Act, 15 U.S.C. 1011(f)—states are given broad authority to regulate mergers involving insurance companies. States have similar authority in other areas in which the states have special regulatory jurisdiction, such as the alcoholic beverages industry.

Mergers of companies with foreign operations or subsidiaries sometimes require review and approval by foreign governments. In addition, some foreign countries (most notably, Canada) have their own premerger notification programs that may have to be complied with.

How does the government gather information about proposed mergers and acquisitions?

The Hart-Scott-Rodino Antitrust Improvements Act of 1976 (the HSR Act) requires the parties to a proposed acquisition transaction to furnish certain information about themselves and the deal to the FTC and the DOJ before the merger is allowed to go forward. The information supplied is used by these governmental agencies to determine whether the proposed transaction would have any anticompetitive effects after completion. If so, in general, they must be cured prior to closing. A mandatory waiting period follows the agencies' receipt of the HSR filings.

What mergers or acquisitions require premerger notification under the HSR Act?

Generally, all mergers and acquisitions that meet certain criteria must be reported under the HSR Act and the related premerger notification rules.[60] See Exhibit 2-14. The "persons" involved include not only constituent corporations, but also any other corporation that is under common control. *Control,* for purposes of the HSR Act, is defined as ownership of 50

Exhibit 2-14 Premerger Notification Thresholds Under Hart-Scott-Rodino

HSR THRESHOLD ADJUSTMENTS AND REPORTABILITY FOR 2019

Based on the website* and press release† from the Premerger Notification Office Staff, Bureau of Competition | Feb 15, 2019

When Congress passed the Hart-Scott-Rodino Antitrust Improvements Act of 1976, it created minimum dollar thresholds to limit the burden of premerger reporting. In 2000, it amended the HSR statute to require the annual adjustment of these thresholds based on the change in gross national product. As a result, reportability under the Act changes from year to year as the statutory thresholds adjust. . . . The Commission recently announced the new HSR thresholds, which will become . . . effective on February 28, 2018.

Rule 1: The correct threshold for determining reportability is the one in effect at the time of closing.

The most significant threshold in determining reportability is the minimum size of transaction threshold. This is often referred to as the "$50 million (as adjusted)" threshold because it started at $50 million and is now adjusted annually. For 2019, that threshold will be **$90 million.** To determine reportability for a deal that will close around the time that the new threshold is effective, look to what the threshold will be *at the time of closing. . . .*

Rule 2: The filing fee is determined by the value of the transaction at the time of filing.

If you determine that a transaction is reportable, the filing fee should be based on the filing fee threshold that is in effect *at the time of filing.* Note that the filing fees themselves do not change, only the thresholds for calculating the correct fee. Here are the new filing fee thresholds, effective February 28, 2018.

Fee	**Size of Transaction**
$45,000	valued in excess of $90 million but less than $180 million
$125,000	valued at $180 million or greater but less than $899.8 million; or
$280,000	valued at $899.8 million or greater

Rule 3: Notification thresholds for subsequent purchases adjust yearly, too.

The HSR Rules contain additional notification thresholds that relieve parties of the burden of making another filing every time additional voting shares of the same person are acquired. So, when HSR notification is filed, the acquiring person has one year from the end of the waiting period to cross the threshold stated in its HSR filing. Under Section 802.21, you must cross the threshold stated in the filing within one year after the end or termination of the waiting period, or you will have to file a new HSR notification in order to cross that threshold. Section 802.21 also specifies that once the filed-for waiting period ends or terminates, you can acquire up to the next threshold over the next five years without filing again.

Here's how this works. If you filed on February 1, 2019, for a $90 million voting securities acquisition that would close sometime in April 2019, you should file to cross the $90 million threshold because that's the $50 million (as adjusted) threshold in effect at the time of closing (See Rule 1). You then have one year from the end of the waiting period to cross the $90 million threshold, even though the $50 million (as adjusted) threshold may be higher next February when the thresholds adjust again.

The next relevant threshold is the "$100 million (as adjusted)" threshold (so called because it started as $100 million and is now adjusted annually). So, after the end of the waiting period for the filing to cross the $90 million threshold, you then have five years to acquire up to the next notification threshold—in this case, the $100 million (as adjusted) threshold—without an additional HSR filing. In each subsequent year of the five-year period under Section 802.21, that threshold will adjust, and you always look to the revised threshold in effect at the time. The revised $100 million (as adjusted) threshold for 2019 is $180 million, but in 2020, it will likely be higher, and you would look to the higher 2020 figure for evaluating additional acquisitions at that time.

* Due to a government shutdown in early 2019 the website had not updated at the time of publication.

† https://www.ftc.gov/news-events/press-releases/2019/02/ftc-announces-annual-update-size-transaction-thresholds-premerger

Source: Federal Trade Commission, February 15, 2019.

percent or more of a company's voting securities or having the contractual power to designate a majority of a company's board of directors. Special control rules apply to partnerships and other unincorporated entities.

What information is required in the HSR premerger notification form?

The form requires a description of the parties and the proposed merger or acquisition, certain current financial information about the parties, and a breakdown of revenues of the parties according to industry codes (North American Industry Classification System).[61] This breakdown of revenues is used by the FTC and the DOJ to determine whether the proposed combination of the businesses would result in anticompetitive effects. The information filed is exempt from disclosure under the Freedom of Information Act, and no such information may be made public except pursuant to administrative or judicial proceedings.

After the premerger notification form has been filed, how long must the parties wait before the merger or acquisition can be consummated?

Where the acquisition is being made by a cash tender offer, the parties must wait 15 days before the purchaser may accept shares for payment. In all other cases, the parties must wait 30 days before the transaction can be completed. If the acquisition raises antitrust concerns, the government may extend the waiting period by requesting additional information from the parties. In that case, the waiting period is extended for 30 days (15 days in the case of a cash tender offer) past the time when the additional information is provided.

The parties may request early termination of the waiting period. Where the acquisition raises no antitrust concerns, the government may grant the request at its discretion.

Are certain mergers and acquisitions exempt from the HSR Act?

Yes. Acquisitions made through newly formed corporate acquisition vehicles are frequently exempt from the reporting requirements of the HSR Act because the vehicle does not meet the size-of-person test; that is, it does not have the threshold amount in gross assets or sales. This is true, however, only where no other person having that amount in gross assets or annual sales owns 50 percent or more of the voting stock of the vehicle or has the contractual power to designate a majority of the vehicle's directors. If the vehicle is not controlled by another person, it will be the only company matched against the threshold size-of-person test. If another company or person does control the vehicle, through either a 50 percent stock ownership or a contractual power to appoint a majority of its directors, that controlling person will be matched against this test. Special rules apply in determining control of partnerships and other unincorporated acquisition vehicles.

Special rules are also used to determine the size of a newly formed corporation, and care must be taken to avoid making contractual commitments for additional capital contributions or for guarantees of the new corporation's obligations until after the formation has been completed.

The assets of a newly formed acquisition vehicle that is not controlled by another person do not include the funds contributed to the vehicle or borrowed by the vehicle at the closing to complete the acquisition.

The HSR Act and FTC rules also provide numerous exemptions for special situations.

How can we tell whether a particular horizontal merger is likely to be challenged by the federal government?

Current administration policy is set forth in the revised Horizontal Merger Guidelines. These guidelines are reprinted at the end of this chapter in Appendix 2C.

As in previous guidelines, horizontal mergers are assessed according to a sliding scale of permissiveness. Thus, the less concentrated the industry, the larger is the permissible merger. The index used to measure concentration, the Herfindahl-Hirschman Index (referred to as the HHI), sums the squares of the individual companies' market shares to measure both postmerger share and the growth in market share resulting from the transaction. Current (2017) levels are:

- Unconcentrated Markets: HHI below 1500
- Moderately Concentrated Markets: HHI between 1500 and 2500
- Highly Concentrated Markets: HHI above 2500[62]

So the more concentrated a market is, the more likely the transaction will be challenged. A score is only one factor to be considered when assessing market concentration.

What about challenges to vertical mergers?

US antitrust regulators have not published guidelines for verticals (called "nonhorizontals") since 1984, and those old guidelines are considered no longer valid.[63] But a recent speech by the FTC official responsible for merger review notes three areas of concern:

- A vertical merger may reduce the likelihood of beneficial entry. Regulators look at whether there is some aspect of the merging firms, such as assets, know-how, or reputation, indicating that having a presence in another vertically related market or in another part of the distribution chain may make it more likely or easier for the merging firms to enter each other's markets, as compared to de novo entry by another firm.
- A vertical merger may result in anticompetitive foreclosure. There can be supplier (called "input") foreclosure. The upstream firm (supplier) may refuse to supply downstream rivals (other customers) or will provide supply only on disadvantageous terms that favor its own integrated downstream business unit. Also, there can be customer foreclosure, which is the inverse of input foreclosure: the downstream firm refuses to buy from competitors of the upstream supplier.
- A vertical merger may lead to anticompetitive behavior due to information sharing about a rival. The integrated firm gains access that it did not previously have to competitively sensitive business information of an upstream or downstream rival, producing various anticompetitive effects.[64]

What might be an example of a merger that would create a highly concentrated industry?

An example would be if an industry of five firms having market shares of 30 percent, 25 percent, 20 percent, 15 percent, and 10 percent, respectively, has an HHI score of $30^2 + 25^2 + 20^2 + 15^2 + 10^2$, or 2,250. If the third and fifth firms merge, the resulting score is $30^2 + 25^2 + 30^2 + 15^2$, or 2,650, and the increase in the score would be 400.

Is the HHI analysis conducted on the acquirer's industry only?

No. An HHI analysis must be performed for each distinct relevant market in which both of the merging companies operate.

What factors would the DOJ and FTC consider beyond the HHI?

The guidelines express an intent to scrutinize mergers that can in some circumstances confer market power on a single firm, even if that firm does not have a sizable market share. If, for example, the two merging firms had previously sold products that were perceived by a substantial number of customers to be close substitutes for one another, the merged firms could raise prices on one product line and risk only some diversion of sales to its other product line.

Whatever the level of concentration, regulators will challenge any merger that is likely to create or enhance one-firm domination of a market. Thus, a leading firm that accounts for 35 percent of the market and that is twice the size of its next largest competitor will normally not be allowed to acquire any firm accounting for even 1 percent of that market.

Types of evidence the antitrust agencies consider include:

- Actual effects observed in consummated mergers
- Direct comparisons based on experience
- Market shares and concentration in a relevant market
- Substantial head-to-head competition
- Disruptive role of a merging party[65]

In addition, analysis of horizontal mergers no longer focuses on the market concentration problem usually associated with monopolies.

It considers instead other real-market factors, including the following:

- Ease of entry into the market (the easier it is for new firms to enter the market, the less the likelihood of challenge)

- The availability of out-of-market substitutes (the more readily available, the less prospect there is of collusion)
- The degree to which the merging firms confront each other within the relevant market (if they occupy separate sectors of the market, the merger is less a cause of concern than if they are head-to-head in the same corner)
- The level of product homogeneity (the more homogeneous the product, the easier it is to collude)
- The pace of technological change (the slower the rate of change, the more likely is collusion)
- The importance of nonprice terms (the more important they are, the harder it is to collude)
- The degree to which firms have access to information concerning their competitors' transactions (the more information available, the greater is the likelihood of collusion)
- The size and frequency of orders (the smaller and more frequent, the greater is the likelihood of collusion)
- Whether the industry is characterized either by a history of collusion or by patterns of pricing conduct that make collusion more likely (if it is, the likelihood of a challenge increases)
- Historical evidence of noncompetitive performance (challenge is more likely)

What about foreign competition?

Market shares are assigned for foreign competitors in the same way they are assigned to domestic competitors. These shares may have to be calculated over a longer period of time to account for exchange rate fluctuations. They may also have to be adjusted to account for import quotas. Finally, market shares may have to be combined if foreign firms appear to be acting in a coordinated or collusive way.

If the FTC and the DOJ either do not investigate a reportable transaction or allow it to proceed after investigation, can the transaction still be challenged afterward?

Technically, the government is not prevented from challenging any merger or acquisition at any time, but challenges are almost unheard of where HSR filings have been made and the waiting period has been allowed to expire or has been terminated. On the other hand, transactions may be challenged in state court, or by private litigants.

A good example of the regulatory review process is Tesoro's acquisition of BP's Southern California business, which began in 2012 and concluded in 2013.[66] When Tesoro (now Andeavor) announced on August 13, 2012, its acquisition of BP's West Coast business, the conventional wisdom was that the FTC would block the transaction. Petroleum refining and retail operations are a politically sensitive sector, and Herfindahl Index calculations suggested market concentration. The FTC together with the California Attorney General's office conducted a nine-month joint investigation, and the waiting period was extended while this was under way. The parties closed the transaction 10 days after the FTC and the AG concluded their investigations. This is described in more detail in Appendix 2D.

CONCLUDING COMMENTS

Strategy is only the beginning of the merger process—only one of many stages to come. Up ahead are structuring, due diligence, negotiating, closing, and integration—not to mention all the perfecting that must be done in areas like pensions, labor, and compensation. But although strategy might take up only 20 percent of the M&A process, it requires fully 80 percent of the energy.

In fact, this phase is a perfect example of the 80/20 law coined by economist Vilfredo Pareto. Buyers, it is worth putting 80 percent of your effort into this important phase. So do your strategic planning. Set up your in-house search program. Hire your brokers, finders, and advisors. And last but not least, study the regulatory factors. All this preparation will pay off down the road.

APPENDIX 2A

Types of Organizational Structure

FUNCTIONAL ORGANIZATION

Widget Company, Inc.

Accounting function
Distribution function
Engineering function
Manufacturing function
Marketing function
Purchasing function
Sales function
- North
- South
- East
- West

PRODUCT/SERVICE ORGANIZATION

Machine Tools Company, Inc.

Product 1

Accounting function
Distribution function
Engineering function

Manufacturing function
Marketing function
Purchasing function
Sales function
    North
    South
    East
    West

Product 2
Accounting function
Distribution function
Engineering function
Manufacturing function
Marketing function
Purchasing function
Sales function
    North
    South
    East
    West

Product 3
Accounting function
Distribution function
Engineering function
Manufacturing function
Marketing function
Purchasing function
Sales function
    North
    South
    East
    West

DIVISIONAL ORGANIZATION

Modern Industries, Inc.
Division 1

Product 1
Accounting function
Distribution function
Engineering function
Manufacturing function
Marketing function
Purchasing function
Sales function
- North
- South
- East
- West

Product 2
Accounting function
Distribution function
Engineering function
Manufacturing function
Marketing function
Purchasing function
Sales function
- North
- South
- East
- West

Division 2

Product 3
Accounting function
Distribution function

Engineering function
Manufacturing function
Marketing function
Purchasing function
Sales function
    North
    South
    East
    West

Product 4
Accounting function
Distribution function
Engineering function
Manufacturing function
Marketing function
Purchasing function
Sales function
    North
    South
    East
    West

Note: These data points can also be organized as block matrixes (two dimensions—products and functions, or products and territories) or cube matrixes (three dimensions—products, functions, and territories).

APPENDIX 2B

Checklist of Assets

Physical Assets*

Equipment (including computer hardware and software)

- Office equipment
- Plant equipment

Inventory

- Finished
- Work-in-process

Land

Materials

Mines

- Production, reserves, locations, development
- Maps

---

* Items with an asterisk appear on the balance sheet. Items without an asterisk do not appear on the balance sheet, or any other traditional financial statement. However, they are usually discussed in the Management Discussion and Analysis section of the 10-K report, along with balance sheet items, especially if they are at risk. Note: This entire list can be used as column D of a spreadsheet as shown in Appendix 2-X. with these column headings: (Col. A) Phase 1: Strategy (subphases are planning, search, valuation, and selection); (Col. B) Phase 2: Transaction (subphases are financing, due diligence, tax structuring, negotiation, and closing); (Col. C) Phase 3: Integration (subphases are integration planning, integration communication, and integration implementation); (Col. D, Assets or "Capitals" to Track (following the framework of Integrated Reporting or "<IR>" (see integrated reporting.org); these may be organized as financial capital, manufacturing capital, human capital, social and relationship capital, intellectual capital, and natural capital.

Real estate
- Branch buildings
- Factory buildings
- Construction in progress

Real estate—Other

Financial Assets

From Balance Sheet

Financial Assets
- Cash
- Investment securities
- Accounts receivable
- Prepaid income taxes
- Other prepaid expenses
- Deferred charges
- Other financial assets
  - Goodwill
  - Long-term receivables
  - Investments in affiliates
  - Goodwill from previous acquisitions
- (*For Banks,* Debt Owed to Bank via Outstanding Loans)

Financial Liabilities and Equity
- Financial Liabilities
  - Accounts payable
  - Debt
- (*For Banks,* Cash Deposits Held by Bank and Owed by Bank to Customer)

Financial Equity
- Common stock outstanding
- Preferred stock outstanding
- Retained earnings

From Income Statement
- Gross Revenues
- Growth trend

Net Revenues
- Growth trend

Off Balance-Sheet Financing (MD&A)

Intellectual Assets

Contracts (if favorable—otherwise, a liability)
- Employment agreements
- Franchise agreements
- Noncompete agreements

Culture
- Reporting relationships (real versus formal)
- Policies and procedures
- [Any other cultural factor not covered elsewhere in this taxonomy]

Marketing Intangibles
- Company name recognition
- Brand name recognition
- Service mark (right to use company signage)
- Trademark (right to use company name)

Production Intangibles
- Copyrights
- Favorable supplier contracts
- Patents
- Product design
- Product quality
- Production costs
- Production speed
- Productions standards
- Software
- Trade secrets

Human Assets (People)

Knowledge, experience, competencies, and leadership and/or teamwork ability of each of the following individuals:

Directors (including chairperson if separate)
CEO/COO/president
Other senior managers
Sales force
Other employees
(See also Human Resources Function under Organizational Assets)

Organizational Assets (Activities)

Quality of the "infrastructure" described as follows:

Contracts and commitments
Relating to all human capital and also to eternal relations
(If the contract is unfavorable and/or broken, it can turn from an asset into a liability.)

Primary Functions

Management Systems
Processes for design, production, and supply
Channels for distribution
Inbound logistics
Receiving
Storing
Material handling
Warehousing
Inventory control
Outbound logistics
Distribution

Manufacturing Function

R&D Function
Laboratory notebooks
Invention disclosure forms

Sales Function
- Established territories

Support Functions
- Accounting Function
  - Bookkeeping
  - Treasury
  - Internal auditing
- Communications/Marketing Functions
  - Marketing
  - Public Relations
- Corporate Administrative Function
  - Headquarters administration
- Facilities Function
  - Facilities management
- Finance Function
  - Financing (issuing equity, borrowing debt)
  - Management of funds (opening/closing deposits; lockbox)
- Human Resources Function
- Rewarding and "incentivizing" performance
  - Base pay
  - Bonus pay
  - Pensions
  - Benefits
  - Special pay arrangements
  - Recognition programs (awards and honors)
- Retention (Retaining key qualities: relevant knowledge, experience, competencies)
- Recruitment (Seeking relevant knowledge, experience, competencies)
- Termination/Retirement
- Performance management
- Career development
- Succession planning
- Training

IT Function

Hardware, software, and systems for internal communications

Email

Telephones (LAN, WAN, routers, switches)

Legal Function

Compliance programs, including internal code of conduct

Internal Financial Controls[67]

Control Environment Risk Assessment

Control Activities

Information and Communication re finances

Monitoring Activities

Mission, Vision, and Strategy

Mission statement

Vision statement

Strategic plan document

External Relationship Assets

(If any of these has a corresponding function, see Organizational Assets—Functions)

Customer relations

Reputation of brands

Reputation of service

Major customers (required under SAS131)

Major geographic areas (SAS131)

Shareholder relations

Reputation for increasing market share/paying dividends

Stability of holdings by shareholders

Bondholder relations

Reputation for repaying debt instruments

Bond rating

Lender relations

Rate of interest charged by lenders

Credit rating

Supplier relations

Favorable contracts

Community relations

Community programs

Public relations

Reputation of company name re public issues—see also Company name recognition under Intellectual Property

Lobbying (if any)—See also Legal under Support Functions

History of fulfilling contracts and commitments

APPENDIX 2C

Horizontal Merger Guidelines[68]

Department of Justice
Federal Trade Commission
August 19, 2010

Overview (Excerpts)

These Guidelines outline the principal analytical techniques, practices, and the enforcement policy of the Department of Justice and the Federal Trade Commission (the "Agencies") with respect to mergers and acquisitions involving actual or potential competitors ("horizontal mergers") under the federal antitrust laws. . . .

The Agencies seek to identify and challenge competitively harmful mergers while avoiding unnecessary interference with mergers that are either competitively beneficial or neutral. Most merger analysis is necessarily predictive, requiring an assessment of what will likely happen if a merger proceeds as compared to what will likely happen if it does not. Given this inherent need for prediction, these Guidelines reflect the congressional intent that merger enforcement should interdict competitive problems in their incipiency and that certainty about anticompetitive effect is seldom possible and not required for a merger to be illegal.

These Guidelines describe the principal analytical techniques and the main types of evidence on which the Agencies usually rely to predict whether a horizontal merger may substantially lessen competition. They are not intended to describe how the Agencies analyze cases other than horizontal mergers. These Guidelines are intended to assist the business community and antitrust practitioners by increasing the transparency of the analytical process underlying the Agencies' enforcement decisions. They may also assist the courts in developing an appropriate framework for interpreting and applying the antitrust laws in the horizontal merger context. . . .

The unifying theme of these Guidelines is that mergers should not be permitted to create, enhance, or entrench market power or to facilitate its exercise. For simplicity of exposition, these Guidelines generally refer to all of these effects as enhancing market power. A merger enhances market power if it is likely to encourage one or more firms to raise price, reduce output, diminish innovation, or otherwise harm customers as a result of diminished competitive constraints or incentives. In evaluating how a merger will likely change a firm's behavior, the Agencies focus primarily on how the merger affects conduct that would be most profitable for the firm.

A merger can enhance market power simply by eliminating competition between the merging parties. This effect can arise even if the merger causes no changes in the way other firms behave. Adverse competitive effects arising in this manner are referred to as "unilateral effects." A merger also can enhance market power by increasing the risk of coordinated, accommodating, or interdependent behavior among rivals. Adverse competitive effects arising in this manner are referred to as "coordinated effects." In any given case, either or both types of effects may be present, and the distinction between them may be blurred.

These Guidelines principally describe how the Agencies analyze mergers between rival suppliers that may enhance their market power as sellers. Enhancement of market power by sellers often elevates the prices charged to customers. For simplicity of exposition, these Guidelines generally discuss the analysis in terms of such price effects. Enhanced market power can also be manifested in non-price terms and conditions that adversely affect customers, including reduced product quality, reduced product variety, reduced service, or diminished innovation. Such non-price effects may coexist with price effects, or can arise in their absence.

When the Agencies investigate whether a merger may lead to a substantial lessening of non-price competition, they employ an approach analogous to that used to evaluate price competition. Enhanced market power may also make it more likely that the merged entity can profitably and effectively engage in exclusionary conduct. Regardless of how enhanced market power likely would be manifested, the Agencies normally evaluate mergers based on their impact on customers. The Agencies examine effects on either or both of the direct customers and the final consumers. The Agencies presume, absent convincing evidence to the contrary, that adverse effects on direct customers also cause adverse effects on final consumers.

APPENDIX 2D

Tesoro Strikes Gold in California[69]

"Tesoro, the West Coast oil refiner, may have pulled off the acquisition of the year when it reached a deal last month to purchase a large California refinery from BP for $1.175 billion. By Tesoro's calculations, it paid virtually nothing for the refinery—in Carson, south of Los Angeles—when considering other assets included in the deal, such as pipelines, other energy infrastructure, gas stations, and the ARCO brand. The refinery could be worth $1.5 billion or more, . . ."[70]

When Tesoro announced on August 13, 2012, its acquisition of BP's West Coast business, the conventional wisdom was that the FTC would block the transaction. Petroleum refining and retail operations are a politically sensitive sector, and all six West Coast senators (California, Oregon, and Washington) frequently write to the FTC to express concerns.[71] The proposed acquisition would add a fourth refinery to Tesoro's West Coast system (which already included Anacortes, Washington, Martinez, California, and Wilmington, California), and on previous occasions in the late 1990s and early 2000s, the Commission had challenged acquisitions in California.[72]

The Herfindahl Index—if calculated based upon refinery capacity in southern California—was well into the Moderately Concentrated band and approaching Highly Concentrated. And the change in the HHI postcombination would signal an increase of more than 400. The FTC's Horizontal Merger Guidelines provide perspective:[73]

- *Moderately Concentrated Markets:* Mergers resulting in moderately concentrated markets that involve an increase in the HHI of more than 100 points potentially raise significant competitive concerns and often warrant scrutiny.
- *Highly Concentrated Markets:* Mergers resulting in highly concentrated markets that involve an increase in the HHI of between 100 points and 200 points potentially raise significant competitive concerns and often warrant scrutiny. Mergers resulting in highly concentrated markets that involve an increase in the HHI of more than 200 points will be presumed to be likely to enhance market power.

And there were other headwinds: Tesoro proposed to combine two immediately adjacent facilities (the Tesoro refinery at Wilmington, California, and the BP refinery at Carson, California). The California Attorney General's office stated[74] that "Acquisitions such as this one often lead to significant layoffs, which are then touted as "synergies" by the companies. Our office was concerned that this acquisition might lead to similar reductions in jobs." And at the same time as Tesoro's announcement, other companies' West Coast refinery outages had caused significant gasoline price spikes which raised the political profile—spurring further Senate demands of the FTC (2, op. cit.): "Since August 6th, gasoline prices have risen 30 cents per gallon, reaching $4.21. As a result, California has the highest gas prices in the continental United States. The increase is more than double the increase in the national average over the same period." Local consumer watchdog groups demanded the Tesoro transaction be blocked.[75]

In this climate, Tesoro undertook a multiple-track approach to address stakeholder concerns including:[76]

- Offering to sell its existing Wilmington refinery if necessary to satisfy competition concerns

- Presenting evidence that the integration would provide cost reduction efficiencies that were primarily in processing and logistics operations, not headcount
- Presenting evidence that the integration would provide significant environmental benefits including specifically quantified reductions in stationary source air emissions
- Presenting evidence that the integration would increase clean product yields

The joint investigation by the FTC and the California Attorney General's office took nine months. On May 20, 2013, the FTC closed its investigation[77] after determining that no further action was required.

The FTC stated that its investigation ". . . left the Commission without a reason to believe this transaction is likely to substantially lessen competition" and specifically citing ". . . evidence that the combination of Tesoro's southern California refinery and the adjacent BP refinery is likely to reduce the cost of manufacturing CARB gasoline."

The California Attorney General's office specifically referred to the benefits that Tesoro had identified with respect to environmental improvement and job security, concluding "At the outset of the investigation, we had significant concerns about the potential effect of the acquisition on competition. Over the course of the investigation the parties and various third parties combined to produce millions of pages of documents and voluminous amounts of data.

We reviewed these documents and data, subpoenaed the parties and numerous third parties for testimony, and secured a leading economist in the field of oil and gas to conduct various analyses of the markets at issue. After a thorough investigation and review of the evidence, many of our initial market competition concerns were addressed, and our office decided that our remaining consumer, environmental, and job security issues were appropriately addressed . . ."

While the specifics of these investigations are not a matter of public record[78] it is clear that the professional approach by staff at both the FTC and AG offices, and the substantial efforts made by Tesoro to provide documents, data, and testimony to address stakeholder concerns, were sufficient to accomplish what the conventional wisdom said could not be accomplished. The stock analysts had hedged their bets pending the regulatory review, with the result that Tesoro's share price—which had jumped sharply on the initial announcement—jumped again upon the news of regulatory clearance.

NOTES

1. The Oxford English Dictionary defines strategy as "a plan of action designed to achieve a long-term or overall aim." Corporate strategies are typically both "long-term" and "overall." https://en.oxforddictionaries.com/definition/strategy.
2. For more on divestitures see Chapter 9, which covers divestitures as an aspect of integration.
3. Jeff Golman of Forbes notes that in recent times, corporate or strategic buyers have dominated the M&A market. https://www.forbes.com/sites/jeffgolman/2017/09/20/corporate-buyers-account-for-an-all-time-high-in-ma-deal-activity/#79c2d3582138.
4. In some cases, the profit may be derived through dividends. In others, it may be gained through resale in whole or in parts to another buyer or buyers, or to the public in a stock offering. The financial acquirer is not alone in seeking profit, of course. From a financial perspective, one could say that strategic planning revolves around the reallocation and redeployment of cash flows from lower-yielding to higher-yielding investments. In most cases, the financial buyer will want to minimize the interrelations of the companies it owns so that each can be refinanced or disposed of without affecting the others.

5. Jeff Golman, "Corporate Buyers Account for an All-Time High in M&A Deal Activity," *Forbes,* September 20, 2017, https://www.forbes.com/sites/jeffgolman/2017/09/20/corporate-buyers-account-for-an-all-time-high-in-ma-deal-activity/#6ecdb2912138.

6. A leading association for middle market advisors is the Alliance of M&A Advisors, http://www.amaaonline.com/join-us/. Michael Nall, founder and managing partner, provided advice on brokers and finders for this chapter.

7. Michael Porter, *Competitive Strategy: Techniques for Analyzing Industries and Competitors* (New York: Free Press, 1998). This second edition of Porter's classic is still in print after 20 years.

8. Mohamad Laid Ouakouak, "Does a Strategic Planning Process That Combines Rational and Adaptive Characteristics Pay Off ? Evidence from European Firms," *Australian Journal of Management,* http://journals.sagepub.com/doi/pdf/10.1177/0312896217721589.

9. Porter, *Competitive Strategy,* p. 50.

10. Resource redeployment is one of 12 aspects of strategic planning identified by Bain and Company in "Strategic Planning," April 2, 2018, http://www.bain.com/publications/articles/management-tools-strategic-planning.aspx.

11. Dag Øivind Madsen, "SWOT Analysis: A Management Fashion Perspective," Buskerud and Vestfold University College, Norway, 2105 white paper available through ResearchGate.net, https://www.researchgate.net/profile/Dag_Madsen/publication/299278178_SWOT_Analysis_A_Management_Fashion_Perspective/links/56f05fee08ae70bdd6c94a74/SWOT-Analysis-A-Management-Fashion-Perspective.pdf.

12. Willard T. Carlton, Robert S. Harris, and John F. Stewart, *An Empirical Study of Merger Motives,* 1980, http://www.worldcat.org/title/empirical-study-of-merger-motives/oclc/5821740. Completed under an interagency agreement with the Federal Trade Commission, this is one of the earliest studies ever done on why companies merge.

13. The author gratefully acknowledges the late J. Fred Weston, Cordner Professor of Money and Financial Markets, University of California-Los Angeles, as the source of this list.
14. This is where the Q ratio often comes in. The Q ratio is the market value of shares divided by the replacement costs of the assets represented by the shares. Of all motives, this may be the most fundamental.
15. For example, to avoid the penalty of depreciation on lower historical costs during a period of inflation, a company might make an acquisition in order to achieve a stepped-up basis for depreciable assets.
16. Alex Lielacher, "Is the Blockchain M&A Wave Starting?," Bravenewcoin.com, August 3, 2018, https://bravenewcoin.com/news/is-the-blockchain-m-and-a-wave-starting/.
17. This discussion of small-cap M&A risk was contributed by Adam J. Epstein, Third Creek Advisors, LLC, based on his blog post, "A Dinner Conversation About the Realities of Small Cap M&A," May 1, 2018, https://www.linkedin.com/pulse/dinner-conversation-realities-small-cap-ma-adam-j-epstein/.
18. The list of assets shown in Exhibit 2-3 were developed by Alexandra Lajoux for publication in *The Art of M&A Integration,* 2nd ed. (New York: McGraw-Hill, 2006). The list of risks has a long history, beginning with a list from Stanley Foster Reed based on wheel-and-fit sessions with hundreds of companies over a period of 30 years. Significantly, they are almost identical to the categories in the Enhanced Business Reporting Framework from the Enhanced Business Reporting Consortium launched in 2005 by the American Institute of Certified Public Accountants. The main categories are *competition, customers, technological change, shareholder relations, capital availability, legal, political,* and *regulatory.*
19. The researchers worked from a "dataset comprising a sample of 472 M&A deals and 886 associated corporate voluntary communications over a five-year period." BasakYakis, et al., "Opening M&A Strategy to Investors: Predictors and Outcomes

of Transparency during Organisational Transition," Strategic Planning, June 2017, http://www.sciencedirect.com/science/article/pii/S0024630116300607.

20. https://www.tesla.com/about.
21. *Report of the NACD Blue Ribbon Commission on Strategy Development* (Washington, DC: NACD, 2014), p. 9. This report was a sequel to *The Role of the Board in Corporate Strategy* (Washington, D.C.: National Association of Corporate Directors, 2006). The discussion here includes timeless insights from both reports.
22. Federal Register, p. 37220, https://www.gpo.gov/fdsys/pkg/FR-2017-08-09/pdf/2017-16735.pdf.
23. The following discussion of M&A strategies draws from the strategy title in The Art of M&A series: Kenneth Smith and Alexandra Reed Lajoux, *The Art of M&A Strategy: A Guide to Building Your Company's Future Through Mergers, Acquisitions, and Divestitures* (New York: McGraw-Hill Education, 2012).
24. The use of "portfolio" in this chapter refers to building a company by buying other companies. It is substantially different from building an investment portfolio by buying stock. Companies, unlike stock, are not liquid or fungible.
25. The term *corporate center* is used by McKinsey. See Stephen Hall, Bill Huyett, and Tim Koller, "The Power of an Independent Corporate Center," *McKinsey Quarterly,* March 2012, https://www.mckinsey.com/business-functions/strategy-and-corporate-finance/our-insights/the-power-of-an-independent-corporate-center.
26. John C. Naman and Bruce McKern, "The Role of the Corporate Center in Global Network Corporations," in *Managing the Global Network Corporation* (New York: Routledge, 2003).
27. For a deeper look, see Aswath Damodaran, "Real Options, Acquisition Valuation and Value Enhancement," January 2012 white paper, http://people.stern.nyu.edu/adamodar/pdfiles

/eqnotes/packet3a.pdf. For books on the subject, see Richard Shockley, *An Applied Course in Real Options* (Thomson South-Western Finance, 2006); Jonathan Mun, *Options Analysis: Tools and Techniques for Valuing Strategic Investment and Decisions,* 2nd ed. (New York: Wiley, 2005); and Thomas Copeland and Vladimir Antikarov, *Real Options: A Practitioner's Guide* (Texere, 2001). All are available on standard bookseller websites.

28. For a checklist, see the list titled "Key Tests for Real Options," in Damodaran, "Real Options," 2012, p. 23.
29. "M&A Forecast: Craft Breweries Headed for Rapid Pace of Rollups," *Food Engineering,* January 29, 2017, https://www.foodengineeringmag.com/articles/96461-ma-forecast-craft-breweries-headed-for-rapid-pace-of-rollups.
30. C. Burkehart, "2016: Another Active Year for Industrial Distribution M&A," January 16, 2017, https://www.inddist.com/article/2017/01/2016-another-active-year-industrial-distribution-m.
31. "Prescriptions for a Successful Healthcare Rollup," *FTI Journal,* May 2017, http://www.fticonsulting.com/insights/fti-journal/prescription-for-a-successful-healthcare-rollup.
32. "The Race for AI: Google, Intel, Apple in a Rush to Grab Artificial Intelligence Startups," February 27, 2018, see https://www.cbinsights.com/research/top-acquirers-ai-startups-ma-timeline/.
33. The US federal antitrust authorities bring an average of 39 merger challenges per year, and most of these involve horizontal mergers. See D. Bruce Hoffman, "Vertical Merger Enforcement at the FTC," speech, January 10, 2018, https://www.ftc.gov/system/files/documents/public_statements/1304213/hoffman_vertical_merger_speech_final.pdf.
34. The "regulations under section 482 [of the US Internal Revenue Code] generally provide that prices charged by one affiliate to another, in an intercompany transaction involving the transfer of

goods, services, or intangibles, yield results that are consistent with the results that would have been realized if uncontrolled taxpayers had engaged in the same transaction under the same circumstances." https://www.irs.gov/businesses/international-businesses/transfer-pricing.

35. According to Hoffman, "Vertical Merger Enforcement at the FTC" (see note 33), vertical deals may "reduce the likelihood of beneficial entry," may "result in competitive foreclosure," and/or may lead to anticompetitive behavior due to information sharing about a rival."
36. Robert B. Little and Joseph Orien, "Determining the Likely Standard of Review in Delaware M&A Transactions," https://corpgov.law.harvard.edu/2017/04/28/determining-the-likely-standard-of-review-in-delaware-ma-transactions-2/.
37. For more on the use of Delphi in WOFC, see "A WOFC Case Study: JT Smith Consultants," in previous editions of this book . This case can also be purchased separately at https://www.thecasecentre.org/educators/products/view&&id=100661. Other recognized methods for group decisions include the Hoy-Tarter Model of Decision Making, Multi-Voting, the Modified Borda Count, Hartnett's CODM Model, and Bain's RAPID Framework, summarized in Paul Newton, *Effective Group Decisionmaking* (2017), http://www.free-management-ebooks.com/dldebk-pdf/fme-group-decision-making.pdf.
38. "What It's Like to Be Owned by Berkshire Hathaway," *Harvard Business Review,* December 14, 2015, https://hbr.org/2015/12/what-its-like-to-be-owned-by-berkshire-hathaway.
39. *Division of Corporation Finance:*
    Standard Industrial Classification (SIC)
    Code List
    The Standard Industrial Classification Codes that appear in a company's disseminated EDGAR filings indicate the company's type of business. These codes are also used in the Division of Corporation Finance as a basis for assigning review responsibility for the company's filings. For example, a

company whose business was Metal Mining (SIC 1000) would have its filings reviewed by staffers in A/D Office 4. http://www.sec.gov/info/edgar/siccodes.htm, accessed June 25, 2011.

40. Description from http://www2.standardandpoors.com/spf/pdf/index/GICS_methodology.pdf, accessed June 25, 2011.
41. Porter, *Competitive Strategy.*
42. *Mergers & Acquisitions: The Dealmakers Journal* is the official publication of the Association for Corporate Growth. It was founded in 1966 by Stanley Foster Reed, the original senior author of this book. For more information visit http://www.themiddlemarket.com.
43. LexisNexis Corporate Affiliations Plus gives access to all the information found in the eight-volume print directory, in electronic format. Its coding enables 29 search criteria, including parent company, subsidiaries, sales/revenue, earnings, assets liabilities, net worth, SIC codes, and number of employees.
44. This database was originally developed by Lockheed, prior to its merger with Martin Marietta (becoming LockheedMartin). The Dialog portfolio of products and services, including Dialog® and DataStar®, offers organizations the ability to precisely retrieve data from more than 1.4 billion unique records of key information, accessible via the Internet or through delivery to enterprise intranets.
45. See http://www.mergent.com/solutions/private-company-solutions/million-dollar-directory-(mddi).
46. See http://www.hoovers.com/sales-leads/list-building.html.
47. Kathy Kristof, "Phone Spam Soars to a New Record," *Moneywatch,* December 19, 2017, https://www.cbsnews.com/news/robocalls-phone-spam-soar-to-a-new-record.
48. Kevin S. Haeberle, "A New Market-Based Approach to Securities Law" (2018), *Faculty Publications,* 1895, https://scholarship.law.wm.edu/facpubs/1895.
49. State law is fairly uniform following the Uniform Fraudulent Transfer Act. Like the other "uniform" acts, this one was

drafted by the National Conference of Commissions of Uniform State Laws (Uniform Law Commissioners), a group of law professors, former judges, and lawyers who have volunteered to set these standards. The Uniform Law Commissioners propose uniform laws to the states for ratification. To date, 43 states have ratified this act. At the federal level, The US Code covers fraudulent transfers under Title 11, in Section 548, "Fraudulent transfers and obligations."

50. This section on brokers and finders benefits from the review of Michael Nall, founder and managing director, Alliance of M&A Advisors, http://www.amaaonline.com/join-us/.
51. Kenneth G. Sam, "The Danger of Paying Finder's Fees to Unregistered Broker-Dealers," Dorsey &Whitney, LLC, March 29, 2017, https://governancecomplianceinsider.com/the-danger-of-paying-finders-fees-to-unregistered-broker-dealers/.
52. "The Lehman Formula is a descending scale and can be structured where the first five million dollars of a deal's value may be charged a certain percentage—say, 6%—the next five million another percentage—say, 3%—and the remaining amount can be charged another percentage—2%, for example" (https://www.firmex.com/uncategorized/ma-fee-guide-2018-2019-download/).
53. Section 501 of the Sarbanes-Oxley Act requested the National Association of Securities Dealers and the New York Stock Exchange to propose rules for curbing conflicts of interest, and in May 2002 the SEC approved them. For a description of the relevant SEC rule on analyst certification (Rule AC) and related rules of the stock exchanges, see https://www.sec.gov/reportspubs/investor-publications/divisionsmarketregbdguidehtm.html#V.
54. For HSR resources from the Federal Trade Commission, see https://www.ftc.gov/enforcement/premerger-notification-program/hsr-resources.
55. According to a January 2018 speech by Bruce Hoffman, acting director of the FTC's Bureau of Competition, the

average number of challenges to mergers since 2000 has been 39 per year—with only one of those per year being a vertical (https://www.ftc.gov/system/files/documents/public_statements/1304213/hoffman_vertical_merger_speech_final.pdf). Typically, the DOJ and FTC together review some 2,000 mergers per year. In fiscal 2017, the two agencies reviewed 1,992 transactions, receiving clearance to investigate 277 of them (14 percent), and taking a second look at 51 of them, or just 3 percent of all transactions (https://www.ftc.gov/system/files/documents/reports/federal-trade-commission-bureau-competition-department-justice-antitrust-division-hart-scott-rodino/p110014_fy_2017_hsr_report_final_april_2018.pdf).

56. *United States v. Bestfoods,* 542 U.S. 51 (1998).

57. For regulatory contact information, see https://www.sec.gov/fast-answers/answersbankreghtm.html.

58. For a study of recent M&A decisions by the US Federal Reserve Board, see Robert C. Azarow, et al., "Bank Lessons Found in 2016," February 15, 2017, https://www.apks.com/en/perspectives/publications/2017/01/bank-m-a-lessons-found-in-2016.

59. According to the European Commission, it "assessed more than 2,000 different product markets and reviewed 2.7 million internal documents" to make its determination (http://europa.eu/rapid/press-release_IP-18-2282_en.htm).

60. For a useful reference, see this Q&A from the FTC: https://www.ftc.gov/enforcement/premerger-notification-program/hsr-resources/most-frequently-asked-hsr-questions.

61. HSR filing instructions can be found at https://www.ftc.gov/system/files/attachments/premerger-notification-program/hsr_form_instructions_090116.pdf.

62. https://www.ftc.gov/sites/default/files/attachments/merger-review/100819hmg.pdf.

63. The FTC notes the following: "The Non-horizontal Guidelines were included in DOJ's 1984 Merger Guidelines and are available at https://www.justice.gov/atr/non-horizontal

-merger-guidelines. While the DOJ and FTC have updated the Guidelines as they relate to horizontal mergers several times since then, most recently in 2010, the Non-horizontal Guidelines have not been updated since 1984, and do not provide useful guidance for vertical mergers today."

64. https://www.ftc.gov/system/files/documents/public_statements/1304213/hoffman_vertical_merger_speech_final.pdf.
65. Ibid.
66. See http://www.andeavor.com/about/company-history/.
67. See COSO, https://www.coso.org/Documents/990025P-Executive-Summary-final-may20.pdf.
68. For the full text of the guidelines, see https://www.ftc.gov/sites/default/files/attachments/merger-review/100819hmg.pdf.
69. *Barron's,* Sept 8, 2012. Tesoro was subsequently renamed Andeavor, and is now being purchased by Marathon Petroleum Company. We use the Tesoro name here to correlate with the citations.
70. Ibid.
71. For example, "6 West Coast Senators Urge DOJ to Investigate Senators' Call for 'Refinery by Refinery Probe,'" https://www.cantwell.senate.gov/news/press-releases/6-west-coast-senators-urge-doj-to-investigate-western-gas-price-spikes.
72. See, for example, Valero Energy Corp., FTC Dkt. No. C-4031 (Dec. 18, 2001) (Analysis of Proposed Consent Order to Aid Public Comment), available at http://www.ftc.gov/os/2001/12/valeroanalysis.htm; Exxon Corp., No. C-3907 (Nov. 30, 1999) (Analysis of Proposed Consent Order to Aid Public Comment), available at http://www.ftc.gov/os/1999/11/exxonmobilana.pdf.
73. https://www.justice.gov/atr/horizontal-merger-guidelines-08192010#5c.
74. https://oag.ca.gov/system/files/attachments/press_releases/AG%20Letter%20to%20CEC%20(Tesoro).pdf.
75. www.consumerwatchdog.orgresourcesagharristesoroltr10-10-12.pdf.

76. Tesoro's 8K filing to the SEC on August 13, 2012: "If the transactions contemplated by this Agreement are enjoined other than through a temporary restraining order (whether preliminarily or permanently) as a result of any injunction or other order in any action or proceeding brought by any Governmental Authority that seeks to prevent the Closing of this transaction as a violation of any antitrust Law as long as the basis of the court order is not solely a violation of Section 7A of the HSR Act, the Buyer must immediately propose to the relevant Governmental Authority to commit to and to effect, by consent decree, hold separate order, trust or otherwise, the sale, license, divestiture or other disposition of the Wilmington Refinery in order to effect the dissolution or lifting of any such injunction or other order. . . ."
77. Statement of the Federal Trade Commission *In the Matter of Tesoro Corporation / BP p.l.c.,* FTC File No. 121-0190.
78. Tesoro's deal lead and the author of this appendix, Bruce Fleming, is presently a member of the Board of M&A Standards. This account was drawn entirely from publicly available information.

CHAPTER 3

Valuation and Modeling

INTRODUCTION

How much is this company worth? What can we buy (or sell) it for?

The purpose of this chapter is to help a buyer (or seller) answer both questions. The first question is about *value*; it is general and abstract. The second question is about *price*; it is specific and concrete.

Some believe that there is no such thing as value; it is all about price. This line of thinking says that a company that sells for a low price has a low value, and the company that sells for a fortune has a high value. Period. It doesn't matter if the low-priced-seller has a century of history, a global customer base, and $600 billion in assets. (Think of the core Lehman Brothers business selling to Barclays for only $250 million in cash and assumption of liabilities back in the panicked market of 2008.) Nor does it matter that the high-priced-seller has little more than a platform and followers. (Consider the $19 *billion* Facebook paid for the then five-year-old WhatsApp in the exuberant market of 2014.) The pricing school of thought shrugs at the discrepancy, rejecting any notion that Lehman was undervalued or WhatsApp overvalued: if the price is set honestly at arm's length (with no fraud or self-interest involved), price is value, value is price.

The previous edition of this book noted that value essentially exists only in the minds of the people setting it, while price reflects real-world market behavior—and it is sometimes the only criterion we have available to estimate an asset's intrinsic value. Yet while price is a key expression of valuation and a meaningful check against theory, *it can never be enough*. To hold price up as the be-all-and-end-all of value would be like saying that public companies are only worth their current stock price, when we all know how volatile stock prices can be—and how much more a buyer will pay for control in the form of a premium. So instead of mere pricing, the more enlightened members of the M&A community support the use and study of *valuation*—and, equally as important, *modeling*, through which abstract concepts become actionable.

Valuation and modeling, as distinct from mere pricing, have great utility for buyers and sellers alike. In a depressed market, a reliable valuation and model combination can help owners hold out for a better buyer. In a manic market, a professional valuation, supported by financial modeling, can help buyers avoid caving in to fads. It is important to remember that it takes two—and that includes *you* (whether you are buying or selling). The price any acquirer pays for a company represents the outcome of a negotiation between what the buyer is willing to pay and what a seller is willing to accept—and behind that final price lie many valid considerations on both sides that do not cease to be true once the price is set.

Although price can be expressed as a single number—the $X that Company A paid for Company B—it is hardly a simple matter. The amount that might be paid for the same company may vary greatly among different buyers at different times. One might say that just as beauty lies in the eyes of the beholder, so value lies in the equations of the buyer and seller. But which equations to use?

There is no limit to the possible approaches one can take to valuation. There are more than a dozen in use. (See Exhibit 3-1.) Which to choose?

Of the models listed in Exhibit 3-1, two dominate: comparable companies and transactions, and discounted cash flow. These are recognized as valid in courts of law when appraisals are challenged.[1] Even so, it is not always easy to use either one. Fortunately, help is available. Investment bankers stand ready to produce fairness opinions to opine on a valuation of a public company transaction that might be challenged by shareholders.

Exhibit 3-1 Valuation Approaches

- Book Value (Liquidation Value): The equity on the balance sheet (assets minus liabilities)
- Comparable Companies: Using multiples or ratios to compare the company to peer companies that have been appraised
- Comparable Transactions: Using multiples or ratios to compare the company to peer companies that have been purchased
- Current Value: Used for start-up technology companies*
- Discounted Cash Flow: Considering the net present value of the company's future cash flows†
- Economic Value Added (EVAC): Calculating the value of Capital Invested in Assets in Place + Present value of EVA from Assets in Place + Sum of present value of EVA from new (postmerger) projects‡
- Enterprise Value: Calculating market capitalization plus debt, minority interest, and preferred shares, minus total cash and cash equivalents§
- Exit value: The amount of money that would be paid if original investors were repaid with a reasonable return on investment
- Leveraged Buyout Value: Same as exit value but assuming repayment of bank loan (debt capital)
- Option Pricing: Use for start-up technology companies with multiple innovations¶
- Owners' Investment Value: Amount of money investors have paid for their shares
- Probability-Weighted Expected Return: Used for start-up technology companies**
- Market value: Number of shares outstanding times current market price
- Replacement value: The amount of money it would take to replicate the company from scratch starting now
- Sunk cost value: The amount of money owners have already spent to create the company
- Venture capital method: Return on Investment (ROI) = Terminal Value ÷ Postmoney Valuation (or conversely postmoney Valuation = Terminal Value ÷ Anticipated ROI)††

* Mark Spaneth, "How Much is Artificial Intelligence Worth?," . http://www.markspaneth.com/blog/2017/how-much-is-artificial-intelligence-worth.

† For an application of this technique to new technology companies, see Mark Goedhart Tim Koller, and David Wessel, blog post, February 2016, https://www.mckinsey.com/business-functions/strategy-and-corporate-finance/our-insights/valuing-high-tech-companies. The blog is excerpted from their bookValuation: Measuring and Managing Value of Companies (Hoboken, NJ: John Wiley, 2015).

‡ http://people.stern.nyu.edu/adamodar/New_Home_Page/lectures/eva.html.

§ https://corporatefinanceinstitute.com/resources/knowledge/valuation/what-is-enterprise-value-ev/.

¶ Option pricing is one of the valuation methods listed here for assessing the value of artificial intelligence in a company, according to Angela Sadang, "How Much Is Artificial Intelligence Worth, blog post, August 4, 2017, http://www.markspaneth.com/blog/2017/how-much-is-artificial-intelligence-worth. For formulas, see "Application of Option Pricng Theory to Equity Valuation" (Stern School of Business, New York University, undated), http://pages.stern.nyu.edu/~adamodar/New_Home_Page/lectures/opt.html.

** http://www.markspaneth.com/blog/2017/how-much-is-artificial-intelligence-worth.

††http://billpayne.com/2011/02/05/startup-valuations-the-venture-capital-method.html.

Appraisers have credentials to value even the most unusual assets—and they can avail themselves of global standards (as discussed at the end of this chapter). And, as for economic analysis, you don't have to be a financial economist yourself to get this work done. Any accredited business school is likely to have a team of them ready, willing, and able to help—at an affordable price, or even pro bono.

But even before consulting a specialist, it is valuable to learn the basics. The purpose of this chapter is to explain how deal price comes about and why.

VALUATION FUNDAMENTALS

Are "valuation" and "price" interchangeable?

Value is the intrinsic worth of an asset, whereas price is what a buyer has actually paid for it. Recall the words of Warren Buffett: "Price is what you pay; value is what you get." Prices change daily; value is more stable.

The key point is that the price paid for an asset—or a company, for that matter—does not always reflect its underlying value, but rather the zone of agreement between a buyer and a seller at a given point in time. Confusing "valuation" and "price" is an easy trap to fall into—we inadvertently do it ourselves more often than we care to admit. However, it is important to at least keep in mind how the two are differentiated. A good example of the role of valuation can begin with the notion of a valuation multiple.

What exactly is a valuation multiple?

A *valuation multiple* is simply a means of expressing a firm's market value relative to one or more key financial metrics that presumably relate to that value. It can also be called a *valuation ratio*, since a ratio is another way of expressing a multiple. For example, if a company with $1 million in revenues is priced at $3 million, the relationship of transaction price to seller's revenues can be expressed as 3:1 or as three times revenues.

To be useful, those metrics—whether sales, earnings, cash flow, or some other measure—must bear a logical relationship to the market value observed. That is, the financial metric should comprise a key driver of that market value. Some industries tend to focus on sales, others on earnings, yet others on particular assets. In each case, multiples can provide a helpful starting point for analysis. But in these real-world terms, it becomes clearer why the appraiser must choose the appropriate sample set and still leave at least some room for interpretation.

Suppose a company is so new that it has no revenue and no profit. How can it be valued?

This is called *pre-revenue valuation*, and there are several techniques for this. The most popular one is the Venture Capital Method defined earlier, but there are several others. While it is beyond the scope of this chapter to discuss pre-revenue valuation, it is an important topic and guidance is available.[2]

What about valuation rules of thumb?

Sometimes a valuation multiple becomes popular in an industry and, rather than being recalculated each time based on new information, becomes an assumption. In many cases, the valuation rules of thumb emerged due to lack of current profitability and low visibility into future profitability—and they proved to be too generous. This said, there are business brokers who rely on them.[3]

What is discounting?

Discounting is the process of determining the present value of cash to be received in the future. Assuming interest rates and/or inflation rates above zero, cash today is worth more than it will be tomorrow. Discounting quantifies this premium.

When you were studying math in school, your teacher probably taught you that a $1 investment, when *compounded* at 6 percent interest, will have a *future value* of $2 in 12.4 years, as that original $1 has earned an additional $1 in interest. What the teacher did not teach you was the reciprocal corollary: that $2 to be paid out 12.4 years from now, when *discounted* at 6 percent, has a *present value* of only $1 today. Most M&A investments revolve around projecting how much an investment will yield in some future time horizon and figuring out what that amount of money is worth now. The business of estimating M&A investment risk involves including in the discount rate the certainties and uncertainties of receiving a future stream of earnings or cash flows from your M&A investment. The lower the certainty, the higher the discount rate; the higher the certainty, the lower the discount rate.

What are hurdle rates?

A *hurdle rate* is the discount rate, usually set by the board of directors or other governance of a corporation, that must be applied to a projected earnings stream to determine whether the investment is likely to generate at least a minimally acceptable return. If the expected return does not exceed the hurdle rate, the investment is unlikely to be approved. Most companies set the hurdle rate as equivalent to their own cost of capital. Special situations then call for documented reasons to add points to the discount rate—for inexperience in the field, for high deviation rates on historical earnings for the target or its industry, or for other risk-related reasons. For example, executives may develop different hurdle rates for entries into different industries that coincide with the comfort level of the executives' personal "feelings" about the industry, which, upon investigation, may turn out to coincide with their familiarity with the industry. This approach appears rational but is not at all a proper proxy for risk, because those assessing the risk are not necessarily the ones who will be managing the acquisition.

What about time horizons?

Any valuation involving future value will include a *forecast period*. These vary widely by industry, based in part on how long it takes to bring a product to market. In the pharmaceutical industry, because it takes many years to develop drugs and then obtain approval for them, it is not uncommon to use a 10-year forecast period.[4] By contrast, in the field of information technology, a three-year horizon is typical.[5] And in the subfield of artificial intelligence (deep learning, machine learning, natural language processing, and speech recognition) the window may be a matter of months.[6] In parts of the world struggling with economic or political uncertainty, even that is too long. Tomorrow is charted on a deal-by-deal basis.

Nearly every company, and almost every industry, that we encounter today will eventually fade away as others come into focus. Yet despite the perishability of their subjects, valuation and modeling are still possible. One need only focus on the task at hand, considering how changes in various factors such as financial and environmental factors might have a material impact on the business or the industry over a reasonably foreseeable investment horizon.

This is where a few financial skills can really help a dealmaker. One of the benefits of "sensitivity analysis" is to discover the effects of different time horizons on a target company's present value. Unfortunately, in the current environment, many dealmakers are shortening their forecast period just because conditions are uncertain—even when the uncertainties they face are not random. (One might say that they are *known unknowns*.) This shortening is a poor substitute for factoring in quantifiable risk. In many cases, with a little work, the uncertainties can be converted to probabilities.

CHOOSING A VALUATION APPROACH

How does an acquirer choose a valuation approach?

The kind of financial analysis the acquirer conducts—multiples from comparable companies or transactions, discounted cash flow (DCF), a combination of these, or another approach entirely—will depend in part on the strategic reason for buying the company. There are many possible reasons one company would want to buy another. Here are some primary ones:

- *Growth*. To lessen economic vulnerability and/or increase latitude for strategic choices by increasing the size of the company and thus potential revenues and/or profits. A growth-oriented acquirer may consider valuation multiples focusing on ratios that involve sales, such as earnings before interest, taxes, depreciation, and amortization (EBITDA) to sales.

- *Diversification*. To hedge against risk in current industries by investing in others. A diversification-oriented acquirer may choose DCF as a valuation model because it lends itself to comparability across industries.
- *Progress*. To accomplish strategic goals more quickly and more successfully by buying an operating company that is already doing what is envisioned in the buyer's strategy, or that could provide some missing piece of the buyer's strategic puzzle. A progressive acquirer will rarely value the target company by itself but will value the future combined company—typically with DCF, using postcombination scenarios.
- *Vertical synergy*. To achieve economies of scale or other economic benefits by buying a customer or supplier. An acquirer interested in this kind of financial synergy will recast the financial statements showing a different cost structure postmerger and then create a DCF statement from that.
- *Horizontal synergy*. To increase market share ("market power") or reduce competition by buying an actual or potential competitor. Since this kind of acquisition involves a company that is similar to the acquirer, both multiples and DCF are relevant modes of valuation.
- *Financial offset*. To smooth financial performance by combining companies with different cash flow cycles, tax profiles, and/or debt capacities. Here, the emphasis is not so much on the amount of cash flow in the future as on its timing, so multiples may be the natural choice.
- *Efficiency*. To realize a return on investment by buying a company with less-efficient managers and making them more efficient or replacing them. This is a natural candidate for DCF analysis, since the acquirer is relying on a new and different scenario; current and historical multiples will be meaningless.
- *Bargain hunting*. To take advantage of a price that is low in comparison to current stock prices, or in relation to the cost the buyer would incur if it built the company from scratch. Regarding current stock prices, this is clearly a candidate for multiples (e.g.,

price/earnings, earnings per share). As for cost to build, this is a cost-based approach unrelated to multiples and DCF. This is not so much valuation as appraisal—a subject in its own right.

- *Control*. To assert control in an underperforming company with dispersed ownership by acting as an agent for the owners. Here any multiple or ratio involving stock price and/or dividends is most relevant, such as total shareholder return (TSR).

With these types of goals in mind, let us now take a deeper look at the two valuation approaches emphasized in this book: comparable companies and transactions, and DCF.

COMPARABLE COMPANIES AND TRANSACTIONS

What is the comparable companies and transactions approach?

The *comparables* approach is a two-step process. First, we compare one company to other companies. Second, we compare one transaction to other transactions. Both of these comparisons involve a series of questions that deal with valuation multiples.

What are the basic types of valuation multiples?

There are two basic types of valuation multiples: multiples that relate to a company's equity value and multiples that relate to a company's enterprise value.

- *Equity multiples* refer to the value of shareholders' ownership and/or claims on the assets and cash flow of a business. An equity multiple therefore expresses the value of this ownership relative to a financial metric that applies to shareholders only. The best example would be a company's net income (sometimes also referred to as its earnings), defining *net income* as the residual income left after payments to creditors, minority shareholders, and other nonequity claimants.

- *Enterprise value multiples* refer to the value of the entire enterprise, or the value of all claims on a business—both the equity value and *net debt* (gross debt less cash on hand), as well as other nonequity claimants. An enterprise value multiple therefore calculates the value relative to a financial metric that relates to the entire enterprise; a prime example might be sales or EBITDA.

Why would someone want to use valuation multiples to ascribe a value to a business?

There are three key reasons to use valuation multiples in the context of M&A analysis:

- *Objectivity.* Valuation is partly a subjective process. Multiples can provide a useful framework for introducing a level of objectivity to the process. That is, multiples provide helpful information about relative value when used properly. At a minimum, valuation multiples can serve as the proverbial rule of thumb to double-check other valuation measures. For example, if a DCF analysis were to peg the value of a business at $100 million, the analyst could calculate earnings-based multiples (for example, the price of the company in relation to EBITDA, as in "five times EBITDA," commonly written as 5× EBITDA) and then ask how those multiples compare with similarly situated companies in the industry.
- *Ease of use.* The very ease of calculation makes multiples an appealing and user-friendly method of assessing value. Multiples can help the analyst avoid potential misperceptions of other, more "precise" approaches, such as DCF. Valuations such as these can sometimes create a false sense of comfort unless they are triangulated with other valuation analyses.
- *Relevance.* Valuation multiples focus on the key metrics that investors use. Key examples include a business's revenue, EBIT, EBITDA, and earnings. Since investors in aggregate make the

market—and thus dictate relative value—the most commonly used metrics and multiples will have the most impact.

What about the disadvantages of using valuation multiples? What should I keep in mind?

Despite their advantages, multiples have several disadvantages that one should consider when evaluating the worth of a particular company. Some of the principal criticisms levied against multiples can be summarized as follows:

- *Overly simplistic.* A valuation multiple is a deceptively complex variable; it seeks to distill a tremendous amount of information—including both known and unknown data—into a single figure or series of numbers. At times, this can be an overambitious objective! By combining many value levers into a single-point estimate, multiples may make it difficult to disaggregate the effect of different drivers. Consider the following real estate example: a 100-acre farm in Pennsylvania arguably is worth $530,000 based upon the average value per acre for farm real estate of $5,300. However, this single variable neglects to consider the location, condition, and potential uses of the property. Clearly, these variables can have a tremendous influence on the intrinsic value of the land. The lesson learned, then, is not to rely on just one or even a handful of valuation multiples to dicate value. Dig deeper.
- *Static.* A multiple represents a snapshot of a firm's value at a given point in time. However, clearly every business and industry has a life cycle. Moreover, the economic backdrop is constantly changing, which typically will have a carryover effect on the worth of a particular enterprise. Valuation multiples often fail to capture the ever-changing nature of business and competition. The takeaway: consider how the market valued an asset over an extended period of time, not just on any given day.

- *Potentially misleading.* Multiples are primarily used to make comparisons of relative value. However, comparing multiples is an inexact art, as there are many reasons that multiples can differ. If we were to extend the aforementioned farm example, a $530,000 valuation might be grossly high if the land is, in fact, pasture (which, at $2,700 per acre, is worth only $270,000) or a bit on the low side if the parcel is cropland (which, at $5,700 per acre, might be valued at $570,000). There are even more subtle ways in which valuation multiples might differ between two seemingly similar businesses, not all of which relate to true differences in value. For instance, even modest changes in accounting policies can result in diverging multiples for otherwise identically operating businesses. For these reasons, the selection of truly comparable companies is critical. Where there are differences, the analyst may need to make adjustments to the implied multiples. Exhibit 3-2 summarizes the key advantages and disadvantages of valuation multiples.

COMPARING ONE COMPANY WITH OTHER COMPANIES

What is comparable companies analysis?

The *comparable companies* approach to valuation is the most widely used methodology in corporate finance. It involves contrasting the financial metrics and valuation multiples of a peer group of companies (generally publicly traded) to those of the business being appraised, known as the *target*. The foundation of this approach is the concept that the market should ascribe similar valuations to businesses with similar characteristics. To select the appropriate peer group—also called the *universe of comps*, or just *comps* for short—the analyst must understand the target's business. Comparable companies should comprise companies that are similar to the target; that is, the comps should be from a similar industry, of approximately similar size, with similar growth trajectories, and so on.

The analyst will calculate the peer group's average margins, financial returns, growth prospects, and—most important—valuation multiples to arrive at a group mean and median. The analyst will then apply these

Figure 3-2 Advantages and Disadvantages of Valuation Multiples

Advantages	Disadvantages
■ *Objective.* Can be robust tools that filter out subjective assumptions, such as future growth rates. Can provide useful information about relative value. ■ *Easy to use.* Are relatively simple to calculate, particularly with widely available data. Their wide use makes them a "common language" for dealmakers. ■ *Relevant.* Are based on key metrics that investors use.	■ *Overly simplistic.* Can combine multiple value drivers into a single point estimate. Difficult to disaggregate the effects of different value drivers. ■ *Static.* Only measure value at a single point of time. Do not fully capture the dynamic nature of business and competition. ■ *Potentially misleading.* Can vary for many reasons, not all relating to true differences in value. Can result in misleading "apples-to-oranges" comparisons among companies.

metrics to those of the target to arrive at an approximate valuation. This process underscores a key difference between comparable companies and DCF as valuation techniques: whereas DCF evaluates companies on an individual basis, the comparable companies approach considers valuation relative to the target's peers.

It is important to recognize that the valuation determined through comparable companies analysis does *not* reflect any premiums or discounts that might apply—such as the control premium a buyer typically pays in an M&A transaction, or the discount that either the public or private capital markets might apply to a bankrupt entity to reflect the future operating uncertainty. However, the analysis will provide a useful starting point for the M&A analysis, or a confirmational datapoint for a more exhaustive DCF analysis.

Why are publicly traded stocks typically used as the comps? Why not private companies?

The comparable companies analysis typically uses publicly traded stock prices to drive the process because public companies generally provide the most transparent valuations. Privately held businesses, in contrast, do not publish their financial statements and do not trade on stock exchanges, yielding limited public data. In addition, a publicly traded company's current stock price is generally viewed as one of the best valuation metrics because it represents a balance of the subjective views of numerous investors on various factors affecting the company's future performance. In this sense, the comparable companies methodology provides an up-to-date judgment on the company's risk profile, competitive pressures, cyclicality, and business prospects.

Which financial metrics and valuation multiples do M&A analysts typically focus on?

The answer partly depends on a particular company's industry and stage of development, among other factors.

As a practical matter, investors or acquirers in different industries may scrutinize entirely different financial metrics. As described in greater detail later in this chapter, an acquirer of an early-stage company in an emerging industry such as AI might focus on assets or revenue, rather than earnings—particularly if the target has incurred heavy up-front costs and is not yet profitable but is now on a tremendous growth trajectory. In contrast, the potential buyer of an established company in a mature industry, such as newspaper publishing, might be more concerned with cash flow and less about revenue, as the would-be purchaser may be more concerned with sustainability than growth.

Likewise, a commodity-driven business, like a gold mine or natural gas producer, might typically be valued as a multiple of its reserves. That may be because the market might choose to focus primarily on the business's current production capacity and the bankable value of what the producer has in the ground and assume that production will cease once the reserves are depleted. However, one would not necessarily expect an auto manufacturer to be valued as a multiple of its production capacity, but rather as a multiple of EBITDA or some other more standard financial measure.

These extremes aside, there is a reasonably finite list of financial metrics and valuation measures from which acquirers are likely to start.

From a valuation standpoint, the most popular valuation multiples involve the following:

- EBITDA
- Earnings or earnings per share (EPS)
- Sales or revenue
- Cash flow
- Book value

Profitability can likewise be benchmarked many different ways. However, the most common measures include gross margins, operating and/or EBITDA margins, pretax margins, and net margins. Other key metrics that acquirers will examine include the company's growth trajectory—whether measured in unit sales, revenue, earnings, or some other figure—and the target's financial returns—such as return on equity (ROE), return on invested capital (ROIC), or return on assets (ROA).

The preceding examples, while popular, only scratch the surface of possible financial ratios. If you consider the number of balance sheet and income statement required by the Code of Federal Regulations items, there are some 53 financial realities that companies must report—32 for the balance sheet and 21 for the income statement.[7] In theory at least, each of these can be compared with each of the others, both within the same statement and across statements. Mathematically, therefore, this yields *2,756 possible ratios*. Adding the dimension of time (rate of change) only multiplies the possibilities!

Lastly, the buyer might look at variables that fall beyond the company's financial statements—such as its sales per employee or (as noted) mining reserves. Much depends on the facts and circumstances of a particular situation.

Which is more common: EV/EBITDA or P/E?

As previously outlined, it largely depends on the particular industry. However, the fact is that the price-to-earnings (P/E) ratio is an equity metric—

that is, it only looks at the equity portion of the company and ignores debt and preferred shareholders—whereas enterprise value divided by EBITDA (EV/EBITDA) is an enterprise metric. As such, P/E is highly dependent upon a particular company's leverage. All else equal, two identical companies with different capital structures can have markedly different P/E ratios. This can cloud the valuation process.

EV/EBITDA is capital structure neutral. The mix of equity and debt does not change the EV calculation, but it can dramatically skew a company's P/E. Ultimately, then, it doesn't matter how you slice the pie between debt and equity—total enterprise value remains unchanged. Accordingly, EV/EBITDA generally results in more comparable multiples among various companies.

When might P/E represent a better valuation yardstick than EV/EBITDA?

The question that the analyst should consider is whether interest expense is an operating expense or a *financing expense* of the target company. An *operating expense* is an expense incurred in carrying out an organization's day-to-day activities. For example, interest is a cost of doing business for companies such as banks, leasing companies, and other financial institutions. These businesses borrow money at one rate and lend it out at a higher rate. As such, interest expense is directly related to operations. For these companies, P/E is the best valuation measure.

A *financing expense* is an expense triggered by how a particular company is capitalized—that is, how much debt it chooses to carry. One illustration would be an auto parts manufacturer; the amount of debt—and therefore interest expense—a company carries is a balance sheet decision and really has no impact on operations. In a case such as this, EV/EBITDA is preferable.

The other instance in which P/E might be a better measure is in industries that carry negligible amounts of debt. Prime examples include tech companies and those with highly volatile business models, such as biotech firms. In these situations, the extra effort of calculating EV/EBITDA might not provide any additional useful information and therefore isn't worth the extra step.

When using EBITDA as a metric, how can an acquiror make sure that the earnings number used in the formula is a sustainable number and not just some unusual and temporary result?

It is important to consider the quality of earnings in all financial analysis, including those based on EBITDA.[8] Following is just a sample of the types of adjustments found in a quality of earnings (Q of E) analysis:

- Litigation settlement or expenses
- Management fees to private equity owners
- Owner personal expenses
- Unusual bad debts or inventory write-offs
- Severance or other restructuring expenses
- Unusual or nonrecurring incentive compensation
- Gains or losses on the sale of assets
- Insurance recoveries and reimbursements
- Departures from US GAAP
- Unrecorded proposed audit adjustments
- Impact of year-end adjustments (true-ups) on interim periods
- Corporate allocations versus proposed transition services agreement (carve-out)
- Reversal of reserves built in prior periods
- Income statement misclassifications (operating items recorded in other income/expense)
- Impact of acquisitions or divestitures

With so many potential valuation and financial metrics to consider, how do I narrow the alternatives to those that are the most important to my target's industry?

From a practical standpoint, there are three sources of information that M&A practitioners historically have found to be useful starting points—once the analyst has identified the relevant industry and peer group:

- *Sell-side analyst reports*. Most major investment banks and brokerage firms employ entire departments of equity research analysts that publish reports on stocks in specific industry sectors. Once highly guarded publications, sell-side analyst reports are becoming increasingly available to retail investors through various websites (or, frankly, by simply researching the analysts' names and contacting them directly). In particular, ask for "initiation reports," "industry primers," or "deep dives"—these terms are analyst jargon for the firm's most comprehensive reports. See how the analyst critiques and values the businesses in his or her sector. Inevitably, these insights will advance your research quickly.

- *Company 10-Ks, annual reports, sustainability reports, and investor presentations*. As is commonly known, all publicly traded companies are required to publish annual reports (on Form 10-K) containing a minimum level of financial disclosures as well as a Management Discussion and Analysis (MD&A) section detailing risks. Many companies supplement their 10-Ks with an additional annual report telling the company's story in more detail, using illlustrations aimed at retail investors. In addition, a growing number of companies provide in-depth information on their nonfinancial performance—either within their annual reports (thus called an "integrated report") or in a separate report (often called a "sustainablity report"). All these are posted on the company's website under investor relations, along with transcripts from recent earnings calls or analyst presentations, which management has used to communicate its business fundamentals to current and potential investors in the stock. Taken together, these reports can be a gold mine of information.

- *Industry benchmarking surveys*. Finally, the M&A analyst might track down trade associations and/or consulting firms that specialize in the relevant sector for benchmarking surveys. Benchmarking involves comparing a given company's process and/or performance metrics to industry norms or best practices from within or outside the given industry. Trade associations often provide benchmarking surveys, either for free or at a relatively modest price, as a member benefit. Consulting firms, in contrast, sometimes create such surveys, generally for a price, to demonstrate their industry expertise and attract clients. One example is IHS, a publicly traded company that sells industry-specific forecasts and strategy tools. In any event, the M&A analyst can learn volumes from how these industry experts measure companies in a given sector.

Exhibit 3-3 summarizes the most common multiples used for selected sectors and provides the rationale behind each selection.

Which companies are comparable?

As noted, in constructing a comparable companies analysis, the analyst typically chooses a peer group of firms from the same industry as the target. These firms should also have similar fundamental characteristics, such as revenues, profitability, credit quality, and so on. While this analysis should ideally target direct competitors, it is often necessary to include a broader array of firms as a practical matter. One example would be where there are only a handful of publicly traded peers. The analysis should also adjust the capital structures of each comparable company in order to more accurately compare them with the corporation being valued (see Exhibit 3-4).

It's easy to overlook the last category in Exhibit 3-4: business model. However, that should not discount its significance. The Delaware Chancery Court tackled the issue of differing business models in *ONTI, Inc. v. Integra Bank,*[9] a frequently cited 1999 case. This case was cited for example in In Re Oxbow Carbon LLC Unitholder Litigation, C.A. No. 12447-VCL (Del. Ch. Aug. 1, 2018). Reversal by the Delaware Supreme Court **in 2019** did not affect the precedent set by the ONTI court, which agreed with plaintiffs that the seemingly similar physician practice management companies being compared were too different because one was less equipment intensive and derived more revenues and profits from pharmaceuticals.

Exhibit 3-3 Common Multiples Used in Selected Sectors

Sector	Multiples Used	Rationale
Cyclical manufacturing	P/E, relative P/E	Consider using normalized earnings
Growth firms	PEG ratio	Big differences in growth rates
Young growth firms with losses	Revenue multiples	Few other choices
Infrastructure	EV/EBITDA	Early losses, substantial D&A
REITs	Price/Cash flow to equity*	Large depreciation charges on real estate
Financial services	Price/Book value	Works better if book value is marked to market
Retailers	Revenue multiples	Margins equalize sooner or later

*Cash flow to equity, also known as CFE, is defined as net income plus depreciation.

Source: Professor Aswath Damodaran, New York University.

How many comparable companies should the analysis use?

While there is no formal requirement, practical experience suggests that the analyst should choose approximately four to eight comparable companies to form a representative group for performing the valuation analysis. If few or no companies exist that are both comparable and publicly traded, then the analyst might want to broaden how he or she is defining the industry.

Consider, for example, the potential purchase of a regional chain of vitamin stores. If the analyst defines the industry sector that narrowly—retailers of vitamins—the analyst will only find two public comps: Vitamin Shoppe, Inc. (VSI) and Vitacost.com Inc. (VITC). That's not really enough to create a thoughtful comparable companies analysis. What's more, Vitamin Shoppe, with a market capitalization of more than $1 billion, might be too large to be truly relevant as a valuation comp, depending on the size of the target. However, if the M&A analyst were to broaden the

Exhibit 3-4 Comparable Companies Checklist

Look for similarity in:

- Industry
- Size (revenues)
- Profitability
- Rate of growth
- Credit quality
- Capital structure (debt/equity and related ratios)
- Business model

industry definition to specialty retailers—particularly those that are both regional and in the small- or micro-cap segment of the market—several more options open up: indeed, a quick online screen yields well over a dozen candidates with market caps ranging from $100 million to $500 million.

Ultimately, if the broadened industry definition still yields too few results, the comparable companies valuation methodology fails, and the analyst should apply other methods instead. For example, in *In re Radiology Assoc., Inc. Litigation,*[10] the bankruptcy court held that differences between proposed comparable companies were so large that any comparable companies comparison was meaningless.

After identifying the list of comparable companies, the comparable valuation multiples are applied to the company being valued to establish a relative valuation range. Multiplying the mean or median price-to-earnings ratio of the comparable companies by the earnings of the company being valued to establish a relative valuation can be helpful to pinpoint a specific valuation but may be misleading. A better approach is to consider the relative strengths and weaknesses of the target.

Over what time period should multiples be measured?

Ideally, the time period selected for multiples should be long enough to correct for cycles that occur in the elements being measured. In some industries, such as those that are consumer driven (e.g., restaurants), this cycle might coincide with the macroeconomic cycle. In other industries, such as so-called short-cycle markets like semiconductors, there can be multiple inventory stocking and destocking periods within a single macroeconomic cycle. As always, the answer depends on the facts and circumstances of a particular situation. However, there are a couple of criteria to keep in mind:

- Any multiple that includes stock price as an element should be measured during a period that will not be distorted by a bull or bear market. A valid period could be the most recent market cycle from its start to end points, typically a three- or four-year period, though this may vary.
- Any multiple that includes revenue or earnings as an element should be measured over a time period long enough to correct for cycles of boom and bust in the company's industry (e.g., four years in the construction industry or seven years in aerospace).

Why might multiples vary across seemingly similar businesses?

There are a number of ways of answering this question, but arguably there are four primary reasons why multiples may vary: (1) the businesses might have varying levels of quality; (2) the companies might use different accounting approaches; (3) the firms might be encountering short-term or cyclical fluctuations in financial performance; and (4) the market might simply be mispricing the two enterprises.

How do differences in business quality impact valuation multiples?

All else equal, higher-quality businesses deserve higher valuation multiples. Invariably, there will be qualitative differences in the underlying drivers of a firm's valuation—management experience and depth, the business's opportunity set, its specific strategy, and so on. Converting these qualitative factors into measurable statistics is challenging, although four metrics worth considering are the business's return on capital, cost of capital, rate of growth, and duration of growth.

What about variations in accounting? How do they impact valuation?

Differences in accounting policies that do not affect cash flow do not impact the intrinsic value of the business. However, differences in accounting policies *can* impact the business's reported sales, earnings, financial returns, and so on. From a practical standpoint, then, these policy differences can drive a range of reported financial results that have a carryover impact on valuation multiples. Unless these variations in accounting are normalized, the differences in valuation multiples can paint a misleading picture of relative valuation.

Consider, for example, two companies—A and B—with identical revenue, operating expenses, tax rate, share count (e.g., shares outstanding), and stock prices. In fact, the two businesses are identical operationally but have one accounting difference. Both companies carry $50 million of goodwill on their balance sheets; however, Company A does not amortize it, whereas Company B expenses this item over 10 years (or $5 million annually). How might this one accounting difference impact the companies' relative valuation?

Exhibit 3-5 illustrates the outcome. Company B's amortization expense of $5 million results in $35 million of operating income compared to Company A's $40 million. There is no impact to cash, mind you, as goodwill amortization is a noncash expense. If we progress down the income statement through book taxes and shares outstanding, Company A has $2.40 of EPS compared to Company B's $2.10. The stock market, however, isn't fooled in this case by the difference—shares of both companies are trading at $35. *In effect, the market is looking through these accounting differences and ascribing the same value to both stocks.* A natural question might be, why is this so? After all, why should two stocks with comparable growth prospects trade at the same price if one has an EPS of $2.40 while the other has an EPS of $2.10? The answer is cash flow. Amortization is a noncash accounting expense. Either way, the two companies are

Exhibit 3-5 Variations in Accounting May Affect Valuation Multiples*

	Company A	Company B
Revenue	$100	$100
Operating Expenses	(60)	(60)
Amortization	—	(5)
Operating Income	40	35
Taxes @40%	(16)	(14)
Net Income	**$24**	**$21**
Shares Outstanding	10	10
Earnings per Share	$2.40	$2.10
Share Price	$35	$35
P/E Multiple	**14.6×**	**16.7×**
Valuation "premium"		*14%*

Is Company B really trading at a 14% premium to Company A?

* $ in millions, except per-share data

delivering the same amount of cash to shareholders. However, the implied P/E multiples are meaningfully different—Company A is trading at 14.6 times (14.6×) reported earnings, while Company B is trading at 16.7×. If an M&A analyst had not dug into the details, he or she might have concluded that Company B is worth 14 percent more than its counterpart based on a high-level P/E analysis. However, this premium is actually mere accounting fiction; it would be wrong to conclude that Company A is cheaper than Company B.

How commonly do accounting differences impact a firm's reported financials and, consequently, valuation multiples?

Accounting differences are not a one-off issue. Many different factors can drive variations in a company's reported profits. As was the case in the example used in Exhibit 3-5, these accounting differences can also impact valuation multiples. Although not all differences in profit measurement are material enough to move the needle, accounting differences are clearly not a trivial issue.

How might an analyst adjust a company's financial results in response to accounting differences?

There are practically an infinite number of accounting decisions that the management of any particular company can make. While it is virtually impossible to completely eliminate the impact of different accounting methodologies, there is still much that the analyst can do to mitigate their impact and produce data relevant to M&A analysis. In particular, there are two steps the analyst can take when these differences have the potential to unreasonably influence the valuation results: (1) restate accounting data in a common format; and (2) focus on key metrics that are less affected by accounting differences.

What are some of the most common accounting adjustments that analysts make?

Accounting adjustments can be acutely industry sensitive—for instance, accounting standards for companies in the energy industry differ substantially from those in the insurance industry, the biotech space, and the transportation sector. However, there are a few key issues that can be analyzed across industries: depreciation, extraordinary items, and leases. Although these items may be more common in some industries than others, they are calculated in the same way across the board (with some global differences as noted later). Other, more complex issues to consider include deferred tax assets, pensions and postretirement health benefit plans, and provisions such as those for doubtful accounts.

- *Depreciation.* How a business depreciates its property, plant, and equipment is a prime example of how there can be significant differences in accounting policies. There are several standard methods of computing depreciation expense, including fixed percentage, straight line, and declining balance methods.

Moreover, it is entirely reasonable for two different firms to adopt different economic lives for similar assets. Any of these variables can drive a meaningful difference in a company's annual depreciation expense. Study each company's depreciation policies. If possible, adopt a standardized methodology across each company, and calculate whether the change to net income would be material for each. If the data do not permit a standardized methodology, the analyst should at least keep these differences in mind when building the valuation model.

- *Extraordinary items.* Nonrecurring gains and losses are given a variety of names such as extraordinary, exceptional, unusual, or one-time. Unfortunately, the type of item included in this category, as well as its presentation in the income statement, varies. All such "exceptional" items should be excluded from EBIT and adjusted net income figures. These items include gains and losses on capital transactions and all truly one-off operating items, such as the cost of restructuring.
- *Leases.* There can be material differences in lease accounting across different companies, even those that are similarly situated. These differences are particularly important in capital-intensive industries with heavy use of leasing, such as airlines, construction, equipment manufacturing, and real estate. The primary area to consider is the classification of a capital lease (or finance lease, called Type A) versus an operating lease (called Type B) under US generally accepted accounting principles (GAAP) accounting. In a capital lease, the underlying asset is considered purchased; the transaction gives rise to an on-balance-sheet debt obligation with a corresponding interest charge. In an operating lease, in contrast, the underlying asset is considered rented and does not necessarily create a liability. Under new US leasing standards, most recently amended with ASU 2018-20: Leases (Topic 842), which became effective January 1, 2019, leases with a term of more than 12 months must make a balance sheet disclosure. Comparability would improve, particularly with respect to balance sheet and

enterprise value ratios, by consistently capitalizing all lease obligations. The biggest challenge is that disclosure can be inconsistent, adding subjectivity to some adjustments. As a result, many analysts do not automatically adjust for leases unless leasing is highly material. For companies with non-US operations, the new leasing standard IFRS 16 from global standard setters, also effective January 1, 2019, may apply.

Which financial metrics are less affected by accounting differences?

As noted, it is generally impossible to eliminate all accounting differences between two companies—particularly when the analyst does not have complete access to the internal books of one or both businesses. Consequently, the M&A analyst should supplement the adjusted valuation multiples with multiples that are less likely to be distorted by accounting assumptions. The be-all and end-all financial measure is cash flow: after all, either the cash is there or it is not. After that, measures such as EBITDA and, to a lesser extent, sales are commonly used for valuation multiples.

- *Cash flow.* Cash flow is a helpful basis for valuation because cash, when calculated properly, is entirely independent of accounting assumptions. Indeed, this is one key reason why DCF is generally considered the best valuation methodology. However, even this metric should be interpreted with care, as cash flows naturally vary from year to year, and any single year's results may not be indicative of a company's true earnings potential. To some degree, this volatility is mitigated if the analyst uses the next 12 months' forecasted cash flows as the basis for valuation. This does require that the analyst construct cash flow estimates for each company that is used in the comparables group. It goes without saying that predictions of the future can fall prey to error and bias.
- *EBITDA.* EBITDA is often used as a proxy for cash flow and is arguably the most common measure of financial performance

and value that purportedly overcomes the challenge of accounting differences. This is partly true, particularly when it comes to varying accounting assumptions used for depreciation, amoritization, and deferred taxes. However, even if EBITDA has been reviewed to correct for any issues for quality (as discussed earlier) there are other accounting problems with EBITDA as a valuation methology, particularly when EBITDA is presumably being used as a proxy for cash flow. That is, EBITDA ignores capital expenditures and taxes (remember, it is before interest, taxes, depreciation, and amortization). The cost of these items certainly *does* have an impact on value. More subtly, however, EBITDA shares many of the challenges that proliferate with GAAP—revenue and cost recognition, pension accounting, and so on.

- *Sales.* Sales, or revenue, has some appeal for valuation, as it speaks to a company's sales volume and, potentially, market share. Also, it is probably the second-least vulnerable financial metric after cash flow. This is because line items at the top of the income statement, such as sales, generally have fewer assumptions underpinning them. However, even these are open to at least some accounting interpretation—as is evident from the FASB's current standard for revenue recognition, ASU 2014-09: Revenue from Contracts with Customers (Topic 606). Furthermore, revenue says nothing of the company's profitability and cash flow–generating capabilities. Sales, in a vacuum, therefore may be of relatively minimal importance to the valuation discussion. As such, revenue multiples are less popular than EBITDA multiples and are often used only as a last resort if some of the other, more relevant, profit measures are unavailable or unreliable.

How do fluctuations in financial performance impact valuation multiples?

A valuation multiple based on a firm's profits is only meaningful if the profitability measure used is representative of the true earnings power of the business over time. What if, for instance, the target booked a large, windfall gain from multiyear litigation? Likewise, what if the target had experienced a substantial operating loss from a union strike? Clearly, the analyst would not want to put a multiple on these sums, as they are unlikely to recur each year. Rather, the analyst might make adjustments to a target's financial results to reflect unusual or nonrecurring gains or expenses such as these.

Sometimes, however, the fluctuation in a company's financial performance might reflect a cyclical downturn in earnings. Consider the impact to aluminum company Alcoa from a slowdown in auto sales, housing starts, or some other macroeconomic variable. Even a modest downturn in auto sales might have a disproportionate impact on Alcoa's earnings in a particular year, given Alcoa's relatively high fixed costs and, thus, operating leverage. Clearly, auto sales are not Alcoa's sole earnings driver; other variables will also impact results. The point, however, is that some companies—even entire industries—are more vulnerable than others to shorter-term fluctuations in demand.

So does that mean that Alcoa's intrinsic value should mirror the peaks and valleys of a volatile factor such as auto sales? Most analysts would agree that the answer is no. If it did, a buyer could just wait for an inevitable blip in demand, swoop in to acquire businesses like Alcoa on the cheap, wait 12 to 24 months for demand to rebound, and then sell the company. If only it were that easy! A multiple is only meaningful if the profit on which it is based is indicative of the target's future profit potential. Where this is not the case, the analyst should smooth out earnings over a reasonable period of time (three to five years often works).

Is it possible that inconsistencies in valuation multiples might simply reflect market mispricings?

Yes. If the analyst cannot reconcile differences in multiples by the companies' relative business quality, accounting differences, or profit/cyclical fluctuations, then it is at least possible that the market may be mispricing the asset. Indeed, market inefficiencies such as these are what nearly every active manager of publicly traded stocks and bonds seeks.

Furthermore, the M&A market, which involves control, is a less efficient market than the publicly traded securities market as a whole, so it is even more likely that, yes, mispricings can, and do, happen. (For more about the role of control premiums, see the discussion of comparable transactions analysis in the following section.) Just as identifying mispricings is the rallying cry of most asset managers, so too is it the objective of many M&A practitioners. In our experience, if the work is exhaustive and accurate, and a business still appears mispriced, it probably is. This is what we work for! It is the M&A analyst's task to identify such mispricings; the analyst's skill is in distinguishing between differences from underlying fundamentals—which are therefore justifiable—and those from market inefficiencies.

Can you use the comparable company approach for distressed companies?

Comparable companies analysis is not easy for a distressed entity, because the trailing earnings and cash flow for a business in bankruptcy will be low (perhaps even negative) relative to its normalized earnings power. However, this might only be a temporary dip—at least until the company is able to stabilize operations and/or its balance sheet. Accordingly, it may be difficult to apply comparable company multiples to the distressed entity's most recent results. Instead, it is frequently necessary to apply the multiples to projected financial results (one to two years is typical) and, if applicable, discount the implied valuation back to the present. If applying the comparable companies analysis to projected financial results, be sure to calculate forward multiples using projected financial results of comparable publicly traded companies.

Are there other times when a particular comp should not be used?

Yes—beware of outliers. Sometimes, a valuation multiple might look unusually high when the denominator is very small relative to the numerator. A good example might be the P/E of an emerging-growth Internet company with a stock price of $50 per share but an EPS of only a small amount, say, \$0.25 per share. The P/E ratio in this case would be 200×. Think about that—on its surface, it would appear that the market is willing to capitalize 200 years' worth of the tech company's current-year earnings! Of course, what the market is more likely doing is looking through the near-term EPS of \$0.25 and anticipating significant earnings growth in the near future. If, for instance, the tech company were on a path to improve earnings tenfold over the next five years, a \$50 stock price would essentially be discounting \$2.50 of EPS for a more reasonable 20× P/E five years out.

Still, this does little to help our universe of valuation comps today. When an output value is very large relative to the peer group, try to determine the reason, mark the multiple as "NM" (not material) in your spreadsheet, and exclude the outlier from the calculation of summary statistics.

What does a comparable companies analysis look like?

To build a comparable companies peer group for a potential acquisition target in any industry, the first step is to develop a list of industry comps and gather their relevant valuation and financial metrics. The analysis would summarize the equity capitalization, enterprise value, and book value of each comp. It would also look at revenue, EBITDA, and EPS for each comp, comparing them side by side. Data points such as these can provide insight into the quality of a particular company or market segment. The data gathered can be used to calculate each company's valuation multiples. There can be a relatively wide dispersion of valuation multiples. As described earlier in this chapter, there are a variety of factors that might be at play: varying levels of quality, different accounting standards and policies, short-term or cyclical fluctuations, and/or market mispricings.

COMPARABLE TRANSACTIONS ANALYSIS

What about comparable transactions? How can they be used to value a business?

At the root of *comparable transactions analysis*, also known as *precedent transactions analysis*, is that an analyst can estimate the value of a business based upon the prices paid by acquirers of similar companies in similar circumstances. This analysis provides useful information on valuation multiples that acquirers have paid for companies in the past in a specific sector.

The purpose and process are similar to what an acquirer would undertake in the case of a comparable companies analysis. Recall that the foundation of the comparable companies approach is the concept that businesses with similar characteristics should have similar valuations in the marketplace. This logic carries over to precedent transactions analysis—similar companies should sell at similar multiples—so the M&A analyst can approximate valuation for a particular target by researching the multiples paid in comparable deals. In effect, historical multiples represent an index of recent market prices paid by other acquirers and accepted by sellers. From a potential seller's perspective, these multiples suggest a price range within which buyers have been willing to transact. For potential buyers, the multiples represent price ranges that have been acceptable to sellers. At times, sharing this information can help bridge expectation gaps between the two sides.

The biggest difference between comparable companies and comparable transactions is the control premium embedded in transaction prices. As described earlier in this chapter, the comparable companies analysis generally does not reflect the control premium that a buyer typically pays in an M&A transaction. This control premium typically means that transaction multiples (i.e., those implied by a comparable transactions analysis) will generally be higher than trading multiples (i.e., those implied by a comparable companies analysis).

Strategic considerations for the future combined companies often take precedence over stand-alone valuation and cause companies to pay more than the company would attract from general investors. For example, in scenarios in which the buyer and seller have substantial geographic and product overlap, there may be greater prospects for cost synergies. This allows the buyer to increase its purchase price. Similarly, companies will often pay more in a competitive bidding situation to ensure a strategic asset does not fall into the hands of a competitor. Buying a company may also be a way of reserving a future opportunity that may or may not occur—an approach that can be valued as a "real option." (Real options are discussed in Chapter 2. See note 30 in that chapter.) Accordingly, a thoughtful comparable transactions analysis will provide at least some insight into what premium past acquirers have been willing to pay to gain control of a target. Note, however, that when comparing premiums paid in stock transactions, it may be necessary to make adjustments for inconsistencies in the date chosen for the stock value—for example, the date of announcement versus some earlier date. Preannouncement rumors can drive stock price up, reducing the premium if calculated at announcement date.[11]

Earlier you said that comparable companies analysis typically considers only publicly traded businesses. Is that true for comparable companies, as well?

Not necessarily. Recall that transparency was the key reason why comparable companies analysis typically uses public comps; the stock market ascribes a specific value on a stock at any given time, discounting a tremendous amount of economic and industry data into a single-point price. Also, the Securities and Exchange Commission (SEC) requires publicly traded companies to publish a minimum level of financial detail to public investors, making the data collection process a little easier for an M&A analyst.

M&A transactions involving two privately held businesses can be just as relevant to a given situation as deals involving two publicly traded companies. As before, though, the level of price transparency can pose challenges—it can be difficult to obtain sufficient financial data for private deals. In contrast, where at least one of the parties to a deal is public, there is likely to be a press release or quarterly filings on Form 8-K with at least high-level financial data. Often, the only data available in smaller acquisitions by public companies are the purchase price and target's revenue. However, even this can offer at least some perspective on valuation—despite the shortcomings of price-to-sales multiples, described earlier in this chapter.

As a practical matter, then, the data underlying M&A transactions involving at least one public company will be easier to obtain. Consequently, it would not be unusual for a precedent transactions analysis to be skewed toward those involving either a publicly traded buyer or seller.

What are the advantages of incorporating comparable transactions into the M&A valuation process?

Similar to its valuation cousin, comparable companies, the precedent transactions analysis is helpful because it is based on publicly available data and reflects real-world situations. Just as a comparable companies analysis is meaningful because it shows how the financial markets value publicly traded stocks, so too is the comparable transactions analysis helpful because it illustrates past transactions that successfully closed at certain valuation levels.

A thorough comparable transactions analysis yields a secondary, but equally important, benefit to the M&A practitioner: by researching who paid what for which companies or assets, the M&A analyst is building valuable market research into which industry players are the highly acquisitive consolidators versus rugged stand-alones committed to internal growth and into the underlying market demand for different types of acquisition targets. For instance, the frequency of transactions, trend of multiples paid, structure of transactions, and so on, can help suggest whether M&A demand is building or waning in a particular sector.

What should I be wary of when building a precedent transactions analysis?

Unfortunately, there are some limitations to using comparable transactions to estimate the value of a target. Here again, precedent transactions share several of these disadvantages with their comparable company brethren. Arguably, the biggest question to ask is whether the public data on past transactions are "clean" or whether they might be limited and/or misleading. Consider the following questions in any transaction comps that you might consider including in your M&A universe:

- What was the state of the financial markets at the time of the deal? Was the stock market particularly strong or weak? Could that have had an impact on the price paid?

- Where were we in the business cycle when the transaction closed? Were the target's earnings peakish, normal, or at trough levels? Did the target recently report any one-time gains or losses that might have skewed reported earnings? How might these factors have been accounted for in the takeout price?
- What was the sale process? Did the acquirer source the transaction through its proprietary deal flow, or was it a competitive auction run by an investment bank?
- How competitive was the M&A market for businesses like this at the time of the deal? Was there some scarcity value attributable to the asset? At the other end of the spectrum, was this a distressed sale or some other form of motivated seller?
- How strategic was the target to the acquirer? What cost savings and/or revenue synergies were discounted into the deal? Are these assumptions representative of most deals in the industry, or was this deal special?
- Were there unique structuring details to this transaction that we should consider? Was there future, contingent consideration that we should add back? Was there a unique tax angle, such as net operating loss carryforwards that represented hidden value?
- How much time has elapsed since the deal? Understandably, recent M&A transactions may more accurately reflect the values that buyers are currently willing to pay than would acquisitions that happened in the distant past. In addition to the fact that business cycles are always changing, industry fundamentals are similarly in constant evolution.

The key takeaway is that precedent transactions are rarely comparable. Nearly every deal represents a unique set of circumstances. It is the role of the M&A analyst, then, to tear into the details behind each deal and understand at least the high-level strategy behind each deal. This will help explain *why* the deal happened and, consequently, how representative the transaction might be as a clean-deal comp.

Which transactions are comparable?

The reader faced a similar challenge earlier in this chapter when thinking through which companies are comparable enough to be grouped together as a peer group. *In re Sunbelt Beverage Corp. Shareholder Litigation*, a decision by Chancellor William B. Chandler in the form of a letter to counsel, offers a cautionary tale in company valuation using comparable transactions.[12] In this case, the plaintiff contended that members of the Sunbelt board of directors violated their fiduciary duties in cashing them out at an unfair price ($45.83 per share), based on a flawed comparison of other transactions. Like the *Onti* case mentioned earlier with respect to comparing companies, it is clear that a target's size and industry may not represent narrow enough criteria when selecting which transactions are truly comparable. As one commenter noted, it is not enough to simply apply the median implied multiple from a set of transactions involving companies in the same general industry: "A comparable transaction analysis is much more likely to be a meaningful indicator of value, and to therefore withstand serious scrutiny, if the unique attributes of each transaction are fully understood and accounted for in applying the data to the subject company."[13]

As previously discussed, comparable transactions should share a number of characteristics: similar industries, fundamental characteristics (margins, credit quality, etc.), and size. In addition to these factors, which are shared by the comparable companies analysis, deal comps should also consider transaction-specific characteristics, such as those described in the preceding question. The M&A analyst should understand the background to the deal and why it occurred. In addition to the questions listed previously, the analyst should know whether the buyer was strategic or financial (with financial buyers more likely to pay a "pure" multiple), domestic or international, and whether the acquirer sourced the transaction through a full-blown auction process (which tends to drive up prices) or through proprietary channels (likely resulting in a more negotiated, middle-of-the-road multiple).

Exhibit 3-6 contains a checklist of variables to consider in gauging the comparability of two M&A transactions.

Exhibit 3-6 Comparable Transactions Checklist

Look for similarity in:

- Industry group
- Size (revenues, assets, market cap)
- Timing
- Business mix (products, markets served, distribution channels, etc.)
- Geographic location
- Profitability
- Rate of growth
- Credit quality
- Capital structure (debt/equity and related ratios)
- Business model

You mentioned cost savings and revenue synergies here and in Chapter 2, "Strategy." How exactly do these synergies impact transaction multiples?

Cost savings are typically the biggest value driver in most M&A transactions, although the magnitude can vary dramatically from situation to situation.The point of raising cost savings in this chapter is to emphasize that you should comb through press releases, investor presentations, and other sources to understand what might have been discounted into the M&A transaction. This will help you to normalize the implied transaction multiple.

In the event that the parties have not quantified the expected cost savings in the public disclosure, but you are reasonably confident that they were a key driver of the deal's pricing, there are a few rules of thumb that you can try, to see if they normalize the multiples. For instance, many investment bankers in industrial deals will assume cost savings of approximately 3 percent of revenue. In other cases in which there are material back-office and production savings, advisors may assume that 20 to 25 percent of costs are eliminated. Like everything else in M&A, however, these rules of thumb should not be viewed in a vacuum—they should be considered in the context of the facts and circumstances of the specific situation.

What about revenue synergies? How do they factor into deal pricing?

We often read about potential revenue synergies in M&A announcements. In the classic case, the acquirer anticipates a healthy amount of cross-selling between the buyer's and seller's customer lists. In other circumstances, the purchaser might have strong distribution but limited product, whereas the seller has strong product and weak distribution. It seems fairly intuitive.

It is wise to be skeptical of these assumptions. To be sure, such situations can and do arise. However, they often look better on paper than they do in practice. For instance, consider the time a manufacturer of aluminum wheels for heavy-duty trucks bought out a manufacturer of brake kits for the same kind of truck. Both suppliers made components for the same *type* of truck, but for different original equipment manufacturer (OEM) customers. In theory, combining the two businesses seemed like a home run: cross-sell into each other's customers, and, potentially, even eliminate some redundant sales resources. The problem, however, was that the purchasing managers for wheels and brake kits at the OEM customers were two completely different people! So the fact that the wheel manufacturer sold into "Joe at Peterbilt" really had no benefit to the brake kit manufacturer, since he really needed to talk to "Mike at Peterbilt." This company ultimately filed for bankruptcy, and while the transaction itself did not cause this, it certainly didn't help matters—the point being, beware of overly optimistic revenue expectations.

Indeed, while revenue synergies often populate M&A press releases, rarely do you read about potential revenue *attrition*. That is, how much revenue do the combined companies expect to *lose* to competitors as a result of this deal? Although not discussed frequently, revenue attrition is seen at least as often as revenue synergies.

Which party generally pays more for an acquisition: strategic buyers or financial sponsors?

At the risk of making broad generalizations, the conventional wisdom is that strategic buyers can generally pony up more for a target because they perceive greater synergies and/or cost savings. In addition, financial sponsors are generally more price sensitive because they will typically target a five-year annualized return of 20 to 25 percent before making an investment. Strategic buyers may also face hurdle rate requirements from their boards of directors—perhaps 15 percent, 20 percent, or more. However, a strategic buyer, all else equal, has more leeway to deviate from these return criteria for a target that's, well, "strategic."

Of course, there are exceptions. If a financial sponsor is consolidating a particular segment, it might have all the same cost savings opportunities as a strategic buyer. Also, the sponsor might consider a particular target as a "platform deal" of a certain size that creates follow-on acquisition opportunities. Some financial sponsors will use these points to rationalize paying up for a deal—and, in some cases, rightly so.

One other comment: it's no surprise to financial sponsors that strategic buyers can afford to pay more. This has some influence on the behavioral aspects of the M&A cycle. For instance, financial sponsors are more likely to buy into segments that are out of favor—where EBITDA, deal multiples, and competition for acquisitions are all depressed. Also, financial sponsors will often pay all cash, whereas a strategic buyer might need to incorporate a large amount of stock as transaction consideration. This can be a deal advantage to the financial buyer when the sellers are highly focused on liquidity. Lastly, some financial sponsors will understandably point out to a seller that a strategic buyer can pay more because it's likely to take out costs (i.e., fire people). The prospect—whether fairly or unfairly cast—of an industry competitor potentially dismantling an entrepreneur's life work can motivate some prospective sellers to select a financial buyer, even at a lower price.

So what's the process for constructing a comparable transactions analysis?

As noted, the process is similar to that used in a comparable companies analysis. The process basically involves five steps:

1. Research the universe of M&A deals involving companies in similar industries and of approximate size as the potential target.

2. Refine this universe to a list of, ideally, 5 to 10 acquisitions.
3. Calculate the implied valuation multiples, based on the most commonly used metrics in the target's particular industry. As was the case with comparable companies, this list will typically involve EV/EBITDA, P/E, price to cash flow, and, potentially, price to sales.
4. Strip out the transaction-specific factors that might skew the multiples in other deals.
5. Apply the resulting multiples to the target to broadly estimate its change-of-control value.

Where should I look for transaction details?

If you have access to a database such as Bloomberg, Capital IQ, FactSet, Zephyr, Mergermarket, or Reuters, this step is easy. If you do not have access to these types of resources, you will have to find annual reports, conduct Google searches, or track down sell-side analyst reports to gather your data.

What does a precedent transaction analysis look like?

Much of the process is similar to the comparable companies analysis outlined earlier in this chapter. As a result, this chapter will not go into the same level of detail for precedent transactions. In any event, a deep dive may not be necessary, because a "picture is worth a thousand words." Exhibit 3-7 summarizes seven hypothetical deals in the managed-care industry and what the output might look like. The most common datapoints to include are the following:

- Names of the buyer and seller in each deal.
- For public sellers, pricing, including offering price per share and percentage premium over recent closing prices. (As mentioned earlier, however, this is a tricky area, as premium metrics vary greatly.)[14]

Exhibit 3-7 Summary of Precedent Transactions*

		Pricing Data for Public Sellers		Enterprise	Enterprise Value Multiples			Equity Multiples		
Acquirer	Target	Per-Share	One-Day Premium	Value	Sales	EBITDA	EBIT	Earnings	Book Value	Contingent Consideration
Delta Logistics	Mom & Pop Trucking	N/A	N/A	$230	1.5x	4.3x	5.6x	8.3x	1.0x	$20 million in Year 4
Eagle Freight	U Store It Ltd.	$34.00	18%	$1,267	1.2x	8.0x	10.4x	15.4x	1.2x	N/A
Expedited Process	Fox Enterprises	N/A	N/A	$356	1.6x	3.5x	4.6x	6.7x	0.9x	$15 million over three years
XTP Delivery	Keytouch Logistics	N/A	N/A	$337	1.4x	4.0x	5.2x	7.7x	1.1x	None.
Delta Logistics	Global Freight	$45.50	21%	$773	1.7x	5.0x	6.5x	9.6x	1.1x	N/A
Eagle Freight	Big Sky Leasing	$77.25	35%	$2,227	1.2x	8.5x	11.1x	16.4x	1.3x	N/A
United Express	Ivy Track	N/A	N/A	$135	1.7x	4.5x	5.9x	8.7x	1.0x	$25 million in Year 5
Delta Logistics	Forever Freight	$36.70	26%	$665	1.3x	6.0x	7.8x	11.5x	1.2x	N/A
		Mean	**25%**	**$749**	**1.5x**	**5.5x**	**7.1x**	**10.5x**	**1.1x**	
		Median	**24%**	**$511**	**1.5x**	**4.8x**	**6.2x**	**9.1x**	**1.1x**	

*$ in millions, expected per-share data

- The equity value and enterprise value at the offering price.
- The implied EV/EBITDA and P/E multiples (which, in this case, are calculated as last 12 months [LTM], current year, and next year).
- The mix of transaction considerations (not shown here, but occasionally included in notes).
- For an accurate view of pricing, whether there was an earnout or some other contingent consideration. (As an aside, transactions involving public sellers do not have contingent consideration. It would be too difficult mechanically to allocate subsequent payments to formerly public shareholders long after the deal has closed.)

Why do takeout multiples in one market segment or geographic region sometimes appear conservative compared with precedent transactions in other geographic regions?

The concept that M&A transaction multiples can vary widely across different market segments and geographic regions is sometimes a bit surprising, given how global the financial markets and economic forces are. Nonetheless, these variations can, and do, happen. A prime example is the long-standing gap between bank acquisition multiples in Canada versus the United States.

When these wide ranges in valuation multiples materialize, it is helpful to consider whether there are structural differences in the various regions or market segments. For instance:

- Does one market face a more difficult regulatory environment? The more likely it is that industry regulators might challenge a deal, the more likely it is that the deal will crater, which can narrow the list of potential buyers. To compensate, many acquirers will ultimately reduce takeout multiples.
- Does one market represent a mature oligopoly, while the other is in the early stages of consolidation? In a mature market, there

will likely be more targets than acquirers, thus reducing price competition. In contrast, a market in the early stages of consolidation may offer many possible suitors for quality targets, thus providing the targets more leverage. This competition pushes takeout multiples up and, as a consequence, risks nudging postdeal value creation down.

- Are targets in one geographic market more profitable and/or better capitalized than in the competing market? This may have two impacts on M&A valuations: (1) the stronger industry dynamics of the "better" region might attract more buyers and, therefore, increase competition for deals; and (2) the publicly traded acquirers in that "better" region might have higher stock prices and, therefore, a lower cost of capital. This can allow them to "stretch" more for acquisition prices.

What if there are too few (or no) transactions that are comparable or the only comparables are dated?

This is a real-world problem. A key difficulty with the comparable transactions approach is the limited availability of financial data regarding past deals involving one or more private companies. That said, it is always possible to do an analysis of transactions that are not exactly comparable and to give a discount or premium to adjust their values. Ultimately, however, the precedent transaction approach is generally used in conjunction with other valuation techniques, including DCF and comparable companies analysis. As a result, leaving comparable transactions out of a valuation report is certainly permissible.

Can comparable transactions be used in valuing distressed companies?

The comparable transactions approach (similar to the comparable companies approach discussed earlier) is not ideal for distressed transactions unless it is comparing two distressed entities.

Comparing companies, and comparing transactions, can be challenging—since no two companies, and no two transactions, are exactly alike. Therefore, to be complete, valuations should include other valuation approaches. Another commonly accepted approach is the DCF method. The next section offers a primer for this all-important subject.

How can the disadvantages of valuation comparison be mitigated?

In addition to looking at the company in relation to others at a single point in time, look at the company at present in relation to itself at multiple future points in time. This is the purpose of discounted cash flow analysis.

DCF ANALYSIS

What exactly is DCF analysis?

DCF analysis is a widely used analytical framework for measuring the present value of multiyear cash flows. In its simplest application in the world of M&A, a DCF analysis estimates the value of a business based on projections of how much cash the business will generate in the future. These cash flows are "discounted" because a dollar earned in the future is worth less than a dollar earned today, given the time value of money. Tweaking the analysis, DCF also enables an acquirer to explore whether a particular target is likely to generate sufficient risk-adjusted returns.

Although this text discusses DCF in the context of M&A, the analysis is not limited solely to that application. Rather, the framework can apply to nearly any financial decision-making process: whether to buy a stock, whether the purchase of a new piece of equipment makes financial sense, what the value of a piece of real estate should be, and so on. Accordingly, the analyses described throughout are relevant for many other applications.

How is a DCF analysis different from a multiples analysis?

Discounted cash flow looks at *one* company, and it looks into the *future*. It predicts how well the company will do in terms of future free cash flow (money left over after paying necessities). It skips historical analysis in favor of basics: cash is cash, and cash is good!

Multiples analysis looks at *many* companies, and it looks at the *past*. It tells you what kind of ratios have held true for comparable companies in past years. Also, multiples analysis uses a variety of accounting numbers—times sales, times profits, and so on—that may or may not indicate true economic value.

Moreover, DCF has some advantages over static, point-in-time approaches—such as multiples analysis—in that it adds more flexibility and more precision to the investment analysis.

Using all of these approaches in combination can be a helpful cross-check.

How does DCF stack up against other valuation approaches?

In many ways, cash flow–based valuation is the granddaddy of all valuation techniques. This is because, at the end of the day, all valuation measures are directly or indirectly focused on answering the same question: How much cash do I expect this business to generate during the relevant measurement period?

As its name suggests, DCF analysis is a form of analysis that anticipates a company's future net operating cash flow and discounts it to present value. The purist approach counts only "free" cash flow—that is, cash that is available to spend; it is calculated after capital expenditures and dividends are paid during the period.

Many analysts believe that the DCF method is the best way to value a going company, but it is not the only way. A thorough valuation can look not only at cash flow but also at assets, earnings, and stock price—as well as a variety of ratios and methodologies based on these fundamentals and, of course, a discount rate to reflect cost of capital.

What is the basic equation for DCF?

$$DCF = [CF/(1 + r)^1] + [CF/(1 + r)^2] + [CF/(1 + r)^3] + ... + [CF/(1 + r)^n]$$

Where:

CF = Cash Flow in the period
r = discount rate (or interest rate)
n = period number

What are the primary inputs into a DCF model?

To run a basic DCF model, a number of basic assumptions must be made to "drive" the calculations. These include the target's cash flows over a certain period of time, the target's projected capital structure, the appropriate discount rate, and the target's long-term value. How, precisely, the analyst arrives at these assumptions depends on a large number of variables: the target's particular industry, the stage of the company's life cycle, market conditions, the acquirer's requirements, capital structure, and so on.

The number of input variables and the level of detail will also vary, depending on a deal's complexity and the nature of the decision for which the DCF analysis is being conducted. Consequently, forgoing a "plug-and-chug" template model benefits the analyst not only because the analyst will understand the inner workings of the model better, but also because the model can better be customized to the specific target.

How do I build a DCF analysis?

A basic DCF analysis is composed of four major steps, each of which in turn involves a number of assumptions and calculations. These are illustrated in Exhibit 3-8 and include the following:

1. *Forecast the target's free cash flow.* This involves identifying the components and drivers of free cash flow, building out the complete set of historical financial statements, determining the appropriate forecast horizon as well as operating assumptions

Exhibit 3-8 Overview of the DCF Analysis Process

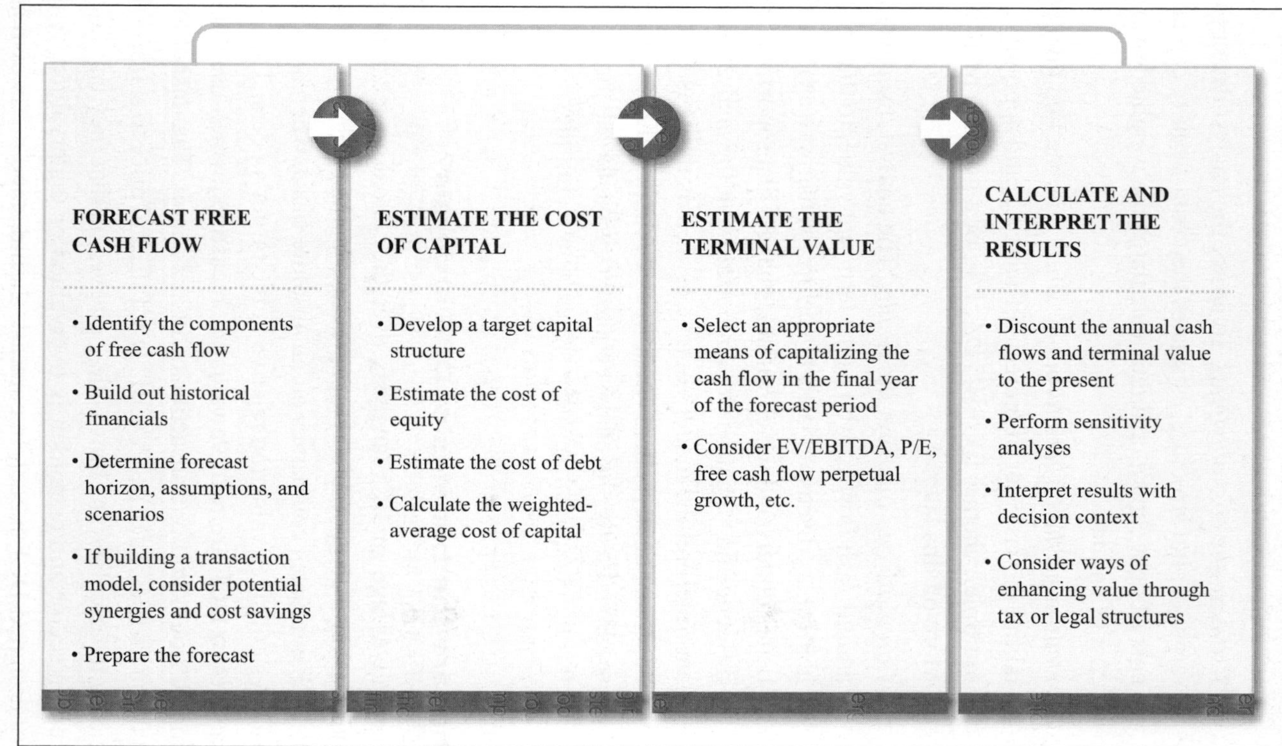
FORECAST FREE CASH FLOW
• Identify the components of free cash flow
• Build out historical financials
• Determine forecast horizon, assumptions, and scenarios
• If building a transaction model, consider potential synergies and cost savings
• Prepare the forecast
ESTIMATE THE COST OF CAPITAL
• Develop a target capital structure
• Estimate the cost of equity
• Estimate the cost of debt
• Calculate the weighted-average cost of capital
ESTIMATE THE TERMINAL VALUE
• Select an appropriate means of capitalizing the cash flow in the final year of the forecast period
• Consider EV/EBITDA, P/E, free cash flow perpetual growth, etc.
CALCULATE AND INTERPRET THE RESULTS
• Discount the annual cash flows and terminal value to the present
• Perform sensitivity analyses
• Interpret results with decision context
• Consider ways of enhancing value through tax or legal structures

and scenarios, and layering in potential synergies and cost savings (if building a transaction model).

2. *Estimate the cost of capital.* To do so, the analyst develops a target capital structure, estimates the cost of equity capital and cost of debt capital, and then calculates the weighted-average cost of capital.
3. *Determine the target's terminal value.* One method involves taking the last year of projected financials and applying a multiple, whether EV/EBITDA, P/E, or a growing perpetuity. More on this later.
4. *Calculate and interpret the results.* The analyst discounts each annual cash flow, as well as the terminal value, to the present. It's helpful, as discussed later, to perform sensitivity analyses to better understand which variables have a disproportionate influence on valuation. It is important that the analyst consider and interpret the model's output, as well as the sensitivity analyses, in a broader context (i.e., does the valuation make sense?). Lastly, the analyst considers ways of enhancing value through tax, legal, or other structuring techniques.

What are the benefits of DCF analysis?

A key advantage of DCF analysis over the valuation techniques introduced earlier—comparable companies and comparable transactions—is that DCF evaluates companies on an absolute basis, whereas other methodologies consider valuation relative to the target's peers. That is, the alternatives to DCF are relative valuation measures, which use multiples to compare stocks and/or transactions within a sector. The upshot to relative valuation metrics, such as EV/EBITDA, P/E, and price to sales, is that they are easy to calculate; the downside, however, is that they can fall short if an entire sector and/or market is overvalued or undervalued. A thoughtfully designed DCF model, in contrast, should stand on its own and steer you clear of opportunities that look inexpensive—but only against overvalued peers.

A second and equally valuable benefit of DCF analysis is that the approach is rooted in cash flow, rather than more subjective financial measures, such as EBITDA, earnings, and even sales. As discussed earlier, these noncash line items are all subject—to varying degrees—to accounting interpretation. For instance, a company's reported earnings may change dramatically based on what depreciation or amortization assumptions the business uses. Exhibit 3-5, seen earlier, illustrates how a minor change to a company's amortization schedule changed its net income by 14 percent. EBITDA, likewise, can change based on how inventories are tracked, among other assumptions. Cash, in contrast, is independent of accounting assumptions. Either the cash is there or it is not.

Consider, for instance, a manufacturer of injection-molded plastics in an environment of rapidly rising oil and resin prices. The manufacturer's EBITDA may look markedly different depending on whether the company tracks inventories on the basis of last-in, first-out (LIFO) or first-in, first-out (FIFO). Even sales figures depend on when and how the company recognizes revenue. For instance, does the aforementioned manufacturer recognize a sale upon shipment to a distributor, or is the product shipped considered contingent stock, with title passing only upon a follow-on sale to a retailer? These seemingly minor differences in accounting assumptions can result in dramatic differences to the company's income statement and, therefore, valuation multiples.

Furthermore, the DCF framework is flexible enough that it can be used to value a company as a stand-alone operation or in the context of a business combination. In the case of a stand-alone valuation, the analyst can forecast the cash flows for two separate businesses over a certain period of time, layer in the terminal values, and arrive at estimated values for each business as is. Then, the analyst can develop a pro forma forecast for the cash flows of the *combined* businesses—that is, including cost savings, revenue synergies, tax savings, and other transaction benefits—layer in a terminal value, and calculate the expected value of the combined businesses. If the present value of the combined businesses exceeds the combined value of the constituent companies on a stand-alone basis, the deal creates value and should proceed to the next stage in the process. Exhibit 3-9 summarizes the advantages of DCF analysis.

Exhibit 3-9 Advantages of DCF Analysis

- Absolute, rather than relative, valuation
- Rooted in cash flow, a more objective basis than earnings-based measures
- Highly flexible in application

Finally, DCF analysis can serve as a sanity check to the valuation that the analyst's multiples analysis produces.

Let's assume that, after a full multiples analysis, an acquirer is inclined to value an auto parts manufacturer at 7× next year's EBITDA of $100 million, for a $700 million enterprise value. Where did the 7× multiple come from? "Well," the acquirer may respond, "the peer group was trading at 6× EBITDA, and this particular manufacturer is growing 15 to 20 percent faster than those peers." Is this a reasonable valuation? What if the peer group was overvalued at the time of the multiples analysis? Or what if industry sales were below trend? Such factors might temporarily skew the peer group's valuation multiples to a figure that is either too high or too low.

Complementing this multiples analysis with a DCF model will help the acquirer think through how quickly the target must grow to achieve its $700 million valuation. DCF analysis requires the acquirer to think through such factors as where we are in the auto cycle, price-downs from OEM customers, obsolescence risk, and unionized labor costs. The acquirer must also consider the discount rate, which depends on the risk-free interest rate, the acquirer's cost of capital, and so on. These considerations should enhance the likelihood that the acquirer is ascribing a realistic price tag to the target. In this way, the DCF framework can help acquirers identify where a company's value is coming from and whether the proposed purchase price is justified.

What are the drawbacks of DCF analysis?

Just as DCF certainly has its merits, so too does it have its share of shortcomings. Some readers will be familiar with the phrase "garbage in, garbage out." The output to a model is only as strong as the quality of its inputs. A DCF model really boils down to three broad assumptions: free cash flow forecasts, terminal value, and discount rate. Depending on the analyst's beliefs around how the company will operate and how the industry will advance, DCF valuations can fluctuate widely. If the model's inputs—cash flows, terminal value, and discount rate—miss the mark materially, so will the resulting analysis. Garbage in, garbage out.

Even when the assumptions are reasonable at the time, small changes can result in material changes to valuation. One such example is illustrated in the discussion accompanying Exhibit 3-25, later in this chapter, where a change of one percentage point in the future expected growth rate has a 12.5 percent impact to valuation. Imagine! Granted, the example used here is an extreme one—but the point is that, like all other valuation analyses, no one approach is sacrosanct. The output from one analysis should be compared to those from other analyses.

Similarly, the DCF approach is enormously sensitive to the discount rate that is used. Because the discount rate can be influenced by many subjective factors, the valuation method is criticized at times as being ripe for manipulation. For instance, one of the first steps in calculating a discount rate is selecting a peer group of comparable publicly traded companies to establish "beta," a component of the weighted average cost of capital calculation defined later in this chapter. Which companies are, or are not, included in this peer group is entirely the decision of the individual conducting the analysis.

Another issue with DCF analysis is that the terminal value may be too large a portion of the total value (e.g., 90 percent). If the terminal value is too large in proportion to the overall value, then the DCF analysis may be meaningless because the interim cash flows that the DCF is supposed to be valuing have become insufficiently relevant. In particular, the higher the perpetuity growth rate discounted into the analysis, the higher the terminal value.

Consequently, it is good practice to constantly update one's assumptions in a DCF model. DCF analysis is a moving target that demands constant rethinking and modification. No model is set in stone; the analyst must adjust inputs and assumptions upon any meaningful development, such as a negative trend in earnings, the financial distress of a customer or vendor, or even a material change in interest rates. If expectations change,

Exhibit 3-10 Disadvantages of DCF Analysis

- Is it sensitive to cash flow projections, which may be inherently difficult to predict.
- Validity of the discount rate depends on assumptions for beta and the market risk premium.
- Terminal value may be distorted by incorrect estimations.

valuations change. This might not necessarily be the case, at least to the same degree, with valuation approaches that look at companies on a relative basis. Exhibit 3-10 summarizes the disadvantages of DCF analysis.

Which inputs into the DCF model can influence the output the most?

This is an important question, particularly given the preceding discussion about "garbage in, garbage out." The fact is, it depends—on the industry, on the company, on what growth assumptions are reflected in the model, and so on. However, of the three key inputs into a DCF model—cash flows, discount rate, and terminal value—a company's cash flows will typically have the least influence on the final valuation. The biggest driver is typically either the terminal value assumed or the discount rate used.

So when is the terminal value a bigger driver of the valuation than the discount rate? The longer the forecast period, the less impact the terminal value will generally have. Most DCF analysis will involve a forecast period of about five to seven years. When the forecast period is less than five years, the risk that the tail may wag the dog starts to increase.

How can I ensure that the assumptions I'm using in my DCF model are reasonable?

Many variables in a DCF analysis are interrelated, with many of the outcomes, such as internal rate of return (IRR), highly sensitive or elastic in response to changes in a number of key variables. Several steps can be taken to address this caveat:

- *Input validation.* The analyst should spend considerable time researching the set of assumptions and their relevance to the particular target being analyzed.
- *Sensitivity analysis.* In addition to crunching a core set of numbers, the analyst should explore the stability of the outputs and metrics generated by a DCF in response to changes in assumptions, scenarios, or "states of nature." More will be revealed in the "Forecasting Free Cash Flow" discussion later in this chapter.
- *Monte Carlo simulations.* While sensitivity analysis is helpful, in some cases the use of "best-case" and "worst-case" scenarios may provide misleading indications of risk. This is due to the fact that the scenario approach fails to recognize the interdependencies and probabilities that a worst-case or best-case scenario could be realized. That is, in many cases the joint probability of all things going bad, or all things going well, at the same time is infinitesimally small, and thus the use of worst-case or best-case scenarios provides false cues. The use of Monte Carlo simulations through specialized applications or spreadsheet add-ins can improve the quality of decision support provided by static DCF analysis.
- *Attribution analysis.* A final form of analysis that can help qualify the outputs generated by DCF models is the application of attribution analysis. Briefly, this technique focuses on identifying the key input assumptions that have the most impact on the outputs and performance measures. Once the critical assumptions have been identified, they can be subjected to more scrutiny through additional research.

How far out should I forecast annual cash flows before ascribing a terminal value?

As noted, the analyst should ideally forecast out at least five years—or else the terminal value comprises a disproportionate percentage of the enterprise value. Five to seven years is probably the most common horizon, although plenty of models look out 10 years. However, the ultimate test comes down to visibility; the analyst should forecast future cash flows as far out as there is a reasonable degree of confidence and until the business has matured and settled into slower growth.

This is not to say that the analyst must have 100 percent conviction in the forecast. After all, nobody has a crystal ball, and so each flow will be an estimate. However, there should be some reasonable basis to each year's view, with an explanation for how the analyst arrived at the particular forecast. Consequently, the acquirer's ability to make effective forward-looking projections is critical—or else the DCF will be particularly vulnerable to error.

Can DCF be used to value company divisions and subsidiaries, and how important is it to do this?

It is possible to perform DCF analysis on individual business units, but it can very much be a do-it-yourself job. Unit-level cash flow statements are not required under current accounting rules, although this has arisen as a suggestion in discussions of FASB Accounting Standards Codification Topic 280, Segment Reporting. The current accounting rules require separate income statements for company units but do not require cash flow statements, which must be estimated based on other data.

Divestitures are often made under duress, whether to gain needed cash or to comply with an antitrust order,[15] but there is strategic value in the case of companies that have diversified too far beyond their strategic core. While diversification makes sense for a financial portfolio, it can be risky for an operating company. Some become not so much conglomerates as *ag*glomerates—an assortment of disparate operations, each paying a fee for what often proves to be headquarters hindrance rather than headquarters help. The benefits of association—synergies such as the smoothing of cash flows effected by joining countercyclical operations—are often more than offset by the headquarters stultification of the entrepreneurial process so necessary for successful growth. The agglomerators are discovering that their disparate operations will generally do better as stand-alones if they cannot be integrated with similar operations.

FORECASTING FREE CASH FLOW

What exactly is free cash flow?

Free cash flow is the cash that a company throws off during a particular measurement period after all cash expenses have been paid. Free cash flow represents the actual amount of cash that a target has left from its operations that could be used for investing or financing activities. Examples of such activities include paying dividends and buying back stock.

In predicting future cash flows can I just use current cash flows and grow them from there?

M&A deals typically involve millions, if not billions, of dollars at risk. In our view, this is not the time for back-of-the-envelope work.

Ideally, the process of forecasting cash flows starts with the M&A analyst building a full set of three-part financial statements, including the income statement, balance sheet, and statement of cash flows. Although it is tempting to start with the target's most recent EBIT or EBITDA and run a quick top-down cash flow analysis, as described later, the analyst risks missing the true insight that can be gleaned from building a full model from the ground up.

In our experience, the only way an analyst can really understand how a company operates is by digging into the detail of forecasting revenues, margins, working capital, and so on—using perspective from the target's historical results. Building a full model also forces the analyst to consider economic and industry cycles, as well as shifts in product mix and customer base. Understandably, there are times when only a high-level analysis is required, making a full set of financials seem like a waste of time. But those who choose this route should be aware that the results are unlikely to accurately represent the target's financial future.

How do you calculate free cash flow?

There are two ways of calculating free cash flow: the top-down approach and the bottom-up approach. Exhibits 3-11 and 3-12 supplement the definitions that follow.

Exhibit 3-11 Defining Free Cash Flow—Top-down Approach

Financial Statement Line Item	Comments
EBIT	
Add depreciation and amortization	*Includes all depreciation and amortization subtracted from EBITDA to arrive at EBIT.*
EBITDA	
Subtract (add) increases (decreases) in working capital	*Includes changes in accounts receivable, inventory, prepaid expenses, accounts payable, accrued liabilities, etc.* *In some cases, it may be appropriate to include as working capital the minimum amount of cash necessary for operational purposes.*
Subtract capital expenditures	*Going forward, should include one-time, non-recurring cash flows to the extent they are planned.*
Equals free cash flows to the [unlevered] firm (FCFF)	***Cash flows available to both debt and equity holders***
Subtract cash interest paid	*May differ from interest expense due to noncash interest charges.*
Add interest tax shield	*Calculated by multiplying marginal tax rate by interest expense.*
Add (subtract) increases (decreases) in debt, preferred stock, and minority interest	*Increases in non–common equity sources of capital, net of principal repayments, result in greater cash for common equity holders.*
Subtract preferred dividends	*Any cash payments to non–common equity claimholders result in less cash to common equity holders.*
Equals free cash flows to the common equity (FCFCE)	***Cash flows available only to common equity holders. Assumes that all cash flows to the common equity are distributed (i.e., not reinvested) to ensure that retained earnings are not double-counted.***

Exhibit 3-12 Calculating Free Cash Flow—Example of Top-down Approach ($000s)

Financial Statement Line Item	Amount
EBIT	**$12,880**
Add depreciation and amortization	2,576
EBITDA	**15,456**
Changes in working capital	(1,546)
Subtract capital expenditures	(2,190)
FCF to the unlevered firm	**11,721**
Cash interest paid	(586)
Add interest tax shield	234
Changes in debt, preferred stock, and minority interest	—
Preferred dividends	—
FCF to the common equity	**$11,369**

The *top-down approach* (Exhibit 3-11) starts with the target's EBIT; it adds back depreciation and amortization, which are noncash expenses, to arrive at EBITDA. The analyst then adds or subtracts changes in working capital (depending on whether working capital was a source or use of cash during the period) and subtracts capital expenditures. This arrives at *free cash flows to the unlevered firm* (FCFF). FCFF are the cash flows, generated by the target, that are available to both debt and equity holders. From here, the analyst subtracts financing expenses—both interest and preferred dividends—to calculate *free cash flows to the common equity* (FCFCE). This is the residual cash flows available to common shareholders after required financing expenses are paid to creditors and preferred shareholders.

Exhibit 3-12 illustrates a top-down calculation of free cash flow for an auto parts manufacturer.

In contrast, the *bottom-up approach* (Exhibit 3-13) starts with the target's reported net income (i.e., GAAP earnings) and adds back noncash expense and other flows. For instance, the bottom-up approach either adds

Exhibit 3-13 Defining Free Cash Flow—Bottom-up Approach

Financial Statement Line Item	Comments
Net income	***Net income as reported***
Add (subtract) noncash expenses (income)	*Includes depreciation and amortization, deferred taxes, and other noncash items but excludes noncash interest expense.*
Subtract (add) increases (decreases) in working capital	*Includes changes in accounts receivable, inventory, prepaid expenses, accounts payable, accrued liabilities, etc.* *In some cases, it may be appropriate to include as working capital the minimum amount of cash necessary for operational purposes.*
Equals adjusted cash flow from operations	
Add interest expense	*Includes noncash interest expense. As long as you assume that initial excess cash and all interim cash flows are distributed to shareholders (i.e., no cash other than minimum cash balances accumulates in the forecast period), it is appropriate to exclude interest income on excess cash balances from the free cash flow calculation.*
Subtract interest tax shield	*Calculated by multiplying marginal tax rate by interest expense. If the company has net operating losses (NOLs) or is not expected to be a taxpayer within the forecast horizon, there should be no interest tax shield.*
Subtract capital expenditures	*Going forward, should include one-time, non-recurring cash flows to the extent they are planned.*

Equals free cash flows to the unlevered firm (FCFF)	***Cash flows available to both debt and equity holders***
Subtract cash interest paid	*May differ from interest expense due to noncash interest charges.*
Add interest tax shield	*Calculated by multiplying marginal tax rate by interest expense.*
Add (subtract) increases (decreases) in debt, preferred stock, and minority interest	*Increases in non–common equity sources of capital, net of principal repayments, result in greater cash for common equity holders.*
Subtract preferred dividends	*Any cash payments to non–common equity claimholders result in less cash to common equity holders.*
Equals free cash flows to the common equity (FCFCE)	***Cash flows available only to common equity holders. Assumes that all cash flows to the common equity are distributed (i.e., not reinvested) to ensure that retained earnings are not double-counted.***

to or subtracts from net income (depending on the aggregate flows) such noncash expenses as depreciation, amortization, and deferred taxes, as well as changes in working capital. The resulting figure is the target's cash flows from operations. From here, the analyst adds back the tax-effected interest expense (i.e., interest expense less the tax shield) and subtracts capital expenditures to arrive at FCFF. The bridge from FCFF to FCFCE is identical under both the top-down and bottom-up approaches.

Exhibit 3-14 illustrates a bottom-up calculation of free cash flow for the same auto parts manufacturer discussed earlier.

Which approach for calculating cash flow is preferable: top-down or bottom-up?

Mathematically, the two approaches should generate the same FCFF and FCFCE. (If they do not, your model is wrong!) Thus, it doesn't *really* matter which method the analyst selects; it's a matter of personal preference.

Exhibit 3-14 Calculating Free Cash Flow—Example of Bottom-up Approach ($000)

Financial Statement Line Item	Amount
Net income	**$7,376**
Add (subtract) noncash expenses (income)	7,728
Changes in working capital	(1,546)
Adjusted cash flow from operations	**13,559**
Add interest expense	586
Subtract interest tax shield	(234)
Subtract capital expenditures	(2,190)
FCF to the unlevered firm	**11,721**
Subtract cash interest paid	(586)
Add interest tax shield	234
Changes in debt, preferred stock, and minority interest	—
Subtract preferred dividends	—
FCF to the common equity	**$11,369**

As a practical matter, however, the choice might partly depend on whichever valuation multiples the acquirer is most focused on, for example, EV/EBITDA or P/E (as described earlier). If the valuation discussion is generally focused on a multiple of EBITDA (i.e., 7× EBITDA for an auto parts manufacturer), most of the discussion will revolve around that financial metric. In this case, dealmakers generally prefer to use the top-down approach because it has EBIT or EBITDA neatly at the top of the column.

If, in contrast, the valuation multiples are focused largely on earnings or net income, then it probably makes more sense to use the bottom-up approach because it leads with net income. A good example might be a specialty lender, for which interest is a "real expense." Such companies are more likely to sell for a multiple of book value or a multiple of earnings, rather than a multiple of EBITDA, since interest is actually an operating expense in such cases.

OK, I understand the mechanics of how cash flows are calculated. How do I go about evaluating whether they are reasonable?

Projecting cash flow is the most difficult and usually the most subjective part of constructing a DCF model. It requires addressing a myriad of questions, including the following:

- Is the forecast substantially different from management's projections? If so, why?
- Has the company been able to meet its projections in the past?
- What are the industry's prospects?
- How secure is the company's competitive position?
- Is this business cyclical? If so, do the projections properly take this into account?
- What are the company's growth or expansion plans?
- What are the working capital and fixed asset requirements to achieve these plans?
- Is the business seasonal? If so, what are the seasonal working capital needs?
- What events (strikes, currency fluctuations, foreign competition, loss of suppliers, etc.) could affect the projected results?
- Does the company have any excess assets or divisions that can or should be sold?
- How long would it take to make these sales, and how much money would they generate?
- Are there any other potential sources of cash?
- What can go wrong in all this, and does the company have any contingency plans?

This list is far from exhaustive, and it can take anywhere from a few hours to several weeks or months of due diligence to get a good feel for the cash flow. Once this has been done, the acquirer will be able to reasonably estimate the total financing needed at the closing date and prospectively for a five- to ten-year period thereafter.

How do you avoid undue optimism in cash flow projections?

At least two sets of projections should be made: the *base case* and a *reasonably worst case*. The base case tends to have some optimistic thinking in it, and the reasonably worst case is one in which management believes it has a 90 percent chance of meeting its targets. The buyer's decision to pursue a deal and the amount of money he or she targets to borrow is dependent on that 90 percent case. If the buyer relies on the reasonably worst-case projection, everything need not fall exactly into place for the target to meet its debt obligations.

CALCULATING THE DISCOUNT RATE

What is a discount rate?

Recall that the fundamental concept behind the DCF method is that the value of a business is the sum of all future cash flows of that business, discounted back to the present. Since a dollar in the future is worth less than a dollar today, future cash flows are discounted using a *discount rate*. The formula to calculate the value of future cash flows is summarized in Exhibit 3-15.

Exhbit 3-15 Present Value Formula

$$PV = \frac{FV}{(1 + i)^n}$$

Where:

PV = Present value of the future payment
FV = Future amount of the money that must be discounted
i = Discount rate used
n = Number of periods (typically in years)

Consider an example. If you were to offer me a guaranteed payment of \$100 one year from today, what would be the value of that payment today (known as the *present value*)? If we were to assume a 10 percent discount rate, the present value of that payment would be \$90.91. Mathematically, the equation would look like the following:

$$PV = \frac{\$100}{(1 + 10\%)^1}$$

In contrast, if we were to assume a 12 percent discount rate, the present value would be only \$89.29. Note the inverse relationship between the two: a *higher* discount rate results in a *lower* present value, whereas a *lower* discount rate drives a *higher* present value.

$$PV = \frac{\$100}{(1 + 12\%)^1}$$

Sometimes it is more intuitive to think about a discount rate being the corollary to an interest rate. For example, let's assume I have a \$100 debt that comes due one year from today. If I were to put \$90.91 in the bank today at a fixed interest rate of 10 percent, the account would be worth \$100 in the future. But let's say I shop around a bit and find a competing bank willing to offer me a 12 percent rate. How much must I deposit today to have \$100 in a year? Only \$89.29; the higher interest rate requires a lower present value.

The previous examples calculate the present value of only one future payment. My DCF model has several years of future cash flows. How does that work?

This is typical of most DCF models—the analyst is calculating the *net present value*, or NPV, of a stream of future cash flows. In effect, the value of each period's cash flow is discounted to today.

Let's revisit the first example. Let's assume a guaranteed payment of \$100 every year for three years, starting one year from today. If we were to assume a 10 percent discount rate, the analysis would look like the following:

$$NPV = PV1 + PV2 + PV3 = \frac{100}{(1.10)^1} + \frac{100}{(1.10)^2} + \frac{100}{(1.10)^3}$$

$$= \$90.91 + \$82.65 + \$75.13 = \$248.69$$

So what is the correct discount rate to use in a DCF analysis?

There really is no "correct" rate to use. Selecting which discount rate to use is a subjective process. But if we were to rephrase the question as "What is the *appropriate* discount rate to use?," there would probably be (at least) two ways to answer this question: the academic approach and the practical approach. As with most things academic, it is important that the student understand the theory behind the textbook answer. By understanding the theory, the student has a better appreciation for when to tweak the rules. For nothing in M&A is as much an art as valuation.

The textbook DCF analysis uses a firm's after-tax, nominal *weighted average cost of capital*—more commonly referred to as its WACC—to discount the after-tax, nominal unlevered free cash flows to the firm. WACC is the weighted average of the debt and equity costs of capital (including preferred stock), using market value weights for capital structure components.

How do I calculate a company's WACC?

The weighted average cost of capital is calculated as shown in Exhibit 3-16.

The cost of equity capital is the return a firm theoretically pays to its shareholders to compensate for the risk such shareholders undertake by investing their capital. Likewise, the cost of debt capital is the return a firm pays to its creditors for a loan. Both the cost of equity and cost of debt are typically expressed as a rate of return. So the shareholders of a particular company might target a 20 percent annual return before investing in a company, whereas lenders might only need an 8 percent return. The cost of equity capital, in this case, is 20 percent, while the cost of debt capital is 8 percent.

Exhibit 3-16 WACC Formula

$$WACC = K_E\,(E/V) + K_D\,(1 - T)\,(D/V) + K_P\,(P/V)$$

Where:

K_E = Cost of common equity capital
E/V = Ratio of market value of common equity to total firm value
K_D = Cost of debt capital
T = Corporate marginal tax rate
D/V = Ratio of market value of debt to total firm value
K_P = Cost of preferred equity capital
P/V = Ratio of market value of preferred equity to total firm value

We can extend this example to calculate the company's WACC. Assume the company described here is 20 percent debt financed and 80 percent equity financed. For the sake of simplicity, we will assume the equity is common, that is, no preferred shares. As noted, this particular company has a cost of common equity capital of 20 percent and a cost of debt capital of 8 percent. Its marginal tax rate is 40 percent. To reiterate the formula from Exhibit 3-16:

$$WACC = K_E\,(E/V) + K_D\,(1 - T)\,(D/V) + K_P\,(P/V)$$

Where:

K_E = 20% (cost of common equity capital)
E/V = 80% (ratio of market value of common equity to total firm value)
K_D = 8% (cost of debt capital)
D/V = 20% (ratio of market value of debt to total firm value)
T = 40% (corporate marginal tax rate)

Accordingly, the company's WACC is 16.6%:

$$WACC = 20\%\,(80\%) + 8\%\,(1 - 40\%)\,(20\%) = 16.0\% + 0.6\% = 16.6\%$$

This makes sense if I'm doing a stand-alone valuation. But what if I'm combining two companies? Whose WACC should I use?

In valuing an M&A target, the analyst should use the WACC of the target company rather than the WACC of the acquirer.

How do I calculate a company's cost of debt capital?

Estimating a company's cost of debt capital is relatively straightforward when the company already has debt outstanding and the capital structure is static; the interest rate charged on the existing debt should be an accurate proxy, provided that the rate is arm's-length and not below market (i.e., from an intercompany or shareholder-provided loan).

The current interest rate on the debt might not be an accurate proxy if circumstances have changed since the time the company secured the debt. Have macroeconomic conditions improved or worsened? What about the company's financials? Has its industry fallen out of favor? If the debt is publicly traded, these factors are likely discounted into the debt's effective yield. If, however, the debt is privately held, the stated interest rate may be misleading. Accordingly, it is important that the analyst consider changes in both macroeconomic and microeconomic factors.

What about changes in the target's capital structure? How does that impact its WACC?

WACC does not take into account a dynamic capital structure; therefore, the analyst should generally assume a constant capital structure (i.e., the target's existing leverage or the industry average). For a company with a rapidly changing capital structure (i.e., a leveraged buyout [LBO]), it may be appropriate to use a different WACC in each year of the forecast as financial leverage changes.

Consider, for instance, a private equity firm that's evaluating a target with a debt-to-capital (debt-to-cap) ratio of 20 percent and current borrowing costs of 8 percent. The target's borrowing costs would likely increase meaningfully from 8 percent currently if the private equity firm were to increase the target's debt-to-cap ratio to 80 percent. As the private equity firm repays the loan, the target's borrowing costs would presumably decline—which would drive the WACC lower. As an aside, this changing capital structure may impact not only the cost of debt capital but also the cost of equity capital. That is, capital providers demand higher returns for riskier investments or they will place their capital elsewhere. As a company's risk increases (decreases), its cost of capital increases (decreases)—from both a debt and an equity standpoint.

What about a company's cost of equity capital?

While a company's present cost of debt capital is relatively easy to estimate by its current interest rate, the company's cost of equity is more difficult to estimate because the cost of equity is unobservable. However, equity capital is still a cost despite the fact that it might not have a fixed and stated price that a company must pay. Equity investors will have an expected return on the capital they invest in the company; if the company cannot meet this expected return, the company's stock price will go down. This declining stock price may be obvious if the company's shares are public traded. In the case of a privately held company, this deteriorating equity value may not be apparent until management seeks to raise new equity capital.

There are multiple models—derived both in academia and in practice—for estimating a company's cost of equity capital. The granddaddy of these is the *capital asset pricing model*, or CAPM, which estimates a company's cost of equity based on the risk-free rate plus a company-specific premium for equity risk. To be sure, CAPM is a deeply rooted methodology, although at times the analyst might choose to blend the CAPM results with one or more other methods; these include the Gordon Model (which is based on dividend returns and an eventual capital return from the sale of the investment) and/or the Bond Yield Plus Risk Premium (which incorporates a subjective risk premium added to the company's long-term debt interest rate).

How do I estimate a company's cost of common equity using CAPM?

The formula for the cost of common equity is defined in Exhibit 3-17.

The fundamental idea behind CAPM is that an investment must reward investors in two ways: time value of money and risk. The time value of money is represented in the formula by the risk-free rate (R_F); this compensates investors for allocating capital to any investment over a period of time. Risk is captured in the formula by estimating the premium that the investor requires for taking on a specific investment opportunity. This premium is calculated by taking a risk measure (ß, or beta) that compares the returns of the asset to the market over a period of time and to the market premium ($R_M - R_F$).

Of the three variables—the risk-free rate, beta, and the market risk premium—beta is probably the least intuitive. As noted, *beta* is a measure of the risk of a particular stock or other investment. It measures the stock's relative volatility, that is, how much a stock's price is expected to rise or fall as the stock market rises or falls:

- *Beta equal to 1.0.* A stock with a beta equal to 1.0 would be expected to track the overall stock market in lockstep—if the market rises (or falls) by 10 percent, the stock would be expected to rise (or fall) by 10 percent.
- *Beta higher than 1.0.* A beta of more than 1.0 implies that the stock would be more volatile than the overall market. For example, a stock with a beta of 1.5 would be 50 percent more volatile than the market. If the market rises (or falls) by 10 percent, the shares would be expected to rise (or fall) by 15 percent.
- *Beta lower than 1.0.* A beta lower than 1.0 (but greater than 0.0) implies that the stock would be less volatile than the market. Accordingly, a stock with a beta of 0.8 would be 20 percent less volatile than the market. Accordingly, if the market rises (or falls) by 10 percent, the shares would be expected to rise (or fall) by 8 percent. Companies with betas lower than 1.0 tend to

Exhibit 3-17 Cost of Common Equity Formula

$$K_E = R_F + \beta [R_M - R_F] + S$$

Where:

R_F = Risk-free rate
β = Beta of the security
R_M = Market risk premium

be stable; a milk or bread producer might be one example. Demand for such consumer staples is unlikely to swing dramatically from year to year, even as external conditions change.

Beta values are calculated and published regularly (e.g., Bloomberg) for all stock exchange–listed companies. The problem here is that uncertainty arises in the value of the expected return because the value of beta is not constant, but rather changes over time. For relatively stable, mature companies, one can use a stock's five-year historical beta with monthly observations. For targets that are in dynamic, high-growth industries, or for recently restructured companies, consider using a shorter period—e.g., two years using weekly observations.

The biggest drawback to using beta as a risk measure is that it implicitly assumes that all of a company's risk can be distilled to only one market factor. This is rarely the case. Nevertheless, those who feel strongly about beta's biggest drawback might consider developing a multifactor model to increase the formula's relevance to a particular situation.

From a practical standpoint, how do I calculate the three inputs for my CAPM model?

This is a key question, because seemingly minor changes in a CAPM model can drive substantial changes in a company's cost of equity capital. Accordingly, the assumptions that an analyst uses in a CAPM model are subject to our favorite adage: garbage in, garbage out. Choose wisely.

- *Risk-free rate.* The widely accepted basis for the risk-free rate is the current yield on the government bond whose duration most closely matches the time horizon in the DCF model. For instance, a 10-year DCF would typically use the current yield on 10-year US Treasuries as its basis for the risk-free rate. As will likely become clearer subsequently, this assumption is the least subjective of all those in the CAPM process and likely to be the source of the least debate when it comes to the valuation of a particular company.
- *Beta.* If the company that you are valuing is publicly traded, simply use the published beta for its stock. For companies that are privately held, or that have short operational histories, restructured operations, or leverage that departs significantly from the industry average, it may be appropriate to use an industry average beta rather than an individual company beta—provided good comparable companies are available. In calculating the industry average beta, use the market cap weighted average unlevered beta for a group of comparable, publicly traded companies. Lastly, the proliferation of industry-specific exchange-traded funds (ETFs) adds a new option; consider using the ETF's beta if the fund's underlying components are representative of the valuation target.
- *Market risk premium.* As noted, the market risk premium is an estimate of the excess returns an investor can expect to receive as compensation for bearing equity risk (i.e., investing in the market portfolio rather than a risk-free instrument). The market risk premium is calculated by taking an average of data points over time in order to incorporate a large sample of events and mitigate measurement error. The appropriate time frame over which to calculate the market risk premium is a matter of debate. On the one hand, a long horizon helps smooth out short-term fluctuations; on the other hand, a short horizon is arguably more relevant in current circumstances. This is an academic debate that could rage on for years. Our approach is a bit more pragmatic: the market risk premium should be based on the

same duration as that used to calculate the risk-free rate. Lastly, those analysts who are looking for a "quick and dirty" starting point for arriving at a reasonable market risk premium can look to the experts. Duff & Phelps's helpful text, *Valuation Handbook—Guide to Cost of Capital*, which is updated annually, has suggested in recent years an equity market risk premium of 5.0 percent,[16] while KPMG sets a slightly higher level at 5.5 percent.[17] These seem reasonable.

What if the valuation target is substantially smaller than its public peers? Does this change the analysis in any way?

Yes, consider adding a *size premium* (also sometimes known as a *small company premium*) to the CAPM-derived discount rate. Accordingly, the CAPM formula is restated as $K_E = R_F + \beta\ (R_M - R_F) + S$, where S is the size premium.

The theory behind the size premium is that smaller companies are often more capital constrained and/or do not have the scale and competitive advantages of larger competitors. Investors in smaller companies, the logic goes, will require a higher return on equity investments into such companies to compensate for these added risks. The higher the size premium, the higher the cost of equity and, consequently, the lower the DCF value, all else equal.

To calculate historical size premiums, the analyst should construct portfolios of publicly traded stocks by size. The size premiums are computed as the average returns for each size portfolio less the average of the returns predicted by CAPM for the stocks in each portfolio. The results are then divided into quartiles, quintiles, deciles, and so on. Exhibit 3-18 shows how such analysis might be displayed.

As can be seen from Exhibit 3-18, companies with small market capitalizations can command larger-size premiums, whereas companies with large market caps often command only modest-size premiums. One way of using this table is to apply no size premium to companies with market capitalizations above \$6.8 billion. Discount rates for companies with market caps between \$1.8 billion and \$6.8 billion would include a 1.20

percent size premium. Similarly, discount rates for companies between roughly $478 million and $1.8 billion would include a 1.98 percent size premium. And discount rates for companies with market capitalizations below $478 million would include a 4.07 percent size premium.

Exhibit 3-19 illustrates these results graphically. Notice that the relationship is not entirely linear. Moreover, the substantial size premiums observed for very small companies lead many to question whether the lower end of the sample set contains an unusual number of statistical outliers. One argument, for instance, is that the lowest end of the market contains the largest number of financially distressed firms. As described earlier, capital structure is a key component of how portable assumptions in CAPM are. Accordingly, it would be wise to disregard the results for 10y and 10z in most cases.

It is important to understand the theory behind the process. However, many practitioners also value general rules of thumb. To this end, a typical small company premium is around 25 percent; that is, the appraiser might increase a CAPM-driven discount rate of, say, 13.6 percent by 25 percent

Exhibit 3-18 Chart Showing Size Premiums by Quartile and Decile ($000s)

Quartile Group	Size Premium (Quartile)	Decile Group	Size Premium (Decile)	Size of Largest Company in Decile
Large cap (1 and 2)	N/A	1	–0.38%	$314,623
		2	0.81%	15,080
Mid-cap (3–5)	1.20%	3	1.01%	6,794
		4	1.20%	3,711
		5	1.81%	2,509
Small cap (6–8)	1.98%	6	1.82%	1,776
		7	1.88%	1,212
		8	2.65%	772
Micro-cap (9–10)	4.07%	9	2.94%	478

Source: Morningstar. (*Ibbotson SBBI Valuation Yearbook.* Morningstar has discontinued this yearbook, but these figures from 2011 can serve as a graphic example of how to display data.)

Exhibit 3-19 Chart Showing Size Premiums by Decile

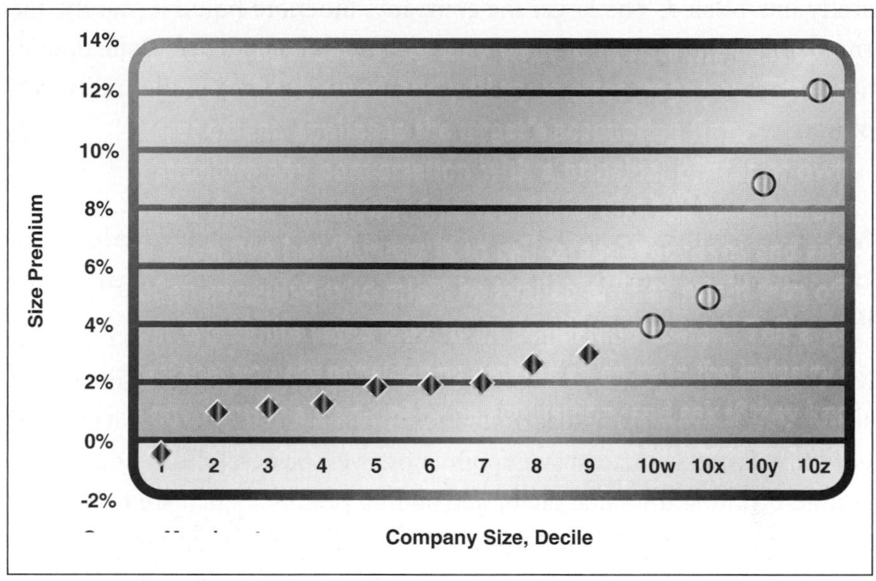

Source: Morningstar.

to 17.0 percent. This benchmark is not based on any scientific survey, mind you, just historical perspective. As such, use it with discretion.

What if the valuation target is privately held? How is this reflected in the valuation?

This touches on a subject that is closely related to a target's size premium—namely, whether an illiquidity premium is appropriate. An *illiquidity premium* is the additional return that an investor requires when a particular security cannot be easily converted into cash.

For example, assume an investor is evaluating the purchase of stock in one of two companies that are identical except for one factor: the shares of the first company are publicly traded, whereas the shares of the second company are privately held. The shares of the second company are said to be *illiquid* because there's no active market for the investor to subsequently sell the shares, should the investor later decide to exit. Accordingly, the investor will not be willing to pay as much for the shares of the second company.

From a practical standpoint, a company's size and liquidity are generally interrelated. The larger the company, the more liquid its equity; the smaller the company, the less liquid its equity. From a CAPM standpoint, the discount rate of an illiquid target increases to reflect its illiquidity premium.

My target is a lower-middle-market, privately held business. Should I apply both a size premium and an illiquidity premium?

Many commentators argue that an appraiser should add premiums to a small private company's discount rate to reflect both its size *and* its lack of liquidity. From a practical standpoint, however, be careful that you are not double-counting the same factor and adding premiums that are too high.

For example, Exhibit 3-18 shows historical size premiums for companies across a wide range of market capitalizations—from mega-cap to micro-cap. However, somewhere embedded in the size premiums is each stock's liquidity; that is, the size premiums shown reflect not only each company's size, but also how liquid the shares are. Micro-cap stocks are less liquid than mega-cap stocks; investors will understandably require a higher return on an equity investment in an illiquid stock to compensate for the added risk of not being able to pull the capital out when needed. However, this risk is generally reflected in the size premium calculated, unless the analyst has created a two-factor model.

Accordingly, adding an illiquidity premium *in addition to* the size premium calculated in Exhibit 3-18 would likely involve some double-counting. This would potentially lead to a discount rate that is unreasonably high and an unusually low valuation under CAPM. Make sure your final outcome "feels" right.

ASCRIBING A TERMINAL VALUE

Why does DCF analysis use a terminal value?

A company is unlike you and me—while it is an entity that is "alive" in the eyes of the law, the simple truth is that a business is not a person; it goes through cycles, and ultimately it may mature, but it *theoretically* has an infinite life. Accordingly, a business valuation that is rooted in cash flows should reflect the present value of those cash flows forever.

This is an excellent example of why theory does not always carry over into reality: it is simply impractical to forecast a company's cash flows into infinity. Frankly, it is hard enough to predict next year's flows, let alone those 10, 20, or 30 years from now. However, if we do not include the value of long-term cash flows, we are, in effect, assuming that the company will stop operating at the end of the projection period. Clearly, this is not the case.

Consequently, the DCF approach to valuation involves estimating cash flows over the forecast period and then estimating a *terminal value* to capture the value at the end of the period. This terminal value is intended to approximate the discounted, lump-sum value of the target's cash flows after the forecast period—that is, when the business has matured and settled into middle age.

How do I calculate a company's terminal value?

There are three primary ways of estimating a firm's terminal value: liquidation value, the exit multiple approach, and the constant growth model:

- *Liquidation value.* This calculation assumes the liquidation of the target's assets in the final year of the DCF analysis by estimating what the market would pay for the firm's assets at that point. The liquidation value approach is most useful when the target's assets are separable and marketable. However, by assuming a firm will cease operations and liquidate its assets at the end of the DCF analysis, this approach is limited, as it does not reflect the earning power of the target's assets.
- *Exit multiple approach.* The exit multiple approach is the easiest to implement but involves traces of the comparable companies approach. This approach uses a multiplier of some income or cash flow measure, such as net income, EBITDA, or free cash flow, which is generally determined by looking at how the

Exhibit 3-20 Exit Multiple Approach to Estimating Terminal Value

Assume that the target is expected to generate $15 million of EBITDA in year 10. The target is expected to have $20 million of debt at that time. Multiplying $15 million of EBITDA by a projected EV/EBITDA multiple of 8.0× produces a terminal enterprise value of $120 million. Subtracting $20 million of debt results in $100 million of terminal equity value.

Terminal value:	
EBITDA	$15 million
EV/EBITDA multiple	8.0×
Enterprise value	$120 million
Less:	
Debt	$20 million
Equity value	$100 million

market values comparable companies. Recall that a key benefit of DCF analysis is that it focuses more on a company's absolute value and less on relative value. Accordingly, in order to keep the terminal value "pure," the terminal value multiple should have some basis beyond trading multiples. Also, if the multiple relates to enterprise value, don't forget to subtract the projected debt. Exhibit 3-20 illustrates the exit multiple approach to estimating terminal value.

- *Constant growth model.* Some commentators consider the constant growth model to be the soundest technically. However, it does require the analyst to make judgments about when the firm's growth rate will decline to a mature level and what its sustainable rate is. At a minimum, the constant growth model should be used to check the reasonableness of the exit multiple assumption for the terminal value.

Analytically, the terminal value calculation for a company generally looks like the formula for a growing perpetuity: the expected cash flow next period, divided by the firm's discount rate, less the expected growth rate of those cash flows. This formula is illustrated in Exhibit 3-21.

Exhibit 3-21 Terminal Value Model Assuming Constant Growth

$$\text{Terminal Value} = \frac{\text{Expected Cash Flow Next Period}}{(r - g)}$$

Where:

r = Discount rate
g = Expected growth rate

Intuitively, the analogy to a perpetuity makes sense. After all, the concept of terminal value is rooted in the view that the life of a company is infinite—much like a perpetuity that pays dividends forever. So what would an investor pay for a perpetuity that pays $100 per year, assuming that investor cost of capital is 10 percent? The answer, of course, would be $1,000, as illustrated in Exhibit 3-22.

What if the annual payment from the perpetuity were to start at $100 and grow 2 percent annually thereafter? Again assuming a 10 percent cost of capital, the value of the perpetuity would increase to $1,250, as demonstrated in Exhibit 3-23.

As described in the discussion that follows, a firm's terminal value follows the same logic.

How do I estimate a company's constant growth rate?

Many companies can maintain high growth rates for extended periods, but they will all approach stable growth at some point in time. The primary questions, as noted, are when the company will see its growth rate mature and what the longer-term assumed growth should be.

Exhibit 3-22 Perpetuity Value Assuming No Growth in Cash Flows

$$\text{Perpetuity Value} = \frac{\$100}{10\%} = \$1,000$$

Exhibit 3-23 Perpetuity Value Assuming 2 Percent Growth

$$\text{Perpetuity Value} = \frac{\$100}{10\% - 2\%} = \$1{,}250$$

In terms of timing, the M&A analyst might want to choose among three different alternatives:

- That there is no high growth remaining, and that the company is already in constant growth mode.
- That there will be high growth for a period of time, at the end of which the growth rate will drop to the constant growth rate. This is known as a *two-stage model.*
- That there will be high growth for a period of time, at the end of which the growth will decline gradually to a constant growth rate. This is known as a *three-stage model.*

What factors determine a company's growth rate, and how should I factor these into the terminal value model?

There are almost as many drivers for a firm's growth rate as there are for valuation itself. However, there are a handful of factors that rise to the top in terms of importance:

- *Size of the firm.* The larger a company becomes, the harder it becomes for it to maintain the high growth rate it once enjoyed. This is the law of big numbers in action.
- *Current growth rate.* Despite the disclaimers plastered over nearly every stock market–related advertisement, the past *can* be a reasonable predictor for some things. In our experience, there is at least a loose correlation between a company's current growth rate and its future growth rate. Of course, it is up to the analyst to understand whether this growth is due to some

temporary factor. However, it is not an unreasonable starting point to assume that a company currently expanding at 30 percent can probably grow faster for longer than a business currently growing at 10 percent.

- *Barriers to entry and/or structural advantages.* It's difficult, if not impossible, to think about a company's longer-term growth rate without referencing factors such as Michael Porter's five competitive forces and/or barriers to entry. Consequently, the question of how long growth will last and how great it will be can be reframed as a test of the relevant barriers to entry, including how strong they are and how long they are likely to remain in place.
- *Life cycle of the firm and its industry.* As described in greater detail later, every industry—and every market participant in that industry—has a life cycle. Where an industry or company is in this cycle will partly depend upon the barriers to entry and/or structural advantages just discussed. However, there are other reasons why a particular company in an otherwise thriving industry might fade away; key examples include the company's reinvestment rate and management execution.

This final point—low reinvestment and/or poor execution in an otherwise growing market—is key, as it can happen more often, and on a grander scale, than one might think. For instance, it may surprise some younger readers that the most popular fast-food chain after McDonald's used to be a company called Burger Chef. Not only was Burger Chef a dominant player in the fast-food industry, it held the first patent to the flame broiler (now associated with Burger King) and pioneered the value combo, the "Works Bar" (now most commonly seen at Roy Rogers restaurants), and even the "Funmeal" (preceding the McDonald's Happy Meal by many years). Eleven years after opening its first location, Burger Chef sold in 1968 to General Foods, which ultimately was unable to support the company's growth. The chain sold in 1982 to Canadian-based Imasco, the parent company of Hardee's. Most Burger Chef locations were rebranded shortly thereafter, with the once-iconic name disappearing completely by the mid-1990s.

Exhibit 3-24 DCF for a Business Already in Constant Growth Mode

$$\text{Enterprise Value} = \frac{\text{Expected Cash Flow Next Period}}{(r - g)}$$

Where:

r = Discount rate
g = Expected growth rate

Lastly, and on a more technical note, it stands to reason that the constant growth rate cannot be higher than the growth rate of the economy in which the firm operates. So, for example, if you use nominal cash flows and discount rates, the growth rate should also be nominal in the currency in which the valuation is denominated.

How do I conduct the DCF analysis if a company is already in its stable, constant growth mode?

The valuation process, in this case, is easier than in a full-blown DCF: the enterprise value of the business is simply the terminal value component of the broader DCF analysis. That is, it's the expected cash flow for the next period, divided by the discount rate, less the expected growth rate. This is illustrated in Exhibit 3-24.

Consider, for instance, a manufacturer in a slow-growth industry—perhaps no. 2 pencils—with forward-year cash flows of $10 million, a growth rate of 4 percent per annum, and a 12 percent discount rate. The enterprise value of the business, then, would be $125 million, calculated as illustrated in Exhibit 3-25.

As an aside, the example in Exhibit 3-25 illustrates why the assumed growth rate can have a tremendous impact on enterprise value. For in-

Exhibit 3-25 DCF for a No. 2 Pencil Manufacturer

$$\text{Enterprise Value} = \frac{\$10 \text{ million}}{(12\% - 4\%)} = \$125 \text{ million}$$

stance, every one-percentage-point change in the growth rate of the pencil manufacturer has a 12.5 percent carryover impact to valuation. That is, if the manufacturer were expected to grow at a rate of 2 percent, rather than 4 percent, the firm's valuation would plummet to $100 million, a rather striking 25 percent haircut.

Are there circumstances that do not warrant using a terminal value?

The biggest exception to the preceding discussion is a so-called runoff business or wasting asset—one that does, in fact, have a finite life. Some industries simply go into secular decline, whether due to changes to technology, regulation, or social preferences. One solution to this challenge is to use a negative assumption in the aforementioned constant growth rate model. The resulting terminal value would be lower than it would be if the business were growing and would reflect the perception that the business will disappear over time. In circumstances in which the business is expected to disappear in less than, say, 10 years, it might be better not to assume any terminal value, but rather to forecast the annual cash flows through the expected time horizon and discount each back individually.

What is the situation with artificial intelligence? And how can it be valued?

Like many aspects of M&A, it is a buy or build situation. For firms that wish to build their own AI, it is all about hiring the right talent. A June 2017 study from McKinsey Global Institute found that this was running between $5 million and $10 million per expert. For firms that prefer to buy the AI, Amazon, Google, and Microsoft offer enterprise solutions that can supply ready-made in-house capabilities. Of course, both talent and technology are needed, and the value they add to a company will depend on particular circumstances.[18]

Here are some of the questions an acquirer can ask when valuing a company that claims to be an AI company or to own AI solutions:

- Is this truly AI or merely big-data/other technologies with an AI wrapper?
- Where in the company does the value reside (e.g., algorithm, specific part of the tech stack such as middleware, user interface, background of people, team cohesion, vision of founders, etc.)?
- Is the technology stable; does all functionality work the way it is supposed to?
- What is the source and sustainability of any competitive advantage offered? How replicable it is by others in the market?
- How exactly does the AI company bring in direct revenue-enhancing speed to market (e.g, unlocking additional insights, creating a new market, augmenting existing products), and what does the revenue acceleration projection look like?
- How extensible and interoperable is the technology? How will the AI interact with other technology, and can the resulting technology operate at the desired scale? (By analogy, even if an orchestra has all the musical instruments, it may not make good music that can fill Carnegie Hall.)
- Does the AI company create cost efficiencies, productivity gains, and/or meaningful automation, and what part of those can add to the buyer EBITDA and what part of the value can be passed on to the customers? What do those projections look like?
- How and when can the acquired product, feature, or technology create synergy through integration? For example, how much boost would the buyer's existing analytics capability get from the acquired AI, and when will this impact be felt?
- What is the performance and how does it get impacted by scale or change of environment? What is the threshold of impact where it breaks down?
- Does it have a risk of obsolescence?
- Is it truly representing its valuation, that is, if the target says it is a SaaS product, is it a real SaaS with multitenancy, and so on?

- What are security features, and how secure are they?
- Is there nonstandard technology used, and what is the impact on maintainability?
- Is the knowledge documented and well understood or is it tribal with few developers and architects?
- What are R&D processes, approval cycles, and investments in future features?
- Does the AI pose compliance risks (for example, with laws on cybersecurity and privacy)?
- How much open source is used, and what risks do they bring to the company?

CONDUCTING SENSITIVITY ANALYSES

What is a sensitivity analysis?

As the term suggests, in sensitivity analysis we try to ascertain the impact of changes to inputs on outcome. In other words, it is a way to predict the outcome—or range of outcomes—of a decision if a situation turns out to be different compared to a key prediction. Several methods of conducting sensitivity analyses are built into Microsoft Excel's "what-if" analysis tools.

Why should I conduct a sensitivity analysis?

Despite best intentions, forward-looking assumptions may not always hold true. In fact, there's an old saying among financial analysts: The question is not whether your forecast is wrong, it's *how* wrong it is and in *what direction*. Nobody has the proverbial crystal ball, so of course forecasting errors will occur. The use of sensitivity analysis, through a scenario manager, is a great way to incorporate several different performance possibilities into your financial model. This allows the analyst to "stress-test" the financial results, because the reality is, expectations can and usually will change over time. Because the future cannot be predicted with certainty, it is never a good idea to take your financial model's results and claim, either to your boss or to your client, that these results are final. This is where the sensitivity, or "what-if," analysis comes into play!

What can a thoughtful sensitivity analysis of my DCF analysis tell me?

A thorough sensitivity analysis will allow you to do the following:

- Test the robustness of the results of the DCF model in the presence of uncertainty
- Increase the understanding of the relationships between input and output variables in the model
- Focus attention on those variables that have the most impact on the valuation
- Search for errors in the model (by encountering unexpected relationships between inputs and outputs)
- Simplify the model by fixing model inputs that have no effect on the output or by identifying and removing redundant parts of the model structure

Which inputs to my DCF model should I subject to a sensitivity analysis?

While the answer ultimately depends on the facts and circumstances of a particular situation, we suggest a rigorous testing of the following interrelated assumptions: (1) discount rate, (2) long-term growth rate, and (3) terminal value.

THE IVS FRAMEWORK

Is there an international standard for valuation, and if so, what is it?

Yes, there is an International Valuation Standards (IVS) Framework, most recently updated in 2017 by the International Valuation Standards Council.[19] The IVS 2017 Framework proposes three approaches to enterprise value:

- *Market Approach.* The IVS 2017 framework states that this approach provides an indication of value by comparing the asset with identical or comparable (that is, similar) assets for which price information is available. An example of this is the comparable transactions approach, with adjustments for companies that are not publicly held.
- *The Income Approach.* The IVS 2017 framework states that this approach provides an indication of value by converting future cash flow to a single current value, often referred to as discounted cash flow, or DCF. Under the income approach, the value of an asset is determined by reference to the value of income, cash flow, or cost savings generated by the asset.
- *The Cost Approach.* The IVS 2017 framework states that this approach indicates value by using the economic principle that "a buyer will pay no more for an asset than the cost to obtain an asset of equal utility." This can occur by either purchase or by construction (buy or build), unless undue time, inconvenience, risk, or other factors are involved. The cost approach calculates the current replacement or reproduction cost of an asset, making deductions for physical deterioration and all other relevant forms of obsolescence.

What does the IVS base value on?

According to the IVS standard, there are several possible bases for value.

- *Market Value.* The IVS 2017 framework defines this as " the estimated amount for which an asset or liability should exchange on the valuation date between a willing buyer and a willing seller in an arm's length transaction, after proper marketing and where the parties had each acted knowledgeably, prudently, and without compulsion."[20]

- *Equitable Value.* The IVS 2017 framework defines this as "the estimated price for the transfer of an asset or liability between identified knowledgeable and willing parties that reflects the respective interests of those parties." (As the IVS framework notes, "Equitable Value requires the assessment of the price that is fair between two specific, identified parties considering the respective advantages or disadvantages that each will gain from the transaction. In contrast, Market Value requires any advantages or disadvantages that would not be available to, or incurred by, market participants generally to be disregarded."[21])
- *Investment Value/Worth.* The IVS 2017 framework defines this as "the value of an *asset* to a particular owner or prospective owner for individual investment or operational objectives," noting that this is "an entity-specific basis of value. Although the value of an asset to the owner may be the same as the amount that could be realised from its sale to another party, this basis of value reflects the benefits received by an entity from holding the asset and, therefore, does not involve a presumed exchange. Investment Value reflects the circumstances and financial objectives of the entity for which the valuation is being produced."[22]
- *Synergistic Value.* The IVS framework defines this as "the result of a combination of two or more *assets* or interests where the combined value is more than the sum of the separate values." The framework notes that if the synergies are available to only one specific buyer, then "Synergistic Value will differ from Market Value, as the Synergistic Value will reflect particular attributes of an *asset* that are only of value to a specific purchaser."[23]
- *Liquidation Value.* The IVS 2017 framework defines this as "the amount that would be realised when an *asset* or group of *assets* are sold on a piecemeal basis. Liquidation Value *should* take into account the costs of getting the *assets* into saleable condition as well as those of the disposal activity. Liquidation Value can be

determined under two different premises of value: (a) an orderly transaction with a typical marketing period (see section 160), or (b) a forced transaction with a shortened marketing period (see section 170)." The valuer should indicate which kind is in play.

- *Fair Value.* The IVS 2017 framework breaks out four versions: International Financial Reporting Standards (IFRS), Organisation for Economic Co-operation and Development (OECD), United States Internal Revenue Service (US-IRS), and the general Legal/Statutory approach (considering whatever prevailing law may be).
- *The Cost Approach.* The IVS 2017 framework states that this approach "provides an indication of value using the economic principle that a buyer will pay no more for an *asset* than the cost to obtain an *asset* of equal utility, whether by purchase or by construction, unless undue time, inconvenience, risk or other factors are involved. This approach provides an indication of value by calculating the current replacement or reproduction cost of an asset and making deductions for physical deterioration and all other relevant forms of obsolescence."

CONCLUDING COMMENTS

Valuation and modeling results, along with the seller's goals, will determine the price paid for an acquired company—and, to state the obvious, price matters. The amount of money that an acquirer pays for a target can make a major difference in the performance of the postdeal company going forward, because the financial legacy of the transaction will stay with the acquirer, no matter what kind of financing the acquirer chooses. If the acquirer borrows money for the transaction, the transactional legacy takes the form of debt. If the acquirer pays out of its own cash, the legacy will be lower cash reserves. And if the acquirer pays stock, the aftereffect will be dilution of equity value. Therefore, it is important not to overpay, no matter how great a target may seem. Chapter 4, "Financing and Refinancing," explores these alternatives in greater depth.

NOTES

1. https://www.law360.com/articles/798432/how-courts-view-valuation-methods-in-appraisal-litigation.
2. http://vtknowledgeworks.com/sites/all/themes/vtknowledgeworks/files/Valuation_Models_for_Pre-Revenue_Companies.pdf.
3. See http://businessreferenceguide.com/buy-the-business-reference-guide/.
4. Philip McDuff, "A Global Technology Roadmap for Biopharmaceutical Manufacturing: An Update from BPOG," bBiogen, November 2016, https://www.biophorum.com/wp-content/uploads/2016/11/Technology-Roadmapping-update_ISPE-F0F_1.5_website-version.pdf.
5. "The five-year planning horizon that used to be typical of traditional strategic plans is no longer feasible. The pace of changes in technology and changes in the business environment warrant no more than three years' planning horizon." Anita Cassidy, A Practical Guide to Information Systems Strategic Planning, 2nd ed., (Boca Raton, FL: CRC Press, 2016), p. 26.
6. For a running tally of acquisitions of AI firms, see https://index.co/market/artificial-intelligence/acquisitions.

7. See Title 17, Chapter II, Sections 210.5-02 and 201.5-03. The website is https://www.gpo.gov/fdsys/pkg/CFR-2013-title17-vol2/pdf/CFR-2013-title17-vol2-sec210-5-03.pdf.
8. This answer is provided by Tony Enlow, Partner, Transaction Advisory, BDO, based on his previous writings, including his article "Purchase Price Wars: EBITDA vs. Adjusted EBITDA and Why It Matters, BDO," 2016.
9. https://law.justia.com/cases/delaware/court-of-chancery/1999/14514-3.html.
10. https://law.justia.com/cases/delaware/court-of-chancery/1991/611-a-2d-485-3.html.
11. Note: when comparing premiums paid in stock transactions, make adjustments for an inconsistency in the date chosen for the stock value, for example, the date of announcement versus some earlier date. Preannouncement rumors can drive stock price up, reducing the premium calculated. See Sangwon Lee and Vijay Yerramilli, "Relative Values, Announcement Timing, and Shareholder Returns in Mergers and Acquisitions," C. T. Bauer College of Business, University of Houston, May 2018, https://www.bauer.uh.edu/yerramilli/LeeYerramilli.pdf.
12. https://law.justia.com/cases/delaware/court-of-chancery/2010/131480-1.html.
13. Ibid.
14. Lee and Yerramilli, "Relative Values, Announcement Timing, and Shareholder Returns in Mergers and Acquisitions," 2018.
15. http://clsbluesky.law.columbia.edu/2017/03/03/paul-weiss-discusses-an-ftc-study-on-merger-remedies/.
16. https://costofcapital.duffandphelps.com/.
17. Equity Market Risk Premium: Research Summary, October 2018, https://assets.kpmg.com/content/dam/kpmg/nl/pdf/2018/advisory/equity-market-risk-premium-research-summary-september-2018.pdf.
18. Craig Aidis and Alex Purcell, "Valuation Issues in Acquiring Artificial Intelligence Companies," The Recorder, October 30,

2018, https://www.law.com/therecorder/2018/10/30/valuation-issues-in-acquiring-artificial-intelligence-companies/.

19. International Valuation Standard 2017, https://www.ivsc.org/.
20. Ibid.
21. Ibid.
22. Ibid.
23. Ibid.

CHAPTER 4

Financing and Refinancing

INTRODUCTION

Of all aspects of the merger/acquisition/buyout process, perhaps none is as critical as financing. There is no such thing as a free merger: it takes money to buy a company, and the money must come from somewhere. At the simplest level, all transactions are paid for in the form of cash, stock, and/or notes, but behind these three basic modes of payment lies a complex universe of funding sources and issues.

- If the deal is funded by *stock,* will the stock come from existing shares, a public offering, or a private placement? Will a private equity firm be involved in the deal and, if so, how much control will it want over the company's operations going forward?
- If the deal is funded from *cash,* will the cash be generated internally from profits, or will it be borrowed? If it is borrowed, will it come from a traditional commercial bank or from a less traditional source, such as a commercial finance company, a leasing company, or a life insurance company? How many lenders will be involved under what terms?
- Will the seller accept *promissory notes* as part of the payment? Can part of the price be paid out as a contingency payment,

based on company performance? Will the terms of any loan agreements or notes unduly restrict the acquirer's plans to pay the lender or seller back?

In the dynamic terrain of financial dealmaking, what matters most is how the money will be structured, not where it will come from. In this highly creative field, much depends on written agreements between buyers, sellers, and various third parties (including, but not limited to, commercial bankers), all of whom are betting on the future. Creativity, negotiating skills, and a keen eye for detail can make the difference between success and failure here.

This chapter begins with an overview of financing sources, followed by a brief discussion of equity sales as a source of capital. The remainder of this chapter will focus on debt. We will focus on highly leveraged transactions (HLTs) with an emphasis on leveraged buyouts (LBOs)—that is, taking publicly held companies or units private using borrowed cash. Some of the principles described here are also applicable to the less-leveraged acquisitions, but we will not take pains to point out such broad applications.

FINANCING OVERVIEW

How does the size of a target company affect the ability of a buyer to obtain financing?[1]

One would think that the smaller the target, the easier it might be to find financing. However, this is not the case. Many sources of capital have a minimum below which they will not go in financing a deal—for example, $10 million.

How can a buyer find money to make acquisitions?

The art of M&A (merger-and-acquisition) financing is a subject worthy of an entire book. (In fact, McGraw-Hill Education's Art of M&A Series includes one.[2]) This is because there are literally hundreds of specific sources of capital, ranging from an accounts receivable credit line to a wraparound mortgage. The simplest source, of course, is the cash the company already has in its bank accounts. Beyond this, financing sources vary greatly by size of business, as described later in the chapter.

All these different modes of financing, and hundreds more, can be divided into *equity, debt,* and *hybrids* of the two.

FINANCING INSTRUMENTS: EQUITY VS. DEBT VS. HYBRIDS

What exactly is equity and how does it work as an M&A financing source?

Equity is the book value of a company, shown in a balance sheet as net worth after liabilities have been subtracted from assets. It is expressed in units called shares or, collectively, stock. Shares of stock can be sold as a security—a financial instrument "secured" by the value of an operating company or a government.

Under normal circumstances, the value of equity can be realized either as dividends the company pays its stockholders or as gains stockholders can make by selling shares. When a company is insolvent (bankrupt), equity represents claims on assets after all other claims have been paid.

There are two types of equity-financed M&A deals. A company can sell its equity and use the money to buy another company. Or it can simply offer its own shares to the buyer as a mode of payment for a company.

If a company wishes to remain private, it can do a *private offering* of equity or debt securities. A private offering is a sale of securities that does not involve registering with the Securities and Exchange Commission (SEC). It is made possible through an exemption from requirements in the Securities Act of 1933, still the dominant securities law (along with the Securities Exchange Act of 1934) after nearly a century. According to a recent report from the SEC, the total amount of funding raised through private offerings of debt and equity for 2012 through 2016 exceeded the total amount raised through public offerings of debt and equity over the same time period by some 26 percent.[3] Depending on the amount of money to be raised and the purpose of the offering, it may qualify for certain exemptions from the requirement to register. There are two main regulations for this, Regulation A[4] and Regulation D[5] (this lettering has no particular significance; there are no significant exemptions titled B or C):[6]

- *The Regulation A exemptions* from registration requirements were expanded under the JOBS Act of 2012, earning the title Regulation A+. This exemption occurs in two tiers: offerings of up to $20 million and offerings of up to $50 million. This type of offering requires numerous conditions; it is considered more complicated than an offering under Regulation D, described in the following list as "limited" or "private."
- *Limited offerings.* Rule 504 under Regulation D, which became effective January 20, 2017, provides an exemption for offerings to any investors (including nonaccredited ones) as long as the amount to be raised does not exceed $5 million.[7] Companies may not use this exemption, however, if they "have no specific business plan or have indicated their business plan is to engage in a merger or acquisition with an unidentified company or companies."[8]
- *Private offerings.* Rule 506b under Regulation D provides an exemption for offerings to accredited investors, with no limits to the amount of money to be raised.[9] In such an offering, securities may not be sold to more than 35 nonaccredited investors. If all of the investors are accredited, the issuer can solicit broadly under Rule 506c.[10]
- *Crowdfunding.* This alternative allows private companies to offer and sell up to $1 million in equity securities during a 12-month period to any investor in small amounts through a broker or funding portal, with accompanying disclosure requirements and investment limitations.

A public offering of securities, including any securities issued in connection with a merger or acquisition, must be registered with the SEC. Public offerings—both initial public offerings (IPOs) and secondary offerings after that—are managed by an underwriter, usually an investment banking firm (described later in the chapter). Once the public owns stock in a company (and thus establishes a market value) it is generally easier for the issuer to use its shares as an acquisition currency. Alternatively, the company can have a secondary public offering or a debt offering and use that cash for acquisitions. (For more about registration of equity and debt securities, see the discussion about registration rights later in this chapter.) The market for initial public offerings has shown some long-term declines but appears to be on a rebound as of 2019.[11]

What exactly is debt and how does it work as an M&A financing source?

Debt is a promise to repay a certain sum by a definite time. The promise is made in the form of an agreement, also called (in multilender deals) a facility. To raise capital via debt, a company can do two basic things:

- It can take out a loan from a creditor such as a commercial bank.
- It can sell a bond, note, or commercial paper to an investor such as a pension fund.

Whether debt capital is obtained by borrowing from a lender or by selling a debt security to an investor, interest is charged either in fixed or in variable rates. The interest rate(s) for the typical loan—for example, a standard term loan—can be determined by the lender's cost of funds as well as the following rates, listed from highest to lowest: the bank prime rate, the federal funds rate, and/or the London Interbank Offered Rate (LIBOR).[12] Under normal circumstances, the value of debt can be realized through the rate of interest charged.

What are some examples of financial instruments that have both equity and debt (hybrid) characteristics?

Securities may be issued as equity securities (shares of company stock) or as debt (company or government bonds, notes, or paper). Common stock typically grants its owners the right to vote and (if authorized by the company's board of directors) receive dividends. Preferred stock is a hybrid security with characteristics of both debt and equity. Payments to preferred stockholders are called preferred dividends. Being based on a contract promising payments of fixed size, preferred dividends are similar to interest payments on debt (albeit taxed differently).

Why does it matter whether an instrument is characterized as debt versus equity?

The characterization of an instrument as debt vs. equity can change how the company accounts for a transaction (e.g., impact of debt vs. equity on balance sheet), as well as how taxes are paid. For more details, see Chapter 5, on structuring.

In addition to accounting and tax considerations, what other considerations might come into a decision to use debt or equity financing?

Market conditions matter, and these are ever-changing. To take the most obvious example, companies using their stock to buy other companies generally prefer to do so when their stock prices are up—a difficult call in a volatile market. Debt markets, too, have their ups and downs. For example, recently, preferred equity has had a boost in popularity over and above taking out mezzanine loans.[13] Meanwhile, a late 2018 increase in bond yields and corresponding drop in bond prices[14] caused some to speculate that insurance companies, pension funds, and other buyers of corporate debt would dump their holdings, driving bond prices lower.[15]

FINANCING SOURCES

What are some common sources of equity and debt financing?

As mentioned, there are literally hundreds of sources of financing. Here are some of the most common ones:

- Asset-based lenders, which make loans based on a company's hard collateral, such as real estate.
- Business development companies, which are closed-end investment funds that invest in small private companies and distressed firms. These are different from usual investment companies in that nonaccredited investors are allowed to buy into the fund.[16]
- Commercial and community banks, which make term loans or offer credit cards, a source of funding for very small companies.
- Commercial finance companies, which make term loans (but unlike banks cannot take deposits).
- Employees, who can buy a company's stock through an employee stock ownership plan, a special type of private stock offering.[17]
- Family offices, which in recent years have joined other nontraditional investors as a source of capital for M&A deals.[18]
- Insurance companies, which are permitted to make loans collateralized by insurance policies.
- Investment banks, which serve as underwriters by working with brokerage firms as buyers and resellers of issues of equity and debt. They, in turn, sell to institutional investors such as pension funds, which buy stocks and bonds for their beneficiaries, and investment companies.
- Merchant banks, which are like investment banks, but which invest their own money as principals in a transaction. They do private placements of equity, often taking partial ownership in companies. They also offer trade financing services such as letters of credit.
- Mutual funds, a type of investment company, which buy stock in publicly traded companies to create portfolios for customers.
- Private investment firms, such as private equity firms or venture capital firms, which buy debt or equity securities of privately held companies as an investment.

- Sovereign wealth funds, through which nations can make equity investments in the hopes of strong returns for beneficiaries[19]

There is a thin line between an investment company (subject to the Investment Company Act of 1940) and a private investment firm, which may or may not be subject to that law. A list of private investment firms (some of which may also qualify as investment companies, depending on circumstances) includes:

- *Crossover funds.* Funds that invest in both public and private equity.
- *Exchange-traded funds.* Funds that can be traded on a stock exchange. Most exchange-traded funds track an index, for example, the SPDR Dow Jones Industrial Average. (See also Index funds.)
- *Fund of funds.* Funds that invest in other funds. Types include master-feeder and multiple-class funds.
- *Hedge funds.* Funds of investors (usually institutional) and wealthy individuals exempt from many investment company rules and able to use regulations, and can thus use aggressive investment strategies that are unavailable to mutual funds, including selling short, leverage, program trading, swaps, arbitrage (investing in companies that have made and/or received acquisition tender offers), and derivatives—all ways of hedging investments.
- *Index funds.* Funds that track an index such the S&P 500 Index. These funds are generally sold through a mutual fund broker; they are not generally considered to be exchange-traded funds (although some exchange-traded funds do track an index).
- *Leasing funds.* Funds that invest in leases. Some funds focus on a particular kind of lease, such as aircraft leasing.[20]
- *Mezzanine funds.* Funds that invest in relatively large loans that are generally unsecured (not backed by a pledging of assets) or have a deeply subordinated security structure (e.g., third lien). These funds provide mezzanine financing, which is considered

to be a hybrid between debt (at the highest level of financing) and equity (at the lowest level)—hence the term *mezzanine.*[21]

- *Pledge funds.* Funds created through multiple pledges from individual investors.
- *Private equity (LBO/MBO) funds.* Funds that buy all the stock in a public company, or buy a unit of a public company, and thus take the company or unit private. See further discussion later in this chapter.
- *Real estate funds.* Funds that invest in real estate, often structured as real estate investment trusts (REITs).
- *SBIC funds.* Funds that qualify as Small Business Investment Companies (SBICs) under a Small Business Administration (SBA) program to encourage small business investing. See further discussion later in this chapter.
- *Venture capital funds.* Funds that manage money from investors who want to buy stock in smaller companies with potential for growth.

Interest rates charged vary greatly by size of the loan, and by source of the financing.[22]

Note that the use of these sources varies by company size.

- Financing sources for small businesses include personal savings, personal loans (from family members), loans from banks (including small community banks), credit cards, loans backed by the SBA, and loans from credit unions. If a small company decides to buy another one, it is likely to use one of these sources to expand. (Bear in mind that the great majority of M&A transactions are valued at under $50 million.)
- At the other extreme, the large multinational company will raise capital through a variety of debt and structured finance transactions, including syndicated loans, leveraged loans, high-yield bond offerings, mezzanine financing, project finance, equipment financings, restructurings, and securitizations. These

sources, too, can be used to fund mergers—generally through commercial and/or investment banks.

What is the difference between a commercial bank and an investment bank?

Today the word bank is used broadly to cover a great range of financial institutions, including commercial banks and investment banks, merchant banks, so-called nonbank banks, and, of course, savings banks. What most ordinary citizens think of as a bank, however, remains the commercial bank—the bank that makes loans and lets customers make deposits that can be withdrawn on demand (demand deposits).

An *investment bank* is neither an investor nor a bank. It does not invest its own money, and it does not take deposited funds. Rather, an investment bank is an intermediary between saving and investing. An investment bank, in its broadest definition, is a financial institution that helps companies find the money they need to operate and/or grow. Although investment banks do not make loans directly, they can be a bridge to lending. Investment bankers may also serve as finders or brokers in locating and approaching company buyers or sellers.

The distinction between commercial banks and investment banks has been blurred ever since the repeal of the banking law known as Glass-Steagall. Although the Dodd-Frank Act of 2010 included a provision that banned proprietary trading and fund sponsorships by commercial banks, this "Volcker rule," named after former Federal Reserve chair Paul Volcker, has been amended since passage, and is still under review as part of deregulation under the Trump Administration.[23]

As of 2019, the distinction between commercial banks and investment banks remains blurred.

- Companies other than commercial banks (including industrial companies with no past financial experience) have made inroads into the services traditionally offered by commercial banks, such as loans. There are even nonbank banks, which may provide depositary services or make loans (but not both).

- Conversely, many commercial and investment banks have formed holding companies that own other kinds of financial institutions, broadening their scope of services.

How can a company decide which kind of source to use for financing?

Every company has a unique capital structure and network of relationships that will determine the kind of financing that would be most advantageous for it and the sources that would be the most likely to provide funding.

Start by deciding the appropriate kind of financing you want, based on the company's current financial condition, and then begin approaching sources. The important thing is to avoid preconceived notions about what these sources can and cannot do. For example, don't think that because you are a small private firm, you cannot sell equity in your business.

There are four main types of underwriting:

- *Firm commitment.* An arrangement in which an underwriter assumes all the risks of bringing new securities issues to market by buying the issue from the issuer and guaranteeing the sale of a certain minimum number of shares to investors.
- *Dutch auction.* Offers come in and determine highest beginning price. The bank buys a set amount for a specific value. Clearing price is determined by investor demand, as revealed through the bidding process, rather than set in advance as in the firm commitment.
- *Best efforts.* An underwriting in which an investment bank, acting as an agent for an issuer, agrees to do its best to sell an offering to the public, but does not buy the securities outright or guarantee any particular financial result from the issuance. Over the past 20 years, this has become the standard, rather than the firm, offering.
- *Bought deal.* One investment bank buys the entire offering and resells it.

Sometimes bankers keep their initial purchase conservative and add an overallotment provision in the underwriting agreement of an IPO. The provision allows the underwriting syndicate to buy up to an additional 15 percent of the shares at the offering price if public demand for the shares exceeds expectations and the stock trades above its offering price. This provision, nicknamed "green shoe" after the first company to use it (The Green Shoe Company), can be used in both IPOs and private offerings.[24]

Suppose a small private company—say, a $10 million company—wants to get funding for an acquisition without doing a public offering. What would be a possible source?

One possible source can be SBICs, which are like investment companies but have special privileges under the tax code (and so are thought of as "government venture capital" although they are owned and controlled privately). SBICs make loans and charge interest, take equity positions, or may insist on holding options or warrants that allow the holder of them to buy stock at predetermined prices for a predetermined period of time. As of the end of fiscal 2016, there were 313 operating, managing $28 billion in assets, providing $6 billion in financing to 1,200 small businesses in 2016 alone.

Companies that meet the SBA's definition of small (or, better yet, smaller) are eligible for SBIC financing, with certain restrictions.[25] For example, SBICs can invest only in small businesses, currently defined as businesses with a tangible net worth of less than $19.5 million and an average of $6.5 million (or less) in net income over the previous two years at the time of investment. A business may also be deemed "small" based on SBA's own code standards under the National Association of Investment Companies (NAIC). Also, SBICs must invest at least 25 percent of their capital in smaller businesses, defined as those with tangible net worth of less than $6 million and an average of $2 million (or less) in net income over the previous two years.

Most SBICs concentrate on a particular stage of investment (i.e., start-up, expansion, or turnaround) and identify a geographic area in which to focus:

- *Securities SBICs* typically focus on making pure equity investments but can make debt investments as well.
- *Debenture SBICs* focus primarily on providing debt or debt with equity features. Debenture SBICs will typically focus on companies that are mature enough to make current interest payments on the investment.

HIGHLY LEVERAGED TRANSACTIONS

What is a highly leveraged transaction?

The answer varies by jurisdiction and by agency. In the United States, banking regulators have varying definitions.

In March 2013, the three main US bank regulators—the Board of Governors of the Federal Reserve Bank (Fed), the Federal Deposit Insurance Corporation (FDIC), and the Office of the Controller of the Currency (OCC)—issued *Interagency Guidance on Leveraged Lending,*[26] which stated that the policies of financial institutions should "include criteria to define leveraged lending that are appropriate to the institution." Each of the regulators has made its own statements on this matter, according to its role.[27] As an example of such a policy, the joint guidance noted that definitions of leveraged lending typically contain some combination of the following:

- Proceeds used for buyouts, acquisitions, or capital distributions
- Transactions where the borrower's total debt divided by EBITDA (earnings before interest, taxes, depreciation, and amortization) or senior debt divided by EBITDA exceed 4.0× EBITDA or 3.0× EBITDA
- A borrower recognized in the debt markets as a highly leveraged firm, which is characterized by a high debt-to-net-worth ratio
- Transactions when the borrower's postfinancing leverage, as measured by its leverage ratios (e.g., debt-to-assets, debt-to-net-worth, debt-to-cash flow, or other similar standards common to particular industries or sectors), significantly exceeds industry norms or historical levels

In September 2013, the FDIC put forth its own definition as follows:

> A highly leveraged transaction means an extension of credit to or investment in a business by an insured depository institution where the financing transaction involves a buyout, acquisition, or recapitalization of an existing business and one of the following criteria is met:
>
> - The transaction results in a liabilities-to-assets leverage ratio higher than 75 percent; or
> - The transaction at least doubles the subject company's liabilities and results in a liabilities-to-assets leverage ratio higher than 50 percent; or
> - The transaction is designated a highly leveraged transaction by a syndication agent or a federal bank regulator. [28]

In Europe, a leveraged transaction occurs in any type of loan or credit exposure where the borrower's postfinancing level of leverage exceeds a total debt to EBITDA ratio of 4.0×, or all types of loan or credit exposures where the borrower is owned by one or more financial sponsors.[29]

(For banks in the United States, Europe, and elsewhere, there is an additional complication, as they themselves must avoid a highly leveraged financial structure under the commonly accepted guidance of the Committee on Banking Supervision, housed in the Bank of International Settlements in Basel Switzerland—currently under the nickname Basel III.[30])

US and European definitions of highly leveraged transactions include some mention of M&A and/or a financial sponsor. How does this aspect work?

It is one thing for an operating company to borrow money to buy another operating company. In such a case, the banker bases its decision on the good credit of the acquirer, and related assets and cash flow. But when an investment company borrows money to buy a company, the analysis is different. The main objective of the leverage maestro is to finance as large a part of the cost of an acquisition as possible by borrowing against the assets and the future cash flows of the *acquired* company. In extreme examples, leveraged buyers have been able in some cases to reduce their equity investment to as little as 5 percent or less of the acquisition price. Success depends in part on the quality of assets to be purchased from the acquired company.

How can a buyer finance the acquisition with the acquired company's assets and revenues?

As this question implies, LBOs seem to defy conventional buy-sell wisdom. How, one may ask, can the buyer borrow against the assets of the acquired company when it is a different entity and needs the money as a precondition to the acquisition? Really, it is no more mysterious than a mortgage loan. Lenders don't mind lending against a house as long as they own the house until the loan is repaid. The key concept here is assets—the left side of the balance sheet. The typical leveraged acquisition is based on collateral a lender would consider desirable. So a key structuring objective is to cause the assets and revenues (cash flow) of the acquired company to be located in the buyer-borrower. This can be achieved in three different ways:

- The buyer can acquire the assets and business of the company.
- The buyer can acquire the stock of the company and immediately thereafter merge with it. (The question of which entity survives the merger is important for tax, and occasionally other, reasons; see Chapter 5.)
- Skipping the stock acquisition stage, the buyer and the company can simply merge directly.

If the buyer and company merge, a problem of timing arises at the closing: payment for the stock purchased by the buyer must be made *before* the merger places the assets of the acquired company in the buyer's possession, but the loan to the buyer cannot be funded until *after* the merger is consummated. To resolve this problem, the parties to the closing agree that all transactions will be treated as occurring *simultaneously* or, for the sticklers, that the seller of the stock will get a promissory note, which is repaid minutes later when the merger documents are filed. Sometimes lenders prefer to have both the buyer and the company named as borrowers on the acquisition loan. Tax or contract compliance questions may be raised by these timing issues (see Chapter 5), and they should be thought through carefully.

Why would a buyer want to do a highly leveraged transaction? Doesn't this leave the acquired business in a financially exposed position?

Certainly it does—this was the great lesson of the 1980s, the era of overleverage, which drove a number of companies into bankruptcy. Even today, heavy debt servicing can compete against operating excellence as dollars once marked for needed research and development or plant and equipment go to interest payments, often with dire consequences for the acquired company and eventually its community.

Prudently undertaken, however, a high level of debt need not harm postmerger performance. Pro-leverage forces point to the successes and say that having a large amount of debt on the balance sheet provides survival incentive for managers to perform efficiently. Management, say these LBO boosters, will focus on making the core business profitable, minimizing the use of capital and maximizing cash flow, rather than on building personal empires.

Indeed, there is some evidence that mergers financed with cash (including borrowed cash) do as well or better than mergers financed through stock[31] (although this evidence was gathered before the Tax Cuts and Jobs Act of 2017 put a limit on deductibility of interest payments). Furthermore, as a mode of payment, debt is an equalizer. Few have the cash or stock already in hand to buy a company, but many can borrow; debt financing enables a buyer with limited resources—in particular, a management group—to own a company. It also gives an investor a chance to reap a high return on equity. The Gibson Greeting Cards LBO, which returned several thousand percent to its equity suppliers, is a classic example. Other LBO successes range from the many successful small and midsized investments by Forstmann Little to the blockbuster $25 billion RJR Nabisco deal that enriched its promoter, Kohlberg Kravis & Roberts (KKR). Other notable KKR deals include Duracell Inc., Owens-Illinois Inc., Safeway Stores Inc., and, in more recent times, Gibson and Lyft.[32]

In any event, if the buyer plans to impose heavy financial leverage on a company, the buyer must be sure that the company can bear the interest and paydown burdens and must minimize operating risks. This is particularly true now in 2019 and beyond, due to the new US tax law. As one headline has stated, "U.S. Tax Curbs on Debt Reduction to Sting Buyout Barons."[33]

How will the new US tax law affect LBOs?

The Tax Cuts and Jobs Act of 2017 reduces incentives to take on leverage. It states in Section 3301 that the amount allowed as a deduction under this chapter for any taxable year for business interest shall not exceed the sum of—''(A) the business interest income of such taxpayer for such taxable year, (B) 30 percent of the adjusted taxable income of such taxpayer for such taxable year, plus the floor plan financing interest of such taxpayer for such taxable year."[34] Disallowed amounts can be carried forward to the following year (except in the case of partnerships) and there are exemptions for some small businesses, but the net result is that debt is not as tax-friendly as it used to be. For more on this matter, see Chapter 5 (and, as always, consult with qualified counsel).

What kinds of businesses lend themselves to financial leverage?

Look for mature businesses that generate cash flow on a steady basis. High growth potential is not necessarily a prerequisite; more probably, suitable candidates will show only moderate growth and will be easier to buy. LBO candidates should be on the far end of the spectrum, opposite from venture capital operations, which tend to be early-stage, growth companies.

Such companies, unless they are too small to attract any outside financing beyond the personal sphere, are financed predominantly through equity.

Producers of basic products or services in stable markets are the best LBO candidates. Start-ups and highly cyclical companies should be avoided. So should companies whose success is highly dependent on forces beyond the control of management. Oil and gas deals that depend on fuel prices are thus not suitable for highly leveraged deals, in contrast to oil pipeline or trucking companies, which receive a steady, stable payment for transportation charges and do not speculate on oil prices. In any industry, stable management offers an important element of reassurance. When evaluating the likelihood of repayment, lenders want to see a team of managers who work well together and who have weathered several business cycles.

MINIMIZING BORROWING

How can a buyer minimize borrowing?

A buyer's first thought in financial planning should be a very simple one: the less we have to lay out at closing, the less we have to borrow.

The financing needs to be met at the closing can be calculated as follows:

- The purchase price of the stock or assets of the acquired company.
- Plus any existing debt that must be refinanced at closing.
- Plus any working capital needs of the acquired company. (These amounts need not actually be borrowed, but the credit line must be large enough to cover them.)
- Plus administrative costs to effect the acquisition.
- Plus postacquisition payments that may be necessary because of settlement of litigation.
- Less cash or cash equivalents of the acquired company.
- Less any proceeds from partial divestitures of the acquired business.

(Seller takeback financing also reduces the closing payment, but is analyzed here as part of the borrowing program because of the many interconnections between it and other financing layers.)

The next step in our analysis is to explore how to minimize each of the cost elements and minimize the closing payment.

How can the buyer minimize the purchase price?

Most sellers have multiple objectives, including price, speed, and certainty of closing. Thus, a buyer need not necessarily offer the highest price in order to gain the contract. It should also offer the seller noncash incentives for the deal, such as the following:

- "We can close faster."
- "We have a good track record in obtaining financing and closing similar transactions."
- "We can offer a substantial deposit on signing the acquisition agreement."
- "We can work well with you and your management."

Other incentives that can make a deal attractive include good terms for management such as shares in the company, favorable employment contracts, profit-sharing plans, and the like. When the transaction involves the sale of a privately owned company, there is no limit to the value and utility of such social considerations. In the sale or merger of a public company, however, it is good to exercise caution. There may be the appearance of self-dealing at the expense of shareholders. Even companies that have maintained a strong reputation for ethics can be tainted by this brush.

One of the most delicate questions of buying (or buying out) a company is whether to obtain a lower price by assuming substantially greater risks or to accept significant defects in the candidate. Such risks or defects can loom very large in the eyes of the acquisition lenders, and the timing of negotiations does not always permit them to be checked out with a lender before signing the contract. Here is a cardinal rule: negotiate and sign *fast* when the price is right. The willingness to close expeditiously can bring a lower price. (Some of the most spectacularly successful deals have been achieved when a buyer saw that management and a lender could live with a minor flaw the seller thought was major.)

Another way to lower the purchase price is to buy only some of the assets or divisions of a company, or to buy all of them with a firm plan for postmerger sell-offs in mind.

When planning postdeal sell-offs, how easy is it for an acquirer to pick and choose among acquired assets?

It is desirable—but often difficult—for a buyer to be selective about what it acquires. The seller may be packaging some "dogs" together with some "stars" (to use some old terms from Boston Consulting Group). Therefore, the buyer should consider gaming the offer out from the seller's point of view and making a counterproposal. Crucial for such selection is knowing the seller's business better than the seller does—not impossible if the seller is a large conglomerate of which the target is a small part, and management is the buyer or is already on the buyer's side. The offer of sale may include several businesses, some of which are easier to finance than others, or assets used in part by each of several business operations. The buyer may have a choice, for example, between buying and building a computer system or merely leasing it.

Sometimes a deal can be changed to the buyer's advantage after the main price and other negotiating points have been determined. The seller may then be receptive to either including or excluding what appear to be minor ancillary facilities as a last step to signing. To encourage the seller, the buyer may guarantee the resale price of unwanted assets or share any losses realized on their disposal. Taking or not taking these minor assets may become the key to cash flow in the critical first two years after the buyout.

Can a buyer always finance all or part of a transaction through partial divestments or spin-offs?

Not necessarily. This is possible only when the business acquired consists of separate components or has excess real estate or other assets. The buyer must balance financial and operational considerations; there should always be a good business reason for the divestment. Consider selling off those portions of the business that are separable from the part that is most desirable.

As indicated earlier, not all businesses generate the cash flow or have the stability necessary for highly leveraged transactions, yet many cash-rich buyers are available for such businesses. A solid domestic smokestack (industrial) business with valuable assets, itself highly suitable for leveraged financing, may have a subsidiary with foreign manufacturing and distribution operations, a separate retail division, and a large timberland holding—all candidates for divestiture. The foreign operations are accessible to a whole new set of possible buyers, the retail division could function better as part of another company's nationwide chain, and the timberland does not generate cash flow.

Many buyout transactions are undertaken in order to divest assets at a profit. These transactions are better called restructurings or breakups. For example, the acquisition of Beatrice Foods by KKR at the height of the LBO boom of the 1980s resulted in the disbanding of its senior management and the sale of most of its assets to ConAgra. In 2007, the brand revived in a new company operating under the Beatrice name.[35] Meanwhile, the Canadian division of Beatrice, which was not a part of the KKR buyout, remained intact, growing through acquisition until getting acquired by Parmalat, S.A., in 1997, surviving as a division of Parmalat to this day.[36] The divergent paths of the two Beatrices (in the United States and in Canada) illustrate the range of strategic and financing options available to acquirers—much as studies of twins can help us understand heredity versus environment. (See Exhibit 4-1.)

There is a question of timing here; it is not advisable to start beating the bushes for a purchaser of a company's division or subsidiary without a signed contract for the purchase of the company as a whole. On signing an agreement, however, looking for division buyers is perfectly appropriate. Indeed, it is not uncommon to have an escrow closing of the divestiture in advance of the closing to minimize the risk of last-minute holdups. Even if the deal does not close simultaneously with the main acquisition, the presence of the divestiture agreement of such presold assets may make possible a bridge loan to be taken out at the closing.

Exhibit 4-1 The LBO of Beatrice and Its Aftermath

- 1894: Founded as "Haskell and Bosworth."
- 1898: Incorporated as "Beatrice Creamery Company."
- 1946: Beatrice Creamery changes its name to "Beatrice Foods Co."
- 1984: Beatrice Foods changes its name to "Beatrice Companies, Inc."
- 1984: Beatrice Companies acquires Esmark, Inc.
- 1986: Kohlberg, Kravis and Roberts (KKR) acquire Beatrice Companies, and spend the next four years dismantling the company.
- 1987: BCI Holdings spins off Beatrice Consumer Products Corporation, which becomes E-II Holdings.
- 1987: BCI Holdings sells the original company business operations, Beatrice Dairy Products, Inc., to Borden, Inc.
- 1987: Beatrice International Foods, which included Beatrice Foods Canada Ltd., is sold to corporate attorney Reginald Lewis and becomes TLC Beatrice International.
- 1987: KKR creates new company called Beatrice Company. This is not the same entity as Beatrice Companies, Inc., or Beatrice Foods Co., and was specifically created to include Beatrice Cheese, Inc., Beatrice-Hunt/Wesson, Inc., and Swift-Eckrich, Inc., business units.
- 1990: KKR sells Beatrice Company to CAGSUB, Inc., a subsidiary of ConAgra, Inc., which merged the assets and liabilities (including legal exposures) into its operations.*
- 1997: The Canadian division of Beatrice is sold to Paralmalat.
- 2007: After a hiatus, Beatrice Companies, Inc., is reactivated.
- 2010: Beatrice forms new business unit for commodities called Beatrice Mercantile Exchange.
- 2011: Beatrice creates new business called Zyclopz, which is to handle business virtual directory services, and later website design and web hosting.
- 2011: Beatrice U.S. Food Corporation changes name to Beatrice Foods Co.
- 2018: The website providing this history (beatriceco.com) features the Beatrice logo and the company name Beatrice Companies, Inc.

* The only mention of Beatrice in the 2017 ConAgra annual report pertains to the legacy of environmental lawsuits stemming from ConAgra's 1991 acquisition of the company. http://www.beatriceco.com/bti/porticus/conagra/pdf/2017CAGar_Complete.pdf.

Source: A history of the company appears at http://www.beatriceco.com/about_investor/.

What cash can a buyer find in the company?

Cash can be found on the balance sheet, as well as in more unusual places. Does the acquired company have a lawsuit pending against a third party that can be settled quickly and profitably? Does it have excess funded reserves? Is its employee benefit plan overfunded, and if so, can it be terminated or restructured? Can its pension plan acquire any of the company assets? Typically, pension plans can invest a portion of their assets in real estate of a diversified nature, including real estate acquired from the company. Has the company been acquiring marketable stock or debt of unrelated companies? Does it have a valuable art collection that can be cashed in at the next Sotheby's auction?

Keep track of changes in the company's cash position between signing the acquisition agreement and closing. The terms of the acquisition agreement can ensure either that the buyer retains cash at the closing or that all cash goes to the seller. (See Chapters 3 and 9.)

Before selling a division, is it advisable to take the cash out of it?

It depends on how the sale is structured. In most sales, there's no obligation to include cash among the assets. It is perfectly ethical to move the cash to a corporate account and sell the assets without the cash. This would be the exact equivalent of selling the cash as an asset at face value. However, in most stock sales, the seller must acknowledge that the value of the stock includes the value of the cash and make appropriate adjustments when pricing the transaction if the cash is removed.

DETERMINING STRUCTURE IN DEBT FINANCING

After the need to borrow is minimized, the next step is to organize and orchestrate the borrowing program. The art of structuring a financing is to allocate the revenues and assets of the acquired company to lenders in a manner that does the following:

- Maximizes the amount loaned by the most senior and highly secured and thus lowest-interest-rate lenders
- Leaves sufficient cash flow to support, if needed, a layer of subordinated, higher-interest-rate mezzanine debt, as well as any seller takeback financing
- Provides for adequate working capital and is consistent with seasonal variations and foreseeable one-time bulges or dips in cash flow
- Permits the separate leveraging of distinct assets that can be more advantageously set aside for specialized lenders, such as sale-leasebacks of office buildings or manufacturing facilities
- Accommodates both good news and bad—that is, permits debt prepayment without penalty if revenues are sufficient and permits nonpayment and nonenforcement of subordinated debt if revenues are insufficient
- Avoids and, where necessary, resolves conflicts between lenders

Customarily, these results are achieved through layering of debt.

What types of debt are typically used in an LBO?

Although sometimes only one secured lender is needed (or in the case of a very simple business with strong cash flow, only a single unsecured lender), multiple tiers of lenders are normally necessary for large transactions. The multilender LBO may include several or all of the following layers of debt, in rough order of seniority:

- *Senior revolving debt,* secured by a first lien on current assets (inventory and accounts receivable), a first or second lien on fixed assets (property, plant, and equipment, or PPE), liens on intangibles, and perhaps a pledge of stock of the acquired company or its subsidiaries. This debt typically provides a part of the acquisition financing and working capital, including letter of credit financing, and is generally provided by commercial banks or similar institutional lenders. It is often referred to as "commercial paper."

- *Senior term debt,* secured by a first lien on fixed assets, a first or second lien on current assets, and liens on intangibles and stock of the company and subsidiaries, to provide acquisition financing. Sometimes—but not very frequently—this debt is subordinated to the senior revolving debt. It is normally provided by commercial banks in conjunction with senior revolving debt, or by similar commercial lenders or insurance companies.
- *Senior subordinated debt,* or mezzanine debt unsecured or secured by junior liens on the assets securing the senior debt, used for acquisition financing. These instruments, known as high-yield debt by promoters and junk bonds by detractors, are mainly placed by investment bankers, the principal purchasers being insurance companies, pension and investment funds, and financial institutions.
- *Sale leasebacks or other special financing arrangements* for specific facilities or equipment. These arrangements may range from installment purchases of office copiers or long-term computer lease-purchases to sales of the target's real estate to an independent investment partnership, which then net leases such real estate back to the target.
- *Seller's subordinated note or warrant,* secured or unsecured, perhaps convertible to stock.

Beneath all of these in seniority are various forms of equity. These types of financing instruments have a relatively low priority on the financing totem pole and will not be discussed in the remainder of this chapter, which focuses largely on debt financing.

We will discuss senior debt from both banks, high-yield/junk bonds, LBO investment funds, and seller takeback financing in greater detail later in this chapter. First, however, we should consider how much debt can be obtained at each of these layers.

How are the amounts of the different layers of debt determined?

The initial decision is, of course, the lender's. As discussed later in this chapter, the lender for each layer of the financing will indicate to the buyer a range or approximation of the amount it is prepared to lend. The lender's decision (or, if there are several lenders, each lender's decision) will be based largely on amount, interest rate, and payback period, but also on ability to perform. A basic objective is to maximize senior debt, which bears the lowest interest rate. At the same time, senior debt also requires relatively favorable coverage ratios; therefore, there will be excess cash flow left over after servicing senior debt to support high-yield/junk bonds or other mezzanine debt. After mezzanine debt is covered, something should still remain to persuade the seller that its takeback financing has a reasonable chance of payment.

The process is not exact. Each lender evaluates the cash flow and assets of the target differently, and uses a different formula for setting the loan amount. The term lender may be willing to lend $10 more if the revolving lender lends $8 less, but the buyer may be reluctant to explore that possibility for fear that the term lender had not previously focused on the exact amount being loaned by the revolving lender, and a second review by the term lender's credit committee could result in a decision not to make the loan at all.

When resources and time permit, the best course of action for a buyer will probably be to obtain bids from several lenders on each layer, and then to select, at the moment when the lenders' commitment letters are about to be signed, the optimum combination and present it to each approved lender as a *fait accompli,* burning no bridges to the unsuccessful lenders until the package has been accepted by all the intended players. In this way, commitments can be entered into with the optimum combination of lenders. The competitive nature of the process will discourage objections by the lender fortunate enough to be selected. In addition, lenders tend to leave to the later stages of the closing a full investigation of the other lenders' terms, by which time they may be less likely to rethink the terms of their loan.

How does a senior lender decide how much to lend in an acquisition?

A number of considerations are key to a bank's lending decision:

- Liquidation value of the collateral
- Credibility of the borrower's financial projections
- Whether the borrower's projections show enough cash flow to service the debt (including junior debt)
- Whether proposed asset liquidations are likely to take place in time and in sufficient amount to amortize the term debt (or reduce the revolver commitment)
- Potential company profitability and industry prospects
- The amount of junior debt (and capacity of the junior creditor to assist the borrower with additional funds in a workout scenario)
- The amount of equity

SENIOR DEBT

When should the senior lender in a transaction enter the picture?

Ideally, the senior lender should be brought into the transaction as early as possible, and thus one of the first steps a buyer takes is to prepare his presentation of the deal to lenders. Many lenders are reluctant to review a proposed acquisition unless they already have a formal or informal agreement to go through with the transaction, or at least to cover their costs and, perhaps, a fee. Thus, the presentation is quickly followed by a commitment letter.

The senior lender's loan will usually represent the single largest portion of the cash to be raised for the transaction. If the senior lender is not willing to finance, the deal cannot be done. For that reason, the buyer must be sure to make a correct judgment about the financeability of the transaction before he or she incurs the considerable expense of negotiating an acquisition agreement.

What form does senior debt take?

Typically, senior debt is part term loan and part revolving loan, with the term loan used to finance the purchase price, and the revolving loan used to provide working capital (although a portion of the revolving loan is often used to finance the purchase price as well). Usually, senior debt is provided by banks or their affiliates, and thus we often use the term bank to refer to a senior lender.

What is demand lending?

It is becoming more and more common for senior debt to be provided by banks in a demand format quite different from traditional local bank financing, which relied primarily on the personal guarantees of the business owner, had a fixed term and limited covenants, and kept its nose out of the borrower's business. By contrast, demand lending gives the initial impression to a borrower of being intrusive and one-sided: the bank may have the right to call the loan at any time, make revolving loan advances only at its discretion, require all business receipts to be applied immediately to repayment, and have a bristling array of protective covenants that require bank consent for almost any action not in the ordinary course of business. The appropriate trade-offs for these provisions are absence of personal guarantees and a willingness to lend relatively large amounts.

Because this style of lending is unfamiliar to many borrowers and lenders, the logic of the trade-offs may not be observed: the bank may require a demand loan and guarantees as well, or the borrower may seek a high loan limit but refuse to consider demand repayment. Borrower and bank need to clearly understand their relationship from the start. Success depends on both players recognizing that the relationship will be a close one involving cooperation and mutual dependency.

Can lenders be arbitrary?

No. A borrower can take considerable comfort in the principle of "commercial reasonableness" that binds lenders and should thus understand that many of the rights the bank obtains on paper it cannot exercise in practice. A number of cases have held that if a bank makes a loan on terms that give it extensive power over a company's financial affairs, it cannot use that power arbitrarily and may in fact be liable for consequential damages if the company is put out of business or otherwise damaged because of an unreasonable refusal to lend. (See the summary of the *K.M.C.Co., Inc. v. Irving Trust Co.* case cited in the legal case summaries in the final section of this book.)

SALE-LEASEBACKS

What are sale-leasebacks and what are the pros and cons of using them?

A sale-leaseback involves the sale of the seller's real estate or equipment to a third party, which then net leases the real estate or equipment back to the company. In essence, a company takes out a mortgage on a property in the form of a sale-leaseback. The ownership remains with the original entity, yet the lender is taking a lien on the assets of the surviving company as collateral on the loan. This type of financing is ideal for leveraged buyouts, where companies are often looking for ways to replace expensive unsecured debt or equity debt with less expensive secured debt as a means of raising cash or controlling capital debt structure.

A sale-leaseback may be structured as an installment contract, as an operating lease, or as a finance lease. These distinctions have important tax and accounting ramifications and should always be kept in mind. Topic 842, Leases, a change in GAAP that came about in 2016, will have a major impact on this type of financing, as described in more detail in Chapter 5.[37] When a leaseback is structured as a finance lease, which is considered a type of capital lease under US accounting rules, the acquirer as lessee can make a case as owners of the asset for tax and accounting purposes. The lending source (lessor) generally retains title and takes a perfected first security interest in the equipment. (A security interest, e.g., lien on collateral, is perfected when it is registered with the appropriate statutory authority, which makes it legally enforceable; any subsequent claim on that asset is given a junior status.) The lessee raises cash from the sale-leaseback.

Acquirers should note several points:

- Price can be negotiable. If the value of the leaseback is expressed as a percent of the equipment price, beware. The lessor will most likely want to only value the equipment at its liquidation value, which may be significantly different from any remaining depreciation or book value of the equipment.
- In a true sale-leaseback, if title is in the lessee's name, it must pass to the leasing company so applicable sales taxes can be accounted for.
- A finance lease acts the same as a loan against the asset. Thus, the obligation and the yield or rate of the transaction might be greater than the borrowers' incremental borrowing rate at its primary bank. The acquiring entity must weigh the benefits of leasing (conservation of capital and credit lines for unsecured lending, etc.) as a way to manage their cost of funds or available capital instead of pledging the same assets in other forms of borrowing.
- In any leaseback scenario, there are tax and accounting implications. These must be reviewed and weighed toward the benefits of the transaction.

Some sale-leasebacks offer an option to buy. How does this type of transaction affect an acquirer?

In this type of leaseback, the leasing company is purchasing the equipment at a fixed amount, then leasing back to the entity. In this type of deal, the stream of payments may or may not equal the value of the equipment and interest charged over the term. In this instance there is a residual position in the equipment on behalf of the leasing company (the lease is not a full-payout lease). Thus, at the end of the term of the lease, the leasing company is looking for one of two things to happen:

- For the original entity to make them whole on their residual position

- For the original entity to return the equipment so the leasing company can remarket the equipment to another user, thus recapturing its residual position

Why would an acquirer want to do a leaseback?

Let's say an acquirer has bought a company that has assets suitable for a sale-leaseback, and has found a leasing company that is willing to take a residual position on the equipment. Let's also assume that the acquirer is able to sell the equipment for 100 percent of its value to the leasing company and promises a stream of payments, not including the end purchase option that equals only 90 percent of the transaction. At the end of the lease, the lessee must either exercise its purchase option or return the equipment. If the lessee elects to return the equipment (then, in effect, use the leasing company as a remarketing agent as well as a funding source), it has raised relatively inexpensive capital by only paying the stream rate versus the full yield of the transaction (stream plus residual). Here is the math for a three-year sale-leaseback with a 10 percent purchase option (written as a finance lease):

Asset value at time of sale-leaseback:	$100,000
Residual position at 3 years taken by leasing company	$10,000
All-in yield required by leasing company including residual	12%
Payment terms	
36 payments @	$3,089
Purchase option	$10,000
Total payments made if lessee does not exercise purchase option*	$111,214
Thus, effective interest rate paid by lessee would be	7.9%
Total payments if lessee exercises purchase option	$121,214
Thus, effective interest rate paid by lessee would be	12.00%

*Leasing company remarkets the equipment looking for at least its residual position plus remarketing expenses.

What paperwork is involved in a sale-leaseback?

To prepare for a sale-leaseback, a detailed appraisal, an as-built survey, and title insurance of the real estate must be ordered, preferably at least six weeks in advance of closing. The other loan documents must be drafted to permit the sale-leaseback. The sale-leaseback may be financed by a mortgage loan. The lease and the mortgage loan documents must clarify that the borrower/tenant continues to own, and the senior lender continues to enjoy a first and prior lien upon, all equipment and fixtures used in the borrower's/tenant's business.

PROS AND CONS OF PRESERVING DEBT AND LEASE OBLIGATIONS

What are the pros and cons of keeping existing debt in place?

Review carefully the existing debt of the target and determine whether prepayment may be necessary or advisable. In some cases, the acquisition may entitle the lender to prepayment, perhaps at a premium. In other cases, even where prepayment is not required, it might be a good idea to repay existing debt because of high interest rates or burdensome covenants in leases, loan agreements, or indentures.

What should a buyer look for in a new debt agreement?

Restrictive covenants in leases or loan agreements may prohibit a sale of assets without the lessor's or lender's consent, a condition that could hamper postmerger restructuring or spin-offs. Restrictions on sale of assets provide important protection to a lessor or lender who otherwise cannot prevent major changes in the structure or operations of its lessee or debtor, and courts have interpreted such restrictions liberally in favor of lessors and lenders. Although many covenants use the language "all or substantially all" in describing this restriction, even modest asset sales may be challenged. Any sale of more than 25 percent of the assets raises questions, particularly if the assets being sold constitute the major revenue-producing operations of the historical core business.

Indentures for unsecured borrowings also typically contain covenants prohibiting the imposition of liens on assets of the lessor or debtor and may prohibit more than one class of debt or interlayering (for example, both senior and subordinated debt). Such financing must be done on an unsecured basis and without recourse to some of the techniques for layering of debt discussed later in this chapter.

Debt agreements of this unsecured kind are deceptively simple. It may first appear that the lack of elaborate and specific covenants, such as those contained in the typical secured loan, offers many opportunities to substantially restructure the company without lenders' consents. But the canny buyer, when analyzing such loan agreements, will realize that the broad prohibitions on making dividend payments or selling assets can defeat most financing plans. Whereas technically tight, detailed loan agreements can encourage and even legitimize the use of loopholes based on technicalities, so the broadly written loan agreement makes lawyers and other technicians cautious about arrangements that may violate the spirit of the existing debt agreement.

In addition to restrictions on sales of assets or liens on assets, the selling company may also be subject to preexisting covenants prohibiting a change of control of the lessee or debtor. In such cases, preservation of existing debt may require changing the structure of the acquisition. A common legal issue that arises in such cases is whether the merger of the lessee or debtor into another corporation constitutes a transfer of ownership requiring the lessor or lender's consent. In most cases, it is possible to conclude that the merger is not a transfer to another entity, because the original lessee or debtor continues as part of the surviving entity, although the conclusion varies according to state law.

How common is it for an acquired company to have a lot of leases, and how important are they?

In recent decades, leasing has increased as a source of financing, as companies (particularly smaller ones) lease their equipment, vehicles, and other valuable property, in order to leverage their cash and equity. Although such lease obligations are not material to the overall balance sheet position of large companies, they can greatly affect the value of small and midsized firms.

Suppose an acquirer wants to buy a company that has a lot of valuable leases, but the leases contain a lot of fine print about cancellation in the event of a change of control. How serious is such fine print?

The seriousness of the fine print, as with everything in M&A life, depends first and foremost on the size and nature of the entities involved and the past relationship between them. Beyond this general rule, the situation will vary according to whether the company being acquired is a heavy lessee, a lessor, or both.

What advice do you have for the acquirer of a heavy lessee?

If the company being acquired has signed one or more important lease agreements as a lessee, the first decision to be made will be whether or not the acquirer will be assuming the lessee's obligations. This is usually what happens. Note, though, that the original lessee will almost always need to get approval from the lessor before it can assign its lease obligations or sublease to a new owner.

Therefore, the first order of business for any acquirer will be to contact the lessor and inform it of the pending transaction. The lessee should also contact the lessor. Almost every lease requires that the funding source must be notified if there is a change in ownership. (This is to enable the lessor to look at the credit history and worthiness of any new owners before allowing the previous ownership to assign their obligations over to it.) On almost any lease, *non-notification of change in ownership or location of the equipment is generally considered a technical default of the terms of the lease.* If the new and old owners are in technical default, the funding sources may call the remaining payments due.

Of course, if the company that is leasing survives, and is as strong as it was or stronger before the merger, there won't be any issues. At the end of the day, it isn't as much the change in ownership but the change in credit risk that is of concern. Ordinarily the credit of the acquiring company is better than the existing entity, so the acquirer can make its own decision as to whether or not to assume the lease, renegotiate it, or pay it off.

But in cases where the lease that must be assigned and the credit of the acquiring company is not sufficient, there is a chance that the original lessee, especially in small privately held companies, will be required to remain as a guarantor of the lease or find some structure to assure the funding source that they will continue to receive timely and complete payments.

In LBOs, the financial ratios of the selling company might change dramatically, making the creditworthiness of the new entity insufficient for the original funding source. In this case, the lessor may have to repay the funding source through a prepayment of the lease with monies raised in the leveraged buyout or may need to pledge additional collateral in order to give the funding source sufficient comfort from a credit perspective in what they may see as a new transaction.

Differing funding/lending sources have different policies for lease rewrites, buyouts, and refinancing. Lessors responsible for any significant lease need to understand these policies and learn about options for early lease termination.

What advice do you have for the acquirer of a heavy lessor with major lease receivables?

Buying a company with major lease receivables raises a different set of issues. Many companies have contracts with customers whereby those customers agree to pay for their equipment in a lease or lease-type transaction. Some companies that have a consumable component to their sales may rent equipment with their consumables in order to tie their customers up over time. In this type of company, an acquirer will find accounts receivable from bundled lease papers or installment contracts. Also, companies that manufacture capital equipment may offer a lease alternative to customers that can't afford to pay up-front cash. In such companies, acquirers will also find significant lease receivables carried on the balance sheet.

In either case, prospective acquirers should perform due diligence on the portfolio of leases. Before starting, it is important not to reinvent the wheel when dealing with a public company. The advisors doing the acquirer's due diligence in this area or any other area of risk can simply ask for management's most current report on internal financial controls. Under Section 404 of the Sarbanes-Oxley Act, companies are required to include in their annual reports a report of management on the company's "internal control over financial reporting." It is safe to say that in the aftermath of Sarbanes-Oxley, the quality of lease portfolios, like any other object of due diligence, is more likely to stand up to scrutiny due to stronger internal controls in many public companies.

On the upside, there may be options to discount the leases to third parties, generating a possible premium—or at least a vehicle to reevaluate the asset values of the receivables given by the company being acquired. On the downside, leases might not be included in the lessor's accounts for delinquency, days sales outstanding, or bad debt, thus giving a higher level of performance of the overall company than they should. For example, some capital equipment leases are really sales that the lessor would not take for credit or documentation reasons—so, as a liquid asset, they are suspect.

Sometimes the accounting for the leases varies and how the company books them may not give a true picture of the company's balance sheet or revenue stream. For instance, say the company being acquired is a subsidiary of a large entity with a low cost of capital, and that this subsidiary historically wrote contracts with its customers as leases at current market rates, but booked the deals by discounting the stream at its (much lower) cost of funds. Since the company books these transactions by discounting the paper, the booked sales amount or present value amount might in fact be higher than the actual sales price.

One company that looked great as an acquisition candidate delivered disappointing financial results after the deal because of such a practice. This company leased internally about 15 percent of its capital sales, and then discounted the stream up front at the corporate cost of funds. This elevated the apparent sales amount by 110 percent! The company's good-looking revenues, which indicated a great deal, didn't take into account a differing cost of funds. Revenues after the acquisition were lower since the new entity couldn't borrow at the same rates and/or discount the deals below market.

SELLER TAKEBACK FINANCING

Many leveraged acquisitions involve contingency payments structured with a takeback by the seller of debt or stock. This is particularly likely to occur if the seller is a major corporation divesting a minor operation. In such deals, the seller takes only part of the money, with the understanding that it will be paid more if certain conditions (contingencies) are met. In return, the seller gets a note from the buyer. If the note is subordinated to other debt, it is called a seller's subordinated note.

If debt is taken back, it may be structured as a simple installment sale, or it may involve accompanying warrants. In either case, the claims of the seller are generally junior to those of other creditors, such as the senior lenders to the buyer. A seller takeback is not always possible. In particular, it may be necessary to pay stockholders of publicly held companies the acquisition price entirely in cash because of the delays and disclosures involved in offering them debt or other securities that require a prospectus registered under federal security laws.

Why do sellers consider takeback financing, including junior class financing?

Sellers are generally reluctant to take back stock or debt that is junior to all other debt. Still, a seller benefits from such subordinated financing by receiving an increased purchase price, at least nominally, and obtaining an equity kicker or its equivalent. The seller may well be aware, and should be prepared to face the fact, that the note or stock will realize full value only if the acquired company prospers, and that there is a real risk that this part of the purchase price will never be paid.

By the same token, however, the upside potential that the seller can realize if the transaction is successful can be much greater than it could receive if no part of its purchase price were contingent or exposed. There may also be cosmetic advantages to both buyer and seller in achieving a higher nominal price for the target company, even though a portion of that price is paid in a note or preferred stock with a market value and a book value below face. Thus, for example, if a seller has announced that it will not let its company go for less than $100 million, but has overestimated its value, the seller may eventually be pleased to settle for $60 million cash and a $40 million 10-year subordinated note at 4 percent interest. The note will go onto the seller's books at a substantial discount. (The amount of the discount will be useful for the buyer to discover if he or she later wishes to negotiate prepayment of the note in connection with a restructuring or a workout.)

What are the relative advantages of subordinated debt and preferred stock?

Preferred stock has the advantage of increasing the equity line on the balance sheet and thus helps protect the highly leveraged company from insolvency and makes it more attractive to senior and junk bond lenders. Remember that an insolvent corporation cannot transfer its property to anyone else without receiving full consideration. To do otherwise would be to defraud its creditors—that is, to deprive them of access to its assets. Thus, if solvency is an issue, the seller and lenders may feel more comfortable in including some preferred stock on the balance sheet.

Subordinated debt offers considerable advantages to the seller, however. Payments are due whether or not there are corporate earnings, unless otherwise restricted by subordination provisions. Negotiators may have been told to sever completely the seller's connection with the company. Taking back a note bespeaks a greater degree of separation and greater apparent certainty that the amounts due will be paid. The seller may intend to sell the paper it takes back and can get more for a note than it could get for preferred stock. The seller may be able to obtain security interests in the acquired company's assets, junior of course to the liens of the acquisition lenders, but no such security interest accompanies preferred stock.

From the buyer's point of view, a note has the major advantage of generating deductible interest payments rather than nondeductible dividends. Preferred stock has the important disadvantage of preventing a buyer from electing pass-through tax status as an S corporation. For both reasons, be sure that if a note does emerge, it is not subject to reclassification as equity by the IRS. Seller preferred stock can also have other adverse tax consequences (see Chapter 5).

Absent unusual circumstances, if the buyer can persuade the senior and junk bond lenders to accept a seller's subordinated note rather than preferred stock, the seller should have no objections. If not, the lenders and seller may accept preferred stock convertible into a note at buyer's option once the company achieves a certain net worth or cash flow level. As a last resort, the buyer may persuade the seller, six months or a year after closing when debt has been somewhat reduced, to convert the preferred stock into a note.

How can a seller obtain an equity kicker in the company it is selling?

Sometimes, as mentioned before, a takeback note has the same effect as an equity kicker because it serves to inflate the sales price beyond the company's real present worth, and it can only be paid if the company has good future earnings. It is also quite possible for the seller simply to retain common stock in the acquired company. In the alternative, the seller can obtain participating preferred stock, in which dividend payments are determined as a percentage of earnings or as a percentage of dividend payments made to common stockholders, and in which the redemption price of the preferred stock rises with the value of the company. Some of these choices have tax consequences (see Chapter 5).

WARRANTS

How exactly do warrants work?

One increasingly popular alternative to preferred or common stock is a warrant to acquire common stock at some time in the future. This has the double advantage for the buyer of not making the seller a common stockholder entitled to receive information and participate in stockholders' meetings during the immediate postacquisition period, and of not adversely affecting the target's eligibility for S corporation status. S corporations may not have more than 35 stockholders, and, with minor exceptions, all stockholders must be individuals. A corporate seller cannot remain as a stockholder of an S corporation, but it can remain as a warrant holder. It is important, however, that the warrants not be immediately exercisable, since their exercise will cause a loss of S corporation status. Thus, certain triggers are established as preconditions to their exercise. These are basically events that entitle the stockholder investors to extract value from their stock: a public sale of stock, a sale of substantially all the stock or assets, or a change of control of the target. Once one of these events occurs, S corporation status is likely to be lost anyway, and it is logical to let the warrant holder cash in and get the benefit of equity ownership.

What are the key terms generally found in warrants?

Key provisions will address how many shares can be acquired upon exercise of the warrant: the amount of the "exercise price" (the amount to be paid to acquire the shares); the period of time during which exercise may occur (which, to prevent interference with any future sale of the company, should not extend beyond the date of any such sale); any restrictions on transfer of the warrant; and any rights, discussed more extensively later, when the warrant holder may have to register shares or participate in registrations by the company for a public stock offering under the securities laws. There are also lengthy and technical provisions providing for adjustment in the number of shares for which the warrant can be exercised to prevent dilution if there are stock splits or dividends or if shares are sold to others at less than full value.

Does the seller ever receive security interests as a subordinated lender?

Occasionally, but not typically. The seller may take a subordinated note either on an unsecured basis or with security. Security interests strengthen a seller's bargaining power with senior lenders in the event of bankruptcy or refinancing. The collateral gives the seller a right to foreclose as well as a seat at the bankruptcy table, even if under the subordination provisions the seller has no immediate right to payment. Possession of a security interest also gives the subordinated lender leverage to initiate and influence a refinancing.

Suppose that an acquisition candidate is leasing a facility under terms that guarantee purchase for a nominal price at the end of the lease (say, under a tax-exempt bond deal). How easy is it for an acquirer to assume the lease and get the same purchase rights?

This is very hard to answer as a general rule. Most leases issued under tax-exempt funding involve very large sums of money, and, as with all large transactions, each lease tends to have some unique terms and conditions. A few points of advice may be in order here nonetheless.

First, it should be noted that the nominal end-of-term price generally does not matter as much as the original structure and reason for issuing the tax-exempt funds. Changes in ownership more often than not signal changes in the conditions of the lessee and, thus, the primary reason tax-exempt funding was available. Remember, just because an entity is tax exempt does not always mean that it is qualified to receive tax-exempt leasing or funding. For these reasons, under the terms of most agreements, the issuing authority must be notified of any changes in the status of the lessor.

In general, both the lessor and the lessee will hope for continuation of a lease of this type. Although tax exemption was given originally to the lessee, it winds up (through the economics of leasing) being enjoyed by the lessor. Tax-exempt leases enable the lessor to offer a lower cost of funds to the lessee, since the lessor does not have to pay tax on the profit from the interest charges within the lease.

What issues arise in leases extended to tax-exempt organizations?

When a company leases a piece of equipment, it must pay taxes including personal property tax, sales tax, and/or use tax. Many different tax authorities may require that the tax be paid up front, and some require the tax to be paid on the payments over the term of the lease. In tax-exempt situations where an entity is exempt from items such as sales and use taxes, this may also be in effect on its current leases. (But check with a tax attorney: even tax-exempt organizations may have to pay unrelated business income tax [UBIT] under some circumstances.) If a company is acquired by an entity that does not qualify from a tax standpoint, or if a change of control changes the tax-exempt status, the leasing company can't always be relied upon to recognize this during the transfer of the lease from one entity to another. Though leases specify that the leasing entity is liable to collect and submit any taxes owed, some leases state that the lessee is also liable. Thus, the acquiring entity needs to raise the issue of possible changes in its tax-exempt status and tax payment obligations to the leasing company. Such concerns should be incorporated into the assignment of obligations in the acquisition agreement—and possibly in the deal's payment structure as well.

WORKING CAPITAL DEBT OF THE SELLER

What is working capital debt? Should an acquirer leave it in place or refinance it?

Working capital debt of the target before the acquisition is likely to appear in any of at least four forms:

- A secured revolving credit loan from an outside lender
- A parent's intercompany transfers, either with or without interest
- Bank letters of credit or guarantees to secure purchases from suppliers, principally for foreign sourcing
- More or less generous payment terms from suppliers

The first two kinds of debt will almost certainly have to be refinanced at the acquisition closing. A secured revolver, or even an unsecured one, will inevitably tie up assets and stand in the way of any plans for secured acquisition financing, and the parent/seller will not want to retain what are probably short-term, rather informal financial arrangements of an in-house nature. There may, however, be some room for a buyer to argue for at least some short-term financing through a seller takeback of existing intercompany loans.

Refinancing the third type of debt is also common, but risky for all parties. A senior revolving credit acquisition lender often provides letter of credit financing after the acquisition and will probably insist upon doing this financing as part of the deal. Sometimes this can be trouble, because while the new acquisition lender is learning the ropes, there can be awkward slipups in a sensitive area. One possible solution is to explore including the existing letter of credit lender in the lending group where its expertise will be accessible.

As for the fourth type of debt, it usually should not be a problem to retain existing relationships and favorable terms with suppliers. They will probably be relieved to find that the buyer doesn't plan to close the business or move it elsewhere. In some cases, suppliers have relied on the presence of a deep-pocket parent company as added security and may be looking for special assurances difficult for the postacquisition company to provide. In other cases, it is possible to structure the acquisition so that a subsidiary that purchases on trade credit has a better debt-to-equity ratio than its parent and can retain favorable trade terms.

What should be done if existing debt includes tax-exempt industrial development bonds?

Tax-exempt industrial development bonds give the borrower the advantage of low interest rates but also carry disadvantages: they encumber assets better used to support new borrowings, and they may carry with them old parent company guarantees that must be lifted as a condition of the acquisition. Often these bonds can be "defeased" under the terms of their trust indentures; that is, high-quality obligations (usually issued or guaranteed by the US government) can be deposited with the trustee bank for the bond issue in an amount high enough to retire the bonds over their term through scheduled payments on the obligations. If the interest rate on the bonds is low enough, the amount of obligations required to defease them may be less than their face amount, and once the bonds are defeased, their covenants and liens cease to have any effect. Note, however, that the defeasance of high-interest-rate bonds is expensive, and the defeasance of variable-rate bonds is impossible because they lack a predictable interest rate for which a sufficient sum for certain can be set aside. In addition, tax problems can arise: Are the earnings on the defeasance fund taxable, and does the defeasance give rise to discharge of indebtedness income for the borrower?

Tax-exempt bond issues are likely to be complex, and any transactions involving them may require special attention from the bank serving as bond trustee and the issuer's original bond counsel. Such issues involve a two-step process: the funds are borrowed by a governmental body and are then reloaned to the company to build a facility or are used to construct a facility that is leased to the company, normally but not necessarily on terms that permit a purchase for a nominal price at the end of the lease term. Check with a tax or leasing expert for hidden problems.

THE BANK BOOK AND COMMITMENT LETTER

How is an LBO transaction presented to prospective lenders?

The normal medium of the LBO transaction is the so-called bank book, a brief narrative description of the proposed transaction and the target company. The bank book indicates what financing structure is contemplated and includes projections of earnings sufficient to cover working capital needs and to amortize debt, along with a balance sheet setting forth the pledgeable assets. (Since the balance sheet will typically value assets based on GAAP, an appraisal of actual market and/or liquidation value, if available, may be attached or referenced.)

What happens after the bank book is presented to a lender?

If the loan officer believes that the bank may be willing to make a loan that meets the dollar amount and general terms requested by the buyer, he or she will seek to obtain as much information as possible about the company from the buyer. This information will include proxy statements, 10-Ks, and 10-Qs if the target is a public company, and audited financials or tax returns if it is not. The loan officer will also send out a team of reviewers to visit the company's facilities and interview its management and will obtain an internal or outside appraisal of the assets. This review can take from half a week to a month or more. Banks are aware that they are in a competitive business and generally move quickly, particularly if the loan is being simultaneously considered by several of them.

The loan officer will then prepare a write-up recommending the proposed loan and will present it to the bank's credit committee. The committee may endorse the recommendation as made, approve it with changes (presumably acceptable to the buyer), or turn it down. If the proposal is approved, the bank will prepare a commitment letter (sometimes with the assistance of its counsel, but often not) setting forth the bank's binding commitment to make the loan. This letter thereafter becomes the bank officer's governing document in future negotiations.

What does the commitment letter contain?

Apart from the bare essentials (the amount of the loan, how much will be term and how much revolver, the maturity of the term loan and amortization provisions, and interest rates), the commitment letter will also set forth the bank's proposals on the following:

- Fees to be paid to the bank
- Voluntary prepayment rights and penalties under the term loan
- What collateral is required; whether any other lender may take a junior lien on any collateral on which the bank has a senior lien, and whether the bank is to receive a junior lien on any other collateral subject to another lender's senior lien
- How the funds are to be used
- The amount of subordinated debt and equity that may be required as a condition to the making of the senior loan
- Payment of the bank's expenses

The commitment may also set forth in some detail lists of covenants, default triggers, reporting requirements, and conditions to closing, including legal opinions to be furnished by counsel to the borrowers; it also usually contemplates additional closing conditions and covenants that may be imposed by the bank as the closing process evolves. The commitment letter will also contain an expiration date, typically a very early one. For example, it may provide that the offer to make the loan will expire in 24 hours if not accepted in writing by the borrower, or it may allow as much as two weeks.

The commitment letter, if it provides for a revolving line of credit (usually called a revolver), will generally state both the maximum amount that may be borrowed under the line (the cap) and a potentially lower amount that the bank would actually lend, sometimes expressed as a percentage of the value of the collateral pledged to secure the revolver. This lower amount is called the borrowing base. The difference between the amount actually borrowed on the revolver at any time and the amount that could be borrowed (i.e., the lower of the cap or the borrowing base) is called availability.

How is the borrowing base determined?

If receivables are pledged, the commitment letter may distinguish between "eligible receivables" and other "receivables." Both are subject to the bank's lien, but only the former may be used to enhance the amount of availability; that is, they may constitute assets against which borrowings may be made.

In a typical situation, eligible receivables will be those that are not more than 90 days old or past due, have been created in the normal course of business, arise from bona fide sales of goods or services to financially sound parties unrelated to the borrower or its affiliates, and are not subject to offset, counterclaim, or other dispute. The bank will lend up to a specified percentage (typically 70 to 90 percent) of eligible receivables. This percentage is known as the advance rate. Thus, notwithstanding the maximum amount of the line theoretically available to the borrower, revolving loans outstanding may not at any time exceed that stated percentage of eligible receivables, determined monthly or even weekly.

Inventory is also usually used as collateral. To be eligible, inventory will generally have to be of the kind normally sold by the borrower (if the borrower is in the business of selling goods) and will be limited to finished goods boxed and ready for sale, not located in the hands of a retail store or in transit. An advance rate of 50 percent is not uncommon in such circumstances. In addition, some banks will lend against work in process or raw materials. However, a rather low advance rate—perhaps 15 percent—will be applied against such unfinished goods because of the problem a bank would experience in attempting to liquidate such collateral. The bank may also impose an "inventory sublimit"—an absolute dollar ceiling on the amount of inventory-based loans.

What does this method of determining the amount of the loan imply for company operations?

It is important to have accurately calculated the need for working capital at the time the loan is committed for and then to operate within the ceiling and borrowing formulas imposed by the revolving loan. A heavy penalty falls on the manager who allows inventory to build up, and a lesser but still significant penalty falls on the one who fails to collect receivables promptly. Only 50 or 60 cents can be borrowed for every dollar tied up in finished inventory, and every dollar of uncollected receivables costs the company 10 to 30 cents of inaccessible revenues. Financing practices of the preacquisition company may have been much looser, particularly if it was part of a well-heeled conglomerate or run as a family business, and untried chief financial officers can get in trouble very quickly after the closing if they don't understand the business implications of their loan terms.

Are the terms of the commitment letter negotiable?

Yes, but the best, and often the only, time to negotiate is when early drafts of the commitment letter are circulated, or when the loan officer sends the buyer an initial proposal letter before credit committee approval. Buyers should be careful to involve their lawyers and other advisors at that stage, and not wait until later to get into details. Be sure to understand the lender's procedures. The proposal letter may be the only opportunity to negotiate a document in advance; sometimes commitment letters appear only after the credit committee has met. Afterward, expectations of the lender become set, and the loan officer will find it awkward to resubmit the proposed loan to the credit committee. The borrower typically does not know how much latitude the loan officer has to modify the commitment without returning to the credit committee. Because time is of the essence in the typical LBO, and a new credit action can result in delay, it is also frequently not in the interest of the borrower to return to the credit committee.

Once the commitment letter is signed, how long will the commitment remain open?

The lender's commitment to make a loan will typically provide that definitive documentation must be negotiated, prepared, and signed by a certain date. Sometimes the time allowed is quite short: 30 or 45 days. Sometimes closing on the LBO will be protracted because of the need to obtain administrative consents, such as FCC (Federal Communications Commission) consents to change of ownership of television stations. In such cases, the termination date of the commitment must be pushed back to allow reasonable time to accomplish all of the actions necessary to effect the closing of the acquisition.

OTHER PRINCIPAL ISSUES IN SENIOR LOAN AGREEMENTS

What fees are typically charged by banks for lending services?

Bank fees tend to be as varied as the ingenuity of lenders can devise and as high as borrowers can accept. In some cases, the lender may charge a fee upon the delivery of the commitment letter signed by the bank (the "commitment letter fee") and a second commitment letter fee upon its execution by the borrower. Both such fees will probably be nonrefundable, but they may be credited against a third due from the borrower at closing on the loan (the "closing fee").

If the loan has been syndicated, the bank may charge an agency or management fee for its services in putting together the syndicate. This will typically be an ongoing fee (as opposed to the one-time commitment letter and closing fees), payable quarterly or monthly as a percentage of the total facility (0.25 percent per annum is not uncommon).

The total amount of fees charged by a bank at the closing ranges between 1 and 2.5 percent. The percentage depends on the speed demanded of the bank, the complexity of the transaction, the size of the banking group (the more lenders there are, the more expensive it is), and the degree of risk. A short-term bridge loan will probably involve a higher front-end fee than a long-term facility, since the bank has less opportunity to earn profit by way of interest over the life of the loan. Usually, the New York money center banks charge fees at the higher end of this range. In addition to the front-end fees, there will usually be a commitment fee or facility fee (typically, 0.5 percent) on the amount from time to time undrawn and available under the revolver.

If the borrower will need letters of credit, the bank will typically assess a letter of credit fee (typically 1 percent to 1.5 percent per annum) on the amount committed under a standby or commercial letter of credit.

Finally, the bank will often seek early termination fees on the unpaid balance of the term portion of the financing. These are intended to compensate the bank for economic losses it may suffer if the borrower terminates the term loan prior to its maturity because of a cheaper financing source, thus depriving the bank of the anticipated profit on the loan for the balance of the term. These fees may step down in amount the longer the term loan is outstanding. It is usually possible to get the bank to drop these termination fees or at least limit them to terminations occurring in the first year or two. This is worth spending some chips to achieve. If the company does well, the buyer will probably want to refinance the senior loan as quickly as possible to escape a whole panoply of burdensome covenants, and these fees are likely to be a problem.

What bank expenses is the borrower required to pay?

Typically, whether the loan is made or not, the commitment letter will require that the borrower be liable for all of the lender's out-of-pocket expenses and obligations for fees and disbursements of the bank's outside counsel. This provision is not negotiable; banks never expect to pay their own counsel for work done in connection with a loan. Such fees are always assessed against the borrower or, if the loan does not close, the intended borrower.

What interest rates do banks charge for LBO loans?

Typically, a bank will charge 1.5 to 2 percent over the prime rate or base rate. Contrary to popular belief, prime does not necessarily mean the lowest rate a bank charges its customers, as the loan agreement will often admit. Rather, the prime or base rate will be whatever the lending bank from time to time says it is.

Are reference rates other than prime ever used in floating-rate loans?

Yes, and the loan agreement may permit the borrower to switch back and forth between two references, or to charge a premium above a reference rate. The amount of the premium charged by the bank above the reference rate will depend on which reference rate is used, and the present and anticipated differentials between the bank's own prime and the alternative third-party reference rate or rates; premiums are generally about 100 basis points greater for Eurodollar rate loans than they are for prime-rate loans. This is largely, but not completely, offset by the fact that LIBOR is usually a lower rate than prime; the net effect of selecting LIBOR is probably to increase rates about 25 to 50 basis points. LIBOR is more responsive to interest rate changes and will move more quickly. A change in prime represents a significant political decision for a bank, and thus changes in prime come less frequently and in bigger steps.

Are there problems in having more than one lender participate in a loan?

Frequently LBO loans are made by groups of banks, or syndicates. In some cases, the banks involved in making the loan will all be parties to the loan agreement, with one of their number designated as the agent bank. In other cases, only one bank will sign the loan agreement, but it will sell off participation interests to other banks. Although the number of participants in a loan makes no difference to the borrower from a legal standpoint, the practical implications of having to deal with multiple lenders can be serious and troublesome.

Because of the high degree of leverage involved, LBO lenders tend to limit their risks by imposing an intrusive array of covenants—negative and affirmative, financial and operational—upon the borrower.

These covenants are designed to ensure that the business will be conducted as represented to the bankers and in accordance with the financial projections submitted to the bankers by the borrower. Any deviation, any change in the manner of operation of the business, or any bad financial development is likely to trigger a default. Because it is not always possible for a buyer to foresee all future developments in the way the business will be conducted, it is generally not possible, even in the absence of bad financial news, to operate at all times within the requirements imposed by the loan covenants. Hence, the borrower will generally find it necessary, from time to time, to go back to the lenders to have certain covenants waived or amended. If only one lender is involved, the process can be relatively simple. If the consent of a dozen or more is involved, the process can be expensive, time consuming, and painful.

Do all the members of a lending group have to approve every waiver and amendment?

Generally, no. But the provisions that relate to interbank matters, such as the percentage of lenders needed to grant waivers, are generally contained in a document (sometimes called the participation agreement) to which the borrower is not a party and which, frequently, the borrower may not even be allowed to see. Although lender approval arrangements are various, it is not unusual for them to provide that certain changes in the loan (such as changes in interest rates, due date, and principal amount) are so fundamental that all lenders must consent, whereas other changes can be approved by banks holding at least a 51 percent interest (or in some cases, a 66.6 percent interest) in all loans outstanding or in lending commitments.

Can junior lenders ever be paid back before senior lenders?

Not generally. Under a long-standing principle in bankruptcy law called the absolute priority rule, junior creditors may not go ahead of senior creditors. There are exceptions—such as the "new capital" exception for junior lenders who invest—but the rule generally prevails.

What is a negative pledge covenant, and why do lenders seek them?

A negative pledge is an undertaking by the borrower not to pledge to someone else assets that may be subject to the bank's lien or to no lien. It generally is used to bar junior liens on collateral that is subject to the bank's senior lien. Although in theory the rights of a junior loanholder should not impinge on the senior lender's rights in the collateral, in practice lenders strongly prefer not to be accountable to a second loanholder with regard to their stewardship over the collateral on which they have a first lien. A junior loanholder is, in the eyes of a senior lender, someone who can second-guess your actions in realizing upon the collateral and sue you if you slip up, or even if you don't.

What kinds of problems are most likely to be encountered in attempting to perfect liens on collateral?

- Prior unsatisfied liens may be discovered. (For this reason, as well as for general due diligence considerations [see Chapter 6], it is prudent to begin a lien search as promptly as possible in all jurisdictions in which record filings may have been made affecting the collateral.)
- Liens on patents, trademarks and trade names, and copyright assignments require special federal filings, which may be time consuming and require the services of specialized counsel.
- Collateral assignments of government contracts and receivables from the US government require federal approval, which involves a potentially time-consuming process.
- Uniform Commercial Code (UCC) filings giving notice to the world of security interests must be made at state and, sometimes, local government offices where the target and its assets are located. Filing requirements in Puerto Rico and Louisiana, the two non-UCC jurisdictions in the United States, are markedly different from, as well as more elaborate than, filing

requirements in other US jurisdictions. Local counsel should be contacted early and will play key roles.

- Security interests in real estate and fixtures require separate documentation and recordation in the localities and states in which they are located. Lenders will often require title insurance and surveys, both of which involve considerable lead time.
- Lenders will often want local counsel opinions as to perfection and priority of liens, and obtaining these can be a major logistical task.

For interest rate and fee calculations, bankers typically treat the year as having only 360 days. Why?

Because it produces a slight increase in yield over the stipulated rate or fee. This practice has acquired the status of a convention and is not generally subject to negotiation.

What is collateral position?

Collateral position describes where a lender is in relation to other lenders with respect to particular collateral. A senior lender in a two-lender deal would have the first collateral position, while the junior lender would have the second collateral position.

The term also refers to the relationship between the value of collateral pledged in a loan and the borrower's rate of repayment. In this sense, banks typically operate under policies that dictate a minimum collateral position. To avoid driving a lender to this point, borrowers should maintain awareness of the bank's collateral position with respect to the bank's collateral.

What are default rates?

Loan agreements typically provide for an increase in interest rates in the event of default, or at the time of acceleration of the loan. A premium of 2 or 3 percentage points above the rate normally in effect is not uncommon. A borrower should try to have a default rate go into effect only after the lender makes a formal declaration of default, since minor technical defaults are all too easy to stumble into and should not be a source of profit to the lender.

Why are mandatory prepayment obligations imposed by lenders?

Reasons for mandatory prepayment requirements vary depending on the bank's perception of the transaction. In some transactions, the lender is anxious to recoup and redeploy its money as swiftly as possible. This desire, and the anticipated availability of cash derived from cash flow projections, will tend to drive in the direction of an aggressive amortization schedule on term debt. (In some cases borrowers may also be asked to amortize revolving lines of credit as well by accepting scheduled reductions in availability over a period of time and making any principal payments required by such reductions.)

In addition, a bank may schedule amortization payments to match the buyer's plans for selling off assets or terminating pension plans, in effect forcing the buyer to honor his or her promises to break up and sell off parts of the acquired business or to terminate such pension plans as represented to the bank. Finally, lenders may require that all or a portion of excess cash flow be paid down to reduce senior term debt. Although the bank may permit distributions of dividends to stockholders of an S corporation for the purpose of paying federal, state, and local income taxes on income of the company and retaining some earnings for capital expenditures, it may also require that the buyer use everything left over after paying off junior debt to pay off any outstanding balance on the term loan.

Why do banks insist on applying prepayments first to the last installments due (in inverse order) rather than the other way around?

Banks reverse the order of LBO loan payments in order to keep the flow of cash coming into the bank and to get the loan paid off as swiftly as possible. If borrowers could prepay the next payments due, they would, in effect, be buying themselves a payment holiday. Sometimes prepayments may result from sale of income-producing assets (or the bank's application of casualty insurance proceeds to prepay principal in lieu of making such proceeds available to the borrower), because such events can reduce the subsequent capacity of the borrower to pay debt service. In such cases, the loan should be recast to lower proportionately the combined total of subsequent interest and principal payments.

Can a letter of credit facility be combined with an LBO loan?

Yes. If the business uses letters of credit in its ongoing operations (for purposes such as ensuring payment for raw materials or foreign-sourced goods), it can generally obtain a commitment from the lenders to provide such letters of credit up to a stipulated aggregate amount. The letter of credit facility will typically be carved out of the revolving line of credit, will be collateralized by the same collateral that secures the revolver, and will have the effect of limiting availability under the revolver to the extent of the aggregate letter of credit commitment. Draws on letters of credit will be treated, in such circumstances, as draws on the revolver. Separate fees (frequently ranging from 1 to 1.5 percent per annum) will be charged from time to time by the lenders for outstanding standby letters of credit.

Sometimes companies have a practice of issuing a large letter of credit for all shipments in a certain period and then securing specific orders as they arise. In such cases, it may be possible to limit availability by the amount of claims that can be or have been made against the letter of credit for specific orders, and not by the larger unused balance of the letter of credit.

LBO loan agreements typically contain a lengthy list of conditions to closing. Are there any that are likely to be particularly troublesome?

Although points of sharpest contention vary from transaction to transaction, there are some that crop up regularly. They include the following:

- *Requirements regarding perfection and priority of security interests in collateral.* If, for example, first liens are to be given to the lenders on inventory in various jurisdictions, certain events must occur: *first,* lien searches have to be completed and reports received and reviewed (there are professional companies that can be hired to conduct computerized searches of liens on record in any state or county office); *second,* documents terminating old liens have to be prepared, signed, and sent for filing; and *third,* documents perfecting new liens have to be prepared, signed, and sent for filing.
- *Related filing schedules.* Once all that has been done, filing must be coordinated in each of the jurisdictions so that it occurs contemporaneously with the funding of the new loan and the payoff of the old loan. In a complex, multijurisdictional transaction, such coordination, if it is to be done successfully, requires a combination of monumental effort and plain old good luck. Not infrequently, lenders have some flexibility about the filing of termination statements in connection with the old loan being discharged and will allow a reasonable period after closing for this to be accomplished.
- *Counsel opinions.* Few deals crater over the failure of counsel for the borrower to deliver required opinions, but it is not unheard of for a closing to be delayed while final points in the opinions are negotiated between counsel for the bank and the borrower. Problems typically occur in local counsel opinions and relate to the validity of the bank's lien in a particular jurisdiction. There is no magic solution, but early involvement of local counsel for the borrower is always a good idea.
- *Auditors' opinions.* Auditors are becoming increasingly reluctant to opine as to the solvency of borrowers or the reliability of financial projections provided by the borrower to the bank. By contrast, they now routinely make assessments of internal controls, because of the requirement under Section 404 of the Sarbanes-Oxley Act as described previously.

- *Governmental consents and approvals.* In certain transactions, approval of a governmental entity is a central element in the transaction. For example, a sale of a television station cannot be effected without requisite approvals from the FCC. The timing of such approvals, even if they are reasonably ensured, is outside the power of the parties, and the failure of a governmental agency to act when expected can wreak havoc on the schedule for closing an LBO.
- *Material litigation and adverse changes affecting the company.* Some loan agreements give the buyer and/or lender the right to back out if the target gets hit by a major lawsuit that, if successful, could seriously harm the company's business. If this contingency does occur, the burden is on seller's counsel to persuade both the buyer and the bank that the suit is unlikely to succeed or, if successful, would not be material to the company or its operations. Similarly, bad economic news can cause either the buyer or the bank to halt the process, resulting either in a negotiated price reduction or a termination.

Are there continuing conditions that apply to subsequent draws on the revolving line of credit?

Yes. In most loan agreements, the bank's obligation to honor subsequent draws upon the revolver is subject to a variety of conditions. Chief among them is reaffirmation by the borrower that the original warranties and representations made in the loan agreement are still true (including those stating that there have been no material adverse changes in the business since a date generally preceding the closing date) and a requirement that no covenant default exists. If the foregoing conditions are not met, the bank is not required to lend.

What purposes do the representations and warranties in the loan agreement serve?

The representations and warranties are intended to corroborate and complete the acquired company information upon which the lender based its credit decision. They constitute, in effect, a checklist of potential problem areas for which the borrower is required to state that no problem exists, or to spell out (by way of exceptions or exhibits) what the problem is. Thus, typical warranties will state the following:

- The financial statements of the borrower that have been submitted to the bank are correct. (Although it is comforting to have this conclusion backed by an auditor's certification, usually the auditor's report is laced with qualifications.)
- There are no liens on the borrower's assets, except as disclosed to the bank or permitted pursuant to the loan agreement.
- The transactions contemplated will not conflict with laws or any contracts to which the borrower is a party or by which it is bound (the "noncontravention representation").
- There are no lawsuits pending or threatened against the borrower that are likely to have a material adverse effect on it if decided against the borrower, except as disclosed to the bank.
- The loan will not violate the "margin rules."
- The borrower has no exposure under the Employee Retirement Income Security Act (ERISA).
- The borrower is not a regulated public utility holding company or investment company (since, if it were, various governmental orders would be required).
- The borrower is "solvent" (so as to mitigate concerns about risks of "fraudulent conveyance," discussed later in this chapter).
- The borrower's assets (and principal office) are located in the places specified. (This information is needed to ensure that perfection of security interests in the collateral is effected by filing notices in the correct jurisdictions.)

What happens if a representation is wrong?

A breached representation can have two practical consequences for a borrower: (1) if such a breach occurs, the bank may refuse to make a requested advance, either at or after the closing, and (2) breach of a representation or warranty can trigger a default under the loan agreement.

The first consequence—bank refusal to fund—should not be surprising. The truth and accuracy of the representations is typically a condition to the initial loan made at the time the loan agreement is signed and also to any subsequent draws on the revolving line of credit. If, for example, the borrower has warranted in the loan agreement that it has no significant environmental problems, and subsequently it is discovered that it has been guilty of illegal dumping of hazardous wastes, the bank will probably have the right under the loan agreement to shut off further draws on the line of credit. Such a decision could be catastrophic for a company precluded from financing itself from cash flow because its loan agreement also provides for the "lockboxing" of revenues and mandatory paydown—that is, a requirement that they be deposited in a lockbox under the lender's control and used to pay off bank debt.

The second consequence—a default under the loan agreement—triggers the remedies a lender generally has under a loan agreement, one of which is the right to accelerate the loan, that is, to declare all moneys loaned immediately due and payable, even though the amounts due under the term portion may not be otherwise due for several years, and the revolver may not expire until the end of the current year.

The right to accelerate is, in a practical sense, the right to trigger the bankruptcy of the borrower and for that reason is unlikely to be exercised except in those cases where a lender determines that its interests will be better protected by putting the borrower in bankruptcy than through other means. Since bankruptcy is viewed by most secured lenders as risky, slow, and a last resort (and potentially liability producing for the bank), a breached warranty is generally unlikely to bring the house down. But unless the breach is waived by the lender, its existence in effect turns what was originally conceived of as a term loan into a demand loan, callable by the bank at any time. Frequently, highly leveraged transactions result in the bank having a demand loan even in the absence of a default, so going into default does not make matters much worse; also, some lenders and their counsel try to negotiate loan agreements that are so tight that the company is arguably in default from the moment the agreement is entered into. Banks also impose default rates of interest in some cases, so that the cost of borrowing can go up on a warranty breach. This is a more effective sanction for the bank, provided that the company's fiscal health is not endangered.

Covenants in LBO loan agreements frequently appear more intrusive than those in most commercial loan agreements. Why?

Because in a typical leveraged acquisition the lenders are significantly more at risk than they are in a normal business loan. Both from a balance sheet standpoint (because of the absence of a substantial equity pad under the senior debt) and an operating standpoint (because of the burden that debt service will place on the borrower's cash flow), the lender is likely to view itself as significantly exposed. Lenders attempt to address this problem by imposing covenants on the borrower to achieve the following five results: first, to obligate the borrower, by express contractual provision, to operate the acquired business in accordance with the business plan submitted to and approved by the bank; second, to provide early warning of divergence from the business plan or of economic bad news; third, to protect the collateral; fourth, to prevent the leakage of money and property out of the borrower, whether as "management fees" or other payments to related parties, costs of new acquisitions, capital expenditures, or simply as dividends; and fifth, to enable the bank to exercise its remedies at as early a stage as possible if things go awry by exercising its right to declare a default as a result of a covenant breach.

What are the covenants a borrower is most likely to be confronted with?

When borrowing funds in a leveraged transaction, the buyer is often asked to sign off on promises that it will comply with the business plan, provide early warning of potential economic trouble, protect collateral, and control expenditures.

How can a seller in a contingency payment deal make sure the buyer will comply with the business plan?

The buyer is typically asked to promise to:

- Use the proceeds of the loan only for the stipulated purposes
- Engage only in the kinds of business contemplated by the lenders
- Refrain from merging or selling all or substantially all of its assets, or any portion thereof in excess of a specified value, without the bank's consent
- Limit capital expenditures, lease payments, borrowings, and investments in affiliates and third parties to agreed amounts
- Prevent change in ownership or control of borrower without lenders' consent
- Bar acquisitions of other businesses
- Make changes in the acquisition agreement, subordinated debt instruments, or other material documents

What about covenants designed to give early warning of economic trouble?

The seller involved in a contingency payment deal typically asks the buyer to promise to:

- Remain in compliance with financial covenants (discussed subsequently)
- Provide periodic (monthly, quarterly, annual) financial reports, with annual reports to be audited

- Give prompt notice of any material adverse development affecting the operations of the business
- Provide revised and updated projections, on at least an annual basis, prior to the commencement of each new fiscal year
- Permit visits and inspections by bank representatives

How can the seller in a contingency payment deal protect its collateral?

The buyer must typically promise to:

- Keep the business and property adequately insured
- Limit sales of property to merchandise sold in the ordinary course of business
- Require property to be kept free of liens (a "negative pledge")
- Bar leases of property by the borrower
- Provide key person life insurance for principal executives of the borrower

What loan agreement covenants can discourage financial leakage out of the borrower?

Lenders will often ask the borrower to agree to:

- Cap executive compensation and management fees
- Limit, or often prohibit (at least for a specific time period, or until specified financial tests are satisfied), dividends and other distributions to equity holders
- Prohibit transactions with affiliates, except as expressly agreed upon and except for those provided on an arm's-length basis for services definitely required by the borrower
- Lend money or guarantee the obligations of other parties

What kinds of financial covenants are likely to be imposed?

The financial covenants that lenders are most concerned with relate to the company's cash generation and cash distribution. Lenders are vitally concerned about monitoring the company's ability to service current and future obligations to the lender. Thus, in general, they want to limit unnecessary cash outflows such as dividends, excessive capital expenditures, and future payment obligations (that is, additional debt) until their claims are satisfied. In addition, lenders want sufficient advance information about the company's cash inflow relative to debt service requirements. If this ratio starts to deteriorate and approach default levels, the lender will increase monitoring activity and notify management of relevant default consequences. Therefore, the borrower may be required to maintain stipulated ratios for:

- Interest coverage (earnings before interest and taxes to interest expense)
- Debt to net worth
- Current assets to current liabilities
- Fixed charges to net income (or cash flow)

In addition, the borrower may be required to attain stipulated minimum goals for:

- Net worth
- Cash flow

The borrower may also be required not to exceed stipulated maximum limits for:

- Capital expenditures
- Total debt

How do lenders determine financial covenant levels?

Lenders use information provided by the borrower and their own lending experience combined with regulatory guidelines to set financial covenant levels. The projected financial statements serve as the basic data for estab-

Exhibit 4-2 Sample Company's Cash Flow and Debt Service Requirements (in thousands of dollars)

Year	1	2	3	4	5
Loan balance at 1/1	$2,000	$1,700	$1,250	$800	$350
Interest	240	204	150	96	42
Principal payments	300	450	450	450	350
Total debt service	540	654	600	546	392
Projected cash flow	1,000	1,200	1,400	1,600	1,800
Projected coverage ratio	1.85	1.83	2.33	2.93	4.59

lishing covenant levels. Since financial covenants are usually designed as early warning devices, lenders want covenants that are good indicators of debt service capability. Contrary to popular belief, lenders do not want financial covenants as high as possible. What they try to achieve is an effective filter system, identifying problem loans that merit special attention. If covenants are too high, the lender may waste valuable administrative time on a relatively low-risk situation.

For example, assume a senior lender provides $2,000,000 at 12 percent fixed interest to be paid over five years. The company's projected cash flow and debt service requirements appear in Exhibit 4-2. The projected coverage ratio is calculated by dividing projected cash flow by total debt service.

Given these data, the lender will make a judgment about the projected volatility of the company's cash flow. Assuming the company's prospects satisfy the senior lender's loan committee, a projected coverage ratio covenant must be determined. The level selected will probably be a simple discount on expected performance that still provides the lender with reasonable security. Once the company is out of the woods, the lender should be comfortable and should not keep increasing the level of required performance even if the projections indicate that it can be achieved.

The covenant level will probably rise over time to reflect the lender's desire to see the company's cash flow continue to increase. A sample covenant and the resulting minimum cash flow to prevent default appears in Exhibit 4-3. The covenant levels shown in this exhibit require the company in effect to increase cash flow each year until the last, when the lender's risk has been significantly reduced.

Exhibit 4-3 Sample Covenant (in thousands of dollars)

Year	1	2	3	4	5
Covenant ratio	1.4	1.4	1.8	2.1	2.5
Minimum cash flow (covenant ratio × debt service)	$756.0	$915.6	$1,080.0	$1,146.6	$980.0

Borrowers are faced with an interesting dilemma when presenting a prospective lender with the target company's projected financial performance. A borrower may be motivated to make the target's future performance look good in order to obtain the loan. However, these same projections will form the basis for the lender's financial covenants. If the projected performance were inflated, the company could continually be in default on the loan agreement. On the other hand, if the borrower downplays the future performance of the target company to avoid this possibility, the borrower runs the risk of making the loan relatively unattractive to the lender. Ultimately, both sides benefit the most when forecasts are submitted that genuinely reflect the buyer's expectations for the target.

When are financial covenants usually negotiated?

Very late in the process, usually just before closing. The typical buyer prefers to get the commitment for the loan before negotiating these provisions in detail. Often the most reliable financial projections become available only at the last moment, and they provide the base for the covenants. Sometimes, the bank sets the covenants too tightly at the closing, and the negotiating process continues through the initial months of the loan in the form of waivers. This should be avoided if possible.

What events typically trigger default?

- Breach of one or more of the covenants described here (sometimes subject to a right to cure certain breaches within a specified cure period and/or to the qualification that the breach be "material" or have a "material adverse effect" on the borrower).

- Payment defaults (failure to pay interest, principal, or fees when due or, in the case of interest and fees, sometimes within a stipulated grace period—see next question).
- Breach of a representation or warranty (sometimes subject to the qualification that the breach be material—see next question).
- Cross default (default in the loan agreement triggered by a default in another loan document, such as a security agreement, or in another unrelated but material agreement to which the borrower is a party, such as a subordinated debt instrument). Typically, for a cross default to be triggered, the default in the other instrument must be mature, that is, all cure periods must have expired and the other lender must have the right to accelerate. In addition, defaults on other debts below a specified dollar threshold may be expressly exempted from a loan agreement's cross-default provisions.
- Insolvency or voluntary bankruptcy, or involuntary bankruptcy, if not discharged by the borrower within a stipulated period (typically 60 days).
- An adverse final court judgment above a stipulated dollar amount that is not discharged or stayed on appeal within a prescribed period.
- The imposition of a lien (other than a lien permitted pursuant to the loan agreement) on assets of the borrower.
- The occurrence of an event triggering ERISA liability in excess of a stipulated amount.
- The death of the chief executive officer or an individual guarantor or other termination of the employment of certain specified managerial employees.

What techniques can be used to take some of the bite out of default provisions?

There are basically two default softeners: the use of grace or cure provisions and the concept of materiality.

A *grace period* is a period of time, following the due date for the making of a payment, during which payment may be made and default avoided. It is rare, but not without precedent, for a grace period to be accorded to a principal repayment obligation. More common are grace periods for interest payments or fees. Five days' grace beyond the due date is not uncommon; sometimes 10 or even 15 days may be granted.

Cure periods apply to defaults triggered by covenant breaches. Generally, the lender will attempt to limit their application to those covenants that are manifestly susceptible of cure (the duty to submit financial reports at specified dates) but deny them for covenants designed to provide early warning of trouble (breach of financial ratios). Sometimes, the cure period will not begin to run until the lender has given the borrower notice of a failure to perform; in other cases, the cure period will begin to run when the borrower should have performed, whether the lender knew of the borrower's failure or not. Cure periods vary greatly from transaction to transaction and from provision to provision. However, 5-day, 10-day, and 30-day cure periods are seen from time to time, and sometimes the concept of counting only "business days" is used to extend the period by excluding Saturdays, Sundays, and nationally recognized holidays.

The concept of materiality is more commonly applied in the case of defaults triggered by warranty breaches. The borrower will assert that default should not be triggered if a representation turns out to be untrue, but the effect of such inaccuracy is not materially adverse to the borrower or the collateral, or to the lender's position. The concept of a cure right for misrepresentations is not at all common but is not illogical in many cases. In some cases, where the loan agreement does not afford the borrower the right to cure a breached covenant, it is sometimes provided that such a breach will nevertheless not trigger a default if the effect is not material and adverse.

So far, we have been talking about commercial bank loans. What other major sources of financing are there?

In addition to commercial banks, leveraged acquirers can turn to insurance companies (for loans),[38] underwriters (to do high-yield/junk bond issues or to make bridge loans), and equity investment funds or other funds, all discussed next.

HIGH-YIELD (A.K.A. "JUNK") BONDS

What are junk bonds?

Junk bonds are medium-term to long-term obligations that (1) are subordinated to its senior debt, (2) are normally unsecured, and (3) bear high interest rates. Their rather inelegant name, reportedly coined by Michael Milken in a conversation with Rik Riklis,[39] comes from the fact that they are riskier than senior debt: they get a below-investment-grade rating from one or more of the bond rating services. They generally deserve a better label, however, and are thus called by some underwriters "high-yield securities." Indeed, the term junk arguably had the effect of discounting the price, which helped some purchasers realize enormous returns, to the detriment of issuers. Junk bonds are normally not prepayable for an initial period (three to five years), and thereafter are only prepayable at a premium.

The main purpose of junk bonds is to provide mezzanine financing for acquisition transactions, filling in the gap between senior secured debt, which pays a lower interest rate, and the seller's takeback financing or the buyer's equity financing, which is the last to be paid back. There is sometimes more than one layer of junk debt—one being senior subordinated and the other junior subordinated debt. A fairly recent example is the $1 billion offering for cereal maker Post Holdings, redeeming more expensive debt and backing the acquisition of Bob Evans Farms.[40]

To whom and how are junk bonds sold?

They are commonly sold to large financial institutions—insurance companies, pension funds, and mutual funds, including overseas investors—usually in blocks of $500,000 or more, and are primarily for the sophisticated investor. Funds that invest in junk bonds often attract supersophisticated money managers, who are known to go in and out of the junk bond market rapidly, causing volatility in prices. Often, but not necessarily, the offerings are registered under the federal securities laws to increase their marketability and are sold in a package with warrants to acquire common stock in the target. If they are privately placed, they often carry registration rights that will enable the holders to require the borrower to register the debt for sale in a public offering. (See the discussion of registration rights later in this chapter.)

How do warrants relate to junk bonds?

As mentioned earlier, warrants are rights to buy stock from the company at a specified price for a future period of time. Junk bonds offer some of the same high-risk/high-reward characteristics of equity, so it is natural to offer them together with an equity kicker in the form of warrants. Frequently, the institutions buying the bonds sell the warrants (sometimes back to the underwriter), thereby obtaining the junk bonds at a discount.

What is a bond indenture?

The indenture is the basic agreement setting forth the terms of the junk bonds and is entered into between the borrower and a bank, acting as trustee for the bondholders. It serves the same function as the credit or loan agreement executed with the senior secured lender and the note purchase agreement executed with an institutional mezzanine lender. The indenture contains the covenants, events of default, and other material terms of the transaction, including the various responsibilities and rights of the issuer, trustee, and bondholders. If the bonds are issued or subsequently sold pursuant to a public offering, the indenture must qualify under the Trust Indenture Act of 1939, as amended. Much of the boilerplate in the indenture is derived from requirements under that law.

The covenants have several principal objectives:

- To prevent disposition of the assets of the borrower (unless the sale proceeds are reinvested in assets used in the same business by the borrower or used to pay off the junk bonds or senior debt)
- To ensure that if any merger, consolidation, or change of the borrower occurs, the successor entity is obligated to repay the bonds on the same terms and is in as strong a financial position after the transaction as before

- To limit the creation of additional debt and liens (particularly secured debt senior to the bonds)
- To limit payments of dividends and distributions to stockholders (restricted payments), and to restrict transactions with affiliates

What covenants do junk bonds normally contain?

Compared with senior debt agreements, unsecured junk bond indentures are simpler, fitting the classic bond indenture mold. Unlike senior debt instruments, which provide for total information flow to lenders, hair-trigger default provisions, and, in theory, extensive second-guessing and approval of management decisions, junk bond indentures tend to rely more on the borrower's good judgment and the value of the company as a going concern and limit themselves to protecting against major restructurings or asset transfers or increases in amounts of senior or secured debt. This difference in approach reflects the longer-term nature of such debt and the impracticality of obtaining consents from a large, diverse group of public bondholders. In the very rare case that the junk bonds are secured, however, a more elaborate set of covenants relating to the protection of collateral will be included.

What should borrowers look for in agreeing to covenants?

Generally, borrowers should try to limit the financial covenants in junk bond issues to *incurrence* tests rather than *maintenance* tests. In other words, the covenants should not require that any specified level of financial health be maintained; rather, the covenants should be breachable only by certain prohibited actions, such as:

- Paying a prohibited dividend
- Incurring prohibited debt
- Merging or combining with another company or selling assets unless certain tests are met
- Dealing with affiliates at less than arm's length

These covenants will often closely restrict operating subsidiaries of the borrower to ensure that all debt is incurred on the same corporate level.

In many transactions the covenants go much further. They may include detailed financial maintenance covenants relating to net worth, current ratios, interest coverage and the like, limitations on investments, and application of asset sale proceeds.

Which bond covenants are particularly subject to negotiation?

The following key issues should be covered in the indenture:

- *Restrictions on mergers and asset sales.* There are a variety of such restrictions. The most onerous require that the surviving entity in the merger or the purchaser of all or substantially all the assets have a net worth not lower than the borrower had before the merger and that the fixed charge coverage ratios (generally the ratio of debt payments to cash flow [pre–debt service]) equal a certain percentage of the ratio that pertained before the merger. The effect of this type of provision is to preclude a sale of the business in a leveraged buyout that will cause a material increase in total debt of the company after the merger. The borrower thus has fewer means available for disposing of the business.

  Some indentures require the borrower to offer to prepay junior debt from asset sale proceeds that are not used to prepay senior debt. (It must be an offer because the debt is usually not prepayable without the consent of the lender.) Senior lenders object to this provision because they believe that it may be necessary for the proceeds to be left in the business, particularly if there is trouble and the asset sale was used to gain needed liquidity for the business. The dispute can usually be solved by allowing, until the senior lender is paid in full, a limited amount of such proceeds to be left in the business before a prepayment offer must be made.

A borrower should always check in advance to learn what the investment banker's standard format is (best done by reviewing indentures from previous transactions). Once you've locked in with an investment banker, you'll hear over and over again that it can't market the debt without the restrictions it is used to. Be prepared with examples of other junk debt with less onerous provisions. If you have any specific plans to sell off assets, be sure they don't violate this provision.

- *Debt incurrence.* Many junk bond indentures have very tight restrictions on debt incurrence by the issuer. The simplest form of restriction is that the issuer cannot issue "sandwich debt" or "interlayer debt," that is, debt subordinated to the senior debt but senior to the junk debt. This restriction allows the issuer to borrow as much senior debt or debt junior to the junk debt as the lenders are willing to lend. The holders of the junk debt are relying on the limitations senior lenders will place on the amount of senior debt that can be incurred.

  Other types of restrictions limit the incurrence of debt to a percentage of the original amount of debt or require the achievement of certain financial ratios before incurring additional debt. The ratios, and any particular provisions necessary for a particular business plan, are all subject to negotiation with the lender. The senior lender will want the borrower to be able to incur new senior debt somewhat in excess of the unpaid amount of the existing senior debt in order to permit minor workout arrangements and to finance some expansion.
- *Restrictions on prepayments.* Most junk bonds preclude prepayments for several (often five) years and thereafter may permit prepayments only on payment of substantial premiums. This restriction is not as troublesome if the covenants in respect of mergers and debt incurrence are not too strict. A long nonprepayment period means that the issuer can't rid itself of the debt except through defeasance of the bonds, if the covenants become too burdensome.

- *Subordination provisions.* See section under the heading "Subordination Issues."
- *Restricted payments.* These restrictions prohibit dividends and other distributions as well as stock redemptions unless specified conditions are satisfied. The conditions usually prevent payments until a specified minimum net worth level has been attained; thereafter, payments may not exceed a certain percentage (25 to 50 percent) of accumulated net income.

  Be careful of this provision; it may have the effect of precluding a sale of the company through an LBO unless the junk bonds are also prepaid. Such a buyout normally requires the borrower, or a successor obligor under the junk bond indenture, to borrow the acquisition debt and pay the proceeds to the target's shareholders. Such payments probably constitute a restricted payment that may not be made unless the tests are satisfied (and in most such cases they won't be). Even if all the other tests for the merger are satisfied (such as net worth and coverage ratios), this test may present an often insurmountable hurdle.

But won't it be possible to just waive these covenants if they prove to be too restrictive?

No. Prepaying the junk bonds will very likely be either impossible or very expensive because of prepayment restrictions and penalties. In addition, unlike the case of senior lenders, it is often impossible, or at the least very difficult, to obtain waivers of covenants from a multitude of public bondholders. Therefore, the restrictions contained in the junk bond indenture should be something the borrower can live with for a long time. Special care must be taken to ensure that the covenants fit the long-term plans of the company with respect to acquisitions, dispositions of assets, expansions, and so on. Once the covenants are in place, you'll have to live with them pretty much unmodified.

What about default rates for junk bonds?

It varies over time, with a very low chance of default for a year or so, then a higher likelihood in years three and four, and then a decreasing chance after four years. The current outlook for default rate is 1.5 percent for 2019, which is relatively low in comparison to recent decades.[41]

What is a quasi-junk bond?

A quasi-junk bond is a bond that gets a split rating—where one credit rating service gives it a lowest investment grade and another calls it junk.

What recourse do bondholders have in the event of poor bond performance?

Creditor lawsuits against parties involved in failed LBOs have targeted numerous parties, including issuers of junk bonds. Many of these cases are filed under state fraudulent conveyance laws (discussed later in this chapter). Few are brought to trial. Many are settled out of court. Junk bondholders often have a say in restructuring or changes of control.

Is there ever insider trading in junk bonds?

Some investors believe there is widespread insider trading—trading based on material nonpublic information—in various debt securities including junk bonds, municipal bonds, government securities, commodities, and futures. A common symptom of such trading, often seen in junk bonds, is a sharp increase in price prior to a positive announcement. Investigation, pursuit, and punishment of such trading has been limited to date, though, because the federal agency with explicit authority to go after insider trading in securities, the SEC, fears that it may not have jurisdiction to pursue such cases. There are also detection problems. Junk bond trading, done only over the counter, is more difficult to track than equity trades, which occur on the major stock exchanges.

BRIDGE LOANS

Underwriters will sometimes offer a buyer immediate short-term financing for an acquisition in exchange for the right to replace that financing with a later junk bond issue.

The risk in bridge lending is that the market will go sour before the loan is repaid and the bonds are sold.

What should be the interest rate on the bridge loan?

The interest rate on the bridge loan, being short-term financing, should initially be 5 to 8 points over the Treasury or federal funds rate, lower than the expected rate on the junk bonds that will be sold to repay the bridge loan. This rate should rise by 0.5 percent or more per annum if the underwriter cannot refinance the bridge loan in a three- to six-month period. The increasing interest rate compensates the underwriter for the bridge financing risk, as does a warrant for a small amount (normally 3 to 5 percent) of the common stock of the target. The underwriter will also receive substantial fees: commonly 2 percent—1 percent upon execution of a commitment letter for the bridge loan and another 1 percent or more when the loan is funded.

What issues arise in the negotiation of a bridge loan/junk bond financing?

The bridge lender is most concerned about ensuring that it will be able to market the refinancing debt, that is, the junk debt that will be used to repay its loan. Thus, it will seek to clarify in advance any potential issue that could arise with the borrower or with other lenders. The bridge lender will also seek utmost flexibility in the terms of the refinancing debt that it can offer (such as interest rate and equity kickers such as warrants) and will further require that the borrower use its best efforts to get the offering done as soon as possible. The bridge lender's prime concern is to get its debt refinanced, and it will seek to build into the contract strong incentives to motivate the borrower toward that end.

The borrower, on the other hand, wants to be sure, if possible, that its permanent mezzanine debt is borrowed on terms it can repay. The borrower should seek to place limits on the terms of the refinancing debt and also to ensure that the bridge lender's debt will roll over into longer-term debt if the refinancing debt can't be placed.

These general concerns are reflected in the following specific points of negotiation:

- *The term of the bridge loan.* In many cases, the bridge loan falls due at the end of a fixed period, usually three to nine months. If the refinancing debt is not placed by then, the bridge loan is in default. The senior lenders are often unwilling to accept this risk, and the borrower should be concerned as well. The refinancing debt may not be marketable on reasonable terms even though the company is doing extremely well; the problem may simply be a failure of the markets (as in the post–October 1987 and 1989 periods) or in the marketing efforts of the bridge lender. The other parties will have made financial commitments based on the confidence level of the investment banker that the refinancing debt would be available.

  For the foregoing reasons, the bridge lender can often be persuaded (particularly in a competitive environment) to commit to a longer-term investment if the refinancing debt doesn't get placed. This often takes the form of a rollover provision where the terms of the note change after the maturity date and it becomes long-term subordinated debt with covenants and other provisions, similar to subordinated junk debt. Another technique is to cast the original bridge note as a long-term note that the borrower is obligated to prepay with the proceeds of refinancing debt or other cash proceeds such as equity offerings. In either case, the extended bridge note will have higher than normal, or increasing, interest rates to encourage refinancing of the bridge debt at the earliest possible time.

- *The terms of the refinancing debt.* The borrower should obtain reasonable limits on the terms of refinancing debt that it will be obligated to accept. The usual formulation is something like "at prevailing market rates and terms," subject to limitations on the interest rate, the term, scheduled principal payments, and the amount of equity that the purchasers of the refinancing debt will be entitled to receive. The borrower may seek a limitation on the amount of cash interest payable annually or, alternatively, on the average yield on the instrument, although it is difficult to bar access of the bridge lender to takeout financing, even if there has been a major interest rate move in the market. The senior lender also will be interested in ensuring that the terms of the refinancing debt don't violate its expectations about coverage ratios and limits on other indebtedness.

- *The covenants and events of default of the bridge loan.* The senior lender and the borrower will generally try to make the bridge loan covenants, events of default, and subordination provisions similar to the refinancing debt that will take out the bridge loan. They resist, often successfully, attempts by the bridge lender to make the bridge loan agreement a tighter, more restrictive document or to have the bridge lender ride on the covenants of the senior lender. Avoidance of overly tight default triggers is especially important where the obligation of the bridge lender to sell the refinancing debt is conditioned on absence of a default under the bridge note. The tighter the covenants, the greater the risk of a default that could prevent the rollover into the longer-term note and thus could put the company into a financial crisis soon after the acquisition.

EQUITY INVESTMENT FUNDS

Suppose a small group of managers wants funding to buy out a division of a company. What happens then?

One solution might be a private equity fund, also called a buyout fund. Such funds are often used to provide the mezzanine level of financing in a management buyout. The investment fund raises capital from private investors and uses the money to make equity and subordinated debt investments in a portfolio of companies that are in need of mezzanine financing, including companies that have gone private in an MBO. In return for their capital, investors in an investment fund typically receive income from the debt the fund provides to its portfolio of companies and the potential for capital appreciation from the fund's equity investments.

As of late 2018, based on capital raised over the last five years, the largest buyout funds were:

- The Carlyle Group
- Blackstone
- KKR
- Apollo Global Management
- CVC Capital Partners
- Warburg Pincus
- EQT
- Neuberger Berman
- Silver Lake
- TPG

How are MBO investment funds structured and who invests in them?

Generally, MBO investment funds are organized as limited partnerships. The interests in the partnerships are considered securities under federal and state securities laws and, consequently, are offered and sold in a registered public offering or in reliance on an exemption from the registration requirements.

Most commonly, the private equity investment funds have been marketed to a limited number of sophisticated, wealthy individuals; financial institutions; and public and private pension funds in a private placement offering. Proceeds of the offering are used by the investment fund to acquire common equity, preferred stock, and subordinated debt in a series of management buyouts. Investment funds generally make majority investments, although there have been exceptions.

How do the fund investors share in the benefits of the investment?

Fund investors do not directly own any stock or other interests in the company to be acquired. Instead, each participant, or investor, in an investment fund contributes capital to each acquisition vehicle formed and will become a limited partner in the acquisition vehicle, receiving a return on investment in accordance with the partnership agreement.

Are the acquisitions in which the fund will invest identified in advance?

No. Investment funds are typically structured as "blind pools," meaning that the portfolio of companies in which a fund will invest will not be identified or known at the time each investor purchases his or her interest in the fund. The general partner of the fund will have complete discretion in selecting the companies in which the fund will invest. Generally, the funds do not invest in companies where management is opposed to the acquisition.

What kind of time frame and returns can an investor in an equity fund expect?

Private investment funds are often structured so that each investor enters into a commitment, for an average period of five to six years, to make a capital contribution upon the request of the general partner. The commitment is usually quite large, on the order of $10 million; however, investors have control over use of their capital until it is actually invested in a particular acquisition vehicle upon request of the general partner. Returns on equity fund investments vary, especially between equity and debt investors.

What other investments do funds make besides mezzanine and equity financing?

Occasionally, an investment fund will provide bridge financing rather than mezzanine financing. Bridge financing is provided for a short term, typically nine months or less, to supply funds during the interim period before permanent financing is arranged. After the bridge loan is repaid, the fund remains with an equity interest in the acquired company and can roll the loan proceeds over into another acquisition.

In addition, investment funds may be structured to allow the fund to use its capital to finance a friendly tender offer for stock of a publicly held company whereby 51 percent of the stock is acquired in the tender offer and the remaining stock is acquired in a cash merger. This structure permits leveraged purchases of public companies, despite the margin requirements that prohibit acquisition financing secured by more than 50 percent of the value of the securities acquired. The initial 51 percent of the stock acquired in the tender offer is financed half by borrowings and half by equity from the fund. When the cash merger occurs, the additional financing can be supported by the assets of the target, and all or a part of the initial equity investment can be repaid. (See Chapter 10, on public companies.)

What regulatory controls are imposed on investment funds?

The main federal law affecting funds is the Investment Company Act of 1940, which is likely to apply to any investment fund that raises money from the public (IPOs, secondary offerings) and uses the proceeds to acquire securities of other companies in order to achieve passive income.

Mutual funds such as the Fidelity funds are the most obvious example of investment funds covered by the Investment Company Act. But the law can apply even if no investment fund is involved, especially if the buyer uses the proceeds of publicly held junk bonds for financing.

The law requires a primarily equity-based capital structure raised from public sources, prohibits dealing with affiliates, and imposes various public reporting and fiduciary obligations on the fund's principals. To avoid the effect of the Act, most leveraged buyout funds raise their capital from private placements.

The law does not apply to equity funds that buy controlling shares in operating subsidiaries and manage them in a classic holding company manner. But anyone who is in the business of buying companies, holding them short term (particularly under two years), and selling them, all without actively engaging in their day-to-day management, should check to be sure he or she is not subject to regulation as an investment company under the law. Furthermore, equity funds that are structured as limited partnerships are subject to a growing body of state and federal law governing these structures.

REGISTRATION RIGHTS

What are registration rights?

Registration rights are rights given to an owner of debt or equity securities (1) to require the issuer of the securities to register such securities for public sale under federal and state securities laws or (2) to participate in any such public sale initiated by the issuer or another securityholder. They are key provisions of warrants, preferred stock, and privately placed subordinated debt issues and thus deserve special attention here. They also appear in stockholders' agreements and agreements with management. (See relevant portions of Chapter 5 on structuring transactions.)

Why do securityholders want registration rights?

Registration rights give securityholders more liquidity. Absent such rights, debt or equity privately placed in connection with an acquisition usually cannot be resold freely to the public. Any such resale either must be made by another private placement or otherwise pursuant to an exemption from the applicable registration provisions of federal and state securities laws or must comply with the holding period and other limitations of Rule 144a of the Securities Act of 1933, which restricts the amount of control, the amounts of restricted or unregistered securities that can be sold at any one time, and the manner in which those securities may be sold.

These restrictions are more than just an administrative nuisance and, because of the decrease in the liquidity of the investment represented by such securities, may reduce substantially their market value. In order to minimize the effect of these restrictions, holders of acquisition debt or equity, particularly holders of privately placed junk bonds, preferred stock, warrants for common stock, or common stock, are usually interested in obtaining from the buyer a promise to include the securities in a registration statement under the Securities Act at the securityholders' request.

Note that shelf registration is not an all-or-nothing process: each registration statement relates only to a particular, specified number of shares or amount of debt obligations of a particular type, and thus some securities of a company may be freely available for sale while others, even if otherwise identical, may still be restricted. In order to protect a securityholder, it is not enough to require that securities of the kind of security held by the holder be registered; rather, the holder's particular securities must be registered.

Why wouldn't the buyer automatically grant registration rights?

There are considerable costs to the company in granting registration rights. The registration process involves substantial expense for preparation of the registration statement, including the fees of accountants, attorneys, and financial printers. These costs usually amount to several hundred thousand dollars. In addition, the registration process is an arduous one for the issuing company and its officers and directors, and it requires company employees to spend a significant amount of time and attention that would otherwise be focused on management of the company and its business.

Perhaps most important of all, the buyer wants to control when and if the company goes public. The exercise of registration rights may cause the company to become a "reporting company" under the Securities Act, necessitating the filing of periodic reporting documents with the SEC and resulting in additional expenses. Through the registration process, the target subjects itself to various potential liabilities as well as a host of regulations under federal and state securities laws. If the registration rights relate to common or preferred stock, the buyer will, furthermore, not want to go to the public market until its acquisition debt has been paid down and it is sure that the offering will be a success.

What are demand registration rights?

"Demand" registration rights entitle a holder of securities of a company to cause the company to register all or a part of such securities for resale by the securityholder. Usually, the company is required to effect such registration promptly upon demand of the securityholder, or within some other reasonable time frame.

What are piggyback registration rights?

"Piggyback" registration rights entitle a securityholder to cause the company to include all or a part of its securities in a registration of the same or other classes of securities of the company undertaken at the request of a third party, such as a lender. Piggyback registration rights might allow a lender holding warrants, for example, to have the shares of common stock for which his warrants can be exercised included in a registration of common stock or subordinated debt of the company that was undertaken by the company with a view toward raising additional capital.

Piggyback registration rights generally are not exercisable, however, in the issuance of securities in connection with an acquisition or exchange offer, or pursuant to employee benefit plans, including employee stock ownership plans (ESOPs).

How many times should securityholders be entitled to exercise their registration rights?

Generally, the number of registration rights that securityholders receive is a function of the relative bargaining powers of the buyer-borrower and its securityholders. It is fairly common for lenders with common stock warrants or privately placed junk bonds to receive one or two demand registration rights. It is often the case, however, that for demand registration rights other than the first demand, certain other terms and conditions of the registration rights, such as payment of expenses and limitations on the number of shares allowed to be included, become more restrictive with respect to the securityholder and more favorable to the borrower.

A greater or unlimited number of piggyback registration rights are often granted to securityholders, with the primary limitations being the time during which such rights are exercisable and the amount of securities that the securityholder can include in the registration.

What time restrictions should apply to demand registration rights?

The company's desire for a period of stability after the acquisition must be balanced against the selling securityholder's desire for liquidity. Therefore, demand registration rights usually will not be exercisable for some fixed period of time, often several years, after the acquisition. In addition, demand registration rights are often not exercisable until after the company has conducted its own initial public offering of its common stock. In this manner the company can control the key decision whether and when to go public. Sometimes, if the company has not gone public before a certain extended deadline, perhaps the date on which warrants will expire, the securityholder can compel registration.

Registration rights should not be exercisable during a stated period, usually six to nine months, following a prior registration of securities by the company. This helps prevent an overhang problem—marketing of the prior offering can be hurt if a large block of additional securities is entitled to go to market in the near future.

Securities are sometimes registered by a company for a sale to take place at a future time but the exact date and terms of the sale are not yet determined. Such a registration is referred to as a *shelf registration* because the securities are put on the shelf for later sale, with most of the work on the registration process already done. Demand registration rights usually do not entitle a securityholder to demand registration of its securities in a shelf registration until after the company has already effected such a shelf registration of its own securities, if at all.

What about timing for piggyback registration rights?

Piggyback registration rights raise additional timing issues, since they may be exercisable upon a registration by the company of securities of a type other than the securities to which the rights attach. A holder of common stock, for example, could require inclusion of some or all of its shares in a registration statement that covers debt securities of the company. In the acquisition context, in which the company's ability to sell debt securities during the first months or years after the acquisition may be crucial, care must be taken that piggyback rights do not create competition for the company's own offering. It is thus normal for piggyback registration rights to be restricted only to registrations of equity securities for several years after the acquisition.

When do registration rights terminate?

The exact termination date for registration rights is a matter for negotiation, but it is common for such rights to terminate under any of the following conditions: when the securities of the issuing company are widely held; when the securityholders could otherwise make use of the existing market for such securities to sell their shares without significant limitations; or when a securityholder has sold, or has had the opportunity through piggyback rights to sell, a specified percentage of securities held.

What benefits can accrue from registration rights agreements?

Registration rights agreements usually provide that the holders of a certain percentage of the securities, often as high as a majority, must join together in order to exercise their demand registration rights. The agreements may also provide that a threshold dollar amount must be reached before the offering will be large enough to be marketed efficiently by underwriters. Demand registration rights are usually not exercisable unless the aggregate offering price of the securities to be registered (or market price, if a market exists for such securities) exceeds a certain amount, which may be $5 million or more.

Without such agreements in place, the company could be forced to undertake the expensive and time-consuming process of registration for relatively small amounts of securities. Conversely, even with such agreements in place, the company can forestall an offering by persuading a substantial number of securityholders that an offering would be inadvisable at any particular time.

What amount of securities may each securityholder include on a demand or piggyback basis in any particular registration statement?

This issue arises when the number of securities sought to be included in the registration is so great that the underwriter cannot place such a large number of securities at a suitable price. Registration rights agreements usually provide that the underwriter is the final arbiter of the question of just how many securities may be included in the registration statement. In such a case, an orderly system for priorities with respect to inclusion of securities in the registration statement must be spelled out in the registration rights agreement.

If the registration is being carried out pursuant to a demand registration right, those making the demand usually have priority. Securityholders with piggyback registration rights often have the next priority, the includable shares being allocated among them on a pro rata basis, depending on the relative bargaining positions of the securityholders. In demand registrations, the company is often the last one that is able to participate and thus may be unable to sell for its own account.

These priorities usually change, however, with respect to registrations of securities initiated by the company in which securityholders are exercising piggyback rights. If the registration involves an underwritten distribution of securities, then the priorities will generally be as follows: first, securities that the company proposes to sell for its own account (this is important in order to permit the company to raise needed capital); and, second, shares of selling securityholders, who may be either members of the investor/management control group or outside securityholders exercising piggyback registration rights. Such selling shareholders will generally participate pro rata according to the relative numbers of shares held by them or the relative number of shares sought to be included in the registration statement by them, although it is a matter of negotiation between the control group and those with piggyback rights as to who gets priority.

Who pays the expenses of registration?

The company generally pays the expenses of registering securities pursuant to demand registration rights. This is true at least with respect to the first demand registration right exercised by a securityholder. These expenses include SEC filing fees, accountants' and attorneys' fees, and expenses of financial printers. The securityholders including securities in the registration statement will, if such shares are sold by an underwriter, have to pay underwriters' and broker–dealers' commissions from the sale of their shares, as well as applicable stock transfer fees. An open item for negotiation is the payment of any applicable fees and expenses relating to the sale of securities under various state securities laws ("blue sky" fees).

Responsibility for payment of expenses of registering securities pursuant to exercises of demand registration rights (other than the first such exercise) are often the subject of negotiation. They may be payable in whole or in part by the securityholder demanding registration, in order to put some limitation on the exercise of such subsequent demand rights. Sometimes state blue sky commissioners will insist that selling stockholders pay a pro rata share of expenses, particularly if they feel that insiders would otherwise get a free ride; such a possibility should be provided for in the registration rights provision.

Expenses incurred in registering securities included in a registration pursuant to the exercise of piggyback rights are usually relatively small and, except for underwriters' and brokers' commissions, are typically paid by the company.

What indemnification will a securityholder seek in negotiating a registration rights agreement?

Registration rights agreements, because of the potential liabilities involved under federal and state securities laws, generally provide that the company will indemnify the securityholders, including their shares in a registration statement, against liabilities arising through any misstatement or omission of a material fact in the registration statement and the prospectus. This indemnification should not, however, include statements supplied by the selling securityholders themselves for inclusion in the registration statement or prospectus.

A mirror image of this indemnification should be included in the registration rights agreement to provide for indemnification of the company by the securityholders including securities in the registration statement with respect to the information provided by them. The SEC and several court decisions have maintained that indemnification against liabilities under federal and state securities laws are against public policy and therefore unenforceable. In the event that such indemnification is unenforceable, "contribution" (that is, a right to require pro rata sharing of liabilities) between the company and the securityholders may be allowed, however, and is customarily included in the registration rights agreement as an alternative to indemnification.

Who picks the underwriter?

The company. This is customary even in demand registrations, although sometimes an institutional securityholder will try to get this right.

What special problems arise with respect to registration rights of debt securities and preferred stock?

The company and the debt holders may have planned from the start to sell the debt publicly, in which case the initial placement is really a bridge loan pending the registration, and the registration rights provisions serve to lay out the next stage in the proposed financing sequence. In the alternative, the debt holders may plan to continue to hold the debt, but with a shelf registration in place so as to be able to sell publicly at any time. Under either circumstance, the registration rights provision presents no problems, and the subordinated debt should be issued from the start in a publicly held junk bond format with appropriate covenants and other indenture provisions.

Sometimes, however, the mezzanine debt has been structured to be privately held. The covenants may be tight, so that the company knows that it can operate only on the basis of repeated requests for waivers. This is particularly likely to occur if the subordinated debt holder has also taken a substantial equity position in the company and plans to operate effectively as a business partner of the company. Under such circumstances, the loan agreement with the subordinated debt holder must be completely rewritten before a public registration can occur. It will be necessary either to negotiate in advance and include an entire alternate indenture in the registration rights provisions or have a brief, more informal, understanding that registration of the debt can occur only under certain conditions—for example, only if the loan covenants are adjusted to a conventional format for a public issue and/or the company has otherwise issued some class of publicly held securities.

Preferred stock raises some of the same issues, since a private placement of preferred stock may contain provisions, such as special exchange or redemption rights, not suitable for publicly held preferred stock. In addition, demand or piggyback registration rights create marketing problems when they compel the simultaneous offering of different classes of securities, particularly at the time of an initial public offering of common stock. The company should consider offering the preferred stock holder a right to redeem preferred stock from a specified percentage of the proceeds of the common stock offering in lieu of granting preferred stock registration rights. In the alternative, a demand preferred stock registration should not be permitted until a reasonable time (120 to 180 days) following an initial public offering of common stock, and no piggyback rights should arise on such initial public offering or thereafter without the approval of the common stock underwriter.

INTERCREDITOR ISSUES

What are intercreditor issues?

Intercreditor issues are legal and business conflicts arising between lenders. The major areas of difference relate to (1) subordination provisions and (2) rights to collateral.

Do not underestimate the importance of these issues. Intercreditor issues can give rise to serious negotiating problems and can even imperil the deal itself. Unlike buyers and sellers, both of whom usually have a strong stake in achieving a closing and therefore considerable negotiating flexibility, lenders may feel less impelled to close the deal and may condition their participation on compliance with a rather narrow and specific set of security and return criteria.

Once misunderstandings or conflicts arise as to who is to get what collateral or how subordinated the junior debt will be, they are often very difficult to resolve. For example, if two lenders' negotiators have sold the deal to their loan committees on mutually inconsistent bases, misunderstandings can take weeks to straighten out. Competitor banks or insurance companies, rather than focusing on closing the deal, may try to settle old scores to prove their negotiating skills, to win points with their superiors, or to meet the not-always-appropriate standards of their lending manuals. Nothing can be more alarming and frustrating for buyer and seller than watching lenders' loan officers or counsel come to loggerheads over major or even minor points where neither lender has much incentive or institutional flexibility to accommodate or withdraw gracefully. The situation becomes worse when each lender is not a single entity but a syndicate of banks or insurance companies. For these reasons, transactions should be structured and planned to minimize and resolve intercreditor conflicts as rapidly and as early as possible.

Why doesn't the buyer simply make clear to each lender from the start which security rights and priorities each will have?

Most intercreditor problems arise when two creditors are negotiating subordination rights or rights over collateral and encounter an issue that has not been raised and resolved as part of their respective loan commitments. Consequently, solution number one is to identify as fully as possible at the commitment stage which priorities, assets, or kinds of assets will be allocated to each lender. Some areas are clear and well accepted: revolving lenders get a first lien on current assets; term lenders get a first position in property, plant, and equipment. Less clear is who gets the first position in intangibles, other than those (such as patents) necessary to use a particular piece of equipment, or licenses necessary to sell inventory, which go with the tangible assets to which they relate.

The buyer may, however, choose to keep this point unclear as a matter of negotiating tactics—the buyer may not want to deprive one lender of a particular piece of collateral unless he or she is sure that another lender will insist on getting it. The lender may be more easily persuaded to get along without the additional collateral once its loan officers are fully involved and appraisals and due diligence have been satisfactorily completed. The buyer may also be trying to keep some assets unencumbered.

Or the buyer may simply miss the point. There is likely to be a lot of time pressure at the stage at which loan commitments are being negotiated, and the buyer may have landed the target by promising to close in two weeks. Furthermore, even if all the major terms can be worked out between the parties, the commitment letter won't cover minor issues, such as how much time the term lender will give the revolving credit lender to complete processing of or to remove the inventory (revolving credit collateral) from the premises before being free to close down and sell the plant (term lender collateral). Even these questions can be troublesome sources of delay or conflict at the late hours of the closing.

How can such intercreditor problems be avoided?

There are two cardinal rules for borrowers to follow in minimizing intercreditor issues: (1) try to resolve the major issues in advance while there is still competition between potential lenders and before substantial commitment fees are paid; and (2) try for as long as possible to negotiate the issues via shuttle diplomacy between the lenders, forestalling direct negotiation between them.

How do you identify and solve intercreditor issues early in the process?

Prior to signing the commitment letter, the borrower should seek to obtain from each potential lender copies of its most recent executed (as opposed to draft) intercreditor documents. The executed documents will reflect concessions that the drafts will not. The documents should be compared to see which senior and junior lender has the most reasonable provisions, and these should be used as the basis for negotiating with all of the lenders. A comparison of the junior and senior documents will reveal the areas most likely to create material conflicts, that is, those that could imperil the deal, as opposed to those that are susceptible to easy resolution in the course of negotiations.

If the borrower has decided which junior lender it will use and is choosing among competing senior lenders, it is often useful to present the typical language that the junior lender has agreed to with respect to the major intercreditor issues for review by the potential senior lenders. Before the commitment is made final, the borrower should seek senior lender approval of the most important parts of the typical junior lender language. The same process works in reverse if the senior lender has been chosen and there are several potential junior lenders.

Once the conflict areas are identified, the borrower must make a judgment about whether the differences are so great that the issues must be resolved at this stage of the negotiation. This would be the case, for example, where one lender requires provisions that are novel or likely to be provocative.

Where subordinated debt is to be sold in a public offering, investment bankers will often insist on subordination provisions that, they assert, the market expects and demands. If the investment banker is making a bridge loan that depends for its takeout upon having easily marketable junk debt, it will be particularly insistent on the inclusion of these basic provisions in the junk debt. If the senior lender expects substantially different provisions, you are in for big problems. Iron them out at this stage, while you still have time to get a new lender if necessary.

Nothing helps more on such a negotiation than having an in-depth knowledge of the current practices in the marketplace. It's always easier to decide to postpone resolving an issue if you know you can make the argument later to your senior lender that all or most other lenders give in on this point.

Remember that you are engaged in a balancing act between the desire to resolve intercreditor issues early and the other more crucial economic terms of the loan, such as interest rate, fees, term, and prepayment schedule. It is foolish to press hard unnecessarily on intercreditor issues before you have commitments on basic terms, when the result could be adverse trade-offs on material terms. On the other hand, great economic terms are meaningful only if the deal actually closes.

Shouldn't lenders work out intercreditor questions between themselves?

Typically, no—at least not in the initial stages of negotiation. Especially early on, the buyer should try to avoid having the lenders communicate directly with each other about these issues. The buyer will have much more control over the negotiating process if he or she filters the proposals of each party. More important, there is a much better chance of reaching agreement if the buyer can formulate a compromise position and sell it to each party. This is especially true because the intercreditor meetings can involve a cast of thousands—each tier of lenders, the borrower, and sometimes trustees and their respective counsel, each of whom brings its own group of partners and associates. It is far harder to achieve major concessions in such a crowded environment with everyone's ego on display. If you're forced to agree to direct intercreditor negotiation, try to minimize the size of the meeting.

By the late stages of negotiating the loan agreements and the intercreditor agreement the lenders are more likely to come into direct contact, and if the transaction is well advanced and the personalities and relationships of the lenders are suitable, the final minor issues can often be resolved most efficiently directly between them. Even then, however, the buyer should be ready to continue the shuttle diplomacy process right up to the end if any of the lenders or their counsel are difficult or the negotiating atmosphere is tense.

The one exception to the no-early-direct-negotiations rule can arise when the lenders involved have worked together successfully in prior deals and agreed precedents exist between them for resolving intercreditor issues. If one lender says, when you mention the identity of the other, "Oh, is Jim doing it? We'll use the Amalgamated format," you can relax a little. But still keep a close eye on them.

SUBORDINATION ISSUES

What are subordination provisions?

Subordination provisions basically determine who among the lenders gets paid first if the borrower has insufficient money to pay all of the lenders. The subordinated lender (often referred to as the junior lender) is the one who gets paid after the lender to which it is subordinated (the senior lender). A distinction is commonly made between "substantive" subordination (who gets paid first in the event of trouble?) and "procedural" subordination (when and how can the subordinated lender proceed against the borrower if there is a default in the subordinated loan?). Priority of payment under subordination provisions is different from lien priority, which relates only to the question of which lender has first access to proceeds of sale or foreclosure on the particular asset covered by the lien.

What are the principal subordination provisions?

- In the event of any insolvency or bankruptcy proceeding, the junior lender agrees that the senior lender will be paid in full before the junior lender receives any payment.
- Payment of the junior debt is prohibited if the senior debt is in default. Sometimes only defaults in payment (or certain major financial covenants of senior debt) will block payments of junior debt, or blockage will only occur, in certain types of default, for a limited period. Since any major default in the senior debt can lead to an acceleration of the debt, in theory the senior lender can convert any major covenant default into a payment default, if necessary, to prevent payment of junior debt. However, senior lenders do not want to be forced into taking the extreme step of acceleration, which can quickly lead to bankruptcy. Much negotiation of subordination provisions arises from the senior lender's desire to keep the junior lender from (1) being paid even if the senior debt is not accelerated, and (2) being able to force the senior lender to accelerate.

- The junior lender agrees to hold in trust for, and pay over to, the senior lender any amount received by the junior lender not in accordance with the subordination provisions. This clause, known as a "hold and pay" provision, gives the senior lender a direct right to recover from the junior lender without going through the borrower.

What issues arise in negotiating substantive subordination provisions?

- *Principal payments on junior debt.* The financing is almost always arranged so that no principal payments are scheduled to be made on junior debt until after the final maturity date on the senior debt. The senior loan agreement normally prohibits payments of junior debt ahead of schedule. A common exception to this rule is that senior lenders will often permit prepayment of junior debt with the proceeds of equity offerings or other junior debt. Also, the borrower is often allowed to prepay the junior debt to the extent it could otherwise make dividend or similar payments to shareholders. Where there are notes to the seller, the parties are sometimes able to negotiate financial tests that, if satisfied, will permit principal payments on the notes. This is especially true where the note involves contingent payments to the seller.
- *Priority of ancillary obligations to the senior lender.* The senior lender will often seek (and get) the right to have all of its penalties, fees, and expenses of collection paid before the junior lender gets any payments. If there is conflict with the junior lender over this point, it can usually be resolved by setting a cap on the fees.
- *Priority of refinancings of senior debt.* A very important clause for the borrower in a typical subordination agreement is one that provides that the junior lender continue to be junior to any refinancing or refunding of the acquisition debt. Refinancing eventually occurs in at least half of all leveraged buyouts, and

borrowers want to be sure they can replace a senior lender with another one on more favorable terms. They don't want such a transaction to become an opportunity for the seller or any other junior lender to make trouble. This provision is more often an issue with sellers in seller takeback financings than it is with junior institutional lenders, who tend to accept rather broad definitions of senior debt. Senior debt is usually defined in junk bond subordination provisions as any debt for borrowed money that is not expressly made subordinated to the junior loan. Seller subordinated debt is more likely to define senior debt in terms of specific debt instruments and any refinancings or refundings thereof. Sellers sometimes exclude from the definition of senior debt any debt owed to the buyer or its shareholders.

Both seller and junk bond subordination provisions often will limit the amount of debt to which the junior loan is subordinated to a fixed amount, say 125 to 150 percent of the senior debt on the original date of borrowing. This limitation is designed to prevent the junior lender from being buried under a growing burden of senior debt that could substantially reduce its chances of getting paid.

- *Priority of trade debt.* This issue, again, is particularly likely to arise with sellers. Trade debt is particularly important in buyouts because in a typical LBO the buyer is purchasing a company that has been under the credit umbrella of its parent. Company management has never worried about its trade credit security because everybody knew that it was a subsidiary of a great big parent with all the money in the world, and now it has become a separate, heavily leveraged company on its own. All parties should consider at an early stage the impact that the acquisition will have on all the target's suppliers. It may be necessary in order to preserve supplier relationships that the seller be willing to remain below the suppliers in loan priority. The senior lender may insist on this feature in order to ensure that the company can retain its suppliers if financial storm clouds start to gather.

What issues arise in negotiating procedural subordination provisions?

These tend to be particularly difficult. They can best be divided into blockage and suspension provisions.

What is blockage?

The blockage provisions are those parts of the subordination agreement that prevent the borrower from making payments to the junior lenders under certain circumstances. Seller subordinated notes frequently provide that, if there is any default of any kind to a senior lender, no payments may be made on the seller note. In the case of institutional and junk bond lenders, payments on the junior debt are usually barred indefinitely when there is a payment default on the senior loan, and for a limited period of time (anywhere from 90 to 270 days, but usually around 180 days) when a nonpayment default exists, unless the senior lender accelerates its debt, in which case the blockage continues. Such periods of blockage are often available only once each year.

The fact that a payment is blocked does *not* mean that there is no default under the junior loan. The blockage provisions do not by themselves prevent the junior lender from declaring a default, accelerating its loan, and, if appropriate, forcing an involuntary bankruptcy on the borrower, although the "suspension" provisions discussed next may prevent this. Such provisions are merely an agreement between the lenders and the company that no matter what action the junior lender takes, during the blockage period the company may not make the proscribed payments. Because a blocked payment will constitute a default on the junior debt and entitle the junior lender to accelerate the loan, unless prevented by the suspension provisions, a senior lender is likely to waive its right to blockage unless the company is in serious trouble.

What are the suspension provisions?

These are the parts of the subordination agreement that limit a junior lender's rights to take enforcement actions if there is a default on the junior loan. These provisions are prevalent in privately placed subordinated debt. Enforcement actions include suing the borrower, accelerating the loan, and declaring the entire amount due or putting the borrower into bankruptcy. Depending upon the type of loan, these rights may be severely restricted until the senior debt is paid in full or for a significant length of time, or they may be subject to few or no restrictions.

The suspension provisions are also important where both lenders have security interests in the same collateral (that is, a senior and junior lien on fixed assets). In such a case it is not uncommon for the junior lender to be required to refrain from taking any action against the collateral until the earliest to occur of (1) the expiration of a fixed period of time, (2) acceleration of the loan by the senior lender, or (3) the full payment of the senior lender.

What rights do the senior and junior lenders want to have if the borrower defaults?

The senior lender wants to be as certain as possible that its superior position is meaningful in a practical sense. It wants no money leaving the corporation if there is any default on its loan, and it wants to control the timing, pace, and final resolution of any workout including possible asset sales or restructuring of the business. For that reason it wants to restrict the junior lender to relatively few events of default (generally only those that are a signal of substantial financial difficulties, such as a payment default on the junior loan or acceleration of other significant debt) so that the junior lender will have fewer opportunities to force the borrower into a workout or, worse, bankruptcy. If there are fewer possible events of default under the junior loan, a senior lender may be able to keep the junior lender on the sidelines by keeping the interest payments on the junior debt current while it arranges a workout with the borrower. Once there is actually a default on the junior loan, the senior lender seeks the suspension provisions to forestall efforts by the junior lender to sue the borrower, accelerate the maturity of the junior loan, or throw the borrower into bankruptcy. The effect of all these provisions is to reduce the negotiating leverage of the junior lender.

The junior lender wants to minimize the time it is not participating in the workout and the ability of the senior lender to work out matters with the borrower without its consent or, at least, participation. It basically wants a seat at the table of any workout as soon as possible. It also wishes to keep the blockage periods as short as possible and minimize suspension provisions so that it can pressure the senior lender not to block payments on the junior debt. To gain negotiating leverage, the junior lender will also seek to structure the subordination provisions so that, once there is a default, it can threaten to accelerate its loan and bring down the financial house of cards. In actuality, however, the junior lender is unlikely to accelerate, since it would probably have more to lose than the senior lender in a bankruptcy.

What about the borrower?

The typical borrower is trapped in the middle. It is mainly concerned with not letting these issues kill the deal. It also has a strong interest in having the subordination provisions not create a situation where it will have little or no time or leverage to work out problems with the senior lenders before financial Armageddon arrives. The borrower does not favor an unrestrained senior lender who can sell off all the assets and close down the business to pay its own loan off rather than live with an extended workout that offers a better chance for ultimate survival of the borrower. And it particularly wants to be sure that the seller will be tied down without the ability to compel action by the institutional lenders, both senior and junk bonds. A deeply subordinated seller is more likely to accept 10 cents on the dollar and go away—often a key step in a workout if the borrower's stockholders are to have any incentive to make the additional effort and investment necessary to save the company.

What does the senior lender require with respect to defaults on the junior loan?

A basic objective of the senior lender is to eliminate or at least minimize opportunities for the junior lender to declare a default. Thus, the senior lender will be likely to strongly oppose a "cross-default" provision in favor of the junior lender; that is, that any default under the senior loan is a default under the junior loan. If such a provision is given, it should at least be narrowed to certain specific senior loan defaults and should provide that any waiver by the senior lender or cure of the default terminates the default and rescinds any resulting acceleration on the junior loan as well. The senior lender will also wish to be sure that any default on the junior loan is a default on the senior loan; that is, the senior lender will have a cross-default provision running in its favor, so that the junior lender is never in a position to take enforcement action against the borrower at a time when the senior lender cannot. The senior lender should not object, however, to a "cross-acceleration" clause permitting the junior lender to declare a default and accelerate its loan if the senior lender accelerates the senior loan.

Are subordination provisions generally the same for all junior loans?

Definitely not. First, the subordination provisions and all other intercreditor issues are the subject of negotiation, and rarely are two deals exactly the same. Second, the subordination provisions vary greatly depending upon the type of junior lender and whether the junior debt is privately placed or sold in a public offering. The range of junior debt subordination includes (from most deeply subordinated to least) seller's notes, institutional mezzanine lenders and other privately placed funded debt, and public junk bonds.

Typical provisions for public junk debt, for privately placed institutional debt, and for seller paper are set forth in the appendixes at the end of this chapter. Note that there are almost no suspension provisions in the case of public debt and very extensive ones for seller debt.

The public debt provisions are worth special note because of their prevalence in today's transactions. In almost all cases, if a senior lender has plans to deviate from the current norms for blockage periods or other customary provisions, the borrower will run into serious problems in getting a bridge loan from an investment banker. The areas where negotiations do occur are typically: (1) the number of days in a blockage period

(120 to 180 days has been customary) and the number of blockage periods that can occur in any 365-day period; (2) notice periods before the junior loan can be accelerated; and (3) rescission of acceleration by the junior lender resulting from cross-acceleration provisions if the other lender has rescinded its acceleration.

For how long is the subordinated debt subordinated?

Usually the junior debt is subordinated throughout its term or until the senior debt, including refinancings, is paid in full.

Is preferred stock subordinate to all debt?

Preferred stock is subordinated in liquidation to all debt. But preferred stock is a creature of contract between the company and its preferred stockholders, and if it is to be subject to payment restrictions imposed by lenders, the company's articles of incorporation should specifically say so.

In what agreement do subordination terms appear?

Very often, subordination provisions are found in the junior debt instrument itself, but in many cases the lenders prefer to have a separate subordination agreement. This is especially true where the junior lender doesn't want some or all of the subordination provisions to apply after the particular senior loan has been repaid. The borrower must be careful here because if the subordination provisions fall away, the borrower may have a hard time refinancing its senior loan. As discussed previously, it is customary to expect and get continuing subordination of some kind on the part of the junior lenders.

How are subordination issues affected by corporate structure?

Corporate structure has a powerful effect on relative rights and priorities of lenders, and sometimes is deliberately taken advantage of to keep intercreditor relationships and, thus, problems to a minimum, or to enhance one lender's position against another's. An oversimplified example will illustrate how this works. Suppose the target is a retail company in the form of a parent corporation with a principal operating subsidiary. The revolving credit and term lender could lend to the operating subsidiary, secured by its current and fixed assets, except the stores. The stores could be financed through loans to a separate partnership that owns them and leases them to the subsidiary. The subsidiary can obtain its working capital by selling certain categories of its accounts receivable to a separate corporation, which would finance the purchase with notes secured by the accounts. The mezzanine debt could be loaned to the parent corporation. The result is shown in Exhibit 4-4.

Because each lender lends to a different entity, there is minimal contact between lenders and their security rights, and relative priorities are determined by the assets and corporate structure of their respective borrowers. The revolving credit and term lender to Corporation B is in the senior position, except that its rights do not extend to the stores, which are owned by Partnership D, or accounts receivable, which are sold to Cor-

Exhibit 4-4 Subordination and Corporate Structure

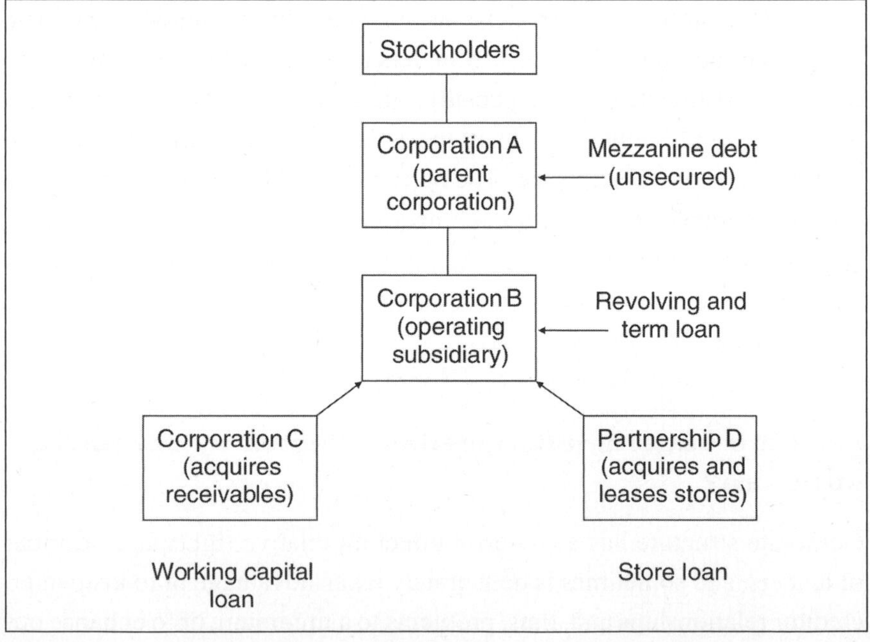

poration C. Proceeds from the sale of accounts receivable are used to pay down both the revolving and term loan and to pay rent on the stores; after these needs are met, the proceeds can be paid out as dividends to Corporation A, which then can pay the mezzanine debt.

To the extent that the revolving loan is paid down, Corporation B gains working capital financing through its ability to borrow again under the revolver, assuming sufficient availability. Because no dividends will be paid if Corporation B's revenues cannot cover its debts to the revolving and term lender and Partnership D, the mezzanine debt is automatically subordinated to both the revolving and term lender and Partnership D. Such a structure makes the relationships between lenders clear from the start and minimizes opportunity for conflict between them.

This method of structuring priorities can, at least in theory, give one lender a very strong advantage over another in bankruptcy. (We say "in theory" because no one can predict the behavior of a bankruptcy judge, who has ample power to disregard corporate layers and combine bankruptcy proceedings of different corporations so as to sweep away even the most elegant structural devices.) If, in our example, Corporation B goes bankrupt, the revolving and term lender will be deemed its sole creditor, other than trade credit and Partnership D (but only to the extent of overdue rent). The revolving and term lender can thus control the bankruptcy proceeding without even giving the mezzanine lender a place at the creditor's table. For that reason, the mezzanine debt, which is unsecured, is even more deeply subordinated than it would be if all loans were made to the same entity but subject to the subordination provisions discussed earlier in this chapter. Junior lenders may, consequently, object strongly to being required to lend at the parent level if the senior debt is at the operating level. (For more about bankruptcy, see Chapter 11.)

Lending at different levels can also present state tax problems. Some states do not permit consolidation of parent and subsidiary tax returns. Consequently, in those states, the deductions derived by Corporation A from interest payments on the mezzanine debt cannot be netted against the operating income received by Corporation B. In addition, care must be taken to be sure that loan agreements and corporate laws permit the necessary dividends to be paid so that funds can flow as required between the different corporations. (See also Chapter 5.)

INTERCREDITOR AGREEMENTS

What is an intercreditor agreement?

This is an agreement among lenders to a particular borrower to which the borrower may or may not be a party. It governs, among other things, the priority rights of lenders in collateral and proceeds of collateral and sets forth which lender or group of lenders shall have the right to make decisions about collateral. It is normally drafted by the most senior lender.

What issues are most likely to come up in negotiations of an intercreditor agreement?

- *Issues of equal or fair treatment.* When one lender has a first priority in some assets and another lender in other assets, each should have parallel rights as to priority, initiation of foreclosure proceedings, exercise of other remedies, payment for related expenses, and the like. A senior lender may seek to write in overbearing provisions with respect to junior liens. It may, for example, try to grant itself the right to foreclose on or sell collateral whether or not at market price. Such provisions should be avoided because they are probably not enforceable and raise the hackles of junior lenders.

  Preserving the form of equal treatment between lenders can be very important. In one situation where the term and revolving lenders had been at each other's throats and the intercreditor agreement was expected to be very difficult to negotiate, no problem arose because, despite great differences in the quality and amount of the collateral, the lawyer for the senior lender was careful to keep the clauses of the intercreditor agreement in strict parallel—for every grant of a right to the revolving lender there was a similar (if less valuable) grant for the term lender.
- *Rights of one lender to amend its loan agreement without the consent of another lender.* It is not uncommon for a junior lender to be barred from shortening amortization schedules or the weighted average life of a financing, since senior lenders

will not want subordinated lenders paid off while senior debt is still outstanding. Nor will one lender permit another lender to increase interest rates or rate formulas without its consent, because these terms may affect the company's ability to service all of its debt. However, a borrower should be able to agree with any one lender to ease terms of payment or to amend covenants or waive defaults without involving other lenders. Subordinated lenders frequently require that the borrower may not enter into amendments to its loan agreement that could "materially and adversely affect" the junior lender. This is a vague provision that will tend to make the senior lender cautious but leaves leeway for the run-of-the-mill adjustments and corrections that normally are needed in a loan agreement after the closing. It often provides a reasonable compromise.

- *Changes in status between lenders.* Sometimes one lender is prepared to take a lower priority against another only for a limited period of time or until some external event occurs. If one lender ceases to be secured, another lender may also be willing to release its security. If a senior lender agrees to extend the term of its loan past a certain date, the subordinate lender may demand the right to gain equal seniority, that is, to become *pari passu*.
- *Allocation of shared rights over collateral.* If an intangible right, such as a patent or copyright, is needed for realization of value for assets pledged to two different lenders, or if exercise of its rights by one lender blocks another lender's rights (as, for example, if the term lender's right to foreclose on a factory building blocks the revolving lender's right to remove or complete processing of inventory), these matters should be covered.
- *Voting rights of creditors and other rights in bankruptcy.* Senior lenders try very hard to have control of creditors' committees in bankruptcy. Although such rights may not be enforceable, they may seek to require junior creditors to waive contests of bankruptcy plans, marshaling questions and issues of interpretation of the intercreditor agreement.

FRAUDULENT CONVEYANCE AND OTHER LITIGATION CONCERNS

Lenders worry about fraudulent conveyances in LBOs. Why?

Leveraged acquisitions and buyouts have an unfortunate tendency to attract lawsuits. When buyouts are successful, parties may sue to get a larger share of success; when unsuccessful, parties may sue to reduce their exposure to the failure. Parties suing or sued may include bondholders (senior and junior), shareholders (majority and minority), underwriters, lenders, and officers and directors of the selling company.[42] A bank that lends money to finance the acquisition of a business needs to be assured that, in the event of a bankruptcy of that business, its lien on the assets will secure the loan, and the note given by the acquired company will be enforceable. However, the lien will be set aside and voided, and even the note can be rendered worthless, if the pledge of assets and the giving of the note are determined to be "fraudulent conveyances or transfers" under the Federal Bankruptcy Code or under comparable state law—either the Uniform Fraudulent Conveyance Act (UFCA) or its successor, the Uniform Fraudulent Transfer Act (UFTA), discussed at length in Chapter 11 of this book. Shareholders in leveraged buyouts are also at risk: if a transaction is judged to be a fraudulent conveyance, they may have to return the proceeds received from selling their shares.

Can a pledge of collateral, or a note or guaranty, be a fraudulent conveyance even though there is no intent to defraud anyone?

Yes. Both the Federal Bankruptcy Code and comparable provisions of state law permit the voiding of a lien or obligation as "fraudulent" without the requirement of malign intent. These laws may, in effect, be utilized to protect the interests of general creditors of acquired companies where the transactions financed by the banks have the effect of depriving the acquired company of the means to pay its debts to its general creditors, whether those transactions are actually intended to do so or not.

Is there a special risk of creating an unintended fraudulent conveyance in an LBO loan as opposed to an ordinary corporate loan?

Yes. Under Section 548 of the Federal Bankruptcy Code and comparable provisions of state law, a lien given by the acquired company on its assets, or the note secured by that lien, will be deemed "fraudulent" if the company receives less than "reasonably equivalent value" in exchange and one of the following three conditions exists: (1) the company was "insolvent" at the time of such transfer or became "insolvent" as a result of the transfer; (2) the company was left with "unreasonably small capital" as a result of the transfer; or (3) the company incurred or intended to incur debts beyond its ability to pay.

In an LBO loan, no matter how the transaction is structured (whether as a cash merger, stock purchase, or asset purchase), most of what the bank lends winds up not in the hands of the acquired company, but in the pockets of the sellers. On the date after closing, the acquired company is, by definition, "highly leveraged." It has a great deal of new debt, and liens on all its assets, but a large portion of the money raised by such debt (which the company is required to repay) has gone to the previous stockholders. It is not hard to see why an unsecured creditor of the company, viewing the new debt obligations of the company and the encumbrance of its assets, would complain that the company (as opposed to its former owners) did not receive "reasonably equivalent value" in the transaction.

Assuming that the lack of reasonably equivalent value may be a problem in all LBO loans, can't the problem be solved by showing that none of the other three conditions that would trigger a fraudulent conveyance exists?

It can, if each of the three conditions can be shown not to exist, but that is not always easy to do in the typical LBO. Of the three conditions—(1) insolvency, (2) unreasonably small capital, and (3) ability to pay debts—the last two are the easiest to overcome. To the extent that the company and the bank can demonstrate, through well-crafted, reasonable projections, that the company will have sufficient revenues and borrowing capacity to meet its reasonably anticipated obligations (including servicing the acquisition debt), it should be possible to establish that the company's capital, although small, is adequate, and that the company will be able to pay its debts. Solvency, however, is another matter.

Why is it difficult to show that an acquired company is solvent for fraudulent conveyance purposes?

Because the definition of solvency as used in the Federal Bankruptcy Code and state counterpart legislation is different from that used under GAAP. Solvency under GAAP can mean having sufficient assets to pay debts as they mature, or having book assets that are greater than book liabilities. In the typical LBO, at least one of the tests for GAAP solvency can usually be met. But for fraudulent conveyance purposes, a company is solvent only if the "fair, salable value" of its assets is greater than its probable liabilities. In valuing assets, the approach should be conservative, using liquidation value rather than book value or other measures.

Why is the "fair, salable value" test difficult to meet for many companies?

As mentioned, the fair, salable value of assets has to be greater than the value of liabilities. Some companies lack hard assets having "fair, salable value" at least equal to their direct and contingent liabilities. Also, probable liabilities are not limited to GAAP balance sheet liabilities. All probable liabilities, contingent as well as direct, must be considered.

The upper right side of the balance sheet is also becoming more burdened by reporting of pension and healthcare liabilities. Whereas in the past, companies had a degree of flexibility in reporting these, there are stricter standards now.

Is the "fraudulent conveyance" problem inescapable for all LBOs?

Each sophisticated lender who is willing to make an LBO loan has made a bottom-line decision that it can live with the risk of unclear law in this area. The classic case on the subject, *Gleneagles*, actually involved intentional misconduct, although the court's reasoning in that case cast a cloud over innocent LBOs as well. A number of commentators in the late 1980s, supported by some court decisions (*Kupetz*, *Credit Managers*), argued that the fraudulent conveyance doctrine should not be employed as a blunt instrument against LBOs. Courts in recent years have also shown a range of opinions in the matter.

Although it is not possible yet to say how the law will develop in the twenty-first century, a reasonable compromise might be that creditors who predate the acquisition and did not consent to it have a right to exact realistic standards for solvency at the time of the acquisition, while subsequent creditors who knew or could have known of the terms of the acquisition loan and its security arrangements should not be entitled to the benefit of fraudulent conveyance laws.

Are there structural arrangements in LBOs that can trigger fraudulent conveyance problems?

Yes. In addition to the issue of lack of "reasonably equivalent value" to the company, lenders and borrowers can get into trouble in transactions involving multicompany groups. These problems are not unique to LBOs, but they can occur in such transactions. Typically they occur when collateral is provided by a subsidiary to secure a borrowing by its parent (upstreaming) or when collateral is provided by one subsidiary to secure a borrowing by a sister subsidiary (cross-streaming). Similarly, upstream and cross-stream guaranties can run afoul of the fraudulent conveyance prohibitions. By contrast, guaranties and pledges by a parent to support a borrowing by its subsidiary (downstreaming) do not present fraudulent conveyance problems.

Why are upstreaming and cross-streaming bad?

Because the donor entity—the one providing the collateral or the guaranty—is not getting "reasonably equivalent value," which is going instead to its affiliate. Thus, one of the triggers (although not the only one) for fraudulent conveyance is tripped. In addition, each subsidiary is typically asked to guarantee all the senior debt of its parent, yet the assets of the subsidiary represent only a fraction of the total acquisition. The result is that each subsidiary, taken by itself, cannot repay the full acquisition debt and may be rendered insolvent if the guaranty is called against it alone. This illogical result would be avoided if the test of solvency took into account that all the subsidiaries would share in meeting the guaranty obligation. Some cases give support for this conclusion, but the law is unfortunately not clear enough to eliminate the risk.

Are there ways to solve upstreaming and cross-streaming problems?

Yes. If the transaction passes each of the three additional tests—(1) no insolvency, (2) not unreasonably small capital, and (3) ability to pay debts—there is no fraudulent conveyance. However, to guard against the risk of flunking one of the tests, two kinds of additional solutions can be explored: (1) merging the entity providing the collateral or guaranty with the borrower before the acquisition is consummated or (2) dividing up the loan into two or more distinct credit facilities, each collateralized by (and commensurate with) the collateral provided by each borrower. Care should be taken, if the latter course is used, to avoid having the loan proceeds simply pass through one of the borrowers into the hands of another borrower or affiliated entity. The loan proceeds can be used to pay off bona fide intercorporate debt, but if the cash flow among the borrowing entities indicates that the separate loans are shams, the transaction runs the risk of being collapsed in a bankruptcy proceeding. In such a case, the liens and guaranties could be voided.

Are upstream or cross-stream guaranties that are limited to the net worth of the guarantor fraudulent conveyances?

No. Indeed, limiting the guaranty (and the lien collateralizing it) to the amount of the guarantor's net worth at the time of delivery of the guaranty can provide an ingenious way to ensure that the guarantor is not rendered insolvent by delivery of the guaranty and consequently should eliminate any fraudulent conveyance problem. However, the guarantor must have the requisite net worth in the bankruptcy sense, and not just GAAP net worth, in addition to being able to pay its debts and not having unreasonably small capital. Net worth guaranties have yet to be tested in a bankruptcy proceeding, and although they appear conceptually sound, there are no certain predictions on what the courts will say.

REFINANCING ISSUES

Not all financing agreements survive the challenges of postmerger life. Some must be refinanced. Strategies to meet creditor obligations and/or maintain creditor relations include:

- Renegotiating loan terms
- Changing or adding lenders
- Selling or restructuring assets, debt, or stock to gain cash
- Combinations of the above

Although each of these can be employed up front as a way to find initial financing, they are often used after an acquisition or buyout to pay that financing back.

How does one go about renegotiating loan terms? A deal's a deal, isn't it?

Yes, a deal is a deal when it comes to leveraged transactions, as in others, but the higher the loan amount and the more sophisticated the lender, the more likely it is that the terms of a loan can be changed, despite the numerous technical provisions discussed earlier in this chapter. (For ample evidence of the flexibility of creditors when they are hard-pressed, see Chapter 11.) On the other hand, lenders, too, may wish to renegotiate loan terms, particularly during periods of falling interest rates.

What about changing lenders?

Some companies with postmerger debt heirs do change or add on banks, but this is not the only way to switch horses in midstream. In considering a change or expansion of lenders, refinancing teams should not forget corporate sources, including potential future acquirers who might be willing to loan funds or take over loans in exchange for an option to acquire.

How can leveraged buyers sell off assets? Doesn't this violate covenants protecting lender collateral?

Many leveraged acquirers include specific asset sales in their strategic plans approved by lenders. As long as such sales do not come as a surprise and are priced well, they generally meet with lender approval. On the other hand, the kind of wholesale dismantling of going concerns for mere cash flow purposes has fallen into disfavor even at the planning stage. One way to preserve company integrity and still generate cash from assets is to pursue sale-leasebacks.

How can selling debt—corporate paper—help to pay back other debt? Isn't it just another leverage burden?

If a company can sell its paper, this can be preferable from the point of view of interest obligation. Average high-grade commercial paper tends to pay rates lower than the LIBOR, which is a baseline for much bank lending.

So high-grade commercial paper issuers can get away with paying low interest rates. What's the catch? Why don't all companies use this approach?

First, not every company can achieve and sustain a high credit rating from the credit rating agencies. Second, the paper is issued with short maturities, ranging from 14 to 270 days. Issuers must find new buyers or convince present buyers to roll over their investments. This is why many companies take out standby lines of credit from banks to back up their paper in the event that they have trouble in rolling over their commercial paper lines.

What are some ways companies can restructure the debt they issue?

With so many types of corporate debt finding their way to market, opportunities to restructure obligations are limited only by an issuer's imagination and the quality of underlying company values. Some strategies include:

- Offering to buy back debt from holders at less than its original price
- Offering to trade debt for new issues that mature later
- Asking bondholders to trade their holdings for equity

What are the chief benefits and drawbacks of selling stock as a means of refinancing if a company is already a public company?

On the upside, there is financial flexibility. When a company issues stock, it receives cash for it but incurs no obligation. It can seem like free money. On the downside, stock sales may decrease:

- Control of original owners
- Earnings per share (as the shares denominator decreases, the earnings numerator increases)
- Market value (when management sells, the market may, too)

Do refinancing methods differ by industry?

Yes. For example, in the financial services industry there are several creative refinancing techniques that are relatively foreign to other industries. Some commercial banks use a good bank, bad bank technique. This involves placing nonperforming and other lower-quality assets into a collecting bank, or liquidating trust, that is sold or spun off to shareholders. Insurance companies sometimes employ securitization, the sale of several chunks, or tranches, of securities backed by the mortgages or junk bonds held by the insurance company. Insurance companies and savings and loans can raise capital by converting from depositor-owned mutual organizations to stockholder-owned structures, called stocking.

CONCLUDING COMMENTS

The choice to grow through acquisition begins with strategy. What is best for the company and its owners? If a company makes the right strategic choices, the valuation will be well founded and the financing will be forthcoming. In this chapter, we have provided an overview of the kinds of financing available, focusing on debt financing, which is the most easily and broadly available. In the next chapter, we will show how to translate strategic and financial considerations into the actual structure of an M&A transaction.

APPENDIX 4A

Typical Subordination Provisions of Publicly Issued Notes

Section 1.1. Agreement to Subordinate. The Company agrees, and the holders of the Subordinated Notes by accepting the Subordinated Notes agree, that the Indebtedness evidenced by the Subordinated Notes is subordinated in right of payment, to the extent and in the manner provided in this Article, to the prior payment in full of all Senior Debt of the Company and that the subordination is for the benefit of the holders of Senior Debt of the Company, but the Subordinated Notes shall in all respects rank pari passu with all other Subordinated Debt of the Company.

Section 1.2. Default on Senior Debt of the Company. No direct or indirect payment by the Company of principal of or interest on the Subordinated Notes whether pursuant to the terms of the Subordinated Notes or upon acceleration or otherwise shall be made if, at the time of such payment, there exists a default in the payment of all or any portion of principal of or interest on any Senior Debt of the Company (and the Trustee has received written notice thereof), and such default shall not have been cured or waived. In addition, during the continuance of any other event of default with respect to such Senior Debt pursuant to which the maturity thereof may be accelerated, upon the receipt by the Trustee of written notice from the holders of Senior Debt, no such payment may be made by the Company upon or in respect of the Subordinated Notes for a period of [180] days from the date of receipt of such notice; provided, however, that the holders of Senior Debt may give only [one] such notice in any 360-day period, and provided, further, that this provision shall not prevent the payment of an installment of principal of or interest on the Subordinated Notes for more than [180] days.

Section 1.3. Liquidation, Dissolution, Bankruptcy. Upon any distribution of the assets of the Company in any dissolution, winding up, liquidation, or reorganization of the Company (whether voluntary or involuntary and whether in bankruptcy, insolvency, or receivership proceeding or upon an assignment for the benefit of creditors or any marshaling of the assets and liabilities of the Company or otherwise):

1. Holders of Senior Debt of the Company shall be entitled to receive payment in full on the Senior Debt of the Company before the holders of the Subordinated Notes shall be entitled to receive any payment of principal of, or premium, if any, or interest on the Subordinated Notes; and
2. Until the Senior Debt of the Company is paid in full, any distribution to which the holders of the Subordinated Notes would be entitled but for this Article shall be made to holders of Senior Debt of the Company as their interests may appear. Consolidation or merger of the Company with the sale, conveyance, or lease of all or substantially all of its property to another corporation upon the terms and conditions otherwise permitted in this Agreement shall not be deemed a dissolution, winding up, liquidation, or reorganization for purposes of this Article.

Section 1.4. When Distribution Must Be Paid Over. If distributions are made to the holders of the Subordinated Notes that because of this Article should not have been made, the holders of the Subordinated Notes who received the distribution shall hold it in trust for the benefit of the holders of Senior Debt of the Company and pay it over to them as their interests may appear.

Section 1.5. Subrogation. After all Senior Debt of the Company is paid in full and until the Subordinated Notes are paid in full, the holders of the Subordinated Notes shall be subrogated to the rights of holders of Senior Debt of the Company to receive distributions applicable to Senior Debt of the Company. A distribution made under this Article to holders of Senior Debt of the Company that otherwise would have been made to the holders of the Subordinated Notes is not, as between the Company and the holder of the Subordinated Notes, a payment by the Company on Senior Debt of the Company.

Section 1.6. Relative Rights. This Article defines the relative rights of the holders of the Subordinated Notes and holders of Senior Debt of the Company. Nothing in this Agreement shall:

1. Impair, as between the Company and the holders of the Subordinated Notes, the obligation of the Company, which is absolute and unconditional, to pay principal of, premium, if any, and interest on the Subordinated Notes in accordance with their terms; or
2. Prevent the holders of the Subordinated Note from exercising their available remedies upon a Default, subject to the rights of holders of Senior Debt of the Company to receive any distribution otherwise payable to the holder of the Subordinated Notes.

Section 1.7. Subordination May Not Be Impaired by Company. No right of any holder of Senior Debt of the Company to enforce the subordination of the Subordinated Notes shall be impaired by any act or failure to act on the part of the Company or its failure to comply with this Agreement.

Section 1.8. Modification of Terms of Senior Debt. Any renewal or extension of the time of payment of any Senior Debt or the exercise by the holders of Senior Debt of any of their rights under any instrument creating or evidencing Senior Debt, including without limitation the waiver of any default thereunder, may be made or done without notice to or assent from the holders of Subordinated Notes or the Trustee.

No compromise, alteration, amendment, modification, extension, renewal, or other change of, or waiver, consent, or other action in respect of, any liability or obligation under or in respect of any Senior Debt or of any of the terms, covenants, or conditions of any indenture or other instrument under which any Senior Debt is outstanding, shall in any way alter or affect any of the provisions of this Article or of the Subordinated Notes relating to the subordination thereof.

Section 1.9. Reliance by Holders of Senior Debt on Subordination Provisions. The holders of the Subordinated Notes by accepting the Subordinated Notes acknowledge and agree that the foregoing subordination provisions are, and are intended to be, an inducement and a consideration to each holder of any Senior Debt, whether such Senior Debt was created or acquired before or after the issuance of the Subordinated Notes, to acquire and continue to hold, or to continue to hold, such Senior Debt and such holder of Senior Debt shall be deemed conclusively to have relied on such subordination provisions in acquiring and continuing to hold, or in continuing to hold, such Senior Debt.

Section 1.10. This Article Not to Prevent Events of Default. The failure to make a payment pursuant to the Subordinated Notes by reason of any provision in this Article shall not be construed as preventing the occurrence of a Default or an Event of Default. Nothing in this Article shall have any effect on the right of the holders of the Subordinated Notes to accelerate the maturity of the Subordinated Notes.

Section 1.11. Definition of Senior Debt. "Senior Debt" means the principal of, premium, if any, and interest on (1) all indebtedness incurred, assumed, or guaranteed by the Company, either before or after the date hereof, which is evidenced by an instrument of indebtedness or reflected on the accounting records of the Company as a payable (excluding any debt that by the terms of the instrument creating or evidencing the same is not superior in right of payment to the Subordinated Notes) including as Senior Debt (a) any amount payable with respect to any lease, conditional sale, or installment sale agreement or other financing instrument, or agreement that in accordance with generally accepted accounting principles is, at the date hereof or at the time the lease, conditional sale, or installment sale agreement, or other financing instrument or agreement is entered into, assumed, or guaranteed by the Company, required to be reflected as a liability on the face of the balance sheet of the Company; (b) all borrowings under any lines of credit, revolving credit agreements, or promissory notes from a bank or other financial renewals or extensions of any of the foregoing; (c) any amounts payable in respect of any interest rate exchange agreement, currency exchange agreement, or similar agreement; and (d) any subordinated indebtedness of a corporation merged with or into or acquired by the Company and (2) any renewals or extensions or refunding of any such Senior Debt or evidences of indebtedness issued in exchange for such Senior Debt.

APPENDIX 4B

Typical Subordination Provisions of Privately Placed Institutional Notes

Section 1.1. Agreement to Subordinate. The Subordinated Notes shall be subordinated to Senior Debt to the extent set forth in this Article, and the Subordinated Notes shall not be subordinated to any debt of the Company other than Senior Debt.

Section 1.2. Default on Senior Debt of the Company. In the event of a default in any payment of interest or principal in respect of any Senior Debt, whether at the stated maturity, by acceleration or otherwise, then no payment shall be made on account of principal of or interest or premium, if any, on the Subordinated Notes until such default shall have been cured or waived.

Section 1.3. Liquidation, Dissolution, Bankruptcy. In the event of (i) any insolvency, bankruptcy, liquidation, reorganization, or other similar proceedings or any receivership proceedings in connection therewith, relative to the Company or its assets, or (ii) any proceedings for voluntary liquidation, dissolution, or other winding up of the Company, whether or not involving insolvency or bankruptcy proceedings, then all principal of and interest (including postpetition interest), fees (commitment or other), expenses, and premium, if any, then due and payable on all Senior Debt shall first be paid in full, or such payment shall have been duly provided for in the manner set forth in the proviso to the next sentence, before any further payment on account of principal or interest, or premium, if any, is made upon the Subordinated Notes. In any of the proceedings referred to above, any payment or distribution of any kind or character, whether in cash, property, stock, or obligations, which may be payable or deliverable in respect of the Subordinated Notes shall be paid or delivered directly to the holders of the Senior Debt (or to a banking institution selected by the court or Person making the payment or delivery as designated by any holder of Senior Debt) for application in payment thereof, unless and until all Senior Debt shall have been paid in full, provided, however, that in the event that payment or delivery of such cash, property, stock, or obligations to the holders of the Subordinated Notes is authorized by a final non-appealable order or decree which takes into account the subordination of the Subordinated Notes to Senior Debt, and made by a court of competent jurisdiction in a reorganization proceedings under any applicable bankruptcy or reorganization law, no payment or delivery of such cash, property, stock, or obligations payable or deliverable with respect to the Subordinated Notes shall be made to the holders of Senior Debt. Anything in this Article to the contrary notwithstanding, no payment or delivery shall be made to holders of stock or obligations which are issued pursuant to reorganization, dissolution, or liquidation proceedings, or upon any merger, consolidation, sale, lease, transfer, or other disposal not prohibited by the provisions of this Agreement, by the Company, as reorganized, or by the corporation succeeding to the Company or acquiring its property and assets, if such stock or obligations are subordinate and junior at least to the extent provided in this Article to the payment of all Senior Debt then outstanding and to payment of any stock or obligations which are issued in exchange or substitution for any Senior Debt then outstanding.

Section 1.4. When Distribution Must Be Paid Over. In the event that the holder of any Subordinated Note shall receive any payment, property, stock, or obligations in respect of such Subordinated Note which such holder is not entitled to receive under the provisions of this Article, such holder will hold any amount so received in trust for the holders of Senior Debt and will forthwith turn over such payment to the holders of Senior Debt in the form received to be applied on Senior Debt. In the event of any liquidation, dissolution, or other winding up of the Company, or in the event of any receivership, insolvency, bankruptcy, assignment for the benefit of creditors, reorganization or arrangement with creditors, whether or not pursuant to bankruptcy laws, sale of all or substantially all of the assets, or any other marshaling of the assets and liabilities of the Company, holders of Subordinated Notes will at the request of holders of Senior Debt file any claim or other instrument of similar character necessary to enforce the obligations of the Company in respect of the Subordinated Notes.

Section 1.5. Subrogation. Upon payment in full of all Senior Debt the holders of the Subordinated Notes shall be subrogated to the rights of the holders of Senior Debt to receive payments of distributions of assets of the Company applicable to Senior Debt until the principal of the premium, if any, and interest on the Subordinated Notes shall have been paid in full, and, for the purposes of such subrogation, no payments to the holders of Senior Debt of any cash, property, stock, or obligations which the holders of Subordinated Debt would be entitled to receive except for the provisions of this Article shall, as between the Company and its creditors (other than the holders of Senior Debt) and the holders of the Subordinated Notes, be deemed to be a payment by the Company to or on account of Senior Debt.

Section 1.6. Relative Rights. The provisions of this Article are for the purpose of defining the relative rights of the holders of Senior Debt on the one hand, and the holders of the Subordinated Notes on the other hand, against the Company and its property; and nothing herein shall impair, as between the Company and the holders of the Subordinated Notes, the obligation of the Company, which is unconditional and absolute, to pay to the holders thereof the full amount of the principal thereof, and premium, if any, and interest thereon, in accordance with the terms thereof and the provisions hereof, and to comply with all of its covenants and agreements contained herein; nor shall anything herein prevent the holder of any Subordinated Notes from exercising all remedies otherwise permitted by applicable law or hereunder upon Default hereunder or under any Subordinated Note, subject to the rights, if any, under this Article of holders of Senior Debt to receive cash, property, stock, or obligations otherwise payable or deliverable to the holders of the Subordinated Notes and subject to the limitations on remedies contained in sections 1.5 and 1.9.

Section 1.7. Subordination May Not Be Impaired by the Company. No present or future holder of any Senior Debt shall be prejudiced in the right to enforce the subordination of the Subordinated Notes by any act or failure to act on the part of the Company.

Section 1.8. Modification of Terms of Senior Debt. Each holder of Subordinated Notes consents that, without the necessity of any reservation of rights against such holder of Subordinated Notes, and without notice to or further assent by such holder of Subordinated Notes, (a) any demand for payment of any Senior Debt may be rescinded in whole or in part and any Senior Debt may be continued, and the Senior Debt, or the liability of the Company or any other Person upon or for any part thereof, or any collateral security or guaranty therefor or right of offset with respect thereto, and any Senior Debt, may, from time to time, in whole or in part, be renewed, extended, modified, accelerated, compromised, waived, surrendered, or released and (b) any document or instrument evidencing or governing the terms of any Senior Debt or any collateral security documents or guaranties or documents in connection therewith may be amended, modified, supplemented, or terminated, in whole or part, as the holders of Senior Debt may deem advisable from time to time, and any collateral security at any time held by such holder or any collateral agent for the benefit of such holders for the payment of any of the Senior Debt may be sold, exchanged, waived, surrendered, or released, in each case all without notice to or further assent by the holders of Subordinated Notes which will remain bound under this Agreement, and all without impairing, abridging, releasing, or affecting the subordination provided for herein, notwithstanding any such renewal, extension, modification, acceleration, compromise, amendment, supplement, termination, sale, exchange, waiver, surrender, or release. Each holder of Subordinated Notes waives any and all notice of the creating, renewal, extension, or accrual of any of the Senior Debt and notice of or proof of reliance by any holders of Senior Debt upon this Agreement, and the Senior Debt shall conclusively be deemed to have been created, contracted, or incurred in reliance upon this Agreement, and all dealings between the Company and the holders of Senior Debt shall be deemed to have been consummated in reliance upon this Agreement. Each holder of Subordinated Notes acknowledges and agrees that the lenders in any refinancing have relied upon the subordination provided for herein in entering into such refinancing and in making funds available to the Company thereunder. Each holder of Subordinated Notes waives notice of or proof of reliance on this Agreement and protest, demand for payment, and notice of default.

Section 1.9. Limitations on Rights of Subordinated Noteholders to Accelerate. The right of the holders of Subordinated Notes to declare the Subordinated Notes to be immediately due and payable pursuant to this Agreement upon the occurrence and continuance of an Event of Default under this Agreement shall be subject to the following:

1. If such Event of Default shall arise solely out of a default in specified financial covenants, then such holders may only so declare the Subordinated Notes due and payable if the holder of any Senior Debt shall have declared to be due and payable any obligations of the Company in respect of Senior Debt by reason of a default in respect thereof;
2. If such Event of Default shall arise out of a failure to make payments on the senior debt then such holder may not so declare the Subordinated Notes due and payable until the earliest to occur of (a) the continuance of such Event of Default for 180 consecutive days, (b) the day upon which the next payment is actually made of principal of or interest on any Senior Debt, or (c) the day upon which holders of Senior Debt declare to be due and payable before its normal maturity any obligations of the Company in respect of Senior Debt.

Section 1.10. Definition of Senior Debt. "Senior Debt" means Debt which is not by its terms expressly subordinated in right of payment to other Debt.

"Debt" of any Person means (i) all indebtedness of such Person for borrowed money or for the deferred purchase price of property, (ii) all obligations under leases which shall have been or should be, in accordance with generally accepted accounting principles (GAAP, as defined herein), recorded as capital leases in respect of which such Person is liable as lessee, (iii) all indebtedness referred to in clause (i) or (ii) above secured by (or for which the holder of such indebtedness has an existing right, contingent or otherwise, to be secured by) any lien, security interest or other charge or encumbrance upon or in property (including, without limitation, accounts and contract rights) owned by such Person, (iv) all indebtedness referred to in clause (i) or (ii) above guaranteed directly or indirectly in any manner by such Person, or in effect guaranteed directly or indirectly by such Person through an agreement to pay or purchase such indebtedness or to advance or supply funds for the payment or purchase of such indebtedness, or to otherwise assure a creditor against loss, and (v) liabilities in respect of unfunded vested benefits under Plans and withdrawal liability incurred under ERISA by such Person or by such Person as a member of the Controlled Group to any Multiemployer Plan, provided that Debt shall not include trade and other accounts payable in the ordinary course of business in accordance with customary trade terms and which are not overdue for a period of more than 60 days, or, if overdue for a period of more than 60 days, as to which a dispute exists and adequate reserves in accordance with GAAP have been established on the books of such Person.

APPENDIX 4C

Typical Subordination Provisions of Seller Notes

Section 1.1. Agreement to Subordinate. The obligations of the Company in respect of the principal of and interest on the Subordinated Notes shall be subordinate and junior in right of payment, to the extent and in the manner set forth in this Article, to any indebtedness of the Company in respect of Senior Debt.

Section 1.2. Default on Senior Debt of the Company. No payment of principal of or interest or distribution of any kind on the Subordinated Notes shall be made at any time when a default has occurred and is continuing under any Senior Debt, and, if any such payment or distribution is made, then the holder of the Subordinated Notes will hold the same in trust and pay it over to the holders of the Senior Debt.

Section 1.3. Liquidation, Dissolution, Bankruptcy. (a) In the event of any insolvency or bankruptcy proceedings, and any receivership, liquidation, reorganization, arrangement, readjustment, composition, or other similar proceedings in connection therewith, relative to the Company or to its creditors, as such, or to its property, or in the event of any proceedings for voluntary liquidation, dissolution, or other winding up of the Company, whether or not involving insolvency or bankruptcy, or in the event of any assignment by the Company for the benefit of creditors or in the event of any other marshaling of the assets of the Company, then the holders of Senior Debt shall be entitled to receive payment in full of all principal, premium, interest, fees, and charges on all Senior Debt (including interest thereon accruing after the commencement of any such proceedings) before the holder of the Subordinated Notes is entitled to receive any payment on account of principal or interest upon the Subordinated Notes, and to that end the holders of Senior Debt shall be entitled to receive for application in payment thereof any payment or distribution of any kind or character, whether in cash or property or securities, which may be payable or deliverable in any such proceedings in respect of the Subordinated Notes.

(b) In the event that the Subordinated Notes are declared due and payable before their expressed maturity because of the occurrence of an Event of Default (under circumstances when the provisions of the foregoing clause (a) shall not be applicable), the holders of the Senior Debt outstanding at the time the Subordinated Notes so become due and payable because of such occurrence of such Event of Default shall be entitled to receive payment in full of all principal of, and premium, interest, fees, and charges on, all Senior Debt before the holder of the Subordinated Notes is entitled to receive any payment on account of the principal of, or the interest on, the Subordinated Notes.

Section 1.4. Relative Rights and Subrogation. The provisions of this Article shall not alter or affect, as between the Company and the holder of the Subordinated Notes, the obligations of the Company to pay in full the principal of and interest on the Subordinated Notes, which obligations are absolute and unconditional. In the event that by virtue of this Article any amounts paid or payable to the holder of the Subordinated Notes in respect of the Subordinated Notes shall instead be paid to the holders of Senior Debt, the holder of the Subordinated Notes shall to this extent be subrogated to the rights of such holders; provided, however, that no such rights of subrogation shall be asserted against the Company until the Senior Debt has been paid in full.

Section 1.5. Subordination May Not Be Impaired by the Company. No present or future holder of Senior Debt shall be prejudiced in his right to enforce the subordination of the Subordinated Notes by any act or failure to act on the part of the Company. This subordination of the Subordinated Notes, and the rights of the holders of Senior Debt with respect thereto, shall not be affected by any amendment or other modification of any Senior Debt or any exercise or nonexercise of any right, power, or remedy with respect thereto.

Section 1.6. Modification of Terms of Senior Debt. The holders of Senior Debt may, at any time, in their discretion, renew or extend the time of payment of Senior Debt so held or exercise any of their rights under the Senior Debt including, without limitation, the waiver of defaults thereunder and the amendment of any of the terms or provisions thereof (or any notice evidencing or creating the same), all without notice to or assent from the holder of the Subordinated Notes. No compromise, alteration, amendment, modification, extension, renewal, or other change of, or waiver, consent, or other action in respect of any liability or obligation under or in respect of, any terms, covenants, or conditions of the Senior Debt (or any instrument evidencing or creating the same) and no release of property subject to the lien of the Senior Debt (or any instrument evidencing or creating the same), whether or not such release is in accordance with the provisions of the Senior Debt (or any instrument evidencing or creating the same), shall in any way alter or affect any of the provisions of the Subordinated Notes.

Section 1.7. Restrictions on Holders of Subordinated Notes. (a) The terms of the Subordinated Notes shall not be modified without the prior written consent of the holders of the Senior Debt.

(b) The holder of the Subordinated Notes shall not take any action against the Company with respect to any Event of Default until and unless (i) any event described in Section 1.3(a) has occurred, or (ii) a holder of Senior Debt shall have accelerated payment of any Senior Debt obligation of the Company, or (iii) the Senior Debt shall have been paid in full.

(c) The holder of the Subordinated Notes shall provide to the Company, at any time and from time to time, at the Company's request and at no expense to the holder of the Subordinated Notes, a written acknowledgment by the holder of the Subordinated Notes addressed to any holder of Senior Debt to the effect that such holder is a holder of Senior Debt, provided that prior to furnishing such acknowledgment, the holder of the

Subordinated Notes shall have received from the Company such information as the holder of the Subordinated Notes shall reasonably request demonstrating to the holder of Subordinated Notes reasonable satisfaction that such holder is a holder of Senior Debt.

Section 1.8. Definition of Senior Debt. "Senior Debt" means (i) any indebtedness of the Company in respect of a certain Revolving Credit and Security Agreement between the Company and [the specific Lender], including any advances or readvances under refunding or refinancings with the same or other lenders of the aforementioned loan agreement, (ii) [specific existing long-term indebtedness of the Company] and (iii) all trade debt of the Company.

NOTES

1. This question and answer was provided by Rob Baker, founder, Tecaq, Houston, Texas.
2. See Alexandra R. Lajoux and J. Fred Weston, *The Art of M&A Financing and Refinancing: Sources and Instruments for Growth* (New York: McGraw-Hill, 1999).
3. Steven T. Mnuchin, Secretary of the Treasury, and Craig S. Phillips Counselor to the Secretary, *A Financial System That Creates Economic Opportunities: Capital Markets: US Department of Treasury Report to President Donald J. Trump, Executive Order 13772 on Core Principles for Regulating the United States Financial System,* October 2017, p. 24, https://www.treasury.gov/press-center/press-releases/Documents/A-Financial-System-Capital-Markets-FINAL-FINAL.pdf.
4. https://www.law.cornell.edu/cfr/text/17/230.2516.
5. https://www.law.cornell.edu/cfr/text/17/230.500.
6. For an overview of exemptions from the Securities and Exchange Commission, see https://www.sec.gov/smallbusiness/exemptofferings. See also *Report to Congress: Access to Capital and Market Liquidity As Directed by the Explanatory Statement to the Consolidated Appropriations Act, 2016*

(P.L. 114-113) (Washington, DC: Securities and Exchange Commission, Division of Economic Risk Analysis, August 2017), https://www.sec.gov/files/access-to-capital-and-market-liquidity-study-dera-2017.pdf; Steven T. Mnuchin and Craig S. Phillips, *A Financial System That Creates Economic Opportunities: Capital Markets,* https://www.treasury.gov/press-center/press-releases/Documents/A-Financial-System-Capital-Markets-FINAL-FINAL.pdf.

7. Exemption for offerings not exceeding $5 million—Rule 504 of Regulation D, https://www.sec.gov/smallbusiness/exemptofferings/rule504. For more information, see Rule 504 of Regulation D: A Small Entity Compliance Guide for Issuers, https://www.sec.gov/divisions/corpfin/guidance/rule504-issuer-small-entity-compliance.html.
8. Ibid., https://www.sec.gov/smallbusiness/exemptofferings/rule504.
9. Exemption for private offerings, Regulation D, Rule 506b of Regulation D, https://www.sec.gov/smallbusiness/exemptofferings/rule506b.
10. https://www.sec.gov/smallbusiness/exemptofferings/rule506c.
11. "Global initial public offering activity during full year 2018 totaled US$200.2 billion, an 11% increase compared to last year and the strongest full year period for global IPOs since 2014. Proceeds from US IPO listings surpassed US$50 billion for the first time since full year 2014 . . ." http://dmi.thomsonreuters.com/Content/Files/4Q2018_Global_Equity_Capital_Markets_Review.pdf. Annual numbers of IPOs appear in this source: https://www.ey.com/Publication/vwLUAssets/ey-global-ipo-trends-report-q4-2018/$FILE/ey-global-ipo-trends-report-q4-2018.pdf.
12. The lender's *cost of funds* is the dollar cost of the interest paid or accrued either on funds acquired from various sources within a bank or on borrowed funds acquired from other banks. The *prime rate* is the "reference or base rate" that banks use to set the price or interest rate on many commercial loans and

some consumer loans. The *federal funds* rate is the rate banks charge. The overnight rate for LIBOR has ranged from as high as 6.65125 to as low as 0.08650 0 from 2001 to present, with a sustained low period from 2009 through 2016, according to the Federal Reserve Bank of St. Louis. https://fred.stlouisfed.org/series/USDONTD156N.

13. "Many borrowers also are turning to preferred equity over mezzanine, even though preferred equity is more expensive to the borrower. . . . Preferred equity has the edge because many preferred equity managers now are issuing evergreen securities that have no mandatory redemption date. By contrast, mezzanine debt generally matures in three years to five years." Arleen Jacobus, "Mezzanine Managers Losing Places at Table," Pensions and Investments, February 19, 2018.
14. As the US Financial Industry Regulatory Authority notes on its website, "Price and yield are inversely related: As the price of a bond goes up, its yield goes down, and vice versa." For more on the topic, see http://www.finra.org/investors/bond-yield-and-return. J.P. Morgan Chase offers this example: A £1,000 bond with a 3% coupon pays £30 in income each year (£1,000 (0.03). If the bond's price rises to £1,100, the yield falls to 2.73% (£30/£1,100). Thus, when price goes up, yield goes down—and vice versa. This is known as an inverse relationship. https://am.jpmorgan.com/blob-gim/1383243044660/83456/the-relationship-between-yields-and-prices.pdf.
15. Sunny Oh, "Junk Bonds—No Longer 2018's Darling—Flip to Red as the Corporate Debt Climate Deteriorates," November 19, 2018, https://www.marketwatch.com/story/junk-bonds-no-longer-2018s-darling-flip-to-red-as-the-corporate-debt-climate-deteriorates-2018-11-19.
16. For current examples of business development companies, see "9 Ways to Invest in Business Development Companies," by Jeff Reeves, Contributor, USA Today, June 28, 2018.
17. For more on employee funding, see https://www.esop.org.

18. "Family offices are getting more involved in venture capital and funding earlier stage deals than they have previously, according to new figures from Pitchbook, a private markets data provider." Alecia McElhaney, "The Hot Asset Class for Family Offices," *Institutional Investor,* July 10, 2018. See also Justin Abelow and Houlihan Lokey, "New Breed of Family Offices Disrupts Field, Upends Old Verities," PE Hub Network, February 26, 2018, https://www.pehub.com/2018/02/new-breed-family-offices-disrupts-field-upends-old-verities/#.
19. "Sovereign Wealth Funds Embrace Their Growing Ambitions," *New York Times,* October 8, 2018.
20. https://www.wsj.com/articles/private-equity-makes-leasing-planes-a-hot-commodity-1530715021.
21. *Financial Times* defines mezzanine funding as "a type of financing that combines debt and equity characteristics." http://lexicon.ft.com/Term?term=mezzanine-finance.
22. See Dr. Craig R. Everett, *2017 Private Capital Markets Report,* Pepperdine University, 2017, https://bschool.pepperdine.edu/about/people/faculty/appliedresearch/research/pcmsurvey/content/private-capital-markets-report-2017.pdf.
23. The Economic Growth, Regulatory Relief, and Consumer Protection Act of 2018 exempts smaller banks from compliance with the rule. See "Banking Policy Issues in the 116th Congress," Congressional Research Service, February 21, 2019, p. 608, https://fas.org/sgp/crs/misc/R45518.pdf.
24. See "Over-Allotment Option" at Westlaw, 2018, https://content.next.westlaw.com/Document/Ibb0a12aeef0511e28578f7ccc38dcbee/View/FullText.html?contextData=(sc.Default)&transitionType=Default&firstPage=true&bhcp=1.
25. https://www.sba.gov/sbic/general-information/program-overview.
26. https://www.federalreserve.gov/supervisionreg/srletters/sr1303a1.pdf.
27. The Fed supervises state-chartered banks that opt to be members of the Federal Reserve System, as well as bank

holding companies, thrift holding companies, and the nondepository institutions and subsidiaries of these institutions; and nonbank financial companies designated for enhanced supervision by the Financial Stability Oversight Council. The FDIC insures the deposits of all banks and thrifts that are approved for federal deposit insurance, and supervises state-chartered banks that are not part of the Fed system. The OCC supervises national banks and federal savings associations. Most banks are state-chartered, so the OCC has a relatively limited jurisdiction compared to the Fed and the FDIC.

28. https://www.law.cornell.edu/cfr/text/12/303.207. Note: The full definition ends with an exclusion as follows: "Loans and exposures to any obligor in which the total financing package, including all obligations held by all participants is $20 million or more, or such lower level as the FDIC may establish by order on a case-by-case basis, will be excluded from this definition."
29. https://www.bankingsupervision.europa.eu/ecb/pub/pdf/ssm.leveraged_transactions_guidance_201705.en.pdf.
30. The group develops standards for prudential banking that are followed by banks around the globe. The most recent set of standards is called Basel III, developed after the global financial crisis of 2008 and still being refined. (Previous Basel standards were published in 1988 [Basel I] and 2005 [Basel II]). (Basel standards address issues important to banks' internal financial structure, and do not set guidelines for transactional lending. In October 2017, the three major US bank regulators (Fed, FDIC, OCC) proposed a simplification of these rules that would enable banks to take on more leverage. https://www.fdic.gov/news/board/2017/2017-09-27-notice-dis-b-fr.pdf.
31. See Anand M. Vijh and Ke Yang, "The Acquisition Performance of S&P 500 Firms," which finds that "acquirer returns increase with the relative deal size, are *higher for cash deals* [and] decrease with cash flow." The study defines cash deals as "those financed with cash, liabilities, and newly issued notes," and stock deals as "those financed with acquirer stock that has full

voting rights or inferior voting rights." (p. 28). https://www.biz.uiowa.edu/faculty/avijh/S&P%20500%20Vijh%20and%20Yang.pdf.

32. For current investments see: http://www.kkr.com/businesses/kkr-portfolio. For an historical list of KKR investments, see http://www.kkr.com/historical-list-portfolio-companies.
33. Joshua Franklin, "U.S. Tax Curbs on Debt Deduction to Sting Buyout Barons," Reuters, December 21, 2017, https://www.reuters.com/article/us-usa-tax-privateequity/u-s-tax-curbs-on-debt-deduction-to-sting-buyout-barons-idUSKBN1EF1G5.
34. For the full text of the 2017 tax law, see http://docs.house.gov/billsthisweek/20171218/CRPT-115HRPT-466.pdf.
35. A history of the company appears at http://www.beatriceco.com/about_investor/.
36. http://corporate.parmalat.ca/our-brands/beatrice/.
37. Charlie Shannon, "How Will the New Lease Accounting Standards Impact Loan Covenants?" September 2016, "https://www.mossadams.com/articles/2016/september/lease-accounting-and-loan-covenantshttps://www.mossadams.com/articles/2016/september/lease-accounting-and-loan-covenants.
38. See "Four Things You Should Know About Life Insurance Company Financing," http://psrs.com/insights/four-things-you-should-know-about-life-insurance-company-financing/ and "Life Company Loans for Commercial Real Estate," https://www.commercialrealestate.loans/life-company-loans/.
39. Michael Milken is the financier who rediscovered and popularized junk bonds in the 1980s. Through him, his employer Drexel Burnham Lambert became famous—and then notorious. Meshulam "Rik" Riklis is CEO of Rapid American Corp. Their story is chronicled in Connie Bruck, *The Predators' Ball* (New York: Penguin Books, 1989).
40. High Yield Bond archives at LeveragedLoan.com, accessed January 1, 2018.
41. "Fitch Sees US Leveraged Loan, High-Yield Default Rates Near Decade Lows in 2019," October 4, 2018, https://www

.spglobal.com/marketintelligence/en/news-insights/trending/y14jnmvvwnbzbofrf9vrlq2. This prediction may be optimistic. Historically, the rate has been 4.17 percent, according to H. Peter Nesvold, Jeffrey M. Anapolsky, and Alexandra R. Lajoux, *The Art of Distressed M&A: Buying Selling, and Financing Troubled and Insolvent Companies* (McGraw-Hill Education, 2011), pp. 17–19.

42. For a recent case, consider *Weisfelner v. Blavatnik* (*In re Lyondell Chemical Company*), 2017 BL 131876 (Bankr. S.D.N.Y. Apr. 21, 2017), described here in "Lyondell Chemical: A Long and Winding Road for Creditors in Leveraged Transaction Cases," http://www.lawjournalnewsletters.com/sites/lawjournalnewsletters/2017/08/01/lyondell-chemical-a-long-and-winding-roadmap-for-creditors-in-leveraged-transaction-cases/?slreturn=20180001035850, and updated here: https://www.wsj.com/articles/judge-dismisses-lyondellbasell-creditors-clawback-lawsuit-1504655066.

CHAPTER 5

Structuring Transactions: General, Tax, and Accounting Considerations

INTRODUCTION

The structuring of a transaction—the determination of what legal and financial form it will take—is often the most challenging aspect of any deal. The range of available forms (asset sales, stock transfers, mergers of a variety of types, and so on), coupled with the variety of relevant factors (legal, accounting, tax, and so on), gives dealmakers both tools to use and traps to avoid as they respond to the many and often conflicting goals of buyers, sellers, investors, and lenders—not to mention taxing authorities.

This chapter can help managers determine the most efficient and desirable form of each transaction they plan. It will be particularly instrumental in structuring friendly transactions involving privately owned companies. (Issues unique to change of control in public companies, particularly hostile tender offers and proxy contests, are covered in Chapter 10.)

Although the first part of this chapter discusses general structuring factors, the final choice of transaction structure often depends on specific tax and accounting considerations. For example, structuring a transaction as an asset sale can enable a buyer to avoid assuming the financial and legal liabilities of the seller and inheriting any pending disputes about them. But in some industries, structuring a transaction as an asset sale may be impossibly impractical because of tax or accounting issues. It is

Exhibit 5-1 A Guide to US (Federal) and State Codes

NAME	ACRONYM	COVERS
Code of Federal Regulations	CFR	US rules and regulations
United States Code	USC	US laws (including laws in IRC)
Internal Revenue Code	IRC	US tax laws
Uniform Commercial Code	UCC	State laws impacting commerce

imperative to retain professional advisors for guidance in these matters. Tax and accounting pros know their way around the various regulations that can be involved in a transaction—including the United States Code (USC)[1] that codifies all US general and permanent laws, including the tax laws that are included in the USC's Title 26, known as the Internal Revenue Code (IRC). In addition, qualified professional advisors will be familiar with the Code of Federal Regulations (CFR) that codifies all rules and regulations under all these laws. (See Exhibit 5-1.)

A word to the wise: do not skip this chapter's sections on taxes and accounting simply out of fear that they may be arcane or complex. They are designed to accommodate both the neophyte and the old hand. Of particular importance in this edition of *The Art of M&A* is a more detailed discussion of tax issues triggered in the United States by the Tax Cuts and Jobs Act (TCJA) of 2017.[2] While the law left untouched most tax law provisions addressing M&A structuring,[3] some aspects of the new law do affect structural considerations. These aspects include the lowering of the maximum corporate tax rate to 21 percent, new limits on interest deductibility, a stricter limitation on deductibility of executive pay under 162(m), new rules on use of net operating losses (NOLs), a higher percentage for depreciation of newly acquired or constructed tangible property, and rules for treatment of foreign income.[4] This chapter concludes with a discussion of structuring matters unique to management buyouts, including special tax considerations affecting management compensation, employee benefits, and stock ownership. *One caveat:* All tax laws and accounting principles are subject to change. In some areas, the pace of change is glacial. In others, it can happen with lightning speed. Keep an eye out for all major changes in the tax law—they almost always affect merger taxation. And *always* consult with qualified tax and accounting professionals. (If dealing with a major accounting firm, remember that nearly every local office has an M&A specialist and sometimes a special department at headquarters. This also applies to law firms. Make sure your legal counsel has recent experience in the M&A area.)

GENERAL CONSIDERATIONS

When one company acquires another, what are the various forms that the transaction can take?

Three general forms can be used for the acquisition of a business: (1) a purchase of the assets of the business, (2) a purchase of the stock of the company to be acquired (aka target) owning the assets, and (3) a statutory merger of the buyer (or an affiliate) with the target. It is possible to combine several forms so that, for example, some assets of the business are purchased separately from the stock of the company that owns the rest of the assets, and a merger occurs immediately thereafter between the buyer and the acquired company. Or a transaction may involve the purchase of assets of one corporation and the stock of another, where both corporations are owned by the same seller.

STRUCTURING ASSET TRANSACTIONS

What happens in an asset transaction?

The target transfers all of the assets used in the business that is the subject of the sale. These include real estate, equipment, and inventory, as well as intangible assets such as contract rights, leases, patents, and trademarks. These might be all or only part of the assets owned by the selling company. The target executes the specific kinds of documents needed to transfer the specific assets, such as deeds, bills of sale, and assignments.

When is an asset transaction necessary or desirable?

Many times, the choice of an asset transaction is dictated by the fact that the sale involves only part of the business owned by the selling corporation. Asset sales are generally the only choice in the sale of a product line that has not been run as a subsidiary corporation with its own set of books and records.

In other cases, an asset deal is not necessary but is chosen because of its special advantages:

- Where the seller will realize a meaningful taxable gain from the sale (that is, where the "tax basis" of the assets in the acquired company is materially lower than the selling price), the buyer generally will obtain significant tax savings from structuring the transaction as an *asset* deal, thus stepping up the assets' basis to the purchase price. (An asset's tax basis, as explained more fully later in this chapter, is the value at which the taxpayer carries the asset on the tax balance sheet. An asset's basis is initially its historical cost to the taxpayer.)
- Conversely, if the seller will realize a tax loss, the buyer is generally better off inheriting the tax history of the business by doing a *stock* transaction, and thus keeping the old high basis.

Taxes tend to be a zero-sum game: what is best for the buyer might not be best for the seller, who might lose tax advantages by structuring the deal in favor of the buyer. This conflict can and should give rise to lively negotiations—and even an adjustment of price in favor of the conceding party. Concepts of stepped-up versus carryover tax basis will be discussed in greater detail later in this chapter.

As mentioned, as a legal matter, the buyer in an asset sale generally assumes only the liabilities that it specifically agrees to assume. This ability to pick and choose among the liabilities generally protects the buyer from undisclosed liabilities of the seller. Exceptions do apply, however.

In an asset purchase, will the buyer be able to avoid all liabilities that it doesn't expressly agree to assume?

The general rule is yes, but there are three general exceptions:

- Mere continuation (when the purchaser is basically the same company as the seller)

- A fraudulent transaction through which the seller is avoiding its liabilities[5]
- A consolidation or merger of the buyer or seller—by law (de jure) or in fact (de facto)

What is a de facto merger?

In certain jurisdictions, if a buyer buys an entire business and the shareholders of the seller become the shareholders of the buyer, even if the transaction is not classified as a merger, some courts may apply a doctrine known as the de facto merger doctrine that treats the transaction as a merger.[6] (In a merger transaction, the buyer takes on all of the seller's liabilities.) This is undesirable for the buyer because it increases the buyer's liabilities. (Note, however, that the de facto merger doctrine is generally not applicable in Delaware, where most major US corporations are incorporated.)

In addition to getting classified as a de facto merger, what other conditions might shift liabilities to an acquirer in an asset purchase?

At least three common conditions can cause liabilities to shift from the seller to the buyer.

- In certain jurisdictions, most notably California, the courts require the buyer of a manufacturing business to assume the tort liabilities for faulty products manufactured by the seller when it controls the business.
- Also, buyers cannot usually terminate a collective bargaining contract under any structural condition, including even an asset sale.
- Finally, the acquirer in an asset purchase may have to contend with the bulk sales law, set forth in the Uniform Commercial Code[7] (UCC), and applicable in one form or another in all jurisdictions in the United States except Louisiana.[8] If the

parties fail to comply with that law, and there is no available exemption, the buyer can be held responsible for certain liabilities of the seller.

What is the bulk sales law, and what effect does it have on asset transactions?

The bulk sales law, subject to variations among states, applies to transactions in which a company sells all or a major part of its material, supplies, merchandise, or other inventory to a buyer, effectively emptying out the seller's inventory. The law requires the buyer to give a certain amount of advance notice of the sale (typically at least 10 days' notice) to each of the seller's creditors. The buyer must also notify state tax authorities.[9] The notice must identify the seller and the buyer and state whether or not the debts of the seller will be paid as they become due. If orderly payment will not be made, further information must be disclosed. In addition, many states require the buyer to ensure that the seller uses proceeds from the sale to satisfy existing debts, and to hold in escrow an amount sufficient to pay any disputed debts.

Although the law's requirements are straightforward, its applicability to particular sellers and to specific transactions can be ambiguous. Also, states can amend or repeal this law as they so choose.[10] Acquirers should consult qualified legal counsel to ensure compliance when and if necessary.

What are the disadvantages of an asset sale?

First and foremost is its potentially high tax cost. An asset acquisition is frequently subject to double taxation (a corporate-level tax for the seller if it is a C corporation, as well as capital gains under certain scenarios.[11] The 2017 tax law did not change this basic fact, although it did make such double taxation less onerous by reducing the maximum corporate tax rate to 21 percent.[12]

Second, an asset transaction is usually more time consuming and significantly more costly than the alternatives because of legal, accounting, and regulatory complications, such as the complications from bulk sales laws previously mentioned. An asset transaction requires a legal transfer of each asset. In certain industries, this might not be feasible.

- For instance, in wholesale distribution, hundreds of exclusive distribution agreements might be in force, and the costs of preparing a large number of new contracts with manufacturers might be prohibitive.
- As another example, in the oil and gas industry, each pipeline requires numerous permits, and land rights can be complex, involving both surface and subsurface rights.
- Many industries involve real estate, and real estate transfers are often subject to significant state and local transfer and recordation taxes. Such transfers may also motivate local tax assessors to increase the assessment of the property and thereby significantly increase the real estate tax burden on the company. If the property is spread over numerous jurisdictions, different forms might be required for each jurisdiction.

Third, many leases might not be assignable without the consent of the other party to the transaction. Assuming the other party is willing to consent (and this is rare), you can expect this consent to exact a price. This can be true especially where the seller has leases providing rent below the then-prevailing rental rates. It is possible that consent might then be obtained only by agreeing to significant rent increases. The same is true of other types of contracts with terms that are favorable for the target. The loan agreements of the target must also be carefully reviewed to ensure that the asset transaction will not trigger default provisions.

Fourth, many businesses have local licenses needed to operate, and a transfer of ownership may involve lengthy hearings or other administrative delays as well as a risk of losing the license. Similarly, some businesses may be exempt from local ordinances such as zoning restrictions that include a "grandfather" clause exempting them. The asset transfer route can require the implementation of costly improvement programs to conform to such rules.

For these reasons, before plunging into an asset transfer, be sure to conduct an in-depth review of all of the legal arrangements of the business to determine whether such a deal is feasible. If problems are discovered, the parties must negotiate to decide who should bear the costs, such as the expense of obtaining consents. Usually, it is the buyer's responsibility, because the purchase price has been premised upon certain cash flows that might be impaired without the consents. Increasing rents or other fees can lower the value of the company and might require renegotiation of the purchase price.

Are any stockholder approvals required for an asset transaction?

Yes. Under Delaware law, for example, a sale of all or substantially all of the assets requires the approval of a majority (more than 50 percent) at a meeting of stockholders that have voting rights (common stockholders), who must receive 20 days' notice of the meeting. Also, in some cases, the company's charter and/or bylaws might even require a higher percentage (known as a supermajority provision).[13]

Where is a supermajority provision more likely to be found–in the charter or in the bylaws?

Such a provision is likely to be found in the bylaws document, rather than in the charter document. Charters, more technically known as articles of incorporation, are filed in the state of incorporation as a matter of public record. As such, they do not generally contain substantial detail beyond the name of the company, its location, the nature of its business, state of incorporation, shares issued, powers to amend bylaws or elect directors, and director and officer indemnification. Bylaws, which can run five times the length of charter documents, cover the rules a corporation sets for itself. They typically repeat charter language but provide more detail and outline additional areas. In general, neither document can be amended without shareholder approval.

Does an asset transaction always involve a cash payment to the seller?

No. Payment for the assets can be made in any form of consideration acceptable to the seller, including the stock of the buyer.

STRUCTURING STOCK TRANSACTIONS

What happens in a stock transaction?

The seller transfers its shares in the target to the buyer in exchange for an agreed-upon payment. Usually the transfer involves all company shares. Although the buyer may buy less than all of the stock in a public company (through a tender offer), this rarely occurs in purchases of private corporations. Such partial acquisitions of private companies usually happen only when some previous stockholder decides to stay (or become) active as a manager of the company and retains a stock interest.

When is a stock transaction appropriate?

A stock transaction is appropriate whenever the tax costs or other problems of doing an asset transaction make the asset transaction undesirable. As explained earlier, asset transfers may produce too onerous a tax cost in many major transactions. Apart from tax considerations, a stock deal might be necessary if the transfer of assets would require unobtainable or costly third-party consents, or where the size of the company makes an asset deal too inconvenient, time consuming, or costly.

Sellers frequently prefer a stock deal because the buyer will take the corporation's entire business including all of its liabilities. This may not offer as big an advantage as it appears, though, because in negotiating the acquisition agreement, the buyer will usually seek to be indemnified against any undisclosed liabilities. (See Chapter 7, on negotiating the acquisition agreement.)

Will a stock deal always avoid the problem of obtaining third-party consents that often arise in an asset transaction?

No. The pertinent documents must be carefully reviewed for "change of control" provisions. Many leases, for example, require consent if there is a change in the control of the tenant. Other contracts or local permits or leases might have similar requirements.

What are the disadvantages of a stock deal?

There are two major disadvantages:

- First, it might be more difficult to consummate the transaction if the company's stockholders are parties to a stockholder's agreement that gives them certain rights. Assuming that the buyer wants to acquire 100 percent of the company, it may have to enter into a contract with each of the selling stockholders, and any one of them might refuse to enter into the transaction or might refuse to close. The entire deal might hinge on one stockholder. Minority shareholder rights under states law may provide special protections in such cases.[14] As will be shown later in this chapter, the parties can achieve the same result as a stock transfer through a merger transaction and obviate the need for 100 percent agreement among the stockholders.
- The stock transaction lacks the tax basis step-up that occurs in an asset acquisition. Under Section 338 of the Internal Revenue Code (IRC), however, it is possible to have most stock transactions treated as asset acquisitions for federal income tax purposes. Under a so-called Section 338 election, the tax benefits can be achieved while avoiding the nontax pitfalls of an asset transaction.

STRUCTURING MERGER TRANSACTIONS

What happens in a merger transaction, and what is the difference between a reverse merger and a forward merger?

A *merger* is a transaction in which one corporation is legally absorbed into another, and the surviving corporation succeeds to all of the assets or liabilities of the absorbed corporation. There are no separate transfers for the assets or liabilities; the entire transfer occurs by operation of law when the certificate of merger is filed with the appropriate authorities of the state.

In a *forward merger,* the target merges into the buyer or a subsidiary of the buyer, and the target shareholders exchange their stock for the agreed-upon purchase price. When the transaction is complete, the buyer owns all the assets and liabilities of the target. For federal income tax purposes, such a transaction is treated as if the target sold its assets for the purchase price, and then made a liquidation distribution (that is, as if it liquidated the company and distributed the money to the target's shareholders). Where the consideration consists of stock in the buyer and other requirements are met, the merger may qualify as a tax-free reorganization.

In a *reverse merger,* the target absorbs the "buyer," in the form of a newly formed subsidiary of the buyer (called a reverse subsidiary merger). The buyer—as shareholder of the merging subsidiary in the reverse subsidiary merger—gets all the stock in the target, and the shareholders of the target receive the agreed-to consideration. For example, in an all-cash deal, the shareholders of the target will exchange their shares in the target for cash. At the end of the transaction, the old shareholders of the target are no longer shareholders, and the buyer, or shareholders of the buyer, own the target. For federal tax purposes, a reverse merger is often treated essentially like a stock deal.

What exactly is a subsidiary merger–and is it also characterized as forward or reverse?

A *subsidiary merger,* also called a *triangular merger,* is a merger where the buyer corporation incorporates an acquisition subsidiary that merges with the target. For a chart depicting types of subsidiary mergers (explained in more detail later in this answer) see Exhibit 5-2.

In a *forward subsidiary merger,* the target is merged into the acquisition subsidiary; in a *reverse subsidiary merger,* the acquisition subsidiary merges into the target. The key difference here is the fate of the target. In a forward subsidiary merger, the target ceases to exist. In a reverse subsidiary merger, the target continues to exist as an entity as a wholly owned subsidiary of the acquiring company—just as if the acquiring company had purchased all shares of stock of the target.[15] Generally speaking, in taxable deals, no one does forward subsidiary mergers; they are generally to be avoided. Forward subsidiary mergers are most often seen in the world of tax-free reorganizations.

Both kinds of subsidiary mergers offer the benefit of speed. Generally speaking, mergers must be approved by the stockholders of each corporation that is a party to the merger, but this requirement does not usually apply to a merger of a subsidiary into its parent or with an unrelated corporation.[16] Although state corporation laws typically require that the board of directors approve the transaction on behalf of the acquiring entity, such approval is not necessarily required from shareholders.

Another benefit of subsidiary mergers is legal segregation. After a subsidiary merger, the buyer owns the target's business in a subsidiary. This has the effect of keeping the businesses legally separate and not subjecting the assets of the parent to the liabilities of the acquired business.

Exhibit 5-2 Forward Subsidiary Merger (FSM) vs. Reverse Subsidiary Merger (RSM)

Forward Subsidiary Merger	**Reverse Subsidiary Merger**
Target merges into acquisition subsidiary	Acquisition subsidiary merges into target
Target ceases to exist	Target continues to exist
Asset transfer restrictions may apply	Asset transfer restrictions do not apply
Section 388 election not possible.	Section 338 election possible

Source: Alexandra R. Lajoux with Michael J. Kliegman, November 2018.

Although both forward and reverse forms of merger convey the target's assets to the buyer in some manner, the forward merger is considered more challenging because the acquirer, not the target, is the surviving entity.[17] (Remember, in a forward merger, the target ceases to exist.) In certain jurisdictions, the transfer of target assets to a new entity might violate lease and other contract restrictions the same way a direct asset transfer does. Similarly, in some jurisdictions, so-called recordation taxes might be due after a forward merger when the buyer seeks to record the deeds in its name to reflect the merger.

The reverse subsidiary merger form, by contrast, provides ease and avoids other contract restrictions because the target is the surviving corporation, albeit now a subsidiary of the buyer. Finally, the reverse subsidiary merger offers the special advantage of enabling the acquirer to make a Section 338 election, described earlier.

What steps must be taken to effect a merger?

Generally, the board of directors of each corporation that is a party to the merger must adopt a resolution approving a merger agreement. Shareholders owning a majority of the stock must also approve the transaction. In some cases, the corporate charter and/or bylaws might require a higher percentage for shareholder approval under a supermajority provision. The merger becomes effective upon the filing of a certificate of merger. Under Delaware law, the approval of the surviving corporation's stockholders is necessary unless its certificate of incorporation will not be amended by the merger and the shares of the survivor issued to the sellers comprise more than 20 percent of the outstanding shares of the survivor, among other exceptions.[18]

The agreement between buyer and seller in the case of a merger is essentially the same as in a stock or asset deal, except that the means of transferring the business will be the statutory merger as opposed to a stock or asset transfer.

What are the advantages of using a merger?

A merger transaction has many of the advantages of a stock deal: it is simple and will generally avoid the problems of an asset transaction.

In fact, a merger agreement is even simpler than a stock purchase agreement, because a merger agreement is executed only with the target company—not with its owners. Although mergers generally must be approved by a majority or some specified higher percentage of the stockholders, unlike an asset deal, it does not depend upon reaching an agreement with each individual stockholder. The stockholders who dissent from the transaction are forced to go along as a matter of law, subject to certain statutory protections against so-called squeeze-outs of minority investors who do not approve a transaction. Many state statutes confer *dissenters' rights* to protect minority shareholders in such situations. Such provisions say that in a share-for-share merger or acquisition voted in by a majority, the losers have a right to receive a cash payment for the fair value of their shares.

In a leveraged buyout that uses a merger structure, mergers are the best form of transaction from the secured lender's point of view. In this format, the lender lends to the surviving corporation (either directly or to a holding company that owns it[19]) and obtains a security interest in the assets of that corporation; the loan proceeds are used to satisfy the obligation to pay off the stockholders of the target.

Can a transaction combine a merger and a stock acquisition? If so, how does this work?

In certain cases, a stock deal is combined with a merger transaction in a two-step transaction. The first step is an acquisition of the target's stock (usually at least a majority); the second step is a merger with the target.

Such transactions are useful if the buyer wishes to pay a majority stockholder a premium for the control block, a payment that generally is permissible under most state laws. The buyer purchases that stock separately and then, in a second vote, a majority of stockholders approves a merger transaction. The selling shareholders exchange the balance of their stock (i.e., the shares the buyer did not obtain in the first step) in the merger for a lesser purchase price that reflects the absence of a control premium. For publicly held targets, offerors must conform to Rule 14d-10(a)(1) of the Securities Exchange Act of 1934, which says that offers to purchase a class of securities must be open to all holders of the securities in that class, and the consideration paid to any securityholder for securities tendered in the tender offer is the highest consideration paid to any other securityholder for securities tendered in the tender offer.[20]

Another use for two-step transactions arises where part of the consideration consists of notes or preferred stock in the survivor and there is a desire to limit the persons to whom the noncash payments are to be made. The first step would consist of a stock deal with certain of the stockholders where the consideration includes noncash payments. The second step would be an all-cash merger.

This might be important, for example, if there are many individual shareholders and the distribution of the securities to all of them would constitute a public offering that would require the filing of a registration statement under the securities laws. This also might be useful where some of the sellers want to encourage a positive vote of the stockholders by absorbing the risk of holding notes or equity in the target and allowing the other stockholders to receive the full purchase price in cash.

Two-step transactions are very common in public company acquisitions where the first step is the acquisition of a control block through a tender offer and the second step is a merger in which the minority is bought out. Tax treatment of step transactions varies depending on circumstances and policy changes over time.[21]

What is the most typical form for a leveraged buyout?

The buyer usually creates an acquisition vehicle solely for the purpose of merging with the acquired company. Usually, the acquisition vehicle does a reverse merger into the acquired company. If the buyer wants a holding company structure—that is, wants the acquired company to be a subsidiary of a holding company—it forms a holding company with an acquisition corporation subsidiary. After the merger, the holding company will own all of the stock of the acquired company, and the buyer will own all of the stock of the holding company. For an example of a leveraged buyout structure, see Exhibit 5-3.

The senior lender in such a transaction might prefer to have a transaction structured in a holding company arrangement. In such a structure, a holding company borrows money from a senior lender to purchase the

Exhibit 5-3 Anatomy of a Merger, Acquisition, and Buyout Transaction

In 2017, ClubCorp was acquired by investment funds affiliated with Apollo Global Management (Apollo funds).* This transaction involved a **merger**, an **acquisition**, and a **buyout**, all in one ownership transfer.

On July 9, 2017, ClubCorp filed a Form 8-K filing with the Securities and Exchange Commission disclosing that it was party to an "Agreement and Plan of Merger" involving Constellation Club Parent, Inc., a Delaware corporation ("Parent"); Constellation Merger Sub Inc., a Nevada corporation and a wholly owned subsidiary of Parent ("Merger Sub"); and the Company, after which the Merger Sub would merge with and into the Company, with the Company surviving as a wholly owned subsidiary of Parent."† Apollo used an investment vehicle to effect the change of ownership via a **merger** that resulted in ClubCorp being privately owned.

Money changed hands through an **acquisition**. On September 15, ClubCorp shareholders approved the sale of their shares for $17.12 per share (a premium of more than 30 percent) to the Apollo affiliate, the acquirer of the shares.‡ As part of the deal, the Apollo affiliate also made a tender offer to buy notes issued by ClubCorp.§

As a result of the merger via investment vehicle, and acquisition via tender offer, ClubCorp is now a private company. Because its shares were bought out from the public, this is also referred to as a buyout transaction.

* https://globenewswire.com/news-release/2017/07/09/1041784/0/en/ClubCorp-Enters-into-a-Definitive-Agreement-to-be-Acquired-by-Certain-Investment-Funds-Affiliated-with-Apollo-Global-Management-in-an-All-Cash-Transaction-Valued-at-1-1-Billion.html

† https://www.sec.gov/Archives/edgar/data/1577095/000157709517000103/holdings-20170707x8xk.htm

‡ https://globenewswire.com/news-release/2017/09/15/1123427/0/en/ClubCorp-Stockholders-Approve-Acquisition-By-An-Affiliate-of-Certain-Funds-Managed-By-Affiliates-of-Apollo-Global-Management-LLC.html

§ https://www.businesswire.com/news/home/20170725006631/en/Constellation-Merger-Announces-Tender-Offer-Consent-Solicitation

stock of the acquired corporation. The senior lender obtains a senior security interest in the stock of the acquired company, and if there are loan defaults, the lender can foreclose and sell the stock to pay off the debt. For this structure to succeed, all the layers of financing must be made at the holding company level.

In addition, the senior lender in a holding company structure will often ask for a secured guarantee from the acquired corporation, notwithstanding the fraudulent conveyance risks. Junior lenders often ask for a backup guarantee in such a case. This adds a layer of complexity to the intercreditor negotiations, and to the structure of financing and refinancing.

What is the role of federal and state securities laws in acquisition structuring?

State securities laws tend to have their greatest impact when the acquired corporation is publicly traded. But these laws also affect the structure of corporate acquisitions of private companies. When a buyer issues consideration other than cash—say, notes, stock, and/or warrants—or where the merger agreement provides that the stockholders of the target will receive noncash payment in exchange for their stock, the noncash consideration will almost certainly be classifiable as a security for federal and state securities law purposes.[22]

When the sellers receive securities in connection with a merger or a sale of assets requiring approval of the acquired corporation's stockholders (because securities will be distributed to them), this is considered to be an offer to sell securities under Rule 145.[23] If the offer constitutes a public offering, the transaction might not take place unless there is a registration statement that has been declared effective under the Securities Act. Rule 145 would apply, for example:

- Where a buyer uses a reverse merger and where the acquired company survives as a subsidiary of the buyer, and the acquired company's stockholders receive notes or preferred stock or warrants of the acquired company or of the buyer (if the buyer is a corporation)
- Where the buyer sets up a corporation that buys the stock of the acquiree in exchange for cash and notes or other securities of the corporation

What is a private placement?

A *private placement* is a transaction in which securities are offered and sold in reliance on an exemption from the registration requirements under federal and state securities laws. Typically, the entity selling its securities (the *issuer*) will rely on the exemption from registration provided by Rules 501 to 508 of Regulation D of the Securities Act of 1933. The registration procedure requires the preparation and filing of documents that provide detailed information about the issuer, the offering, and the securities being sold. Rules 501 through 503 set the ground rules, followed by exemptions under Rule 504 (for transactions of $5 million or under), Rule 506 (limited offerings), and other general exemptions.[24]

In a private placement, a brief notice of sale on federal Form D must be filed with the SEC for informational purposes. There is, however, no federal review or comment process for a Regulation D private placement.

Recent changes to Regulation D broadened the availability of the exemption from registration by permitting up to 35 nonaccredited investors to participate in a Regulation D private placement and an unlimited number of accredited investors. An *accredited investor* is defined under Rule 501(a) of Regulation D to include wealthy individuals, entities with substantial net worth, certain institutional investors, and executive officers and directors of the issuer.[25] Anyone who does not fit within the definition of *accredited* is considered nonaccredited.

Suppose participants in a private placement want to sell the stock they bought?

Rule 144 of the Securities Act of 1933 allows public resale of restricted and control securities (including so-called Regulation D securities) if a number of conditions are met—such as holding the securities for at least six months, in some cases.[26] Filing with the SEC is required prior to selling restricted and control stock, and the number of shares that may be sold is limited. Rule 144A is an additional safe harbor for resale of certain restricted securities to "qualified institutional buyers."[27] For other exemptions, such as Rule 506 of Regulation D, a company may sell its securities to any accredited investor.

GENERAL ACCOUNTING CONSIDERATIONS

How do acquirers account for their acquisitions under US generally accepted accounting principles (US GAAP)?

US GAAP require a method known as the acquisition method. The relevant principles are codified by the Financial Accounting Standards Board as Accounting Standards Codification (ASC) Topics under several types of "broad transactions."[28] These include business combinations (ASC Topic 805) and consolidation (ASC Topic 810/812).[29]

ASC Topic 805 describes steps to use for the acquisition method of accounting for a business combination:[30]

- Step 1: Identifying the acquirer—the entity that attains control of the target.
- Step 2: Determining the acquisition date—generally the closing unless agreements state otherwise.
- Step 3: Recognizing and measuring the identifiable assets acquired, the liabilities assumed, and any noncontrolling interest in the target.
- Step 4: Recognizing and measuring goodwill or, conversely, gain from a bargain purchase. (Goodwill is recorded when the net amount of assets acquired, liabilities assumed, and noncontrolling interest is lower than the total consideration paid; conversely, a bargain purchase occurs when those values exceed total consideration paid.

The rules for business combinations apply only when a *business* is purchased, not when mere assets are purchased. The FASB defines a business as one or more inputs (such as human or intellectual capital or raw materials) that undergo a process to produce an output.[31] For such acquisitions, additional FASB guidance—such as standards on consolidation, fair value measurement (ASC Topic 820),[32] or intangibles (ASC Topic 350)[33]—may also apply. Many audit firms and financial educators have explained accounting rules in simple language. The following updates our original text with help from these resources.[34]

ALLOCATING THE PRICE OF A TRANSACTION FOR ACCOUNTING PURPOSES

An important step in accounting for a transaction (after identifying the acquirer and determining the acquisition date) is to allocate the purchase price. This is done by valuing the individual assets acquired and liabilities assumed, for example:

- Net working capital
- Tangible assets (personal property and real property)
- Identifiable intangible assets/liabilities
- Liabilities assumed (e.g., assumed debt, contingent consideration, noncontrolling interests)
- Goodwill (calculated as the unallocated portion)

Acquirers then allocate the total amount of consideration to these categories, including goodwill. Companies then describe these allocations in their annual reports to shareholders. (For an example, see Exhibit 5-4.)

Fair value measurements of these items must be made as of a certain date. For M&A accounting that is the day on which the acquirer obtains control of the target—typically the date of closing—ideally at the end of the month.[35] (See Chapter 8.) Any deferred costs (such as contingency payments if probable and measurable) are also reported at fair value by discounting the amounts payable to their present value at the date of acquisition, including any applicable premium or discount.

DIFFERENCE BETWEEN ACCOUNTING AND TAX TREATMENTS

Accounting treatment differs from tax treatment in many respects. For example, when computing purchase price for the purposes of financial reporting, the acquirer includes deferred taxes, accrued liabilities, and

Exhibit 5-4 Description of Acquisition Allocation from Emcor Group, Inc.

ACQUISITIONS OF BUSINESSES

On January 4, 2017, March 1, 2017, and November 1, 2017, we acquired three companies for a total consideration of $109.3 million. One company provides fire protection and alarm services primarily in the Southern region of the United States. The second company provides millwright services for manufacturing companies throughout the United States. Both of their results have been included in our United States mechanical construction and facilities services segment. The third company provides mobile mechanical services within the Western region of the United States, and its results have been included in our United States building services segment. In connection with these acquisitions, we acquired working capital of $9.8 million and other net assets of $2.3 million and have preliminarily ascribed $40.6 million to goodwill and $56.6 million to identifiable intangible assets. We expect that all of the acquired goodwill will be deductible for tax purposes. The purchase price allocations for the businesses acquired in March and November of 2017 are still preliminary and subject to change during their respective measurement periods. The purchase price allocation for the business acquired in January 2017 has been finalized during the fourth quarter of 2017 with an insignificant impact. The acquisition of these businesses was accounted for by the acquisition method, and the prices paid for them have been allocated to their respective assets and liabilities, based upon the estimated fair value of their assets and liabilities at the dates of their respective acquisitions by us.

Source: Emcor Group, Inc. 10-K statement for 2017.

contingent consideration and liabilities, but not transaction costs. Tax reporting is very different; it includes some transaction costs but not the other costs, except for some accrued liabilities. And, of course, there is only purchase price allocation for tax if there is an actual or deemed asset purchase. (See Exhibit 5-5.)

Digging a little deeper, in tax reporting, why are contingent consideration and liabilities included?

Liabilities in each case are treated as part of the consideration paid, and contingent consideration is included as purchase price paid for tax reporting purposes. The taxpayer waits until the full amount is paid rather than up front, generally.

Exhibit 5-5 Differences in the Purchase Price Computation

Topic	Financial Reporting	Tax Reporting
Transaction Costs	Not included	Includes certain costs
Deferred Taxes	Included	Not included
Accrued Liabilities	Includes all	Includes some
Contingent Consideration and Liabilities	Included and measured at fair value	Included
Debt Measurement	Measured at fair value	Measured at face value

How should transaction costs be recorded under GAAP and reported for tax purposes?

GAAP and tax treatment differ. Costs associated with an acquisition can be divided into three categories:[36]

- Direct costs of the transaction, which may include due diligence services, accountants, attorneys, investment bankers, and so on.
  —Accounting treatment: Transaction costs are not considered part of the fair value exchanged between the buyer and seller and are therefore expensed as incurred.
  —Tax treatment: The tax treatment of these costs varies. The timing and nature of the expenditure impact the treatment. Costs incurred during the investigative phase of an engagement but before a letter of intent is signed may be currently deductible, while costs incurred to pursue the transaction after a letter of intent is signed are generally capitalized. These capitalized costs are added to the tax basis of the assets and typically amortized of the life of the underlying asset(s).
- Financing costs or debt issuance costs, which may need to be segregated from direct transaction costs, include the cost to issue debt that is included in the opening balance sheet.

—Accounting treatment: Debt issuance costs are not expensed. These costs are "deferred" or netted against the proceeds of the debt liability and amortized of the term of debt.
—Tax treatment: Tax treatment is generally the same as the book treatment.

- Equity or stock issuance costs relate to fees paid to obtaining new capital by issuing stock that is classified as permanent equity.
  —Accounting treatment: Stock issuance costs should be considered a reduction of the related proceeds and recorded net with the amount received in equity. These costs are not amortized.
  —Tax treatment: Tax treatment is generally the same as the book treatment.

The transaction costs that must be expensed under GAAP, according to ASC Topic 805,[37] include:

- Finders fees
- Accounting, advisory, legal, valuation, and other professional services
- General administrative costs including the cost of maintaining and internal M&A department

Are transaction costs tax deductible?

This is an interesting question that highlights the basic difference between treating an item as an expense on the income statement and treating it as a capital expenditure (on an asset) on the balance sheet. (An item is capitalized when it is recorded as an asset, rather than an expense.)

Under GAAP, Topic 805, as mentioned, transaction costs are expensed. But the IRS requires taxpayers to capitalize amounts paid to facilitate a business acquisition or reorganization transaction.[38]

An amount paid to integrate the business operations of the taxpayer with the business operations of another may be expensed, as it is *not* considered a facilitative cost regardless of when the integration activities occur. Employee compensation and overhead costs may be expensed and, furthermore, the expenses may be deducted from the company's tax return as deductible, nonfacilitative costs. This can include any transaction bonuses directly related to the transaction.

Examples of deductible integration costs include costs to:

- Relocate personnel and equipment
- Pay severance benefits to terminated employees
- Integrate records and information systems
- Prepare new financial statements for the combined entity
- Reduce redundancies in the combined business operations

TAX CONSIDERATIONS

What are the principal goals of tax planning for a merger, acquisition, or divestiture?

From the purchaser's point of view, the principal goal of tax planning is to minimize, on a present-value basis, the total tax costs of not only acquiring, but also operating, and even selling the acquired corporation or its assets. In addition, effective tax planning provides various safeguards to protect the parties from the risks of potential changes in circumstance or in the tax laws. Moreover, the purchaser should attempt to minimize the tax costs of the transaction to the seller in order to gain advantage as a bidder. (Of course, to realize this advantage, the buyer needs to point out the advantages to the seller, who may not be familiar with tax implications of particular structures.)

From the seller's point of view, the principal goal of tax planning is to maximize, on a present-value basis, the after-tax proceeds from the sale of the acquired corporation or its assets. This tax planning includes, among other things, deciding how to structure the transaction, developing techniques to provide tax benefits to a potential buyer at little or no tax cost to the seller, and structuring the receipt of tax-deferred consideration from the buyer.

Are the tax planning goals of the buyer generally consistent with those of the seller?

No. More often than not, the most advantageous tax plan for the buyer is the least advantageous plan for the seller. The phrase win-win usually cannot apply. For example, the tax benefit of a high basis in the assets of the acquired corporation might be available to the purchaser only at a significant tax cost to the seller. (For more on basis, see the next section.) But buyers rarely if ever pursue tax benefits at the seller's expense, because the immediate and prospective tax costs of a transaction are likely to affect the price. Generally, the parties will structure the transaction to minimize the aggregate tax costs of the seller and buyer, and allocate the tax burden between them through an adjustment in price.

What tax issues typically arise in an acquisition or divestiture?

There is no definitive checklist of tax issues that might arise in every acquisition or divestiture. The specific tax considerations for a transaction depend upon the facts and circumstances of that particular deal. Certain tax terms and issues, however, many of which are interrelated, are more common than others:

- To have a useful impact on tax matters, participants in a transaction must grasp certain concepts, such as *earnings and profits* or *distribution,* discussed later in this chapter.
- A primary issue is the *basic structure of the transaction:* whether the transfer is devised as a stock acquisition or an asset acquisition (explained earlier), and whether the transaction can be structured as a tax-free reorganization or if the transfer will be immediately taxable. As mentioned earlier, the optimal structure is generally the one that maximizes the aggregate tax benefits and minimizes the aggregate tax costs of the transaction to the acquired corporation, the seller, and the buyer.

- Another initial question to be resolved in many acquisitions is the *choice of entity* issue: whether the operating entity will be a C corporation, an S corporation, a general or limited partnership, a limited liability company (LLC), or a trust.
- The tax implications of the *financing* (cash, debt, and/or equity) must also be analyzed.
- The issue of *management participation and compensation* should also be addressed. Top-level managers of the company being acquired might be invited to purchase stock, or they might be granted stock options, stock appreciation rights, bonuses, or some other form of incentive compensation. Different structures of management participation can create vastly different tax results.
- In addition, tax advisors (particularly for the purchaser) should examine the *tax effects* that the proposed structure will have on the postacquisition operations of the company. For example, consideration should generally be given to NOLs, amortization of intangible assets (other than goodwill), planned asset dispositions, elections of taxable year and accounting methods, integration of the company's accounting methods into the buyer's existing operations, foreign tax credits, and the interrelationships among the differing tax systems of the countries in which the combining companies do business.
- Tax advisors should also give attention to other matters, including the effects of *state tax laws,* the tax consequences of future *distributions* of the acquired company's earnings, and the ultimate *disposition* of the acquired company or its assets.

These issues should be analyzed with an eye on pending and recent M/A/B-related tax legislation, keeping retroactivity in mind.

Does the Internal Revenue Service (IRS) play a direct role in the review or approval of business acquisitions?

Generally speaking, no. Advance approval from the IRS is not required before consummating an acquisition, divestiture, or reorganization. Ordinarily, the IRS will not have occasion to review a transaction unless and until an agent audits the tax return of one of the participants.

An important and often useful exception to this rule is that the parties to a transaction can often obtain a private letter ruling issued by the National Office of the IRS. Such a ruling states the agency's position with respect to the issue raised and is generally binding on the IRS. Requesting such a ruling is a serious business and should never be undertaken without expert legal help.

BASIC TAX CONCEPTS AND DEFINITIONS

What is basis?

A taxpayer's basis in an asset is the value at which the taxpayer carries the asset on its tax balance sheet. An asset's basis is initially its historical cost to the taxpayer. This *initial basis* is subsequently increased by capital expenditures and decreased by depreciation, amortization, and other charges, becoming the taxpayer's adjusted basis in the asset.[39] Upon the sale or exchange of the asset, gain or loss for tax purposes is measured by the difference between the amount realized for the asset and its adjusted basis.

The basis of the asset represents, in effect, the amount at which the cost of the asset may be recovered free of tax through depreciation deductions and adjustments to gain or loss upon disposition.

What are earnings and profits?

The phrase *earnings and profits* is a term of art in IRC. For financial reporting purposes, the amount of a corporation's earnings and profits is roughly equivalent to a corporation's net income and retained earnings as distinguished from current or accumulated taxable income. The primary purpose of the earnings and profits concept is to measure the capacity of a corporation to distribute a taxable dividend. If the IRS believes that a corporation, by virtue of its current and accumulated earnings and profits, can pay a taxable dividend, it may view certain nonliquidating distributions as dividends and tax them as such—even if the corporation does not (and never has) issued a dividend.

What is a distribution?

A *corporate distribution* means an actual or constructive transfer of cash or other property (with certain exceptions) by a corporation to a shareholder acting in the capacity of a shareholder. (The phrase, "shareholder acting in the capacity of a shareholder" is admittedly a mouthful, but it essentially means that the shareholder receives the payment because of the status as an owner of the corporation.) Rules for ordinary nonliquidating distributions are set under Section 301[40] of the US Code, a consolidation and codification by subject matter of the general and permanent laws of the United States.[41] For tax purposes, a transfer of property to a shareholder acting in the capacity of an employee or lender, in contrast, is not a corporate distribution.

What is a liquidation?

Corporate liquidation occurs when a corporation ceases to be a going concern. At this point, its actions are limited to winding up its affairs, paying its debts, and distributing its remaining assets to its shareholders. A liquidation for tax purposes may be completed prior to the actual dissolution of the corporation under state law.

What is a liquidating distribution?

A *liquidating distribution* is generally a distribution (or one of a series of distributions) made by a liquidating corporation in accordance with a plan of complete liquidation.

What is a nonliquidating distribution?

A *nonliquidating distribution* is any distribution by a corporation to a shareholder that is not a liquidating distribution. A nonliquidating distribution is generally either a dividend or a distribution in redemption of some (but not all) of the corporation's outstanding stock.

What are the tax consequences to corporations of distributions of property to their shareholders?

The taxation of corporate distributions involves myriad complex rules, many with exceptions and qualifications. In general, however, the tax consequences to corporations of distributions of property depend upon three factors: (1) whether the property distributed is cash or property other than cash, (2) whether the recipient shareholder is an affiliated corporation, and (3) whether the distribution is a liquidating or nonliquidating distribution.

Distributions of cash, both liquidating and nonliquidating, generally have no tax consequences to the distributing corporation, except that the amount distributed reduces the corporation's earnings and profits.

Distributions of appreciated property, both liquidating and nonliquidating, generally trigger the recognition of gain to the distributing corporation to the extent of the appreciation in the asset.

What is an affiliated group of corporations?

An *affiliated group of corporations* consists of two or more member corporations where the parent corporation controls, directly or indirectly, the stock of each of the subsidiary corporations. More precisely, the parent corporation must generally own a certain percent (usually 80 percent) of the voting power and equity value of at least one of the subsidiary corporations. Other members of the group have similar ownership levels in the other subsidiaries. Certain corporations, such as foreign corporations, are not permitted to be members of an affiliated group.

What is a consolidated federal income tax return?

It is a single federal income tax return made by an affiliated group of corporations in lieu of a separate return for each member of the group. Subsidiaries consent to such treatment by filing a Form 1122 to the IRS.[42]

What are the advantages of filing consolidated federal income tax returns?

The principal advantages of a consolidated return are as follows:

- Losses incurred by one member of the group may be used to offset the taxable income of another member.
- The tax consequences of many intragroup transactions are either deferred or wholly eliminated.
- Earnings of the subsidiary corporations are reflected in the parent's basis in the stock of the subsidiary, so that such earnings are not taxed again on the sale of such stock by the parent.

Is there such a thing as a consolidated state income tax return?

Yes, but not all states allow an affiliated group of corporations to file a combined (consolidated) tax return. Some states do not allow combined returns at all; others allow them only in limited circumstances.

What is a tax year?

Every entity and individual that is required to file a tax return must do so on the basis of an annual accounting period. For individuals, the annual accounting period is almost always the calendar year. For other entities, however, the tax accounting period may be either a calendar year or a fiscal year ending on the last day of a month other than December. An entity's tax year need not coincide with its fiscal year for purposes of financial accounting. Extensive rules govern the selection of tax years other than calendar years by C corporations, S corporations, LLCs, partnerships, and trusts.

What is the current US federal income tax rate structure for corporations?

The federal tax rate is 21 percent for corporate income tax. In addition, there are state taxes. Most (44 of the 50) US states levy corporate income taxes, ranging from 3 percent in North Carolina to 12 percent in Iowa. The average state corporate income tax rate (weighted by population) is 6 percent, according to the Tax Foundation, a nonprofit tax policy think tank.[43]

The 2017 tax law also set a new 20 percent deduction for the business income of some pass-through entities, sole proprietorships, partnerships, and S corporations, subject to various restrictions.[44] Professional service firms, such as law and accounting firms, may qualify for the deduction if owners are under an income threshold.[45] These new rules could be adjusted by subsequent legislation or clarified through guidance by the Treasury Department and the IRS.

Is the distinction between capital gains and ordinary income still relevant in tax planning?

Yes. The 2017 tax law retained the myriad rules and complexities in the tax code pertaining to capital gains and losses.[46] While at any given time, it is typical for members of Congress to propose bills to lower the capital gains tax,[47] it currently remains bracketed at 0, 15, and 20 percent.[48] More important for tax planning is that the IRC, including new provisions from the 2017 tax law, retains various limitations on the use of long-term capital losses to offset ordinary income. So M/A/B planners must still pay attention to the characterization of gains or losses as long-term capital versus ordinary. (Short-term capital losses are taxed the same as ordinary income, which can be taxed up to 37 percent.)

What about the tax on dividends?

The IRS considers dividends to be income, so taxpayers generally pay tax on them, even if the taxpayer reinvests them. There are two kinds of dividends, ordinary and qualified. The dividend tax rate that the taxpayer pays on ordinary dividends is the same as his or her regular income tax rate. Qualified dividends are taxed at the capital gains rates, which are generally lower.

What is the significance of the relationship between the corporate and individual tax rates?

Corporations can be used to accumulate profits when the tax rate on the income of corporations is less than the tax rate on the income of individuals. (Offsetting this benefit is the double tax on corporate earnings—paid once by the company and then by the stockholders receiving the company's dividends.) Conversely, noncorporate pass-through entities can be used to store profits when the tax rate on the income of corporations is greater than the tax rate on the income of individuals.

How does capital gains tax fit in?

A shareholder's tax on the sale or liquidation of interest in the corporation is determined at preferential capital gains rates (long-term capital gains rate).

Is the tax treatment different for debt versus equity?

Yes. Some debt interest may be deductible for tax purposes, but the TCJA and subsequent IRS pronouncements have put limits on such deductions.[49] However, dividends paid on common stock are not deductible in calculating income for tax purposes.

How does the double tax on corporate earnings work?

The IRC sets forth a dual system of taxation with respect to the earnings of corporations. Under this system, a corporation is taxed as a separate entity, unaffected by the tax characteristics of its shareholders. The corporation's shareholders are subject to tax on their income from the corporation if and when corporate earnings are distributed to them in any form.

What are the practical consequences of the dual system of corporate taxation?

The primary consequence of the dual system of taxation is that corporate earnings are generally taxed twice—first at the corporate level and again at the shareholder level when and if there are dividends or other distributions. The shareholder-level tax may be deferred but not eliminated when the corporation retains its earnings rather than paying it out in dividends. Under some circumstances, the shareholders may have to pay a second level of tax when they sell their interests in the corporation.

Leverage can reduce the negative effect of double taxation of corporations when the borrower can deduct part of the interest payment, as mentioned earlier.

It is very important to remember, however, that the IRS might take the position that a purported debt is actually equity, as discussed later in this chapter.

What is the alternative minimum tax, or AMT?

The alternative minimum tax was enacted in 1969 to curb exploitation of deductions and preferences by certain high-income individuals and corporations. In later tax legislation, Congress amended the minimum tax provisions and created a rather severe regime of alternative minimum tax, particularly for corporations. The AMT for corporations was eliminated by the TCJA; the rate for individuals is determined by computing taxable income under the regular method (with certain adjustments), and adding back certain deductions or "preferences" to obtain AMT income. The AMT rate for individuals or for corporations is applied to this amount."

The taxpayer is required to pay the greater of the regular tax or the AMT.

BASIC TAX STRUCTURE: TAXABLE TRANSACTIONS

How does an asset acquisition for tax purposes differ from a stock acquisition for tax purposes?

The basis a purchaser takes in the assets acquired is the primary distinction between an *asset acquisition* and a *stock acquisition* for tax purposes. When a purchaser directly acquires the assets of another corporation, and the acquired company is subject to tax on the sale or exchange of the assets, the basis of the assets to the purchaser is their cost. This is called *cost* or *stepped-up basis.* When a purchaser indirectly acquires the assets of another corporation through the acquisition of stock, the basis of the assets in the possession of the corporation is generally not affected. This is called *carryover basis* because the basis of an asset in the acquired corporation carries over on the change of stock ownership.

With the exception of a stock acquisition governed by the provisions of Section 338 of the IRC, the acquisition of all or part of the stock of a corporation does not alter the bases of the assets owned by the corporation. (In a Section 338 transaction—which is an indirect asset acquisition—the acquisition's cost basis in each asset is generally its fair market value.) With the exception of an asset acquisition governed by the IRC's tax-free reorganization provisions, the acquisition of the assets of a corporation will produce a cost basis to the purchaser.

A cost basis transaction is, therefore, often referred to as an *asset acquisition for tax purposes* (or as an *asset acquisition,* for short), and a carryover basis transaction is often referred to as a *stock acquisition for tax purposes* (or a *stock acquisition,* for short). Neither of these terms necessarily reflects the actual, legal structure of the transaction.

What types of transactions are carryover basis, or stock, transactions?

As a general rule, a carryover basis, or stock, acquisition includes any transaction where the stock or assets of the acquired corporation are acquired by the purchaser, and the bases of the assets of the acquired company are not increased or decreased on the change of ownership. There are several types of stock or carryover basis transactions. The direct purchase of the acquired corporation stock in exchange for cash and debt is the most straightforward stock acquisition. Another transaction that is treated as a sale of stock for tax purposes is the merger of the acquiring corporation into the acquired corporation—a reverse merger—where the shareholders of the acquired corporation relinquish their shares in exchange for cash or debt in a fully taxable transaction. Another common stock transaction is the purchase of the stock or assets of the acquired corporation in a transaction free of tax to its exchanging shareholders.

What types of transactions are cost basis, or asset, transactions?

As a general rule, a cost basis, or asset, acquisition includes any transaction where the preacquisition gains and losses inherent in the assets acquired are triggered and recognized by the acquired corporation. There are several types of cost basis transactions. The direct purchase of the assets from the acquired corporation in exchange for cash or indebtedness is the quintessential asset acquisition. Another common asset transaction is the statutory merger of the acquired corporation into an acquiring corporation—a forward cash merger—where the shareholders of the acquired corporation exchange their shares for cash or other property in a fully taxable transaction. In certain circumstances, a corporation may acquire the stock of another corporation and elect under Section 338 of the IRC to treat the stock acquisition, for tax purposes, as an asset acquisition.

What is the significance to the purchaser of the basis of the assets in the acquired corporation?

The basis of the assets in an acquired corporation may have a significant and continuing effect on the tax liabilities and, therefore, the cash flow of either the purchaser or the acquired corporation. The basis of an asset represents the extent to which the asset may be depreciated or amortized (if at all), thereby generating noncash reductions of taxable income. Basis also represents the extent to which the consideration received in a taxable sale or exchange of an asset may be received by the seller free of tax.

What is the prospective cost basis of an asset to the purchaser?

The *prospective cost basis* of an asset to the purchaser is the price that it will pay for the asset, directly or indirectly, which is presumed to be its fair market value.

What is the prospective carryover basis of an asset to the purchaser?

The prospective carryover basis of an asset to the purchaser is simply the adjusted basis of the asset in the possession of the acquired corporation prior to its acquisition. As explained previously, the adjusted basis of an asset is generally its historical or initial cost, reduced or adjusted by subsequent depreciation or amortization deductions.

What is meant by stepped-up basis?

Where the basis of an asset is increased from the acquired corporation's lower initial basis (or adjusted basis, if different) to a basis determined by a purchaser's cost or fair market value, the basis of the asset is said to have been *stepped up.* The term may refer, however, to any transaction in which the basis of an asset is increased. In most asset, or cost basis, transactions, the basis of the assets of the acquired corporation is stepped up to the purchaser's cost. An acquisition in which the basis of the assets of the target corporation is increased is referred to as a step-up transaction.

Who benefits from a cost (stepped-up) basis?

Generally, the buyer. High tax basis in an asset is always more beneficial to its owner than low basis. The higher the basis, the greater the depreciation or amortization deductions (if allowable), and the lower the gain (or the greater the loss) on the subsequent disposition of the asset. An increase in these deductions and losses will reduce the tax liabilities of the purchaser or the acquired corporation during the holding period of the assets, thereby increasing after-tax cash flow. For the same reasons, a high basis in the acquired corporation's assets will enhance their value to a potential carryover basis purchaser.

The purchase of another company should generally be structured to maximize the basis of the assets of the acquired corporation. If a purchaser's prospective cost basis in the assets of the acquired corporation exceeds its prospective carryover basis, an asset acquisition or step-up transaction is generally more beneficial to the purchaser than a stock acquisition. If a purchaser's prospective carryover basis exceeds its prospective cost basis in the assets of the acquired corporation, a stock acquisition is generally more beneficial to the purchaser than an asset, or cost basis, acquisition.

The primary exceptions to this general rule are the situations where (1) the purchaser would acquire beneficial tax attributes—NOLs, tax credits, or accounting methods—in a carryover basis transaction that would be lost in a step-up transaction, and (2) the value of such tax attributes to the purchaser exceeds the value of the stepped-up basis in the acquired corporation's assets that it would have obtained in a cost basis transaction.

How does goodwill fit in here?

From a tax perspective, an asset acquisition can be better for a buyer compared to a stock acquisition because it can provide an increase, or step-up, in the tax basis of the assets acquired, based on the purchase price. For certain assets, this increased tax basis may be depreciated or amortized by the buyer, offering a potential tax benefit. For example, in the case of acquired goodwill (resulting from the difference between the book value of a company and its purchase price) is this kind of asset: its tax basis may be amortized over 15 years. By contrast, when there is a step-up in corporate stock tax basis resulting from a stock acquisition (in a transaction that is not treated as a deemed asset acquisition under the tax laws) this does not result in increased depreciation or amortization, because stock is not considered to be an amortizable asset.[50]

Will a purchaser's cost basis in an asset generally be greater than its carryover basis?

Yes. Where an asset has appreciated in value, or where the economic depreciation of an asset is less than the depreciation or amortization deductions allowed for tax purposes, a purchaser's prospective cost basis in the asset will exceed its prospective carryover basis. The depreciation and amortization deductions allowed for tax purposes for most types of property are designed to exceed the actual economic depreciation of the property. As a result, the fair market value of most assets, which represents the prospective cost basis of the asset to a purchaser, generally exceeds adjusted tax basis. The aggregate difference between the purchaser's prospective cost and carryover bases of the acquired corporation's assets is often substantial.

Will a purchaser generally receive greater tax benefits by acquiring another corporation through a cost basis transaction than through a carryover basis transaction?

Yes. A purchaser will generally acquire a higher basis in the assets of the acquired corporation through a cost basis transaction than through a carryover basis transaction because the cost or fair market value of the assets acquired is generally greater than the adjusted basis of the assets prior to the transaction. In that circumstance, a cost basis transaction will step up the basis of the assets of the acquired corporation. The amount of the increase in basis—the excess of cost basis over carryover basis—is referred to as the *step-up amount.*

Do all asset, or cost basis, transactions step up the bases of the acquired corporation's assets?

No. Where the purchase price of the assets of the acquired corporation, which is presumed to equal their fair market value, is less than the carryover basis of the assets, a cost basis, or asset, transaction will result in a net reduction of basis. In such cases, the transaction should generally be structured as a carryover basis, or stock, acquisition.

In what circumstances are carryover basis transactions more beneficial to a purchaser, from a tax standpoint, than cost basis transactions?

There are two situations where a carryover basis, or stock, transaction may be more beneficial to the purchaser than a cost basis, or asset, acquisition. The first is where the carryover basis of the acquired corporation's assets to the purchaser exceeds their cost basis. This excess represents potential tax benefits to the purchaser—noncash depreciation deductions or taxable losses—without a corresponding economic loss. That is, the tax deductions or losses from owning the assets may exceed the price paid for such assets. The second is where the acquired corporation possesses valuable tax attributes—net operating loss carryovers, business tax credit carryovers, or accounting methods, for example—that would inure to the benefit of the purchaser. Situations where carryover basis transactions are preferable to the purchaser over cost basis transactions, however, are more the exception than the rule.

What is Section 338 of the IRC?

Section 338 of the IRC applies to taxable acquisitions. The provision enables an acquirer to treat a purchase of stock as a purchase of assets for tax purposes.[51] This election can be attractive to the acquirer because the buyer obtains a stepped-up basis in the selling company's assets. This step-up, in turn, provides the acquirer with a higher depreciable tax base in the assets and generates higher tax deductions in future years.

After a Section 338 acquisition, must the purchaser retain the acquired company as a subsidiary?

The purchasing corporation is permitted to liquidate the company in a tax-free liquidation as soon after the qualified stock purchase as it wishes. Such a liquidation may be structured as a statutory merger.

What are loss carryovers and carrybacks?

If a corporate taxpayer has an excess of tax deductions over its taxable income in a given year, this excess becomes a net operating loss (NOL) of that taxpayer. Section 172 of the IRC, as amended with the TCJA, allows that taxpayer to use its NOL to offset taxable income in subsequent years (a carryover or carryforward) for an indefinite period starting in the first taxable year after December 31, 2017. However, it does not allow the taxpayer to offset taxable income in earlier years (a carryback).[52] It also limits reduction of taxable income by NOL; for taxable years beginning after December 31, 2017, only 80 percent of taxable income in any given year can be reduced by NOLs.

Under other provisions of the IRC, certain tax losses or tax credits that are unusable in a given year may be carried forward or carried back to other tax years. Generally, IRC provisions for a company's ability to use NOL carryovers apply as well to these other items. For purposes of simplicity, all of these items tend to be grouped together with loss carryovers.

Generally speaking, each state has its own NOL carryback and carryforward rules, which might not necessarily match the federal rules. Therefore, an acquired corporation might have different amounts of available federal and state NOLs.

What role do loss carryovers play in mergers and acquisitions?

As stated previously, a potential advantage in carryover basis acquisitions (both taxable stock purchases and tax-free reorganizations) is the carryover of basis and of favorable tax attributes in the hands of the buyer. To the extent that a buyer can purchase an acquired corporation and retain favorable NOL carryovers, it can increase the after-tax cash flow generated by the activities of the acquired corporation and, to some extent, use those losses to offset tax liability generated by the buyer's own operations.

Over the course of many years, Congress and the IRS have imposed various limitations on the use of loss carryovers by persons other than those who owned the entity at the time that the loss was generated. For example, after a substantial ownership change, an acquiring corporation can deduct the NOLs of the acquired corporation only up to a certain limit, called a *Section 382 limitation,* and must meet a *continuity of business enterprise* requirement. Continuity of business enterprise means the continuation of a significant business of the acquired corporation's business assets. These rules have achieved a level of complexity that is extreme even by the standard of the tax laws generally.[53]

What happens when corporations having loss carryovers acquire other corporations that generate taxable gains?

The IRC covers this in Section 384, which limits a company's ability to offset its losses against taxable gains recognized by the subsidiaries that it acquires (and with which it files a consolidated tax return).[54] Loss carryovers of the acquiring corporation include unrealized built-in losses.

What are the tax consequences of a cost basis, or asset, acquisition to the acquired corporation?

The general rule is that the basis of an asset in the possession of an acquired corporation may not be stepped up to cost or fair market value without the recognition of taxable gain to the corporation. In a cost basis transaction, the acquired corporation will generally be subject to an immediate tax on an amount equal to the aggregate step-up in the bases of the assets. In addition, the sale or exchange of an asset may trigger the recapture of investment or business tax credits previously taken by the acquired corporation on the acquisition of the asset.

What are the tax consequences of a cost basis, or asset, acquisition to the shareholders of the acquired corporation?

The shareholders of the acquired corporation will be subject to tax upon the receipt of the asset sales proceeds (net of the corporate-level tax) from the acquired corporation, whether the proceeds are distributed in the form of a dividend, in redemption of the shareholders' acquired corporation stock, or in complete liquidation of the acquired corporation. If the asset sale's proceeds are retained by the acquired corporation, then the value of those proceeds is indirectly taxed to the shareholders upon the sale or exchange of the stock of the acquired corporation.

In what circumstances will an acquired corporation and its shareholders be subject to double tax on a cost basis, or asset, acquisition?

The acquired corporation and its shareholders will typically be subject to double tax where (1) the acquired corporation sells, or is deemed for tax purposes to sell, its assets to the purchaser in a taxable transaction; (2) the shareholders of the acquired corporation will ultimately receive the proceeds of the sale, either directly or indirectly through the sale of their stock in the acquired corporation; and (3) the receipt of the proceeds by the shareholders of the acquired corporation will be taxable to them. The cost basis transaction in these circumstances causes the proceeds of the sale to be taxed twice, first to the acquired corporation and again to its shareholders. There are several significant exceptions to this general rule.

The most common exception is those situations where a selling shareholder of the acquired corporation stock is a C corporation: the proceeds from the sale of the acquired corporation's stock by a corporate shareholder will likely be taxed again upon their ultimate distribution to noncorporate shareholders.

On balance, from a tax perspective, which type of structure is preferable: an asset or a stock acquisition?

Generally, a stock acquisition is preferable to an asset acquisition because of the adverse tax consequences to the seller. The immediate tax cost to the target corporation and its shareholders on the basis step-up amount of asset acquisition is generally greater than the present value of the tax benefits to the acquirer.

What are the circumstances in which a cost basis, or asset, acquisition transaction is justifiable for tax purposes?

An asset, or cost basis, transaction is generally advisable for tax purposes in situations where double tax is inevitable regardless of the structure, and in situations where the double-tax burden to the seller can be partially or wholly avoided. For instance, the seller may be able to avoid the double-tax burden where tax losses from other corporate activities can offset the taxable gains that arise from the sale of assets. Alternatively, where the sales price of the assets is less than the seller's tax basis in those assets, the seller may actually generate a tax benefit from structuring the deal as an asset sale rather than as a stock sale.

Previously you said that a pass-through entity isn't subject to double taxation like a C corporation is. Can a seller avoid the double tax by converting the acquired corporation to a pass-through entity immediately prior to a sale?

No. In general, a corporation can convert to a pass-through entity only by first undergoing a taxable liquidation. For all practical purposes, such liquidations are taxed the same as an asset sale.

The new lower corporate tax rates have caused some pass-throughs to consider converting to C corporations. What are the pros and cons of this move in an M&A context?

By converting to a C corporation from a pass-through, a company can take advantage of a lower tax rate. The problem is that if, later on, the company wants to go back to being a pass-through, it will be difficult. Selling a business as a pass-through has certain advantages, including:

- A single layer of tax
- A build-up in basis for the accumulated earnings not distributed
- Lower likelihood of net investment income tax[55]

How can a seller reduce tax costs?

The simplest way to reduce the seller's tax bill is to postpone the recognition of gain. This may be accomplished in a tax-free or partially tax-free acquisition or via the installment sale route.

What are installment sales and how can they help in structuring a merger, acquisition, or buyout?

Basically, an installment sale is a sale or exchange for a promissory note or other debt instrument of the buyer. In the case of an installment sale, the gain on the sale is recognized, pro rata, whenever principal payments on the note are received, or if earlier, upon a disposition of the installment obligation. For example, if A sells property to B for a note with a principal amount of $100 and A's basis in the property was $60, A realizes a gain of $40. Because the ratio of the gain recognized ($40) to the total amount realized ($100) is 40 percent, this percentage of each principal payment received by A will be treated as taxable gain. The other $60 will be treated as a nontaxable return of capital.

What kinds of transactions are eligible for installment sale treatment?

The installment method is generally available for sales of any property other than installment obligations held by a seller, and other than inventory and property sold by dealers in the subject property. Subject to certain exceptions, installment treatment is generally available to shareholders who sell their stock or to corporations or other entities that sell their assets. Installment treatment is not available for sales of stock or securities that are traded on an established securities market.

BASIC TAX STRUCTURE: TAX-DEFERRED TRANSACTIONS

What exactly is a tax-deferred transaction and how does it differ from a tax-free transaction?

The term *tax-free* in its purest sense means that no tax is ever paid on the transaction, while the term *tax-deferred* means that the tax is paid later. Colloquially, many professionals use the terms interchangeably. Technically, *tax-deferred* is more accurate for all transactions. Also, most tax-deferred transactions take the form of reorganizations—this is because, for tax purposes, the IRC views such transactions as a mere reshuffling of assets.

Could you give an example of a so-called tax-free reorganization that in reality only defers taxes?

In the classic tax-free acquisition, Al Smith (Smith) owns all of the stock of Mom and Pop Grocery, Inc. (Grocery), which is acquired by Supermarkets, Inc. (Supermarkets). In the transaction, Smith surrenders to Supermarkets all of his stock in Grocery solely in exchange for voting stock of Supermarkets. This is a so-called tax-free transaction known as a Type B reorganization, in which Smith recognizes no immediate gain or loss.

In other words, Smith obtains a basis in his Supermarkets stock equal to his basis in the Grocery stock surrendered (substituted basis) and continues his old holding period in the stock. Similarly, Supermarkets takes a basis in the Grocery stock acquired equal to Smith's basis (carryover basis) and also picks up Smith's holding period. Because the seller will have a basis in the buyer's stock that is the same as the seller's old basis in the acquired corporation's stock (a substituted basis), *tax is deferred only until the acquired corporation's stock is ultimately sold.* Nonetheless, this type of transaction is widely called tax-free, a terminology used here.

What are the advantages of tax-free transactions to sellers and buyers in this sense?

By participating in this type of transaction, the seller is provided the opportunity to exchange stock in the acquired corporation for stock of the buyer without the immediate recognition of gain. Where the acquired corporation is closely held and the buyer is publicly held, the seller may obtain greatly enhanced liquidity without a current tax.

Additionally, although both death and taxes are said to be inevitable, a seller participating in a tax-free transaction may use the former to avoid the latter. Under a long-standing IRC rule, an individual's estate and beneficiaries may take a new, fair market value basis in the decedent's properties upon death (or, alternatively, the FMV of the property on an alternate valuation date if the executor of the estate chooses to use the alternate valuation).[56] Thus, a seller may avoid the payment of any tax on the buyer's stock received in exchange for the old acquired corporation stock by holding this new stock until the seller's death.

For the buyer, there are two principal advantages to a tax-free acquisition. First, if the buyer can use stock in the transaction, significant acquisition-related debt may not be incurred (although debt might be assumed on the balance sheet of the acquired corporation at the time the deal closes). If the buyer wants equity financing anyway (as opposed to debt financing or internal growth), a business acquisition is a good way to get it. Second, the acquired corporation's tax attributes will remain usable after the acquisition (subject to some limitations).

What kinds of transactions may qualify for tax-free treatment?

Every transaction involving an exchange of property is taxable unless otherwise specified in the IRC. Thus, corporate acquisitions are generally taxable to the seller of stock or assets. However, several types of acquisition transactions may be tax-free to the seller, but only to the extent that the seller receives stock in the acquiring corporation (or in certain corporations closely affiliated with the acquiring corporation).

In general, tax-free acquisitions fall into three categories:

- Statutory mergers
- Exchanges of stock for stock
- Exchanges of assets for stock

Two IRC sections set conditions for tax-free mergers.

One is Section 351, which states, "No gain or loss shall be recognized if property is transferred to a corporation by one or more persons solely in exchange for stock in such corporation and immediately after the exchange such person or persons are in control (as defined in section 368(c)) of the corporation."[57] Section 351 of the IRC provides nonrecognition treatment on the transfer of property to a corporation by one or more parties in exchange for stock or stock and securities of the transferee corporation, provided the transferors possess 80 percent control of the transferee corporation immediately after the transaction. Although designed for the initial incorporation of a previously unincorporated business, Section

351 can be used as an alternative to the reorganization provisions in order to allow nonrecognition of gain to some of the acquired corporation shareholders.

All other available tax-free corporate acquisition transactions are provided under Section 368, which makes possible more than a dozen different varieties of acquisition reorganizations (including hybrids).

The most commonly used forms of reorganizations under Section 368 are the Type A, B, C, and D reorganizations. (Others are E, F, and G reorganizations, and various hybrids.) See Exhibit 5-6.

How does a transaction qualify as tax-free under Section 368?

To qualify as tax-free reorganizations under Section 368, all acquisitive reorganizations must meet three nonstatutory requirements:[58]

- First, the reorganization must have a *business purpose.* That is, a transaction must be motivated by a legitimate business purpose other than tax avoidance. Associated with this requirement is a requirement to have a plan of reorganization. This requirement arises most frequently in the context of divisive reorganizations. (See the first example in Appendix 5A.)
- The second, probably the most burdensome, is the *continuity of proprietary (ownership) interest* requirement. One test of this is the *step transaction doctrine* described later in this chapter.
- Third, the acquiring corporation must satisfy the *continuity of business enterprise* requirement.

What is continuity of proprietary interest?

Continuity of proprietary interest is a legal doctrine that frequently arises in applying the IRC's tax-free reorganization rules to a specific transaction. The general reasoning behind the continuity of interest doctrine is that a reorganization is the amalgamation of two corporate enterprises. Accordingly, the equity owners of both enterprises must continue to be

Exhibit 5-6 Section 368: Types of Reorganization

(A) a statutory merger or consolidation*;

(B) the acquisition by one corporation, in exchange solely for all or a part of its voting stock (or in exchange solely for all or a part of the voting stock of a corporation which is in control of the acquiring corporation), of stock of another corporation if, immediately after the acquisition, the acquiring corporation has control of such other corporation (whether or not such acquiring corporation had control immediately before the acquisition);

(C) the acquisition by one corporation, in exchange solely for all or a part of its voting stock (or in exchange solely for all or a part of the voting stock of a corporation which is in control of the acquiring corporation), of substantially all of the properties of another corporation, but in determining whether the exchange is solely for stock the assumption by the acquiring corporation of a liability of the other shall be disregarded;

(D) a transfer by a corporation of all or a part of its assets to another corporation if immediately after the transfer the transferor, or one or more of its shareholders (including persons who were shareholders immediately before the transfer), or any combination thereof, is in control of the corporation to which the assets are transferred; but only if, in pursuance of the plan, stock or securities of the corporation to which the assets are transferred are distributed in a transaction which qualifies under section 354, 355, or 356;

(E) a recapitalization;

(F) a mere change in identity, form, or place of organization of one corporation, however effected; or

(G) a transfer by a corporation of all or part of its assets to another corporation in a title 11 or similar case; but only if, in pursuance of the plan, stock or securities of the corporation to which the assets are transferred are distributed in a transaction which qualifies under section 354, 355, or 356.

*This is described as follows in the regulation:
(A) All of the assets (other than those distributed in the transaction) and liabilities (except to the extent such liabilities are satisfied or discharged in the transaction or are nonrecourse liabilities to which assets distributed in the transaction are subject) of each member of one or more combining units (each a transferor unit) become the assets and liabilities of one or more members of one other combining unit (the transferee unit); and
(B) The combining entity of each transferor unit ceases its separate legal existence for all purposes.

(*Source:* 26 CFR 1.368-2 - Definition of terms. https://www.law.cornell.edu/cfr/text/26/1.368-2#b_1_ii_A)

Source: 26 U.S. Code § 368 - Definitions relating to corporate reorganizations, https://www.law.cornell.edu/uscode/text/26/368.

owners following the transaction. This rule is intended to prevent transactions that aren't really sales from being accorded tax-free treatment. Stock typically maintains a shareholder's continuity of proprietary interest in a business, while debt and cash do not.

What is continuity of business enterprise?

Continuity of business enterprise is a second legal doctrine that frequently arises in applying the IRC's tax-free reorganization rules to a specific transaction. Generally, the doctrine requires that the acquirer either (1) continue the acquired corporation's "historic business" or (2) use a "significant portion" of the acquired corporation's "historic business assets" in a business. The term *significant portion* takes a relative meaning—that is, the portion of assets that are considered significant are relative to their importance in the operation of the acquired corporation's business. However, all other facts and circumstances, such as the net fair market value of those assets, are also considered. If the acquired corporation has more than one line of business, the acquirer is only required to continue one of the selling company's lines, although the transaction is still subject to the significant portion requirement. Alternatively, the IRC generally permits the acquirer to use the selling company's assets in *any* business—not just the acquired corporation's historic business. For examples, see Appendix 5A.

What is a Type A reorganization?

A *Type A reorganization* (named after its alphabetic place in Section 368 of the IRC) is very simply "a statutory merger or consolidation."[59] This type of reorganization has other, more complex names—such as a *reorganization not solely for voting stock,* as distinct from a *B reorganization,* which is solely for voting stock. It is also referred to as a *tax-free forward merger,* as opposed to the taxable forward merger and taxable reverse merger forms discussed previously (there is no tax-free reverse merger).

To qualify for a Type A, the most important consideration is whether the shareholders of the selling corporation (dubbed the target, or T, in this chapter) maintain continuity of proprietary interest by owning stock in the acquiring corporation (called the acquirer, or A, in this chapter). In order to satisfy the IRS's advance ruling requirements, the parties generally should structure the transaction so that the acquirer pays at least 50 percent of the transaction consideration in the form of A stock—which can be either voting or nonvoting stock, and may be common or preferred shares. The rest of the consideration (up to 50 percent) can be in the form of cash, debt, or property (commonly referred to as *boot* in tax law nomenclature).

If the acquirer is a subsidiary of another corporation, may it use its parent's stock as transaction consideration in a Type A reorganization?

Yes. In the event the acquirer is a controlled subsidiary of another corporation (the acquirer's parent or, in tax parlance, a "controlling corporation"), target shareholders can receive parent stock for their shares if (1) no acquirer (i.e., subsidiary) stock is used in the transaction, and (2) the transaction would have otherwise qualified as a Type A reorganization if acquirer stock had been used instead of parent stock. This alternative is particularly attractive if the parent is publicly traded but the acquirer-subsidiary is not. In addition, if the parent is a holding company of other subsidiaries, the parent company stock may offer more diversification to the sellers.

How long must the target shareholders hold their new shares under a Type A reorganization?

The IRC generally permits the target's shareholders to sell or otherwise dispose of their shares after the transaction. The one exception to this is where there is a planned sale of shares to the acquiring corporation or a related party, in which case the IRS may collapse all the transactions (i.e., view all steps of a transaction as a single, integrated transaction) in applying the continuity of interest test and treat that portion of the consideration as if it had been cash rather than stock in the acquiring corporation. There is no limitation on planned shares to third parties. This process is also known as the *step transaction doctrine,* and is a fact-based test not subject to mechanical application of the IRC.[60]

What is a creeping transaction?

A *creeping transaction* (sometimes also referred to as *creeping control*) is generally defined as two or more purchases by the acquirer of target stock as part of the same overall plan (i.e., to which the *step transaction doctrine* applies). Without the creeping transaction doctrine, the parties to a Type A reorganization could easily circumvent the spirit of the IRC's reorganization rules. For example, the acquirer could structure a two-step transaction in which (1) Step 1 involved a taxable purchase of an otherwise prohibited percentage of target stock, say 75 percent, and (2) Step 2 involved a statutory merger that would otherwise qualify under the Type A reorganization rules. Where the two-step transaction is used as an overall plan, the IRS will generally evaluate the continuity of propriety interest and other requirements as if the transactions all occurred at the same time. In cases in which multiple transactions are not part of the same overall plan, however, the IRS will treat the prior purchases as "old and cold" (in tax parlance) and apply the continuity of propriety interest test to only the relevant transaction(s). As with the step transaction doctrine, the IRS makes a fact-based determination in evaluating a potential creeping transaction.

What is a drop down, and does it preclude a transaction from qualifying under the Type A rules?

In a *drop down,* the acquirer transfers all or part of the recently acquired assets of the target to a subsidiary that the acquirer controls. The IRC permits a drop down in a transaction that otherwise qualifies as a Type A reorganization.[61]

Must all target shareholders in a Type A reorganization receive the same mix of consideration?

No. The tax rules analyze whether the target's shareholders as a group—not individually—maintain continuity of propriety interest. As a result, the acquirer may pay some target shareholders in cash or debt, but others in stock, so long as the minimum percentage is met overall. This point adds a degree of flexibility to the potential transaction structure and can allow the acquirer to meet the objectives of differing shareholder classes. It should be noted, however, that shareholders receiving cash or other forms of boot will be taxed on a pro rata portion of their shares. The taxation of boot consideration is discussed later in this chapter.

May the acquirer sell a portion of the target's historic operating assets following a Type A reorganization?

Generally, yes. A transaction will still qualify as a Type A reorganization notwithstanding the sale of a portion of the target's assets after the merger and as part of a plan that includes the merger, where the proceeds from the sale continue to be held by the surviving corporation.

Does federal tax law ever permit the acquirer to pay less than 50 percent of the transaction consideration in stock and still qualify as a Type A reorganization?

In some older tax case law, courts have permitted acquirers to pay less than 50 percent of the transaction consideration in stock. In a 1935 Supreme Court decision, for example, the Court permitted tax-free treatment to a transaction that involved 38 percent of the consideration paid in preferred stock.[62] IRS regulations provide that continuity of proprietary interest is satisfied where at least 40 percent of the consideration consists of stock. If the transaction is found to not qualify as a Type A reorganization, all of the transaction consideration will be taxable to the target's shareholders. This can create a tax-inefficient scenario for the sellers, and the acquirer would lose the target's tax characteristics.

How is nonstock consideration taxed in a Type A reorganization?

To the extent that the T shareholders receive boot (i.e., consideration other than stock, such as cash or debt), such shareholders must recognize realized gain on the nonstock consideration. The shareholder recognizes gain to the extent of the boot received.

What is a Type B reorganization?

A *Type B reorganization* is a stock-for-stock exchange in which one company buys the stock of another company using only ("solely") its own stock. Under a Type B reorganization, the target becomes a subsidiary of the acquirer, which must control the target immediately after the transaction. Under Section 368(a)(1)(B) of the IRC, the term *control* is defined as ownership of 80 percent or more of the target's voting power and 80 percent or more of each class of the target's voting stock.

Must the acquirer purchase 80 percent of the target's voting power and stock in one transaction?

No. The Type B reorganization rules do not require a purchase of 80 percent or more of the target's voting power and stock all at once, but rather only require that the acquirer control the target immediately following the deal. If the acquirer uses only voting stock as the transaction consideration, the acquirer may purchase target stock in one or more traunches. If more than one purchase is made, only the transaction that pushes the acquirer over the control threshold (80 percent) can qualify for tax-deferred treatment under the Type B reorganization rules.

What kind of stock may the acquirer use in a Type B reorganization?

The acquirer may use only voting stock in a Type B reorganization, and generally even the smallest amount of nonvoting stock or other consideration will disqualify Type B treatment altogether. The voting rights associated with these shares cannot be restricted to just extraordinary corporate events such as merger, but extend unconditionally to votes on routine corporate matters.

Can the target or the target's selling shareholders receive cash under any circumstances in a Type B reorganization?

Yes, in some instances. There are three principal scenarios in which the IRC permits the target or the target's shareholders to receive cash in a Type B reorganization: (1) the redemption of fractional shares by the acquirer; (2) payment of the target's transaction expenses (but not the target shareholders' transaction expenses), such as accounting, legal, and other reorganization costs; and (3) buyouts of dissenting minority shareholders that object to the transaction. Under this third exception, only the target or other target shareholders may purchase the dissenting shareholders' stock—not the acquirer—nor may the acquirer indirectly provide the funds for these purchases. To the extent that the T shareholders receive boot, such shareholders must recognize realized gain on the nonstock consideration. The pro rata portion of the transaction that involves boot is generally treated as a taxable stock acquisition, discussed previously in this chapter.

What about earnouts, holdbacks, or other forms of contingent consideration? Are those permitted under a Type B reorganization?

Generally speaking, the IRC permits contingent consideration in Type B reorganizations, assuming, of course, that the contingent consideration is paid only in voting stock. In an *earnout,* the selling shareholders are entitled to additional consideration if the target meets certain financial milestones postclosing.[63] In a *holdback,* the selling shareholders are entitled to additional consideration, assuming that a certain representation made at the time of closing is later confirmed to be accurate.

Does the step transaction doctrine apply to a Type B reorganization?

Yes. Accordingly, if the acquirer redeems a selling shareholder's shares for cash after the reorganization, the redemption may disqualify the entire transaction from Type B treatment if the acquirer agreed to redeem the target shareholder's shares as part of the broader transaction.

Are drop downs permitted in a Type B reorganization?

Assuming the transaction otherwise qualifies as a Type B reorganization, the acquirer is permitted to transfer the target's stock or assets to a controlled subsidiary after the reorganization.

If the acquirer is a subsidiary of another corporation, may it use its parent's stock as transaction consideration in a Type B reorganization?

Yes. Similar to a Type A reorganization, the acquirer may exchange the voting stock of a controlling corporation (i.e., the acquirer's parent) for target stock, assuming (1) no acquirer stock is used in the transaction, and (2) the transaction would have otherwise qualified as a Type B reorganization if acquirer stock had been used instead of parent stock.

What is a Type C reorganization?

A *Type C reorganization* is a transaction in which one company buys substantially all of the assets of another company using its own voting stock, and the target corporation subsequently liquidates. The IRS defines *substantially all* as either (1) 90 percent of the target's net assets (i.e., assets less liabilities—the book value of the assets acquired), or (2) 70 percent of the target's gross assets (measured at fair market value). In some situations, courts have approved Type C reorganizations that involved asset percentages below these thresholds, particularly where the target retains liquid assets such as cash in order to pay creditors. However, if the target redeems stock held by dissenting shareholders for assets, the IRS may count such assets toward the "substantially all" test (assuming the redemptions are part of the overall reorganization). Extraordinary distributions by the target prior to the acquisition could prevent the target from passing the substantially all requirement.

There is also a qualitative definition of *substantially all,* as courts consider the nature of the assets retained and the reasons for retaining them. Extraordinary distributions by T before the acquisition may impair satisfaction of the substantially all requirement.

A Type C reorganization is also sometimes referred to as a practical merger because, although the transaction consideration flows into the target (and not directly to the target's shareholders), the IRC generally requires the target to liquidate following the reorganization and distribute the acquirer stock and the target's remaining assets and liabilities to the target's shareholders.

Can the target receive any consideration other than voting stock of the acquirer under any circumstances in a Type C reorganization?

While the acquirer generally must use voting stock to compensate the target, there are a number of exceptions (sometimes referred to as *boot relaxation rules*) in which the acquirer may use consideration other than voting stock. First, the acquirer can assume liabilities of the target without violating the "solely for voting stock" requirement. Second, the acquirer can use stock of its parent as transaction consideration. Third and finally, the acquirer may use cash or other non-voting-stock consideration if the transaction involves assets with at least 80 percent of the fair market value of the target's total assets. In the case of this third exception, the dollar value of any liabilities assumed by the acquiring corporation, and the dollar value of any liability to which any asset acquired by the acquiring corporation is subject, shall be treated as cash paid to the target corporation.

Can creeping acquisitions arise in a Type C reorganization?

Yes, though the area is not well settled from a legal perspective. While a Type C reorganization is by definition a stock-for-assets exchange, a creeping acquisition can occur in two scenarios. First, a creeping acquisition may arise where the acquirer purchases more than 20 percent of the target's assets for non-voting-stock consideration, and then subsequently acquires some or all of the remaining assets solely for voting stock. In this case, the best advice is to follow the step transaction doctrine—if both the first and second transactions were part of the overall same plan, the IRS would probably disqualify the second transaction for Type C reorganization treatment.

Second, a creeping acquisition may arise in certain historical transactions where the acquirer already owns more than 20 percent of the target's stock, it acquires all of the target's assets solely for voting stock, and the target subsequently liquidates and distributes the acquirer stock to the target's shareholders.

Are drop downs permitted in a Type C reorganization?

Assuming that the transaction otherwise qualifies as a Type C reorganization, the acquirer is permitted to transfer the target's assets to a controlled subsidiary after the reorganization.

If the acquirer is a subsidiary of another corporation, may it use its parent's stock as transaction consideration in a Type C reorganization?

Yes. Similar to Types A and B reorganizations, the acquirer may exchange the voting stock of a controlling corporation (i.e., parent) for target stock, assuming (1) no acquirer stock is used in the transaction, and (2) the transaction would have otherwise qualified as a Type C reorganization if acquirer stock had been used instead of parent stock.

What is a forward triangular merger, and when might an acquirer consider using the structure?

A *forward, or direct, triangular merger* (also known as a *forward, or direct, subsidiary merger*) is a form of tax-free reorganization. The structure generally involves the acquirer (A) creating a new, wholly owned acquisition subsidiary (S) into which A contributes A stock tax-free under Section 351 of the IRC. The target (T) is then merged into S under state law (and dissolves), with the former T shareholders receiving A stock in exchange for their T stock. S is the surviving corporation after the reorganization and remains a wholly owned subsidiary of A.

An acquirer might structure a forward triangular merger if it wishes to keep the target corporation's liabilities segregated in a separate subsidiary, as even using a drop-down structure can potentially open up the acquirer to legal liability beyond the target's book value. In addition, A's shareholders are not required to vote on the deal because A is technically not a party to the deal. Because A is the only shareholder of S, the structure can streamline the shareholder approval process and cut down on considerable time and expense—particularly if A is a widely held corporation.

What are the requirements to qualify for a forward triangular merger?

A forward triangular merger functions like a hybrid of Types A and C reorganizations (acquiring 90 percent of net assets or 70 percent of gross assets), so it might not come as a surprise that the requirements are similar. In order to qualify for tax-free treatment, the transaction must meet the following requirements:

- S must acquire substantially all of the assets of T, with *substantially all* being defined in the context of a Type C reorganization.
- The reorganization would have qualified as a Type A, but for the fact that T is merged into S instead of its controlling corporation A.
- S may not use its own stock, only that of A, as consideration in the transaction. Consistent with the Type A reorganization requirements, S may generally use its own debt securities, cash, or other property for up to 50 percent of the consideration. To the extent that the T shareholders receive boot (i.e., consideration other than stock, including cash or debt) such shareholders must recognize realized gain on the nonstock consideration. The pro rata portion of the transaction that involves boot is generally treated as a taxable asset acquisition, discussed previously in this chapter.

What is a tax-free spin-off?

A *spin-off* is a wholly or partly tax-free division of a single corporation into two or more corporations. The division typically involves converting a preexisting company division into a wholly owned subsidiary and distributing the stock in the subsidiary pro rata to all shareholders in the original company. By contrast, an ordinary divestiture or sell-off is the sale (often taxable) of the stock or assets of a business unit to another company or to an investment group. Assuming the transaction qualifies under Section 355 of the IRC, a spin-off is tax-free to both the issuer and its shareholders.

CHOICE OF ENTITY

What types of entities may operate the business of an acquired company?

Choosing the appropriate legal form for operating the business of the acquired company depends on the unique circumstances of the constituent parties and is important for tax, liability, financing, and other purposes. Though an exhaustive discussion is outside the scope of this chapter, the business may generally take the legal form of nearly any business entity, such as (1) a C corporation, (2) an S corporation, (3) a partnership, either general or limited, or (4) a limited liability corporation (LLC). An LLC is a more recent kind of hybrid entity, authorized in 1988 by the IRS. It offers the legal insulation of a corporation and the preferred tax treatment of a partnership. Today, all 50 states and the District of Columbia permit LLCs.

What are the primary differences among the four types of business entities?

A regular, or C, corporation is a separate taxpaying entity. Therefore, the corporation pays taxes on its earnings, and shareholders pay taxes on their dividends. Partnerships, S corporations, and LLCs, in contrast, are generally not separate taxpaying entities.

Because S corporations, partnerships, and LLCs are generally exempt from tax (but rather pass the tax liability with respect to such earnings directly through to their owners) these entities are commonly referred to as pass-through entities. The earnings of pass-through entities are taxed directly at the partner or shareholder level, whether or not distributed or otherwise made available to such persons. Moreover, pass-through entities may generally distribute their earnings to the equity owners free of tax. The TCJA included a deduction on the business income of up to 20 percent for pass-throughs, as mentioned earlier.

What kinds of pass-through entities are there?

There are generally three types of pass-through entities: (1) a partnership, both general and limited, (2) an LLC, and (3) an S corporation. The earnings of an S corporation, with certain exceptions, are subject to taxation only at the shareholder level. The earnings of a partnership are also subject to a single tax. However, note that where a C corporation is a partner, its share of the earnings will ultimately be subject to double taxation. (In some rare cases, a C corporation can get a pass-through treatment,[64] but, generally speaking, they do not.)

What is a C corporation?

The IRC defines a *C corporation* as any corporation that is not an S corporation. The term *C corporation* as used in this chapter, however, excludes corporations granted special tax status under the IRC, such as life insurance corporations, regulated investment companies (mutual funds), or corporations qualifying as real estate investment trusts (REITs).

What is an S corporation?

An *S corporation* is simply a regular corporation that meets certain requirements and elects to be taxed under Subchapter S of the IRC. Originally called a *small business corporation,* the S corporation was designed to permit small, closely held businesses to be conducted in corporate form, while continuing to be taxed generally as if operated as a partnership or an aggregation of individuals. As it happens, the eligibility requirements under Subchapter S, keyed to the criterion of simplicity, impose no limitation on the actual size of the business enterprise.

To qualify for S corporation status, the corporation must meet the following requirements:

- Be a domestic corporation
- Have only allowable shareholders
  —May be individuals, certain trusts, and estates
  —May not be partnerships, corporations, or nonresident alien shareholders
- Have no more than 100 shareholders
- Have only one class of stock
- Not be an ineligible corporation (i.e., certain financial institutions, insurance companies, and domestic international sales corporations)[65]

It should be noted that not all states recognize the S corporation. For those that do not, the corporation pays state income taxes as if it were a C corporation. For those states that do recognize S corporations, both resident and nonresident shareholders of the state where the corporation does business must file returns and pay taxes to that state. In such cases, a shareholder's state of residence will usually (but not always) provide a credit against its own tax.

What is a partnership for tax purposes?

Except under rare circumstances, a *partnership for tax purposes* must be a bona fide general or limited partnership under applicable state law. Generally, LLCs are treated as partnerships for tax purposes, unless elected to be treated as corporations for tax purposes.

What considerations are key to choosing the appropriate legal form of the operating entity?

Where there are many considerations the parties need to keep in mind, there are four key points that often drive the choice of legal form for the operating entity:

- *Limitations on liability.* Frequently, the most important consideration in choosing a business entity is the limitation of investors' liability. Where the owners select a limited liability entity, their risk of capital loss is capped at the amount of capital actually invested into the entity (with limited exceptions, as briefly discussed in the following). Where the owners select a different entity, their liability may be unlimited.

  Business entities that afford the owners limited liability include corporations (both C corporations and S corporations), limited liability companies, limited liability partnerships, and, to some degree, limited partnerships. By contrast, a general partnership does not offer limited liability. However, under principles of general corporate law, owners of limited liability entities can in rare circumstances be held personally liable for the actions and/or obligations of their businesses. These circumstances are known as *piercing the corporate veil.*
- *Financing alternatives.* The financing plans of the owners of the operating entity may preclude certain entities from consideration. In particular, an S corporation election usually offers the shareholders the least amount of flexibility regarding financing alternatives. For example, an S corporation would not be an appropriate choice if one of the potential shareholders is a corporation, due to legal restrictions that generally limit shareholders to individuals only. Similarly, an S corporation would not be an efficient choice if the parties plan to take the operating entity public in the foreseeable future—S corporations cannot qualify for publicly traded status because, among other reasons, the number of S corporation shareholders is limited to 100. Finally, S corporations cannot have more than one class of

stock. As a result, the choice of entity does not accommodate a preferred stock structure.

For these reasons and others, partnerships and LLCs are frequently the entity of choice for operating the acquired company. An LLC, for example, allows multiple classes of stock, which facilitates institutional shareholdings. In addition, both partnerships and LLCs offer tremendous flexibility in structuring creative profits allocation among the partners (see the following). They also allow corporations as partners or as members (in the case of an LLC), and generally are not subject to a tax penalty upon conversion to a C corporation.

- *Taxation.* The owners of the operating entity must consider the tax implications of forming, operating, and exiting the operating entity. As discussed previously, forming a new business entity is usually (although not always) considered a nontaxable event. The choice of entity and precise structure of the operating entity can impact whether a partner's exit from the entity is nontaxable, tax deferred, or taxable at ordinary income rates or capital gains rates. It is beyond the scope of this chapter to detail all the differences distinguishing different entities; here are some notable ones:

  Partnerships: Business entities classified as partnerships for tax purposes are usually considered pass-through entities and are usually subject to only one level of federal taxation. (Note, however, that some state and local tax regimes might still apply to partnerships.) Income and/or losses are taxable to partners as the business entity earns income, regardless of whether the operating entity makes any distributions, and such income or losses retain their character (depreciation, charitable contributions, capital gains, etc.). Undistributed income from the operating entity generally increases the basis of each partner's interest in the operating entity. This minimizes the likelihood of double taxation of the partner's interest if the partner subsequently sells the ownership position. When distributions are made, the payments are not taxable to the extent the partner has sufficient adjusted basis in the partnership interest. (After the partner works down the adjusted basis, subsequent distributions are usually considered a nontaxable return of capital and capital gains.) Tax law usually requires a partnership to adopt a calendar tax year rather than a noncalendar, fiscal tax year.

- *C corporations:* In contrast, business entities structured as C corporations usually isolate tax consequences related to the operating entity to the entity level rather than passing them through to the owner level. However, as mentioned earlier, C corporations are subject to two levels of taxation: one at the operating entity level as the entity generates income, and one at the shareholder level as the entity pays out dividends. Finally, unlike a partnership, a C corporation is usually permitted substantial flexibility in adopting a fiscal tax year that does not end on December 31.
- *Financial allocation and governance provisions.* Some entities such as partnerships and LLCs offer substantially more flexibility than corporate structures (both C corporations and S corporations) regarding allocation, distribution, and governance provisions.

Therefore, unless differential tax rates would dictate the choice of a C corporation, in most cases, a form of partnership (either general or limited) or an LLC structure is the preferable legal form, given the relative flexibility of these structures.

When should an S corporation be considered?

Typically, an S corporation should be considered where the acquired corporation is, or will be, a freestanding domestic operating corporation owned by 100 or fewer US individual shareholders. There is no limit on the size of the business that may be conducted in an S corporation. Assuming the business entity has at least one individual shareholder, the corporate parties to the operating entity have a variety of alternatives to stay under the 100 limit. For example, the operating entity could issue the nonindividual warrants, other options, or convertible debt. These must be carefully constructed to avoid the appearance or reality of de facto corporate entity holders.

Nonetheless, just because a large company can use an S corporation does not mean it should. The S corporation requirements intentionally encourage simple structures; they are not inherently user-friendly vehicles for larger, complex operations. With the emergence of LLCs, and other business entities with both limited liability and partnership tax treatment, it is frequently not worthwhile pursuing the S corporation alternative.

When should a partnership be considered?

The partnership is an alternative to the S corporation, with several notable advantages. First, it is always available without restriction as to the structure or composition of the acquired corporation's ownership; therefore, it can be used when the S corporation is unavailable for technical reasons. In addition, the partnership is unique in enabling the partners to receive distributions of loan proceeds free of tax. Finally, if the acquired business is expected to generate tax losses, a partnership is better suited than an S corporation to pass these losses through to the owners (unless they do not wish to recognize such losses). The last two advantages result from the fact that partners, unlike S corporation shareholders, may generally include liabilities of the partnership in their basis in the partnership.

In addition to the choice of entity, what major structural issue should be considered?

From a tax standpoint, probably the most important issue is whether the buyer should seek to obtain a cost basis or a carryover basis in the assets of the acquired corporation. Because of the potential for obtaining either of these results regardless of whether assets or stock are actually acquired, the determinations of the tax goal and the actual structure may initially be made on a separate basis.

What are the mechanics of achieving a cost vs. carryover basis?

This may be a good time to review an earlier point. A cost basis transaction is often referred to as an *asset acquisition for tax purposes* (or as an *asset acquisition,* for short), and a carryover basis transaction is often referred to as a *stock acquisition for tax purposes* (or a *stock acquisition,* for short). And, as mentioned earlier, neither of these terms necessarily reflects the actual, legal structure of the transaction.

In a taxable acquisition, carryover basis can be achieved only through a stock acquisition. For federal tax purposes, however, stock may be acquired in two ways: first, through a direct purchase of seller's stock and, second, through a reverse cash merger.

As indicated previously, a cost basis can be achieved by purchasing either assets or stock from the seller. As in the case of a stock purchase, the tax law permits an asset purchase to be effected in two ways: first, through a direct purchase of the seller's assets and second, through a forward cash merger. In the context of a stock acquisition, a cost basis can be achieved by making an election under Section 338 of the IRC.

Is it possible to obtain a cost basis in some of the assets of the acquired company and a carryover basis in other assets?

If structured carefully, it is possible to obtain a cost basis in some of the assets and a carryover basis in others.

Are there any complications involving the sale of stock between related parties?

Section 304 of the IRC addresses a tax avoidance technique involving the sale of stock in one related corporation to another related corporation. Under the prohibited structure, a common shareholder could withdraw cash or property from his corporations while retaining undiminished ownership. The classic case involves Individual A, who owns all of the stock of corporations X and Y, and who sells some or all of the X stock to Y for cash. In such a case, Section 304 recharacterizes the transaction and treats it as a dividend from Y accompanied by a nontaxable contribution of X stock to Y, instead of merely a sale of X stock that would qualify as capital gain.

The reach of Section 304 goes far beyond this example, however. It encompasses any situation in which there is direct or indirect control by the selling shareholders of the stock of both the acquiring corporation and the corporation being acquired. *Control* is defined here as 50 percent of the voting power or 50 percent of the value of a corporation's stock (including pure preferred). Control of the buyer acquired in the transaction itself is included.

How are purchase price allocations made for tax purposes?

Although businesses are usually bought and sold on a lump-sum basis, for tax purposes each such transaction is broken down into a purchase and sale of the individual assets, both tangible and intangible. There is no specific requirement under the tax laws that a buyer and a seller allocate the lump-sum purchase price in the same manner. Because each party has tended to take positions most favorable to it, and because the IRS has an interest in maintaining consistent principles in this domain, the IRS has litigated reallocation issues fairly often over the years. At the same time, courts and, to a lesser extent, the IRS have tended to defer to allocations of purchase price agreed upon in writing between a buyer and seller in an arm's-length transaction.

Are there any rules governing the allocation of purchase price?

Yes. If the seller transfers assets constituting a business and determines its basis as the consideration (e.g., purchase price) paid for the assets, then this transfer is considered a Section 1060(c) *applicable asset* acquisition.[66] Both buyer and seller in such a transaction must use the *residual method* to allocate the purchase price received in determining the buyer's basis or the seller's gain or loss. This method, which is also used for a stock purchase, requires that the price of the assets acquired be reduced by cash and cash-like items; the balance must be allocated to tangible assets, followed by intangibles, and finally by goodwill and going-concern value. IRS regulations state that both buyer and seller are bound by the allocations set forth in the acquisition agreement.

What about amortization of intangibles following an acquisition?

Section 197 of the IRC sets a uniform standard of 15 years for amortization of intangibles at a rate of 100 percent. Intangibles acknowledged under Section 197[67] include the following:

- Goodwill
- Going-concern value
- Workforce in place
- Business books and records, operating systems, or any other information base, including lists or other information concerning current or prospective customers
- A patent, copyright, formula, process, design, pattern, know-how, format, or similar item
- A customer-based intangible
- A supplier-based intangible
- Any item similar to items (3) through (7)
- A license, permit, or other right granted by a governmental unit or agency (including issuances and renewals)
- A covenant not to compete entered into in connection with the acquisition of an interest in a trade or business
- Any franchise, trademark, or trade name
- A contract for the use of, or a term interest in, any item in this list

The IRS notes that items 1 through 8 must be acquired, not created, by the taxpayer.[68]

Exceptions include the following under Section 197:[69]

- *Financial interests.* Any interest in a corporation, partnership, trust, or estate, or under an existing futures contract, foreign currency contract, notional principal contract, or other similar financial contract.

- *Land.* Any interest in land.
- *Computer software,* defined in the section as "any program designed to cause a computer to perform a desired function." (The term does not include any proprietary database, which may in fact be considered a Section 197 intangible.)
- Certain interests or rights acquired separately. The law lists these particular interests, including, notably, interests in a patent or copyright.
- *Interests under leases and debt instruments.* An existing lease of tangible property, or, with some exceptions, any debt.
- *Mortgage servicing.* Any right to service indebtedness that is secured by residential real property unless this right is acquired in a transaction (or a series of related transactions) involving the acquisition of assets (other than rights described in this paragraph) constituting a trade or business or a substantial portion of one.
- *Certain transaction costs in stock deals.* Any fees for professional services, and any transaction costs, incurred by parties to a transaction that with respect to which any part of the gain or loss is not recognized under the relevant part of the tax code.[70]

These exceptions are treated with either longer periods (e.g., land) or shorter periods (e.g., computer software). In general, Section 197 benefits acquirers of companies that have intangibles with a long life that normally would have to be amortized over a longer period. In general, businesses like to write off intangibles as quickly as possible, as this creates cash in hand from tax savings and rids the company of a drag on profits. However, a noncompete is amortized over 15 years regardless of the term.

TAX CONSEQUENCES IN STRUCTURING ACQUISITION DEBT FINANCING

What is debt financing, technically speaking?

Debt is an obligation to repay money that is loaned. The purest kind of debt is called straight debt, which (1) is an unconditional obligation to repay principal and interest, (2) has a fixed maturity date not too far removed, (3) is not convertible, and (4) has not attached warrants, options, or stock. A straight debt instrument ordinarily does not include interest that is contingent on profits or other factors, but it may provide for a variable interest rate. It will not have a principal that is subject to contingencies. In short, straight debt is an instrument without significant equity features.

Straight debt instruments are generally classified as debt for tax purposes. Accrued interest on a straight debt instrument is partly deductible by the borrower and taxable to the lender. A key tax issue in straight debt financing is the computation of the accrued interest.

The IRC and related regulations contain an extremely complex set of comprehensive rules regarding interest accruals. These rules generally require that interest must accrue whether or not a payment of interest is made. Thus, interest may be taxed, or deducted, before or after interest is paid.

More generally, the IRC has generated complex rules concerning what is debt versus what is equity under IRC section 385, since this can have tax implications. In 2016, the IRS issued final documentation regulations, but these were cut back in 2018 as part of a deregulatory movement.[71]

What are the principal tax issues that arise in structuring acquisition debt financing?

Some of the issues to consider are:

- Whether the IRS might recharacterize the debt as equity
- How much of the interest payments will be deductible (including whether the acquirer risks maxing out its interest deductions, or otherwise is not in a position to fully use the benefits of debt financing)

- If the target will be part of an affiliated group filing a consolidated return post-transaction[72]

How is debt distinguished from equity for tax purposes?

A few useful generalizations can be made. Virtually all of the litigation and activity by the IRS has been in the recharacterization of purported debt as equity, and not the other way around. Therefore, it is quite safe to say that recharacterization is not a problem when one is dealing with a purported equity instrument.

In examining a purported debt instrument, the courts look for evidence that the parties intended a true debtor-creditor relationship. In particular, they have placed great weight on whether the instrument represents an unconditional promise to pay a certain sum at a definite time. Other significant factors that are considered include whether the loan was made by shareholders of the borrower, the borrower's debt-equity ratio, whether the loan is subordinated to third-party creditors, and whether it has a market rate of interest.

While a thorough discussion of the circumstances under which the IRS might take this position are outside the scope of this book, a key consideration is whether the leveraged company has enough equity underpinning the debt to adequately support it (i.e., thinly capitalized). While there is no bright-line test, a debt-equity ratio higher than 1.5:1 might draw attention. This was one of the threshold conditions for disqualifying interest deductions prior to the TCJA.[73] If the debt is reclassified as equity, interest and repayment of principal might be taxable as dividends.

A corporation can minimize the likelihood of IRS scrutiny and reclassification by (1) adequately documenting the debt instrument, (2) structuring reasonable debt terms, such as a market interest rate and a definite maturity rate, (3) adhering to the debt repayment schedule, (4) not structuring payments that are contingent on earnings, and (5) as previously noted, maintaining a prudent debt-equity ratio. Other red flags to consider are if shareholders hold similar pro rata positions of debt and equity or if the use of funds is for start-up operations.

What about debt issued to third-party investors?

Debt issued to third-party investors for cash is not likely to be recharacterized as equity, even though the debt may be subordinated to senior debt, convertible into common stock, or part of a capital structure involving a high ratio of debt to equity. This will at least be true where the instrument contains the common indicia of indebtedness—that is, a certain maturity date that is neither unduly remote nor contingent, a reasonable interest rate, and creditors' rights upon default. Note, however, that even if these criteria are met, the IRS is likely to argue for equity characterization if the conversion features of the instrument are such as to make it economically inevitable from inception that the instrument will be converted into stock.

What are the tax consequences if debt with equity features is recharacterized as equity?

The tax consequences of recharacterization of purported debt into equity may be quite severe.

First, interest payments with respect to recharacterized debt will be treated not as interest but as distributions to a shareholder and, therefore, will not be deductible. Repayment of debt principal is tax-free to the debt holder, but if treated as a redemption of stock, it may be taxed as a dividend.

Second, the recharacterization may destroy the pass-through status of the issuer. When debt is recharacterized as equity, it is ordinarily expected to be treated as a kind of preferred stock. Because an S corporation may not have two classes of stock, a recharacterization of debt into equity can create a second class of stock, invalidating the S election and causing a corporate-level tax. If the issuer is a member of a consolidated group, the recharacterized debt will most likely be treated as preferred stock that is not pure preferred stock. As such, the company may be disaffiliated from the consolidated group if, after taking into account the newly recharacterized stock, the members of the consolidated group own less than 80 percent of the company's stock.

Third, a recharacterization of debt into equity may completely change the structure of the deal. For example, the recharacterization may invalidate an election to have a stock transaction treated as an asset transaction under Section 338 of the IRC. For a valid Section 338 election, the buyer and the acquired company must be affiliated at the time of the election. If the recharacterization of a purported debt into equity disaffiliates the two companies, the election is invalid. In the case of purchase money notes, the conversion of debt into stock consideration may convert a taxable acquisition into a tax-free reorganization.

What are the new rules for interest deductions?

Under current law (following TCJA) the amount allowed as a deduction may not exceed the sum of business interest income for the taxable year, plus 30 percent of the adjusted taxable income for that year.[74] Adjusted taxable income means earnings before interest, taxes, depreciation, and amortization (EBITDA) before 2022, but starting in 2022 it means earnings before interest and taxes (EBIT). Disallowed business interest may be carried forward the next year.

What if the acquired company's operations are to be held in an affiliated group of corporations filing a consolidated federal income tax return? How is postacquisition debt treated then?

In such a case, the acquisition debt will often be issued by the parent. Therefore, for federal income tax purposes, the group is treated as a single taxpayer, in which the parent's interest deductions offset the operating income of the subsidiaries. From the point of view of the various states in which the subsidiaries do business, there is no consolidation with the parent; therefore, the parent's interest payments, even though funded by cash flow from the subsidiary, will not reduce the subsidiary's state income tax liability.

In such cases, deal planners should consider, where feasible, passing the parent's interest deductions to the subsidiaries by having them assume portions of the parent's indebtedness directly, or indirectly via bona fide intercorporate indebtedness owed to the parent by the respective subsidiaries. The parent must exercise great care to avoid adverse tax treatment under federal law—or under state law (in its own state of residency)—as a result of such restructuring.

From a tax standpoint, when might preferred stock be more advantageous than subordinated debt?

When an issuer does not need additional interest deductions (for example, when it expects to generate or otherwise have available NOLs), it might have no reason to use debt, and preferred stock might be a sensible alternative.

The most common tax reason for using preferred stock over debt is to enable an acquisition to qualify as a tax-free reorganization. As discussed previously, shareholders can obtain tax-free treatment on the receipt of nonvoting, redeemable preferred stock, and such stock will qualify in satisfying the continuity of interest requirement.

More generally, preferred stock can be used to provide tax-free treatment to an acquired company's shareholders while still effectively converting their interest to that of a passive investor or lender. Although preferred stock dividends are not deductible to the issuer, the corporate holder may exclude from its taxable income a portion of the dividends received, called the *dividends-received deduction* (DRD). This is a tax benefit that the wise dealmaker will not want to ignore.[75]

Can an ESOP be used to provide favorable financing in a leveraged buyout?

An employee stock ownership plan (ESOP) is a type of qualified employee benefit plan that invests primarily in stock of the employer. In order to encourage the use of ESOPs, Congress has provided a variety of special tax benefits both to stockholders who sell their stock to an ESOP and to lenders providing financing for so-called leveraged ESOPs. Shareholders who sell their stock to an ESOP may qualify for nonrecognition of gain, Section 1042 of the IRC.[76]

MANAGEMENT BUYOUT TAX BASICS

What is a management buyout?

A *management buyout* (MBO) is a transaction in which a company, or subsidiary or division, is acquired by a new company in which management of the acquired business holds a significant, if not controlling, equity stake. The purchaser is typically privately held and has not been an operating company or a subsidiary of one. Its funds typically consist of borrowed money, so most MBOs are also LBOs.

How is an MBO typically structured?

In brief, management, together with any financial partner, forms a new company to acquire the target business. The acquiring company might purchase either all the assets or stock of the target, or it may merge with the target. Often, management forms a holding company and engages in a forward or reverse merger with the selling company. If management owns stock, it can either have the acquiring company repurchase its existing shares or contribute its equity in the target business to the acquiring company. These methods have different tax consequences.

How should an MBO be structured?

MBOs are usually structured either as tender offers or as mergers. In the first case, managers buy company stock using cash or stock. In the second case, they do the same thing but then merge the purchased entity into another company. Each structure—the tender offer versus the merger—has its disadvantages.

A stock purchase via a tender offer is the fastest method to purchase a majority of any public company's stock. A tender offer can be made in cash or stock, and timing is about the same. Under current rules, exchange offers can start upon filing, which enables bidders to solicit the tender of stock from securityholders. This so-called fast-track review allows exchange offers to compete with their cash counterparts.

However, tender offers have certain disadvantages. Tender offers can force buyers to spend money prior to gaining access to the target company's cash flow, and without any assurance of ever tapping it. The margin rules of the Federal Reserve Board (Regulation U) restrict a purchaser from borrowing more than half of the purchase price against the pledge of publicly traded securities.[77] Because the margin rules complicate financing, acquisitions of public companies are often done as mergers or use unsecured financing.

The merger form for an MBO usually requires approval of the stockholders. In noncash transactions, approvals are needed from the shareholders of both entities. In cash transactions, approval must come from the shareholders of the nonsurviving corporation. A merger transaction involving a public company will require the filing of proxy materials with the SEC and a registration statement complying with federal and state securities laws where securities are to be issued. A stock purchase can be done where ownership of the target's shares is concentrated in the hands of a few persons, but it typically must be consummated contemporaneously with a merger to obtain the required financing.

What special tax issues ordinarily arise in an MBO?

For the most part, an MBO raises the same tax issues as any other LBO. In addition, there are a few categories of issues that pertain specifically to acquisitions with equity participation by management. These issues relate primarily to the manner in which management's investment will be paid for or financed and generally involve questions of whether significant amounts of compensation income will be deemed to be received by management. Where members of management already own stock or stock rights in a selling company, special care must be taken in structuring the transaction to allow a tax-free conversion of these existing equity rights.

A discussion of management equity participation in a buyout inevitably leads to a broader discussion of executive compensation. The focus here is primarily on management's direct equity participation in an acquisition. To the extent management does obtain a direct ownership interest in the company, the mindset of managers may become more long term. Equity-based remuneration is a longer-term incentive (more than one-year performance measurement period) and is forward looking, while a bonus plan is short term, typically considering performance for one year, and is backward looking (past year).

An MBO will likely require a greater cash investment than most of the management participants will have available from personal resources. Unless the management pays for the stock, in cash, at fair market value, there may be taxable income to the employee when stock is obtained. The employee and the corporation will have some control over when the taxable income is treated as being received. Their interests may differ. The tax consequences of the alternative ways of making this investment are governed by the basic rules under Section 83 of the IRC. [78]

What is the basic rule for taxation of an employee who receives or purchases stock in an MBO?

As a general rule, under Section 83 an employee receives taxable compensation to the extent that the value of any property received from the employer exceeds the amount the employee pays for that property. To the extent that the employee has taxable income, the employer is entitled to a deduction and is required to withhold tax on the same basis as if regular salary were paid. These rules apply whether the employee is receiving stock or other kinds of property. If an employee has not paid full value for the stock and is thus taxed on the receipt of the stock, the employee will obtain a basis in the stock equal to the amount actually paid for it, plus the amount of taxable income recognized. If an employee has paid full value for the stock, the employee will have a basis in the stock equal to the cost and will have no compensation income. In either case, when the employee later sells the stock, the employee will have capital gain or loss measured by the difference between the sale proceeds and the basis in the stock.

There is an important exception to the general rule. If the stock is not substantially vested in the employee, there is no tax to the employee and no deduction to the employer until such time as the stock does become substantially vested.[79] Stock is substantially vested if it: is not subject to a "substantial risk of forfeiture," is transferable by the employee, or if there are no vesting provisions attached to the shares (e.g., no time-based or performance-based vesting provisions).

When the risk of forfeiture or the restriction on transferability lapses, rendering the property substantially vested, the employee will be required to pay tax on the excess of the stock's value at the time the property vests over the amount paid for the stock, unless the employee takes an 83b election at the time of grant.[80]

This rule will apply even if the employee originally paid full value for the stock, and it cannot be avoided unless the employee otherwise elects under Section 83(b).[81]

Here is how it works. Assume that a management employee will acquire 100 shares of company stock in the MBO. The employee buys the stock for $100, which is the full fair market value of the stock. If the stock is then fully vested and transferable, the employee recognizes no taxable income. If, two years later, the stock is worth $150, there will be no impact on the employee; only if the stock is actually sold for $150 will the employee have $50 in long-term capital gain. The company will have no deduction. But if the employee acquires the stock subject to a substantial risk of forfeiture that does not lapse for a two-year period, the result is different. There is still no income at the outset. Two years later, when the stock is worth $150, the risk of forfeiture lapses. The employee must then recognize taxable income of $50 (which is the difference between the $150 fair market value of the stock at that time and the $100 paid for the stock two years earlier), even if the employee has not sold the stock and has no cash proceeds to pay the tax. At that time, the company is entitled to a $50 deduction.

Are there circumstances that might impel an employee to forfeit stock?

Yes. Many typical "golden handcuff" techniques create a substantial risk of forfeiture and can therefore undermine the tax plans. The receipt of stock may be subject to forfeiture if the employee will be required to return the stock upon the occurrence of a particular event or the failure to satisfy some condition. The typical example of a provision creating a substantial risk of forfeiture is one requiring that the employee return the stock to the company in the event that the employee terminates employment with the company within a certain period after the receipt of the stock. A requirement that the employee return the stock unless certain earnings goals are met also creates a substantial risk of forfeiture.

There is not, however, a substantial risk of forfeiture where the company is required to pay the employee full value for the stock upon a termination of employment, unless the termination is "for cause." (Most employee stock plans have this provision as a rule.) Also, where the event that will produce a forfeiture is peculiarly within the control of the employee, such as dismissal for cause or taking a job with a competitor of the company, there will not be a substantial risk of forfeiture. A special rule applies if the sale of the stock could subject the employee to litigation alleging violation of Section 16(b) of the Securities Exchange Act of 1934. This is the so-called *short-swing* rule, which makes profits on sales in a six-month period illegal. In such a case, the employee's rights in the property could be subject to a substantial risk of forfeiture. Consequently, when the six-month period ends, the employee's interest vests and the employee becomes subject to tax on any increase in value of the stock over what was paid for it.

If the employee sells the stock before the risk of forfeiture lapses, the employee will have taxable income equal to the excess of the amount realized on the sale over the amount paid for the stock. The employer can take a deduction in this amount.

Will receipt of stock by a management investor always be treated as receipt of stock by an employee?

Technically, Section 83 applies to the receipt of stock or other property by an employee only if it was received in connection with the performance of services. This includes past, present, and future services. In some circumstances, a reasonably strong case can be made that the employees are not receiving stock in connection with the performance of services but are receiving stock on the same basis and in the same context as other members of an investor group. In spite of this commonsense analysis, most tax advisors recommend that planning in this area proceed on the assumption that the IRS will apply Section 83 in determining the tax consequences to members of an investor group who are employees of the company.

May employees elect to recognize any taxable income currently?

If an employee receives stock that is substantially nonvested, the employee may elect under Section 83(b) to take any gain into income at the time of receipt of the stock. The election allows employees essentially to prepay a tax liability based on an expected low valuation, with an assumption that the equity value increases in the subsequent years. The employee will recognize compensation income in the amount of the excess, if any, of the stock's value over the amount paid for it. The employer receives a deduction at that time, equal to any compensation income recognized. The election must be made, no later than 30 days after the receipt of the stock, by filing a form with the IRS service center at which the employee files tax returns. The employee must also file a copy of the election with her tax return. The IRS is quite strict in applying the 30-day filing deadline, and one should not expect any flexibility on this point. Additionally, once such an election is made, it may not be revoked. This essentially means that if the stock depreciates, the employee will have overpaid the tax associated with the stock grant.

Note that a Section 83(b) election may be made even where the effect of making the election will be to recognize no income because at the time the stock was issued there was no spread between its value and the amount paid. Thus, such an election can be useful for an employee who does pay full value at a time when the prospects for subsequent appreciation in the stock are significant. The employee described previously, with $100 in forfeitable stock, could have filed an 83(b) election, recognized a gain of zero, and avoided the $50 gain when the risk of forfeiture lapsed.

Where management is purchasing stock in an acquiring entity or in a selling company that is the subject of a leveraged buyout at or before the acquisition closing and at the same price as other investors, it can usually be comfortably argued that the amount paid for the stock at the inception of the transaction is equal to its fair market value. In such a case, there will be no compensation income to the management participants under Section 83, provided that either the stock is substantially vested or the management participants file Section 83(b) elections.

If the employee's stock purchase is financed with a note, is Section 83 income avoided?

Management rarely has enough cash to buy as large an equity interest as it would like. The stock acquisition of management is usually financed by the company, the investor partner, or a third party. A promissory note from the employee will be treated as a bona fide payment for the stock in an amount equal to the face amount of the note, provided it meets two important requirements. First, the note should provide for adequate stated interest at least equal to the applicable federal rate. Second, the note should be with recourse to the employee.

What happens when management borrows from third-party investors rather than from the company itself?

Where stock of the company or a nonrecourse loan to buy stock in the company is made available to an employee from a party that is a shareholder in the company, the Section 83 rules make it clear that the employee will suffer the identical income tax results as if the stock or loan were made available directly from the company itself. As to the shareholder who makes the stock or loan available to the employee, any value transferred to the employee thereby is treated as having been contributed to the company by the shareholder on a tax-free basis. The only benefit obtained by the shareholder will be an increase in the basis in her stock of the company.

Can some of the employee's assets be protected from the recourse loan?

Typically, even in the most highly leveraged transactions, the amount of money required for management to purchase its shares cannot be repaid if the buyout does not succeed, without having a fairly severe impact on the lifestyle of the employee. Given a high level of confidence in the venture, and a relatively low stock purchase price, a management participant should be willing to risk his capital in a meaningful way, albeit not with personal bankruptcy as the consequence. In such cases, it might be worthwhile to consider a loan that gives the lender recourse to the borrowing employee, but specifically excludes recourse with respect to certain assets—for example, a house.

Although there is no authority on this question, one would have to stretch the Section 83 regulations substantially to treat such partially nonrecourse loans as nonqualified options. As long as the debt, and the personal liability of the employee thereon, is bona fide and real, it should probably be respected as such for tax purposes.

What other techniques provide management with full equity rights at a lower cost than the cost to third-party investors?

The most direct and effective means of reducing the cost of management stock relative to that purchased by other investors is through some multiclass arrangement. There are numerous variations on this theme. Here is an example of the most straightforward: Assume that a leveraged buyout is to be capitalized with $5 million in common equity, and that third-party investors are willing to put up this entire sum. The third-party investors could be given a preferred stock with a liquidation preference of $5 million and some reasonable preferred dividend rights. For a relatively nominal sum, both the third-party investors and management would purchase all of the common shares of the company.

By providing the third-party investors with preferential rights equal to virtually the entire shareholders' equity of the corporation, the book value, and arguably the fair market value of the common stock, will be nominal.

There are two problems with this arrangement. First, the IRS can argue that the preferred stock was in fact worth less than $5 million and that in any event the common stock was worth more than the nominal value ascribed to it because of the very low risk-reward ratio of the investment. Second, having more than one class of stock will prevent the company from electing to be an S corporation. Where S corporation status is desired, the purchase price of the common stock can be reduced by having third-party investors purchase deeply subordinated debt instruments in addition to their common stock.

If management already owns stock, how can management convert its existing stock ownership into stock in the buyer on a tax-free basis?

There are several tax-free ways in which management (as well as other shareholders) of a selling company may exchange existing equity in the target for a participating interest in the acquiring company in a leveraged buyout. Depending upon the other structural goals and requirements, a tax-free rollover may occur in the context of a recapitalization of the acquired company, some other tax-free reorganization, or a Section 351 National Starch transaction.

Achieving a tax-free rollover of management's equity can adversely affect other aspects of the tax structuring of the transaction. Most notably, if the management buyout is intended to be treated for tax purposes as a cost basis asset acquisition, overlapping ownership between the selling company and the buyer may thwart such a characterization.

If cash is received as part of the exchange, how is it treated?

Because LBOs involve a significant reduction in the value of the target's equity through increased debt financing, a target shareholder who wishes to retain an equity interest will either realize a significant increase in her percentage ownership of the outstanding stock or receive cash or other nonequity consideration in addition to the stock. In the latter case, management's tax advisors must analyze the facts to ensure that the receipt of nonstock consideration will be treated as capital gain rather than a dividend to the participant. One key difference between a dividend and capital gain is that under the latter characterization the shareholder will be permitted to reduce taxable income by her basis in the stock.

Do the same rules apply where management owns nonqualified options or substantially nonvested stock?

No. In the case of both nonqualified options and restricted stock subject to a substantial risk of forfeiture for which a Section 83(b) election has not been made, the exchange of the option or stock for stock in the buyer that is not subject to a substantial risk of forfeiture will give rise to compensation income under Section 83 in an amount equal to the value of the target stock involved. If the employee holds restricted stock for which he has made a Section 83(b) election, the employee will be eligible for tax-free treatment.

POSTACQUISITION TAX ISSUES

What is the principal tax planning goal in postdeal asset dispositions?

Postdeal asset disposition, if structured properly, can reduce or eliminate taxable gain.

It is helpful to illustrate this point with a simple scenario. Purchaser corporation P wishes to acquire target corporation T from selling corporation S in an LBO for $100. The operations of T consist of two divisions, T1 and T2. The purchase price for the T stock has been financed largely through borrowed funds. S has a tax basis in its T stock of $20, and T has a tax basis in the T1 and T2 assets of $0. To pay down acquisition debt, P must dispose of the T2 division to a third party shortly after the acquisition of T. Although the two divisions of T are of approximately equal value, P believes that it will be able to sell the T2 division alone for $60.

Proposition: If P has purchased all of T for $100, it should be able to dispose of all of T immediately thereafter for $100 and recognize no taxable gain. What should follow is that if P disposes of the T2 division, constituting one-half of the value of T, for $50, then no gain should be recognized there as well.

As a general matter, whether or not this proposition will be true depends upon whether P has purchased the assets of T or the stock of T.

The general rule is that the assets of T may not be disposed of by T without the recognition of a tax on the appreciation in those assets, notwithstanding that a buyer may have obtained a cost basis in the stock of T. The most direct and sure means of eliminating a second tax on built-in gain inside a target is to obtain a cost basis in the target's assets through a direct asset acquisition, forward cash merger, or Section 338 transaction.

OTHER TAX ISSUES

What role do state and local taxes play in structuring mergers, acquisitions, and buyouts?

State and local taxes generally play a secondary role in planning M/A/B transactions. First, most state income tax systems are based largely on the federal system, particularly in terms of what is taxable, to whom, when, and in what amount. Second, when the company being acquired operates in a number of states, it can be inordinately difficult to assess the interaction of the various state tax systems. On the other hand, tax planners cannot afford to ignore a transaction's state tax consequences. Although a detailed discussion of state income tax consequences deserves a book of its own, several extremely important state tax issues will be mentioned throughout the following discussion.

First and foremost, there are income taxes. These vary from state to state and may affect companies located outside the state. Beyond income taxes, there are numerous taxes imposed by states and localities that may affect an acquisition. Although these rarely amount to structural prohibitions or incentives, they often increase costs. For example, when real estate (including in some cases, leases) gets transferred, the buyer may owe taxes.[82]

Purchases of assets might not be exempt from a state's sales tax. Many states offer exemptions, but this should not be taken for granted. Check it out.

Certain types of state and local taxes not directly associated with an acquisition can be significantly affected by an acquisition or by the particular structure of the acquisition. For example, a state's real property and personal property taxes are based on an assessment of the value of the property owned by a taxpayer. Often, a transfer of ownership of the property will trigger a reassessment of the value of the property.

What is pro forma financial information?

Pro forma financial information reflects the impact on historical financial statements of a particular business combination and its financing as if the transaction had been consummated at an earlier date. While it is considered a non-GAAP measure, it is permitted under certain circumstances.[83] Pro forma information ordinarily includes (1) a description of the transaction, the entities involved, and the periods for which the pro forma information is presented, and (2) a columnar presentation of historical condensed balance sheet and income statements, pro forma adjustments, and pro forma results.

Pro forma adjustments to the income statement are computed assuming that the transaction was consummated at the beginning of the fiscal year and include adjustments that give effect to events that are (1) directly attributable to the transaction, (2) expected to have a continuing impact on the registrant, and (3) factually supportable.

Pro forma financial information might appear in both the private M&A and public M&A contexts. In the private M&A context, a seller might show how the selling company's financial results would have been reported if the company were controlled by a different shareholder. A typical adjustment in this case might include above-market compensation to a CEO or controlling shareholder. A selling company might present such information to prospective buyers in order to maximize the perceived earnings power and, hence, acquisition price of the target.

In the public M&A context, the acquiring corporation frequently might be required by GAAP to publish pro forma financial data in its 10-Q to reflect the acquisition. The most common adjustments to the acquiring corporation's actual results would include any adjustments under purchase accounting, as well as interest expense on acquisition or assumed debt, for the full reportable period, rather than just the period during which the target was part of the acquirer's actual results.

How should the fair value or carrying amount of preferred stock issued in business combinations be determined?

The distinctive attributes of preferred stock make some preferred issues similar to debt securities, whereas others are more similar to common stock, with many variations between the extremes. Determining the appropriate carrying value to assign to preferred stock issued in a business combination will be affected by its characteristics.

Even though the principle of recording the fair value of consideration received for stock issued applies to all equity securities, preferred as well as common, the carrying value of preferred securities may be determined in practice on the same basis as debt securities. For example, the carrying value of a nonvoting, nonconvertible preferred stock that lacks characteristics of common stock may be determined by comparing the specified dividend and redemption terms to debt securities with similar terms and market risks.

What is pushdown accounting?

Pushdown accounting refers to the establishment of a new accounting and reporting basis in an acquired company's separate financial statements, resulting from the purchase and substantial change of ownership of its outstanding voting equity securities. The buyer's purchase price is "pushed down" to the target and used to restate the carrying value of its assets and liabilities. For example, if all of a target's voting equity securities are purchased, the assets and liabilities of the acquired company are restated using fair market values so that the excess of the restated amounts of the assets over the restated amounts of the liabilities equals the buyer's purchase price.

In what circumstances should pushdown accounting be applied?

The SEC permits the use of pushdown accounting by public enterprises with respect to target corporations that are substantially or wholly owned.[84] As mentioned, under US GAAP, an acquirer of a target initially recognizes most of the assets and liabilities it acquires at liabilities at fair value. If the target prepares separate financial statements, the assets and liabilities could theoretically be presented in one of two ways: either the historical basis of the target or the "stepped-up basis" of the acquirer, meaning that the acquirer establishes a new basis for the assets and liabilities of the acquired company. This is called a "pushdown" of the acquirer's stepped-up basis. Pushdown accounting often results in higher net assets for the acquired company on the acquisition date because the assets and liabilities are stepped up to fair value and goodwill is recognized. This in turn usually results in lower net income after the acquisition because of higher amortization, higher depreciation, and potential impairment charges.[85]

CONCLUDING COMMENTS

Deal structuring is not for the faint of heart. It requires current, professional-grade knowledge of accounting standards, securities law, and tax law. Dealmakers should call on expert advisors with current M&A experience. At the same time, dealmakers should not shy away from learning about the structuring of their transaction. That way they can be sure that the transaction they are handling remains linked to the other aspects of their deal—including due diligence, the subject of the next chapter.

TRANSACTION DIAGRAMS

Exhibits 5-7 to 5-17 illustrate graphically many of the transactions discussed in this book. In each diagram, "SH" represents a shareholder, a square is a corporation, and a circle represents corporate assets. Vertical and diagonal lines indicate the ownership of stock or assets, and arrows represent the flow of cash, assets, stock, and so on.

Exhibit 5-7 Stock Purchase

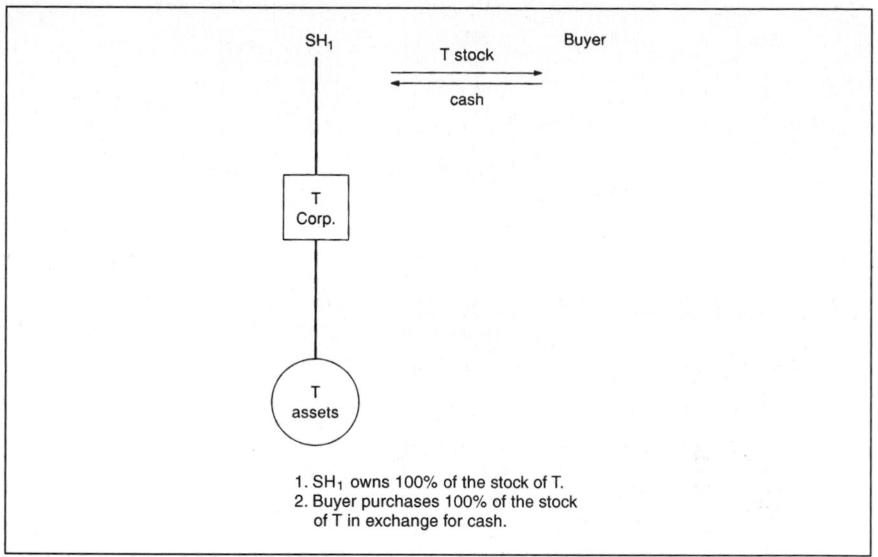
SH$_1$
Buyer
T stock
cash
T
Corp.
T
assets
1. SH$_1$ owns 100% of the stock of T.
2. Buyer purchases 100% of the stock of T in exchange for cash.

Exhibit 5-8 Asset Purchase

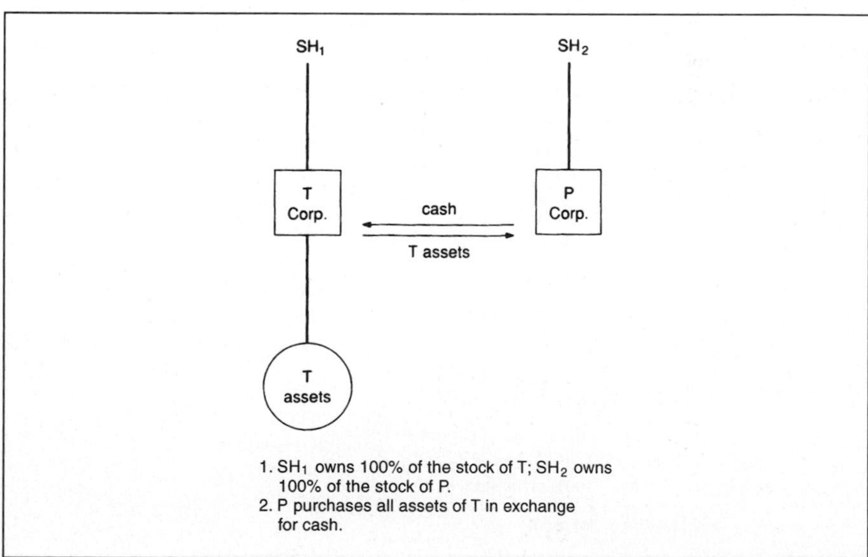
SH$_1$
SH$_2$
T
Corp.
cash
T assets
P
Corp.
T
assets
1. SH$_1$ owns 100% of the stock of T; SH$_2$ owns 100% of the stock of P.
2. P purchases all assets of T in exchange for cash.

Exhibit 5-9 Taxable Forward Merger

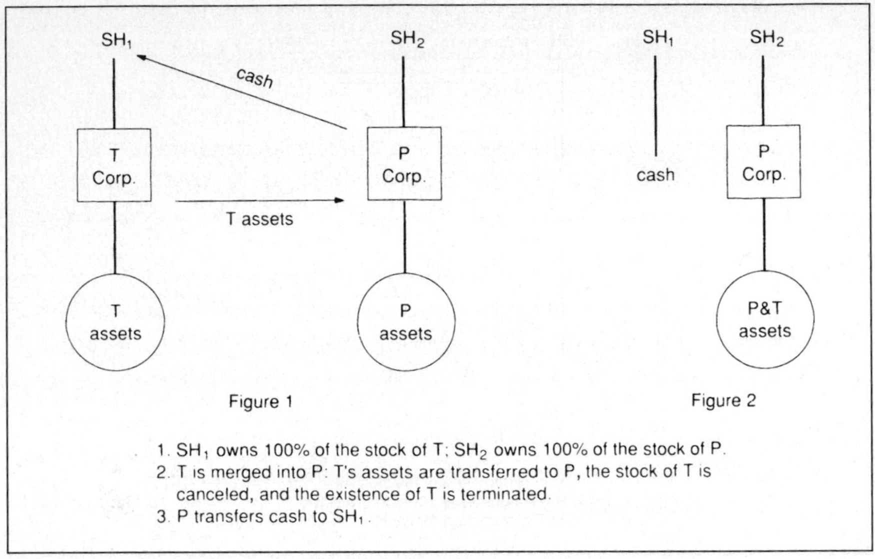
SH1
SH2
cash
T Corp.
P Corp.
T assets
T assets
P assets
Figure 1
SH1
SH2
cash
P Corp.
P&T assets
Figure 2
1. SH1 owns 100% of the stock of T; SH2 owns 100% of the stock of P.
2. T is merged into P: T's assets are transferred to P, the stock of T is canceled, and the existence of T is terminated.
3. P transfers cash to SH1.

Exhibit 5-10 Taxable Reverse Merger

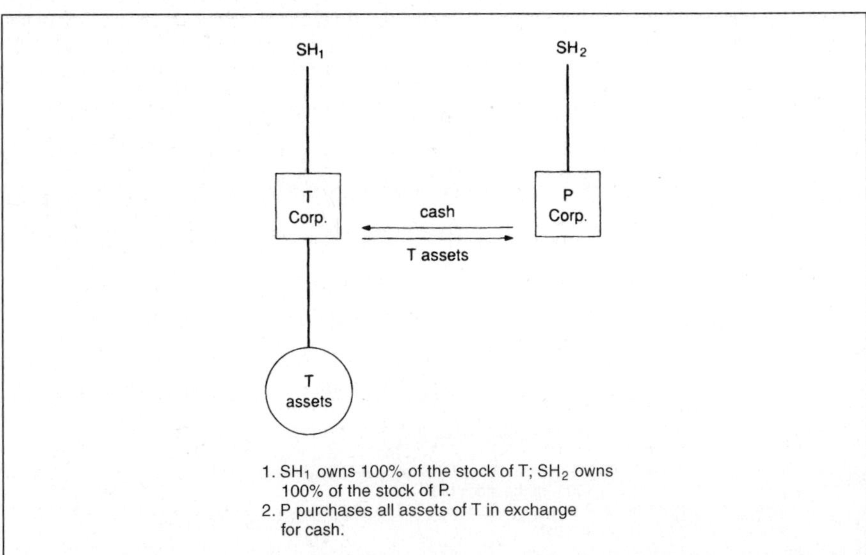
SH1
SH2
T Corp.
cash
P Corp.
T assets
T assets
1. SH1 owns 100% of the stock of T; SH2 owns 100% of the stock of P.
2. P purchases all assets of T in exchange for cash.

Exhibit 5-11 Taxable Forward Subsidiary Merger

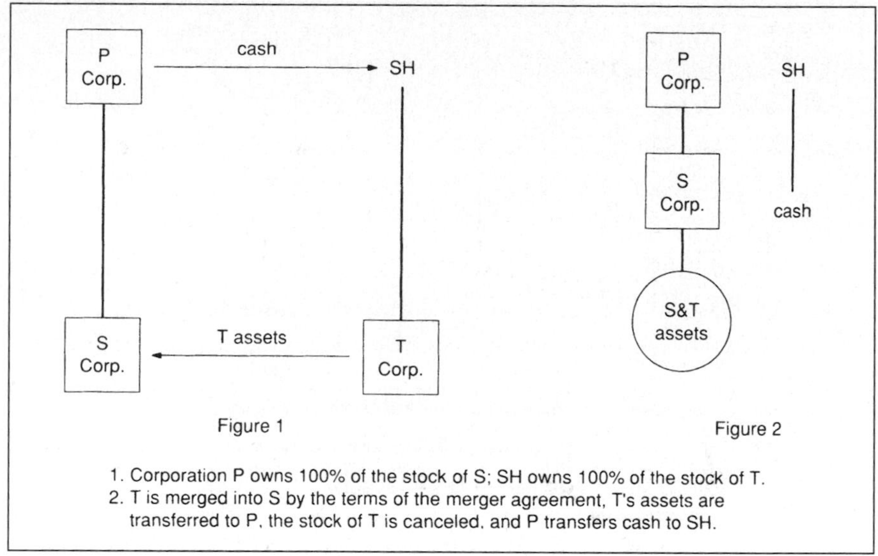

1. Corporation P owns 100% of the stock of S; SH owns 100% of the stock of T.
2. T is merged into S by the terms of the merger agreement, T's assets are transferred to P, the stock of T is canceled, and P transfers cash to SH.

Exhibit 5-12 Tax-Free Forward Merger (A Reorganization)

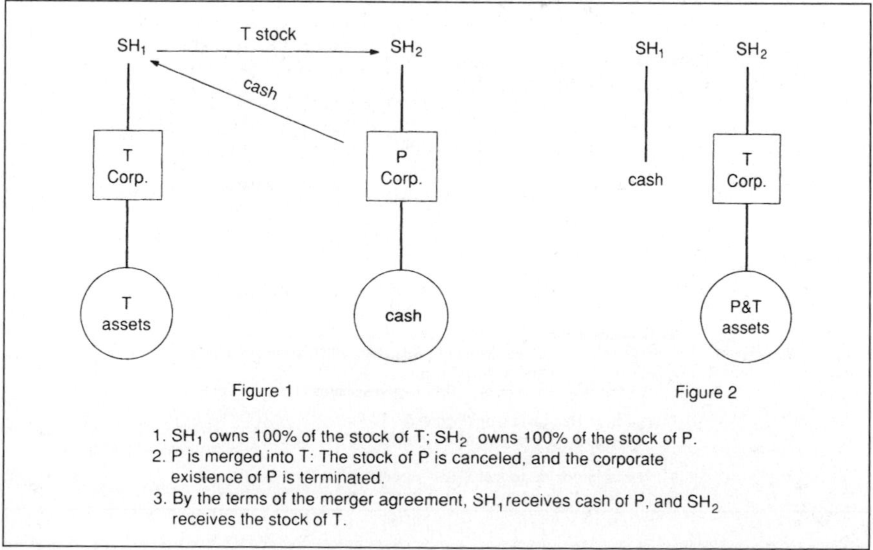

1. SH_1 owns 100% of the stock of T; SH_2 owns 100% of the stock of P.
2. P is merged into T: The stock of P is canceled, and the corporate existence of P is terminated.
3. By the terms of the merger agreement, SH_1 receives cash of P, and SH_2 receives the stock of T.

Exhibit 5-13 Tax-Free Forward Triangular Merger

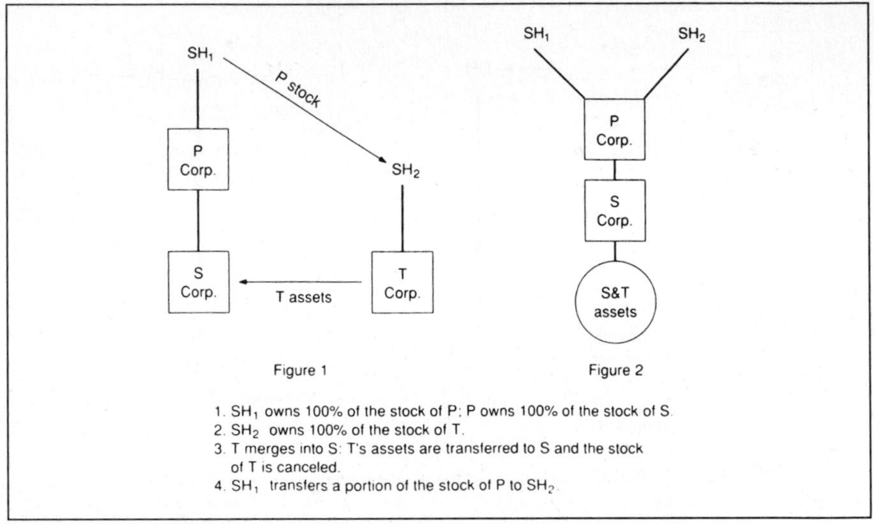

Exhibit 5-14 Tax-Free Acquisition of Stock for Voting Stock (B Reorganization)

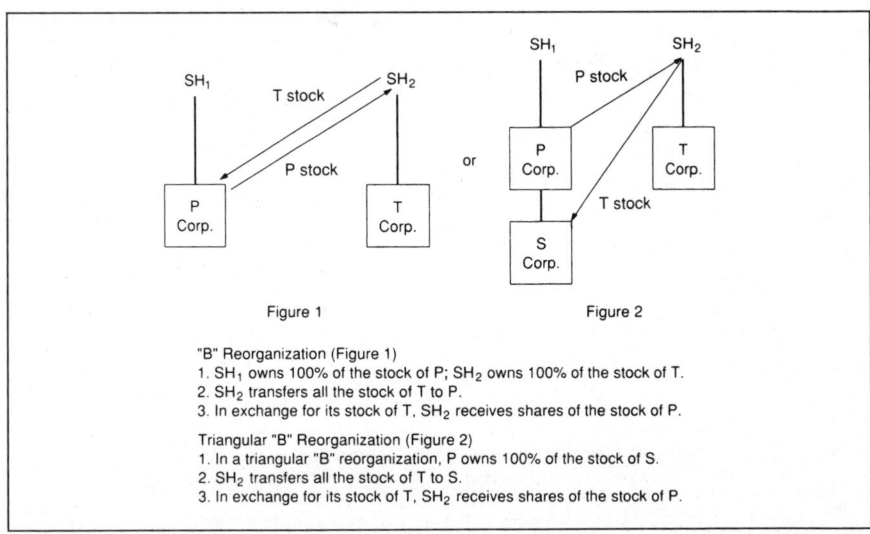

SH1
T stock
SH2
P stock
P Corp.
T Corp.
Figure 1
or
SH1
SH2
P stock
P Corp.
T Corp.
T stock
S Corp.
Figure 2
"B" Reorganization (Figure 1)
1. SH1 owns 100% of the stock of P; SH2 owns 100% of the stock of T.
2. SH2 transfers all the stock of T to P.
3. In exchange for its stock of T, SH2 receives shares of the stock of P.
Triangular "B" Reorganization (Figure 2)
1. In a triangular "B" reorganization, P owns 100% of the stock of S.
2. SH2 transfers all the stock of T to S.
3. In exchange for its stock of T, SH2 receives shares of the stock of P.

Exhibit 5-15 Acquisition of Property for Voting Stock (C Reorganization)

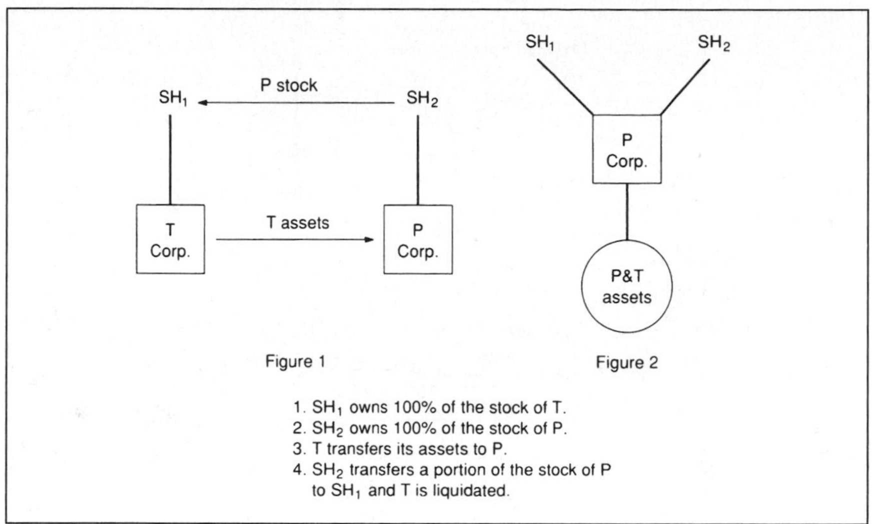

1. SH_1 owns 100% of the stock of T.
2. SH_2 owns 100% of the stock of P.
3. T transfers its assets to P.
4. SH_2 transfers a portion of the stock of P to SH_1 and T is liquidated.

Exhibit 5-16 Acquisition of Property for Voting Stock (D Reorganization)

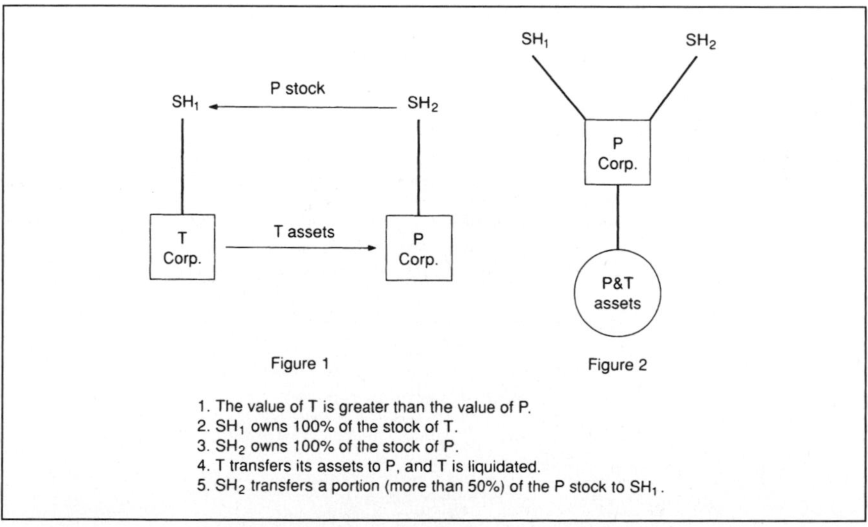

1. The value of T is greater than the value of P.
2. SH_1 owns 100% of the stock of T.
3. SH_2 owns 100% of the stock of P.
4. T transfers its assets to P, and T is liquidated.
5. SH_2 transfers a portion (more than 50%) of the P stock to SH_1.

Exhibit 5-17 National Starch Transaction (Section 351 Acquisition)

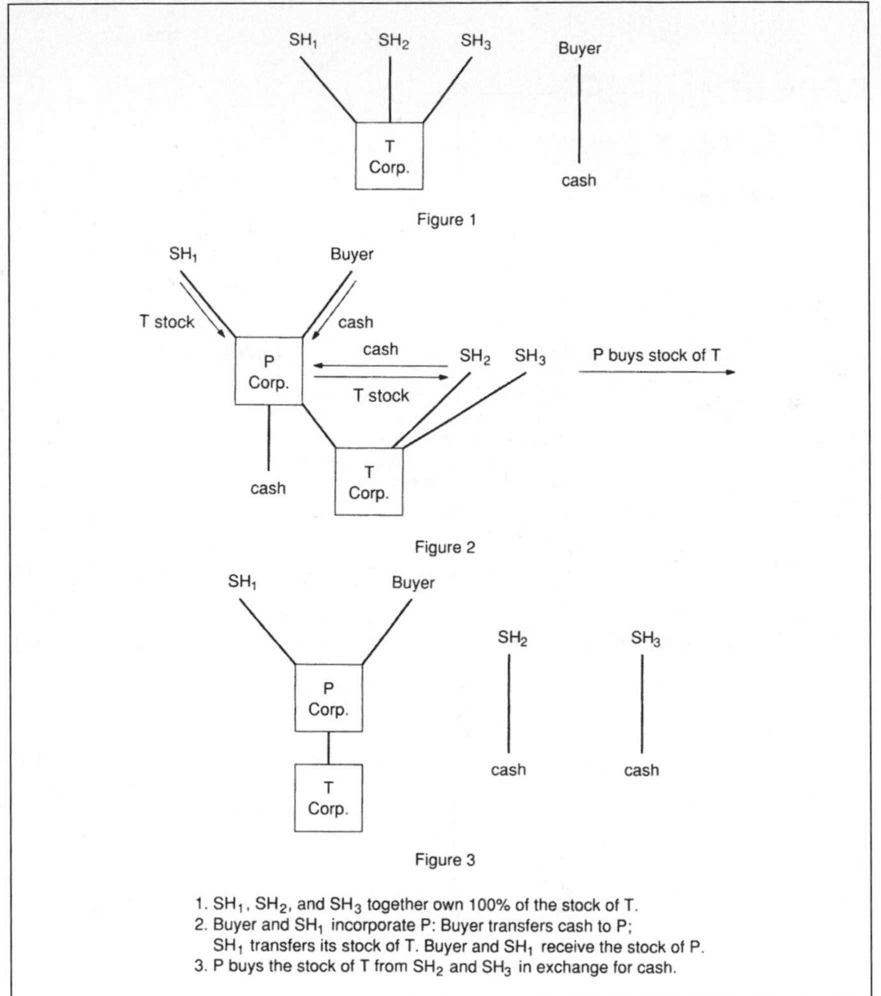

1. SH_1, SH_2, and SH_3 together own 100% of the stock of T.
2. Buyer and SH_1 incorporate P: Buyer transfers cash to P; SH_1 transfers its stock of T. Buyer and SH_1 receive the stock of P.
3. P buys the stock of T from SH_2 and SH_3 in exchange for cash.

APPENDIX 5A

Meeting the Reorganization Test: US Examples from the Internal Revenue Service

The following examples illustrate the rules of paragraph (b)(1) of [section 368 of the Internal Revenue Code]—namely, whether or not the transaction qualifies as a statutory merger or consolidation. In each of the examples, except as otherwise provided, each of R, V, Y, and Z is a C corporation. X is a domestic limited liability company. Except as otherwise provided, X is wholly owned by Y and is disregarded as an entity separate from Y for Federal income tax purposes. The examples are as follows:

Example 1. Divisive transaction pursuant to a merger statute.

(i) Facts. Under State W law, Z transfers some of its assets and liabilities to Y, retains the remainder of its assets and liabilities, and remains in existence for Federal income tax purposes following the transaction. The transaction qualifies as a merger under State W corporate law.

(ii) Analysis. The transaction does not satisfy the requirements of paragraph (b)(1)(ii)(A) of this section because all of the assets and liabilities of Z, the combining entity of the transferor unit, do not become the assets and liabilities of Y, the combining entity and sole member of the transferee unit. In addition, the transaction does not satisfy the requirements of paragraph (b)(1)(ii)(B) of this section because the separate legal existence of Z does not cease for all purposes. Accordingly, the transaction does not qualify as a statutory merger or consolidation under section 368(a)(1)(A).

Example 2. Merger of a target corporation into a disregarded entity in exchange for stock of the owner.

(i) Facts. Under State W law, Z merges into X. Pursuant to such law, the following events occur simultaneously at the effective time of the transaction: all of the assets and liabilities of Z become the assets and liabilities of X, and Z's separate legal existence ceases for all purposes. In the merger, the Z shareholders exchange their stock of Z for stock of Y.

(ii) Analysis. The transaction satisfies the requirements of paragraph (b)(1)(ii) of this section because the transaction is effected pursuant to State W law and the following events occur simultaneously at the effective time of the transaction: all of the assets and liabilities of Z, the combining entity and sole member of the transferor unit, become the assets and liabilities of one or more members of the transferee unit that is comprised of Y, the combining entity of the transferee unit, and X, a disregarded entity the assets of which Y is treated as owning for Federal income tax purposes, and Z ceases its separate legal existence for all purposes. Accordingly, the transaction qualifies as a statutory merger or consolidation for purposes of section 368(a)(1)(A).

Example 3. Merger of a target S corporation that owns a QSub into a disregarded entity.

(i) Facts. The facts are the same as in Example 2, except that Z is an S corporation and owns all of the stock of U, a QSub.

(ii) Analysis. The deemed formation by Z of U pursuant to § 1.1361-5(b)(1) (as a consequence of the termination of U's QSub election) is disregarded for Federal income tax purposes. The transaction is treated as a transfer of the assets of U to X, followed by X's transfer of these assets to U in exchange for stock of U. See § 1.1361-5(b)(3) Example 9. The transaction will, therefore, satisfy the requirements of paragraph (b)(1)(ii) of this section because the transaction is effected pursuant to State W law and the following events occur simultaneously at the effective time of the transaction: all of the assets and liabilities of Z and U, the sole members of the transferor unit, become the assets and liabilities of one or more members of the transferee unit that is comprised of Y, the combining entity of the transferee unit, and X, a disregarded entity the assets of which Y is treated as owning for Federal income tax purposes, and Z ceases its separate legal existence for all purposes. Moreover, the deemed transfer of the assets of U in exchange for U stock does not cause the transaction to fail to qualify as a statutory merger or consolidation. See § 368(a)(2)(C). Accordingly, the transaction qualifies as a statutory merger or consolidation for purposes of section 368(a)(1)(A).

Example 4. Triangular merger of a target corporation into a disregarded entity.

(i) Facts. The facts are the same as in Example 2, except that V owns 100 percent of the outstanding stock of Y and, in the merger of Z into X, the Z shareholders exchange their stock of Z for stock of V. In the transaction, Z transfers substantially all of its properties to X.

(ii) Analysis. The transaction is not prevented from qualifying as a statutory merger or consolidation under section 368(a)(1)(A), provided the requirements of section 368(a)(2)(D) are satisfied. Because the assets of X are treated for Federal income tax purposes as the assets of Y, Y will be treated as acquiring substantially all of the properties of Z in the merger for purposes of determining whether the merger satisfies the requirements of section 368(a)(2)(D). As a result, the Z shareholders that receive stock of V will be treated as receiving stock of a corporation that is in control of Y, the combining entity of the transferee unit that is the acquiring corporation for purposes of section 368(a)(2)(D). Accordingly, the merger will satisfy the requirements of section 368(a)(2)(D).

Example 5. Merger of a target corporation into a disregarded entity owned by a partnership.

(i) Facts. The facts are the same as in Example 2, except that Y is organized as a partnership under the laws of State W and is classified as a partnership for Federal income tax purposes.

(ii) Analysis. The transaction does not satisfy the requirements of paragraph (b)(1)(ii)(A) of this section. All of the assets and liabilities of Z, the combining entity and sole member of the transferor unit, do not become the assets and liabilities of one or more members of a transferee unit because neither X nor Y qualifies as a combining entity. Accordingly, the transaction cannot qualify as a statutory merger or consolidation for purposes of section 368(a)(1)(A).

Example 6. Merger of a disregarded entity into a corporation.

(i) Facts. Under State W law, X merges into Z. Pursuant to such law, the following events occur simultaneously at the effective time of the transaction: all of the assets and liabilities of X (but not the assets and liabilities of Y other than those of X) become the assets and liabilities of Z and X's separate legal existence ceases for all purposes.

(ii) Analysis. The transaction does not satisfy the requirements of paragraph (b)(1)(ii)(A) of this section because all of the assets and liabilities of a transferor unit do not become the assets and liabilities of one or more members of the transferee unit. The transaction also does not satisfy the requirements of paragraph (b)(1)(ii)(B) of this section because X does not qualify as a combining entity. Accordingly, the transaction cannot qualify as a statutory merger or consolidation for purposes of section 368(a)(1)(A).

Example 7. Merger of a corporation into a disregarded entity in exchange for interests in the disregarded entity.

(i) Facts. Under State W law, Z merges into X. Pursuant to such law, the following events occur simultaneously at the effective time of the transaction: all of the assets and liabilities of Z become the assets and liabilities of X and Z's separate legal existence ceases for all purposes. In the merger of Z into X, the Z shareholders exchange their stock of Z for interests in X so that, immediately after the merger, X is not disregarded as an entity separate from Y for Federal income tax purposes. Following the merger, pursuant to § 301.7701-3(b)(1)(i) of this chapter, X is classified as a partnership for Federal income tax purposes.

(ii) Analysis. The transaction does not satisfy the requirements of paragraph (b)(1)(ii)(A) of this section because immediately after the merger X is not disregarded as an entity separate from Y and, consequently, all of the assets and liabilities of Z, the combining entity of the transferor unit, do not become the assets and liabilities of one or more members of a transferee unit. Accordingly, the transaction cannot qualify as a statutory merger or consolidation for purposes of section 368(a)(1)(A).

Example 8. Merger transaction preceded by distribution.

(i) Facts. Z operates two unrelated businesses, Business P and Business Q, each of which represents 50 percent of the value of the assets of Z. Y desires to acquire and continue operating Business P, but does not want to acquire Business Q. Pursuant to a single plan, Z sells Business Q for cash to parties unrelated to Z and Y in a taxable transaction, and then distributes the proceeds of the sale pro rata to its shareholders. Then, pursuant to State W law, Z merges into Y. Pursuant to such law, the following events occur simultaneously at the effective time of the transaction: all of the assets and liabilities of Z related to Business P become the assets and liabilities of Y and Z's separate legal existence ceases for all purposes. In the merger, the Z shareholders exchange their Z stock for Y stock.

(ii) Analysis. The transaction satisfies the requirements of paragraph (b)(1)(ii) of this section because the transaction is effected pursuant to State W law and the following events occur simultaneously at the effective time of the transaction: all of the assets and liabilities of Z, the combining entity and sole member of the transferor unit, become the assets and liabilities of Y, the combining entity and sole member of the transferee unit, and Z ceases its separate legal existence for all purposes. Accordingly, the transaction qualifies as a statutory merger or consolidation for purposes of section 368(a)(1)(A).

Example 9. State law conversion of target corporation into a limited liability company.

(i) Facts. Y acquires the stock of V from the V shareholders in exchange for consideration that consists of 50 percent voting stock of Y and 50 percent cash. Immediately after the stock acquisition, V files the necessary documents to convert from a corporation to a limited liability company under State W law. Y's acquisition of the stock of V and the conversion of V to a limited liability company are steps in a single integrated acquisition by Y of the assets of V.

(ii) Analysis. The acquisition by Y of the assets of V does not satisfy the requirements of paragraph (b)(1)(ii)(B) of this section because V, the combining entity of the transferor unit, does not cease its separate legal existence. Although V is an entity disregarded from its owner for Federal income tax purposes, it continues to exist as a juridical entity after the conversion. Accordingly, Y's acquisition of the assets of V does not qualify as a statutory merger or consolidation for purposes of section 368(a)(1)(A).

Example 10. Dissolution of target corporation.

(i) Facts. Y acquires the stock of Z from the Z shareholders in exchange for consideration that consists of 50 percent voting stock of Y and 50 percent cash. Immediately after the stock acquisition, Z files a certificate of dissolution pursuant to State W law and commences winding up its activities. Under State W dissolution law, ownership and title to Z's assets does not automatically vest in Y upon dissolution. Instead, Z transfers assets to its creditors in satisfaction of its liabilities and transfers its remaining assets to Y in the liquidation stage of the dissolution. Y's acquisition of the stock of Z and the dissolution of Z are steps in a single integrated acquisition by Y of the assets of Z.

(ii) Analysis. The acquisition by Y of the assets of Z does not satisfy the requirements of paragraph (b)(1)(ii) of this section because Y does not acquire all of the assets of Z as a result of Z filing the certificate of dissolution or simultaneously with Z ceasing its separate legal existence. Instead, Y acquires the assets of Z by reason of Z's transfer of its assets to Y. Accordingly, Y's acquisition of the assets of Z does not qualify as a statutory merger or consolidation for purposes of section 368(a)(1)(A).

Example 11. Merger of corporate partner into a partnership.

(i) Facts. Y owns an interest in X, an entity classified as a partnership for Federal income tax purposes, that represents a 60 percent capital and profits interest in X. Z owns an interest in X that represents a 40 percent capital and profits interest. Under State W law, Z merges into X. Pursuant to such law, the following events occur simultaneously at the effective time of the transaction: all of the assets and liabilities of Z become the assets and liabilities of X and Z ceases its separate legal existence for all purposes. In the merger, the Z shareholders exchange their stock of Z for stock of Y. As a result of the merger, X becomes an entity that is disregarded as an entity separate from Y for Federal income tax purposes.

(ii) Analysis. The transaction satisfies the requirements of paragraph (b)(1)(ii) of this section because the transaction is effected pursuant to State W law and the following events occur simultaneously at the effective time of the transaction: all of the assets and liabilities of Z, the combining entity and sole member of the transferor unit, become the assets and liabilities of one or more members of the transferee unit that is comprised of Y, the combining entity of the transferee unit, and X, a disregarded entity the assets of which Y is treated as owning for Federal income tax purposes immediately after the transaction, and Z ceases its separate legal existence for all purposes. Accordingly, the transaction qualifies as a statutory merger or consolidation for purposes of section 368(a)(1)(A).

Example 12. State law consolidation.

(i) Facts. Under State W law, Z and V consolidate. Pursuant to such law, the following events occur simultaneously at the effective time of the transaction: all of the assets and liabilities of Z and V become the assets and liabilities of Y, an entity that is created in the transaction, and the existence of Z and V continues in Y. In the consolidation, the Z shareholders and the V shareholders exchange their stock of Z and V, respectively, for stock of Y.

(ii) Analysis. With respect to each of Z and V, the transaction satisfies the requirements of paragraph (b)(1)(ii) of this section because the transaction is effected pursuant to State W law and the following events occur simultaneously at the effective time of the transaction: all of the assets and liabilities of Z and V, respectively, each of which is the combining entity of a transferor unit, become the assets and liabilities of Y, the combining entity and sole member of the transferee unit, and Z and V each ceases its separate legal existence for all purposes. Accordingly, the transaction qualifies as the statutory merger or consolidation of each of Z and V into Y for purposes of section 368(a)(1)(A).

(For foreign examples, see Chapter 12.)

NOTES

1. http://uscode.house.gov/.
2. https://www.congress.gov/bill/115th-congress/house-bill/1/text; see also https://www.congress.gov/115/bills/hr1/BILLS-115hr1enr.pdf.
3. A client memo from Skadden Arps states: "The TCJA generally does not change the tax-free reorganization rules or the rules related to other types of corporate transactions, including spin-offs, corporate liquidations and incorporation transactions. For example, the same rules that previously determined whether a particular acquisition would qualify as a tax-free reorganization, such as the relative mix of stock and cash consideration, continue to apply following the enactment of the TCJA. Similarly, the requirements for a spin-off or split-off to qualify as tax-free to both the distributing corporation and its shareholders are unchanged."
4. For an overview of these changes, see "Impact of US Tax Reform on Mergers and Acquisitions: New Opportunities and Pitfalls," Skadden, January 18, 2018, https://www.skadden.com/insights/publications/2018/01/an-in-depth-look-at-the-impact-of-us-tax-reform. See also note 54 for a subsequent update on NOLs.

5. These four default exceptions are cited in Stephen M. Procter, "Another Illinois Case Decides When an Asset Purchaser Is Responsible for Liabilities as a Mere Continuation of the Seller," Masuda Funai, June 1, 2017, https://www.masudafunai.com/articles/another-illinois-case-decides-when-an-asset-purchaser-is-responsible-for-liabilities-as-a-mere-continuation-of-the-seller.
6. Gary Matso, "De Facto Merger: The Threat of Unexpected Successor Liability," ABA Business Law Today, https://businesslawtoday.org/2018/03/de-facto-merger-the-threat-of-unexpected-successor-liability/.
7. The Uniform Commercial Code is produced by the American Law Institute and the National Conference of Commissioners on Uniform State Laws. Its nine articles cover general provisions, sales, leases, negotiable instruments, bank deposits and collections, funds transfer, letters of credit, bulk sales and bulk transfers, documents of titles, investment securities, and secured transactions. For the full text, see https://www.law.cornell.edu/ucc.
8. Louisiana has adopted all of the UCC, with the exception of UCC Article 2 "Sales," UCC Article 2A "Leases," and UCC Article 6 "Bulk Sales." "Louisiana Oddities in Secured Transactions," American Bar Association 2017 Business Law Section, Spring Meeting, April 6, 2017, presented by R. Marshall Grodner and Kristi W. Richard, McGlinchey Stafford, apps.americanbar.org/webupload/commupload/CL190016/...files/spring_2017.pdf.
9. For an example of the procedure of notification, see http://www.state.nj.us/treasury/taxation/faqbulksale.shtml.
10. For example, in January 2018, New Jersey amended the law with respect to real estate transactions among nonincorporated individuals. http://www.state.nj.us/treasury/taxation/faqbulksale.shtml.
11. There will be capital gains if the target liquidates, and otherwise, generally, a dividend. At the present time, if the

target is a US company, US individual shareholders get capital gain rate on dividends, but no basis offset.

12. See Zoe Henry, Inc., "Under New Tax Law, Should Your Business Restructure as a C Corporation?," December 21, 2017, https://www.inc.com/zoe-henry/new-tax-law-startups-re-structure-c-corp.html.
13. Delaware General Corporation Law, Title 8, Subchapter X. Sale of Assets, Dissolution and Winding Up, Section 271, http://delcode.delaware.gov/title8/c001/sc10/index.shtml.
14. See "What Rights Do Minority Shareholders Have in a Dispute?," Bashian & Farber, LLP, March 19, 2018, https://www.bashianfarberlaw.com/blog/2018/03/what-rights-do-minority-shareholders-have-in-a-dispute.shtml.
15. In a reverse triangular merger, the private equity buyer forms a "Newco" group, which has two levels: a holding company that receives the consideration paid by the buyer, and a merger subsidiary, which merges with and into the target, with the target surviving the merger. The International Comparative Legal Guide to Private Equity,. https://www.srz.com/images/content/1/5/v2/150389/The-International-Comparative-Legal-Guide-to-Private-Equity-2017.pdf.
16. For example, Delaware law states that, among other conditions, "[U]nless expressly required by its certificate of incorporation, no vote of stockholders of a constituent corporation shall be necessary to authorize a merger with or into a single direct or indirect wholly-owned subsidiary of such constituent corporation if: [the] constituent corporation and the direct or indirect wholly-owned subsidiary of [the] constituent corporation are the only constituent entities to the merger." See Chapter 1, General Corporation Law, Subchapter IX. Merger, Consolidation or Conversion, Section 251 (g), http://delcode.delaware.gov/title8/c001/sc09/index.shtml.
17. "When it comes to nontax issues, forward triangular mergers are usually less favorable than reverse triangular mergers. They can have a big impact on the target company's licenses and

contracts, because third parties can withhold consent to the assignment of contracts and licenses to the acquirer, and seek a price for providing such consent." InvestorsHub, May 17, 2018, https://investorshub.advfn.com/boards/read_msg.aspx?message_id=140857515.

18. Title 8 Corporations, Chapter 1. General Corporation Law, Subchapter IX. Merger, Consolidation or Conversion, § 251 Merger or consolidation of domestic corporations, http://delcode.delaware.gov/title8/c001/sc09/index.shtml.
19. Delaware law defines *holding company* as follows: "The term 'holding company' means a corporation which, from its incorporation until consummation of a merger governed by this subsection, was at all times a direct or indirect wholly-owned subsidiary of the constituent corporation and whose capital stock is issued in such merger."
20. The citation for this rule in the Code of Federal Regulations is 17 CFR 240.14d-10—Equal treatment of security holders, https://www.law.cornell.edu/cfr/text/17/240.14d-10.
21. See "IRS issues step transaction guidance on 'north-south' transactions," PWC, May 5, 2017, https://www.pwc.com/us/en/tax-services/publications/insights/assets/pwc-irs-step-transaction-guidance-on-%27north-south%27-transactions.pdf.
22. The SEC issues no-action, interpretive, and exemptive letters in particular cases where questions arise about what constitutes a security, and what constitutes the sale or exchange of a security, among other matters. These letters are listed at https://www.sec.gov/divisions/corpfin/cf-noaction.shtml#2a3.
23. The text of Rule 145 appears in the Code of Federal Regulations (CFR) at https://www.law.cornell.edu/cfr/text/17/230.145.
24. Rule 505 has been repealed. Rule 506(b) prohibits general solicitation and limits sales to no more than 35 nonaccredited investors. Rule 506(c) permits general solicitation where all

purchasers of the securities are accredited investors and the issuer takes reasonable steps to verify that the purchasers are accredited investors. Securities issued pursuant to Rules 506(b) and 506(c) are deemed restricted securities. https://www.sec.gov/rules/final/2016/33-10238.pdf.

25. https://www.law.cornell.edu/cfr/text/17/230.501.
26. According to the SEC, "Rule 144 permits the resale of restricted securities if a number of conditions are met, including holding the securities for six months or one year, depending on whether the issuer has been filing reports under the Exchange Act." https://www.sec.gov/smallbusiness/exemptofferings/faq.
27. https://www.law.cornell.edu/cfr/text/17/230.144A.
28. For the FASB's discussion of broad transactions, see https://asc.fasb.org/area&trid=2122744.
29. The Financial Accounting Standards Board (FASB) is currently planning on giving most of the content in Topic 810 a new number, Topic 812. The reference here is to both numbers—810 to reference the current number as this book goes press, and 812 to reference the number that is likely to be official in 2019 and beyond.
30. ASC 805, Section 10 Overall, https://asc.fasb.org/section&trid=2899126.
31. Accounting Standards Update (ASU) No. 2017-01, *Business Combinations: Clarifying the Definition of a Business.*
32. ASC 820, Fair Value Measurement, https://asc.fasb.org/topic&trid=2155941.
33. Topic 350, Intangibles—Goodwill and Other, https://asc.fasb.org/topic&trid=2144416.
34. The author acknowledges with special gratitude the guidance found in the following resources: Michelle Brower and Jay Wachowicz, "Acquisition Accounting," presentation for Financial Executives International, September 12, 2017, https://www.financialexecutives.org/getattachment/Events/Event

-Builder/FEI-Presentation-(September-2017-Webinar)-091117.pdf.aspx?lang=en-US; and "Consider Financial Reporting Issues Before Closing," http://www.bakertilly.com/insights/business-combinations-consider-financial-reporting-issues-before-closing/. For IFRS accounting, the following is recommended: "Investment Banking Manual of the Corporate Finance Institute" (2018), in its section on Purchase Accounting for Merger or Acquisition, (undated), at https://corporatefinanceinstitute.com/resources/ebooks/investment-banking/purchase-accounting-merger-acquisition/.

35. In a blog titled "Don't Fall in the GAAP" (July 2015), Brian West, CPA, writes: "A close not occurring at month-end can present accounting departments with several financial statement concerns. The primary issue: Most accounting departments aren't set up to close in the middle of a month. Systems may not be prepared to provide reports for this period. There are also other issues, including adjusting controls over the cutoff of receivables and payables or the counting of inventory. In most circumstances, closing at month-end is advisable. If this is not possible or there are circumstances that cause delays, it's important to include your accounting department and audit firm in these discussions early, so they can make necessary adjustments and preparations."

36. John Nicklas, *Accounting for Acquisition Transaction Costs*, Meaden and Moore, April 25, 2018.

37. Common Pitfalls of Business Combination Accounting, https://www.dhgllp.com/Portals/4/ResourceMedia/publications/Common-Pitfalls-of-Business-Combination-Accounting-1.pdf.

38. See https://www.law.cornell.edu/cfr/text/26/1.263(a)-1, https://www.irs.gov/businesses/corporations/examination-of-transaction-costs-in-the-acquisition-of-businesses, BNN, https://www.bnncpa.com/resources/library/tax_treatment_of_merger_acquisition_costs.

39. Topic Number 703—Basis of Assets, IRS, February 1, 2018, https://www.irs.gov/taxtopics/tc703.
40. 26 U.S. Code § 301—Distributions of property, https://www.law.cornell.edu/uscode/text/26/301.
41. http://uscode.house.gov/.
42. "About Form 1122, Authorization and Consent of Subsidiary Corporation to be Included in a Consolidated Income Tax Return," https://www.irs.gov/forms-pubs/form-1122-authorization-and-consent-of-subsidiary-corporation-to-be-included-in-a-consolidated-income-tax-return.
43. https://taxfoundation.org/us-corporate-income-tax-more-competitive/.
44. See "Focus on New Tax Law: Section 199A Pass-Through Deductions and Restrictions on Interest Deductions," *Tax Update* (2018), no. 2.
45. For the restrictions and how some may resolve them, see Lydia O'Neal, "How Firms Could Sidestep Tax Law's Pass-Through Deduction Limits," BNA, March 27, 2018, https://www.bna.com/firms-sidestep-tax-n57982090462/.
46. A KPMG guide titled *Tax Reform: KPMG Report on the New Tax Law* (2018) notes that in the new tax law "tax rates for capital gains and dividends are left unchanged. Also left unchanged is the 3.8 percent net investment income tax." https://home.kpmg.com/content/dam/kpmg/us/pdf/2018/02/tnf-new-law-book-feb6-2018.pdf.
47. Consider, for example, the S.2688—Capital Gains Inflation Relief Act of 2018, introduced by Senator Ted Cruz, April 17, 2018. https://www.congress.gov/bill/115th-congress/senate-bill/2688/text?q=%7B%22search%22%3A%5B22capital+gains%22%5D%7D&r=4.
48. The TCJA retains the 0 percent, 15 percent, and 20 percent rates on long-term capital gains and qualified dividends. However for the period 2018–2025, these rates have their own brackets,

which are no longer tied to ordinary personal income brackets. Here are the 2018 brackets for LTCGs and dividends.

	Single	Joint	Head of household
0% tax bracket	$0–38,600	$0–$77,200	$0–$51,700
Beginning of 15% tax bracket	$38,601	$77,201	$51,701
Beginning of 20% tax bracket	$425,801	$479,001	$452,401

After 2018, the amounts in these brackets will be indexed for inflation.

Higher-income individuals are still exposed to the 3.8 percent NIIT. So such an individual could owe 18.8 percent (15% + 3.8% for the NIIT) or 23.8 percent (20% + 3.8%) to the federal government instead of the basic 15 percent or 20 percent.

49. The TCJA amended section 163(j) of the IRC. See Initial Guidance Under Section 163(j) as Applicable to Taxable Years Beginning After December 31, 2017, Notice 2018-28: "For any taxpayer to which section 163(j) applies, section 163(j)(1) now limits the taxpayer's annual deduction for business interest expense to the sum of: (1) the taxpayer's business interest income (as defined in section 163(j)(6)) for the taxable year; (2) 30 percent of the taxpayer's adjusted taxable income (as defined in section 163(j)(8)) for the taxable year; and (3) the taxpayer's floor plan financing interest (as defined in section 163(j)(9)) for the taxable year." https://www.irs.gov/pub/irs-drop/n-18-28.pdf. Until 2021, the taxpayer's annual business interest expense is generally limited to: business interest income; 30 percent of adjustable taxable income (equivalent to earnings before interest, taxes, depreciation, and amortization, or EBITDA). From 2022 on, depreciation and amortization will not be taken into account, so the deductible expense will be based on 30 percent of earnings before interest and taxes (EBIT), with an exception applying to certain regulated public utilities and small businesses.

50. Credit for this Q&A goes to Dr. Solange Charas, founder, Charas Consulting, and the opening sections of Pepper Hamilton, LLP, "Personal Goodwill: Opportunities for Buyers and Sellers," *Tax Update* (2018), no. 5, https://www.jdsupra.com/legalnews/personal-goodwill-opportunities-for-48114/.
51. https://www.law.cornell.edu/uscode/text/26/338.
52. See "Net operating losses (NOLs) after the Tax Cuts and Jobs Act, Understanding the limitation on future use and carryback of NOLs," updated March 29, 2018, https://rsmus.com/what-we-do/services/tax/washington-national-tax/net-operating-losses-after-the-tax-cuts-and-jobs-act.html.
53. For a recent twist on this issue, see IRS notice 2018–30 effective for any ownership changes (as defined in section 382(g)) that occur after May 8, 2018, https://www.irs.gov/pub/irs-drop/n-18-30.pdf. For an explanation of this notice, see "Section 382 recognized built-in gains, losses determined without regard to section 168(k)," May 8, 2018, https://home.kpmg.com/us/en/home/insights/2018/05/tnf-notice-2018-30-section-382-recognized-built-in-gains-losses-determined-without-regard-to-section-168k-immediate-expensing.html.
54. See 26 U.S. Code § 384—Limitation on use of preacquisition losses to offset built-in gains, https://www.law.cornell.edu/uscode/text/26/384.
55. "M&A Impact of Pass-Through Conversion," Grant Thornton, February 2018, https://www.grantthornton.com/library/articles/tax/2018/M-and-A-impact-pass-through-conversion.aspx.
56. In some cases, the executor must provide a statement identifying the FMV of certain inherited property to the individual receiving that property. Internal Revenue Service, "Gifts and Inheritances," https://www.irs.gov/faqs/interest-dividends-other-types-of-income/gifts-inheritances/gifts-inheritances.
57. 26 U.S. Code § 351—Transfer to corporation controlled by transferor, https://www.law.cornell.edu/uscode/text/26/351.

Note that abuses of Section 351 are officially recognized as "Recognized Abusive and Listed Transactions" by the IRS. See https://www.irs.gov/businesses/corporations/listed-transactions#12.

58. As noted by CPA firm Peterson Sullivan LLP (which expresses these requirements in five categories), "If even one of the requirements above is not met, the transaction will fail to qualify for tax-free treatment under §368." https://www.pscpa.com/time-for-a-change-tax-free-reorganizations/.
59. 26 CFR 1.368-2—Definition of terms, https://www.law.cornell.edu/cfr/text/26/1.368-2#b_1_ii_A.
60. For recent application in a partnership context, see Tax Court (T.C.) Memo 2018-59 for a case involving two trading companies. https://www.ustaxcourt.gov/USTCInOP/OpinionViewer.aspx?ID=11634.
61. For commentary on dropdowns, see Nick Niermann, "Minimizing Taxes in Designing the Sale of a Business," McGrath North, 2018, https://www.mcgrathnorth.com/publications/minimizing-taxes-in-designing-the-sale-of-a-business/. He states, "Private equity groups like PEG often encourage—and sellers often want—to leave part of their target company ("T") stock in the deal. Sellers want this to be a tax-deferred rollover, i.e. they want no tax on their retained shares until they are sold in the future. The PEGs want to step-up the basis in T's assets to the amount of the transaction price. This allows for higher future depreciation and amortization tax deductions." He notes some complications with this structure.
62. *John A. Nelson Co. v. Helvering,* 296 U.S. 374 (1935), https://supreme.justia.com/cases/federal/us/296/374/case.html.
63. For a memo to IRS examiners on milestone payments, see "Updated Guidance on the Examination of Milestone Payments in the Acquisition of Businesses," https://www.irs.gov/businesses/updated-guidance-on-the-examination-of-milestone-payments-in-the-acquisition-of-businesses.

64. A C corporation that files a consolidated income tax return with its corporate parent can get a pass-through treatment. The earnings of all C corporations are subject to double taxation, but the consolidated return provisions generally permit the earnings of subsidiary members of the consolidated return group to be taxed to the ultimate parent only. The earnings of an S corporation, with certain exceptions, are subject to taxation only at the shareholder level. The earnings of a partnership are also subject to a single tax, though where a C corporation is a partner, its share of the earnings will ultimately be subject to double taxation.
65. Internal Revenue Service, S Corporations, https://www.irs.gov/businesses/small-businesses-self-employed/s-corporations.
66. 26 U.S. Code § 1060—Special allocation rules for certain asset acquisitions, https://www.law.cornell.edu/uscode/text/26/1060.
67. USC 26 U.S. Code § 197—Amortization of goodwill and certain other intangibles, https://www.law.cornell.edu/uscode/text/26/197.
68. Internal Revenue Service, Publication 535, Section 197, "Intangibles Defines IRS Tax Map," https://taxmap.irs.gov/taxmap/pubs/p535-042.htm#TXMP6f4f46f2.
69. https://www.law.cornell.edu/uscode/text/26/197.
70. Specifically, the law states: "not recognized under part III of subchapter C." This is a short citation referring to the USC, Title 26, Subtitle A, Chapter 1, Subtitle C, Part III. That part of the IRC states, in section 351: "No gain or loss shall be recognized if property is transferred to a corporation by one or more persons solely in exchange for stock in such corporation and immediately after the exchange such person or persons are in control (as defined in section 368(c)) of the corporation. https://www.law.cornell.edu/uscode/text/26/351.
71. "Proposed Regulations: Removal of Section 385 "Documentation Regulations," KPMG, September 21, 2018, https://home.kpmg.com/us/en/home/insights/2018/09/tnf-prop-regs-removal-of-section-385-documentation-regulations.html.

72. See Domingo Vasquez, "How the New Tax Law Impacts M&A Activity," which states: "Another consideration is that the limits on interest deductibility reduce the advantage of financing M&A transactions with debt. The cost of debt-financed acquisition will be higher under the new law. Also, carryforward of disallowed interest is an item considered for certain corporate acquisitions described in Code Sec. 381 and is treated as a 'pre-change loss' subject to limitation under Code Sec. 382. This means that highly leveraged corporations will be considered loss corporations and will be subject to Code Sec. 382 solely because they have disallowed interest." https://ct.wolterskluwer.com/resource-center/articles/new-tax-law-and-mergers-and-acquisitions.
73. "Prior to the Act, section 163(j) disallowed a deduction for disqualified interest paid or accrued by a corporation in a taxable year if two threshold tests were satisfied. The first threshold test was satisfied if the payor's debt-to-equity ratio exceeded 1.5 to 1.0 (safe harbor ratio). The second threshold test was satisfied if the payor's net interest expense exceeded 50 percent of its adjusted taxable income (generally, taxable income computed without regard to deductions for net interest expense, net operating losses, domestic production activities under section 199, depreciation, amortization, and depletion). "Initial Guidance Under Section 163(j) as Applicable to Taxable Years Beginning After December 31, 2017, Notice 2018-28, https://www.irs.gov/pub/irs-drop/n-18-28.pdf.
74. Under USC Title 26, Subtitle A, Chapter 1, Subpart B, Part VI, Section 163 at provision j, https://www.law.cornell.edu/uscode/text/26/163.
75. USC, Title 26, Subtitle A, Chapter 1, Subchapter B, Part VIII, Section 243—Dividends received by corporations, https://www.law.cornell.edu/uscode/text/26/243.
76. See Patrice Radogna, "ESOPs and the New Tax Act," FEI, April 30, 2018, https://www.financialexecutives.org/FEI-Daily

/April-2018/Employee-Stock-Ownership-Plans-and-the-Tax-Act.aspx.

77. Regulation U: Credit by Banks or Persons Other than Brokers or Dealers for the Purpose of Purchasing or Carrying Margin Stocks, https://www.federalreserve.gov/bankinforeg/regucg.htm.
78. https://www.law.cornell.edu/uscode/text/26/83.
79. This is the case unless the employee elects to take an "83b election," whereby he or she recognizes the "income" event at the time of grant even though the employee is not fully vested in the stock. The employee pays taxes at the time of the election on the then fair market value of the stock (again, without having full vesting) and establishes basis in the stock. At the time of vesting, there is no taxable event. The next time there is a taxable event is when the employee sells the shares and the tax due will be considered capital gains on the difference between the basis established at the time of the 83b election and the fair market value at the time of stock disposition.
80. https://www.law.cornell.edu/uscode/text/26/83.
81. Ibid.
82. See Asel T. Mukeyeva, "Tax Due Diligence in Asset Acquisitions," American Bar Association, https://www.americanbar.org/groups/young_lawyers/publications/the_101_201_practice_series/tax_due_diligence_in_asset_acquisitions.html?cq_ck=1513351205239.
83. The SEC's landing page on Non-GAAP Financial Measures has a Q&A about this: "If reconciliation of a non-GAAP financial measure is required and the most directly comparable measure is a 'pro forma' measure prepared and presented in accordance with Article 11 of Regulation S-X, may companies use that measure for reconciliation purposes, in lieu of a GAAP financial measure?" The answer is yes. https://www.sec.gov/divisions/corpfin/guidance/nongaapinterp.htm.

84. See “Pushdown accounting now optional; New guidance applicable to all companies,” PWC, https://www.pwc.com/us/en/cfodirect/assets/pdf/in-depth/us2014-08-pushdown-accounting-optional.pdf.
85. Ibid.

CHAPTER 6

The Due Diligence Inquiry

INTRODUCTION

The basic function of *due diligence,* in any merger or acquisition, is to assess the potential risks of a proposed transaction by inquiring into all relevant aspects of the past, present, and predictable future of the business to be purchased. The term is also used in securities law to describe the duty of care and review to be exercised by officers, directors, underwriters, and others in connection with public offerings of securities.

Although the term *due diligence* is applied in *securities law*—statutory law set by legislatures—the term itself originated in *common law,* also known as *case law*—the law that develops through decisions of judges in settling actual disputes. The common-law system arose in medieval England after the Norman Conquest, and is still in use there as well as in the United States, among other countries. In this type of law, as opposed to law passed by legislatures, judges use the precedents of previous case decisions in order to render their own decisions. Much of US common law has been codified in the statutes of individual states, and in the U.S. Uniform Commercial Code (UCC, introduced in Chapter 5).

The due diligence effort in a merger transaction should include basic activities to meet diligence standards of common law and best practices. These activities include the following:

- *Financial statements review*—to confirm the existence of assets, liabilities, and equity in the balance sheet, and to determine the financial health of the company based on the income statement.
- *Management and operations review*—to determine quality and reliability of financial statements, and to gain a sense of risks and contingencies beyond the financial statements.
- *Legal compliance review*—to check for potential future legal problems stemming from the target's past.
- *Document and transaction review*—to ensure that the paperwork of the deal is in order and that the structure of the transaction is appropriate.

Careful scrutiny in all these areas can prevent problems after the transaction is over and the new company's life begins. So let's get started!

GETTING STARTED

When does due diligence begin?

The due diligence process begins from the moment a buyer senses a possible acquisition opportunity. The buyer then starts to examine the information that is readily available at this early time about the company. For public companies, this information is usually derived from public documents—including press reports, filings with securities regulators, and any debt or equity offering memorandums the company or its bankers might have prepared for potential buyers.

This initial stage of due diligence review based on public documents usually starts during the strategy, valuation, financing, and structuring phases, described in the previous chapters. During these phases, the acquirer has asked and answered four opening questions:

- Is it in our stockholders' long-term interests to own and operate this company?
- How much is it worth?
- Can we afford it?
- How should we structure this acquisition?

When the parties are ready to go forward and to set a tentative price and structure for the deal, the buyer should engage attorneys and accountants to conduct a more thorough study of the company to be acquired. This "dirty linen" phase of the due diligence inquiry—discovering what's wrong with the company—can never start too early. Buyers often neglect this phase, because they do not want to offend sellers, but they must proceed. Buyers need to ask and answer the tougher questions such as:

- Do the firm's financial statements reveal any signs of insolvency or fraud?
- Do the firm's operations show any signs of weak internal controls?
- Does the firm run the risk of any major postmerger litigation by the government or others?

Two milestones marking the official onset of due diligence are the signing of a *confidentiality agreement* and a *letter of intent* to buy the company. Formal due diligence usually does not begin until these two documents are signed. More details are specified in the *acquisition agreement.* (For a sample confidentiality agreement, see Appendix 6A at the end of this chapter. For a sample letter of intent and acquisition agreement, see Chapter 7.)

What does the acquisition agreement typically say about due diligence?

Among other items, the acquisition agreement should:

- State the time available for due diligence
- Promise the buyer access to the selling company's personnel, sites, and files

Here is sample language about due diligence from an acquisition agreement:

Investigation by Buyer. The Seller and Target shall, and the Target shall cause its Subsidiaries to, afford to the officers and authorized representatives of the Buyer free and full access, during normal business hours and upon reasonable prior notice, to the offices, plants, properties, books, and records of the Target and its Subsidiaries in order that the Buyer may have full opportunity to make such investigations of the business, operations, assets, properties, and legal and financial condition of the Target and its Subsidiaries as the Buyer deems reasonably necessary or desirable; and the officers of the Seller, the Target, and its Subsidiaries shall furnish the Buyer with such additional financial and operating data and other information relating to the business operations, assets, properties, and legal and financial condition of the Target and its Subsidiaries as the Buyer shall from time to time reasonably request.

Prior to the Closing Date, or at all times if this Agreement shall be terminated, the Buyer shall, except as may be otherwise required by applicable law, hold confidential all information obtained pursuant to this Section with respect to the Target and its Subsidiaries and, if this Agreement shall be terminated, shall return to the Target and its Subsidiaries all such information as shall be in documentary form and shall not use any information obtained pursuant to this Section in any manner that would have a material adverse consequence to the Target or its Subsidiaries.

The representations, warranties, and agreements of the Seller, the Target, and its Subsidiaries set forth in this Agreement shall be effective regardless of any investigation that the Buyer has undertaken or failed to undertake.

The first paragraph of this clause is called an *investigation covenant.* It ensures that the seller will cooperate with the buyer by granting access and logistical support for the buyer's due diligence review of the seller and its subsidiaries. This is one of the most valuable parts of any acquisition agreement.

The second paragraph, sometimes nicknamed a *burn or return* provision, may help allay the seller's fears about confidentiality. Note, however, that the seller will often require the prospective buyer to enter into a separate confidentiality agreement.

The third paragraph makes a statement that removes the burden of perfect investigation from the acquirer. Without such a statement, the seller can avoid liability following a breach of contract. The seller can disclaim responsibility for representations, arguing that the buyer could have discovered the breach during the investigation of the seller's company.

Who conducts due diligence?

Typically, outside counsel to the acquirer directs the due diligence review with help from a team of professionals employed or retained by the acquirer. As mentioned, the review has financial, operational, and legal aspects. Each of these parts can benefit from specialized attention. The financial and legal sides each have separate and distinct responsibilities, although they may, and indeed should, communicate with one another.

The financial statement review requires attention from the acquirer's financial and accounting personnel, such as the chief financial officer and, if the company has one, the chief internal auditor. The operations review will involve risks inherent in the company's conduct of its business—for example, weak defenses against cyberattacks.

The legal compliance review requires external and, if available, internal counsel. The acquirer may also bring in asset appraisers, cybersecurity experts, environmental experts, and a host of other professional talent during the review.

The party directing the review should be clear from any conflicts of interest. Any party paid a contingency for the completion of the transaction—for example, an investment banker having such an arrangement—may have a conflict of interest, and that fact should be considered in the acquirer's decision as to who should direct the review. Also, if a firm has a financial relationship or consulting engagement with the company it is studying, it may also have a conflict of interest with respect to the transaction. This would include any audit firm that has financial, employment, or business relationships in addition to the audit, among other conditions that may suggest lack of independence.[1]

Cybersecurity is a major risk today. What advice do you have for detecting such risk during a due diligence?

Cybersecurity audits should be a very comprehensive review of the existing digital environment of the target company that includes a wide variety of different platforms and tools.[2] IT infrastructure, including firewalls, firewall rules, intrusion detection, and intrusion remediation tools and processes are typical areas to review. This should include both current and past environments, including a review of the intrusions and remediations that occurred, both in the past and in the present. With the trend toward the use of cloud technologies, where key information resides with one or more third parties, the analysis can get complex. Knowledge that the cloud provider has acceptable security is not enough information, since the target company could have chosen to bypass some of the available security and use, for example, just a simple password scheme, which would not be an acceptable secure environment. And, for target companies that support a bring your own device (BYOD) environment for their employees, the analysis should include considerations to properly protect the infrastructure environment from devices that may contain dangerous malware.

The analysis of key application software, including data content such as customer information, financial information, and intellectual property rights (IPR) information is a second key focus area, including what information is digitized and made available online to authorized users. And, with the growing use of applications that span organizations across customers, suppliers, and third-party environments, the review can get complex. With the advent of cloud-based applications, it is essential to understand the use of applications not under IT control, but where business personnel have contracted directly with third-party providers to use applications (often referred to as "shadow IT").

Third, the review of software tools such as email and document management should be analyzed to thoroughly review the target company's environment. Included in this area would be online applications and websites, including those that are not current or used anymore but still exist, since they could have embedded vulnerabilities, which could lead to intrusions.

Fourth, a review should include the IT and cybersecurity organization and personnel, for responsibilities and adequacies to properly protect the digital environment of the target company.

Fifth, a review of the use of social media by the target company is also crucial in understanding the cybersecurity environment and possible vulnerabilities.

Sixth, with the growing concern about data privacy, a review of data privacy information is recommended, especially in deals involving multinational targets and target companies that are located in different countries. The European Union's General Data Protection Regulation (GDPR), which went into effect May 25, 2018, has wide-ranging effects. The law requires—with some exceptions—affirmative opt-in and usage notices for any data collection in the European Union (EU) by any organization with 250 or more employees based anywhere in the world. Vendors to these companies may also be affected by this law. The GDPR affects not only European companies collecting data within the EU, but also large non-European companies with "data subjects" based anywhere in the EU. Since most organizations today engage in digital commerce that includes data collection, and since digital commerce per se has no geographic boundaries, the directive has the potential to affect many businesses.

What is the best way to get information about a company during due diligence?

Internet research is a good way to start. Around the world, public companies that use the eXtensible Business Reporting Language (XBRL) are literally posting a searchable database about themselves for all to explore.[3] In the case of a US publicly traded company, there are a wealth of filings to study, including annual reports on Form 10-K, quarterly reports on Form 10-Q, and many more. The SEC has more than 100 different forms that a public company may have to file, depending on circumstances.[4] These are a gold mine of information for due diligence. Some filings may include key agreements, contracts, and other significant company documents filed as exhibits. Of particular note in the United States are the Management Discussion and Analysis (MD&A) section of the annual report on Form 10-K, listing key risks. Even still, the acquirer will undoubtedly want to go into deeper detail than what's available publicly. Accordingly, the acquirer will typically provide the target with a due diligence request list around the time that it appears if there is mutual interest in pursuing a corporate discussion.

In the case of private companies, the process is much more difficult, as most information is unpublished. Most companies today do have websites, and this is a good place to begin. For more guidance on obtaining information about private companies, see Chapter 2, in the section titled "The Search Process."

How can the professionals conducting due diligence keep the process on track?

Two main practices can keep due diligence on track: first, a checklist of items to seek and, second, a means of storing documents in accessible and secure format. Ideally, the two will interrelate in the use of a virtual data room (VDR) that has a customizable document request checklist also used as a list of categories for storing documents. The old-school "checklist" of yesterday is today a set of search terms, tags, and headings in a customizable database.

(See Exhibit 6-1 for a VDR menu screen shot; see Appendix 6C for a longer list.)

What is a virtual data room, or VDR?

A virtual data room is a place in cyberspace, either in the cloud or on an in-house server, where due diligence and other deal documents can be stored and accessed. This function can be constructed in-house but is often outsourced to data management companies with VDR products. (See Exhibit 6-2 for a list of vendors.)

The full-service data room will have, among other features:

- Indexing template for document upload (checklist categories)
- Apps to support mobile access

Exhibit 6-1 VDR Menu Screen Shot

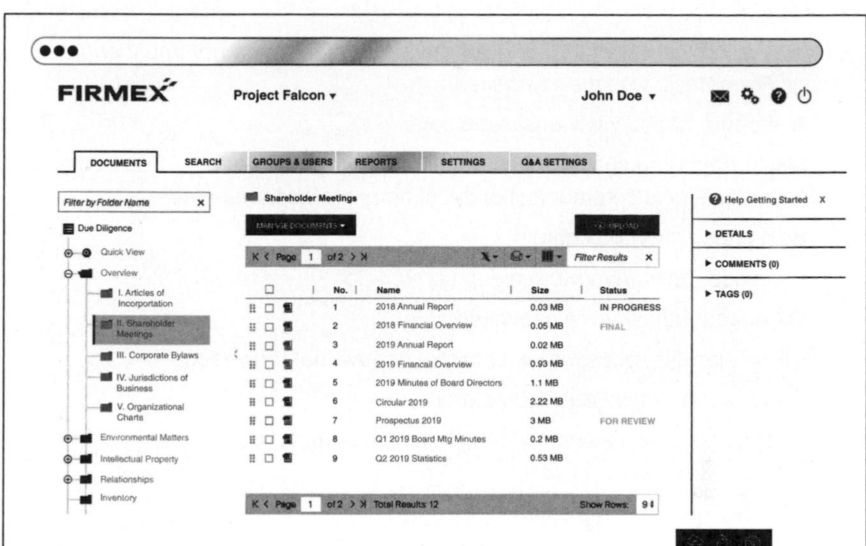

Source: Firmex, Toronto/London, 2019.

- Integration with the user's document system (e.g., Microsoft Office)
- Security including encryption, administrative controls, and firewall protection
- Deal platforms to share documents for specific transactions
- Support and security for multiple file formats (PDFs, Word documents, etc.)
- Visual document tracking

What items should be included in a typical due diligence checklist?

A typical checklist will include a list of key assets, both tangible and intangible. In parallel, the acquisition agreement will often indicate which of these assets will be appraised. (For a sample due diligence checklist,

Exhibit 6-2 A Representative List of Virtual Data Room Providers

This alphabetical list of virtual data room providers does not imply endorsement. For details, visit their websites.

Ansarada, https://www.ansarada.com/

Blackberry Workspaces (was Watchdox), https://www.blackberry.com/us/en/products/communication/blackberry-workspaces-efss

Box, https://www.box.com

Brainloop, https://www.brainloop.com/en-gb/

Caplinked, https://www.caplinked.com/

Citrix Sharefile, https://www.sharefile.com/virtual-data-room

DataRooms, https://datarooms.org/

Deal Interactive (TransPerfect), https://securetrial.dealinteractive.com/public/index.html

Drooms, https://drooms.com

EthosData, https://www.ethosdata.com/

Firmex, https://www.firmex.com/

ForData, https://fordata.pl/en/products/fordata-virtual-data-room/

HighQ, https://highq.com/

iDeals, idealsvdr.com

Intralinks, https://www.intralinks.com/

Merrill Datasite, https://www.merrillcorp.com/en/

OneHub, https://www.onehub.com/

RR Donnelly Venue, https://venue.dfsco.com/venue/

SecureDocs, https://www.securedocs.com/

Sharevault, https://www.sharevault.com/

Smartroom, https://smartroom.com/virtual-data-room/

V-Rooms (also called Vault Rooms),- https://www.vaultrooms.com/

The authors acknowledge the following source for many of the names on this list: https://datarooms.org/vdr-providers/.

see Appendix 6B.) There should be a match between the due diligence appraisal checklist and the language of the acquisition agreement with respect to assets. Each informs the other. Take, for example, Section 4.8 of the sample acquisition agreement at the end of Chapter 7, on the subject of inventory (a key asset category), which states:

> ***Section 4.8. Most Recent Inventory.*** The inventories of the Target and the Subsidiaries on a consolidated basis as reflected on the Most Recent Balance sheet consist only of items in good condition and salable or usable in the ordinary course of business, except to the extent of the inventory reserve included on the Most Recent Balance sheet, which reserve is adequate for such purpose. Such inventories are valued on the Most Recent Balance Sheet *at the lower of cost or market* in accordance with GAAP.

As the language of this provision implies, it is important for the buyer to know whether the valuation of inventory on the financial statements reflects its actual value. In some cases, the buyer may include a representation that a particular dollar amount is the minimum value of the target's inventories—a representation that is more common in an asset purchase. To find this dollar amount, the services of an appraiser can be helpful.

What exactly should an appraiser study during an appraisal of the target's assets?

- The first priority will be to appraise any assets *used in the business* that are *independently marketable,* such as machinery, real property, or inventories. This kind of appraisal is mandatory for asset-based lenders, who set the amount of their loans based on the market value of the assets available as security.
- It is also advisable (but not mandatory) to appraise *other assets* (i.e., those not used in the business and/or that cannot be marketed independently). These include unused real property, marketable securities, excess raw material, investments in nonintegrated subsidiary operations, and reserves in the extracting industries.
- Finally, the acquirer can appraise the company's *operations* and *intangibles* such as the "bench strength" of the company's

management, its core technology supporting operations, including any third-party or internally developed software that may be employed, especially software involving artificial intelligence (AI), as well as patents or trademarks that support an earnings stream. For a checklist of questions to ask about AI, see Chapter 3 on valuation and modeling.

Another important aspect of management to assess is the company's culture, which is a force that influences what people believe, think, and do.[5] in an organization. It can shape:

- Attitudes/mental processes (how people feel and think)
- Behavior (what actions get performed and rewarded)
- Functions (how people do things)
- Norms (what rules get enforced)
- Structures (how the previous items get organized and repeated)
- Symbols (what images and phrases have special meaning)
- History (what stories and traditions get passed on to future generations)[6]

(For more on culture after a merger, see Chapter 9, "Postmerger Integration and Divestitures.")

What should be in the due diligence checklist and resulting VDR categories?

A due diligence checklist will often parallel the structure of the representations and warranties that the seller makes in the acquisition agreement. These are essentially written assurances from the seller that things are as they seem—for example, the buyer must require that the seller state that the consolidated financial statements of the target fairly represent the financial condition of the target in accordance with GAAP.

In creating a workable checklist, acquirers should concentrate on areas of relevance to the transaction at hand. For example, inquiries regarding the frequency and extent of customer complaints and returned goods would be most relevant to a consumer goods retail business, while questions regarding environmental violations would be most appropriate in a manufacturing firm. Data protection would be most relevant to companies where data processing is a core function of the business or where the data handled is of particular sensitivity—especially if the business has customers in Europe where data protection policies are extremely stringent.[7]

Depending on the size of the acquisition, the checklist may or may not reflect a threshold of materiality. For example, a checklist may include only capital expenditures above $50,000, or will set a limit of five years back for certain documents. Acquirers should agree to limits of this kind carefully, bearing in mind that any ground given at this point is likely to limit the scope of the seller's representations and warranties in the acquisition agreement.

Some items on the checklist will require the seller to provide documentation. For this, there can be a separate checklist. (See Appendix 6C.) Not everything has to be a document from the seller. Some sellers will not welcome requests for information that require creating new documentation; if possible, the buyer might attempt to obtain data through interviews with the seller's officers or other key employees. This information can be stored in memo form in the VDR and then captured in the acquisition agreement signed by buyer and seller. New documentation might reasonably be necessary depending on the thoroughness and accuracy of the seller's information retention.

Remember, though, the checklist (or VDR starting template) should be used as a reminder rather than a sequential road map. Investigators should focus their investigation on the particular issues as they arise. Due diligence will often unfold as a series of independent mini-investigations with respect to the key issues.

DURATION OF DUE DILIGENCE

How long should the due diligence process take?

The due diligence process occurs throughout the acquisition process, which lasts from a few weeks to a year or more. Surprisingly, the due diligence process does not slow the pace of the acquisition negotiation in most cases; sometimes the buyer accelerates the process by doing extensive investigation before making the first offer. At the other extreme, management-led acquirers, who know (or believe they know) their own company may want to skip some categories—for example, quality of the management team. If the parties are eager to deal, they may substitute extensive warranties for the due diligence process.

When buyers do initiate a formal, organized due diligence investigation, they should put it on a fast track. Speedy due diligence ensures minimal disruption to ongoing business activities and the minimization of out-of-pocket costs to both parties. Another benefit can be smoother relations between the parties.

The most valuable result of fast-track due diligence is timely information to the buyer, who can quickly determine whether the acquisition is of interest and, if so, on what terms and conditions. The buyer can then focus attention on determining the appropriate structure for the transaction; the basis for calculation of the purchase price; what representations, warranties, and covenants should be negotiated into the final acquisition agreement; and what conditions to closing need to be imposed. (In fact, the earlier the draft of the schedule "Conditions Precedent to Closing" is generated, the better. Somehow, with that document on the table and under constant revision as the due diligence proceeds, the probability that the deal will close seems to improve.)

DUE DILIGENCE LEVELS

How thorough must due diligence be?

The due diligence conducted must be reasonable, but it need not be perfect. Companies are complex entities operating in a complex world; no investigation can uncover all the potential risks of an acquisition. Even if an expert can later find fault, the expert's ability to poke holes in the diligence of investigators does not automatically create liability.

In court decisions, diligence and negligence are opposite qualities; the presence of one can prove the absence of the other. (Later on, this chapter will go into more depth on the subject of due diligence as a defense against charges of negligence during a transaction.)

The level of due diligence necessary in any given transaction depends on the companies involved. Due diligence in public companies is far more complex than it is in private companies. Manufacturers might have greater legal exposure than many service companies, although service companies might require a deeper examination of the employee base than a manufacturing business, given the intangible nature of a service company's key assets. The due diligence work in the acquisition of large companies that are diversified and global looms larger than the work necessary for small firms that are monoline and domestic. Finally, transaction type can limit the due diligence effort, since stock purchases trigger more due diligence responsibilities than do asset purchases.

How far a buyer wishes to go in the due diligence process depends in part on how much time and money the buyer has to investigate the enterprise. This will depend to some extent on the status of the enterprise in the community, the years it has been in business, whether it has been audited by a major firm for some years, whether executive turnover is low, and other factors that would establish the basic stability of the firm, such as long-term customer retention.

The thoroughness of due diligence also depends to some extent on what information the seller is willing to give in the form of representations and warranties to be included in the purchase agreement. Beware the seller who resists making any written representations or warranties, insisting on less formal assurances. Such deals are high-risk transactions and are rarely the bargains they appear to be. There are risks of insolvency and litigation.

Even if buyers decide to rely on the sellers' representations and warranties, they must nevertheless still conduct at least enough due diligence to be assured that there will be a solvent company and/or seller to back the representations and warranties. If there is any doubt, acquirers must establish cash reserves.

And in any event, if stockholders' money is involved, shareholder lawsuits are likely to follow if things go wrong. Possibilities for litigation include charges of fraudulent conveyance under state law and federal bankruptcy law[8] based on a variety of standards set by state and federal securities laws.

SECURITIES LAWS AND DUE DILIGENCE

What do securities laws say about due diligence?

The two fundamental federal securities laws, the Securities Act of 1933[9] and the Securities Exchange Act of 1934,[10] do not contain the term due diligence themselves, but their statutory provisions and related rules have generated expectations of due diligence by regulators and courts, generally in connection with disclosure issues. Both laws emphasize the importance of accurate and timely disclosure of material nonpublic information; as such, claims under federal securities laws, including those alleging inadequate due diligence, often have a disclosure component.[11]

Both of the two main securities statutes mandate a certain level of diligence with respect to the registration and exchange of securities. This is especially true for a defense against violations of Section 11 of the 1933 Act, which does not require knowledge (scienter) of the false or misleading statement. For more discussion of the key sections of federal securities laws with respect to M&A litigation, see Chapter 10. Of these, Section 14 is currently the dominant one in M&A securities class actions under federal law, according to Cornerstone Research, which limits its annual count of M&A claims to Section 14 claims, as seen in Exhibit 6-3. See also Chapter 10 for an overview of public company issues.

Exhibit 6-3 Some Typical Plaintiff Claims in M&A Litigation

Securities Act of 1933

- Section 11—Plaintiffs claim material misstatements or omissions in a registration statement. (Claim does not require scienter—due diligence defense applies.)
- Section 12—Plaintiffs claim scienter of fraud in a registration statement.

Securities Act of 1934

- Section 10—Rule 10(b)5—Plaintiffs claim *scienter* of fraud in the purchase or sale of a security.
- Section 14—Plaintiffs in 14(a) claim fraud in a proxy statement; plaintiffs in 14(e) claim *scienter* of fraud in a tender offer.

Exhibit 6-4 Venn Diagram Showing Interrelationship of M&A, Due Diligence Standards, and Securities Law

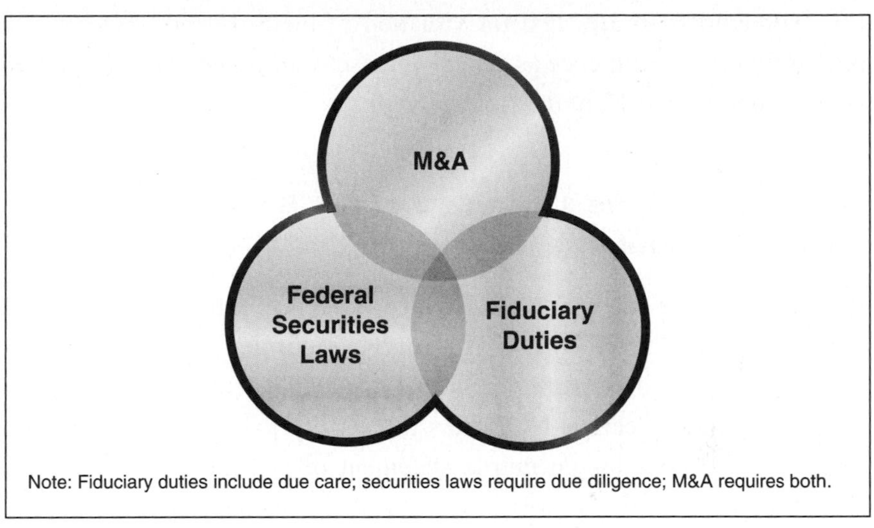

Note: Fiduciary duties include due care; securities laws require due diligence; M&A requires both.

Note, however, that when state courts interpret compliance with federal statutes, they may draw upon legal precedent that refers to other legal mandates, such as the fiduciary duties expected of directors and officers under state law. M&A standards, federal securities laws, and fiduciary duties are interconnected but not equivalent. See Exhibit 6-4.

How does the Securities Act of 1933 mandate due diligence?

The *Securities Act of 1933* (Securities Act) applies primarily to disclosures made when registering securities (debt or equity) for sale to the public, but it has broader implications. Some concepts in the Securities Act, and in rules promulgated under it, have had far-reaching influence in court decisions. Therefore, mastering the disclosure principles in the Securities Act can help companies, both public and private, maintain good business practices.

The Securities Act applies to companies that register securities in a variety of situations, including M&A. Publicly traded companies must file a registration statement on Form S-4 when undergoing an exchange offer or when registering securities to be used as consideration in a deal.[12] These forms contain a good amount of information about a proposed merger, and the information needs to be accurate.

Directors who are sued for violation of the Securities Act can use proof of their due diligence as a legal defense.[13] Of particular interest here are Sections 11 and 12 of the Act.

What do Sections 11 and 12 of the Securities Act of 1933 say about due diligence?

Both sections are relevant to M&A due diligence, although neither addresses the topic directly. Section 11 of the Securities Act requires accurate and complete disclosure of material facts in an offering's registration statement. Under Section 11, issuers are strictly liable for a registration statement that contains an untrue statement of a material fact or omits to state a material fact required to make the statements not misleading. If a registration document contains misstatements or omissions of material facts, shareholders can sue the underwriters, accountants, and/or directors—and may prevail even without any proof of *scienter* (or intent or knowledge of wrongdoing). However, all defendants except the issuer have a due diligence defense that they have no grounds to believe the statement had a misstatement or omission. Accordingly, Section 11 is a significant source of liability for directors of public companies in general, and must be regarded with a great deal of attention—particularly the so-called expertised portions of the statement. In the language of a report from a commission chaired by former Delaware Supreme Court Chief Justice Norman Veasey, "When evaluating the reliability of the parts of the registration statement (or other disclosures) based on expert authority, directors should be satisfied that the expert is qualified and fully informed, and should remain alert for any red flags that would raise doubts about the reliability of those experts' authority."[14]

How does the Securities Exchange Act of 1934 mandate due diligence?

The *Securities Exchange Act of 1934* (Exchange Act) is the sequel to the Securities Act. Whereas, as their respective names suggest, the Securities

Act covers the registration of securities, the Exchange Act covers their exchange. Since many mergers involve the exchange of securities, the so-called due diligence portions of this law are particularly important for acquirers to master.

Like the Securities Act, the Exchange Act does not use the term *due diligence* anywhere, but individuals accused of violating certain parts of the Exchange Act can use due diligence as a defense. In particular, a due diligence defense may be useful in defending against charges relating to Section 10(b) of the Exchange Act, particularly Rule 10b-5.[15] It may also be useful in defending against charges involving Section 14 of the Exchange Act concerning the proxy statement.

What does Rule 10(b)5 say in connection to M&A?

Rule 10b-5 forbids certain practices deemed to constitute intentional fraud in connection with the purchase or sale of a security—including one bought or sold in connection with a change of control. The fraudulent behavior must be engaged in knowingly (*scienter*). Legal complaints can come from any buyer or seller of a security who claims to be harmed by such a fraud—not just from the government.

The text of 10b-5, as amended, reads as follows:

> It shall be unlawful for any person, directly or indirectly, by the use of any means or instrumentality of interstate commerce, or of the mails, or of any facility of any national securities exchange:
>
> (a) To employ any device, scheme, or artifice to defraud,
>
> (b) To make any untrue statement of a material fact or to omit to state a material fact necessary in order to make the statements made, in the light of the circumstances under which they were made, not misleading, or
>
> (c) To engage in any act, practice, or course of business which operates or would operate as a fraud or deceit upon any person, in connection with the purchase or sale of any security.[16]

The due diligence defense cannot be used in all 10b-5 cases. If the fraud came from a conscious intent to deceive, the due diligence defense does not apply. The defense applies only in cases where the plaintiff alleges that the fraud in question stemmed from extreme negligence or recklessness. (As mentioned earlier, diligence is the opposite of negligence.)

Recklessness may be deemed a type of *scienter* fraud, thus making 10b-5 lawsuits a threat to acquirers who have insufficient due diligence in the conduct of acquisitions involving public companies.[17] One of the best ways to ensure and demonstrate strong due diligence is to obtain independent verification of facts.

What do Sections 14(a) and 14(3) of the Exchange Act say about M&A due diligence?

Again, these do not address the topic directly, but a strong due diligence process can lower the likelihood of such litigation in an M&A context. Section 14(a) prohibits corporate management (the issuers of the securities in question) from soliciting proxies by the use of deceptive or misleading statements. Directors and officers who are aware of the due diligence efforts in an M&A transaction are more likely to spot inaccuracies in a proxy statement.

Section 14(e) sets forth a similar expectation for those involved in making a tender offer for a company's shares. It prohibits those making a tender offer (the buyers of the securities in question) from making a false statement of material fact or an omission and participating in any deceptive, manipulative, or fraudulent activities.

What are some key lessons from these various laws and rules?

The key lesson is that, after establishing lack of intent to defraud (if relevant to the underlying claim) it may be important to show diligence in approving a purchase or sale of a security. For an acquirer, this means establishing a good due diligence process in which to study a target company, including hiring independent experts to verify alleged facts in communications to existing or prospective shareholders.

What does independent verification of facts entail?

In conducting a due diligence investigation, attorneys (or others) need to obtain independent verification of facts wherever reasonable. Reasonable, independent verification, based on accepted wisdom concerning due diligence in securities offerings, usually means referencing information sources outside, as well as inside, the company.

The famed case of *Escott v. Barchris Construction Co.* (1976) stated that it is not sufficient "to ask questions, to obtain answers which, if true, would be thought satisfactory, and to let it go at that, without seeking to ascertain from the records whether the answers in fact are true and complete."[18]

The plaintiffs in both the Enron and WorldCom bankruptcies (in late 2001 and mid-2002, respectively) sued directors and officers on multiple issues, including one of particular interest in the due diligence context, namely an alleged violation of Section 11 of the Securities Act, which imposes strict liability for errors in a prospectus, even without *scienter*.[19] Consistent with this argument, the final investigative reports faulted the board members and advisors who allegedly failed to pay adequate attention to warning signs of financial troubles.[20] Generally speaking, directors can avoid liability under Section 11 by adopting the so-called due diligence defense, which can protect defendants who establish that they: believed the statements were true and free from material omissions, had reasonable grounds for their belief, and undertook a reasonable investigation of the matters at issue. This defense went to trial in WorldCom but the court rejected it,[21] and subsequent courts have followed suit, leading to an increase in Section 11 litigation ever since.[22] Given this rise in Section 11 claims, many of them originating in M&A cases, it is more important than ever to prepare a strong due diligence case.[23] Chapter 10 discusses this matter in context (see Exhibit 10-1).

Chapter 10 delineates the four standards of review for decisions to sell, but here we note that directors and officers may still be exculpated from claims under any of these standards, assuming no conflicts of interest.[24] Such cases get dismissed before they are settled. But while many M&A lawsuits are dismissed or settled, enough are litigated to strike a note of caution—particularly on the target company side, where most case law occurs.[25] Even if buyers decide to rely on the sellers' representations and warranties, they must nevertheless conduct at least enough due diligence to be assured that there will be a solvent company and/or seller to back the representations and warranties. If there is any doubt, acquirers must establish cash reserves.

RED FLAGS

What are some red flags in a due diligence investigation?

Acquirers should be alert to certain warning signs in each of the due diligence areas previously listed (from financial statements review to transaction review). All of the following are warning signs that need to be investigated to some degree.

- *Financial red flags* include resignation of external or internal auditors, change in accounting methods, sales of stock by insiders, and unusual ratios. These may indicate fraud and/or insolvency.
- *Operational red flags* include very high or very low turnover and poor or inadequate reporting of important nonfinancial programs (quality, compliance). These may indicate unstable operations.
- *Liability/compliance red flags* include potential exposure to litigation from various stakeholders, including regulators, consumers, employees, stockholders, and bondholders and other creditors.
- *Transactional red flags* include conflicting accounting and tax goals. These need to be resolved as early as possible.

RELATIONS WITH THE SELLER

How can a buyer obtain seller cooperation during due diligence?

The seller is more likely to cooperate when the buyer (or the buyer's counsel) conveys the important message that full exploration of facts and risks benefits everyone—and can help protect against the risk of an even more adversarial process via cross-examination in court, if either the seller or the buyer is sued after the transaction closes. For example, just as a buyer can be sued for paying too much money for an acquisition, a seller may be sued for accepting too little money.

Sellers may wish to conduct their own due diligence—both of themselves in anticipation of all of the buyer's requests, and also of the buyer. For obvious financial reasons, the seller will need to conduct due diligence of the buyer when the buyer is paying in stock, particularly if the buyer is offering stock in a closely held company. Finally, it is in the interests of sellers to investigate the buyer to the extent that the seller or the seller's key people will be working for the buyer or otherwise receiving an income stream from the buyer (e.g., in a sale that is financed in part by buyer notes).

Suppose the seller refuses to produce the requested documentation but offers access to its files?

Then the buyer must organize an on-site document review effort, which will typically entail traveling to the entity's corporate headquarters and, potentially, satellite operations. Investigators will be using the previously mentioned acquisition checklist. The seller should be willing to direct the buyer to employees with knowledge of each subject of inquiry detailed on the checklist or, at least, to the relevant files.

As mentioned, the acquisition agreement should include the seller's representation (promise) to the buyer that the buyer will have access to all relevant files for requested information. A refusal to support due diligence could look bad if the acquisition ever had to undergo judicial review for any reason.

As a courtesy to the seller and to avoid confusion between or among documents, which can vary in format from company to company, the buyer should make two copies of each document—one for itself and one for the seller. In any event, some identification system involving numbering should be devised to keep track of the documents produced, especially of those that are copied.

Throughout the process, the buyer should be sensitive to the stress on its own personnel and on its relationship with the seller. The due diligence effort is a disruption of the ordinary business routine and may be viewed by the seller as a sign of unwarranted suspicion by the buyer and disregard for the seller's interests. The seller may fear adverse consequences for the conduct of its business and its future sale to others if the contemplated deal does not close. Indeed, many potential transactions do fall through because of the rigors of the due diligence process, which alienates the seller, the buyer, or both.

Thorough due diligence can substantially increase pretransaction costs and can absorb the attention of key employees who have other jobs to do. Nonetheless, the distractions are largely unavoidable. The key is to make the process thorough, yet reasonable.

LOCATION OF DUE DILIGENCE RESEARCH

Where should due diligence take place?

The buyer's examination of the seller's assets occurs both on-site (tire-kicking) and off-site (record-hunting). On-site inquiries may involve discussions with officers and employees as well as inspections of real property, machinery, equipment, and inventory. In conducting interviews with key executives and employees, the investigator seeks to fill in the gaps in the documentation and to ascertain whether there may be areas of potential concern or liability (or definable assets) not identified in the due diligence checklist.

Good interview notes will include the following:

- Time and place of the interview
- Name and title of the person interviewed
- Scope of the interview
- Significant disclosures made during the interview

Depending on the size and structure of the transaction and the importance of the specific assets, the buyer may wish to use a real estate appraiser to value any owned real property involved, an engineer to inspect plant and equipment, and an accounting team to review inventory. The accountants should also review the seller's financial statements with respect to these items.

Off-site investigations may include the search of public records about the company and discussions with parties with whom the acquisition target has significant relationships. These include customers and suppliers, private lenders, and former key employees including directors and officers. Key people to interview are those who have won major suits against the target—especially former employees and stockholders.

What are some potential problem areas when talking about a company with third parties?

This is a very sensitive area. Discussions with third parties may, if correctly conducted, be the source of valuable information. But they can also give rise to tensions between buyer and seller if the seller believes that the discussions may impair its ability to carry on future business or that the buyer might use the information when and if it buys a competitor. Discussions with the buyer's lenders may be particularly sensitive in this regard. Guidelines for third-party discussions should be covered in the confidentiality agreement (see the end of this chapter) and the letter of intent (see the end of Chapter 7).

Another delicate area is that of *standing agreements.* The buyer should begin fairly early to negotiate with parties to existing supplier or customer agreements, requiring that they be assigned to the buyer when and if it acquires the business. If the supplier or customer refuses, this may be the basis for a claim that there has been a material adverse change (MAC), also known as or material adverse effect (MAE) in the affairs of the business between the execution of the acquisition agreement and the closing. The acquisition agreement should include a clause that allows the buyer to lower price or even back out of a deal in the event of a MAC.

What public records should be checked?

The first concern to be satisfied in the due diligence search is basic: the buyer must confirm that the corporation was legally formed and continues to exist. To do so, the buyer will establish the jurisdiction of the company's incorporation and document the company's organization by finding and examining the articles of incorporation, including any amendments such as name changes. The Due Diligence Checklist in Appendix 6B begins with these basics.

Articles of incorporation are public documents that may be obtained (in the form of certified copies) from the secretary of state of the jurisdiction of incorporation. Acquirers of privately held companies should also request, from the same office, evidence of the corporation's continuing status in good standing there. This is pretty easy to do online: if the buyer types the name of the state in which the target is located and the words "business entity search," the relevant state agency's website should pop up, where the buyer can check on whether the target's business status in that state is still active. It is also necessary to review carefully the relevant state statutes and corporate minute books to establish that the articles and amendments have been properly adopted and that no action has been taken to dissolve the corporation. An examination of the minute book should also ascertain that it is up-to-date and that the election or appointment of the corporation's directors and officers is duly reflected there. (For public companies listed on major exchanges, the need for this additional step may be lower, due to the many safeguards there are for public company conduct.)

Having established that the corporation was indeed duly formed, the buyer's due diligence team then examines the company's qualifications to do business in jurisdictions other than its state of incorporation—in other words, in whatever other states or countries it may conduct business. To be thorough in wrapping up this initial due diligence stage, the buyer must seek out good standing certificates and tax certificates from each of the states and foreign jurisdictions in which the seller operates. This process was further complicated by *South Dakota v. Wayfair, Inc.*, in which the US Supreme Court held that states within the United States have the right to collect sales tax on purchases made by out-of-state sellers, even if the seller does not have a physical presence in the taxing state.[26]

Once corporate formation, qualification, good standing, and tax certificates are established, a search should be made for liens, encumbrances, and judgments that may exist against the company or any of its assets. Sources to be searched in uncovering such obligations include the following:

- The offices of the secretary of state of the state where the company's principal office is located and of other relevant states and, sometimes, county clerk offices where filings are made to disclose creditors' interests in assets under the UCC
- All relevant recorder of deeds offices
- All relevant courts, including federal, state, and local
- Any special filing jurisdictions[27]

With respect to the last item, check out the present and previous corporate names, URLs, and all trade names, service marks, and trade dress registrations. Ownership information about a website URL is often available at www.whois.net, unless the owner has paid a fee for this information to be kept private. If you are buying a company because of its trademarks, be sure the company in fact owns them. This is a relatively straightforward exercise at the US Patent and Trademark Office's (USPTO) website, www.uspto.gov. One of the authors of this book was considering an investment in a privately held consumer products company. A simple search on the USPTO's site revealed that the target's trademarks had been canceled because its legal counsel had neglected to respond to a USPTO inquiry. The target initially was incredulous but subsequently learned it was true—which unfortunately decreased the value of the business.

EVALUATING ASSETS

How much information can a buyer get about a target that is a corporate subsidiary or division?

It depends on whether the company is private or public, and, if public, what percentage of its revenues comes from the subsidiary.

Private corporations may not have to make any public disclosure of subsidiary or divisional performance, depending on their states of incorporation (some states do require the filing of such data). Public corporations must make such disclosure (as *line of business* reports) for units generating 5 percent or more of corporate revenues.

Some companies, private and public, make voluntary public disclosure of all subsidiary and divisional financials, however, and all well-managed companies report such results on an internal basis. Lastly, highly regulated industries, such as airlines, may require selected financial disclosures from all industry participants—whether publicly traded or privately held.

LITIGATION ANALYSIS

Is there any do-it-yourself approach for litigation analysis?

As a starting point, summary information about federal lawsuits is available for a fee through an electronic service called PACER. While the results are not exhaustive and they do not include lawsuits filed in state courts, one of the authors of this book has uncovered valuable information in multiple situations for only a few dollars on PACER.

How should a buyer analyze existing or potential litigation against an acquisition candidate?

A thorough litigation analysis of acquisition candidates requires a special procedure, usually conducted by trained litigation analysts. Management or its counsel can ask an attorney who specializes in commercial or corporate litigation and is familiar with the seller's industry to determine the validity of and exposure on existing claims.

The individual primarily responsible for the litigation risk review must first determine the parameters of the review and identify the litigation or administrative actions that warrant particular scrutiny. The primary reviewer must obtain a schedule of all litigation, pending and threatened, and must arrange to receive copies of all relevant pleadings.

Before reviewing specific cases, the primary reviewer should ascertain what cases the seller believes are covered by liability insurance and then determine what cases, if any, are in fact covered. Because the two do not always coincide, it is critical to review all insurance policies.

The individual responsible for the litigation analysis must have a working knowledge of both the structure of the transaction—for example, whether it is to be a stock or asset purchase—and the corporate and tort law rules concerning successor liability for debts and torts, especially with regard to compensatory and punitive damages. These are then applied case by case. Any reviewer should have at hand the latest trends on director and officer (D&O) litigation.[28]

Who might be suing (or planning to sue) a company, and what are some of the issues that give rise to lawsuits against companies?

Customers—as well as competitors, suppliers, and other contractors—might sue over:

- Contract disputes
- Cost, quality, and/or safety of a product or service
- Debt collection, including foreclosure
- Deceptive trade practices
- Dishonesty or fraud
- Extension or refusal of credit
- Lender liability
- Other customer and client issues
- Restraint of trade

Employees—including current, past, or prospective employees or unions—might sue over:

- Breach of employment contract
- Defamation
- Discrimination
- Employment conditions
- Harassment or humiliation
- Pension, welfare, or other employee benefits
- Wrongful termination

Regulators might sue over:

- Antitrust (in suits brought by government)
- Environmental law
- Health and safety law

Shareholders might sue over:

- Contract disputes (with shareholders)
- Divestitures or spin-offs
- Dividend declaration or change
- Duties to minority shareholders
- Executive compensation (such as golden parachutes)
- Financial performance or bankruptcy
- Financial transactions (such as derivatives)
- Fraudulent conveyance
- General breach of fiduciary duty
- Inadequate disclosure
- Insider trading
- Investment or loan decisions
- M&A scenarios (target, bidder)
- Proxy contents
- Recapitalization
- Share repurchase
- Stock offerings

Suppliers might sue over:

- Antitrust (in lawsuits brought by suppliers)
- Business interference
- Contract disputes
- Copyright or patent infringement
- Deceptive trade practices

What general rules govern the buyer's potential liability for the target's debts and torts?

The traditional rule is that where one company sells or otherwise transfers all its assets to another company, the successor is not liable for the debts and tort liabilities of the predecessor; rather, these debts and liabilities remain the responsibility of the selling entity. In fact, this is one of the key advantages to the buyer of structuring an asset purchase rather than a stock purchase, as discussed in Chapter 5. Nevertheless, even in an asset purchase, the successor may be liable under the following circumstances:

- If it has expressly or implicitly agreed to assume liability
- If the successor is deemed a mere continuation of the predecessor
- If the transaction was fraudulently designed to escape liability

A further exception exists for labor contracts. If the successor buys the predecessor's assets and keeps its employees, the successor will probably also be bound to recognize and bargain with unions recognized by the predecessor, and to maintain existing employment terms with such employees. Existing contracts may also create successorship problems. State law may vary with respect to assumption of debts and liabilities, so the reviewer must be cognizant of the specific statutory or case law that will govern the transaction.

Courts are increasingly likely to find successor liability, particularly with respect to product liability claims, under the "continuity of product line" or "continuity of enterprise" exceptions to the general rule of nonliability. The first of these exceptions applies where the successor acquires a manufacturer in the same product line. The second exception applies where the successor continues the predecessor's business.

Faced with an increasingly aggressive plaintiffs' bar in search of ever-deeper pockets, with the public and the courts searching for someone to blame, someone to shoulder the costs of injury to plaintiffs with no other course for recovery, the courts are exacting from corporate successors product liability damage awards, including in some instances punitive damages. This trend is particularly egregious in the case of asbestos manufacturers, whose decades-long struggle to achieve a class settlement continues to this day. Accordingly, the due diligence reviewer must be aware of the current state of the law concerning successor liability for both compensatory and punitive damages.

What about insurance policies and cases being handled by insurance companies?

Each and every insurance policy must be reviewed to ensure that pending claims for compensatory damages will be covered. What is the deductible? What are the liability limits per occurrence and in total? Are punitive damages excluded by the policy or by state law? Does the policy contain regulatory or other exclusions? For large companies, there may be overlapping policies; all policies must be reviewed in light of these questions. (This can be subcontracted to firms specializing in the area of insurance-based risk analysis, *provided* that they are reviewed for their deal-killing potential before being retained.)

Another consideration when reviewing insurance policies is whether they are for claims incurred or for claims made. Coverage under a claims-incurred policy continues after the cancellation or termination of the policy and includes claims that arose during the period of insurance coverage, whether or not those claims are reported to the insurance company during that period. Claims-made policies cover only those claims actually made to the insurance company during the term of the policy. In addition, under some policies, coverage will continue only if a *tail* is purchased. A tail is a special policy purchased to continue coverage that would otherwise be terminated. It is important that the reviewer identify the nature of the seller's policies and determine any potential problems that may result from a failure to give the insurance company notice of claims during the policy period or from a failure to purchase a tail.

Also, cases being handled by insurance companies should be scrutinized. The reviewer should determine if the insurer has undertaken the representation under a reservation of rights (that is, where the insurer agrees to pay for or provide legal representation, without prejudice to its right to later deny coverage), if the insurer has preliminarily denied coverage, or if the damages claimed include punitive or treble damages, which may not be covered.

How does counsel determine whether particular litigation is material to the acquiring company in the due diligence context?

Before gathering information through a due diligence request, counsel must determine what litigation is *material.* The materiality determination for litigation, as for other aspects of due diligence, will be relative. A $5 million lawsuit, even if it has merit, may have little significance in the context of a $1 billion deal. On the other hand, even a case with little financial exposure may jeopardize a $20 million deal if the buyer and seller cannot agree on how to handle that case.

When evaluating litigation pending against a midsized company, a materiality cutoff point of $250,000 might be reasonable. In addition, certain types of cases might merit close attention, whatever the financial exposure. For example, a product liability case that looks like it might be the first of many should receive close attention, even if the financial exposure on that one case is insignificant.

In assessing the potential cost of potential litigation, companies should consider the option of settling out of court. Lately, more and more companies have discovered that much litigation is wrongly created and stubbornly maintained by their executive staff, internal and external legal advisors, and even some corporate directors. Many firms, such as Motorola, have set up special groups to reduce litigation costs and are exploring the possibilities of alternative dispute resolution (ADR), a field of law where minitrials that bypass or supplement the courts are held to quickly resolve disputes at a fraction of the usual legal costs. This may also yield hidden income, as many companies maintain expensive legal actions that can be replaced by inexpensive ADR processes, and cases are easily, quickly, and inexpensively settled even in the course of an acquisition negotiation.

What material information should the litigator review?

In the due diligence request, counsel should seek a summary of all pending or threatened actions that satisfy the materiality standard that has been established. The summaries should include the following:

- Names and addresses of all parties
- The nature of the proceedings
- The date of commencement
- Status, relief sought, and settlements offered
- Sunk costs and estimated future costs
- Insurance coverage, if any
- Any legal opinions rendered concerning those actions

A summary should also be provided for the following:

- All civil suits by private individuals or entities
- Suits or investigations by governmental bodies
- Criminal actions involving the target or any of its significant employees
- Tax claims (federal, state, and local)
- Administrative actions
- All investigations

In addition, counsel should request copies of all material correspondence during the past five years with government agencies such as the Department of Justice (DOJ), Environmental Protection Agency (EPA), Federal Trade Commission (FTC), Internal Revenue Service (IRS), Occupational Safety and Health Administration (OSHA), Department of Labor, and any other regulatory agency (city, county, state, or federal) to which the seller is subject. If the company sells stock through a stock exchange or stock market (New York Stock Exchange, Nasdaq, etc.), all material correspondence with the listing body should be gathered. If the target itself has subsidiaries, all relevant information should be requested for the subsidiaries as well.

After all this information has been gathered, how is the litigation analysis conducted?

Before the actual analysis begins, the individual in charge of the review must determine who will analyze which claims. Highly specialized claims should be assigned for review to attorneys with the most knowledge of the area involved.

The individual reviewer must arrange to receive pleadings and documents concerning any additional relevant claims. Also, the reviewer should have access to the attorneys representing the target in those matters. This may be difficult, however. Even in an acquisition characterized by cooperation, obtaining all the relevant pleadings can be challenging. This is particularly true if the target is represented by more than one law firm.

The individuals responsible for this aspect of the litigation analysis must establish a particularly good working relationship with the attorneys representing the target company. In some instances, communications with outside counsel should be handled gingerly because that firm may see some portion of its legal work disappearing as a result of the acquisition. More often, with larger target companies, litigation is being handled by several firms around the country; all those firms will have to be consulted.

In some cases, it will be sufficient to review the case file and consult briefly with the target's outside counsel. In other cases, outside counsel will have to become more involved in the analytic process. The reviewer should be particularly cautious accepting the representations made by the target's outside counsel currently handling the case; those representatives may be overly optimistic.

Finally, each pending material case should be systematically evaluated. Some number should be assigned to the pending liability or recovery, and should include the costs of executives' time. For litigation being handled on the target's behalf by outside law firms, the reviewer should evaluate whether the case is being capably handled. Even a meritless case can create significant exposure if handled by an inexperienced or incompetent firm or practitioner.

What cases should the reviewer consider first?

The reviewer should concentrate only on the worst cases—those that, if lost, could have a negative ripple effect on the acquired company's business operations in general. The investigation should also identify and study other known cases involving other companies in the same industry. For example, suppose a court decides that a business practice of one company in the industry constitutes a deceptive trade practice or other violation of law. If the target is in the same industry and engages or might engage in the same practice, this can have a significant impact on the future business of the company, even if it is not a party to the litigation in question.

What are the hot topics today in litigation?

Environmental law remains particularly treacherous. The primary federal law governing this area is the Comprehensive Environmental Response, Compensation, and Liability Act (CERCLA), also known as *Superfund.* This law focuses on environmental liability stemming from land and water use. Some states have enacted environmental protection statutes that create a *superlien* on property of those persons liable for pollution. The existence of such far-reaching remedies requires that state and federal environmental laws be considered during due diligence and that the reviewers be familiar with the state of environmental law.

In addition, there is an area of law where environmental concerns combine with concerns for consumer or worker safety with regard to products or the manufacturing process. Some hot-button areas include:

- Asbestos, which has been subject to lawsuits for over three decades. Some companies have suffered extensive punitive damages claims.
- Paints and adhesives, which can give rise to claims of personal injury alleged from exposure to volatile organic compounds.
- Pesticides, which can be subject to litigation based on allegations of poisoning.
- Other chemicals such as beryllium (used in manufacturing lightweight alloys incorporated into aerospace and defense

items), formaldehyde, carbon monoxide, hydrocarbon and isocyanate (oil companies have been sued because of inhalation), silica, and toluene diisocyanate.

This list is by no means comprehensive. Almost anything chemical can be subject to a health claim. Some states still make it too easy for workers and consumers to sue manufacturers for product flaws even if the manufacturer maintains high safety standards. Some states have enacted reforms but there are still judicial hellholes—jurisdictions where litigation is heavy and verdicts and sentencing is harsh.

What about danger areas for pharmaceuticals?

Litigation-intensive areas include antibiotics, diet drugs, vaccine injury, and hormone replacement therapy, among others.

In assessing a company's potential exposure to environmental liability, where should an acquirer start?

Before getting into details, an acquirer should conduct a broad environmental exposure analysis. Generally speaking, there are two kinds of environmental problems to be feared in a proposed acquisition: those that adversely affect the balance sheet and those that adversely affect the financial projections. Either can destroy the economic benefits the buyer hopes to achieve.

What is the difference between a balance sheet environmental problem and a financial projection environmental problem?

Balance sheet problems result from liabilities, either disclosed or undisclosed, that the buyer becomes subject to as a result of acquiring the business. Such liabilities typically include the cost of cleaning up a mess caused by the seller or one of the seller's predecessors. The costs can include charges for removing contaminated soil or purifying tainted groundwater and can cover not only the site purchased by the buyer but also adjoining properties or remote locations on which hazardous substances generated by the business were dumped.

Moreover, under the Superfund, officers, directors, and even stockholders can be personally liable for cleanup costs, and the liability of companies that contributed to the pollution of a common dump site are jointly and severally liable for such cleanup costs. Finally, even secured lenders that wind up operating or controlling the contaminated property can be liable for such cleanup costs. As a result, the buyer must approach these problems not just from his own point of view; the buyer must also consider how the lender will react.

In addition to cleanup costs, a company can be liable to third parties who have become ill or died as a result of drinking contaminated groundwater, or whose property has been contaminated by pollution emanating from the company's facilities.

Financial projection problems adversely affect the company's ability to achieve its projected cash flow and earnings goals. They typically arise in situations in which the acquired company has a history of noncompliance with applicable air or water emissions standards. Where the due diligence process discloses such a history of operating problems, the prospective purchaser needs to calculate the cost of bringing the company into compliance and keeping it in compliance. This may involve significant unbudgeted capital costs (to procure needed emissions control equipment) or heightened operating costs (to ensure that the offending equipment is operated in conformity with applicable environmental standards) or both. In extreme cases, the buyer's diligence may disclose that the company (or a particular plant) cannot be economically operated in compliance with environmental law.

What kinds of acquisitions are most likely to present significant environmental problems?

The classic asset-driven LBO, involving a manufacturer, arguably is most at risk of presenting elevated environmental concerns. However, environmental problems are by no means limited to the manufacturing sector. Warehouses, retail businesses, and service companies may own structures that contain asbestos in wall insulation or pipe wrapping, electrical transformers filled with polychlorinated biphenyls (PCBs) may be found in many types of facilities, and underground motor fuel tanks may exist in any business that operates or has operated a fleet of trucks or cars. All of these situations are common environmental troublemakers, making environmental problems a common "skeleton in the closet" for many acquirers.

What are the principal environmental trouble spots to look for in an acquired company?

Any diligent buyer should work from a comprehensive environmental checklist in performing due diligence on a target company or retain an environmental consultant to do so. But be sure to do a thorough background check on the consultant. Due diligence requires the buyer or its representative to be sensitive to certain key areas of potential concern:

- Were any toxic or hazardous substances used or generated by the target business? Those most commonly encountered are PCBs, used in electrical transformers and commercial solvents such as those found in paint thinner and degreasing agents, which are potent carcinogens and which migrate readily into groundwater if spilled. Also considered toxic or hazardous are heavy metals (such as lead, arsenic, and cadmium) from various industrial processes and paints.
- Were any hazardous wastes shipped off-site for disposal?
- Are there lagoons or settling ponds that may contain toxic wastes?
- Are there underground tanks that may have leaked and discharged their contents (heating oil, gasoline) into the groundwater?
- Is asbestos present in any structure (as insulation in walls, pipe wrapping, or other application)?

Why should the buyer worry about hazardous wastes shipped off the premises?

If they were shipped to a dump that has been or may be declared a federal Superfund site, the buyer might inherit a potential liability that could be substantial. This liability may flow through to the buyer even if it purchases assets rather than stock. Moreover, the buyer may be liable even though it expressly does not assume the liability, if in fact the buyer does not intend to continue the same business as the predecessor.

What special problems are posed by Superfund liability?

First, Superfund can pierce the corporate veil. Officers, directors, and even shareholders can be held personally liable. Second, cleanup costs can be enormous—well beyond the value of the assets purchased. Third, liabilities of companies that generated wastes dumped in a common site are joint as well as several; every contributor of hazardous waste to that site is theoretically liable for the whole cleanup. Fourth, it can take years before liability is finally determined.

What can the buyer do to protect against environmental litigation after an acquisition?

- Due diligence requires that an acquirer hire an environmental consulting firm to do an environmental liability audit of the target company. Lenders increasingly require delivery of such an audit report, showing an essentially clean bill of health, as a condition to lending. Although the EPA has relaxed lender liability under Superfund, lenders still remain cautious.
- Make sure that the seller's warranties are broad enough to cover (1) environmental liabilities arising as a result of on-site or off-site pollution, and (2) all actions causing pollution, whether or not at the time such actions were taken they were in violation of any law or standard. The latter point is critical because

Superfund liability can reach back to actions taken before the adoption of modern environmental protection laws, when the shipment of such wastes by unlicensed carriers to unlicensed sites was not illegal.

- Make sure environmental warranties and any escrows or offset rights survive as long as possible. It may take years before the pollution is discovered and traced back to the company.

Are environmental clearances typically required?

Yes. Federal, state, and local permits and consent decrees relating to water quality, air emissions, and hazardous wastes should be checked carefully to make sure they remain effective after closing. In addition, in at least one state (New Jersey), state approval of a cleanup plan or any cleanup process must be granted or formally waived in connection with the transfer of virtually any kind of industrial or commercial facility in order for the seller to pass an effective title to the buyer.

EMERGING LEGAL ISSUES

What are some of the emerging legal issues to be concerned about in a due diligence investigation—issues that a buyer might never think of but that could hurt the company later?

Such issues crop up constantly as courts around the country offer legal theories, set new precedents, and abolish old ones. No list of such new legal theories could be complete, but here are a few questions to consider:

- To what extent can the head of a company be held accountable for the wrongful acts of subordinates? This agency theory is constantly being tested.
- To what extent can advisors rely on the word of management? To what extent can management rely on advisors? The nature of attorney-client privilege is changing rapidly, with courts demanding more skepticism on both sides.

- How many times can a company be sued for the same action? Is there a limit to the number of plaintiffs who can ask for punitive damages?
- What areas are the trial lawyers targeting? Visit the website of the American Association for Justice (justice.org; formerly the American Trial Lawyers Association) if you dare and see what hot topics they are discussing.
- Will fulfillment of change of control provisions give a departing or incoming CEO compensation that is unreasonable? If so, regulators (e.g., IRS) or shareholders could try to sue directors and officers on the basis of a failure to fulfill their fiduciary duty of care. Since excessive CEO salaries are a concern right now, make sure you avoid perpetuating the problem with your transaction.

What are the factors considered by regulators and courts when determining whether executive compensation is reasonable?

Regulators usually don't get involved in executive compensation unless tax authorities are challenging the deductibility of the compensation. They can challenge compensation paid to a shareholder of a private company if the pay is excessive. The following are questions used by tax courts to determine whether compensation paid to shareholders is reasonable, according to the AICPA:

- Would an unrelated outside investor consider the compensation reasonable?
- How does the amount of compensation compare with the amount of dividends paid?
- How does the compensation compare with the profit performance of the corporation?
- Was the level of compensation arranged in advance, or was it based on corporate profit?

- What is the typical level of compensation in the corporation's industry?

A compensation package is likely to withstand IRS scrutiny if it approximates the amount that would be paid in an arm's-length transaction.

What about golden parachute payments?

A *golden parachute* is compensation paid to officers, shareholders, or other highly compensated individuals contingent on the change of ownership or control of a corporation. The part of the payment that exceeds three times the recipient's base amount is not deductible as compensation by the corporation, under Section 280G of IRC. (The base amount is average annualized compensation payable for the five years prior to the change in ownership or control.) So, for example, if an officer had been receiving a salary over the past five years that averaged $500,000 per year, and his parachute was for $2 million, the corporation could only deduct $1.5 million of that parachute amount as salary expense. Also, the recipient would be assessed a 20 percent tax on the excess amount. Finally, it is notable that any compensation paid over $1 million is generally not tax deductible to the corporation under Section 162(m) of the IRC, as amended by the 2017 tax act. (For more on the subject of compensation in the context of mergers, see Chapter 9 on integration.)

DUE DILIGENCE AFTER CLOSING

When does the due diligence process properly end?

As important as it is for due diligence to be completed rapidly, the due diligence effort really should extend up to, through, and beyond closing. The discipline imposed by the process—dealing with the realities of the complications of business—should never be abandoned, and it is a rare deal that does not have, on closing day, a revision to the acquisition agreement covering unfinished items of due diligence inquiry.

Many acquisition agreements contain a bring-down condition to assure the buyer that, on the closing date, the target will be the same target, from a legal and financial perspective, that the buyer bargained for in the contract. The bring-down condition requires, as a condition to closing, that the seller extend its representation that there has been no material adverse change through the date of the closing.

The buyer's bring-down list can be extensive and makes both buyers and sellers nervous because it provides for a subsequent effective closing. Many prefer to wait until everything is completed and then sign the acquisition agreement right at closing (rather than before closing).

Under most acquisition agreements, the buyer will not be required to close if:

- The seller has breached any of its covenants
- Any of the representations and warranties of seller and target were not true when made or are not true on the closing date, or as if made on the closing date

This condition provides an escape for the buyer if the representations and warranties were true on the date of signing but are no longer true as of the closing date, either because of events that occurred after the signing or because breaches were discovered after the signing.

The significance of final due diligence at closing is twofold:

- First, individuals who had hands-on involvement in the due diligence process will have a particularly good insight into the operational areas they studied, and they may be called upon during the initial postacquisition "re-start-up" period under new ownership to answer questions or provide guidance. There are always items of unfinished business that grow out of the due diligence process that must be resolved after closing. They should be listed and assigned to people to solve with completion dates attached, and someone should be assigned to follow up.
- Second, in the event of a claim by the buyer or the seller against the other, the resolution of the claim may go back to a due diligence issue—that is, whether one party disclosed or made available to the other the documents or pertinent facts. Insofar as

the acquisition agreement fails to identify the information the defendant is supposed to know, the due diligence process must be examined to determine where liability lies. For this reason, it is absolutely essential to maintain complete written reports on due diligence processes and results.

What happens if a lawsuit arises after closing?

If a lawsuit arises after the signing, the conditions to closing clause will not apply. That is why it is so important to conduct a liability exposure analysis prior to closing, and to continue bring-down due diligence right up to the last minute.

In our example, the seller only guaranteed that no lawsuits existed as of the date of the acquisition agreement. Since the representation was true when made, there is no breach of the litigation representation as a result of the postsigning events. A bring-down condition will obligate the seller to make the same representation as of the closing date, however. On the basis of such a condition, the buyer will be able to terminate the agreement if interim events such as new litigation, liabilities, or other postsigning occurrences reduce the value or viability of the target. For more about this topic, see Chapter 7.

Does diligence continue to be significant after closing?

Yes. The postclosing significance of the due diligence effort is twofold.

First, individuals who had hands-on involvement in the due diligence process will have a particularly good insight into the operational areas they studied, and they may be called upon during the initial postacquisition re-start-up period under new ownership to answer questions or provide guidance.

Second, in the event of a claim by the buyer or the seller against the other, the claim's resolution may go back to a due diligence issue, that is, whether one party disclosed or made available to the other the documents or pertinent facts. Insofar as the acquisition agreement fails to identify the information the defendant is supposed to know, the due diligence process must be examined to determine where liability lies. For this reason, it is absolutely essential to maintain complete written reports on due diligence processes and results.

Ultimately, the purpose of due diligence is to minimize risk. To anticipate and protect itself from future financial, operational, and legal problems, the acquirer must first check for problems common to all acquisitions, and then for problems common to the target's industry, and finally, to risks in the target company. In seeking acquisition candidates in the first place, the acquirer can favor companies that have in place strong programs for risk management and legal compliance. In addition, the acquirer can try to minimize the risk of the transaction in other ways:

- The acquirer can consult with a broker of *liability insurance* that protects directors and officers (D&O) of the acquiring company against acquisition-related risks, and to enter into an agreement with an insurance provider. Since D&O liability insurance providers employ actuaries who specialize in predicting risk, acquirers can learn a lot from talking to them. Insurance vendors are natural allies to those who seek to limit risk.
- Furthermore, the acquirer can make sure that its due diligence phase includes all the steps generally considered to show *due care* under common law.
- If suspicions arise during standard due diligence, acquirers can employ the services of private investigators to confirm them.
- The acquirer can include protective clauses in the documents that record the agreements between the parties.
- The acquirer can structure the transaction to minimize its risk.
- The acquirer can make sure that the various deal-related agreements it signs include adequate protections against postacquisition losses stemming from preacquisition conditions.
- Finally, the acquirer can obtain representations and warranties insurance whereby the acquirer can recover directly from an insurer for losses arising from breaches of the seller's representations and warranties in the deal documents.

Together with thorough due diligence, such steps can help to ensure the long-term success of any acquisition.

CONCLUDING COMMENTS

Due diligence provides two distinct benefits to any acquirer:

- First, individuals who have had hands-on involvement in the due diligence process will gain good insight into the financial, operational, and legal areas they investigated. They may be called upon during the postacquisition re-start-up period under new ownership to answer questions or provide guidance. (There are always items of unfinished business growing out of the due diligence process that must be resolved after closing. They should be listed and assigned to people to solve with completion dates attached, and someone should be assigned follow-up.)
- Second, in the event of a claim by the buyer or the seller against the other, the resolution of the claim may go back to a due diligence issue—that is, whether or not one party disclosed certain facts or made available certain documents. Insofar as the acquisition agreement fails to identify the information the defendant was supposed to know or learn, the due diligence process gives a paper trail for determining where liability lies. Acquirers that have conducted a thorough due diligence process, and that have kept records of their efforts, will be prepared to meet this challenge—as well as the more important challenge of meeting the newly combined company's future risks and opportunities.

APPENDIX 6A

Sample Confidentiality Agreement

STRICTLY PRIVATE AND CONFIDENTIAL

[Date]

Acquisition, Inc.
Corporate Office Towers
New York, New York
To the Board of Directors:

In connection with your consideration of a possible transaction with Seller, Inc. (the "Company") or its stockholders, you have requested information concerning the Company so that you may make an evaluation of the Company to undertake negotiations for the purchase of the Company. As a condition to being furnished such information, you agree to treat any information (including all data, reports, interpretations, forecasts, and records) concerning the Company which is furnished to you by or on behalf of the Company and analyses, compilations, studies, or other documents, whether prepared by you or others, which contain or reflect such information (herein collectively referred to as the "Evaluation Material") in accordance with the provisions of this letter. The term "Evaluation Material" does not include information which (i) was or becomes generally available to the public other than as a result of a disclosure by you or your directors, officers, employees, agents, or advisors, or (ii) was or becomes available to you on a nonconfidential basis from a source other than the Company or its advisors provided that such source is not bound by a confidentiality agreement with the Company, or (iii) was within your possession prior to its being furnished to you by or on behalf of the Company, provided that the source of such information was not bound by a confidentiality agreement with the Company in respect thereof, or (iv) was independently acquired by you as a result of work carried out by an employee of yours to whom no disclosure of such information has been made directly or indirectly.

You hereby agree that the Evaluation Material will not be used by you in any way detrimental to the Company. You also agree that the Evaluation Material will be used solely for the purpose set forth above, and that such information will be kept confidential by you and your advisors for five (5) years provided, however, that (i) any such information may be disclosed to your directors, officers, and employees, and representatives of your advisors who need to know such information for the purpose of evaluating any such possible transactions between the Company and you (it being understood that such directors, officers, employees, and representatives shall be informed by you of the confidential nature of such information and shall be directed by you to treat such information confidentially and shall assume the same obligations as you under this agreement), and (ii) any disclosure of such information may be made to which the Company consents in writing. You shall be responsible for any breach of this agreement by your agents or employees.

In addition, without the prior written consent of the Company, you will not, and will direct such directors, officers, employees, and representatives not to disclose to any person either the fact that discussions or negotiations are taking place concerning one or more possible transactions between either the Company or its stockholders, on the one hand, and you, on the other hand, or any of the terms, conditions, or other facts with respect to any such possible transactions, including the status thereof. The term "person" as used in this letter shall be broadly interpreted to include without limitation any corporation, company, group, partnership, or individual.

In addition, you hereby acknowledge that you are aware, and that you will advise your directors, officers, employees, agents, and advisors who are informed as to the matters which are the subject of this letter, that the United States securities laws prohibit any person who has material, nonpublic information concerning the matters which are the subject of this letter from purchasing or selling securities of a company which may be a party to a transaction of a type contemplated by this letter or from communicating such information to any other person under circumstances in which it is reasonably foreseeable that such person is likely to purchase or sell such securities. You consent that you will not, and you will cause each of the aforementioned persons to not, violate any provisions of the aforementioned laws or the analogous laws of any state.

You hereby acknowledge that the Evaluation Material is being furnished to you in consideration of your agreement (i) that neither you nor any of your affiliates nor related persons under your control will for a period of three (3) years from the date of this letter make any public announcement with respect to or submit any proposal for a transaction between you (or any of your affiliates) and the Company or any of its securityholders unless the Company shall have consented in writing in advance to the submission of such proposal, nor will you, directly or indirectly, by purchase or otherwise, through your affiliates or otherwise, alone or with others, acquire, offer to acquire, or agree to acquire, any voting securities or direct or indirect rights or options to acquire any voting securities of the Company, for a period of three (3) years from the date of this letter without such permission, and (ii) that you will indemnify any director, officer, employee, or agent of the Company and any "controlling person" thereof as such term is defined in the Securities Act of 1933, for any liability, damage, or expense arising under federal and state securities laws from an actual or alleged breach of this agreement by you or your directors, officers, employees, representatives, or affiliates. You also agree that the Company shall be entitled to equitable relief, including an injunction, in the event of any breach of the provisions of this paragraph.

In the event that you do not proceed with the transaction which is the subject of this letter within a reasonable time, you shall promptly redeliver to the Company all written material containing or reflecting any information contained in the Evaluation Material (whether prepared by the Company or otherwise) and will not retain any copies, extracts, or other reproductions in whole or in part of such written material. All documents, memoranda, notes, and other writings whatsoever, prepared by you or your advisors based on the information contained in the Evaluation Material, shall be destroyed, and such destruction shall be certified in writing to the companies by an authorized officer supervising such destruction.

Although we have endeavored to include in the Evaluation Material information known to us which we believe to be relevant for the purpose of your investigation, you understand that we do not make any representation or warranty as to the accuracy or completeness of the Evaluation Material. You agree that you shall assume full responsibility for all conclusions you derive from the Evaluation Material and that neither the Company nor its representatives shall have any liability to you or any of your representatives resulting from the use of the Evaluation Material supplied by us or our representatives.

In the event you are required by legal process to disclose any of the Evaluation Material, you shall provide us with prompt notice of such requirement so that we may seek a protective order or other appropriate remedy or waive compliance with the provisions of this agreement. In the event that a protective order or other remedy is obtained, you shall use all reasonable efforts to ensure that all Evaluation Material disclosed will be covered by such order or other remedy. Whether such protective order or other remedy is obtained or we waive compliance with the provisions of this agreement, you will disclose only that portion of the Evaluation Material which you are legally required to disclose.

This agreement shall be governed by and construed and enforced in accordance with the laws of the state of New York, U.S.A.

Any assignment of this agreement by you without our prior written consent shall be void.

It is further understood and agreed that no failure or delay by the Company in exercising any right, power, or privilege hereunder shall operate as a waiver thereof nor shall any single or partial exercise thereof preclude any other or further exercise of any right, power, or privilege.

If you are in agreement with the foregoing, please so indicate by signing and returning one copy of this letter, whereupon this letter will constitute our agreement with respect to the subject matter hereof.

Very truly yours,

SELLER, INC.

By: Its:

Confirmed and Agreed to:

ACQUISITION, INC.

By: Its:

Date:

APPENDIX 6B

Due Diligence Checklist

Note: This is a sample only; it should not be used as an exhaustive guide and should be modified for every transaction as appropriate (e.g., a public offering versus a private acquisition). For example, due diligence into the capitalization of a company may be less significant in an asset sale than in a stock sale. This document request list does not contain specialized sections dealing with intellectual property, environmental, and employment matters, and so forth. For a checklist including those elements, see Alexandra R. Lajoux and Charles M. Elson, *The Art of M&A Due Diligence: Navigating Critical Steps and Uncovering Crucial Data* (New York: McGraw-Hill, 2009).

DOCUMENTS

Corporate Documents

Certificate of Incorporation (CI) Including All Amendments, Name Changes, Mergers. The CI is particularly helpful in determining what name to search for title to real estate. Special care should be taken not to overlook name variations, for example, "Rocket Airlines Inc.," "Rocket Air Lines, Inc.," and "Rocket Airlines Corp." These are quite likely to be very separate legal entities. The date and state of incorporation are also critical. There may be different companies with identical names incorporated in different states.

Bylaws. Look for change of control provisions. Many bylaws contain "poison pill" provisions designed to place restrictions on changes in control, or to make such changes very expensive to the potential acquirer.

Minutes. Look in particular for information on past acquisitions or mergers and other transactions affecting capital; this will help trace ownership of assets and equity. Make certain the election and appointment of current directors and officers is duly reflected in board minutes, and that the issuance of all outstanding stock has been properly authorized.

Financial Statements

Develop breakdowns, by location, of assets (land, buildings, equipment, inventory, vehicles, and, if not billed out of a central office, receivables). Consider whether those provided are adequate for use in possible SEC filings and whether pro forma financials are needed. Examine footnotes as a source of information for more detailed inquiries into existing debt, leases, pensions, related party arrangements, and contingent liabilities. Especially in leveraged acquisitions, consider the target's debt.

Engineering Reports

Try to find "as-built" drawings, especially if surveys are not available. Review for environmental problems or other concerns that might require major capital expenditures.

Market Studies/Reports on Company's Product

These may be written in-house or by outside consultants. In the case of public companies, if findings are material, they may be mentioned in the company's Management Discussion and Analysis section of its annual report/10-K. Check the 10-Ks and proxies, too.

Key Intangibles

Patents, Trademarks, Trade Names, and Copyrights. These items generally involve "registered" or "filed" rights that can be searched for at the US Patent and Trademark Office and, for copyrights, at the Library of Congress, Washington, D.C. However, such rights may not have been filed for. Also, corporations frequently have other key intangibles that are not filed for anywhere, such as trade secrets. This is especially true of companies that deal in high technology (including AI), software, and the like. Due diligence would call for inquiry as to the status of and the methods of protection for these items. Review all related trade secrets, know-how, and license agreements. (For more on AI, see the checklist that appears in Chapter 3, on valuation and modeling.)

Licenses. Whether granted by the government or by a private third party, licenses may be absolutely essential to the ability of a corporation to continue legally to conduct its business. The buyer should ensure that all such necessary licenses are current and in good order and that these licenses will be readily transferable, or remain valid, in the context of the acquisition transaction. It is generally useful to obtain the advice of special counsel or experts in the particular field (for example, FCC counsel in the case of broadcasting licenses).

Key Tangibles

Mortgages. If these are significant, request closing binder. Look for notes or other evidence of indebtedness. In the case of International Development Bank (IDB) or other quasi-public financing, request the closing binder, and be sure to review indenture, and so on.

Title Documents to Real Estate and Personal Property. Review title policies and documents creating any encumbrance upon title and deeds or bills of sale by which the company acquired assets. If assets were acquired by stock purchase or merger, find evidence of filing of appropriate corporate documents in jurisdiction(s) where assets are located as well as in state(s) of incorporation.

Real Property and Assets Identification. Ask seller to give the complete address (including county) of every facility or piece of real estate owned or leased by the company, and describe each such facility using the following list of categories (indicate more than one category if appropriate):

- Corporate offices
- Production, manufacturing, or processing facilities
- Warehouses, depots, or storage facilities
- Distribution facilities
- Sales offices
- Repair/warranty work facilities
- Apartments or other residential real property
- Undeveloped real property
- Any other facilities

If *owned,* the seller should indicate as "O" and provide full legal name in which title is recorded. If *leased,* seller should indicate as "L" and provide full name of lessor. The seller should indicate whether there is any *inventory* at any such facility by "I."

The seller should indicate whether any goods, products, or materials at any such facility are there on consignment from a supplier, as "Supp C." Ask the seller to provide the complete address (including county) of every site not described above where any of the company's assets are located, including every facility of any customer, or processor at which the company has raw materials, goods, products, or inventory on consignment, and the name of the party in possession of such assets, including any such customer or processor.

Compare actual documents to title insurance. Look for encumbrances, easements, rights of third parties, and personal property encumbrances appearing on UCC records that should be checked. When in doubt, send someone to the site. (Remember Cascade International, whose founder, Victor G. Incendy, disappeared in 1991 following the discovery that the company had overstated not only its sales and profits but the number of stores and cosmetic counters it owned. By comparing financial records to state tax records and to industry rules of thumb, outside sources were able to determine that the exaggeration was at least 300 percent. Later investigation found that this was a conservative estimate.)

Contracts

Supply and Sales Agreements. Do these meet the company's future business requirements? Review as to assignability, term, and expenditures required. (Some long-time distribution contracts will survive a merger but not an acquisition of assets.)

Employment and Consulting Agreements. These relate both to the current key employees the acquirer wishes to retain and to exposure to claims of past employees or those the acquirer does not wish to retain. They should also be reviewed to discover if they restrict the retaining of proprietary information such as customer lists.

Leases. Get legal descriptions. Have particular concern as to term and expiration dates and renewal rights, rent, and special provisions concerning assignment that may include change of corporate ownership.

License and Franchise Agreements. Look for correspondence concerning extension, expansion, disputes, and estoppels. Franchise relationships are likely to be stormy. Is there a franchise organization? Note assignment clauses and clauses creating a landlord's lien. Are any prior consents required? Are these sufficient for the business's requirements?

Loan Agreements. Review terms, intention, and assignability provisions as to any need to refinance or to obtain consents to an acquisition from lenders. Schedules and exhibits should be reviewed to glean useful information regarding the company's assets and structure.

Shareholder Agreements. Review provisions and their effect on the proposed transaction and, if the agreement will survive, its effect on future transactions, that is, registration rights and antidilution or dissenters' rights.

Sponsorship Agreements. Are these tax deductible to the giver and tax-free to the receiver?

Agreements with Labor. Obtain and study all agreements for unusual provisions that would unduly constrain management's options. Review benefits, severance, and plant closing provisions.

- Will the agreements terminate at sale or are they binding on the buyer?
- Do the agreements provide for arbitration?[29]
- Do they have provisions that restrict the buyer?
- Is the company presently in compliance with the agreements?
- Do any of the agreements expire soon? Will the buyer want to renegotiate them? (Notice may be required.) Is a strike likely?
- Are there any grievances that raise general issues of contract interpretation?

Agreements with Management

- Are there golden parachutes?
- Is there excessive compensation? (Compare with current compensation studies by executive compensation firms.)

Security Agreements or Other Agreements Giving Other Parties the Right to Acquire Assets of the Company. Review financing statements or other evidence of perfected security interests. Lien searches conducted by professional services engaged in this business are usually the most efficient way of uncovering UCC financing statements of record, but it is also sometimes necessary to check for third-party interests recorded against particular assets of the seller, rather than against the name of the seller itself. For example, security interests in assets such as vessels or aircraft are recorded in special registries (outside of the scope of the usual UCC lien search) against the particular vessel or aircraft itself, rather than against the owning company.

Sales and Product Warranty Agreements. Review for provisions that vary from the description or understanding of such documents that are provided or held by management. Review for provisions that may be illegal and/or unenforceable. Review for indemnity obligations of the company.

Selected Correspondence. This is a useful means of uncovering past problems that may recur.

Acquisition Agreements. Review prior acquisition agreements concerning surviving provisions, that is, noncompete clauses and indemnification obligations.

Pension and Profit-Sharing Plans. Check out the fine print in all plans and trust documents and review the personnel handbook and any policy manual.

- Form 5500
- Summary Plan Description (SPD)
- Actuarial valuation
- Auditor's report and accompanying management reports
- Investment manager agreements
- Fiduciary insurance and bonds
- Investment contracts
- Investment policy
- Accrued, unfunded liabilities
- Fringe benefits

Welfare Benefit Plans. Be aware that potential liabilities in this area can be substantial and that valuation of plans requires expert guidance. Check out fiduciary insurance and bonds.

Multiemployer Plans. As shown in Chapter 7, these can be a major problem.

Deferred Compensation Plan and Stock Option Plan. The TCJA created a new IRC provision, section 83(i), that can delay the taxation of compensation paid to employees of "eligible corporations" in the form of "qualified stock" for up to five years. An eligible corporation is a private company that has a written plan in place to grant stock options or restricted stock units (RSUs) to at least 80 percent of all its full-time, US-based employees. Qualified stock must be received by an employee of the corporation in connection with the exercise of stock options or the settlement of RSUs.

Supplemental or Excess Pension Plan

- Is the plan exempt from ERISA?
- Will future law affect costs or benefits?
- Are large claims anticipated?
- Are reserves on company books adequate?
- Can the plan be terminated or amended?
- Are there any benefits in pay status?
- Are the benefits in effect funded with insurance?

Insurance Policies

Review all policies and ask at least these questions:

- Do policies cover the areas of risk exposure? (Consider a risk analysis consultant to review this very technical area.)
- What is the deductible?
- What are the liability limits per occurrence? In total?
- Are punitive or treble damages excluded by the policy or by state law?
- Are policies written for claims incurred or claims made?
- Must a tail be purchased to extend coverage?
- Is there a reservation of rights clause?
- Is there a regulatory exemption clause?
- What about coverage for director and officer liability?
- What about environmental liability?

KEY INFORMATION FROM THE COMPANY'S MANAGEMENT

Financial Information. Perform an analysis of the company's past operating and financial performance. Document any planned substantive changes. In conducting such an analysis keep in mind the latest tax and accounting changes. For example, under current Financial Accounting Standards Board rules, companies may report their projections of how current losses may offset future gains, even if it is not certain the losses will trigger an offsetting tax benefit. Under previous rules, companies could not report such projections on the grounds that they were not certain to materialize. (See also Chapter 5.)

Relative Profitability of the Company's Various Classes of Products and Business Segments. Compare to comspanies of similar size in the industry.

Ownership of Company's Securities. Trace title of present owners of corporation (if privately held). Review for existing pledges or liens that must be released to permit transaction.

Litigation Matters

Potential Defaults Under Existing Contracts or Potential Litigation. Identify as many as possible and obtain waivers, consents, and so on. Ask for summary of all pending or threatened legal actions that are material:

- Names and addresses of all parties
- The nature of the proceedings
- The date of commencement
- Current status
- Relief sought
- Estimated actual cost
- Insurance coverage, if any
- Any legal opinions rendered concerning those actions

Summaries should also be provided for the following:

- All civil suits by private individuals or entities
- Suits or investigations by governmental bodies
- Criminal actions involving the target or any of its significant employees
- Tax claims (federal, state, and local)
- Administrative actions
- All investigations
- All threatened litigation

Ask for copies of all material correspondence during the past five years with government agencies. In rough order of likely importance, these include the following:

- Department of Justice
- Internal Revenue Service
- Securities and Exchange Commission
- Environmental Protection Agency
- Department of Labor
- Federal Trade Commission
- Occupational Safety and Health Administration
- Equal Employment Opportunity Commission
- Public Utility Commissions
- Federal Energy Regulatory Commission

Recent or Pending Changes in Laws or Regulations That Might Affect the Company's Business. Evaluate risk and potential existing noncompliance. Don't forget state laws, particularly tax laws. These can carry surprises for new owners. Consider Proposition 13, a 1978 amendment to the California constitution still in effect more than four decades later. It set property taxes at 1 percent of assessed valuation, rolled back assessments to 1975 levels, and limited increases to 2 percent per year. When property is under new ownership, it is reassessed and the buyer pays taxes based on the purchase price.

Product Backlogs, Purchasing, Inventory, and Pricing Policies. Is the company accurately tracking the flow of goods in a company? Falsification of records can abet fraudulent schemes of massive proportions. Classic cases in point include Crazy Eddie Stores, where founder Eddie Antar created a "giant bubble" of a company according to the US attorney in Newark, New Jersey, and Miniscribe Corporation, where managers shipped bricks to distributors and booked them as sales.

Pending Negotiations for the Purchase or Disposition of Assets or Liens. The buyer may want to drop real property that it is planning to dispose of into another entity (such as an affiliated partnership) to avoid gain recognition or to provide for means of early investment return to acquiring persons.

Charitable Contributions Claimed. Are valuations accurate? If not, this can lead to IRS challenges.

KEY INFORMATION FROM OUTSIDE SOURCES

Market and Product Studies. Whether or not the company has conducted market and product studies, it's always a good idea to consult independent research. (See Chapter 2 for a list of sources.) Try also to obtain product test data from regulatory agencies. Contact major customers to determine their level of satisfaction and copies of test programs they have run.

Capital Confirmation. Confirm outstanding capitalization from the company's stock transfer agent.

Lien Search

Acquirers will want to confirm the absence of liens or judgments via searches of public records. Note that names of debtors to be searched are often difficult to determine.

- Prior names—four-month rule regarding after-acquired collateral—cannot rely on creditor
- Fictitious names or other false information
- Continuation statements

Sometimes a search must be conducted at the state or local level. In such cases it may be necessary to do the following:

- Coordinate between the search firm and title company (sometimes not done)
- Consult Uniform Commercial Code (UCC) and related procedures to determine if state(s) at issue has additional or unusual search requirements
- Obtain the lender's or borrower's approval

Ordering a Search. Send a letter to the search firm or title company listing names, location, cost, and deadline, and request copies of all liens found. Send a copy to the client and lender's or borrower's counsel.

Reviewing a Search. What is your client buying, selling, liening, or loaning against? Are certain equipment, goods, and intangibles supposed to be free and clear? Are they vital to the business? To the closing? If so, watch for liens against those items.

- If certain secured debt is to remain in place, one would expect related UCC-1s to show up on the search report.
- If secured debt is to be paid off at closing, the seller must produce UCC-3 or other required forms of releases from the relevant parties.
- What does the appraisal say? What does the commitment or finance package say?

Check the report for names and jurisdictions. Review the UCC-1s sent for:

- Debtor
- Secured party
- Date (five-year rule)
- Description of collateral

Compare against schedules to be incorporated into loan documents, contracts, and bills of sale. Often, local counsel will need copies of lien searches in order to deliver a priority opinion.

Bring-down of Search. A search bring-down is a telegram or telephone update of lien searches and of corporate good standing certificates. It is often difficult to obtain closer than a few days before closing, but every effort should be made to close on the basis of the most recent bring-downs possible.

Creditor Check

Assumption of Debt. If secured debt is not to be paid off, get security documents to see if, for example, incurring of acquisition debt, imposition of related liens, merger, change of control, or sale of assets is permitted. Are there burdensome covenants? Is prepayment permitted, with or without penalty? (See Chapter 4.)

Confirm absence of defaults from the principal lenders.

Confirm absence of defaults from lessors (landlords).

Recognizing the Unusual or the Potential Problem. The key here is detail and curiosity.

- Is the affiliate of the seller named as a secured party?
- Are the names of the debtor not exactly right, but must be related?

Other Searches

- Patent and trademark searches for possible infringement of products or product names
- Certificates of good standing for all corporate subsidiaries whether active or inactive
- Title search/acquisition of title insurance
- Appraisals of company-owned real property and improvements
- Any equipment appraisals made by or for insurance companies

DOCUMENT LIST

Preliminary Document and Information Request List for [Name of Company]

PRIVILEGED AND CONFIDENTIAL

[Draft (Date)]

All references in the following list to the "Company" include [Name of Company] and each of its subsidiaries or divisions.

I. Corporate Records

1. Charter documents and bylaws of the Company, as amended to date.
2. Minute books of the Company for the last five years (including copies of reports to members not set forth in the minutes).
3. Stock books, stock ledgers, and other records of the issuance of stock by the Company.
4. A copy of the most current organizational chart available for the Company, including all entities or investments in which the Company owns less than a 100 percent interest.
5. Schedule showing for the Company and each of its subsidiaries: name, jurisdictions where qualified to do business, and jurisdictions where it owns or leases real property.

II. Public Filings and Financial Information

1. Audited consolidated financial statements and the notes thereto for the past five years (or the earliest date available) for the Company.
2. Interim financial statements for quarters since the last audit for the Company.
3. Most recent internal financial statements for the Company (i.e., for the period since the last quarterly statements).

4. Audited financial statements for any enterprises merged with, or acquired by, the Company in the last five years.
5. Current internal budget, operating and financial plans and projections, and any reports or papers relating to any long-term budget, capital development, restructuring program, or strategic plan, including any plans regarding systems and operations, of the Company.
6. Any private placement memoranda or offering circulars prepared and used by the Company in the last five years.
7. All annual or other letters or reports from the Company's independent public accountants or internal auditors to management during the last five years regarding accounting control systems, methods of accounting, and other procedures. Any other reports prepared by the Company, its internal auditors, counsel, or others regarding similar accounting matters.
8. List of tax returns of the Company and the years thereof which have been audited by state or federal tax authorities, and copies of the determination letters related thereto. List of tax years open. Specify whether the Internal Revenue Service or similar authorities have indicated that there may be a claim relating to open tax years.

III. Corporate Agreements

1. All agreements or documents evidencing borrowings (including bank lines of credit) or guarantees by the Company or any partnership in which the Company holds interests, or security related to borrowings or guarantees of the Company.
2. All documents and agreements evidencing other financial arrangements of the Company, including sale and repurchase or leaseback arrangements, capitalized leases, real estate and other installment purchases, equipment leases, and so on.
3. Any agreement to loan funds or to provide working capital to non–wholly owned subsidiaries, partnerships in which the Company owns an interest, or other third parties.

4. Material correspondence of the Company with lenders during the past five years, including any compliance reports prepared by the Company or its auditors and any waivers provided by the lenders.
5. Any agreements (other than those previously described) that restrict additional indebtedness or the sale, lease, or transfer (by dividend or otherwise) of the assets or capital stock of the Company.
6. All contracts relating to the Company's securities to which the Company is a party, or among shareholders of the Company, or between shareholders and the Company, including (i) any agreements relating to the purchase, issuance, transfer, or voting of securities of the Company (e.g., stock option plans, forms of stock option agreements, private placement agreements, registration rights agreements, or subscription agreements); (ii) all stockholders' agreements, voting trusts, or other restrictive agreements relating to the sale or voting of shares of the Company; and (iii) any agreements under which any person has any rights concerning issued or unissued securities of the Company (e.g., rights of purchase or sale, preemptive rights, rights of first refusal, registration rights, options, warrants, or convertible securities).
7. Any joint venture, shareholders', partnership, or other management, operating, or consulting agreements to which the Company is a party.
8. All divestiture or acquisition agreements and related documents entered into by the Company in the last five years (or earlier if the Company has any material ongoing commitments in respect of any divestiture or acquisition), including all documents relating to any proposed material divestiture or acquisition by the Company.
9. List of material customers of the Company, giving annual dollar amounts purchased during the last three years, and copies of contracts with such persons.

10. List of all distribution agreements and copies of material distribution contracts (or any form contracts) to which the Company is a party.
11. List of material suppliers and volume of purchases made from each listed source in the last two fiscal years. Copies of material supply contracts of the Company and any correspondence with material suppliers, including the agreements and correspondence with sole source suppliers. Copies of any reports or internal memoranda relating to potential supply or inventory problems.
12. List of all principal properties owned or leased by the Company. Copies of all material leases of real property and personal property to which the Company is a party either as lessee or lessor. Copies of all mortgages and related agreements or other security agreements concerning properties owned or leased by the Company.
13. List of all patents, trademarks, trade names, copyrights, and so on ("Intellectual Property") owned or used in the business of the Company, giving brief descriptions of the use, registration numbers, and dates of issuance of registration, names of any persons to or from whom such Intellectual Property is licensed, and brief descriptions of such arrangements. Description of any claims asserted or threatened by any third party with respect to any intellectual property.
14. Copies of all material agreements relating to competition, noncompetition, nonsolicitation, licensing, territorial arrangements, distributorships, or franchises to which the Company is a party, and any Hart-Scott-Rodino filings.
15. Copies of tax-sharing agreements among the Company and any of its affiliates or subsidiaries.
16. Schedule of material insurance policies of the Company.
17. Form of product warranties of the Company.
18. Records relating to customer complaints during the last two years.

19. Material research and development reports prepared by the Company in the last three years.
20. Any material contracts and agreements, not otherwise described previously, to which the Company is a party.

IV. Employees

1. All material employment agreements, consulting agreements, retention agreements, agency agreements, noncompete agreements, collective bargaining agreements, and similar agreements to which the Company is a party, including employment contracts of executive officers.
2. All bonus, retirement, profit-sharing, stock option, incentive compensation, pension, and other employee benefit plans or agreements of the Company. Provide a schedule of all outstanding options and warrants, identifying the holders thereof; issue dates, exercise price, expiration date, price of underlying shares at time of issue, and other material terms.
3. List of any strikes, unusual labor relationships, work stoppages, or employment-related proceedings during the last five years.
4. All contracts or agreements with or pertaining to the Company and to which directors, officers, or beneficial owners of more than 5 percent of the common shares of the Company are parties. All documents relating to any other transaction between the Company and any director, officer, or beneficial owner of more than 5 percent of the common shares of the Company.
5. Indemnification arrangements with officers and directors of the Company, including a description of any pertinent insurance policies.

V. Governmental Regulation and Environmental Compliance

1. List of all material government permits, licenses, and so on, of the Company (obtained or pending).
2. Any correspondence with, reports filed with, or other communications between the Company and regulatory authorities

within the last five years with respect to significant regulatory matters, including any correspondence, memoranda, or other communication relating to [specific regulatory authority].

3. Any correspondence, memoranda, or other communications relating to existing or pending governmental regulations affecting the Company's businesses, including any correspondence, memoranda, or other communications relating to any proposed legislation.
4. Any information concerning environmental matters and compliance with environmental law and governmental regulations, including descriptions of any contaminated properties, spills, liabilities to third parties, current or prospective environmental remediation efforts, potentially responsible party letters, and administrative orders.
5. Copies of waste-generation records including generation registration, hazardous waste manifests, and any correspondence, directions, or orders relating to waste disposal sites, including PCB waste disposal sites.
6. Copies of all environmental audits, inspections, surveys, questionnaires, and similar reports (internal or external) relating to the Company, including any commissioned by legal counsel to the Company.

VI. Legal Matters

1. A schedule and status report of any material litigation, administrative proceedings, or governmental investigation or inquiry, pending or threatened, affecting the Company or any of its respective officers or directors, including a brief description (amount in controversy and name of attorney handling matter, etc.) of all such pending or threatened matters.
2. Any memoranda of or correspondence with counsel with respect to pending or threatened litigation or litigation settled or otherwise terminated within the last three years.
3. Any material consent decrees, judgments, other decrees or orders, settlement agreements, or other agreements to which the

Company or any of its officers or directors is a party or is presently bound, requiring or prohibiting any future activities.

4. All letters from the Company or from counsel for the Company to the Company's independent public accountants or to any regulatory authority in the last three years regarding material litigation in which the Company or any of its respective officers or directors may be involved, including updates thereof to the most recent practicable date.

VII. Other Material Information

1. Any recent analyses of the Company prepared by the Company, investment bankers, commercial bankers, engineers, management consultants, accountants, federal or state regulatory authorities, or others, including appraisals, marketing studies, future plans, credit reports, and other types of reports, financial or otherwise.
2. Copies of customer profile studies and any other major research projects conducted, undertaken, or completed in the last three years.
3. Press releases issued during the last three years.
4. Any reports or communications to shareholders for the last three years.
5. Responses to the directors' and officers' questionnaires.
6. Product brochures and other marketing material.
7. Backlog and order summary records for the last fiscal year.
8. Copies of accident reports for the Company for the last three years.
9. Any other documents or information which, in the judgment of the officers of the Company, are significant with respect to the business of the Company or which should be considered and reviewed in making disclosures regarding the business and financial condition of the Company.

Note: Add additional specific requests according to the type of company involved in the transaction.

APPENDIX 6C

An Annotated Initial Document and Information Request List

Junior associates in law firms are often handed a document request list similar to the Annotated Initial Document and Information Request List that follows and are instructed to begin due diligence. Unfortunately, this is often done without much explanation as to why certain documents are requested and for what type of information the associate should be looking. To help associates facing this situation, this book has annotated a sample request list to assist associates in understanding why they are looking at certain types of documents and what type of information is important to cull from such documents. Often, associates are not looking for specific information but any information that seems unusual or curious—so-called red flags. In addition, associates should review all documents with an eye toward provisions of a burdensome nature that may prohibit or inhibit the deal or the company's future plans—a.k.a. obstacles. Red flags and obstacles should be brought to the attention of the other team members and, generally, the client.

I. CORPORATE DOCUMENTS

A. Certificates of incorporation with all amendments and restatements to date of each of Parent, Inc. (the "Company"), its direct and indirect subsidiaries (the "Subsidiaries"), and predecessor companies.

- You should obtain all documents on file with the secretary of state of the Company's state of incorporation (e.g., long-form good standing certificate). You should compare documents received from the secretary of state with documents received from the Company to check for discrepancies. Obtain a good standing certificate at the beginning of your investigation as well as at the closing.
- Compare the certificate of incorporation to the relevant corporate statute.
- The certificate of incorporation is the first document that should be reviewed, as it will provide important information such as the Company's legal name, the duration of its corporate existence, the Company's powers, the history of the Company's authorized share capital, existence of preemptive rights, and restrictions upon stock issuances or business combinations. In addition, the charter serves as an important basis for checking what the Company's minutes show as to dates and amounts of authorized stock.
- For the Company, it will be very important to understand its capital structure, including amount of voting stock, voting rights, and preferences, particularly if stockholder approval is required for the transaction. For example, you need to know whether a supermajority vote of stockholders is required for the transaction at hand. You should also check applicable state law regarding shareholder approval requirements.
- With regard to the Subsidiaries, your firm may be asked to opine that the Company owns as much of each Subsidiary as it claims. Knowing the amount of authorized capital stock is the first step in supporting this opinion.
- If your firm has been asked to opine that the target or issuer is duly incorporated, you should compare the charter and bylaws with the law of the state of incorporation in effect at the time the Company was incorporated as well as at the time the charter or bylaws were amended, if amended. You

must determine whether these documents were properly adopted and amended under the state law governing at that time and if they are in full force and effect.

- You should check closely provisions concerning preemptive rights and rights of first refusal. If such provisions exist, review each issuance of stock. The preemptive rights of the stockholders must have been duly waived or taken into account.
- Check to make sure that the charter contains no restrictions on corporate actions, for example, upon sales or other transfers of stock, issuance of certain types of securities, incurrence of debt, anti-takeover provisions, or other obstacles to your transaction. These types of restrictions may also impact any future plans your client may have.
- Depending on the transaction, you may have to amend or eliminate certain provisions in the certificate of incorporation.

B. Bylaws of the Company and the Subsidiaries.

- The bylaws usually contain a significant amount of information about corporate procedure. Read the bylaws of each of the Companies closely to make sure there are no procedural obstacles to your transaction.
- You need to be aware of the procedure for amending the bylaws, the powers of the corporate officers, whether shareholders and directors may act by written consent, and indemnification of directors and officers.
- Check also for vote requirements, the notice required for meetings, whether notice can be waived, whether telephone meetings are permitted (all for both shareholders and directors), the types of action for which shareholder approval is required, and the general mechanics of how the company is governed.
- It will also be important to understand the procedures for electing, removing, and replacing directors and officers. You will need to verify that the directors and officers have been duly elected, have approved minutes and resolutions

regarding the transaction (in the case of directors), and have signed transaction documents (in the case of officers).

- Compare the bylaws to the relevant corporate statute.
- Depending on the transaction, you may have to amend or eliminate certain provisions in the bylaws.

C. Minute books and all materials distributed in connection with any meetings of the Company and each of the Subsidiaries for the last five years.

- You should review the minutes of meetings of the board of directors and any committees as well as meetings of stockholders.
- Prior to reviewing minutes, you should be familiar with any stockholders' agreements or voting agreements that may contain restrictions on corporate actions, vote requirements, and so on.
- You are checking to see whether the actions taken by the directors and shareholders were taken in accordance with the charter, bylaws, stockholders' agreements, and state law.
- If your firm will be opining as to the Company's due incorporation, examine the minutes from organizational meetings and the state law in effect at the time of incorporation to determine whether the incorporation procedure in effect at the time of incorporation was followed, that the certificate of incorporation was properly adopted, that the bylaws were properly adopted, that the subscription agreement was properly approved, and that the initial issuance of stock was properly approved.
- Be sure you understand how the Company was formed, who were the initial stockholders or contributors, and what they contributed. There should be clean receipts, canceled certificates, and so on, for everything. Did the Company receive the consideration it was supposed to receive?
- Whenever directors have authorized or issued securities (including options and warrants), have amended the charter

or taken other significant action (such as approvals of material contracts, employment and severance arrangements, pension plans, loans, acquisitions, and transactions involving officers, directors, and principal stockholders), verify that the procedures prescribed by applicable securities laws, state law, the charter, and bylaws were followed, including that the directors were properly elected, each of the meetings was duly and properly called, a proper quorum was present, and a proper percentage of votes favorable to the action was recorded (this applies to both director and stockholder meetings).

- Verify that the current directors and officers have been elected in strict accordance with the charter, bylaws, and state law in effect at the time of election.
- If the Company keeps detailed board minutes, the minute books can provide a good overview of the company's operations, material transactions and agreements, litigation, and other business affairs. Keep an eye out for red flags. If the Company does not keep detailed board minutes, that fact alone can be a red flag.
- If there are consents in lieu of meetings, check that the requisite vote was met.
- Verify that no action has been taken to dissolve the Company or its Subsidiaries.
- If you find actions that have not been taken properly, cleanup work will be necessary through ratification action by directors or stockholders.

D. Stock books, stock ledgers, and other records of the issuance of the Company and each of the Subsidiaries.

- You are checking to see whether the outstanding stock of the Company has been duly authorized, validly issued, and fully paid and nonassessable.
- The goal is to track stock issuances, transfers, cancellations, and exchanges. Sometimes it is helpful to create a flowchart. Check to see if stock issuances were properly

authorized by the board, and were in accordance with the charter bylaws and federal and state securities laws.
- Has the stock described in the minute books as having been issued in fact been appropriately recorded?
- Does the total number of shares indicated in the stock books as outstanding conform to the number of shares indicated as outstanding in the Company's financial statements?
- If there is a corporate transfer agent or registrar, obtain a certificate showing the number of outstanding shares and compare it to the numbers in the financial statements.
- Were there any stock repurchases? Were they completed in accordance with the state law?
- Obtain a certificate from the Company's independent public accountant that the stock is fully paid; otherwise, you will have to review the Company's financial statements from past years.

E. List of all jurisdictions in the United States and elsewhere in which the Company is qualified to do business.
- You should obtain good standing certificates from each foreign jurisdiction to check that the Company is duly qualified.
- Also, you should check the state laws for all requirements imposed on the Company by foreign jurisdictions.
- Consider whether you need to withdraw from any state or qualify in a new state as a result of the transaction.
- You may also need to check with local counsel in foreign jurisdictions if the Company does business in other countries.

F. A copy of the most current organizational chart available for the Company, including all Subsidiaries and any other entities or investments in which the Company owns less than a 100 percent interest.
- The organizational chart provides a basic understanding of how the Company and the Subsidiaries are structured and

operated. It will become invaluable during your investigation in figuring out who can provide you with certain documents and who would be helpful to interview regarding certain issues.

G. Any and all agreements among shareholders of the Company, or between shareholders and any of the Companies, relating to the management, ownership, or control of the Companies, including voting agreements, rights of first refusal, preemptive rights, and registration rights.

- Look for potential obstacles to the contemplated transaction such as voting agreements, rights of first refusal, preemptive rights, and registration rights. These agreements may affect the potential change of control of a company or the transferability of its stock. Look to see whether the deal will trigger any of these burdensome provisions. In closely held companies, there may be complex agreements between shareholders, including agreements to buy back shares, issue more shares, and so on. Nearly all such agreements have complex registration rights upon a public offering.
- If the contemplated transaction is a sale of stock, determine whether the purchaser will be required to enter into such types of agreements (e.g., voting agreement) or, if appropriate, whether such agreements are assignable.
- Review any shareholder rights plans.

H. Reports or other material communications to shareholders of the Company for the last five years.

- Read these communications to make sure that you and your client are aware of all the material information that has been disclosed to stockholders.
- Look for red flags.

II. FINANCIAL INFORMATION

A. [If the Company is public: All filings by the Company and Subsidiaries with the Securities and Exchange Commission during the last five years.] [If the Company is not public: Audited consolidated financial statements and the notes thereto for the past five years and interim financial statements for quarters since the last audit for the Company and the Subsidiaries.]

- These documents will help you understand the Company's business.
- In the case of public companies, you will review annual reports (a Form 10-K) and quarterly reports (a Form 10-Q). The 10-Ks and 10-Qs will contain a significant amount of disclosure about operations, financials, and management's view of these results [the Management's Discussion & Analysis of Financial Condition and Results of Operations (MD&A)]. Public companies also file a proxy statement annually. In addition to these periodic filings, public companies must disclose extraordinary events on Form 8-Ks. Review these documents to make sure that you and your client are aware of all the material information that has been disclosed to stockholders and the public. Look for red flags.
- The footnotes to the financial statements will contain information on stock options, debt, and capital structure; be sure you understand all footnotes and that you have reviewed all agreements discussed in the footnotes.
- You should look for and obtain explanations of any significant losses or unusually good years.

B. Any private placement memorandum or offering document prepared and used by any of the Companies in the last five years.

- Again, these documents provide useful information in understanding the Company and should be reviewed, with the most recent documents getting the most attention.
- Pay attention to the risk factors section. Use it as a checklist to be sure you have caught all potential problems.

C. If the Company is public: any Schedule 13D* or 13G† filed with the Company in the last five years.

- In an acquisition, the buyer will want to know who owns stock in the target and how much stock each stockholder owns. Such information will assist the buyer in analyzing the probability of obtaining stockholder consent to the transaction.
- Use these filings as a check to understanding the Company's capital structure.

D. Current internal budget, operating and financial plans, and projections and any reports or papers relating to any long-term budget, capital development, restructuring program, or strategic plan, including any plans regarding systems and operations.

- Internal budgets and forecasts are useful in understanding what management thinks the Company's current and future prospects are, and for highlighting areas of concern to management. Look for red flags.
- Check to see if the internal budget matches what the Company has stated publicly. Are the assumptions overly optimistic? Is the Company ignoring or covering up problems? This review may reveal disclosure issues, such as product backlog.

E. Audited financial statements for any enterprises merged with, or acquired by, the Company or any of its Subsidiaries in the last five years.

- Focus especially on the footnotes. They can provide a checklist for just about everything about the Company, including credit agreements, debt structure, capital

---

* A Schedule 13D is a form that must be filed under the Securities Exchange Act of 1934. Generally, this form must be filed within 10 days after an acquisition that brings a stockholder above the 5 percent ownership threshold. It requires disclosure concerning the identity and background of the acquirer, the purpose and funding of the acquisition and the acquirer's plans, agreements, and understandings regarding the issuer.

† A Schedule 13G is a form that must be filed under the Securities Exchange Act of 1934. Generally, this form must be filed and updated annually by every beneficial owner of 5 percent of a registered class of voting securities. This form requires disclosure of the owner's identity and size of holdings.

structure, compensation, options, and leases. This holds true for all reviews of financial statements.

F. All annual or other letters or reports from each of the Companies' independent public accountants or auditors to management during the last five years regarding each of the Companies' accounting control systems, methods of accounting, and other procedures.

- Look for red flags, especially in terms of hesitancy, qualified opinions, or warnings.

G. Any reports prepared by any of the Companies, their internal auditors, counsel, or others regarding material accounting matters (such as memoranda relating to a change in the Companies' accountants, inventory markdowns, increases in reserves for doubtful accounts, or other reports prepared for the board of directors).

- These reports are helpful as they highlight problems that the Company has had in the past. Look for red flags. As part of your investigation, you will want to note what steps have been taken to resolve the problems and to prevent their reoccurrence.

H. List of returns of the Company and the years thereof which have been audited by state or federal tax authorities, and copies of the determination letters related thereto. List of tax years open. Indicate whether the Internal Revenue Service or similar authority has indicated that there may be a claim relating to open tax years.

- Look for significant potential liabilities either in the operations of the Company being investigated or in connection with the specific proposed transaction.
- Bring these documents to the attention of the tax specialist on your team.
- Do a search of tax havens. Several search firms have a service that can provide this type of search. Remember, though, that havens, while legal, can attract negative public attention. Factor in the potential reputation risk.

III. MATERIAL CORPORATE AGREEMENTS

There may be agreements that could materially affect the Company's operations or the proposed transaction. Your goal is to find business and legal risks. In most cases, you want to make sure the material agreements will remain in effect. Some of the items that you should consider are the following: (i) what is the term; (ii) what are the Company's obligations and liabilities under the agreement; (iii) how is corporate action restricted; (iv) what are the events of default; (v) what are the consequences of a material breach (for example, cross defaults, termination); (vi) is the contract assignable; (vii) how can the agreement be terminated; (viii) are there any changes in control provisions; (ix) are any consents required; (x) are any notice provisions triggered; (xi) what is the total exposure; and (xii) what types of indemnification provisions are there, and so on. Also consider obtaining an officer's certificate certifying that the material agreements are still in effect and have not been amended or modified (otherwise than as set forth in subsequent amendments). Also, if need be, material contracts can be verified with the counterparty. When reviewing minutes, you should double-check that material contracts were approved and authorized by the board of directors. Finally, make sure you have reviewed fully executed copies of the material agreements and that the copies are complete. In the context of a public offering you will have to determine which material agreements should be filed as exhibits to the registration statement.

A. All agreements or documents evidencing borrowings (including bank lines of credit) or guarantees by the Company, each of its Subsidiaries, or any partnership of which the Company holds partnership interests.

- First, it is important to determine the amount of money the Company owes or has guaranteed, the terms of the debt, and the amount and timing of the payments. What are your client's plans? Will it repay debt? Check the repayment and prepayment provisions. Any penalties?
- Second, review these documents to make sure there are no obstacles to the transaction. For example, the contracts may not be assignable, or certain covenants may restrict the transaction. Events of default may be triggered by the

transaction. When working on a financing, keep in mind that often the sale of securities is deemed an assignment of the agreement. In these documents, you are looking for obstacles. If there are obstacles, your client may have to renegotiate the terms.

- Identify any consents that may be required and ensure that any such consents or waivers that have been previously obtained are in proper form.
- Debt instruments usually contain affirmative and negative covenants (for example, restrictions on combinations, offering, asset sales, payment of dividends, etc.) that can significantly restrict your client's plans for the Company's operations or the pending transaction itself.

B. Material correspondence of the Company and each of its Subsidiaries with lenders during the past five years, including any compliance reports prepared by the Company or any of its Subsidiaries or their auditors.

- Review this correspondence to verify that the Company is not in default on its loans and that there are no outstanding issues with lenders. Look for red flags.

C. All contracts relating to the Company's securities to which the Company is a party, including stock option plans, forms of stock option agreements, private placement agreements, registration rights agreements, subscription agreements, voting agreements, warrant agreements, and so on.

- Review these documents to verify that your client is aware of their existence, as well as the significant provisions thereof. Look for obstacles and red flags.
- You should be familiar with the total outstanding amount of options or other rights to acquire stock of the Company.
- What are the Company's obligations under these documents?

D. Copies of all mortgages or other security agreements that are material to the Company or any of its Subsidiaries.

- Depending upon the target or issuer, there may be a few mortgages or several thousand. If there are many mortgages, before reviewing all of these agreements, discuss with the other team members whether there is an efficient way to reduce the number of mortgages examined. For example, you might decide to examine only mortgages involving a certain minimum dollar amount. Another option is to examine a randomly selected percentage of mortgages.
- Summarize the key terms of the mortgages, including location and character of property owned, term of debt, payment amounts, due dates of payments, and any covenants or obstacles that may impact the transaction.
- Determine whether there are any disputes under the material mortgages.
- Undertake UCC searches to check for liens in the company's state of incorporation, the state where its executive office is located, and the state where major operations are conducted or facilities are located.
- Note that for certain assets such as aircraft, there are special registries that should be checked.
- Review financing statements.
- Which are the assets in which your client is most interested? Check for liens against those assets.

E. Any agreement to lend funds or provide working capital to non-wholly owned Subsidiaries, partnerships in which the Company owns an interest, or other third parties.

- Look for red flags, obstacles—do any agreements involve related parties?
- What is the total exposure to the Company?

F. All documents and agreements evidencing other financial arrangements, including sale and repurchase or leaseback arrangements, capitalized leases, real estate and other installment purchases, equipment leases, and so on.

- Look for red flags, obstacles—do any agreements involve related parties?

- Has the Company agreed to perform or not perform certain actions in the future?
- What is the Company's exposure?

G. Any joint venture, partnership, or other material management, operating, or consulting agreements to which the Company or any of its Subsidiaries are a party.

- What are the Company's obligations and liabilities? How will the pending transaction affect these agreements?

H. All divestiture or acquisition agreements entered into by the Company in the last five years.

- Which provisions survive?
- What are the Company's continuing obligations (e.g., indemnification, noncompetition)?

I. List of material customers and vendors of the Company and each of its Subsidiaries, giving annual dollar amounts purchased or sold during the last five years, and copies of contracts with such persons.

- Often material relationships may not be documented and you will need to interview company officials. Consider whether your client will want to document these relationships.
- Are there possible disruptions to sales or supplies? Are prices expected to increase or decrease?
- Look to see whether any single customer or vendor accounts for a large percentage of the total amount purchased or sold annually. What are the terms of the contracts with such customers or vendors? What would happen if these relationships were terminated? Any such concentration should be brought to the attention of the buyer or disclosed in the prospectus.
- Review the contracts for red flags and obstacles.

J. List of all distribution agreements and copies of material distribution contracts (or any form contracts) to which the Company or any of its Subsidiaries is a party.

- *See* III.1.
- Review the contracts for red flags and obstacles.

K. List of material suppliers and copies of material supply contracts and any correspondence with material suppliers, including the agreements and correspondence, if any, with sole source suppliers.

- *See* III.1.
- Are the Company's requirements for the future covered by these contracts?

L. List of all principal properties. Copies of all material leases of real and personal property to which the Company or any of its Subsidiaries is a party, either as a lessee or lessor.

- If real estate is a significant asset, a real estate lawyer should review these documents.
- Actual documents should be compared against title insurance.
- You are checking for encumbrances, rights of third parties, and so on.
- With regard to leased properties, summarize the key terms of each lease (for example, term, rent, and the square footage of the property).
- Review whether the proposed transaction triggers any provisions in the leases that would be obstacles to the deal.
- Are there renewal rights? What happens upon a change of control?

M. Copies of all material agreements relating to competition, noncompetition, licensing, territorial arrangements, distributorships, or franchises to which the Company or any of its Subsidiaries is a party.

- Obstacles and red flags—does the Company have burdensome obligations or is it relying on unenforceable provisions?
- You may wish to consult an antitrust lawyer.
- Will these agreements cover the Company's needs in the future?

N. Copies of tax sharing agreements among the Company and any of its Subsidiaries.
- These documents should be brought to the attention of the tax specialist on your team.

O. Schedule of material insurance policies of the Company and its Subsidiaries currently in effect.
- Are all areas of risk covered (for example, environmental, product liability, directors and officers)?
- You should review each material insurance policy.
- What is the deductible?
- Are there liability limits?
- What types of exclusions exist?
- Sometimes a firm specializing in risk analysis should be engaged.

P. Form of product warranties of the Company and its principal Subsidiaries.
- Look for red flags such as material contingent liabilities.
- What are the Company's indemnification obligations?

Q. Company records relating to customer complaints during the last two years.
- Look for red flags, such as patterns of complaints.

R. Any material foreign currency exchange agreements, including, without limitation, any hedging agreements, and a summary of derivative trading.
- Given the times, you must make sure you understand these agreements and the exposure and risks to the Company.

S. All material contracts and agreements, not otherwise previously described, to which the Company or any of its Subsidiaries is a party.
- Make sure that you have asked the target or issuer to provide you with copies of any documents that you may have overlooked or any agreements or relationships that are not documented.

T. All contracts or agreements with or pertaining to the Company or the Subsidiaries to which any director or officer of the

Company or the Subsidiaries or any beneficial owner of more than 5 percent of the common stock of the Company and the Subsidiaries is a party.

- The concern with respect to affiliate transactions is that the agreements may be on terms more favorable than an arm's-length agreement. If that is the case, the termination of such agreement may adversely affect the Company's business.
- Review these documents as you would any similar document that does not have an insider or large stockholder as a party.

U. All documents pertaining to any receivables from, or payables (including loans) to, any director or officer of the Companies or any beneficial owner of more than 5 percent of the common stock of the Company.

V. Indemnification arrangements with officers and directors of any of the Companies, including any pertinent insurance policies.

IV. GOVERNMENTAL REGULATION

You must understand the significant regulations affecting the Company's business and operations, and the proposed transaction. Are any regulatory approvals or consents required? Are any regulatory issues presented by the transaction and/or the Company's business that must be addressed? Are there any regulatory proceedings pending or threatened that may materially affect the Company's business?

A. Filings with regulatory authorities for the past five years.

- Are any filings or approvals required in connection with the transaction?

B. Any correspondence or other communications with regulatory authorities within the last five years with respect to significant regulatory matters, including any correspondence, memoranda, or other communication relating to the applicable regulatory authorities.

- You should review all material correspondence with regulatory authorities.

C. Any correspondence, memoranda, or other communication relating to existing or pending governmental regulations affecting the Company's business, including any correspondence, memoranda, or other communication relating to any proposed legislation.

- What effects may proposed legislation have on the Company's business?
- What will the cost of compliance with any such new legislation be?

D. A list of all governmental permits, licenses, and so on, of the Company and its Subsidiaries.

- You will usually have to consult with expert counsel—FCC, FDA, environmental, and so on.
- What is the impact of the transaction on the permits, licenses, and so on? Can the permits and licenses be transferred? Must your client reapply for such permits and licenses?

V. LEGAL MATTERS

A. A schedule and status report of any material litigation, administrative proceedings, or governmental investigation or inquiry (including, without limitation, tax and customs matters), pending or threatened, affecting any of the Companies or any of their officers or directors, including brief descriptions (amount in controversy and name of attorney handling matters, etc.) of all such pending or threatened litigation, proceedings, and so on.

- The primary reason for reviewing litigation documents is to determine the total amount of contingent liability and the likelihood of liability. Also look for any patterns of suits. What types of problems does the Company seem to have?
- You want to understand the scope of any ongoing material lawsuit, investigation, or inquiry, and the potential consequences, including monetary damages. You probably will have to consult with the litigation counsel handling the case.

- You may have to review complaints and pleadings and discuss exposure with litigation counsel. If the claims are very specialized, you may have to consult expert counsel in that area (e.g., environmental).
- Many times you cannot rely on the information provided to you, and you also should do an independent search through one of the search services.
- Is the potential liability covered by insurance?

B. Any memoranda of counsel or correspondence with counsel with respect to pending or threatened litigation or litigation settled or otherwise terminated within the past five years.

- If you are told a matter has been resolved, make sure you review signed settlement agreements.

C. Any material consent decrees, judgments, other decrees or orders, settlement agreements, or other agreements to which any of the Companies or any of their officers or directors is a party or is bound, requiring or prohibiting any future activities, regardless of when issued.

- Look for obstacles to the transaction. In addition, in acquisitions, you need to understand whether there are any activities in which the Company may not engage. This is important, as your client may have plans to the contrary.

D. All letters from the Companies or from the attorneys or from any of the Companies to the Companies' accountants or to any federal or state regulatory authority for the last five years regarding material litigation in which the Companies (or any of their officers or directors) may be involved, including any and all updates thereof to the most recent practicable date.

VI. OTHER MATERIAL INFORMATION

A. Any recent analyses of any of the Company or Subsidiaries prepared by any of the Companies, investment bankers, engineers, management consultants, accountants, federal or state regulatory authorities, or others, including appraisals, marketing studies, future plans and projections, credit reports, and other types of reports, financial or otherwise, including reports detailing plans for new divisions for the Company or any of the Subsidiaries.

- These documents will give you insight into how others view the company. Review these analyses for red flags.

B. Any other documents or information which, in the judgment of officers of the Company, are significant with respect to the business of the Companies or which should be considered and reviewed in making disclosures regarding the business and financial condition of the Companies.

- Look for red flags and obstacles.

C. Copies of press releases, issues, or significant articles written about the Companies during the last five years.

- Look for red flags.

D. Copies of responses to the most recent officers' and directors' questionnaires.

- With regard to public offerings, you generally must include information on the Company's officers and directors, their remuneration and employee benefits, and material transactions which they have had with the Company underwriters, and issuer's counsel should review the completed questionnaires and compare them with the disclosure in the registration statement.

E. Product brochures and other marketing material.

- Look for any red flags. Try to determine whether anything in these materials seem misleading or inaccurate.
- If applicable, compare more technical materials to sales-oriented documents. Engineers can often be more frank about a key product's shortcomings.
- Information about customers may not be in writing; interviews of marketing people may be necessary to be sure of the strength of the Company's customer base.

APPENDIX 6D

Sample Index of VDR Documents[30]

NOTES:

VDR File names have been color coded as follows:

Green: Open access. Yellow: Access limited to due diligence team.
Red: Accessed only by internal and external counsel.

A. ACCOUNTING DATA

Yellow A.1	Consolidating Balance Sheet 2018
Yellow A.2	Consolidated Balance Sheet 2018
Yellow A.3	Consolidating Balance Sheet 2019
Yellow A.4	Consolidated Balance Sheet 2019

E. ENVIRONMENTAL

Overview

E.1 File: Overview Manual

Green	Facility Overview
Red	Facility Descriptions
Green	Emissions Data
Red	Accident & Injury Data

E.2 File

Green	Plant Description
Red	General Information
Yellow	Permits
Red	Audit Report

F. FACILITIES
Plant Facilities

F.4 File

Green	Key Facts
Green	Photo
Green	Major Equipment
Green	Production Process
Green	Manufactured Products
Green	Operating Permits Listing

H. HUMAN RESOURCES
Benefits Information

Green H.1	Long-Term Disability Plan Document
Green H.2	Medical Reimbursement Plan Document
Green H.3	Dependent Reimbursement Plan Document
Green H.4	Retirement Income Plan Document
Green H.5	Personal Plan Document
Yellow H.6	Retirement Income Plan for Hourly Employees (in progress of being amended)
Green H.7	Dental Plan Benefit Summary—Comprehensive Medical Plan

I. INTERNATIONAL INDEX
FRANCE

Debt/Credit Arrangements

Green 1.1	Debt/Credit Arrangement—Loan Documentation (Loans to Company)
Green 1.2	Debt/Credit Arrangement—Guaranties/Comfort Letters/Promissory Notes/Pledges/Mortgages/Other Liens

Taxes

Green 1.3	Tax—Taxes Paid

Employment

Green 1.4	Employment Head Count
Green 1.5	Employment Total Compensation (by division/function)
Green 1.6	Employment Payroll List (showing compensation for management personnel)

L. LEGAL

L.1 File: Product Liability Litigation

Red	US Product Liability Overview
Red	US Product Liability History—Legal Fees
Red	US Pending Litigation Legal Fees
Red	Litigation Expenses
Red	Case Summaries
Red	Claim Summaries
Red	Letter of Credit

L.2 File: Miscellaneous Litigation/Claims (See also related Trademark File)

Red	Bankruptcy Litigation
Green	Worker's Compensation Claims Experience

L.3 File: Selected Regulations Affecting Business Operations

Yellow	Fair Packaging and Labeling Act
Yellow	Federal Hazardous Substances Act

LEASES

Yellow L.6	Lease
L.7–L.12	Not Used

Personal Use Equipment

Yellow L.14	Company-Issued Mobile Phones
Yellow L.15	Company-Issued Laptops

CONTRACTS

Green L.20	R&D Contract
L.21	Not Used
L.22	Not Used
L.23	R&D Contract

Data Processing (including licenses)
SOFTWARE LICENSES

L.24	Not Used
Green L.25	R&D Contract—List of Confidentiality Agreements
L.26–L.27	Not Used
Green L.28	Software License—Software—Accounts Payable System

ACQUISITIONS/MERGER DOCUMENTATION

L.618–L.633	Not Used
Yellow L.634	Acquisition of XYZ Company
Yellow L.635	Acquisition of ABC Company
Yellow L.636	Purchase of Certain Assets of New York Company (2019)
Yellow L.637	Purchase of Certain Assets of New Jersey Company (2015)
Yellow L.638	Certificates of Merger Merger of UV, Inc., and X, Inc.
	Corporate Records
Yellow L.639	Corporate Records—(2 Volumes, 1 Book of Stock Certificates & 1 Stock Transfer Ledger)
L.640–L.650	Not Used
Yellow L.651	Corporate Records (2 Volumes)
L.652	Not Used
Yellow L.653	Corporate Records (3 Volumes)
L.654	Not Used
Yellow L.655	Corporate Records (2 Volumes)

P. PATENTS

Red	P. I Listing of Patents

R. RESEARCH & DEVELOPMENT

R.1 File: Research & Development Overview

Green	Overview
Green	Building Facilities
Green	Product Development Process
Green	R&D Capabilities
Green	R&D Organization

T. TRADEMARKS

Red T.1 File

1. Printout (and update) of worldwide trademark registrations and applications of marks (by marks; by owner; updates)
2. Printout of trademarks

Red T.2 File: Printout of pending conflicts (Selected trademarks pertaining to products with sales exceeding $5 million)

T.3–T.6 Not Used

Red T.7 File: Encumbrances on trademark: exclusive licenses, consents, and agreements

NOTES

1. The definition of auditor independence is found in Title 17, Chapter II, Part 210, Section 210.2-01, https://www.law.cornell.edu/cfr/text/17/210.2-01. Note that on May 2, 2018, the SEC issued a proposed rule to clarify the rules surrounding auditor independence with regard to loans and creditor-debtor relationships (proposing the elimination of arrangements that arguably do not affect independence). https://www.sec.gov/rules/proposed/2018/33-10491.pdf.
2. This answer was provided by Bill Blandford, Manager of M&A, Retired, Nokia, and a member of the Board of M&A Standards, as introduced in the preface to this book.
3. XBRL is the universal language for financial information, used in securities disclosure and for other purposes, such as transactional information along an accounting supply chain. Currently, 29 stock exchanges use it, involving a total of 22,000 companies (https://www.xbrl.org/the-standard/why/xbrl-for-securities-filing/). In the United States, some smaller public companies may become exempt from the requirement to use XBRL, if the Small Company Disclosure Simplification Act of 2018 becomes law (https://www.congress.gov/bill/115th-congress/house-bill/5054.

4. https://www.sec.gov/forms.
5. This definition is based on the writings of John H. Bodley, author of *Cultural Anthropology: Tribe, State, and the Global System,* 6th ed. (Lanham, MD: AltaMira Press, Rowman & Littlefield Publishers, 2018).
6. Ibid.
7. See the General Data Protection Regulation, decreed April 27, 2016, and effective May 25, 2018. https://eur-lex.europa.eu/legal-content/EN/TXT/HTML/?uri=CELEX:32016R0679&from=EN.
8. Most states base their statutes regarding fraudulent conveyance on the Uniform Fraudulent Transfer Act, a model law developed by the National Conference of Commissioners on Uniform State Laws. As for federal bankruptcy law, this is found in Title 11, Chapter 5, Subchapter III, § 548, Fraudulent transfers and obligations.
9. See in the USC Title 15, Chapter 2A, Subchapter I (Domestic Securities), Sections 77a and ff. https://www.law.cornell.edu/uscode/text/15/77a and ff. https://www.law.cornell.edu/uscode/text/15/78a.
10. USC Title 15, Chapter 2B (Securities Exchanges). https://www.law.cornell.edu/uscode/text/15/chapter-2B.
11. In the Delaware Chancery case of *In re Trulia, Inc. Stockholder Litigation,* 2016 WL 270821 (Del. Ch.), the court stated that it would no longer accept pleadings alleging merely a violation of a disclosure law; claims henceforth would need to include additional allegations. This had the effect of sharply reducing settlements in such cases (as all were dismissed) but pushed disclosure-only cases away from Delaware to other states or to federal courts. See https://www.law.com/newyorklawjournal/sites/newyorklawjournal/2017/11/13/impact-of-trulia-on-merger-litigation-in-state-and-federal-courts/.
12. Form S-4 states: "This Form may be used for registration under the Securities Act of 1933 ("Securities Act") of securities to be issued (1) in a transaction of the type specified in paragraph

(a) of Rule 145 (§230.145 of this chapter); (2) in a merger in which the applicable state law would not require the solicitation of the votes or consents of all of the security holders of the company being acquired; (3) in an exchange offer for securities of the issuer or another entity; (4) in a public reoffering or resale of any such securities acquired pursuant to this registration statement; or (5) in more than one of the kinds of transaction listed in (1) through (4) registered on one registration statement." https://www.sec.gov/files/forms-4.pdf.

13. For a good overview of claims and defenses in M&A litigation, see Kaufman, Gildin, and Robbins, LLC, *Securities Litigation: Claims and Defenses,* 2018. This source lists more than a dozen securities law sections that may be raised in M&A litigation, as well as several defenses against them, including due diligence. https://www.securitieslosses.com/Securities-Arbitration-and-Litigation_PC/Securities-1-Securities-Arbitration-and-Litigation_PC.shtml.
14. *Director Liability: Myths, Realities, and Prevention—Report of the NACD Blue Ribbon Commission* (Washington, D.C.: NACD, 2006, 2013).
15. CFR Title 17, Chapter II, Part 240, Subpart A, Section 240.10b-5, https://www.law.cornell.edu/cfr/text/17/240.10b-5.
16. Ibid.
17. See Ann M. Olazabal and Patricia S. Abril, "Recklessness as a State of Mind in 10(b) Cases," *New York University Journal of Law and Public Policy,* vol. 18, 2015, pp. 305 ff., http://www.nyujlpp.org/wp-content/uploads/2015/09/Olazabal-Recklessness-As-a-State-of-Mind-in-10b-Cases-18nyujlpp305-.pdf.
18. The full quote is as follows: "Is it sufficient to ask questions, to obtain answers which, if true, would be thought satisfactory, and to let it go at that, without seeking to ascertain from the records whether the answers in fact are true and complete? I have already held that this procedure is not sufficient. . . ." https://law.justia.com/cases/federal/district-courts/FSupp

/283/643/1906035/scott v. BarChris Construction Corporation, 283 F. Supp. 643 (S.D.N.Y. 1976).

19. See *In re WorldCom, Inc.,* Securities Litigation 294 F. Supp. 2d 431 (S.D.N.Y. 2003), http://worldcomlitigation.com/courtdox/2005-03-21OrderDenyRobertsSJMot.pdf. Note that some Enron litigation also included Section 11 allegations (see, for example, this pleading: http://securities.stanford.edu/filings-documents/1020/ENE01/2002610_r19x_013624.pdf). For an analysis shortly after the Enron and WorldCom cases, see Richard A. Spehr, et al., *Securities Act Section 11: A Primer and Update of Recent Trends,* Mayer, Brown, Rowe & Maw LLP, Washington Legal Foundation, 2006, http://www.wlf.org/upload/0106CLNSpehr.pdf.

20. The directors' report on Enron (William C. Powers, Jr., et al., *Report of Investigation by the Special Investigative Committee of the Board of Directors of Enron Corp.,* February 1, 2002) states, in part: "The Board, and in particular the Audit and Compliance Committee, has the duty of ultimate oversight over the Company's financial reporting. While the primary responsibility for the financial reporting abuses discussed in the Report lies with Management, the participating members of this Committee believe those abuses could and should have been prevented or detected at an earlier time had the Board been more aggressive and vigilant" (http://news.findlaw.com/wsj/docs/enron/sicreport/cover.html). Further relevant commentary is provided by the Permanent Subcommittee on Government Investigations, Governmental Affairs Committee of the US Senate, *Role of the Board of Directors in Enron's Collapse* (July 8, 2002), which states, in part: "The Board's lack of knowledge of certain aspects of the Raptor transactions, however, does not justify its handling of these transactions. At best, it demonstrates a lack of diligence and independent inquiry by the Board into a key Enron liability," and further, the board's "duty of care requires a director to be diligent and prudent in managing the corporation's affairs" (citing *Gearheart Industries*

v. Smith International, 741 F.2d 707, 719 (5th Cir. 1984). For a report from independent directors on WorldCom, see Dennis R. Beresford, et al., *Report of Investigation by the Special Investigation Committee of WorldCom Inc.* (March 31, 2003), concluding that there was a failure of oversight (http://news.findlaw.com/wsj/docs/worldcom/bdspcomm60903rpt.pdf). For a subsequent independent report about WorldCom, see Richard Breeden, "Restoring Trust" August 26, 2003, https://www.sec.gov/Archives/edgar/data/723527/000119312503044064/dex992.htm.

21. The court in *In re Worldcom, Inc. Securities Litigation,* No. 02 Civ. 3288 (DLC), 2005 U.S. Dist. LEXIS 4193 (S.D.N.Y. Mar. 21, 2005), denied an independent director's motion for summary judgment on due diligence grounds. See D. Anthony Rodriguez, *Building the Section 11 "Due Diligence" Defense for Outside Directors,* American Bar Association, https://www.americanbar.org/publications/blt/2012/07/02_rodriguez.html.
22. See *Containing the Contagion: Proposals to Reform the Broken Securities Class Action System,* US Chamber of Commerce Institute for Legal Reform, February 2019, https://www.instituteforlegalreform.com/uploads/sites/1/ContainingtheContagion_Paper_WEB_FINAL.pdf. See also Recent Trends in Securities Class Action Litigation: 2017 Full Year Review, http://www.nera.com/content/dam/nera/publications/2018/PUB_Year_End_Trends_Report_0118_final.pdf. An earlier paper also showed an increase. "An Empirical Study of Securities Litigation after WorldCom," Rutgers Law Journal, vol. 40, no. 2, 2009. https://papers.ssrn.com/sol3/papers.cfm?abstract_id=1303634.
23. For guidance tailored to independent directors, see D. Anthony Rodriguez, *Building the Section 11 "Due Diligence" Defense for Outside Directors.*
24. The standards are Revlon (duty to get best price for shareholders once company is in play), Unocal (enhanced scrutiny to see if decision was reasonable and proportional),

entire fairness (to make sure it is fair to both minority and majority shareholders), and the business judgment rule (duty of care and loyalty). But for any of these to succeed, litigants must get past the barrier of exculpation, where the company's officers and directors are shielded from liability if they are nonconflicted. As noted by Francis Pileggi of Eckert Seamans, "The court cited the recent Delaware Supreme Court decision of *In re Cornerstone Therapeutics, Inc., Stockholder Litigation,* 115 A.3d 1173, 1175—76 (Del. 2015), for the proposition that whether *Revlon* or *Unocal* or the entire business standard or the Business Judgment Rule applies, a plaintiff seeking only monetary damages must still plead non-exculpated claims against the director who is protected by an exculpatory charter provision to survive a motion to dismiss." See his blog dated May 26, 2017, titled "See Unocal Claim Does Not Satisfy Rule 23.1."

25. Even in 2018 it is still the case that, as Foley & Lardner (now since April 1, 2018, Foley Gardere) opined a decade ago (in "The Board's Role in M&A," 2007): "The amount of case law addressing the particular duties of directors on the buy side of a transaction pales in comparison to the large number of cases addressing the duties of a target company's directors."
26. http://www.scotusblog.com/case-files/cases/south-dakota-v-wayfair-inc/.
27. "Subject matter" jurisdiction may include bankruptcy, maritime issues, intellectual property, or Internet communication. Regarding jurisdiction generally, for filing lawsuits, see Jonathan I. Blackman, "Supreme Court Reaffirms Corporate Defendants Subject to Personal Jurisdiction Only 'At Home,'" Cleary Gottlieb Steen & Hamilton LLP, June 14, 2017, https://corpgov.law.harvard.edu/2017/06/14/supreme-court-reaffirms-corporate-defendants-subject-to-personal-jurisdiction-only-at-home/. For application to non-US parties, see Lanier Saperstein, "The Reach of the U.S. Courts: Long-Arm Jurisdiction and Notions of International Comity," Dorsey &

Whitney, January 10, 2018, https://www.dorsey.com/~/media/files/uploads/images/cle—20180110-presentation-to-visiting-delegationv5.pdf?la=en.

28. A leading source for this information is Willis Towers Watson. See "Insurance Marketplace Realities: Directors and Officers Liability," April 12, 2018, at https://www.willistowerswatson.com/en/insights/2018/04/directors-officers-insurance-marketplace-realities.
29. The US Supreme Court case of *Epic Systems Corp. v. Louis,* decided May 21, 2018, found that such agreements are enforceable. This decision is considered positive for employers, who tend to prefer arbitration to its riskier and more costly alternative, litigation. https://www.supremecourt.gov/opinions/17pdf/16-285_q8l1.pdf.
30. Adapted from a checklist from Battle Fowler, New York.

Note: The documents stored in a virtual data room, along with a menu describing them, provide concrete evidence of due diligence, which US regulators consider to be an important aspect of corporate compliance. As stated in the landmark US Department of Justice guidance document *Evaluation of Corporate Compliance Programs* (US Department of Justice, Criminal Division, April 2019), p. 8, "A well-designed program should include comprehensive due diligence of any acquisition targets. Pre-M&A due diligence enables the acquiring company to evaluate more accurately each target's value and negotiate for the costs of any corruption or misconduct to be borne by the target." The url for the document is https://www.justice.gov/criminal-fraud/page/file/937501/download.

CHAPTER 7

Negotiating the Letter of Intent and Acquisition Agreement

INTRODUCTION

The legal centerpiece of any acquisition transaction is the acquisition agreement. Although negotiations begin earlier with the crafting of the letter of intent (or an abbreviated version of it, called the term sheet), it is the acquisition agreement that is most likely to make or break a deal.[1]

This is not to downplay the importance of the letter of intent. Although some lawyers dislike letters of intent and will insist on going directly to the final agreement, this is generally the exception and not the rule. Therefore, this chapter begins with a discussion of the purpose and uses of that vital document as it is employed in the acquisition context, and Appendix 7A contains a sample letter of intent. The majority of this chapter, however, is devoted to the acquisition agreement and the most basic negotiation issues it raises. Appendix 7B contains the principal provisions of a typical merger agreement, together with analytical comments discussing the basis for their inclusion, and highlights the alternatives available to the buyer and the seller.[2] Numerous issues must be negotiated in connection with these complex agreements. Some of these are purely legal issues that are best left entirely to counsel, and others are business issues that lawyers normally do not and should not be asked or expected to address. This chapter will emphasize the latter while presenting the major themes of M&A negotiation. As always, there is no substitute for experienced legal counsel.

The sample agreement analyzed in this chapter is one that would be prepared by a buyer; it is comprehensive and contains many provisions that favor the buyer. Accordingly, many of these provisions may not appear in a document prepared by a seller. Indeed, unless the seller is represented by highly inexperienced counsel, there is no way the buyer should expect to get everything that is in this sample contract. But from a buyer's perspective, it is a good starting point. In addition, a document used for the acquisition of a public company is likely to be quite different from the one set forth in this chapter. Those differences will be noted, both in the general discussion and, where appropriate, in the context of the agreement itself.

Before getting started, it may be helpful to note the emergence of what some call the "smart contract." In fact, this new technology is not a true, traditional human contract concerning a transaction (which remains indispensable in M&A) but rather a string of computer programs designed to automatically execute certain steps in that transaction.[3] For example, if a traditional contract contains a clause stating that the seller will receive an earnout based on future profits, there could be a "smart contract" or computer program set up that would make that happen through automatic bank withdrawals.[4]

For guidance on the use of electronic signatures, see Chapter 8, "Closing."

LETTER OF INTENT

What is a letter of intent?

A *letter of intent,* or LOI (also known as a *memorandum of understanding*) is a written instrument that defines the respective preliminary understandings of the parties about to engage in contractual negotiations. In most cases, such a letter is not intended to be binding except with respect to certain limited provisions—for example, provisions ensuring confidentiality, assigning expenses, or banning negotiations with other parties (an *exclusivity* or *no-shop provision*). The terms of a typical letter of intent are set forth in Appendix 7A at the end of this chapter. Every transaction is different, so the scope of letters of intent varies. This said, however, Appendix 7A can serve as a checklist of items that usually appear in letters of intent.

What is the purpose of the letter of intent?

The letter of intent memorializes in writing the basic terms of the transaction, which up to that point have been the subject of discussions and early negotiations between the parties. The letter typically will set forth the proposed structure of the transaction; the price and how it will be paid (cash, notes, stock); the terms of notes or stock to be conveyed as part of the price; and other important, but general, features of the transaction such as proposed timing, scope of the representations and warranties, and termination provisions.

The letter of intent also sets forth the conditions for consummating the transaction including, among others, the need for regulatory approvals, collateral agreements, legal opinions, and, most important, the completion of due diligence and the execution of mutually satisfactory definitive documentation.

Does the letter of intent create a binding legal obligation?

Not necessarily. Most letters of intent specifically state that the letter does not create a binding obligation to close the transaction. But simply declaring that the letter is nonbinding in a given area may not be enough to make it nonbinding. The legal test for the binding character of an agreement is the intent of the parties as determined from the circumstances. Some courts have held that a party to an otherwise nonbinding letter of intent has a duty of good faith to negotiate definitive agreements with the other side, even where no such duty is specified in the letter.

In addition, in cases where the parties have agreed on most substantive issues and do not anticipate many closing contingencies, they may consider entering into a fully binding letter of intent—although legal counsel will often advise against this. Also, even with respect to nonbinding letters, the parties typically seek to create binding obligations with respect to the provisions governing such things as confidentiality and the bearing of expenses, and such things as no-shop provisions (see discussion that follows).

If the letter of intent is not binding, is it really needed? Why not proceed directly to the contract itself?

Except in rare cases, use of a letter of intent is recommended.

First, sometimes the parties are not ready for a formal contract—for example, if an acquirer is waiting for financing, a letter of intent can secure the option of a deal.

Second, it can keep the deal from going to a third party. Because the parties have agreed in principle on basic deal terms at this stage, they have an incentive to protect the time and expense they have invested in the transaction, and certain binding provisions of a letter of intent afford them the opportunity to do so. For example, experienced buyers do not want to serve as a stalking horse while the seller shops an offer around to other potential buyers. Thus, the buyer may wish to obtain a no-shop agreement from the seller, as mentioned earlier. This is accomplished through a provision requiring the seller to refrain from negotiating with other parties for a specified period of time in order to give the buyer a proper chance to negotiate a binding agreement.

Third, it can prevent misunderstanding down the line. The parties will have to expend a considerable amount of time and money to complete due diligence and negotiate and draft a contract. A letter of intent agreement enables them to agree on basic terms before incurring the expense of negotiating definitive documentation. Later on in the process, a carefully drafted letter can often be used by a party in the negotiation of a definitive agreement to establish initial positions and to rebuff the opposing party's efforts to retake lost ground. The document discourages attempts to "retrade" long-settled terms, which can lead to ill will between the parties even before they come to the closing table.

Finally, it can help to seal the deal. Although the letter of intent is not typically a binding agreement, its execution often has the effect of creating a moral commitment to use good-faith best efforts to consummate the transaction in accordance with the outlined terms. After investing the energy to negotiate a letter of intent, neither party wants to be the one to walk without a very good reason.

The nonbinding nature of a letter of intent can have some drawbacks, though. Because the document is not intended to be binding, some parties will gloss over the details or rush the document to preclude another party from snatching away the opportunity. If one side is hasty, it may overlook details that it did not realize were in the document. When these details resurface subsequently in definitive documentation, it can be viewed as a sign of bad faith if one were to retrade the deal from the LOI. In this way, the old saw is true: haste makes waste.

Is it ever a good idea to skip the letter of intent?

In some rare situations, yes. If having a letter of agreement will complicate or slow things down unnecessarily, or if there is some risk of a leak to target employees, it can be best to go straight to a formal agreement. Also, if either of the parties is a public company, the signing of a letter of intent may be considered material and require a public announcement—a scenario that might not be appealing to one or both parties until the deal is finalized.

When should the letter of intent be executed?

In most circumstances, the parties execute the letter after the acquirer has completed its basic financial due diligence but before it embarks on the other aspect of due diligence (management and operations, legal and compliance, and transactional). This timing reduces the likelihood of incurring substantial expenses before the parties have reached an agreement in principle as to basic business terms. Nevertheless, there are some industries in which the buyer realistically cannot take a sharp pencil to the financial terms without more comprehensive due diligence. These might include services-related industries where the key assets are people-related and thus intangible, or where there exists a substantial amount of uncertainty or contingencies around the business.

What can happen if buyer and seller have different expectations regarding the letter of intent?

The *Texaco v. Pennzoil* decision from 1987, still cited today,[5] highlights the magnitude of problems that can result when buyer and seller have a different understanding of their respective obligations arising from the letter of intent. The primary question before the court was whether Pennzoil's memorandum of understanding with Getty Oil via Gordon Getty, a major shareholder in Getty Oil, was a binding contract for Pennzoil to acquire Getty Oil. Thinking that the deal was not yet binding, Texaco swooped in to acquire Getty at a higher valuation. The court found that Pennzoil's memorandum of understanding was, in fact, binding, rendering a $10.2 billion judgment against Texaco for tortious interference. After a series of appeals by Texaco, which was forced into bankruptcy over the event, the case was settled for $3 billion.

What other court cases are instructive in this regard?

Similar questions arose in a cluster of cases from the late 1990s: *Krauth v. Exec. Telecard, Ltd.* (1995),[6] finding a letter of intent binding based on a multifactor analysis; *Hoxeng v. Topeka Broadcomm, Inc.* (1996),[7] finding a letter of intent binding because the parties' actions reflected an intent to be bound; and *S. Colo. MRI, Ltd. v. Med-Alliance, Inc.* (1999),[8] which found a letter of intent binding because the parties effectively waived the requirement of a final written agreement.[9]

Likewise, the Delaware Supreme Court's recent decision in *SIGA Technologies, Inc. v. PharmAthene, Inc.,* established a right under Delaware law to seek damages for bad faith breaches of an agreement to negotiate (in the form of a nonbinding term sheet). Such outcomes are common enough to suggest a need for caution when drafting a letter of intent, term sheet, or memorandum of understanding.[10]

How can negotiators maintain their freedom to back out of a deal without getting sued?

When writing the letter of intent, the parties should define the terms under which it is and is not acceptable to withdraw from negotiations and, in the case of an unacceptable withdrawal, the amount of the liquidated damages, if any. The parties should also agree in advance on their freedom to undertake parallel negotiations, defining the contract nonexclusive (rather than including no-shop language). Inclusion of such clauses in the letter of intent may help to avert tort liability, as they support the conclusion that the parties did not intend the letter to be a binding agreement in respect of the terms of their transaction.

THE ACQUISITION AGREEMENT

Who usually drafts the final acquisition agreement?

Customarily, the buyer controls the drafting of the agreement, and it is in the buyer's interest to safeguard this prerogative. The drafter sets the initial framework of discussions and can regulate the pace of negotiations by controlling the pace of drafting. Also, the drafter can be sure to include all the most crucial provisions and safeguards—and prevent an opposing party from sowing the seeds of subsequent legal destruction.

As a buyer, do not be surprised if the seller tries to wrestle control of the documents from you and put its own team to work. The explanation can sound convincing: "We respect your normal prerogative as the buyer to draft the document, but our business is so complex, and we anticipate such substantial changes that it just seems to make more sense to draft it ourselves."

Do not fall for this argument, however well-meaning the seller may be. It is important for the buyer to protect its customary right to control the drafting of the documents, and for the buyer's attorneys to be skillful about pressing the point and forestalling attempts to usurp control. It is the shortsighted buyer who tries to save legal fees by letting the other team do the drafting. First, the savings in fees are illusory because substantial redrafting will be necessary to make the agreement work from the buyer's perspective if the sellers are allowed to do the drafting. Moreover, the change in the tone of the negotiation and the loss of control over its pace is likely to cost the buyer more in the long run. Every time new sections of the agreement are negotiated, the buyer is left to the less-than-tender mercies of the seller's attorney to draft the changes. Even well-intentioned lawyers may have a hard time shedding their adversarial instincts to include things that will protect the buyer's interests.

Suppose there are multiple buyers, in an auction. Who drafts the agreement then?

When a company is sold in an auction process, which has become the norm today, it is customary for the seller to submit the first draft of the contract for comment by the buyer. The buyer submits a bid for the target together with its comments on the draft. In such cases, there is typically no letter of intent; the parties go straight to an acquisition agreement.[11]

What is the main purpose of the acquisition agreement?

A definitive agreement will set forth almost all of the legal understandings of the buyer and seller about the transaction. Ideally, it accomplishes five basic goals:

1. It sets forth the structure and terms of the transaction.
2. It discloses all the important legal, and many of the financial, details of the target's operations, as well as the comments of each party prior to closing.
3. It obligates both parties to do their best to complete the transaction and obligates the seller not to change the target in any significant way before the deal closes.
4. It governs what happens if, before or after the closing, the parties discover problems that should have been disclosed earlier either in the agreement or in discussions, but were not properly disclosed.

5. It contains the final conditions to each party's closing (what must happen before the deal is final), as well as the comments of each party prior to closing.

Unlike the typical letter of intent, an acquisition agreement is a completely binding agreement. Once it is signed, a party that fails to consummate the transaction without a legally acceptable excuse can be liable for damages.

The negotiation of the agreement is, in large part, an effort by the parties to allocate the risk of economic loss attributable to legal (and certain financial) defects in the target that surface before or after the closing. A question might arise, for example, if the parties discover legal problems after the contract is signed (such as a major lawsuit against the target, or identification of the main plant site of the target as a toxic waste dump[12]): Should the buyer still be required to close the transaction and thus bear the risk of loss, or will the seller suffer the loss because the buyer is not required to close?

The same question can be asked if the bright financial prospects of the target are suddenly dimmed by a new set of import tariffs affecting the target's entire industry. Similarly, if after the closing the buyer discovers a liability that existed at the time of the closing but that was not properly disclosed in the agreement, will the buyer suffer the loss, or will it be able to recover damages from the seller pursuant to indemnification provisions in the definitive agreement? A comprehensive agreement will make the answers clear. The representations and warranties section of the agreement is particularly important here, and will receive emphasis in this chapter.

What are the buyer and seller really concerned about when negotiating the acquisition document?

The seller and buyer come from two different places, as Exhibit 7-1 illustrates.

Once the parties agree to the key substantive aspects of the transaction (price and terms), the seller wants to be as certain as possible of at least two things: that the closing will occur as soon as possible after the

Exhibit 7-1 Seller vs. Buyer Key Goals

SELLER	BUYER
Closing ASAP	Freedom to walk
No refunds—sale as is	Money back for bad surprises

agreement is signed and that no postclosing events will require a refund of any of the purchase price.

The buyer's concerns are the converse of the seller's. The buyer would like flexibility to abandon the transaction in the event that it discovers any legal, financial, or business defects in the target. After closing, the buyer would like to know that it will be compensated penny for penny for any economic loss resulting from legal or financial problems that were not disclosed to it beforehand. This is not to be confused with the business risk of operating the target after the closing: general economic downturns, new competition, and failures of management after the closing are business risks that any sensible buyer knows it assumes when it acquires a business. But the buyer will seek to protect itself against hidden flaws in the target's business; these include any pending litigation, liabilities, or environmental problems—to name only a few—that were not disclosed before the closing and that undermine the target's intrinsic value compared to the agreed-upon purchase price.

With such diametrically opposed goals, buyer and seller will rarely agree. Without fail, the buyer will try to increase its flexibility to withdraw from the transaction before the closing. However, with such flexibility, the contract is simply an option to acquire the target and not a contract that legally binds the buyer to acquire the target. If the buyer really wants to buy the target, it should be willing to be legally obligated, within reason, to do so.

On the other hand, the seller can never be certain that the transaction will close, simply because there are too many conditions beyond the control of both buyer and seller that must be satisfied before any transaction can close. (These conditions are discussed in greater detail next.) Moreover, although the seller invariably would like to sell the target on an as-is basis, the vast majority of private companies are sold with at least modest postclosing protection. Thus, the reasonable seller will typically, grudgingly, give the buyer a modicum of protection in the event that the target is not what the seller represented it to be.

In this process of risk allocation, who should bear the risk of loss associated with undisclosed legal defects in the target discovered after the closing–the buyer, the seller, or both? Is there one correct answer?

This is a matter of negotiation. The smart seller will say:

> "Look, before you sign anything, we'll show you everything we have. Talk to our management, our accountants, and our lawyers. Kick the tires to your heart's content. If you discover problems, we'll negotiate a mutually fair resolution in the agreement. Then tell us how much you'll pay on the assumption that any unknown problems are simply your risk of buying and owning the business. Once we close, the business and the risk are yours."

The canny buyer's answer will be along the following lines:

> "Our contractual arrangements should be structured to provide both of us with strong incentives to unearth problems before the closing. You will have a strong incentive to uncover all the issues only if you share some or all of the risk of undisclosed problems. Anyway, if the target suffers a dollar loss attributable to undiscovered problems after our mutual diligent efforts, and if the buyer bears the entire risk of loss, we will effectively be paying an additional purchase price. In the end, we may be paying more than the target is worth. Our price is

premised upon the target's not having any material undisclosed problems. We're willing to do our share of tire kicking, but at some point it's absurd for us to absorb a loss that surfaces notwithstanding our extensive due diligence, a loss that is so large as to make our price far exceed the value of what we acquired. Surely, you don't want to exact an unfair price under these circumstances."

The real issue is: *What is a fair price for the target?* The answer hinges on the assumptions of the parties when the transaction was negotiated. The buyer can either (1) determine a price based upon assuming the risk, that is, an as-is deal, which presumably would be less than the price that would be paid if the seller retains some or all of the risks; or (2) determine a higher price premised on the seller's retention of some part of the risk, as shown in Exhibit 7-2.

The first alternative (as-is, low price, low safeguards) may be acceptable to a buyer comfortable with its familiarity with the target, or where the target doesn't engage in activities that could give rise to extraordinary

Exhibit 7-2 The Safeguards-Price Negotiating Matrix

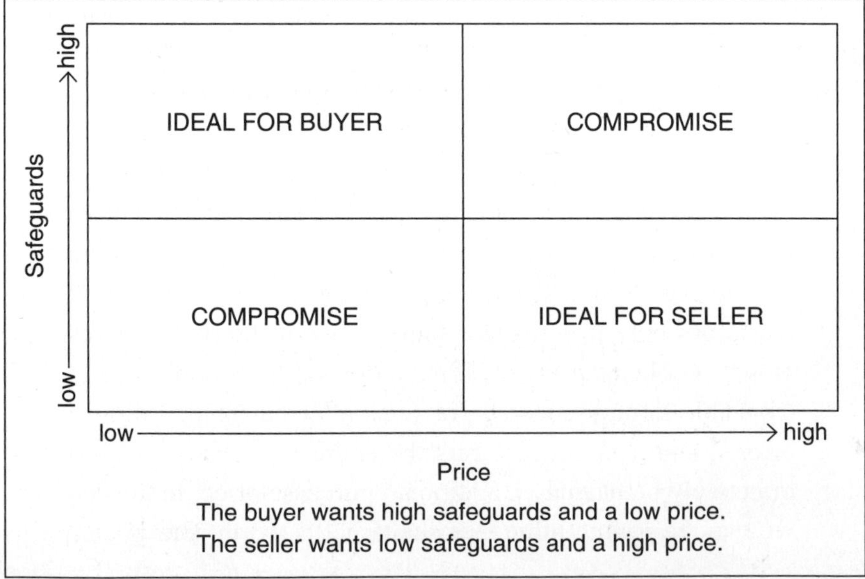
Safeguards
low
high
IDEAL FOR BUYER
COMPROMISE
COMPROMISE
IDEAL FOR SELLER
low
high
Price
The buyer wants high safeguards and a low price.
The seller wants low safeguards and a high price.

liabilities (for example, violations of environmental laws or product liabilities). However, it is a gamble.

The second alternative (high price, high safeguards) is much more common. In most sales of private companies, the seller bears a significant portion of the risk of target defects, and the deal is priced accordingly.

This said, however, the seller should not be pestered incessantly about relatively insignificant items that prove not to be true about the target. Everyone knows going into an acquisition that no company is perfect and that in due course blemishes on its legal and financial record will undoubtedly surface. Accordingly, although seller accountability is the general rule, that accountability is usually limiting by specifying the time during which it can be held liable and by requiring the buyer to limit its claims to significant problems.

Does the customary practice of adding safeguards to justify a maximum price make sense? Yes, for three reasons:

- First, an as-is transaction may force the buyer to reduce the purchase price *even though the likelihood of a claim is insubstantial.* A seller's concern about postclosing hassles would typically not be serious enough to justify the trade-off in price that might result from forcing a buyer to price the deal on an as-is basis.
- Second, having the seller share in the risk along with the buyer will provide both buyer and seller with a strong incentive to discover problems before the agreement is signed or the deal is closed. Thorough investigation by both parties that have a stake in the outcome reduces the likelihood that a claim will arise.
- Third, if the problem were discovered before the closing, it probably would result in a price adjustment, even to an as-is deal. Logically, the result should not be different because the problem arises after closing.

This does not mean that every seller should cave in on this issue and agree to take on all the postclosing risk. In certain circumstances, the seller may prefer taking a lower price to avoid the risk of postclosing adversities.

Nor should one assume that the pricing will necessarily reflect the risk of an as-is approach. In the case of a deal-hungry buyer, or a buyer that has confidence in its assessment of the risk of loss, the seller may get the best of both worlds—a high price with little or no postclosing risk. This is especially true in a competitive bidding situation. In the end, the allocation of risk will depend more on the bargaining power and negotiating skills of the parties than the niceties of pricing theories.

COMPONENTS OF THE AGREEMENT

What are the major parts of the agreement?

The major segments of a typical agreement are as follows:

1. Introductory material
2. The price and mechanics of the transfer
3. Representations and warranties of the buyer and seller
4. Covenants of the buyer and seller
5. Conditions to closing
6. Indemnification
7. Termination procedures and remedies
8. Legal miscellany

How are the general concerns of the buyer and seller reflected in the acquisition agreement?

The major concerns of the parties are focused on two sections of the agreement: the Conditions section and the Indemnity section. The former lists the conditions that must be satisfied before the parties become obligated to close the transaction and thus controls whether the buyer or seller can "walk" from the deal with impunity. The Indemnity section establishes the liability, if any, of each party to the other for problems relating to the target that are discovered after the closing. Both sections are generally keyed to two earlier parts of the agreement: the Representations and Warranties and the Covenants.

INTRODUCTORY MATERIAL

What is covered in the introductory material and pricing mechanics of a transfer?

It is often useful in a legal document to describe the intentions of each of the parties. If set out in the agreement, the parties' intentions may aid in interpreting the agreement in the event of a dispute. Therefore, it has become customary to introduce the agreement with a series of *recitals,* which are statements that set forth the purpose of, and parties to, the agreement. The legal significance of the introductory material is usually secondary to the anecdotal description of the parties' objectives at the time they executed the agreement.

The next sections of the agreement set forth the most significant substantive business points of the agreement, the price and the mechanics of transfer. This section identifies the structure of the transaction as a stock disposition, an asset disposition, or a merger, and describes the mechanics to be utilized to transfer the property from seller to buyer. The parties may also provide in this section the requirement for a deposit by the buyer, or other security for the buyer's obligations to close.

In the case of an asset acquisition, this section identifies exactly which assets are to be conveyed to the buyer and, often more important, which liabilities of the seller will be assumed by the buyer. In the case of a merger, these sections contain the consideration per share to be received by the exchanging shareholders, as well as all of the other terms of the merger, including the identity of the surviving corporation, the articles of incorporation and bylaws governing the surviving corporation, the composition of its board of directors, and the names of its officers. For both asset purchases and mergers, this section will, of course, also identify the nature of the consideration to be received by the seller as well as the timing of its payment.

Frequently, this section will contain provisions regarding intercompany liabilities, and how they must be satisfied by the surviving company or forgiven by the seller and capitalized as additional equity in the transaction.

For a detailed discussion of issues relating to pricing, see Chapter 3.

REPRESENTATIONS AND WARRANTIES

What is the purpose of the representations and warranties section of the agreement?

In this section of the agreement, the seller makes detailed statements about the legal and financial condition of the target, the property to be conveyed, and the ability of the seller to consummate the transaction. The representations and warranties reflect the situation as of the date of the signing of the agreement and, together with the exhibits or schedules (see the discussion of exhibits and schedules), are intended to disclose all material legal, and many material financial, aspects of the business to the buyer. The seller also gives assurances that the transaction itself will not have adverse effects upon the property to be conveyed. Some of the representations and warranties are not related to the legal condition of the target but serve to provide the buyer with information. For example, the seller might represent that it has attached a list of all the major contracts of the target. The buyer makes similar representations and warranties about its legal and financial ability to consummate the transaction and certain other limited representations and warranties.

The buyer should be aware that lenders providing acquisition financing will require the buyer to make extensive representations and warranties about the target as a condition to funding. To the extent that the acquisition agreement does not contain comparable representations from the seller, with appropriate recourse in the event of a breach, the buyer will take on the dual risk of a loan default and any direct loss as a result of the seller's breach. In some cases, it may be more difficult to obtain adequate financing if there are insufficient representations and warranties about the business. The buyer should make every effort to anticipate the representations and warranties that the lenders will require and attempt to include language in the acquisition agreement to obtain coverage for these areas.

A buyer or seller will be able to back out of the agreement if it discovers that the representations or warranties of the other party are untrue to any material extent. Thus, the fewer the items represented to, the less is the risk that the other party will be able to back out of the agreement. Also, the seller must indemnify the buyer for problems that surface after the closing only if the seller breached a representation or warranty in the agreement. Again, the fewer the representations and warranties and the narrower their scope, the less is the exposure to the seller. For these reasons, a great deal of the negotiation of the agreement centers around the scope of the representations and warranties.

How can a seller narrow the scope of its representations and warranties?

There are several ways in which the seller can attempt to reduce its exposure attributable to representations and warranties. First, the seller may steadfastly refuse to make any representation or warranty about specific items, for example, accounts receivable or the financial condition or liabilities of certain subsidiaries.

Second, the seller may refuse to make representations and warranties about matters not *material* to the transaction or the target, or may attempt to make representations and warranties only to the "best of its knowledge." To protect itself, the seller can seek to insert the word *material,* or phrases with the same effect, in every place in the representations that it can. For example, it can state that it is disclosing only "material liabilities," or "material litigation," or that it knows of no violations of law by the company that will constitute a *material adverse change* (MAC) or that will have a *material adverse effect* (MAE) on the company.

What does the term *material* mean when it appears in representations and warranties?

It is often said that materiality is in the eyes of the beholder. Although the courts have defined material information in specific cases, the concept remains vague, and changes in accounting concepts over time have added to the mystery. (See Exhibit 7-3, on the Financial Accounting Standards Board [FASB].) Generally, the case law holds that *material* means important to a normal, prudent investor in determining whether to make a given

Exhibit 7-3 The FASB on Materiality

The FASB has advanced three definitions of materiality since 1980 and has reinstated the first.

Con 2. The earliest definition, valid from 1980 to 2010 (and likely to be revived in 2019), appeared in Statement of Financial Accounting Concept No. 2, which defined materiality as a measure of "the magnitude of an omission or misstatement of accounting information that, in the light of surrounding circumstances, makes it probable that the *judgment of a reasonable person relying on the information would have been changed or influenced by the omission or misstatement.*"

Con. 8. That definition was replaced in 2010 with the narrower (entity-specific) Statement of Financial Accounting Concept 8 (Con 8), which stated that "Information is material if omitting it or misstating it could influence decisions that users make on the basis of the financial information of a specific reporting entity. In other words, materiality is an entity-specific aspect of relevance based on the nature or magnitude or both of the items to which the information relates in the context of an individual entity's financial report."

Con 8—Proposed Amendment. Then in 2015, the FASB proposed an amendment to Con 8 as follows: "Materiality is a legal concept. In the United States, a legal concept may be established or changed through legislative, executive, or judicial action. The Board observes but does not promulgate definitions of materiality. Currently, the Board observes that the U.S. Supreme Court's definition of materiality, in the context of the antifraud provisions of the U.S. securities laws, generally states that information is material if there is a substantial likelihood that the omitted or misstated item would have been viewed by a reasonable resource provider as having significantly altered the total mix of information." This 2015 update drew from two landmark legal cases: *TSC Industries, Inc. v. Northway, Inc.,* 426 U.S. 438 (1976), and *Basic Inc. v. Levinson,* 485 U.S. 224 (1988). Investors pushed back against this approach on the grounds that it put materiality into the domain of law rather than accounting.*

Con 2—Reinstated. In November 2017, the FASB voted to "Amend the current definition of materiality in Chapter 3, *Qualitative Characteristics of Useful Financial Information,* of FASB Concepts Statement No. 8, *Conceptual Framework for Financial Reporting,* with language similar to that of the definition in FASB Concepts Statement No. 2, *Qualitative Characteristics of Accounting Information.*"† This change became final in August 2018.

And so it is that in this very important issue of materiality, the FASB has come full circle.

* *https://www.sec.gov/news/speech/deane-speech-rulemaking-process.*

† https://www.fasb.org/jsp/FASB/FASBContent_C/ActionAlertPage&cid=1176169442224&rss=1 &pf rue. This discussion pertains only to the United States. For a global history of materiality, see H. Gin Chong, "A Review on the Evolution of the Definitions of Materiality," *International Journal of Economics and Accounting* 6 (2015): 15–32.

investment.[13] In many contracts the parties agree that a "*material*" *fact must be material to the business* of the target and any subsidiaries taken as a whole. The purpose of the emphasized language is to ensure that the importance of the fact relates to the entire enterprise acquired and not solely to the parent corporation or to a single subsidiary.

In order to reduce the opportunity for disagreement, the parties often set a dollar threshold that defines materiality in particular circumstances. For example, rather than asking for representations about material contracts, the buyer will substitute a request for disclosure about all contracts involving payments above a specified dollar amount. Similarly, the buyer may request disclosure of all liabilities greater than a certain sum. Use of numbers tends to fine-tune the disclosures and in many ways provides protection for the seller as well. If there is a dollar threshold of, say, $100,000 for liabilities, the seller can be assured that a $95,000 undisclosed liability will not be deemed material in a later dispute.

How and to what degree can the buyer resist the narrowing of the scope of the representations and warranties?

Generally speaking, it is in the buyer's interest to have the broadest possible representations and warranties. However, unreasonable requests for disclosure can threaten a deal. Pressuring the seller of a large, complex target to make comprehensive disclosures may cause the seller to fear that it will inadvertently fail to disclose minor matters, jeopardizing the transaction or leading to unfair liabilities after the closing.

Moreover, anyone buying a business must recognize that no business is more perfect than the human beings who conduct it. Therefore, there are bound to be a variety of problems in connection with the operation or ownership of the business, including litigation, liabilities, or violations of law, which the buyer must accept as part of the package of owning the business. As a result, in most transactions the buyer will permit the seller to limit the scope of the matters that are being represented to those things that are material, individually or in the aggregate, but—where appropriate—will negotiate over dollar threshold amounts to require more, rather than less, disclosure.

What different motivations might a seller have for narrowing representations and warranties?

For negotiation purposes it is important for the buyer to understand the seller's real concerns. The seller may be concerned simply about the time and expense necessary to uncover a lot of detailed information that in its view should not matter to a buyer or that, under the time pressure of the deal, just cannot be obtained. Or the seller may be far more concerned about making representations and warranties that will increase the risk that the buyer will be able to back out of the transaction. Alternatively, the seller's most significant concern may be with postclosing liabilities for breaches of representations, warranties, and covenants in the agreement.

How can a buyer address these different motivations?

Concern about time and expense is legitimate only to the extent that the buyer is asking for truly inconsequential or irrelevant representations or warranties. Remember that the seller's negotiator on these points is likely to be an in-house lawyer or technician more worried about being imprecise than about the broad scope of the deal. Where time is truly a crucial factor (as opposed to a negotiating point for the parties), the buyer's lawyer should exercise care and use good judgment to pare down the more burdensome, yet noncrucial, representations and warranties.

The buyer should, however, address the more legitimate concerns of the seller. The buyer can address the risks of the deal's failing to close or of postclosing liability while still including very broad representations and warranties with low dollar thresholds. The buyer can explain to the seller that it wants very broad, in-depth disclosure of items so that the buyer can determine on its own what is material. Most buyers prefer to determine the materiality of information themselves rather than leaving it up to the lawyers or officers of the seller in the target, whose idea of materiality may differ from the buyer's, and who may not be aware of the buyer's specific concerns about certain legal or financial aspects of the target or the assets to be acquired.

The seller should be assured that extensive disclosures will not increase the risk of a terminated transaction or postclosing liability. The buyer may provide the requisite assurance by agreeing not to terminate the transaction, and by stating that the seller need not indemnify the buyer, except in the event of material breaches of representations, warranties, or covenants. In summation, the buyer must look through the stated position of the seller, determine its real interests, and deal creatively with those concerns, rather than simply viewing negotiations as an argument over whether or not the word *material* is going to modify a particular representation or warranty.

What is the purpose of the phrases "best of knowledge" and "ordinary course of business" often found in representations and warranties?

These phrases are simply other ways in which the parties can agree to narrow the scope of the representations and warranties required of the seller. The phrase *ordinary course of business* is usually found in representations and warranties to exclude certain things from the representations. For example, the seller may not be required to disclose supply contracts entered into in the ordinary course of business, or may not be required to disclose liabilities accrued in the ordinary course of business. The definition of *ordinary course of business* will depend upon the normal practice of the specific business being acquired and the industry of which it is a part, including the normal character and size of routine transactions. It can be generally defined not to include business activities that the seller does not engage in on a regular and consistent basis. For greater clarification, the parties could enumerate in the acquisition agreement the seller's ordinary practices. An important point is that any transactions that are extraordinary in nature, price, or size will be included in such representations and warranties.

The phrase *best of knowledge* (also known as a *knowledge qualifier*) serves a similar function. A seller may ask that its representation as to litigation be limited to the litigation about which it has knowledge, so that it will not be required to represent and warrant absolutely that there is no material litigation. The seller often argues that the phrase should modify other representations and warranties.

At each juncture the buyer should ask, Is the "best of knowledge" modification appropriate? Usually it is not, but it is often agreed to in respect to the existence of threatened litigation and infringements by third parties of copyrights and patents. Beyond those few customary areas, the buyer should vigorously resist efforts to base the representations on the knowledge of the seller. Because such a representation and warranty tells the buyer only that the seller is unaware of any problems, it protects the buyer only if problems known to the seller are not disclosed. Thus, "best of knowledge" representations have the effect of allocating to the buyer all the risk of defects no one knows about.

From a philosophical perspective, the knowledge of the seller is not pertinent to the key question of the buyer: "Am I getting what I am paying for?" The fact that the seller didn't know that the buyer was overpaying is of little comfort to a buyer who discovers significant defects in its acquisition. Thus, the "knowledge" caveat should be used sparingly unless the buyer is willing to accept a substantial risk in connection with breaches of representations and warranties.

"Best of knowledge" qualifiers may be presented as a compromise to a seller who adamantly refuses to indemnify the buyer for breaches discovered after closing. At the very least, an indemnity should be forthcoming in respect to problems the seller knew about but didn't disclose.

There are other issues in connection with the phrase *best of knowledge.* First, whose knowledge are we talking about? Careful sellers will attempt to limit the knowledge to a narrow group of people, such as the executive officers of the target. Theoretically, the argument will go something like this: "We don't want to be held responsible if one of the loaders on the trucking platform happens to overhear something bad about the target or knows something bad about the target and we didn't seek his information about the transaction." Aside from the fact that any proposition reduced to that level can become absurd, there is some merit to the idea that a large organization ought to be careful about making representations about what the corporation knows. Consequently, a buyer accepting a "best of knowledge" representation will often permit the seller to limit the persons whose knowledge will be tested. The buyer ought to be certain that everyone who has material information about the target is included in the selected circle of officers. This will force the seller to quiz the officers whose knowledge will be pertinent for purposes of the agreement.

Another issue is whether the phrase *best of knowledge* implies any obligation of the seller to look into the matter; that is, does it assume that the knowledge is based upon a reasonable effort to ascertain the existence of any problems? The general answer is that the seller's inquiry would be limited to information already in the seller's possession. A buyer wishing to impose a duty on the seller to make reasonable investigations into the matters represented to the buyer should augment the *best of knowledge* phrase with the words *after due inquiry.*

What if the seller claims to have no knowledge, or ability to get knowledge, about an area that is the subject of a representation or warranty?

In this era of rapidly changing ownership of companies through restructurings and leveraged buyouts, the seller often has not had a chance to become acquainted with the details of the business it is selling. It is not unusual to hear the seller say, "I really don't know that much about this company, so I don't want to take much risk on these representations and warranties. I don't want to make representations about too many matters or in too much detail."

This may be reasonable from the perspective of the seller, but the buyer should not give the argument much weight. In every transaction, the seller will want to reduce its exposure to losses attributable to breaches of representations or warranties. That concern may be heightened by the insecurity of not knowing enough about the target, and possibly not having enough time to become acquainted with the details of the operations of the target. Nevertheless, the knowledge of the seller is not necessarily relevant to a logical allocation of the risks associated with breaches of representations and warranties. As noted, if the loss due to a breach is absorbed by the buyer, the buyer pays an increased purchase price. The knowledge of the seller should not bear upon the buyer's resolution of the question whether an increased price makes sense.

An appropriate response to the seller might be the following:

> "We certainly understand your concern, but we have even less of a basis for intimate knowledge of the target's operations. The real issue is, Who should absorb the risk in the event that there are undisclosed material defects in the business? We have different views, of course, of who should bear the risk, but let's really talk about what matters, not about what each of us knows about the company right now. The agreement between us ought to be structured to provide incentives for both of us to do the best job possible to unearth problems and to increase our knowledge of the company now, before we close, rather than wait for problems to surface afterward. Then, if something does surface later, either after we sign or after we close, we need to decide where the risk should reside."

This response addresses the real interest of the parties and will prevent digressions into who knows most about the company or who can know the most about the company.

Sometimes the seller is leery of making legally important statements without being absolutely certain of their truth. It is important for both sides to recognize that the representations and warranties are not a test of the integrity of the parties making them. A party cannot properly be accused of dishonesty if it makes a representation about which it is not certain (provided, of course, that it has no knowledge that the representation is in fact untrue). In order to reduce legal exposure, it makes sense to try to verify the accuracy of the representations and warranties as much as possible. There will always be, however, some degree of uncertainty. But if the parties recognize that the representations are not a test of integrity but a legal device for allocating risk, the process becomes more manageable and less subject to emotional decision making.

When might the knowledge of the parties about the target be relevant?

The traditional format under which the seller assumes the risks associated with breaches of representations and warranties might be attributable to the fact that the seller, rather than the buyer, is in the position to know the most about the target. The seller is the logical candidate for assessing and bearing the risk of loss arising from any breach of the representations and warranties.

There may be unique circumstances, however, where the seller will be in a position to argue persuasively that the buyer has much more knowledge about the target and should be more willing to accept the risk associated with the sale. For example, in an MBO, where management will own the lion's share of the target and has operated the target for several years, it is very possible that management could be persuaded to accept the risk of inaccuracy in the representations and warranties of the target because management is in the best position to assess that risk and make a business decision based upon it. As has been discussed in relation to pricing, the shift of the risk to management is not necessarily fair or logical. If a latent problem causes a loss, the management buyers absorbing the loss are paying an additional purchase price. The fairness of that result has little to do with the state of management's knowledge.

Moreover, this line of reasoning will not apply in most MBOs because a promoter, investment bank, or the lenders—and not the management group—typically end up owning the majority of the equity. They, unlike management, have no basis for certainty with respect to the accuracy of the representations and warranties, and they should be much less willing to accept the risk that management inadvertently neglected to properly assess the accuracy of the representations and warranties.

Are some representations and warranties more important than others?

Yes. The representations regarding financial statements, litigation, undisclosed liabilities, and taxes are usually the most important. If a buyer is pressed to get indemnities only for what it absolutely needs, it should, at a minimum, argue vociferously for solid representations and warranties on these points. Protection for breaches of the representations on financials should be the last point the buyer concedes; the buyer should make this concession only if it is fully apprised of, and is committed to taking, the associated risk. In general, the audited financial statements represent the best picture of the target as a whole, and any undisclosed material problems will cause that representation to be breached.

What is the role of exhibits or disclosure schedules?

The exhibits are an integral part of the representations and warranties. Each exhibit is usually keyed to a specific representation or warranty and sets forth any exceptions to the statements made in the representation. For example, a representation might provide that there are no undisclosed liabilities of the target "except as set forth on Exhibit A," or state that there is no litigation that might have an adverse effect on the target "except as set forth on Exhibit B." Another representation might state that "except as set forth on Schedule C," there are no contracts of a "material nature," or there are no contracts involving amounts in excess of a fixed sum, say $100,000. Schedule C would contain a list of all the contracts that meet the criteria in the representation, that is, contracts that either are material or involve dollar amounts above the threshold.

By design, then, the exhibits list all of the items the buyer needs to investigate in its due diligence effort in anticipation of pricing and financing the deal. The exhibits are a crucial part of that due diligence; because they require the seller to make statements about all of the pertinent aspects of the target, the schedules constitute a succinct legal and business synopsis of the target.

The use of exceptions to create exhibits might seem odd, but it is merely a practical drafting device. The alternative would be to incorporate each of the target's documents in the acquisition agreement, which would make the agreement unwieldy. The basic contract and the exhibits, because the former contains the terms of the parties' agreement and the latter provides vital information about the target, are a simpler and more practical method.

Time needed to prepare lengthy exhibits can often be used by the seller as an argument to reduce the scope of the representations and warranties. When the seller has prepared the agreement, it will have prepared its exhibits, usually skipping representations and warranties.

When the buyer submits proposed changes, including significant beefing up of the representations and warranties, the seller will say:

> "Look, if we want to sign in this milieu, we can't possibly prepare exhibits based on these representations and warranties. We'll have to recirculate questionnaires to all the officers of each member of the target's corporate group (often scattered around the world) and review once again all the pertinent documents (and, of course, there are hundreds of documents) to make sure we don't violate these tighter representations and warranties."

Where there is a need to sign quickly, this tactic pressures the buyer's lawyers, whose client will ask, "Are we really asking for a lot of unnecessary garbage?" First, the lawyer should be aware of applicable time pressures in preparing the representations and warranties. Having done so, he or she must be ready to defend the relative importance of the various requests. One way to deal with the problem is to sign the contract but give the seller additional time to prepare the exhibits. The buyer would reserve the right to abandon the deal if the revised exhibits reveal any material problems. A word of caution: don't leave too much time or you'll be getting revised schedules the night before the closing.

Should exhibits be used if the target is, or will become, a public company?

In the event that the target is a public company, or the buyer has intentions to take the target public, the buyer would be well advised to use a disclosure statement as opposed to an exhibit or disclosure schedule in order to avoid the public disclosure of information about the target. The utility of a disclosure statement is that it is a separate document that otherwise sets forth all of the items that would be listed in exhibits or schedules to the acquisition agreement. However, since the disclosure statement is a document separate from the acquisition agreement, the target may not be required under the securities laws to file the disclosure statement with the SEC.[14]

COVENANTS

What is the major purpose of the covenants?

The Covenants section of the agreement defines the obligations of the parties with respect to their conduct during the period between the signing and the closing. For negotiation purposes, the most significant covenant relates to the obligation of the seller to conduct the business in the ordinary course, with such exceptions as are agreed upon by the parties between the time of signing and closing. In the representations and warranties, the seller assures the buyer of the legal characteristics of the target as of the date of the signing of the agreement; in the Covenants section, the seller in essence agrees not to do anything to change that picture in any material way, except as necessary in the normal operations of the business.

Typically, changes other than those that are specifically permitted under the agreement can be made only with the consent of the buyer. However, it is often necessary to limit the restrictions by requiring the buyer not to "withhold consent unreasonably." This limitation should be used sparingly to ensure that it achieves its limited purpose; that is, in narrow circumstances the seller may be required to take certain actions in order to preserve the business, and the buyer should not be allowed to prevent them unless such actions have a material impact on the transaction.

Many attorneys feel that this limitation is never appropriate because, provided that the conditions to closing are fulfilled, the buyer is obligated to purchase the target. The buyer should therefore have control over any extraordinary actions pending closing. That position, however, must be tempered with the following consideration: if there is a specific area of business conduct about which the seller has a great deal of concern, liberalizing the restriction may be the only way to close the gap between the parties. If the phrase *reasonable consent* is troublesome, it is often possible to craft language that more carefully defines the circumstances under which the seller should be permitted to do things not otherwise permitted by the agreement.

CONDITIONS TO CLOSING

What role do the conditions to closing play in the acquisition agreement?

The form agreement appearing as Appendix 7B at the end of this chapter contains the typical conditions that must be satisfied before the buyer or the seller is obligated to close.

The agreement typically sets forth separate closing conditions for each of the parties. If a condition to the buyer's obligation to close is not satisfied, the buyer will have the right to terminate the agreement without being liable for damages to the seller. Similarly, if one of the seller's conditions is not satisfied, the seller will not be obligated to close. Under appropriate circumstances, a condition might be established that applies to both parties. One mutual condition might be the receipt of certain key governmental consents; another is the absence of litigation or any administrative ruling that precludes the closing. Either party may waive a condition and proceed to close the acquisition notwithstanding the failure of the other party to satisfy each condition.

How do the conditions to closing affect the key concerns of the buyer and seller?

The Conditions to Closing are the first part of the agreement that addresses one of the two major concerns of the parties. The Conditions section sets forth the ability of each party to terminate the contract with legal impunity. For example, if any condition is not met by the target or the seller, the buyer will be free to terminate the contract.

The most significant condition is the *bring-down condition,* which makes the buyer's obligation to close contingent upon two factors: the buyer will not be required to close if (1) the seller has breached any of its covenants or (2) any of the representations and warranties of seller and target were not true when made or are not true on the closing date, or as if made on the closing date. This condition provides an escape for the buyer if the representations and warranties were true on the date of signing but are no longer true as of the closing date, either because of events that occurred after the signing or because breaches were discovered after the signing.

In a typical representation, the seller warrants that the target's financial statements, which always predate the signing, represent a true and accurate picture of the target. In a different representation, the seller must state that there has been no *material adverse change* in the financial condition, operations, or prospects of the target between the date of the financial statements and the date of signing. The bring-down condition requires, as a condition to closing, that the seller extend its representation that there has been no *material adverse change* through the date of the closing.[15]

The effect of the bring-down condition is to assure the buyer that, on the closing date, the target will be the same target, from a legal and financial perspective, that the buyer bargained for in the contract. Because the buyer is not required to close the transaction if any bring-down condition is not satisfied, the condition allocates to the seller the risk of loss attributable to any adverse change during the period between signing and closing. Interim losses probably reduce the value of the target, and the bring-down condition allows the buyer to renegotiate a lower price reflecting the changes.

The form agreement requires a corporate officer to certify that the representations and warranties are accurate in all material respects as of the closing date, providing this certificate is a condition of closing, but it has another very important effect: it is a restatement of all the representations and warranties as of the closing date.

If the certificate is not accurate, the inaccuracy will constitute a breach of a representation or warranty and may give rise to liability from buyer to seller under the Indemnity section of the agreement. In the absence of an officer's certificate, a buyer might be unprotected against certain adverse events occurring between signing and closing. For example, if a material liability arises and is discovered before closing, a closing condition will be unsatisfied, and the buyer can walk from the deal. But if it is not discovered, the parties may close because to their knowledge each closing condition—including the condition that the representation and warranty about undisclosed liabilities is true—was satisfied. Clearly, the buyer needs more than a condition to closing to fully insulate it from undiscovered problems. Requiring the seller to represent that the closing condition is satisfied allows the buyer to treat the seller's failure to satisfy the condition as a breach of the representations. If the buyer is indemnified for losses attributable to such breaches, the buyer, by virtue of the certificate, will be protected against losses resulting from undiscovered problems.

What is a financing out condition and when is it appropriate?

The *financing out condition* (sometimes also referred to as a *financing contingency*) provides that the buyer need not close if it is unable to finance the transaction. It is a very broad exception to the buyer's obligation to close the deal, and the seller must be wary of allowing such a condition. The seller may have kept the target off the market for a long period of time and incurred substantial expenses only to find out that the buyer failed to obtain the necessary financing. For these reasons a seller should resist the use of a financing condition or narrow the risk if there must be one.

The seller's initial position should be that, if the buyer is confident of the financing, it should be willing to take the risk that the financing will not be available; that is, there should be no financing out. Next, the seller can attempt to require the buyer to have its financing commitments in place before the contract is signed. This strategy limits the seller's risk to those cases where the lenders refuse to consummate the transaction. In addition, the parties will know in advance that the basic transaction is acceptable to the lenders who propose to finance the transaction. Another alternative is to require the buyer to provide financing commitments (or executed loan agreements) within a specified number of days after the contract is signed. After that period, the financing condition falls away. This approach may be preferable to a buyer that doesn't want to incur what can be very costly commitment fees to lenders before it has a contract signed. In addition, the seller should attempt to require the buyer to pay the seller's expenses if the transaction is abandoned because the commitments could not be obtained.

At the very least, the seller should know what the proposed financing structure will be. For example, how much equity will be invested? How much mezzanine and senior debt will be necessary? What are the buyer's assumptions about the lender's interest rates and equity demands? With this information, the seller's financial advisers can assist in evaluating the feasibility of the proposed financing. It should go without saying that the buyer should be required in a covenant to use its best efforts to obtain the necessary financing.

Many contracts do not contain a financing out because the buyer is a shell company with no assets. Even if the buyer breaches the contract, a lawsuit by the seller will not yield significant damages. For this reason, a seller should investigate the buyer's financial strength and inquire who will stand behind the buyer's contract obligations.

All this being said, the buyer has a strong interest in obtaining a financing out. Often, financing can fall through for reasons beyond the control of the buyer, and it needs protection in such a case. Moreover, in periods of volatile interest rates, a transaction that is financeable when the contract is signed may not be when the time for closing arrives because new rates may place too high a financial burden on the target. The buyer, forced to put more equity in the transaction, may not have the required funds or may no longer find the deal attractive. When all else fails, the buyer should try to obtain a dollar limit on its exposure, in the form of a liquidated damages clause, in the event it refuses to close a deal in which there is no financing out.

This controversial provision generally should be addressed by the seller as early as possible, usually in the letter of intent. The buyer, on the other hand, is better off letting this issue ride until the seller becomes emotionally committed to the deal by signing the letter of intent. Once the letter of intent is signed, the seller also may be bureaucratically (if not legally) committed to selling and may be more amenable to compromise on the point. The parties must approach this problem by crafting a solution that is carefully tailored to the specific concerns of the parties. Compromise can often be reached by adjusting (1) the time within which financing commitments must be provided and (2) the consequences of the buyer's failure to finance the transaction.

What is a material adverse change?

One of the typical conditions to closing for the buyer is that there has been no *material adverse change* in the financial condition of the seller. Who bears the risk if there is a general business downturn or a specific problem in the industry of the seller that causes a deterioration in its financial condition—and what if the adverse change will clearly occur, but only after the closing?

The buyer's right to abandon the deal usually does not depend upon the reason for the deterioration in the target's financial condition. Some sellers try to shift to the buyer the risk of general or industry-specific economic reversals, but buyers are usually successful in resisting the attempt. The seller's argument is not fatuous, however. The buyer clearly gets the benefit of unanticipated improvements in the financial condition due to such factors because the seller still must close; why not the downside as well as the upside?

This issue stems from the signing of a contract binding the parties to close the transaction before they are ready to close. The seller benefits because the buyer is legally obligated to close unless material seller's problems surface. The buyer, on the other hand, has the deal locked up; yet if significant problems arise, the buyer can terminate or renegotiate the acquisition. But from the seller's perspective, it has given up the upside (which should be reflected in the purchase price) but still retains the economic downside until the deal closes. Thus, if the parties' expectations prove untrue—for example, because oil is discovered on the property—the buyer gets the benefit. But if a new material lawsuit arises, the buyer can walk. In other words, once the contract is signed, the buyer is the owner, but only if things continue to look good.

It is for this reason that many sellers lately have attempted to shift the date of the transfer of risk from the seller to the buyer to the date the contract is signed. Their theory is that the buyer has to accept a balanced economic deal—it gets both the good and the bad occurring after the signing. So long as (1) the representations and warranties as of the signing date are accurate on the closing date and (2) the seller doesn't breach its covenants concerning the conduct of the business pending closing, the buyer is getting what it bargained for.

The argument has logical appeal, particularly if there will be a great deal of time between the signing and closing, say, on account of the need for regulatory approvals. If the seller is going to push this point, it must also be willing to give up any earnings during the interim period.

Logic notwithstanding, the seller has an uphill battle. This is one of those situations where one custom is worth a thousand arguments. A buyer can be expected to resist strenuously: "Deals just aren't done this way," "Hey, you still control the operation of the business," or "My price doesn't take into account this type of risk." Because tradition is on the buyer's side, the seller can expect to have to give up something significant to win this point. Where the time span between signing and closing is customarily 30 to 60 days, it may not be worth the fight.

The seller's argument may prove too much. The buyer rarely is expected to assume the risk of other postsigning adverse changes, such as new lawsuits, major undisclosed liabilities, or major uninsured casualty losses. There is no logical basis for distinguishing financial deterioration resulting from a general recession from other types of risks. In any event, the buyer must resist this attempt by the seller, because the buyer may not be able to close its financing in the face of negative events. It does not seem fair to tag the buyer with damages for failing to close in this situation, particularly if the seller knows it is selling in a highly leveraged transaction and if the buyer has obtained financing commitments in advance.

In order to govern events that occur before closing that will harm the financial condition of the company afterward, the conditions to closing should require that there be no *material adverse change* in the "prospects" of the target. In the absence of such a provision, the buyer would be obligated to close under these circumstances. The seller often argues that the word *prospects* is too vague. The proper response is to be more specific, but not to eliminate the concept and shift the risk to the buyer. Of course, there is no one correct answer as to who should bear the risk of loss associated with clear changes in the prospects of the target, and the buyer may be willing to undertake the risk of adverse events.

What happens if the buyer is aware of a material breach in a representation or warranty and nevertheless proceeds to close?

The buyer would be stopped from asserting a claim for damages based on the material breach because it had notice. In that circumstance, the buyer has most likely negotiated the price accordingly or does not consider the breach of the representation or warranty as substantially altering the basic terms or desirability of the transaction.

INDEMNITY SECTION

Why is there an indemnity section?

The purpose of the indemnification section is to set forth the circumstances under which either party can claim damages or take other remedial action in the event the other party to the agreement has breached a representation or warranty or failed to abide by its covenants. This section usually includes provisions concerning the procedural aspects of indemnity claims and the rights of the parties to take part in any legal proceedings that could give rise to an indemnity claim. In effect, the Indemnity section supplements the parties' general legal rights because the section typically provides specificity regarding the kinds of recovery to which the parties may be entitled.

Indemnity sections are considered especially necessary and desirable in agreements involving private company targets for two reasons. First, these companies do not routinely disclose their risks publicly, so buyers typically want some assurance that they will not be blamed when those risks materialize. Second, private companies by definition have a small number of owners, and these can be held accountable under an indemnity section. The opposite is true for public company targets, where there is generally no indemnity because of the seller's dispersed ownership, and because public disclosure already provides some protection.[16] Indemnity sections are also increasingly rare in private equity (PE) agreements where dealmakers want to emulate public deals.

Why is there a need for an indemnity section? Can't the parties simply rely on their general legal rights?

The parties would have the right to collect damages or take other legal action in the event of a breach of a representation or warranty or a specific legal covenant. However, those rights are often vague and do not always include the kinds of recovery to which the parties may feel entitled. For example, it is typical for the indemnity provision to provide specifically that all losses, including reasonable attorney fees and out-of-pocket expenses, will be recovered by the indemnified party. This is often not the result under general case law. In addition, the indemnification provisions contain specific rules governing the involvement of the indemnifying party in proceedings that could give rise to indemnification claims, as well as specific provisions governing the length of time that the representations and warranties will survive the closing.

The Indemnity section also governs items that do not constitute a breach of a representation or warranty because they were specifically disclosed to the buyer at the time of the signing or closing but in respect of which the buyer nevertheless wishes protection. For example, the seller might, in the course of its due diligence, discover that there is a significant potential environmental claim under the federal Superfund laws, or that there is a continuing stream of uninsurable litigation claims attributable to a specific product manufactured by the target. Because the seller disclosed this fact to the buyer, there is no breach of a representation or warranty in connection with these items. However, the indemnification provisions may allocate to the seller the risks associated with disclosed items.

For what period of time is the buyer protected under the indemnity?

This issue is generally expressed in a different way: how long do the representations and warranties survive after the closing? Without a specific provision to the contrary, it is not clear that the representations and warranties survive at all. Consequently, the duration of the indemnity term is often the subject of substantial negotiation. Theoretically, the statute of limitations applicable to actions for breach of contract could govern the claims under the contract, but in most cases the sellers feel that the statutory period is too long.

The buyer should request at least a two-year indemnity period. As a fallback position if the seller resists (and it will), the buyer can suggest that the indemnity continue until the buyer receives audited financial statements of the target for a full fiscal year of operations after the acquisition. Because of the time necessary to prepare the target's financials for its first full fiscal year, the buyer may obtain an indemnity period as long as 15 months after the acquisition closes.

One further point: it is important to provide that each party will be indemnified for all breaches discovered during the indemnity period, not merely for losses actually realized during that period. For example, a lawsuit brought by a third party during the period might not be finally resolved by the end of the period. The indemnified party should nevertheless be entitled to recover so long as the claim arose during the survival period.

Should the time limitation for recovering under the agreement apply to all claims under the contract?

The time limitation should not apply to breaches of covenants that involve a willful act, or to willful breaches of representations or warranties. The seller shouldn't be offered reduced exposure for purposeful breaches. Representations and warranties about taxes customarily survive for the full period of limitation under applicable federal, state, or local law.

Are there any limitations as to how and when a buyer can file a claim for indemnified losses?

Typically, there are. The seller usually does not want to deal with a handful of small-ticket claims postclosing; rather, it is easier if the buyer aggregates any purported losses until they reach a minimum amount. Thus, the parties will usually agree to an *indemnification basket,* which is the dollar amount set forth in the indemnification provision as the loss that must be suffered by the buyer before it can recover damages under the indemnity provisions. The buyer is often successful in arguing that the seller should indemnify losses resulting from breaches of covenants or willful breaches of representations and warranties without regard to the basket amount.

The basket closes the gap between the buyer and the seller and permits reasonable negotiation of the postclosing liability issue. The typical argument that the seller will make is, "You're buying my business, warts and all." The standard buyer's response to this is, "We understand that we are accepting the risks of operating the business on a going-forward basis, but we fully expect to get what we paid for without any significant deviation from the target described in the representations and warranties."

Both parties must assume that there will be problems with the business and realize that dollar-for-dollar compensation for imperfections is not realistic. The purchase price should take into account material deviations from the expectations of the parties about the target. However, significant damages flowing from the breach of the representations or warranties may cause the buyer to overpay for the target. The happenstance that the problem arises after the signing or the closing rather than before should not put the buyer in a substantially worse position than if both parties knew of the problem in advance of the closing.

The dollar amount of the basket and the exact mechanics of its operation are often the subject of a great deal of negotiation between the buyer and the seller. It is unwise for the parties, particularly the buyer, to commit to an exact amount early in the negotiation process, since basket flexibility can become a negotiating tool. Seemingly intractable issues can often be resolved by adjusting one feature or another of the basket, including the dollar amount, even when the problematic issue is unrelated to the basket. For example, differences over the representations and warranties can be resolved if the parties negotiate the minimum amount of the claims, the basket amount, how claims are aggregated, or the length of the survival period.

What are the kinds of issues that most frequently arise in connection with a basket?

The first question is the size of the basket. The median basket on small transactions historically was around 10 percent, but baskets are correlated with deal size, with larger transactions having lower baskets (for example, 1 percent of the purchase price, e.g., $1 million for a $100 million deal).[17]

The next question about the basket is whether the buyer or the seller should absorb the amount of the basket once the threshold is crossed. In a *tipping basket,* the seller is liable for all cumulative losses, starting at dollar one, once the basket amount is hit. For example, if a tipping basket is $1 million and the buyer suffers $1.5 million in damages, is the seller liable for the full $1.5 million? In contrast, the parties might agree to a *deductible basket*—meaning that the seller is liable only for the losses over and above the threshold amount. For example, if a deductible basket is $1 million and the buyer suffers $1.5 million in damages, is the seller liable for only the $500,000 over the basket amount?

There is a cogent argument that buyer and seller ought to split the losses up to the basket amount. The basket is an incentive for the buyer to be thorough in its due diligence, since the basket provision requires the buyer to absorb a significant part of any losses due to breaches of representations and warranties. Splitting liability for the basket amount has the same due diligence incentive for the seller, because if the basket threshold is passed, the seller will be required to pay some part of the initial basket amount. If the basket amount is not split, the buyer may have a legitimate concern that the seller will not be diligent in unearthing problems because it is protected by the basket, especially if the basket amount is large.

Another issue relates to minimum claims. Because the seller does not want to be bothered with small claims—however many of them there might be—the seller often asks for the following additional protection: no claim can be brought if the claim is for less than a specified amount (the "minimum amount"). The seller may insist that such claims not even count toward meeting the basket amount. Of course, the buyer should be expected to resist this approach, particularly if the minimum amount is significant in light of the size of the target's business. In addition, the buyer will likely request that these smaller claims be subject to the indemnity if in the aggregate they are a significant amount.

What is the relationship between the basket amount, the minimum amount, and the word *material* when used in connection with representations and warranties?

As discussed, in order to limit the exposure of the seller to frivolous claims or claims that are normal to the business being acquired, many of the representations and warranties require disclosure only of material items, or items that are material to the business of the target and its subsidiaries taken as a whole. In the absence of a specific dollar threshold to define what is material, it is unclear exactly how much damage the buyer must incur before it can claim that there has been a breach of a representation containing a materiality limitation. These materiality limitations can create an unfair result for the buyer if there are several legal problems for the target that cause a significant aggregate loss for the buyer but there is no single breach that has a material adverse effect on the business.

The precise effect of the basket amount on all of this is uncertain. It might be argued that the basket amount is a numerical definition of the word *material.* Thus, if the basket amount is $1 million, a loss of less than $1 million arising from a breach of a single warranty might not be viewed by a court interpreting the agreement as material to the business as a whole. But what if there are claims in five areas covered by representations and warranties, averaging $750,000 each? If the agreement is construed to mean that only a loss of more than $1 million is material, the buyer will suffer $3.75 million of damage and will have no recourse against the seller. The result may not be sensible, but in the absence of any other guidance it is, unfortunately, plausible. If the parties do not wish the basket amount to be used as a definition of material, they should state so in the agreement.

Can use of a basket and a minimum amount provision eliminate the need for including materiality limitations in the representations and warranties?

It is possible to resolve the ambiguity of using *material* by using the concepts of the basket amount and minimum amount in the following manner: a representation or warranty would not be breached unless the resulting loss exceeded the minimum claim amount (say, $50,000), and there would be no recovery by the buyer until all of the potential claims add up to the basket amount. This way, the seller is assured that relatively minor imperfections in the business will not result either singly or in the aggregate in exposure for indemnity claims, and both parties will have a much better idea of the expectations surrounding the indemnity provisions.

The seller must exercise care here. The materiality limitations in the representations and warranties serve another function: They limit the ability of the buyer to terminate the transaction without penalty between the time of signing and closing. If the materiality limitations are eliminated altogether, the buyer could point to a minor legal defect in the business causing a loss equal to the minimum amount and say that the representations and warranties were not "true as of the closing date." This problem can be remedied either (1) by leaving the materiality limitations in the agreement solely for this purpose, as is often the case, or (2) by leaving them out and requiring that potential losses equal the basket amount or some other agreed-upon figure before the buyer would be permitted to terminate the transaction.

The latter solution can be very risky for the buyer. The basket amount is frequently the subject of negotiation and manipulation having little or nothing to do with the concept of materiality as incorporated into individual representations or warranties. The buyer may assess the risk of an unknown or undisclosed problem arising after the closing as small because it knows the target or the industry extremely well, or because it has tremendous faith in the management coparticipants in the acquisition. The buyer may also feel that it is getting a bargain. In this situation, and because of the speculative nature of the losses, the buyer may be willing to agree to a very large basket amount.

On the other hand, the buyer might well feel that if problems actually arise before the closing, it should be free to reevaluate the wisdom of its decision to buy the target long before its losses reach the basket amount. To meet this concern, either a different threshold amount should be established for the Conditions to Closing section or, as is most often the case, the materiality caveats should remain in place in the representations and warranties for purposes of the Conditions to Closing section.

Is the indemnity sufficient protection for the parties, or are escrows or setoff rights necessary?

The indemnity alone is meaningless unless the indemnifying party is creditworthy. The parties should take care to satisfy themselves about the financial strength of indemnifying parties. This is achieved, in part, by the representations and warranties made by the buyer and its owners about their respective financial conditions. Where there are doubts about the ability of the seller to meet its obligations, or where the target has many stockholders, it may be advisable to place a portion of the purchase price in escrow to serve as security for the seller's obligations under the indemnity. Under a typical escrow, which often (but not always) lasts as long as the survival period, the buyer has access to the escrowed funds after it is finally determined that the seller is liable under the indemnity portion of the contract.

Another device that is useful when the seller has a right to receive deferred payments is to give the buyer a right to set off any damages it suffers for breach of the contract against payments due the seller. Agreements may permit a setoff either after a final determination of liability or when a loss is suffered despite the fact that the buyer has not yet established the seller's liability. The latter arrangement reverses the normal posture of the parties negotiating a claim for indemnification—normally the indemnifying party has control of the money, and the party who has suffered damages must sue to get it. For this reason, an immediate setoff right is fiercely, and usually successfully, fought off by the seller.

In the absence of a specific setoff provision, in most jurisdictions it does not appear that a buyer has the legal right to withhold payments from the seller until there is a final determination of liability under the indemnity. If note payments to the seller are withheld before such a determination, it is probable that a court would grant a summary judgment to the seller and force the buyer to pay principal and interest on the note in accordance with the terms, even if the buyer has a separate claim under the contract.

Are there any special concerns of the seller in connection with the indemnity?

Most of the issues for the seller are covered in the preceding text since the basket amounts, survival period, and minimum amount are all issues of great concern to both parties. Obviously, the seller will try to avoid all indemnity completely.

In the case of a privately held target, the major thrust of the seller's argument is often to reinforce the basic argument outlined here about who assumes the risk of owning a business with the additional argument that if the target were a public company the representations and warranties would not survive the closing. This argument is more persuasive if there are public securities issued by the target so that it has been regularly filing public reports with the SEC and has a relatively long history of audited financial statements. One major reason for the different treatment of public companies is the impracticality of bringing suits against hundreds or even thousands of stockholders. This burden is not usually present in the sale of a closely held private company. Nevertheless, the apparent willingness of buyers in the public arena to live without indemnities, together with the sale of companies through auction procedures (discussed later), has allowed sellers to avoid indemnities in an increasing number of situations.

When there are several selling stockholders, the sellers ought to (1) try to limit each stockholder's liability to "several" liability, meaning that one stockholder is not liable if another is unable to satisfy its liabilities under the indemnity, and (2) be certain that breaches of representations and warranties that are specific to a stockholder, such as a stockholder's failure to have or convey good title to its shares being sold, will not create liability for other stockholders.

The sellers also should argue that there should be a limit on liability. Most buyers will agree to limit liability to the purchase price paid, and some sellers have been successful in arguing for a lower cap on liability—sometimes even limited to the amount held in escrow (although not in such cases of fraud or deceit).

Finally, the sellers ought to pay close attention to the terms of notes they accept as part of the payment. In order to placate senior lenders, seller notes are often deeply subordinated (see the discussion in Chapter 4) and contain provisions that limit the ability of the seller to sue if there is a payment default. A buyer should not be permitted to take advantage of this provision to hold back payments (that is, create a payment default) when there is a potential claim under the indemnity. The subordination provisions are for the benefit of the senior lenders and are not designed to allow the buyer to use the seller's funds to finance indemnity claims; the limitation on the seller's remedies under the note ought not to apply to a constructive setoff by the buyer because of potential indemnity liabilities.

Are there any special items that a buyer is indemnified for even if they are disclosed, such as litigation?

Yes. In the course of due diligence, the buyer will often uncover items for which it will either seek a price adjustment or request specific indemnification. Typical examples are unusual litigation that is not insured or reserved for on the balance sheet, and major environmental problems.

What about litigation arising after the closing based on business conducted before the acquisition?

In an asset transaction, the buyer usually does not assume the risk of such litigation and will obtain a specific indemnity against any losses from the seller.

In the case of a merger or stock acquisition, many contracts contain indemnities specifically protecting the buyer against this type of loss. Even in the absence of specific protection, it is at least arguable that such litigation is an unmatured and contingent undisclosed liability that constitutes a breach of the warranty, or an undisclosed liability to which the general indemnity applies.

Before engaging in lengthy negotiation about this issue, the parties should focus on litigation-specific insurance coverage for this type of loss. In this area, the availability of insurance coverage may render the parties' exposure immaterial. In most cases, insurance is on a "claims made" basis; that is, the insured is protected against losses from claims made during the insurance period. If so, the target's insurance policy will provide protection in the ordinary course, and it would be unfair to expect the seller to cover such losses. It is critical to avoid an insurance coverage gap during which neither the old policy (because it is a claims-made policy) nor the target's new policy (because it only insures claims based on events occurring during the insurance period) will make good on a legitimate claim. A gap is more likely to arise when the target is part of a conglomerate and coinsured under a single umbrella policy covering all members of the seller's corporate group. In this situation, the target must take out separate policies effective as of the closing date.

Are there any circumstances that might make it challenging or undesirable for the buyer to enforce an indemnification claim against the seller?

Yes. It could be that there are a large number of selling shareholders that would be difficult to track down in the event of a claim (and a holdback or escrow is not a reasonable option, for whatever reason), or it could be that the sellers are expected to manage the business posttransaction or the parties will have ongoing business relationships. In other cases, the buyer might want indemnification protection for a longer period of time than what the sellers might be reasonably willing to agree to. All of these scenarios present challenges when it comes to postdeal disputes and indemnification collections. Of course, the buyer would still want to be reimbursed for its losses. Accordingly, it might make sense for one or both parties to consider representation and warranty insurance.

What is representation and warranty insurance? How does it work?

Representation and warranty insurance (RWI) protects the insured against unintentional and unknown breaches of a seller's representations and warranties made in the transaction agreement. RWI can enhance an indemnification package or it can serve as the buyer's sole source of recovery. The financial product has been around approximately 15 years, but has gained substantial momentum in recent years. A dealmaker might not ordinarily enter transaction discussions having RWI in mind. However, RWI might look increasingly attractive to the acquirer as the scope of business risks becomes clearer during the deal process.

In exchange for a fixed upfront payment to cover the premium and related expenses, a policy may reduce or eliminate the need for seller accruals, reserves, or collateral for contingent liabilities. Also, the buyer can recover directly from the insurance company rather than the sellers, which can be helpful when the creditworthiness of the sellers is low or when the sellers are "friendly sellers" with which the buyer must maintain a positive working relationship going forward. Lastly, as mentioned earlier, the acquisition of a publicly traded company typically would not have indemnification protection from the sellers. However, the acquirer could purchase RWI to achieve a similar result.

What are typical terms for RWI?

There are generally two primary components to the cost of RWI: the insurance premium and the size of the deductible. Ancillary upfront costs may include underwriting or diligence fees and other governmental taxes and fees (e.g., state surplus line taxes).

At least in the present market, premiums of 2 percent to 3 percent are relatively common, although they can range as high as 6 percent. The actual amount will depend upon the insurer's assessment of risk, the quality of the representations and warranties, the retention, the coverage limit, and the policy period. The policy might typically be subject to a deductible of 1 percent to 3 percent of enterprise value. In terms of duration of coverage for fundamental representations and warranties, RWI insurance might typically run five years or longer—meaning for more than the 12- to 24-month duration that would be typical in a seller indemnification. So, if an acquirer were to price out $10 million of coverage on a $100 million transaction, it might expect to pay a $200,000 to $300,000 premium for protection against losses in excess of $2 million, with a $10 million cap and a five-year term.

What is the purpose of the termination section of the agreement?

The Termination section of the agreement sets forth the circumstances under which either party may terminate the transactions and the consequences of such termination. This section normally includes a date by which the closing must occur. If the closing fails to occur by that date as a result of the action or inaction of one party, the party that was capable of closing typically can elect to terminate the contract and sue the other party for breach of contract.

The section also allows a party to terminate if it discovers a material breach by the other of a representation, warranty, or covenant that would cause the bring-down condition to be unsatisfied. A party should not have to wait until the termination date to terminate if it is clear that it won't be obligated to close in any event.

This section will also set forth any limitation on damages that can be collected by the successful litigant for breach of the contract and any special remedies, such as specific performance, of which a nonbreaching party may avail itself. The requirements for security for the buyer's obligations as well as the condition under which the seller can resort to the security are set forth often in this section.

What are the advantages and disadvantages of arbitration provisions in the agreement?

The oft-stated benefits of arbitration—such as quick and inexpensive resolution of disputes—may make arbitration a satisfactory mechanism by which parties to an acquisition agreement can enforce their rights. As discussed in Chapter 6, alternative dispute resolution (ADR) is gaining acceptance by both courts and companies. It should be noted, however, that the benefits of arbitration can be offset by its risks.

Arbitration is best suited for resolution of disputes of little economic consequence or of technical issues, such as valuation of inventory, not readily within the ken of a trial judge. Even in the latter situation, the parties should consider whether the savings in time and money by arbitration are outweighed by the protections of judicial resolution, particularly where the amounts involved potentially constitute a significant multiple of litigation costs. Where the benefits of arbitration outweigh its disadvantages, the arbitration clause should be drafted to minimize the negative aspects of arbitration.

One factor that contributes to prompt resolution by arbitration is the use of a nonjudicial or extrajudicial decision maker. An arbitrator's schedule will usually be more open and flexible than that of a court. However, an arbitrator may have biases or lack sufficient knowledge of the law or subject area to reach a proper decision. This disadvantage can be minimized by careful drafting. For example, if the agreement designates arbitration under the rules of the American Arbitration Association (AAA), the parties will have to choose an arbitrator from one or more lists of names provided to them. These arbitrators may be unsatisfactory. To avoid this situation, the acquisition agreement can designate another means of choosing an arbitrator, such as having each party choose its own arbitrator, and then having these select a third arbitrator.

A second factor that contributes to the speed of arbitration, as well as its lower costs, is the absence of discovery. In certain situations, the lack of discovery may not be a serious disadvantage. For example, if each party has sufficient familiarity with, or access to, the company's books and records, discovery may not be necessary to resolve a dispute concerning those documents. Even if discovery is necessary with regard to a particular issue, arbitration may still be a viable alternative to court proceedings. The parties can draft the agreement to allow some discovery but not so much as to make the arbitration process comparable to a judicial one. Furthermore, the extent of discovery can be made subject to decision of the arbitrators.

In drafting an arbitration agreement, the parties should attempt to anticipate all future disputes. If arbitration is broadly required for all disagreements, the parties may be barred from seeking emergency injunctive relief from a court. A narrow arbitration clause, however, may result in requiring counterclaims to be filed in court, thereby compounding, rather than simplifying, resolution of disagreements.

The parties should also draft the arbitration agreement with the controlling law of the relevant jurisdiction in mind. Certain jurisdictions, such as California, are less likely than others to limit the scope of the arbitration clause. In those jurisdictions, courts tend to interpret narrow arbitration provisions to require arbitration of issues that the parties neither mentioned nor intended to be arbitrated.

One caveat: in the M&A area, arbitration proceedings, even before an AAA tribunal, can be very expensive if they are pursued by lawyers normally involved in litigative court proceedings. Both sides should recognize that the services of law firms specializing in ADR are now widely available and resolution of disputes using their services is highly efficient.

Do auction procedures for selling companies have any effect on the contract negotiation process?

Yes, they may have a significant effect. In an auction process, a seller hires an investment banker to sell the target on a bid basis. The investment banker prepares a "book" describing the target, sends this book to multiple prospective acquirers (sometimes more than 100), and solicits bids from these potential buyers. After the investment banker winnows out unacceptable initial bids, the remaining buyers may receive a form contract and be told that the bid should be accompanied by the form contract together with any changes to it required by the buyer. The buyer is expressly warned that extensive changes will be considered negatively in evaluating the competitive nature of the bid. Often, the buyer is offered limited access to the target's management and carefully controlled opportunities for due diligence before the initial bid must be made. Needless to say, the form contract typically provides the buyer no indemnities and only limited representations and warranties. Typically, extensive changes are required to make the contract similar to a typical and reasonable buyer's contract.

How should a buyer respond in this process? There is simply no clear answer. The response will depend entirely upon the strength of the buyer's desire to buy the target and its confidence that it knows the target well enough to take the risk of an as-is transaction. Even if the buyer is willing to take such risks, certain points should be addressed in the contract, and the buyer must insist upon the opportunity to conduct thorough due diligence for the following reasons:

- First, the buyer must remember the twofold purpose of representations and warranties. The representations and warranties not only provide the basis for indemnities but also establish the buyer's right to refuse to close a deal if legal defects are discovered before the closing. The buyer should get representations and warranties ensuring that if the buyer finds legal problems, it may terminate the contract without penalty.
- Second, the buyer has the right to protect itself against overpaying. The question is how far to carry the aforementioned actions.

The bid process often has an intended psychological effect on many buyers. The purchaser's lawyer is likely to hear: "Don't give me the world's most perfect contract. I want the absolute minimum protection I need. Don't overlawyer and get me knocked out in the first round." The buyer, who often believes that the contractual protections are overkill by lawyers, gets spooked and doesn't want the lawyers to lose the deal. Assuming that (1) the first two points previously listed are accounted for in the contract, (2) the deal is priced on an as-is basis, and (3) the buyer is fully informed of the risks, the buyer may indeed be wise to keep it simple.

If additional protection is desired, the buyer might require indemnification for breaches of representations and warranties made regarding the financial statements, undisclosed liabilities, taxes, and litigation. This requirement can be made easier for the seller to accept with generous minimum amount and basket provisions.

As a final word, the buyer should not be fooled by the putative formality of the bid procedures and the investment banker's stern admonitions. Most buyers do submit changes to the contract along the lines described earlier, and in the end the insiders will tell you that the price and a credible ability to close, and not the contract terms (provided they are reasonable), will dictate the results in most cases. A buyer that has concerns about the legal aspects of the target or its business should not hesitate to say that it reserves the right to submit further changes after it has been given complete access to management and an opportunity for full due diligence. It is not unusual for the buyer to submit a solid bid and indicate that it would like the opportunity to negotiate the terms of the contract with the seller face-to-face. Typically, the buyer would also indicate the several areas where it would require changes.

Another favored approach is to do a relatively extensive markup and suggest that the contract can be watered down in face-to-face negotiations after due diligence is completed. This approach is constructive because the seller will usually negotiate the contract with the two or three top bidders. Whatever the buyer sends in will be the starting point for negotiation. Even if the buyer is willing to accept only minimum protection, it is important to start ahead of where the buyer wants to end up.

What are the main advantages of auction procedures?

Auctions are still generally believed to be the best way of ensuring that the highest possible price is obtained—at least during bull markets. The same sentiment probably drives the seller to use auction methods for sales of divisions or subsidiaries of companies. Also, who can fault a corporate executive for the price he or she agrees to if it was the result of a competitive bid procedure?

The auction process also saves the seller the time and effort of dealing sequentially with dozens of potential buyers, many of whom may be shoppers that never buy anything, and bringing it down to serious negotiations with two or three serious potential buyers. Sellers must be very careful to supervise the way the investment bankers deal with the bidders. The seller should be involved in the negotiations because most serious buyers are justifiably put off by having to negotiate substantive points through an intermediary who may or may not have the authority to cut a deal.

ACQUISITIONS FROM AN AFFILIATED GROUP

Are there any special aspects to be negotiated when the buyer is acquiring the assets of a division or the stock of a subsidiary that is a part of a larger corporate group?

There are numerous issues that arise under such circumstances that should be addressed:

- Is the buyer getting all of the assets needed to operate the company as a separate business or are some critical assets located elsewhere in the group?
- Are there any special, advantageous contractual or administrative relationships with the seller that must be continued (for example, supply or purchase contracts), or are there unfavorable ones that must be terminated? This can be a crucial aspect of a transaction for the buyer or the seller. As part of the pricing and as an inducement to complete the transaction, one party can offer a favorable long-term contract to the other.
- Are there administrative services provided to the target by the group that should be continued for a period of time? In many cases the seller's group provides legal, accounting, billing, and other administrative support as well as shared office and warehouse space. Unless replacements will be available at closing, the agreement should contain provisions to continue those services at an agreed-upon cost for a specified period of time.
- Finally, is it clear that the target financial information upon which the deal is based takes into account the need to provide for the services or other arrangements described in the previous paragraphs?

TRANSACTIONS INVOLVING PUBLIC COMPANIES

Are acquisition agreements different when the target is a public company?

Yes. The acquisition agreement in a public company transaction is very different from the type of agreement used for a privately held target. The differences may be divided into two categories: (1) provisions that are present in agreements involving private companies but are typically absent from agreements involving public companies, and (2) provisions that are typically absent from private company agreements but are present in public company agreements.

What provisions common to private company agreements will be missing from agreements involving public companies?

One of the biggest difficulties in acquiring a public company rather than a private company is that it is impossible, from a practical standpoint, to track down all the public selling shareholders in the months and years following the close of the deal. This has several impacts on the acquisition agreement. In agreements involving public companies, the representations and warranties do not survive the closing of the transaction; the buyer is not protected in the event breaches are discovered in postclosing. In short, there is no indemnity provision, mainly because an indemnity against hundreds or thousands of shareholders is considered impractical. The buyer therefore must rely on the substantial disclosure required under federal securities laws as the basis for evaluating the legal and financial risks of ownership. It is generally assumed that those disclosures, which if materially inaccurate can give rise to criminal and civil liability on the part of the officers and directors, together with a history of audited financial statements that are also required under the securities laws provide a reliable rendition of the legal/financial history of the target.

Because the representations and warranties don't survive anyway, and because of the extensive public disclosures, the representations and warranties tend to be far briefer in a public company deal. They serve more as a means of organizing due diligence. The buyer shouldn't get too carried away, however, with agreeing to gut the representations and warranties. As repeated so often in this chapter, these provisions serve another function—they provide the basis for a buyer's terminating the transaction if the representations, warranties, and covenants are breached in a material way. Therefore, although many of the detailed disclosures are eliminated, the key concepts must be retained. The key sections that would be retained in a public deal agreement are discussed in the introduction to the form agreement at the end of this chapter.

What are some of the provisions that appear only in the public deal acquisition agreement?

First, the agreement will contain specific representations and warranties to the effect that the parties have complied with all applicable securities laws and, specifically, that the disclosures made pursuant to those laws are all materially accurate.

Second, the agreement will set forth the specific form of the transaction, for example, a merger or a tender offer or a combination of the two, and what the responsibilities of the various parties will be for preparing, reviewing, and filing the documents that must be filed with the SEC.

NEGOTIATING AND DOCUMENTING AN MBO

What is the course of negotiation between a management group and an outside financial or investor group?

The typical MBO involving an outside financial partner requires at least three separate but coordinated negotiations: (1) the negotiation between management and the financial partner as to the nature of their relationship, (2) the acquisition negotiation between a team consisting of management and the financial partner on the one side and the seller on the other, and (3) the negotiation with lenders, in which the financial partner usually plays the lead role but management participates because of its knowledge of the business and its financing needs, and the lenders' desire to keep management involved.

Because both the second and third negotiations demand close coordination between management and the financial partner and a considerable amount of mutual trust, the first negotiation should, to the extent possible, be completed at the earliest possible stage but is often delayed. MBOs, like most LBOs, normally take place under acute time pressure, and management and the financial partner may have met for the first time and for the sole purpose of doing the acquisition. The issues between them are difficult and go to basic questions of allocation of benefits and burdens and management self-esteem.

It is often difficult for management to accept how much equity the financiers want to receive when they don't even know how to run the company. Therefore, it is likely that management and the financial partner are working out their relationship at the same time that they are negotiating with the seller and the lenders. To some extent, this is unavoidable, even with ample time and advance contact, because the terms negotiated with the seller or the obligations imposed by a lender cannot be entirely foreseen and will involve changes in the allocations of responsibilities or benefits between the acquirers. It may even be beneficial, as during the course of negotiations both management and the financial partner begin to appreciate how essential each is to the other in bringing the deal to a proper closing.

The first step is reaching an understanding of the terms of management and the financial partner's relationship. Although this is often an oral agreement, occasionally management and its financial partner may enter into a written preincorporation agreement.

What issues should the preincorporation agreement address?

The four main issues are as follows:

1. The terms on which the acquisition will be conducted: that each party will bear its own expenses or how they will be shared; that neither will be liable to the other if the transition is not

consummated; that neither will negotiate with another party; that information about the other will be kept confidential; that each will use its reasonable efforts to accomplish the acquisition; and the responsibilities that each party will have in negotiating the acquisition (that is, the financial party will probably commit to obtain financing on a best-efforts or reasonable-efforts basis)

2. The share each party will have in the ownership of the acquired company
3. The voting power or veto power each party will have over the business operations of the acquired company and over sale or refinancing of the company
4. The makeup of the board of directors

Are there any provisions a preincorporation agreement should not contain?

The lender, as part of its due diligence, may well insist upon seeing any written preincorporation agreement. Some will advise that details, such as contingency plans specifying which of the parties will provide personal guarantees for the loan, if necessary, be based on handshakes rather than memorialized in the written agreement, which dilutes their position with lenders.

How is a manager-investor understanding expressed if there is no preincorporation agreement?

These arrangements are then handled as a matter of oral understanding and custom that ultimately, after the acquisition, may be reduced to writing in various agreements such as employment, consulting, and stockholder agreements, and in the target's articles of incorporation and bylaws. Informal agreements are often indicators of a more healthy and successful relationship between the management and the investor group, since the key elements in most MBOs are trust and cooperation. Getting everything in writing at an early stage is nearly impossible anyway since the parties are dealing, in part, with ephemera, and attempts to reduce verbal agreements to precise language can lead to arguments, delays, mistrust, and perhaps the breakup of the deal before it's had a chance to get going.

What are typical allocations of control over corporate decisions?

Again, allocations vary greatly according to which party controls the deal, how badly they need each other, and how much they trust each other. Discussions tend to reflect a basic division of interest: management tends to think in terms of preservation, expansion, and meeting operating needs of the company, whereas the financial partner tends to think of satisfying a lender in order to achieve the acquisition and, thereafter, realizing value by payment of dividends, sale of stock, or divestitures.

Management will presumably make "ordinary course of business" decisions, subject to the board of directors, which may be equally divided between the parties at first but will swing one way or the other depending on events. Sometimes, board membership is divided proportionate to stockholdings. If management has less than 50 percent of the stock, it may have the protection of a supermajority provision for stockholder votes affecting major transactions, such as sale of the company, public issuances of stock, or refinancings. If the financial partner does not have a majority of the stock, it may insist on the ability to sell its interest or to take the company public after a certain period of time if certain conditions are met. A financial sponsor with a minority stake will also negotiate certain information rights and governance provisions to at least create guardrails for how the business is to be run.

How can the value of management be locked in—for example, if key people leave or die?

Two very important factors in a management LBO are:

- Employment contracts with key personnel for three-year or five-year terms
- Key-executive life insurance

Compensation and equity participations can be structured through employment and stockholder agreements so that key managers have everything to gain and nothing to lose by staying; therefore, the risk of voluntary departure can be minimized.

Key-executive life insurance should always be part of any MBO planning. No group of financial wizards will substitute for a strong CEO who knows the business, particularly if the plan is to place the company deeply into debt to finance the acquisition. Lenders will frequently require life insurance on the chief executive and perhaps one or two others. Even if they don't require it, any financial group working with management probably will. The senior author of this book was advising a seller some years ago and noticed at the closing that the buyer/CEO was smoking and coughing very heavily. The author insisted successfully that the closing not occur without obtaining key-executive (then called "key-man") life insurance in the amount of the acquisition loan. The closing was delayed until the insurance was obtained. Two weeks later, the buyer/CEO died.

EMPLOYMENT AGREEMENTS

In addition to equity, what other benefits are typically made available to management?

Prior to trying to sell a division or subsidiary to a third party or to managers, a seller must be sure that its managers have signed employment agreements and they conform with what is actually happening and adequately cover bonuses, vacations, stock options, and so on. Such agreements keep managers with the company while the business is being offered for sale.

Should an MBO manager enter into an employment agreement?

Generally, managers should accept such agreements, as they often offer protection against precipitous termination by a new owner. Further, those financing the deal, including lenders, may insist on it. On the other hand, managers should be wary of signing off on broad *covenants not to compete* (also known as *noncompete provisions*) that will prevent them from working for competitors for long periods of time. If an employee must agree to such provisions, which is likely given the strong interest the company will have in protecting its business, he or she will want to be compensated during the noncompete period if it results in hardship and will want to limit the period, for example, to one year, and perhaps limit the territory affected. Even still, the legal trend in many states—such as California—is to not enforce noncompete provisions unless the employee received a very substantial payment on the basis that people should be free to earn a living. In such proemployee states, sponsors are better off obtaining nonsolicitation agreements that restrict the manager's right to poach the company's clients (or customers), employees, and so forth, should the manager resign from the business.

After purchasing the business, key members of management will want to have new employment agreements replacing those entered into before the sale of the business. Such an agreement will at the least provide a term, a specified salary, and noncompetition or nonsolicitation provisions. Management's partner or its bank lenders will usually also want key management to have such agreements.

What are the typical terms of a postbuyout employment agreement with managers involved in an MBO?

An employment agreement should specify the term of employment, the amount of compensation and bonuses, and the conditions under which an executive can be terminated.

Employment agreements can be for a fixed term of years or can be extended from year to year under an "evergreen" provision unless one party gives notice to the contrary to the other within a limited period before the start of each year.

The agreement will specify a base salary. The agreement can provide that the salary can be increased by specified increments or by an adjustment such as a rise in the Consumer Price Index. The agreement may also require that the executive receive a percentage of the excess of the company's pretax earnings or net income over projected levels of earnings or income. The agreement might also incorporate an existing bonus plan, as well as special pensions or stock plans, and might guarantee specific benefit levels.

Most employees are at-will, meaning that an employer may terminate the employee at any time for any reason and with few, if any, further obligations. In employment agreements that limit the employee's ability to terminate the employee arbitrarily, the employer still will have the right to terminate the employee for just cause, which usually includes at minimum willful misconduct or gross negligence in the course of employment, fraud in the course of employment, or the conviction for a crime. Just cause may include other matters, but the employee's interest is in limiting the bases for termination for just cause. If the employer has the right to terminate an employee without just cause, the employee might be compensated by receiving his or her base salary through a specific date in a lump sum or periodic payments, or by receiving payments in addition to his or her base salary. Even in circumstances in which an employee is not entitled to severance, it is good practice for the employer to offer a payment of some sort—provided that the employee signs a release forgoing the right to sue the employer in the future for matters predating the release. In any event, the basis for the terms of the severance agreement should be anticipated in the employment agreement. For instance, if the employee gets a new job, his or her salary may or may not reduce the amount that must be paid under these provisions by the terminating employer.

The agreement protects the employer and the employee if the employee is disabled for a continuous period of time. If an employee is disabled or dies, the employee or his estate may be entitled to receive benefits after disability or death.

What other provisions may be included in an employment agreement?

Other employment agreement provisions may stipulate that:

- The executive work in a specified city and not be required to relocate
- The executive receive a company car
- The company pay for country club memberships and other expenses

- Other special benefits be provided, such as guaranteed vacation leave policies or the right to run for public office

An employee may also negotiate for a deferred compensation agreement. Deferring income can have financial and tax benefits to individuals. The employee may be able to negotiate funded deferred compensation, with amounts payable out of insurance or a special trust.

A word of caution: Make sure that you do not inherit agreements that contain provisions that can award compensation that can be viewed as excessive. Such provisions can do reputational harm, as seen in the case of the Walt Disney Corporation when 52 percent of shareholders in 2018 cast a (nonbinding) vote against CEO Bob Igor's $36.3 million pay package. At a congressional hearing in May 2019, heiress Abigail Disney called the pay a "moral issue."

What are the benefits and detriments of a deal-induced severance agreement?

Occasionally, an employee who is not offered an employment agreement or is resistant to entering into an employment agreement will enter into a severance agreement instead. The severance agreement, sometimes called a "golden parachute," will provide that the employee receive two or three times his or her annual salary if he or she is terminated as the result of a change in control of the company. The employee may also be entitled to receive substantial severance benefits if he or she chooses to leave under such circumstances. Such agreements are more prevalent in public companies than in the private companies that emerge from an MBO.

Such agreements can harm the employer by giving the employee a strong incentive to become uncooperative and even disruptive in order to cause termination and trigger the severance payment. It is not uncommon for management to be asked to give up or scale back its golden parachute protections as part of the price for participating in an MBO.

Golden parachutes can have significant tax consequences to the employer. (See the following paragraphs.) But they can trigger corporate governance concerns, as well. Management compensation (including severance pay) is a common theme in shareholder resolutions every proxy season.[18]

What are the tax penalties for golden parachute payments?

Under current law, if a corporation makes an "excess parachute payment" to an employee, the payment may not be deducted by the corporation, and the employee will be subject to a 20 percent nondeductible excise tax on the excess parachute payment in addition to any regular income tax.

The definition of an excess parachute payment is complex. Generally an excess parachute payment is made to a high-level management employee, is exceptional in relation to the employee's previous compensation, and is contingent upon a change of control of the company. The definition of change of control is broad enough to include circumstances in which a friendly buyer enters into a compensation arrangement with the employee. Management equity participation that results in taxable compensation under Section 83 of the IRC will be taken into account along with all other compensation under the golden parachute rules and thus may be subject to additional tax as an excess parachute payment.

STOCKHOLDERS' AGREEMENTS

At or shortly following the acquisition closing, it is usually advisable for the acquirers to enter into a stockholders' agreement. If the postacquisition entity is a partnership, the partnership agreement will contain comparable provisions.

What are the main reasons for the buyers of a business to enter into a stockholders' agreement?

To the extent that they have not already done so in a preincorporation agreement, a stockholders' agreement will allow the buyers to do the following:

- Obtain advance commitments for additional equity or debt
- Exercise control over who the owners of the business will be
- Specify their respective legal rights over the governance of the business

Why might the buyers want to exercise control over who the owners of the business will be?

Presumably, one of the main reasons the buyers completed the transaction was their particular individual and collective strengths. They wanted to be in business together rather than with other persons or entities. In an MBO (with or without an outside investor group), equity ownership by the persons who will be running the business is a key ingredient of the future success of the enterprise. Therefore, especially in the early period following the acquisition closing, the buyers will want to limit the ownership of the business to those who are active employees or members of the initial investor group. Moreover, the acquisition lenders will have similar concerns and usually will require that the equity ownership of management and the initial investor group be maintained at certain levels for as long as their loans are outstanding.

What are some of the typical ways to limit the equity ownership of the target?

The stockholders' agreement will contain "restrictions on transferability," which are limitations on the persons or entities to whom the stockholders may transfer their stock, the time periods during which the stock may be transferred, or the manner in which the stock may be transferred. For example, the stockholders may agree that, in order to give themselves an opportunity to put the business on a solid footing, for a specified period of time, usually from one to five years after the closing, no stockholder will be allowed to transfer stock to anyone other than to an affiliate in the case of a corporate stockholder or to a spouse or child in the case of a stockholder who is a natural person. Management stockholders may even be locked in for a longer period, perhaps as long as they continue to be employed by the corporation.

Conversely, in the case of a management stockholder, the stockholders' agreement may also provide that upon termination of his or her employment, the corporation or the other stockholders will have the option to purchase the terminated employee's stock. One benefit of a provision like this is that the purchased stock could then be sold to another employee of the corporation, including the terminated employee's replacement, enhancing his or her incentive to perform well. Another benefit is that the stock need not remain in the hands of a fired or otherwise disgruntled former employee.

Are such restrictions on transferability legally enforceable?

Generally speaking, yes, assuming that there is a valid business purpose for the restriction, the restriction is reasonably related to a business purpose, and no stockholder has been induced by deception or forced into agreeing to the restriction. However, the more expansive the restriction, the greater is the risk that a court will find the restriction to be an "unlawful restraint on the alienation of property." In addition, most states' laws require the existence of transfer restrictions be noted in the form of a legend on the stock certificate in order for those restrictions to be enforceable against third-party transferees who have no knowledge of their existence.

Are there any other ownership restrictions that management may want to have in a stockholders' agreement?

Where management is in a minority position vis-à-vis the other stockholders, it may want some protection against dilution of its interest or some influence over when, and to whom, additional stock may be issued.

Through the stockholders' agreement, management could be given an option to purchase such additional stock, or a proportion thereof, for the same price and terms on which they would otherwise be sold to a third person or entity. It could also be given certain consensual rights over the issuance of such additional stock (see the following discussion).

How may a stockholders' agreement create the framework by which the corporation will be governed?

The stockholders' agreement may contain provisions (1) whereby the stockholders commit themselves in advance to vote their shares to maintain a certain governing structure, (2) that require that certain matters normally within the province of the board of directors or the president shall be regulated by the stockholders, or (3) that require that, under certain circumstances, normal majority rule by the board or the stockholders, as applicable, will not be sufficient.

An example of the first type of provision is where the stockholders agree that they will exercise their power to adopt and amend the corporation's bylaws to maintain a board of directors of a particular number and that they will vote to elect as directors representatives nominated by various groups of stockholders. In the case of a typical MBO in which the majority of stock is held by an investor group, the stockholders' agreement would provide that the stockholders will at all times vote their shares so as to maintain a board of directors of, say, five members, three of whom shall be nominated by the investor group and two of whom shall be nominated by the management group.

An example of the second type of provision is where the parties agree that the stockholders must approve the dismissal of certain executive officers, or any contracts with affiliates of the corporation, or the issuance of stock—activities that are usually handled by the board of directors.

An example of the third type of provision is where the stockholders agree that the corporation cannot engage in certain major transactions, such as a merger or a sale of substantially all the assets of the corporation, without the approval of all of the stockholders or some greater proportion of the stockholders than the proportion required under the applicable state corporation statute.

In most, if not all, states it will also be necessary for the second and third types of provisions to be stated in the certificate of incorporation or bylaws of the corporation. For example, Delaware Code Sections 141 and 216 provide, respectively, (1) that the business and affairs of every Delaware corporation shall be managed by its board of directors unless the corporation's certificate of incorporation provides otherwise and (2) that unless the corporation's certificate of incorporation or bylaws provide otherwise, all matters, other than election of directors, subject to stockholder approval shall be approved by majority vote, and by plurality vote in the case of the election of directors. In this case the stockholders' agreement should also provide that the stockholders will vote their shares to adopt and maintain these types of provisions as part of the company's certificate of incorporation or bylaws, as applicable.

How long are voting agreements enforceable?

This matter is governed by the corporation statutes of the state in which the company is incorporated. In Delaware, for example, such agreements are valid for only 10 years, but at any time within 2 years prior to expiration of a voting agreement, the stockholders may extend such agreement for as many additional periods, each not exceeding 10 years, as they desire. It is possible, however, through the use of devices such as irrevocable proxies, to lock in stockholder votes for a longer period than that permitted for voting agreements.

What kinds of additional financial commitments are usually found in stockholders' agreements?

Because in most cases, especially LBOs, the buyers do not intend to make further equity contributions to the corporation, the stockholders' agreement usually does not contain any provision for additional capital calls. However, where the corporation is in a volatile industry, or where the acquisition is highly leveraged, serious consideration should be given to requiring the stockholders to commit themselves to contributing additional equity to, making loans to, or extending personal guarantees on behalf of the corporation. In addition to the conditions under which such a commitment will be triggered, the extent to which any group of stockholders, such as the investor group, will assist the other stockholders in obtaining the funds to meet their commitment should also be incorporated in the stockholders' agreement.

What are some of the exit strategies typically embodied in a stockholders' agreement?

The following are the major kinds of provisions relating to opportunities for the stockholders to liquidate their investment:

- Voting provisions pursuant to which the stockholders agree to vote their shares in favor of any arm's-length merger or asset sale recommended by a certain group of stockholders (such as the investor stockholder group) or a certain percentage of all the stockholders
- The right to sell stock to any third-party person or entity, subject to the right of the corporation or the other stockholders to purchase the stock for the same terms offered by the third party (a "right of first refusal")
- The right of any stockholder to sell stock to any other stockholder
- The right of a stockholder to "tag along" with other stockholders, that is, to require a third-party offeror to purchase a pro rata portion of each stockholder's stock rather than purchase the same number of shares from the original offeree
- The right of any stockholder or group of stockholders to force along the other stockholders, that is, to sell their shares to a third-party offeror
- The right of a stockholder or his or her heirs to sell his or her stock to the corporation in the event of death, disability, or termination of employment
- The right of a stockholder to require the corporation to register his or her shares in a public offering

From management's point of view, what are the important negotiation points of a "buy/sell" arrangement upon termination of employment?

The following are crucial:

- *Mandatory versus optional requirement.* Management wants a mandatory obligation or, preferably, a "put," particularly in the case of death or disability.
- *Price.* Management wants fair market value, preferably at all times, but at least in the case of death, disability, retirement, or termination without cause.

- *Determination of price.* Management at least wants an opportunity to get an independent appraisal at the time a buyback is triggered.
- *Payment terms.* Management wants the payout period to be as short as possible, preferably in cash at the closing (particularly in case of death or disability).
- *Security for payment.* Unless premium payments would cripple the company, where the buyout price is significant or where acquisition loan agreements have low caps on the amount of noninsured buybacks the corporation can make, management wants the corporation to purchase life insurance and, if possible, disability insurance, to fund the buyback. In other cases involving deferred payments, management wants protections such as an opportunity to get the stock back free of transfer restrictions in the event of uncured payment defaults and prepayments out of the proceeds of public offerings.

As is the case with every contractual arrangement, each party must carefully consider the tax consequences associated with the various provisions under negotiation.

CONCLUDING COMMENTS

The documentation of a merger, acquisition, or buyout presents an opportunity to record the most important aspects of the transaction for the future. By following the guidance in this book, dealmakers can ensure that expectations are clear—a good start for any venture.

APPENDIX 7A

Sample Letter of Intent

STRICTLY PRIVATE AND CONFIDENTIAL
[Date]

Target Corporation
Corporate Office Park
New York, New York

To the Board of Directors:

This letter of intent sets forth the basic terms and conditions under which Acquisition, Inc. (the "Purchaser") will enter into a definitive merger agreement (the "Merger Agreement") with Target Corporation (the "Company") for the merger of the Purchaser with and into the Company (the "Merger"). It is anticipated that the consummation of the Merger will occur on or before ______, or on such other date to which the parties may agree.

Purchase Price

Pursuant to the Merger Agreement, upon consummation of the Merger, the selling stockholders of the Company will receive in exchange for each share of the

Company's common stock and preferred stock (the "Stock") outstanding as of the date of this letter:

(5)__________________ Dollars ($_______) in cash; and

(6) One share of preferred stock ("Preferred Stock") of the surviving corporation of the Merger with a liquidation preference in the amount of __________ Dollars ($______) and containing the terms set forth on Exhibit A hereto.

Conditions to Closing

The consummation of the Merger shall be subject to the satisfaction of the following conditions:

(a) the parties shall have received all required approvals and consents from governmental authorities and agencies and third parties;

(b) the Purchaser and the Company shall have executed on or prior to __________, a definitive Merger Agreement containing mutually acceptable provisions relating to, among other things, representations, warranties, conditions and indemnification;

(c) the truth and accuracy of all representations and warranties and the satisfaction of all conditions;

(d) the consummation of the Merger on or prior to ______________;

(e) Purchaser and certain members of management of the Company designated by Purchaser having entered into mutually satisfactory employment contracts simultaneously with the execution of the Merger Agreement;

(f) since ______________, [date of last audited balance sheet] the business of the Company and its subsidiary shall have been conducted in the ordinary course, and there shall have been no material adverse change in the business, prospects, operations, earnings, assets or financial condition of the Company and its subsidiaries;

(g) Purchaser shall have obtained financing in an amount and upon terms satisfactory to it to consummate the Merger; [and]

(h) there shall have been no dividend, redemption or similar distribution, or any stock split, recapitalization or stock issuance of any kind, by the Company since ________________, [date of last audited balance sheet] other than regularly scheduled dividends on the preferred stock.

General

After executing this letter and until _________________, the Company agrees, and shall use its best efforts to cause its officers, directors, employees, agents and stockholders, not to solicit or encourage, directly or indirectly, in any manner any discussion with, or furnish or cause to be furnished any information to, any person other than Purchaser in connection with, or negotiate for or otherwise pursue, the sale of the Stock of the Company or the capital stock of its subsidiaries, all or substantially all of the assets of the Company or its subsidiaries or any portion or all of its business or that of its subsidiaries, or any business combination or merger of the Company or its subsidiaries with any other party. You will promptly inform Purchaser of any inquiries or proposals with respect to the foregoing. [In the event that the agreements in this paragraph are violated by the Company or its officers, directors, employees, agents or stockholders, and Purchaser does not consummate the Merger, then, in addition to other remedies available to Purchaser, Purchaser shall be entitled to receive from the Company all out-of-pocket expenses (including reasonable attorneys' fees and expenses relating to the financing), which Purchaser has incurred.]

Neither of the parties to this letter shall disclose to the public or to any third party the existence of this letter or the proposed sale described herein other than with the express prior written consent of the other party, except as may be required by law.

From and after the date hereof, upon reasonable prior notice and during normal business hours, the Company will grant to each of Purchaser and its agents, employees and designees full and complete access to the books and records and personnel of the Company and its subsidiaries. Except as may be required by law or court order, all information so obtained, not otherwise already public, will be held in confidence.

[Except as provided herein,] each party will be responsible for its own expenses in connection with all matters relating to the transaction herein proposed. If this proposed transaction shall not be consummated for any reason other than a violation of the agreement not to solicit other offers or negotiate with other purchasers, neither party will be responsible for any of the other's expenses.

Each party will indemnify, defend and hold harmless the other against the claims of any brokers or finders claiming by, through or under the indemnifying party.

Except for matters relating to (i) the confidentiality of this proposal and the business operations of the Company and its subsidiary, (ii) the agreement not to negotiate with others for or otherwise pursue the sale of the Company or its subsidiary, and (iii) the agreement that each party will bear its own expenses in connection herewith, this letter does not create a binding, legal obligation on any party but merely represents the present intentions of the parties.

In the event that for any reason the definitive Merger Agreement is not executed by _______________, any party may discontinue negotiations and terminate this letter without liability to any other party.

Your signature below shall indicate your agreement with the foregoing letter of intent. We look forward to working with you on this transaction.

Very truly yours,

Acquisition, Inc.
By: ________________________________
Its: Vice President, Strategic Planning

Agreed to and Accepted this ______ day of _______________,

Target Corporation
By: _________________________
Its: __________________________

APPENDIX 7B

Typical Merger Agreement and Commentary

The following articles and sections typify the content of an acquisition agreement used in a merger.

RECITALS

ARTICLE I **THE BUSINESS COMBINATION**

Section 1.1	The Merger
Section 1.2	Stockholders' Meeting
Section 1.3	Filing of Articles of Merger; Effective Time
Section 1.4	Effect of Merger
Section 1.5	Certificate of Incorporation and Bylaws
Section 1.6	Directors
Section 1.7	Officers
Section 1.8	Alternate Structure of Merger
Section 1.9	Taking of Necessary Action

ARTICLE XIII	**NONCOMPETE**
ARTICLE XIV	**TERMINATION**
Section 14.1	Termination for Failure to Close on Time
Section 14.2	Default; Remedies
Section 14.3	Specific Performance
ARTICLE XV	**MISCELLANEOUS**
Section 15.1	Definitions
Section 15.2	Payment of Expenses
Section 15.3	Modifications or Waivers to the Agreement
Section 15.4	Assignment
Section 15.5	Burden and Benefit
Section 15.6	Brokers
Section 15.7	Entire Agreement
Section 15.8	Governing Law
Section 15.9	Notices
Section 15.10	Counterparts
Section 15.11	Rights Cumulative
Section 15.12	Severability of Provisions
Section 15.13	Further Assurance
Section 15.14	Confidential Information
Section 15.15	Writings and Disclosures

ARTICLE I: THE BUSINESS COMBINATION

The following is a discussion of the material items that are usually included in Article I of a merger agreement (the "Agreement"). The following section headings provide the topics frequently covered in this article.

Section 1.1	The Merger
Section 1.2	Stockholders' Meeting
Section 1.3	Filing of Articles of Merger; Effective Time

Section 1.4 Effect of Merger
Section 1.5 Certificate of Incorporation and Bylaws
Section 1.6 Directors
Section 1.7 Officers
Section 1.8 Alternate Structure of Merger
Section 1.9 Taking of Necessary Action

Article I of the Agreement typically (a) describes how the merger will be accomplished (the "Merger"), (b) identifies which corporation's legal existence will cease and which corporation will be the "Surviving Corporation" in the merger, and (c) identifies the state laws that will govern the surviving corporation's legal existence. This section also contains the agreement of the parties to meet the corporate legal requirements of the states of incorporation of the respective parties in order to obtain approval of the Merger.

The disappearing corporation frequently commits itself to call a special meeting of stockholders and to use its best efforts to obtain stockholder approval of the merger. These undertakings tend to be more elaborate where the disappearing corporation is a publicly held corporation and therefore must provide a proxy statement or information statement to its stockholders.

Once the stockholders of the disappearing corporation have approved the merger and the additional corporate actions and the conditions contained in Articles IX and X of the Agreement are satisfied, the Agreement provides that the articles of merger will be filed in the respective offices of the secretary of state (or comparable authority) of the states in which each corporation is incorporated. The merger will become effective upon such filing. The effect of the merger is described by reference to a section of the business corporation laws governing the corporate existence of each corporation involved in the transaction. Some states require the surviving corporation to appoint an agent for service of process if the surviving corporation will no longer be present or resident within the state following consummation of the merger. This requirement is intended to enable creditors in the state to continue to have recourse against the disappearing corporation. The merger will have no effect on the rights of creditors or on any liens on the property of either company; liens and debts of the disappearing corporation will become the obligations of the surviving corporation.

The parties stipulate in this article which corporation's articles and bylaws will apply to the surviving corporation and whether any changes or amendments to these documents will be made upon the consummation of the merger. The officers and directors of the surviving corporation may also be identified.

In order to preserve structural flexibility, the buyer can suggest the inclusion of language that gives the buyer the right to restructure the transaction for tax, financial, or other reasons. Because a change in the structure of the transaction could have a significant adverse impact on the seller if, for example, the direction of the merger were to be changed from downstream to upstream, the buyer and seller must reach a resolution that satisfies each of their concerns.

ARTICLE II: CONVERSION AND EXCHANGE OF SHARES

The following discussion pertains to the mechanics of the conversion of shares of the merging corporations and the transfer of the purchase price. The following section headings provide the topics generally covered in this article.

Section 2.1	Conversion of Shares
Section 2.2	Dissenting Stockholders
Section 2.3	Stock Transfer Books
Section 2.4	Surrender and Exchange of Stock Certificates
Section 2.5	Determination and Payment of Merger Payment

This article describes the manner in which shares in each of the merging corporations will be converted or, in the case of the surviving corporation, the number of shares that remain outstanding upon consummation of the merger. It also describes the nature of the cash or securities consideration to be received by each holder of stock of the nonsurviving corporation.

Where the disappearing corporation has a diverse group of stockholders, the buyer may wish to consider the potential effects of stockholders' exercise of their dissenters' or appraisal rights under the laws of a particular jurisdiction. In transactions where exercise of dissenters' rights may occur, the buyer should include a provision that describes the effect of the merger on such stockholders' rights and imposes an obligation upon the seller and target to give the buyer notice of any communications by stockholders with respect to their dissenters' or appraisal rights. The notice obligation is frequently included in the covenant section. The buyer should also attempt to procure for itself the opportunity to direct all negotiations and proceedings concerning these rights.

Also included in this article is the method of surrender and exchange of stock certificates that enables the stockholders of the disappearing corporation to receive the merger payment. For a closely held target this may simply involve the seller's surrender of the certificates to the buyer and the buyer's payment to the seller of the agreed-upon merger consideration. However, in the case of a public target or where the target has a significant number of stockholders, the method for surrender of certificates is somewhat more complicated. The buyer and target will agree that the stock transfer books of the target will be closed as of a particular time, usually the time of the filing of the certificate of merger with the secretary of state, and that stockholders must surrender their certificates to a paying agent that will be responsible for the disbursement of the merger payment. Typically, the buyer will agree that simultaneously with the consummation of the merger it will transfer the entire amount of the merger consideration to an account that will be administered by a paying agent. Funds in the account are then disbursed to the target's stockholders upon the surrender of their stock certificates. See Chapter 5 for a discussion concerning the timing of the payment of the merger consideration and the filing of the certificate of merger.

In the event that the target has outstanding preferred stock, options, warrants, or securities convertible into common stock, the buyer should make provision in this article for the effect that the merger will have on such securities. The buyer's preeminent concern in dealing with these securities is to extinguish through the merger, to the extent possible, any right that a third party may have to receive common stock of the surviving corporation and not be subject to any dilution as a result of the exercise or conversion of any such securities. This assures the buyer that it will hold 100 percent of the common stock of the surviving corporation immediately after the merger. In certain cases the terms of such securities require the surviving corporation to honor the holder's right to receive common stock; other securities merely fail to provide for their termination in the event of a merger. The buyer should always attempt to include, as a condition to the buyer's obligation to close the transaction, the agreement of all holders of such securities to surrender their securities for cancellation at the closing.

ARTICLE III: CLOSING

This article provides the date, time, and place for the closing of the transaction (the "Closing"). Typically, the parties agree to close the transaction at the offices of the legal counsel for the buyer. Closings generally commence early in the morning so that wire transfers of funds can be accomplished prior to the afternoon close of the federal wire. The parties further agree that at the closing the parties will deliver all of the documents and instruments required to be delivered by the acquisition agreement. (The date that the certificate of merger is filed with the appropriate officials governing the merger is referred to as the "Closing Date.") For a more detailed discussion of closing procedures, see Chapter 8.

ARTICLE IV: REPRESENTATIONS AND WARRANTIES OF SELLER AND TARGET

The representations and warranties included in this article are extremely comprehensive and may, in some instances, be inappropriate in light of the size of the transaction or the nature of the target's business.

In an acquisition of a publicly traded target, it would not be customary to include all of these representations and warranties. As previously mentioned, the reason for fewer representations and warranties in a public company context is that there is usually no one to sue after closing for a misrepresentation or breach of warranty. It is unrealistic for the buyer to expect to recover from thousands of public stockholders. Accordingly, some of the representations and warranties, which are of less importance to the buyer or not directly related to the buyer's ability to terminate the acquisition agreement because of certain adverse changes in the target, are frequently omitted. For example, the following seller/target representations and warranties are typically omitted in the acquisition of a publicly traded target:

Section 4.4	Title to Securities of Target and Subsidiaries
Section 4.9	Solvency
Section 4.10	Debt
Section 4.12	Product and Service Warranties and Reserves
Section 4.13	Reserves for Public Liability and Property Damage Claims
Section 4.18	Intellectual Property
Section 4.19	Assets Necessary to the Business
Section 4.21	Customers and Suppliers
Section 4.22	Competing Lines of Business
Section 4.23	Restrictive Covenants
Section 4.24	Books and Records
Section 4.25	Bank Accounts
Section 4.35	Investment Purpose
Section 4.36	Dealership and Franchises

The following language is typical of the seller/target representations and warranties sections in a merger agreement.

The Seller and the Target represent and warrant to Buyer as follows:

> ***Section 4.1. Organization; Subsidiaries and Other Ownership Interests.*** The Target and the Seller are each corporations duly organized, validly existing and in good standing under the laws of the jurisdiction of their incorporation. Section 4.1 of the disclosure statement of even date herewith delivered to Buyer by Seller (the "Disclosure Statement") sets forth the name of each Person (as defined in Article XII) in which the Target or any other Subsidiary (on a combined basis) owns or has the right to acquire, directly or indirectly, an equity interest or investment of ten percent (10) or more of the equity capital thereof or having a book value of more than ______________ Dollars ($_________) (a "Subsidiary"). Each Subsidiary

is duly organized, validly existing and in good standing under the laws of its jurisdiction of incorporation or organization. Each of the Target and the Subsidiaries has the corporate or other necessary power and authority to own and lease its properties and assets and to carry on its business as now being conducted and is duly qualified or licensed to do business as a foreign corporation or other entity and is in good standing in each jurisdiction in which the properties owned or leased by it or the nature of the business conducted by it makes such qualification or licensure necessary except where the failure to be so qualified or licensed and in good standing would not have a Material Adverse Effect. For purposes of this Agreement, the term Material Adverse Effect shall refer to any event which would have a material adverse effect on the financial condition, business, earnings, assets, prospects or condition of the Target and its Subsidiaries taken as a whole. Section 4.1 of the Disclosure Statement sets forth the name of each jurisdiction in which the Target and each Subsidiary are incorporated and is qualified to do business. The Target has delivered to the Buyer true and correct copies of its Certificate of Incorporation and Bylaws and true and correct copies of the certificate of incorporation or comparable charter documents and bylaws of each of the Subsidiaries. Except as set forth in Section 4.1 of the Disclosure Statement, neither the Target nor any Subsidiary owns any equity investment or other interest in any Person other than the equity capital of the Subsidiaries which are owned by the Target or a Subsidiary.

It is customary in acquisition agreements to have the seller and target warrant that the seller, the target, and its subsidiaries are duly organized, and that each is qualified to do business in every jurisdiction in which each is required to qualify. If the seller or the target is not duly organized, the acquisition agreement may not be binding against it since it will not have the authority to execute the document in a corporate capacity. The utility of this representation is often debated in a theoretical context but is rarely heavily negotiated. Underlying the debate is the following question: If the agreement is not binding on the seller or the target, whom do you sue and for what? The answer is not carved in stone; the buyer could probably sue the person who signed the document in an individual capacity for misrepresentation, although a sizable recovery is unlikely. More important, the buyer would certainly have the right to walk from the deal, and that right is the primary reason the buyer should require this representation.

It is also prudent for the buyer to know that the subsidiaries are duly organized and qualified to do business in order to be assured of the subsidiaries' ability to conduct business or maintain a suit in a particular jurisdiction.

The definition of subsidiaries in this provision is extremely broad, as it includes entities in which the target may only have a small equity interest. Depending upon the particular situation, the seller may want to increase the 10 percent ownership requirement in order to avoid making representations and warranties about entities with which it may not be overly familiar. In addition, the seller may wish to specifically exclude from this definition entities that are not material to the target.

> ***Section 4.2. Authorization.*** The execution, delivery and performance of this Agreement and any instruments or agreements contemplated herein to be executed, delivered and performed by Target or Seller (including without limitation [list important agreements to be executed on or before the Closing]) (the Related Instruments), and the consummation of the transactions contemplated hereby and thereby, have been duly adopted and approved by the Board of Directors and the Stockholders of the Target and the Board of Directors of the Seller, as the case may be. The Target and the Seller have all requisite power and authority to execute, deliver and perform this Agreement and the Related Instruments, as applicable, and to consummate the transactions contemplated hereby and in the Related Instruments. This Agreement has been and as of the Closing Date, and each of the Related Instruments will be, duly and validly authorized, executed and delivered on behalf of the Seller and the Target. This Agreement is and the Related Instruments will be as of the Closing Date, the valid and binding obligation of the Target and Seller, as applicable, enforceable against the Target or Seller, as the case may be, in accordance with their respective terms.

It is customary for the seller and target to represent to the buyer that the Agreement is properly authorized and enforceable. Certainly, the buyer is entitled to know that the seller and target have taken all the steps that are necessary to authorize the agreement and any documents that are material to the consummation of the transaction (referred to as the "Related Instruments") in order to ensure that such documents are binding. The Related Instruments might include a noncompete agreement, a separate purchase agreement relating to certain other assets, and other documents containing agreements between the parties that are special to the transaction and therefore are not specifically covered by a stock purchase, asset purchase, or merger agreement.

The most important aspect of this representation relates to enforceability of the agreement and Related Instruments, as this will directly affect the buyer's rights under these documents.

A similar issue arises here as was discussed in connection with Section 4.1. What damages would be recoverable by the buyer if the seller breached this representation? If the breach arises because the signatory to the document on behalf of the seller or the target did not have authority to bind that party, the buyer may have a cause of action against the signatory (if the signatory misrepresented his or her authority) or against the party on whose behalf the signatory executed the document (if such party knew of the misrepresentation, or if the acts of such party created the appearance of authority on the part of the signatory). In addition, the buyer faced with a seller or target who refuses to close the deal because the Agreement was not signed by an authorized agent may be able to force the seller or target to close the transaction if its acts created an appearance of authority, or if it ratified the Agreement after it was signed. Partial performance of the terms of the deal—application for regulatory approval, permitting continued due diligence investigation, or complying with representations requiring the consent of the buyer to certain actions by the target, for example—may provide convincing evidence of such ratification. In any event, the buyer would definitely have the right to refuse to close the transaction.

In a representation by the seller that an agreement is enforceable, the seller may request the inclusion of an exception for certain future events that are beyond its control. For example, a court applying bankruptcy laws or equitable principles may not honor the express terms of the documents if such terms are not in accordance with the principles of bankruptcy or equity. Although the seller may have a basis for arguing for the inclusion of this exception, it seems unfair for the buyer to bear this risk. If the documents prove to be unenforceable in some respect against the seller, the buyer should be able, at least, to attempt to recover damages for this misrepresentation, rather than be forced to waive rights in the case of bankruptcy.

Section 4.3. Capitalization of Target and Subsidiaries.

(i) The authorized, issued and outstanding shares of the Target's capital stock consist of ____________________ shares of common stock, $ ____________________ par value per share, of which __________ shares are issued and outstanding [and any other shares, such as preferred stock] (the "Company Capital Stock"). The issued and outstanding shares of the Company Capital Stock are duly authorized, validly issued and fully paid and nonassessable and were not issued in violation of the preemptive rights of any person or of any agreement, law or regulation by which the issuer of such shares at the time of issuance was bound. The authorized, issued and outstanding equity capital of each Subsidiary is listed in Section 4.3(i) of the Disclosure Statement. The outstanding shares of, and the outstanding units of equity capital of, the Subsidiaries have been duly authorized, validly issued and are fully paid and non-assessable. Neither the Target nor any Subsidiary has issued any securities, or taken any action or omitted to take any action, giving rise to claims for violation of federal or state securities laws or the securities laws of any other jurisdiction.

(ii) Except as set forth in Section 4.3(ii) of the Disclosure Statement, at the date hereof there is no option, warrant, call, convertible security, arrangement, agreement or commitment of any character, whether oral or written, relating to any security of, or phantom security interest in, the Target or any Subsidiary, and there are no voting trusts or other agreements or understandings with respect to the voting of the capital stock of the Target or the equity capital of any Subsidiary.

A representation that requires that a seller set forth the capitalization of the target and its subsidiaries is rarely negotiated. Rather, discussions between the buyer and seller generally involve the factual circumstances surrounding the matter being represented. In order for a buyer to understand the effect of its purchase of the capital stock of the target (including the capital stock of the subsidiaries), it must be aware of the capital structure of the target and its subsidiaries.

Section 4.4. Title to Securities of Target and Subsidiaries.

(i) Except as set forth in Section 4.4(i) of the Disclosure Statement, the Seller has good and valid title to all of the issued and outstanding shares of the Company Capital Stock free and clear of all claims, liens, mortgages, charges, security interests, encumbrances and other restrictions or limitations of any kind whatsoever (other than pursuant to this Agreement). The

Seller is not party to, or bound by, any other agreement, instrument or understanding restricting the transfer of such shares.

(ii) Except as set forth in Section 4.4(ii) of the Disclosure Statement and other than pursuant to this Agreement, the issued and outstanding units of equity capital of each of the Subsidiaries are owned by the Persons listed as owner on Section 4.4(ii) of the Disclosure Statement, in each case free of preemptive rights and free and clear of all claims, liens, mortgages, charges, security interests, encumbrances and other restrictions or limitations of any kind whatsoever.

Generally, a buyer entering into an acquisition agreement is acquiring the entire company. Therefore, it is essential that the buyer know that it is purchasing all of the outstanding capital securities of the target, and that no one can challenge its ownership thereof after closing.

Section 4.5. Financial Statements and Projections.

(i) Seller has furnished to Buyer true and complete copies of the audited consolidated financial statements (including balance sheets, statements of income, statements of changes in stockholder's equity and statements of changes in financial position) of the Target and its Subsidiaries as of and for the years ended [fill in fiscal year-end for last five years] accompanied by the related opinions of the Target's official independent auditors as of such dates and for such periods (collectively, the "Financial Statements"). The Financial Statements, together with the notes thereto, fairly present the consolidated financial position of the Target and its Subsidiaries at the dates of, and the combined results of the operations and the changes in stockholders' equity and financial position for each of the Target and its Subsidiaries for the periods covered by, such Financial Statements in accordance with generally accepted accounting principles ("GAAP") consistently applied with prior periods except as indicated in the accompanying opinion of the official independent auditors. Seller has furnished to Buyer true and complete copies of the unaudited consolidated and consolidating balance sheets of the Target and its Subsidiaries as at [fill in the date of the most recent quarterly or fiscal period then ended] (the "Most Recent Balance Sheet") and the related consolidated and consolidating statements of income, statements of changes in stockholders' equity and statements of changes in financial position of the Target and its Subsidiaries as of and for the period then ended (collectively, the "Unaudited Financial Statements"). The Unaudited Financial Statements fairly present the financial position of the Target and its Subsidiaries at the date of, and the consolidated results of the operations and the changes in stockholders' equity and financial position for the Target and of its Subsidiaries for the period then ended. Such Unaudited Financial Statements have been prepared in accordance with GAAP consistently applied with prior periods, except that the Unaudited Financial Statements do not contain any or all of the footnotes required by GAAP, are condensed and are subject to year-end adjustments consistent with prior practice.

(ii) Seller has delivered to Buyer true and correct copies of the projected balance sheets of the Target for the fiscal years ending [fill in appropriate information], and the related statements of projected earnings and projected cash flow for the periods then ended (the "Projected Financial Statements"). The Projected Financial Statements are reasonable and mathematically accurate, and the assumptions underlying such projections provide a reasonable basis for such projections. The factual data used to prepare the Projected Financial Statements are true and correct in all material respects.

Generally, the most important representation that a buyer must require of the seller is that the consolidated financial statements of the target fairly present the financial condition of the target in accordance with GAAP. Almost every other representation in an acquisition agreement is in some way related to the financial statements of the target. For example, representations relating to receivables, inventory, real property, and tangible and intangible assets and liabilities concern items that are included on the balance sheet of the target to the extent required by GAAP. Accordingly, although the financial statement representations are somewhat standard in their format, they are vital to the buyer because the buyer has based its entire investment decision on either the overall financial condition of the target or certain financial characteristics of the target such as operating performance or net assets. As a result, the financial statements are usually the basis for fixing the purchase price of the target. Although situations exist where financial statements are less vital to the buyer's investment decision (for example, in the purchase of a start-up company), such statements are usually of critical importance.

The financial statement representation is usually not the subject of intense negotiation. The most frequently negotiated aspects of this representation relate to the kind of financial statements to be included in this representation and the periods to be covered by such financial statements. For example, will the financial statements that are the subject of the representation include balance sheets, operating statements, statements of changes in financial position, and stockholders' equity? Will the seller warrant the accuracy of historical financial statements covering a five-year period? Another area of discussion may relate to specific problems in preparing the financial statements that require the buyer to grant certain exceptions from GAAP. This problem usually arises when the buyer is already aware of the target's accounting problems. However, exceptions from GAAP can have the effect of diminishing the reliability of the financial statements. The determination whether the buyer is entitled to certain financial statements or should accept statements not prepared in accordance with GAAP depends on what information about the target was provided to the buyer prior to striking a deal with the seller, and what the buyer honestly relied on when it made its decision to purchase the target.

In many circumstances, the seller has provided the buyer with projected financial statements of the target. In such cases, if the buyer has relied on them, it is prudent for the buyer to have the seller warrant the reasonableness of the assumptions used in the preparation of the projected financial statements and the accuracy of the financial data underlying such projections. This representation is frequently negotiated and will certainly be more difficult to obtain from the seller than representations regarding the historical financial statements of the target. The reason for this is that projections, no matter how reasonable the assumptions that underlie them, are always the subject of hindsight. For example, a buyer might claim a breach of this representation if, one year after Closing, the target fails to meet its projections. The buyer would argue that the projections were obviously based upon unreasonable assumptions given the postclosing performance of the target. The decision whether or not this representation should be pursued is, like decisions related to historical financials, largely dependent on the degree of the buyer's reliance on these projections in its decision to buy the target. If the buyer is heavily relying on the projections, which may very well be the case if the target is a company that does not have a long operating history, then this representation should be vigorously pursued. In addition, this representation will commonly be found in loan agreements and lenders will be able to gain some additional comfort from the buyer's right of action back to the seller on this representation.

Section 4.6. Absence of Undisclosed Liabilities. As of the date hereof and as of the Closing Date, except as and to the extent reflected, reserved against or otherwise disclosed on the Most Recent Balance Sheet or the notes thereto, or set forth in Section 4.6 of the Disclosure Statement, or otherwise properly disclosed in any other Section of the Disclosure Statement and except for those incurred in the ordinary course of business, the Target and its Subsidiaries did not have and do not have, any indebtedness or liability of any nature, whether accrued, absolute, contingent or otherwise, whether due or to become due, which is in excess of _______________ Dollars ($_____________).

The absence of undisclosed liabilities is by and large a representation that serves as a catchall for any and all liabilities of the target and its subsidiaries that were not reflected on the Most Recent Balance Sheet of the target or the notes thereto, or were not otherwise disclosed pursuant to any of the other representations in the acquisition agreement. A smart seller should never agree to this representation without some resistance. To begin with, why should the seller (after having made numerous representations about the target) now be asked to warrant something the buyer may have failed to ask the seller to disclose? The answer is one that relates to a shifting of risk. Who should bear the risk of the buyer's omission? There is no clear answer, except that if the seller has agreed to the concept that it will generally warrant that the Most Recent Balance Sheet includes all liabilities of any kind or nature, then this representation does little more than provide additional comfort for the buyer.

If the seller had not made that general warranty, the buyer should be aware that many liabilities need not be disclosed on a balance sheet of the target prepared in accordance with GAAP. For example, when the amount of a liability cannot be determined because of its nature, such as a lawsuit the outcome of which is uncertain, GAAP would not require its disclosure. (See ASC 450.)[19] If the target is subject to off-balance-sheet liabilities, this representation provides the buyer with much more than an additional assurance.

Another aspect of this representation that may be difficult to negotiate with the seller is the period of time to be covered by the representation. A buyer often wants protection against material liabilities beyond the date of the Most Recent Balance Sheet. This may be a problem for the seller, since it has no financial statements to rely on for that period. The seller may be able to supply a balance sheet that is current as of the closing. If this is not possible, and if the buyer fails to persuade the seller to warrant the period after the date of the Most Recent Balance Sheet, the buyer must rely on the covenants (operation of the business in the ordinary course; see Section 6.1) or the conditions (material adverse change; see Section 9.6) as its way of addressing undisclosed liabilities.

In light of the nature of this representation it would be overreaching not to incorporate an exclusion for minimal undisclosed liabilities. Accordingly, the form of representation set forth here contains a blank amount for such an exclusion. The dollar amount of this exclusion is negotiable and usually depends upon the size of the target and its subsidiaries. For example, in an acquisition of an extremely large company, the buyer would find it extremely difficult to justify an exclusion of only $1,000 for undisclosed liabilities.

> ***Section 4.7. Accounts Receivable.*** Seller has delivered, or shall deliver at Closing, to Buyer a list of all accounts receivable of the Target and its Subsidiaries as at [fill in appropriate date] (the "Accounts Receivable"), which list is true, correct and complete in all material respects and sets forth the aging of such Accounts Receivable. All Accounts Receivable of the Target and its Subsidiaries represent sales actually made or services actually performed in the ordinary and usual course of their business consistent with past practice. Since the date of the Most Recent Balance Sheet, (A) no event has occurred that would, under the practices of the Target or the Subsidiary in effect when the Most Recent Balance Sheet was prepared, require a material increase in the ratio of (I) the reserve for uncollectible accounts receivable to (II) the accounts receivable of the Target or the Subsidiary, and (B) there has been no material adverse change in the composition of such Accounts Receivable in terms of aging. There is no contest, claim or right of set-off contained in any written agreement with any account debtor relating to the amount or validity of any Account Receivable, or any other account receivable created after the date of the Most Recent Balance Sheet, other

than accounts receivable which do not exceed, in the aggregate, the reserve for uncollected accounts. At the date of the Most Recent Balance Sheet, as of the date hereof and as of the Effective Time of the Merger, all accounts receivable of the Target and the Subsidiary, if any, were, are and will be, respectively, unless previously collected, valid and collectible and there is no contest, claim or right of set-off contained in any written agreement with any maker of an account receivable relating to the amount or validity of such account or any note evidencing the same.

In instances where the Most Recent Balance Sheet reflects a significant amount of receivables, the buyer should require this representation in order to get specific protection that the receivables of the target and its subsidiaries are collectible. A representation with respect to the receivables of the target is sometimes unnecessary depending upon the type of company that is being acquired. For example, if the company that is being acquired entered into a factoring arrangement with respect to all of its receivables, then this representation may be altogether unnecessary or to a great degree simplified. Conversely, the buyer purchasing assets may, in circumstances where the collectability of the accounts is in doubt, require the seller to guarantee the buyer's ability to collect the receivables.

Section 4.8. Most Recent Inventory. The inventories of the Target and the Subsidiaries on a consolidated basis as reflected on the Most Recent Balance Sheet consist only of items in good condition and salable or usable in the ordinary course of business, except to the extent of the inventory reserve included on the Most Recent Balance Sheet, which reserve is adequate for such purpose. Such inventories are valued on the Most Recent Balance Sheet at the lower of cost or market in accordance with GAAP.

In the event that the company to be acquired is engaged in manufacturing or is otherwise involved in the distribution of goods whether retail or wholesale, it is extremely important for the buyer to have the seller make a specific representation with respect to the inventory of the target and its subsidiaries. A buyer needs to understand the relationship between the value of the inventory reflected on the Most Recent Balance Sheet and the condition of the inventory. Items that are or may become obsolete should be reserved against on the Most

Recent Balance Sheet. In addition, it is important for the buyer to know whether the valuation of inventory on the financial statements reflects its actual value. Accordingly, the seller's representation that inventories are valued at the lower of cost or market in accordance with GAAP will assure the buyer that the inventories are valued in the most conservative fashion. In some cases, the buyer may include a representation that a particular dollar amount is the minimum value of the target's inventories. That type of representation is more common in an asset purchase.

> ***Section 4.9. Solvency.*** The Seller and each of the Target and its Subsidiaries is on the date hereof, and immediately prior to the Closing Date will be, Solvent. "Solvent" shall mean, in respect of an entity, that (i) the fair value of its property is in excess of the total amount of its debts and (ii) it is able to pay its debts as they mature.

Aside from the obvious pricing implications of acquiring an insolvent corporation, one of the primary purposes of obtaining a solvency representation from a seller regarding the target and its subsidiaries is that lenders providing acquisition debt often require such a representation from the buyer. Especially in leveraged buyouts, one of the principal concerns of lenders is the solvency of the leveraged company because transfers (for example, security interests granted to lenders) from insolvent companies are voidable as fraudulent conveyances. Although the leveraged surviving corporation may certainly be in a more precarious position than the target, this representation provides the initial base from which the buyer will attempt to satisfy its lenders on the solvency issue.

The solvency representation regarding the seller is intended to protect the buyer against the risk of acquiring the target and its subsidiaries in a transaction that could be characterized as a fraudulent conveyance by the seller. A buyer's decision to include the seller in the solvency representation must be based upon the financial condition of the seller, the extent to which the target and its subsidiaries constitute a substantial portion of the seller's assets and the seller's ability to pay its debts as they mature after the sale of the target and its subsidiaries.

> ***Section 4.10. Debt.*** Set forth in Section 4.10 of the Disclosure Statement is a list of all agreements for incurring of indebtedness for borrowed money and all agreements relating to industrial development bonds to which the Target is a party or grantor, which list is true and correct in all material respects. Except as set forth in Section 4.10 of the Disclosure Statement, none of the obligations pursuant to such agreements are subject to acceleration by reason of the consummation of the transactions contemplated hereby, nor would the execution of this Agreement or the consummation of the transactions contemplated hereby result in any default under such agreements.

This representation serves to break down the debt components of the Most Recent Balance Sheet that relate to debt for money borrowed. It also requires the seller to identify debt items that may be accelerated by reason of the consummation of the transactions contemplated by the Agreement. Because this representation has an information-gathering purpose, it is not usually negotiable.

> ***Section 4.11. Fairness Opinion.*** The Target has received an opinion of [name of independent and nationally recognized investment banker], dated the date hereof, addressed to the Target and has delivered a copy of such opinion to Buyer to the effect that, as of the date of the Agreement, the consideration per share to be received by the holders of the Target's Common Stock in the Merger is fair to the holders of the Target's Common Stock from a financial point of view. The Target believes that it is justified in relying upon such opinion.

The buyer should attempt to include this representation where the target has a significant number of stockholders or is a publicly traded company. The buyer should require the target to obtain a fairness opinion because, after consummation of the merger, the buyer will succeed to the target's liabilities, including liabilities that may result from stockholder suits against the target or its officers and directors alleging that the merger price was inadequate. Liabilities could result where stockholders have exercised dissenter's or appraisal rights and sued the target directly or have instituted a derivative suit against officers or directors who are indemnified by the target.

The last sentence of the representation regarding reliance is intended to elicit from the target any facts that might undermine the validity of the opinion, such as facts not disclosed to the investment bankers or knowledge of conflicts of interest that might tend to bias the opinion. Several factors make this reliance representation important. First, investment bankers typically require indemnification in connection with rendering fairness opinions, and the buyer will succeed to any liability of the target to its investment bankers after the merger. Second, although a target might argue that the buyer is in a position to evaluate the reasonableness of the opinion based on the representations of the target in the Agreement and on its own financial investigation of the target, the buyer is not privy to all the circumstances involving the preparation and delivery of the fairness opinion. Consequently, the buyer should not be reticent about making inquiries into the fairness opinion process and the manner in which the target has attempted to satisfy itself that the opinion rendered is reasonable.

> ***Section 4.12. Product and Service Warranties and Reserves.*** Except as disclosed in Section 4.12 of the Disclosure Statement, the amount of any and all product warranty claims relating to sales occurring on or prior to the Most Recent Balance Sheet Date shall not exceed the amount of the product warranty reserve included on the Most Recent Balance Sheet, which reserve was prepared in accordance with GAAP consistently applied and which the Target believes is adequate in light of any and all circumstances relating to its warranties of which it was aware and the amounts actually paid by it for product warranty claims. The only express warranties, written or oral, including without limitation [insert warranty], with respect to the products or services sold by the Target and its Subsidiaries, are as set forth in Section 4.12 of the Disclosure Statement.

One area that may expose a buyer to tremendous liability is product and service warranties made by the target or any subsidiary. A seller is required under GAAP to have "adequate" reserves on its balance sheet to cover such liabilities, but this standard is a very subjective one. Accordingly, a prudent buyer should have the seller specifically warrant the accuracy of this element of the Most Recent Balance Sheet. In addition, the buyer should be apprised of any and all of the warranties made and reserves held by the target so that the buyer can make its own determination of the adequacy of the target's reserves. In certain situations, a buyer may require specific representations setting forth the annual amount paid in satisfaction of claims under a particular product warranty. Gambling on the law of averages, the buyer may derive some degree of comfort.

> ***Section 4.13. Reserve for Public Liability and Property Damage Claims.*** The amount of the public liability, property damage and personal injury reserve included on the Most Recent Balance Sheet was prepared in accordance with GAAP consistently applied and the Target reasonably believes such reserve is adequate.

A buyer may be concerned about this type of liability if it is foreseeable that the target or a subsidiary could have exposure above and beyond the limits of its insurance policies. Similar to the product warranty reserve discussed in Section 4.12, the adequacy of this reserve is a subjective judgment.

> ***Section 4.14. Insurance.*** Set forth in Section 4.14 of the Disclosure Statement is a complete and correct schedule of all currently effective insurance policies or binders of insurance or programs of self-insurance which relate to the Target and its Subsidiaries, which insurance is with financially sound and reputable insurance companies, against such casualties, risks and contingencies, and in such types and amounts, as are consistent with customary practices and standards of companies engaged in businesses similar to the Target and its Subsidiaries. The coverage under each such policy and binder is in full force and effect, and no notice of cancellation or nonrenewal with respect to, or disallowance of any claim under, or material increase of premium for, any such policy or binder has been received by the Target or its Subsidiaries, nor to the Seller. Neither the Target, the Seller nor the Subsidiaries has knowledge of any facts or the occurrence of any event which (i) reasonably might form the basis of any claim against the Target or the Subsidiaries relating to the conduct or operations of the business of the Target or the Subsidiaries or any of the assets or properties covered by any of the policies or binders set forth in Section 4.14 of the Disclosure Statement and which will materially increase the insurance premiums payable under any such policy or binder, or (ii) otherwise will materially increase the insurance premiums payable under such policy or binder.

A representation with respect to the insurance policies of the target is important to the buyer in order to safeguard the assets it is buying against a variety of damage claims. Since the buyer may be unaware of what type of insurance should be carried by the target, the seller should warrant that the target has all of the insurance that is customary for the business of the target and its subsidiaries. The seller will not usually quarrel about this part of the representation; what troubles the seller most is the buyer's desire for assurances that the premiums for such insurance will not increase dramatically because of an event or claim that the seller may be aware of. How can the seller be certain what events will increase the premiums? In a clear case—where the seller has recently become aware that its product is carcinogenic, for example—the seller should be aware that its insurance premiums will obviously increase dramatically when this fact comes to the attention of its insurance companies. The buyer should also investigate whether such policies will survive after the acquisition, since many policies lapse on a change of control of the target or, in some cases, a buyer may be prudent to include a representation by the seller stating that such policies will survive after the acquisition.

A second important consideration is whether the insurance policies are "claims made" or "claims incurred" policies. The difference between these types of policies is that a "claims made" policy covers only those claims that are made to the insurance company while the policy was in full force and effect, whereas a "claims incurred" policy covers all claims made at any time, provided that the events giving rise to a liability occurred during the time the policy was in full force and effect.

Lastly, if insurance is an important aspect of the business and a certain portion of the insurance consists of self-insurance, the buyer should factor this in when analyzing the cost of running the business. In the event the buyer wishes to continue to self-insure, the buyer should require the seller's cooperation in obtaining any regulatory approvals necessary to continue to self-insure the operations of the target.

> ***Section 4.15. Real Property Owned or Leased.*** Section 4.15 of the Disclosure Statement sets forth a complete and accurate list or description of all real property (including a general description of fixtures located at such property and specific identification of any such fixtures not owned by the Target or any Subsidiary) which the Target or any Subsidiary owns

> or leases, has agreed (or has an option) to purchase, sell or lease, or may be obligated to purchase, sell or lease and any title insurance or guarantee policies with respect thereto, specifying in the case of leases, the name of the lessor, licensor or other grantor, the approximate square footage covered thereunder, the basic annual rental and other amounts paid or payable with respect thereto and a summary of the other terms thereof. True copies of all such leases for real property with aggregate annual rental payments (excluding payments to third parties on account of real estate taxes (or increases therein), insurance, operating costs, or common area expenses), individually in excess of __________________ Dollars ($___________) (including all amendments thereof and modifications thereto) have been delivered to Buyer prior to the date hereof. Except as set forth in Section 4.15 of the Disclosure Statement, no consent to the consummation of the transactions contemplated by this Agreement is required from the lessor of any such real property.

The scheduling of real property serves to support the buyer's due diligence efforts by identifying each property owned or leased by the target or any subsidiary. In requesting disclosure of leases, consideration should be given to the dollar threshold in annual rental payments that identifies a lease that the target must disclose. For smaller targets, it may be appropriate to include no threshold at all, requiring the disclosure of all leases of real property.

This representation is also designed to elicit disclosure of both (i) obligations for periodic payments or capital commitments that have been incurred by the target or any subsidiary, and (ii) those leases where landlord consents may be required to avoid lease terminations by virtue of the acquisition. Rental commitments and agreements to purchase will have an impact on the cash flow requirements of the target but may not have been apparent to the buyer from a review of the target's financial statements.

The buyer should require the annual lease payment information in order to prepare a cash flow analysis. In addition, this disclosure will aid a buyer who is trying to determine the financeability of the target's and subsidiaries' real estate and the necessity of obtaining appraisals of the real estate to assist its financing efforts.

Section 4.16 Fixed Assets; Leased Assets.

(i) Section 4.16(i) of the Disclosure Statement sets forth a complete and accurate list or description of all equipment, machinery and other items of tangible personal property which the Target or any Subsidiary owns or leases, has agreed (or has an option) to purchase, sell or lease, or may be obligated to purchase, sell or lease having a book value of _____________ Dollars ($__________) or more or requiring annual rental payments in excess of ______________ Dollars ($ __________), specifying in the case of leases, the name of the lessor, licensor or other grantor, the description of the property covered thereby, the basic annual rental and other amounts paid or payable with respect thereto and a summary of the other terms thereof. True copies of all leases for such assets with aggregate rental payments individually in excess of ______________ Dollars ($ __________) (including all amendments thereto and modifications thereof) have been delivered to Buyer prior to the date hereof. The book value of all such assets owned or leased by the Target and its Subsidiaries not included on such list does not, in the aggregate, exceed ______________ Dollars ($ __________) at the date hereof.

(ii) Except as set forth in Section 4.16(ii) of the Disclosure Statement, no consent to the consummation of the transactions contemplated by this Agreement is required from the lessor, licensor or other grantor of any such tangible personal property.

As with the representation relating to real estate in Section 4.15, this representation elicits disclosure of each item of tangible personal property owned or leased by the target or any subsidiary that has a value or annual cost in excess of a given dollar threshold. Unlike the real property representation, where the buyer may reasonably request and be interested in information on each piece of real property owned by the target or any subsidiary, requesting disclosure of every item of tangible personal property absent a dollar threshold would impose an unreasonable burden on the seller and would subject the seller to the risk of misrepresentation in the event an asset were inadvertently omitted.

This risk will motivate the seller to negotiate for a higher dollar threshold. A buyer may determine that it can live with a dollar threshold on the book value of owned assets but must require a lower amount in respect of lease obligations since the latter will have a direct impact on cash flow projections. The buyer, in any event, should base its threshold on the individual value of assets that it deems relevant to any financing that may be necessary for it to finance the purchase price.

Section 4.17. Title and Related Matters.

(i) Subject to the exceptions contained in the second sentence of this Section 4.17, the Target or a Subsidiary has, and immediately after giving effect to the transactions contemplated hereby will have, good and marketable title (or, in jurisdictions where title insurance policies insuring good and marketable title are not available, good and indefeasible title, or good and merchantable title or some quality of title substantially equivalent thereto) to or a valid leasehold interest in (a) all of the properties and assets reflected in the Most Recent Balance Sheet or acquired after the date of the appropriate Most Recent Balance Sheet by the Target or a Subsidiary, (b) all properties or assets which are subject to operating leases as defined in ASC 842 and are not reflected in the Most Recent Balance Sheet, and (c) all other properties and assets owned or utilized by the Target or any Subsidiary in the conduct of their respective businesses. All properties and assets referred to in the preceding sentence are presently owned or held by the Target or a Subsidiary, and at and immediately after the Closing Date, will be held by the Target or a Subsidiary, free and clear of all title defects or objections, mortgages, liens, pledges, charges, security interests, options to purchase or other encumbrances of any kind or character, except: (v) liens for current taxes not yet due and payable; (w) liens, imperfections of title and easements which do not, either individually or in the aggregate, materially detract from the value of, or interfere with the present use of, the properties subject thereto or affected thereby, or otherwise materially impair the operations of the entity which owns, leases or utilizes such property or materially impair the use of such property by such entity; (x) mortgages and liens securing debt which is reflected as a liability on the Most Recent Balance Sheet; (y) mechanics,' carriers,' workmen's, repairmen's and other similar liens arising or incurred in the ordinary course of business; and (z) as set forth in Section 4.17(i) of the Disclosure Statement.

(ii) All the plants, structures, facilities, machinery, equipment, automobiles, trucks, tools and other properties and assets owned or leased by the Target and the Subsidiaries, including but not limited to such as are reflected in the Most Recent Balance Sheet or acquired after the respective dates of the Most Recent Balance Sheet by the Target or a Subsidiary are structurally sound with no defects known to Seller and in good operating condition and repair (except for routine immaterial maintenance in the ordinary course of business) and usable in a manner consistent with their current use.

(iii) All leases pursuant to which the Target and the Subsidiaries lease (as lessee) real and/or personal property are valid and enforceable by the Target or a Subsidiary in accordance with their respective terms; other than with respect to property which has been sublet by the Target or the Subsidiaries as noted on Section 4.17(iii) of the Disclosure Statement, the Target or a Subsidiary has been in peaceable possession since the commencement of the original term of each such lease; except for the tenancies in respect of property being sublet, as specified in the second clause of this sentence, there are no tenancies or other possessory interests with respect to any real or personal property owned by the Target or any Subsidiary; all rents due under, or other amounts required to be paid by the terms of, each such lease have been paid; and there is not under any of such leases, to Seller's knowledge, any default (or event which, with the giving of notice, the passage of time or both, would constitute a default), waiver or postponement of any of the Target's or any Subsidiary's obligations thereunder.

(iv) Except as stated in Section 4.17(iv) of the Disclosure Statement, none of the real property owned or leased by the Target or any Subsidiary is subject to any governmental decree or order to be sold and there is no condemnation or eminent domain proceeding pending, or, to the best of Seller's knowledge, threatened, against any real property owned or leased by the Target or any Subsidiary or any part thereof, and neither Target nor any Subsidiary has made a commitment or received any notice, oral or written, of the desire of any public authority or any entity to take or use the real property owned or leased by the Target or any Subsidiary or any part thereof, whether temporarily or permanently, for easements, rights-of-way, or other public or quasi-public purposes, or for any other purpose whatsoever, nor is there any proceeding pending, or threatened in writing or by publication, or, to the best knowledge of the Seller, threatened, which could adversely affect, as to any portion of any parcel of the real property owned or leased by the Target or any Subsidiary, the zoning classification in effect on the date hereof. On the Closing Date, the real property owned or leased by the Target and its Subsidiaries shall be free and clear of any management, leasing, maintenance, security or service obligations other than utilities and except those incurred in the ordinary course of business.

(v) All rights-of-way, easements, licenses, permits and authorizations in any manner related to the location or operation of the business of the Target and the Subsidiaries are in good standing, valid and enforceable in all material respects in accordance with their respective terms. Except as stated in Section 4.17(v) of the Disclosure Statement, neither the Target nor any Subsidiary is in violation of any, and each has complied with all, applicable zoning, building or other codes, statutes, regulations, ordinances, notices and orders of any governmental agency with respect to the occupancy, use, maintenance, condition and operation of the real property owned or leased by the Target and its Subsidiaries or any material portion of any parcel thereof, and the use of any improvements for all purposes for which the real property owned or leased by the Target and its Subsidiaries is being used on the date hereof will not violate any such code, statute, regulation, ordinance, notice or order. The Target and the Subsidiaries possess and shall maintain in effect all licenses, certificates of occupancy, permits and authorizations required to operate and maintain the real property owned or leased by the Target and its Subsidiaries for all uses for which the real property owned or leased by the Target and its Subsidiaries is operated on the date hereof. Except as stated in Section 4.17(v) of the Disclosure Statement, no equipment installed or located in any part of the real property owned or leased by the Target and its Subsidiaries violates any law, ordinance, order, regulation or requirement of any governmental authority which violation would have an adverse effect on the real property owned or leased by the Target or any Subsidiary or any portion of any parcel thereof.

Title to the property owned by the target and its subsidiaries is important for the purpose of verifying the value and financeability of the assets acquired. It is useful to include within the scope of the title representations assets leased under operating leases, as these assets will generally not be disclosed on a balance sheet and may represent significant value if the target's rental payments are below market rates, especially if the target's leasehold interest is mortgageable.

An acquisition lender advancing funds on a secured basis will require the buyer to make extensive representations regarding the quality of its title to the assets securing the loan. The buyer should therefore attempt to obtain as much comfort on the existence of liens and encumbrances from the seller as possible. Not only is it important to elicit in the Disclosure Statement all liens that might have an impact on the buyer's ability to obtain sufficient financing, but the buyer must also carefully review the liens disclosed and assess the degree to which the liens impair financeability of the assets of the target and its subsidiaries. Close scrutiny may reveal the existence of liens that limit marketability and prevent the buyer from providing its lender with a first priority security interest. Once these liens have been identified, the buyer may wish to require as its condition to closing that certain liens be discharged.

As an alternative to having the seller schedule existing liens (as is the approach in the second sentence of paragraph (i)), the buyer could permit an exception for "liens, imperfections of title and easements which do not, either individually or in the aggregate, materially detract from the value of, or interfere with the present value of, the properties subject thereto or affected thereby, or otherwise materially impair the operations of the entity which owns, leases or utilizes such property or materially impair the use of such property by such entity." In addition, the materiality standard might be made more definite by referring to a lien or imposition in excess of a specified dollar amount. However, although a materiality exception may provide sufficient protection to the buyer vis-à-vis the seller, a lender may find it unacceptable. The buyer employing the exception must be willing to take on the risk that a lender may, through certain loan representations and covenants, require the discharge of liens that are not material to either the seller or the buyer.

The representations in paragraphs (ii) and (iii) are intended to assure the buyer that the assets to be acquired are in good operating condition and that the target's and subsidiaries' leases are enforceable and not in default.

Paragraphs (iv) and (v) attempt to verify that no violations or proceedings exist that might prevent the buyer from using the real estate acquired as it had been used in the past by the target and the subsidiaries. The seller may seek to limit the statement about existing violations by imposing a materiality standard. A buyer might well concede this point; a useful compromise position might be to require the representation that any violation would not result in an award of damages, or require expenditures to remedy the violation, in excess of a specified dollar amount.

Section 4.18. Intellectual Property.

(i) Section 4.18(i) of the Disclosure Statement sets forth a complete and accurate list, including, where applicable, the date of registration or expiration, serial or registration number or patent number, of all United States (including the individual states and territories of the United States) and foreign registered trademarks, service marks and trade names; unregistered trademarks, service marks and trade names; trademark, service mark and trade name applications; product designations; designs; unexpired patents; pending and filed patent applications; current and active invention disclosures; inventions on which disclosures are to be prepared; trade secrets; registered copyrights; and unregistered copyrights (collectively, the "Intellectual Property"), which the Target or any Subsidiary owns or licenses, has agreed (or has an option) to purchase, sell or license, or may be obligated to purchase, sell or license. With respect to each of the foregoing items, there is listed on Section 4.18(i) of the Disclosure Statement (a) the extent of the interest of the Target and its Subsidiaries therein; (b) the jurisdictions in or by which each such patent, trademark, service mark, trade name, copyright and license has been registered, filed or issued; (c) each agreement and all other documents evidencing the interest of the Target and its Subsidiaries therein, including, but not limited to, license agreements; (d) the extent of the interest of any third party therein, including, but not limited to, any security interest or licenses; and (e) each agreement and all other documents evidencing the interest of any third party therein.

(ii) Except as set forth in Section 4.18(ii) of the Disclosure Statement, the right, title or interest of the Target and its Subsidiaries in each item of Intellectual Property is free and clear of material adverse Liens.

(iii) Except as set forth in Section 4.18(iii) of the Disclosure Statement, the Target and its Subsidiaries have all right, title and interest in all inventions, trade secrets, proprietary information and have all other intellectual property rights necessary in any material respect for the non-infringing manufacture, use or sale, as the case may be, of all of the products, components of products and services which the Target or any Subsidiary manufactures, uses or sells in their business as currently conducted or which the Target or any Subsidiary contemplated manufacturing, using or selling in connection with the preparation of the Projected Financial Statements.

(iv) Except as set forth in Section 4.18(iv) of the Disclosure Statement, the Target and its Subsidiaries have all right, title and interest in all trademarks, service marks, trade names and product designations necessary for the non-infringing use of all such marks and trade names which the Target or any Subsidiary uses in their business as currently conducted or which the Target or any Subsidiary contemplated using in connection with the preparation of the Projected Financial Statements.

(v) Except as set forth in Section 4.18(v) of the Disclosure Statement, the Target and its Subsidiaries have all right, title and interest in all material copyrights necessary for the non-infringing publication, reproduction, preparation of derivative works, distribution, public performance, public display and importation of all copyrighted works which the Target or any Subsidiary in their business as currently conducted or as contemplated in connection with the preparation of the Projected Financial Statements, publishes, reproduces, prepares or has prepared a derivative of, distributes, publicly performs, publicly displays or imports.

(vi) Except as set forth in Section 4.18(vi) of the Disclosure Statement, neither the Target nor any of the Subsidiaries has, whether directly, contributorily or by inducement, within any time period as to which liability of the Target or the Subsidiaries is not barred by statute, infringed any patent, trademark, service mark, trade name or copyright or misappropriated any intellectual property of another, or received from another any notice, charge, claim or other assertion in respect thereto or committed any actions of unfair competition.

(vii) Except as set forth in Section 4.18(vii) of the Disclosure Statement, neither the Target nor any of the Subsidiaries has sent or otherwise communicated to another person any notice, charge, claim or other assertion of, or has any knowledge of, present, impending or threatened patent, trademark, service mark, trade name or copyright infringement by such other person, or misappropriation of any intellectual property of the Target or any of the Subsidiaries by such other person or any acts of unfair competition by such other person.

(viii) No product, license, patent, process, method, substance, design, part or other material presently being sold or contemplated to be sold or employed by the Target or any Subsidiary infringes on any rights owned or held by any other person; (b) no claim, litigation or other proceeding is pending or threatened against the Target or any Subsidiary contesting the right of such entity to sell or use any such product, license, patent, process, method, substance, design, part or other material and no such claim is impliedly threatened by an offer to license from a third party under a claim of use; and (c) no patent, formulation, invention, device, application or principle nor any statute, law, rule, regulation, standard or code, exists or is pending or proposed that would have a Material Adverse Effect.

(ix) No filing or recording fees, stamp or transfer taxes or other fees, costs or taxes of any kind are payable by the Target or any Subsidiary in respect of the Intellectual Property and no such filing or recording fees, stamp taxes or other fees, costs or taxes of any kind will be payable by the Target, any Subsidiary or Buyer in connection with the Merger except as set forth in Section 4.18(ix) of the Disclosure Statement.

The intellectual property representation requires the disclosure of all intellectual property that the target or any subsidiary uses in its business and is designed to assure the buyer that the intellectual property, or the target's or its subsidiaries' use thereof, does not infringe upon the rights of third parties. The representation has been drafted to cover any intellectual property rights that may exist or are pending that would adversely affect the target or its subsidiaries. This representation may be extremely important if, for example, the value of the target's business is largely dependent upon its possession of a particular patent or its ability to market its product under a particular trademark.

Subparagraph (ix) is intended to elicit information as to filing or transfer fees that might be incurred in connection with the transaction. Where the target and its subsidiaries have extensive foreign intellectual property holdings, these fees can be of sufficient magnitude that the buyer may desire to attempt to obligate the seller to pay a portion of these costs.

Section 4.19. Assets Necessary to the Business. Except as set forth in Section 4.19 of the Disclosure Statement, the Target and the Subsidiaries collectively own or lease, directly or indirectly, all of the assets and properties, and are parties to all licenses and other agreements, in each case which are presently being used or are reasonably necessary to carry on the businesses and operations of the Target and the Subsidiaries as presently conducted, and none of the stockholders of the Target, the Seller nor any of their affiliates (other than any of the Target and the Subsidiary) owns any assets or properties which are being used to carry on the business or operations of the Target and the Subsidiaries as presently conducted.

Notwithstanding all of the other representations made by the seller about the specific assets, liabilities, and other agreements, rights, and obligations that the target and its subsidiaries may have, a buyer has no way of knowing that it is getting everything that it needs to operate the business of the target and its subsidiaries as presently conducted without this broad representation. This type of representation is critical if the buyer is purchasing a company by means of an asset acquisition or a business that has been operated as a division of another company. If, for example, certain equipment or services necessary to the business of the target or its subsidiaries were provided by the seller or its affiliates, the buyer would be unable to operate the business without replacing such equipment or services, most likely at a cost that far exceeds the cost at which they were provided by the seller or its affiliates.

Section 4.20. Additional Contracts. In addition to the other items set forth in the Disclosure Statement attached hereto pursuant to the other provisions of this Agreement, Section 4.20 of the Disclosure Statement identifies as of the date hereof the following:

(i) each agreement to which the Target or any Subsidiary is a party which involves or may involve aggregate annual future payments (whether in payment of a debt, as a result of a guarantee or indemnification, for goods or services, or otherwise) by the Target or any Subsidiary of ______________ Dollars ($__________) or more;

(ii) each outstanding commitment of the Target or any Subsidiary to make capital expenditures, capital additions or capital improvements in excess of ______________ Dollars ($__________);

(iii) any contract for the employment of any officer or employee or former officer or employee of the Target or any Subsidiary (other than, with respect to any employee, contracts which are terminable without liability upon notice of 30 days or less and do not provide for any further payments following such termination) pursuant to which payments in excess of ______________ Dollars ($__________) may be required to be made at any time following the date hereof;

(iv) any stock option or stock appreciation rights plan or arrangement of the Target or any Subsidiary;

(v) any mortgage or other form of secured indebtedness of the Target or any Subsidiary;

(vi) any unsecured debentures, notes or installment obligations of the Target or any Subsidiary, the unpaid balance of which exceeds _______________ Dollars ($__________) in the aggregate except trade payables incurred in the ordinary course of business;

(vii) any guaranty of any obligation of the Target or any Subsidiary for borrowings or otherwise, excluding endorsements made for collection, guaranties made or letters of credit given in the ordinary course of business, and other guaranties which in the aggregate do not exceed _______________ Dollars ($__________);

(viii) any agreement of the Target or any Subsidiary, including options, for the purchase, sale, disposition or lease of any of its assets (other than inventory) having a book value of more than _______________ Dollars ($__________) for any single asset or _______________ Dollars ($__________) in the aggregate or for the sale of inventory other than in the ordinary course of business;

(ix) any contract to which the Target or any Subsidiary is a party pursuant to which the Target or any Subsidiary is or may be obligated to make payments, contingent or otherwise, exceeding _______________ Dollars ($__________) in the aggregate, on account of or arising out of the prior acquisition of businesses, or all or substantially all of the assets or stock, of other companies or any division thereof;

(x) any contract with any labor union of which the Target or any Subsidiary is a party;

(xi) any contract or proposed contract, including but not limited to assignments, licenses, transfers of exclusive rights, "work for hire" agreements, special commissions, employment contracts, purchase orders, sales orders, mortgages and security agreements, to which the Target or any Subsidiary is a party and which (A) contains a grant or other transfer, whether present, retroactive, prospective or contingent, by the Target or any Subsidiary, of any rights in any invention, trade secret, proprietary information, trademark, service mark, trade name, copyright or other intellectual property by whatever name designated, without regard to whether such invention, trade secret, proprietary information, trademark, service mark, trade name, copyright, material object or other intellectual property was in existence at the time such contract was made, or (B) contains a promise made by the Target or by any Subsidiary to pay any lump sum or royalty or other payment or consideration in respect to the acquisition, practice or use of any rights in any invention, trade secret, proprietary information, trademark, service mark, trade name, copyright, material object in which an original work of authorship was first fixed or other intellectual property by whatever name designated and without regard to whether such lump sum, royalty payment or other consideration was ever made or received;

(xii) any contract with the Seller or any officer, director or employee of the Target or any Subsidiary of the Seller (A) involving at least ______________ Dollars ($__________) in aggregate payments over the entire term thereof or more than ______________ Dollars ($__________) in any 12-month period or (B) the terms of which are not arms-length; or

(xiii) any other contract, agreement or other instrument which the Target or any Subsidiary is a party not entered into in the ordinary course of business which is material to the financial, business, earnings, prospects or condition of the Target or the Subsidiaries and not excluded by reason of the provisions of clauses (i) through (xii), inclusive, of this subsection.

Except as otherwise agreed to by the parties as set forth in Section 4.20 of the Disclosure Statement, true and complete copies of all contracts, agreements and other instruments referred to in Section 4.20 of the Disclosure Statement have heretofore been delivered, or will be delivered at least ten business days prior to Closing, to Buyer by the Seller. All such contracts, agreements and other instruments are enforceable by the Target or the Subsidiaries which is (are) a party thereto in accordance with their terms except as to enforceability thereof may be affected by applicable bankruptcy, reorganization, insolvency, moratorium or other similar laws now or hereafter in effect, or by general equity principles.

This is an information-gathering representation that is designed to identify all the important contractual relationships of the target and its subsidiaries. Depending upon the type of deal being negotiated, a seller may be reluctant to make this representation because of the inordinate amount of work required to satisfy the disclosure obligation. The seller may instead tell the buyer that it is welcome to review all the contracts and other agreements at the offices of the seller. However, like any other representation that is founded on access as opposed to identification, the buyer takes responsibility at its own peril. Therefore, a prudent buyer will demand that the seller identify all such documents and, if need be, offer to assist in the seller's preparation of the Disclosure Statement.

The amount of the dollar thresholds in this representation are deal-specific and the same considerations previously discussed are appropriate here.

> ***Section 4.21. Customers and Suppliers.*** Section 4.21 of the Disclosure Statement sets forth (i) a true and correct list of (A) the ten largest customers of the Target and each of the Subsidiaries in terms of sales during the fiscal year ended [fill in date of most recent fiscal year end] and (B) the ten largest customers of the Target and each of the Subsidiaries in terms of sales during the three (3) months ended [fill in the most recent quarter end], showing the approximate total sales to each such customer during the fiscal year ended [fill in date of most recent fiscal year end] and the three (3) months ended [fill in most recent quarter end]; (ii) a true and correct list of (A) the ten largest suppliers of the Target and each of the Subsidiaries in terms of purchases during the fiscal year ended [fill in date of most recent fiscal year end], and (B) the ten largest suppliers of the Target and each of the Subsidiaries on a consolidated basis in terms of purchases during the three (3) months ended [fill in most recent quarter end], showing the approximate total purchases from each such supplier during the fiscal year ended [fill in date of most recent fiscal year end], and the three (3) months ended [fill in most recent quarter end], respectively. Except to the extent set forth in Section 4.21 of the Disclosure Statement, there has not been any material adverse change in the business relationship of the Target or any Subsidiary with any customer or supplier named in the Disclosure Statement. Except for the customers and suppliers named in Section 4.21 of the Disclosure Statement, neither the Target nor any Subsidiary had any customer who accounted for more than 5 of its sales during the period from [insert appropriate period of 12 to 18 months prior to date of Agreement], or any supplier from whom it purchased more than 5 of the goods or services purchased by it during such period.

Depending upon the nature of the target's and the subsidiaries' businesses, the buyer may agree to require disclosure of the largest customers and suppliers on "a consolidated basis." The principal reason for this representation is to identify the dependence of the business on a single or small group of customers or suppliers.

> ***Section 4.22. Competing Lines of Business.*** Except as set forth in Section 4.22 of the Disclosure Statement, no affiliate of the Seller owns, directly or indirectly, any interest in (excepting not more than 5 stockholdings for investment purposes in securities of publicly held and traded companies), or is an officer, director, employee or consultant of, or otherwise receives remuneration from, any person which is, or is engaged in business as, a competitor, lessor, lessee, customer or supplier of the Target or any Subsidiary.

In certain situations, it may appear unnecessary to require a seller to enter into some sort of noncompete agreement because of the nature of the seller's business. However, it still may be useful for the buyer to assure itself that there are no hidden companies that the seller operates or controls that compete with the target or a subsidiary. The protection afforded by this representation is limited; the seller may be able to adversely affect the business of the target or a subsidiary in light of the seller's inside knowledge or simply because it has greater resources. The buyer should be forewarned that, despite its receipt of this representation, a seller may remain a competitor given the practicalities of a particular situation.

> ***Section 4.23. Restrictive Covenants.*** Except as set forth in Section 4.23 of the Disclosure Statement, neither Target nor any Subsidiary is a party to any agreement, contract or covenant limiting the freedom of the Target or any Subsidiary from competing in any line of business or with any person or other entity in any geographic area.

A buyer must be aware of agreements that constrain the operation of the target and its subsidiaries. Many buyers purchase targets with the expectation that the business of the target can be expanded geographically. In some cases, the buyer may be relying on this expectation to the point of including such expansion in its projections. Therefore, the buyer should carefully review any agreements that are disclosed as a result of this representation.

> ***Section 4.24. Books and Records.***
>
> (i) The books of account and other financial records of the Target and its Subsidiaries are in all material respects complete and correct, and have been maintained in accordance with good business practices.

(ii) The minute books of the Target and its Subsidiaries, as previously made available to the Buyer and its counsel, contain accurate records of all meetings and accurately reflect all other material corporate action of the stockholders and directors and any committees of the Board of Directors of the Target and its Subsidiaries.

(iii) The Buyer has been or will be prior to the Closing Date, afforded access to all such records referred to in subparagraphs (i) and (ii) above.

Section 4.25. Bank Accounts. Section 4.25 of the Disclosure Statement contains a true and correct list of the names of each bank, savings and loan or other financial institution, in which the Target or its Subsidiaries has an account, including cash contribution accounts, or safe deposit boxes, and the names of all persons authorized to draw thereon or to have access thereto.

Sections 4.24 and 4.25 are representations that confirm the accuracy of information usually furnished to the buyer in connection with its due diligence efforts.

Section 4.26. Employee Benefit Plans; Labor Relations.

(i) The term "Employee Plan" shall mean any pension, retirement, profit-sharing, deferred compensation, bonus or other incentive plan, any medical, vision, dental or other health plan, any life insurance plan, or any other employee benefit plan, including, without limitation, any "employee benefit plan" as defined in Section 3(3) of the Employee Retirement Income Security Act of 1974, as amended ("ERISA") and any employee benefit plan covering any employees of the Target or any Controlled Entity in any foreign country or territory (a "Foreign Plan"), to which the Target or any Controlled Entity contributes or is a party or is bound and under which employees of the Target or any Controlled Entity are eligible to participate or derive a benefit, except any government-sponsored program or government-required benefit. Section 4.26(i) of the Disclosure Statement lists each Employee Plan and identifies each Employee Plan (other than a Foreign Plan) which, as of the date hereof, is a defined benefit plan as defined in Section 3(35) of ERISA (a "Defined Benefit Plan") or is a multi-employer plan within the meaning of Section 3(37) of ERISA (a "Multi-Employer Plan"). In the case of each Defined Benefit Plan, the unfunded accrued liabilities of such plan as of [insert date], determined on an ongoing plan basis by the actuaries for such plan using the actuarial methods and assumptions used in the latest actuarial valuation of the plan, do not exceed the assets of the plan. Section 4.26(i) of the Disclosure Statement identifies each of the Employee Plans which purports to be a qualified plan under Section 401(a) of the Internal Revenue Code (as defined below). In the case of each Multi-Employer Plan, Section 4.26(i) of the Disclosure Statement sets forth the Target or Controlled Entity contributions made to such Plan for the 12 months ended on the last day of its most recent fiscal year. In the case of each Foreign Plan, Section 4.26(i) of the Disclosure Statement sets forth the Target or Controlled Entity contributions made to such Plan for the last plan year ending prior to the date of this Agreement. The Target has delivered, or will deliver prior to the Closing, to Buyer the following documents as in effect on the date hereof: (a) true, correct and complete copies of any Employee Plan, other than a Foreign Plan, including all amendments thereto, which is an employee pension benefit or welfare benefit plan (within the meaning of Sections 3(1) or 3(2) of ERISA), and, in the case of any unwritten Employee Plans, descriptions thereof, (b) with respect to any plans or plan amendments described in the foregoing clause (a), (1) the most recent determination letter issued by the Internal Revenue Service (the "IRS") after September 1, 1974, if any, (2) all trust agreements or other funding agreements, including insurance contracts, (3) with respect to each Defined Benefit Plan, all notices of intent to terminate any such Employee Plan and all notices of reportable events with respect to any such Employee Plan as to which the PBGC has not waived the thirty (30) day notice requirement, (4) the most recent actuarial valuations, annual reports, summary plan descriptions, summaries of material modifications and summary annual reports, if any, and (5) a true, correct and complete summary of the benefits provided under each Foreign Plan, together with the most recent actuarial valuation of financial information relative thereto.

(ii) As of the date hereof:

(a) Each of the Employee Plans that purports to be qualified under Section 401(a) of the Internal Revenue Code, as amended (the "Code") is qualified as of the Closing Date and any trusts under such plans are exempt from income tax under Section 501(a) of the Code. The retroactive cure period with respect to any plan amendments not yet submitted to the IRS has not expired. The Employee Plans each comply in all material respects with all other applicable laws (including, without limitation, ERISA, the Age Discrimination in Employment Act, the Americans with

Disabilities Act, the Family Leave Act, and the Tax Cuts and Jobs Act) of the United States and any applicable collective bargaining agreement. Other than claims for benefits submitted by participants or beneficiaries or appeals from denial thereof, there is no litigation, legal action, suit, investigation, claim, counterclaim or proceeding pending or threatened against any Employee Plan.

(b) With respect to any Employee Plan, no prohibited transaction (within the meaning of Section 406 of ERISA and/or Section 4975 of the Code) exists which could subject the Target or any Controlled Entity to any material liability or civil penalty assessed pursuant to Section 502(i) of ERISA or a material tax imposed by Section 4975 of the Code. Neither the Seller nor the Target, nor any Controlled Entity, nor any administrator or fiduciary of any Employee Plan (or agent of any of the foregoing) has engaged in any transaction or acted or failed to act in a manner which is likely to subject the Target or any Controlled Entity to any liability for a breach of fiduciary or other duty under ERISA or any other applicable United States law. The transactions contemplated by this Agreement and the Related Instruments will not be, or cause any, prohibited action.

(c) No Defined Benefit Plan has been terminated or partially terminated after September 1, 1974.

(d) No plan termination liability to the Pension Benefit Guaranty Corporation ("PBGC") or withdrawal liability to any Multi-Employer Plan that is material in the aggregate has been or is expected to be incurred with respect to any Employee Plan or with respect to any employee benefit plan sponsored by any entity under common control (within the meaning of Section 414 of the Code) with the Target or a Controlled Entity by reason of any action taken by the Seller, the Target or any Controlled Entity prior to the Closing Date. The PBGC has not instituted, and is not expected to institute, any proceedings to terminate any Employee Plan. Except as described in Section 4.26(ii)(d) of the Disclosure Statement, there has been no reportable event since [insert date] (within the meaning of Section 4043(b) of ERISA and the regulations thereunder) with respect to any Employee Plan, and there exists no condition or set of circumstances which makes the termination of any Employee Plan by the PBGC likely.

(e) As of the date hereof, as to each Employee Benefit Plan, all filings required by ERISA and the Code have been timely filed and all notices and disclosures to participants required by ERISA or the Code have been timely provided.

(iii) Except as indicated in Section 4.26(iii) of the Disclosure Statement, the Target and each Controlled Entity has made full and timely payment of all amounts required under the terms of each of the Employee Plans that are employee pension benefit plans, including the Multi-Employer Plans, to have been paid as contributions to such plans for the last plan year ended prior to the date of this Agreement and all prior plan years. No accumulated funding deficiency (as defined in Section 302 of ERISA and Section 412 of the Code), whether or not waived, exists with respect to any Employee Plan (other than a Foreign Plan) as of the end of such plan year, provided contributions owed with respect to such plan year are timely paid. Further, the Target and each Controlled Entity has made or shall make full and timely payment of or has accrued or shall accrue all amounts which are required under the terms of the Employee Plans to be paid as a contribution to each such Employee Plan that is an employee pension benefit plan with respect to the period from the end of the last plan year ending before the date of this Agreement to the Closing Date in accordance with [insert covenant cross-reference] hereof.

(iv) No state of facts exists with respect to a Foreign Plan, the effect of which would have a material adverse effect on the business, assets, earnings, financial condition or prospects of the Target and the Controlled Entities taken as a whole.

(v) All contributions made to or accrued with respect to all Employee Plans are deductible under Section 404 or 162 of the Code. No amounts, nor any assets of any Employee Plan are subject to tax as unrelated business taxable income under Sections 511, 512 or 419A of the Code.

(vi) No facts exist which will result in a material increase in premium costs of Employee Plans for which benefits are insured or a material increase in benefit costs of Employee Plans which provide self-insured benefits.

(vii) No Employee Plan provides medical, disability, life or other benefits to retired former employees.

(viii) Except as described in Section 4.26(v) of the Disclosure Statement, no union has been recognized as a representative of any or all of the Target's or any Subsidiary's employees. There are no agreements with, or pending petitions for recognition of, a labor union or association as the exclusive bargaining agent for any or all of the Target's or any Subsidiary's employees; no such petitions have been pending at any time within two (2) years of the date of this Agreement and, to the best of the Seller's knowledge, there has not been any organizing effort by any union or other group seeking to represent any employees of the Target or any Subsidiary as their exclusive bargaining agent at any time within two (2) years of the date of this Agreement; and there are no labor strikes, work stoppages or other troubles, other than routine grievance matters, now pending, or, to the best of Seller's knowledge, threatened, against the Target or any Subsidiary, nor have there been any such labor strikes, work stoppages or other labor troubles, other than routine grievance matters, at any time within two (2) years of the date of this Agreement.

This particular representation is extremely important in situations in which the target or any subsidiary has a substantial number of employees. Over the past few years, potential liability with respect to employee benefits and related plans has increased dramatically. Therefore, it is important for the buyer to know that the employee plans maintained by the target or any subsidiary are in compliance with existing regulations and are adequately funded. (For a further discussion of employee benefits and other compensation issues, see Chapter 9.)

Section 4.27. Litigation. Except as set forth in Section 4.27 of the Disclosure Statement, there is no action, suit, proceeding or investigation pending or, to the best knowledge after due inquiry of Seller and the Target, threatened, which would be likely to have a Material Adverse Effect; there is no reasonable basis known to the Seller or the Target for any such action that may result in any such effect and that is probable of assertion; and the Target, or any Subsidiary, is not in default in respect of any judgment, order, writ, injunction or decree of any court or any federal, state, local or other governmental department, commission, board, bureau, agency or instrumentality which would be likely to have a Material Adverse Effect.

Generally, a seller will have no problem disclosing to the buyer the existence of any pending or threatened action against the target or a subsidiary that would have Material Adverse Effect. The part of this representation that is more difficult for the seller to make relates to whether the seller has a reasonable basis to know of any action that may result in a Material Adverse Effect. Although there may be no claim pending or action threatened, the buyer wants to know whether the seller, target, or subsidiary has taken any action that would result in a Material Adverse

Effect. For example, if immediately prior to the signing of the acquisition agreement the target were to willfully breach a contract essential to its business, the other party to the contract, unaware of the breach, would not yet have filed a claim. Without this particular representation, the seller would not have to disclose this event. Not surprisingly, the seller is often unwilling to evaluate which of its actions may result in a claim that would have a Material Adverse Effect, or make warranties based on its evaluation. The seller may argue that routine corporate actions could result in a Material Adverse Effect, or the seller may express unwillingness to take on liability for the knowledge of each of its directors, officers, and employees. As with other representations, the issue is risk allocation. A smart buyer will soften this representation to appease the seller but will nonetheless seek disclosure, since the seller should be aware of an action taken that would or may constitute a Material Adverse Effect and can always choose to disclose it rather than guess as to its outcome.

Section 4.28. Compliance with Laws.

(i) The Target and the Subsidiaries comply with, and have made all filings required pursuant to, all federal, state, municipal or local constitutional provisions, laws, ordinances, rules, regulations and orders in connection with the conduct of their businesses as now conducted.

(ii) The Target and the Subsidiaries have all governmental licenses, permits and authorizations necessary for the conduct of their respective businesses as currently conducted (the "Permits"), and all such Permits are in full force and effect, and no violations exist in respect of any such Permits, and no proceeding is pending or, to the knowledge of the Seller, threatened, to revoke or limit any thereof. Except as otherwise disclosed in Section 4.28(ii) of the Disclosure Statement, all such Permits are set forth on the Disclosure Statement.

(iii) Except as set forth in Section 4.28(iii) of the Disclosure Statement, neither the Target nor any Subsidiary has received notice of violation or of any alleged or potential violation of any such constitutional provisions, laws, ordinances, rules, regulations or orders, cured or not, within the last five years or any injunction or governmental order or decree.

(iv) Except as set forth in Section 4.28(iv) of the Disclosure Statement, there are no present or past Environmental Conditions in any way relating

> to the business of the Target or any Subsidiary. For purposes of this Agreement, "Environmental Condition" means (a) the introduction into the environment of any pollution, including without limitation any contaminant, irritant, or pollutant or other toxic or hazardous substance (whether or not such pollution constituted at the time thereof a violation of any federal, state or local law, ordinance or governmental rule or regulation) as a result of any spill, discharge, leak, emission, escape, injection, dumping or release of any kind whatsoever of any substance or exposure of any type in any work places or to any medium, including without limitation air, land, surface waters or ground waters, or from any generation, transportation, treatment, discharge, storage or disposal of waste materials, raw materials, hazardous materials, toxic materials or products of any kind or from the storage, use or handling of any hazardous or toxic materials or other substances, as a result of which the Target or any Subsidiary has or may become liable to any person or by reason of which any of the assets of the Target or any Subsidiary may suffer or be subjected to any Lien, or (b) any noncompliance with any federal, state or local environmental law, rule, regulation or order as a result of or in connection with any of the foregoing.

The buyer might limit the representation contained in paragraph (ii) by excepting "any such licenses, permits and authorizations the failure to obtain which will not have a Material Adverse Effect."

Similarly the buyer might agree to limit the scope of subparagraph (iii) by adding to the five-year limitation the phrase "which would be reasonably likely to result in any liability for penalties or damages exceeding ______________ Dollars ($__________) in the aggregate."

The environmental representation in paragraph (iv) is extremely important in light of the tremendous cost that can be incurred in correcting environmental problems. As a result of significant legislative and judicial developments over the past two decades, unwary buyers may find themselves saddled with obligations to clean up environmental problems caused by their predecessors. Such problems can range from removing asbestos in buildings to expensive groundwater purification programs made necessary by leaks from underground storage tanks.

> ***Section 4.29. Non-Contravention; Consents.*** Except as set forth in Section 4.29 of the Disclosure Statement, the execution, delivery and performance

of this Agreement and the Related Instruments and the consummation of any of the transactions contemplated hereby and thereby by the Seller and the Target do not and will not:

(i) violate any provisions of Seller's or Target's certificate of incorporation or bylaws;

(ii) violate, or result with the passage of time in the violation of, any provision of, or result in the acceleration of or entitle any party to accelerate (whether after the giving of notice or lapse of time or both) any obligation under, or result in the creation or imposition of any lien, charge, pledge, security interest or other encumbrance upon any of the properties of Target or any Subsidiary pursuant to any provision of, any mortgage, lien, lease, agreement, permit, indenture, license, instrument, law, order, arbitration award, judgment or decree to which the Seller, Target or any Subsidiary is a party or by which it or any of its properties are bound, the effect of all of which violations, accelerations, creations and impositions would result, in the aggregate, in subjecting the Target or the Subsidiaries to liabilities in excess of ______________________ Dollars ($__________);

(iii) violate any law, order, judgment or decree to which the Target or any Subsidiary is subject;

(iv) violate or conflict with any other restriction of any kind or character to which Target or any Subsidiary is subject, or by which any of their assets may be bound, the effect of all of which violations or conflicts would result, in the aggregate, in subjecting Target or the Subsidiaries to aggregate liabilities in excess of ______________________ Dollars ($__________);

(v) constitute an event permitting termination of an agreement to which Target or any Subsidiary is subject, if in any such circumstance, individually or in the aggregate with all other such events, could have a Material Adverse Effect; or

(vi) require a consent, license, permit, notice, application, qualification, waiver or other action of any kind, authorization, order or approval of, or filing or registration with, any governmental commission, board, regulatory, or administrative agencies or authorities or other regulatory body.

This representation is quite useful in that it clearly lays out the various items that should be of concern to the buyer in its operation of the business after the consummation of the transactions contemplated by the acquisition agreement. The utility of the representation lies in the ability it gives the buyer to address each adverse consequence of the transaction before the deal is closed. For example, many agreements provide for their termination in the event that there is a change of control of the target or a subsidiary, as the case may be. Advance notice of the number and nature of these agreements gives the buyer the opportunity to put replacement contracts in place. In addition, the disclosure of certain consents may prompt the buyer to condition its obligation to close upon the success of the seller in obtaining such consents.

The buyer should give careful consideration to the amount of the dollar thresholds, as items beneath the threshold will not be disclosed and may result in dollar-for-dollar liability to the surviving corporation.

> ***Section 4.30. Unlawful Payments.*** Neither the Target nor any Subsidiary, nor to the best of the Target's knowledge any officer or director of the Target nor any officer or director of any Subsidiary, nor any employee, agent or representative, of the Target or any Subsidiary has made, directly or indirectly, with respect to the business of the Target or such Subsidiary, any illegal political contributions, payments from corporate funds not recorded on the books and records of the Target or such Subsidiary, payments from corporate funds that were falsely recorded on the books and records of the Target or such Subsidiary, payments from corporate funds to governmental officials in their individual capacities for the purpose of affecting their action or the action of the government they represent to obtain favorable treatment in securing business or licenses or to obtain special concessions or illegal payments from corporate funds to obtain or retain business.

The purpose of this representation is to identify whether the target or any subsidiary has made any payments that violate laws, such as the Foreign Corrupt Practices Act, or any payments that are not accurately reflected on the target's or subsidiaries' books and records. In addition, disclosure of these payments might reveal the tenuous nature of certain aspects of the target's or its subsidiaries' business, or the necessity for continuing such payments in order to obtain favorable treatment.

> ***Section 4.31. Brokers and Finders.*** Neither the Seller, Target or any Subsidiary nor any stockholder, officer, director or agent of the Seller, the Target or any Subsidiary has incurred on behalf of Seller, the Target or any Subsidiary any liability to any broker, finder or agent for any brokerage fees, finders' fees or commissions with respect to the transactions contem-

plated by this Agreement, except to [name of broker or finder]. Such fees and commissions will be paid by Seller.

This representation protects the buyer against obligations of the target or any subsidiary to pay certain fees in connection with the acquisition. Buyer and seller may agree to share some of these fees, but the buyer certainly doesn't want to be obligated to pay any fees of which it is not aware or that are not included in its calculation of the purchase price.

Section 4.32. Absence of Certain Changes or Events. Except as reflected in Section 4.32 of the Disclosure Statement or as specifically set forth herein, since the date of the Most Recent Balance Sheet neither Target nor any Subsidiary has

(i) conducted its business other than in the ordinary course of business;

(ii) issued or sold, or contracted to sell, any of its stock, notes, bonds or other securities, or any option to purchase the same, or entered into any agreement with respect thereto;

(iii) amended its certificate of incorporation or bylaws;

(iv) had or made any capital expenditures or commitments for the acquisition or construction of any property, plant or equipment in excess of __________________________ Dollars ($__________) individually and __________ Dollars ($__________) in the aggregate;

(v) entered into any transaction inconsistent in any material respect with the past practices of its business or has conducted its business in any manner materially inconsistent with its past practices;

(vi) incurred (A) any damage, destruction or similar loss in an aggregate amount exceeding _________________________ Dollars ($_________) and which is covered by insurance or (B) any damage, destruction or loss in an aggregate amount exceeding _________________________ Dollars ($__________) and which is not covered by insurance;

(vii) suffered any loss or, to the best knowledge of the Seller, Target and the Subsidiaries, any prospective loss, of any dealer, customer or supplier or altered any contractual arrangement with any dealer or supplier, the loss or alteration of which would (or would, when added to all other such losses or alterations) have a Material Adverse Effect;

(viii) incurred any material liability or obligation (absolute or contingent) or made any material expenditure, other than such as may have been incurred or made in the ordinary course of business and other than capital expenditures described in clause (iv) of this subsection;

(ix) suffered any material adverse change in the business, operations, earnings, properties, liabilities, prospects, assets or financial condition or otherwise of the Target or any Subsidiary and no event which would have Material Adverse Effect has occurred;

(x) declared, set aside or paid any dividend or other distribution (whether in cash, shares, property or any combination thereof) in respect of the capital stock of the Target or any Subsidiary;

(xi) redeemed, repurchased, or otherwise acquired any of its capital stock or securities convertible into or exchangeable for its capital stock or entered into any agreement to do so;

(xii) except as reflected on the Most Recent Balance Sheet and covered by an adequate reserve therefor, made any sale of accounts receivable or any accrual of liabilities not in the ordinary course of business or written off any notes or accounts receivable or portions thereof as uncollectible;

(xiii) purchased or disposed of, or contracted to purchase or dispose of, or granted or received an option to purchase or sell, any properties or assets having a value greater than ____________________ Dollars ($__________) for any single asset, or greater than ____________________ Dollars ($__________) in the aggregate;

(xiv) except for normal annual increases or increases resulting from the application of existing formulas under existing plans, agreements or policies relating to employee compensation, made any increase in the rate of compensation payable or to become payable to the Target's or any Subsidiary's officers or employees or any increase in the amounts paid or payable to such officers or employees under any bonus, insurance, pension or other benefit plan, or any arrangements therefor made for or with any of said officers or employees;

(xv) adopted, or amended, any collective bargaining, bonus, profit-sharing, compensation, stock option, pension, retirement, deferred compensation or other plan, agreement, trust, fund or arrangement for the benefit of employees;

(xvi) made any change in any material accounting principle, material accounting procedure or material accounting practice, if any, followed by the Target or any Subsidiary or in the method of applying such principle, procedure or practice [except as required by a change in generally accepted accounting principles in the country of domicile];

(xvii) made any provision for markdowns or shrinkage with respect to inventories other than in the ordinary course of business and consistent with past practices or any write-down of the value of inventory by the Target or any Subsidiary of more than _______________ __________ Dollars ($__________) in the aggregate;

(xviii) discharged any lien or paid any obligation or liability (whether absolute, accrued, contingent or otherwise) other than current liabilities shown on the Most Recent Balance Sheet, and current liabilities incurred thereafter;

(xix) mortgaged, pledged or subjected to any lien, except liens specifically excepted from the provisions of Section 4.17 hereof, any properties or assets, real, personal or mixed, tangible or intangible, of Target or any Subsidiary;

(xx) experienced any material shortage of raw materials or supplies;

(xxi) made any gifts or sold, transferred or exchanged any property for less than the fair value thereof; or

(xxii) made or entered into any agreement or understanding to do any of the foregoing.

In order to "bring down" the financial condition of the target and its subsidiaries from the date of the Most Recent Balance Sheet, the buyer should have the seller represent the lack of certain events since such date. As mentioned earlier, the bring-down condition is intended to assure the buyer that, on the closing date, the target will be the same target, from a legal and financial perspective, that the buyer bargained for in the contract. Because there are no financial statements covering the period between the date of the Most Recent Balance Sheet and the Closing Date, it is important for the buyer to understand the operation of the business during this period. In addition, the buyer should require the seller to covenant that it will not breach this representation on or prior to the Closing Date (see Section 6.1). Included in Section 4.32 are representations regarding matters which, although not specifically related to the financial statements, provide vital information about the ongoing business of the target. For example, the representation requires the disclosure of any material shortage of raw materials or supplies. A buyer must, of course, tailor this representation to the business of its target.

Section 4.33. Accuracy of Information Furnished. No representation or warranty by the Seller or Target contained in this Agreement, the Disclosure Statement or in respect of the exhibits, schedules, lists or other documents delivered to Buyer by the Seller and referred to herein, and no statement contained in any certificate furnished or to be furnished by or on behalf of the Seller or Target pursuant hereto, or in connection with the transactions contemplated hereby, contains, or will contain as of the date such representation or warranty is made or such certificate is or will be furnished, any untrue statement of a material fact, or omits, or will omit to state as of the date such representation or warranty is made or such certificate is or will be furnished, any material fact which is necessary to make the statements contained herein or therein not misleading. To the best knowledge of the Seller, the Target and the Subsidiaries, there is no fact which could have a Material Adverse Effect on the Target or any Subsidiary which the Seller has not prior to or on the date hereof disclosed to Buyer in writing.

The buyer will request this representation to provide assurance that the information upon which the buyer has based its evaluation of the target and its subsidiaries is accurate and complete. This representation is typically referred to as a "10b-5 representation" because the language closely parallels Rule 10b-5 promulgated by the SEC.

Similar to the representation made in Section 4.6 with respect to undisclosed liabilities, the last sentence in this representation shifts to the seller the responsibility of providing any information of which the buyer should be aware. The seller, although typically reluctant to make this representation, may derive some comfort from the fact that it has already told the buyer everything it could possibly know about the target and the subsidiaries in the preceding representations.

Section 4.34. Reports Filed with the Securities and Exchange Commission. Buyer has been furnished with accurate and complete copies of each annual report on Form 10-K that Target has filed with the Securities and Exchange Commission, all other reports or documents, including all amendments and supplements thereto, required to be filed by the Seller pursuant to Section 13(a) or 15(d) of the Securities Exchange Act since the filing of the most recent annual report on Form 10-K and its most recent annual report to its stockholders. Such reports do not contain any material false statements or any misstatements of any material fact and do not omit to state any fact necessary to make the statements set forth therein not misleading in any material respect.

This representation is applicable only to targets that are publicly traded corporations required to file reports with the SEC. The buyer must assure itself that the target has discharged its obligations to file reports with the SEC, and that the statements contained in the target's filings are true and are not misleading. Failure to obtain this representation may expose the buyer to significant postclosing liabilities, as the target may be the object of stockholders' suits or SEC enforcement actions.

Section 4.35. Investment Purpose. The Seller's acquisition of the [describe securities of Buyer to be purchased by Seller] is made for its own account for investment purposes only and not with a view to the resale or distribution thereof. The Seller agrees that it will not sell, assign or otherwise transfer or pledge the [describe securities of Buyer to be purchased by Seller] or any interest therein except in compliance with the transfer restrictions set forth on such securities.

When the seller has agreed to accept securities of the buyer in partial payment of the purchase price for the acquisition, the buyer should require certain investment representations from the seller. The representations of the seller are intended to provide the basis for characterizing the sale of securities to the seller as a private placement, thereby exempting the securities from registration under the Securities Act of 1933 and applicable state securities laws. However, this representation is not meant to satisfy all the requirements for exemption under the securities laws, especially in cases where there are more than a handful of persons receiving these securities.

Section 4.36. Dealership and Franchises.

(i) Section 4.36(i) of the Disclosure Statement contains a list of (a) those franchisees or dealers who or which, as of the date of this Agreement, were authorized by the Seller to operate stores under the name "____________," or other similar name associating such franchisee or dealer with the Seller (the "Franchisees"), (b) those Franchisees whose relationship with the Seller, the Target or any Subsidiary has been terminated within one year prior to the date hereof and (c) those persons who have become Franchisees within one year prior to the date hereof. Such list is true, correct and complete and includes the expiration date of each existing Franchise Agreement. The Seller has given Buyer an opportunity to review true and correct copies of each of the agreements between it, the Target or any Subsidiary and each Franchisee. Except as stated in Section 4.36(i) of the Disclosure Statement, each agreement between the Seller, the Target or any Subsidiary and each Franchisee (A) has been duly and validly authorized, executed and delivered by, and is the valid and binding obligation of, such Franchisee, enforceable against such Franchisee in accordance with its terms, except as may be limited by applicable bankruptcy, reorganization, insolvency, moratorium or other similar laws or by legal or equitable principles relating to or limiting creditors' rights generally, and (B) does not violate any law or regulation applicable thereto, and (C) does not conflict with the provisions of any other agreement.

(ii) Except as set forth in Section 4.36(ii) of the Disclosure Statement, there is not, under any agreement between the Seller, the Target or any Subsidiary and any Franchisee, any existing default or event which with notice or lapse of time, or both, would constitute an event of default and which has or would be reasonably likely to have a Material Adverse Effect. The execution and delivery of this Agreement and the performance of the transactions contemplated hereby will not result in any event of default under any agreement between the Seller, the Target or any Subsidiary and any Franchisee.

(iii) Except as set forth in Section 4.36(iii) of the Disclosure Statement, each Franchisee was offered his, her or its franchise in accordance with all applicable laws and regulations, including, without limitation, the regulations of the Federal Trade Commission, and any state and/or local agencies regulating the sale of franchised businesses. The Seller has not offered any person or entity a franchise since [insert a date 18 months prior to date of Agreement].

Where the target has entered into franchise or distributorship arrangements in the conduct of its business, the buyer will want to obtain specific disclosures about the terms of these arrangements. This representation is designed to require the seller to disclose the health of its contractual relations with its franchisees and distributors. A statement certifying compliance with FTC regulations is important, as the target may be liable for any failure to comply with FTC disclosure requirements.

ARTICLE V: REPRESENTATIONS AND WARRANTIES OF THE BUYER

The Buyer represents and warrants to the Seller and the Target as follows:

Section 5.1. Organization. The Buyer is a corporation duly organized, validly existing and in good standing under the laws of the jurisdiction of its incorporation. The Buyer has delivered to the Seller true and correct copies of its Certificate of Incorporation and Bylaws.

Section 5.2. Authorization. The execution, delivery and performance of this Agreement and any instruments or agreements contemplated herein to be executed, delivered and performed by the Buyer (including without limitation, [list important agreements to be executed by Buyer on or before Closing]) (the "Buyer's Related Instruments"), and the consummation of the transactions contemplated hereby and thereby, have been duly adopted and approved by the Board of Directors and the stockholders, of the Buyer. The Buyer has all requisite power and authority to execute, deliver and perform this Agreement and the Buyer's Related Instruments and to consummate the transactions contemplated hereby and in the Buyer's Related Instruments. This Agreement has been and as of the Closing Date, each of the Buyer's Related Instruments will be, duly and validly authorized, executed and delivered by the Buyer. This Agreement is and the Buyer's Related Agreements are or will be, as of the Closing Date, the valid and binding obligation of the Buyer, enforceable against the Buyer in accordance with their respective terms.

Section 5.3. Non-Contravention; Consents. Except as set forth in Section 5.3 of the Disclosure Statement, the execution and delivery of this Agreement and the Related Instruments and the consummation of any of the transactions contemplated hereby and thereby by the Buyer do not and will not:

(i) violate any provisions of the Buyer's certificate of incorporation or bylaws;

(ii) violate, or result with the passage of time in the violation of, any provision of, or result in the acceleration of or entitle any party to accelerate (whether after the giving of notice or lapse of time or both) any obligation under, or result in the creation or imposition of any lien, charge, pledge, security interest or other encumbrance upon any of the properties of the Buyer pursuant to any provision of, any mortgage, lien, lease, agreement, permit,

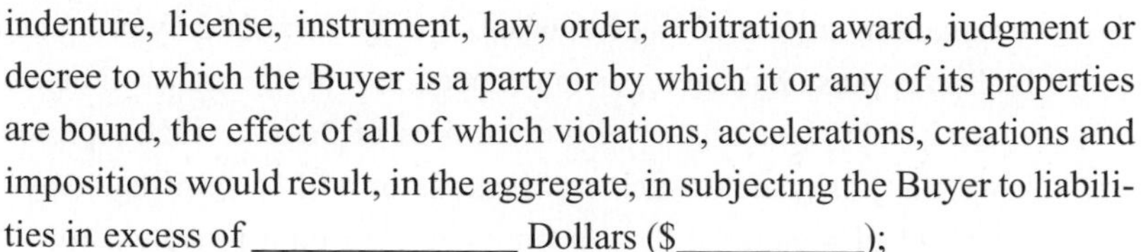

indenture, license, instrument, law, order, arbitration award, judgment or decree to which the Buyer is a party or by which it or any of its properties are bound, the effect of all of which violations, accelerations, creations and impositions would result, in the aggregate, in subjecting the Buyer to liabilities in excess of ______________ Dollars ($__________);

(iii) violate any law, order, judgment or decree to which the Buyer is subject;

(iv) violate or conflict with any other restriction of any kind or character to which the Buyer is subject, or by which any of their assets may be bound, the effect of all of which violations or conflicts would result, in the aggregate, in subjecting the Buyer to aggregate liabilities in excess of ______________ Dollars ($__________); or

(v) require any consent, license, permit, notice, application, qualification, waiver or other action of any kind, authorization, order or approval of, or filing or registration with, any governmental commission, board, regulatory, or administrative agencies or authorities or other regulatory body.

Section 5.4. Litigation. There is no action, suit, proceeding or investigation pending, or, to the best of the Buyer's knowledge, threatened, against or related to the Buyer or its respective properties or business which would be reasonably likely to adversely affect or restrict the Buyer's ability to consummate the transactions contemplated hereby or in the Related Instruments; and there is no reasonable basis known to the Buyer for any such action that may result in such effect and is probable of assertion.

Section 5.5. Brokers and Finders. Neither the Buyer nor any stockholder, officer, director or agent of the Buyer has incurred on behalf of the Buyer any liability to any broker, finder or agent for any brokerage fees, finders' fees or commissions with respect to the transactions contemplated by this Agreement, except to [name of broker or finder], whose fees will be paid by the Buyer.

Section 5.6. Business. The Buyer has not engaged in any activities other than those incident to its organization or as contemplated by the terms of this Agreement.

Section 5.7. Accuracy of Information Furnished. No representation or warranty by the Buyer contained in this Agreement, the Disclosure Statement or in respect of the exhibits, schedules, lists or other documents delivered to the Seller by the Buyer and referred to herein, and no statement contained in any certificate furnished or to be furnished by or on behalf of the Buyer pursuant hereto, or in connection with the transactions contemplated hereby, contains, or will contain as of the date such representation or warranty is made or such certificate is or will be furnished, any untrue statement of a material fact, or omits, or will omit to state as of the date such representation or warranty is made or such certificate is or will be furnished, any material fact which is necessary to make the statements contained herein or therein not misleading.

The representations and warranties of the buyer generally parallel the representations made by the seller and target in Article IV. However, there is no need for the buyer, as the acquirer, to make the vast number of representations and warranties required of the seller and target, because it is the businesses and assets of the seller that are being purchased and in respect of which most representations and warranties therefore apply.

In some instances, the buyer may accomplish its acquisition of the target by utilizing a shell company as the acquirer. If properly structured, this strategy may permit the parties to avoid filing a premerger notification under the Hart-Scott-Rodino Antitrust Improvements Act of 1974. The representation made in Section 5.6 regarding the scope of the business of the buyer is useful to the seller in that it assures the seller that there should be few contractual constraints on the shell company to consummate the acquisition.

In circumstances where the buyer is not a shell company, it may be appropriate for the seller to include additional representations about the buyer. For example, a representation relating to the buyer's financial statements and the absence of certain changes or events since the date of such financial statements might assure the seller of the buyer's ability to consummate the transaction.

ARTICLE VI: COVENANTS OF SELLER AND TARGET

Section 6.1. Conduct of Business. Except as set forth in Section 6.1 of the Disclosure Statement or required to consummate the transactions contemplated hereby, from and after the execution and delivery of this Agreement and until the Closing Date, the Seller shall cause the Target and each of

> the Subsidiaries (a) to use its best efforts to preserve the respective present business organizations of the Target and the Subsidiaries substantially intact; (b) to maintain in effect all foreign, federal, state and local approvals, permits, licenses, qualifications and authorizations which are required to carry on their respective businesses as now being conducted; (c) to use their best efforts to maintain their respective relationships with, and preserve the goodwill of, employees, agents, distributors, franchisees, licensees, customers, suppliers and others having business dealings with them; and (d) without the prior written consent of the Buyer, to take any action which would result in a breach of any of the representations set forth in Section 4.32 hereof.

The "conduct of business" covenant is used by a buyer to ensure that the seller will not do, or cause to be done, anything that would (a) alter the business being purchased, (b) diminish the value of such business to the buyer, or (c) create for the buyer an unanticipated liability or problem with respect to the business it is acquiring. This is important because the buyer has presumably negotiated an acceptable purchase price for the target based on the operations and performance of the business as it presently exists. If the seller were to allow necessary permits or licenses, or business relationships with distributors, employees, or franchisees to lapse, the value of the business could be diminished. If not restricted by such a covenant, the seller could render the buyer's valuation meaningless by taking some action outside of the ordinary course of business that impairs the financial position of the target or the value of the target to the buyer. One issue that often arises is how to define the actions that are in the ordinary course of business. Since most agreements fail to include a definition of this phrase, the buyer should acquaint itself with applicable case law in order to be aware of its usage in the jurisdiction governing the acquisition agreement.

In negotiating this representation, the seller should be certain that, between the signing of the agreement and the closing date, it need not obtain the buyer's consent for anything other than items that would not normally occur in the ordinary course of business of the target or its subsidiaries. Subsection (d) incorporates all of the items represented in Section 4.32 and consequently may require the seller to obtain the buyer's consent for actions to be taken by the target or any subsidiary that are extremely important to the continued operation of the business. A seller would likely request that the buyer agree not to unreasonably withhold its consent in order for the seller to take such actions. Although this language may seem innocuous, it can in certain circumstances have consequences that the buyer did not intend at the time. As state courts have not consistently interpreted the standard of reasonableness, the buyer may be unable to reconcile its business judgments with local case precedent. A common strategy is for a buyer to require unmodified consent in its first draft, and then, if the seller requests it, add the reasonableness standard as a bargaining point or show of good faith.

> ***Section 6.2. Pre-Closing Activities.*** Prior to the Closing Date, the Seller shall cause the Target, with the cooperation of the Buyer where appropriate, and the Target shall and shall cause each Subsidiary to use their best efforts to obtain any consent, authorization or approval of, or exemption by, any governmental authority or agency or other third party, including without limitation, their landlords and lenders and those persons (other than the Target or a Subsidiary) who are parties to the agreements described in Section 4.29 of the Disclosure Statement required to be obtained or made by them in connection with the transactions contemplated by this Agreement and the Related Instruments or the taking of any action in connection with the consummation thereof, including without limitation, any consent, authorization or approval necessary to waive any default under any of the agreements described in Section 4.29 of the Disclosure Statement.

Once the buyer is made aware of the various consents necessary to consummate the acquisition by means of the seller's disclosure in Section 4.29, the buyer typically will attempt to require the seller to use its best efforts to obtain such consents. The seller, who has an interest in getting the deal done, should agree to accommodate the buyer, but only to the extent it is reasonable for the seller to do so under the circumstances. It should make clear that "best efforts" do not extend to spending money.

> ***Section 6.3. Proposals; Disclosure.*** Prior to the Closing Date, the Target and the Seller (i) will not, directly or indirectly, whether through any of their officers, employees, representatives or otherwise, solicit or encourage any written inquiries or proposals for the acquisition of stock, or all or

substantially all of the assets or the business or any portion thereof of the Target or any Subsidiary and (ii) will promptly advise the Buyer orally and in writing of any inquiry or proposal for the acquisition of any stock, or all or substantially all of the assets or business or any portion thereof of the Target or any Subsidiary occurring on or after the date hereof.

This covenant is designed (a) to prevent the seller from shopping for a better deal during the period between signing of the acquisition agreement and the Closing Date, and (b) to keep the buyer apprised of any unsolicited inquiries. From the buyer's point of view, the seller has made a commitment to sell to the buyer and should be concentrating all of its efforts toward a closing with the buyer rather than continuing to court other would-be suitors. In addition, the acquisition agreement represents a binding contract, and the buyer has made a commitment to purchase provided that all conditions to closing are satisfied. The buyer should have the benefit of having made such a commitment as well as the risk of a deterioration in the target's business in the ordinary course of events. One benefit of ownership is the opportunity to sell at a profit. The *Pennzoil v. Texaco* case has highly publicized the fact that this benefit belongs to a potential buyer once a contractual commitment between the seller and the buyer has been put in place.

Section 6.4. Additional Financial Statements. Prior to the Closing Date, the Target shall furnish to the Buyer as soon as practicable but in no event later than ______________ days after the close of each quarterly period or ______________ days after the close of each monthly period (i) for each successive quarterly period ending after the date of the Most Recent Balance Sheet, an unaudited consolidated quarterly balance sheet and related statements of income, stockholders' equity and changes in financial position of the Target and its Subsidiaries and (ii) for each successive monthly period ending after the date of the Most Recent Balance Sheet, an unaudited consolidated monthly balance sheet and related monthly statements of income, stockholders' equity and changes in financial position of the Target and its Subsidiaries. Such financial statements shall be complete, accurate and correct and present fairly the financial condition of the Target and the Subsidiaries, both individually and taken as a whole, as of the end of each such quarterly or monthly period, as the case may be, and shall present fairly the results of operations for each of the quarterly or monthly periods then ended, in accordance with generally accepted accounting principles consistently applied except for the footnotes thereto, normal year-end adjustments consistent with past practices or as contemplated by this Agreement.

Section 6.5. Additional Summaries of Accounts Receivable. Prior to the Closing Date, the Target will deliver to the Buyer, as soon as practicable but in no event later than ______________ days after the close of the appropriate monthly period hereinafter referred to, for each successive monthly period after the date of the Most Recent Balance Sheet a true and correct summary of all accounts receivable of the Target and the Subsidiaries as at the end of each such monthly period.

Sections 6.4 and 6.5 permit the buyer to monitor the operations of the business after the execution of the acquisition agreement by reviewing monthly and quarterly financial statements furnished by the seller. This can be extremely important to the buyer, especially if the financial statements reveal a material adverse change in the business. In this event, the buyer would not be obligated to close, since a customary condition to its obligation to close is the absence of any material adverse changes in the business. For a further discussion of material adverse change, see Section 9.6.

Section 6.6. Investigation by Buyer. The Seller and Target shall, and the Target shall cause its Subsidiaries to, afford to the officers and authorized representatives of the Buyer free and full access, during normal business hours and upon reasonable prior notice, to the offices, plants, properties, books and records of the Target and its Subsidiaries in order that the Buyer may have full opportunity to make such investigations of the business, operations, assets, properties and legal and financial condition of the Target and its Subsidiaries as the Buyer deems reasonably necessary or desirable; and the officers of the Seller, the Target and its Subsidiaries shall furnish the Buyer with such additional financial and operating data and other information relating to the business operations, assets, properties and legal and financial condition of the Target and its Subsidiaries as the Buyer shall from time to time reasonably request. Prior to the Closing Date, or at all times if this Agreement shall be terminated, the Buyer shall, except as may be otherwise required by applicable law, hold confidential all information obtained pursuant to this Section 6.6 with respect to the Target and its Subsidiaries and, if this Agreement shall be terminated, shall return to the Target and its Subsidiaries all such information as shall be in documentary form and shall not use any information obtained pursuant to this Section 6.6 in any manner that would have a material adverse consequence to the Target or its Subsidiaries.

The representations, warranties and agreements of the Seller, the Target and its Subsidiaries set forth in this Agreement shall be effective regardless of any investigation that the Buyer has undertaken or failed to undertake.

The "investigation" covenant ensures that the seller will cooperate with the buyer by granting access and logistical support for the buyer's due diligence review of the target and its subsidiaries. It is important for the buyer to include the last paragraph of this covenant so that the seller cannot attempt to prevent the buyer from taking action against the seller as a result of a material breach of the seller's or target's representations by alleging that, since the buyer discovered or could have discovered the breach during its investigation of the target and its subsidiaries, the seller should be relieved of any responsibility for such misrepresentations.

Section 6.7. Notification. The Seller shall give prompt notice to the Buyer of (i) any notice of, or other communication received by the Seller, the Target or any Subsidiary subsequent to the date of this Agreement and prior to the Closing Date, relating to a default or event which with notice or lapse of time or both would become a default, or which would cause any warranty or representation of the Seller or the Target to be untrue or misleading in any material respect, under this Agreement, or any other material contract, agreement or instrument to which the Target or any Subsidiary is a party, by which it or any of its property is bound or to which it or any of its property is subject, (ii) any notice or other communication from any third party alleging that the consent of such third party is or may be required in connection with the transactions contemplated by this Agreement, (iii) any material adverse change in the business, operations, earnings, prospects, assets or financial condition of the Target or its Subsidiaries, or (iv) any information received by the Seller or Target prior to the Closing Date relating to the operations of the Buyer which, to the best knowledge of the Seller or Target, constitutes (or would be reasonably likely to constitute) or indicates (or would be reasonably likely to indicate) a breach of any representation, warranty or covenant made by the Buyer herein or in any other document relating to the transactions contemplated hereby.

The "notice" covenant places on the seller the onus of notifying the buyer of any potential material breaches of the seller's representations and warranties. Upon such notification, the buyer has the option of asserting a breach and abandoning the deal on the grounds that the conditions to closing are not met. However, a buyer does not have a right to walk from the deal if the breach can be cured by the seller prior to the closing.

Section 6.8. Access to Records. After the Closing, the Buyer shall be entitled to reasonable access to the business and tax records of the Seller relating to the Target and its Subsidiaries for proper business purposes, including the preparation of tax returns. In connection with any such purpose, the Seller agrees to cooperate with the Buyer in the communication of information contained in such records and the handling of examinations, appeals and litigations.

This covenant may be important where many of the records of the target and its subsidiaries are consolidated with those of the seller. It is impossible in such circumstances for the seller to turn over to the buyer such records, since they may also relate to other companies owned by the seller.

Section 6.9. Stockholders' Meeting. The Target, acting through its Board of Directors shall, as soon as practicable and in accordance with its Articles of Incorporation and By-Laws and applicable law:

(1) prepare and distribute proxy materials (the "Proxy Statement") in compliance with applicable law for, and duly call, give notice of, convene and hold, a special meeting (the "Special Meeting") of its stockholders as soon as practicable after the date hereof but not later than [insert the date] for the purposes of considering and voting upon this Agreement in accordance with the [name of business code for Target's state of incorporation] Code;

(2) include in the Proxy Statement (as hereinafter defined) the recommendation of the Board that stockholders of the Target vote in favor of the approval and adoption of this Agreement; and

(3) use its best efforts (a) to obtain and furnish the information required to be included by it in the Proxy Statement, (b) to file a preliminary version of the Proxy Statement with the Securities and Exchange Commission ("SEC") not later than [insert number of days] after the receipt by the Target of its audited financial statement for the year ended [insert year], furnish copies thereof to the Buyer and, after consultation with the Buyer, respond promptly to any comments made by the SEC with respect to the Proxy Statement and any preliminary version thereof, (c) to cause the Proxy Statement to be mailed to its stockholders as early as practicable after the date hereof but no later than [insert number of days], and (d) to obtain the necessary approval of this Agreement by its stockholders. Notwithstanding any consultation with the Buyer in connection with the Proxy Statement, neither the Buyer nor any of its officers, directors, employees or affiliates shall incur any liability to the Target or its stockholders with respect thereto, except with respect to any information contained in the Proxy Statement which any of them has furnished, or confirmed the accuracy of, in writing to the Target.

(4) amend, supplement or revise the Proxy Statement as may from time to time be necessary in order to insure that the Proxy Statement does not contain any statement which, at the time and in the light of the circumstances under which it is made, is false or misleading with respect to any material fact, or omits to state any material fact necessary in order to make the statements therein not false or misleading. Prior to submitting any such amendment, supplement or revision of the Proxy Statement to the stockholders of the Target, such amendment, supplement or revision shall be submitted to the Buyer for its approval. Notwithstanding such approval, neither the Buyer nor any of its officers, directors, employees or affiliates shall incur any liability to the Target or its stockholders with respect thereto, except with respect to any information contained in such amendment, supplement or revision which any of them has furnished, or confirmed the accuracy of, in writing to the Target.

In an acquisition of a target whose equity securities are publicly traded, it is essential that the target comply with all relevant regulations, especially those promulgated by the Securities and Exchange Commission dealing with proxies and required stockholders' meetings. Failure to comply with these regulations can expose the target to stockholder suits or regulatory enforcement actions. The buyer is also desirous of placing an affirmative obligation on the target to solicit proxies and to obtain stockholder approval.

In some circumstances, the buyer may require the seller to deliver a cold comfort letter from the seller's or target's accountants at closing confirming the financial information in the proxy statement. The purpose of this requirement is to reduce the potential for error in the financial information presented in the proxy statement and thereby reduce the chance that a stockholder may prevail in a suit against the surviving corporation.

> ***Section 6.10. Dissenting Stockholders; Notice.*** The Target will promptly advise the Buyer of each notice given or demand made by a dissenting Target stockholder pursuant to [cite relevant section of business law in state where Target is incorporated].

No buyer wants to close a transaction in which a large percentage of the target's stockholders are seeking appraisal rights. If such stockholders were to be awarded a price per share in excess of the price paid by the buyer, it could expose the surviving corporation to an inordinate amount of liability. Therefore, as covered in Section 9.10 and the discussion that follows, in order for a buyer to exercise its right not to consummate the transaction pursuant to Section 9.10, it must be aware of any dissenting stockholders of the target.

ARTICLE VII: COVENANTS OF THE BUYER

> The Buyer shall give prompt notice to the Seller of (i) any notice of, or other communication received by the Buyer subsequent to the date of this Agreement and prior to the Closing Date, relating to a default or event which with notice or lapse of time or both would become a default, or which would cause any warranty, or representation of the Buyer to be untrue or misleading in any material respect, under this Agreement, or any other material contract, agreement or instrument to which the Buyer is a party, by which it or any of its property is bound or to which it or any of its property is subject, (ii) any notice or other communication from any third party alleging that the consent of such third party is or may be required in connection with the transactions contemplated by this Agreement, or (iii) any information

received by the Buyer prior to the Closing Date relating to the operations of the Seller, the Target or its Subsidiaries which, to the best knowledge of the Buyer, constitutes (or would constitute) or indicates (or would indicate) a breach of any representation, warranty or covenant made by the Seller or Target herein or in any other document relating to the transactions contemplated hereby.

Similar to the representations, the seller's covenants usually far outnumber the covenants of the buyer. Typically, a seller would at a minimum require a buyer to give the same "notice" that it is required to give. One useful device (which is advantageous to both buyer and seller) is the requirement that each notify the other in the event that the first party is aware of the other's breach of a particular representation, warranty, or covenant. The utility of this obligation, especially for the seller, is that neither side has a distinct advantage over the other post-closing by reason of a breach that was known about prior to the closing.

ARTICLE VIII: COVENANTS OF BUYER, TARGET AND SELLER

Section 8.1. Governmental Filings. The Buyer, the Target and the Seller shall cooperate with each other in filing any necessary applications, reports or other documents with any federal or state agencies, authorities or bodies (domestic and foreign) having jurisdiction with respect to the Merger, and in seeking necessary consultation with and prompt favorable action by any such agencies, authorities or bodies. Without limiting the generality of the foregoing, the Buyer, the Target and the Seller shall as soon as practicable, and in any event within fifteen (15) days, after the date hereof, make the necessary filings under the Hart-Scott-Rodino Antitrust Improvements Act of 1976 (the "Hart-Scott-Rodino Act") and shall cooperate in attempting to secure early termination of the applicable waiting period.

This covenant requires the buyer, target, and seller to work together in making any governmental filing or application. The buyer and the seller should use a general covenant of this type and then specify the particular filings that must be made (Hart-Scott-Rodino Act filings with respect to a merger, SEC filings, state government filings, and so on).

Section 8.2. Publicity. The Buyer, the Target and the Seller will consult with each other before making any public announcements with respect to the Merger or the Related Instruments or the transactions contemplated hereby or thereby, and any public announcements shall be made only at such time and in such manner as the Seller and the Buyer shall mutually agree, except that either party shall be free to make such public announcements as it shall reasonably deem necessary to comply with foreign, federal or state laws.

The buyer and the seller must be aware of each other's plans with respect to publicity surrounding the acquisition of a target so as to be able to coordinate their efforts. It can be extremely harmful to the transaction or one of the parties to the transaction if there are conflicting reports or misleading statements. For example, conflicting reports in the press can disrupt management of the target or may even damage the ongoing business. More important, where one or both of the entities involved are public companies, liability can arise from premature press reports that might be alleged to have been made to manipulate the market or mislead stockholders and investors. When possible, the buyer and seller should issue joint press releases or, at least, carefully review releases before they are distributed.

ARTICLE IX: CONDITIONS TO OBLIGATIONS OF THE BUYER

The obligations of the Buyer to consummate this Agreement, and the transactions to be consummated by the Buyer hereunder on the Closing Date, shall be subject to the satisfaction, prior to or concurrently with the Closing, of each of the conditions set forth in this Article IX; such conditions may be waived in writing in whole or in part by the Buyer to the extent permitted by applicable law.

Section 9.1. Compliance with Agreement. The Seller and the Target shall have complied with and performed the terms, conditions, acts, undertakings, covenants and obligations required by this Agreement to be complied with and performed by each of them on or before the Closing Date; and the Buyer shall have received from the Seller at the Closing a certificate, dated the Closing Date and signed by the President or a Vice President of the Seller to such effect.

This condition gives the buyer the opportunity to abandon the acquisition if the seller or the target has failed to perform its obligations under the acquisition agreement. Although this condition is less critical than the bring-down of representations and warranties to the closing date that appears in Section 9.2, it provides the buyer a valuable "out" if the seller or the target has breached a covenant that is essential to the buyer's valuation of the target. For example, the duty of the target to endeavor to obtain all regulatory approvals necessary for the transaction would usually arise from a covenant made to the buyer in the acquisition agreement, as would the obligation of the target to conduct business only in the ordinary and usual course. Because failure to perform under these covenants may compromise the value of the target, the buyer must ensure its right to abandon the transaction in these circumstances.

The requirement for an officer's certificate is based upon the belief that prior to any officer's execution of such a certificate, the officer will investigate to ascertain its accuracy, and the certificate can be drafted to include a representation to that effect.

This condition can be drafted without a materiality standard. However, sellers typically demand that the materiality qualifier be incorporated. This position is a reasonable one given the broad language of both the condition itself and the covenants and other agreements to which it refers. Consequently, the buyer should be prepared to accept "performance in all material respects of the terms" of the agreement as adequate protection of its interests. A similar qualifier appears in the condition set forth in Section 9.2, which follows.

Section 9.2. Representations and Warranties True as of Closing Date. All representations and warranties of the Seller and the Target set forth in this Agreement shall be true and correct in all material respects on and as of the Closing Date with the same force and effect as though such representations and warranties had been made on and as of the Closing Date and the Buyer shall have received from the Seller at the Closing a certificate, dated the Closing Date and signed by the President or a Vice President of the Seller to such effect.

The importance of this bring-down condition was discussed earlier in this chapter. A bring-down of the representations and warranties to the closing date is, from the buyer's perspective, insurance that the target it acquires is the target for which it bid and upon which it conducted due diligence.

Section 9.3. Third Party Orders and Consents.

(i) The Seller and the Buyer shall have fully complied with the applicable provisions of the Hart-Scott-Rodino Act and any and all applicable waiting periods thereunder shall have expired, or an opinion, reasonably acceptable to the Buyer, that no such filing is required shall have been delivered to the Buyer.

(ii) All consents and approvals listed in Section 4.29 of the Disclosure Statement hereto shall have been obtained, and the Seller and the Buyer shall have been furnished with appropriate evidence, reasonably satisfactory to them and their respective counsel, of the granting of such consents and approvals.

This condition enables the buyer to abandon a transaction if all necessary consents are not obtained before closing. Failure to obtain the consent of the target's lenders, for example, may prejudice the pricing of the acquisition or its financeability because consummation of the transaction may entitle the lenders to accelerate their debts or impose a lien on the property of the target. Failure to obtain necessary governmental consent to an acquisition may preclude the buyer from operating the business of the target as previously operated.

The seller should attempt to limit this condition to governmental consents necessary in order to consummate the transactions contemplated by the acquisition agreement. The seller could reasonably maintain that any debt instruments that are accelerated by their terms should be refinanced by the buyer. If this limitation is accepted, the obligation of the buyer to close the deal should not be conditioned upon the consent of the holders of such debt. Clearly, the buyer and the seller must agree on exactly what consents must be obtained prior to the closing.

Section 9.4. Corporate Action. The Buyer shall have received:

(i) a copy of the resolution or resolutions duly adopted by the Board of Directors of the Seller and the Target and by the stockholders of the Target authorizing the execution, delivery and performance of this Agreement and the Related Instruments by the Seller and the Target, and authorizing all other necessary or proper corporate action to enable the Seller and the Target to comply with the terms of this Agreement, certified in each case by the Secretary or an Assistant Secretary of the Seller or the Target as the case may be; and

(ii) a certificate of the Secretary or an Assistant Secretary of each of the Seller and the Target, dated the Closing Date, as to the incumbency and signatures of the officers of the Seller and the Target, respectively, executing this Agreement and the Related Instruments and any other documents in connection with the transactions contemplated by this Agreement or the Related Instruments.

A further protection for the Buyer that the acquisition agreement and related documents are properly authorized and delivered is a review of the resolutions authorizing such documents.

Section 9.5. Opinion of the Seller's and Target's Counsel. At the Closing, the Seller shall furnish the Buyer and the banks and/or other financial institutions providing financing for the Merger (the "Acquisition Lenders") with an opinion, dated the Closing Date, of [name of Seller's counsel], in form and substance satisfactory to the Buyer and its counsel and the Acquisition Lenders and counsel to the Acquisition Lenders, to the effect that:

(i) Target (a) is a corporation duly organized, validly existing and in good standing under the laws of its state of incorporation, (b) is duly qualified or licensed to transact business as a foreign corporation and is in good standing in each jurisdiction in which the properties owned or leased by it or the nature of the business conducted by it makes such qualification or licensing necessary, except in those jurisdictions where the failure to be so qualified or licensed and in good standing will not, individually or in the aggregate, have a Material Adverse Effect, and (c) has full power and authority to carry on its business as it is now being conducted and to own the properties and assets it now owns;

(ii) Target has full power and authority to execute, deliver and perform the Agreement and the Related Instruments and to consummate the transactions contemplated hereby and by the Related Instruments; and the execution, delivery and performance of the Agreement and the Related Instruments and the consummation of the transactions contemplated by the

Agreement and the Related Instruments have been duly authorized by all requisite action on the part of the Target;

(iii) the Seller is a corporation duly organized, validly existing and in good standing under the laws of its state of incorporation and has full power and authority to execute, deliver and perform the Agreement and the Related Instruments and to consummate the transactions contemplated by the Agreement and the Related Instruments; and the execution, delivery and performance of the Agreement and the Related Instruments and the consummation of the transactions contemplated by the Agreement and the Related Instruments have been duly authorized by all requisite action on the part of the Seller;

(iv) each of the Subsidiaries (a) is a corporation duly organized, validly existing and in good standing under the laws of its jurisdiction of organization, (b) is duly qualified or licensed to transact business and is in good standing in each jurisdiction in which the properties owned or leased by it or the nature of the business conducted by it makes such qualification or licensing necessary, except in those jurisdictions where the failure to be so qualified or licensed and in good standing will not, individually or in the aggregate, have a Material Adverse Effect and (c) has full power and authority to carry on its business as it is now being conducted and to own the properties and assets it now owns;

(v) the authorized, issued and outstanding equity capital of the Target and each Subsidiary consists solely of (a) in the case of the Target, ______________ shares of Common Stock, of which ______________ shares are issued and outstanding and ______________ shares of Preferred Stock, of which ______________ shares are issued and outstanding and (b) in the case of each Subsidiary, as set forth in Section 4.3 of the Disclosure Statement (the "Subsidiary Stock"). All outstanding shares of the Target Common Stock and the Subsidiary Stock have been duly and validly authorized and issued and are fully paid, nonassessable and free of preemptive rights and based upon an examination of the organizational documents, minute books, stock registers and other similar records of the Target, all of such shares are owned of record and beneficially by (a) the Seller, in the case of the Target and (b) as set forth in Section 4.1 of the Disclosure Statement, in the case of each Subsidiary, in each case free and clear of all claims, liens, mortgages, charges, security interests, encumbrances and other restrictions or limitations of any kind whatsoever, and there are no outstanding options, warrants, calls, convertible securities or other rights relating to unissued shares of capital stock of Target or any Subsidiary;

(vi) the Agreement and the Related Instruments have been executed and delivered by each of the Seller and the Target and constitutes the legal, valid and binding obligations of each of the Seller and the Target, enforceable against each in accordance with their respective terms, except (a) as such enforcement may be subject to fraudulent conveyance, bankruptcy, insolvency, reorganization, moratorium or other similar laws now or hereafter in effect, or by legal or equitable principles, relating to or limiting creditors' rights generally and (b) that the remedy of specific performance and injunctive and other forms of equitable relief are subject to certain equitable defenses and to the discretion of the court before which any proceeding therefor may be brought;

(vii) neither the execution, delivery and performance of the Agreement or the Related Instruments by the Seller or the Target, nor the consummation of the transactions contemplated hereby or thereby will violate any provision of the Certificate of Incorporation or Bylaws of the Seller or the Target or of any of the Subsidiaries or, to the best knowledge of such counsel after due inquiry, will violate, conflict with, or constitute a default under, or cause the acceleration of maturity of any debt or obligation pursuant to, or result in the creation or imposition of any security interest, lien or other encumbrance upon any property or assets of the Target or any of the Subsidiaries under, any contract, commitment, agreement, trust, understanding, arrangement or restriction of any kind to which the Target or any of the Subsidiaries is a party or by which the Target or any of the Subsidiaries is bound or violate any statute or law, or any judgment, decree, order, regulation or rule of any court or governmental authority;

(viii) to the best knowledge of such counsel, none of the Target, the Seller nor any Subsidiary is engaged in or threatened with any legal action or other proceeding or has incurred or been charged with or is under investigation with respect to any violation of any law or administrative regulation which if adversely determined might, in such counsel's opinion, materially adversely affect or impair (a) the business or condition, financial or otherwise, of the Target or any of the Subsidiaries except as specifically disclosed in the Agreement or the Disclosure Statement or (b) the ability of the Target and/or the Seller to consummate the transactions contemplated by the Agreement or the Related Instruments;

(ix) no filing, declaration or registration with, or any permit, authorization, license, consent or approval of, any governmental or regulatory authority is required in connection with the execution, delivery and performance of the Agreement or the Related Instruments by the Seller and the Target or the consummation of the transactions contemplated by the Agreement or the Related Instruments, except as expressly disclosed in this Agreement, all of which have been duly and validly obtained;

(x) no facts have come to the attention of such counsel that cause such counsel to believe that any information provided to the Buyer in writing by or on behalf of the Seller or the Target contained any untrue statement of a material fact or omitted to state any material fact necessary to make the statements therein, in light of the circumstances under which they were made, not misleading, except that counsel may also state that it has not independently verified the accuracy, completeness or fairness of such information, and the limitations inherent in the examination made by it and the knowledge available to it are such that it is unable to assume, and does not assume, any responsibility for the accuracy, completeness or fairness of such information.

As to any matter contained in such opinion which involves the laws of a jurisdiction other than the United States or the State of [state in which such counsel is licensed to practice], such counsel may rely upon opinions of local counsel of established reputation reasonably satisfactory to the Buyer, which opinions shall expressly state that they may be relied upon by the Buyer and the Acquisition Lenders. Such counsel may also expressly rely as to matters of fact upon certificates furnished by appropriate officers of the Seller, the Target and any Subsidiary, or appropriate governmental officials.

Typically, the seller and the target will require an opinion from the buyer's counsel (see Section 10.6) that mirrors many of the provisions included in the opinion given by seller's counsel. Although these opinions may be heavily negotiated by the counsel who must render them, they are useful for a variety of reasons. First, legal opinions serve as a due diligence device and force counsel to closely examine the important aspects of the transaction. Second, counsel's reluctance to deliver an opinion regarding a particular issue raises a red flag, permitting the parties to reexamine that aspect of the transaction. Third, the opinion gives the party to which it is addressed legal recourse against counsel delivering the opinion. In this regard, the buyer may be asked to accept the opinion of general counsel to the seller or target. The buyer should resist this request since the buyer's recourse against the general counsel of the target may be tantamount to recourse against the surviving corporation. In contrast, outside counsel's opinion provides recourse against an independent source, one that may be more diligent in its efforts and less biased in its evaluation as a result of its potential liability and relative "distance" from the seller's management.

In some circumstances, the buyer may be required to accept the opinion of general counsel with respect to certain matters relating to the law of a jurisdiction where it would be impractical or inordinately expensive to retain outside counsel. In addition, outside counsel frequently relies on a backup opinion from the general counsel of the target with respect to matters that pertain to the business of the target in general. For example, general counsel would probably provide a backup opinion with respect to whether the target is qualified as a foreign corporation in each jurisdiction in which the properties owned or leased by it or the nature of the business conducted by it makes such qualification or licensure necessary.

The opinion also may be used as a negotiating tool in the earlier phases of the transaction; counsel's unwillingness to opine that no governmental consent is required in connection with the contemplated transactions or to the enforceability of particular documents may cause the parties to revamp the structure of the transaction.

One opinion that counsel is often reluctant to deliver is expressed in clause (x) on the preceding page. Only rarely will counsel accept such a high level of responsibility. If the acquisition involves a public company, counsel may agree to opine to the accuracy of the proxy statement if counsel oversaw its preparation. Otherwise, despite the buyer's legitimate concern with the accuracy of information provided by the seller, the target, and the subsidiaries, it will not have the comfort of counsel's opinion on the matter. If a party is extremely concerned about the withholding of information or the accuracy thereof, it may be able to persuade the seller's counsel to include clause (x) at the end of its opinion letter without giving it the benefit of being a legal opinion.

> ***Section 9.6. No Material Adverse Change.*** No material adverse change in the business, operations, earnings, prospects, assets or financial condition of the Target or any Subsidiary and no event which would have such an effect shall have occurred.

As discussed, a customary condition to the buyer's obligation to close the transaction is that the target has not suffered any adverse change prior to the closing. The seller should attempt to limit this condition to the target and its subsidiaries taken as a whole since the buyer is not buying the target and its subsidiaries piecemeal. The seller should also focus on the phrase "business, operations, earnings, prospects, assets or financial condition" because, in some instances, the buyer may not have bargained for a certain earnings stream or the prospects of the target. For example, in a transaction based on the net assets of the target, a seller who has not made any projections as to the growth of the business of the target could argue that the target's "earnings" and "prospects" are irrelevant and should be deleted from this condition, since the deal was not priced on a multiple of earnings or discounted cash flow. This appears plausible, since the buyer has based its investment decision only on the value of the net assets. However, most buyers will resist this approach, alleging that future earnings were an important factor in the investment decision.

Conversely, where the buyer has relied on projections, it should specifically include the projections in this condition as a yardstick for measuring the prospects of the target.

What constitutes a material adverse change is unclear and varies from circumstance to circumstance. It's easy to identify an obvious one, such as the single line target that has lost the only supplier of raw materials for the manufacture of its product. But the loss of a customer whose purchase of goods from the target constitutes 5 percent of the target's overall revenues is a less clear-cut situation. The usual vagueness of this condition gives the buyer the opportunity to get out of the deal, even in circumstances where the change is of uncertain harm to the target, because the seller is usually disinclined to bring suit on the basis that no material adverse change has occurred. Of course, the buyer must have some real basis for its belief that a material adverse change has occurred. Usually, the seller and buyer attempt to restructure the transaction in light of any material adverse change.

Section 9.7. Litigation. At the Closing, there shall be no effective injunction, writ or preliminary restraining order or any order of any nature issued by a court or governmental agency of competent jurisdiction restraining or prohibiting the consummation of the transactions provided for herein or any of them or limiting in any manner the Buyer's right to control the Target and the Subsidiaries or any aspect of their businesses or requiring the sale or other disposition of any of the operations of the Target or any Subsidiary or making the consummation of the Merger or the transactions contemplated by this Agreement and the Related Instruments unduly burdensome to the Target or any Subsidiary, and immediately prior to the Closing Date no proceeding or lawsuit shall have been commenced and be pending or be threatened by any governmental or regulatory agency or any other person with respect to the transactions contemplated by this Agreement or the Related Instruments which the Buyer, in good faith and with the advice of counsel, believes is likely to result in any of the foregoing or which seeks the payment of substantial damages by the Target, any Subsidiary or the Buyer.

The utility of this condition is self-explanatory. It is usually triggered in circumstances in which either the acquisition is unfriendly and a potential suitor has brought suit to enjoin the consummation of the transaction contemplated by the acquisition agreement or a governmental agency has attempted to enjoin the transaction because of antitrust or other governmental concerns.

Section 9.8. Financing.

(i) The Buyer shall have received the financing proceeds pursuant to, and on substantially the same terms and conditions as those contained in, the commitment letter from [name of Acquisition Lender].

(ii) The final documentation of such financing arrangements referred to in the commitment letter from [name of Acquisition Lender] shall in all respects be reasonably satisfactory in form and substance to the Buyer.

This provision about financing is appropriate if the buyer has obtained financing commitments before signing the acquisition agreement. Another approach, which is appropriate if the parties have agreed that the buyer must finance the transaction within a certain period of time, is to build in a provision enabling the parties to terminate the acquisition agreement if commitment letters are not obtained or the deal is not closed by a specific date.

> ***Section 9.9. Title Insurance.*** [Insert name of title company], or any other reputable title company reasonably satisfactory to the Buyer (the "Title Company") shall have issued owners,' lessees' and mortgagees' title insurance policies (or unconditional commitments therefor) with respect to, and in the amount of the fair market value of, the real property and the leased real property listed in Section 4.15 of the Disclosure Statement and located in the United States, the United States territories and possessions and Canada, on the current edition of the American Land Title Association (ALTA) Form B[20] (or Loan Policy Form, in the case of mortgagees' title insurance) insuring title, with all standard and general exceptions deleted or endorsed over so as to afford full "extended form coverage," except for the lien of taxes not yet due and payable, and with no further exceptions not reasonably satisfactory to the Buyer. It is hereby agreed that if, in order to delete, or endorse over, standard form or general exceptions so as to afford to owners, lessees or lenders "extended form coverage," the Title Company requires standard form seller's affidavits, the conditions set forth in this Section 9.10 shall be satisfied by an authorized officer of the Seller giving such affidavit. The Buyer shall have received unconditional title insurance commitments reflecting the foregoing matters at least ten (10) days prior to Closing.

This condition provides the buyer comfort that the real property owned or leased by the target is free from defects in title and, consequently, may be used to secure acquisition financing. The seller may demand that this condition be effective only to the extent that Acquisition Lenders require title insurance. On the other hand, the buyer may strengthen the condition to make the existence of a title defect that compromises the business of the target a sufficient basis for abandoning the transaction. To the extent that title insurance is unavailable and the real property is an integral part of the business of the target, this condition gives the buyer the opportunity to renegotiate the price of the acquisition or to walk away from the deal.

Section 9.10. Dissenting Stockholders. Holders of not more than [insert percentage] of the Target's Common Stock shall have elected dissenter's rights as provided in Section [ ] of the [business code of Target's state of incorporation] Code, and the Target shall have taken all action with respect to the rights of dissenting stockholders required of it pursuant to such Code.

In an acquisition of a target with numerous stockholders, a buyer should attempt to limit its exposure to liability in the event that the stockholders of the target achieve a higher price for the value of their shares than that paid by the buyer through an appraisal proceeding brought by such stockholders postclosing. The seller should obviously negotiate a percentage high enough to prevent the buyer from abandoning the deal without good cause, and the buyer should be willing to accept some level of risk. The exact percentage of holders seeking appraisal rights in this condition depends on the circumstances.

ARTICLE X: CONDITIONS TO OBLIGATIONS OF THE SELLER AND TARGET

The obligations of the Seller and the Target to consummate this Agreement, and the transactions to be consummated by the Seller hereunder on the Closing Date, shall be subject to the satisfaction, with the Closing, of each of the conditions set forth in this Article X; which conditions may be waived in writing in whole or in part by the Seller to the extent permitted by applicable law.

Section 10.1. Compliance with Agreement. The Buyer shall have complied with and performed in all material respects the terms, conditions, acts, undertakings, covenants and obligations required by this Agreement to be complied with and performed by it on or before the Closing Date; and the Seller shall have received from the Buyer at the Closing a certificate, dated the Closing Date and signed by the President or a Vice President of the Buyer to such effect.

Section 10.2. Representations and Warranties True as of Closing Date. All representations and warranties of the Buyer set forth in this Agreement shall be true and correct in all material respects on and as of the Closing Date with the same force and effect as though such representations and warranties had been made on and as of the Closing Date and the Seller shall have received from the Buyer at the Closing a certificate, dated the Closing Date and signed by the President or a Vice President of the Buyer to such effect.

Section 10.3. Third Party Orders and Consents.

(i) The Seller and the Buyer shall have fully complied with the applicable provisions of the Hart-Scott-Rodino Act and any and all applicable waiting periods thereunder shall have expired, or an opinion, reasonably acceptable to the Seller, that no such filing is required shall have been delivered to the Seller.

(ii) All consents and approvals listed in Section 4.29 of the Disclosure Statement shall have been obtained, and the Seller and the Buyer shall have been furnished with appropriate evidence, reasonably satisfactory to them and their respective counsel, of the granting of such consents and approvals, and such consents and approvals remain in full force and effect on the Closing Date.

Section 10.4. Corporate Action. The Seller shall have received:

(i) a copy of the resolution or resolutions duly adopted by the Board of Directors of the Buyer and by the stockholders of the Buyer authorizing the execution, delivery and performance of this Agreement and the Related Instruments by the Buyer, and authorizing all other necessary or proper corporate action to enable the Buyer to comply with the terms of this Agreement and the Related Instruments, certified in each case by the Secretary or an Assistant Secretary of the Buyer; and

(ii) a certificate of the Secretary or an Assistant Secretary of the Buyer, dated the Closing Date, as to the incumbency and signatures of the officers of the Buyer executing this Agreement and the Related Instruments and any other documents in connection with the transactions contemplated by this Agreement and the Related Instruments.

Section 10.5. Opinion of the Buyer's Counsel. At the Closing, the Buyer shall furnish the Seller with an opinion, dated the Closing Date, of [name of Buyer's outside counsel], in form and substance reasonably satisfactory to the Seller and its counsel, to the effect that:

(i) the Buyer is a corporation duly organized, validly existing and in good standing under the laws of the state of its incorporation;

(ii) the Buyer has the power and authority to execute, deliver and perform the Agreement and the Related Instruments and to consummate the transactions contemplated by the Agreement and the Related Instruments; and the execution, delivery and performance of the Agreement and the Related Instruments and the consummation of the transactions contemplated by the Agreement and the Related Instruments have been duly authorized by all requisite action on the part of the Buyer;

(iii) this Agreement and the Related Instruments have been executed and delivered by the Buyer and is the legal, valid and binding obligation of the Buyer, enforceable against the Buyer in accordance with their respective terms, except (a) as such enforcement may be subject to fraudulent conveyance, bankruptcy, insolvency, reorganization, moratorium or other similar laws now or hereafter in effect, or by legal or equitable principles, relating to or limiting creditors' rights and (b) that the remedy of specific performance and injunctive and other forms of equitable relief are subject to certain equitable defenses and to the discretion of the court before which any proceeding therefor may be brought;

(iv) neither the execution, delivery and performance of the Agreement and the Related Instruments by the Buyer, nor the consummation of the transactions contemplated by the Agreement and the Related Instruments will violate any provision of the Certificate of Incorporation or Bylaws of the Buyer, or to the best knowledge of such counsel, will violate, conflict with, or constitute a default under, or cause the acceleration of maturity of any debt or obligation pursuant to, or result in the creation or imposition of any security interest, lien or other encumbrance upon any property or assets of the Buyer, any contract, commitment, agreement, trust, understanding, arrangement or restriction of any kind to which the Buyer is a party or by which the Buyer is bound or violate any statute or law, or any judgment, decree, order, regulation or rule of any court or governmental authority;

(v) to the best knowledge of such counsel, the Buyer is not engaged in or threatened with any legal action or other proceeding nor has it incurred or been charged with, nor is it under investigation with respect to, any violation of any law or administrative regulation which if adversely determined might, in such counsel's opinion, materially adversely affect or impair the ability of the Buyer to consummate the transactions contemplated hereby;

(vi) no filing, declaration or registration with, or any permit, authorization, license, consent or approval of, any governmental or regulatory authority is required in connection with the execution, delivery and performance of the Agreement and the Related Instruments by the Buyer or the consummation of the transactions contemplated by the Agreement and the

Related Instruments, except as expressly disclosed in the Agreement or the Disclosure Statement, all of which have been duly and validly obtained;

(vii) no facts have come to the attention of such counsel that cause such counsel to believe that any information provided to the Seller in writing by or on behalf of the Buyer contained any untrue statement of a material fact or omitted to state any material fact necessary to make the statements therein, in light of the circumstances under which they were made, not misleading, except that counsel may also state that it has not independently verified the accuracy, completeness or fairness of such information, and the limitations inherent in the examination made by it and the knowledge available to it are such that it is unable to assume, and does not assume, any responsibility for the accuracy, completeness or fairness of such information.

As to any matter contained in such opinion which involves the laws of a jurisdiction other than the United States or the State of [state in which Buyer's counsel is licensed to practice], Buyer's counsel may rely upon opinions of local counsel of established reputation reasonably satisfactory to the Seller, which opinions shall expressly state that they may be relied upon by the Seller. Such counsel may also expressly rely as to matters of fact upon certificates furnished by appropriate officers of the Buyer, or appropriate governmental officials.

Section 10.6. Litigation. At the Closing, there shall be no effective injunction, writ or preliminary restraining order or any order of any nature issued by a court or governmental agency of competent jurisdiction restraining or prohibiting the consummation of the transactions provided for herein or any of them or limiting in any manner the Buyer's right to control the Target and the Subsidiaries or any aspect of their businesses or requiring the sale or other disposition of any of the operations of the Target or any Subsidiary or making the consummation of the Merger or the transaction contemplated by this Agreement and the Related Instruments unduly burdensome to the Target or any Subsidiary, and immediately prior to the Closing Date no proceeding or lawsuit shall have been commenced and be pending or be threatened by any governmental or regulatory agency or any other person with respect to the transactions contemplated by this Agreement or the Related Instruments which the Buyer, in good faith and with the advice of counsel, believes is likely to result in any of the foregoing or which seeks the payment of substantial damages by the Target, any Subsidiary or the Buyer.

Sections 10.1 and 10.2 afford the seller the same right to abandon the transaction as the buyer has under Sections 9.1 and 9.2. However, since the buyer enters into fewer and less expansive representations and covenants than the seller, this right is typically less valuable to the seller than it is to the buyer.

Sections 10.3, 10.4, 10.5, and 10.6 are the seller's equivalent of the bring-down, consent, and corporate action legal opinions and litigation conditions given the buyer in Sections 9.3, 9.4, 9.5, and 9.7, respectively.

ARTICLE XI: TAX MATTERS

Section 11.1. Representations, Warranties and Covenants. The Seller and the Target each represents and warrants to the Buyer that:

(i) The Seller, the Target, and each of the Subsidiaries have filed or will file when due all federal, foreign, state and local tax returns, tax information returns, reports and estimates for all years and periods (and portions thereof) for which the due date (with extensions) is on or before the Closing Date. All such returns, reports and estimates were or will be prepared in the manner required by applicable law, and reflect or will reflect the liability for taxes of the Target or the Subsidiary filing same in all material respects and all Taxes (as defined in paragraph (v) of this Section 11.1 hereof) shown thereby to be payable and all assessments received by the Target and any Subsidiary have been paid or will be paid when due.

(ii) Section 11.1(ii) of the Disclosure Statement sets forth all jurisdictions in which the Target and the Subsidiaries have filed or will file income or franchise tax returns for each taxable period, or portion thereof, beginning on [insert date] and ending on or before the Closing Date.

(iii) The Target and each Subsidiary have withheld or will withhold amounts from their respective employees and have filed or will file all federal, foreign, state and local returns and reports with respect to employee income tax withholding and social security and unemployment Taxes for all periods (or portions thereof) ending on or before the Closing Date, in compliance with the provisions of the Internal Revenue Code, as amended and currently in effect (the "Code"), and other applicable federal, foreign, state and local laws.

(iv) The Target and the Subsidiaries have paid, or have provided a sufficient reserve on the Most Recent Balance Sheet for the payment of, all federal, state, local, and foreign Taxes with respect to all periods, or portions thereof, ending on or before the date of the Most Recent Balance Sheet.

(v) "Taxes" or "Tax" means all net income, capital gains, gross income, gross receipts, sales, use, ad valorem, franchise, profits, license, withholding, payroll, employment, excise, severance, stamp, occupation, premium, property, or windfall profit taxes, customs duties, or other taxes, fees, assessments, or charges of any kind whatsoever, together with any interest and any penalties, additions to tax, or additional amounts imposed by any taxing authority ("Taxing Authority") upon the Target or any Subsidiary.

(vi) The consolidated federal income tax returns of the Target through the taxable year ended ______________, have been examined by the United States Internal Revenue Service (the "IRS") or closed by applicable statutes of limitations, and any deficiencies or assessments, including interest and penalties thereon, claimed or made as a result of such examinations in respect of the Target and any of the Subsidiaries whose results of operations are includible for such years in the consolidated federal income tax returns of the Target have been paid or provided for.

(vii) Except as set forth in Section 11.1(vii) of the Disclosure Statement, there are no material claims or investigations by any Taxing Authority pending or to the best of the knowledge of Seller threatened against the Target or any Subsidiary for any past due Taxes; and there has been no waiver of any applicable statute of limitations or extension of the time for the assessment of any Tax against the Target or any Subsidiary except as set forth in Section 11.1(vii) of the Disclosure Statement.

(viii) Neither the Target nor any Subsidiary has made, signed or filed, nor will it make, sign or file any consent under Section 341(f) of the Code with respect to any taxable period ending on or before the Closing Date.

(ix) No event has occurred or will occur on or prior to the Closing Date that would require indemnification by the Target or any Subsidiary of any tax lessor under any agreements relating to tax leases executed under Section 168(f)(8) of the Internal Revenue Code or by Seller as to assets of the Target or any Subsidiary.

(x) Any and all consolidated federal income tax (or similar) agreements executed between the Target or a Subsidiary and the Seller, or any other member of the Seller's consolidated group that relate to any payments or liability therefor by or to the Target or a Subsidiary with respect to its federal income and other Taxes and that are continuing in effect will terminate as of the Closing Date, and notwithstanding any provisions contained in such agreements, and on the Closing Date, the Target and the Subsidiaries shall be relieved of all liability and obligation thereunder.

Section 11.2. Payment of Tax Liabilities.

(i) Subject to indemnification by the Seller under Section 11.3(i) hereof, the Target shall pay or cause to be paid at the times required by the relevant Taxing Authority all unpaid separate (unconsolidated) state, local or foreign Tax liabilities, including interest and any penalties thereon, of the Target and any Subsidiary for all periods, or portions thereof, ended on or before the Closing Date.

(ii) The Seller shall pay at the times required by the relevant Taxing Authority all unpaid federal or combined foreign, state or local Tax liabilities, including interest and any penalties thereon, attributable to the Target and the Subsidiaries for all periods, or portions thereof, with respect to which the Target and the Subsidiaries are included in a combined return.

Section 11.3. Indemnification.

(i) The Seller agrees to indemnify, defend and hold the Buyer, the Target and the Subsidiaries harmless against and from (a) all unpaid federal or combined foreign, state or local Tax liabilities of the Target and any Subsidiary for all periods, or portions thereof, ended on or before the Closing Date, together with any penalties and interest attributable to such liabilities, and (b) all unpaid separate (unconsolidated) state, local or foreign Tax liabilities of the Target and any Subsidiary for all periods, or portions thereof, ended on or before the Closing Date, together with any penalties and interest attributable to such liabilities. The amount of the Seller's obligation under this Section 11.3 shall be reduced by the value of any net Tax benefit ("Net Tax Benefit") realized by the Target and/or any Subsidiary by reason of a Tax deduction or loss, basis adjustment, and/or shifting of income, deductions, gains, losses and/or credits. For this purpose, the value of a Net Tax Benefit shall be determined by the accountant of the Target, using reasonable assumptions and methods of valuation.

(ii) The Seller shall indemnify and hold the Buyer, the Target, the Surviving Corporation and each Subsidiary harmless against any loss, liability, damage or expense (including reasonable attorneys' fees) arising out of or resulting from any inaccuracy or misrepresentation in or breach of any of the warranties, representations, covenants or agreements made by the Seller or the Target in this Article XI.

(iii) The Buyer, the Target, the Surviving Corporation and the Subsidiaries shall indemnify and hold the Seller harmless against any loss, liability, damage or expense (including reasonable attorneys' fees) arising out of or resulting from any inaccuracy or misrepresentation in or breach of any of the warranties, representations, covenants or agreements made by the Buyer in this Article XI.

(iv) The Seller and the Buyer shall satisfy their obligations to each other for indemnification hereunder by check or cash within sixty (60) days after written notice thereof from the other respective party.

(v) The Buyer, the Target and each Subsidiary, on the one hand, and the Seller, on the other hand, hereby agree that in the event a claim is made by one party to this Agreement against the other party, the party making the claim shall furnish to the other party all books, records and other information reasonably requested by such other party that relate to such claims.

Section 11.4. Post-Closing Obligations.

(i) The Seller shall include the results of operations of the Target and the Subsidiaries for the period ending on the Closing Date in its consolidated federal income tax return and in any consolidated or combined foreign, state or local income Tax return required to be filed by Seller after the Closing Date; and Seller will pay all federal, state, local and foreign income Taxes (including interest and penalties relating thereto) due for the periods covered by such returns with respect to the Target and each Subsidiary.

(ii) The Buyer shall cause the Target and the Subsidiaries to include the results of their respective operations in any separate (unconsolidated) state, foreign or local income Tax return for any taxable year beginning before and ending on or after the Closing Date. Subject to indemnification by the Seller under Section 11.3 hereof, the Buyer shall pay, or cause to be paid, all state, foreign or local income Taxes (including interest and penalties relating thereto) shown as due on any such return with respect to the Target or any Subsidiary.

(iii) All refunds or credits of Taxes paid by the Seller with respect to the Target or the Subsidiaries for periods ending on or prior to the Closing Date shall be the property of the Seller (except for refunds attributable to the carryback of any credits, losses or deductions arising out of the operation of the Target or the Subsidiaries after the Closing Date), and the Buyer shall forward to or reimburse the Seller for such refunds or credits (except as aforesaid) as soon as practicable after receipt thereof. Any refunds or credits of foreign, federal, state or local income Taxes, paid by the Buyer, the Target, the Surviving Corporation or any Subsidiary in accordance with the provisions of Section 11.4(ii) hereof with respect to the Target or any Subsidiary shall be the property of Buyer, the Target or the Subsidiary, as the case may be, and the Seller shall forward or reimburse the Buyer, the Target, or the Subsidiary for any such refunds or credits as soon as practicable after receipt thereof.

(iv) Any losses, credits or other Tax items of the Target or a Subsidiary, including, but not limited to, net operating losses, capital losses, business, foreign and other tax credits (the "Tax Attributes"), which may be attributable to the operation of the business of the Target or a Subsidiary after the Closing Date, including any carrybacks of such Tax Attributes to any period ending on or before the Closing Date, and any refunds of Taxes attributable thereto, shall belong to the Target. To the extent the Tax Attributes are carried back to the Seller's returns under applicable Treasury Regulations, the Seller will file appropriate refund claims upon receipt from the Target of information to be included in such claims. Any refunds attributable to such refund claims received by the Seller shall be received by the Seller solely as agent for the Target and the Seller shall pay over such refunds to the Target immediately upon receipt thereof. The out-of-pocket expenses incurred by the Seller in filing any such refund claim shall be borne by the Target.

(v) To the extent that any election or other action by the Seller or an audit by the IRS or relevant state revenue agency for taxable years ending on or before the Closing Date results in an increase in the federal, state or foreign income Tax liability of the Target or any Subsidiary for a taxable year ending after the Closing Date, the Seller shall promptly pay the amount of such increase to the Buyer, provided, however, that the Seller shall not be required to make such payment until it receives from the Target reasonable evidence that the increased liability of the Target (or a Subsidiary, as the case may be) is due and payable and provided further that in the event that a subsequent audit by the IRS or relevant state revenue agency of the Buyer, the Target or any Subsidiary results in a reduction or elimination of such increase that resulted in any payment made under this paragraph, the Buyer shall promptly refund such payment or portion thereof, as the case may be, together with interest thereon at the prime rate from the date of such payment through the date of such refund.

(vi) If requested by the Buyer, the Seller shall make or cause the Target, with respect to the Subsidiaries, to make a deemed dividend election as of [______________], the first day of the Target's most recent taxable year, pursuant to consolidated return Treas. Regs. 1.1502-32(f)(2) and, with respect to such Subsidiaries, a consent dividend with respect to the period commencing on [______________], the first day of the Target's most recent taxable year, through the Closing Date pursuant to Section 565 of the Code. The Seller shall also cause the Target and any Subsidiary, to the extent not inconsistent with the requirements of the preceding sentence, to not have an excess loss account, as defined in Treas. Regs. 1.1502-32(e)(1),[21] in the stock of any domestic subsidiary at the Closing Date.

(vii) At the reasonable request of the Buyer, the Seller will furnish to the Buyer, to the extent prepared or available and without representation or warranty, copies of (i) studies on the earnings and profits of the Target and each Subsidiary made pursuant to Treas. Regs. 1.1502-33 and (ii) computations pursuant to Treas. Regs. 1.1502-32 of actual investment adjustments with respect to the stock of, or any ownership interest in, the Target and each Subsidiary through the Closing Date.

(viii) Subsequent to the filing of the Seller's consolidated federal income tax return which includes the taxable period ending on the Closing Date, the Seller shall determine, under the Seller's policy, consistently applied, and pursuant to Treas. Reg. 1.1502-21,[22] the portion of any net operating loss or capital loss carryover, charitable contribution carryover, or business and other credit carryovers, not availed of in the Seller's consolidated federal income tax returns that are allocable to the Target and each domestic subsidiary of the Target when each such corporation ceased to be a member of the Seller's consolidated group.

(ix) In the event that (a) the Target or a Subsidiary pays any separate (unconsolidated) state, local or foreign tax liability, including interest and penalty thereon, pursuant to Section 11.2(i) hereof and (b) the Target is indemnified against such payment by the Seller under Section 11.3(i), then the Seller shall reimburse the Target or the Subsidiary in the following manner: Any reimbursement payment required to be made by Seller to the Target or a Subsidiary pursuant to this Section 11.4(ix) shall be made no later than thirty (30) days after receipt by the Seller of (x) a notice or demand for payments, (y) a copy of the complete return or report to be filed with the Taxing Authority, and (z) copies of all supporting workpapers or other appropriate assurances showing that the Tax liability less the value of any Net

Tax Benefit, as provided in Section 11.3(i), has been correctly computed and apportioned to the Seller.

Section 11.5. Further Assurances and Assistance. From time to time prior to and after the Closing, the Seller and the Buyer will, without further consideration, (i) execute and deliver such documents as the other may reasonably request in order to consummate more effectively the transactions contemplated by this Agreement and (ii) provide such assistance and records as the other may reasonably request in connection with any tax return, tax investigation or audit, judicial or administrative proceeding or other similar matter relating to the Target or any of its Subsidiaries.

There are at least two approaches for dealing with the concerns of the seller and the buyer as to who should control the tax audit. Sections 11.6 and 11.7 are examples of each approach. The first approach is quite straightforward and eliminates any involvement by the buyer provided that the seller completely indemnifies the target from any tax liability relating thereto. The second approach gives the buyer the right to control the tax contest in situations in which the buyer has greater exposure than the seller. The advantages of each of these approaches are discussed in connection with the control of proceedings in the indemnity provisions in Article XII.

Section 11.6. Audit Matters. The Seller will be responsible for and have the right to control, at the Seller's expense, the audit of any Tax return relating to periods ended on or prior to the day of Closing. The Buyer will have the right, directly or through its designated representatives, to approve any settlement, provided, however, that the Seller may settle an audit on any terms by providing the Target with full indemnification against any Tax liability as a result thereof, in form and substance satisfactory to the Buyer.

Section 11.7. Certain Tax Claims for Which Seller May Be Liable.

(i) If a claim is made by any Taxing Authority or, if during the course of an examination by a Taxing Authority, it appears that the examining agent will propose adjustments that will result in a claim (a "Proposed Claim") with respect to the Target or a Subsidiary (the "Target Group"), the party to this Agreement that has the legal right to settle or compromise such Proposed Claim under applicable law (the "Controlling Party") shall notify in writing ("Notice") the other party to this Agreement that may incur any liability in respect of such Proposed Claim under this Article XI (the "Noncontrolling Party") within ten (10) business days of the date of such Proposed Claim. If the Controlling Party is a member of the Target Group, Notice shall be given to the Seller; if the Seller is the Controlling Party, Notice shall be given only to the Target. In the case of any such Proposed Claim, the Controlling Party shall not agree to such Proposed Claim or make payment thereof for at least sixty (60) days (or such shorter period as may be required by applicable law) after the giving of Notice with respect thereto. The Controlling Party need not give Notice of a Proposed Claim if the Controlling Party assumes liability for it. The failure to give Notice as provided hereunder shall not affect a Noncontrolling Party's liabilities under this Article XI unless such failure materially prejudices the ability of the Noncontrolling Party to defend against such Proposed Claim or to seek a refund of amounts paid in regard of such Proposed Claim.

(ii) As to a Tax that would result from a Proposed Claim for which the Controlling Party or the Noncontrolling Party would be solely liable under this Article XI hereof, the party that would be solely liable shall have the right, at its sole cost, to resist the Proposed Claim and if any Tax is paid, to seek the recovery of any such tax ("Tax Contest"). Such party may contest such Tax Contest by any and all appropriate proceedings, whether involving amended tax returns, claims for refund, administrative proceedings, litigation, appeals or otherwise, and in connection therewith, the other party will execute and deliver, or cause to be executed and delivered, to the party conducting the Tax Contest or its designees all instruments (including without limitation powers of attorney) reasonably requested by the party conducting the Tax Contest in order to implement the provisions of this paragraph.

(iii) As to a Tax for which the Noncontrolling Party is liable for a portion hereunder ("Joint Tax"), either the Controlling Party or the Noncontrolling Party shall have the right to institute or maintain a Tax Contest with respect thereto, subject to the provisions of Section 11.7(ii) hereof, as further modified by the following:

(a) If the asserted liability of the Controlling Party hereunder is equal to fifty percent (50) or more of the Proposed Claim, the Controlling Party may elect to conduct all proceedings of the Tax Contest as to such Joint Tax or to tender the conduct of all proceedings to the Noncontrolling Party.

(b) If the asserted liability of the Controlling Party hereunder is less than fifty percent (50) of the Proposed Claim, the Controlling Party shall tender the conduct of all proceedings of the Tax Contest to the Noncontrolling Party.

(c) If the conduct of all proceedings of the Tax Contest is tendered to the Noncontrolling Party and it declines to conduct such proceedings, then the Controlling Party (unless it elects to settle or not to contest as provided below) will conduct such proceedings. All costs of the Tax Contest will be shared as between the Controlling Party and the Noncontrolling Party in the ratio in which the Joint Tax is ultimately assessed.

(d) If the party conducting the Tax Contest (the "Manager") wishes to concede a Joint Tax or wishes and is able to compromise a Joint Tax and so notifies the other, the other party must either concede or agree to such compromise, as appropriate, or else agree to bear any portion of the Manager's tax liability in excess of the conceded or compromised amount. The party not wishing to concede or compromise will then assume responsibility for the conduct of the proceedings relating to the Tax Contest, and shall bear all costs of the Tax Contest thereafter incurred.

(iv) The "costs" of a Tax Contest means all out-of-pocket costs incurred by the Manager during the period it is acting as the Manager and any reasonable costs incurred by the other party for other than routine services or materials requested by the Manager in connection with such Tax Contest.

(v) The Target and the Seller will cooperate fully with each other in connection with any audit examinations of the Target by any Taxing Authority or any Tax Contests, including, without limitation, the furnishing or making available of records, books of account, or other materials necessary or helpful for the defense against the assertions of any Taxing Authority as to any income tax returns (consolidated or otherwise) of the Target and the Subsidiaries.

(vi) The Seller shall not agree to a settlement of any such Tax liabilities which would adversely affect any member of the Target Group in any taxable period ending after the Closing Date to any material extent (including, without limitation, the imposition of income tax deficiencies or the reduction of asset basis or cost adjustments) without the Target's prior written consent, which consent shall not be unreasonably withheld, unless the Seller indemnifies the Target Group against the effects of any such settlement. The Target shall not resolve, settle or contest any tax issue with respect to the Target which would have an adverse material effect on the Seller without the Seller's prior written consent, which consent shall not be unreasonably withheld, unless the Target indemnifies the Seller against the effects of any such settlement.

Many nontax lawyers merely skim the tax section of an acquisition agreement, since they find it extremely esoteric. Although this may be unavoidable, the importance of tax provisions should not be minimized or overlooked. Article XI is used in connection with the acquisition of a target whose federal income tax returns are filed as part of the consolidated tax return of the seller. Although preclosing federal tax liabilities of the target will be automatically included in the seller's consolidated return, the target will itself have liability to various other taxing authorities for periods prior to the closing. Therefore, since the target will file a tax return after Closing that covers a portion of the period prior to closing, the agreement should require the seller to pay any taxes for periods prior to the closing that may be due to various taxing authorities. This is logical, as the seller reaped the benefits of the target's income during this period. It is also necessary for the seller and the buyer to coordinate the filing of tax returns postclosing as well as the handling of tax refunds or credits.

When agreeing to indemnify the target for the target's tax liability covering periods prior to the closing, the seller should require its indemnity obligation to be reduced by the amount of any offsetting tax benefits realized by the target by reason of preclosing tax liability. (See Section 11.3(i).) This is at least theoretically a fair result, since the buyer should not be expected to get a windfall from the indemnity provisions. The principal, and fairly valid, argument against such a provision is that the actual determination of an offsetting tax benefit can be quite difficult in practice.

The representations and warranties set forth in Section 11.1 assure the buyer that it should not be faced with unanticipated tax liabilities of any kind.

In situations in which the target is not a member of the seller's consolidated group, much of Article XI may be unnecessary, and the buyer should instead require a representation by the seller in Article IV as follows:

Tax Matters. For purposes of this Agreement "Taxes" or "Tax" means all net income, capital gains, gross income, gross receipts, sales, use, ad valorem, franchise, profits, license, withholding, payroll, employment, excise, severance, stamp, occupation, premium, property, or windfall profit taxes, customs duties, or other taxes, fees, assessments, or charges of any kind whatsoever, together with any interest and any penalties, additions to tax, or additional amounts imposed by any taxing authority ("Taxing Authority") upon the Target or the Subsidiary.

(i) Except as set forth in Section ______________ of the Disclosure Statement, the Target and the Subsidiary have filed or will file when due all federal, foreign, state and local tax returns, tax information returns, reports and estimates for all years and periods (and portions thereof) ending on or before the Closing Date for which any such returns, reports or estimates were due. All such returns, reports and estimates were prepared in the manner required by applicable law, and all Taxes shown thereby to be payable have been paid when due.

(ii) Section ______________ of the Disclosure Statement sets forth all jurisdictions in which the Target and the Subsidiaries have filed or will file income or franchise tax returns for each taxable period, or portion thereof, ending on or before the Closing Date.

(iii) The Target and the Subsidiaries each has withheld or will withhold amounts from its respective employees and has filed or will file all federal, foreign, state and local returns and reports with respect to employee income tax withholding and social security and unemployment Taxes for all periods (or portions thereof) ending on or before the Closing Date, in compliance with the provisions of the Internal Revenue Code, as amended and currently in effect (the "Code"), and other applicable federal, foreign, state and local laws.

(iv) The Target and the Subsidiaries each have paid, or provided a sufficient reserve on the Balance Sheet for the payment of, all federal, state, local and foreign Taxes with respect to all periods, or portions thereof, ending on or before ______________. The amount of any net operating loss for federal income tax purposes shown on the Target's federal income tax returns has been accurately and properly determined in accordance with the Code and other applicable law without giving effect to the transactions contemplated hereby.

(v) The separate and consolidated federal income tax returns of the Target and its Subsidiaries, through the taxable year ended [insert date], have been examined by the United States Internal Revenue Service (the "IRS") or closed by applicable statute of limitations, and any deficiencies or assessments, including interest and penalties thereon, claimed or made as a result of such examinations in respect of the target and any of its Subsidiaries.

(vi) Except as set forth in Section ______________ of the Disclosure Statement there are no material claims or investigations by any Taxing Authority pending or, to the best knowledge of the Seller and the Target, threatened, against the Target or the Subsidiaries for any past due Taxes; and there has been no waiver of any applicable statute of limitations or extension of the time for the assessment of any Tax against the Target or the Subsidiaries, except as set forth in Section ______________ of the Disclosure Statement.

(vii) Neither the Target nor any Subsidiary has made, signed or filed, nor will it make, sign or file any consent under Section 341(f) of the Code with respect to any taxable period ending on or before the Closing Date.

(viii) Except as set forth in Section ______________ of the Disclosure Statement, no event has occurred or will occur on or prior to the Closing Date that would require indemnification by the Target or the Subsidiaries of any tax lessor under any agreements relating to tax leases executed under Section 168(f)(8) of the Internal Revenue Code as to assets of the Target or its Subsidiaries.

(ix) Neither the Target nor any Subsidiary has ever been, nor is the Target or any Subsidiary currently, a party to any agreement relating to the sharing of any liability for, or payment of, Taxes with any other person or entity.

ARTICLE XII: SURVIVAL OF REPRESENTATIONS; INDEMNIFICATION

Section 12.1. Indemnification by Seller. Notwithstanding any other provision of this Agreement and subject to the terms and conditions of this Article XII, the Seller hereby agrees to indemnify, defend and hold harmless the Buyer, any subsidiary or affiliate thereof (including the Target, the Surviving Corporation and the Subsidiaries) and their respective successors, if any, and their officers, directors and controlling persons (the "Buyer Group"), at any time after the Closing Date, from and against all demands, claims, actions or causes of action, assessments, losses, damages, liabilities, costs and expenses, including without limitation, interest, penalties and attorneys' fees and expenses, which were reasonably incurred by or imposed upon the Buyer Group or any member thereof, net of any insurance proceeds received by any member of the Buyer Group with respect thereto (all such amounts, net of insurance proceeds being hereafter referred to collectively as "Buyer Group Damages"), asserted against, resulting to, imposed upon or incurred by the Buyer Group or any member thereof, directly or indirectly, by reason of or resulting from any misrepresentation, breach of any warranty or nonperformance or breach of any covenant, obligation or agreement of the Seller or the Target or its Subsidiaries contained in or made pursuant to this Agreement, the Disclosure Statement, the Related Instruments or pursuant to any statement, certificate or other document furnished pursuant to this Agreement or the Related Instruments (collectively referred to as the "Indemnity Documents") or any facts or circumstances constituting such a breach. (A claim for indemnification under this Section 12.1 shall be referred to as the "Buyer Group Claims.")

Section 12.2. Indemnification by the Surviving Corporation. Notwithstanding any other provision of this Agreement and subject to the terms and conditions of this Article XII, the Surviving Corporation hereby agrees to indemnify, defend and hold harmless the Seller and their respective successors, if any, and their officers, directors and controlling persons (the "Seller Group"), at any time after the Closing Date, from and against all demands, claims, actions, or causes of action, assessments, losses, damages, liabilities, costs and expenses, including, without limitation, interest, penalties and attorneys' fees and expenses, which were reasonably incurred by or imposed upon the Seller Group or any member thereof, net of any insurance proceeds received by any member of the Seller Group with respect thereto (all such amounts, net of insurance proceeds being hereafter referred to collectively as "Seller Group Damages"), asserted against, resulting to, imposed upon or incurred by the Seller Group or any member thereof, directly or indirectly, by reason of or resulting from any misrepresentation, breach of any warranty, or nonperformance or breach of any covenant, obligation or agreement of the Buyer contained in or made pursuant to any Indemnity Document or any facts or circumstances constituting such a breach. (A claim for indemnification under this Section 12.2 shall be referred to as the "Seller Group Claims.")

The buyer group damages and seller group damages take into account any insurance proceeds that are received by the indemnified party in order to reduce the amount of damages that can be recovered by the indemnified party. Another item that arguably should offset the amount of damages that an indemnified party can claim is the amount of any tax benefits that the surviving corporation has enjoyed as a result of such damages. The difficulty of determining the exact amount of the tax benefit that directly resulted from the damages almost always causes the buyer and seller to overlook this potential windfall.

> ***Section 12.3. Materiality.*** For purposes of determining whether an event described in Section 12.1 or 12.2 has occurred, any requirement in any representation, warranty, covenant or agreement contained in any Indemnity Document that an event or fact be material, meet a certain minimum dollar threshold or have a Material Adverse Effect, which is a condition to such event or fact constituting a misrepresentation or a breach of such warranty, covenant or agreement (a "Materiality Condition"), shall be ignored, if the aggregate Buyer Group Damages or Seller Group Damages, as the case may be, resulting from all such breaches and misrepresentations (determined by ignoring all Materiality Conditions) exceeds the amount of the Basket (as defined in Section 12.5). Notwithstanding the foregoing, an event described in Section 12.1 or 12.2 (other than a claim for indemnification under Article XI) that would otherwise give rise to a claim for Buyer Group Damages or Seller Group Damages, as the case may be, shall not be deemed to have occurred unless the Buyer Group Damages or Seller Group Damages, as the case may be, resulting from the single misrepresentation or breach of warranty, covenant or agreement that constitute such event exceeds Dollars, provided that for the purposes of this sentence, all claims for Buyer Group Damages or Seller Group Damages, as the case may be, arising out of the same facts or events causing any such breach shall be treated as a single claim.

> ***Section 12.4. Survival of Indemnification.*** The right to make a claim for indemnification under this Agreement shall survive the Closing Date for a period of twenty-four (24) months except that a claim for indemnification under (a) Section 4.4 of this Agreement or based upon any misrepresentation or breach of a warranty which was actually known to be untrue by the indemnifying party when made or asserted or to any willful breach of a

covenant, shall continue to survive indefinitely, (b) Article XI shall continue to survive until the latest to occur of (i) the date twenty-four (24) months after the Closing Date, (ii) the expiration date of the statute of limitations applicable to any indemnified liability for Taxes, and extensions or waivers thereof and (iii) ninety (90) days after the final determination of any such Tax liability, including the final administrative and/or judicial determination thereof, and thereafter no party shall have a right to seek indemnification under this Agreement unless a notice of claim setting forth the facts upon which the claim for indemnification is based, and if possible, a reasonable estimate of the amount of the claim, is delivered to the indemnifying party prior to the expiration of the right to make a claim as provided in this Section 12.4. This Section 12.4 shall have no effect upon any other obligation of the parties hereto, whether to be performed before or after the Closing Date. It shall not be a condition to the indemnification with respect to such claim that the loss or liability upon which the claim would be based actually be realized or incurred prior to the date that the indemnifying party is no longer obligated to indemnify the indemnified party pursuant to this Article XII.

The length of time that the seller's indemnification obligations survive the closing date is often heavily negotiated, and its outcome is largely dependent upon the nature of the transaction and the strength of the parties' respective bargaining positions. The buyer should require the seller to indemnify the title to the securities to be purchased by it for an indefinite period of time. For indemnification relating to tax liability, the buyer should require the seller to indemnify the surviving corporation until the target can no longer suffer any loss. In some cases, the buyer may require the seller to indemnify certain items, such as an environmental or product liability concern, beyond the general indemnification period.

Section 12.5. Limitation on Claims and Damages.

(i) No amount shall be payable in indemnification under this Article XII, unless (a) in the case of the Seller, the aggregate amount of Buyer Group Damages in respect of which the Seller would be liable under this Article XII, or (b) in the case of the Surviving Corporation, the aggregate amount of Seller Group Damages in respect of which the Surviving Corporation would be liable under this Article XII, exceeds in the aggregate

__________________________ Dollars ($_______________) (the "Basket"); provided, however, the Basket shall not apply to (a) any Buyer Group Claim or Seller Group Claim, as the case may be, based upon any misrepresentation or breach of a warranty which was actually known to be untrue by the indemnifying party when made or asserted or to any willful breach of a covenant or (b) any claim for indemnity under Article XI. In the event that the Buyer Group Damages or Seller Group Damages exceeds the Basket, the indemnified party shall be entitled to seek indemnification for the full amount of the Buyer Group Damages or Seller Group Damages, as the case may be.

(ii) The maximum amount of Buyer Group Damages for which the Seller may be liable under this Article XII shall be an amount equal to __________________________ Dollars ($________________).

(iii) A party shall not be liable for Buyer Group Damages or Seller Group Damages, as the case may be, under this Article XII resulting from an event relating to a misrepresentation, breach of any warranty or nonperformance or breach of any covenant by the indemnifying party if the indemnifying party can establish that the party seeking indemnification had actual knowledge on or before the Closing Date of such event.

(iv) In any case where an indemnified party recovers from third parties all or any part of any amount paid to it by an indemnifying party pursuant to this Article XII, such indemnified party shall promptly pay over to the indemnifying party the amount so recovered (after deducting therefrom the full amount of the expenses incurred by it in procuring such recovery and any additional amounts owed to the indemnified party by the indemnifying party under this Agreement), but not in excess of any amount previously so paid by the indemnifying party.

(v) The indemnified party shall be obligated to prosecute diligently and in good faith any claim for Buyer Group Damages or Seller Group Damages, as the case may be, with any applicable insurer prior to collecting or indemnification payment under this Article XII. However, an indemnified party shall be entitled to collect an indemnification payment under this Article XII if such indemnified party has not received reimbursement from an applicable insurer within one year after it has given such insurer written notice of its claim. In such event, the indemnified party shall assign to the indemnifying party its rights against such insurer.

(vi) Except in the case of fraud and other than as set forth in Article XI or Section 12.5(vii) hereof, the indemnification and terms thereof provided for in this Article XII shall be the exclusive remedy available to any indemnified party against any indemnifying party for any damages arising directly or indirectly from any misrepresentation, breach of any warranty or nonperformance or breach of any covenant, obligation or agreement pursuant to the Indemnity Documents.

(vii) Nothing in this Article XII or in Article XI shall be construed to limit the non-monetary equitable remedies of any party hereto in respect of any breach by any other party of any covenant or other agreement of such other party contained in or made pursuant to the Indemnity Documents required to be performed after the Closing Date.

The seller, who usually has the most at stake under the indemnification provisions, should require the surviving corporation to pursue collection from an insurance company for the redress of buyer group damages if the insurance policy arguably covers the buyer group damages. In addition, with respect to the covenants in Section 6.7 and Article VII, the seller should not be liable for any buyer group damages if the buyer was aware of the seller's misrepresentation or breach prior to the closing date.

A seller should always attempt to limit its exposure for indemnification. As a practical matter, the seller should not be liable for any amount in excess of the purchase price paid for the target. During negotiations of this ceiling, every argument conceivable is put on the table for consideration. However, its outcome, like that of any other highly controversial provision, rests with the party holding the trump card.

Section 12.6. Claims by Third Parties. The obligations and liabilities of an indemnifying party under any provision of this Agreement with respect to claims relating to third parties shall be subject to the following terms and conditions:

(i) Whenever any indemnified party shall have received notice that a Buyer Group Claim or a Seller Group Claim, as the case may be, has been asserted or threatened against such indemnified party, which, if valid, would subject the indemnifying party to an indemnity obligation under this Agreement, the indemnified party shall promptly notify the indemnifying party of such claim in the manner described in Section 12.4; provided, however, that the failure of the indemnified party to give timely notice hereunder shall not relieve the indemnifying party of its indemnification obligations under this Agreement unless, and only to the extent that, such failure caused the Buyer Group Damages or the Seller Group Damages, as the case may be, for which the indemnifying party is obligated to be greater than they would have been had the indemnified party given timely notice.

(ii) The indemnifying party or its designee will have the right, but not the obligation, to assume the defense of any claim described in Section 12.6(i); provided, however, if there is a reasonable probability that a Buyer Group Claim may materially and adversely affect the Surviving Corporation or any other member of the Buyer Group despite the indemnity of the Seller, the Surviving Corporation or such member of the Buyer Group shall have the right at its option to defend, at its own cost and expense, and to compromise or settle such Buyer Group Claim which compromise or settlement shall be made only with the written consent of the Seller, such consent not to be unreasonably withheld. If the indemnifying party fails to assume the defense of such claim within 15 days after receipt of notice of a claim pursuant to Section 12.6(i), the indemnified party against which such claim has been asserted will (upon delivering notice to such effect to the indemnifying party) have the right to undertake, at the indemnifying party's cost and expense, the defense, compromise or settlement of such claim on behalf of and for the account and risk of the indemnifying party, subject to the right of the indemnifying party to assume the defense of such claim at any time prior to settlement, compromise or final determination thereof and provided, however, that the indemnified party shall not enter into any such compromise or settlement without the written consent of the indemnifying party. In the event the indemnified party assumes defense of the claim, the indemnified party will keep the indemnifying party reasonably informed of the progress of any such defense, compromise or settlement. The indemnifying party shall not be liable for any settlement of any action effected without its consent, but if settled with the consent of the indemnifying party or if there be a final judgment beyond review or appeal, for the plaintiff in any such action, the indemnifying party agrees to indemnify and hold harmless an indemnified party from and against any loss or liability by reason of such settlement or judgment. Any party who does not undertake the defense of a claim may, at its own expense, retain such additional attorneys and other advisors as it shall deem necessary, which attorneys and advisors will be permitted by the party undertaking such defense, and its attorneys, to observe the defense of such claim.

(iii) Any member of the Buyer Group shall give the Seller at least thirty (30) days' prior written notice before such member shall waive the provisions of any statute of limitations as such provisions may apply to the assessment of taxes payable by the Surviving Corporation or any Subsidiary for any taxable year or period (or portion thereof) ending on or prior to the Closing Date.

An area that can be extremely sensitive is control of a proceeding relating to a claim that is the subject of indemnification. If the indemnifying party refuses to acknowledge its obligation to indemnify a claim, then it should certainly have no right to control the proceeding. However, where the indemnifying party has accepted its obligation to indemnify for a claim, the indemnifying party will probably want to control the proceeding in order to be in command of its own destiny. If the buyer is comfortable with the creditworthiness of the seller, this should not pose a serious threat to the buyer. There are, of course, circumstances in which the buyer may want to control the proceedings notwithstanding the creditworthiness of the seller. For example, if the surviving corporation is temporarily enjoined from conducting its business as a result of the action of a third party, the buyer may feel that the seller will not move quickly enough to resolve the matter.

In some cases, the buyer and seller may have a joint interest in the outcome of a certain proceeding. For example, the proceeding may involve numerous claims against the surviving corporation, only one of which relates to a buyer group claim. One approach that may appease both the seller and the buyer in this circumstance is to let the party that has the most to lose control the proceeding.

Section 12.7. Indemnity for Taxes of Indemnified Party. Each party hereto further agrees that, with respect to payment or indemnity under this Article XII, such payment or indemnity shall include any amount necessary to hold the indemnified party harmless on an after-tax basis from all taxes required to be paid with respect to the receipt of such payment or indemnity under the laws of any federal, state or local government or taxing authority in the United States, or under the laws of any foreign government or taxing authority or governmental subdivision of a foreign country.

In circumstances in which the indemnification payment is taxable to the indemnified party, it is common for the seller and the buyer to negotiate the inclusion of a tax gross-up provision. One difficulty with this concept is that the indemnifying party may be grossing up the indemnified party for taxes that it would have been responsible for had no indemnity been necessary.

> ***Section 12.8. Right of Offset.*** In the event the Seller should be required to pay monies to the Surviving Corporation pursuant to Section 12.1 or any other indemnification provision of this Agreement, the Surviving Corporation may offset the amount the Seller owes in indemnification against any outstanding principal balance of the [insert title of instrument under which the surviving corporation has continuing payment obligations].

In an acquisition in which the seller has agreed to accept, as part of the purchase price of the target, a note or other instrument that represents a payment obligation of the surviving corporation, the buyer may attempt to satisfy its right to indemnification by the seller by canceling a portion or all of such payment obligations. A creditworthy seller should resist this provision on several grounds. First, the surviving corporation should have a setoff right only after it has demonstrated, through a final determination from which no appeal can be taken, that the seller is obligated to indemnify the surviving corporation for the buyer group claim. Second, if the seller has sufficient resources, it should be able to choose whether it wants to forgive a portion of the payment obligation or simply pay cash. It is conceivable that the payment obligation may bear an interest rate well in excess of the prevailing market rate. A creditworthy seller should not lose this benefit through an offset provision.

ARTICLE XIII: NON-COMPETE

> The Seller agrees that for the period of three years following the Closing Date (the "Non-Compete Period"), the Seller shall not, without the prior written consent of the Buyer, either directly or indirectly, engage in business of the type presently conducted by the Target or any Subsidiary in the United States or any other jurisdiction in which the Target or any Subsidiary currently conducts business (the "Business"). The Seller may acquire

any entity which, directly or indirectly, engages in the Business or any portion thereof (the "Acquired Entity"), if (i) the total assets and gross revenues attributable to or derived from such Business do not exceed [insert percentage] of the total assets and gross revenues of the Acquired Entity and its subsidiaries in the fiscal year immediately preceding the date of acquisition, or (ii) the Seller uses its reasonable efforts to divest itself of the Acquired Entity within a reasonable time (not to exceed six months), subject to receipt of all regulatory approvals. The Seller also agrees that, after the Closing Date, the Seller will not disclose or reveal to any person or an Acquired Entity any trade secret or other confidential or proprietary information relating to the Business, including, without limitation, any financial information relating to the Target or any Subsidiary, or any customer lists, unless readily ascertainable from public information, and the Seller confirms that after the Closing Date, such information will constitute the exclusive property of the Target and its Subsidiaries. During the Non-Compete Period, the Seller agrees not to, and to cause its affiliates not to, recruit, directly or indirectly, employees of the Target or any Subsidiary for employment with or as a consultant to the Seller or its affiliates. The Buyer and the Seller hereby agree that of the total cash consideration to be paid to the Seller at Closing, $__________ represents the consideration for the covenants of the Seller contained in this Article XIII.

Covenants not to compete can be difficult to enforce if not structured properly. The difficulty arises from a court's reluctance on public policy grounds to give force to a contractual provision restricting the ability of one of the parties to work freely in any way it chooses, even if the party being restricted has voluntarily agreed and has received consideration to be so bound. Courts have invalidated noncompetition provisions (a) that continue for too long a period of time, (b) that are too broad geographically, or (c) that are too indefinite or broad with respect to the restricted activity. Consequently, the buyer must ensure that its noncompetition clause is specific with respect to the term (typically one to five years), extends to a limited geographic area, and restricts a specific activity in the industry. For example, a court would probably accept a provision restricting the seller from selling or distributing aluminum baseball bats in the State of California for a period of two years, but would probably not accept a provision restricting the seller from selling or distributing sports equipment anywhere in the world for a period of twenty years. It is, of course, within these extremes that the enforceability of a covenant not to compete is less clear. The buyer must be cognizant of courts' rulings under the state laws that govern the acquisition agreement and must balance the case law against its need to acquire the target without fear that the seller will acquire or establish a similar business in the same territory and attempt to lure away existing customers of the target.

The seller may also desire to modify clause (ii) above, which requires the seller's divestiture of the acquired entity within a reasonable period of time by providing that the seller is only obligated to divest the acquired entity "at a price which is economically reasonable in light of the circumstances."

ARTICLE XIV: TERMINATION

Section 14.1. Termination for Failure to Close on Time. This Agreement may be terminated upon two (2) days' written notice (i) by the Buyer, on the one hand, or the Seller, on the other hand, at any time after [insert date], or (ii) by the mutual agreement of all parties at any time. In the event of such termination, this Agreement shall be abandoned without any liability or further obligation to any other party to this Agreement unless otherwise stated expressly herein. This Section 14.1 shall not apply in the event of the failure of the transactions contemplated by this Agreement to be consummated as a result of a breach by the Seller, Target or Buyer of a representation, warranty or covenant contained in this Agreement. In such event, the provisions of Section 14.2 hereof shall apply.

Section 14.2. Default; Remedies. This Section shall apply in the event that a party refuses to consummate the transactions contemplated by this Agreement or if any default under, or breach of any representation, warranty or covenant of, this Agreement on the part of a party (the "Defaulting Party") shall have occurred that results in the failure to consummate the transactions contemplated hereby. In such event, the non-Defaulting Party shall be entitled to seek and obtain specific performance pursuant to Section 14.3 or to seek and obtain money damages from the Defaulting Party plus its court costs and reasonable attorneys' fees in connection with the pursuit of its remedies hereunder.

Section 14.3. Specific Performance. In the event that any party shall fail or refuse to consummate the transactions contemplated by this Agreement or if any default under, or breach of, any representation, warranty or covenant of this Agreement on the part of any party (the "Defaulting Party") shall have occurred that results in the failure to consummate the transactions contemplated hereby, then in addition to the other remedies provided in this Article XIV, the non-Defaulting Party may seek to obtain an order of specific performance thereof against the Defaulting Party from a court of competent jurisdiction, provided that it files its request with such court within forty-five (45) days after it became aware of such failure, refusal, default or breach. In addition, the non-Defaulting Party shall be entitled to obtain from the Defaulting Party court costs and reasonable attorneys' fees incurred by it in enforcing its rights hereunder. As a condition to seeking specific performance hereunder, Buyer shall not be required to have tendered the [insert defined term for the total purchase price] but shall be ready, willing and able to do so.

The termination section provides both the mechanism for the termination of, and the remedies available against a nonperforming or defaulting party to, the acquisition agreement. In some cases, a seller may want to modify this section to limit liability for a willful failure to perform. Obviously, there are situations in which the buyer may be disadvantaged by the inclusion of this modifier. Therefore, like other disputed provisions, the outcome rests on the balance of power between seller and buyer.

In an acquisition requiring regulatory approval, the buyer and seller should consider extending the term of the acquisition agreement in Section 14.1 for a certain period of time in case the approval process takes longer than anticipated.

The relief of specific performance afforded the nondefaulting party in Section 14.3 is extremely difficult to enforce in a court of law. If a court can ascertain the amount of monetary damages to award the nondefaulting party, it will not generally grant specific performance.

Special consideration should be given to the termination section in connection with the acquisition of a publicly traded target. For example, an independent committee of the board of directors of the target may determine in light of the circumstances to include a fiduciary out for the target. A fiduciary out is a unilateral right of the target to terminate the acquisition agreement in the event a more favorable offer for the target is received prior to closing. The buyer should in this situation and possibly others, require a "breakup" or "topping" fee to compensate the buyer for its damages and out-of-pocket expenses. The following is an example of a "bustup" fee that covers both buyer and seller:

> ***Damages Upon Default.*** In the event that either Target or Buyer shall fail to refuse to consummate the transactions contemplated by this Agreement or if any default under, or breach of any representation (other than those contained in Section 3.5 hereof), warranty, covenant (other than those contained in hereof) or conditions of, this Agreement on the part of the Target or Buyer shall have occurred that results in the failure to consummate the transactions contemplated hereby, then (i) if Target shall be the defaulting party, Target shall pay to the Buyer Dollars ($), or (ii) if the Buyer shall be the defaulting party, then the Buyer shall pay to Target Dollars ($). In each case such payment shall be in consideration of the expenses incurred by and efforts expended by and opportunities lost by the nondefaulting party. The parties agree that in such circumstances it would be impossible to determine the actual damages which any party may suffer and that therefore such payments shall be in lieu of any such actual damages and shall be full and complete liquidated damages and shall constitute the sole remedy in the event of such default.

ARTICLE XV: MISCELLANEOUS

Article XV contains provisions that govern the interpretation of the agreement and the taking of actions thereunder. Although the bulk of these provisions are generally not negotiated by the parties to the agreement, several sections provide valuable rights to both buyer and seller and may be subject to closer scrutiny by the parties.

Section 15.1. Definitions.

Agreement. ***See Article I.***

Buyer. ***See Article I.***

Closing. ***See Article III.***

Closing Date. ***See Article III.***
Company Capital Stock. ***See Section 4.3(i).***
Disclosure Statement. ***See Section 4.1.***
Financial Statements. ***See Section 4.5(i).***
GAAP. ***See Section 4.5(i).***
Material Adverse Effect. ***See Section 4.1(i).***
Merger. ***See Article I.***
Most Recent Balance Sheet. ***See Section 4.5(i).***
Persons. First used in Section 4.5(ii) but not defined.
Related Instruments. ***See Section 4.2.***
SEC. Defined in paragraph describing Section 4.33.
Seller. ***See Article I.***
Subsidiary. ***See Article I.***
Target. ***See Article I.***

Section 15.2. Payment of Expenses. Buyer shall pay its own expenses and the Seller and Target shall pay their own expenses incident to preparing for, entering into and carrying out this Agreement and the Related Instruments, except as otherwise provided in this Agreement and the Related Instruments.

Section 15.3. Modifications or Waivers to the Agreement. The parties may, by mutual written agreement, make any modification or amendment of this Agreement.

Section 15.4. Assignment. Neither the Buyer, Seller nor Target shall have the authority to assign its rights or obligations under this Agreement without the prior written consent of the other party, except that the Buyer may assign all or any portion of its respective rights hereunder without the prior written consent of the Seller or Target to an entity controlled by, controlling or under common control with it or to any Acquisition Lender, and the Seller, Target and the Buyer shall execute such documents as are necessary in order to effect such assignments.

Section 15.5. Burden and Benefit.

(i) This Agreement shall be binding upon and, to the extent permitted in this Agreement, shall inure to the benefit of, the parties hereto and their respective successors and assigns.

(ii) In the event of a default by the Seller or Target of any of its or their obligations hereunder, the sole and exclusive recourse and remedy of the

Buyer shall be against the Seller or Target and its assets and under no circumstances shall any officer, director, stockholder or affiliate of the Seller or Target be liable in law or equity for any obligations of the Seller or Target hereunder.

(iii) In the event of a default by the Buyer of any of its obligations hereunder, the sole and exclusive recourse and remedy of the Seller or Target hereunder shall be against the Buyer and its assets, and under no circumstances shall any officer, director, stockholder or affiliate of the Buyer be liable in law or equity for any obligations of the Buyer hereunder.

(iv) It is the intent of the parties hereto that no third-party beneficiary rights be created or deemed to exist in favor of any person not a party to this Agreement, unless otherwise expressly agreed in writing by the parties.

The buyer and seller may seek to include a provision, often entitled "Burden and Benefit," limiting the rights of the seller in the event of a breach of the agreement to an action against the buyer and not against any officer, director, or controlling stockholder of the buyer. This provision, assuming the entity purchasing the target has elected to do so through a shell or thinly capitalized corporation, generally should insulate the acquiring entity from liability to the seller in the event the deal goes sour.

Section 15.6. Brokers.

(i) Each of the Seller and Target represents and warrants to the Buyer that there are no brokers or finders entitled to any brokerage or finder's fee or other commission or fee based upon arrangements made by or on behalf of the Seller or Target in connection with this Agreement or any of the transactions contemplated hereby other than the fee due [insert name of any such entity].

(ii) The Buyer represents and warrants to the Seller and the Target that no broker or finder is entitled to any brokerage or finder's fee or other commission or fee based upon arrangements made by or on behalf of the Buyer in connection with this Agreement or any of the transactions contemplated hereby other than fees payable by it in connection with the financing of this transaction.

Section 15.7. Entire Agreement. This Agreement and the exhibits, lists and other documents referred to herein contain the entire agreement among the parties hereto with respect to the transactions contemplated hereby and supersede all prior agreements with respect thereto, whether written or oral.

Section 15.8. Governing Law. This Agreement shall be governed by and construed in accordance with the laws of the State of [insert name of state].

Section 15.9. Notices. Any notice, request, instruction or other document to be given hereunder by a party shall be in writing and delivered personally or by facsimile transmission, or by telex, or sent by registered or certified mail, postage prepaid, return receipt requested, addressed as follows:

If to the Seller: [insert name and address of Seller]
with a copy to: [insert name and address of Seller's counsel]
If to Target: [insert name and address of Target]
If to Buyer: [insert name and address of Buyer]
with a copy to: [insert name and address of Buyer's counsel]
If to the Surviving Corporation: [insert name and address of Target postclosing]
with a copy to: [insert any other desired parties]

or to such other persons or addresses as may be designated in writing by the party to receive such notice. If mailed as aforesaid, ten days after the date of mailing shall be the date notice shall be deemed to have been received.

Section 15.10. Counterparts. This Agreement may be executed in two or more counterparts, each of which shall be an original, but all of which shall constitute but one agreement.

Section 15.11. Rights Cumulative. All rights, powers and privileges conferred hereunder upon the parties, unless otherwise provided, shall be cumulative and shall not be restricted to those given by law. Failure to exercise any power given any party hereunder or to insist upon strict compliance by any other party shall not constitute a waiver of any party's right to demand exact compliance with the terms hereof.

Section 15.12. Severability of Provisions. The parties agree that (i) the provisions of this Agreement shall be severable in the event that any of the provisions hereof are held by a court of competent jurisdiction to be invalid, void or otherwise unenforceable, (ii) such invalid, void or otherwise unenforceable provisions shall be automatically replaced by other provisions which are as similar as possible in terms to such invalid, void or otherwise unenforceable provisions but are valid and enforceable and (iii) the remaining provisions shall remain enforceable to the fullest extent permitted by law.

The provision entitled "Severability," while addressing a purely legal issue, may have great practical impact. The section provides that, in the event particular portions of the document are found invalid, void, or otherwise unenforceable by a court interpreting the agreement, the remaining provisions shall be considered severable from the invalid provisions and shall therefore remain enforceable. This result is of particular concern when the agreement contains ancillary agreements, such as a covenant by the seller not to compete with the buyer after the acquisition. The enforceability of the agreement should not depend on the enforceability of a noncompetition agreement, and the severability provision serves to accomplish this end.

Section 15.13. Further Assurance. The Seller, the Target and the Buyer agree that at any time and from time to time after the Closing Date they will execute and deliver to any other party such further instruments or documents as may reasonably be required to give effect to the transactions contemplated hereunder.

Section 15.14. Confidential Information. The Seller, the Target and the Buyer for themselves, their directors, officers, employees, agents, representatives and partners, if any, covenant with each other that they will use all information relating to any other party, the Target or any Subsidiary acquired by any of them pursuant to the provisions of this Agreement or in the course of negotiations with or examinations of any other party only in connection with the transactions contemplated hereby and shall cause all information obtained by them pursuant to this Agreement and such negotiations and examinations, which is not publicly available, to be treated as confidential except as may otherwise be required by law or as may be necessary or appropriate in connection with the enforcement of this Agreement or any instrument or document referred to herein or contemplated hereby. In the event of termination of this Agreement, each party will cause to be delivered to the other all documents, work papers and other material obtained by it from the others, whether so obtained by it from the others, whether so obtained before or after the execution of this Agreement, and each party agrees that it shall not itself use or disclose, directly or indirectly, any information so obtained, or otherwise obtained from the other hereunder or in connection therewith, and will have all such information kept confidential and will not use such information in any way which is detrimental to any other party, provided that (i) any party may use and disclose any such information which has been disclosed publicly (other than by such party or any affiliate of such party in breach of its obligations under this Section 15.14) and (ii) to the extent that any party or any affiliate of a party may become legally compelled to disclose any such information if it shall have used its best efforts, and shall have afforded the other parties the opportunity, to obtain an appropriate protective order, or other satisfactory assurance of confidential treatment, for the information required to be disclosed.

The confidential information section typically requires each party to keep confidential all information obtained in the course of the transaction. Because the target has already been or will shortly thereafter be the object of an intensive due diligence review when the agreement is signed, the seller is initially more concerned with disclosure issues than the buyer. The seller may take the position that all materials provided to the buyer relating to the target should be returned or destroyed in the event the parties fail to close the transaction.

Section 15.15. Writings and Disclosures. Except as otherwise provided or contemplated herein, each exhibit, schedule, writing or other disclosure described in this Agreement as having been delivered or to be delivered by one party to the other shall be identified by reference to the section of this Agreement to which it relates and shall be signed or initialed on the first page by an officer or legal counsel of the Seller and by an officer or legal counsel of the Buyer and unless so identified and signed or initialed, the party receiving the same shall not be chargeable with notice of its content.

NOTES

1. This chapter owes a debt to attorney Neil D. Falis, deputy corporate secretary, Willis Towers Watson, PLC, for his original comments on deal documentation for *The Art of M&A Structuring: Techniques for Mitigating Financial, Legal, and Tax Risk* (New York: McGraw-Hill, 2004), and Jack Feder, the Lane & Edison attorney who wrote about acquisition agreements in the original edition of *The Art of M&A: A Merger/Acquisition/Buyout Guide* (New York: Irwin, 1989). Alexandra Lajoux served as project manager for that book. The general principles set forth in the original *Art of M&A* remain true and relevant today, and so are carried forward here in this updated text.
2. The updated observations in this chapter were provided by Michael J. Kliegman, Senior Counsel, Akin Gump Strauss Hauer & Feld LLP, New York.
3. For more on this topic, see Richard Stobbe, "How Do 'Smart Contracts' Fit with 'Traditional Contracts,'" Field Law, October 2018, https://www.fieldlaw.com/portalresource/smart-contracts?utm_source=Mondaq&utm_medium=syndication&utm_campaign=View-Original.

4. Mark Bissegger, "Smart Contract Applications in M&A: Earn-Outs," Dealwire, November 22, 2017, https://www.deallawwire.com/2017/11/22/smart-contract-applications-in-ma-earn-outs/.
5. *Pennzoil Co. v. Texaco Inc.,* 481 US 1 (1987).
6. *Krauth v. Exec. Telecard, Ltd.,* 890 F. Supp. 269, 293-95 (S.D.N.Y. 1995).
7. *Hoxeng v. Topeka Broadcomm, Inc.,* 911 F. Supp. 1323, 1331 (D. Kan. 1996).
8. S. *Colo. MRI, Ltd. v. Med-Alliance, Inc.*, 166 F.3d 1094, 1099 (10th Cir. 1999).
9. "Letters of Intent in Corporate Negotiations: Using Hostage Exchanges and Legal Uncertainty to Promote Compliance," *University of Pennsylvania Law Review,* vol. 162 (2014): 1237, https://scholarship.law.upenn.edu/cgi/viewcontent.cgi?referer=https://www.google.com/&httpsredir=1&article=9438&context=penn_law_review.
10. Benton B. Bodaver, "Good Faith: The New Frontier of Agreements to Negotiate," posted by Douglas Warner on the Harvard Law School Forum on Corporate Governance and Financial Regulation, July 3, 2013, https://corpgov.law.harvard.edu/2013/07/03/good-faith-the-new-frontier-of-agreements-to-negotiate/.
11. This insight comes from Michael J. Kliegman, senior counsel, Akin Gump Strauss, Hauer & Feld, LLP, who reviewed this chapter for accuracy and currency.
12. Toxic waste dumps continue to be a concern in M&A in 2018, nearly 40 years after passage of the Comprehensive Environmental Response, Compensation, and Liability Act (CERCLA), aka Superfund, in 1980. For example, in New Jersey today, there are still more than 100 active tox sites. See http://www.nj.gov/dep/srp/community/sites/.
13. See *TSC Industries, Inc., v. Northway, Inc.*, 426 U.S. 438 (1976), which held that "[t]he issue of materiality is a mixed question of law and fact, involving as it does the application

of a legal standard to a particular set of facts, and only if the established omissions are 'so obviously important to an investor that reasonable minds cannot differ on the question of materiality' is the ultimate issue of materiality appropriately resolved 'as a matter of law' by summary judgment." https://www.law.cornell.edu/supremecourt/text/426/438.

14. See Jeffrey B. Morlend, "Filed vs. Furnished," Sullivan & Worcester, September 18, 2017.
15. Verdicts in recent cases show that it can be difficult to cancel a transaction based on material adverse impact. As stated by one legal expert, "Due to the Delaware Court's high materiality standard and parties' traditional preference for vague MAC clause drafting, the historical probability of deal cancellation from MAC provisions is low." John Prinzivalli, "Defining Materiality: Drafting Enforceable MAC Provisions in Business Combination Agreements Following *IBP v. Tyson,*" *University of Puerto Rico Business Law Journal,* vol. 8, August 2017, http://uprblj.org/wp-content/uploads/2017/08/8-UPRBLJ-162-John-Prinzivalli-Defining-Materiality-2017.pdf. This article cites *IBP v. Tyson Foods* (2001); *Frontier Oil Corp. v. Holly Corp.,* C.A. No. 20502, Court of Chancery (April 29, 2005), and *Hexion Specialty Chemicals Inc. v. Huntsman Corp.*, 965 A.2d 715, 738 (Del. Ch. 2008).
16. This insight comes from attorney Michael J. Kliegman, cited earlier, and is confirmed by other published sources. For example, one source states: "Public target—generally no indemnity because public disclosure provides some protection and cannot seek recourse from widely dispersed public stockholders." Ben Willis and Andrew Budreika, "M&A Academy: Indemnification," https://www.morganlewis.com/-/media/files/publication/presentation/webinar/2017/ma-academy/ma_indemnification-issues_5dec17.ashx?la=en&hash=709959FE162629EB2946BFD45168AE7D74A14A2C.
17. Alexander J. Wilson and David P. Creekman, "Indemnification Caps and Baskets in Private Company M&A Transactions:

What's market?," M&A Practice Brief, February 16, 2017, https://www.wyrick.com/news-publications/indemnification-caps-and-baskets.

18. See proxymonitor.org.
19. ASC 450-2-25-2 states that a loss contingency must be reported when it is "probable that one or more future events will occur confirming the fact of the loss," and when "the amount of the loss can be reasonably estimated." https://asc.fasb.org/section&trid=2127173.
20. In addition to the ALTA forms, there are other forms used in specific areas. In New York, California, Texas, and Illinois, there are local forms of title policy. In Florida, unless the insured asks for the owner's Form B title insurance policy, which insures marketability, the insurer will issue a Form A policy, which does not insure marketability. James P. McAndrews, "History of Title Insurance and ALTA Forms," GPSolo Ereport, March 2012.
21. References to Treas. Regs. are to the Code of Federal Regulations, Title 26, Chapter I, Subchapter A, Part 1, and specific sections. The link to the first citation is https://www.law.cornell.edu/cfr/text/26/1.1502-19.
22. https://www.law.cornell.edu/cfr/text/26/1.1502-19.

CHAPTER 8

Closing

INTRODUCTION

As many a disappointed dealmaker can attest, a deal isn't a deal until it closes. Many have felt the heartache of a compelling opportunity stalling out at the last minute—whether due to legal nuances or emotional swings. This chapter discusses the main elements of getting a deal to closing—a kind of symphony performance in which many individual items must be synchronized carefully to produce a harmonious transaction.

THE BASICS OF CLOSING

What happens at a closing?

The typical acquisition closing has two major elements:

- In the typical *acquisition closing,* the seller and the buyer effect the merger or the transfer and delivery of the stock or assets pursuant to the acquisition agreement.
- In the typical *financial closing,* lenders provide funding for the acquisition to the buyer, as borrower, pursuant to a specific loan agreement or other financing documentation; the buyer

simultaneously remits some or all of these funds to the seller in payment of the purchase price.

The process is simpler when the acquirer provides its own funding, in which case there is no financial closing. In the acquirer-funded transaction, the acquisition closing culminates with payment to the seller in the amount named in the signed acquisition agreement.

Is it always necessary for the parties to sign the acquisition agreement prior to the closing?

Not necessarily. Sometimes, the parties will want to execute the agreement at closing, which is often referred to as a *simultaneous signing and closing.* This most often occurs when the buyer is financing the transaction internally, when no governmental approvals are required to consummate the transaction, or when the deal must close very quickly after the parties have reached their initial meeting of the minds—for example, to take advantage of the provisions of a soon-to-expire tax law or to enable a seller to obtain the sales proceeds in time to meet a debt retirement obligation. In some instances, the parties do not intend to sign and close at the same time, but end up doing so because they fail to reach a basic agreement until the closing date.

If the transaction is at all complex and requires governmental approval or third-party financing, the parties will most likely sign a letter of intent, negotiate and execute the acquisition agreement, and then proceed to close when the "conditions precedent to closing" (often a formally drawn document) have been met and when the financing has been made available. Government agencies may require a signed acquisition agreement before they will begin the process of transaction approval. Similarly, lenders may require that the terms of a transaction be established before they commit their resources to evaluating the transaction; in particular, they will want to know what representations and warranties are being made by the seller and the remedies available to the buyer in the event of a breach.

Can financing agreements be signed before closing?

Most financing agreements are entered into at the closing. Before then, however, the borrower and the lenders will have executed a commitment letter, or reached agreement on a term sheet, setting forth the basic terms of the lending arrangements.

How long does a closing take?

The closing process may last for a few hours, or for days or weeks, depending on the amount of negotiation left for the finale and the ability of the parties to satisfy the conditions precedent to closing. The period immediately before the closing is often consumed by final negotiation of the terms and conditions of the operative documents, but this is not always the case. Closings on transactions for which the terms have been negotiated and finalized prior to the closing involve review of documents and confirmation that the conditions precedent to closing have been met, followed by the signing and delivery of documents and, when appropriate, the actual receipt of funding. The simplest of closings may be effected by an exchange of documents signed in counterpart without convening the parties at a single location. In such cases, digital signatures are generally acceptable.[1]

Can a closing be held if either of the parties has not yet met all the conditions to closing?

Yes. This can be done through an *escrow closing,* which allows the parties to go forward subject to satisfaction of the remaining conditions. In this case, transaction documentation can be executed and entrusted to a designated escrow agent, chosen by the parties, who will break escrow and deliver the documents to the parties as soon as the outstanding conditions are fulfilled. An arrangement of this nature will require the negotiation and drafting of an escrow agreement among the parties; the agent must clearly set forth the terms upon which the breaking of escrow may occur, and the actions to be taken if those conditions are not fulfilled.

Alternatively, the parties may close the transaction if the one that set the unsatisfied condition agrees to waive it and proceed. In some cases, it may be possible for the waiving party to exact some additional concession, such as an increase or decrease in the purchase price (as the case may be), or a pledge from the other party that it will satisfy the condition after the closing. If the unsatisfied condition is so critical that the deal would unwind were it not to be fulfilled, the prudent path is not to close, since the cost of unwinding a closed transaction or resolving the unsatisfied condition may be much higher than the cost of failing to close.

Who should attend a closing?

Each person responsible for signing a document at the closing should expect to be present at the closing offices, or to be otherwise available, from the time that the closing is scheduled to the time of actual signing. If the signatory officer is also the businessperson responsible for the transaction, he or she is likely to be engaged throughout the preclosing and closing process. If, on the other hand, the individual with signing authority is not otherwise involved in the transaction, he or she should be willing and able to remain available in the event that there is a delay in the closing process. Each individual sharing responsibility for the transaction should be on hand to review documents and participate in the negotiation of any final changes.

Attorneys for each of the parties to the transaction will typically be required to participate in final negotiations and preparation and review of the closing documents, including, if required, opinions of counsel as to certain matters such as expected tax effects of the deal. The attorneys will also typically coordinate a *bring-down letter,* which is a certificate signed by an officer of one of the constituent companies to the transaction promising that all of the representations and warranties from the signing date are still true and correct as of the closing date.

The participation of parties at other locations may also be required, depending on the nature of the transaction. For example, a transaction involving the transfer of assets (rather than stock) will typically require that certain conveyance documents be recorded at the time of closing at the appropriate federal, state, or local recordation offices in the jurisdiction where those assets are located. Likewise, multistate acquisitions involving real and personal property may require filings in numerous locations. Further, counsel from each of those jurisdictions may have to render an opinion as to the effectiveness of the conveyances as a condition to closing.

If the transaction involves one or more mergers, attorneys or other appropriate persons will have to file merger certificates and other documents at the offices of the secretary of state of each jurisdiction where filing is required to effect those mergers. Finally, if the conveyed assets constitute security for the financing of the transaction, then the security documentation (such as a mortgage, in the case of real estate) will also be recorded, and opinions of local counsel will be given in connection to these. (One important type of security document will be form UCC-1, under the Uniform Commercial Code discussed in Chapter 4.) The effective coordination of all of these off-site events is one of the more significant organizational challenges of a transactional closing.

Where should the closing take place?

The closing should occur at a location most convenient to all parties involved. In the event that a financing is involved, this is almost always the city in which the principal lender is located—often in the offices of the lender's attorneys. Otherwise, the closing is typically scheduled to take place at the offices of counsel to one of the parties.

The offices in which the closing takes place should offer adequate services, space, and electronic communications (scanning, emailing) together with sufficient secretarial (and notarial) staff, to complete the transaction documentation and otherwise consummate the deal. These facilities and services are typically found at transactional law firms that maintain offices for these specific purposes.

The buyer should seriously consider having the corporate closing and the financing closing in separate offices, within the same city, if possible. Having two office locations (or possibly more, if several pieces of large, complex financings are involved) serves the practical purpose of reducing the confusion and tension generated when many people are confined to the same quarters under stressful conditions. It also has tactical significance to the buyer. The most difficult aspect of any closing is last-minute negotiation (and renegotiation) of deal points, both major and minor. Most often, it is in the buyer's best interest to keep the seller and the various lenders physically apart from each other so that the buyer can control the flow of information that each group receives and can broker a consensus on open points of common concern to the buyer's best advantage.

This can be particularly important in the area of intercreditor relationships. As closing approaches, lenders get increasingly nervous about the risks they are about to take, particularly in a highly leveraged deal, and seek to improve their position by getting more collateral to secure their loans or a piece of the equity, or by imposing tighter postacquisition covenants. There is a definite me-too syndrome among lenders; that is, whatever concession one lender wins, the others will demand for themselves. The buyer has a better chance of neutralizing this syndrome if lenders are kept from talking to each other.

How large a staff should support a closing?

Each party should plan to have staff adequate to cover all aspects of the transaction, from negotiating issues that exist or may arise to performing all the mechanical tasks required to complete the transaction. Most of the tasks will be performed by attorneys and other law firm employees. The parties' accountants and various people from the business entities involved in the transaction, particularly the finance department, will also need to be on hand, or be easily reachable.

If the transaction will be financed by third parties, the buyer's attorneys should have separate closing teams for the corporate side of the transaction and each major piece of financing. This will be necessary if the closing is split among several physical locations. Each team should consist of the attorneys who have been primarily responsible for that aspect of the transaction since its inception and other attorneys and legal assistants as required. With adequately staffed teams in place to handle the details, the attorney in charge of the entire matter will be freed up to offer advice on the big picture and to troubleshoot different aspects of the transaction where necessary. Periodic all-hands briefings are a good way to keep everyone abreast of changing events.

PLANNING THE CLOSING

What is the best way to prepare for a closing?

Well in advance of the closing, the parties should prepare one or more closing checklists that set forth the steps and documentation required for closing. Compliance with the checklist and with the conditions precedent to closing set forth in the basic loan or acquisition documents will increase significantly the likelihood that the requirements for closing are met.

This checklist should:

- Set forth each and every task that must be completed in order for the parties to be legally and logistically ready to consummate the transaction, and the date by which such task must be completed
- State, where applicable, the document in which the completion of the task will be embodied
- Set forth the name of one or more persons responsible for the task
- Contain a space for status notes

The closing checklist is both a road map and a progress report of the transaction. It can also be a source of embarrassment and a goad to those responsible for producing or reviewing documents whose failure to meet deadlines is documented in the status notes. Finally, it is the basis for the preparation of a closing memorandum for the transaction.

How should one schedule preclosing tasks?

The first concern should be to deal with documents and actions of parties who either will not be at the closing, will have a limited role in the closing, or are beyond the control of the parties to the transaction.

These persons include directors and shareholders whose authorizations are required; governmental agencies without any incentive to expedite review of applications for regulatory approvals; third parties to critical agreements who may prove recalcitrant when asked for consents, estoppel letters, solvency letters, or legal opinions; actuaries who must give up-to-date valuations of pension assets; and persons who are committed to other tasks but need to be on call to file or record mortgages, UCC financing statements, or merger certificates upon a moment's notice.

The persons responsible for ensuring that the closing takes place on the appointed day must make an accurate assessment of how long it is likely to take to obtain a required document or to accomplish a necessary task, and, working backward from the expected closing date, attempt to develop a realistic schedule for reaching closing.

Should all the parties use the same closing checklist?

At the very least, by the time the parties arrive at the preclosing phase, they should be working from the same closing checklist, with the following exceptions. The seller does not need those portions of the checklist dedicated to the financing of the transaction other than items related to the financing in which the seller has a role (such as delivery of reliance letters from the seller's counsel to lenders allowing them to rely on such counsel's legal opinion, and delivery of the seller's consent to assignments by the buyer to the lenders of the buyer's rights under the acquisition agreement).

The seller and the lenders do not need an expansive checklist relating to the tasks associated with the formation and capitalization of the buying group. Moreover, there may be certain tasks or documents, including side letters, that each party wishes to keep confidential within its own group. As a result, each party may have more than one closing checklist—that is, an expansive one setting forth everything about which it is concerned, and other lists that are abridged versions of the global checklist and are to be shared with one or more of the other parties. These latter lists must be developed along with the other parties so that all agree as to what activities in each phase of the closing will make everyone ready, legally and logistically, to consummate the transaction.

What are the phases of a closing?

The typical complex closing has three distinct phases: (1) the preclosing process, (2) the closing itself, and (3) postclosing matters.

PRECLOSING

What happens during the preclosing process?

During the preclosing process: (1) the parties and their counsel distribute closing documents, including drafts of execution documents, for final review and approval prior to the scheduled date of execution and funding; (2) each party satisfies itself that all conditions to closing have been either satisfied or waived; and (3) the parties negotiate and resolve any open deal points. The size and complexity of the transaction and the number of open points, including new issues that may arise during this final phase, will determine the length of the preclosing phase. A typical complex transaction—that is, one with layers of financing, multistate collateral, and several third-party or governmental consents, can easily involve one or two weeks of preclosing activities.

How do the parties satisfy themselves that the conditions precedent to closing have been satisfied or waived?

With respect to closing conditions that are satisfied through the delivery of documents such as regulatory approvals, landlord waivers, estoppel certificates, and management employment agreements, the parties and their counsel will examine the pertinent documentation and determine whether it comports with the requirements of the acquisition agreement or the relevant financing agreement, as applicable.

In some cases, such as closings that require the previously mentioned legal opinions and bring-down letters, the parties delivering such documents and/or their counsel will have the additional burden of satisfying themselves prior to delivery that the documents listed in the agreement have in fact been delivered, and that the factual and legal matters set forth in those documents are, in fact, true.

For example, prior to delivering its legal opinion, counsel will review documents such as UCC lien searches, corporate resolutions, good-standing certificates, and officers' certifications, and will verify that certain actions such as the filing of merger documents and the recording of mortgages and UCC financing statements have been completed.

With respect to other closing conditions, such as the conditions that there be no pending litigation that threatens to enjoin the consummation of the transaction, and that the target shall not have suffered a material adverse change in its business, the parties must review the results of the due diligence process with respect to such items and, if necessary, conduct further study (for example, reviewing the target's most recently available financial statements). Then the seller may need to make a bring-down representation, consistent with the earlier discussion.

Can you elaborate on the seller bring-down representation?

In the representation made in the acquisition agreement, which always precedes the deal signing (closing), the seller warrants that the financial statements of the company being sold represent a true and accurate picture of the company. In the *new* representation made at the closing, the seller must state that there have been no material adverse changes in the financial condition, operations, or prospects of the target between the date of the financial statements and the date of signing.

The buyer is not required to close the transaction if any bring-down condition is not satisfied, so the condition allocates to the seller the risk of loss attributable to any adverse change during the period between the signing of the acquisition agreement and closing. Interim losses probably reduce the value of the target, so the bring-down condition may allow the buyer to renegotiate a lower price reflecting the changes.

At the closing, a corporate officer must certify (in a certificate) that the representations and warranties are accurate in all material respects as of the closing date. Providing this certificate is a condition of closing, but it has another very important effect: it is a restatement of all the representations and warranties as of the closing date.

If the officer's certificate is not accurate, the inaccuracy will constitute a breach of a representation or warranty and may give rise to liability from buyer to seller under the indemnity section of the agreement. In the absence of an officer's certificate, a buyer might be unprotected against certain adverse events occurring between signing and closing.

For example, if a material liability arises and is discovered before closing, a closing condition will be unsatisfied, and the buyer can walk from the deal. But if it is not discovered, the parties may close because to their knowledge each closing condition—including the condition that the representation and warranty about undisclosed liabilities is true—was satisfied.

Clearly, the buyer needs more than a condition to closing to fully insulate it from undiscovered problems. Requiring the seller to represent that the closing condition is satisfied allows the buyer to treat the seller's failure to satisfy the condition as a breach of the representations. If the buyer is indemnified for losses attributable to such breaches, the buyer, by virtue of the certificate, will be protected against losses resulting from undiscovered problems.

As an aside, it is typical that the officer's certificate be made solely on behalf of the corporation; it should not constitute a personal affidavit. Otherwise, the corporate officer might be personally liable to the buyer if the certificate is proved untrue, even if the corporate officer is not at fault.

How can a buyer or seller ensure that its representations and warranties are true as of the closing date?

Counsel for each party should periodically confirm with the client that nothing material has occurred that makes a representation or warranty of the client untrue. Generally speaking, as soon as any significant event occurs that will make a representation or warranty untrue, such as a loss of a major customer of the seller or the filing of a lawsuit, the warranting party should typically inform the other parties of the development so that appropriate waivers or modifications of terms can be negotiated and resolved in advance of the closing. (Of course, it can sometimes soften the blow if the seller can pair this disclosure with a favorable development in the business.)

In addition, at least two or three days prior to the closing, counsel should review the client's representations and warranties line by line with appropriate employees and representatives of the client. Any facts that deviate from these representations and warranties should be incorporated as exceptions to the client's closing certificate regarding the accuracy of the representations and warranties and be immediately presented to the other relevant parties for their review. If they agree to accept the certificate with such exceptions, they shall be deemed to have waived the condition to closing (although they may not have waived their claims to indemnification for breach of the representation or warranty).

In addition to waiving a condition in an existing document, what other forms do waivers take?

Waivers of conditions to closing may also be made through the acceptance of documents containing terms that differ from the previously negotiated terms, such as legal opinions that take exceptions, make assumptions, or exclude matters not originally contemplated by the parties. Unless these new terms can easily be incorporated into the existing agreement, the best course is to create a new written waiver for the waiving party to execute.

How much renegotiation of the deal really takes place during the preclosing phase?

At times, quite a considerable amount! As is the case in most aspects of M&A, the parties should be prepared for anything and everything, including the following:

- The filing of a lawsuit or the assessment of a tax deficiency against the seller
- A change in the financial condition of the seller

- An unresolved personality conflict between principals in the buying and selling companies
- A demand by lenders that the transaction between the buyer and seller be modified, that additional security be provided, that the buyers raise additional equity, and/or that the lenders be given an equity kicker

These unthinkable events can and do happen and may require the parties to renegotiate fundamental business issues. As a result, the buyer and seller should come to the preclosing phase prepared to compromise where appropriate and to identify what items are nonnegotiable.

Who has the most leverage in closing-week negotiations?

First of all, the convergence of the parties at the various appointed closing offices, added to the resources they have already expended in getting to this phase of the transaction, creates tremendous momentum and incentives for everyone to close. Therefore, there will be some room for compromise by each party. Nevertheless, the parties will not necessarily have equal bargaining strength simply because both sides are fast approaching the finish line. Differences in leverage that developed through the course of prior negotiations are likely to persist during the closing week. However, there are no hard-and-fast rules about the degree to which the power relationships among the parties will, or will not, change.

For example, it would be logical for the buyer to assume that the sweet image of sales proceeds is dancing in the seller's head and, as a result, the seller will bend easily to any changes requested by the lenders. But the seller, in fact, may be having second thoughts about the bargain and resist any modifications of the acquisition agreement as a way of trying to force the buyer into a position where it cannot close. Conversely, the buyer may think (or know) that it is buying the target cheaply and may therefore do whatever is necessary to achieve a quick closing.

What is a preclosing drill?

The preclosing drill is a dress rehearsal for the closing, preferably held no earlier than three days before closing and no later than the night prior to closing. Counsel for the parties conduct the drill; their clients and other persons will be present as needed. It perhaps comes as little surprise that the preclosing process has become more electronic over time—although the fundamental elements of the process remain the same.

Historically, each party would spread all of its closing documents out on the closing room table—with documents inside a series of manila folders, which themselves would sit in long metal file organizers—so that the other appropriate parties could satisfy themselves that the conditions to closing embodied in those documents had been met. To the extent feasible, the parties would execute as many documents as possible during the preclosing drill in order to save time on the closing day and thereby ensure that all conditions to closing would be satisfied early enough to allow any wire transfer of funds or investment of sale proceeds to be completed on the closing day. After review of the closing documents and the closing checklist, the parties would identify tasks that would have to be completed before, legally and logistically, closing could be effected. However, it was not unusual to generate a schedule of minor uncompleted items and agree that they would be resolved postclosing.

Today, most of this process is completed electronically and via email. The attorneys will circulate PDF copies of all the relevant documents, clients will typically sign the documents (here again, often electronically through services such as DocuSign), and the attorneys will exchange signature pages prior to the closing date with the explicit instruction that the attorney receiving such signature pages is to hold the documents in escrow until the attorney transmitting the pages has explicitly authorized their release in writing (typically, through email). So while the days of a "war room" of legal documents may be gone, the overall process is generally the same.

The biggest exception to the trend toward electronic closings is when a deal involves bank financing or the transfer of real estate. Partially because of legacy rules in UCC law, transactions such as these do still require actual signatures—often in multiple copies—that are physically retained and/or filed in the appropriate channels.

Transactions involving third-party financing, lenders, and their counsel may even require two or more preclosing drills, that is, one involving their own financing, one involving review of the corporate side of the transaction, and, if applicable, others involving the other financing pieces of the transaction.

CLOSING

What happens on the closing day itself?

Assuming the parties have conducted a preclosing drill, three things will typically happen:

1. *Document preparation:* The parties and their counsel will review any documents that were revised or newly generated, the parties will execute any previously unexecuted documents, all undated documents will be dated, any required meetings of the board of directors that have not previously been held will be held, and any changed documents or signature pages that must be submitted to local counsel prior to release of their opinions will be transmitted to them.
2. *Document check:* The parties will recheck all the documents lined up on the closing table against the closing checklists.
3. *Funding and document delivery:* When all counsel are satisfied that conditions to closing have been satisfied or waived, they will instruct their clients' respective agents to wire funds or file or record documents (simultaneously or in such order as they have agreed), as applicable, and will deem all the documents on the closing table to have been delivered in the sequence set forth in the closing checklist and other governing agreements.

In the case of a transaction involving third-party financing, what part of the deal closes first?

In theory, all transactions typically are deemed to take place simultaneously. Practically speaking, however, the lenders usually will not release the loan proceeds until they receive confirmation that the corporate portion of the transaction has been completed; that is, stock certificates or bills of sale have been delivered or merger certificates have been filed, and security and title documents have been properly recorded.

How long does it actually take to close a transaction?

Depending on the complexity of the transaction, the number of things that do not go according to plan or schedule, and the goodwill, patience, and ingenuity of the parties and their counsel in devising acceptable bridge arrangements, substitutes, or accommodations, the closing phase may be effected within a matter of an hour or two, or it may stretch over several days.

On what day should the closing take place?

Preferably any day but a Friday or the day before a holiday. The failure to achieve the closing on the scheduled day prior to a weekend or holiday puts the parties in the awkward position of having to work into or through the nonbusiness day, without the ability to transfer or invest funds until the next business day, and with the attendant disruption in the personal lives of all concerned (which can be particularly troublesome for nonprofessional staff).

What are some of the most common logistical snafus that can derail a closing?

Some of the biggest headaches result from failure to:

- Have local counsel on standby to review last-minute changes to documents, because they may contain material inaccuracies caused by the passage of time that will require redating, amendment, or waiver in order to close the transaction
- Provide local counsel with copies of documents or other items that are conditions to release of their opinions
- Have precleared articles of merger with appropriate jurisdictions

- Have persons on standby to file or record documents, including merger documents, UCC forms such as UCC-1s, mortgages, and terminations of UCC-1s required to be removed off-record
- Have adequate support staff to make last-minute revisions in documents
- Have conducted the preclosing drill, including execution of all documents not subject to change
- Have adequate legal staff at closing headquarters to negotiate final documents, including local counsel legal opinions
- Secure funding before transferring title
- Obtain proper wiring instructions for funds transfers
- Ascertain time periods by which wires must be sent or to make arrangements to have banks hold their wires open past normal hours
- Consummate any preclosing corporate reorganizations (such as mergers of subsidiaries into parent companies, dissolution of defunct subsidiaries, or filing of charter amendments) in a timely fashion
- Have tax counsel review the final terms and documentation to ensure that tax planning objectives have not been adversely affected by last-minute restructuring or drafting
- Obtain required bring-down good-standing certificates or other certified documents from appropriate jurisdictions

Proper advance planning can prevent most, if not all, of these failures.

What exactly are UCC forms and where do they have to be filed?

A UCC form is a document filed pursuant to the Uniform Commercial Code, the legislative template produced by the American Law Institute and the National Conference on Uniform State Laws, introduced in Chapter 5, note 7. The most common UCC form is the UCC-1, or Financing Statement, which is used in a secured loan, where the lender uses the UCC-1 to place a lien on a particular piece of collateral or all assets belonging to a business or person.[2]

The UCC allows a creditor to notify other creditors about a debtor's assets used as collateral for a secured transaction by filing a public notice (financing statement) with a particular filing office.[3] The place of filing is usually with the office of the secretary of state in the company's state—that is, the state of organization if the organization is registered with a state. Or it will be a state of the chief executive office (headquarters) if the organization is unregistered and has more than one place of business. Finally, it can be the state where an individual resides in the case of an individual or sole proprietor.

Filing with the office of the secretary of state is required to perfect a security interest or agricultural lien except where a filing is required with the county clerk or other office designated for the filing or recording of a mortgage on the related real property. This is also necessary if the collateral is as-extracted collateral or timber to be cut, or the financing statement is filed as a fixture filing and the collateral is goods that are or are to become fixtures.

In most cases, financing statements are filed at the close of a secured transaction. However, it is advisable to file financing statements and perform a search on the debtor to discover existing filings by other creditors before the loan closing.

WIRE TRANSFERS

What is a wire transfer of funds?

A *wire transfer of funds* is payment through a series of debits and credits transmitted via computers. A domestic wire transfer is made through the Federal Reserve System, which is divided into 12 districts throughout the United States, with each district having one main Federal Reserve Bank and a myriad of branch banks. The actual physical transfer of funds takes place on the books of the Federal Reserve Banks and branches. An international wire transfer of funds is payment through a series of debits and credits transmitted directly among correspondent banks.

How is a domestic wire transfer made?

To make a wire transfer, both the buyer's and the seller's banks must be members of the Federal Reserve System and maintain accounts with a Reserve Bank, or have an account with a member bank. The buyer or lender remitting funds by wire must provide to its bank the name of the seller, the name of the seller's bank, the identity of the account to be credited, and the American Banking Association (ABA) number that identifies the seller's bank in the Federal Reserve System.

Upon the confirmation of customer funds, the originating member bank, or transferor, will notify its Reserve Bank to debit the transferor's account for credit to the member bank transferee. If the transferor and transferee maintain accounts at two separate Reserve Banks, the request for credit will be sent by the transferor's Reserve Bank to the transferee's Reserve Bank for credit to the latter. The transferee's Reserve Bank will then credit the transferee's account via the Federal Reserve Bank's official transfer system, Fedwire, in any amount. The average value of a Fedwire transfer today is $5 million.[4]

How does the originating bank confirm customer funds?

All funds to be remitted must be collected before the wire occurs. Thus, a check deposit covering the wire transfer that has not yet cleared will delay or prevent the transfer. Essentially, the remitting bank is protecting itself from exposure on items subject to stop-payment orders until final payment is effectuated. This includes certified checks and bank checks. Often, reference is made to "immediately available funds" or "federal funds," which signifies that the funds for remittance have been collected.

When is final payment of the wire transfer made?

As soon as the transferee receives notice of the credit—the Fedwire transfer from its Federal Reserve Bank—payment is considered final, and, except as described in the following, the seller has the right to the use of such funds.

Can a transferor revoke the request for a wire transfer of funds once the transferor has notified its Reserve Bank to debit its account?

The Reserve Bank may cease acting on the wire transfer if the transferor's request for revocation allows the Reserve Bank a reasonable opportunity to comply with the requested revocation. If the request is received too late, the Reserve Bank may ask the transferee's Reserve Bank to ask the transferee to return the funds, if the transferor so desires. However, the Reserve Bank will only be liable for lack of good faith or failure to exercise ordinary care. Therefore, it is not responsible if the transferee refuses to return the funds.

What is the deadline for placing a wire transfer order for funds intended to be received by the seller on the same day?

Although no Reserve Bank will guarantee that it will complete a transfer of funds on the day requested, generally speaking, 3:00 p.m. is the originating bank's deadline. Moreover, the Reserve Bank may, at its discretion, process a wire transfer after its closing hour. This will usually occur in an emergency or when large sums of money are being transferred. The deadline for placing an international wire transfer order is generally 12:30 p.m.

What are the differences between the domestic and international wire transfer of funds?

With an international wire transfer, the ease and security of the Federal Reserve are not available. Hence, the transfer generally takes longer. In addition, with international wire there is a problem of provisional payment. Specifically, the bank that debits the customer's account usually reserves the right to withdraw the credit extended to the corresponding bank, if the customer's account is overdrawn in the process. This may create problems in determining when final payment is made.

What are the advantages and disadvantages to a seller in requiring payment through a wire transfer of funds?

Next to actual cash in hand, this is the best way for a seller to have use of the sale proceeds on the closing day, because the Federal Reserve Bank assumes the risk of final payment once the transferor's request is accepted by its Reserve Bank.

One potential disadvantage associated with a wire transfer is a possible delay at the receiving end. The seller's bank may not be required to credit the seller's account immediately upon receiving Federal Reserve credit because of the account agreement. Federal law requires that the transferee *promptly* credit the beneficiary's account. However, what "promptly" means is not clearly specified. The seller is best advised to be familiar with the terms of its bank account agreement. Moreover, the seller could specify in the acquisition agreement that the buyer's duty to deliver funds is completed only when the seller's individual account has been credited.

Are there methods of payment, other than cash or wire transfer, that would be acceptable to sellers at a closing?

There are basically three types of bank-issued checks that are virtually risk-free to a seller who accepts them: (1) the certified check, (2) the cashier's check, and (3) the bank check.[5] Each of these checks has some distinguishing feature, but all of them are designed to offer comfort to the recipient that payment will definitely be made by the designated payor bank.

- Certified checks are instruments that, upon certification by the payor bank, are not subject to an order to stop payment. Under the UCC, the certifying bank becomes personally liable for failure to honor the check, and the customer is then secondarily liable.

- Cashier's checks are similar. When a bank issues a cashier's check, the bank acts as both the payor and the payee for the amount of the check. As with the certified check, a bank is deemed to have accepted a cashier's check for payment at the moment it is issued. The customer cannot stop payment on it. The seller's only risk of nonpayment is if the issuing bank becomes insolvent before payment can be made. Even in that event, if the bank is a member of the FDIC, the check will be insured up to $100,000.
- A bank check does not give a seller the same degree of comfort as either a certified check or a cashier's check, because, unlike the certified and cashier's checks, the issuing bank of a bank check has not accepted the check for payment (that is, committed to pay the stated amount upon demand) at the moment of issuance. Rather, the check will be paid only when presented. Despite this difference, the UCC treats bank checks as cash equivalents, and the only instance in which the issuing bank can stop payment is if it is a direct party to the transaction. The only time a customer ordering a bank check can request that payment be stopped is in the case of fraud or a theft of the instrument.

POSTCLOSING

What are typical postclosing activities?

Postclosing tasks typically fall into one of two categories: document distribution and cleanup.

Document Distribution

Document distribution requires planning. Although each of the parties to a closing generally wants to depart from the closing table (whether that table is physical or virtual) with a complete set of all official closing documents, this is not frequently practical. First, each of the parties has different requirements for closing documents. Some parties should not receive documents that other parties will receive, and some parties need original documents whereas others need only scanned PDFs (or copies of same).

Further, some documents held or executed at other locations may be available at the time and place of closing only by electronic transmission, or not at all. Finally, the sheer number and volume of documents may preclude sorting and scanning of the executed papers swiftly enough to be delivered to the parties prior to their departure from the premises.

At some point, however, each of the participants should receive a complete set of the transaction documents to which it is entitled. Historically, the initial distribution of originals and, as available, copies, in some transactions would be followed by the production of a closing binder containing a complete indexed set of documents in one or more volumes. These binders might have been velobound or, if the expense is approved by the clients, permanently bound in stitched covers with stamped lettering on the spine. The acquisition documents often are bound separately from the financing documents.

Just as the preclosing drill has turned increasingly digital, so too has postclosing document distribution. Today, it is not uncommon to distribute a master PDF file with all of the closing documents, indexed with electronic bookmarks to jump to specific documents. At times, these files can be unusually large and cannot be sent by email. In such cases, it would be typical for files to be sent through a service providing secure transmission of large files.

Regardless of whether the postclosing document distribution is accomplished physically or electronically, the final document assembly and distribution effort will be much easier if a good closing document checklist was in use prior to closing. When completed and updated, the checklist may be turned into a closing memorandum (which may double as an index to the closing document binders), with the addition of a brief narrative chronology of the transactions taken prior to, at, and following the closing to complete the transaction. A common closing memorandum can be used even if the acquisition and financing closings occurred at different offices.

Cleanup

The second principal postclosing effort is the cleanup process, which involves the completion of any tasks left open at closing. This may include items such as:

- Corrections or amendments to ancillary documents
- The termination or transfer of pension plans
- The receipt of consents and approvals not obtainable by closing
- The completion and documentation of a closing date audit for balance sheet pricing adjustment, or the receipt of title insurance commitments or policies as of the closing date from jurisdictions with filing delays

In addition, where many real estate parcels in multiple jurisdictions must be mortgaged, or collateral is located in foreign countries, postclosing may include completion of recordation of mortgages and perfection of security interests, with a deadline for completion set for several months after the closing date.

In both cases, individuals responsible for postclosing efforts should strive to complete their tasks as soon as possible before the pressure of other matters and the passage of time make wrapping up these loose ends more difficult. A postclosing checklist similar in design to the closing checklist should be prepared, and adhered to, by the parties responsible for these activities.

CONCLUDING COMMENTS

The closing of a transaction is often a last chance to check details of that transaction and to make sure all parties understand it. The closing memorandum memorializes the transactional events that have led up to closing day. The sample closing memorandum in Appendix 8A, which is from a very complex transaction, provides a useful template.

APPENDIX 8A

Sample Closing Memorandum (Including a Detailed Schedule of Closing Documents)

MERGER OF TARGET ACQUISITION CORP. INTO TARGET CO. INC.

DECEMBER 31, 2019
9:00 a.m. Eastern Standard Time

I. GENERAL

This memorandum describes the principal transactions that have occurred in connection with the acquisition (the "Acquisition") of Target Co. Inc., a Delaware corporation ("Target"), by Purchaser Holdings, Inc., a Delaware corporation ("Holdings"). Holdings; Target Acquisition Corp., a Delaware corporation and a wholly owned subsidiary of Holdings ("TAC"); and Target and Seller Holdings, Ltd., a Delaware corporation which owns all of the issued and outstanding Stock of Target ("Seller"), have entered into an Agreement of Merger, dated as of October 1, 2019 (the "Agreement"), pursuant to which TAC will be merged into Target pursuant to the Certificate of Merger.

In connection with the capitalization of Holdings to accomplish the Acquisition on the Effective Date, affiliates (the "Investor Shareholders") of Investor Corporation, a Delaware corporation ("IC"), purchased

800,000 shares of the common stock of Holdings for an aggregate amount of $4,000,000. Concurrently, IC loaned $1,000,000 on a recourse basis to certain management personnel at Target (the "Management Shareholders"). The Management Shareholders purchased 200,000 shares of the common stock of Holdings for $1,000,000 and pledged such stock to IC to secure repayment of the loan. TAC then merged into Target.

On the Effective Date, Holdings entered into a Credit Agreement with Lender Bank ("Bank") pursuant to which Holdings obtained a term loan of $40,000,000 and revolving credit loans of up to $10,000,000 (the "Credit Agreement"). Concurrently therewith, Holdings entered into a Bridge Funding Agreement with The Investment Bank Group Inc. ("Investment Bank Group") pursuant to which Holdings obtained a bridge loan of $60,000,000 (the "Bridge Agreement"). Holdings sold warrants for 200,000 shares of its Common Stock (the "Investment Banker Warrants") to Lead Investment Banker Incorporated ("Lead Investment Banker") and its designees for $20,000.

After the Effective Date it is anticipated that Holdings and Lead Investment Banker will enter into a Securities Purchase Agreement (the "Securities Purchase Agreement") pursuant to which Holdings will return the $20,000 to Lead Investment Banker and Lead Investment Banker will return the Investment Banker Warrants to Holdings. Holdings will then sell Warrants for 200,000 shares of its Common Stock to the Purchasers named in the Securities Purchase Agreement (the "Purchasers") for $20,000 (the "Note Purchase Warrants") and deliver to the Purchasers Notes due December 31, 2024, in an aggregate principal amount of $60,000,000 and bearing interest at approximately 14 percent per annum (the "Note") for which Holdings will receive $60,000,000 cash, which it will use to pay off the $60,000,000 bridge loan under the Bridge Agreement.

After the Effective Time and concurrently with the funding of the term loan, the initial revolving loans, and the bridge loan, Holdings contributed to TAC the amount of $100,000,000 as a capital contribution. Seller received $100,000,000 cash less the amount of the intercompany loan to be paid after Closing, Series A Preferred Stock of Holdings having a redemption value of $10,000,000 and a Warrant entitling it to purchase 40,000 shares of the common stock of Holdings (the "Seller Warrant").

The Closing occurred on December 31, 2019 (the "Effective Date"), at 9:00 a.m. Eastern Standard Time. The merger was effective on the Effective Date at the time the Certificate of Merger was filed with the Secretary of State of Delaware (the "Effective Time").

All capitalized terms used herein which are not defined herein and which are defined in the Agreement, the Credit Agreement, the Bridge Funding Agreement, or the Securities Purchase Agreement have the respective meanings attributed to them in the Agreement, the Credit Agreement, the Bridge Funding Agreement, or the Securities Purchase Agreement.

II. TRANSACTIONS PRIOR TO THE CLOSING

The following actions were taken prior to the Closing.

1. On October 1, 2019, the Agreement among Holdings, Target, TAC, and Seller was executed and delivered.
2. On October 1, 2019, TAC, Seller, and Agent Bank (the "Escrow Agent") entered into an Escrow Agreement pursuant to which TAC deposited with the Escrow Agent One Million Dollars ($1,000,000) pursuant to Section 3.3 of the Agreement.
3. On October 1, 2019, the Board of Directors of each of Holdings and TAC approved the terms of the Merger and the Agreement and the Board of Directors of TAC approved the Escrow Agreement.
4. On October 1, 2019, the Board of Directors of each of Target and Seller approved the terms of the Merger and the Agreement and the Board of Directors of Seller approved the Escrow Agreement.
5. On October 2, 2019, Seller issued a press release announcing the Holdings, Target, Seller, and TAC agreement to the terms of the Merger and announcing the execution of the Agreement.
6. On November 16, 2019, Bank delivered to Holdings a commitment letter pursuant to which Bank agreed to provide a $40,000,000 term loan and a $10,000,000 revolving line of credit

to facilitate the Acquisition and to provide working capital thereafter.

7. On November 24, 2019, Lead Investment Banker delivered to Holdings a commitment letter pursuant to which Lead Investment Banker undertook to provide a bridge loan for an aggregate amount of $60,000,000.
8. On November 24, 2019, Holdings delivered to Lead Investment Banker a retention letter pursuant to which Holdings retained Lead Investment Banker to sell the Notes and Note Purchaser Warrants.
9. On December 24, 2019, a date at least three business days before the Closing, Seller delivered to TAC pursuant to Section 4.3 of the Agreement a notice setting forth the amount of the Intercompany Loan to be paid immediately after Closing.
10. On December 28, 2019, the Board of Directors and shareholders of Holdings adopted an amendment of the certificate of incorporation of Holdings to authorize the Series A Preferred Stock.
11. On December 28, 2019, Holdings caused to be filed an Amended and Restated Certificate of Incorporation providing for 1,500 shares of Series A Preferred Stock par value $1.00 per share.
12. As of December 30, 2019, the Certificate of Merger was executed by the President of TAC and attested by the Secretary of such corporation and was executed by the President of Target and sealed and attested by the Secretary of such corporation.
13. On December 30, 2019, the Board of Directors of Holding authorized the issuance of 1,000 shares of Series A Preferred Stock to Seller with the rights designated in the Amended and Restated Certificate of Incorporation of Holdings.
14. On December 30, 2019, Seller, as sole stockholder of Target, consented to the Agreement and Certificate of Merger.
15. On December 30, 2019, Holdings, as sole stockholder of TAC, consented to the Agreement and Certificate of Merger.

III. CLOSING DOCUMENTS AND TRANSACTIONS

The following documents were delivered at or prior to the Effective Date, but all such documents are deemed delivered at the Effective Date. All documents are dated as of the Effective Date and delivered in New York, New York, unless otherwise indicated. All transactions in connection with the Closing shall be considered as accomplished concurrently, so that none shall be effective until all are effective. Executed copies (or photocopies, or conformed copies where necessary) of each document will be delivered after the Closing as follows:

one to IC
one to Holdings
one to Seller
one to Target
one to Bank
one to Lead Investment Banker

with photocopies to be distributed as follows:

one to Investment Banker Counsel (IBC)
one to Seller Counsel (SC)
one to Bank Counsel (BC)
one to Investor Corporation Counsel (ICC)

IV. SCHEDULE OF CLOSING DOCUMENTS

1. Corporate Good Standing, Articles, Bylaws, and Incumbency of Target, Its Subsidiaries, and Seller

1.01. Certificate of Incorporation and all amendments to date of Target certified by the Secretary of State of Delaware on December 3, 2019.

1.02. Certificate of the Secretary of State of Delaware, dated December 3, 2019, certifying that Target is an existing corporation and in good standing under the laws of the State of Delaware.

1.03. Telex from the Secretary of State of Delaware, dated the Effective Date, updating the information described in item 1.02 above.

1.04. Certificates of the Secretaries of State of California and New York dated December 1 and 2, 2019, respectively, certifying that Target is qualified to conduct business and is in good standing in such states.

1.05. Telexes or verbal consents from the Secretaries of State of California and New York, dated the Effective Date, updating the information described in item 1.04 above.

1.06. (a)–(b) Articles or Certificates of Incorporation or other organization documents and all amendments to date of the following Subsidiaries of Target ("Subsidiaries") certified by the appropriate authority of the governing jurisdiction:

(a) New York Target Subsidiary Ltd. (N.Y.)

(b) Delaware Target Subsidiary, Inc. (Del.)

1.07. (a)–(b) Certificates of the authorities described in item 1.06, certifying that each of the Subsidiaries is an existing corporation and in good standing.

1.08. (a)–(b) Telexes or verbal consents of the authorities described in item 1.06, dated the Effective Date, updating the information set forth in item 1.07 above.

1.09. Certificate of Incorporation and all amendments to date of Seller certified by the Secretary of State of Delaware, dated December 3, 2019.

1.10. Certificate of the Secretary of State of Delaware, dated December 3, 2019, certifying that Seller is an existing corporation and in good standing under the laws of Delaware.

1.11. Telex from the Secretary of State of Delaware, dated the Effective Date, updating the information described in item 1.10 above.

1.12. Certificate of Secretary of Target, dated the Effective Date, as to the Certificates of Incorporation and Bylaws of such corporation, the election, incumbency, and signatures of officers of such corporation, and certifying as to the resolutions of the Board of Directors and stockholders of such corporation relating to the transaction pursuant to Section 8.4 of the Agreement.

1.13. Certificate of Secretary of Seller, dated the Effective Date, as to the Certificate of Incorporation and Bylaws of such corporation, the election, incumbency, and signatures of officers of such corporation, and certifying as to the resolutions of the Board of Directors of such corporation relating to the transaction pursuant to Section 8.4 of the Agreement.

2. Good Standing, Articles, Bylaws, and Incumbency of Holdings and TAC

2.01. Certificate of Incorporation and all amendments to date of Holdings certified by the Secretary of State of Delaware on December 21, 2019.

2.02. Certificate of the Secretary of State of Delaware, dated December 21, 2019, certifying that Holdings is an existing corporation and in good standing under the laws of the State of Delaware.

2.03. Telex of the Secretary of State of Delaware, dated the Effective Date, updating the information set forth in item 2.02 above.

2.04. Certificate of the Secretary of State of each of California and New York, dated December 22, 2019, certifying that Holdings is qualified to conduct business and is in good standing in such states.

2.05. Certificate of Incorporation and all amendments to date of TAC certified by the Secretary of State of Delaware on December 10, 2019.

2.06. Certificate of the Secretary of State of Delaware, dated December 21, 2019, certifying that TAC is an existing corporation and in good standing under the laws of the State of Delaware.

2.07. Telex of the Secretary of State of Delaware, dated the Effective Date, updating the information set forth in item 2.06 above.

2.08. Certificate of the Secretary of Holdings, dated the Effective Date, as to the Certificate of Incorporation and Bylaws of such corporation, the election, incumbency, and signatures of officers of such corporation and certifying as to the resolutions of the Board of Directors of such corporation relating to the transaction pursuant to Section 9.4 of the Agreement, Sections 5.01(e), (f), and (h) of the Credit Agreement and the Bridge Agreement.

2.09. Certificate of the Secretary of TAC, dated the Effective Date, as to the Certificate of Incorporation and Bylaws of such corporation, the election, incumbency, and signatures of officers of such corporation, and certifying as to the resolutions of the Board of Directors and stockholders of such corporation relating to the transaction pursuant to Section 9.4 of the Agreement, Sections 5.01(e), (f), and (h) of the Credit Agreement, and the Bridge Agreement.

2.10. Certificate of the Secretary of Target (the Surviving Corporation), dated the Effective Date, certifying as to the resolutions of the Board of Directors of such corporation relating to Sections 5.01(e), (f), and (h) of the Credit Agreement and the Bridge Agreement.

2.11. (a)–(b) Certificates of the Secretaries of the Subsidiaries listed in (a)–(b) of item 1.06 as to the Certificate of Incorporation and Bylaws, the election, incumbency, and signatures of officers and certifying as to resolutions of the Board of Directors of such corporations relating to Sections 5.01(e), (f), and (h) of the Credit Agreement.

3. Principal Documents

3.01. Agreement of Merger, dated as of October 1, 2019.

3.02. Certificate of Merger.

3.03. Escrow Agreement, dated October 1, 2019.

3.04. Certificate No. PA-1-1 evidencing 1,000 shares of Series A Preferred Stock of Holdings.

3.05. Seller Registration Rights Agreement.

3.06. Seller Warrant.

3.07. Credit Agreement, together with Schedules and Exhibits thereto.

3.08. Target Security Agreement, between Bank as Agent and for the Ratable Benefit of Lenders and Target.

3.09. (a)–(b) Subsidiary Security Agreement between Bank as Agent and for the Ratable Benefit of Lenders and each of the Subsidiaries listed in (a)–(b) of item 1.06.

3.10. Holdings Pledge Agreement.

3.11. Certificate No. 8 evidencing 100 shares, constituting all of the issued and outstanding shares of Target together with a stock power duly endorsed.

3.12. Target Pledge Agreement.

3.13. (a)–(b) Certificates evidencing all of the issued and outstanding shares of each of the Subsidiaries listed in item 1.06, together with stock powers or other instruments of transfer duly endorsed.

3.14. Individual Stock Pledge Agreements, executed by each of the Investor Shareholders and Management Shareholders in favor of the Bank.

3.15. Certificates evidencing all of the issued and outstanding common shares of Holdings, together with stock powers from each shareholder duly endorsed.

3.16. Mortgage.

3.17. Joinder Agreement executed by Target.

3.18. Private Placement Memorandum of December 27, 2019.

3.19. Supplement to the Private Placement Memorandum dated December 30, 2019.

3.20. Bridge Agreement.

3.21. Bridge Notes Indenture.

3.22. Senior Subordinated Bridge Note.

3.23. Bridge Note Registration Rights Agreement.

3.24. Warrants issued by Holdings to Lead Investment Banker.

3.25. Subordinated Pledge Agreement between Holdings and Investment Bank Group.

3.26. Intercreditor Agreement between Bank and Investment Bank Group.

4. Documents Relating to the Escrow Agent

4.01. Joint Written Notice executed by Seller and TAC pursuant to Section 4(a) of the Escrow Agreement to the effect that the Merger has been effected and instructing the Escrow Agent to pay the Escrow Deposit and interest accrued thereon to Target.

4.02. Receipt of Target, dated the Effective Date, for funds received from the Escrow Agent in the amount of $1,025,000.

5. Documents Relating to Compliance with Agreement of Merger

5.01. Certificate of the President of Seller, dated the Effective Date, pursuant to Sections 8.1 and 8.2 of the Agreement and as to compliance with and performance of the Agreement and as to the representations and warranties set forth in the Agreement.

5.02. Certificate of the Vice President of TAC dated the Effective Date, pursuant to Sections 9.1, 9.2, and 9.7 of the Agreement as to compliance and performance of the Agreement; the representations and warranties set forth in the Agreement; and its business, financial conditions, and operations.

5.03. Releases executed by each person holding an option to purchase common stock of Target under the Target Stock Option Plan pursuant to Section 8.9 of the Agreement.

5.04. Certificate No. 7 of Target evidencing 1,000 shares of common stock of Target issued to Seller together with such stock transfer tax stamps as may be required.

6. Documents Relating to Compliance with Credit Agreement

6.01. Certificate executed by CEO and CFO of Holdings as to representations and warranties and no event of default pursuant to Section 5.01(d) of the Credit Agreement.

6.02. (a)–(d) UCC-1 Financing Statements covering personal property and appropriate documents for perfecting security interest in US intellectual property as follows:

(a) Holdings—California Secretary of State; Clerk of Los Angeles County, California; New York Department of State; and City Register of New York City;

(b) Target—California Secretary of State; Clerk of Los Angeles County, California; New York Department of State; and City Register of New York City;

(c) New York Target Subsidiary Ltd.—New York Department of State; and City Register of New York City; and

(d) Delaware Target Subsidiary Inc.—Delaware Secretary of State; Clerk of New Castle County, Delaware.

6.03. Certificate of President of Target to the effect that all indebtedness of Target has been paid or refinanced pursuant to Section 5.01(o) of the Credit Agreement.

6.04. Appointments of CT Corporation System in State of California as agent for service of process executed by CT Corporation, Holdings, Target, and the Subsidiaries pursuant to Section 5.01(s) of the Credit Agreement.

6.05. Pro Forma Closing Date Balance Sheet for Holdings and its consolidated Subsidiaries pursuant to Section 5.01(t) of the Credit Agreement.

6.06. Borrowing Base Report, dated not more than two (2) days prior to the Effective Date pursuant to Section 5.01(y) of the Credit Agreement.

6.07. Appraisal of Appraisal Co. as to fair market value and orderly liquidation value of the real and personal property of Target pursuant to Section 5.01(b) of the Credit Agreement.

6.08. Written undertakings, executed by each of Target and the Subsidiaries pursuant to Section 5.01(d) of the Credit Agreement.

6.09. Solvency letters from CFOs and accountants for Holdings and Target pursuant to Section 5.01(k) of the Credit Agreement.

6.10. Bank Credit Audit pursuant to Section 5.01(p) of the Credit Agreement.

6.11. Certificate of Borrower as to consents pursuant to Section 6.03 of the Credit Agreement.

6.12. Evidence of payment of or indemnification against tax liens: City of New York—$10,000,000; State of New York—$500.00.

7. Consents, Waivers, and Estoppel Certificates of Landlords of Target and Real Estate Matters

7.01. Consent of Lessor Ltd., lessor to New York Target Subsidiary, Ltd., with respect to the facility located at One Main Street, New York, New York.

7.02. Owners' title insurance policy with respect to the California property, dated the Effective Date, pursuant to Section 8.8 of the Agreement.

7.03. Lenders' title insurance policy with respect to the California property.

7.04. Title Insurance Questionnaire.

7.05. Estoppel Certificate.

7.06. Survey.

7.07. Indemnities of Seller to the Title Insurance Company.

7.08. Discharges of Trust Company Mortgages.

7.09. Seller Agreement regarding effluent discharge.

8. Insurance

8.01. Insurance endorsements naming Agent as additional insured or loss payee pursuant to Section 5.01(x) of the Credit Agreement.

9. Documents Relating to Compliance with Bridge Agreement

9.01. Certificate of Vice President of Holdings pursuant to Section 3.1.4 of the Bridge Agreement as to the satisfaction of certain conditions of the Bridge Agreement.

9.02. Warrant Repurchase Letter Agreement, dated the Effective Date, between Holdings and Investment Bank Group.

10. Opinions of Counsel

10.01. Opinion of SC, dated the Effective Date, addressed to Holdings, the Agent, Lead Investment Banker, and the Indenture Trustee pursuant to Section 8.5 of the Agreement, Section 5.01(mm) of the Credit Agreement, and Section 3.1.8 of the Bridge Agreement.

10.02. Opinion of ICC, dated the Effective Date, pursuant to Section 9.5 of the Agreement.

10.03. Opinion of ICC, dated the Effective Date, addressed to the Agent pursuant to Section 5.01(c) of the Credit Agreement.

10.04. Opinion of ICC, dated the Effective Date, addressed to Lead Investment Banker and the Indenture Trustee pursuant to Section 3.1.7 of the Bridge Agreement.

10.05. Opinion of California Counsel, dated the Effective Date, addressed to the Agent pursuant to Section 5.01(v) of the Credit Agreement.

10.06. Opinion of Copyright Counsel, dated the Effective Date, addressed to the Agent and Holdings as to the trademark and copyright registrations in the United States pursuant to Section 5.01(w) of the Credit Agreement.

10.07. Opinion of BC dated the Effective Date, addressed to the Lenders pursuant to Section 5.01(u) of the Credit Agreement.

11. Documents Relating to IC and Management Shareholders

11.01. Employment Agreement between Target and John Smith, President of Target.

11.02. Powers of Attorney from each Management Shareholder appointing John Smith Attorney-in-fact.

11.03. Recourse Notes in the aggregate of $1,000,000 executed by each of the Management Shareholders (originals delivered to IC).

11.04. Pledge Agreement executed by Management Shareholders in favor of IC.

11.05. Cross Receipt of IC acknowledging receipt of the notes described in 11.03 and by John Smith as Attorney-in-fact for each of the Management Shareholders acknowledging receipt of an aggregate amount of $1,000,000.

11.06. Stockholders Agreement among Holdings, Investor Shareholders, and Management Shareholders.

11.07. Agreement for Management Consulting Services between IC and Target.

11.08. IC Intercreditor Agreement by and between IC and Bank.

11.09. Letter as to Recourse Promissory Notes in favor of IC, dated the Effective Date, from IC to counsel for the Management Shareholders.

12. Funding of Holdings and TAC and Merger Payment

12.01. Cross Receipt executed by Holdings acknowledging receipt of $4,000,000, and by the Investor Shareholders acknowledging receipt of Certificate Nos. 1–4 evidencing 800,000 shares of the common stock of Holdings.

12.02. Cross Receipt executed by Holdings acknowledging receipt of $1,000,000, and by the Management Shareholders acknowledging receipt of Certificate Nos. 5–8 evidencing 200,000 shares of the common stock of Holdings.

12.03. Cross Receipt executed by Seller, dated the Effective Date, acknowledging receipt of (a) the Cash Portion of the Merger Payment in the amount of $100,000,000 determined pursuant to Section 3.2(b) of the Merger Agreement; (b) the Warrant; and (c) Certificate No. PA-1 evidencing 1,000 shares of Series A Preferred Stock, and by Holdings acknowledging receipt of (i) $10,000,000 as consideration for the issuance of the Series A Preferred Stock and (ii) a certificate evidencing 1,000 shares of Common Stock of Target.

12.04. Receipt executed by IC acknowledging receipt of $3,000,000 as a structuring fee.

13. Funding of Loan and Sale of Warrants

13.01. Term Note in the amount of $40,000,000 (original delivered to Lender).

13.02. Revolving Note in the amount of $10,000,000 (original delivered to Lender) (only $1,000,000 borrowed at Closing).

13.03. Cross Receipt of Lender acknowledging receipt of the Term Note and the Revolving Note and of Holdings acknowledging receipt of $41,000,000.

13.04. Cross Receipt of Investment Bank Group and Lead Investment Banker acknowledging receipt of the Investment Banker Warrants and Bridge Note and of Holdings acknowledging receipt of $60,000,000.

V. FILING OF CERTIFICATE OF MERGER

When all parties and their counsel were satisfied that the documents described in Section IV were complete and in order, the Certificate of Merger was filed in the office of the Secretary of State of Delaware, in accordance with the General Corporation Law of the State of Delaware.

NOTES

1. See Dechert LLP, "M&A Documentation in the USA," Lexology, May 25, 2018, https://www.lexology.com/library/detail.aspx?g=9fd46b1d-d441-4796-906e-099ca04d7125. In the United States, there are two bodies of law governing the legality of electronic signatures and electronic records. At the federal level, there is the Electronic Signature in Global and National Commerce Act of 2000 (ESIGN). At the state level, there are state laws, which are generally based on the Uniform Electronic Transactions Act (UETA), last amended in 1999. See DLA Piper, A Short Primer on Applicable US eSignature Laws, May 2, 2018, https://www.dlapiper.com/en/us/insights/publications/2018/05/esignature-and-epayment-news-and-trends-1-may-2018/a-short-primer-on-applicable-us-esignature-laws/.
2. Daniel W. Lias, "What You Need to Know About Common Uniform Commercial Code (USS) Forms," Wolters Kluwer, June 7, 2018, https://ct.wolterskluwer.com/resource-center/articles/what-you-need-know-about-common-uniform-commercial-code-ucc-forms.
3. The source of this explanation is the Office of the Secretary of

State, Texas, at www.sos.state.tx.us/ucc/index.shtml. Every state has similar explanations. For the State of Delaware, see https://corp.delaware.gov/uccform/.

4. https://www.federalreserve.gov/paymentsystems/fedfunds_qtr.htm.
5. Each of these types has varieties. See Gene Elerding, Partner, Manatt, Phelps & Phillips, LLP, and Ted Teruo Kitada, Senior Company Counsel, Wells Fargo Bank, N.A., May 2012, https://www.jdsupra.com/legalnews/the-check-book-a-guide-for-check-disp-09983/.

CHAPTER 9

Postmerger Integration and Divestitures

INTRODUCTION

After the closing of an M&A transaction, many buyers and sellers feel relieved. They know the work of strategy, valuation, financing, structuring, due diligence, and negotiation is behind them. But for strategic acquirers, the conclusion of an M&A transaction is also the beginning of a new process—combining two companies, usually in their entirety.

A typical acquisition announcement will state that one company is buying another in order to take advantage of a specific resource in the other company—for example, expertise in a new technology, as seen in Cummins Engine's July 2018 acquisition of electrification leader Efficient Drivetrains, Inc.[1] Or the acquirer may seek a broader benefit, as seen in T-Mobile's April 2018 announcement of a merger with Sprint to bring them both into the 5G age.[2]

But whatever the reasons for a transaction, most acquisitions do entail a full-scale integration of all resources, processes, and responsibilities for both companies. Therefore, at the integration phase, many aspects of the acquired company having nothing to do with strategy demand closer attention. Acquirers who had been dreaming about teaming up for scientific breakthroughs find themselves worrying about designing a payroll system—and hundreds of similarly mundane matters. To deal with these details, comprehensive, detailed integration plans are needed.

At the same time, the company and its stakeholders need to prepare for the possibility that some company units or assets may be *sold* following an acquisition. This possibility, too, should be part of postmerger planning.

This chapter briefly explains basic concepts of postmerger integration and divestiture, and gives general guidance for the fiduciary care of key resources, processes, and responsibilities following the closing of an M&A transaction. Our explanation will be at a fairly high board-of-directors level. For close-to-the-ground managerial tools, other books in this series will be helpful.[3]

BASIC CONCEPTS OF INTEGRATION

What is M&A integration?

The term *M&A integration* refers primarily to the art of combining two or more companies—not just on paper, but in reality—after they have come under common ownership: *M&A* refers to the merger or acquisition transaction that leads to the combination, and *integration* refers to a combination of elements that enables the two companies to function as one. To practice the art of M&A integration well, one must learn by doing it—or at least learn from similar companies that have done it.

Of course, for-profit corporations aren't the only entities that get involved in mergers and divestitures. Associations, charities, universities, trade unions, and government agencies can merge too—just to name a few merger candidates. And mergers and acquisitions aren't the only kinds of transactions that can elicit skills in integration. Joint ventures, strategic alliances, or partial acquisitions can require some integration work as well. Finally, sometimes integrations can be extremely complex, involving the integration of multiple companies. For the most part, this chapter will emphasize standard mergers or acquisitions involving two companies, with occasional references to other applications.

Don't all buyers and sellers count on postmerger integration? What would be the point of buying a company without integrating it?

Companies make acquisitions for a variety of motives, as explained in Chapter 2, "Strategy," and not every one involves integration.

The degree and nature of integration necessary after an acquisition depends in part on which goals are to be met. For example, the goal of operating synergy may require more attention to integration than a change in tax status. Nonetheless, for most acquirers, some degree of integration will be necessary.

What are the benefits of integration versus separate management for an acquired company or one of its units?

If the acquirer has a strategic reason for buying the company, some form of integration will be necessary for success. If the acquirer's reason for buying a firm is financial, however, integration may not be particularly helpful. (For more on strategic versus financial acquirers, see Chapter 1.)

What is the difference between a financial and a strategic approach when it comes to integration?

Financial acquirers have no intention of integrating the resources, operations, or technology of the acquired company into their own. These acquirers, which are typically (but not always) buyout funds, do not so much manage as *monitor* the resources they acquire.

Thus, a financial approach treats each acquired company as a separate entity. In such an approach, exemplified by the buyout firm of Kohlberg Kravis Roberts & Company (KKR), the buyer tries to add value through imposing superior, top-down management strategies in a short period of time. Financial acquisitions can be fairly diverse. Although these transactions may build on the acquirers' expertise, they need not be integrated into the acquirers' operations to yield good postmerger returns.

A *strategic approach,* by contrast, treats each acquired company as a new member of its corporate family—whether its industries are diverse (Berkshire Hathaway, General Electric) or focused (Cisco, General Dynamics). Strategic acquisitions (commonly referred to as mergers) often involve combinations of companies in the same or related industries. Mergers within the same industry can reduce costs (usually by increasing purchasing scale or reducing the cost of payroll by laying off employees) and/or increase revenues (usually by increasing the customer base).

THE POSTMERGER PLAN

What is the window of time for implementing a postmerger plan?

No one has ever suggested a minimum, but a number of consulting companies have suggested maximums. Realistically, the integration can take up to a year, but the more successful initiatives are completed in six months, with the most critical phases completed in three months or, more poetically, "100 days."

It stands to reason that the longer the acquirer waits to add value to the unit—presumably through some form of integration—the more expensive it will be to repay the premium paid to purchase the unit.

How successful are mergers generally after the initial windfalls? Is it true that most of them turn out to be failures?

The answer to this question depends on how you define *failure.* If you are not sure about your definition, you are not alone. In the past half century, scholars have published hundreds of studies of postmerger financial performance, and few have defined failure—or, conversely, success—in exactly the same way.

On average, M&A has a neutral effect on share prices, with some companies losing value and others gaining it. A classic study in this regard is one by Darden Business School dean Robert Bruner, whose comprehensive review of M&A research—covering more than 100 studies—found that in general:

- Shareholders of selling firms earn large returns.
- Shareholders from buyers and sellers combined earn significant returns.
- Shareholders of buyers usually earn the required rate of return.[4] A more recent study from the University of Bayreuth in Germany analyzing postmerger returns from 55,399 transactions between 1950 and 2010, extracted from 33 previous M&A studies, stated that "M&A transactions predominantly do not have a positive impact on the success of a company," but noted that "indicates that the type of M&A and the time frame used for measurement influence the success of M&A transactions." An older study by Spencer Stuart and Dr. Sanjai Bhagat of the University of Colorado at Boulder found that the most successful mergers of the period studied (1990–2002) employed "best practices in human capital," such as identifying and rewarding key talent and integrating quickly.[5]

Based on this research, what factors contribute to postmerger—and thus what factors should be emphasized in announcing a merger?

A number of factors can contribute to success. Here is a list of some commonly cited success factors, along with some possible press-release language to use:

- *Strategic motivation.* "Approximately half of the two companies' revenues derive from geographic markets and networks that overlap, creating the opportunity for significant network efficiencies and synergies."
- *Clear relation to core business.* "Our core business is to provide superior customer service in apparel retail. Our purchase of this well-respected apparel franchise helps build our legacy."
- *Economic pricing.* "We will pay $27 per share for this company. This price is based on analysis by our internal financial staff, advised by external experts in this industry."

- *Prudent cash- or debt-based financing.* "The purchase price will be paid in cash. To help finance this transaction, we took out a loan at a favorable lending rate based on our sound credit rating. Our future cash flow will support repayment of the debt."
- *Efficient integration planning.* "This integration will take 100 days. This memo describes the actions we will take, and the people responsible for the actions."

For a sample press release highlighting strategic motivation, see Appendix 9A.

What should be in a postmerger plan?

This varies greatly by industry and by situation. Clearly, however, there should be three elements in the postmerger plan:

- Goals of the new company
- How integration (or, in some cases, divestiture or discontinuation) of resources, systems, and responsibilities will support those goals
- Timetable for the integration

For example, a postmerger plan for two hospitals might say that the two hospitals want to expand the range of services they provide to their local communities. Implementation details might include how the board, management, and staff will be organized; how staff will be credentialed; who will be responsible for clinical policy making; how budgeting, accounting, accounts receivable, and bond covenants will be handled; what clinical services will be changed, expanded, or cut back; and what nursing models will be used. The thorough integration plan might also include how the mission, values, and vision of the two hospitals will be merged. In addition, the plan would include notes on how the information technology of the two companies will be combined and, based on the acquisition agreement, what parties will be responsible for any security issues that arise.

Some plans never get implemented or get implemented poorly. How can postmerger planners avoid this problem?

The following 15-point M&A planning checklist can help integration planners at the senior management level see if they are on the right track:

1. Are the plans consistent with the intrinsic logic of the deal?
2. Do the plans specify how the company will pay for the deal?
3. Are there written plans to cover both the short term (less than five years) and the long term (five years or more)?
4. Do short- and long-term plans mesh?
5. Has the planning process involved both senior managers and employees most affected by the plans?
6. Do the plans take into account the operational and cultural realities of the two companies involved?
7. Have senior managers and the board of directors reviewed the plan documents?
8. Are senior managers and the board using the plans to make their decisions?
9. Are the plans supported by appropriate policies?
10. Are the plans supported by adequate resources (including any needed training)?
11. Do the plans specify measures and milestones of progress?
12. Do the plans identify the individuals or groups accountable for fulfilling them?
13. Have the plans been distributed to all appropriate parties?
14. Is there a program for communicating the plans internally?
15. Is there a program for communicating the plans externally?

The answer to each question should be *Yes!*

COMMUNICATING THE INTEGRATION PLAN

How can buyers and sellers stem the tide of rumors from various stakeholders before, during, and immediately after the deal?

In general, companies that plan to merge should say so publicly as soon as they have reached an agreement to combine. This announcement should go out to all the companies' stakeholders and to the general public.

This initial announcement should be the beginning of a series of regular communications through letters, memos, meetings, and any other available media about each phase of the transaction. Once the transaction is close to completion or completed and a plan is in place, both the acquirer and the acquired firm should disseminate the plan (in brief format) to all stakeholder groups, developing a special position statement for each group.

Prior to day one of the new company, it is important to prepare customer-facing technology on both the selling and the buying side, ranging from the company websites to social media presence. This may be the time for the acquiring company to get control and ownership of social media pages and identities, and to become "mobile friendly" or even "mobile first" in its outreach strategy.

The communications process must continue for the entire period of active integration—generally up to 12 months. The best strategy is to establish, at the front end, a regular process of communications with stakeholders on postmerger progress. Videos with key leaders can help employees assess them—and by implication the cultures they represent—through nonverbal cues.[6]

At every stage of postmerger integration, management of the new company should communicate to all stakeholders in all appropriate media, as shown in Exhibit 9-1.

Exhibit 9-1 Audience Media Communications Matrix

	Media																				
Audiences	Letter	Capabilities Brochure	Special Brochure/Flyer	News Releases	Special Press Kit	Quarterly Report	Annual Report	Special Newsletter	Regular Newsletter	Promotional Item	Magazines/Bulletins	Personal Meetings	Special Event	Advertisement—Financial	Advertisement—General	Advertisement—Trade	Internal Meeting	External Group Meeting	Company Website	Videos	Other
Other Employees																					
Salespeople																					
Vendors																					
Retail Customers																					
Commercial Customers																					
Community Businesspeople																					
Bank(s)																					
Telephone Listings																					
General Public (National)																					
General Public (Regional)																					
Special Interest Groups																					
Elected Officials																					
Local Press																					
Opinion Leaders																					
Securities Analysts																					
Brokers																					
Shareholders																					
Institutional Shareholders																					
Key Investors																					
Board of Directors																					
Advisory Directors																					
Senior Management																					
Subsidiary Officers																					
Subsidiary Nonofficials																					
Retired Employees																					
Financial Media																					
General Business Media																					
Directories																					
Rating Agencies																					
Peer Groups																					
Prospective Acquirees																					
State Regulators																					
Government Agencies																					

Source: Courtesy of Gene Grossman, Siegel+Gale, New York.

COMBINING COMPANY NAMES

What considerations arise when deciding what to name a newly combined company?

A company's name, along with the names of its brands, can constitute a significant percentage of its value. When a company's name is the only brand, the choice of a new moniker is particularly important. One researcher believes that when United subsumed the Continental brand into its own in 2010, it lost a chance to build on the strength of the latter.[7] When one company buys another, it has four basic choices:

- To keep its own name
- To assume the seller's name
- To combine both names into a new name
- To create an entirely *new* name

The first three are the most common, with combinations being the most successful, according to one study.[8]

Why do most acquiring companies keep their names unchanged after a merger or acquisition?

Name changes are generally reserved for deals in which the acquired company has a reputation equal to or more prominent than that of the acquirer. The majority of M&A deals involve purchases of companies that are smaller and less well known than their acquirers.

What are the pros and cons of these four different approaches?

Let's look at them one by one:

- *Keeping the acquirer's name* is the simplest approach, and it is often a wise course for high-profile companies that buy low-profile companies—or for companies that buy firms that are very similar to them, when nothing can be gained from incorporating the target company's brand name.[9] The chief drawback will be a sense of loss by the acquired company's employees. There is also a dollars-and-cents issue for the company as a whole and its owners: if the selling company has name recognition, as most companies worth buying do, the value of this trade name might be diminished, along with any trademark value it may have.

- *Adopting the seller's name* is good for acquirers that need to gain cachet from the seller's company. The chief advantages and disadvantages here are the same as in the first example, but with acquirer and seller roles reversed.
- *Putting the two names together,* with or without acronyms, has the advantage of bolstering the pride of both parties. On the other hand, it poses the challenge of a dual identity to be understood both within and outside the company.
- *Creating an entirely new name* avoids this challenge while creating another one: what to call the new company. Of all the communication challenges facing newly combined companies, this one is paramount. (In fact, the comprehensive communications grid that appears in Exhibit 9-1 was originally developed as a grid to announce company name changes.) In this option, the potential sense of loss is doubled. Employees from both the acquired and the acquiring company may feel a sense of abandonment. And customers may not like—or even recognize—the name of the merged company.

How do buyers and sellers decide whether to use old or new names? And how do they create new names?

Sometimes the best course for naming a newly combined entity will be obvious. If a large, successful company buys a small, struggling firm in its industry, the acquirer's name should probably prevail, unchanged, especially if that acquirer has already changed its name within the past few years. Usually, however, the choice is not so easy.

Exhibit 9-2 Steps for Naming a Newly Combined Company

1. Compare present names with future of company.
2. Determine needs and expectations of stakeholders.
3. Develop criteria for a new name.
4. Develop a long list of names.
5. Review/screen names to make short list.
6. Conduct preliminary legal search.
7. Evaluate attributes, both graphic and linguistic, considering a global market.*
8. Select final candidates.
9. Conduct final legal search.
10. Recommend new name to board and stockholders.
11. Seek approval from board and stockholders.
12. Develop communications plan.

* The old Chevy Nova brand was reportedly mocked in Spanish-speaking markets because "no va" implies that the car will not run.

Merging companies would be wise to appoint a small group of managers to look into this important question. There are basically 12 steps. (See Exhibit 9-2 and the discussion that follows.)

Step 1: Compare Present Names with Future of Combined Company

Managers can ask themselves honestly if the existing company names—separately or in combination—adequately convey the range of the products and services the new company will offer. Is the company expanding? Is it planning to sell off noncore businesses? What qualities does the company want to project?

Step 2: Determine the Needs and Expectations of Stakeholders

Managers or their agents (designated employees or consultants) can then interview representatives of each stakeholder group to find out what they think of the businesses that are combining. This includes customers, suppliers, stockholders, bondholders, lenders, employees, and people in the communities where the companies are headquartered.

Step 3: Develop Criteria for a New Name

In listing criteria, managers should ensure suitability with as many facets of the company as possible. Here is a quick checklist of 10 important attributes of a name:

- *Descriptive* of the combined companies' core business?
- *Suitable* to the products, services, and (if regional) location of subsidiaries?
- *Broad* enough to suit the present while leaving room for growth in the future?
- *Acceptable* to the company's stakeholders?
- *Distinctive* rather than clichéd?
- *Memorable* rather than arcane?
- *Pronounceable* or a tongue-twister?
- *Real-sounding* or outlandish?
- *Self-explanatory* or a stretch?
- Legally available?

Step 4: Develop a Long List of Names

Now is the time for maximum creativity; the decision-making group may wish to include additional employees and/or outside consultants for brainstorming at this point. In generating a list of possible names, managers can use key prefixes, suffixes, and word fragments to imply general image attributes, such as "Uni" for centralization, "Max" for scale, or "Excel" for quality. Some industries favor certain themes. For example, a recent study found that two out of three bank names have one of the following five words in their names: *state, first, national, trust,* and *savings.*[10] To add to the list, a computer can be programmed to generate random names.[11] In the end, the list should include up to several hundred names for a large, complex company.

Step 5: Review Names, Making a Short List

Next, managers should winnow the list down to 25 to 35 acceptable candidates. In this process, they should bear in mind that no single name can fulfill all criteria. It is up to senior management to set priorities. Managers might assign points for each desired attribute—with extra points for the attributes that matter most. They might also decide that failure on certain key points will mean automatic rejection, despite overall score.

Step 6: Conduct Preliminary Legal Search

Although the process of obtaining legal clearances can be long and frustrating, a full corporate designation must be legally cleared, registered, and protected in accordance with statutes governing its use. Depending on the size of the business and its market, a preliminary search must be conducted at the national, state, and/or local level to identify the legal availability of names on the list. (Sometimes the search must be conducted internationally, nation by nation.) It is fairly typical at this point to find that most of the names are already taken. In addition, it is important to secure website URLs. Even if there is no legal entity named "XYZ Inc.," some domain collector might have secured "XYZInc.com."

Step 7: Evaluate Graphic and Phonetic Attributes

In the process of narrowing down the choice, managers should begin to get a feel for what it will be like living with each of the names. At this point, they should begin to pay especially close attention to the way the name looks and sounds. The name selected must be adaptable to a variety of media, both visual and auditory. It will appear in newspapers, magazines, and on the Internet, as well as on a range of forms, stationery, and signage. It will also be heard on radio, over the telephone, and in conversation—sometimes in many languages.

Step 8: Select Final Candidates

By now, a company may have about a dozen name finalists. At this point, it is time to make a final choice. One way to do this is to take two names at a time and select only one each time—a process called pairwise comparison—continuing to evaluate the attributes listed so far. At the end, only one name will survive. For a guide to pairwise comparison (a technique that can be used for many aspects of integration—not just name choices), see Appendix 9E.

Step 9: Obtain Final Legal Clearance for Use of the Name

Having selected a name, managers should ask their legal counsel to begin the paperwork for obtaining the legal right to use the name and any images and URLs associated with it, pending board and stockholder approval. As will be discussed, trademarks and service marks have value, so this is an important step.

Step 10: Seek Approval from the Board and/or Stockholders

In most situations, it will be necessary to seek approval for the name change from a board of directors and from owners. In seeking approval, managers should disclose the criteria and process they used to select the new name, and the benefits that a new name may bring.

Step 11: Create a Graphic System for the New Name

Once the name is selected and approved, it will be time to design a graphic system for it, which will include such visual elements as logos, symbols, and type fonts, as well as color palettes, for the name's expression in all foreseeable applications.

Step 12: Develop a Communications Plan

Managers should decide when to announce the name change, leaving adequate time for reprinting and reordering materials such as forms, stationery, pens, and signs, and for website changes. After the announcement, the company should use only the new supplies. The announcement (which is sometimes coupled with the announcement of the merger itself) should be made not only through the usual channels of communication, but also in special mailings or meetings tailored to specific stakeholder concerns.

The company should be sure to include information about the new name in the part of its website devoted to the merger. One of the FAQs (frequently asked questions) often posted about mergers is "What is the name of the new company?"[12]

In the end, the burden of proof will be on the new owner, who must demonstrate that the values underneath the company name and logo will survive and indeed thrive under a new banner.

INTEGRATING CULTURES

The values wrapped up in a company name could also be called a company's culture or even soul. What happens to these following a merger?

Individuals who believe people have souls can readily believe that companies do. This was the view of the late B. Kenneth West, who wrote eloquently on this subject.[13]

The embodiment of company *soul* lies in culture, which is easier to analyze and manage. Culture, as mentioned in Chapter 6, on due diligence, is a force that influences what people believe, think, and do. As mentioned earlier, in an organization it can shape:

- Attitudes/mental processes (how people feel and think)
- Behavior (what actions get performed and rewarded)
- Functions (how people do things)
- Norms (what rules get enforced)
- Structures (how the previous items get organized and repeated)
- Symbols (what images and phrases have special meaning)
- History (what stories and traditions get passed on to future generations)[14]

All of these elements tend to synchronize within a culture. So, for example, if attitudes are risk averse, so too will be the behavior, functions, norms, structures, symbols, and history.

Is it true that culture clashes often cause postmerger problems?

Yes. For example, cultures often clash over risk. The more risk-averse cultures (older, more mature companies) may be praised as prudent or criticized as passive. Conversely, risk-tolerant cultures (typically belonging to smaller, newer companies) may be either branded as brash or lionized as innovative. One of the greatest challenges in any merger is to find a way to balance the two cultures.

Many mergers are cited for cultural differences—most recently Amazon and Whole Foods (2018).[15] It takes time to see whether the cultural integration is a success or a failure. Some alleged failures include:

- Sprint/Nextel (2005)[16]
- Hewlett Packard and Compaq Computer (2002)
- AOL and Time Warner (2001)
- Daimler-Benz and Chrysler (1998)

In most of these cases, analysts depicted the acquirer (listed first) as being more risk averse than the acquired or merged firm.

Alleged cultural successes include the Renault investment in Nissan, combining French and Japanese cultures, an alliance that is currently heading toward a full-scale merger (as of late 2018). An early case study reported: "Cross training occurred, and culture ambassadors were appointed from each company."[17]

Once an agreement has been reached with a buyer, how should culture alignment be addressed?

A buyer should seek to understand the culture of the company it is buying and develop a plan to align this culture with its own. It should not automatically impose its culture on the acquired company, but instead should strive to carry over cultural aspects deemed important. Benefits such as free coffee or traditions such as "Employee of the Month" may be important to preserve; eliminating them may seem disrespectful. Sensitivity to regional cultures is also important. For example, Silicon Valley employees are much more resistant to employment contracts that include promises to stay on after a merger ("golden handcuffs").[18]

As a tool, the acquirer may wish to use a cultural integration planning matrix, like the one featured in works by Timothy Galpin and Mark Herndon, simplified in the version shown in Exhibit 9-3.

What is "change management" all about for companies involved in merger integration?[19]

Change management addresses the people side of change and, when addressed holistically, can increase the chances of integration success. Some common change management models[20] are:

- Bridges's transition model (letting go, neutrality, new beginning)
- Kotter's theory (eight steps from creating sense of urgency to setting change in stone)
- Kübler-Ross's change curve (denial, anger, bargaining, depression, acceptance)
- Lewin's model (unfreeze, change, refreeze)
- McKinsey's 7-S model (strategy, structure, systems, shared values, style, staff, skills)
- Prosci's ADKAR model (awareness, desire, knowledge, ability, reinforcement)
- Satir's model (old status quo, resistance, chaos, integration, new status quo)
- Thaler and Sunstein's "Nudge" approach (presenting changes incrementally)

According to Prosci, projects that incorporate change management are six times more likely to achieve their objectives.[21] Change management should be woven into the integration plan as opposed to existing as a separate workstream. Whatever approach is used, change management activities should support and reinforce the tasks and actions identified in the integration work.

Exhibit 9-3 A Matrix for Planning Cultural Integration

	Key Similarities	Key Differences	Integration Actions	Integration Timing	Integration Responsibility
Strategy					
Values					
Staffing					
Communications					
Training					
Rules and Policies					
Goals and Measures					
Rewards and Recognition					
Decision Making					
Organization Structure					
Other					

Source: Adapted from Timothy J. Galpin and Mark Herndon, *The Complete Guide to Mergers & Acquisitions: Process Tools to Support M&A Integration at Every Level,* 3rd ed. (San Francisco: Jossey-Bass, 2014).

What are some tips for integration leaders to consider when incorporating change management into their integration plan?

If the integration manager is not a certified change leader or has not had training in change management, it is optimal to find someone in the organization to assist with building out a holistic project plan that incorporates the principles of change management to ensure enablement.

The key to driving meaningful change is to engage leadership early in the process. Educate leaders about the benefits and need for them to support the change-enabling activities. For instance, a welcome message from the acquiring company can begin to build trust with the employees of the acquired company.

Assessing and identifying areas of change resistance is an activity that should be done before integration planning begins. For example, the change leader can draw on insights gained from due diligence and identify gaps in cultural fit that may indicate an area of resistance.

Although there may be a cultural gap, adopting some of the traditions or practices of the acquired company can begin to close that gap. For example, if the acquired company observed a casual dress code on Fridays, perhaps this could be a tradition carried forward across the NewCo organization.

Although change management may seem like a small, insignificant step toward building trust, ultimately it can enable larger, more significant change to happen. That said, it is imperative that communication to the acquired company be transparent, honest, and straightforward. When changes are made in the organization, people will need to be held accountable and change needs to be reinforced. For example, a large global company acquires a small entrepreneurial company. Prior to acquisition, employees had full administrative capabilities to load software onto their business computers. As part of a global company, employees are not permitted to do this. This change could seem restrictive or bureaucratic to the new employees, but understanding the risks and reasons for that policy can help drive change adoption; however, it doesn't stop there. Reinforcing messages, random audits, or removing system admin privileges can ensure that the change is adhered to for the long term.

How does Murphy's law fit in there?

Murphy's law says that if something can go wrong it will. This is why it is important to do scenario planning on your integration project.[22] One of the best tools in project management is Monte Carlo simulation, which will help you think about what can kill your deal. All kinds of random events can occur, and the pace and quantity of results can be ragged. Imagining plausible scenarios and plugging them in will improve your forecasting ability.

INTEGRATING MISSION, POLICY, ETHICS, AND VISION STATEMENTS

What happens to key documents such as mission and vision statements, codes of ethics, or corporate policies after a merger?

First, let's look at some definitions.

The primary purpose of the *mission* statement is to provide identity and focus. A mission statement says, "This is the business we are in today, as exemplified by our present products/services," and it typically has a broad audience that includes the general public as well as all company stakeholders.

Vision statements provide direction and motivation for an organization. A vision statement (sometimes called a *vision and values* statement) says, "Here is the difference we want to make in the world—the vital goal that animates us as we pursue our mission and adhere to our policies." It is fairly rare for this to be longer than a sentence, and it is typically found in a company's proxy statement.[23] Most major companies have comprehensive *codes of ethics.* Indeed, the Sarbanes-Oxley Act of 2002 requires all public companies to have them.

The final rule promulgated under the law defines the term *code of ethics* as written standards that are reasonably designed to deter wrongdoing and to promote:

- Honest and ethical conduct, including the ethical handling of actual or apparent conflicts of interest between personal and professional relationships
- Full, fair, accurate, timely, and understandable disclosure in reports and documents that a registrant files with, or submits to, the Commission and in other public communications made by the registrant
- Compliance with applicable governmental laws, rules, and regulations

- The prompt internal reporting to an appropriate person or persons identified in the code of violations of the code
- Accountability for adherence to the code[24]

Codes of ethics are supported by policy statements. The main goal of any *policy* statement is to ensure ethical and legal behavior. A policy statement says, "This is how we operate our business. All our employees must adhere to these rules." Almost all companies have developed policy statements for some aspects of their business.

Assuming that an acquirer wants to develop and disseminate new mission, policy, ethics, and/or vision statements to suit its new identity, how should it go about this?

Certainly both companies should devote part of their postmerger planning session to this question. Answers will vary according to the two companies' situations.

If the acquirer has fully developed statements that apply perfectly to the acquired company, and if the acquired company has no statement of its own, the job of integration will be easy. This will be merely a matter of educating acquired company employees in the statements of the acquirer. If, on the other hand, both companies have statements, a greater effort may be required.

First of all, management must determine who will be drafting the statements. Each mission statement should be developed by senior line managers, since mission statements pertain to lines of business, whereas policy statements (or a code of conduct) should be developed by senior legal staff. The vision statement should be developed by the chief executive and board of directors, ideally based on the advice of outside experts who have a sense of the company's potential future.

Beyond this, the development of each statement should proceed step by step. The working group that is drafting the statement should obtain comparable statements and work from these, developing a content and style appropriate to the company's circumstances. Mission and vision statements can be brief, but codes of conduct are longer and are often supported by numerous specific policies. Wells Fargo, a bank that is striving to improve in this area, has a code of ethics that references 38 additional policies, as well as an ethics portal on its website.[25]

Do you have any additional guidance on how to draft postmerger mission statements for the new company?

If the companies are in completely different businesses, it is best to leave their respective mission statements undisturbed at least temporarily, for the sake of continuity. If, however, the companies are in related businesses that require integration of their missions, they can and should consider drafting an entirely new mission statement for the newly combined entity.

The creation of a new mission statement should not be from a blank slate. Instead, it should be from the scratch of existing statements. First, the postmerger integration team (or its designated agent, such as a public relations manager or consultant) should inventory all formal self-descriptions the company has generated, including not only mission statements and vision statements, but also advertising slogans.

If the statements have been widely disseminated, it would be wiser to build on them than to scrap them entirely. If, however, they have not received wide distribution, they can be used or discarded, as appropriate to the new situation.

Finally, with past statements as a base, the newly combined entities should then work to develop a new set of statements that can apply to both companies.

INTEGRATING KEY RESOURCES, PROCESSES, AND RESPONSIBILITIES

It's important to think about a company's brand, but what about continuing to do business after a merger? How can an acquirer manage all the details involved?

First, it is important to identify each company's resources, processes, and responsibilities, and decide if they will be integrated. See Appendix 9B for a checklist of assets featuring key resources (human, financial, tangible, and intangible/intellectual), key processes (primary processes such as management systems, support processes such as information technology, and, in a class by itself, internal financial controls), and key responsibilities (commitments to various stakeholders).

Then for each area to be integrated, identify:

- What needs to be done (tasks and subtasks)
- Who must do it (task owner)
- Resources needed (perquisites)
- Information needed (tactical data)
- Insight needed (strategic questions)

See Appendix 9C for an integration planning worksheet on these points, and see Appendix 9D for an integration timeline. Before using these tools, however, more guidance could be helpful. This chapter will give such guidance on how to integrate key resources, processes, and responsibilities. It will also take a closer look at compensation, a phenomenon that involves all three of these company dimensions: it rewards a resource, it entails a process, and it constitutes a responsibility. In conclusion, this chapter will discuss issues pertaining to postmerger divestiture.

INTEGRATING RESOURCES

Integrating Human Resources

What are some general guidelines for managing human resources after a merger?

Following a merger, acquirers need to integrate specific groups of people, such as sales teams, senior management teams, and even the board of directors. Each of these group integrations raises specific issues. It is beyond the scope of this chapter to give templates for this integration, but resources are available.[26]

When do human resources personnel typically get involved in a merger?

Most companies involve HR at the integration stage, but some companies involve HR earlier—even at the planning stage, as well as in due diligence.[27] This is a recommended practice for important financial reasons, as mentioned in those earlier chapters.

This said, HR will do its most intensive work leading up to and during the integration phase. When two companies merge their human resources, they also merge their HR policies, such as approaches to recruitment, retention, compensation, training and development, and (sometimes immediately) outplacement.[28] For a checklist of HR policies, see Exhibit 9-4.

How can an acquirer integrate target company employment policies and data?

A target company may capture its employment policies and employee data in an HR system with a payroll component. The acquirer may want to migrate these data into its own system immediately. But first it must ensure that the data are clean—complete, relevant, and accurate. Meanwhile, people must continue to be paid. So during the initial postmerger phase it may be necessary to maintain two systems—at least for payroll. Eventually, the acquirer's system may be used—and possibly upgraded. This may be a good time to implement "best practice" HR systems with secure employee data in a private or hybrid (not public) cloud.

Benefits, compensation, and payroll are obviously important elements in the HR checklist featured here. For more on merging compensation plans, see the end of this chapter.

Integrating Financial Resources

How can an acquirer and a seller combine financial resources?

This means combining them (e.g., consolidating cash reserves) and then tracking them through both accounting and controls.

Exhibit 9-4 Acquisition Integration Plan for Human Resources Operation

Conduct integration planning kick-off meeting

HR INTEGRATION PLAN

- Standardize HR policy
- Integrate HR processes
  - Employee relations
    - Performance review and evaluation
    - Employee dispute resolution
    - Employee complaint investigation
    - Acquisition integration communication
    - Turnover reporting
    - Employee relations legal/regulatory compliance
    - EEO
    - OSHA
  - Benefits administration
    - Benefits orientation
    - Presentation of compensation/benefits at welcome party
    - Benefits conversion and enrollment
    - Medical
    - Dental
    - Vacation (varies widely across countries)
    - Benefits plan administration
    - Benefits-related legal/regulatory compliance
    - 401(k)
    - Health/welfare
    - New hire process
    - Termination process
  - Compensation
    - Job mapping and redesign
    - Map acquiree and company job positions
    - Set pay scales
    - Manage changes in pay
    - Performance reviews and promotions
    - Equity/noncash compensation
    - Sales compensation
  - Payroll
    - Leave accrual and administration
    - Customer service

- Payroll administration
- Accounting reconciliation
- Communications with treasury
- Pay-cycle disbursement
- Recruiting/staffing
- Facilities management
  - Office/real estate consolidation
  - Update database of site/contracts, leases
  - Assign leases to company
  - Obtain acquiree staffing projections
- Organization development/training
- HR infrastructure integration
  - Employee setup in HRIS
    - Establish department numbers for acquirees
    - Collect acquiree employee information
    - Input acquiree EE data in HRIS database
    - Provide acquirees with company services
    - Provide acquirees with company intranet access
- HR communications plan development
- HR contracts and commitments

Source: HR checklist used by a midsize US telecommunications company acquiring multiple companies. Used with permission.

Combining the financial resources. A company's primary financial resources are cash, stock, and bonds. These exist in the form of bank account balances and stock and bond certificates. Immediately following the closing, acquiring managers must take possession of the acquired company's resources—transferring bank accounts and renaming stock and bond certificates. This is a fairly straightforward matter that can be entrusted to the acquirer's chief financial officer and the CFO's team, as long as the acquiring company has adequate financial controls. Even in a merger of equals, for ease of transfer one company should be designated for the acquirer's role in this sense.

Tracking the financial resources. The optimal value of cash, stock, and bonds, of course, is their ability to move—to be spent or paid (in the case of cash), or to be exchanged (bought or sold, in the case of stocks and bonds). Movements of financial resources at any time, including following a merger, must be tracked and controlled.

- The main tool of financial tracking is financial *accounting.* Chapter 5, on structuring, explains how acquisitions must be reported to conform to certain accounting practices under generally accepted accounting practices (GAAP) as determined by the Financial Accounting Standards Boards (FASB) for public companies.
- The main tool for financial controls is the set of processes known as *internal financial controls.* For more about internal financial controls, see the discussion about integration of key processes.

What does the combination of intangible resources involve?

Following a merger, intangible resources, much like financial resources, must be combined and tracked.

Combining the intangible resources. Appendix 9B lists a number of key intangibles to be considered for combination. Discussing all of them would exceed the scope of this chapter. The next sections discuss what to do about company names and brand names after a merger or acquisition.

Tracking intangible resources. Chapter 5 talks about the accounting issues that arise after purchasing a company that has intangibles.

Integrating Brand Identities

What happens to brand names after a merger? Do they have to change when a company name changes?

As mentioned earlier, often the company name is not the only brand acquired; many companies own additional brands. Companies often build brands by imposing their identity (through a visual logo or by sharing a product title, for example) on a series of different products. Conversely, sometimes a single, powerful brand owned by a company may become the company's name or an important part of its description.[29] (To this day, people define Alphabet as the parent of Google, as the latter is better known.)

In some cases, acquirers choose not to link their corporate identity with any of the brands they develop or acquire. Maintaining separate brand identities for their subsidiaries gives these acquirers more flexibility should they wish to sell the subsidiaries later. Autonomous brands that do not rely on their parents' identities can change hands many times in the lifetime of a consumer, and the consumer will notice only the brand, not its changing owners. This brings the valuable element of continuity to the best product brands. See Exhibit 9-5.

When brand value is independent of the owner's identity, why do acquirers have to work to preserve brand identity after a merger? Can't they just do nothing (so to speak)?

Acquirers need to bear in mind that when they buy a brand (that is, a company that has a branded product or product line) they buy four things: the brand's definition (values it promises); its culture (how the brand's previous owner has honored the brand's promise); its infrastructure (support internally and externally via advertising, distribution, marketing, promotion, and sales networks); and, finally and most apparently, the visual identity as expressed in a name and logo (often protected by a trademark and/or service mark). To the extent that any of these elements change, the brand's value will change. Also, sometimes an acquiring organization fails to recognize the value of a brand it is acquiring.[30]

How can an acquirer preserve brand identity during the postmerger integration process?

An acquirer can preserve brand identity by putting the brand first and integration second. The management of a newly combined company should not say, "Let's combine our advertising efforts" (or other brand support), thinking that what works for one brand will work for another. This can bury a brand. Instead, managers should say, "Let's build this brand." In other words, managers should use integration as a means, not an end. In the process of building a brand, an acquirer should have special reverence for existing names and logos and what they mean to employees and others.

Exhibit 9-5 Three Brand Approaches

Parent Brand ≥ Brands (Parent brand appears on all brands owned)
Parent ≠ Brands stand on their own)
Parent ≤ Brand (Parent renames itself after a brand)

Integrating Tangible Resources

What about tangible resources? How can these be integrated?

From a balance sheet perspective, these will typically be combined. Therefore, in addition to financial assets (for example, cash, marketable securities, and accounts receivable), a consolidated balance sheet will include combined values for plants, equipment, inventories, and land.

In addition to being combined on a balance sheet, are these tangible assets ever actually combined from an operational standpoint?

Plants, equipment, and inventories may be combined in whole or in part when two companies integrate their operations. Land and real estate, of course, cannot be combined physically, but the leasing or ownership terms for the use of the land may be consolidated.

Plants

How can plants be combined operationally (as opposed to merely on the balance sheet)?

First, let's define our key term. A *plant* is a production operation at a defined physical location. It is usually envisioned in a manufacturing context. A plant's major assets include real estate, structures (foundations, buildings, framework, and related improvements), equipment (for production, communication, control, and administration), distribution assets (such as piping, conveyers, and docks), wiring and instrumentation (for electrical supply, communications, and control of operations), and software. In a service context, a plant may be a physical location in which services are performed. Examples of service plants include a computer processing facility, a branch bank facility, and a phone operation.

In both the manufacturing and the service sectors, plants can be consolidated in many different ways, ranging from plant closings to integration of plant operations through common, integrated systems.

What are the main costs associated with plant consolidation?

In consolidating plants, employers may incur costs associated with disposal of assets (including environmental aspects); relocation, termination, and/or recruitment of employees; investments in physical assets or software to support consolidation; and redesign of products and/or services to accommodate integration. In addition, acquirers may have to spend money on new marketing efforts to preserve goodwill if plant consolidation has involved layoffs. Finally, closing or relocating plant operations may cause the loss of a group of customers or increase transportation and distribution costs to a set of customers (see the final section in this chapter on fulfilling commitments to employees).

Equipment

How can equipment be combined operationally?

Physically combining equipment is uncommon unless the equipment is mobile or unattached, such as forklifts, trucks, office equipment, and furniture. Combining companies are often at distant locations. Even when operations are consolidated, it is often preferable (if money permits) to purchase and install new equipment, rather than to remove, transport, and install older equipment from a discontinued operation. Furthermore, in addition to equipment purchased for replacement, some equipment may be purchased for enhancement—for example, to facilitate the integration of systems and operations.

Note also that the owners of the acquired business may retain some equipment, either to keep or to sell separately. They may wish to retain personal property (including equipment) for their own use, and such property will not convey with the sale.

What are the main valuation issues associated with the combination of equipment in a purchase?

All the equipment that will continue to remain in use after the acquisition should be restated at fair market value in use and integrated into the balance sheet accordingly. “Fair market value in use” means that certain delivery, installation, and setup costs should be included in the valuation of the equipment since an acquirer of the equipment would have to bear the costs if each individual unit were acquired separately. Appraisers may consider replacement or reproduction cost as if new (including installation and freight), less economic and physical obsolescence, as an appropriate measure of value.

Most other equipment (especially any equipment being moved or relocated, typically that of the acquired entity) should be valued at fair market value in exchange or, alternatively, stated to reflect the expected value to be realized (possibly negative) upon sale or disposal. The buyer can then expense or capitalize the costs associated with moving and reinstalling the equipment at the new location. The equipment’s fair market value in exchange, plus the cost of bringing it into use in a newly consolidated operation, should equal the fair market value in use of the equipment once it is fully integrated into the new operations.

What are the cost implications of combining equipment?

The value of some equipment held by the acquired entity and/or the acquirer may be written off because of costs associated with disposing of it or transferring it (the aforementioned cost of transportation, installation, and setup that is part of fair market value in use).

Inventories

What tips do you have on valuing and combining inventories on a consolidated balance sheet and in reality?

Inventories of the acquirer are stated, as always, at the lower of cost or market (wholesale) value. If certain units in inventory become obsolete, are likely to be sold at a discount, or will require more time to sell, some downward adjustment in the value of these items in inventory may be appropriate. If significant, the inventories of the acquired entity should be audited during the due diligence process and appraised at the current fair value in exchange (wholesale).

For large inventories—even with heterogeneous units—it is possible to use sampling techniques to value the inventories with reasonable precision by comparing the market value of a set of units sampled to the current book value for those same units. For example, an acquired salvage operation reports $2,560.35 million on its balance sheet as the cost basis of its inventory of used parts. A sample of 5,000 out of 100,000 items (representing $245,199.10 of inventory at original cost) reveals that the current cost (at wholesale auction) of these items would be $250,619.50. This yields a value-to-book ratio of 1.022106. Thus, the overall inventory can be valued based on this cost-to-book ratio at $2,616,751.50.

Land/Real Estate

How can land and/or real estate from two different companies be valued and "combined" on a consolidated balance sheet?

The real estate of the acquired entity should be valued at fair market value. Each tract of real estate is typically valued separately but in connection with any surrounding tracts commonly owned by the same entity.

What are some valuation issues to consider when combining the land and/or real estate of two companies?

It is possible for the value of two adjoining properties to increase as a result of having common ownership. A change in the expected use of a specific piece of real estate may impair the value of that real estate, especially if the property is to be sold after being acquired and the future use of the property would require some modification or remedial efforts. Land associated with a profitable manufacturing operation may be worth more than equivalent value land, especially when it is in full use.

Integrating Technology

What is required to understand before integrating two companies' information technology platforms–obviously a critical resource?[31]

To integrate two companies' technology platforms, it is critical to first understand the deal's rationale. Why did the acquirer buy this company? Is it for the territorial reach of its sales force, covering a new geography? Is it for a complementary technology tool that will enhance your current suite? The answers to these questions will all have different IT integration paths.

Let's explore:

- *Enter new geography:* More than likely the acquirer will want to onboard this sales staff and spend the IT investment on training on your existing platforms and capturing existing customer information through a transfer of data into an existing platform. The most important IT integration milestones would be ensuring that training and tools are provided quickly and thoroughly to the staff and that the new company is aligned with supporting the HR onboarding and employee access requirements, as well as ensuring data is not lost for this staff to retain their customer base.
- *Complementary tool (expanding IT portfolio):* If the acquirer is buying a new tool it is imperative to understand the security of

the tool *prior* to integration to avoid introducing any vulnerabilities to its existing networks. This will include performing a security assessment or third-party code scan.

Of course, there are many other reasons why companies acquire. The general premise of IT integration is first understanding what has been purchased and why, then being certain to maintain the security and integrity of the new environment.

Then, just as important, is developing a team of resources from both separate entities, focused on (and investing in) delivering on the integration strategy. It is critical that resources be identified to help drive the integration activities. These people should be dedicated (paid full-time) if possible, but at minimum have the necessary incentives to complete activities based on integration timelines established.

Lastly, integration budget and timeline for synergy capture is crucial; it is often minimalized, but can pose many problems if not fully understood. Costs to integrate can add up quickly, and without securing proper funding and resource bandwidth, the synergy capture can be impacted.

What are the key IT items to focus on for Day 1–Day 100 as a key milestone?

The first 90 to 100 days of any deal are critical.

- First, this period sets the tone for the new entity—for culture, for employees, and for speed to combine the two entities.
- Second, it typically will involve combined financial reporting.
- Third, this period is usually when combined senior leadership is identified.

Additionally, this time frame is critical for information technology. People need to be able to collaborate effectively, technology platforms need to remain secure, and businesses cannot lose productivity. However, technology is the backbone of all integrations; therefore, it cannot remain stagnant. The balance to achieve this should be the first area of focus post-deal close.

Exhibit 9-6 Sample Plan for 30-, 60-, and 90+-Day Milestones

30 Days	60 Days	90+ Days

• Establish secured temporary network connectivity
• Initial employee platform access
• Email (address book/calendar sync)
• Determine nonexempt time reporting
• Launch assessments:
  • Security
  • Network/telecom
  • Telephony
  • Software license
  • Data center
  • IT inventory
  • Vendors
	• Security remediation: mitigation plan; critical items addressed
	• Long-term network connectivity plan
	• Remediate end-of-life equipment
	• End user support strategy
	• Consolidate telecom billing (typical synergy)
	• IT contract consolidation (typical synergy)
	• SW license exposure/true-up
	• Email migration
		• Security remediation completed
		• Active directory integration
		• End user support strategy implemented
		• Long-term network in place
		• Determine telephony road map
		• Data center plan (closure/ consolidation)

To illustrate this, Exhibit 9-6 shows a sample plan for 30-, 60-, and 90+-day milestones.

For more comments on technology, see the section titled "Some General Postmerger Technology Considerations" later in this chapter.

INTEGRATING PROCESSES

Earlier, when discussing the merging of human resources, you mentioned the merging of HR *processes* as well. What other processes should be considered after an M&A transaction?

First, management structures (reporting lines) are extremely important. They are the means for the sharing of authority and the channeling of communication. Other important processes to merge include processes for product or service design, production, and supply. Finally, internal controls are also a key process. This section will cover all these points.

Merging Management Structures

Merging companies means merging their management structures. What is the best way to do this?

Building a new reporting structure for combining companies requires two things: knowledge of the old companies' past patterns and a sense of the companies' potential patterns as a newly combined company.

To gain knowledge of past structures, managers should try to obtain the latest organization charts for both organizations and check them out via interviews. (If there are no charts, interviews will have to do.) The information from these charts and interviews might seem like old news after the merger, but in fact they are the foundation for the future. Those boxes, lines, and dotted lines reveal not only past experience but future expectations with regard to accountability and relationships.

The next step is to move beyond the past and into the future to build a new structure. A few truisms are in order here. The structure should be based on the business needs of the companies, not on some theory of what makes people happy. "Right" structure is not only a matter of comfort for employees but a matter of fit with the company's economic environment. No structure guarantees behavior; a structure merely makes it easier or harder to get work done. Experience, not theory, will always be the best arbiter here.

What are the basic types of organizational structures and how common are they?

Actual organization structures differ widely (just study the hundreds of representative charts available from the Conference Board in New York), but it is possible to identify five basic types of organizational structure:

- Functional
- Geographic

- Market segment
- Product/service
- Divisional

Any of these structures may coexist with a so-called *cluster framework* that organizes people by projects.

In a *functional* organization, people are assigned to groups according to functions or specialties such as accounting, distribution, engineering, manufacturing, marketing, purchasing, and sales. This is common for small, new companies.

In a *geographic* organization, employees' work is organized by physical territory.

In a *market segment* organization, the customer also determines structure, but it is not the location of the customer that matters; rather, it is the customer's profile. Thus, a financial company might be structured according to institutional versus retail clients.

In a *product/service* organization, functional specialists are grouped according to their responsibilities toward a given product or service.

In a *divisional* organization, families of products are grouped into independent divisions (or strategic business units). This organizational structure, which is highly decentralized, has always been dominant for very large, complex companies.

When two companies have very different reporting patterns, how can they be integrated?

If following the path of least resistance, the pattern with the most complexity will prevail. Thus, a divisional structure will prevail over a product/service or functional structure, and a product/service structure will prevail over a functional structure. These structures are like Russian dolls. Each of them can stand alone, but they can also contain smaller structures. A divisional structure (the biggest doll) can easily contain a product/service structure within it (the next biggest doll), and that structure can easily contain territories and/or functions (the smallest dolls).

But engineering isn't everything. As observed throughout this book, other factors can come into play, such as size. Large acquirers can and usually will impose their structures on the smaller, less powerful units they acquire.

This can provoke disappointment; few employees like change per se. The positive alternative must be a new structure that is sensitive to the expectations arising from the old structures, while serving the needs of the newly combined organization.

Following are some important checkpoints to bear in mind:

- Appropriateness of reporting lines
- Adequacy of staffing and experience levels
- Clarity of delegation of authority and duties

Which organizations tend to be more profitable–those associated with centralized hierarchies or those associated with flatter, more decentralized organizations?

Both can be profitable, but these organizational types derive their income in different ways. Centralization may be associated with cost cutting (e.g., "Headquarters is putting a freeze on new hires"), whereas decentralization may be associated with revenue building (e.g., "The West Coast Division will be heading up a new initiative"). Adding or subtracting management layers intensifies this contrast. If a middle manager has to seek approval before spending money, he will tend to invest less of it—but also to generate less of it. By the same token, if a manager has no restraints on spending money, she may tend to invest more of it and, if successful, generate more.

Which basic option is better for postmerger integration, a hierarchical centralized structure or a flat decentralized structure?

Hierarchy makes integration a lot easier, enabling managers to promulgate universal policies throughout the organization, deliver financial and technological support, and resolve conflicts between and among units. Extreme decentralization, by contrast, can make integration more difficult, unless the organization has identified a position or unit with authority to create and disseminate policies and a network for sharing or redistributing resources.

On the other hand, centralization does not guarantee success. In the case of a *detrimental parent,* the policies of headquarters may be wrong for the organization, or it may fail to deliver enough of the right kind of support to its units. Conversely, a *beneficial parent* knows how to overcome the challenges of decentralization and link units without a centralized, hierarchical structure.[32]

Why don't all corporate parents add value to the units they integrate?

Potential problems include too many rigid controls, not enough communication and support, lack of understanding of the business, a focus on the wrong issues, hiring or promoting the wrong managers, and pressing for the wrong levels or measures of performance.

In short, postmerger management requires the same kinds of judgment calls as other kinds of management, but focusing on the unique challenges of integration with techniques and tools—our next subject.

What can managers actually do to enhance integration?

Following a merger, designated managers can work to ensure that company units share space, goals, standards, and/or services to some useful degree.

Sharing Space

How can sharing space help or hinder M&A integration?

For many years office architects believed that open work spaces would enhance face-to-face communication and, as a result, collaboration and innovation. Recent empirical research suggests the opposite, however. Open architecture, a recent study claims, can "trigger a natural human response to socially withdraw from officemates and interact instead over email and IM."[33]

Sharing Goals

How can sharing goals help M&A integration?

Common goals can serve to integrate two or more units for a period of time. Setting exact timetables and procedures for new product development can impel the different units of the organization to work together in small groups or clusters to accomplish the development by the target date. Or, to cite another example, a five-year plan to improve shareholder value (if employee compensation is linked to stock price) can create unity of purpose in an entire organization for half a decade. The more units that share the goals, and the longer the time span necessary to accomplish the goals, the more integration is accomplished.

Sharing Standards

How can common standards help M&A integration?

Shared standards can create a sense of cohesion throughout the company; they are the very essence of integration. Types of standards useful in M&A integration include operating procedures, technological specifications, ethical values, internal control guidelines, or, most important of all, employee performance yardsticks—setting comparable performance *standards* using comparable *measures* to obtain comparable *rewards* throughout a company.

For example, no matter how a company defines its subunits (be it by function, geographic territory, customer segment, product/service, and/or division), it will need to find a way to measure the financial performance of the identified unit. There is not one set method of doing this. In fact, there are several possible ways—including cost center, profit center, investment center, or producer of residual income.[34]

Sharing Services

How can sharing services help M&A integration?

Sharing services can help eliminate duplication in a decentralized structure. Instead of each unit having its own accounting staff, for example, there may be an accounting staff at headquarters. The same goes for legal, public relations, information processing—the list is virtually infinite.

The classic way to share services is to use common staff, typically located at headquarters. Another way to share services is to create *shared-services units* for nonoperating activities, and to allow other business units to buy services from the unit.

How is using shared services different from using headquarters staff?

When headquarters staff provides services, it is typically under monopoly conditions: all units must use the company's central services at a cost determined by headquarters and borne by the company as a whole. It's the only game in town. The shared-services model, by contrast, puts competition into the equation. Heads of company divisions and their key employees negotiate with the shared-services unit for the services they will receive and the price they will pay. They may go outside for services if they are not satisfied. Unlike headquarters staff, the shared-services unit is not a cost center; it is a profit center. Corporate headquarters still has a role, but this is confined to the high-level areas of strategy and governance.

Integrating Processes for Product or Service Design, Production, and Supply

If two merging companies make and/or distribute the same product and/or service, how should they go about integrating these activities?

First of all, it's a good idea to step back and compare each company's quality control programs. There are several different ways of controlling quality, and if two companies have different systems, these will need to be integrated.

What are some systems for quality improvement that can be used in a postmerger setting to improve operations?

Consider a standard benchmark such as the *ISO 9001 Quality Systems-Model for Quality Assurance in Design, Development, Production, Installation, and Servicing,* most recently updated in 2015.[35] The ISO, which stands for International Standards Organization, is a network of the national standards institutes of 161 countries, with a central office in Geneva, Switzerland, that coordinates the system and publishes the finished standards. There are also other benchmarks used in particular industries in particular countries.[36]

What exactly are the ISO 9001 series standards, and how can they help companies integrate their plant operations?

The ISO 9001 standards are guidelines for ensuring quality of design, manufacturing, and supply systems. They are jointly determined by national standards bodies in countries around the world, drawing on recommendations from technical advisory groups (nearly 3,000 of them). The standards are used by an estimated 100,000 organizations around the world.

The series also has specific applications in sectors such as medical devices; petroleum, petrochemical, and natural gas industries; and software engineering.[37]

How can you consolidate plants?

First, as mentioned, management can *adopt a common set of systems and standards* for activities.

Second, management can *forge closer links* between plants. New links may emerge from common information systems, inventory control, supply relationships, pipelines, or rail links.

Third, management can *pursue more vertical integration,* having different operations focus on different stages of production. Some facilities may specialize in producing specific components or intermediate goods, while other operations become more oriented to producing finished goods, or finishing and packaging goods for local or regional markets.

Fourth, when and if there is excess capacity and/or redundancy in capacity, a company may *close certain operations* and move certain production activities and assets from the closed operations to the other facilities.

Fifth, a company may *shift production allocations* across facilities to allow each operation to become more focused on its production of a subset of products or to serve a narrower geographic region or customer base.

What are the chief benefits and drawbacks of postmerger plant closings?

It depends on the company's situation. If there is excess capacity or significant redundancy, closing plants may make economic sense. However, acquirers should bear in mind the economic costs associated with plant closings, often taken as a significant one-time charge against earnings.

Also, having too few manufacturing sites may be risky and inefficient. Having manufacturing locations at multiple sites may reduce operational risks while increasing flexibility and efficiency. Following the tragic events of September 11, 2001, many corporations started building redundancy in their most critical operations.

Therefore, when demand is low, it may be more efficient to shut down a select number of small units entirely on a temporary basis than to experience a partial, long-term idling of larger, consolidated units.

Finally, there can be reputational costs associated with plant closings—costs that eventually impact a company's bottom line.

Integrating Internal Financial Controls—A Key Process

What exactly are internal financial controls, and why are they important following a merger?

Internal financial controls are the processes a company uses to make sure that its financial statements are reliable. In a mom-and-pop microbusiness, these controls can be as simple as keeping the checkbook balanced and requiring two signatures on every check (from the two owners). In a major public company, they may involve literally thousands of procedures.

The Securities and Exchange Commission defines "internal control over financial reporting" as follows:

> A process designed by, or under the supervision of, the registrant's principal executive and principal financial officers, or persons performing similar functions, and effected by the registrant's board of directors, management and other personnel, to provide reasonable assurance regarding the reliability of financial reporting and the preparation of financial statements for external purposes in accordance with generally accepted accounting principles and includes those policies and procedures that:
>
> (1) Pertain to the maintenance of records that in reasonable detail accurately and fairly reflect the transactions and dispositions of the assets of the registrant;
> (2) Provide reasonable assurance that transactions are recorded as necessary to permit preparation of financial statements in accordance with generally accepted accounting principles, and that receipts and expenditures of the registrant are being made only in accordance with authorizations of management and directors of the registrant; and

(3) Provide reasonable assurance regarding prevention or timely detection of unauthorized acquisition, use or disposition of the registrant's assets that could have a material effect on the financial statements.[38]

Under Section 404 of Sarbanes-Oxley, all public companies must have internal controls and have their managements and auditors assess them. As for management's assessment, SEC rules implementing Section 404 state that "the assessment of a company's internal control over financial reporting must be based on procedures sufficient both to evaluate its design and to test its operating effectiveness."

In particular, "an assessment of the effectiveness of internal control over financial reporting must be supported by evidential matter, including documentation, regarding both the design of internal controls and the testing processes."

Controls subject to such assessment (again quoting verbatim from the SEC final rule) include:

- Controls over initiating, recording, processing, and reconciling account balances
- Classes of transactions and disclosure and related assertions included in the financial statements
- Controls related to the initiation and processing of nonroutine and nonsystematic transactions
- Controls related to the selection and application of appropriate accounting policies
- Controls related to the prevention, identification, and detection of fraud

As for the auditors' assessment of controls and their assessment, the standard is the PCAOB's standard An Audit of Internal Control Over Financial Reporting That Is Integrated with An Audit of Financial Statements (AS 2201).[39]

The Committee of Sponsoring Organizations of the Treadway Commission, or COSO, has a framework for internal control, among other standards.[40,41]

The COSO Framework for Internal Control has five interrelated components:

- Control environment
- Risk assessment
- Control activities
- Information and communication
- Monitoring activities[42]

Clearly all these are important following a merger.

How does COSO define the control environment?

In its 2013 framework, COSO defines the control environment as follows:

- The organization demonstrates a commitment to integrity and ethical values.
- The board of directors demonstrates independence from management and exercises oversight of the development and performance of internal control.
- Management establishes, with board oversight, structures, reporting lines, and appropriate authorities and responsibilities in the pursuit of objectives.
- The organization demonstrates a commitment to attract, develop, and retain competent individuals in alignment with objectives.
- The organization holds individuals accountable for their internal control responsibilities in the pursuit of objectives.

What can the acquirer of a small organization do on Day 1 to hit the ground running with an internal control system, namely with respect to cash?

The day the acquisition is completed, the acquirer should assume control over all cash receipts and disbursements by the acquired business. For each location, a new checking (or lockbox) account should be established and all receipts deposited into this account. Access to this account should be limited to individuals designated by the acquirer. In addition, a separate cash disbursement checking account should be established for payroll and accounts payable.

Having separate accounts for receipts and disbursements makes sense, but it sounds complicated. How exactly does it work?

Typically, the financial management of the acquired company requests a weekly transfer of funds to the disbursement account (the checking accounts for payroll and accounts payable) with appropriate justification, such as payroll or vendor payments (by name and invoice number). The manager designated by the acquirer should collect all receipts and transfer funds to the cash disbursement account as requested.

What other techniques can the acquirer use to establish financial control?

In addition to setting up separate accounts for receipts and disbursement, the acquirer can establish a budgeting process and a signatory level requirement.

The budgeting process will vary from company to company, but it usually involves identifying revenue sources and expenses for the upcoming 12 months, along with a forecast of balance sheet changes. Once the acquirer and the acquired company have agreed on this budget, they can monitor the acquired company's progress each month against the forecast. If there are changes or trends indicating that the budget is inaccurate, the acquirer can ask the budget managers to revise it. If the revisions are not satisfactory, the managers can be replaced.

Signatory levels will also vary from company to company, as levels of materiality differ according to company size. An expenditure of $1,000 might require the signature of an officer in a $1 million company but not in a $1 billion company. Here is a sample signatory requirement for a midsize company with sales levels between these extremes. In this example, the acquired company is operating independently from the acquiring company, with its own senior management team.

Sample Signatory Levels

1. All checks over $5,000 must be signed by the senior financial officer and the chief operating officer of the acquired company.
2. All checks over $25,000 must be cosigned by a staff member of the acquiring company.
3. All sales contracts over $1 million or with potential liabilities over this level will require a signature by the CEO of the acquirer or a manager the CEO designates.
4. All compensation to senior management (defined by job function or by name) must be approved by the CEO of the acquiring company.

This system is ideal for small companies or for units of large companies. A large company with many units will need a more complex system for cash control, and should consult a public accounting firm with experience in relevant standards.

INTEGRATION OF KEY RESPONSIBILITIES

What key responsibilities should be considered after an M&A transaction?

The press release announcing the acquisition should make it clear that the new company will honor commitments to constituencies, including customers, employees, and shareholders. See Appendix 9A for a sample acquisition announcement mentioning these stakeholders.

Commitments to Customers

What commitments to customers will a company typically inherit after a merger?

As mentioned earlier, every company comes to a merger with a unique set of promises it has made to various individuals and groups, including customers. Some of these promises are written, some unwritten. Some are contractual (enforceable by law), some covenantal in nature. As companies merge, they must merge these promises, and the first step is defining what they are.

To fulfill commitments to wholesalers and distributors (who buy directly and in bulk), a first step for the integration team will be to look over all the legal agreements the company has inherited along with these customers. For each product or service, the company will need to know *how much* each company had promised to provide *what customers* at *what price* for *what period of time.* It will also want to know about any *exemptions* or *waivers* that may apply to those conditions.

To fulfill commitments to retail customers (who buy indirectly and in small quantities), the first order of business for the integration team will be to study any promises the company has published to the general public, such as slogans used in space ads. If they have had any value, these slogans are not just words—they are commitments.

More generally, managers might consider a list that appears in the section titled "Respect Stakeholders Beyond Shareholders" in *Principles for Responsible Business,* developed by Caux Round Table for Moral Capitalism. This document, reprinted in full at the end of this chapter in Appendix 9F, is the consensus of leading business executives from the United States, Europe, and Japan, who meet regularly to discuss global business ethics.

Why is it so important to fulfill commitments to existing customers after a merger?

First of all, there is the ethical dimension. Promise-keeping is one of the oldest and most basic moral principles known to humankind. Also, there is the legal dimension: keeping promises is a good way to prevent lawsuits. Last but not least, there is also the economic dimension. Customers are a key driver of a company's economic value, and current customers are worth more than future ones—especially after a merger, when a buyer's market prevails.

It is usually easier and less expensive to maintain an existing relationship than to attract a new one. Business appraisers acknowledge this fact when allocating purchase price to various financial, tangible, and intangible assets. When allocating price to intangibles, they allocate present and future customers differently.

More generally (beyond postmerger price allocation), values assigned to present relationships are much higher than those assigned to future relationships. This is true whether the values are derived from an income approach or a replacement cost approach. Appraisers use an income approach to value customer relationships when they can identify income directly attributable to customers, and a replacement cost approach when they cannot. For replacement cost, they assume that the amount of money a business is willing to spend to attract a new customer equals the value of an existing customer. Similarly, in allocating marketing and selling expenses, the income and/or replacement cost attributable to present relationships is often higher than that attributable to future ones.

What benefits can mergers bring to existing customers, and how can these be communicated?

Merger announcements often claim that the mergers will benefit customers by increasing product range and/or by reducing prices through economies of scale and technology. Sometimes FAQs posted on the new company's website promise benefits to customers in the first question—as to why the merger occurred—and address the all-important question of the bank's postmerger name. See Exhibit 9-7.

Exhibit 9-7 Old Line Bank and Bay Bank Merger FAQ (Excerpts)

Why is Bay Bank merging with Old Line Bank?

Both Bay Bank and Old Line Bank are strong local financial institutions that provide personal, one-on-one service to customers in the state of Maryland. By merging the two organizations, Bay Bank customers will gain additional products and services, as well as access to 26 full service branches across nine Maryland counties.

Has the merger received all required approvals?

Yes, the transaction has been approved by the proper regulatory agencies and the shareholders of both Old Line Bancshares, Inc. and Bay Bancorp, Inc. The Bay Bank branches will open for business as Old Line Bank on April 14, 2018.

Will Bay Bank change its name?

Yes, under the terms of the merger agreement, the name will change to Old Line Bank.

When will I notice the new signs?

On April 14, 2018, you will see the Old Line Bank signs installed at all Bay Bank branches.

Who is Old Line Bank?

Old Line Bank is a Maryland-based bank headquartered in Bowie, Maryland. Old Line Bank was founded in 1989 in Waldorf, Maryland. Since that time, Old Line Bank has charted a path of steady growth with 28 branch locations serving nine counties. Old Line Bancshares, Inc., the parent company of Old Line Bank, is publicly traded on the NASDAQ Capital Market under the symbol OLBK. Old Line Bank's mission is to promote the growth and prosperity of the communities we serve. Our strategic plan is built on the premise of enhancing shareholder value and growth through branching and operating profits.

Why the name Old Line Bank?

The State of Maryland earned her nickname the "Old Line State" in 1776 during the first major battle of the Revolutionary War. The war could have ended that day had it not been for the "Maryland 400," who after General George Washington ordered a retreat, sacrificed themselves, allowing the Continental Army to escape. Maryland's regiment of soldiers referred to as the "Old Line" achieved a reputation as saviors of the Continental Army and the cause of independence. As a tribute to the contributions and heroic sacrifices of those brave Maryland men, Old Line Bank proudly chose its name.

What happens now with my Bay Bank account?

Nothing at this point, it is business as usual. You may continue to conduct your banking as you always have. We plan to integrate the operating systems of both banks on June 1, 2018.

Source: https://www.oldlinebank.com/old-line-bank-and-bay-bank-merger-faq.

Legal Aspects of Customer Relations

What are customer lawsuits usually about?

In addition to antitrust law violations (generally brought by regulators on behalf of customers and/or competitors), issues commonly alleged in such lawsuits include:

- Contract disputes
- Cost/quality of products or service
- Debt collection
- Deceptive trade practices
- Dishonesty/fraud
- Extension/refusal of credit
- Lender liability

Do customers ever sue to block mergers?

This is rare, but it does happen, usually as a private class action lawsuit that shadows a government lawsuit. Government lawyers do most of the litigation work, and then plaintiff attorneys shadow the effort.

Commitments to Shareholders

What commitments does a company typically have to fulfill for its shareholders after a merger?

When issuing stock, a corporation must adhere to certain standards. In privately held companies, these standards are typically expressed in shareholders' agreements. In publicly held companies, standards exist in federal and state securities laws and in stock exchange listing rules. Companies that sell shares to the public must disclose certain information according to certain standards in offering documents prior to listing, and in financial statements after listing. They also have to grant holders of common stock certain voting rights, often exercised by proxy—hence the term *proxy voting.* And beyond these mandatory and legally enforceable promises are some that corporations may make and keep voluntarily as part of their company bylaws, corporate governance guidelines, or other corporate policies.

How exactly can postmerger integration teams make sure that the new company meets these various commitments to shareholders?

In a merger that involves a privately held company, legal counsel (internal or external) should look over all the agreements the company has signed with its owners, asking what rights each company has promised to what owners, under what terms, and for what period of time.

In a merger involving a publicly held company, the advisor will need to know where the company stands with respect to the securities laws for the jurisdiction (for example, in the United States, both state and federal securities laws).

For firms that have a general counsel or other inside attorney, the resources of an organization like Association of Corporate Counsel (acc.com) or the Society for Corporate Governance (societycorpgov.org) can be helpful. When outside counsel is engaged, a resource such as Martindale-Hubbell (martindale.com) can guide the selection of a firm with experience in securities law.

Attorneys specializing in securities law keep abreast of these issues and often send out letters to clients (and potential clients) summarizing major trends. Securities regulators, such as the SEC (sec.gov) in the United States, regularly post new and pending rules.

In addition to compliance with securities law, what are some general ethical considerations?

With respect to the ethics of shareholder relations, postmerger integration managers can benefit from consulting a document such as the *Principles for Responsible Business,* mentioned earlier (see Appendix 9F), as an excellent checklist for essential corporate commitments.

This said, it should be recognized that only a minority of actual stock trades today result from a conscious act by institutions or individuals. Today, index trading, exchange-traded funds, and/or algorithmic trading effectively automate most buy/sell/hold decisions based on predetermined formulas; these trades do not reflect perceptions of a particular company in any holistic sense.[43]

Should postmerger financial reports include non-GAAP financial information? Why or why not?

Postmerger reports should include a range of information that shareholders will find useful. Some of it will conform to GAAP, but some will not. (Consider the shareholder value calculation just discussed.)

Non-GAAP numbers are desirable to shareholders because accounting numbers can be constrained by accounting conventions that may lose economic sense over time. But whenever non-GAAP measures enable abuses—for example, the off-balance-sheet entities that enabled Enron's fraud—they eventually become disallowed or reformed under GAAP. And to cover all bases, securities law requires subordination of non-GAAP to GAAP disclosures, so investors can see them in context.[44]

One exception is forecasts of non-GAAP measures exchanged between the parties in a business combination transaction. If these are material and if their disclosure is required to comply with the antifraud and other liability provisions of the federal securities laws, then the financial measures included in such forecasts would be excluded from the definition of non-GAAP financial measures and therefore not subject to the rules.[45]

Building Shareholder Value

From a general, strategic point of view, how can managers increase shareholder value after a merger?

A number of general strategies appear to build the value of a company's shares, no matter how that value is measured. Here are three to consider:

- *Aim for continued, profitable growth.* When it comes to shareholder value, profitable growth is superior to cost-cutting, and unprofitable growth is superior to downsizing. Companies that grow profitably have a disproportionately higher stock appreciation than do companies that only cut costs: a dollar earned through growth is worth more to shareholders than the same dollar earned through cost-cutting. (Of course, in some cases, cost-cutting and downsizing may be the best option.)
- *Alternate external and internal growth.* In pursuing growth, a company can buy or build. Obviously, by the time a company has reached the integration stage, it has already chosen to buy rather than build in at least one case. But after every major acquisition, a company starts back on square one with the same question: Should we continue to buy rather than build, or should we spend time building instead? Most companies alternate the two strategies, going from periods of acquisition to periods of internal growth, just as farmers rotate crops. These companies take time to integrate major acquisitions before embarking on new ones. (Again, there is not a single correct choice. Some companies may be suited to growth that is entirely internal, others to a steady flow of acquisitions.)
- *Develop and disclose good corporate governance practices.* Corporate boards that practice good governance are likely to have the independence and expertise necessary to oversee

financial performance after a merger. Good governance practices include, but are not limited to, independence of the board and its key committees (such as the audit committee), development and disclosure of processes for senior executive evaluation and compensation, and lack of undue restrictions on shareholder voting. Although individual companies lacking some or all of these practices may be successful for long periods of time, these practices tend to be associated with positive share price performance, and many business catastrophes can be traced in part to the absence of one or more of them.

Are there any model governance guidelines a merging company could consider adopting?

The most comprehensive and stringent governance standards in the United States today are the ones required of New York Stock Exchange companies, namely, *Section 303A: Corporate Governance.*[46] Other countries have similar documents. Globally, organizations such as the International Organization of Securities Commissions (IOSCO)[47] or the Global Network of Director Institutes (GNDI)[48] have issued their own standards summarizing views of their globally diverse memberships.

What postmerger financial indicators are most important to shareholders?

Shareholders will look at sales growth and earnings growth, as well as several key ratios based on numbers from the balance sheet, the income statement, and/or stock prices.

In debt-financed acquisitions, shareholders may focus on ratios involving debt, namely:

- Current ratio (current assets/current liabilities)
- Debt ratio (total liabilities/total assets)
- Debt-equity ratio (total liabilities/total equity)
- Net working capital (current assets minus current liabilities)

If the merger was financed through equity capital, then shareholders may focus on ratios involving equity:

- Earnings per share (net income – preferred dividends/common shares outstanding)
- Price/earnings (market price per common share/earnings per share)
- Equity ratio (total stockholders' equity/total assets)
- Return on common stockholders' equity (net income – preferred dividends/average common stockholders' equity)

If a company issues more shares to pay for a merger, this may dilute the value of shares. How can a company mitigate concerns about this?

First, be straightforward about the dilution. Shareholders will notice it, so you might as well point it out and explain it. If future earnings prospects are good, say so, then explain how they will be achieved.

Are there any rules against dilution?

No, but there are rules that require disclosure and/or approval of potentially dilutive transactions. For example, in the mutual fund area, the SEC requires the board of any mutual fund that merges with a trust fund or account not registered with the SEC to make sure that the interests of the fund's shareholders will not be diluted as a result of the merger.[49]

Could you give an example of a successful postmerger communication about dilution?

Exhibit 9-8 provides excerpts from a postmerger press release addressing the dilution issue.

Exhibit 9-8 Marathon Patent Press Release Addressing the Dilution Issue

April 04, 2018
GLOBAL BIT VENTURES ADDS NON-DILUTIVE ACQUISITION OF SERVERS WITH 15,000 GPU CARDS MORE THAN DOUBLING ITS GPU HASHRATE

LOS ANGELES, April 04, 2018 (GLOBE NEWSWIRE)—Marathon Patent Group, Inc. (Nasdaq:MARA) ("Marathon" or the "Company"), today announced that the Company has amended the terms of the pending acquisition of Global Bit Ventures Inc., a digital asset technology company that mines cryptocurrencies ("GBV").

The Company's Board of Directors determined there were material changes in both companies' operations since the date on which the original merger agreement was executed. Since then, the Company leased 26,700 square feet of a purpose-built facility in Quebec, purchased 1,400 Bitmain Antminer S9 bitcoin miners and put such miners into full production. The Company also purchased four patents related to the transmission and exchange of cryptocurrencies between buyers and sellers. Additionally, the Company now has $5,250,000 in cash.

GBV closed a transaction with Alchimista Inc., a corporation organized under the laws of the Province of Ontario, which included the acquisition of GPU servers with 15,000 GPU cards, of which 11,100 are currently in production. The servers were paid for by GBV in the form of a convertible note which will convert to shares of the Company's common stock upon the closing of the merger with GBV. Such shares will come out of the 70,000,000 shares of the Company's common stock to be issued to GBV's shareholders pursuant to the merger and, therefore, will not result in any further dilution to the ownership of the Company's shareholders. . . .

Source: https://ir.marathonpg.com/press-releases/detail/1176.

One cause of dilution is the use of equity to finance a deal. Could you comment on equity versus debt?

Sure. There are four common ways to finance a merger, as mentioned earlier in this book. In order of frequency, companies use cash, stock, a combination of cash and stock, and a combination of notes and cash and/or stock. Each of these payment strategies will have a different impact on the value of a company's equity.

Equity Impact of an All-Cash Deal

This can vary, depending on whether or not the acquirer used its own cash or borrowed it. Overall, when compared to share-financed deals, cash-financed deals have a more positive impact on share prices over a long (five-year) term. Acquirers should avoid taking on too much debt, though. As explained in Chapter 4, a debt-financed transaction that causes the acquirer to have a debt-equity ratio of 0.75 or more is considered to be a highly leveraged transaction (HLT). Such transactions often have a negative impact on share values.

Equity Impact of an All-Stock Deal

This impact also varies depending on the source (in this case, the source of the stock). In exchanging its stock for the seller's stock, the acquirer can either issue new shares or convince existing shareholders to exchange their shares with the seller's shareholders.

- The first scenario (using new shares) may cause dilution.
- The second scenario (using existing shares) can signal that the acquirer knows its stock is priced high.

Both of these possibilities can explain why share values do not do as well overall following stock deals as following cash deals.

Equity Impact After a Cash-and-Stock Deal

If the acquirer combines cash and stock in the payment, the impact on postmerger compensation may be positive or negative, depending on the sources of these instruments, as previously explained.

Equity Impact of a Contingency Deal

Sometimes acquirers offer notes to the seller promising additional payments or earnouts based on meeting certain financial goals. Obviously, from the shareholders' perspective, this mode of financing, although rare, is ideal. If the goals are not met, the company (and its shareholders) pay nothing. If the goals are met, then the company (and the value of its equity) is bound to improve. This is especially true if the performance goals relate to share price or to ratios that relate to share price.

In summary, an acquisition may have a negative or a positive effect on the acquirer's share prices, and this effect depends in part on how the deal was financed. It is up to postdeal managers to do what they can to ensure the most positive outcome for shareholders, and to admit, explain, and work to correct any negative result to existing shareholders, rather than hoping for a new generation of owners to come along.

COMMITMENTS TO EMPLOYEES

What commitments does a company typically have to fulfill for its employees after a merger?

Once again—as with customers, suppliers, stockholders, bondholders, and lenders—managers should review all outstanding contractual commitments with employees. Ideally, this will be a second review, benefiting from good due diligence (see Appendix 9A).

For a general overview, Caux Round Table's *Principles for Responsible Business* again proves useful.

Of all the Caux lists, this one is the longest, presenting a variety of positive employment values, including job creation, health and safety, well-being, transparency, responsiveness, fairness, inclusion, and training. If the merging companies have made commitments in these areas, the new company must honor them. If the new company has not made commitments in these areas, it should consider doing so for reasons discussed throughout the rest of this chapter.

Why is it important to make and keep commitments to employees?

Once again, as in the case of other stakeholders, the answer involves ethics, law, and economics. Breaking a promise is not only wrong (and sometimes illegal), but it is likely to have negative economic consequences. For example, key employees may leave because they lose trust in the new organization.

If employees leave, can't the new company just hire new people to replace them, or outsource their work?

Yes, but each of these alternatives can be costly. Existing employees have already been recruited and trained. Replacing them with equally qualified employees is not economically neutral, because it usually means that a company must pay for recruitment and training a *second time* for the same positions.

In addition, there are the negative multiplier effects of employee departures, whether voluntary or involuntary. For example, remaining employees may feel guilt with respect to the employees who lose their jobs—either personal guilt because they (as managers) axed jobs or survivor guilt because their own jobs were spared.

Some acquirers turn to outsourcing, but it is not a magic bullet. It takes a lot of management time communicating with a vendor about expectations. Also, vendors have their own overhead to cover, and the hourly rate of their employees or contractors reflects that charge.

What if the target company already outsources its technology management?

The acquirer will need to decide whether to retain any or all of these vendors. Functions that may be outsourced include employee records and pay (HRIS and payroll systems), sales and service (CX software), customer billing (ERP and finance systems), and procurement (supply chain and asset management systems). Retaining these vendors may be critical to the success of the merger.

What is the financial impact of downsizing?

Generally speaking, it is a fairly balanced equation as follows: On the positive side, there are savings from a smaller payroll. On the negative side, there are costs of early retirement packages, termination benefits (usually taken as a one-time charge), disability claims, and so forth. Also, impact on morale is usually negative. Finally, companies with fewer employees generally get less done.

How do pension funds respond to downsizing after mergers? Do they ever vote against mergers because they might cause downsizing?

Pension funds are not supposed to vote for the interests of current employees; they are supposed to vote for the interests of retirees. Under ERISA, which covers funds for employees in the private sector, fiduciaries have an affirmative duty to vote in the interests of beneficiaries. This can mean voting in favor of a merger, even if it will cause layoffs.

When employees sue companies, what do they sue for?

Employee issues in litigation, in rough order of frequency, include:

- Wrongful termination
- Discrimination
- Breach of employment contract (not termination)
- Harassment or humiliation
- Employee benefits
- Defamation
- Workplace safety

What other legal and regulatory issues should managers look out for after a merger?

Pensions continue to be an important area in the United States, where companies have special duties to employees present and past as administrators of their employee pension plans under ERISA. Now, after more than four decades, this law is receiving renewed attention from all three branches of the US government.

- The Supreme Court made it more difficult for plaintiffs to challenge a company pension fund's investment in its own stock in *Fifth Third Bancorp v. Dudenhoeffer,* 134 S. Ct. 2459 (2014).[50] The ruling raised the pleading standard and inspired several subsequent lower court cases to do the same.
- Department of Labor rules effective April 2018 streamline the filing of disability claims under ERISA.[51]
- The FASB voted in March 2018 to change the disclosure requirements for defined benefits plans. For example, it clarified that the disclosure about aggregate information for underfunded (including unfunded) pension plans should be based on both the projected benefit obligation (PBO) and the accumulated benefit obligation (ABO) benchmarks.

How does the existence of collective bargaining agreements affect postmerger management?

Obviously, collective bargaining agreements are a major source of obligations for new management when it comes to working conditions—including hours, safety, and staffing. Also, some agreements stipulate that companies must consult with employees in a change of control. In such cases, employee leverage prior to deal closing may help preserve or improve employee working conditions. Agreements negotiated by labor organizations in the United States are enforced by the National Labor Relations Board (NLRB), which offers alternative dispute resolution as an option for resolving conflicts.[52]

What role can job training and development play in the postmerger phase?

Training programs are the fastest way to reassure employees of both the acquired and the acquiring company that their jobs are secure. These training programs should have two aspects.

First, the management of the newly combined companies can start by educating all employees in the values, vision, and mission of the newly combined companies. These elements should reflect the histories of both companies, even if their framework is derived largely from the acquirer.

Training in information security is particularly critical to prevent cyberthefts during the integration phase, when companies are vulnerable. Employees should be trained to refrain from opening suspicious emails or sharing passwords. From day one of the merged company, there should be continuous monitoring of the corporate network.

What are some relocation issues newly combined companies should consider?

Five questions will arise in the relocation of a company's headquarters, plant, or branch. In order of importance, these are: *Why* is it relocating? *Where* is it going? *Who* will be asked to relocate? *How* will the acquirer handle relocation? *What* support will be provided? Also, facts and figures about the new locations should be disseminated. Comparative information can lessen the shock and trauma of relocation—and may even make it appealing. At the very least, it will enable employees to make good decisions.

In any event, the acquirer should establish a detailed relocation policy that includes adequate reimbursement of expense and job security following the move. Several companies provide such information. One established company, Economic Research Institute (ERI) of Irvine, California, provides cost-of-living comparisons between any 9,000 Canadian and US cities.[53]

What would be an example of a relocation policy?

GM's relocation policy offers a good example. Under its current contract with the United Auto Workers, GM pays a minimum of $5,000 for a standard relocation, and $30,000 for an enhanced relocation.[54]

POSTMERGER COMPENSATION: A COMPLEX ISSUE

When integrating pay plans (or designing new ones), what are the various pay elements and pay arrangements that postmerger planners should consider?

There are basically four pay elements:

- *Base pay,* otherwise known as *salary,* is a fixed amount of cash. It is typically determined annually and paid on a weekly or (in small companies) monthly basis. For most employees, this is the dominant portion of pay (though to large-company senior executives, who receive a high percentage of pay in the form of performance-based incentive compensation, it is of minor importance).
- *Bonus pay* is a lump-sum award in cash and/or stock paid to an employee for past performance. Bonus pay is typically determined and paid on an annual basis. Some companies call their bonuses *incentive pay,* but compensation purists reserve that term for pay that is awarded according to a predetermined plan, not after the fact.
- *Incentive pay* is compensation awarded to employees because they (or their team, division, or company) have met a predetermined performance target. This pay, which may be in cash and/or stock (either outright grants or options), is truly variable; it might not be paid at all. It may be awarded annually and/or long-term, with the term defined by the company. Incentive pay is often awarded as *deferred compensation.* Funds are usually put into an escrow account that appreciates according to a standard interest rate (such as Treasury bills).
- *Benefits* include plans for pensions, healthcare, employment security, vacation time, and, at the board level, liability insurance. Benefits may also include extras or *perquisites* such as use of a company car.

In addition, there is a potentially infinite universe of *special pay arrangements* that can come up during or after a merger.

- Through *noncompete agreements,* companies can take the first of many steps in keeping key executives—not only retaining their talent, but also preventing them from joining (or becoming) competitors of the new company.
- Through *signing bonuses* (called *golden handshakes*), companies can increase the motivation of executives they wish to hire.
- Through *severance agreements,* companies can promise to compensate employees in the event of job loss.
- Through *change-of-control plans* (offered in addition to plain-vanilla severance agreements), a company agrees to pay employees in the event of job loss following a merger or acquisition. At the senior level, these M&A-related severance packages are called golden parachutes. At lower levels, they are called *tin parachutes.*
- Through retention agreements (also called golden handcuffs), companies promise rewards if an employee stays a stated length of time.
- Finally, an acquirer may give an *integration bonus* to all employees following a successful combination resources, as did Alaska Airlines in 2018, following its successful integration of Virgin America.

The sum total of all basic pay elements and all special compensation arrangements is generally referred to as *total compensation.* Most consultants today offer services in total compensation planning.

When two companies merge, to what extent should they merge their compensation plans?

It depends on whether or not the new companies will be integrated or managed separately. As explained earlier in this book, not all acquisitions lead to integration. If an acquirer has only a financial (as opposed to a strategic) reason for buying a company, it may choose to keep its pay plans separate. And even if an acquirer has a strategic reason to buy a company and does plan to integrate resources and systems, the company's leaders may still decide to keep some aspects of pay separate (especially if they are venturing outside their company's core industry).

Given all of these factors, the burden of compensation design is generally shared between the acquirer parent company and its units. In a typical situation:

- The parent company will determine a policy for how much of senior management pay will be in stock (for example, five times salary) and how managers will receive it (by award or purchase, and, if the latter, whether the purchase will be mandatory or voluntary). The division will encourage and enforce compliance with the parent's stock ownership policy.
- The parent company will determine the desired competitiveness of base pay (below market, at market, above market), while the unit will identify the labor market in which it will be competing (local, regional, national).
- The parent company will decide on a policy for bonuses, while the unit will decide who will receive them.
- The parent company will set targets for incentive pay. Achievement of the targets can be based on various metrics (including accounting ratios, stock price, qualitative factors, and/or discretionary factors) and valuation methodologies (economic value added, cash flow return on investment, or other model), while the unit will select whether to award the incentive pay based on unit, team, or individual performance. The parent is also responsible for ensuring that pay plans do not incentivize short-term performance at the expense of ethical behavior.
- The parent company will decide on a benefits policy, while the unit will administer the policy, making occasional exceptions as necessary by contract or law.

Parents have the power to set uniform policies and targets, and they should do so to the extent possible, although there may be exceptions to this rule.

Why would a newly combined company want to have different pay plans for its units?

- Because the units may have very different pay environments.
- Base pay may differ from industry to industry for similar jobs. Also, a company in a mature industry will have a greater percentage of pay in base pay as opposed to variable pay from bonuses or incentives.
- There may be regional differences in pay.
- Bonus pay may be hard to align following a merger between one firm with huge bonuses and another one with none.
- Incentive pay targets vary by type of company. Large public companies are generally expected to link their CEO pay to total shareholder return over one to three years,[55] whereas a new start-up will tend to focus more on sales growth.
- Incentive plans may reflect differences in managerial philosophy, valuing the formal versus the informal, and the quantitative versus the qualitative.
- Benefits are another area where postmerger disparity may be necessary. Suppose that in the negotiation phase, the acquirer agreed to let the selling company's senior management keep certain perquisites, knowing full well that it would not extend these same perks to its own senior team. If that was the deal, the acquirer has no choice but to live with these strings attached, and to explain them as a *grandfather clause* to the envious. Furthermore, there may also be regulatory restrictions on merging certain benefits, such as retirement plans.

All these differences can add up, resulting in sharp contrasts between companies and, once merged, units. For example, a mature, centralized, business with heavy capital investments, stable profit margins, little technological change, and few competitors should strive for the following:

- Senior management depth
- Predominantly fixed compensation
- Moderate incentives
- Moderate equity participation
- Discretionary evaluations

At the other end of the spectrum, a changing, decentralized business with low capital investments, pressured profit margins, significant technological change, and many competitors should strive for the following:

- Little senior management depth
- Predominantly variable compensation
- Heavy incentives
- Heavy equity participation
- Objective evaluations

Aren't there some general principles of compensation that apply in any type of company? If so, what are they?

Yes, there are universal principles for good pay planning. Here is a list of principles already widely accepted in corporate and compensation circles.

Do

- Encourage real share ownership at all levels
- Link pay to performance
- Reward executives for both shareholder value and quality of products/services
- Make sure that pay is competitive in local markets

- Communicate appreciation of an employee through promotion and recognition as well as through pay

Don't

- Award excessive, repriceable stock options to senior management
- Keep increasing pay no matter what
- Use a variety of benchmarks, not just accounting measures (which can be manipulated) or stock price (which can be influenced by external events)
- Rely too heavily on benchmarks such as quartiles, which by their very nature keep rising as long as everyone tries to stay at the top
- Agree to compensation contracts that can pay very large amounts under some scenarios

What generally happens to senior management pay levels after a merger, and why?

Pay levels per employee tend to go up following a merger. This is not surprising, since mergers make companies bigger, and bigger companies tend to pay their top managers more than smaller companies do. Size is not the only factor, though. Companies that have expanded by takeover have systematically higher top management pay growth than same-size peers that are expanding by internal growth.

There are two reasons for postmerger pay inflation. First, postmerger equality is easier to achieve through pay raises than pay cuts. If senior executives from Company A and Company B are doing similar work, but Company A executives are getting paid more, it is more likely that B executives will be raised to A levels than the other way around.

Second, there are the special M&A compensation arrangements mentioned earlier, such as golden handshakes, golden parachutes, and golden handcuffs. Total costs for these elements, under various scenarios, can run in the tens and even hundreds of millions.

How did the Tax Cuts and Jobs Act of 2017 affect pay practice in the United States?

The main effect was to lower both corporate and individual tax rates, as mentioned in Chapter 5, but there are other effects—for example, changes to the $1 million cap on pay deductibility in force for more than a quarter century. Under previous law, Section 162(m) of the IRC prevented companies from deducting any compensation they award to certain officers above $1 million per person, unless it was incentive pay approved by an independent compensation committee. The new tax law maintains Section 16(m), but eliminates the incentive pay exception to the cap. It also expands the number of officer roles affected by the rule, and the number of companies affected.

What is the current situation with golden parachutes?

Section 280G of the IRC defines an *excess parachute payment* as one that equals or exceeds three times the executive's average W-2 compensation over the previous five years. Section 4999 of the IRC imposes in such cases a 20 percent excise tax[56] on the amount exceeding average annual compensation and denies the company a tax deduction for that amount.[57] Shareholders have made their views known with the advent of "say on golden parachutes" and "say on pay"—up or down votes since 2011 on parachutes as well as on the main compensation plan appearing in the proxy statement. While say on pay votes are generally positive, failure rates for golden parachute approvals have been rising in recent years, from single to double digits.[58] This result appears to stem from vote-no proxy advisory recommendations, based primarily on the presence of tax gross-ups in the parachutes rejected.[59]

What about stock purchase rights or options that get triggered in a change of control? Do they count as part of a parachute?

Yes. If a stock option will be granted or vested because of a change in control, this may constitute a parachute payment under Revenue Procedure 2003-68, which provides guidance on the valuation of stock options for this purpose. This could include any shareholder rights (poison pill) antitakeover arrangements that function as golden parachutes.[60]

If an acquirer gives signing bonuses (golden handshakes) to acquired company managers, what prevents the managers from walking away with the gold the very next day?

An acquirer can prevent a golden handshake from becoming a golden escape hatch by adding either a *back-end* provision or a *take-back* provision to the manager's contract. In a back-end provision, a company defers part of the promised sums, making them payable late in the contract period. In the take-back provision, an acquirer states in the manager's employment agreement that he or she will have to repay all or part of the bonus in the event of departure prior to contract expiration. This second strategy can be layered, with heavier penalties for earlier departure. For example, a four-year contract might set the following penalties for repayment of a $4 million signing bonus:

- Year 1: $4 million repayment
- Year 2: $3 million repayment
- Year 3: $2 million repayment
- Year 4: $1 million repayment

These retention provisions are often referred to as the aforementioned *golden handcuffs*. Another type of golden handcuff is the noncompete agreement, discussed previously.

PLANNING PAY INTEGRATION: A STRATEGIC OVERVIEW

Assuming that two companies want to combine their pay systems, how should they do this?

One very simple way is to chart the basic elements of compensation (base pay, bonus pay, incentive pay, and benefits) against the past approaches of each of the merging companies and the future needs of the combined enterprise in the view of senior management. By weighing these, planners can come up with a bridging strategy that takes both into account (see Exhibit 9-9).

How can a planner ensure the financial viability of a new play plan?

Planners need to consider the financial condition of the newly combined company. Although this condition will be based in part on the previous condition of the two merging companies, the new entity will have its own financial dynamics.

Aside from the merger price tag and related charges (which can be substantial, as explained in Chapter 5), the new company's condition will naturally be affected by the way the deal is financed.

There are four common ways to finance a merger. In order of frequency, these are cash, stock, a combination of cash and stock, and a combination of notes and cash and/or stock. Each of these payment strategies can have an impact on the financial condition of the new company—and therefore on the new company's compensation system.

1. *Pay after an all-cash deal.* If the acquirer uses its own cash to finance the deal, depending on the amount of cash used, the impact on compensation planning may be slight, especially if the cash used came from a full treasury. In such a case, planners have a clean slate for their creations. If the acquirer borrows cash to finance the transaction, the deal may be a highly leveraged transaction, or HLT. *Highly leveraged transaction* means an extension of credit to or investment in a business by an insured depository institution where the financing transaction involves a buyout, acquisition, or recapitalization of an existing business and one of the following criteria is met:
   - The transaction results in a liabilities-to-assets leverage ratio higher than 75 percent.

Exhibit 9-9 Sample Matrix for Postmerger Compensation Planning

Compensation Elements	Past Approach of Company A	Past Approach of Company B	Future Needs of Company AB	Bridging Strategy
Base pay	Below market	At market	At market	Raise A's salaries; keep B's on course.
Bonus pay	None	Generous	Minimal	Finish out year keeping status quo. Then start modest awards for all based on B's system, but reduced.
Incentive pay	None	None	Generous	Design pay-for-performance system. Employees: Additional 20 percent on base if goals for unit profits met. Senior management: Additional 30 percent on base if goals for company ROA met.
Benefits	Average benefit plans (cafeteria); generous, flexible benefit plans; no perks	Below average in health and retirement; lavish perks	Average health and retirement; modest perks	Improve B's health and retirement plans. Cut B's perks. Upgrade health coverage. Harmonize vacation policies over 5 years, reducing maximum European times from 6 weeks to 4 weeks, and increasing US times from 2 weeks to 4 weeks. Offer cashout option.
Special	1-year severance	6 months' severance	1-year severance	Extend B's severance.

Note: This is a sample, not a paradigm. Planners should use their own terminology and make their own choices.

- The transaction at least doubles the subject company's liabilities and results in a liabilities-to-assets leverage ratio higher than 50 percent.
- The transaction is designated an HLT by a syndication agent or a federal bank regulator.

Pay packages following HLTs should not be cash-heavy, since the company will need cash to pay debt. Incentive pay should be paid in stock or stock options and based on improvements in cash flow.

2. *Pay after an all-stock deal.* If the acquirer finances the deal through an exchange of stock using newly issued shares, the transaction may cause dilution. In such a scenario, pay planners should be conservative about granting more stock or stock options to managers, unless the company can buy back its own stock (which is difficult following a pooling of interests). Companies facing potential dilution by using stock-based pay might consider *phantom* stock grants (payments based on stock performance).

3. *Pay after cash-and-stock deal.* If the acquirer combines cash and stock in the payment, the impact on postmerger compensation may be nil, unless the cash is borrowed (in which case, the HLT caveats may apply) or the stock is generous (in which case, beware of dilution).

4. *Pay after a contingency deal.* If the acquirer offered notes to the seller, promising additional payments or earnouts based on contingencies (such as 20 percent sales growth), postmerger compensation should be structured to give managers a chance to make good on those targets. Managers who were owners of the merged company (and therefore noteholders after the merger) will be most concerned about being given the authority, autonomy, and resources they need to meet performance targets. Obviously, the performance targets in pay-for-performance plans should be in sync with the targets set in the earnout notes.

Finally, how can planners make sure that a new compensation plan will be, as you say, emotionally viable?

Mergers bring up many negative emotions: loss, anxiety, jealousy. Planners need to make sure their pay plans signify the opposite: gain, security, fairness. One of the best ways to do this is to strive for *positive comparability.* Employees of the newly merged firm may not get the same compensation they did before, but it should be similar or better.

Consider employees of Company AB (shown previously in Exhibit 9-9). The employees who worked for old Company A will rue the decline in their benefits, and employees in old Company B will dread the phaseout of their bonuses, even though both groups stand to benefit from other, positive adjustments in the total pay package. For example, in this scenario, A employees have a lot to gain: raises, bonuses, and additional incentive pay. Company B employees gain in the areas of incentive pay and benefits.

It is up to management to help employees focus on the positives, not the negatives. In this example (and in the case of any postmerger pay plan worth its salt), the message is this: "Your pay package is not the same as it was in the past, but it is comparable, and in some ways it is better." (In other words, don't just practice your compensation philosophy, preach it!)

Of course, change doesn't end with a new plan. As time goes on, managers will want to continually adjust their pay practices to meet changing realities. A word of advice, though: Compensation is a very expensive way to tell employees they are valued. Pay can do only so much to attract, retain, and motivate people. Meaningful work, a sense of worth, and a chance to advance must also come into play. If these are absent, no amount of raises, bonuses, incentives, benefits, and special deals can take their place. The best and brightest will take their talents elsewhere.

How can planners make sure a new pay plan is technically viable?

Compensation rules change frequently. Every day, some new rule or some new interpretation of a rule appears to change the technical nuances of a pay plan. Therefore, compensation planners should rely on specialized experts inside and, often, outside their companies to find out the latest appropriate changes in accounting and legal treatment of base, bonus, incentive, and benefits pay.

Benefits pay is particularly complex, so much so that many employers use outside vendors to keep records for their benefit programs. But outsourcing does not free an employer of its obligations, whether longstanding or newly acquired. Buyers and sellers alike often fail to realize how many different kinds of benefits there are, and what obligations each benefit entails.

MERGING BENEFITS PLANS

What are the different types of pension plans?

There are two types of pension plans: *qualified* (meaning that they meet certain federal standards and qualify for tax-favorable treatment) and *nonqualified.* Furthermore, there are two types of qualified pension plans: a *defined benefits plan* and a *defined contributions plan.*

A *defined benefits plan* is a pension plan that determines the total value of benefits by a formula and requires the employer to meet certain actuarially determined standards in making contributions to the plan. Contributions must be enough to pay obligations when they fall due.

A *defined contributions plan* is a pension plan with shorter-term requirements. Minimum contributions are required year by year for each year in which the plan is in existence. These plans can take the form of profit-sharing plans with or without salary deferral (the well-known 401(k) plan) and usually have variable contribution levels.

Both of these qualified, defined plans are subject to a contribution cap under tax law. More broadly, they are subject to rules set forth under the IRC, administered by the Department of Treasury, and ERISA, administered by the Department of Labor.

If a buyer and seller both have defined contribution plans, how can these be merged?

This is a complex area best understood on a plan-by-plan basis. Let's take the example of the most common defined contribution plan, the 401(k). It depends on whether the acquirer bought the stock of the acquired company or its assets. In an asset acquisition, plans must remain separate, and the acquired company plan must be managed by the seller. In a stock acquisition, three approaches are possible: maintaining separate plans, terminating the acquired plan, or merging the two plans.

- To maintain separate plans, the acquirer simply has to make sure that each group files its own forms (Form 5500) and satisfies federal requirements for the nature and extent of coverage. One benefit of maintaining separate plans is that there is no break in coverage, as both plans continue to exist. If plan years are the same, the acquirer can take a full calendar year to come into compliance. (If plan years are different, the acquirer should check on its timetable; it may be shorter.)
- Terminating the seller's plan requires a one-year waiting period. The IRS's *successor plan rule* says that an acquired company's plan will be disqualified if more than 2 percent of its employees participate in another defined contribution plan (except for an employee stock option plan) within one year of the acquisition. And even if an employer respects the 2 percent limit, it must pay sanctions to prevent those employees from being taxed.
- Merging the two plans can save administrative expense, but can be complicated. Assets from the old plan move to the new one. While this is done, employees are locked out of their plans for a period of time—typically two weeks to four months. During this time the old record keeper runs a final tally on the account, the shares are sold, and the money is moved to the new record keeper. Employees may have to select new investments when they can again access the plan. Sometimes the money is automatically invested in the nearest matching fund in the new

plan. During the lockout period, employees typically aren't allowed to take a loan or withdrawal or pick new investments. However, their contributions and loan obligations and repayments continue. The pension fund blackout provisions of Sarbanes-Oxley added restrictions.

Obviously, pension plans in US companies are subject to a good deal of federal law. What about other benefits?

Like pension plans (but to a lesser degree), health and welfare plans are also subject to the tax code and ERISA.

Aside from these laws, what others apply?

There is no real body of compensation law, but there is considerable employment law, and the pay planner must master its fundamentals. Adhering to both state and federal law, companies must pay minimum wage or better, make proper withholdings, pay proper taxes, honor contracts, avoid discriminatory practices, and so forth. Many of the laws establishing these principles are well known and have no special relevance to the postmerger scene.

Can the Internal Revenue Service or others sue a company for paying excessive compensation to executives?

Yes. It is common for the IRS to monitor corporate deductions for wages paid to employee-shareholders, especially in closely held corporations. The IRS can claim compensation is not reasonable and force the company to recharacterize the amounts as nondeductible dividends.

There are no specific dollar amounts that courts can use as guidelines to determine the actual value of services. Determinations are made on a case-by-case basis.

What do the IRS and courts look at when determining whether compensation is reasonable?

Courts ask the following questions to determine whether compensation paid to shareholders is reasonable:

- Would an unrelated outside investor consider the compensation reasonable?
- Is the amount of compensation consistent with the amount of dividends paid?
- Is it consistent with the profit performance of the corporation?
- Was the level of compensation based on corporate profit (rather than being set in advance)?
- Is the pay consistent with pay awarded in the corporation's industry?

The more "yes" answers to these questions, the more likely it is that the pay package will withstand IRS scrutiny.

SOME GENERAL POSTMERGER TECHNOLOGY CONSIDERATIONS[61]

What kind of tools are there to enhance employee collaboration after a merger?

Postmerger success depends in part on employee productivity and collaboration, and both in turn depend on technology. Fortunately, the number and accessibility of technology tools to increase collaboration have increased in recent years. Today teams can communicate not only via email and teleconference, but also by video (e.g., Skype or Zoom) or group messaging apps. Fortunately, many of these new technologies are relatively easy to set up after Wi-Fi and network access are established.

What guidance do you have for Wi-Fi postmerger?

The technology plan should enable employee use of Wi-Fi networks within at least 30 days. This should be done securely (top priority) and as quickly as possible. The postmerger period, with its high level of change and potential for confusion, can be particularly vulnerable to cyberattacks. Therefore, a careful plan to allow or deny network access is recommended.

What about employee access?

Likewise, there must be a careful plan to allow new employees into corporate enterprise systems, including financial systems in the case of accounting and finance staff. To be productive, employees in the merged company must be able to access the information they need to do their work.

If two companies use different cloud infrastructures, what happens then?

In the first six months, there should be an assessment of the merged company's cloud infrastructure. Existing cloud infrastructure for companies can be maintained, or there can be a careful and secure migration to the acquiring company's cloud infrastructure. But the merger can be an opportunity to implement to a new cloud infrastructure for merged companies. These may be private, public, or hybrid, but in any case must be monitored for security.

What are some of the databases that must be managed after the merger?

There are basically three main data sets: employees, vendors, and customers.

Employee Databases

Most companies today use a human resource information system (HRIS)—and sometimes more than one. If the acquirer is far larger than the target company, it simply maintains its HRIS. But in mergers of equals, there may need to be a hybrid approach, where some systems of the acquirer remain and some are replaced with target systems. In addition, new systems are also possible.[62]

Vendor Databases

Companies with many critical vendors, such as global manufacturing companies, typically manage those relationships with the help of a vendor database. A tool such as this has become even more important as a result of conflicting mineral rules in the United States following the Dodd-Frank Act of 2010, which are still in force despite an enforcement cutback due to a successful legal challenge.[63] These rules and similar regulations elsewhere have motivated companies to keep tabs on suppliers all along their supply chain. These are often supplemented by systems to track logistics (logistics systems) and assets (asset management systems), which should be selected based on current practical considerations (related to integration and operations) as well as strategic considerations.

Customer Databases

In the initial months after closing, the best course may be to maintain existing customer databases. But later in year one or in year two, the merged company may want to establish a *master customer database.* (Establishing this will take time, to clean data.) And if not already implemented at the merged company, a best practice is to move master data to a system that fosters a positive customer experience (CX). Part technology, part operations, a CX system seeks to analyze and optimize the customer's entire interaction with a business, and the customer's resulting perception of the company. CX systems enable salespeople, customer service representatives, and managers to optimize customer interactions. The CX system selected for the merged company should look beyond the here and now; it should meet global needs and plan for the customer experience in the future.

Is it always necessary to merge databases?

Until there is accurate and trusted data, it may be best for acquiring and target companies to maintain separate finance systems. But once data on employees, vendors, and customer data sets are cleaned and optimized, they can be put into a holistic system. With accurate employee and vendor data, and with a master customer database in place, the merged company may be ready for an enterprise resource planning (ERP) system for finances, often located in a secure cloud. To accomplish this, there must be an accurate chart of accounts—a list of all the general ledger accounts used to record transactions. The accounts can be coded using numbers, letters, or both.[64]

Another requirement is an accurate master customer database, which is necessary before integrating to one customer experience system.

Why and how can an acquirer harmonize IT practices following a merger?

Increasing the productivity of employees in the merged or acquired organization should be a goal. In the first six months, efforts should be made to harmonize IT practices (e.g., brand choice) for PCs, mobile phones, and other devices. In many cases, these practices default to one of the companies—typically the acquirer. In such cases target company employees receive PCs, phones, and devices from the acquirer—often brand-new ones to ensure secure access to corporate systems and technology.

What kind of documentation is necessary in this process?

As the technology network, systems, and databases are developed and selected, it is important to document applications, databases, systems, hardware, servers, licenses, networks, and vendors. This is the beginning of documenting the enterprise architecture of the merged company. And with clean(er) data, there is an opportunity to implement meaningful data governance in the merged company—with protocols around collecting, retaining, using, and protecting data, especially personal data subject to regulation (e.g., the European Union's General Data Protection Regulation).

Any final words on postmerger technology?

First, it's not just about technology; it's about people. When planning for retention, it is important to prioritize technology staff with the experience and knowledge to implement technology at the merged company. On the other hand, as noted earlier, certain high-technology cultures such as Silicon Valley are resistant to golden handcuff–type restrictions.

It is unlikely that the first-year plan of the merged company will be ideal. But a plan updated annually will become reasonably solid. Eventually, the merged companies should develop a robust business continuity plan with the updated business processes and selected systems.

At that point there will be an opportunity to implement robust analytics to mine additional revenue opportunities—including those already anticipated to justify the merger. With clean(er) data and systems, there is increased likelihood to find new customers, to increase share-of-wallet for existing customers, and to build new customer experiences. Finally, analytics can also be used to find operational efficiencies that will decrease the cost.

DIVESTITURES

We've spoken about letting employees go after a merger. What about letting entire company units go by selling them? How often does this happen?[65]

It depends on how long a timeline for divestiture you are considering. Few companies divest units immediately following an acquisition (unless they are compelled by antitrust regulators to do so), but many companies divest them eventually. This process is very hard to trace over a significant period of time, since companies and their units are always undergoing restructuring and renaming.

Companies generally review their businesses and alignment to their overall corporate strategy, which itself changes over time, and identify those businesses or teams that no longer fit the strategy and are subject to divestment. In a 2018 survey of 1,000 senior executives by Deloitte, 70 percent of the respondents said they planned to divest businesses within the next year.[66]

In any given year, nearly half of acquisitions occur because the sellers are divesting a company unit. Given the fact that most major companies grow both externally and internally, it would be reasonable to assume that about half of these divestitures stemmed from acquisitions—as opposed to internal growth. According to this logic, we would conclude that over time, about one-fourth of all acquisitions are eventually divested. Yet in major companies, the level appears to be lower. In a 20-year follow-up study for the 10 largest mergers of 1985, an author of this book (Lajoux) found that only a minority of the deals had ended in a divestiture even after two decades—and most of the divestitures were partial.

What kinds of divestiture are there?

There are three basic types of divestiture: sell-offs, spin-offs, and split-ups. Some of these may necessitate a continuing involvement—a strategy referred to as a *satellite launch.*

What is a sell-off?

A *sell-off,* by far the most common type of divestiture (and usually referred to as a *divestiture*), is the sale of one or more company units to another company. For example, in 2017, Abbott Laboratories sold its medical optics business to Johnson & Johnson, and Medtronic sold its patient monitoring and recovery business to Cardinal Health.

What is a spin-off?

A *spin-off* is a series of transactions through which a company divests or "spins off" one or more units—typically a small portion of its business with some common theme—by turning them into an independent company and selling the company's shares to the investing public. Recent US examples include Hewlett-Packard spinning off its enterprise businesses to create Hewlett-Packard Enterprise, and Abbott Laboratories, which spun off its branded pharmaceutical business to become AbbVie.

Sometimes spin-offs precede mergers, and sometimes they follow them.

Spun-off units may be sold in separate spin-offs or may be combined into a single spin-off. This process usually begins with a pro rata distribution of stock to shareholders in the form of a special dividend, followed by (or combined with) an initial public offering of the unit's shares. A common type of spin-off is the IPO carve-out in which the company goes straight to the IPO without the distributions to stockholders. If the parent retains interest in an IPO carve-out, this may be termed a *divestiture IPO.*

What is a split-up?

A *split-up* is the breakup of a company into two or more separate companies. It is different from a sell-off or a spin-off because it involves the entire company, not just a unit or two.

The most famous split-ups have involved AT&T. In 1984, AT&T broke up under order from the Department of Justice Antitrust Division, dividing into a telecommunications company (today's AT&T) and regional Bell companies (a.k.a. *Baby Bells*) to handle local calls. Then in 1996, having grown through acquisition, AT&T divided itself again—this time voluntarily—citing business complexities that outweighed the benefits of integration. One of the surviving units, interestingly, followed this split-up with the spin-off of a unit, Lucent Technologies, in 1996, while another unit, AT&T Wireless, after spinning off in 2001, merged into Cingular in 2005, and then later, in 2007, reasserted its name to become AT&T Mobility. In 2007, Cingular rebranded as AT&T.

Another good example is Motorola Inc., which executed a breakup of itself by spinning off its cellular handset and cable set-top box businesses to form Motorola Mobility, divested its cellular infrastructure business to Nokia Siemens Networks, and renamed its remaining public safety business Motorola Solutions Inc. Motorola Mobility was later acquired by Google, and subsequently sold to Lenovo.

What usually motivates postmerger divestitures?

Reasons for divestitures vary. A unit may be sold off, spun off, or split up because it is performing poorly and the seller wants to stem its tide of losses. Conversely, it may be sold as a crown jewel because it can fetch a good price. Finally, and least appealingly, it may be tagged for sale to appease regulators—for example, the Antitrust Division of the Department of Justice or the European Union—which may set this as a condition for regulatory approval of a merger. For example, when Dow Chemical merged with E.I. du Pont de Nemours & Company ("DuPont"), the European Union required the sale of certain assets in order to approve the deal.

How can an acquirer decide what to divest and when?

Companies often purchase other firms with the intent of selling off some units eventually, holding this divestiture option open until the businesses in question develop further or until the industry consolidates to the point that it becomes a seller's market. Assigning a quantitative value to each divestiture option may seem coldhearted, as the divestiture decision can bring disruptive change into the lives of people and communities—not always for the better. Yet, as in any decision, it is valuable to engage the head as well as the heart. If a divestiture is in the cards, it will happen sooner or later; the humane acquirer won't avoid it, but rather will bring it about in a human fashion, in accordance with the responsibilities discussed earlier in this chapter. A purely mathematical approach, while incomplete in and of itself, can help acquirers make the decision of keeping versus selling. It can also help set an appropriate price for the purchased company. The option to divest has quantifiable value and can be calculated easily (see Exhibit 9-10).

As illustrated in Exhibit 9-10, a comprehensive analysis, based on the strategy of the company and how each business unit contributes to that strategy, forms the basis for deciding which business units to divest, if any. Once a business unit is designated for divestiture, a business case should be prepared, outlining the justification for the divestiture decision. The business case would include the strategic reasons for the divestment, the financials to support the divestment, and the specifics of the unit to be divested, including which assets, services, and people will be included with the business unit to be divested. Once the business case gets approval within the company, the process to begin the execution of the divestment can begin, usually assigned to the company's M&A function.

Exhibit 9-10 Valuing the Divestiture Option

The option to divest has quantifiable value, according to Dr. Ken Smith, Managing Partner, Dundee Associates, Limited, Toronto, Canada, and Professor Alexander Triantis, Dean, Robert H. Smith School of Business at the University of Maryland.

Consider the case of PJP,* a large conglomerate contemplating the acquisition of another firm with substantial real estate holdings. If the acquisition goes through, PJP plans to develop a particular piece of centrally located real estate for a distribution facility in two years. Based on its projected use, PJP has valued this piece at $20 million. Market conditions will of course cause the value of this real estate to fluctuate over the next two years. However, if the firm's business outlook turns sour and the distribution facility is projected to be unprofitable, the firm would be able to sell off this land quickly for at least $15 million.

To account for the value of this divestiture option in its valuation of the acquisition, PJP's management uses a simple two-year binomial model. Management assumes that the value of the real estate to the firm (without taking into account the divestiture option) will either appreciate by 50 percent or depreciate by 40 percent each year. In the worst-case scenario, the land would be worth only $7.2 million to the company after two years. In effect, the divestiture option established a $15 million floor for the value of the real estate after two years, thus mitigating the risk of the acquisition.

Even though the value to PJP of the real estate as a site for its distribution facility may be only $12 million at the end of the first year, it is still not optimal for the firm to sell it at that time for $15 million if it can sell it for that price at the end of the second year. The firm would prefer to retain the option to develop the land at the end of the second year should business conditions improve (at which point the value of the land as a distribution site would rise to $18 million).

The incremental value of waiting to divest amounts to $710,000 at the end of the first year. Overall, the divestiture option increases the current value of the land from $20 million to $21.77 million. In practice, of course, the resale price of an asset is not guaranteed, and more sophisticated option-pricing techniques would be required. The logic behind the valuation and exercise of a divestiture option, however, is still instructive.

* PJP is a fictional composite based on real cases. This text is updated from Alexandra Lajoux, *The Art of M&A Integration: A Guide to Merging Resources, Processes, and Responsibilities* (New York: McGraw-Hill, 2006), and is here adapted with permission from Kenneth W. Smith and Alexander J. Triantis, "Untapped Options for Creating Value in Acquisitions," *Mergers & Acquisitions,* November/December 1994, p. 22.

Can an acquirer simply divest at will? What kinds of restrictions might come into play here?

As the new owner of an acquired company, the acquirer has a great deal of flexibility in how it integrates or separates from the resources it has acquired. Certain restrictions can and often do apply, however. The most common restrictions stem from contracts signed prior to the merger by either the seller or the buyer.

In terms of human resources, the selling company may have signed a labor agreement limiting or penalizing layoffs, and this agreement may extend to a future change of control. In terms of physical assets, the seller may have pledged not to sell assets used as collateral. Other restrictions stem from federal or state law protecting the interests of various stakeholder groups. Ideally, all of these restrictions will have been faced and resolved during the due diligence process prior to closing.

Isn't the divestiture process the same as the acquisition process, except in the reverse direction?

While many steps are similar to the acquisition process, the preparation for a divestiture can be much more complex, as the business unit must be carved out from the existing organization, functions, and services of the selling company and transitioned to the buyer and its functions and services. A key step in this preparation for sale is to identify all shared services, such as those typically provided to business units within the company, for example, IT, HR, and finance. Depending on the structure of the company, business units could share engineering, manufacturing, and procurement, which should be analyzed for inclusion in the list of shared services.

This should be done by establishing a small team under nondisclosure representing each functional area providing services to the business unit, and possibly a senior member of the business team to be divested. This team should identify all these services, as well as preparing a sell-side due diligence, in anticipation of what a potential buyer will ask, possibly using the questions the selling company would ask if they were buying the business unit to be divested.

Sometimes the business unit to be divested provides services to a selling company's business units that are not being divested. In this case, those services should also be identified and plans put in place to replace those services within the company that is selling the business unit.

How are these shared services documented?

All the services that the small team identified can be listed in a document called a Transition Services Agreement, or TSA. For each service, it is important to define exactly what the service is, what it costs the business unit (probably found in the business unit's budget/financial numbers), and a suggested date for when the service will be terminated for the business unit being transitioned.

What is the transition services agreement used for when dealing with the buying company?

The transition services agreement can be used as an education and negotiation item, instructing the potential buyer what services of the business unit to be sold need to be transitioned to the buyer's services, how much the business unit being sold pays for that service, and the suggested date for termination of the service. The buyer gets educated on the shared services of the business, and the cost the business unit pays, and can then negotiate with the selling company on what services are to be provided and for what duration. In some cases, this will include services that the business unit to be sold provides back to the selling company.

For the shared services provided to the business unit to be sold, what can be done before the actual sale to minimize the services and/or minimize the time to transition to the buying company?

Since the potential divestiture is not yet known to people other than on the small team formed to prepare for the divestiture, some clever projects can many times be started to make the service part of the business unit to be sold without disclosing the divestiture. For instance, a project could be started in the name of cost reduction to implement a decentralized approach to a shared service/tool, and selecting the unit to be divested as the first unit to be implemented on the new service/tool.

How should the people being moved to the buyer be treated during the transition process?

The name of the game here is communicate, communicate, communicate. In one case, a business unit that had many long-serving employees was being sold to a buyer, which was headquartered in a different country. Central business functions from both the selling and the buying companies, such as HR, IT, and real estate, did a thorough job of defining what would change, if anything, on day 1 and beyond, created websites documenting the changes, and held town hall–type meetings to introduce the changes. However, many employees were still very worried about the impact to them individually, and they expressed their worry to management. To respond, the business functions held informal lunchtime sessions, where the people could show up and ask questions or comment about what was on their minds. While no new information was needed, that hands-on interaction significantly reduced the fear and worry among the impacted employees. Bottom line: communicate, communicate, communicate!

If a company's senior management knows that the company may divest a unit, should it disclose this to employees or wait until it makes a final decision?

In this area, silence is golden. True, employees deserve full, current, and constant information about all material matters before, during, and after the merger—but speculative information is not considered to be material. It would not be covered, for example, by the WARN Act, which requires six-month notification of employees for certain kinds of layoffs (see Exhibit 9-11). Hypothetical information about the possible divestiture of a unit falls into the "don't ask, don't tell" category.

Similarly, many European countries have Workers' Councils, with specific requirements and processes to follow that are designed to protect impacted employees.

Exhibit 9-11 The WARN Act: Basic Provisions/Requirements

WARN protects workers, their families, and communities by requiring employers to provide notification 60 calendar days in advance of plant closings and mass layoffs. Advance notice gives workers and their families some transition time to adjust to the prospective loss of employment, to seek and obtain other jobs, and, if necessary, to enter skill training or retraining that will allow these workers to compete successfully in the job market. WARN also provides for notice to state dislocated worker units so that they can promptly offer dislocated worker assistance.

A covered plant closing occurs when a facility or operating unit is shut down for more than six months, or when 50 or more employees lose their jobs during any 30-day period at a single site of employment. A covered mass layoff occurs when a layoff of six months or longer affects either 500 or more workers, or at least 33 percent of the employer's workforce when the layoff affects between 50 and 499 workers. The number of affected workers is the total number laid off during a 30-day (or in some cases 90-day) period.

WARN does not apply to closure of temporary facilities, or the completion of an activity when the workers were hired only for the duration of that activity. WARN also provides for less than 60 days' notice when the layoffs resulted from closure of a faltering company, unforeseeable business circumstances,* or a natural disaster.

Employee Rights

Workers or their representatives and units of local government may bring individual or class action suits. US district courts enforce WARN requirements. The court may allow reasonable attorneys' fees as part of any final judgment.

Compliance Assistance Available

For general information about WARN, a fact sheet and employer's guide are available from the Employment and Training Administration (ETA) website.

Specific requirements of WARN may be found in the act itself, Public Law 100-379 (29 USC 2101 et seq.).

For additional assistance, contact the ETA at https://www.doleta.gov/lay-off/warn.cfm.

Penalties/Sanctions

An employer who violates the WARN provisions is liable to each employee for an amount equal to back pay and benefits for the period of the violation, up to 60 days. This may be reduced by the period of any notice that was given, and any voluntary payments that the employer made to the employee.

Exhibit 9-11 *(Continued)*

An employer who fails to provide the required notice to the unit of local government is subject to a civil penalty not to exceed $500 for each day of violation. The employer may avoid this penalty by satisfying the liability to each employee within three weeks after the closing or layoff.

Relation to State, Local, and Other Federal Laws

WARN does not preempt any other federal, state, or local law, or any employer/employee agreement that requires other notification or benefit. Rather, the rights provided by WARN supplement those provided by other federal, state, or local laws.

* Jeffrey Rhodes, "WARN Act Liability Requires Probability of Closure," *SHRM,* September 13, 2017, https://www.shrm.org/resourcesandtools/legal-and-compliance/employment-law/pages/bankruptcy-warn-act.aspx.

Note: For the full text of the WARN Act, see Public Law 100-379 (29 USC 2101 et seq. Text can be found at Cornell University's Legal Information Institute, www4.law.cornell.edu/uscode/html/uscode29/usc_sec_29_00002101——000-.html.

Source: US Department of Labor, *The Employment Law Guide.*

If managers must address this issue (to handle information leaks, for example), here are some principles to keep in mind if divestiture plans are in the making:

- *Honesty.* When asked, never deny. (A "No comment" is sufficient.) Depending on the situation, another answer is to say that the company's Strategy team (assuming there is one) is always reviewing the company's strategy and the impact of selling every business unit if it no longer sits with that strategy. So hearing a rumor does not mean that a rumored business will be sold.
- *Discretion.* Don't volunteer nonessential information.
- *Utility.* Keep your communications useful. For example, if a divestiture decision hinges on a unit's productivity or profitability, these factors should be flagged for employees' urgent attention.

If senior management knows that it will divest a unit, when should it tell employees, and how much should it tell them?

The principles of honesty, discretion, and utility apply here as well, but *not* the rule of silence. Once a plan is certain, silence is *not* golden. Immediate, complete, and frequent disclosure is the rule here.

What should be done to prepare for the first day when the business unit being sold is no longer part of the selling company and is now part of the buyer (often referred to as day 1)?

Divestiture preparation is a key requirement to successfully accomplish a divestiture. Planning for day 1, when change of control happens, should be done in great detail. Not only does the actual deal execution and exchange of funds, if any, need to be defined, but details for HR (e.g., how people will be paid after day 1), IT (how people will log on to their computers, and what they will be able to access at the selling company and the buyer), and Finance/Operations (e.g., how business will be processed from day 1 through the transition period) must be carefully defined. These detailed plans can have separate steps for each hour preceding day 1, and subsequent to the change of control, and involve resources from the buyer, the seller, and impacted employees.

What can be done with the locations that the business unit being sold occupies with other business units of the selling company?

Ideally, the business unit being sold would move from any shared site shortly after day 1. However, depending on the location, it may not be economically possible to move the business unit and, in fact, may dictate that the shared site be "subdivided" to support both companies for a longer period of time. In this case, detailed analysis and planning, including physical security such as separate entrances, separate badging and badge readers, separate phone and IT infrastructure, and separate signage identifying both companies, must be considered and defined.

How is the transition period after day 1 managed to ensure a successful transition?

Management of the transition process after day 1 until the successful transfer of shared services is required by both the seller and the buyer. A typical process includes an overall Senior Transition Team, made up of senior executives from both the buyer and the seller, responsible for managing the transition, reviewing transition costs, resolving issues, and so on. Each functional area, such as HR, IT, Finance, and Operations should also have shared teams that manage the transition of each of their respective functions and services within those functions.

CONCLUDING COMMENTS

Whether an acquirer keeps all the assets of a company or divests some of them, some responsibilities do remain ethically and legally, and these must be carefully weighed. Corporate social responsibility benefits all stakeholders, including shareholders, over time.

APPENDIX 9A

Sample Postmerger Press Release Highlighting Strategic Motivation

News Release

Company A Buys Customers and Networks of Company B

Acquisition of Customers and Networks Expand Service Area, Solidify Acquirer's Market Strength

City, Date.—Company A, a provider of local, long-distance, and Internet services for small and midsize businesses, today announced that it has signed an agreement to purchase Company B for $213 million in cash plus the assumption of approximately $4 million in capital lease obligations.

Under the terms of the agreement, A will purchase B, including its assets and customers, from the Owner. The parties expect to complete the transaction in the third quarter of 2019 upon obtaining necessary governmental and other approvals.

Acquisition Solidifies Market Strength

With the acquisition of Company B's network assets and customer base, Company A will become the most cash profitable and one of the largest competitive local exchange carriers (CLECs) in the West. Combined, the companies will have more than $300 million in annual revenue and more than $100 million in pro forma 2019 EBITDA, before any merger synergies. *Approximately 60 percent of the two companies' revenues derive from geographic markets and networks that overlap, creating the opportunity for significant network efficiencies and synergies.* The acquisition will increase the number of Company A's metropolitan service areas from 18 to 23 and expand the number of states in which it serves from five to eight.

Most important, the combined companies will enjoy important strategic advantages resulting from Company B's eight-market, 2,200-route-mile (160,000 fiber miles) metropolitan area network, with direct fiber access into over 580 major commercial buildings. Many other competitive local exchange carriers are scrambling to find network alternatives in response to recent FCC rules that increase the cost of leasing network. Company A, by acquiring B's metropolitan area network, becomes one of the first to insulate itself from this unpredictable landscape of telecom regulation.

"These robust metropolitan fiber networks will substantially *increase our operating strength and provide a meaningful and sustainable competitive cost advantage over other local carriers,*" said John Doe, chief executive officer of Company A.

In addition to the metropolitan area networks, Company A will also own and operate B's unique long haul network—one of the largest of its kind in its region. The value of this network is evidenced by a blue-chip list of other carriers that lease connectivity from Company B to access their customers.

"We are eager to enhance this network and strengthen our relationships with those that rely on the connectivity we provide," added Doe.

Benefits to Customers

"I'm delighted for our customers," continued Doe. "*We will be offering a stronger regional and local telecommunications network alternative, and we will be better equipped to offer unique and powerful high-bandwidth data products, which are increasingly important to the business customers we serve.*"

Upon completing the integration, Company A will expand the product sets and services currently offered by Company B to include those offered by A, including those that are tailored to the smaller business customer. Doing so will increase the addressable markets in the important new service areas that come with the acquisition. "We look forward to introducing Company B customers to Company A's brand of service, where we staff customer service locally in each major market we serve," said Doe.

"This is an excellent opportunity for Company B employees and customers," said Bob Smith, executive vice president and chief operating officer of Company B. "Company A is a carrier we respect, with a proven track record of success."

Note: This press release is modeled on an actual press release of a midsize merger.

APPENDIX 9B

Sample "Assets" Checklist of Resources, Processes, and Responsibilities

Every corporation is composed of valuable resources, processes, and responsibilities. Following the acquisition of a company, it is important to make sure that management does not neglect any of these "assets" (using the term broadly). Every company will have its own list of assets, but this checklist may be helpful.

PHYSICAL ASSETS

Equipment* (including computer hardware and software)
- Office equipment
- Plant equipment

Inventory*
- Finished
- Work-in-process

Land*

Materials

Mines
- Production, reserves, locations, development
- Maps

Real estate
- Branch buildings*
- Factory buildings*
- Construction in progress

Real estate—other*

FINANCIAL ASSETS

From Balance Sheet

Financial Assets*
- Cash
- Investment securities
- Accounts receivable
- Prepaid income taxes
- Other prepaid expenses
- Deferred charges
- Other financial assets
  - Goodwill
  - Long-term receivables
  - Investments in affiliates
  - Goodwill from previous acquisitions
  - *For banks,* debt owed to bank via outstanding loans

For other common balance sheet assets, such as Property, Plant, and Equipment, see "Physical Assets."

Financial Liabilities and Equity*
- Financial Liabilities
  - Accounts payable
  - Debt
  - *For banks,* cash deposits held by bank and owed by bank to customers
- Financial Equity*
  - Common stock outstanding
  - Preferred stock outstanding
  - Retained earnings

From Income Statement

Gross revenues
- Growth trend

Net revenues
- Growth trend

INTELLECTUAL ASSETS

Contracts (if favorable—otherwise, a liability)
- Employment agreements
- Franchise agreements
- No-compete agreements

Culture
- Reporting relationships (real versus formal)
- Policies and procedures
- Any other cultural factor not covered elsewhere in this taxonomy

Marketing intangibles
- Company name recognition
- Brand name recognition
- Service mark (right to use company signage)
- Trademark (right to use company name)

Production intangibles
- Copyrights
- Favorable supplier contracts
- Patents
- Product design
- Product quality
- Production costs
- Production speed
- Production standards
- Software
- Trade secrets

HUMAN ASSETS (PEOPLE)

Knowledge, experience, competencies, and leadership and/or teamwork ability of each of the following individuals:

Directors (including chairperson if separate)
CEO/COO/president
Other senior managers
Sales force
Other employees

See also "HR function" under "Organizational Assets."

ORGANIZATIONAL ASSETS (ACTIVITIES)

Quality of the "infrastructure" described here
Contracts and commitments
Relating to all human capital and also to external relations
If a contract is unfavorable and/or broken, it can turn from an asset into a liability.

Primary Functions

Management systems
Processes for design, production, and supply
Channels for distribution
Inbound logistics (for manufacturing; see also "Purchasing function" under "Support Functions")
Receiving
Storing
Material handling
Warehousing
Inventory control
Outbound logistics
Distribution
Manufacturing function

Quality control policies applied to production R&D function
- Laboratory notebooks
- Invention disclosure forms

Sales function

Established territories

Support Functions

Accounting function
- Bookkeeping
- Treasury
- Internal auditing

Communications/marketing function(s)
- Marketing
- Public relations

Corporate administrative function
- Headquarters administration

Facilities function
- Facilities management

Finance function
- Financing (issuing equity, borrowing debt)
- Management of funds (opening/closing deposits; lockbox)

HR function
- Rewarding and giving incentives for performance
  - Base pay
  - Bonus pay
  - Pensions
  - Benefits
  - Special pay arrangements
  - Recognition programs (awards and honors)
- Retention (retaining key qualities: relevant knowledge, experience, competencies)
- Recruitment (seeking relevant knowledge, experience, competencies)
- Termination/retirement
- Performance management

Career development
Succession planning
Training
IT function
Hardware, software, and systems for internal communications
Email
Telephones (LAN, WAN, routers, switches)
Legal function
Compliance programs, including internal code of conduct (see also "Regulatory relations" in "External Relationship Assets")
Purchasing function—Policies pertaining to vendor relations
Internal Financial Controls
Control environment*
Appropriateness of the entity's organizational structure and its ability to provide the necessary information to manage its activities
Adequacy of definition of key managers' responsibilities and their understanding of these responsibilities
Adequacy of knowledge and experience of key managers in light of their responsibilities
Appropriateness of reporting relationships
Extent to which modifications to the structure are made in light of changed conditions
Sufficiency of numbers of employees, particularly in management and supervisory capacity
Risk assessment
Control activities
Information/communication re finances
Monitoring

Mission, Vision, and Strategy

Mission statement
Vision statement
Strategic plan document

EXTERNAL RELATIONSHIP ASSETS

If any of these has a corresponding function, see that function under "Organizational Assets."

Customer relations
- Reputation of brands
- Reputation of service
- Major customers (required under SAS131)
- Major geographic areas (SAS131)

Shareholder relations
- Reputation for increasing market share/paying dividends
- Stability of holdings by shareholders

Bondholder relations
- Reputation for repaying debt instruments
- Bond rating

Lender relations
- Rate of interest charged by lenders
- Credit rating

Supplier relations
- Favorable contracts (see also "Production intangibles" under "Intellectual Assets")

Community relations
- Community programs

Public relations
- Reputation of company name re public issues—see also "Company name recognition" under "Intellectual Assets"
- Regulatory Relations Lobbying (if any)—see also "Legal function" under "Support Functions"

History of fulfilling contracts and commitments

* Items with an asterisk appear on the balance sheet. Items without an asterisk do not appear on the balance sheet or any other traditional financial statement. However, they are usually discussed in the Management Discussion and Analysis section of the 10-K report, along with balance sheet items, especially if they are at risk.

APPENDIX 9C

Integration Planning Worksheet

The following two pages provide a simple template for applying project management principles to acquisition integration.

Key Business Process:						
Primary Integration Activities*	Priority	Tasks/Subtasks	Task Owner	Prerequisites	Required Tactical Data	Relevant Strategic Questions
	• Day 1	1.				
	• 100 days	2.				
	• 6 months	3.				
	• Year 1	4.				
	• Eventually	5.				
		6				
		7				
		8				
		9.				
		10.				
	• Day 1	1.				
	• 100 days	2.				
	• 6 months	3.				
	• Year 1	4.				

(Continued)

Key Business Process:

Primary Integration Activities*	Priority	Tasks/Subtasks	Task Owner	Prerequisites	Required Tactical Data	Relevant Strategic Questions
	• Eventually	5.				
		6.				
		7.				
		8.				
		9.				
		10.				
	• Day 1 • 100 days • 6 months • Year 1 • Eventually	1.				
		2.				
		3.				
		4.				
		5.				
		6.				
		7.				
		8.				
		9.				
		10.				

APPENDIX 9D

Integration Timeline from a Midsized Acquirer*

Sample Mission, Team, and Timeline for Acquisition

Team Mission

To facilitate a smooth assimilation of employees of newly acquired organizations into Company XY and to effect a smooth transition of their functional transactions into XY business plans, objectives, and strategies.

*Source: Midsized company in Florida. Names fictional. Used with permission 2018. Reviewed and enhanced by John Hotta, Cofounder, Capital Expert Services, LLC.

Acquisition Integration Team

- Cross-Functional Team Members

–Mary Davis >> Payroll/Benefits Integration and Organizational Charts

–Sharon Peters and PR firm >> Marketing Communications

–Alma Rivers

>>Computer Requirements/Voice data interface/Network/Cloud Infrastructure

–Jeff Coates

>>ISO 9000/Customer Service/Contracts/Facility/Environmental

–Sam Wilson/Tony Robins

>>Transaction Integration and Sales Expectations

–Bob Smith

>>Financial Institution Changes

–Felix Hernandez

>>Website Integration and Transaction Modeling

–Susan Ivory

>>Integration Progress Tracking/Single Point Contact for Acquirees

Acquisition Integration Team

- Roadblocks*

–Confusing, duplicate communication with acquirees

  –Solvable through good internal processes

–Firedrills at time of acquisition for employee integration

  –Solvable through closer communication with dealmakers

–Connectivity issues—email and Internet accessibility

  –Solvable through synchronizing Rivers/Wilson/Ivory on timing

–Cultural Integration

  –Solvable through more resources in HR and continued good communication from Sales Management

–Development of overall company database

  –Need overall systems to facilitate faster access to customer community

–Communication of requirements/sales goals for each facility to implementation team

  –Responsiveness to needs

* Notes from team meeting held to plan integration.

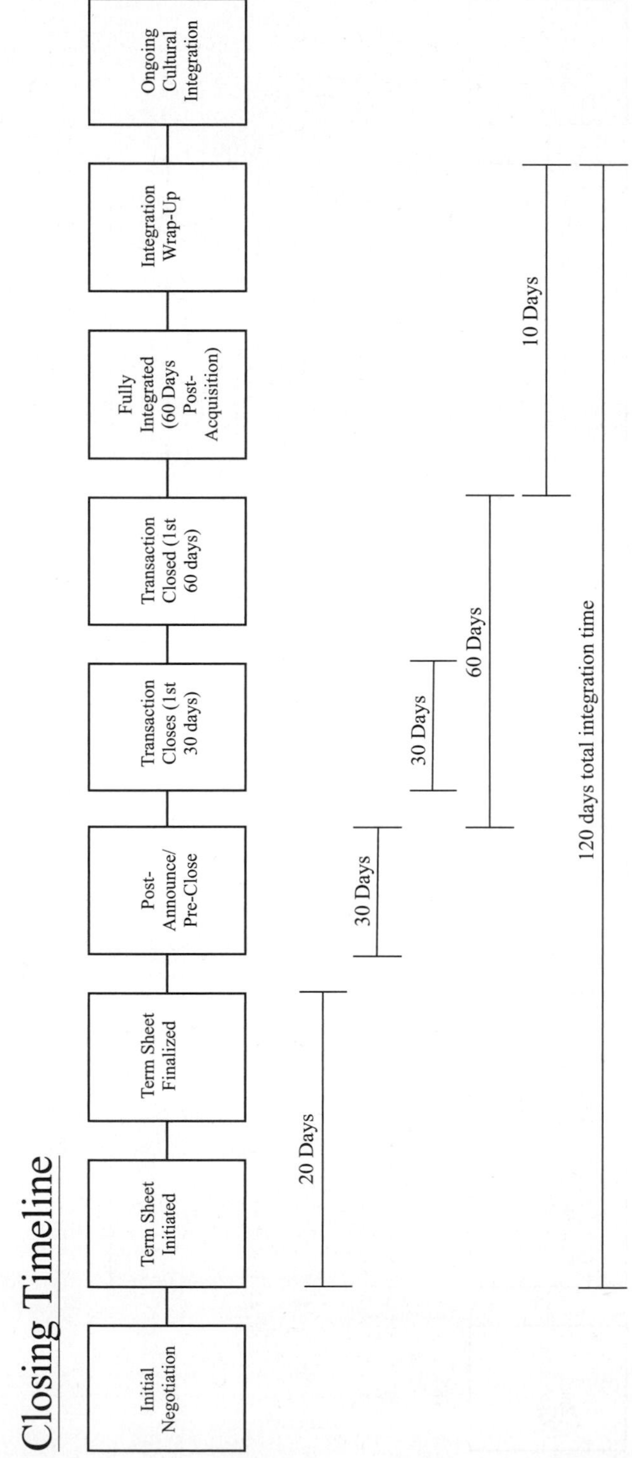
Acquisition Integration Process Timing
Closing Timeline
Initial Negotiation
Term Sheet Initiated
Term Sheet Finalized
Post-Announce/ Pre-Close
Transaction Closes (1st 30 days)
Transaction Closed (1st 60 days)
Fully Integrated (60 Days Post-Acquisition)
Integration Wrap-Up
Ongoing Cultural Integration
20 Days
30 Days
30 Days
60 Days
10 Days
120 days total integration time

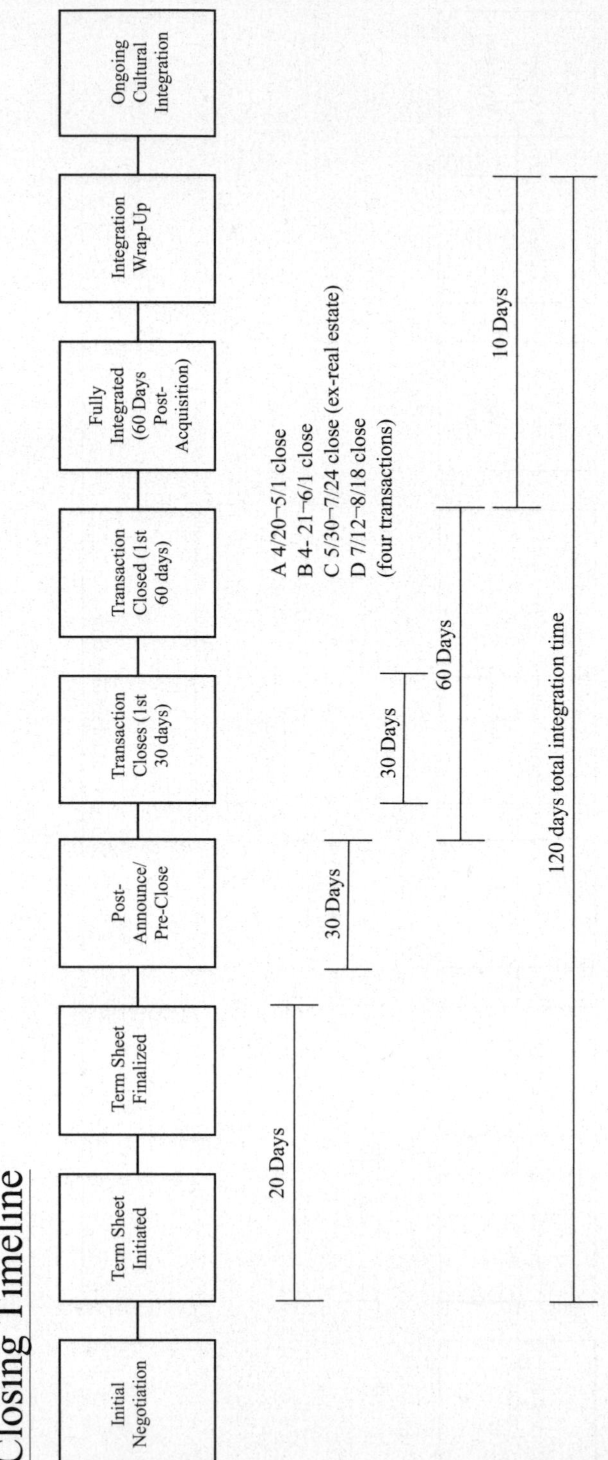
Acquisition Integration Process Timeline
Closing Timeline
Initial Negotiation
Term Sheet Initiated
Term Sheet Finalized
Post-Announce/ Pre-Close
Transaction Closes (1st 30 days)
Transaction Closed (1st 60 days)
Fully Integrated (60 Days Post-Acquisition)
Integration Wrap-Up
Ongoing Cultural Integration
20 Days
30 Days
A 4/20–5/1 close
B 4- 21–6/1 close
C 5/30–7/24 close (ex-real estate)
D 7/12–8/18 close
(four transactions)
30 Days
60 Days
10 Days
120 days total integration time

Acquisition Closing Timeline

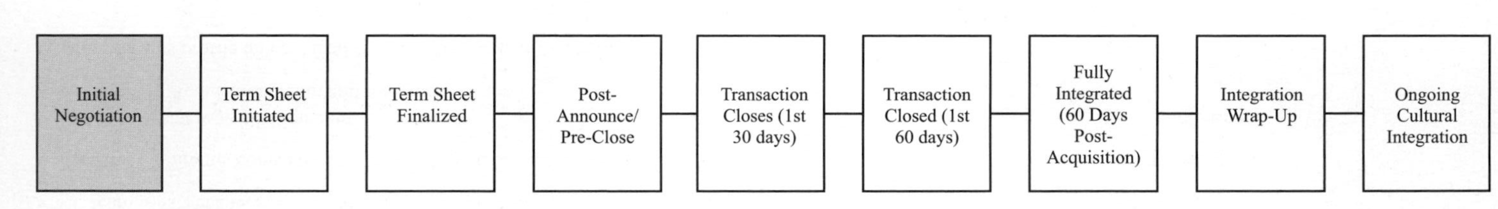

Correlated Integration Activities

During Initial Negotiation Process:	Comments:
• Notification from James to Ivory and Davis (on alert)	-A - Complete -B - Complete -C - Complete -D - Complete

Acquisition Closing Timeline

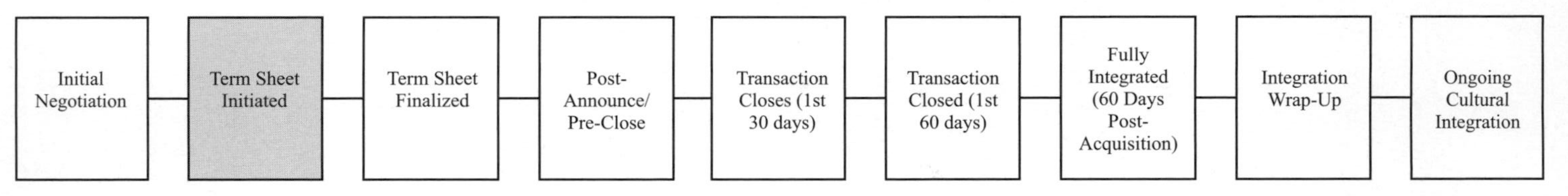

Correlated Integration Activities

During Term Sheet Initiation:	Comments:
• James notifies Ivory and Davis	Complete through D
• HR information collected (current employee and payroll info) (Davis)	Open: D
• Notify acquirees of initial on-site orientation (Davis)	Open: C and D
• Marketing/Communications (MC) team prepares press release and customer letters (Peters)	Open: C and D
• MC team uses website, social media, and video to communicate key messages to stakeholders	Open: C and D
• IT addresses Internet connectivity and orders circuits required (Rivers)	See Attached Plan
• Ivory updates new acquisition contact sheet and distributes to Acquisition Team and Integration Team	Open: Add C and D
• Sales prepares profile on new facility to Integration and Acquisition Teams	Open: A, B, C, D

Acquisition Closing Timeline

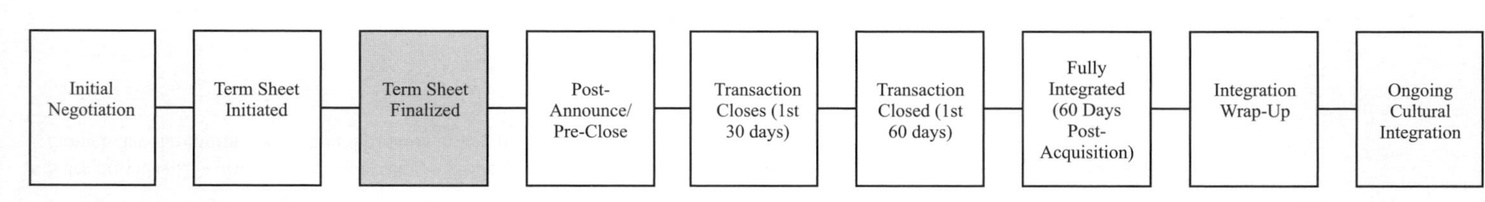

Correlated Integration Activities

Once Term Sheet Is Finalized:	Comments:
• Announcement date determined by James and communicated to Ivory/Davis	Open: C, D
• Conference call scheduled with newly acquired employees (Davis)	Open: C,D
• Internal announcement from Management to current employees regarding acquisition and significance (Davis)	Open: C,D
• Finalize dates for initial on-site employee orientation (Davis)	Open: C,D
• Marketing Communications sends letter to current and newly expanded customer database (Peters and PR firm)	Open: B,C,D
• Marketing Communications releases announcement to public (Peters and PR firm)	Open: B,C,D

Acquisition Closing Timeline

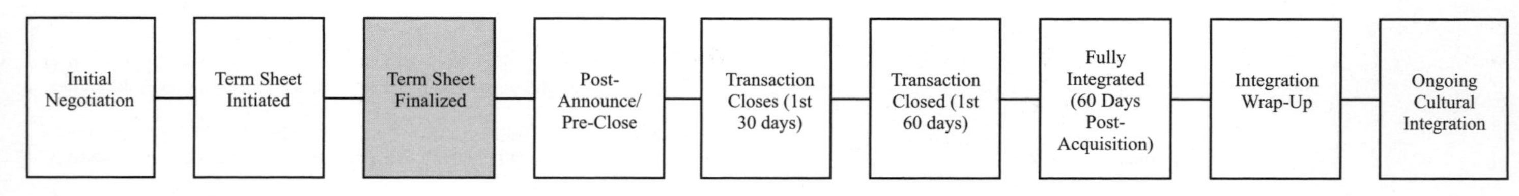

Correlated Integration Activities

Once Term Sheet Is Finalized:	Comments:
• Sales provides requirements for connectivity to IT (city/state/zip/contact name/phone #) (Wilson)	Open: ALL
• Finance orients acquirees on financial institution process, timing and logo use for transactions (James/Smith)	Open: B,C,D.
• Integration Handbook to new acquirees (Ivory/Davis)	Open: ALL
• Ivory established as primary integration contact	Open: D
• Sales provides IT with new employee name, job title, email access, laptop or desktop PC through new-hire form completion. IT places order appropriately (Wilson)	Open: ALL

Acquisition Closing Timeline

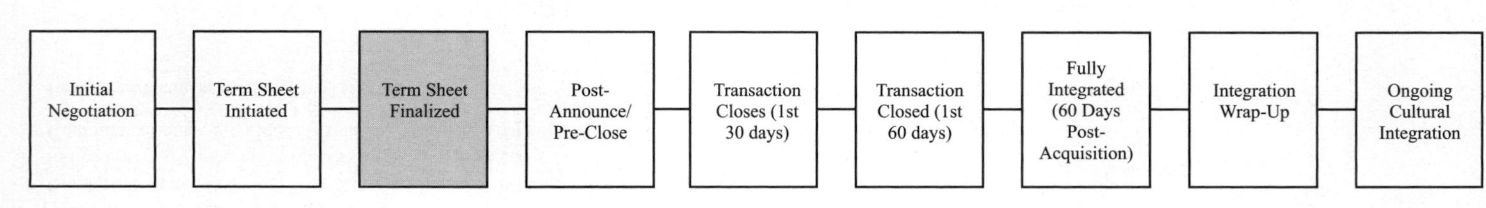

Correlated Integration Activities

Once Term Sheet Is Finalized:	Comments:
• IT sets up training dates for new employees for computer/ email orientation (Rivers)	Open: ALL
• Ivory updates facility chart and distributes to Acquisition and Integration Teams	Open: C,D

Acquisition Closing Timeline

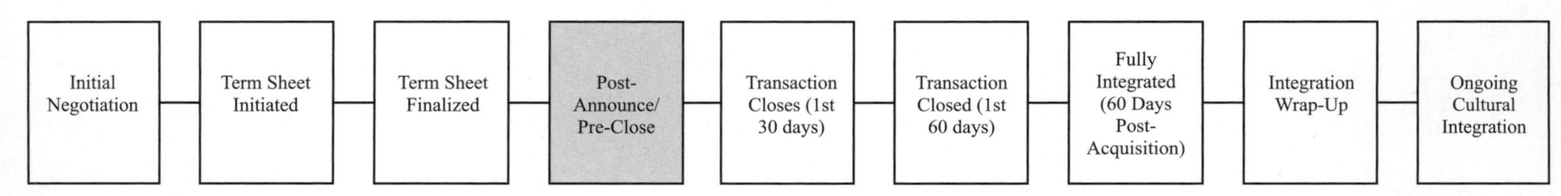

Correlated Integration Activities

During Postannouncement/Preclose Phase:	Comments:
• Conduct initial on-site employee meeting (Davis, Ivory)	Open: C,D
• Present XY business strategy, significance of new acquiree to strategy, key contacts, organizational charts, and XY locations	Open: ALL
(distribute facilities list to all employees) (Wilson, Davis, Ivory)	Open: D
• Distribute/discuss Assimilation Handbook internally (Davis, Ivory)	Open: ALL
• Conduct Acquiree Principal "Expectation Meeting" in Florida (Sales/Forecasts/Integration Process/Org Chart/Marketing Communications—logo/identity manual) (Wilson/Ivory)	Open: C,D
• Letterhead/business cards ordered (Partridge)	Open: B,C,D

Acquisition Closing Timeline

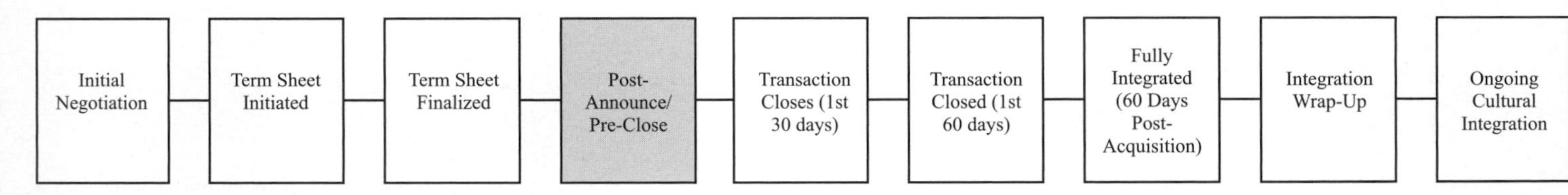

Correlated Integration Activities

During Postannouncement/Preclose Phase:	Comments:
• Determine customer service call routing with principals and determine plan (Coates)	Open: ALL
• Physical Facility plan (including signage) initiated including ISO 9000 regulations and environmental concerns (Coates)	Open: ALL
• Determine Contracts Administration plan (Coates)	Open: ALL
• Hernandez evaluates transactions and makes recommendations to Robins	Open: D
• Marketing Assessments for demographics initiated (Hernandez)	Open: ALL
• Travis Robins develops plan for transaction integration	Open: C,D

Acquisition Closing Timeline

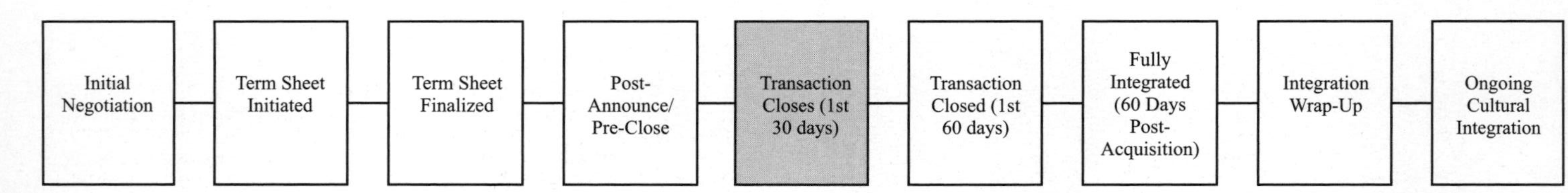

Correlated Integration Activities

Once Transaction Is CLOSED (1st 30 days):	Comments:
• Establish bank accounts for acquiree (Smith)	Open: C,D
• Transaction integration implemented (Sales, Robins)	Open: C,D
• Letterhead issued (Partridge)	Open: C,D
• Business cards issued (Peters)	Open: C,D
• Logo changes instituted (all paperwork) (Peters/Smith)	Open: ALL

Acquisition Closing Timeline

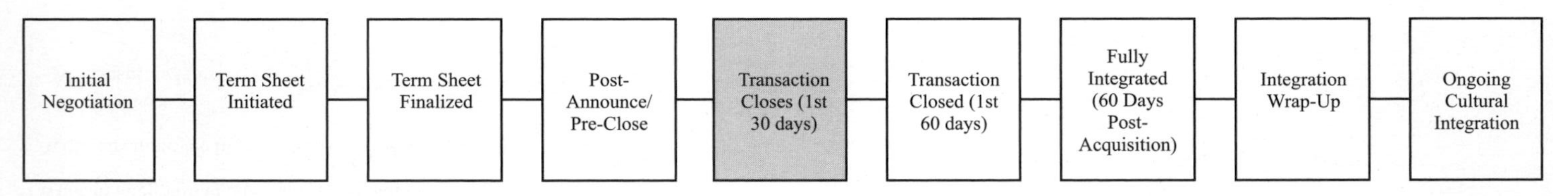

Correlated Integration Activities

Once Transaction Is CLOSED (1st 30 days):	Comments:
• Phone answering training initiated for all acquirees (Coates)	Open: ALL
• New Contract Administration Plan becomes effective (Coates)	Open: ALL
• Physical structure changes begin and ISO 9000 process becomes effective (Coates)	Open: ALL
• Computers installed and email training conducted for on-site employees (Rivers)	Open: ALL
• Voicemail additions established/training for newly acquired employees (Coates)	Open: ALL
• Employee training on business processes and on the technology that supports them	Open: ALL
• Employee training on how to prevent cyber breaches	Open: ALL

Acquisition Closing Timeline

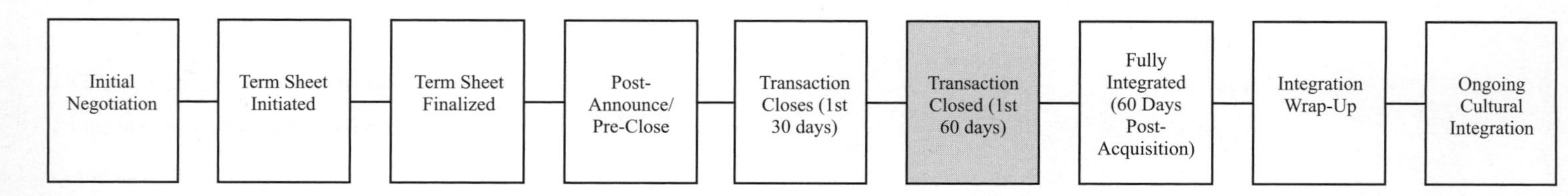

Correlated Integration Activities

Once Transaction Is CLOSED (1st 60 days):	Comments:
• Registration and Insurance Evaluation/Compliance (James)	Open: C,D
• Building • Vehicles	
• P&S Notification (James)	Open: ?
• Website integration addressed (Hernandez)	Open: ?
• Acquiree employee training on (Wilson/Ivory)	Open: ALL
• XY Products • XY Business Plan	

Acquisition Closing Timeline

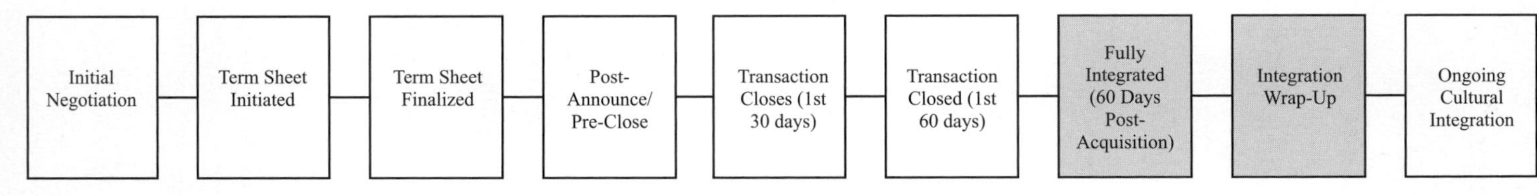

Correlated Integration Activities

Once Fully Integrated:	Comments:
• Close-out meeting scheduled to review	Open: ALL
• Process with acquiree principal in Florida (Wilson/Ivory)	
• Distribute feedback surveys on integration or other concerns to new acquirees (Wilson/Ivory)	Open: ALL
• Collect, collate, and distribute results and open issues to Sales, Executive Management, and acquiree principal (Wilson/Ivory)	Open: ALL

APPENDIX 9E

Pairwise Comparison

During integration, it is important to prioritize actions. One way to do this is to consider proposed actions in a series of pairs, picking the most important one, pair by pair, and in that way creating a ranking. The following primer on pairwise comparison (using a stepladder as an example) can be useful.

Introduction

Pairwise comparison is a kind of divide-and-conquer problem-solving method. It allows one to determine the relative order (ranking) of a group of items. This is often used as part of a process of assigning weights to criteria in design concept development.

Consider the evaluation of a stepladder. In that problem, the following criteria were deemed pertinent:

- Functionality
- Durability
- Quality
- Affordability
- Fabricability
- Usability

- Maintainability
- Safety
- Marketability

In order to weigh these criteria, we could simply tackle the problem all at once and, for example, discuss what weights should be assigned to each criterion. This can be very difficult; it can become an insurmountable task in more complex problems where there may be dozens of criteria. An alternative is to divide the problem of assigning weights into two parts:

1. Determine *qualitatively* which criteria are more important (i.e., establish a ranking of the criteria).
2. Assign each criterion a quantitative weight so that the qualitative ranking is satisfied.

Pairwise comparison can be used for Step 1. Here's how it would work.

Step 1: Identify the Criteria to Be Ranked

This is already done. Typically, the criteria can be derived from the functional requirements and product characteristics (PCs) determined during the development of a product design specification (PDS). Assuming you keep the PDS very handy while you evaluate concepts, you can just use the main PCs as the criteria, as we've done here.

Step 2: Arrange the Criteria in an $N \times N$ Matrix

For the ladder design problem, the matrix would look like Exhibit 9-E.1. Obviously, we need only one triangle of the matrix. That is, since the rows and columns contain exactly the same things in the same order, one triangle of the matrix will contain exactly the same cells as the other triangle.

Furthermore, the diagonal itself does not matter—it simply doesn't make sense to consider how important one criterion is with respect to itself! So now we have Exhibit 9-E.2.

Exhibit 9-E.1 Setting Up the Pairwise Comparison Matrix

		A	B	C	D	E	F	G	H	I
Functionality	A									
Durability	B									
Quality	C									
Affordability	D									
Fabricability	E									
Usability	F									
Maintainability	G									
Safety	H									
Marketability	I									

Step 3: Compare Pairs of Items

For each row, consider the item in the row with respect to each item in the rest of the row. In the example, we begin with functionality versus durability. Which is more important?

In the corresponding cell of the matrix, we put the letter that we consider most important in each pairwise comparison. If we really, really think the

Exhibit 9-E.2 Identifying the Useful Part of the Matrix

		A	B	C	D	E	F	G	H	I
Functionality	A	–								
Durability	B	–	–							
Quality	C	–	–	–						
Affordability	D	–	–	–	–					
Fabricability	E	–	–	–	–	–				
Usability	F	–	–	–	–	–	–			
Maintainability	G	–	–	–	–	–	–	–		
Safety	H	–	–	–	–	–	–	–	–	
Marketability	I	–	–	–	–	–	–	–	–	–

Exhibit 9-E.3 Filling the Useful Part of the Matrix

		A	B	C	D	E	F	G	H	I
Functionality	A	–	A	C	D	A	F	A	AH	I
Durability	B	–	–	C	D	B	B	B	H	BI
Quality	C	–	–	–	D	C	F	C	H	C
Affordability	D	–	–	–	–	D	F	D	D	I
Fabricability	E	–	–	–	–	–	F	E	H	E
Usability	F	–	–	–	–	–	–	F	FH	I
Maintainability	G	–	–	–	–	–	–	–	H	I
Safety	H	–	–	–	–	–	–	–	–	H
Marketability	I	–	–	–	–	–	–	–	–	–

two criteria are equally important, we put both letters in the cell. There are, of course, other ways to fill the cells. The point is that whatever way is chosen, it must represent which of the items is more important.

Note that the comparison is *pairwise*—we completely ignore all other criteria.

Say we determine that functionality is more important than durability. We would put an *A* in cell (2,4) of the matrix. We continue doing this until all of the first row is complete. We then proceed to the second row and repeat until the upper triangle of the matrix is filled. We could end up with Exhibit 9-E.3.

Note the double letters. We have used this convention to indicate that there is no difference in importance between the items being compared.

Step 4: Create the Ranking of Items

Now we simply create an ordered list of the items, ranked by the number of cells containing their flag letter. This leads to:

1. Safety (7)
2. Usability (6)

3. Affordability (6)
4. Quality (5)
5. Marketability (5)
6. Functionality (4)
7. Durability (4)
8. Fabricability (2)
9. Maintainability (0)

Conclusion

We now have a ranked list of the relative importance of the various criteria. Given this, we can now begin considering the actual weights we wish to attach. This is the extent of the pairwise comparison technique, but we can take this particular problem one step further and consider how we could assign the actual weights.

Consider the constraints on the problem of assigning weights.

1. The total of all the weights must be 100 percent.
2. The weights must obey the qualitative ranking given above.

We can either begin to wrestle with the problem in a strictly ad hoc manner, or we can try to structure our solution. It's inevitable that some iteration will be required, so there's no point in looking for a method that will give us actual weights in one pass.

However, we can try to set up an initial set of values that does satisfy the constraints, and then tweak the values until they are satisfactory to all stakeholders.

One very easy way to get that initial set of values is to assume a linear proportion between all the weights and solve the following equation:

$$100 = 7x + 6x + 6x + 5x + 5x + 4x + 4x + 2x + 0x$$

Therefore, $x = 2.56$ (approx.), where the coefficients are the number of occurrences of each criterion in the matrix. This leads to:

- Safety: $7x = 18$
- Usability and affordability: $6x = 15$
- Quality and marketability: $5x = 13$
- Functionality and durability: $4x = 10$
- Fabricability: $2x = 5$
- Maintainability: $0x = 1$

Note: The "1" for maintainability arose by gathering all the round-off from the other calculations.

There are obviously problems with this. For example, the lowest-ranked item in a pairwise comparison will, strictly speaking, *always* end up with zero importance. This means that we cannot assume that zero importance implies we can omit it altogether. If, for example, we omit handling because it ranked zero, and redo the pairwise comparison, we will then find that readability and portability will now rank zero. This would quickly lead to a set of *no* criteria at all.

Still, there is now a baseline from which meaningful discussion can ensue. It is noted that we can get the actual weights shown in the concept evaluation matrix by taking a few points away from each criterion and giving them to the handling criterion. This may be enough.

Whatever is done, however, it is *essential that all stakeholders in the project agree to the actual weights.*

Provided by Professor Filippo A. Salustri (salustri@ryerson.ca), Assistant Professor, Mechanical Engineering, Ryerson University, Toronto, Canada.

APPENDIX 9-F

Principles for Responsible Business

INTRODUCTION

The Caux Round Table (CRT) *Principles for Responsible Business* set forth ethical norms for acceptable businesses behavior.

Trust and confidence sustain free markets and ethical business practices provide the basis for such trust and confidence. But lapses in business integrity, whether among the few or the many, compromise such trust and hence the ability of business to serve humanity's needs.

Events like the 2009 global financial crisis have highlighted the necessity of sound ethical practices across the business world. Such failures of governance and ethics cannot be tolerated, as they seriously tarnish the positive contributions of responsible business to higher standards of living and the empowerment of individuals around the world.

The self-interested pursuit of profit, with no concern for other stakeholders, will ultimately lead to business failure and, at times, to counterproductive regulation. Consequently, business leaders must always assert ethical leadership so as to protect the foundations of sustainable prosperity.

It is equally clear that if capitalism is to be respected, and so sustain itself for global prosperity, it must be both responsible and moral. Business therefore needs a moral compass in addition to its practical reliance on measures of profit and loss.

THE CRT PRINCIPLES

The Caux Round Table's approach to responsible business consists of seven core principles as detailed below. The principles recognize that while laws and market forces are necessary, they are insufficient guides for responsible business conduct.

The principles are rooted in three ethical foundations for responsible business and for a fair and functioning society more generally, namely: responsible stewardship; living and working for mutual advantage; and the respect and protection of human dignity.

The principles also have a risk management foundation—because good ethics is good risk management. And they balance the interests of business with the aspirations of society to ensure sustainable and mutual prosperity for all.

The CRT *Principles for Responsible Business* are supported by more detailed Stakeholder Management Guidelines covering each key dimension of business success: customers, employees, shareholders, suppliers, competitors, and communities. These Stakeholder Management Guidelines can be found at Attachment A below.

PRINCIPLE 1—*RESPECT STAKEHOLDERS BEYOND SHAREHOLDERS*

- A responsible business acknowledges its duty to contribute value to society through the wealth and employment it creates and the products and services it provides to consumers.
- A responsible business maintains its economic health and viability not just for shareholders, but also for other stakeholders.
- A responsible business respects the interests of, and acts with honesty and fairness toward, its customers, employees, suppliers, competitors, and the broader community.

PRINCIPLE 2—*CONTRIBUTE TO ECONOMIC, SOCIAL, AND ENVIRONMENTAL DEVELOPMENT*

- A responsible business recognizes that business cannot sustainably prosper in societies that are failing or lacking in economic development.
- A responsible business therefore contributes to the economic, social, and environmental development of the communities in which it operates, in order to sustain its essential "operating" capital—financial, social, environmental, and all forms of goodwill.
- A responsible business enhances society through effective and prudent use of resources, free and fair competition, and innovation in technology and business practices.

PRINCIPLE 3—*BUILD TRUST BY GOING BEYOND THE LETTER OF THE LAW*

- A responsible business recognizes that some business behaviors, although legal, can nevertheless have adverse consequences for stakeholders.
- A responsible business therefore adheres to the spirit and intent behind the law, as well as the letter of the law, which requires conduct that goes beyond minimum legal obligations.
- A responsible business always operates with candor, truthfulness, and transparency, and keeps its promises.

PRINCIPLE 4—*RESPECT RULES AND CONVENTIONS*

- A responsible business respects the local cultures and traditions in the communities in which it operates, consistent with fundamental principles of fairness and equality.

- A responsible business, everywhere it operates, respects all applicable national and international laws, regulations, and conventions, while trading fairly and competitively.

PRINCIPLE 5—*SUPPORT RESPONSIBLE GLOBALIZATION*

- A responsible business, as a participant in the global marketplace, supports open and fair multilateral trade.
- A responsible business supports reform of domestic rules and regulations where they unreasonably hinder global commerce.

PRINCIPLE 6—*RESPECT THE ENVIRONMENT*

- A responsible business protects and, where possible, improves the environment, and avoids wasteful use of resources.
- A responsible business ensures that its operations comply with best environmental management practices consistent with meeting the needs of today without compromising the needs of future generations.

PRINCIPLE 7—*AVOID ILLICIT ACTIVITIES*

- A responsible business does not participate in, or condone, corrupt practices, bribery, money laundering, or other illicit activities.
- A responsible business does not participate in or facilitate transactions linked to or supporting terrorist activities, drug trafficking, or any other illicit activity.
- A responsible business actively supports the reduction and prevention of all such illegal and illicit activities.

Attachment A

STAKEHOLDER MANAGEMENT GUIDELINES

The Caux Round Table's (CRT) Stakeholder Management Guidelines supplement the CRT *Principles for Responsible Business* with more specific standards for engaging with key stakeholder constituencies.

The key stakeholder constituencies are those who contribute to the success and sustainability of business enterprise. Customers provide cash flow by purchasing goods and services; employees produce the goods and services sold; owners and other investors provide funds for the business; suppliers provide vital resources; competitors provide efficient markets; communities provide social capital and operational security for the business; and the environment provides natural resources and other essential conditions.

In turn, key stakeholders are dependent on business for their well-being and prosperity. They are the beneficiaries of ethical business practices.

1. <u>Customers</u>

   A responsible business treats its customers with respect and dignity. Business therefore has a responsibility to:

   a. Provide customers with the highest-quality products and services consistent with their requirements.
   b. Treat customers fairly in all aspects of business transactions, including providing a high level of service and remedies for product or service problems or dissatisfaction.
   c. Ensure that the health and safety of customers is protected.
   d. Protect customers from harmful environmental impacts of products and services.
   e. Respect the human rights, dignity, and the culture of customers in the way products and services are offered, marketed, and advertised.

2. Employees

A responsible business treats every employee with dignity and respects their interests. Business therefore has a responsibility to:

a. Provide jobs and compensation that contribute to improved living standards.

b. Provide working conditions that protect each employee's health and safety.

c. Provide working conditions that enhance each employee's well-being as a citizen, family member, and capable and caring individual.

d. Be open and honest with employees in sharing information, limited only by legal and competitive constraints.

e. Listen to employees and act in good faith on employee complaints and issues.

f. Avoid discriminatory practices and provide equal treatment, opportunity, and pay in areas such as gender, age, race, and religion.

g. Support the employment of differently abled people in places of work where they can be productive.

h. Encourage and assist all employees in developing relevant skills and knowledge.

i. Be sensitive to the impacts of unemployment and work with governments, employee groups, and other agencies in addressing any employee dislocations.

j. Ensure that all executive compensation and incentives further the achievement of long-term wealth creation, reward prudent risk management, and discourage excessive risk taking.

k. Avoid illicit or abusive child labor practices.

3. Shareholders

A responsible business acts with care and loyalty toward its shareholders and in good faith for the best interests of the corporation. Business therefore has a responsibility to:

a. Apply professional and diligent management in order to secure fair, sustainable, and competitive returns on shareholder investments.
b. Disclose relevant information to shareholders, subject only to legal requirements and competitive constraints.
c. Conserve, protect, and increase shareholder wealth.
d. Respect shareholder views, complaints, and formal resolutions.

4. Suppliers

A responsible business treats its suppliers and subcontractors with fairness, truthfulness, and mutual respect. Business therefore has a responsibility to:

a. Pursue fairness and truthfulness in supplier and subcontractor relationships, including pricing, licensing, and payment in accordance with agreed terms of trade.
b. Ensure that business supplier and subcontractor activities are free from coercion and threats.
c. Foster long-term stability in the supplier relationships in return for value, quality, competitiveness, and reliability.
d. Share information with suppliers and integrate them into business planning.
e. Seek, encourage, and prefer suppliers and subcontractors whose employment practices respect human rights and dignity.
f. Seek, encourage, and prefer suppliers and subcontractors whose environmental practices meet best practice standards.

5. Competitors

A responsible business engages in fair competition, which is a basic requirement for increasing the wealth of nations and ultimately for making possible the just distribution of goods and services. Business therefore has a responsibility to:

a. Foster open markets for trade and investment.
b. Promote competitive behavior that is socially and environmentally responsible and demonstrates mutual respect among competitors.
c. Not participate in anticompetitive or collusive arrangements or tolerate questionable payments or favors to secure competitive advantage.
d. Respect both tangible and intellectual property rights.
e. Refuse to acquire commercial information through dishonest or unethical means, such as industrial espionage.

6. COMMUNITIES

As a global corporate citizen, a responsible business actively contributes to good public policy and to human rights in the communities in which it operates. Business therefore has a responsibility to:

a. Respect human rights and democratic institutions, and promote them wherever practicable.
b. Recognize government's legitimate obligation to society at large and support public policies and practices that promote social capital.
c. Promote harmonious relations between business and other segments of society.
d. Collaborate with community initiatives seeking to raise standards of health, education, workplace safety, and economic well-being.
e. Promote sustainable development in order to preserve and enhance the physical environment while conserving the earth's resources.
f. Support peace, security, and the rule of law.
g. Respect social diversity including local cultures and minority communities.
h. Be a good corporate citizen through ongoing community investment and support for employee participation in community and civic affairs.

NOTES

1. The company's press release stated that "EDI's advanced portfolio of plug-in hybrid and full electronic technologies paired with Cummins' industry leadership and focus on innovation will allow us to deliver best-in-class products, service, and support worldwide." See "Cummins Announces Acquisition of Electric and Electric and and Hybrid Powertrain Provider," July 2, 2018, https://www.cummins.com/news/releases/2018/07/02/cummins-announces-acquisition-electric-and-hybrid-powertrain-provider.
2. "Only the combined company will have the network capacity required to quickly create a broad and deep 5G nationwide network in the critical first years of the 5G innovation cycle," stated the T Mobil press release. "T-Mobile and Sprint to Combine, Accelerating 5G Innovation & Increasing Competition," April 29, 2018, http://investor.t-mobile.com/file/Index?KeyFile=393237761.
3. The Art of M&A series has individual titles on strategy, valuation, financing, structuring, due diligence, and integration as well as distressed M&A and bank mergers. This chapter is based in part on the series title *The Art of M&A Integration: A*

Guide to Merging Resources, Processes, and Responsibilities, 2nd ed. (McGraw-Hill, 2006).

4. Robert F. Bruner, "Does M&A Pay," *Applied Mergers & Acquisitions* (New York: McGraw-Hill, 2004), pp. 30–66. See also Robert F. Bruner, *Deals From Hell: M&A Lessons That Rise Above the Ashes* (John Wiley & Sons, 2005).
5. Reinhard Meckl and Falk Röhrle, "Do M&A Deals Create or Destroy Value? A Meta-Analysis, ResearchGate, December 2016 (University of Bayreuth, Bayreuth, Germany), https://www.researchgate.net/publication/322217484_Do_MA_deals_create_or_destroy_value_A_meta-analysis. The SpencerStuart/Bhagat study appears as an appendix ("Smart Money and Smart Bidders") in Dennis C. Carey and Dayton Ogden (with Judith Roland), *The Human Side of M&A: Leveraging the Most Important Factor in Deal Making* (Oxford University Press, 2004).
6. See, for example, this video on the T-Mobile and Sprint merger announced in 2018 (pending as we go to press January 2019): https://www.youtube.com/watch?v=1nsbmtwMrgY.
7. "Rebranding After a Merger or Acquisition: Lessons from Brands Outperforming Market Averages," Cardwell Beach, August 26, 2015, http://www.cardwellbeach.com/rebranding-after-a-merger-or-acquisition-lessons-from-brands-outperforming-market-averages/.
8. See Jonathan Knowles et al., "Why Fusing Company Identities Can Add Value," *Harvard Business Review,* September 2011, https://hbr.org/2011/09/why-fusing-company-identities-can-add-value.
9. See Tommy Hsu, "Should the Acquired Brand Be Dumped After the Merger?" *Journal of Business Studies Quarterly,* vol. 9, no. 1 (2017). The author states that his research results suggest that "if the acquiring and acquired firms are perceived to be similar by consumers (like Continental Airlines and United Airlines), the acquiring firm should discontinue the acquired brand and just keep its own brand. On the other

hand, if consumers think that the two firms are different (like Amazon.com and Zappos.com), both brand names should be kept to serve two distinct markets." http://jbsq.org/wp-content/uploads/2017/09/September_2017_1.pdf.

10. Carol Gilhawley, "Time to Bank on a Name Change," *ABA Marketing,* July 11, 2017. Also see Brandon Kochkodin, What's in a Hedge Fund Name," Bloomberg, May 16, 2018, https://www.bloomberg.com/news/articles/2018-05-16/what-s-in-a-hedge-fund-name-apparently-booze-boats-and-boston.
11. See Stanislav Sinitsky, "Naming a Business: 7 Popular Business Name Generators," blog post, January 10, 2017, https://anadea.info/blog/7-popular-business-name-generators.
12. See, for example, this FAQ from Berkshire Hathaway about one of the companies in its real estate portfolio that merged with another one and kept its name: http://www.bhhscarolinas.com/pdf/FAQPress.pdf.
13. See B. Kenneth West, "Does the Corporation Have a Soul?" *Directors Monthly,* February 2003. For a discussion of company soul in the context of M&A, see Lajoux, *The Art of M&A Integration,* op. cit., note 3, p. 192.
14. This definition is based on the writings of John H. Bodley, author of *Cultural Anthropology: Tribe, State, and the Global System,* 6th ed. (Lanham, MD: AltaMira Press, Rowman & Littlefield Publishers, 2018).
15. Kate Patrick, "Mackey: Marriage to Amazon Poses Challenges as Cultures Mesh," Supply Chain Dive, October 16, 2017, https://www.supplychaindive.com/news/john-mackey-marriage-amazon-challenge-whole-foods-merger-culture/507300/.
16. This was named as a culturally troubled deal in Darcy Jacobsen, "Six Big Mergers That Were Killed by Culture," globeforce.com, September 26, 2012, https://resources.globoforce.com/globoforce-blog/6-big-mergers-that-were-killed-by-culture-and-how-to-stop-it-from-killing-yours.
17. The source for the Renault-Nissan case is Steven H. Appelbaum, "Cultural Strategies in M&As: Investigating Ten

Case Studies," *Journal of Executive Education,* vol. 8, issue 1 (October 2013), https://digitalcommons.kennesaw.edu/cgi/viewcontent.cgi?referer=https://www.google.com/&httpsredir=1&article=1031&context=jee.

18. Tekla S. Perry, "No-Poaching Pacts Broke with Silicon Valley Culture," *IEEE Spectrum,* May 8, 2014, https://spectrum.ieee.org/view-from-the-valley/at-work/tech-careers/nopoaching-deal-didnt-just-break-the-law-it-broke-with-silicon-valley-culture.
19. This answer and the following one were contributed by Ellen Owens, director of business transformation at Avnet, a global technology company. She is a member of the Board of M&A Standards, as referenced in the front matter of this book.
20. For more on these models, see Ben Mullholland, "Eight Critical Change Management Models to Evolve and Survive," https://www.process.st/change-management-models/.
21. Time Creasey, "The Correlation Between Change Management and Project Success," in an undated blog citing a 2016 study. https://blog.prosci.com/the-correlation-between-change-management-and-project-success.
22. Alexandra R. Lajoux and Antonio Nieto Rodriguez, "'Project M&A'—10 Ways to Apply the Science of Project Management to the Art of M&A," *Financier Worldwide,* August 2016, https://www.financierworldwide.com/project-ma-10-ways-to-apply-the-science-of-project-management-to-the-art-of-ma/#.W99__pNKjIU.
23. An example of a vision statement appears in PepsiCo's 2018 proxy statement, as follows: "Performance with Purpose is our vision to deliver top-tier financial performance over the long term by integrating sustainability into our business strategy, leaving a positive imprint on society and the environment." https://www.sec.gov/Archives/edgar/data/77476/000120677418000850/pep_courtesy-pdf.pdf.
24. See Disclosure Required by Sections 406 and 407 of the Sarbanes-Oxley Act of 2002, March 3, 2003, www.sec.gov/rules/final/33-8177.htm.

25. Our Code of Ethics and Business Conduct, Wells Fargo, 2018, https://www08.wellsfargomedia.com/assets/pdf/about/corporate/code-of-ethics.pdfhttps://www08.wellsfargomedia.com/assets/pdf/about/corporate/code-of-ethics.pdf.
26. For specific guidance on integration of sales teams, senior management teams, and boards of directors, see Lajoux, *The Art of M&A Integration,* op. cit., note 3, pp. 119–127. Regarding board integration, there are three studies of note: Kevin McLaughlin and Chinmoy Ghosh, *The Dynamics of Post-Merger Boards: Retention Decisions and Performance Effects* (posted in 2019 on ResearchGate); DHR International, *Risks and Realities of Post-M&A Board Reorganisation: Just How Vulnerable Are Directors Following a Merger?* (a DHR International white paper, July 2016); Johanne Bouchard and Ken Smith, "Advice for Effective Board Mergers," *NACD Directorship,* September/October 2014.
27. Frank Roebroek, "Early HR Involvement Is Critical for the Success of M&A Deals," *Trends in HR,* April 24, 2017.
28. This chapter benefited from comments by Wendy Parkes, Managing Director of Human Resources, Global Acquisitions and Divestitures, BMO Financial Group, retired.
29. This is what Consolidated Foods did in 1985 when it renamed itself Sarah Lee Corporation after one of its acquired brands. Today the company is part of Tyson Foods.
30. For example, one observer expressed the opinion that despite United Airlines' use of the Continental logo, it lost an opportunity to capitalize more on the Continental brand following the acquisition. See Beach, "Rebranding After a Merger or Acquisition," op. cit., note 7.
31. The answer to this question was provided by Jennifer Lee, Vice President, McKesson Corporation.
32. These terms were first introduced in a National Science Foundation study by Professor Alok Chakrabarti, of the New Jersey Institute of Technology, in "Organizational Factors in Post-Acquisition Performance," *IEEE Transactions in*

Engineering Management, vol. 37, no. 4 (November 1990), pp. 259ff. Today Dr. Chakrabarti is Distinguished Professor and Foundation Professor Emeritus at the New Jersey Institute of Technolgy. http://management.njit.edu/people/chakrabarti.php.

33. Ethan S. Bernstein and Stephen Turban, "The Impact of the 'Open' Workspace on Human Collaboration," *Philosophical Transactions of the Royal Society B,* July 2, 2018, https://royalsocietypublishing.org/doi/full/10.1098/rstb.2017.0239.
34. The source of this insight is Lawrence Gordon, Y Alumni Professor of Managerial Accounting and Information Assurance at the University of Maryland Robert H. Smith School of Business. http://scholar.rhsmith.umd.edu/lgordon/home?destination=home.
35. https://www.iso.org/news/2015/09/Ref2002.html.
36. https://www.iso.org/about-us.html.
37. https://www.iso.org/iso-9001-quality-management.html.
38. US Securities and Exchange Commission, "Management's Reports on Internal Control Over Financial Reporting and Certification of Disclosure in Exchange Act Periodic Reports," www.sec.gov/rules/final/33-8238.htm#iia. For current SEC FAQs on the topic, see https://www.sec.gov/info/accountants/controlfaq.htm.
39. AS 2201: An Audit of Internal Control Over Financial Reporting That Is Integrated with an Audit of Financial Statements, effective since 2007, https://pcaobus.org/Standards/Auditing/Pages/AS2201.aspx.
40. For example, in addition to its framework for internal control, it has one for risk management. The COSO ERM framework is organized into five interrelated components: governance and culture; strategy and objective-setting; performance; review and revision; and information, communication, and reporting. Enterprise Risk Management Integrating with Strategy and Performance, COSO, June 2017, https://www.coso.org/Documents/2017-COSO-ERM-Integrating-with-Strategy-and-Performance-Executive-Summary.pdf.

41. The current COSO standard can be conceptualized as lines of defense. The first line of defense is the internal control system set by management. The second line of defense is an additional set of controls: Financial Control Security Risk Management Quality Inspection Compliance. The third line of defense is an internal audit function, checked finally by the external auditor and by regulators. "Leveraging COSO Across the Three Lines of Defense," https://www.coso.org/Documents/COSO-2015-3LOD.pdf.
42. Internal Control: Integrated Framework, COSO, 2013, https://www.coso.org/Pages/ic.aspx.
43. As noted by one reporter, "[A]t any given time, a majority of the market is now determined not by humans making decisions but by computers trading with one another based on programs. There are no hard and fast numbers, though JP Morgan recently estimated that only 10 percent of trading now consists of people trading with people based on fundamental decisions about company A or company B." Zachary Karabell, "How Technology Unsettled the Stock Market," *Wired,* March 3, 2018, https://www.wired.com/story/how-technology-unsettled-the-stock-market/.
44. "When a registrant presents a non-GAAP measure it must present the most directly comparable GAAP measure with equal or greater prominence." See US Securities and Exchange Commission, "Non-GAAP Financial Measures," https://www.sec.gov/divisions/corpfin/guidance/nongaapinterp.htm.
45. Ibid.
46. http://wallstreet.cch.com/LCM/.
47. Report on Corporate Governance, International Organization of Securities Commissions (IOSCO), October 2016, http://www.iosco.org/library/pubdocs/pdf/IOSCOPD544.pdf.
48. See "Guiding Principles of Good Governance," May 6, 2015, under Papers, at Global Network of Director Institutes, gndi.org.
49. See "Valuation of Portfolio Securities and Other Assets Held by

Registered Investment Companies—Select Bibliography of the Division of Investment Management" at https://www.sec.gov/divisions/investment/icvaluation.htm.

50. Joseph C. Faucher and Dylan R. Rudolph, "ERISA Stock Drop Cases Since Dudenhoffer: The Pleading Standard Has Been Raised," Trucker Huss, APC, December 13, 2017, https://www.truckerhuss.com/2017/12/erisa-stock-drop-cases-since-dudenhoeffer-the-pleading-standard-has-been-raised/.
51. "New Regulations Introduce Major Changes to ERISA Disability Benefits Claims Procedures," American Bar Association, May 1, 2018, https://www.americanbar.org/groups/labor_law/publications/ebc_news_archive/new-regulations-introduce-major-changes-to-erisa-disability-bene.html.
52. "NLRB Launches Pilot of Proactive Alternative Dispute Resolution Program," NLRB, July 10, 2018, https://www.nlrb.gov/news-outreach/news-story/nlrb-launches-pilot-proactive-alternative-dispute-resolution-program.
53. https://www.erieri.com/geographicassessor.
54. UAW-GM Center for Human Resources Joint Activity System (JAS), https://www.uawgmjas.org/j/.
55. The pay-versus-performance rule proposed in 2015 and still pending as of late 2018 defines performance as average annual TSR over a three-year-period. https://www.sec.gov/rules/proposed/2015/34-74835.pdf.
56. Companies that exceeded these amounts have offered tax gross-up payment so the employee did not have to pay those extra taxes—a practice unpopular with shareholders.
57. For the current explanation from the Internal Revenue Service, see https://www.irs.gov/pub/irs-utl/goldenparachuteatg.pdf.
58. "[T]he failure rate for Say on Golden Parachute Votes has increased each year for the same period, with 22.5% of Russell 3000 companies failing to win approval of a majority of their shareholders for such golden parachute proposals in the first nine months of 2017 (compared to 7% of companies in 2015

and 11% of companies in 2016)." Joseph M. Yaffe and Lindsay Docto, "Market Trends: Say on Pay, Frequency, and Golden Parachute Payments," Skadden Arps Meagher and Flom, 2018.

59. Albert H. Choi, et al., "Shareholder Voting on Golden Parachutes: Determinants and Consequences," Virginia Law and Economics Research Paper No. 2018-13 (posted August 20, 2018). See note 56 for context on tax gross-ups. https://corpgov.law.harvard.edu/2018/08/20/shareholder-vote-on-golden-parachutes-determinants-and-consequences/.
60. See Matthew M. Friestedt and J. Michael Snypes, Jr., "Section 280G: The Law and Lore of the Golden Parachute Excise Tax, Part I: The Structure and Operation of Section 280G," *Journal of Compensation and Benefits,* July-August 2017, https://www.sullcrom.com/files/upload/Friestedt_Journal_Compensation_Benefits_July_August_2017.pdf.
61. This section was provided by John Hotta, cofounder, Capital Expert Services, LLC, and retired senior executive, Microsoft Corporation.
62. For a wealth of guidance on the merging of HRIS systems, visit shrm.org. (Membership required.)
63. See US Securities and Exchange Commission, "Updated Statement on the Effect of the Court of Appeals Decision on the Conflict Minerals Rule," April 7, 2017, https://www.sec.gov/news/public-statement/corpfin-updated-statement-court-decision-conflict-minerals-rule.
64. For a sample set of codes for a chart of accounts, see https://www.sba.gov/sbic/sbic-resource-library/accounting-valuation-standards/chart-accounts-sbics.
65. This closing section owes a great debt to Bill Blandford, Manager of M&A (retired), Nokia, and Board of M&A Standards board member.
66. The State of the Deal: M&A Trends 2018, Deloitte, 2018, https://www2.deloitte.com/content/dam/Deloitte/us/Documents/mergers-acqisitions/us-mergers-acquisitions-2018-trends-report.pdf.

CHAPTER 10

Special Issues for M&A in Public Companies

INTRODUCTION

So far, this book has discussed transactions involving all kinds of companies, whatever their ownership status (private, closely held, or public). This chapter should serve as a guide through the unique legal and business considerations that affect acquisitions of public companies, with an emphasis on US securities laws.

Public companies offer distinct challenges for M&A. By definition, the equity in such companies is held by the public—large numbers of owners, including powerful institutional owners holding large blocks of stock. Also, by definition, these companies are heavily regulated, as state and federal regulators see themselves as the protectors of the public interest.

This chapter begins with general and legal principles relevant to M&A of public companies. It then covers the two main ways to gain control of a public company—the *tender offer* and the *proxy challenge*. (A tender offer is a general, publicized bid by an individual or group to buy shares of a publicly owned company at a price significantly above the current market price for cash, stock, or a combination of both. A proxy challenge is an effort to effect a change of control by getting shareholders to vote their shares for a dissident slate of directors via proxy at a shareholders meeting.) A section on how to disclose changes of control follows.

In conclusion, readers will find a brief discussion of takeover defenses and state laws that enable them. (For international considerations, see Chapter 12.)

The bulk of this chapter will focus on friendly transactions involving the voluntary, negotiated sale of public companies in whole or in part. Most of the rules and regulations cited here, however, apply as well to *hostile acquisitions* pursued directly with shareholders via a tender offer or proxy solicitation rather than negotiated with the target's board of directors. This is important to note, since virtually every company selling equity securities to the public (out of 8,800 companies in the United States as of 2019,[1] roughly half sell equity on US stock exchanges[2]) is vulnerable in this regard. So if you are a director, officer, employee, or advisor involved with a public company, this chapter is must reading.

GENERAL CONSIDERATIONS

What exactly is a "public" company and why would a company's "public" status affect an acquisition?

Generally speaking, a public company is one that sells securities (stocks and/or bonds) to the general public. Because of their impact on society, publicly held companies are subject to a relatively high number of federal and state securities laws, compared to privately held companies.

What exactly is a security?

The Securities Act of 1933 defines security broadly as follows:

> The term "security" means any note, stock, treasury stock, bond, debenture, evidence of indebtedness, certificate of interest or participation in any profit-sharing agreement, collateral-trust certificate, preorganization certificate or subscription, transferable share, investment contract, voting-trust certificate, certificate of deposit for a security, fractional undivided interest in

oil, gas, or other mineral rights, any put, call, straddle, option, or privilege on any security, certificate of deposit, or group or index of securities (including any interest therein or based on the value thereof), or any put, call, straddle, option, or privilege entered into on a national securities exchange relating to foreign currency, or, in general, any interest or instrument commonly known as a "security," or any certificate of interest or participation in, temporary or interim certificate for, receipt for, guarantee of, or warrant or right to subscribe to or purchase, any of the foregoing.[3]

When a company sells securities to the general public, it becomes subject to securities laws. These laws also affect transactions involving public companies, including M&A transactions.

What are the main differences between buying a public company and buying a private company?[4]

First, let's note similarities. In both kinds of transaction, the board of directors of both the buying and the selling companies must fulfill their fiduciary duties of care and loyalty under state law. Furthermore, basic principles of all the phases discussed earlier in this book—planning, valuation, financing, structuring, due diligence, and closing—apply to both kinds of transactions.

As far as differences go, transactions involving public companies tend to be more complex. The structure, timing, financing, and negotiation of the purchase of a public company are all greatly affected by federal and state securities laws. To understand and negotiate a public company acquisition, the first step is to gain a working understanding of the basic federal securities laws that govern the transaction. These include not only the rules on acquiring a controlling interest in a company (through a partial acquisition or a tender offer for all shares) but also rules on disclosure of negotiations, insider trading, and certain filings upon the acquisition of a 5 percent or more holding of common equity in the target. Because of these rules, any acquisition of a public company is conducted in a fishbowl, as most aspects of the transaction quickly become public knowledge.

Also, the financing of tender offers is subject to certain unique rules that make this kind of financing somewhat more difficult than the normal financing. Moreover, the necessary statutory and practical delays in closing the transaction provide ample opportunity for a new bidder to arrive on the scene. In fact, the board of directors of the selling company may be required under state securities law to provide information to a competing bidder. This can mean the board may no longer be required (or even allowed) to recommend the agreed-upon transaction to stockholders once a better, credible offer is on the table. In any event, the stockholders will be free either to vote against the proposed merger with the buyer or to tender their shares into a more desirable tender offer. Thus, in a public company transaction, an agreement by the board on behalf of the company has only limited value when another bidder appears on the scene with a bid that seems more favorable.

The biggest challenge is the fact that the stock of the target company *continues to trade during the period of the offer.* Once the acquirer makes an offer to current owners, the price of the stock goes up. Then arbitrageurs buy the shares, hoping to sell out at a higher price later. These purchases effectively reduce the premium that is being paid above market price. Also, as a result of the publicity surrounding its offer, the buyer becomes a stalking horse to attract other bidders. This can put the first bidder at a disadvantage, as it will have incurred substantial transaction expenses such as legal and accounting fees and it may have laid out significant sums as commitment fees to lenders to arrange for financing. The first buyer may have also passed up other investment opportunities while pursuing the acquisition of the target.

Ironically, the individuals making the decision in a public company acquisition are often people who will not be there for the long haul to ensure that the company succeeds or to benefit from its success. In a tender offer, for example, the shareholders who enable the transaction are shareholders who sell their shares to the acquirer. By definition, they will not be there to own the resulting company. Thus, they may be indifferent to postmerger performance and its repercussions on remaining shareholders and on employees, communities, and other parties. Thanks to state laws protecting "other constituencies" (discussed at the end of this chapter), these additional interests may be considered by boards as they respond to offers.

Could you give an overview of federal and state laws that apply when buying a US public company?

The United States has a federalist system of government with both federal and state components.

At the federal level, securities laws are encompassed in two main laws: the previously mentioned Securities Act of 1933 (commonly referred to as the Securities Act), which sets forth registration requirements for public companies, and the more extensive Securities Exchange Act of 1934 (commonly called the Exchange Act), which sets the disclosure and filing requirements. Securities Act rules are found in the US Code, Title 17, Part 230,[5] while Exchange Act rules are found in the US.Code of Federal Regulations, Title 17, Part 240.[6]

The basic text of these federal laws has been amended and expanded over time under the aegis of the SEC, the independent federal agency created to promulgate and administer rules and regulations under the Securities Act and the Exchange Act. The two main sections of federal securities laws most likely to create liability are Section 11 and Section 12 of the Securities Act, pertaining to the offering of securities, and Section 10(b) and Section 14 of the Exchange Act, pertaining to the exchange of securities. Another very well traveled legal section in M&A is Section 16(b) of the Exchange Act, which restricts "short-swing" trading—that is, selling stock within six months after receiving it.

The most significant expansion of securities laws affecting mergers was the Tender Offer Act of 1968, known as the Williams Act, after its original sponsor. The Williams Act and amendments became Exchange Act Sections 13(d) and 14(d) (discussed later in this chapter).

At the state level, where corporations must incorporate, state laws govern corporate charters and bylaws. State corporate statutes set forth minimum requirements for the charters of companies in the state, including the duties and responsibilities of company directors and officers, such as their fiduciary duties of care and loyalty in conducting business.

There is some uniformity, thanks to the influence of Delaware, which is often used as a prototype for state corporate statutes. Another source of influence is the Model Business Corporation Act, a suggested template that is continually updated under the auspices of a committee of the American Bar Association (ABA).[7]

What is the current state of shareholder litigation over M&A?

Major public company mergers commonly attract lawsuits alleging violation of securities laws. See Exhibit 10-1. This exhibit highlights a few of more than a dozen federal securities provisions that may be cited in an M&A claim.[8]

What is the current state of shareholder litigation over M&A?

Major public company mergers commonly attract lawsuits alleging violation of securities laws. In general, securities class action lawsuits may be

Exhibit 10-1 Some Typical Plaintiff Claims in M&A Litigation

SECURITIES ACT OF 1933

- Section 11—Plaintiffs claim material misstatements or omissions in a registration statement. (Claim does not require scienter —due diligence defense applies.)
- Section 12—Plaintiffs claim scienter of fraud in a registration statement.

SECURITIES ACT OF 1934

- Section 10—Rule 10(b)5—Plaintiffs claim scienter of fraud in the purchase or sale of a security.
- Section 14—Plaintiffs in 14(a) claim fraud in a proxy statement; plaintiffs in 14(e) claim scienter of fraud in a tender offer.

sparked by some current event such as the Chinese credit crisis, cryptocurrency failures, or the credit crisis, but at a technical legal level, lawsuits typically allege a violation of one of the following: Section 11 of the Securities Act of 1933 regarding the securities prospectus, or any of the following sections of the Securities and Exchange Act of 1934: Section 10(b) regarding fraud or deceit in relation to buying or selling a security; Section 12(a) for registration requirements; or Section 14(a) for proxy solicitations. Any of these alleged violations can be named in a lawsuit over a merger, but in recent federal class actions the dominant allegation has been violation of Section 14(a).

M&A class action lawsuits under Section 14 spiked in federal courts in 2017 when Delaware and other states limited disclosure-only cases, and the trend continued since then. In 2017 and 2018, nearly half of shareholder class actions in federal court involved mergers and invoked Section 14.[9] See Exhibit 10-2.

Exhibit 10-2 Federal Class Actions on M&A 2010–2018

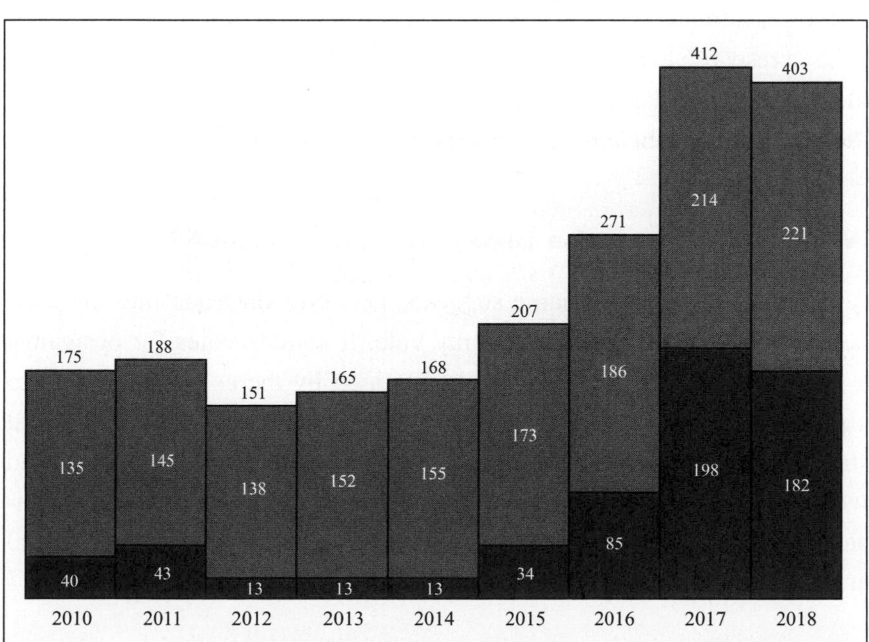

Based on data in Cornerstone Research, 2019, https://www.cornerstone.com/Publications/Reports/Securities-Class-Action-Filings-2018-YIR.

PROXY VOTING

How does the proxy voting system work?

The shareowner receives a proxy statement that lists matters up for a shareholder vote, and votes on these matters. Then the votes are counted to determine the outcome of the various matters. The process sounds simple, but it is in fact quite complex—involving proxy solicitors, proxy advisors, proxy voting services, transfer agents, vote tabulators, and vote inspectors, among others. Many, including the staff of the SEC, say it needs reform.[10] In late 2018, the SEC held a roundtable to discuss, among other topics, voting process, retail shareholder participation, shareholder proposals, and proxy advisory firms, requesting comments on these topics.[11]

What is the role of a proxy advisor?

A proxy advisor gives recommendations to shareholders on how they should vote on the various issues that are in the proxy card for a vote every year. Funds that hold shares in many companies use these services to save research expense. They sometimes provide their own general voting guidelines and ask the proxy advisor to apply it in particular cases, or they may rely on the advisory's own view of a matter.

What is the role of a proxy solicitor in M&A?

A proxy solicitor, as its name suggests, performs outreach into the market to affect the outcome of a proxy vote. It solicits votes for or against a proxy matter. Such a firm may be retained by the company subject to a proxy challenge, or by the challenger. A solicitor may provide general strategic advice, or specific research on who is in the shareholder base and what they are doing. A solicitor can also help with shareholder communications, proxy advisor relations, and ongoing relations with institutional and retail shareholders.

What is the role of a transfer agent?

Transfer agents keep track of the individuals and entities that own a company's stocks and bonds. Sometimes a company can act as its own transfer agent, but most transfer agents are banks or depository trust companies. Transfer agents issue and cancel certificates to reflect changes in ownership, and they handle lost, stolen, or destroyed certificates. A transfer agent may also serve as the company's paying agent to pay out interest, cash and stock dividends, or other distributions to stock- and bondholders. In addition, transfer agents act as proxy agents by sending out proxy materials, exchange agents by exchanging a company's stock or bonds in a merger, tender agents by tendering shares in a tender offer, and/or mailing agents by mailing the company's quarterly, annual, and other reports. Many of these functions are now digitized, changing the nature of the transfer agent's work.[12]

DODD-FRANK, SARBANES-OXLEY, AND M&A

How did the Dodd-Frank Act impact mergers?

Dodd-Frank, signed into law July 2010 after a financial crisis in which global equity shares lost half their value in less than a year and a half,[13] included numerous provisions regulating banks, including, notably, large banks considered to be systemically important financial institutions (SIFIs). One research paper found a post-Dodd-Frank rise in consolidation among large banks near or just over the SIFI threshold.[14] Then, when the administration of President Donald Trump began deregulating banks,[15] there were predictions of another rise in bank consolidation.[16]

How did Sarbanes-Oxley impact mergers?

The Sarbanes-Oxley Act of 2002, and the new disclosure rules and stock exchange listing standards it required, focused attention on the importance of internal audit controls, the external auditor, and the audit committee. (In fact, the formal name of the law is Accounting Reform and Protection Act of 2002.) Auditing, in essence, means having accounting double-checked by an independent expert.

The overall impact of all of these audit-focused rules has been to add more paperwork and cost to everything, but at the same time to reduce the likelihood of business failure due to undetected risk. As mentioned in Chapter 9, in a discussion on due diligence, acquirers have generally benefited from Section 404 of the act, since it increased the level of attention to and documentation of internal controls. This has helped acquirers streamline the financial aspect of their due diligence prior to closing.

Notably, one section in Sarbanes-Oxley (Section 306(a)) requires administrators of corporate pension plans to give 30 days' advance notice to plan participants and beneficiaries if there will be any "blackout" period, during which no plan access is permitted. However, there is a more lenient standard for companies involved in mergers, which are not required to give such a long advance notice.[17]

DUTIES OF CARE AND LOYALTY

How do the fiduciary duties of care and loyalty under state law apply in M&A?

In general, they mean that directors and officers must exercise care in making the decision to buy or sell, and in doing so, they must in good faith serve the company's interests, not their own, in approving a transaction. Meanings of these three concepts develop over time as various courts make decisions in particular matters.

To elaborate, a director owes a *duty of care to the company,* which means acting on behalf of the company and its owners by making informed decisions after obtaining all reasonably available information required to make an intelligent decision and after evaluating all relevant circumstances—including, arguably, whether a company has a workable system for reporting and compliance, as implied in the famous *Caremark* case.[18] A director of a corporation also owes a *duty of loyalty* to act in the best interests of the corporation and its shareholders, for which he or she is a fiduciary. As such, the director is prohibited from entering into a transaction that is tainted by fraud or bad faith, or in which the director has a personal interest. If it appears that a director has a personal interest in a particular corporate transaction, a court often will shift the burden of proof to the director to show that the transaction is fair and that it serves the best interests of the corporation and its shareholders. In the June 2018 case of Certisign Holding, the court defined the duty of loyalty as a "public policy, existing through the years [that] demands of a corporate officer or director, peremptorily and inexorably, the most scrupulous observance of the duty, not only affirmatively to protect the interests of the corporation committed to his charge, but also to refrain from doing anything that would work injury to the corporation."[19]

As part of the duty of loyalty, a director owes a *duty of good faith.* In the August 2005 Disney case before the Delaware Court of Chancery, Chancellor William Chandler wrote about this duty in a broad sense. "The good faith required of a corporate fiduciary includes not simply the duties of care and loyalty, in the narrow sense that I have discussed them above, but all actions required by a true faithfulness and devotion to the interests of the corporation and its shareholders."[20] However, a later case (*Stone v. Ritter,* 2006) opined that the duty of good faith was not a third duty, but rather a subset of the duty of loyalty.[21] If directors and officers meet their fiduciary duties of care and loyalty, their business decisions, even if flawed, receive protection from lawsuits in state court, under a judicial concept called the business judgment rule, a judicial doctrine applied by courts in cases where shareholders have sued directors for violating their fiduciary duties to the corporation. The rule is that the board of directors will be protected unless the shareholders can prove that in making a business decision a director did not act with due care and loyalty to the corporation. The business judgment rule protects directors from liability if they act in a manner consistent with their duties of due care and loyalty.

Nuances of legal interpretation have made fiduciary duties and the business judgment rule complex. The leading legal treatise on the topic is more than 6,000 pages long![22] Most major law firms offer very good guidance on these concepts and the latest cases involving them.

Because fiduciary duties are owed primarily (although not exclusively) to shareholders, most cases alleging failure to fulfill the duties are brought by shareholders, and most of these cases involve public companies, which by definition have more dispersion of equity ownership than private companies. For cases involving fiduciary duties of directors and officers in a merger, see the final chapter of this book, "Landmark and Recent M&A Legal Cases."

DIRECTOR RESPONSIBILITIES IN RESPONDING TO UNSOLICITED BIDS

What standards do courts use to judge the decisions of boards that vote to sell a company?

Directors have four main standards for their conduct in an M&A situation, depending on circumstances.[23] Each of the standards has been the subject of detailed expert analysis beyond the scope of this chapter. Here is a simple explanation of each, listed from least stringent to most stringent:

1. *Business judgment rule.* Under this general standard, the court will not second-guess the board's decision.
2. *Unocal.* Under this standard, from *Unocal v. Mesa Petroleum Co.* (1985), which applies in a contest for corporate control (i.e., a takeover threat), directors can receive protections of the business judgment rule only if their response to a perceived threat is "reasonable in proportion to the threat posed."[24]
3. *Revlon.* This standard, deriving from the case *Revlon, Inc. v. MacAndrews & Forbes Holdings* (1986), applies once a company is for sale. It requires that directors attempt to obtain the best sale price for the company.[25]
4. *Entire fairness.* This standard, which is triggered when one of the parties to a transaction is "interested" (e.g., owns controlling shares), is the strictest of all. It is a legal doctrine that says a transaction must be completely fair to all parties involved; it requires both a fair price and a fair process. This standard may be waived when a transaction includes protection for minority shareholders.

What are the primary responsibilities of a corporate board of directors upon receipt of a takeover bid?

The director's primary responsibility is to evaluate all bona fide offers and to recommend corporate action; in the case of a hostile bid, to also recommend shareholder action. Under the *Unocal* standard mentioned earlier, they may take reasonable protective measures to maintain company independence. This said, directors cannot refuse to consider reasonable offers and expect protection from the business judgment rule.

In the *Revlon* case mentioned earlier, the court described the role of the board of directors as that of a price-oriented "neutral auctioneer" once a decision has been made to sell the company. (In a private company the people making the decision to sell to a particular buyer are themselves the owners, so the *Revlon* duty would be a moot point.) In general, this means that boards should give preference to the bidder most likely to deliver superior returns to shareholders, to whom directors owe their primary fiduciary duty. There are exceptions, though. State "constituency" statutes and shifting interpretations of the business judgment rule can give boards more decision-making discretion in responding to tender offers.

How does a director's duty of care apply in responding to a tender offer bid?

Under this standard, the directors' duty is not merely to try to arrive at the best possible decision for the corporation but to make their decision only after careful, informed deliberation. Both the process of decision making and the substantive decisions themselves are taken into consideration by courts in evaluating whether directors acted with due care.

The 1985 Delaware case of *Smith v. Van Gorkom* dealt a blow to the business judgment rule when the Delaware court found that the board of directors of Trans Union and, in particular, Trans Union's chief executive officer, Jerome Van Gorkom, were personally liable for actions taken in connection with approving and recommending to shareholders a cash-out merger proposal. The court held that they were not entitled to the protection of the business judgment rule even though Van Gorkom and the other board members may well have been highly qualified to make their decisions and had obtained a substantial premium over the market price for the shares of Trans Union.

The significant element in *Van Gorkom* is that the court did not concern itself primarily with the ultimate decision (which was arguably a very good one for the shareholders of Trans Union) but instead emphasized the importance of the correct decision-making process. Directors must make informed decisions and take careful steps to ensure that they are acting responsibly.

What are "material" facts?

Material facts are those that are important enough to influence the buying or selling decisions of an ordinary investor. Dealmakers involved with public company transactions must understand materiality. This chapter, for example, uses the term *material* as an adjective a few dozen times. Yet like many important concepts in securities law, *material* does not have a hard-and-fast definition. In its current Statement of Financial Accounting Concept No. 8, the FASB states: "Materiality is a legal concept. In the United States, a legal concept may be established or changed through legislative, executive, or judicial action. The Board observes but does not promulgate definitions of materiality." By contrast, in its earliest definition, Financial Accounting Concept No. 2, the Board noted:

> The omission or misstatement of an item in a financial report is material if, in the light of surrounding circumstances, the magnitude of the item is such that it is probable that the judgment of a reasonable person relying upon the report would have been changed or influenced by the inclusion or correction of the item.

After undergoing several revisions and challenges, the FASB has declared that its next definition of materiality, to be released in 2019, will be based on this definition. (See Exhibit 7-3 in Chapter 7 for the history.)

What impact do fiduciary duties have on M&A transactions of public companies?

First, these duties affect timing. The need for the board to act with due care will restrict the board's ability to act quickly even on a friendly offer. It is considered recommended practice to have a special committee and to obtain a fairness opinion.

Second, the duties, as interpreted by the courts may limit the ability of the board to take action that either eliminates the possibility of a competing bid—so-called lockups—or other arrangements (breakup and topping fees and "no shop" clauses) that are designed (in part) to frustrate the efforts of other bidders. These arrangements are among the most negotiated provisions of the public deal.

For the aforementioned reasons, the buyer will try to minimize the risk of a successful competing bid and will look for ways to get compensated if it loses to another bidder. The next several questions deal with these issues in the context of the board's fiduciary responsibilities to the shareholders.

When is it appropriate for a selling company to appoint a special committee of its board of directors to review a proposed transaction?

It is always a good idea to appoint such a committee, especially if the transaction is a major one. In addition, it is critical to do so if some members of the board of directors have or could have a personal interest in the proposed merger (for example, if there are members of management who would benefit personally from buying or selling). A special committee is also appropriate where a proposed transaction is complex enough to require careful study for the board to act responsibly. Having a special committee with adequate authority over the transaction will tend to shift to a plaintiff the burden of showing that the transaction is unfair. If the plaintiff has that burden, this makes it more difficult for it to get a court to hold a hearing and issue "injunctive relief" against the merger (order the companies to refrain from going through with it).

What is the role of counsel to the special committee?

Counsel should advise the members of the special committee about the current interpretation of the business judgment rule in the company's jurisdiction of incorporation. In addition, counsel should advise the committee of any potential liability for its actions and the extent to which it may be indemnified or otherwise protected under the company's charter and bylaws and directors' and officers' liability insurance.

Counsel should attend each meeting of the special committee and should prepare or review minutes of each meeting. These minutes should be reviewed for accuracy by each member of the committee. In the event that the proposed transaction may attract other offers, counsel to the special committee should be prepared to advise the committee about the duty of the directors to obtain the best possible price for all shareholders. Counsel should also advise the committee of the extent of its obligations to consider such offers and techniques that it may and may not employ to enhance or limit bidding opportunities.

Which directors are appropriate members of a special committee?

A special committee should consist of independent or disinterested directors. Such directors must not have any financial or personal interest in the proposed transaction that would inhibit their ability to act in an unbiased manner.

What are the benefits of a special committee?

Although there is no guarantee that a special committee will legitimize board action, such a committee may be extremely helpful in, and perhaps essential to, providing directors with the protection of the business judgment rule. It should be noted, however, that courts will closely scrutinize the facts surrounding the actions of the board, and that the mere formation of a special committee will not protect the directors from liability for careless actions.

What steps should a special committee take to ensure that it is acting responsibly and effectively?

The special committee should examine all information about the proposed transaction. This examination must be thorough, and members of the special committee should question carefully the persons supplying such information to be sure the information is complete and accurate. The committee should also take care not to act hastily and should make sure that it documents its deliberations. Recent judicial decisions have indicated that directors who make decisions without adequate deliberation may have difficulty in establishing that they acted with the care necessary to provide the protection of the business judgment rule.

To be most effective, the special committee should have access to and seek the perspective of the investor relations officer in the company. If IROs are doing their job, they have their fingers on the collective pulse of the owners—particularly the major institutional owners.

Should a special committee retain independent advisors?

In the context of mergers and acquisitions, the special committee of a board of directors should retain independent legal counsel and financial advisors.

Should a special committee obtain a fairness opinion?

Yes, but the opinion must be from a qualified, independent source (such as an investment banking firm, a commercial bank, or an appraiser) and must be supplemented by board deliberations. The fairness opinion can be a useful tool both in determining whether to accept an offer and in obtaining the protection of the business judgment rule. However, when there is a potential or actual conflict of interest in a transaction, courts will also examine the transaction to determine its *entire fairness,* mentioned earlier in this chapter as the most stringent test for a transaction.

Because fairness generally depends on the price to be received by the target company's shareholders, having a fairness option from an expert source such as an investment banker can be invaluable to the board. It is, however, necessary for a board of directors to question the experts to determine that they have a reasonable basis for their opinion and that they are free from conflicts of interest. Reliance on a fairness opinion alone may not suffice as proof of the exercise of due care.

What should a fairness opinion say?

A fairness opinion should describe the process the experts used in making their determination of fairness, and should indicate what matters have been investigated and independently verified and what matters have not been verified independently. The opinion should also describe the fee or fees being paid and all possible conflicts of interest. The firm offering the opinion should not accept contingent compensation for the fairness opinion or for the transaction that is the subject of the opinion, because doing so suggests a lack of independence.

What happens if a court determines that a price and/or a process is unfair?

If the court completes the entire fairness inquiry and concludes that the transaction was unfair, it must then identify which duty (care or loyalty) is the basis for liability.[26]

How can an acquirer increase chances of having its bid favored over bids from other companies?

One mechanism employed by companies to give the favored bidder an edge is a lockup option. The lockup agreement may be granted with respect to stock or assets.[27]

In the stock lockup, the bidder receives an option to purchase authorized but unissued shares. This option favors the bidder in two ways: if the option is exercised, either the bidder may vote the shares in favor of the transaction or, if another bidder wins the contract for the company, the favored bidder may realize a profit by tendering the stock to the higher bidder. A variation on the lockup is the reverse lockup, where stockholders or management agree not to tender their shares to a rival bidder. For the same reason, a buyer will attempt to obtain options to acquire the stock of stockholders, typically those that have significant holdings. Stock lockup agreements with the target have received mixed results from courts applying the business judgment doctrine. The courts' main concern is that the lockup may prevent competitive bidding and thereby limit the premiums stockholders would otherwise receive from buyers.

Courts are most likely to approve lockups granted at the end of the bidding process rather than at the beginning, particularly if there are no other bidders contending for the company.

In the asset lockup (or "crown jewel" lockup), the company grants the bidder the option to acquire a particularly attractive asset at a price that may or may not be commensurate with its full market value. Such an option may discourage other bidders if they were also interested in the crown jewel or if the loss of the asset would considerably change the financial position or prospects of the company. Asset lockup agreements have received generally negative treatments from courts, as discussed next.

Can directors adopt a lockup agreement without violating their fiduciary duties?

Yes. A lockup agreement is not illegal per se. However, court decisions hold that a lockup arrangement generally must advance or stimulate the bidding process, not retard it or cut it off. That is, a board can tilt the playing field toward a bidder if the purpose is to elicit a higher bid from that bidder or to otherwise stimulate the competition.

If the purpose of the lockup agreement is to completely stifle competitive bidding by definitively preferring one bidder over another, however, the board will likely be found to have breached its duty of loyalty to the shareholders.

This was the case with *Revlon.* Cases after *Revlon* have indicated clearly that a court will not permit a board to grant a crown jewel lockup option to one bidder that would have the effect of cutting other bidders out of the process while bidding is still active.

Will a lockup agreement subject the bidders to liability for short-swing trading profits?

As previously mentioned, short-swing trading is not permitted under Section 16(b) of the Exchange Act. A bidder's profits will not be subject to short-swing restriction under Section 16(b) unless the bidder "beneficially owned" more than 10 percent of the target's stock prior to the purchase of the stock pursuant to the lockup agreement. Once a bidder achieves insider status as a beneficial owner of more than 10 percent of the stock, all subsequent transactions will be subject to Section 16(b).

What is a beneficial owner?

A beneficial owner of equity is a person or group of persons possessing "voting power" or "investment power" over a security as defined in Rule 13d-3 of the Exchange Act. Thus, shares beneficially owned include not only shares directly owned but all shares with respect to which a person has or shares direct or indirect power to vote or sell. For instance, all shares subject to a shareholders' voting agreement become beneficially owned by each person who is a party to the agreement. The concept of beneficial ownership is especially important in view of the 5 percent threshold to the filing requirements under Schedules 13D and 13G. Thus, if each member of a group of five persons owns 1 percent of the shares of a class of a company, that group must file a Schedule 13D (or 13G if the group has agreed to vote or dispose of those securities as a block). Also, a person is deemed to own beneficially any security that he or she, directly or indirectly, has the right to acquire within 60 days, whether such acquisition is pursuant to a purchase contract, exercise of a warrant or option, or conversion of a convertible security (Rule 13d-3).

Ironically, leaders of public companies in the United States, unlike other countries such as the United Kingdom, have no absolute right to know who their beneficial owners are. When individuals or institutions buy stock through a broker, they have an opportunity to sign a form saying whether they want their identity to remain private. Unless they specifically indicate that they are Non-Objecting Beneficial Owners (NOBOs), they are treated as Objecting Beneficial Owners (OBOs) and their identities remain private. (Brokers reportedly check the "objecting" box for their clients, to make sure brokers stay in the loop.) Owners then receive any communications from the broker rather than the company, which does not have their direct contact information. The Business Roundtable, National Investor Relations Institute, National Association of Corporate Directors, and other groups have requested that the SEC review this policy, which prevents effective relations between companies and their owners.

If a merger or acquisition involves the issuance of securities to the target's shareholders, may such securities be resold freely, or are sales restricted?

Generally, such securities are similar to restricted securities in that Rule 145 under the Securities Act, which deems that an *offer, offer to sell, offer for sale,* or *sale* occurs when securityholders receive a plan or agreement that asks them to accept a new or different security in exchange for their existing security.[28] Under Rule 145, transactions that are subject to the registration requirements of the Securities Act include reclassifications, mergers or consolidations, and transfers of assets. When a shell company is involved, participants are deemed to be underwriters. This said, there are exemptions available. As in all legal matters, the advice of qualified counsel should be sought.

What are topping and breakup fees?

Although these terms are used interchangeably, they each have a special meaning:

- A *breakup* fee is payable if the transaction is terminated by either party (other than for cause).
- *A topping* fee is an agreement with the target to compensate the buyer for potential losses if a new bidder usurps the deal. Because these fees are liabilities of the target, the winning bidder will have to bear their economic burden. This burden has

the effect of increasing the cost of, and thus discouraging, other bids.

- Another arrangement is for the payment of *breakup* fees if the transaction is terminated by the target, other than for cause. (When a buyer pays a fee to a target, this is called a *reverse termination fee.*)

The fees are designed, at the very least, to reimburse the buyer for all of its out-of-pocket expenses. More often, the arrangements include an additional payment for lost time and opportunity. Delaware courts have found that fees in the range of 3 or 4 percent of transaction value in larger transactions are not unreasonable, with even higher amounts approved in smaller transactions.[29]

Aren't breakup fees subject to legal challenge?

Yes. The size of the fee must not be so large that it substantially discourages other bidders or it may be struck down by a court as a disguised lockup arrangement. Provided that the fee is not excessive, under current case law it is very likely to withstand judicial scrutiny if the agreement to pay the fee is viewed as reasonably necessary to attract the bidder or keep it interested in the target in the face of competition. The defensibility of the fee will be enhanced if it is granted by the target in exchange for a "fiduciary out" clause (discussed later) or if the buyer permits the board to "shop" the company for a period of time, that is, to try to find other bidders. Note also that creditors—particularly in the case of companies that are in bankruptcy proceedings—may challenge such fees in court.

What is a no-shop agreement, and when can it be used?

A no-shop agreement is a provision either in the acquisition contract or in a letter of intent that prohibits the board of directors from soliciting or encouraging other bids. It is always found in private company acquisition agreements and, far more often than not, in the acquisition agreement for public company transactions.

The buyer should always be expected to request such an agreement at the letter of intent stage, and the seller will usually agree to it if it has chosen the bidder as the result of either an auction process or a completed bidding war. Under certain circumstances, however—such as when the buyer is the first on the scene or is a member of management or a "white knight" whose bid was solicited to fend off a hostile takeover—such an agreement should be avoided or at least mitigated by adding a "fiduciary out" clause in the agreement.

Although there is no legal requirement that a company be shopped before a definitive agreement to sell is executed, the courts do not look kindly on no-shop provisions, alone or as part of a package (such as with lockups), when the effect of such provisions is to frustrate the role of the board as a neutral auctioneer or where they may result in a bargain price to corporate insiders, such as management. The absence of shopping, coupled with the existence of such provisions, may provide the basis for an argument that the price was not determined fairly, with the result that the transaction could be enjoined by a court at the behest of a competitor or an aggrieved stockholder.

In especially egregious situations, members of the board of directors can be subject to liability if the price is too low or the board has not performed its duties. (See *Van Gorkom* in the last chapter of this book, "Landmark and Recent M&A Legal Cases.") When a board is required to defend the process and result as fair to the stockholders, the fact that it has unsuccessfully solicited better offers is telling evidence of the fairness of the transaction.

The buyer, of course, will argue that it needs the no-shop provision to avoid incurring expenses for a deal that doesn't succeed because the board attracts a higher bidder. The response: give the buyer a breakup fee.

Finally, the board must determine whether the bidder will refuse to enter into the transaction without the no-shop clause. If so, and if the board is comfortable with the fairness of the price, the no-shop agreement may be advisable to secure for the shareholders the benefit of a good sale price.

Once the letter of intent stage is passed, the buyer certainly should expect a no-shop clause in the definitive agreement. Otherwise, why sign an agreement? Notwithstanding the clause in the agreement, because of its fiduciary responsibilities the board should avoid agreeing that it may not provide a competing bidder with the same information given to the buyer.

It is worth reiterating that the decision about whether to grant a no-shop agreement falls within the purview of the business judgment of the board of directors. Thus, the timing of the offer, the surrounding circumstances (hostile bidders, management buyers, and the like), other evidence of fairness, and the necessity of the clause to get the best deal for the stockholders all must be considered. There is no hard-and-fast rule.

What is a fiduciary out clause?

A fiduciary out clause is a provision in an agreement that enables the target to terminate a merger agreement in the event that a more favorable offer is made. In some cases the clause merely allows the board to back out of its obligation to recommend the agreement in the face of a more favorable offer. Although the law is unclear, the latter provision may be unnecessary because the board may have a fiduciary duty to refuse to continue its recommendation if a more favorable offer has been made. Furthermore, from a buyer's perspective, the insertion of a fiduciary out clause in an agreement may not matter, because if a clearly more favorable bid is made, the chances are great that the stockholders won't approve the buyer's offer or will refuse to tender their shares to the buyer in its tender offer.

Fiduciary out clauses are subject to close legal review, and issues are far from clear. In April 2003, when the Delaware Supreme Court issued its opinion in *Omnicare v. NCS HealthCare* (2003), its close (3–2) vote showed a difference of judicial opinion. The majority held that a target company board violated its fiduciary duties by approving a merger agreement with no fiduciary out because in combination with other factors, such as a lockup agreement, the absence of a fiduciary out ensured stockholder approval of the transaction. But in subsequent years, this decision has been criticized to the point of being called the "worst Delaware opinion" ever.[30]

M&A FORMS

What forms must an acquirer of a public company and/or its target file?

Here is a list of the schedules most commonly filed in a merger, acquisition, or buyout (including a going-private transaction).[31]

The following list includes the major forms or "schedules" (hence, the SC label),[32] along with endnotes referring the reader to the content required in each form.

For a Current Report of Significant Events Such as a Merger Agreement

Form 8K—Public companies must file an 8K within four business days of "significant events." One of those is entry into a definitive agreement (Item 1.01); another is the acquisition or disposition of assets (Item 2.01).

For a Tender Offer or Acquisition

SC 13D[33]—This form discloses "beneficial ownership" of a public company's stock (defined earlier in this chapter). Any person or group of persons who has acquired more than 5 percent of a class of equity securities—whether through a tender offer or through other means—must file it within 10 days of the triggering purchase. Note: A Schedule 13D must be amended "promptly" upon the occurrence of any "material change" in the information contained in the original Schedule 13D.

SC 13G[34]—This form is a short version of the same form for those such as banks that are buying as a passive investment, and that do not intend to establish control.

SC 14D2-9[35]—This form is filed by the target of a tender offer within 10 days of the offer, indicating its response to the offer. (If the target is in Canada, SC 14D-9F is filed.)

For Going Private

SC 13E-3[36]—This is a transaction statement with respect to a public company or affiliate going private. (See also SC TO-I.)

Communications to Shareholders via the Proxy Statement

SC 14A[37]—This form lists the information required in the proxy statement, which may be a merger proxy or a challenge proxy.

SC 14N[38]—Filed by a nominating shareholder or group to request inclusion of the group's nominee or nominees in the company's proxy materials.

Additional Tender Offer Schedules

SC TO[39]—Filed when a purchase will result in ownership of 5 percent or more. There are three types of SC-TO:

- *SC TO-C*—Filed if an accepted offer would result in a party's owning more than 5 percent of a class of the target company's securities. (The "C" stands for "Communication.")
- *SC TO-I*—Filed if a company repurchases its own securities. (The "I" stands for "issuer.")
- *SC TO-T*—Filed if someone other than the issuer is tendering the offer. (The "T" stands for "Third Party.")

Stock Offerings Resulting from a Tender Offer or Other Transactions

S-4[40]—This form is used to register securities in connection with business combinations and exchange offers.

TENDER OFFER BASICS

Technically speaking, what is a tender offer?

A typical tender offer (TO) is a broad solicitation by a company to purchase a substantial percentage of another company's publicly traded equity shares for a limited period of time at a fixed price (e.g., $23 per share) that represents a premium over the current market price (e.g., 20 percent), and is contingent on shareholders tendering a fixed number of their shares.[41]

One problem for a company seeking to gain control of a public company through open market purchases of stock is that such purchases may, under certain circumstances, be deemed to constitute a tender offer.

What is a mini tender offer?

A mini tender offer is a tender offer to buy less than 5 percent of a company's shares at a price that, unlike a regular tender offer, is not a premium price, but rather is below market. Once a shareholder agrees to tender shares, as in a regular tender offer it is not possible to back out. Targets of mini tenders, as well as the SEC, have warned investors to decline such offers.[42] These tender offers, unless full-scale tenders, are rarely preludes to an acquisition, but rather are strategies on the part of trading-oriented buyers to buy low and sell high.

How exactly is control transferred in a tender offer or other type of public company acquisition?

A public company acquisition can be accomplished through either a *one-step* or a *two-step* transaction.

In the one-step acquisition, the buyer organizes an acquisition subsidiary that will merge into the target. Upon consummation of the merger, the stockholders of the target receive cash (and possibly notes promising additional cash) and the stockholders of the acquisition subsidiary receive all the stock of the target. The merger will require the approval of the stockholders of the target; the exact percentage of stockholder approval required will depend upon the articles of incorporation of the target and could be as low as a majority of the voting power of the common stock. To gain the approval, the target will be required to solicit proxies from the stockholders and to vote the proxies at a stockholder's meeting called for the purpose of voting on the transaction. The proxy solicitation must comply with the federal securities laws.

A two-step acquisition involves a tender offer followed by a merger.[43]

- In the first step, the buyer organizes an acquisition subsidiary that makes a tender offer for the shares of the target. The acquisition subsidiary may or may not be recognizable as the buyer.[44] Usually, the offer is conditioned upon enough shares being tendered to give the buyer sufficient voting power to ensure that the second-step merger will be approved. For example, if approval by a majority of the voting stock of the target is required, the offer is conditioned on the buyer obtaining at least a majority of the target stock in the tender offer.
- In the second step, the buyer obtains stockholder approval, the acquisition subsidiary is merged into the target, the stockholders of the acquisition subsidiary become stockholders of the target, and the original stockholders of the target who did not tender their shares receive cash. If the buyer obtains sufficient stock of the target (90 percent in Delaware), the merger will not require approval of the target's remaining stockholders (a "short form merger").[45]

In a public transaction, must the stock be acquired only through a tender offer or a merger?

No. The buyer may precede its tender offer or the merger with ordinary purchases through the stock market (open market purchases) or may acquire, or enter into arrangements to acquire, stock from the target or from some of its major stockholders (lockup arrangements). The timing and method of such purchases, however, must respect federal securities laws, which preclude certain transactions after a tender offer begins and also may characterize certain open market purchases as tender offers.

What are the major advantages and disadvantages of the tender offer versus a proxy solicitation?

Timing is the major advantage. The tender offer can close as early as 20 business days from the date of commencement, sometimes earlier,[46] and there is no requirement that the tender offer documents be filed with the SEC prior to commencement. At the conclusion of the tender offer, the buyer will have control of the target.

This contrasts sharply with a proxy solicitation. Proxy materials must be submitted for review by the SEC; the review takes from 10 to 30 days. The materials are rarely sent to shareholders before completion of the SEC review. The shareholders meeting usually won't occur until at least 20 days (depending upon state law and the bylaws of the target) after the proxy materials are sent out. Twenty days is usually a minimum to ensure that the shareholders get the material and have a chance to review it and to submit their proxy. Generally, the time to gain control is 45 to 60 days after the proxy materials are initially submitted to the SEC.

In the friendly two-step transaction, at what point do the parties enter into the merger agreement?

The merger agreement is entered into before the tender offer is commenced. There are several reasons for this. First, if the merger agreement is entered into before commencement of the tender offer, the acquisition subsidiary will be able to use certain types of unsecured loans to finance the transaction that would otherwise be unavailable. Second, the buyer often wants to finalize agreements relating to expense reimbursement, breakup fees, lockup arrangements, and so on, before incurring the expense and risk of a tender offer. Also, under the target's articles of incorporation the percentage of stockholder votes required for approval of the second-step merger may depend upon board approval prior to the tender offer. The board approval, in turn, may hinge upon the buyer's agreeing to make the same payments to all stockholders in the tender offer and the second-step merger. Third, the target board would like to ensure fair treatment for all stockholders by binding the buyer to accomplish the merger promptly after the tender offer.

Generally, how long after the closing of the tender offer will the second-step merger occur?

If the parties are Delaware corporations, and the buyer acquires at least 90 percent of the stock of the target, the merger usually can be accomplished shortly after the tender offer closes. If less stock is acquired, the buyer must cause a stockholders' vote to be taken to approve the merger.

In almost every case, the buyer will not require any favorable votes from the other stockholders because it will own enough stock to assume approval after the tender offer, so no proxies will be solicited. Nevertheless, the buyer must submit an "information statement" to the SEC and cause it to be distributed to the stockholders. The distribution cannot occur until 10 days after the information statement is sent to the SEC in the case of a cash tender offer, or 15 in a noncash tender offer.[47] The stockholders must receive the information statement at least 20 calendar days before the corporate action approving the merger. The result is that the minimum waiting period for a merger following a tender offer is 30 days.[48]

What are tender offer premiums, and how are they measured?

A tender offer premium is the "plus factor" in an offer—it is the incremental amount paid for securities in excess of an established market price as of a stated date. The premium, however, is a moving target. For example, a target stock may be selling for $10 per share and an acquirer may intend to offer $15 per share—a 50 percent premium. But by the time the formal announcement is made, the price of the stock may have risen due to preannouncement trading in the stock based on rumors, guesses, or insider tips about nonpublished inside information (that is, illegal insider trading). Such trading tends to boost the target's stock price prior to a merger, so premiums—unless measured well in advance—can appear to be smaller than they really are. And then after the announcement, the market price may rise, reducing the premium even more. When an acquirer is offering to pay $15 per share for stock that is selling at $14.50 a share, the incentive to sell drops considerably.

What is considered to be an acceptable premium for a company?

In a perfect market, an acceptable premium would be whatever the market will bear. More reasonably, it would be one that exceeds target management's own projections for share price appreciation in the reasonably near term.

In a tender offer, how do shareholders decide whether or not to sell?

The investor needs to determine two things:

- How the premium compares to likely future returns from the company via higher stock price and/or dividends
- How long the investor is willing to wait for those returns

If an investor has a short time frame, it may accept a low premium, even if it believes that the company will eventually provide a higher return; a long-term holder is more likely to wait for that return. See Exhibit 10-3.

What are some of the practical considerations in commencing a tender offer?

The first steps in commencing a tender offer are the formation of a team and the creation of a timetable indicating each planned activity and the person responsible for it.

Exhibit 10-3 Likely Responses to Tender Offers vs. Management Promises

LONG-TIME HOLDERS

Low Premium, Long Time MAYBE	High Premium, Long Time YES
Low Premium, Short Time MAYBE	High Premium, Short Time MAYBE

SHORT-TIME HOLDERS

Low Premium, Long Time NO	High Premium, Long Time MAYBE
Low Premium, Short Time MAYBE	High Premium, Short Time YES

(In responding to a tender offer, shareholders choose between a premium now from the TO versus a premium later from management. This chart shows a contrast between long-time holders and short-time holders in choosing between what they think TOs offer in the short term versus what they think management promises in the long term.)

The formation of the team should begin with the retention of a dealer-manager/investment banker and an independent accountant. Initially, the dealer-manager and accountant will help in the review of the target company's financials and business and advise as to the desirability/feasibility of the proposed transaction. The dealer-manager will also be responsible for the solicitation of large stockholders and for the communications with the financial community and may also assist the buyer in accumulation of a significant stock position prior to the commencement of the actual tender offer.

Experienced lawyers who will prepare the many legal documents required in conjunction with the tender offer are essential members of the team. The lawyers should be familiar with federal and state securities laws, antitrust laws, and numerous other areas of the law that may apply to a specific transaction.

Additionally, as litigation is often a by-product of tender offers, the lawyers on a tender offer team should come from a law firm with a strong, experienced litigation department.

Other members of the team will generally include a proxy solicitor that will arrange for delivery of tender offer materials and will contact shareholders to solicit their shares, and a depository trust bank that will receive and pay for tendered securities.

Tender offer teams also usually include a securities transfer or forwarding agent that will receive shares as an agent for tendering stockholders and a financial printer with the ability to prepare tender offer documents quickly and provide the confidential treatment necessary to avoid premature disclosure of the proposed transaction.

Must the bidder contact the target company's management prior to commencement of a tender offer?

Not necessarily—although failure to do so moves a transaction out of the friendly or neutral category and into the hostile camp. Although a tender offer can be commenced with no prior disclosure to the target company's management, this approach puts significant pressure on the target by allowing it the least amount of time to respond to the offer or to develop a workable defense strategy.

A tender offeror may also choose to contact the target's management and request a meeting at the same time it makes a public announcement of its intention to commence a tender offer. At this meeting, the tender offeror may attempt to obtain the approval and cooperation of the target company's management for the proposed transaction and may also apply additional pressure by indicating that unless the management of the target company approves the transaction, the tender offer will be made at a lower price. In any event, making a public announcement that a tender offer will be made requires the offeror to proceed with or abandon the offer within five days of its announcement.

When does a tender offer begin?

A tender offer commences at 12:01 a.m. on the date when the bidder does one of the following:

- Publishes a long-form publication of the tender offer, containing required information, in a newspaper or newspapers[49]
- Publishes a summary advertisement of the tender offer, disclosing certain information, in a newspaper or newspapers
- Publishes, or provides to shareholders of the target, definitive copies of tender offer materials
- Publicly announces certain information: the identity of the bidder, the identity of the target, the amount and class of securities sought, and the price or range of prices being offered

When must an acquirer file a Schedule 13D?

The Exchange Act provides for disclosure concerning the accumulation of blocks of voting equity securities if that accumulation might represent a potential change in corporate control regardless of how such securities are accumulated. Any person who is the "beneficial owner" of 5 percent or more of the shares of a class of voting equity securities registered under Section 12 of the Exchange Act is required to file a Schedule 13D with the SEC (and each securities exchange on which the securities are traded) containing specified information concerning the filing person. Schedule 13D must be filed with the SEC and sent to the issuer and to each exchange where the security is traded within 10 days after a person acquires 5 percent or more of an outstanding voting equity security.

This requirement is somewhat relaxed for certain institutional investors (such as banks, broker-dealers, or insurance companies) whose purchases are made in the ordinary course of their business without the purpose or effect of changing or influencing the control of the issuer, and for investors that owned their shares prior to the time the company became subject to the Exchange Act. Such investors need only file a Schedule 13G, which is a substantially shorter form than Schedule 13D, 45 days after the end of the calendar year in which the threshold ownership interest was acquired.

If, however, such an institutional securityholder changes its intention and decides to influence control of the company, it must file a Schedule 13D within 10 days of making that decision.[50] During the 10-day period, the shares already owned may not be voted, and the owner may not buy any additional shares of the target company.

Is a written agreement necessary for a group to exist?

No. The existence of a written agreement is not required; circumstantial evidence of an agreement in itself may be enough. Section 13(d) states, in part, that "when two or more persons act as a partnership, limited partnership, syndicate, or group acquiring or disposing of securities of an issuer, such syndicate or group shall be deemed a person for the purposes of this subsection."

When two or more persons acquire a security together, only one of them need file.[51]

At what stage of an acquisition is a group formed?

It can be formed as soon as the members of the group reach an agreement, even if the agreement is merely preliminary. In a 2017 enforcement action against an activist investor group (Lone Star Value Management LLC and two others), the SEC charged the group with inadequate disclosure because it did not make prompt disclosure of its formation as a group as it targeted Analysts International Corp.[52]

Is an agreement to acquire additional shares necessary to form a group?

No. An agreement among shareowners who together hold a total of 5 percent or more of a class of voting stock to act together in the future to further the group's purpose may be enough to form a group regardless of whether acts to carry out the agreement (such as voting and acquiring stock) occur after the date of the agreement.

Does the management of the company to be acquired constitute a group subject to Section 13(d)?

Yes. The target's management could be considered a group if it acts as such to acquire shares and if its members own more than 5 percent of the company. A management group would have to comply with all reporting requirements.

Must members of a group file jointly, or may individual members file separately?

A group may file one joint Schedule 13D, or each member may file individually. An individual filing jointly is not responsible for the information concerning other members of the group unless the individual knows or has reason to know that the information pertaining to another group member is inaccurate.

What can happen if the buyer fails to comply with Section 13(d)?

In most cases, both shareholders and target companies may sue for damages for violations of Section 13(d). The SEC can issue a "cease and desist" order under Section 13(d) for failures to switch from Schedule 13G to Schedule 13D when the investors could no longer be deemed to be "passive," or for failures to disclose on Schedule 13D the group's plans, failures to file on Schedule 13D as a group with greater than 5 percent beneficial ownership, and failures to timely amend Schedule 13D to disclose group holdings.[53]

The enforcement action may lead to a rescission (order to rescind the transaction) or a forced divestiture; however, the SEC usually will not take such action while corporate control is being contested.

What materials are sent to shareholders?

The shareholders receive an "offer to purchase" that sets forth the material terms of the offer and a "letter of transmittal" that the shareholder sends back to accept the offer. The contents of the offer to purchase must reflect the requirements of Rule 14d-6.[54] The bidder is also required to publish, send, or give to shareholders notice of any material change in the tender offer materials.

Do the tender offer materials need to disclose any projections that may have been provided by the target to the acquirer?

The courts that have considered this question have taken different approaches, but generally they have held either that there is no duty to disclose projections in tender offer documents or that there is a duty to disclose only when the projections are substantially certain. Because projections are inherently uncertain, this latter test may in practice result in no duty to disclose financial projections. However, the SEC staff has taken the position that the purchaser must disclose any financial projections it receives from the seller in its tender offer documents. As a result, most buyers make some disclosure of projections furnished by the target in the offering materials.

Is there a way to avoid filing certain documents with the SEC?

No. However, it is possible to avoid the public disclosure of certain material if it can be demonstrated that the disclosure of such material would be detrimental to the operations of the company and that the disclosure of the material is unnecessary for the protection of investors. A company seeking to avoid the public disclosure of such information must seek an Order of Confidential Treatment from the SEC. Generally, if appropriate grounds for relief are asserted, the SEC will grant confidential treatment of such information for a limited period of time.

What kind of disclaimers should an offeror run in announcing its offer?

A typical disclaimer, often appearing in italics at the top of a tender offer announcement, reads as follows:

> *This communication is for informational purposes only, is not a recommendation to buy or sell shares of [the Target's] common stock, and does not constitute an offer to buy or the solicitation to sell shares of [this] common stock. The tender offer described in this communication has not yet commenced, and there can be no assurances that [the Acquirer] will commence the tender offer on the terms described in this communication or at all. The tender offer will be made only pursuant to the Offer to Purchase, the related Letter of Transmittal and other related materials that [the Acquirer] expects to file with the Securities and Exchange Commission ("SEC") upon commencement of the tender offer.*[55]

How long must a tender offer remain open?

A tender offer must remain open continuously for at least 20 business days. This 20-day period commences upon the date the tender offer is first published, sent, or given to the target company's shareholders. Once an offeror has made a public announcement that it intends to commence a tender offer, the tender offer must commence or be abandoned within five days.

Additionally, a tender offer must remain open for at least 10 business days following an announced increase or decrease in the tender offer price or in the percentage of securities to be bought.

If any other change in the tender offer terms is made, the offeror should keep the offer open for five business days to allow dissemination of the new information in a manner reasonably designed to inform shareholders of such changes.

May the offering period be extended?

Yes, but the buyer must announce the extension not later than 9:00 a.m. on the business day following the day on which the tender offer expires, and the announcement must state the approximate amount of securities already purchased.

Once a shareholder tenders his or her shares, may the shareholder withdraw them?

Shareholders who tender shares may withdraw them at any time during the tender offer period unless the shares are actually purchased.

Tendered shares may also be withdrawn at any time after 60 days from the date of the original tender offer if those shares have not yet been purchased by the bidder.

When must payment for tendered securities be made?

An offeror must either promptly pay the consideration offered or return the tendered securities.

May a bidder make an offer for less than all of the outstanding shares of a target company?

Yes. However, if more shares are tendered than the offeror wishes to purchase, the offeror must purchase the desired amount of shares on a pro rata basis from among those shares tendered.

May an offeror quickly acquire control of the target's board of directors after purchasing shares in the tender offer?

Yes. The tender offeror and the target frequently agree that, after a successful tender offer, the offeror may elect a majority of directors to the board of the target. Such an agreement permits the offeror to obtain control of the target's board of directors without holding a meeting of shareholders. Ten days before the newly elected directors are permitted to take office, the target company must file with the SEC and transmit to the holders of its voting securities information about such directors that would be required to be provided to shareholders if such persons were nominees for election as directors at a meeting of the target's shareholders.

Must all shareholders in a tender offer be treated equally?

Yes. The same consideration must be paid to all tendering shareholders. The offer must be open to all shareholders of the class of securities subject to the offer. However, while the bidder does not need to pay the same type of consideration to each shareholder, it must afford each the opportunity to elect among the types offered. In addition, each shareholder must receive the highest consideration paid to any other shareholder receiving the same type of consideration. Therefore, if the tender price is increased at any time during the period, the increased amount must be paid to all tendering shareholders, including those who tendered before the price increase and those whose shares have already been purchased.

What is "short tendering" during a tender?

Short tendering is short selling during a tender offer. It occurs when a shareholder in a partial tender offer tenders more shares than he or she actually owns in the hope of increasing the number of shares that the bidder actually will accept pro rata.

A person is prohibited from tendering a security unless that person, or the person on whose behalf he or she is tendering, owns the security (or an equivalent security) at the time of the tender and at the end of the probation period. A person is deemed to own a security only to the extent that he or she has a net long position in such security. SEC rules also prohibit "hedged tendering." Hedged tendering occurs when a shareholder tenders securities in response to more than one offer or tenders some securities while selling others in the open market.

How do risk arbitrageurs work, then?

Risk arbitrageurs buy, sell, borrow, or tender shares or options on shares in the hope that a change in their price, typically through an offer or a rumor of an offer, will yield a profit. They must work within securities laws. Some, however, have gained an unfair and illegal advantage from receipt of inside information concerning specific offers.

May an offeror purchase shares during a tender offer other than pursuant to the tender offer?

No. During a tender offer, the offeror may not directly or indirectly purchase or arrange to purchase, other than pursuant to the tender offer, securities that are the subject of that offer. This prohibition also includes privately negotiated purchases until the tender offer is concluded or withdrawn.

Purchases made before a public announcement are generally permissible, even if a decision has been made by the purchaser to make the tender offer, but purchase agreements scheduled to close during the offering period are illegal no matter when they were or are made.

When a transaction is closed, and the new company wants to publish a "tombstone" ad about it, what rules apply?

Tombstone ads are considered to be "communications not deemed a prospectus," covered by Rule 134 under the Securities Act.[56] They must contain only basic information, and may not include photographs.[57] These requirements, along with tradition, account for their resemblance to grave markers.

PROXY SOLICITATIONS

What about groups seeking control through a proxy fight?

They must adhere to the proxy rules promulgated under Section 14 of the Exchange Act, which defines solicitation, requires companies to give copies of their shareholders' lists to dissidents (candidates running for board seats that have not been nominated by the board), and requires disclosure of voting results. Section 14 includes several exemptions.

How is solicitation defined under proxy rules?

Narrowly. The rule says that a shareholder can publicly announce how he or she intends to vote and why, without necessarily having to comply with proxy rules. Major institutional investors, such as the California Public Employees' Retirement System (CalPERS), have used this technique to encourage other shareholders to follow their lead.

The current rules offer a broad exemption from the proxy statement "delivery and disclosure" requirements for shareholder communications—unless the person soliciting is seeking proxy authority and has a substantial interest in the matter subject to a vote or is otherwise ineligible for the exemption. On the other hand, public notice—through publication, broadcast, or submission of written materials to the SEC—of soliciting activity is required of all beneficial owners of more than $5 million worth of stock.[58]

May shareholders solicit proxies via the mass media? May they bypass the SEC altogether?

Yes to the first question; no to the second. A person who has a proxy statement on file with the SEC is permitted to solicit votes without delivering a copy of the proxy statement to all shareholders in the audience. Soliciting parties can start a solicitation on the basis of a preliminary proxy statement publicly filed with the SEC, as long as they don't send a proxy voting card to the solicited shareholders until after the dissemination of a definitive proxy statement and final prospectus.[59]

Can shareholders vote for both dissident and management candidates as individuals, or do they have to take sides with slates?

Current proxy rules require voting for one slate or the other. Only individuals present in person at the annual meeting can mix and match. The notion of a universal proxy card that would allow this on the proxy card is still under SEC review at this time.[60] Under current rules, if a dissident proposes a short slate (electing a minority of the board), it may include one or more of management's nominees, if they have given their consent. (The dissident's proxy form and proxy statement may not include the names of management's nonconsenting nominees.)

Under what circumstances must companies give dissidents their shareholder lists?

Registered companies engaged in roll-ups or going-private transactions must provide shareholders, under certain conditions and upon written request, with a list of shareholder names, addresses, and positions, including names of consenting beneficial owners, if known. In all other cases, registrants can either give such a list to the requesting shareholders or mail materials for them.

What is the current status of proxy voting disclosure?

Several forms—including 10-K, 10-Q, and Schedule 14A—require disclosure of voting results and of the vote needed for passage of resolutions presented to shareholders. This disclosure must include the number of abstentions on resolutions and on votes for director elections, and a statement of how exemptions are treated under applicable state law charter and bylaw provisions.

GOING PRIVATE

What is “going private”?

Going private means getting out of public equity markets. More technically, it is a Rule 13e-3 transaction in which certain of the existing stockholders or affiliates of a public target become stockholders of the entity surviving the acquisition of the target and the target is no longer subject to Section 12(g) or Section 15(d) of the Exchange Act. Because certain stockholders may be on both sides of the transaction, Rule 13e-3 requires additional disclosures to the public stockholders in order to demonstrate the overall fairness of the transaction. These disclosures include full-blown discussions of any fairness opinions and appraisals obtained in connection with the transaction and statements by the target as to the fairness of the transaction.

In addition, if anyone buys a public company and takes it private it needs to file a schedule SC 13E-3, mentioned earlier in the list of forms. This schedule must be filed by certain persons engaging in going-private transactions. The schedule must be filed by any company or affiliate of a company who engages in a business combination, tender offer, or stock purchase that has the effect of causing a class of the company’s equity securities to be held by fewer than 300 persons, or be delisted from a securities exchange or market.

Determining whether a particular transaction may constitute a 13e-3 transaction largely depends upon the percentage of stock that the existing stockholders own in the target or the relationship of such affiliates to the target and the percentage ownership that such persons may have in the surviving entity.

MERGER DISCLOSURE ISSUES

Under what circumstances may a public company deny that it is engaged in merger negotiations?

Only if it is not so engaged. That was the gist of the Supreme Court’s 1988 decision in *Basic Incorporated v. Levinson.* In this landmark case, the Court said that outright denial of negotiations is improper even if the negotiations in question are discussions that have not yet resulted in an agreement on the price and structure of a transaction. The appropriate response to inquiries about such a matter is either "no comment" or a disclosure that negotiations are, in fact, taking place.

Prior to the *Basic* decision, the court of appeals for the Third Circuit had held that merger proposals and negotiations were not "material" until the parties had reached agreement in principle on the price and structure of a transaction. In *Basic,* the Supreme Court rejected this so-called bright line test and held that the materiality of merger negotiations must be evaluated on a case-by-case basis after considering all relevant facts and circumstances. Another important aspect of the *Basic* decision was its assertion that material information makes markets move, and that withholding it can constitute a fraud on the market. Some believe that this concept has led to meritless litigation, but the concept was upheld in the 2014 Supreme Court decision of *Halliburton v. Erica P. John Fund,* 134 S.Ct. 2398 (2014).

The Regulation Fair Disclosure (Regulation FD) has drawn a bright line with respect to the timing of disclosures. If a person knows an important or "material" fact about the company that the public does not yet know—and if this person then tells this to another person, the company must make immediate public disclosure of the fact. This principle would obviously apply to any statements about a possible merger.

When does a company have a duty to disclose merger negotiations?

Generally, the timing of disclosure of material information is at the discretion of the company and will be protected by the business judgment rule. Nevertheless, a company that is the subject of takeover speculation or whose stock is trading erratically typically finds itself pressured by brokers, news services, stock exchange officials, securities analysts, and others to disclose merger proposals and negotiations. The *Basic* decision accelerated the trend toward voluntary disclosures in these circumstances, although it is still acceptable under certain circumstances for a company to adopt a policy of silence or state that no comment will be made with respect to merger proposals or rumors.

However, a company may not remain silent where (1) there is an affirmative disclosure rule (such as the tender offer regulations), (2) the company is about to purchase its own shares in the public market, (3) a prior public disclosure made by the company is no longer accurate (such as when a company has publicly denied that merger negotiations with a party were occurring), or (4) rumors that have been circulating concerning the proposed transactions are attributable to a leak from the company.

Disclosure may also be appropriate when it is apparent that a leak has occurred, even if the leak is not from the company. In such a situation, consideration should be given to a variety of factors, including the requirements of any agreement with a stock exchange, the effect of wide price fluctuations on shareholders generally, and the benefits to the market provided by broad dissemination of accurate information. If the company does elect to disclose either the existence or the substance of negotiations, it must take care that its disclosures are neither false nor materially misleading.

It should be noted that if the company refuses to respond to a stock exchange's request for disclosure or issues a "no comment," it may be subject to disciplinary action by the exchange. This disciplinary action may include public notice of a violation, temporary suspension of trading in the corporation's stock, or delisting.

Is management required to disclose inquiries about a possible merger or acquisition?

There is no specific obligation to disclose mere inquiries or contacts made by those interested in acquiring the corporation or its stock. If they are pursued, however, the aforementioned complexities apply. Once an agreement in principle has been reached, a disclosure is required.

INSIDER TRADING

Who or what is an insider, and what is insider trading?

An insider is an officer, a director, or a principal shareholder (generally, any beneficial owner of more than 10 percent of the company's equity securities). An insider may also include any employee who, in the course of his or her employment, acquires material nonpublic information about a publicly traded corporation. These individuals owe a fiduciary duty to the employer and its securityholders not to trade on this information prior to its release and absorption by the market. In addition, outsiders may become temporary insiders if they are given information in confidence solely for a corporate purpose. Attorneys, accountants, consultants, investment bankers, financial printers, and underwriters are examples of temporary insiders who are involved in a merger or acquisition.

Insider trading is trading by insiders. Not all insider trading is illegal; only insider trading based on nonpublic information. A common type of insider trading involves trading on knowledge of mergers and acquisitions. This may be closely scrutinized by the SEC and may result in criminal prosecutions and very substantial civil penalties. The first major crackdown in insider trading occurred in the 1980s in New York courts under then district attorney Rudolph Giuliani, who later became the city's mayor. Books written about this era remain bestsellers for their insights into the dark side of equity markets.[61]

What US laws prohibit insider trading?

Most insider trading cases are covered by one well-known rule promulgated by the SEC under authority of the Exchange Act, Rule 10b-5, which prohibits fraudulent or manipulative conduct in connection with the purchase or sale of securities. The reach of 10b-5 on "Employment of Manipulative and Deceptive Devices" is very broad, but its text is extremely short. In its entirety it reads as follows:

> It shall be unlawful for any person, directly or indirectly, by the use of any means or instrumentality of interstate commerce, or of the mails, or of any facility of any national securities exchange:
>
> (a) To employ any device, scheme, or artifice to defraud,
> (b) To make any untrue statement of a material fact or to omit to state a material fact necessary in order to make

> the statements made, in the light of the circumstances under which they were made, not misleading, or
>
> (c) To engage in any act, practice, or course of business which operates or would operate as a fraud or deceit upon any person, in connection with the purchase or sale of any security.

Additional interpretation of this rule appears in the Insider Trading and Securities Fraud Enforcement Act of 1988, passed by Congress as part of a crackdown against insider trading over merger information. Relevant guidance is also found in the Securities Litigation Uniform Standards Act of 1998 (SLUSA).

Which has priority in a securities class action lawsuit, federal or state law?

On March 21, 2006, in *Merrill Lynch, Pierce, Fenner & Smith, Inc. v. Dabit,*[62] the Supreme Court ruled that SLUSA preempts "covered class actions" purportedly brought under state law on behalf of persons who neither purchased nor sold securities, but instead claim that they were defrauded into refraining from purchasing or selling securities. In doing so, the Supreme Court reaffirmed long-standing policy considerations underlying the application and interpretation of the federal securities laws, which recognize that "litigation under Rule 10b-5 presents a danger of vexatiousness different in degree and in kind from that which accompanies litigation in general."

What other laws prohibit insider trading in a tender offer?

Rule 14e-3 prohibits trading on the basis of inside information in the context of a tender offer, whether as an insider or as the "tippee" of an insider. Also, Section 16(b) of the Exchange Act prohibits any officer or director, or any shareholder owning more than 10 percent of the issuer's stock, from profiting from a purchase and sale or a sale and purchase (a short sale) of securities of the issuer within a six-month period. This is known as the short-swing profit rule. Any profits from such a purchase and sale or sale and purchase must be paid to the issuer. The short-swing profit rule applies whether or not that person was in possession of material inside information.

Can a shareholder who has exchanged his or her stock in a company for the stock of the company's acquirer sue for Section 16(b) violations?

Yes. In the 1991 case of *Gollust v. Mendell,*[63] the US Supreme Court affirmed the legal standing of the plaintiff, a shareholder of Viacom International, Inc., to sue Coniston Partners for alleged 16(b) violations in connection with its 10 percent holding in the company, which was later merged into Viacom, Inc. (today part of Paramount, Inc.). The court ruled that the plaintiff's ownership of stock in the parent corporation, whose only asset was the stock of the issuer, gave it standing to sue. Securities tax specialists have noted, however, that "the Court's reasoning could result in the opposite outcome if a merger were solely for cash."

Must a tender offeror file under Section 16 of the Exchange Act?

Yes. Once a tender offeror becomes a beneficial owner of 10 percent of the target's securities, it is an insider for purposes of Section 16 and must file a Form 3 with the SEC within 10 days of becoming an insider. The amount and type of ownership interest of the offeror must be disclosed on Form 3. An offeror must file a Form 4 upon any subsequent change in its beneficial ownership of the target's securities. The Form 4 must be filed within 10 days after the end of any month in which change in beneficial ownership occurred. Forms 3 and 4 must be filed with the SEC and the exchange on which the target securities are traded. All persons required to file Forms 3 and 4 are subject to Section 16(b).

Are there any exemptions from Section 16(b) liability that apply to mergers and acquisitions?

Yes. Under Rule 16b-7 an insider is exempt from liability under Section 16(b) if it acquires or disposes of shares pursuant to a merger or consolidation of companies and one of the companies owns 85 percent or more of the stock or combined assets of the other.[64] Rule 16b-7 usually applies to second-stage mergers after completion of a partial tender offer.

Also, a transaction that does not follow a typical sale-purchase or purchase-sale sequence may be exempt from the automatic liability provisions of Section 16(b). Unorthodox transactions, such as option transactions, stock conversions and reclassifications, and mergers of a target into a white knight and other corporate reorganizations are frequently judged by a pragmatic or subjective test that may enable an insider to avoid liability when the automatic rules of Section 16(b) might otherwise apply. Under this alternative test, liability may be avoided if the insider did not have access to inside information or if the insider did not have a control relationship with the issuer of the securities.

What is the "disclose or abstain" theory, and how is it applied?

The disclose or abstain theory applies when an individual possesses material nonpublic information about a corporation to which he or she owes a fiduciary duty. The individual must either disclose the information to the market or abstain from trading in securities of the affected company. In the classic *Texas Gulf Sulfur*[65] case of 1968, the Second Circuit Court of Appeals in New York ruled that anyone who possesses material inside information must either strive to tell all (and trade if they wish) or tell nobody and refrain from trading.

In practical terms, disclose or abstain means *abstain.* To be effective, disclosure of a material development affecting a security must result in dissemination broad enough to inform the entire public trading in that security. Most individuals cannot adequately disseminate such information themselves, and disclosure itself may constitute a breach of fiduciary duty. If the inside information is incomplete or inaccurate, disclosure could be misleading to other investors and result in separate liability under other SEC disclosure rules.

What is the misappropriation theory, and how is it applied?

The misappropriation theory of liability holds that an individual violates the securities laws when he or she secretly converts information given to him or her for legitimate business or commercial purposes by trading on the information for personal benefit.

The Supreme Court upheld the misappropriation theory of liability in a case involving *Wall Street Journal* reporter R. Foster Winans. Winans was charged with, among other offenses, violating the securities laws by misappropriating information from his employer, even though the information was not about his employer and was not used to trade in his employer's securities.[66] In the Winans case, the misappropriated information was the content and timing of publication of Winans's influential "Heard on the Street" column in the *Wall Street Journal* about market information.

Can an insider be convicted of insider trading if the insider is unaware that information he or she is trading on is material and confidential?

Traditionally, the answer has been no. Section 10(b) has a *scienter* requirement. This means that to be found liable for violating Rule 10b-5, an insider must have either "actual knowledge" of the fraud or omission or have acted with "recklessness and disregard of the truth."[67] Furthermore, judicial interpretation of 10b-5 has often centered on the issue of fiduciary duty of the tipper to the issuer of the securities or some other party. But another key insider trading rule, Rule 14e-3, does *not* contain such a requirement.

How does Rule 14e-3 operate?

Rule 14e-3(a) prohibits an individual from trading while he or she possesses material nonpublic information concerning a tender offer if the individual knows or has reason to know that such information is nonpublic and has been obtained, directly or indirectly, from any of the following: the entity making the tender offer, the corporation that is the subject of the tender offer, any persons affiliated with these entities, or any person acting on behalf of either entity. The transfer of such information from a tipper to a tippee violates laws against tipping.

What is tipping, and what laws prohibit it?

Tipping is the selective disclosure of material nonpublic information for trading or other personal purposes. Courts have interpreted Rule 10b-5 to prohibit tipping, although the rule does not address the issue directly. Rule 14e-3, which supplements Rule 10b-5, does contain an antitipping provision that applies in the context of a takeover. However, neither of these Rules contains the term *tipping.* The Insider Trading Sanctions Act of 1984 expressly imposes civil penalties for tipping.

What is a tipper?

A tipper is a person who, in return for some direct or indirect benefit, provides material nonpublic information to another person who then trades in that security.

What is a tippee?

A tippee is a person who receives material nonpublic information about a security and then trades in that security. Note that a tippee may also become a tipper if he or she then divulges the information to another person (who becomes a second-level tippee, and who might then tip to another person, and so on).

How does Rule 10b-5 treat tipping?

Tipping is only prohibited by Rule 10b-5 if two tests are met: (1) the tipper has breached a duty that he or she owed to the corporation or its shareholders (for example, a fiduciary duty to a company and its shareholders as an officer and director), and (2) the insider will receive a personal benefit, directly or indirectly, from the disclosure.

If the tipper gains no personal benefit, can he or she still be accused of tipping?

No. But the interpretation of "benefit" is very broad. Obvious examples of personal benefit include not only monetary gain but also any enhancement of the tipper's reputation that might translate into increased future earnings. However, the Supreme Court has stated that divulging inside information to a relative or friend who then trades and returns a gift or a portion of the proceeds resembles trading by the tipper him- or herself.

Under Rule 10b-5, must a tippee have such a fiduciary relationship with the tipper?

No, the typical tippee has no such relationship. However, if the tippee knows or should have known of the tipper's breach of duty and participates in the violation through silence or inaction, the tippee becomes liable as an aider and abettor if he or she then trades or divulges the information to one who trades.

How does Rule 14e-3 treat tipping?

In contrast to Rule 10b-5, Rule 14e-3(d) contains clear antitipping provisions in the context of tender offers (although even in Rule 14e-3, the word *tipping* is not used). Rule 14e-3(d) makes it unlawful for certain persons to "communicate material, nonpublic information relating to a tender offer . . . under circumstances in which it is reasonably foreseeable that such communication is likely to result in [improper trading or tipping]." This portion of the rule expressly excludes communications "made in good faith to certain individuals."

When are the antitipping provisions of Rule 14e-3 triggered?

Rule 14e-3 is triggered when any person has taken a "substantial step" to commence a tender offer, even if the offer never actually begins. A substantial step includes the offeror's directors voting on a resolution with respect to the tender offer, the offeror's formulation of a plan to make an offer, arranging financing for a tender offer, authorizing negotiations for a tender offer, and directing that tender offer materials be prepared.

Suppose a tipper or tippee doesn't make money?

This can make a court more lenient, since the amount earned is one factor that courts, particularly appellate courts, weigh in rendering decisions.

FINANCING THE TWO-STEP PUBLIC TRANSACTION WITH DEBT

Is the financing of a public company acquisition very different from the financing of the acquisition of a private company?

The financing of a one-step transaction, involving the merger of an acquiring company into the target, is essentially the same as the financing of any other acquisition (see Chapter 4). The financing of a two-step acquisition (a tender offer followed by a merger of the acquiring company into the target) is somewhat different.

How is the financing of a two-step transaction different?

The financing of the first step, the tender offer, is subject to Federal Reserve margin rules. These rules generally prohibit lenders, including banks, brokers, and others, from making loans secured directly or indirectly by margin stock (most publicly traded stock) if the loan exceeds a specified percentage of the value of the collateral (generally, 50 percent).

For example, if the acquisition subsidiary intends to acquire stock of a target worth $100 million in a tender offer, the maximum secured loan that can be made would be $50 million. This means that the other $50 million has to be financed by other than secured loans, such as unsecured debt or equity investments. The unsecured loans may be, for example, bridge loans from investment bankers or privately placed debt. Assets of the target are, of course, not available to secure the financing until after the merger.

It is important to know that the margin rules apply even to indirectly secured debt; the substance, not the form, of the transaction will govern the application of the rules. Therefore, if the borrower has no assets other than the target stock and has agreed with the lender not to pledge the stock to any other lender, the loan may be deemed to be indirectly secured by the stock.

If the acquisition subsidiary is a shell corporation, can it freely incur unsecured debt and not violate the margin rules?

No. The position of the Federal Reserve has been that if lenders make unsecured loans to a shell subsidiary for purposes of a tender offer, the loan will be presumed to be secured by margin stock subject to the 50 percent of value limitation. There is an important exception to this rule: the presumption does not apply if a merger agreement with the target is signed prior to the closing of the tender offer. Thus, in the case of a friendly two-step transaction, it is important that a merger agreement be signed *before* the tender offer in order to facilitate the financing of the tender offer. If there is no merger agreement, the amount that can't be financed under the margin rules may have to be financed by preferred or common equity or by loans guaranteed by other entities that have substantial assets.

TAKEOVER DEFENSES

What does the directors' duty of loyalty require when responding to an unsolicited tender offer?

When considering the response to an unsolicited tender offer, the board of directors of a target corporation owes a duty of loyalty to the corporation's shareholders to adopt defensive measures to defeat a takeover attempt that is contrary to the best interests of the corporation and its shareholders. However, the board must be careful to adopt defensive measures only when motivated by a good-faith concern for the welfare of the corporation and its shareholders.

Does it violate the duty of loyalty if a board adopts a defensive tactic in part to retain management control?

No. Defending a corporation against hostile takeovers to maintain control, among other motives, does not violate the duty of loyalty. However, it is improper if a director's sole or primary motive for implementing a defensive tactic is to retain control of the company.

What factors should a board of directors consider before it decides to defend itself against a tender offer?

Before deciding to defend a company against a potential tender offer, directors should take into account the following considerations:

- The attitudes of existing major shareholders about the defenses
- The present and future impact of defenses on the value of the company's stock
- The ability of the company to pursue a negotiated transaction with friendly bidders (white knights) if the defensive measures are implemented
- The reasonableness of the defenses in relation to the threat posed

On what basis can directors reject an acquisition offer?

There are generally three reasons why an offer can be rejected and defenses implemented: (1) the offer is inadequate (that is, the target company's directors have information that enables them to make a reasonable judgment that the company's outstanding capital stock is worth more than what is being offered), (2) the offer is unfair in that those stockholders not tendering their shares will receive less consideration at a later date (such as in the case of a front-end-loaded, two-tier offer), or (3) the company determines that it is better served by remaining independent.

What defenses are commonly adopted against hostile takeovers?

Of some 40 varieties of defenses available to companies, the most common are antitrust defenses, restructuring defenses, "poison pills," charter and bylaw amendments, defensive sales or acquisitions, and defensive payments. State antitakeover statutes can also play an important role in defending against a hostile takeover.

What is an antitrust defense?

In a typical antitrust defense, the target accuses a bidder of violating antitrust rules by tendering for it. For example, a target can request a delay in a takeover bid by claiming the two companies were in the same market segment—electrical products.

What are the main types of restructuring defenses?

Common restructuring defenses include recapitalizations, self-tenders, and master limited partnerships.

How do recapitalizations work as a takeover defense?

A recapitalization substitutes portions of the outstanding capital stock held by the public with cash, debt instruments or securities, or preferred stock. These transactions may increase the percentage of voting stock held by management and employee benefit plans. They may also increase ownership levels of individual stockholders who retain their stock instead of selling into the company buyback. (Indeed, a recapitalization has been likened to a public leveraged buyout because the number of outstanding shares decreases as they are purchased by the company, thereby increasing the percentage holdings of remaining stockholders.)

There are basically three ways to accomplish a recapitalization:

- Through a tender offer for the company's own stock.
- Through a transaction such as a merger, where a subsidiary merges into the company when the plan becomes effective.
- Through a reclassification amendment of the company's charter. (This requires shareholder approval and may involve the issuance of options to shareholders to purchase shares of the recapitalized company upon the occurrence of certain events.)

It is also sometimes possible to issue massive dividends to stockholders, financing such a transaction through debt. Any one of these actions can cool off even the most ardent of pursuers.

Each type of recapitalization has its advantages and disadvantages. In a tender offer situation, speed is the primary advantage because no stockholder vote or proxy statement is required. The company may also issue securities without filing a registration statement with the SEC because Section 3(a)(9) of the Securities Act permits the exchange of securities without registration if it only affects existing securityholders, and no remuneration is paid for soliciting the exchange.

Recapitalizations have generally withstood court challenges. However, courts will not uphold recapitalizations that appear coercive, that is, leave the stockholders without a real option to decline participation.

How can a company recapitalize using an employee stock ownership plan (ESOP)?

An ESOP may be used as a tool in a recapitalization. An ESOP purchases stock in the open market or from the company, allowing its employees and management to own part of the company. By borrowing to acquire the shares, an ESOP can help finance a recapitalization; it can also purchase shares directly from unrelated parties at a premium, which allows it to purchase shares from a hostile bidder. The disadvantage of ESOP participation is this: it can dilute the public's percentage of ownership in the company if the company issues new shares to the ESOP.

An ESOP is managed by trustees who have the duty to act in the best interests of its beneficiaries. If the trustees are also the company's directors, a hostile bidder may assert a conflict of interest by the directors and question their motives for initiating an ESOP during a takeover attempt. The suggestion would be that the directors, as trustees, implemented the ESOP not in the interest of the beneficiaries, but to fend off the bidder and preserve management.

There may also be a conflict of interest issue when the ESOP is in place before a hostile bid, if the trustees decide to purchase more of the company's stock immediately preceding or during such a bid. However, if the trustees can justify their decisions on the basis of acting in the best interests of all the ESOP's participants and demonstrate the requisite detached judgment, legal challenges can be overcome.

What are some of the concerns involved in a recapitalization?

A company that has undertaken a recapitalization that has caused it to become highly leveraged or cash poor may no longer have the financial resources to weather unexpected economic conditions or even to carry on its intended business. The recapitalization plan that engenders such consequences is subject to the federal fraudulent conveyance and transfer laws, the Federal Bankruptcy Code, and state laws (see Chapters 4 and 11). Creditors and stockholders alike may contend that the company has become insolvent or is no longer able to function with the remaining working capital, or that the company has incurred debts that are beyond its capacity to repay.

Most states impose limitations upon a company's ability to make dividend distributions and to repurchase or redeem its own stock if such transactions would impair the company's capital. These corporation statutes may affect the kind of recapitalization a company might initiate.

How do self-tenders work?

A self-tender is a defensive measure implemented to defeat an unsolicited tender offer or at least to obtain a higher price. The company announces its intentions to repurchase its own outstanding stock, or a portion thereof, to prevent the offeror from acquiring a controlling interest in the company. Stock repurchases are seldom effective as a defensive tactic if not combined with other techniques, such as stock purchases by management, by ESOPs, or by other major stockholders, which tend to lock up substantial blocks of stock in friendly hands.

How can open market repurchases dissuade hostile takeovers?

By repurchasing its own shares on the open market without making a formal tender offer, not only can a company boost its level of ownership, crowding hostile acquirers, but it can also maintain or increase its stock prices and thereby make itself less attractive to a bidder. Such purchases, whether financed by cash flow, asset sales, or borrowing, tend to reduce the benefits of a potential buyer while increasing the burdens.

What legal considerations are there in a repurchase?

In implementing a repurchase plan, directors must satisfy the business judgment rule and comply with various other state and federal laws, including, in particular, Rule 10b-18, which regulates the purchase of registered equity securities by an issuer.

How do poison pills work?

A poison pill, the nickname for what is technically called a shareholders' rights plan, involves the issuance to stockholders of rights to acquire securities. These rights can be exercised only under certain circumstances (such as a takeover attempt) and may be redeemed by the company at a nominal price until the occurrence of such events. The primary objective of poison pills is to give management leverage in negotiating bids in order to avoid unfair treatment of stockholders (in coercive two-tier takeovers or partial tenders) and ensure a minimum price in any takeover.

Although poison pills normally do not require stockholder approval, shareholders at some companies have put forth successful proxy resolutions recommending a change in company bylaws to require shareholder approval of their company's shareholders' rights plan, or redemptions in full.

There are two common kinds of poison pills: flip-over and back-end. These may be combined in one defensive plan. Less frequently seen, and not described here, are flip-in, convertible preferred stock, and voting rights poison pills.

The use of poison pills as a defensive measure has generally been upheld by courts, but some plans have been enjoined because of their specific provisions and purposes. In implementing these plans, directors must be able to prove that the measure was adopted in good faith after reasonable investigation and is reasonably related to the threat posed.

What are flip-over plans?

In this plan, each common stockholder receives for each share owned a right to purchase shares of the surviving corporation upon the occurrence of a triggering event. Triggering events are typically the acquisition by a single purchaser or group of a specified amount of stock or the commencement of a tender offer for a specified percentage of the company's stock. Following the occurrence of a triggering event, the company issues certificates to stockholders that allow them to exercise and trade their rights. Because the rights issuance is in the nature of a dividend, it does not generally require shareholder approval, although company bylaws may mandate this.

The rights usually allow the certificate holder to purchase stock of the surviving entity for half price after the merger has been consummated, so the effect of the flip-over is to reduce the acquirer's equity. There is a plus and minus here. Because the rights usually may be redeemed for a nominal amount before the triggering event (and often within a short period of time thereafter), a bidder has an incentive to negotiate with management before the actual takeover attempt. But there is a catch: once the takeover bid has occurred and the rights become redeemable, they may adversely affect the company's ability to negotiate with a white knight, as they would dilute the white knight's future potential equity.

Thus, a flip-over plan should also include a provision that a transaction approved by the directors will not result in the stockholders' rights becoming exercisable even though the triggering events have occurred. Such a provision allows the company to seek a white knight.

What are back-end plans?

A back-end plan is similar to a flip-over plan, although its objectives differ. Holders of the company's common stock receive a right for each share owned that entitles them, upon the occurrence of certain triggering events (for example, a 20 percent acquisition by a bidder), to exchange each share for a note that matures typically within a short period of time (such as one year). Alternatively, the right may be exchanged for cash or preferred stock, or a combination of the three. The value of the right may be fixed at the outset or may be calculated from a formula based on the highest price per share paid or offered by a bidder during the takeover attempt.

The purpose of the plan is to maximize stockholder value in the event of a merger or business combination by ensuring a minimum acceptable price and to protect stockholders from the adverse effects a significant minority interest can have on other bidders even if no merger results. A back-end plan is not designed to prevent a takeover but to ensure a proper negotiated value for the company and its stockholders.

The plan will usually provide that the rights will not be exercisable if the acquirer, upon reaching a certain level of ownership, offers to purchase the remainder of the outstanding shares at the price set by the plan. The rights are usually redeemable for a specified period of time (for example, 120 days) to allow a bidder to express its intentions to complete the transaction as specified.

Such a plan will likely be upheld by the courts if (1) it is not designed to prevent all takeovers, (2) the back-end price is reached with the advice of investment bankers and reflects the realizable value over the plan's life (for example, one year), (3) the plan is a reasonable response to the threat perceived by the directors (for example, a possible second-step merger), and (4) the plan is plausibly related to the goal of shareholder wealth maximization.

How do charter and bylaw amendments help companies deter takeovers?

Charter and bylaw amendments will generally not prevent takeover attempts, but they do provide protection from coercive and abusive acquisition tactics. These amendments may also slow down the acquisition process, giving the company's directors more time to react and negotiate. Proposed amendments must be approved by stockholders.

Any amendments adopted by the stockholders will apply equally to the company's management and any bidder who acquires shares. There is another important consideration in adopting amendments: if the stockholders reject the proposals, the company may seem—and indeed may be—more vulnerable to takeovers by bidders.

What kinds of defensive charter and bylaw amendments are there?

The most widely used charter and bylaw amendments include supermajority provisions, fair price provisions, contingent cumulative voting provisions, staggered board provisions, defensive consent requirements/notice of business and special meetings provisions, and special classes of stock.

What are supermajority provisions?

A company may adopt a charter amendment to require more than a simple majority (a supermajority) of its stockholders to approve certain matters, such as any merger or business combination. There are several effective variations of this defense, one of which is a requirement that a majority of the disinterested stockholders—a majority of the minority—approve the transaction. To protect the supermajority provisions, there should be a provision that would require a supermajority to modify the supermajority provisions of the charter.

What are the drawbacks of supermajority provisions?

One of the disadvantages of supermajority provisions is that they apply to friendly as well as hostile takeovers. Therefore, to the extent such provisions may deter hostile bidders, they may also make it more difficult to negotiate a friendly takeover. As a partial cure, such a provision may be coupled with one specifying that a simple majority is sufficient if the directors approve the merger.

Some companies can find themselves stuck with supermajority provisions that are unnecessarily broad.

What are fair price provisions?

A fair price provision is a variation of a supermajority requirement that would require a specified supermajority to approve a proposed merger unless the bidder pays the minority stockholders a fair price. Usually a fair price means a price that equals or exceeds the highest price paid by the bidder in acquiring shares of the company before the merger. The purpose of this provision is to ensure fairness to stockholders in a two-tier acquisition.

How does contingent cumulative voting work as a defense?

Cumulative voting permits a stockholder to vote the number of shares owned by him or her multiplied by the number of directors being elected; all of a stockholder's potential votes may be added together and cast for a specific director.

Contingent cumulative voting, if coupled with a staggered board of directors, may provide the minority stockholders who disfavor the merger with a tool to block or delay the election of a slate of the bidder's directors. For example, a charter amendment may provide that when and if a bidder acquires a certain specified percentage of the company's stock (for example, 35 percent or more), cumulative voting goes into effect. In this case, the minority stockholders may be able to elect or retain more directors than if the charter amendment were not in place.

What effect does a staggered board have on a target company?

The election of directors on a staggered basis—usually one-third of the directors are elected each year for a three-year term—prevents a bidder from electing a new slate of directors in a single meeting of stockholders and thereby gaining immediate control of management.

By itself, the staggered board (or "classified board") provision would not deter a takeover, but in conjunction with contingent cumulative voting, staggered elections may give a company more flexibility in dealing with unwanted bidders. Only 10 percent of S&P 500 firms had staggered boards in 2018, but the practice is more widespread in smaller public companies.[68]

How do "consent requirements" provisions work?

Many states' corporation laws provide that a majority of stockholders may, without calling a meeting, act by written consent. A company that does not amend its charter to provide otherwise may be susceptible to a bidder acquiring a majority interest and then immediately amending its charter to remove other impediments to control.

To combat this possibility, the company may, by charter amendment, eliminate the written consent provisions entirely or require that all stockholders consent before actions can be approved without a meeting unless state law prohibits the elimination of the consent procedure. If the consent procedure cannot be eliminated, the company may consider amending its charter or bylaws to require stockholders wishing to take action by written consent to notify the board of directors and request that it establish a record date to determine which stockholders are entitled to sign a consent. The passage of such an amendment would also permit the directors a reasonable opportunity to prepare a response and oppose the proposed action, by soliciting proxies, if necessary. Such an amendment might also contain specified periods for consent revocation and consent validity.

What about special classes of stock?

Until 1988 many corporations defending against takeovers created special classes of stock that gave superior voting rights to management. In that year the SEC approved Rule 19c-4, the "one share, one vote rule" that banned such a technique. Some exchanges—the New York Stock Exchange (NYSE) and Nasdaq—have similar rules. In 1990 in *Business Round Table v. SEC,* the US Court of Appeals for the Second Circuit overturned Rule 19c-4, and companies returned to this practice. Although the NYSE does have a rule against multiple classes of stock, it has limited application. Berkshire Hathaway, Ford Motor Company, and the *New York Times* have all had such a structure.

What kinds of defensive sales are there?

A company may sell a crown jewel to avoid being taken over, may radically downsize itself, or may sell its stock to a white squire or white knight.

What is the crown jewel defense?

The crown jewel defense is the sale of particularly attractive assets by the target company to dissuade a bidder from pursuing its takeover attempt. Such sales may also give the company flexibility and resources to fend off a bidder by generating capital and/or reducing costs. On the other hand, if a bidder is interested in a specific asset, such as a subsidiary, and is willing to acquire the entire company for it, the asset may be very valuable to the company as well, and its sale may be detrimental over the long term.

As discussed earlier, courts will generally view with disfavor an asset or crown jewel lockup that has the effect of stopping or discouraging the bidding process.

What is a white squire?

To remain independent, the company may determine that its best course of action is to sell a large block of its stock to a friendly investor, a white squire, that the company does not believe is a threat. The more well-known white squires are investment vehicles such as Warren Buffett's Berkshire Partners or Goldman Sachs's GS Capital Partners V, L.P., but white squires can also be operating companies. The obvious danger here is that relations between the white squire and the company may take a turn for the worse, and the white squire may decide to acquire control of the company at a later date.

To prevent the white squire from becoming a hostile bidder, companies typically use standstill agreements. A standstill agreement imposes certain limitations on the investor that assure the company that the stock will not find its way to a hostile bidder. Typically, the stock purchase agreement will limit the percentage of stock the white squire may acquire in addition to the shares in question for a specific period of time. It will also contain restrictions on the resale of the minority interest to third parties, which is usually coupled with a right of first refusal by the company. The voting rights relating to the block of shares sold also may be limited.

The directors' decision to enter into such an arrangement and the provisions of the standstill agreement will be evaluated under the business judgment doctrine. These arrangements are generally upheld if the court finds that entrenchment is not the directors' sole or primary purpose.

What is a white knight?

A white knight is a friendly acquirer sought by the target as a positive alternative to a hostile acquirer. Unless the friendly acquirer pays as much or more than a hostile acquirer, however, this kind of defensive sale is vulnerable to legal challenge.

What is in it for the white knight?

White knights can make money in the right deal. A. Alfred Taubman, for example, made an estimated profit of $275 million on his gallant purchase of Sotheby's Holdings, Inc., the auction house.

May a company make an acquisition or agree to a merger to avoid being acquired?

Yes. A company may combat an unwanted bidder by acquiring other companies or divisions that make it less attractive to the bidder. The company may also acquire assets that may precipitate an antitrust problem for the bidder if the transaction is completed. The effectiveness of antitrust barriers is mitigated by the fact that government agencies are generally willing to consider proposed curative measures by the bidder (that is, a promise to sell the unit[s] in question) before rejecting a merger.

What is the Pac-Man™ strategy of defense?

When a company learns it is the object of a tender offer, it may respond by tender offering for the stock of the hostile bidder. In this eat-or-be-eaten strategy, named after a video game popular in the early 1980s, the company undertaking the counter tender offer thereby concedes that the business combination is desirable but indicates that it should control the resulting entity. It also forgoes certain defenses it might otherwise bring, such as antitrust and other regulatory barriers that concern the legality of the combination.

The disadvantages of the Pac-Man defense are that the original target company's stockholders will not receive any premium (the original target company may actually give the other company's stockholders a premium), it is very costly, and it may damage the company, even if successful. When considering the legality of this defense, courts will apply the business judgment rule.

What kinds of defensive payments may a target make?

Two ways to spend a company out of immediate danger are *greenmail* and *golden parachutes.* Both, however, entail risks.

What are the potential risks of greenmail as a takeover defense?

Bidders sometimes accumulate stock and threaten to initiate a tender offer with the ultimate purpose of reselling those shares to the company at a premium rather than obtaining control of the company. Greenmail is a payment to purchase such stock at a premium.

Paying greenmail is largely ineffective in protecting the interests of the target (other greenmailers may surface once the company has succumbed the first time), discriminatory (other holders of the same class of stock may not share in the premium), and legally questionable (there have been stockholder lawsuits with various degrees of success to recover greenmail payments as corporate assets). Furthermore, greenmail is relatively unpopular with stockholders.

Finally, greenmail payments are expensive for both the payor and the payee. Not only are the premiums high, but they may be taxable. Section 5881 of the IRC imposes a 50 percent excise tax on greenmail payments, payable by the recipient.[69]

What are golden, lead, and tin parachute payments?

These are the nicknames given to severance payments promised to top management, middle management, and workers, respectively, in the event of their dismissal during or immediately subsequent to a change of control.

STATE LAWS RELATED TO TAKEOVER DEFENSE

What provisions of state law limit director and officer liability for defensive measures?

Charter opt-in provisions authorize corporations to pass a charter or bylaw provision eliminating or reducing the personal liability of directors for money damages. This provision is particularly significant in takeovers, since many shareholder suits against defensive target boards do request money damages.

Several states have raised the threshold of liability to require more than proof of simple negligence by board members. Gross negligence, or recklessness, generally must be proved by the plaintiff for personal liability to attach.

Other provisions protecting directors include expanded indemnification for derivative suits against the board, expanded provisions permitting corporations to provide benefits other than indemnification, and provisions that permit directors to base their decision to reject an offer on considerations other than price, for example, the effect of the transaction on the community and other corporate constituencies.

What states have passed antitakeover statutes?

As of mid-2019, 43 states had passed antitakeover statutes—all states except Alabama, Alaska, Arkansas, California, Montana, New Hampshire, and West Virginia. Washington, D.C., where some public companies are incorporated (although it is not a state), has no antitakeover statutes, either. Common wisdom said that antitakeover laws could be a draw for incorporation, but recent research indicates that governance flexibility is more important.

Antitakeover statutes apply generally to corporations organized within the state. However, some states (for example, Massachusetts) have statutes asserting that companies not incorporated in the state will still be subjected to the statute's provisions under certain circumstances—for example, if the companies have substantial operations there (such as executive offices), if the bulk of their workforces or assets are in the state, if at least 10 percent of the shares are owned by state residents (excluding brokers or nominees), or if 10 percent of the shareholders reside in the state.

What are the most common state antitakeover statutes?

State antitakeover statutes may offer one or more of several protections. In approximate order of popularity, these are laws: banning *freeze-outs;* protecting the right to honor *other constituencies,* also called *stakeholder* statutes or *nonstockholder* or *nonmonetary considerations;* setting a *control share* requirement; requiring *fair prices;* and allowing *poison pills.* Others include antigreenmail provisions, labor contract or severance pay requirements, cash-out requirements, recapture of profits, and classified board mandates for staggered terms of board service.

How does a freeze-out provision work?

It freezes deals at least temporarily by stating that acquirers of companies incorporated in the state must wait a certain period—from two to five years—before completing the second step of their desired merger with resistant targets, under a defined supermajority vote for the merger initially.

What about "other constituency" statutes?

These impose a different standard of care on directors in evaluating any business combination. Directors must examine and consider the long-term effects of an offer on the company, its stockholders, the affected community, and other corporate constituencies.

What is a "control share" statute?

This is a statute regulating a "control share acquisition," typically defined as the acquisition of enough shares in a target company to give the acquirer control over more than a specified percentage of the voting power of the target. The triggering level of share ownership is usually defined as an acquisition that would bring the bidder within a certain range of voting power—with thresholds variously defined as more than 10, 20, 33.3, or 50 percent, with share purchases exceeding these levels defined as controlling. Most control share acquisition laws state that shares acquired in a control share acquisition shall not have voting rights unless the shareholders approve a resolution granting voting rights to the acquirer's shares.

What is a fair price statute?

These require any bidder who is rebuffed by a board to pay a defined fair price to all shareholders unless a supermajority approves the bid.

How do poison pill and antigreenmail provisions work?

Poison pill provisions authorize corporate boards to enact shareholders' rights plans. Without such authorization, poison pills may not be instituted or may be more vulnerable to legal attack by regulators or shareholders.

Conversely, antigreenmail provisions effectively ban, rather than protect, another popular antitakeover measure. These bar the repurchase of a specified percentage of shares at a premium from an investor who has held the shares for less than a specified amount of time, unless the same premium is offered to all shareholders, or all shareholders approve it.

Could you describe antitakeover provisions governing labor contracts?

Some states force acquirers to honor labor contracts, providing severance pay for employees who lose their jobs as a result of a takeover. Some states have adopted cash-out provisions requiring the acquirer of a certain percentage of a company's shares to buy the shares of remaining shareholders at a statutorily defined fair price.

Do any states ban specific antitakeover practices?

Yes. Some states have enacted statutes prohibiting companies from granting nonroutine increases in compensation such as golden parachutes or special bonuses while a tender offer is open.

CONCLUDING COMMENTS

Leaders of public companies engaging in merger transactions need to retain advisors who know the regulations surrounding public company mergers.

They also need to build positive relations with their shareholders and other constituencies, including employees, customers, and bondholders. If they master these two Rs (regulations and relations), their companies are more likely to avoid problems such as poor economic performance. Unfortunately, however, this is a risk for every company, public or private. The next chapter will consider what happens in public and private companies when a company faces insolvency.

NOTES

1. The 8,000 number for companies registered with the SEC is from the 2019 budget of that agency. See US Securities and Exchange Commission, Fiscal Year 2019 Congressional Budget Justification Annual Performance Plan, 2, stating that "the SEC is responsible for selectively reviewing the disclosures and financial statements of over 8,000 reporting companies, of which approximately 4,100 are exchange listed." Source: Fiscal year 2019 Congressional Budget Justification Annual Performance Plan, p. 3 https://www.sec.gov/files/secfy19congbudgjust.pdf.
2. The number of companies listed on stock exchanges has dropped by half during the past two decades. In 1996, more than 8,000 companies listed on US stock exchanges. In 2016, the number was 4,333. And the trend is worldwide, with 20 to 60 percent of stock listings lost in that period. See Gary D. Halbert, "Number of U.S. Companies Falls by Over 50 Percent," July 31, 2018, https://www.valuewalk.com/2018/07/number-of-us-public-companies-fall-50/ Number of US Public Companies Falls By Almost 50%.
3. US Securities Act of 1933, Section 2(a)1.

4. The author acknowledges the expertise of Robert D. Ferris, Managing Director, R. F. Binder, retired, who provided the answer to this question, and who reviewed this entire chapter, adding many insights related to his expertise in communications.
5. https://ecfr.io/Title-17/pt17.3.230.
6. https://ecfr.io/Title-17/cfr240_main.
7. The most recent revision was published in 2016. See https://www.americanbar.org/news/abanews/aba-news-archives/2016/12/aba_releases_firstc.html.
8. For a list of more than a dozen securities law provisions that may be cited in M&A litigation, see Kaufman, Gildin, and Robbins, LLC, "Securities Litigation: Claims and Defenses," 2018, https://www.securitieslosses.com/Securities-Arbitration-and-Litigation_PC/Securities-1-Securities-Arbitration-and-Litigation_PC.shtml.
9. In 2018, plaintiffs filed 403 federal securities class action lawsuits, and of these, 182 (45 percent) involved allegations of Section 14 violations in the context of an M&A transaction. "Securities Class Action Filings: 2018 Year in Review," Cornerstone Research, 2019, https://www.cornerstone.com/Publications/Reports/Securities-Class-Action-Filings-2018-Year-in-Review.
10. https://www.barrons.com/articles/proxy-voting-is-broken-and-needs-to-change-1530924318.
11. For submitted comments, see https://www.sec.gov/comments/4-725/4-725.htm.
12. See "Transfer Agent Overview," Computershare, 2014, https://www.computershare.com/us/Documents/TA_Overview_WhitePaper.pdf.
13. Gerald P. Dwyer, "Stock Prices in the Financial Crisis," Federal Reserve Bank of Atlanta, September 2009, https://www.frbatlanta.org/cenfis/publications/notesfromthevault/0909.

14. Hailey Ballew, et al., "Regulatory Asset Thresholds and Acquisition Activity in the Banking Industry," SSRN, June 20, 2017, https://papers.ssrn.com/sol3/papers.cfm?abstract_id=2910440.
15. See "Financial Regulation in the U.S.: As the World Turns and as the Pendulum Swings," *Financier Worldwide,* September 2018, https://www.financierworldwide.com/financial-regulation-in-the-us-as-the-world-turns-and-the-pendulum-swings/#.W4B1sOhKjIU.
16. Ben Walsh, "Expect More Bank Mergers After Dodd-Frank Rollback," Barron's, May 26, 2018, https://www.barrons.com/articles/expect-more-bank-mergers-after-dodd-frank-rollback-1527292801.
17. US Department of Labor, Final Rule Relating to Notice of Blackout Periods to Participants and Beneficiaries, January 24, 2003. "Section 101(i)(3) of ERISA provides that in any case in which a blackout period applies only to one or more participants or beneficiaries in connection with a merger, acquisition, divestiture, or similar transaction involving the plan or plan sponsor and occurs solely in connection with becoming or ceasing to be a participant or beneficiary under the plan by reason of such merger, acquisition, divestiture, or similar transaction, *the 30-day advance notice requirement shall be treated as met if the notice is furnished to such participants and beneficiaries to whom the blackout period applies as soon as reasonably practicable.*" https://www.gpo.gov/fdsys/pkg/FR-2003-01-24/pdf/03-1430.pdf. See also this rule as of August 2018 that states, in part, that "The requirement to give at least 30 days advance notice . . . shall not apply in any case in which . . . [t]he blackout period applies only to one or more participants or beneficiaries solely in connection with their becoming, or ceasing to be, participants or beneficiaries of the plan as a result of a merger, acquisition, divestiture, or similar transaction involving the plan or plan sponsor." https://www.law.cornell.edu/cfr/text/29/2520.101-3.

18. *In re Caremark Int'l Inc. Derivative Litigation,* 698 A.2d 959 (Del. Ch. 1996).
19. In *CertiSign Holding, Inc. v. Kulikovsky,* C.A. No. 12055-JRS (Del. Ch. June 7, 2018). https://courts.delaware.gov/Opinions/Download.aspx?id=274090. In a blog about this case, attorney Francis Pileggi observes: "This case addressed several issues in connection with claims and counterclaims involving a complex web of inter-related companies and business relationships. The court provided a graphic chart describing how the 12 entities involved were inter-related. Among the claims described in this 83-page opinion were breaches of the fiduciary duty of loyalty by refusing to cooperate to correct corporate records for solely personal reasons, as well as related claims."
20. *In re: The Walt Disney Company Derivative Litigation,* No. 411/2005.
21. *Stone v. Ritter,* 911 A.2d 362, 370 (Del. 2006).
22. Nancy E. Barton, Dennis J. Block, and Stephen A. Radin, *The Business Judgment Rule,* 6th ed. (New York: Wolters Kluwer Law & Business, 2009).
23. See Director Essentials: Strengthening Oversight of M&A, NACD, 2016.
24. *Unocal v. Mesa Petroleum Co.*, 493 A.2d 946 (Del. 1985): "If a defensive measure is to come within the ambit of the business judgment rule, it must be reasonable in relation to the threat posed."
25. *Revlon, Inc. v. MacAndrews & Forbes Holdings, Inc.,* 506 A.2d 173 (Del. 1986).
26. This was the court's view in *Emerald Partners v. Berlin,* 787 A.2d 85 (Del. 2001). The court said, "The directors of Delaware corporations have a triad of primary fiduciary duties: due care, loyalty, and good faith. Those fiduciary responsibilities do not operate intermittently. Accordingly, the shareholders of a Delaware corporation are entitled to rely upon their board of directors to discharge each of their three primary fiduciary duties at all times." And further, "To demonstrate entire

fairness, the board must present evidence of the cumulative manner by which it discharged all of its fiduciary duties."

27. For recent commentary on lockups, see Anna T. Pinedo and Meyer Brown, "United States: Market Trends 2017–2018: Lockup Agreements," Mondaq, August 15, 2018, http://www.mondaq.com/unitedstates/x/727702/Shareholders/Market+Trends+201718+LockUp+Agreements.
28. https://www.law.cornell.edu/cfr/text/17/230.145.
29. Carl F. Barnes, "A Reminder on Break-Up Fees in M&A Transactions," Morse Barnes-Brown Pendleton, February 17, 2015. This article cites the Chancery Court in *In re Answers Corporation Shareholders Litigation,* Consol. C.A. No. 6170-VCN (April 11, 2011), which called a breakup fee equal to 4.4 percent of equity value "near the upper end of a 'conventionally accepted' range," but noted that, in the context of a relatively small transaction "a somewhat higher than midpoint on the 'range' is not atypical." The article also notes that the court, in *In re The Topps Company Shareholder Litigation,* Consol. CA. No. 2786-VCS (June 14, 2007), "determined that, although a break-up fee, including payment of the bidder's expenses, of 4.3% was 'a bit high in percentage terms,' it was 'explained by the relatively small size of the deal.'"
30. Sean J. Griffith and Natalia Reisel, "Dead Hand Proxy Puts and Shareholder Value," *The University of Chicago Law Review,* Summer 2017; citing is Sean J. Griffith, "The Omnipresent Specter of Omnicare," 38 J Corp L 753, 754 nn 2, 5 (2013). See https://chicagounbound.uchicago.edu/cgi/viewcontent.cgi?article=6041&context=uclrev.
31. For a complete list, see https://www.sec.gov/divisions/corpfin/ecfrlinks.shtml.
32. See https://www.sec.gov/divisions/corpfin/guidance/cdi-tender-offers-and-schedules.htm.
33. https://www.law.cornell.edu/cfr/text/17/240.13d-101.
34. https://www.law.cornell.edu/cfr/text/17/240.13d-102.
35. https://www.law.cornell.edu/cfr/text/17/240.14d-101

36. https://www.law.cornell.edu/cfr/text/17/240.13e-100.
37. https://www.law.cornell.edu/cfr/text/17/240.14a-101.
38. https://www.law.cornell.edu/cfr/text/17/240.14n-101.
39. This series replaced 14 D-1. https://www.law.cornell.edu/cfr/text/17/240.14d-100.
40. https://www.law.cornell.edu/cfr/text/17/239.25.
41. See https://www.sec.gov/fast-answers/answerstenderhtm.html.
42. See "General Electric Company Recommends Shareholders Reject 'Mini-Tender' Offer by Ponos Industries LLC," GE Newsroom, August 24, 2018, "http://www.genewsroom.com/press-releases/general-electric-company-recommends-shareholders-reject-"mini-tender"-offer-ponos. For an example involving TRC Capital, see https://investor.lamresearch.com/news-releases/news-release-details/lam-research-corporation-lam-research-recommends-stockholders. For the SEC's warning, see https://www.investor.gov/additional-resources/general-resources/glossary/mini-tender-offers.
43. For a recent resource on this deal structure, see Piotr Korzynski, "Forcing the Offer: Considerations for Deal Certainty and Consent Agreements in Delaware Two-Step Mergers," Baker McKenzie LLP, April 2, 2018, https://corpgov.law.harvard.edu/2018/04/02/forcing-the-offer-considerations-for-deal-certainty-and-support-agreements-in-delaware-two-step-mergers/. Note: a two-step tender offer is not the same as a two-tier offer. This is an offer in which the bidder, generally a hostile one, sets a deadline for an initial high price. Those who sell their stock to the bidder after the deadline get a second, lower price, an abusive practice that is no longer used.
44. Simon Clark, "How J.D. Power Was Acquired by a Chinese Company Shrouded in Mystery," *Wall Street Journal,* January 31, 2018, https://www.wsj.com/articles/how-j-d-power-was-acquired-by-a-chinese-company-shrouded-in-mystery-1517426465. See also Jonathan Ramsey, "In Chinese purchase of J.D. Power, Backers and Motives Remain

a Mystery," Autoblog.com, February 5, 2018, https://www.autoblog.com/2018/02/05/jd-power-mystery-chinese-purchase/.

45. See Steven M. Haas and Charles L. Brewer, Hunton & Williams, LLP, "Nonvoting Common Stock: A Legal Overview," Harvard Law School Forum on Corporate Governance and Financial Regulation, November 30, 2017, https://corpgov.law.harvard.edu/2017/11/30/nonvoting-common-stock-a-legal-overview/.
46. Jones Day notes: "See Rule 14e-1(a) under the Exchange Act of 1934. In practice, the use of certain structural features can effectively result in tender offers being substantially complete in 10 U.S. business days. In addition, any-and-all cash tender offers for nonconvertible debt securities that satisfy certain criteria can be conducted in as little as five U.S. business days." "Sovereign Bond Offerings and Liability Management Exercises—U.S. Perspectives," Jones Day, July 3, 2018.
47. https://www.law.cornell.edu/cfr/text/16/801.30.
48. For a merger agreement that includes timing elements, see Agreement and Plan of Merger by and Among Pisces Mido, Inc., Pisces Merger Sub, Inc., and Ply Gem Holdings, Inc., January 31, 2018. https://www.sec.gov/Archives/edgar/data/1284807/000114420418005006/tv484510_ex2-1.htm.
49. In some cases, the newspaper must be national, metropolitan, and/or regional to qualify. https://www.law.cornell.edu/cfr/text/17/240.13e-4#d_1.
50. https://www.law.cornell.edu/cfr/text/17/240.13d-1#b.
51. https://www.law.cornell.edu/cfr/text/17/240.13d-1.
52. "Recent SEC Enforcement Actions Target Inadequate Disclosure in M&A Transactions and Shareholder Activist Campaigns," Hunton & Williams, March 2017, https://www.huntonak.com/images/content/2/8/v3/28632/recent-sec-enforcement-actions-target-inadequate-disclosure-marc.pdf.
53. Eleazer Klein and Adriana Schwartz, "Section 13 and Section 16 Enforcement Actions—A Guide for Staying in Compliance,"

BNA, June 2, 2017, https://www.bna.com/section-13-section-n73014451906/.

54. See https://www.law.cornell.edu/cfr/text/17/240.14d-6.
55. Excerpted from AbbVie Inc., Schedule TO including earnings call material, April 26, 2018, http://investors.abbvie.com/static-files/feed01b9-071a-4ceb-99a2-73dca0eccc1e.
56. https://www.law.cornell.edu/cfr/text/17/230.134.
57. https://www.sec.gov/divisions/corpfin/guidance/securitiesactrules-interps.htm.
58. https://www.sec.gov/corpfin/proxy-rules-schedules-14a-14c-cdi.
59. "Exchange Act Rule 14a-4(f) prohibits the delivery of proxy cards unless the security holders concurrently or previously received a definitive proxy statement filed with the Commission. Further, because a vote on the transaction described also would amount to a sale of the securities being registered, no proxy card can be sent until after the Form S-4 is declared effective and the final prospectus has been furnished to security holders. SEC Question 126.04, May 11, 2018, https://www.sec.gov/corpfin/proxy-rules-schedules-14a-14c-cdi.
60. A reform proposed in 2016 (https://www.sec.gov/news/pressrelease/2016-225.html) is still pending as of late 2018.
61. See James B. Stewart, *Den of Thieves* (New York: Simon & Schuster, 1991). Other books about the era include Ken Auletta, *Greed and Glory on Wall Street: The Fall of the House of Lehman* (New York: Warner Books, 1986); Sarah Bartlett, *The Money Machine: How KKR Manufactured Power & Profits* (New York: Warner Books, 1991); Connie Bruck, *The Predator's Ball: The Inside Story of Drexel Burnham and the Rise of the Junk Raiders* (New York: Penguin Books, 1989); Michael Lewis, *Liar's Poker: Rising through the Wreckage on Wall Street* (New York: Penguin Books, 1990); and Michael Lewis, *The Money Culture* (New York, London: W. W. Norton & Company, 1991).

62. *Merrill Lynch, Pierce, Fenner & Smith, Inc. v. Dabit,* 126 S. Ct. 1503, 1513 (2006).
63. *Gollust v. Mendell,* No. 90-659 (June 10, 1991).
64. https://www.law.cornell.edu/cfr/text/17/240.16b-7.
65. *Texas Gulf Sulphur,* 401 F.2d 833 (2d Cir. 1968)(en banc).
66. *Carpenter v. United States,* 484 U.S. 19 (1987).
67. See discussion of remote tipping in Christopher Lavigne and Brian Calandra, "Insider Trading Laws and Enforcement," *Practical Compliance and Risk Management for the Securities Industry,* May-June 2016, https://www.shearman.com/-/media/Files/NewsInsights/Publications/2016/06/PCRM_0316_LaVigneCalandra-(2).pdf.
68. Christine LaFollette, et al., "Top 10 Topics for 2018: Shareholder Activism," Akin Gump, January 10, 2018, https://www.akingump.com/en/experience/practices/corporate/ag-deal-diary/top-10-topics-for-directors-in-2018-shareholder-activism.html.
69. https://www.law.cornell.edu/uscode/text/26/5881.

CHAPTER 11

Workouts, Bankruptcies, and Liquidations

INTRODUCTION

Every year, workouts, bankruptcies, and liquidations become final options for thousands of distressed businesses—small and large, new and old. This is not surprising: business is by nature risky—and certain types of risks, if not anticipated and prevented, can lead to financial problems.

But in business, as in life, destiny is determined as much by people's responses to events as by the events themselves. Financial problems may not mean the end of a business; they can signal a new beginning. Indeed, no business activity shows the power of new ownership as clearly as a successful workout or bankruptcy. By structuring such arrangements properly, the owners or acquirers of a business can help a company avoid—or emerge from—bankruptcy, thus bringing it back from financial death into long-lasting financial life.

M&A can play either a negative or a positive role in this drama. Doing the wrong M&A deal can lead a firm into insolvency, but doing a good one can help a company avoid it or emerge from it unscathed. Indeed, many a company involved in bankruptcy has found an exit through a buyer taking advantage of US bankruptcy law (for example, Section 363, discussed later in this chapter).

This chapter shows how to achieve a corporate resurrection by performing a workout or bankruptcy, especially by reorganizing a business under Chapter 11 of the US Bankruptcy Code (a special legal code pertaining to insolvent companies and individuals).[1]

Readers will also encounter a brief discussion of dos and don'ts of liquidation. This chapter also provides guidance on dealing with claims stemming from leveraged transactions that result in insolvency. Emphasizing the M&A angle, the following pages address some specific financial and accounting/tax issues to consider when crafting an agreement to buy an insolvent entity in whole or in part. This is a very important aspect of bankruptcy. Indeed, there are few stand-alone reorganizations today, as most Chapter 11 plans include a 363 sale to a buyer.[2]

GENERAL CONSIDERATIONS

What is bankruptcy?

A debtor (individual or entity) is, generally speaking, one that may be unable to make timely payment of its obligations to creditors. In a narrower, more technical sense, bankruptcy is the condition of an individual or entity that has filed for protection from creditors under bankruptcy law. (Indeed, one bankruptcy attorney has claimed, "Bankruptcy is no longer a sign of true insolvency or liquidation. It's often a strategic tool [used] by management."[3] In any given year, most bankruptcy filings are made by individuals rather than by entities. This chapter focuses on workouts and bankruptcies involving insolvent entities.[4]

What is insolvency? How do the regulatory and accounting authorities define it?

The Bankruptcy Code defines the term *insolvent,* as it applies to a corporation, as a "financial condition such that the sum of [the] entity's debts is greater than all of such entity's property, at a fair valuation."[5] (Debts include contingent liabilities under this definition.)[6] This is referred to as the *balance sheet* or *accounting* definition of insolvency. The Bankruptcy Code does not define "fair valuation" or "fair value," delegating this mat-

Exhibit 11-1 Definitions of Bankruptcy

	BANKRUPTCY CODE	UVTA	STATE LAWS	COURT CASES
Liabilities greater than assets	x	x	x	x
Inability to pay debts when due		x	x	x

ter to the bankruptcy courts. Case law has defined a *fair valuation* of an entity's property as the amount of cash that could be realized from a sale of the property "during a reasonable period of time."[7] A "reasonable period of time" is the time "a typical creditor would find optimal: not so short a period that the value of goods is substantially impaired via a forced sale, but not so long a time that a typical creditor would receive less satisfaction of its claim, as a result of the time value of money and typical business needs, by waiting for the possibility of a higher price."[8]

The Uniform Voidable Transactions Act uses a two-pronged definition. It says a debtor is insolvent "if at a fair valuation, the sum of the debtor's debts is greater than the sum of the debtor's assets," *or* if the debtor "is generally not paying . . . debts when they become due."[9] This latter definition is sometimes referred to as the *equity definition* or *cash flow definition* of insolvency (as opposed to the *balance sheet* or *accounting definition* in the Bankruptcy Code and in the first prong of the Voidable Transactions Act).[10] Most state laws use a balance sheet definition, as in the Bankruptcy Code, but some states (e.g., New York) follow the equity definition.[11] See Exhibit 11-1.

Why is the definition involving debt payments referred to as the "equity" definition?

As mentioned, the equitable definition of insolvency refers to being able to meet one's obligations as they fall due, rather than a strictly legal definition of assets versus liabilities. The latter often gets into difficulty around determination of value, that is, how much the assets are worth, valued on what basis (fire sale, orderly liquidation, going-concern), and so forth. The equity definition is simpler and focused on fairness.

The term *equity* here does not refer to balance sheet equity; rather, it refers to the role of the bankruptcy court as a court of equity, as distinct from statutory law.[12] In England, the source of American legal tradition, there were two kinds of courts: courts of equity and courts of law. Courts of law accorded money damages, while courts of equity dispensed other remedies, such as injunctive relief (making someone stop a certain behavior). Courts of equity are often less concerned with statutory language or legal precedent, and more with concepts of fundamental fairness. Since bankruptcy courts often have to fashion remedies other than "A must pay $X to B," they are considered courts of equity.

Why is it important to know how regulatory authorities define insolvency?

It is important to know how relevant authorities define insolvency because the duties of officers, directors, and other parties might change in the case of insolvency. Also, certain authorities have heightened powers in the affairs of insolvent corporations—and may assume control of them in certain circumstances.

When does a pattern of late payments cross the line into a state of insolvency?

Generally, insolvency begins when creditors stop trusting the entity to pay in an acceptable time frame. One or even two or three missed debt payments may not trigger a response from creditors if there is no history of financial difficulty or misdoing. However, a recurring pattern of missed payments will usually trigger some kind of action. The creditor may serve notice that the borrower is default. The action will vary depending on the type of debt involved.

- If the debt is a bank loan, a loan officer will point out that the borrower is in violation of a loan agreement and ask for an immediate meeting, which usually includes someone from the bank's workout department.

- If the debt is a commercial bill for merchandise, usually someone from the accounts receivable department will inquire about the missed payment or payments.

What are the various alternatives available to an entity that cannot meet its current debt structure with its current cash flow?

Several alternatives are available to a distressed entity, including but not limited to an out-of-court *workout* (often combined with a managerial *turnaround*), a filing for *bankruptcy* protection, and (the least desirable alternative) a total *liquidation.* This chapter discusses workouts and bankruptcy, which involve structuring concerns, but not liquidation, which is a fairly straightforward sale of assets that does not require any complex transactional structuring in our sense of the term.

WORKOUTS

What is a workout?

A *workout,* also called a *debt restructuring,* is a process through which a defaulting entity negotiates a payment schedule or plan with its creditors outside the courts. It is a strictly voluntary process controlled by the parties involved. In a workout, one or more creditors refrain from forcing immediate payment from a defaulting entity and instead agree to an organized payment schedule. A formal workout generally involves multiple creditors—and, often, a committee to represent them.

What are the advantages of a workout?

The major advantages of a workout—compared with the other alternatives such as formal bankruptcy cases—include greater control over the business entity by the participants, faster solutions to problems as they arise, and substantially lower administrative costs. Perhaps the most important advantage of a workout is its confidentiality. Because there are no public hearings and no public records, the company can preserve its public reputation, subject to its disclosure obligations if it has publicly traded securities outstanding.

How does a workout operate?

Typically, a business burdened with heavy debt or declining revenues halts some payments to its creditors and suppliers and asks to meet with the affected creditors in private. (Secured creditors are not usually invited to meetings held by distressed entities with unsecured creditors, and are generally dealt with separately.)

At the meeting, the company presents the current status of its operations and details of its financial condition. In addition, it distributes a plan detailing how it intends to meet its current and future financial obligations. The plan may include a capital restructuring, and sometimes a drastic restructuring of operations under some new management as well.

This restructuring is generally referred to as a *turnaround.* In a typical turnaround, in many cases, an outside manager steps in, often serving as an interim chief executive officer, chief financial officer, or chief restructuring officer (CRO), to help the company return to financial health. The turnaround manager may be hired as a consultant, a temporary employee, or a permanent employee. Some executive recruiting firms have special expertise in locating qualified turnaround executives or other interim managers.[13]

An important part of the presentation of a workout plan is a realistic estimate of the recovery that the creditors—both secured and unsecured—could expect if the company were forced into liquidation. The number should not be unrealistically low—but at the same time, it should account for the cash drain from the administration of the bankruptcy filing itself. Usually the news is not pretty. A senior lender may get 50 cents on the dollar, but a subordinated lender may get pennies, though generalities and averages have little bearing on any actual situation. See Exhibit 11-2 for historic rates from Moody's.[14]

Exhibit 11-2 Average Corporate Debt Recovery Rates Measured by Ultimate Recoveries, 1987–2018

	Emergence Year 2018	**2017**	**1987–2018**	**Default Year 2018**	**2017**	**1987–2018**
Priority Position Loans	85.0%	83.3%	80.3%	85.0%	84.3%	80.3%
Senior Secured Bonds	53.8%	68.0%	62.1%	55.0%	65.7%	62.1%
Senior Unsecured Bonds	38.4%	56.4%	47.7%	35.4%	58.3%	47.7%
Subordinated Bonds	0.0%	51.2%	28.0%	n.a.	62.8%	28.0%

Source: Moody's Investors Service *Annual Default Study,* February 1, 2019; updated February 21, 2019.

Obviously, the lower the estimate of liquidation recovery is, within reason, the more motivated creditors will be to agree to a workout plan. They might reason that if the defaulting entity files for bankruptcy protection, they may not receive any funds whatsoever, because the costs of administration, including fees for legal and accounting services, may eat up what little equity might remain. By contrast, the workout allows the defaulting entity to remain an ongoing business concern, which might continue to be a source of future business and profits for them. However, if the estimate of turnaround recovery is too low or slow, creditors might want to liquidate rather than work matters out. Many such plans will portray both a forced or fire sale liquidation value as well as the expected values realized from going through the workout process.

What are some of the types of concessions that defaulting entities may ask their creditors to accept?

Most of the time, the debtor tries to exact the largest concessions from a bank and/or a lead lender, asking them for partial forgiveness of the debt along with a reduced interest rate and more money. The predominant concession seems to be debt restructuring, such as acceptance of stock (either common or preferred) for debt, lower coupon rates, and, most important, debt stretchouts (increases in the length of the debt payment schedule).

From an operations point of view, what must a distressed entity do in order to orchestrate a workout successfully?

A distressed entity must, above all, be honest with its creditors and demonstrate that it understands the sources and uses of its cash. The entity must devise a realistic budget in sync with the concessions the creditors must provide. Even more important, the distressed entity must control its accounts payable and prove to creditors that it has the will and the way to reduce expenses and to bring cash expenses into line with cash receipts. Company management should communicate often with creditors in order to build the trust necessary for cooperation. No downside surprises!

What are some well-known workouts?

Unlike bankruptcy filings, which are formal events known to the general public, workouts are private matters that do not always make the news. A recent headline involved the high-end retailer Neiman Marcus, rumored to be restructuring its debt in 2018.[15] If successful, the company would join the likes of Castle & Cooke and Revlon Inc., which remained independent by successfully restructuring themselves with the cooperation of their creditors short of formal bankruptcy proceedings.[16]

What happens when the creditors do not go along with a workout proposal and either accelerate the loan or start to enforce it?

The distressed entity has three choices beyond finding the funds needed to satisfy the creditors:

1. It can file for bankruptcy protection under federal law.
2. It can file for insolvency proceedings under state law.
3. It can liquidate itself (subject to laws such as bulk sales laws if no one files against the liquidation by pleading a so-called involuntary petition).

BANKRUPTCY

What, exactly, is bankruptcy protection?

In the United States, protection for debtors is accomplished under the *automatic stay* provisions of US laws governing bankruptcy. The main text of these laws is found as part of the US Bankruptcy Code, which is Title 11 of the US Code.[17] An automatic stay means creditors cannot seize the filer's assets or otherwise seek to enforce their rights without US bankruptcy court permission. If the court accepts the bankruptcy petition, the entity legally becomes the "debtor in possession" and is given a period of time, subject to its ability to finance its operations, to develop and submit a proposed plan of reorganization to its creditors and the court. While developing the plan, the debtor operates under the supervision of the court. Subject to various court reporting requirements, it can make decisions deemed to be within the "ordinary course" of business affairs. Unusual transactions such as asset sales or new debt issuance must be disclosed to all creditors and recognized parties in interest, and approved by the court. If the plan of reorganization ultimately presented is not confirmed, the entity can propose other plans or liquidation, or it may lose its exclusive right to file such a plan and contemplate the possibility of a competing plan being confirmed.

Who can file for bankruptcy, and where can they file?

Under the US Bankruptcy Code, with certain exceptions for banks, insurance companies, and the like, any individual, corporation, partnership, or other entity may file for bankruptcy or have a bankruptcy case filed against it. Under Section 101(12) of the Bankruptcy Code, these parties are called *debtors,* or in case of a Chapter 11, the debtor is called a *debtor in possession,* unless and until the debtor is displaced by a Chapter 11 trustee, working under the United States Trustee Program.[18]

As for location, there are 94 federal bankruptcy courts, and each one maintains its own website.[19] Generally, companies must commence bankruptcy cases in the district of their headquarters, principal assets, or incorporation—or the districts of their affiliates.

How common are bankruptcies, and who files them?

Every year brings about 1 million new bankruptcy filings in the United States, most of them filed by consumers. In the United States, for the past 20 years, fewer than 4 percent of bankruptcies filed each year have involved businesses; 96 percent or more were consumer bankruptcies. (See Exhibit 11-3.) Research suggests that as many as 15 percent of personal bankruptcies come from business ventures; the actual number of business bankruptcies is more than 100,000 annually.

In any event, insolvency is a constant risk for businesses in general. Bankrupt businesses represent about 1 percent of the business population in any given year.[20]

Could you explain the chapters of the Bankruptcy Code as they pertain to businesses?

In the United States, bankruptcy filings are governed by the US Bankruptcy Code. This code is part of the US Code, which is nearly the full

Exhibit 11-3 Business vs. Consumer Bankruptcies

Year	Total	Business	Consumer	Consumer as % of Total
2007	850,912	28,322	822,590	96.67%
2008	1,117,771	43,546	1,074,225	96.10%
2009	1,473,675	60,837	1,412,838	95.87%
2010	1,593,081	56,282	1,536,799	96.47%
2011	1,410,653	47,806	1,362,847	96.61%
2012	1,221,091	40,075	1,181,016	96.72%
2013	1,071,932	33,212	1,038,720	96.90%
2014	936,795	26,983	909,812	97.12%
2015	844,495	24,735	819,760	97.07%
2016	794,960	24,114	770,846	96.97%
2017	789,020	23,157	765,863	97.07%
2018	773,418	22, 232	751,186	97.13%

Source: Administrative Office of the US Courts, January 29, 2019.

set of laws enacted by the US Congress. The bankruptcy portion of the US Code is Title 11, which itself contains 13 chapters, including the well-known Chapter 11, discussed subsequently. This title was added to the US Code following passage of the Bankruptcy Reform Act of 1978.[21]

The current Bankruptcy Code contains eight operating chapters.

- Chapter 1 contains general provisions.
- Chapter 3 describes case administration.
- Chapter 5 explains rules for handling creditors, debtors, and estates.
- Chapter 7 covers liquidation, or the orderly sale of the assets of a debtor, which may be an individual or a corporation; in the case of individuals, some assets to be liquidated may be businesses such as sole proprietorships.[22]
- Chapter 9 covers the debts of municipalities.
- Chapter 11 enables corporations to organize through either corporate reorganization (creating a new entity) or administrative reorganization (moving people and property around). Because the debtor maintains control of the entity's assets, under court supervision, it is called a *debtor in possession* unless and until a Chapter 11 trustee is appointed.
- Chapter 12 provides for relief of family farmers.
- Chapter 13 provides a process by which an individual with regular income may repay all or a portion of his or her indebtedness.

There are no even-numbered chapters except for Chapter 12. The chapters used for business bankruptcies are Chapters 7 and 11. Debtors can apply to change their status from one to the other during the course of their insolvency. This chapter concentrates on Chapter 11 bankruptcies.

What are the ground rules for implementing these different types of bankruptcies?

Federal rules of bankruptcy procedure are meant to ensure a "just, speedy, and inexpensive determination of every case and proceeding" under the bankruptcy code. They are transmitted from the US Supreme Court to Congress at the end of each year.[23]

The rules comprise nine clusters, with rules numbered according to the clusters (the 1000s are in Part I, the 2000s are in Part II, and so forth).

- Part I Commencement of case: proceedings relating to petition and order for relief
- Part II Officers and administration; notices; meetings; examinations; elections; attorneys and accountants
- Part III Claims and distribution to creditors and equity interest holders; plans
- Part IV The debtor; duties and benefits
- Part V Bankruptcy courts and clerks
- Part VI Collection and liquidation of the estate
- Part VII Adversary proceedings
- Part VIII Appeals to district court of bankruptcy appellate panel
- Part IX General provisions

What are some examples of recent changes to the rules of procedure

Changes that became effective December 1, 2017, include the following:

- Amended Rule 3002(a), stating that a secured creditor is now required to file a proof of claim to receive any distribution (although failure to do so does not void the creditor's lien)
- Amended Rule 3012, stating that a request to determine the amount of a secured claim may now be made by motion, and further stating that a request to determine the priority amount of a claim can be made only by motion after the claim is filed or in a claim objection[24]

When it comes to claims and distributions to creditors and equity holders, isn't it true that creditors have a higher priority than shareholders?

Yes. There is a concept called the "absolute priority rule," also called "mandatory priority," which states that senior claims, such as secured lenders, have priority over unsecured claims, such as common stock.[25] The rule refers to ensuring a fair and equitable distribution to all creditors by requiring that more senior creditors be paid in full before more junior creditors receive any recoveries. This is dealt with in several sections of the Bankruptcy Code:

- Section 506 (a) (1) states that the value of secured claims is equal to the allowed amount of their liens, with the balance becoming unsecured claims.[26]
- Section 510 states that in distributions made by a bankrupt entity, certain claims (including many types of claims that might be asserted by an equity holder) "will be subordinated to all claims or interests that are senior to or equal the claim or interest represented by such security, except that if such security is common stock, such claim has the same priority as common stock."[27]
- Section 1129 (b) (2) codifies the absolute priority rule by restating the priority of senior over junior creditors.[28]

These sections, in essence, put unsecured sources of capital such as shareholders at the end of the claims line in a bankruptcy.[29] Note, however, that recent amendments to rules of procedure now require that secured creditors file a proof of claim.[30]

What is the exact status of bankruptcy law right now?

Bankruptcy law is a fairly stable area of law, especially where businesses are concerned. Most of the bills before the current (115th) Congress focus on the reform of laws affecting consumer bankruptcy. The laws controlling business bankruptcy would be made less hospitable under currently proposed legislation, but would still allow for reorganization.

As mentioned, the current bankruptcy code was enacted in 1978 under the Bankruptcy Reform Act of that year. That law established the United States Trustee Program as a component of the Department of Justice responsible for overseeing the administration of bankruptcy cases. The following laws have amended (but not replaced) the 1978 law:

- The Bankruptcy Judges, United States Trustees, and Family Farmer Bankruptcy Act of 1986 (which added an item for Chapter 12 of Title 11).
- The Bankruptcy Reform Act of 1994. This law, considered to be the most comprehensive piece of bankruptcy legislation since the 1978 act, contained provisions to expedite bankruptcy cases and to help creditors recover claims against bankrupt estates. It also created a National Bankruptcy Review Commission, which issued a report in 1997 and then ceased to exist. [31]
- The Bankruptcy Abuse Prevention and Consumer Protection Act of 2005. This get-tough bill was an outgrowth of the final 1997 report of the National Bankruptcy Review Commission formed for that purpose.
- The Tax Cuts and Jobs Act of 2017 affected net operating loss carryforwards, as explained in Chapter 5.[32]
- As of late 2018 more than 50 bills mentioning "bankruptcy" in the title or summary were pending in the 115th Congress (2017–2018), including some that could carry over to the 116th Congress (2019-2020).[33]

What is Chapter 11 reorganization?

Chapter 11 is an administrative process. It allows a financially distressed entity (i.e., one that is unable to pay its debts as they become due) to reorganize to improve its financial condition. This kind of bankruptcy is designed to facilitate the successful reorganization of an entity that is temporarily distressed but otherwise economically viable and worth more as a going concern than in liquidation. If the entity is not economically viable, or if the owners cannot afford to file for Chapter 11,[34] then it is liquidated under Chapter 7 of the US Bankruptcy Code or out of court.

What is the main purpose of Chapter 11 bankruptcy?

The main purpose of Chapter 11 is to save jobs and American enterprise. It protects a defaulting entity from its creditors while it works its way (through many kinds of reorganization) into sound financial health. This works to the ultimate benefit of creditors because it provides an orderly environment to allocate the entity's value. US bankruptcy law is different from the law of other countries, where creditors' rights take precedence over debtor potential. Outside the United States, there is far less gray area between the life and death of a business—and thus few if any stories of a corporate phoenix rising from ashes.

What does it cost to file for Chapter 11?

The typical minimum cost for a smaller organization is $50,000 for basic filing and reorganization plan assistance. For larger organizations, the amounts can run in the millions. Bankruptcy filings reflect the complexity of the situations that precipitate them. In some Chapter 11 cases, literally thousands of separate creditors have claims against the entity.

Not surprisingly, the need for professional assistance rises with each level of complexity.

These are some of the professionals that might be needed:

- Accountants (to provide auditing services)
- Appraisers (to give appraisals of assets for presentation to the court)
- Attorneys (to make the filing and to help draft and present to the court a Chapter 11 reorganization plan)
- Investment bankers (to render financial advice and find possible sources of financing and/or new capital)
- Turnaround managers, who, as mentioned previously, often serve as interim CEOs or CROs

Many of these professionals specialize in working with entities in insolvency. The American Bankruptcy Institute (abiworld.org) has more than 12,000 dues-paying members, who refer to themselves as bankruptcy professionals or "insolvency practitioners."

What happens in a company with multiple subsidiaries in various states of financial health? Must they all file for bankruptcy?

If a parent and its subsidiaries file for bankruptcy protection in the same court, they might be treated collectively by that court.[35] In other instances, a parent and its subsidiaries may not be in the same court. That is, the parent and subsidiary may not be incorporated in the same jurisdiction and legally may not be able to file in the same court. The applicable accounting standard is covered in ASC 810, Consolidation. The bankruptcy status of entities in a consolidated group may affect whether the entities continue to be consolidated. Consolidation considerations include:

- The status of the bankruptcy proceedings
- The parent's relationship with the subsidiary (e.g., majority shareholder, priority debt holder, single largest creditor)
- Expectations about length of bankruptcy
- Expectations about who will control the subsidiary after emergence

For sample scenarios, see Exhibit 11-4.

When considering scenarios, several options are possible. Sometimes a parent company starts a Chapter 11 reorganization case, while subsidiaries, carrying on day-to-day business, may, at least for a period of time, remain outside Chapter 11. In some cases, many affiliates of the Chapter 11 debtor-in-possession remain outside of Chapter 11 for long periods and, in some instances, reorganize outside of Chapter 11 in tandem with the reorganization plans of the Chapter 11 debtors-in-possession. In large part this is because creditors recognize that they can obtain greater value by proceeding in this manner. Doing so, however, requires the de-

Exhibit 11-4 Some Common Consolidation Scenarios Applying ASC 810

Entity Filing Bankruptcy	Consolidation Implication
Subsidiary only	Parent deconsolidates subsidiary
Parent only	Parent continues to consolidate subsidiary
Parent and subsidiary (different jurisdictions)	Parent deconsolidates subsidiary
Parent and subsidiary (same jurisdiction)	Parent continues to consolidate subsidiary

Source: Ernst & Young, *Bankruptcies, Liquidations and Quasi-Reorganizations,* May 2018.

velopment of governance/financial protocols for dealing with conflicting interests.

What are some bankruptcies of historical note?

Before 1970, very large company bankruptcies were rare. When Penn Central failed in 1970 and W.T. Grant failed in 1975, these events sent shock waves throughout business. (Indeed, many attribute the modern "corporate governance" movement to these pivotal events. Corporate governance advocates favor independent corporate boards and active shareholders, both of which can serve as checks on management.) In 1980, Chrysler (today part of Fiat Chrysler) narrowly avoided bankruptcy with a government bailout.

Since the 1980s, major bankruptcies have become more common. Companies have been filing for bankruptcy in record numbers. Over the past half century (as the website bankruptcy.com reports), a number of household names bit the financial dust, including Allied Stores, Continental Airlines, Drexel Burnham Lambert, Eastern Airlines, Federated Department Stores, General Motors, Greyhound, Lehman Brothers, LTV, R.H. Macy, Maxwell Communication, Olympia & York, PanAm, and Texaco. The most infamous bankruptcy in recent years was Enron, which filed for protection from creditors under Chapter 11 in December 2001, eclipsing in importance some of the other high-profile public company bankruptcies of that year, such as Bethlehem Steel, Pacific Gas and Electric, Reliance

Exhibit 11-5 The 10 Largest Bankruptcies in the United States (by Total Assets Pre-Bankruptcy)

1. Lehman Brothers Holdings (9/15/2008) $639.1 billion
2. Washington Mutual (9/26/2008) $327.9 billion
3. WorldCom (7/21/2002) $103.9 billion
4. General Motors (6/1/2009) $91.0 billion
5. CIT Group (11/1/2009) $80.4 billion
6. Enron (12/2/2001) $65.5 billion
7. Conseco (12/18/2002) $61.4 billion
8. Energy Future Holdings (2014) $40.9 billion
9. MF Global Holdings (2009) $40.5 billion
10. Chrysler (4/30/2009) $39.3 billion

Source: https://s3.amazonaws.com/abi-org/Newsroom/Bankruptcy_Statistics/Total-Business-Consumer1980-Present.pdf.

Holdings, and W.R. Grace. The Enron bankruptcy was not only large (at nearly $66 billion) but also complex. A total of 75 entities (the parent company and 74 subsidiaries) all filed for bankruptcy, affecting numerous creditors. (The petitions specifically name 20 major unsecured creditors.) The implosion of Enron was quickly followed by the failure of WorldCom the following year, linking the two forever in infamy.

Yet the Enron and WorldCom crashes, while devastating, were not the largest bankruptcies in history. That distinction belongs to the $639 billion bankruptcy of Lehman Brothers in September 2008. Exhibit 11-5 shows Enron and WorldCom in historical context.

What can acquirers learn from the bankruptcies of Enron, WorldCom, and Lehman Brothers?

Lessons learned from these bankruptcies are captured in the reports written about them after the fact: respectively the so-called Powers report, the Breeden report, and the Valukas report.

- *The Powers report.* On February 1, 2002, William C. Powers, Jr., presented to the Enron board of directors the Report of the

Investigation by the Special Investigative Committee of the Board of Directors on Enron Corp. Powers chaired the special investigative committee. The main message of the report is that the board of directors should have exercised stronger oversight of the company's special financial arrangements (largely off-balance-sheet arrangements involving insiders). These undisclosed arrangements hid the conditions that led to Enron's bankruptcy, and also contributed to it.

- *The Breeden report.* On August 26, 2003, Richard C. Breeden, delivered "Restoring Trust: Corporate Governance for the Future of MCI, Inc." to the US district court judge overseeing the bankruptcy of WorldCom, renamed MCI during this period. Breeden, former chairman of the SEC, served as corporate monitor of MCI-WorldCom, subsequently acquired by and absorbed into Verizon. The report included a "Governance Constitution" with 78 specific corporate governance recommendations that the company had to implement before emerging from bankruptcy.
- *The Valukas report.* According to a report for the bankruptcy court prepared by examiner Anton R. Valukas, "Lehman failed because it was unable to retain the confidence of its lenders and counterparties and because it did not have sufficient liquidity to meet its current obligations." The Valukas report goes on to explain that among other problems, a series of investments in real estate had left the company with heavy concentrations of illiquid assets with deteriorating values.[36]

What are the chances of long-term recovery from a Chapter 11 bankruptcy?

According to the Administrative Office of the US Courts, Chapter 11 filings in Court Year 2017 totaled 7,442. The federal courts do not keep statistics on how many firms emerge from Chapter 11, but one expert has opined that "the bigger the company, the more likely they are to re-emerge."[37] Some that reemerge from Chapter 11 wind up filing again.

Companies that file Chapter 11 a second time are sometimes referred to jestingly as filing "Chapter 22."

Suppose an entity has assets in many jurisdictions. Where can it file for bankruptcy?

Within the United States, according to Section 1408 of Title 28 of the US Bankruptcy Code, an entity must file its bankruptcy petition in the district where the entity is domiciled, where it has its principal place of business, where its principal assets are located, or where any of its affiliates have filed.

Given the fact that there are multiple bankruptcy courts within the United States and, more broadly, many places where a company might conceivably be headquartered, there is obviously a great deal of flexibility in venues.

This multiplicity of forums for bankruptcy cases has led to a certain amount of "forum shopping"—as companies look for jurisdictions favored by debtors or their lenders based on rulings making postpetition reorganization and lending more likely. For instance, within the United States, the US Bankruptcy Court for the Southern District of New York has a reputation for fostering reorganization. A substantial percentage of the largest US bankruptcies have been filed in that district.[38]

What, exactly, happens in a Chapter 11 filing?

In a Chapter 11 filing, the debtor entity initially has the exclusive right to file a Chapter 11 plan, with a window of at least 120 days and no more than 18 months.[39] The steps of the plan are as follows:

1. The debtor develops a plan with its main constituencies: secured creditors and the statutory creditors' committee for unsecured claimholders.
2. The company prepares a reorganization plan and files the proposed plan with the court.

3. The company files a disclosure statement, which must be approved by the bankruptcy court as having adequate information before creditors and shareholders can work on the plan.
4. The court holds a hearing on confirmation of the plan to determine whether it satisfies all legal requirements.
5. If confirmed, the plan proponent carries out the plan by distributing any payments or securities called for by the plan.

What does the reorganization plan entail?

The plan identifies the assets of the entity and explains how the assets will be allocated. If the debt involves bondholders who are governed by a bond indenture agreement, 90 percent of the bondholders must approve the plan, although their decision can be challenged in court for unfairness, for example, if it violates the absolute priority rule mentioned earlier.[40]

The plan should devote some of the assets in the short term to the insolvent entity so that it can continue operating, thus generating revenues and, eventually, profits, to pay its debts. The plan must also factor in repayment to creditors. Debtors will have a natural tendency to allocate as little as possible to creditors, while creditors will want to allocate as much as possible to themselves.

As mentioned earlier, debtors have a period of time in which they have the exclusive right to file a reorganization plan. If the court accepts the plan within that time period, no one else may file a plan. After the time period elapses, creditors may file their competing plans. The exclusive period generally has a window of at least 120 days and no more than 18 months.[41] In unusual cases, some judges have extended filing periods by as much as four years among secured claims, unsecured claims, and equity. Customers also have a say in matters.

A good recent example is Sears. In September 2018, ESL Investments, Inc., a major investor in Sears Holdings presented a plan to the Sears board, urging the company to restructure in order to avoid bankruptcy. Then on January 14, 2019, Sears began an auction for the sale of the company's global assets, and determined that the offer submitted by

ESL's holding company (Transform Holdco, LLC) to acquire "all or substantially all" of the company's global assets, was the highest or best offer. The new owner will be settling claims and resuming business in 2019 and beyond. Claims must be filed on or before September 3, 2019.[42]

What if one or more creditor classes reject the plan?

Before a plan can be confirmed, at least one impaired creditor class must accept it. If one or more classes accept it while one or more classes reject it, the plan may sometimes be confirmed if the rejecting classes receive at least as much as they would in liquidation and no classes junior to them participate.

How can shareholders get a committee to represent their interests in a reorganization plan under Chapter 11?

On request, the US trustee may appoint a shareholders' committee, also called an equity committee.[43] If one is not appointed, the court may order its appointment if shareholders may have a real interest in the case, although many courts are reluctant to do so given the typical increase in both case administration expense and litigation.

Also, as long as the company is not hopelessly insolvent, shareholders can ask the judge of the bankruptcy court to appoint an equity committee that would extend the focus of the court beyond creditors. This is a rare practice, but it is becoming more common.[44] The goal of such a committee and its advisors would be to obtain as much equity as possible.

During a reorganization, what happens to the board of directors of the debtor company?

There are no particular requirements for changes. Sometimes, the board remains the same. At other times, there is a change in the identity of the chairperson, CEO, and/or directors, or a change in the structure of the board. For example, the board may decide to combine or split the chairperson and CEO roles, may decide to appoint a lead director, or may decide to replace the entire board. These matters are decided on a case-by-case basis, depending on decisions of the board itself, the bankruptcy court, and the creditors' committee (and shareholders' committee, if there is one).

What say does the board of an insolvent company have in the choice of an acquirer?

Plans of reorganization are increasingly being used to effect a proposed sale to a third party, because they offer an orderly process through which acquirers strive to limit their liability through gaining the formal approval of the transaction by the court and the parties in interest.

What is a prepackaged bankruptcy?

A prepackaged bankruptcy, or *prepack,* authorized under Section 1126(b) of the Bankruptcy Code, is a type of bankruptcy filing known for its speed and simplicity.[45] It requires that a fully developed plan of organization be negotiated and agreed on by the debtor and its parties in interest out of court. it is required to have received the approval of only a minimum of 51 percent of the creditors holding at least 66 percent of the debt.[46] Prepacks are generally practical only when the number of parties involved is small.

How are prepackaged bankruptcies structured?

Generally, old debt is exchanged for a package that includes new debt instruments, equity, and sometimes cash. Heavily leveraged companies may, for example, persuade their bondholders and other creditors to exchange high-yield bonds for a package of lower-yielding debt and equity.

Are there any other alternatives available to a distressed entity if it does not want to go through an out-of-court workout or a bankruptcy reorganization?

Yes. It may in some circumstances opt for state insolvency procedures as an alternative.

STATE INSOLVENCY PROCEEDINGS

What is a state insolvency proceeding?

In this kind of proceeding, a distressed entity voluntarily begins an action in which it assigns its property to its creditors for liquidation, leading to a total discharge of its debts in that state. It is a good choice for an entity that wants to liquidate its assets—but note that it may have to be subordinated to federal bankruptcy laws.[47]

What are the main advantages and disadvantages of a state insolvency proceeding?

The main advantage of a state insolvency proceeding is that it is inexpensive and fast. The main disadvantage is that the discharge of debts is not binding on creditors located in other states. This can be a major disadvantage to a distressed entity with creditors outside its home state, as their claims will not be discharged. By contrast, in a Chapter 7 bankruptcy proceeding under federal law, all claims within the United States will be discharged.

INVESTING OPPORTUNITIES: STRUCTURING THE PURCHASE OF A TROUBLED COMPANY

What are some of the ways a buyer can structure the acquisition of a troubled company?

It can buy the company in part (by buying shares in an insolvent entity or by investing in a fund that invests in such entities) or in whole (by acquiring all the assets or shares of the entity).

In cases where the entity is merely distressed and has not yet filed for bankruptcy, the buyer can purchase shares of the company on the open market. Once the company files for bankruptcy, purchases of the company must go through bankruptcy court.

The buyout of a bankrupt entity need not be structured as a purchase of shares, though. As long as the seller has made a proper effort to market the assets and there is no otherwise feasible plan for the bankruptcy court to consider, an asset sale may be approved. It would normally be structured as a purchase of assets under Section 363 of the Bankruptcy Code.

What is Section 363?

Section 363 is part of the Bankruptcy Code. Under Section 363(f), a bankruptcy trustee or debtor-in-possession may sell the bankruptcy estate's assets "free and clear of any interest in such property" under certain conditions.[48] In theory, this means that the claims on any assets used as collateral will be suspended, and buyers (i.e., the new owners) will not inherit any old liabilities. Courts have consistently held that a buyer of a debtor's assets pursuant to a Bankruptcy Code section 363 sale takes "free and clear from successor liability relating to the debtor's business."[49]

However, there are some limitations when the sale is structured as the sale of a corporation. In buying a corporation—not merely its assets—under Section 363, a buyer may still inherit the corporation's indebtedness. This was the finding in *Amphenol Corp. v. Shandler* (2006). The bankruptcy court found that an Insilco subsidiary, PCM, following the stock sale to Amphenol, remained subject to the $1 million preference claim by the liquidating trustee.[50]

Are there funds that buy insolvent entities?

Yes. Several kinds of funds have formed for the purchase of distressed entities, called variously *reorganization funds, turnaround funds, vulture funds,* or *workout funds*. By whatever name, their focus is the same: to invest at bargain rates in an entity that is undergoing financial distress or is already bankrupt and then to reap the benefits when the company emerges from this state, often by having taken control of the company.

Guides for purchasing distressed entities are available, including *The Art of Distressed M&A: Buying, Selling, and Financing Troubled and Insolvent Companies* (McGraw-Hill Education, 2011), a book in the McGraw-Hill Art of M&A series that began with the first edition of this book 30 years ago.

What is the quality of information available on a troubled company?

If the company is merely in the zone of insolvency but not yet in a formal bankruptcy, the information can range from excellent to poor—even fraudulent. In a typical negative scenario, a company reports good performance, then shows signs of troubled performance, triggering an investigation (typically internal) that reveals that the trouble is far worse than previously reported.

Once the worst is over, though, and a company has filed for bankruptcy, the quality of information improves. All formal financial reporting in a bankruptcy is done under oath, and there are criminal penalties for falsification of records and statements. Furthermore, by law, the debtor must file detailed reports on its finances, which are a matter of public record. Also, debtors may be compelled to testify in more detailed examinations dictated by Bankruptcy Rule 2004.[51]

Bankruptcy Rule 2004 states that "on motion of any party in interest, the court may order the examination of any entity."[52] Further, it says that this examination may relate to "the acts, conduct or property or the liabilities and financial condition of the debtor, or to any matter which may affect the administration of the debtor's estate, or to the debtor's right to a discharge." In some cases, such as Chapter 11 cases, "the examination may also relate to the operation of any business and the desirability of its continuance, the source of any money or property acquired or to be acquired by the debtor for purposes of consummating a plan and the consideration given or offered [for this money or property], and any other matter relevant to the case or to the foundation of a plan."

Information on bankrupt entities is so good, in fact, that securities issued to creditors in a federal bankruptcy in some circumstances are tradable without registration (enabling some forms to go public without the expense of a registration).

Of course, in a transaction with a distressed entity, all the normal deal imperatives apply, including the necessity of having thorough financial, legal, operational, and transactional due diligence. This subject is beyond the scope of this book; buyers are urged to hire experts in this area and to master it themselves to the extent possible.

Is there a preferred time when an investor should get involved?

Success is possible at all stages of bankruptcy—before, during, and after—but there are pros and cons to each.

Investing *before or during* the filing is generally not advisable, because pre-petition shareholders are generally very low in any plan to receive any postfiling disbursements after the filing. (It might be better to lend money, buy a loan, or purchase bonds, rather than buy stock, because lenders and bondholders rank higher than shareholders.)

However, prefiling investment might make sense in the case of a company that has a relatively high chance of emerging from bankruptcy.

- First, anyone who is a shareholder prior to the filing can ask to be represented by a committee, as mentioned earlier.
- Also, an investor who wants to buy a controlling position might be in a stronger position to make an offer if that investor is an insider and has influence on the bids being presented to the bankruptcy court. Once the court has accepted a bid, it is very difficult to challenge this decision.
- Third, a two-phase strategy, moving from bonds to stock, is also possible if one gets in on the ground floor of a Chapter 11 filing. Several successful fund managers have purchased the bonds of a distressed entity at the time of its bankruptcy filing in anticipation of equity ownership or a cash-out down the line. The distressed entity's plan of reorganization could swap the interest-bearing bonds for a package of new equity or cash.

There are also options *during* the bankruptcy process, between the time of the filing for relief under Chapter 11 and confirmation of the plan of reorganization as the company emerges from bankruptcy. At the time that its plan of reorganization becomes effective, a company usually issues new shares of stock—often at bargain prices. Once it is evident that the company has survived the bankruptcy process, the price of the shares may rise.

Also, in many situations, the court-approved plan will include a provision for the exchange of old bonds or old preferred stock for new shares of common stock. The best time to purchase these post-petition shares is before the plan of reorganization is confirmed. However, because of the headaches caused by bankruptcy, many creditors will want to sell off the shares received. Some investors buy up these shares when they are offered, contacting the company's creditors to ask if their shares are for sale. Others wait until the activity dies down to see how the company is operating and how it is being perceived in the marketplace.

Will the SEC protect investors in a bankruptcy?

Generally, the SEC's role is limited to reviewing the disclosure document filed with the proposed plan of reorganization to determine if the company is telling investors and creditors the important information they need to know.

Although the SEC does not negotiate the economic terms of reorganization plans, it may take a position on important legal issues that will affect the rights of public investors in other bankruptcy cases as well. For example, the SEC might step in if it believes that the company's officers and directors are using the bankruptcy laws to shield themselves from lawsuits alleging securities fraud.

STRUCTURING A BUYOUT TO MINIMIZE INSOLVENCY RISK

When financing a go-private transaction, what ratio of debt to equity is safe?

As mentioned in Chapter 5, "Structuring Transactions," a ratio of 1.5 to 1 (60 percent) or lower is considered conservative.[53] How much higher a company can go depends on its industry and other factors. Each situation is unique. Consider the bankruptcies following debt-financed M&A activity including Energy XXI, Hawaiian Telecom, and Tropicana Entertainment. They all went into bankruptcy following debt-financed M&A, but in each case industry and/or timing factors also played a part.[54] Although these companies have all emerged from Chapter 11 bankruptcy as viable enterprises, their near-death experiences provide cautionary tales on the perils of overleverage.

Could you give specific details on the type and level of debt involved in a bankruptcy?

On February 8, 2019, Ditech Holding Corporation had entered into a restructuring support agreement (RSA) with lenders holding more than 75 percent of Ditech Holding's term loans. The RSA provided for a restructuring of the company's debt while the company continued to evaluate strategic alternatives. Under the RSA, the company said it planned to pursue a recapitalization that would deleverage its capital structure by extinguishing over $800 million in corporate debt, and obtaining appropriate working capital facility at emergence. As contemplated by the RSA, the company would continue to consider a broad range of options, including but not limited to potential transactions such as a sale of the company and/or a sale of all or a portion of the company's assets, as well as potential changes to the company's business model.

The company's SEC filing included these details on how various creditors would be treated:[55]

- *Term loan claims.* Holders of term loan claims will receive their pro rata share of new term loans under an amended and restated credit facility agreement in the aggregate principal amount of $400 million, and 100 percent of the company's stock, which will be privately held.
- *Second lien notes claims.* On the effective date, the holders of the company's 9.00% Second Lien Senior Subordinated PIK Toggle Notes due in 2024 will not receive any distribution.
- *Go-forward trade claims.* With consent of the requisite term lenders, vendors identified as being integral to and necessary for the ongoing operations of New Ditech will receive a distribution in cash in an amount equaling a certain percentage of their claim, subject to an aggregate cap.

- *Existing equity interests.* On the effective date, holders of the company's existing equity would have their claims extinguished.

Clearly, in this bankruptcy filing, there were winners and losers—which is one reason that the procedure can take so long, as various parties argue for their due.

Clearly highly leveraged transactions, such as leveraged buyouts, can result in postacquisition insolvency. How can creditors protect their interests in such a situation?

A leveraged buyout may be structured in a variety of ways—as a cash merger, a stock purchase, or an asset acquisition. However an LBO is structured, it will by definition use the value of the target company (value of assets minus liabilities) to finance the acquisition of the target company. As a consequence, creditors are involved because they have claims on those assets that are both leveraged and transferred.

Depending on the way the leveraged buyout *entity* is structured, the transaction will have an impact on creditors unless it is specifically structured to lack such an effect.

- The simplest LBO structure has an *impact on creditors.* In this structure, the deal architect would insert all or part of the newly created acquisition debt into the target (or its successor), which also takes possession of the assets and pledges them as collateral for the debt. As a result, the claims of the target's preacquisition creditors will be on a par with any new unsecured debt of the target and/or will be subordinate to any new secured debt.
- To structure a transaction that will have *no impact on creditors,* the deal architects must take an extra step. They must leave the target's assets in a separate corporation (generally the original target corporation) that does not assume any liability for the newly created LBO debt. The LBO debt in this structure is the obligation of a separate entity, usually the company that purchased the target's stock (such as a leveraged buyout fund).

The creditors that have claims against the assets are not disadvantaged, because the assets used as collateral have not been diminished and the liabilities have not increased. To illustrate this important point, the end of this chapter features a transaction diagram showing ways to structure the entities and relationships involved in a leveraged buyout transaction. One shows a safe way (Exhibit 11-6) and six show risky ways (Exhibits 11-7 to 11-12).

- There is also the issue of how the actual *financing* is structured. Some financial structures can create such problems, while other financial structures can help prevent them.
- The practices of upstreaming and cross-streaming pose dangers to creditors. *Upstreaming* occurs when a subsidiary provides collateral to secure a borrowing by its parent. *Cross-streaming* occurs when collateral is provided by one subsidiary to secure borrowing by a sister subsidiary. Both of these can weaken the financial integrity of a corporate structure.
- By contrast, downstreaming poses no particular danger to creditors. Downstreaming occurs when a parent makes guarantees and pledges to support borrowing by a subsidiary.

Upstreaming and cross-streaming pose risks to creditors because the donor entity—the one providing the collateral or guaranty—is not getting "reasonably equivalent value," which is going instead to its affiliate. (*Reasonably equivalent value* has technical meaning in the context of fraudulent conveyance law, as discussed subsequently.)

In addition, each subsidiary is typically asked to guarantee all the senior debt of its parent, and yet the assets of the subsidiary represent only a fraction of the total acquisition. The result is that each subsidiary, taken by itself, cannot repay the full acquisition debt and may be rendered insolvent if the guarantee is called against it alone.

Preserving creditors' claims through the proper entity and financing structures can help prevent the entity's owners from being sued for "fraudulent conveyance." If the target becomes insolvent, and preacquisition creditors become disadvantaged as a result of the transaction, creditors can invoke fraudulent conveyance laws to improve their creditor standing. (In fact, a forward-looking bankruptcy trustee, debtor-in-possession, or court-authorized creditor or creditor's committee can avoid the transfer in the first place by appealing to Section 548 of the US Code on "fraudulent transfers and obligations.")[56]

What, exactly, are fraudulent conveyance laws, and what deal attributes can cause a company to run afoul of these laws?

Fraudulent conveyance laws stem originally from English common law. Originally called Statute of Elizabeth laws, after Queen Elizabeth I, they are now enshrined in the US bankruptcy law (Section 548 of the Bankruptcy Code) and the Uniform Voidable Transactions Act.[57] All states have adopted fraudulent conveyance laws based on this uniform act or its predecessors, or on common law.

Under the US Bankruptcy Code and comparable provisions of state law, a transfer of property (such as a lien given by the acquired company on its assets, or the note secured by that lien), may be deemed "fraudulent" under certain conditions, enabling interested parties to avoid a transfer or to sue over it.

A court may find fraud if the debtor transfers property with an actual intent to hinder, delay, or defraud creditors. Alternatively, a court may find fraud if an acquirer of the property receives "*less than reasonably equivalent value*" in exchange *and* if one of the following three conditions exists:

1. The company was insolvent at the time of such transfer or became insolvent as a result of the transfer.
2. The company was left with unreasonably small capital as a result of the transfer.
3. The company incurred or intended to incur debts beyond its ability to pay.

"Less than reasonably equivalent value" is a somewhat ambiguous term. It does not necessarily refer to market value. Instead, it may be as simple as the price *actually paid for a property in a foreclosure,* as long as state foreclosure laws (pertaining to notice of intent to foreclose, etc.) are otherwise respected. State foreclosure laws, by the way, are basically the law of mortgages (since any foreclosure essentially ends a mortgage agreement). In the United States, mortgage law is mainly governed by state statutory and common law. When a mortgage is a negotiable instrument, it is governed by Article 3 of the Uniform Commercial Code (UCC), which covers negotiable instruments.[58] Legal treatment of a mortgage depends in part on the identity of the entity holding the mortgage (the mortagee). Thus, although mortgage law is handled at the state and common-law level, as noted, institutions that are chartered by the federal government may fall under federal law.

Who can be sued under fraudulent conveyance laws or be forced to give up funds if a company goes bankrupt after it is acquired?

Courts may impose these penalties on any party who knew that the loan proceeds would be paid to the target's original shareholders while debt was being imposed on the target's assets.

- *The entity that emerges from bankruptcy* may be liable for the full amount of the conveyance (the purchase price of the company).
- *Target shareholders* might have to refund the purchase price for their stock.
- *Lenders* in the know might have to subordinate their claims to the claims of other creditors or be asked to refund any loan payments received.
- *Professionals* advising the transaction might have to refund their fees, or be sued for negligence.

Suppose that through sophisticated structuring, a transaction gives the appearance of providing adequate consideration. Won't a court respect that at face value?

No. The courts are smarter than that. They have developed something called the *step-transaction* doctrine to see through such tricks. This doctrine developed out of common law but is now enshrined in US tax law. Decisions citing this doctrine vary greatly, but according to one expert tax lawyer, the applicability of the step-transaction doctrine (i.e., the collapsibility of the structure containing the steps) depends on four factors:

1. *The degree of interdependence of the steps.* The higher the degree of interdependence, the more likely the steps may be collapsed.
2. *The extent of any binding commitments.* The fewer the binding commitments, the more collapsible the structure.
3. *The elapsed time between the various steps.* The shorter the time, the more collapsible the structure.
4. *The end result or intention of the parties.* The more the structure appears to be engineered for a specific outcome, the more likely it is to be collapsed.

In addition to fraudulent conveyance laws, what other laws give legal exposure to parties in a transaction with a company that is or becomes insolvent?

Even if a transaction would not violate fraudulent conveyance laws, it might be considered a breach in fiduciary duties under common law—with respect to both the law of corporations and the law of trusts.

Corporation law varies slightly from state to state, but the laws of all states assert a *duty of due care* and a *duty of loyalty.*

- Exercising due care means acting on behalf of the company's stockholders in good faith and with the level of care that reasonable directors would exercise under similar circumstances, paying attention therefore to the likely effects of the transaction.

- Exercising loyalty means avoiding conflicts of interest. State courts have found that directors and officers breach the duty of loyalty when they appropriate a corporate asset or opportunity or use their corporate office to promote, advance, or effectuate a transaction (between the corporation and themselves or a party related to themselves) that is not substantively and entirely fair to the corporation.

These duties of care and loyalty are owed primarily to stockholders, whom directors represent as fiduciaries, and are generally protected by the so-called business judgment rule, which protects director decisions as long as they are made with care and loyalty.

However, in insolvency, things change. The duties of care and loyalty are focused on multiple constituencies, not just stockholders, who in fact rank lower than creditors in the distribution of postfiling funds. Also, some legal experts say that the business judgment rule may not apply to board decisions made outside court-supervised proceedings. An added twist in any complex transaction is the law of trusts, also called the *corporate trust fund doctrine.* In general, this doctrine provides that, once insolvent, a company's assets are to be managed as though held in trust for the benefit of its creditors. Under this doctrine, directors and officers of a financially distressed company should avoid intermingling of funds and other assets, among affiliated companies or within the same company, where different groups of creditors may have different claims on the assets.

According to basic trust law principles, a fiduciary may not mingle assets in a way that weakens the claims against any of those assets.

FINANCING ALTERNATIVES FOR COMPANIES WITH LOSSES

If an entity is having trouble meeting its obligations because it has a lot of debt that has claims on assets, what are its chances of borrowing more money from lenders?

Banks are reluctant to take on any term debt for companies with a weak balance sheet (i.e., a high ratio of total funded debt to earnings before interest, taxes, depreciation, and amortization, or EBITDA). But a new level (or *tranche*) of junior secured debt has emerged to fill the gap left by the traditional lenders. Hedge funds, distressed-debt funds, or specialized high-yield funds are structuring this new debt with a junior lien behind the senior lender on all of the borrower's assets and, on occasion, a senior lien on some of the borrower's assets that are considered to be *boot collateral* (assets securing the loan with no advance provided by the senior lender).

This debt is known by many names, such as a *tranche B loan, junior secured loan, last-out participation,* or *second-lien loan.* Regardless of what it is called, this junior secured loan provides incremental liquidity and leverage to borrowers who are tapped out with their existing senior lenders.

A tranche B lender looks to two broad categories to secure its loans: excess liquidation value from the borrower's assets or enterprise value that exceeds the amount of the senior loan. Credit criteria relating to these two underwritings are entirely different.

- In the liquidation value approach, the lender secures the loan based on the liquidation value of the company's assets. This loan is based on balance sheet considerations. (For more on asset-based lending, see the section on liquidation later in this chapter.)
- In the enterprise value approach, the lender secures the loan based on the intangible value of a company, including brand names, customer relations, and proprietary product lines. This

loan is based on the going-concern value of a business or on the value of its various product lines.

Could you give an example of a tranche B loan based on asset liquidation value?

A borrowing base for a company may provide for an advance in the range of 80 to 85 percent of the net going-out-of-business (GOB) liquidation value. A tranche B loan can provide for an incremental advance of 10 to 15 percent or more of the liquidation value.

Tranche Bs can also be major. For example, as part of its bankruptcy proceedings, United Airlines, Inc., entered into a new senior secured revolving credit facility and term loan (or *exit facility*) provided by a syndicate of banks and other financial institutions. The exit facility provided for a total commitment of up to $3.0 billion, consisting of two separate tranches:

1. Tranche A, consisting of up to $200 million revolving commitment available for tranche A loans and for standby letters of credit to be issued in the ordinary course of business of United Airlines or one of its subsidiary guarantors
2. Tranche B, consisting of a term loan commitment of up to $2.45 billion available at the time of closing and additional term loan commitments of up to $350 million

ACCOUNTING/TAX ISSUES FOR COMPANIES WITH LOSSES

Can an acquirer structure a transaction as an asset or stock purchase, and, if so, which is the best option for the acquirer of a company with losses?

Buyers have a great deal of discretion in how they structure the acquisition of any particular company. The best treatment depends on the basis the acquirer wants.

When a purchaser directly acquires the assets of a target corporation, and the target is subject to tax on the sale or exchange of the assets, the basis of the assets to the purchaser is their cost. This is called *cost basis.*

When a purchaser indirectly acquires the assets of the target through the acquisition of stock, the basis of the assets in the possession of the target corporation is generally not affected. This is called *carryover basis,* because the basis of an asset in the target corporation "carries over" on the change of stock ownership.

A cost basis transaction is, therefore, often referred to as an *asset acquisition,* and a carryover basis transaction is often referred to as a *stock acquisition.* Neither of these terms necessarily reflects the actual structure of the transaction.

How do loss carryovers and carrybacks figure into M&A transactions with troubled companies?

First, let's review some of the material on net operating losses covered in Chapter 5, on general tax principles. As explained earlier, if a corporate taxpayer has an excess of tax deductions over its taxable income in a given year, this excess becomes a net operating loss (NOL) of that taxpayer. Section 172 of the IRC, as amended with the TCJA, allows that taxpayer to use its NOL to offset taxable income in subsequent years (a carryover or carryforward) for an indefinite period starting in the first taxable year after December 31, 2017. However, it does not allow the taxpayer to offset taxable income in earlier years (a carryback).[59] It also limits reduction of taxable income by NOL; for taxable years beginning after December 31, 2017, only 80 percent of taxable income in any given year can be reduced by NOLs.

Are expenses incurred in a reorganization tax deductible?

No. Instead of being expensed, these costs must be capitalized, as they pertain to the long-term value of the company. The only bankruptcy-related expenses that may be deductible will be those to settle tort claims.

What is the tax treatment of the cancellation of debt?

Generally, the rule in the IRC is that a debtor has taxable income when a debt is canceled. However, one of the exceptions to this general rule occurs when a taxpayer is still insolvent after realizing a discharge of indebtedness. (As mentioned earlier, under the tax code, a business is insolvent when the taxpayer's liabilities exceed the fair market value of the taxpayer's assets.)

If the business is still insolvent after the cancellation of a debt, the entire discharged amount is excluded from gross income. This is a very important rule. If a business is insolvent and the cancellation of a creditor's debt returns the business to solvency, then it must report income. But if the company is still insolvent after the cancellation, it does not have to report any income.

There is a catch, however. When a discharge of debt is excluded from gross income, the cancellation must be used to reduce (on a dollar-for-dollar basis) any NOLs. In essence, this defers tax rather than lowering it.

If a company is an S corporation, however, the situation is more favorable for the tax treatment of canceled debt. Shareholders of S corporations may increase their corporate basis by "items of income" that are identified in the tax code. These items include tax-exempt income, losses, and deductions. This prevents double taxation. A shareholder's basis in S corporation stock is decreased when losses and deductions are "passed through." However, shareholders cannot take corporate losses and deductions on their personal tax returns when those items exceed the shareholder's basis in the stock and his or her share of the debt of the S corporation. The amounts of those items that exceed the shareholder's basis are "suspended" until the shareholder's basis increases enough to allow the deduction. The forgiveness of debt is income that would be excluded from gross income if the taxpayer were insolvent. Shareholders can then "pass through" this "item of income" to increase their corporate basis. The taxpayers could then deduct any losses that were previously suspended because there had not been sufficient corporate basis to deduct the losses.[60]

LIQUIDATION

What is a liquidation?

A liquidation is a sale of assets that ends the existence of a going concern.

What is a partial liquidation?

A partial liquidation is a sale of the assets of one business within a larger network of businesses (such as a subsidiary). The proceeds of the liquidation are typically distributed to shareholders.

If a company buys an insolvent company, may it liquidate that company without incurring any special legal exposure?

Directors are under no special obligation to file for bankruptcy if a corporation is insolvent.

But although directors are free to liquidate assets, they must get a reasonable value for them. Indeed, if a corporation is insolvent but does not go through bankruptcy proceedings or otherwise place itself under the supervision of the courts, directors have an enhanced duty to "protect" the value of corporate assets and "account for waste," if any.[61] Fortunately, however, in a liquidation, directors' decisions on priority of creditor payments is protected by the business judgment rule. Other liabilities related to the insolvent company purchase must be carefully considered, however, as there may be many that the acquiring company will inherit.

How are liquidations treated under the US tax code?

If a company buys another company, adopts a plan of liquidation, and liquidates the company, then the liquidation will be tax-free under Sections 332 and 337 of the IRC. Chapter 5 discusses Section 332 in more detail.

Also, under certain circumstances (in a partial liquidation) although gain is fully recognized at the corporate level, a shareholder (other than a C corporation) receiving the proceeds avoids dividend taxation in addition to receiving certain tax benefits. To qualify, the corporation or affiliated group of corporations doing the partial liquidation must have been operating at least two separate businesses (including, of course, the one liquidated) for at least five years.

CONCLUDING COMMENTS

Workouts, bankruptcies, and liquidations exemplify the importance of careful structuring in any transaction—especially transactions with entities that are undergoing financial difficulty. Buyers who make a diligent effort to repay creditors and preserve value for shareholders can reap substantial rewards over the long term.

These rewards are all the more valuable and vulnerable in the new global economy. In many bankruptcies today, assets are located in more than one country. Fortunately for US companies, Chapter 15 of the US Bankruptcy Code allows for the cooperation between United States courts, foreign courts, and other authorities involved in cross-border insolvency cases. Cross-border insolvency law involves rules on choice of law, jurisdiction rules, and the enforcement of judgment.[62] Let us now consider the global scene for dealmaking—for both distressed and healthy companies.

DIAGRAMS SHOWING VARIOUS STRUCTURES FOR REORGANIZATIONS AND WORKOUTS OF INSOLVENT COMPANIES

In the transaction depicted in Exhibit 11-6, a venture capitalist lends $1 million in equity to Newco, the acquirer, while banks lend $9 million. The acquirer takes the resulting $10 million and buys Target from the shareholders. Target, which already has $2 million in liabilities, remains a separate subsidiary of Newco after the transaction and does not guarantee or otherwise assume liability for the $9 million loaned to Newco. This transaction structure would not point to fraudulent conveyance, even if T becomes insolvent after the transaction, because it does not increase the debt load of the target company.

In Exhibit 11-7, a venture capitalist forms Newco by investing $1 million for an equity stake in Target, which becomes a Newco subsidiary, and

Exhibit 11-6 Structure Posing No Fraudulent Conveyance Risk: Newco Purchases Target Stock

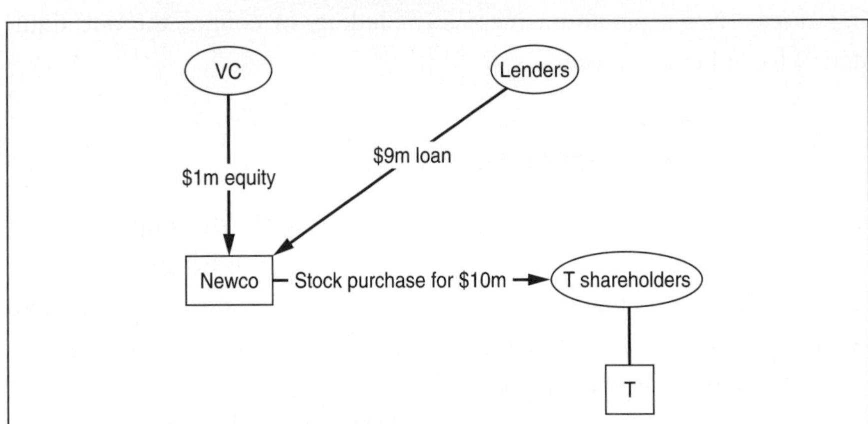

guarantees Newco's $9 million debt. If Target, which already has $2 million in liabilities, becomes insolvent as a result of the transaction, this structuring technique could ***point to fraudulent conveyance****.*

In Exhibit 11-8, a venture capitalist forms Newco by investing $1 million for an equity stake. Target, which already has $2 million in liabilities, borrows $9 million, and reloans it to Newco. If Target becomes insolvent as a result of the transaction, this structuring technique could ***point to fraudulent conveyance****.*

Exhibit 11-7 Structure Posing Fraudulent Conveyance Risk via Guarantee: Target Guarantees Newco Debt

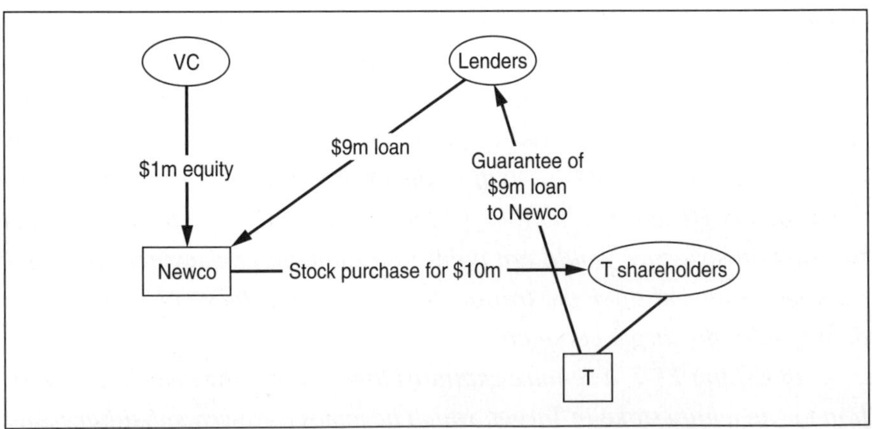

Exhibit 11-8 Structure Posing Fraudulent Conveyance Risk via Transfer of Loan Recipient: Target Does the Borrowing

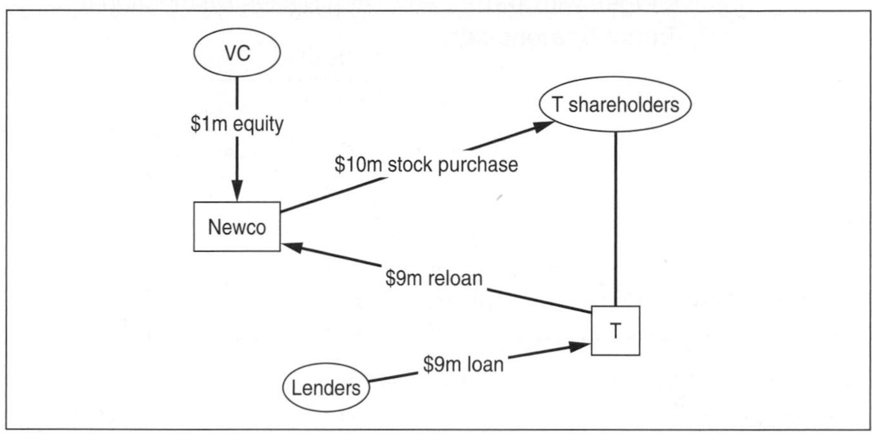

In Exhibit 11-9, a venture capitalist forms Newco by investing $1 million for an equity stake. Newco borrows $9 million and buys the Target stock, merging with Target completely (through a liquidation of Target, an upstream merger of Target into Newco, or a downstream merger of Newco into Target) and assuming Target's liabilities. If the newly combined com-

Exhibit 11-9 Structure Posing Fraudulent Conveyance Risk via Simple Merger: Newco Purchases the Target's Stock and the Two Combine

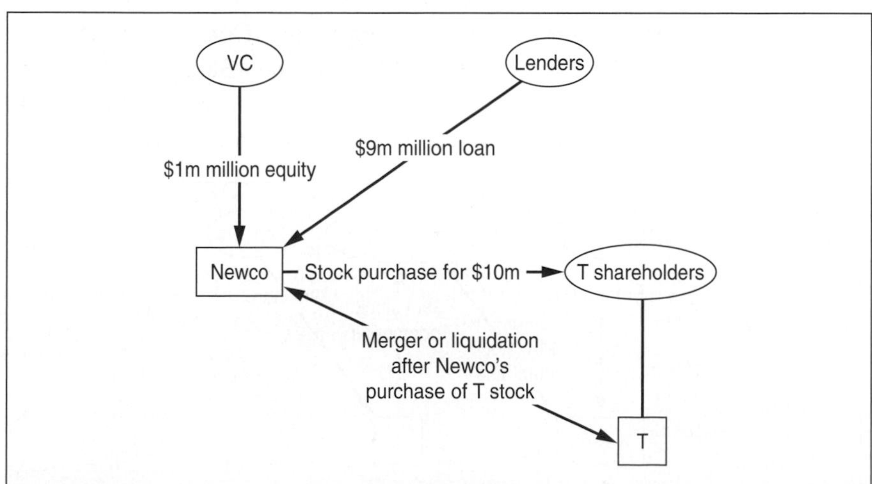

Exhibit 11-10 Structure Posing Fraudulent Conveyance Risk via Distribution to Shareholders: Newco Buys Target Stock/ Merges with Target, and Then Makes Distribution to Target Shareholders

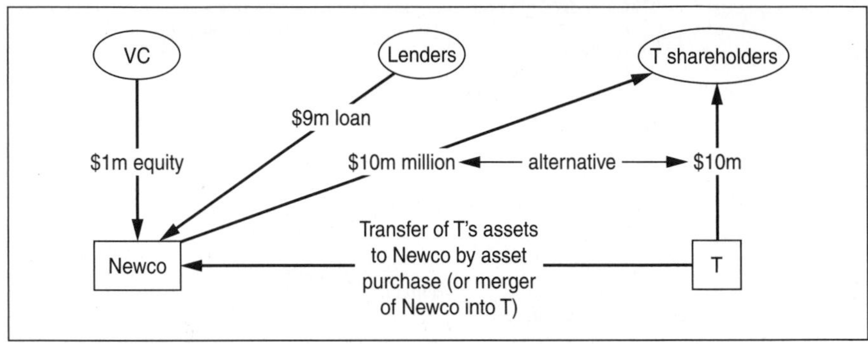

pany becomes insolvent as a result of the transaction, this structuring technique could ***point to fraudulent conveyance****.*

In Exhibit 11-10, a venture capitalist forms Newco by investing $1 million for an equity stake, and Newco borrows another $9 million. Newco then takes the $10 million and does one of two things: (1) purchases Target's assets for $10 million and assumes Target's $2 million in liabilities, and then liquidates, distributing $10 million to shareholders; or (2) merges with Target (with either Newco or Target surviving the merger)

Exhibit 11-11 Structure Posing Risk of Fraudulent Conveyance in Multistep Transaction Involving Small Stock Purchase and Large Loan: Newco Purchases Part of the Target's Stock and Target Borrows to Redeem the Rest of the Stock

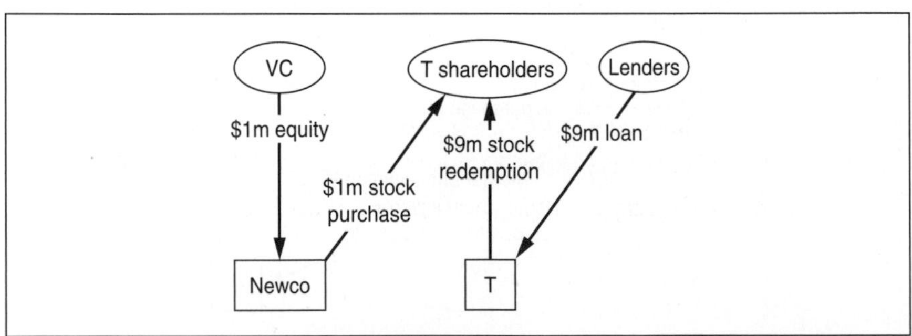

Exhibit 11-12 Structure Posing Fraudulent Conveyance Risk via Transfer of Risk to a Subsidiary: Newco Acquires Target via Forward or Reverse Subsidiary Merger

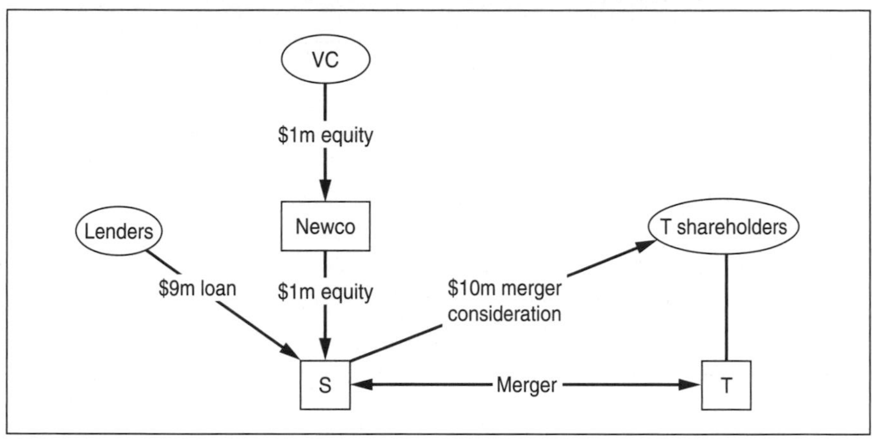

and distributes $10 to Target shareholders pursuant to the merger plan. If Target's creditors fail to be paid what they are owed following this transaction, the transaction could ***point to fraudulent conveyance****.*

In Exhibit 11-11, a venture capitalist forms Newco by investing $1 million for an equity stake. Newco uses the money to buy 10 percent of Target's stock. At the same time, Target borrows $9 million, which Target uses to redeem the rest of the stock. If the newly combined company becomes insolvent as a result of the transaction, this structuring technique could ***point to fraudulent conveyance****.*

In Exhibit 11-12, a venture capitalist forms Newco by investing $1 million for an equity stake. Newco contributes the $1 million to its wholly owned subsidiary S. S borrows $9 million and then merges into T (in a reverse subsidiary merger) or T merges into S (in a forward subsidiary merger). T's shareholders receive $10 million pursuant to the plan of merger (the $1 million of equity plus the $9 million of S acquisition debt). If the resulting company becomes insolvent as a result of the transaction, this structuring technique could ***point to fraudulent conveyance****.*

NOTES

1. Technically, the Code is cited as the United States Code (USC), Title 11, Chapter 11. The US Code has 54 titles, each devoted to a particular aspect of US federal law. It is supplemented by the Code of Federal Regulations (CFR). See Chapter 6, on due diligence, for more details.
2. The general framework of this chapter is based on earlier titles in the series, *The Art of M&A Structuring* and *The Art of Distressed M&A.* See Alexandra Reed Lajoux and H. Peter Nesvold, *The Art of M&A Structuring: Techniques for Mitigating Financial, Tax, and Legal Risk* (New York: McGraw-Hill, 2004); and H. Peter Nesvold, Jeffrey M. Anapolsky, and Alexandra Reed Lajoux, *The Art of Distressed M&A: Buying, Selling, and Financing Troubled and Insolvent Companies* (New York: McGraw-Hill, 2011). However, all material in this chapter is updated to reflect recent developments in bankruptcy law and accounting. The author thanks Deborah Hicks Midanek Bailey for her guidance.
3. Jonathan Rosenthal, advisor to the shareholder committees of Adelphia and Kmart, in a *Business Week Online* interview posted on the Turnaround Management Association website

(turnaround.org). See note 13 for more information about this association.

4. For a good general article about this topic, see Andrea Saavedra and Christopher Hopkins, "The Statutory Definition of 'Insolvent'–Part One," https://business-finance-restructuring.weil.com/valuation/the-statutory-definition-of-insolvent-part-one/.
5. 11 U.S.C. § 101(32)(A), https://www.law.cornell.edu/uscode/text/11/101. (Part II of this article covers the bankruptcy of municipalities under Chapter 9 of the bankruptcy code.)
6. A claim under Chapter 11 is called a "right to payment, whether or not such right is reduced to judgment, liquidated, unliquidated, fixed, contingent, matured, unmatured, disputed, undisputed, legal, equitable, secured, or unsecured." https://www.law.cornell.edu/uscode/text/11/101.
7. Travellers International AG v. Trans World Airlines, Inc. (In re Trans World Airlines), 134 F.3d 188, 194 (3d Cir. 1998), cert. denied, 523 U.S. 1138 (1998).
8. Ibid. at 195.
9. Uniform Voidable Transactions Act, Sections 2(a) and (b). This act is a revision and renaming of the Uniform Fraudulent Transfer Act. Note: Failure to pay debts when they become due is sometimes referred to as "equitable insolvency."
10. http://www.uniformlaws.org/shared/docs/Fraudulent%20Transfer/2014_AUVTA_Final%20Act_2016mar8.pdf.
11. New York Business Corporation Law, § 102(a)(8), defines *insolvent as* "being unable to pay debts as they become due in the usual course of the debtor's business." https://newyork.public.law/laws/n.y._business_corporation_law_section_102.
12. Thanks go to Howard Brownstein, of Brownstein Corp., for his explanation of the equity definition of insolvency.
13. A good source for these executives is the Turnaround Management Association, which has 9,000 members in 49 chapters around the world: https://turnaround.org/about-tma.

14. https://www.researchpool.com/download/?report_id=1751185&show_pdf_data rue.
15. "Neiman Marcus Seeks Debt Restructuring to Avoid Bankruptcy," Retail Touchpoints, October 25, 2018, https://www.retailtouchpoints.com/features/news-briefs/neiman-marcus-seeks-debt-restructuring-to-avoid-bankruptcy.
16. The 2007 edition of this book also listed American Airlines, Chrysler Corp., and Daewoo, but all three filed for bankruptcy following that year.
17. As mentioned in Chapter 5, the United States Code is a consolidation and codification by subject matter of the general and permanent laws of the United States. It is prepared by the Office of the Law Revision Counsel of the US House of Representatives. http://uscode.house.gov/search/criteria.shtml.
18. https://www.justice.gov/ust/bankruptcy-fact-sheets/us-trustees-role-chapter-11-bankruptcy-cases.
19. For links to bankruptcy courts and other important bankruptcy sources, visit the website of the American Bankruptcy Institute, particularly on this landing page: https://www.abi.org/membership/bankruptcy-links. The source of jurisdiction is found in Title 28 of the US Code, § 1334—Bankruptcy cases and proceedings. See https://www.law.cornell.edu/uscode/text/28/1334.
20. In the United States, some 6 million entities file taxes as going concerns every year. See https://www.irs.gov/pub/irs-soi/13CorporateReturnsOneSheet.pdf. Furthermore, the total number of bankruptcy filings, including personal filings, is less than 60,000. (The number of business filings, as mentioned, is about 40,000, but some entity owners use personal bankruptcy to resolve the claims against their business, so the total number of business bankruptcy filings is higher than 40,000.)
21. Public Law 95-598, Title 1, Section 101, Nov. 6, 1978, Statute 2549.

22. Experian states that "Chapter 7 is an option for consumers with limited income" (https://www.experian.com/blogs/ask-experian/what-is-chapter-7-bankruptcy/). On the other hand, as noted by Nolo.com, "Small business owners have the option of filing Chapter 7 on behalf of their business or for themselves personally. If, however, you're a sole proprietor, both your business debt and your personal debt will be resolved in the same Chapter 7 bankruptcy case," noting further that "many business owners choose to file only an individual bankruptcy because it will wipe out an individual's responsibility to pay the business debt" (https://www.nolo.com/legal-encyclopedia/chapter-7-chapter-13-bankruptcy-small-business-owners.html).
23. Federal Rules of Bankruptcy Procedure (December 1, 2017). http://www.uscourts.gov/sites/default/files/bankruptcy-rules-procedure-dec2017.pdf.
24. See "The Year in Bankruptcy," https://www.jonesday.com/the-year-in-bankruptcy-2017-02-02-2018/?utm_source=Mondaq&utm_medium=syndication&utm_campaign=View-Original.
25. The absolute priority rule provides that creditors recover in full before equity holders recover any of their investment. Or as the US Supreme Court has stated, "Bankruptcy courts may not approve structured dismissals that provide for distributions that do not follow ordinary priority rules without the consent of affected creditors." For affirmation via the US Supreme Court, see *Czyzewski v. Jevic Holding Corp.*, No. 15-649, 2017 U.S. LEXIS 2024, at *21 & *7 (Mar. 22, 2017), https://www.supremecourt.gov/opinions/16pdf/15-649_k53m.pdf.
26. https://www.law.cornell.edu/uscode/text/11/506.
27. https://www.law.cornell.edu/uscode/text/11/510.
28. https://www.law.cornell.edu/uscode/text/11/1129.
29. As stated by Mark G. Douglas, the section "provides a mechanism designed to preserve the creditor/shareholder risk allocation paradigm by categorically subordinating most types of claims asserted against a debtor by equityholders in

respect of their equity holdings." "In Brief: Second Circuit Reaffirms Broad Scope of Bankruptcy Code's Subordination of Shareholder Claims, August 15, 2017," Jonesday.com, July/August 2017. In the case *In re Lehman Brothers Holdings Inc.,* 855 F. 3d 459 (2d Cir. 2017), the court affirmed this subordination clause when applying it to restricted stock units received by employees. https://www.jdsupra.com/legalnews/in-brief-second-circuit-reaffirms-broad-89938/.

30. Rule 3002(a) of the US Federal Rules of Bankruptcy Procedure (http://www.uscourts.gov/sites/default/files/bankruptcy-rules-procedure-dec2017.pdf) now requires a secured creditor to file a proof of claim in order to gain allowance for a secured claim. See Joshua D. Morse, "Beware Secured Creditors: The Newly Amended US Federal Rules of Bankruptcy Procedure Now Require Filing a Proof of Claim," DLA Piper, December 21, 2017, https://www.dlapiper.com/en/us/insights/publications/2017/12/restructuring-global-insight-december/beware-secured-creditors/.

31. The Commission archive is here: http://govinfo.library.unt.edu/nbrc/.

32. As noted earlier, if a corporate taxpayer has an excess of tax deductions over its taxable income in a given year, this excess becomes a net operating loss (NOL) of that taxpayer. Section 172 of the IRC, as amended with the TCJA, allows that taxpayer to use its NOL to offset taxable income in subsequent years (a carryover or carryforward) for an indefinite period starting in the first taxable year after December 31, 2017. However, it does not allow the taxpayer to offset taxable income in earlier years (a carryback). It also limits reduction of taxable income by NOL; for taxable years beginning after December 31, 2017, only 80 percent of taxable income in any given year can be reduced by NOLs.

    Under other provisions of the IRC, certain tax losses or tax credits that are unusable in a given year may be carried forward or carried back to other tax years. Generally, IRC provisions for a company's ability to use NOL carryovers apply as well to these other items. For purposes of simplicity, all of these items tend to be grouped together with loss carryovers.

33. See Congress.gov, using the search terms *bankruptcy* and *selecting bill title* and *bill summary.*
34. For a description of hurdles faced by small businesses contemplating Chapter 11, see "Adviser to Businesses Laments Changes to Bankruptcy Law," *New York Times,* February 29, 2012.
35. This answer is adapted from *Bankruptcies, Liquidations and Quasi-Reorganizations: A Comprehensive Guide,* part of the Financial Reporting Developments series, revised May 2018, http://www.ey.com/ul/en/accountinglink/frd-bb1840-bankruptcies--liquidations-and-quasi-reorganizations.
36. *In re Lehman Brothers Inc., et al., Debtors,* Chapter 11, Case No. 08-13555 (JMP), Report of Anton R. Valukas, https://web.stanford.edu/~jbulow/Lehmandocs/VOLUME%201.pdf.
37. David Skeel, a professor of corporate law at the University of Pennsylvania Law School, quoted in Brian Tumulty, "History Shows Corporations Can Survive Bankruptcy" May 29, 2000, https://abcnews.go.com/Business/story?id=7712263&page=1.
38. For example, as of late 2018, this court was overseeing 71 mega cases. http://www.nysb.uscourts.gov/megaCases.
39. http://www.uscourts.gov/services-forms/bankruptcy/bankruptcy-basics/chapter-11-bankruptcy-basics.
40. "[T]he fact that the vast majority of the security holders have approved the plan is *not* the test of whether the plan is a fair and equitable one," said the court in *Case v. Los Angeles Lumber Prods.*, 308 U.S. 106 (1939). Cited in Mark J. Roe, "The Three Ages of Bankruptcy," *Harvard Business Law Review,* March 7, 2017, http://www.hblr.org/wp-content/uploads/2017/11/HLB203_crop.pdf. See also Jason B. Binford et al., "The Top 10 Cases That Every Bankruptcy Practitioner Should Know (Plus Certain Honorable Mentions)," *The Federal Lawyer,*

February 2010, "http://www.fedbar.org/Resources_1/Federal-Lawyer-Magazine/2010/The%20Federal%20Lawyer%20-%20February%202010/The-Top-Ten-Cases-That-Every-Bankruptcy-Practitioner-Should-Know.aspx?FT=.pdf.

41. http://www.uscourts.gov/services-forms/bankruptcy/bankruptcy-basics/chapter-11-bankruptcy-basics.
42. Case information for Sears Holdings Corporation (18-23538) https://restructuring.primeclerk.com/sears/.
43. According to one source, the goal of such a committee and its advisors would be to obtain as much equity as possible. Shivani Shah, "For Equity's Sake: The Appointment of Equity Committees in Bankruptcy Cases," Client Letter, March 16, 2018, http://www.nortonrosefulbright.com/knowledge/publications/163866/for-equitys-sake-the-appointment-of-equity-committees-in-bankruptcy-cases.
44. Ibid.
45. See https://www.law.cornell.edu/uscode/text/11/1126.
46. http://www.uscourts.gov/services-forms/bankruptcy/bankruptcy-basics/chapter-11-bankruptcy-basics.
47. As stated by one scholar, "Generally, federal bankruptcy law takes state law property and contract rights as it finds them, although subject to an important caveat of countervailing federal bankruptcy purposes." See *Butner v. United States,* 440 U.S. 48, 54 (1979). John A. E. Potow, "Fiduciary Duties in Bankruptcy and Insolvency," University of Michigan Scholarship Repository, https://repository.law.umich.edu/cgi/viewcontent.cgi?article=1246&context=law_econ_current.
48. See 11 U.S. Code § 363—Use, sale, or lease of property, https://www.law.cornell.edu/uscode/text/11/363.
49. Cited in the Debtor's Motion for Constellation Enterprises LLC et al., Case No. 16-11213 (CSS), filed May 5, 2016, http://bankrupt.com/misc/Constellation_Ent_88_Sale_M.pdf. Appeals of the court's decision in this matter were dismissed. https://www.courtlistener.com/recap/gov.uscourts.ded.62335/gov.uscourts.ded.62335.58.0.pdf.

50. *Amphenol Corp. v. Shandler* (*In re Insilco Technologies, Inc.*), Adv. Proc. No. 05-52403 (Bankr. D. Del., Sept. 18, 2006). This case is a "reminder that a U.S. Bankruptcy Court cannot grant an order delivering up title to the assets of a non-party subsidiary of a Chapter 11 debtor 'free and clear' of liens." "U.S.-Canadian Cross-Border Restructurings: What's New," May 2007, https://mcmillan.ca/101513.
51. "Rule 2004 authorizes a court to order the examination of any entity, provided that the examination concerns ' . . . the acts, conduct, or property or to the liabilities and financial condition of the debtor, or to any matter which may affect the administration of the debtor's estate, or to the debtor's right to a discharge.'" See Andrew C. Kassner and Joseph N. Argentina, Jr., "Fishing in the Waters of Bankruptcy Rule 2004," *The Legal Intelligencer,* September 16, 2018, https://www.law.com/thelegalintelligencer/2018/09/06/fishing-in-the-waters-of-bankruptcy-rule-2004/?slreturn=20180902175530.
52. https://www.law.cornell.edu/rules/frbp/rule_2004.
53. "Initial Guidance Under Section 163(j) as Applicable to Taxable Years Beginning After December 31, 2017," Notice 2018-28, https://www.irs.gov/pub/irs-drop/n-18-28.pdf. Note: 30 years ago, when the first edition of this book was published, so-called leveraged buyouts, or LBOs, had higher ratios. Up to 90 percent of a transaction might be financed by debt, leaving a debt-heavy balance sheet. In too many cases, insolvency was the result.
54. For more on these examples, see George Schultze, "Chapter 11 Is Not the End of the Game," *Forbes,* September 10, 2018, https://www.forbes.com/sites/georgeschultze/2018/09/10/chapter-11-is-not-the-end-of-the-game/#417560212eb4.
55. The press release can be found here: http://ditechholding.com. The SEC filing can be found here: https://www.sec.gov/Archives/edgar/data/1040719/000119312519032940/d705469d8k.htm.
56. https://www.law.cornell.edu/uscode/text/11/548.
57. As noted by the American Bar Association, "The Uniform

Voidable Transactions Act (UVTA) was recently adopted by the Uniform Law Commission (Commission) as the successor to the Uniform Fraudulent Transfer Act (UFTA). UFTA was itself an update of its predecessor, the Uniform Fraudulent Conveyance Act (UFCA). UFCA was revised to conform the act to the Bankruptcy Reform Act of 1978." https://www.americanbar.org/publications/probate_property_magazine_2012/2015/july_august_2015/2015_aba_rpte_pp_v29_3_article_foster_boughman_uniform_voidable_transactions_act.html.

58. The UCC is developed and maintained by the National Conference of Commissioners on Uniform State Laws (NCCUSL), (also known as the Uniform Law Commission), a nonprofit organization. For more on the UCC, see Chapter 5.
59. See "Net Operating Losses (NOLs) After the Tax Cuts and Jobs Act: Understanding the Limitation on Future Use and Carryback of NOLs," RSM, updated March 29, 2018, https://rsmus.com/what-we-do/services/tax/washington-national-tax/net-operating-losses-after-the-tax-cuts-and-jobs-act.html.
60. That was the finding of the US Supreme Court in *Gitlitz, et al. v. Commissioner of Internal Revenue* (*2001*), 531 U.S. 206 (2001). The case dates from 1991, when PDW&A, Inc., of Colorado, an insolvent S corporation, of which David Gitlitz and Philip Winn were shareholders, excluded over $2 million in discharge of indebtedness from gross income, under Section 108 of the IRC. On their personal returns, shareholders Gitlitz and Winn increased the basis in their S corporation by the amount of the discharge. Gitlitz and Winn claimed additional corporate losses and deductions because of the increase in basis. The court held that the IRC permits taxpayers to increase the basis in their S corporation stock by the amount of an S corporation's discharge of indebtedness excluded from gross income.
61. See *N.Y. Credit Men's Adjustment Bureau v. Weiss,* 305 N.Y. 1 at 7.
62. https://corporatefinanceinstitute.com/resources/knowledge/other/us-bankruptcy-code/.

CHAPTER 12

Global Deals: Structuring for Success

INTRODUCTION

Today, more than ever before in their history, business buyers and sellers operate in a global economy. According to Thomson-Reuters, cross-border M&A activity totaled US$1.6 trillion during 2018, a 32 percent increase compared to 2017. This was the strongest first nine months for cross-border M&A since 2007—the date of the fourth edition of this book. Cross-border M&A accounted for 38.9 percent of the 2018 M&A activity, again the strongest first nine months percentage since 2007, when cross-border M&A accounted for 44 percent of overall dealmaking.[1]

The myriad opportunities and risks (including cyber risks)[2] inherent in global cyberspace have made it virtually impossible for any business to operate outside our economically and technologically unified world. Despite "new nationalism" and global trade wars, the world has seen a steady rise in global trade in the decade following the 2008–2009 financial crisis.[3] Today, US firms' annual overseas exports exceed $1.5 trillion, suggesting confidence in global markets,[4] even as heavier imports (more than $2 trillion) show a continued dependency on global suppliers. Moreover, companies are engaging in an increasing variety of international mergers, acquisitions, and other investment activities—much of it contributing to the boom in global trade. [5]

Of the some $4 trillion spent on M&A annually,[6] more than a 40 percent ($1.7 trillion) is spent to buy firms in the United States.[7] Yet the United States has no monopoly on dealmaking. Many of the largest transaction announcements in recent times have been transborder deals that do not involve US companies, including Takeda Pharmaceutical Co. Ltd. and Shire PLC (Japan/Ireland), which closed in January 2019 for $62.2 billion.[8]

These buyers and sellers are doing their deals in an increasingly fluid financial environment. Around the world, stock exchanges have opened up their listings to foreign issuers, providing 24-hour trading to accommodate global buying and selling. The World Federation of Exchanges now includes 200 market infrastructure providers, listing 45,000 companies with equities valued at $82.5 trillion.[9] Meanwhile, language barriers are falling as more companies print annual reports in multiple languages.

A quick note on terminology. By *foreign,* we mean located outside the corporation's country. Thus, to a French-incorporated company, a British acquirer would be foreign, even if it is in the same region. We are not using this term to indicate transactions across state lines within a multistate country. Since the Internal Revenue Code (IRC) uses the term *foreign* in various ways, we will define them at each usage.

This chapter is divided into two parts: nontax and tax. It makes a distinction in each of those areas between issues relating to foreign investment in the United States (inbound transactions) and those relating to US investment overseas (outbound transactions). It includes information useful to companies acquiring other US companies with international components and useful to US companies wishing to finance their domestic or foreign activities through international techniques and sources.

NONTAX INBOUND: ISSUES REGARDING FOREIGN INVESTMENT IN THE UNITED STATES

US Limitations on Foreign Ownership

Are there any limitations under US law regarding the form of business association in which a foreign person can participate?

Generally, US laws impose no limitations on the form of business association a foreign person can use to create or conduct a business or own business interests. The type of business association a foreign person decides to use is often dictated by the particular needs of the enterprise and the impact upon that enterprise of federal and state laws—particularly tax laws, which may be an incentive to use one particular structure and a disincentive to use another. Any foreign person would be well advised to check with local counsel on the impact of all relevant tax, business, securities, and related laws prior to deciding on the most favorable form of business association to achieve his or her specific goals.

Must the parties forming a new corporation be citizens of the United States and residents of the state of incorporation?

Not necessarily. The ease and simplicity of corporate formation in the United States may come as a surprise to those accustomed to the formality of incorporating under certain foreign systems. In the absence of express requirements in state corporation statutes, these parties, called *incorporators* (not synonymous with *stockholders*), are merely legal instruments used to organize a corporation. They need not be citizens or residents of the state under whose laws the formation of the corporation will be formed. For example, Delaware Corporation Law Section 101(a) states the following:

> Any person, partnership, association, or corporation, singly or jointly with others, and without regard to his or their residence,

> domicile, or state of incorporation, may incorporate or organize a corporation under this chapter by filing with the Division of Corporations in the Department of State a certificate of incorporation which shall be executed, acknowledged, and filed in accordance with Section 103 of this title.[10]

If everyone owning and operating a corporation that is incorporated under the laws of a state of the United States is a non-US citizen, isn't the corporation considered foreign?

No. A corporation formed under the laws of any state is simply a corporation of that state. However, the business activities of that corporation may be restricted because its owners are not US citizens, and its owners may have to pay additional taxes because of their foreign citizenship (see "International Tax and Disclosure Considerations" later in this chapter).

What type of federal restrictions apply to foreign ownership of US businesses?

There are no blanket restrictions on the ownership of US businesses by foreign persons. There are, however, certain federal regulations restricting or limiting foreign ownership in particular industries or in certain circumstances. The following laws, listed in chronological order by year of original passage, control foreign investment and activity in specific industries or circumstances:

- The *General Mining Law of 1872* (along with the *Mineral Lands Leasing Act of 1958*) requires that anyone owning a mine be a US citizen. This category can include a US incorporated entity that is owned by non-US persons, but this information must be disclosed. The *Mineral Lands Leasing Act* requires that any corporation applying to the secretary of the interior for a federal lease to develop certain natural resources of the United States disclose the identity and citizenship of shareholders owning more than 10 percent of its stock, in which case the lease will be granted only if US persons can obtain reciprocal licenses or leases from the home governments of such foreign shareholders.[11]

- The *Edge Act of 1919* limits foreign ownership of corporations chartered by the Federal Reserve Board to engage in international banking and finance.[12]
- The *Merchant Marine Act of 1920,* which includes the better-known *Jones Act,* restricts the registration and licensing of vessels to those vessels owned, chartered, or leased from the secretary of commerce by a US citizen, or a corporation, partnership, or association organized in the United States and controlled by US citizens.[13]
- The *Communications Act of 1934* bars aliens, foreign governments, certain US corporations controlled by foreign interests, and corporations organized outside the United States from possessing a broadcast or common carrier license.[14]
- *The Defense Production Act of 1950,* Section 721, grants authority to the US president to suspend or prohibit certain transactions deemed threatening to national security. This section was strengthened through the *Exxon-Florio Act of 1988,* and more recently with the *Foreign Investment Risk Review Modernization Act of 2018.*
- The *Outer Continental Shelf Lands Act of 1953* stipulates that offshore leases for the development of energy resources be held only by citizens, nationals, and permanent resident aliens of the United States or by business associations thereof. However, because the Department of the Interior considers any corporation organized in the United States an entity suitable for an award of a lease, foreign possession of leases is possible through incorporation of a US subsidiary.[15]
- The *Federal Aviation Act of 1958* prohibits any foreign air carrier, or person controlling such an entity, from acquiring "control in any manner whatsoever" of any US entity or enterprise substantially engaged in the aeronautics business.[16]

In addition to the aforementioned US statutes, additional executive branch measures have been taken to monitor or control foreign investment in and trade with the United States.

In 1975, the Committee on Foreign Investment in the United States (CFIUS) was formed by executive order. The mandate of this committee is to review investments by foreign governments in the United States that, in the judgment of CFIUS, may have an effect on the national interests of the United States. The committee, however, has no power to block or modify investments by foreign governments. That power belongs to the president of the United States under the Defense Production Act and subsequent laws amending it, as previously mentioned.

Are there any special federal requirements that apply to US businesses owned or controlled by foreign persons?

Yes, in addition to tax requirements (discussed later in this chapter), these are primarily disclosure requirements. First, disclosure requirements generally applicable to acquisitions, such as requirements under the Hart-Scott-Rodino Act (see Chapter 2) and the Williams Act (see Chapter 10), apply to foreign as well as US investors. Second, the following federal laws establish specific disclosure requirements for foreign investors or have other requirements pertaining to foreign investments:

- The *International Investment and Trade in Services Survey Act of 1976*[17] requires US business enterprises to report to the Department of Commerce, within 45 days, the acquisition of a voting interest of 10 percent or more in such enterprise by one or more foreign persons if the interest was acquired for a price exceeding US$1 million. Under this law, if the enterprise has annual sales, assets, or net income passing a certain threshold, periodic reporting is also required.[18] In addition to the reporting requirements of foreign investors, the act also requires reporting by any citizen of the United States who assists or intervenes in the acquisition of a voting interest of at least 10 percent by a foreign person or by one who enters into a joint venture with a foreign person to create a US business enterprise.

- The *Agricultural Foreign Investment Disclosure Act* of 1978[19] requires a foreign person or entity to file a report within 90 days following the acquisition or transfer of any interest, other than a lien or security interest, in US farming, ranching, or timberland.[20]
- The *Foreign Investment in Real Property Tax Act of 1980* grants the secretary of the treasury the authority to require reporting by foreign persons holding direct investments in US real property interests meeting a certain threshold of value.[21]

Finally, there are many general business laws that apply generally to anyone acquiring a US company or listing stock in US markets. These include, of course, the blockbuster US laws of this century, as follows:

The Sarbanes-Oxley Act of 2002 set stronger financial controls in the wake of the bankruptcies of Enron and WorldCom. For example, Section 404 requires companies to assess the strength of their internal controls and requires auditors to do the same, following a detailed standard.

The Dodd-Frank Act of 2010 was passed in an effort to prevent the reoccurrence of the global financial crisis of 2008–2009, and for other broad social purposes. It requires federal agencies to set some 400 new rules for the companies under their jurisdictions, including not only many rules affecting the capital structure and disclosure requirements for banks, but also provisions that mandated disclosure rules affecting a variety of public companies—for example, the rule requiring companies to disclose whether or not their products contain conflict minerals.[22] (The European Union passed a similar law in 2017, to be effective January 1, 2021.)[23]

Must foreign investors be concerned about specific state regulations as well as US federal law when acquiring a US business interest?

In general, states do not restrict foreign investment, except with respect to specific industries, such as banking and insurance. Most states have passed antitakeover laws (see Chapter 10), but these apply equally to US and foreign acquirers. Some states restrict land ownership with respect to certain types of property, and the exploitation or development of natural resources by foreign investors. A foreign person desiring to acquire a business interest in the United States should seek legal counsel to ensure that there are no special restrictions imposed by the state in which the target business is domiciled, as well as under the federal law.

Do any of the foregoing restrictions apply to US businesses in which foreign persons hold debt rather than equity?

No. In the United States, the percentage of equity owned is the exclusive means of measuring the extent of a foreign investor's control of a US corporation. Debt holdings are not considered. Note, however, that, as discussed in Chapter 5, the distinction between debt and equity interest is not always clear-cut.

Does federal or state law limit the ability of a US company to guarantee the indebtedness of a foreign affiliate?

There are no federal limitations on the ability of a US company to guarantee foreign indebtedness. Any state limitations on a corporation's ability to guarantee indebtedness would be set forth in the state's corporation statutes, but such limitations are relatively rare. Where limitations do exist under state law, these limitations apply regardless of the nationality of the person on whose behalf the guarantee is given.

Are there legal limitations under US law on the ability of a US company to pledge its assets to a foreign lender?

The power of a corporation to acquire, utilize, and dispose of assets arises from state corporation statutes and is not dependent on the identity of other parties to the transaction. For example, Section 122 of the Delaware General Corporation law empowers any Delaware corporation to "[p]urchase, receive, take by grant, gift, devise, bequest or otherwise, lease, or otherwise acquire, own, hold, improve, employ, use and otherwise deal in and with real or personal property, or any interest therein, wherever situated, and to sell, convey, lease, exchange, transfer, or otherwise dispose of, or mortgage or pledge, all or any of its property and assets, or any interest therein, wherever situated."[24] Federal law in the United States imposes no restriction on the pledge of assets by US individuals or entities.

Does the United States impose any restrictions on the amount of dollars that can be paid by a US business to a foreign investor?

There is no limit, under current US law, on the amount of money that can be taken out of the United States by either US or foreign investors. In fact, it is the lack of such restrictions in the United States and many other countries that has led to the development of a large foreign exchange market with operations centers in financial markets around the world, as discussed later in this chapter.

Restrictions Imposed by the Acquirer's Home Country

Do most countries have laws that affect their citizens' acquisitions in other countries?

Many industrialized nations impose certain domestic laws and/or additional external investment laws on foreign companies acquired by their citizens. The acquirer must be aware of how these domestic and external investment laws might affect its investment.

An example of one area of concern is trade policy. Whereas the target company's country may want to increase exports, the parent company's country may wish to restrict imports. In addition to general national trade policy concerns, there may be licensing requirements for imports and exports, and other trade barriers such as quotas and tariffs. When countries have many trading partners, such as the United States and China, their trade wars can have broad repercussions across the global supply chain.

NONTAX OUTBOUND: ACQUISITIONS INVOLVING ASSETS LOCATED OUTSIDE THE UNITED STATES

What are the main differences between acquisitions that are confined geographically to the United States and those that are international in whole or in part?

One of the advantages that the United States offers dealmakers is that it is a large, homogeneous area that runs on the same basic accounting, legal, and cultural principles. A buyer from Washington state making an acquisition in Florida, or a company in Arizona selling to a firm in Vermont, negotiates from a great deal of shared knowledge, shared perceptions, and shared business practices.

This is not true when a buyer goes abroad, even if only part of a transaction is international. It may seek to find the foreign equivalent of a particular transactional structure in a particular jurisdiction only to find that there is no such equivalent. For example, a buyer of a corporation in a particular country may assume it can offer its lenders warrants as part of its financing package. However, warrants may not be contractual obligations enforceable against corporations in that country. Therefore, the buyer would have to find other devices to give its lender the same or similar economic and legal rights as those embodied in a warrant.

In the United States, a management team and board of directors might decide on a transaction for strategic reasons and then call in the accountants and lawyers. However, they are basing the planned transaction on a great deal of law, tax, and accounting they already know and take for granted. When dealing in the international arena, managers will need a background on the meaning and reliability of information about the target and the country in which it is located.

International dealmaking often forces buyers or sellers to learn an entirely different cross-border vocabulary—even in the same language, identical concepts may be expressed in different words—for example, turnover and remuneration in the United Kingdom versus revenue and compensation in the United States.

Similarly, the American concept of antitrust takes on a different meaning in Europe. Whereas the primary aim of US antitrust law has been to maintain economic efficiency, antitrust law in the European Union has multiple goals, including fairness, European integration, and encouragement of competition through the protection of rivals.[25] In both Europe and Japan, strong cross-shareholdings render the terms *shareholders' rights* and *investor activism* virtually untranslatable.

On the tax and regulatory front, in some countries an acquirer may find that the seller has the government as a silent partner. Many foreign countries reserve the right to review and amend the contracts between a domestic seller and a foreign buyer, in some cases to protect their citizens against overreaching by more sophisticated foreign businesspeople and in others to ensure that the transaction promotes economic development or other governmental policies.

Furthermore, accounting standards differ around the globe despite attempts at convergence. Currently, most developed economies use some version of IFRS in Europe, with the exceptions being China, Japan, and the United States, each of which has its own standards.[26]

When it comes to consolidation of acquired entities, FRS consolidation principles differ from those of US GAAP in some respects, and these differences can cause changes in company structure, causing some companies to deconsolidate entities, or to consolidate entities that were not consolidated under US GAAP.[27] Subsidiaries that previously were excluded from the consolidated financial statements are to be consolidated as if they were first-time adopters on the same date as the parent. Companies also will have to consider the potential data gaps of investees to comply with IFRS informational and disclosure requirements.

Finally, an American firm acquiring abroad will encounter a new cultural and ethical framework. Differences in forms of government, legal systems, language, and economic approaches must be considered and generally understood by potential cross-border investors. Furthermore, a country's identity is a product of its historical, religious, and social underpinnings, all of which have played a role in the development of that nation's business culture.

What are some of the principal issues a US company should know about in connection with the acquisition of a non-US business or a US business with significant foreign assets?

Some of the key areas to focus on are as follows:

- Differences in rights accorded to employees
- Laws and beliefs pertaining to financing—for example, the Islamic principle under sharia (Islamic law) that it is wrong to charge or pay interest
- The ability to use foreign assets to support financing from lenders
- Regulatory requirements and limitations with respect to the acquisition itself and with postacquisition operations
- Ownership requirements for businesses operating within a country's borders
- Need for notification and/or approval of purchase of stock or assets and/or any other contractual arrangements between the parties, such as licensing of intellectual property

US and Foreign Laws Affecting US Acquisitions of Foreign Companies/Assets

Are there many restrictions on the form in which one can do business outside the United States?

Generally speaking, one has the same options as those available in the United States, that is, through a branch or division located in a foreign country, a subsidiary corporation, or a partnership, although it may be necessary to form the corporation or partnership within the foreign country in accordance with local laws. The joint venture is another common form of business association. In fact, in some countries, such as most nonmarket economies, it is the only investment vehicle available to foreigners.

What is the current stance of US antitrust law with regard to US outbound acquisitions?

Unless the product manufactured or distributed by the foreign entity enters into the stream of commerce in, or causes a direct anticompetitive effect inside, the United States, US antitrust laws will not apply to the acquisition or to the operations of the entity thereafter. This is true whether the manufacturing or distributing entity is a wholly owned foreign concern or a foreign subsidiary of a US corporation. If, however, the product does enter the stream of commerce or cause an anticompetitive effect in the United States, then US antitrust laws will apply in the same manner as if the foreign entity were located in the United States, although enforcement is difficult. Even where US courts might find that an act overseas is causing an anticompetitive effect within the United States, the jurisdiction of US courts will usually not reach within the boundaries of another sovereign nation. The Department of Justice (DOJ) and Federal Trade Commission (FTC) have issued guidelines that deal with these kinds of international antitrust concerns.

What do the DOJ and FTC joint guidelines on international antitrust say about US acquisitions of foreign entities?

The *International Guidelines for International Enforcement and Cooperation,* issued January 2017,[28] generally follow the domestic Merger Guidelines periodically issued by the DOJ and FTC—most recently in 2010.[29] Consistent with those domestic guidelines, the international guidelines say that in making investigative and enforcement decisions, the agencies focus on whether there is a "sufficient connection" between the alleged anticompetitive conduct and the United States. In such a case, federal antitrust laws could apply and the agencies would attempt to "redress harm or threatened harm to US commerce and consumers." The guide includes illustrative examples of the kinds of situations that might trigger a US federal antitrust investigation. The final two situations involve a merger, as follows:

- *Situation:* Corporation 1 and Corporation 2 each manufacture Product X and Product Y. Corporation 1 and Corporation 2 enter into an agreement to merge. The proposed merger meets the threshold for premerger notification in the United States under the HSR Act and the thresholds for premerger notification in several other jurisdictions. Corporation 1 and Corporation 2 inform the US Agency reviewing the merger as well as reviewing foreign authorities that the merger will be notified or reviewed in multiple jurisdictions. Prenotification consultations and premerger filings are timed to facilitate communication and cooperation among reviewing authorities at key decision-making stages of their respective investigations.
- *Situation:* After investigating the merger as outlined [above], the US Agency finds that the merger is likely to substantially lessen competition in the US market for Product X, and therefore that the merger would violate Section 7 of the Clayton Act. The US agency determines that these competitive concerns likely can be addressed through a divestiture of Corporation 1's assets related to Product X. Countries Alpha, Beta, and Gamma also find that the merger will harm competition in their markets for Product X, and Country Gamma has additional concerns about a reduction of competition in Gamma's market for Product Y.

What are some other examples of US laws that can affect outbound foreign acquisitions?

Of particular concern to US companies acquiring overseas are the following laws, among others:[30]

The *Trading with the Enemy Act of 1917* prohibits unlicensed trade between US persons and any individual, partnership, or other body of individuals that is (1) resident within the territory of any nation with which the United States is at war or (2) engaged in business within such territory. Unlicensed trade with corporations incorporated under the laws of an enemy nation is also prohibited, as is unlicensed trade with any party determined to be an ally of a nation with which the United States is at war.

The *International Investment and Trade in Services Survey Act of 1976* requires US companies investing overseas to file certain reports with the Department of Commerce. The filing of reports is mandatory if a US person, including a US corporation, has more than a 10 percent ownership interest in a foreign business enterprise and such enterprise has significant assets, sales, or after-tax income. Moreover, there is a proposal that, if adopted, would require a US company that sells services to or purchases services from an unaffiliated foreign person, including legal and accounting services, to file reports.

The *US Foreign Corrupt Practices Act of 1977* (FCPA) requires all US companies to "devise and maintain a system of internal accounting controls sufficient to provide reasonable assurances" that its bookkeeping will adhere to GAAP. It also makes it unlawful for any company "to make use of the mails or any means or instrumentality of interstate commerce corruptly in furtherance of [a payment] . . . while knowing or having reason to know" that the payment will be used to influence a foreign official to assist the company in obtaining or retaining business. The US parent will be responsible for a failure of a foreign subsidiary to comply with these requirements. In the four decades since the FCPA's enactment, the Department of Justice and the Securities and Exchange Commission have increased their enforcement actions under this law.[31]

The Export Administration Act of 1979, as promulgated, has antiboycott provisions that empower the president to issue regulations to prevent US companies engaged in interstate or foreign commerce and their subsidiaries from taking any action intending to comply with a boycott by a foreign country against another country with which the United States maintains friendly relations, as long as the company engages in activities in interstate or foreign commerce.

What regulations beyond national securities commissions govern international equity investment?

The central organization for equity involvement regulation is the International Organization of Securities Commissions (IOSCO). Currently headquartered in Madrid, Spain, it is composed of 220 regulatory agencies in 115 jurisdictions around the world. Although stock market rules vary considerably from country to country, the very existence of IOSCO points to a core of values. Moreover, the group and its individual members could gain more importance as the definition of what constitutes a "security" is brought into focus. And securities commissions are working together more often through IOSCO.

What about the merger regulations of the European Union?

Each member has its own comprehensive merger laws, but these are superseded by any directives intended for the EU. For example, the EU's European Commission (which we will refer to here as the "EU commission") put a new regulation into effect.[32] Ten years later, the EU commission published a white paper with suggested improvements to the law,[33] followed by required annual reports on competition policy.

In October 2018, the European Parliament received a motion for a resolution on competition policy urging the Parliament to view competition more broadly, "in a way that does not focus on narrow, price-centric consumer welfare but that considers the need for social and environmental efficiency, by encouraging horizontal coordination in order to improve the environmental and social sustainability of the supply chain; points out that the efficiencies generated by such agreement in a relevant market must be sufficient to outweigh the anti-competitive effects that they produce in either the same or an unrelated geographical market."[34]

Globally, how common are laws against insider trading based on nonpublic information?

Most jurisdictions outlaw the practice, at least in principle. This is in part because they are members of IOSCO and have signed on to the core principles listed in IOSCO's "Objectives and Principles of Securities Regulation," published in 1998 and most recently updated in 2017.[35] Furthermore, most IOSCO members have signed a multilateral memorandum of understanding for enforcement cooperation.[36] Note also that the World Bank and the International Monetary Fund use the IOSCO core principles in assessing the financial risk of countries.[37]

What is the general status of antibribery legislation around the world?

In the United States, the most well known law is the Foreign Corrupt Practices Act of 1988, still going strong after more than 30 years.[38] As of 2018, this policy still stands, as incorporated into the 2018 Justice Manual produced by the Department of Justice under then Deputy Attorney General Rod Rosenstein.[39] On the deregulatory side, the new Justice Manual incorporates a May 2018 policy that strives to avoid a piling on of punishment in multinational cases. If one country is already penalizing a behavior, it is not necessary for others to mete punishment for the same act.[40]

In addition, the United Kingdom's antibribery law has a broad reach with respect to both application and jurisdiction.[41] The regulatory burden on those in the financial sector is compounded with the Senior Managers and Certification Regime coming online to the United Kingdom in 2019.[42] Under that regime, if an illegal act such as bribery occurs at a low organizational level, a senior manager will be held responsible.

What about privacy legislation? What are significant global developments in this domain?

As mentioned in Chapter 6, The European Union's General Data Protection Regulation, which went into effect May 25, 2018, has wide-ranging effects. The law requires—with some exceptions—affirmative opt-in and usage notices for any data collection in the European Union (EU) by any organization with 250 or more employees based anywhere in the world. A similar law, the California Consumer Privacy Act of 2018, will take effect January 1, 2020.

FOREIGN EXCHANGE

Briefly, what is the foreign exchange market?

The foreign exchange market is a free, unregulated market operating out of global financial centers that enables the exchange of currency and of information about exchange rates.[43]

What are foreign exchange control laws, and how can they affect postacquisition operations?

Foreign exchange control laws restrict the amount of a country's local currency that can be converted into foreign currencies. These laws can operate either to completely restrict or to partially limit the ability of a foreign investor to remove any funds from the target's country to the foreign investor's home country (*repatriation*) or, if it may withdraw funds, to take its profits in its own currency.

What are some current trends in foreign exchange policies in developed countries?

Generally speaking, countries want currency markets to be free of government intervention. In the United States, the Trade Facilitation and Trade Enforcement Act of 2015 (the "2015 Act") requires the secretary of the treasury to provide semiannual reports on the macroeconomic and foreign exchange rate policies of the major trading partners of the United States. Section 701 of the 2015 Act requires that the Treasury Department analyze exchange rates and policies for each major trading partner "that has—(1) a significant bilateral trade surplus with the United States, (2) a material account surplus [defined as a surplus equaling more than 3 percent of GDP], and (3) engaged in persistent one-sided intervention in the foreign exchange market." The U.S., in October 2018, found no trading partner that had met all three conditions because none had been manipulating their currency. However, six partners showed bilateral and account surpluses, including China, which had the largest bilateral surplus.[44]

Are there any risks involved in doing business in a foreign country because of currency differences between the US parent and a foreign subsidiary or affiliate?

Yes, fluctuating exchange rates pose two types of risk to the investor. First, there is the purely economic risk (1) that a deteriorating exchange rate will require US parent companies to pay more for foreign currency–

denominated obligations than was originally anticipated when the obligation was approved or (2) that a relative increase in the value of a foreign currency will cause US creditors to be repaid a lesser amount in satisfaction of US currency–denominated obligations to them. Second, there is an accounting risk that the balance sheet, which must express the value of assets and liabilities denominated in a US currency at the exchange rate in place on the balance sheet date, will lose value in the translation from the local currency to US dollars.

What are the rules for choosing a currency for reporting financial results?

Under ASC 830, a company must report results using the functional currency of the entity. It states that the assets, liabilities, and operations of a foreign entity shall be measured using the functional currency of that entity. An entity's functional currency is the currency of the primary economic environment in which the entity operates. Normally, that is the currency of the environment in which an entity primarily makes and spends cash. ASC 830 explains how to measure and report currency values and how and when adjustments may be necessary (as when, for example, a company changes its functional currency).[45]

If a tax authority considers a currency to be inflationary, it may impose special reporting rules. US authorities did this with Argentina, for example.[46]

How can US owners mitigate the risk inherent in fluctuating exchange rates?

To alleviate the risk of economic losses due to exchange rate volatility, two forms of hedging contracts have developed: the forward purchase contract and the forward sales contract—in essence, a *put* and a *call.* Both are derivative instruments, or "swaps," that can be risky. Forward purchase contracts are used to protect a US debtor who is obligated to repay a certain amount in a foreign currency at a future date. When the value of the foreign currency rises relative to the US dollar, the debtor will have to spend more dollars to obtain the necessary amount of foreign currency to repay its debt. The forward purchase contract locks up the price at which the debtor may acquire the needed amount of currency at the necessary time for a fixed price determined at the time the forward purchase contract is entered into. It is, in effect, a *call* on foreign currency.

Similarly, a US creditor who is afraid that rising exchange rates may cause it to lose the value of its foreign-denominated receivables may hedge against such loss through a forward sales contract. In this case, the creditor contracts to sell the foreign currency to be received at a future date for US dollars at a fixed rate determined at the time the forward contract is entered into. This is a *put* equivalent.

In addition to these currency swaps, owners can use currency options. Options to purchase various currencies at a fixed price are available on many foreign and domestic securities exchanges. Currency options are listed on the exchanges at a particular fixed price (the *strike price*) in accordance with the length of the option period, which is generally 30, 60, or 90 days. The hedging party pays a premium for the ability to purchase the optioned currency at the relevant strike price at any time up to the termination date of the option. If the actual price for one unit of foreign currency exceeds the strike price, the hedging party can exercise its option and receive the currency at a cheaper price per unit. If the actual price never exceeds the strike price for the currency during the option period, the hedging party loses its premium paid for the option but is not required to take delivery of (or pay for) the actual currency.

This feature is the distinguishing factor between forward contracts and options, because forward contracts obligate one to take physical delivery of the currency at an agreed-upon date in the future. The degree of certainty of a hedger's need for a specific amount of foreign currency, plus the difference in the fixed price per unit of foreign currency between forward contracts and options at any given time, will dictate which form of hedging technique will be used.

In addition to currency hedging through swaps or options, US companies can consider shifting production and/or fulfillment to countries where currencies are weakening. The foregoing arrangements add to the cost of the overseas investment, and both legal and accounting experts should be consulted with respect to the tax and financial reporting consequences of such hedging methods.

OTHER GLOBAL REALITIES

In addition to foreign exchange, what are some more global realities dealmakers must master?

These can be classified as repatriation, performance requirements, local content regulations, labor requirements, and technology transfer restrictions.

After a foreign acquisition, can the investor repatriate profits or investment capital from its business interests located in a foreign country without limitations or restrictions?

As a general proposition, most developing and newly industrialized countries have some form of repatriation restrictions, and some other nations that impose exchange controls also regulate repatriation.

Repatriation restrictions or requirements are usually imposed for the same purposes as exchange controls, that is, to acquire or retain foreign currency in a country, to monitor foreign investment, and to police potential tax evasion. Many countries regulating repatriations also provide tax incentives for investors to reinvest profits.

Repatriation restrictions are generally accompanied by some form of additional restriction or reporting requirements, such as (1) registration of foreign capital with corresponding restrictions on withdrawal of such capital from the host country and (2) notification of amounts of foreign capital invested in the host country. For special issues related to the 2017 US tax law (such as deemed repatriation), see "International Tax and Disclosure Considerations," later in this chapter.

What do performance requirements entail?

Performance requirements include setting minimum export levels on the one hand and maximum import levels (such as quotas) on the other. Export-level requirements are designed to promote the flow of foreign currency into a country by permitting a foreign person to invest in a particular local enterprise provided that a minimum percentage of its finished product will be exported rather than distributed locally. Countries may also impose import restrictions, usually expressed as a maximum percentage of the cost of goods produced locally that can be imported, to encourage use of local products and industries.

How do local content regulations work?

Local content regulations specify minimum levels of domestic raw materials or component parts to be used in manufacturing, limitations on the type of products that can be manufactured, and restrictions on product distribution within the country and in the world market. Such limitations are often tied to economic incentives such as government subsidies or tax breaks and, if not imposed by statute, can be negotiated with the host country. Various countries relate local content requirements to specific industries to ensure that local companies do not suffer from the foreign presence.

Countries concerned with unemployment will usually require foreign companies to employ a certain percentage of local labor in both unskilled and managerial jobs. Failure by the investor to accede to such demands can cause the host country government to withhold required approval of the acquisition itself.

Restrictions on technology transfers usually take the form of limitations on royalty or profit remittances, technical assistance, and payments for transfers of technology, especially between related entities. These regulations are encountered most frequently in the developing and newly industrialized nations, although they also exist in any country that desires to promote a particular high-technology domestic industry. Technical assistance and royalty payments are frequently subjected to restrictions because they could potentially be used to circumvent dividend remittance regulations, especially to foreign parent companies.

What about employee rights? How do these affect global M&A?

First of all, the acquirer should ascertain whether the employees have any rights to approve the proposed acquisition. For example, most workers in Europe have the right to information and consultation when management contemplates major changes or plans. This right emanates from national industry sector collective bargaining agreements that set minimum standards and specific company agreements with employee representatives or trade unions.

Second, the acquirer should familiarize itself with rights of employees with respect to the governance of the enterprise. For example, Europeans have had decades of experience with various forms of so-called co-determination, imposed by law or won through collective bargaining. Worker participation in management may include the right to information, to obligatory consultations, or even to a veto in decision making.

The most well known example of co-determination is found in Germany, where employee participation is built into business life.

- All companies with five or more employees have the right to have a works council (*Betriebsrat*), which, once established, has the power to approve or reject proposed plans such as staff layoffs following a merger. German companies also have a management board, called a *Vorstand*.[47]
- Companies with 500 or more employees in Germany must have a supervisory board (*Aufstichtsrat*), electing at least one-third of the board members (or at least half in companies of more than 2,000 employees).

In the Netherlands, any company of medium size or larger must consult with its Works Council before implementing any decision affecting investments, dismissals, and pensions. The Works Council also has the power to challenge corporate decisions in court if its advice is not followed.[48]

Third, the acquirer should understand the nature of employee benefits afforded in a particular country and take the cost of such benefits into account in evaluating the merits of a potential acquisition. For example, the majority of European workers have, under certain conditions, the right to not be unfairly dismissed. In most European countries, an employee is entitled to redundancy compensation—that is, continued payment even though there may no longer be work for him or her. Moreover, unemployment compensation rights in the European Union generally are more substantial than in the United States. Aside from these legislated rights, an employee can also avail him- or herself of the usual breach-of-contract remedies, which may include damages and specific performance—forcing the employer to honor the written contract that is required between the two parties outlining employment terms covering pay scales, work hours, pensions, holidays, and so on. Finally, in several European countries unfair or "abusive" dismissal is actionable, giving affected employees a claim for damages against the companies that dismissed them.

FINANCING OUTBOUND TRANSACTIONS

Once a suitable acquisition of a foreign concern has been identified, how can an acquirer obtain financing for it?

For the most part, the methods of financing an international acquisition will not be very different from those used in a purely domestic deal. Various types of debt, ranging from standard commercial bank debt to subordinated debt (junior/senior/mezzanine) to debt secured by a variety of assets, can be used in the international context. This debt financing can be obtained from both public and private sources. Equity financing through the sale and issuance of new securities is also possible in the global deal. Whatever sources of financing an acquirer uses will have a global dimension.

In considering an international transaction, the potential acquirer may find it necessary to call on a variety of different currencies and to operate within several international jurisdictions. The acquirer must learn how such financial transactions can be affected by regulations imposed by its own government, as well as the governments of the target country, the countries in which investors and lenders reside, and the countries in which banks and securities exchanges may be located. Key areas of concern include the process for perfecting lenders' security interests and global trade agreements.

What issues are involved with perfection of lender security interests abroad?

As mentioned in Chapter 4, it is common to use assets as collateral, and to perfect the lien on the assets by asking for a legal authority to recognize the lien. But some assets cannot easily be subject to a lien or to perfection of such as lien. Some examples include motor vehicles, certain intent to use trademarks, and real property located in a flood zone.[49] Nonperfectable situations are also prevalent with certain non-US subsidiaries of a US entity and US subsidiaries that hold no substantial assets other than equity and/or debt of the non-US subsidiaries. There can be material tax consequences under Section 956 of the US Internal Revenue Code if these entities provide guarantees or security in support of an obligation of a US entity, or if more than 65 percent of the equity interests of any such entity are pledged as collateral for the obligations of a US entity.

What is the relevance of global trade agreements?

In addition, the rules of certain supranational or regional institutions, such as the United Nations, the EU, or the Organization of American States, or agreements such as the North American Free Trade Agreement[50] may apply. Despite a recent move toward national sovereignty and away from multilateral agreements in recent years, the world still hosts some 15 major regional trade agreements via the World Trade Organization.[51]

What special public sources of financing are available to the transnational acquirer?

Many countries have loan programs for businesses that wish to expand into overseas markets. Although most of these programs focus on export, they are not limited to this realm. In the United States, the Overseas Private Investment Corp. (OPIC) provides hundreds of millions of dollars in yearly loans and loan guarantees to companies—including small companies—that do business abroad. In some cases, the borrowers have used their funds to invest in foreign concerns.[52]

Suppose a seller demands to be paid in a currency that is different from the operating currency of the acquirer. How can the acquirer accomplish this?

Any acquirer wishing to obtain a foreign currency can do so through the foreign exchange (forex) market. This is the most actively traded market in the world, with more than $5 trillion in currencies traded on average every day—25 times the level of equities trading.[53]

Forex trading occurs "over the counter," through exchanges by institutions using electronic platforms and telephone lines. This happens outside of stock exchanges, except in the case of futures and options contracts, which constitute only a small part of foreign exchange activity (about 3 percent).[54]

The US dollar is involved in most currency pairs traded because it is the reserve currency of the world, featured in 90 percent of all forex trades, and constituting 64 percent of all central bank foreign exchange reserves.[55]

But it is not always necessary to convert currency. Indeed, a large international banking market has developed as an alternative to currency conversion. An example of such a system is the Eurodollar market, that is, the deposit or redeposit of US dollars into a large pool on foreign territory without the conversion of the funds into the local currency. The transaction is recorded by book entry, and there is no physical importation of the dollars into the foreign country. The entity into which dollars are deposited may be either a foreign branch of a US banking institution or an independent foreign bank, both of which have become known as *Eurobanks*. The Eurobanks can make short-, medium-, or long-term loans for acquisitions or working capital and participate in a wide variety of interbank lending activities. Eurobank deposits also exist for offshore deposits of Japanese yen, British pounds, and a multitude of other currencies in demand. The prefix *Euro* is meant to indicate an external status—see Exhibit 12-1 for sample terms. (Similarly a Eurobond, also called an external bond, is a

Exhibit 12-1 Examples of Eurocurrencies

Eurodollar—US dollar deposited in countries outside the United States

Euroeuro—Euro deposited outside the European Community

Europound—British pound deposited in countries outside the United Kingdom

Euroyen—Japanese yen deposited in banks outside Japan

Euroyuan—Chinese yuan held outside China

Note: The prefix *Euro* in this context means outside the country of jurisdiction.

bond issued in a currency different from the one used in the market where the bond was issued.)

Because offshore banking in different currencies has not been heavily regulated by any jurisdiction (e.g., Eurobanks are not subject to the same reserve requirements as domestic banks), offshore banks are able to have a much higher percentage of bank funds committed to corporate and other loans.

How are interest rates on funds borrowed in the Eurocurrency market calculated?

Generally, interest rates in the Eurocurrency market are tied to the London Interbank Offered Rate (LIBOR),[56] with the exception of Asian monetary units, which are tied to the Singapore Interbank Offered Rate (SIBOR).[57] The interbank offered rate is the interest rate charged by an offshore depository of a particular currency for funds lent in that currency to another offshore banking facility. This rate is used in international finance in the same way the prime rate is used in the United States, that is, as a reference rate from which the individual interest rate of a particular loan is created. LIBOR, SIBOR, and other interbank rates are listed in many of the world's financial newspapers.

What happens when one bank, whether an onshore or an offshore facility, does not have adequate funds to meet an acquirer's lending needs?

This is the function of the international syndicated loan market, which is particularly useful for onshore banks that must maintain a high ratio of capital reserves to borrowed funds, or for banks that do not want to bear the entire risk of a large international loan by themselves.

How do international syndicated loans work?

The principles behind international syndication are generally the same as in a purely domestic syndicated loan, with the added considerations of differing currencies, interest and exchange rates, tax and other government regulatory schemes, supranational currency controls, and the like. In recent times, syndications have explored using blockchain technology to effect group lending.[58]

Syndicated loans, also called consortium loans, are loan agreements entered into by several banks with a single client under identical conditions.[59] They are an efficient financing tool starting from about $50 million or for the consolidation of bilateral limits of several banks. Banks help arrange syndicated loans at fair market rates and place them with third-party banks. After the transaction is executed, they can also handle the administration as an "agent" bank for the borrower.

A bank can underwrite a syndicated loan for a confidential transaction and place it at its own risk. As an alternative, a syndicated loan can be placed on a "best effort" basis with any interested banks, without a need for underwriting.

In an international syndication, a group of lenders will pool its funds via a network of selling participations and other agreements until the required borrowing amount is obtained. There is only one loan agreement between the borrower and the syndication, which is negotiated among the parties to fit the particular needs of the transaction. Funds can flow from either onshore or offshore currency markets.

Typically, the funds borrowed under an international syndicated loan agreement will include at least five charges to the borrower: (1) interest, which can be tied to an international reference rate such as LIBOR or SIBOR, plus a spread; (2) a management fee, which is paid to the lead bank for arranging and managing the syndication; (3) a commitment fee, which is based on the undrawn portion of the loan to compensate the bank for the contingent liability; (4) an agent's fee, which is usually paid to the lead bank for negotiating the loan and acting as agent on behalf of the other members of the syndicate; and (5) any expenses associated with putting together the loan, which can include legal and accounting fees, travel costs, and the like.

A very typical situation is one in which a US company wants to finance the acquisition of another US company that has significant overseas operations. In this case, the lead bank will usually be the primary domestic lender, which may use syndication as a means of bringing in foreign lenders familiar with the business and economic climates of the countries where the target's overseas operations are concentrated. Such syndication will reduce the risk of a US lender that otherwise may be reluctant to lend overseas, but lenders will need to work out a variety of intercreditor issues, including the priority of assets securing the acquisition funding.

Are banks the only institutions that can participate in an international loan syndication?

No. International syndications may include large-scale investors willing to take the risk of lending for corporate acquisitions or refinancings. Such entities could include commercial banks, investment banks, and government-sponsored investment pools, as well as hedge funds, private equity funds, mutual funds, pension funds and endowments, insurance companies, and finance companies. Whether a particular entity can participate in a syndicated loan may be governed by national regulations in force in the country where the potential participant is domiciled.[60] In some cases, participants in the syndicated loans are dual holders, holding the status of both a lender and a shareholder.[61]

What types of requirements will the syndicating lenders generally request from the borrower?

The covenants and representations required by the lenders in an international syndication today are generally not much different from a domestic US syndicator's requirements, although historically, international loans have tended to be unsecured. Today, more and more foreign lenders are looking to corporate fixed assets, inventories, and accounts receivable as security for international syndicated loans. Most syndication agreements include, at minimum, a negative pledge clause (whereby the borrower promises not to encumber any future assets) and a pari passu clause, stating that the priority of the lending banks' rights will be pari passu, or equivalent, compared to any other creditor of the same class. The loan agreement may also contain financial covenants and other restrictions on the borrower that are typically found in domestic loans.

Are traditional loans the only kind of financing that can be syndicated?

No; lenders may also wish to use syndication to spread the risk of large letters of credit or guarantees backed by offshore currency deposits or international commercial paper programs.

Can an acquirer's international merger and acquisition activities be funded by issuing private or public debt securities?

Yes. Companies can issue private or public debt to serve investors who desire long-term, fixed-interest debt instruments.

The offshore currency markets have funded individual corporate debt issues in a multitude of currencies, facilitating investment in corporations located all over the world. The most overwhelming example of this has been the Eurobond market, which has been expanding at an astounding rate. The volume of new Eurobond issues has risen dramatically in the past 25 years.

Eurobonds can be denominated in any currency, but are issued offshore and are usually structured to be sold outside the jurisdiction of the nation whose currency is used or where the issuer resides. For example, in the United States unregistered debt securities may be issued overseas by US issuers, but must not be sold or offered for sale to any US person or anywhere within the United States until a 90-day "rest abroad" period passes. The SEC imposes certain requirements on US issuers designed to ensure that no such sales are made during the rest abroad period, including the placement of a restrictive legend on the bond itself.

Offshore bonds are generally issued in bearer form, and many can have provisions that exclude the interest paid thereon from withholding taxes imposed by countries where the bonds are distributed. They may be privately or publicly traded and often appear on the stock exchanges of the major financial centers from London to Tokyo. Again, the use of international syndicates of underwriters and lending institutions will be instrumental in issuing offshore corporate bonds.

What other types of debt financing are available?

The list is long, thanks to two factors: borrowers' and lenders' needs for greater liquidity. These twin needs have led to the development of a whole spectrum of international negotiable instruments, the utility of which depends on the needs and repayment abilities of borrowers.

Negotiable medium-term or long-term fixed-rate notes (FRNs) are bearer notes evidencing the obligation of the maker of the notes to pay a stated principal amount upon maturity of the note, with periodic payments of interest at a fixed rate. This type of note may be more convenient than conventional banknotes, which usually require the principal to be amortized over the life of the note rather than deferring payment until maturity. Sale of the FRNs is accomplished through subscription agreements, which provide for investors to buy a note or notes worth a certain stated amount on fulfillment of various conditions or the making of certain representations and warranties by the issuer. Terms and conditions appear on the reverse of the notes.

Suppose an acquirer encounters a group of multinational investors, all of whom want to lend, and be repaid, in their own currencies rather than in offshore funds?

One fairly recent innovation in promissory notes is the medium-term note (MTN), in which the maker offers a program of notes through one or more agents that place the notes for a commission on a best-effort basis. Initial holders can negotiate the terms of their individual notes to suit such holder's specific repayment requirements with respect to currencies, payment structures, or rates of interest. Therefore, using an MTN program, a maker may have a series of notes outstanding, each one with a different currency, interest rate calculation, or term. This kind of note program allows an issuer to attract a larger pool of investors by catering to their specific needs at a cost that is often less than a comparable underwriter's fee would be for an underwritten offering.

How can an acquirer obtain the different currencies it needs to meet its obligations to its investors?

It could simply convert the currency generated by the target through a foreign exchange broker for a fee or through the use of a swap.

Swaps, a forward contract type of derivative instrument, may be used to exchange currencies or to exchange interest rates, or they may combine the two. A currency swap agreement is a contract calling for the parties to supply each other with a stated amount of currency at specific intervals. For example, one party might agree to pay the other in Eurodollars in exchange for an equivalent amount of yen.

In such a case, an interest rate swap agreement is negotiated in which the borrower corporation and another party with access to various currencies, perhaps through its own subsidiaries, agree to pay each other a sum equal to the interest that would have accrued on a specific amount over a specific period of time at the desired rate. The exchanging party may be a bank or a large corporation with access to various currencies, perhaps through its own subsidiaries. This corporation may have a Eurobond issue outstanding on which it is obligated to pay a fixed rate of interest. In this case, an interest rate swap agreement may be in order, whereby the corporation and another party agree to pay to each other a sum equal to the interest that would have accrued on a specific amount over a specific period of time at a negotiated rate.

Swap agreements should generally be for shorter terms to protect against significant fluctuations in interest rates or currency exchange rates, which can throw off the economics of a swap transaction, with periodic rollover provisions allowing for the continuation of the agreement on the same or renegotiated terms of exchange. From a legal point of view, swap agreements are nothing more than international contracts that will be governed under the contract law of whichever country the parties choose to govern interpretation of contract terms. Swaps are complicated and, some might argue, risky, but as international currency markets have grown, swaps have become more and more important in structuring transnational deals. It is estimated that forex swaps and forwards account for more than $10 trillion annually, equaling or exceeding the liabilities booked on the balance sheet.[62]

Another financing technique is the conversion of debt for equity, or a debt/equity swap. How does it work, and when is its use appropriate?

In the context of corporate debt, as mentioned in Chapter 4, a debt-equity swap occurs when a lender agrees to receive equity instead of cash in repayment of a loan. In essence, the creditor exchanges its loan to a company for a stake in that company's capital. A recent example is the decision by the Industrial and Commercial Bank of China, Ltd., to throw a lifeline to some of its borrowers.[63]

In the context of sovereign (national) debt, a debt-equity swap occurs when a creditor exchanges its loan to a country for an investment in one of that country's companies.[64]

Security Interests in Foreign Assets

Can acquirers obtain security interests on the assets of foreign companies to finance acquisitions?

Yes. Today, most foreign countries have the same or analogous concepts to those of the United States regarding security interests in assets to serve as collateral for borrowing.

There are many differences, however, in the types of assets that can be secured, the methods of accomplishing such a transaction, the type of notice required, if any, and to whom notice must be given. Thus, it is imperative that local counsel be enlisted to complete these transactions.

International LBOs

Can the concept of an LBO be applied in the international context?

Yes. The LBO has become an accepted acquisition structure in the United Kingdom and several European nations, including France and Germany. However, since the global financial crisis of 2008, regulators have become more concerned about leverage. Article 458 of the European Union's Capital Requirements Regulation (CRR) requires authorities entrusted with the national application of that provision to notify the European Banking Authority if the authority identifies changes in the intensity of macroprudential or systemic risk in the financial system that has the potential to have serious negative consequences for the financial system and for the real economy in a specific country, and which the authority considers would be better addressed by means of stricter national measures. In 2018, in the first application of this regulation, French authorities (the Haut Conseil de Stabilité Financière) called for such a measure in France to apply to large nonfinancial corporations.[65] Specifically, the authorities wanted to set a limit for institutions that met the following conditions, among others:

- The leverage ratio (defined as total financial debt less outstanding liquid assets over total equity) is higher than 100 percent.
- The interest coverage ratio (defined as earnings before interest and taxes over interest expenses) is lower than 3 (i.e., interest expenses are more than one-third of EBIT).

As a backstop, the authorities proposed limiting exposure to no more than 5 percent of eligible capital on the exposure. To ensure a focus on large corporations, the French authorities proposed to consider only exposures with a value equal to or above EUR 300 million.

In response, the European Banking Authority expressed the opinion that the proposed French rule was sound and could be considered for other member countries. However, it advised the French authorities to broaden the scope to include all participating company units, not just those in France.[66]

Unequal leverage restrictions aside, the structure employed in Europe would not be vastly different from the structure one would use in the United States, with certain exceptions resulting from the corporate and business laws of the country involved. The financing will usually entail a tripartite structure comprising (1) senior debt from a traditional lending institution, which may or may not be collateralized; (2) middle-tier financing, including subordinated or convertible debt at a higher fixed rate of interest; and (3) straight equity investment by the managers and other investors. Applicable laws in EU countries are, for the most part, sufficiently nonrestrictive to allow creativity in structuring an LBO.

Other than the perfection of security interests, which has already been discussed, are there any other problems a senior lender seeking security might face?

If shares of the foreign parent company's stock are pledged to a foreign lender, the lender may not be able to foreclose on such shares in the event of a default without the prior approval of the French government. In practice, this risk has not been an impediment to accepting such pledges of foreign stock.

INTERNATIONAL TAX AND DISCLOSURE CONSIDERATIONS

This section covers basic tax and disclosure issues that affect the various kinds of acquisition and disposition activities carried on in the United States by foreign nationals and companies (inbound acquisitions), and foreign acquisition and disposition activities carried on by US nationals and companies (outbound acquisitions). Although this chapter will speak generally about the tax laws of many countries, the principal focus of discussion here will be the tax laws of the United States as they apply to transnational relationships. This section is divided into three parts:

1. A discussion of the general tax and disclosure rules that apply to inbound and outbound acquisitions
2. A general discussion of the US tax rules that ought to be considered by a foreign person planning to acquire a US business
3. A general discussion of the US tax rules that ought to be considered by an acquirer planning to acquire a foreign business from a US seller

This section will not discuss US tax consequences to foreign investors of owning US portfolio investments or US properties unless such holdings are directly related to acquisition of operating businesses. It is assumed that the reader is generally familiar with the basic US federal income tax principles that apply to acquisitions in the domestic context. (See Chapter 5.)

Note: The purpose of this section is not to advise readers of specific, current tax rules; readers are urged to consult specialized tax guides such as those published by Matthew Bender or other legal publishers. Rather, our goal is to give a broad overview of the tax issues buyers and sellers should consider when structuring an international transaction.

What are the fundamental tax considerations for an acquirer that apply specifically to international acquisitions?

Generally, whether the transaction involves an inbound or an outbound acquisition, the basic rules governing the tax treatment of the parties involved extend above and beyond those that would apply in the domestic context. In other words, it is rare that an international transaction is excepted from domestic rules. As a result of these rules, the tax planning in the international context will inevitably become more complex.

The most important thing that a buyer or a seller of a business with international components must bear in mind is that at every stage of planning, consideration must be given to the tax rules of each of the countries involved, as well as to the manner in which their tax systems overlap and interact. It is not uncommon to have three or four different tax systems governing parts or all of a single transaction, and this may present both opportunities and traps. Because of the disparities in the tax laws, and because of the existence in many cases of income tax treaties between the countries, it may be possible to structure a transaction so that it results in less overall tax cost than would be the case if the transaction were undertaken in a single country. On the other hand, because there is often overlapping taxing jurisdiction, it is possible, in the absence of careful planning, that the overall tax cost may be greater than if only a single country were involved.

In focusing on the US tax aspects of a transaction, several principles must be borne in mind. First, the United States imposes different tax rules on individuals and corporations depending on whether they are classified as "US persons" or "foreign persons" for US tax purposes. For this reason, a determination should be made early in the planning process regarding the classification of each of the parties and entities involved in a transaction.

Second, generally speaking, the United States imposes an overall income tax on the worldwide income of individuals who are citizens or residents of the United States and on corporations that are formed in the United States.[67] A resident alien is generally subject to tax in the same manner as a US citizen. A resident alien must report all interest, dividends, wages, or other compensation for services, income from rental property or royalties, and other types of income on a US tax return, whether from sources within or outside the United States. In contrast, nonresident alien individuals and foreign corporations are not subject to US taxation except on income that is sourced in the United States. A nonresident alien is usually subject to US income tax only on US source income. Under limited circumstances, certain foreign source income is subject to US tax. Therefore, once it is determined whether a party is a US person or a foreign person, each item of income must be analyzed to determine whether it has its source in the United States or outside the United States, that is, whether it is domestic source income or foreign source income. Different types of income are taxed in different ways.

Third, foreign persons generally are subject to a gross percentage withholding tax on certain kinds of domestic source passive income. The chief exception to this is the tax on income that is effectively connected with a US trade or business or permanent establishment in the case of foreign persons who are engaged in a US trade or business (or maintain a US permanent establishment). In such a case, the foreign person will pay a net income tax on this trade or business income in much the same way that a US person would on its overall income. Additionally, for US nontrade or business income, the taxation will depend on the precise class or category of such income (e.g., dividends, interests, or royalties). Therefore, determinations will have to be made regarding the characterization of any US source income on a fairly specific basis.

As we will see, there are numerous other significant issues of US international taxation that will have to be understood and taken into account in undertaking any inbound or outbound acquisition.

Income Tax Treaties

What is the role of income tax treaties in the acquisition process?

Income tax treaties play a major role in structuring international transactions, generally by minimizing the overall tax costs that may be imposed. The United States has treaties with at least 59 countries at this time.[68] When a tax treaty is applicable to a particular transaction, it is often useful to review the transaction in light of the treaty before focusing on the laws of the particular countries. In many cases, the treaty becomes the "tax law of the transaction." Treaty-related tax planning consists of analyzing the alternative structures for the chain of entities, selecting the tax jurisdictions, and defining the sources and classes of income. At each stage, tax treaties may be used to avoid double taxation or, in certain circumstances, triple taxation.

Most tax treaties provide for the reduction or elimination of withholding taxes on portfolio income, such as interest, dividends, and royalties, by the country from which such income is derived (the so-called *country of source*) and prohibit the country of source from taxing business income of an enterprise resident in the other country, unless the enterprise has a "permanent establishment" in the source country. Furthermore, most tax treaties provide that capital gains derived by a resident of one country from sources in another contracting country will be exempt from tax by the other country. For many years, acquirers were able to take advantage of these tax rules by placing their activities in an entity which was a resident of a country that had a tax treaty with the United States, thus eliminating the tax exposure of their activities. But today most U.S. tax treaties *limitation of benefits* (LOB) provisions prevent general treaty shopping, looking largely to residency of ultimate owners.

What are income tax treaties?

Income tax treaties, or income tax conventions, are international agreements entered into between two or more sovereign nations (and sometimes extended to dependent territories) for the purpose of reducing double taxation on income generated by residents of one of these countries from sources located in the other contracting country. In the United States, an income tax treaty is signed by the executive branch (usually by the secretary of state) and becomes effective, unless modified, after the US Senate ratifies the treaty.

Under the US Constitution, treaties are the supreme law of the land and rank equally with any federal statute. If the terms of a treaty conflict with a federal statute, whichever was most recently adopted will generally control. Case law holds, however, that Congress must clearly specify an intent to override a tax treaty for a later-enacted statute to prevail over the treaty.[69]

In addition to their role in reducing double taxation, income tax treaties provide, through the "competent authority" mechanism, a means to resolve disputes between two tax jurisdictions that claim the right to tax income that arises in one or both of these countries. Treaties may assist in the prevention of fiscal evasion, for instance, by allowing tax information exchanges between the tax authorities of the contracting countries. Sometimes, income tax treaties are used to advance foreign or economic policies of one or both of the countries, for instance, when one of the countries is committed to allow tax breaks for capital investments in preferred industries in the other country.

Can a taxpaying entity avail itself of a particular tax treaty by incorporating a subsidiary in the treaty country?

Tax treaties ordinarily apply to, and can be invoked by, persons who are residents of the respective treaty countries. Although the definition of a *person* may vary from treaty to treaty, it usually includes individuals, corporations, partnerships, estates, and trusts.

A corporation incorporated in a treaty jurisdiction will in most circumstances be considered a resident of such jurisdiction. Generally speaking, by establishing a corporation resident in a treaty country, investors from another country can subject their investments to the benefits available under that country's tax treaties. However, such so-called treaty shopping has in recent years been the subject of increasing scrutiny, and restrictions have been imposed by the US Department of the Treasury and Congress. Specific actions taken have included (1) the termination of existing treaties with tax haven jurisdictions; (2) the renegotiation of existing treaties; (3) the ratification of new treaties that contain "limitation of benefits" provisions; (4) amending the US tax code to allow treaty benefits only to bona fide residents of a treaty country (the LOBs mentioned earlier); and (5) changing treatment of foreign income, such as income earned by companies practicing corporate tax inversion.

What is corporate tax inversion and how is it currently treated under US tax law?

Corporate tax inversion refers to a practice in which a company from a high-tax country buys a company in a lower-tax country, and declares that country as its headquarters. In the United States, a series of changes to taxation—starting with Treasury rules in 2015 and culminating in a new tax law in 2017—removed this incentive.[70]

Entity Classification

How does the United States classify an entity that is formed under foreign law?

The IRS has published guidance on entity classification. The following is a summary.[71]

First, determine whether the entity is a domestic or a foreign business entity. A business entity is domestic if it is created or organized as any type of entity in the United States or under the laws of the United States or of any state.[72] A business entity that is created or organized both in the United States and in a foreign jurisdiction is a domestic entity. A business entity is foreign if it is not domestic.

Next, determine the type of entity. An entity is deemed a corporation if it is so formed under federal or state corporate statutes, or is a type of foreign entity identified by the US Treasury as such.[73] These entities are automatically classified as corporations and are not eligible to elect their classification. All other business entities are eligible to elect their classification. If no election is made, a default classification will apply, depending on the number of owners and, for a foreign entity, on whether the owners have limited or unlimited liability.

With respect to entities not named on the Treasury list, the proper classification of a foreign enterprise under US law may occasionally be a difficult task because foreign countries have forms of business entities that do not have US equivalents.

The US classification principles applicable to foreign entities provide that, as a starting point, local law (i.e., foreign law) will determine the legal relationships among the entity and its members and among the entity, its members, and the public at large. When these legal relationships are ascertained, US tax principles will classify an entity in various ways. It is generally perceived that the IRS does not apply classification principles to foreign entities in the same manner it does to US entities. Therefore, caution must be used before assuming that the foreign entity would be treated for US tax purposes in a similar manner to its foreign treatment. In addition, one should consider whether a tax treaty prohibits the United States from reclassifying the entity for federal tax purposes because of a specific definition in the treaty.

For classification purposes, when is a person considered foreign?

A *US person* is either an individual who is a citizen or resident of the United States, a domestic corporation, a domestic partnership, or a domestic trust or estate. A *foreign person* is a person who is not a US person. Under this definition, a *resident alien* individual can be a US person. Tax treaties may provide different rules.

What is a US, or domestic, corporation?

Under US principles, all organizations incorporated under the laws of the United States or of any state (including the District of Columbia) are treated as domestic corporations for federal tax purposes. For certain purposes, corporations organized in or under the laws of Guam, American

Samoa, Northern Mariana Islands, or the Virgin Islands will not be treated as foreign corporations.

What is a dual resident company?

As far as the United States is concerned, a corporation incorporated in the United States is a US corporation. This corporation, however, could at the same time be treated by country X as a country X corporation if country X employed different criteria to determine whether corporations are resident for its tax purposes. In particular, some countries treat corporations as domestic corporations if they are managed and controlled therein. Thus, a US corporation that is managed and controlled in one of these jurisdictions can also be a resident of the country in question. Such companies are referred to as *dual resident companies.*

Can a foreign corporation be treated as a domestic corporation for US tax purposes?

Yes. IRC Section 269B provides that if a domestic corporation and a foreign corporation are "stapled entities," the foreign corporation will be treated as a domestic corporation.[74] The term *stapled entities* means any group of two or more entities if more than 50 percent in value of the beneficial ownership in each such entity consists of stapled interests (i.e., if by reason of form of ownership, restrictions on transfer, or other terms or conditions in connection with the transfer of one of such interests, the other such interests are also transferred or required to be transferred).

More important, there are a number of situations in which an election may be made to treat a foreign corporation as if it were a domestic corporation. One involves an election under Section 1504(d) of the IRC to treat certain subsidiaries of a US parent located in "contiguous countries" (Canada or Mexico) as domestic corporations eligible to be included in the parent's consolidated return.[75] The other involves an election under the Foreign Investment in Real Property Tax Act of 1980 (FIRPTA), which provides that a foreign corporation holding a US real property interest may elect to be treated as a domestic corporation. Finally, the anti-inversion provisions of Section 7874 of the US tax code will treat a foreign parent as a US corporation if certain requirements are met.

TAX CONSIDERATIONS IN INBOUND ACQUISITIONS

An inbound acquisition is an acquisition of a US enterprise by a non-US person. This acquisition may involve financing through loans made by financial institutions that are either resident in the acquirer's own country or third-country residents or by US financial institutions, or a possible joint venture with US or foreign equity partners. In debt-financed acquisitions, revenues received from the US enterprise will likely be used to pay off acquisition indebtedness. The acquirers may wish at some point in the future to dispose of the entity or parts thereof in a transaction that will generate a profit over the acquisition price. For these and other reasons, US tax considerations may be important in every stage of the acquisition and disposition process.

This inbound-tax section explains how a foreign corporation holding a US real property interest may elect to be treated as a domestic corporation.

FIRPTA

What is FIRPTA?

The Foreign Investment in Real Property Tax Act of 1980, as amended, also known as FIRPTA, was enacted to close a number of perceived loopholes that enabled foreign investors to own and dispose of US real properties without incurring US tax on the appreciation of the property or on the cash flow from the property. Since 1985, FIRPTA has overridden all income tax treaties. Note, however, that there have been modifications to the IRS approach to enforcing FIRPTA in recent years.

FIRPTA applies to dispositions of US real property interests (USRPIs). A USRPI generally includes (1) an interest in real estate located in the United States or the US Virgin Islands, or (2) any interest (other than an interest solely as a creditor) in a domestic corporation unless it can be established that such corporation was at no time a US real property holding corporation (USRPHC).

A domestic corporation is a USRPHC if the fair market value of its USRPIs equals or exceeds 50 percent of its worldwide real estate plus any other trade or business assets. Thus, if the assets disposed of are clearly not USRPIs or interests in certain pass-through entities that own USRPIs, neither the seller nor the buyer of the assets ought to be concerned about FIRPTA. FIRPTA regulations provide elaborate rules concerning the definition of a USRPI. Because many US corporations own significant amounts of real estate, it will often be difficult to conclude at an early planning stage that a given target is not a USRPHC.

What are the general rules regarding FIRPTA, and how are they enforced?

FIRPTA provides that gain or loss of a nonresident alien individual or a foreign corporation from the disposition of a USRPI will be treated as if the gain or loss is effectively connected with a US trade or business of such person. As such, the gain will be taxed at the regular rates applicable to US citizens and residents, or to domestic corporations, as the case may be. Unlike other passive investments, gain recognized in a transaction subject to FIRPTA ought to be reported on a US income tax return. Nonresident alien individuals are also subject to FIRPTA's minimum tax.

FIRPTA compliance is enforced through a withholding system. The IRC generally provides that a transferee of a USRPI is required to withhold and pay over to the IRS 15 percent of the amount realized (i.e., the consideration) on the disposition by the foreign transferor. Partnerships and trusts disposing of real estate are required to withhold 37 percent of the amount allocable to their foreign partners or foreign beneficiaries. There are several exceptions to the withholding rules, but these are beyond the scope of this discussion.

FIRPTA applies to dispositions of interests in partnerships holding real estate and to dispositions of USRPIs by partnerships held by foreigners. Moreover, FIRPTA applies to distributions of USRPIs by foreign corporations to their shareholders and to capital contributions to foreign corporations. In addition, FIRPTA provisions can override the nonrecognition treatment provided by various other sections of the IRC where necessary to ensure that the gain subject to taxation under FIRPTA is not diminished through transactions such as reorganizations and tax-free liquidations.

Who should be concerned about FIRPTA?

Although the FIRPTA provisions may seem to be of little importance in a merger or acquisition that does not involve real estate holding corporations or direct acquisitions of real estate assets, its application is far-reaching. First, as mentioned earlier, the definition of a USRPHC is broad enough to include even a manufacturing company that owns a large plant. A foreign acquirer should take future FIRPTA taxes into account in evaluating a potential acquisition. A domestic as well as a foreign acquirer from a foreign holder is liable as transferee-payor to withhold tax on the consideration paid for the stock if the corporation is a USRPHC and the payee is subject to FIRPTA. Failure to withhold may result in civil and criminal penalties. On the other hand, the foreign transferor (seller) is required to file a US tax return to report his or her gain from the sale. Finally, if a public offering to refinance a portion of the acquisition indebtedness is contemplated, certain foreign holders (5 percent or more) will be subject to US tax on the disposition of their holdings if the corporation is a USRPHC; under certain circumstances, the buyer of publicly traded stock from a 5 percent or more shareholder will be required to withhold FIRPTA tax.

Consequently, in any stock acquisition, consideration should be given to the value of the US realty owned by the acquired entity, vis-à-vis its other assets, and to the tax status of the seller. If the seller provides a certificate that it is not a foreign person, no withholding will be required. In addition, no withholding is required if a domestic corporation furnishes to the transferee an affidavit stating that it is not and has not been a USRPHC during a certain test period.

TAX CONSIDERATIONS IN OUTBOUND ACQUISITIONS

This section will outline the most prominent features of US taxation of the foreign activities of US persons. As explained earlier in this chapter, the

United States asserts taxing jurisdiction over the worldwide income of its citizens, residents, and corporations. As a general rule, the United States taxes only income received or accrued by US taxpayers. In the domestic context, with the exception of a group filing a consolidated return or an S corporation, income earned by a US taxpayer from a controlled corporation is not taxed to the US owner except and to the extent that such earnings are actually distributed to the owner. As we will soon see, the exceptions to the preceding rules in the international context are so voluminous and complex in US tax law as to suggest that the general rules do not apply at all. As a result of long-standing concerns about the avoidance of US taxes through the expatriation of assets and earnings, there is now an extensive patchwork of rules under which the United States seeks to tax, or at least take into account, income generated in foreign subsidiaries of US persons.

Needless to say, in any transaction involving an acquisition of a foreign business, the primary focus of the tax planner's attention must be the tax laws of the country or countries in which the target does business and holds assets and the country or countries in which its shareholders are located. This is all the more true at a time when income tax rates of most industrialized countries significantly exceed those in the United States. There may in fact be significant opportunities to reduce the impact of foreign taxes through the use of tax treaties and the US foreign tax credit system. These mechanisms are inherently imperfect, however, and a great deal of attention must be paid to US tax rules for the international activities of its taxpayers in order to minimize the overall tax costs of US persons engaging in a variety of multinational operations.

Planning the Outbound Acquisition

When planning an outbound acquisition, what information should the purchaser solicit from the seller in order to minimize foreign and domestic tax liabilities?

Today, where an auction process is commonly used to obtain the highest bid for a group of corporations that is for sale, the buyer cannot ignore the tax consequences to the seller resulting from the sale. To obtain a competitive edge over other bidders, the buyer should strive to maximize its own tax benefits without raising the seller's tax costs above its expectations. Alternatively, without sacrificing the purchaser's own goals, it may be possible to structure the offer in a way that reduces the seller's tax costs. With these goals in mind, the purchaser should solicit from the seller the following information:

- A precise organization chart. The chart should describe the holding company (assuming that the target is a parent of a group of corporations) and the stock ownership in all the various tiers of the domestic corporations, if any, and of the foreign corporations or entities (the "group").
- The estimated US and foreign tax bases as of the projected acquisition date that the holding company is expected to have in the various domestic and foreign corporations.
- To the extent feasible, a description of the overall income tax position of the target group and the seller.
- For each of the foreign companies:
  —The taxable year for both foreign and US income tax purposes
  —The actual and projected earnings and profits by taxable period of such corporation as of the acquisition date
  —The creditable foreign income taxes paid or accrued during each taxable period ending on or before the acquisition date
  —The earnings and profits and creditable foreign taxes accumulated prior to the seller's ownership of the company
  —All other information (foreign currency gains and losses, tax accounting elections, distributions, utilization of foreign tax credits, etc.) necessary to determine the tax consequences of a later sale of each corporation
  —The estimated net book value, or pro forma balance sheet, of each foreign company as of the acquisition date
  —A listing of the intercompany receivables and payables, if any

Why would one need an organization chart of the structure of the target?

An organization chart will describe the precise ownership of the group and will inform one of the different tax jurisdictions (and income tax treaties) that may affect the acquisition process and the subsequent disposition of the group or several of its members.

The organization chart will also provide information about whether any of the foreign subsidiaries is, or would be in the purchaser's hands, a "controlled foreign corporation" (CFC). CFC status may have significant US tax consequences to a US shareholder.

What does the most recent (2017) US tax law say about foreign taxes?

The Tax Cuts and Jobs Act of 2017 (TCJA) enhanced certain features of previous law, such as a step-up in basis possible with a Section 338 election (discussed in Chapter 5).[76]

However, this law also introduced several changes to taxation of income originating from foreign sources. The new provisions boosted taxes on income from foreign sources that stay outside the United States, while cutting taxes on income that is repatriated into the US economy. Overall, these changes disincentivize foreign production and/or incentivize domestic production.[77]

Moving up the clock on deferred income. New Code Section 965 increases the Subpart F income[78] of either a controlled foreign corporation[79] or a foreign corporation with at least one 10 percent US shareholder that is a domestic corporation, for its last tax year ending before January 1, 2018.[80] Subpart F is a part of the tax code that was enacted in 1962 to tax foreign income, using a deferral mechanism. Under this part of the IRC, US tax on the income of a foreign corporation is deferred until the income is distributed as a dividend or otherwise repatriated by the foreign corporation to its US shareholders.[81] This new Code section imposes a transition tax on untaxed foreign earnings of foreign subsidiaries of US companies by deeming those earnings to be repatriated.[82] (For more on controlled foreign corporations, see the preceding question.)

Tax exemption for certain foreign-derived dividends. Under new IRC section 245A, eligible dividends a US corporation receives from an eligible foreign corporation (i.e., earnings of foreign subsidiaries of a US corporation) qualify for a deduction equal to the full amount of the dividend sourced to foreign earnings. In essence, this exempts profits paid back to the United States from US taxation.[83]

Lower taxes for intangible income derived from foreign operations—FDII and GILT. New IRC section 250 provides a lower tax rate for a domestic corporation's foreign-derived intangible income (FDII).[84] This provision, aimed at incentivizing exports of intellectual capital, was bolstered with a new provision for global intangible low-taxed income (GILTI). Together these two provisions create a worldwide minimum tax on intangible income.[85]

Base erosion and anti-abuse (BEAT). This new IRC section 59A is designed to prevent the erosion of a company's tax basis that occurs when companies make excess payments to foreign-affiliated corporations.

Foreign Tax Credits

What is the foreign tax credit?

A common theme throughout the tax system is that a person should be relieved of the burden resulting from the imposition of tax by more than one jurisdiction on the same income. One example of this principle is the foreign tax credit. This is valid only under four conditions:[86]

- The tax must be imposed by a foreign country or US possession.
- The tax must have been paid (not merely owed).
- It must be the actual amount paid, minus any refunds.
- The tax must be an income tax (not another kind of tax).

CONCLUDING COMMENTS

This chapter has highlighted some of the many issues one might encounter when embarking on an inbound or outbound transaction. Of course, as in all transactional matters, buyers and sellers should consult qualified professional advisors, including accountants and auditors as well as legal counsel familiar with applicable laws—including special counsel located in the foreign country or countries involved. Fortunately, as the endnotes in this book show, the world's leading accounting and law firms produce an ongoing stream of resources. May they be for you a living update to the enduring framework this book aspires to deliver to dealmakers everywhere.

APPENDIX 12-1

Meeting the Reorganization Test: Foreign. Examples from the Internal Revenue Service

The following examples illustrate the rules of paragraph (b)(1) of section 368 of the Internal Revenue Code—namely, whether or not a transaction qualifies as a statutory merger or consolidation.[87] *It is important to be classified in this way, or the transaction may be treated as a mere acquisition and any related gain may be taxed.*[88] *In each of the examples, except as otherwise provided, each of R, V, Y, and Z is a C corporation. X is a domestic limited liability company. Except as otherwise provided, X is wholly owned by Y and is disregarded as an entity separate from Y for federal income tax purposes.*

Example: Transaction effected pursuant to foreign statutes.

(i) Facts. Z and Y are entities organized under the laws of Country Q and classified as corporations for federal income tax purposes. Z and Y combine. Pursuant to statutes of Country Q the following events occur simultaneously: all of the assets and liabilities of Z become the assets and liabilities of Y and Z's separate legal existence ceases for all purposes.

(ii) Analysis. The transaction satisfies the requirements of paragraph (b)(1)(ii) of this section because the transaction is effected pursuant to statutes of Country Q and the following events occur simultaneously at the effective time of the transaction: all of the assets and liabilities of Z, the combining entity of the transferor unit, become the assets and liabilities of Y, the combining entity and sole member of the transferee unit, and Z ceases its separate legal existence for all purposes. Accordingly, the transaction qualifies as a statutory merger or consolidation for purposes of section 368(a)(1)(A).

Example: Foreign law amalgamation using parent stock.

(i) Facts. Z and V are entities organized under the laws of Country Q and classified as corporations for federal income tax purposes. Z and V amalgamate. Pursuant to statutes of Country Q, the following events occur simultaneously: all the assets and liabilities of Z and V become the assets and liabilities of R, an entity that is created in the transaction and that is wholly owned by Y immediately after the transaction, and Z's and V's separate legal existences cease for all purposes. In the transaction, the Z and V shareholders exchange their Z and V stock, respectively, for stock of Y.

(ii) Analysis. With respect to each of Z and V, the transaction satisfies the requirements of paragraph (b)(1)(ii) of this section because the transaction is effected pursuant to Country Q law and the following events occur simultaneously at the effective time of the transaction: all of the assets and liabilities of Z and V, respectively, each of which is the combining entity of a transferor unit, become the assets and liabilities of R, the combining entity and sole member of the transferee unit, with regard to each of the above transfers, and Z and V each ceases its separate legal existence for all purposes. Because Y is in control of R immediately after the transaction, the Z shareholders and the V shareholders will be treated as receiving stock of a corporation that is in control of R, the combining entity of the transferee unit that is the acquiring corporation for purposes of section 368(a)(2)(D). Accordingly, the transaction qualifies as the statutory merger or consolidation of each of Z and V into R, a corporation controlled by Y, and is a reorganization under section 368(a)(1)(A) by reason of section 368(a)(2)(D).

NOTES

1. http://dmi.thomsonreuters.com/Content/Files/4Q2018_MNA_Financial_Advisory_Review.pdf.
2. In today's interconnected world, almost anyone can start a global business, and almost any foreign hacker can stop one. For a broad study, see Paul Dreyer, et al., "Estimating the Global Cost of Cyber Risk: Methodology and Examples," RAND Corporation, 2018, https://www.rand.org/pubs/research_reports/RR2299.html.
3. "Strong Trade Growth in 2018 Rests on Policy Choices," World Trade Organization, 2018, https://www.wto.org/english/news_e/pres18_e/pr820_e.htm.
4. "U.S. Trade in Goods with World, Seasonally Adjusted" chart shows US exports in excess of $1.5 trillion for 2017, and levels in excess of $126 million per month through August 2018. https://www.census.gov/foreign-trade/balance/c0004.html.
5. "U.S. Trade in Goods with World, Seasonally Adjusted" chart shows US exports in excess of $1.5 trillion and imports in excess of $2.3 trillion in 2017. In 2018 through August, the levels were $1.1 trillion and $1.7, respectively, showing that the

total for 2018 will be comparable. https://www.census.gov/foreign-trade/balance/c0004.html.

6. http://dmi.thomsonreuters.com/Content/Files/4Q2018_MNA_Financial_Advisory_Review.pdf.
7. Ibid.
8. See Lisa Du, "How Takeda's $62 Billion Shire Deal Reshapes Pharma World," Reuters, January 7, 2019, https://www.bloomberg.com/news/articles/2019-01-07/how-takeda-s-62-billion-shire-deal-reshapes-the-pharma-world.
9. https://www.world-exchanges.org/.
10. http://delcode.delaware.gov/title8/c001/sc01/index.shtml.
11. See "Mining Law: 2019," from International Comparative Legal Guides, https://legcounsel.house.gov/Comps/Mineral%20Leasing%20Act.pdfs. *Note:* This law is not to be confused with the Mineral Leasing Act of 2018, which limits oil exports to foreign countries.
12. See Code of Federal Regulations, https://www.gpo.gov/fdsys/pkg/CFR-2018-title12-vol2/xml/CFR-2018-title12-vol2-part211.xml.
13. For guidance on the Merchant Marine Act, see "Jones Act," Legal Information Institute at Cornell University, https://www.law.cornell.edu/wex/jones_act.
14. For recent clarification, see https://www.fcc.gov/document/fcc-clarifies-policy-foreign-investment-broadcast-licensees-0.
15. See Adam Vann, "Offshore Oil and Gas Development: Legal Framework," Congressional Research Service, April 2018, https://fas.org/sgp/crs/misc/RL33404.pdf.
16. "It shall be unlawful [for] any foreign air carrier or person controlling a foreign air carrier to acquire control, in any manner whatsoever, of any citizen of the United States engaged in any phase of aeronautics." https://www.gpo.gov/fdsys/pkg/STATUTE-72/pdf/STATUTE-72-Pg731.pdf.
17. See the current survey required: https://www.federalregister.gov/documents/2018/02/02/2018-02065/international-services

-surveys-be-120-benchmark-survey-of-transactions-in-selected-services-and.

18. Currently, for example, a BE-12A report is required where the US affiliate is majority-owned (50 percent or more) with total assets, sales or gross operating revenues, or net income (loss) greater than $300 million; a BE-12B is required where the US affiliate is (i) majority-owned with total assets, sales or gross operating revenues, or net income (loss) greater than $60 million, but no one of these items was greater than $300 million; or (ii) minority-owned (at least 10 percent, but less than 50 percent) with total assets, sales or gross operating revenues, or net income (loss) greater than $60 million (positive or negative); and a BE-12C is required where the US affiliate is majority- or minority-owned and none of total assets, sales or gross operating revenues, or net income (loss) was greater than $60 million. http://www.klgates.com/the-be-12-is-due-may-31-03-08-2018/.
19. http://www.klgates.com/acquisition-and-dispositions-of-us-agricultural-land-by-foreign-investors-federal-and-state-legislative-restrictions-limitations-and-disclosure-requirements-09-12-2018/.
20. See Marissa M. Bacci, "Acquisition and Disposition of U.S. Agricultural Land by Foreign Investors: Federal and State Legislative Restrictions, Limitations, and Disclosure Requirements," *Journal of Agricultural Law,* September 12, 2018, http://www.klgates.com/acquisition-and-dispositions-of-us-agricultural-land-by-foreign-investors-federal-and-state-legislative-restrictions-limitations-and-disclosure-requirements-09-12-2018/.
21. See https://www.irs.gov/irm/part4/irm_04-061-012#idm140064496021072 and https://www.irs.gov/individuals/international-taxpayers/firpta-withholding.
22. The Dodd-Frank Act defines conflict minerals as columbite-tantalite (coltan), cassiterite, gold, wolframite, or their derivatives, or any other mineral or its derivatives that are

determined by the Secretary of State to be financing conflict in the DRC or an adjoining country. See Pub. L. No. 111-203, § 1502(e)(4). Columbite-tantalite, cassiterite, and wolframite are the ores from which tantalum, tin, and tungsten, respectively, are processed. For a recent report on disclosure results, see "Conflict Minerals: Company Reports on Mineral Sources in 2017 Are Similar to Prior Years and New Data on Sexual Violence Are Available," Government Accountability Office, 2018, https://www.gao.gov/assets/700/692851.pdf.

23. http://ec.europa.eu/trade/policy/in-focus/conflict-minerals-regulation/regulation-explained/.
24. https://codes.findlaw.com/de/title-8-corporations/de-code-sect-8-122.html.
25. See D. Daniel Sokol, "Troubled Waters Between U.S. and European Antitrust," *Michigan Law Review,* vol. 115, issue 6 (2017), https://repository.law.umich.edu/cgi/viewcontent.cgi?article=1654&context=mlr.
26. See "IFRS and US GAAP: Similarities and Differences," PwC, 2018, https://www.pwc.com/us/en/cfodirect/assets/pdf/accounting-guides/pwc-ifrs-us-gaap-similarities-and-differences.pdf.
27. Ibid.
28. See "International Guidelines for International Enforcement and Cooperation," US Department of Justice and Federal Trade Commission, 2017, https://www.justice.gov/atr/international guidelines/download.
29. "Horizontal Merger Guidelines," Department of Justice and Federal Trade Commission, 2010, https://www.justice.gov/atr/file/810276/download.
30. For an in-depth discussion of international antitrust laws, see "International Guidelines for International Enforcement and Cooperation,"op. cit, note 28, https://www.justice.gov/atr/internationalguidelines/download.
31. See "DOJ and SEC Enforcement Actions per Year," Foreign

Corrupt Practices Act Clearinghouse, Stanford Law School, with Sullivan & Cromwell, LLP, http://fcpa.stanford.edu/statistics-analytics.html.

32. Council Regulation (EC) No 139/2004 of January 20, 2004, on the control of concentrations between undertakings (the EC Merger Regulation). https://eur-lex.europa.eu/legal-content/EN/TXT/PDF/?uri=CELEX:32004R0139&from=EN.

33. http://ec.europa.eu/competition/mergers/legislation/regulations.html.

34. European Parliament, Committee on Economic and Monetary Affairs, Motion for a European Parliament Resolution, Draft Report on the Annual Report on Competition Policy (2018/2102(INI)), http://www.europarl.europa.eu/sides/getDoc.do?type=COMPARL&reference=PE-628.570&format=PDF&language=EN&secondRef=01.

35. https://www.iosco.org/library/pubdocs/pdf/IOSCOPD561.pdf.

36. OICU–OSCO Fact Sheet, October 2018, https://www.iosco.org/about/pdf/IOSCO-Fact-Sheet.pdf.

37. See "DOJ and SEC Enforcement Actions per Year," op. cit., note 31, http://fcpa.stanford.edu/statistics-analytics.html.

38. For a current overview of the impact of FCPA in M&A, see "FCPA M&A: Identifying and Mitigating Anti-Corruption Risk in Cross-Border Transactions, https://www.gibsondunn.com/wp-content/uploads/2018/05/WebcastSlides-FCPA-and-Other-Risks-in-MandA-10-May-2018.pdf. Note that compliance with FCPA had been complicated by a policy introduced in 2015 by Sally Yates, deputy attorney general, US Department of Justice, titled "Individual Accountability for Corporate Wrongdoing." However, on November 29, 2018, in a speech at the American Conference Institute's 35th International Conference on the Foreign Corrupt Practices Act, then Attorney General Rod Rosenstein announced changes to the policy. https://www.justice.gov/opa/speech/deputy-attorney-general-rod-j-rosenstein-delivers-remarks-american-conference-institute-0.

39. Katya Jestin, et al., "What's in a Name? That Which We Now Call the Justice Manual Has a Familiar, But Distinctive, Scent," Compliance and Enforcement blog, New York University School of Law, October 2018, linking to: https://www.justice.gov/opa/pr/department-justice-announces-rollout-updated-united-states-attorneys-manual.
40. Rod Rosenstein, "Policy on Coordination of Corporate Resolution Penalties," US Department of Justice, May 9, 2018, https://www.justice.gov/opa/speech/file/1061186/download.
41. https://www.acc.com/legalresources/quickcounsel/UKBAFCPA.cfm.
42. Terry Allen, "Strengthening the Link Between Seniority and Accountability: The Senior Managers and Certification Regime," *Bank of England Quarterly,* Q3, https://www.bankofengland.co.uk/-/media/boe/files/quarterly-bulletin/2018/senior-managers-certification-regime.pdf?la=en&hash=B8F1B89D09E5C1339BD92AAB3E3ADB7103F7197C. This is similar to the Yates memo in the United States, but this was softened in 2018, per note 38.
43. For a succinct guide, see Francisco Javier Fernandez, "The Foreign Currency Market: What It Is and How It Works," Banco Bilbao Vizcaya Argentaria, S.A. (BBVA), May 21, 2017, https://www.bbva.com/en/foreign-currency-market-work/.
44. China, Japan, Korea, India, Germany, and Switzerland are the six countries identified. https://home.treasury.gov/system/files/206/2018-10-17-%28Fall-2018-FX%20Report%29.pdf.
45. https://www.iasplus.com/en-us/standards/fasb/broad-transactions/asc830.
46. "United States Tax Alert: Key Tax Considerations Related to the Argentine Economy Being Classified as Highly Inflationary Under ASC 830," Deloitte, August 13, 2018, https://www2.deloitte.com/content/dam/Deloitte/global/Documents/Tax/dttl-tax-alert-united-states-13-august-2018.pdf.
47. One article notes: "Further, Germany has an employee codetermination/ participation system for virtually all

businesses." "Germany: Taxation of Cross-Border Mergers and Acquisitions," KPMG, April 1, 2018, https://home.kpmg.com/xx/en/home/insights/2018/04/germany-taxation-of-cross-border-mergers-and-acquisitions.html.

48. https://business.gov.nl/regulation/works-council-staff-representation/.
49. This answer is adapted from Scott Forchheimer and Jennifer Kent, "Cross-Border Financial Report," Latham and Watkins, October 2018, https://www.lw.com/thoughtLeadership/cross-border-financing-report-2018-us.
50. This agreement was undergoing review as of late 2018 but is still in force. https://ustr.gov/trade-agreements/free-trade-agreements/north-american-free-trade-agreement-nafta.
51. https://www.wto.org/english/res_e/publications_e/world_trade_report18_e.pdf.
52. https://www.opic.gov/.
53. Nasdaq, https://www.nasdaq.com/forex/education/iishome.aspx#beginning-1.
54. Ibid.
55. The major currencies traded are (listed by symbol, country, and currency):
    - USD: United States/Dollar
    - EUR: Euro Zone/Euro
    - JPY: Japan/Yen
    - GBP: United Kingdom/Pound
    - CAD: Canada/Dollar
    - CHF: Switzerland/Franc
    - AUD: Australia/Dollar

    The most commonly traded currency pairs are:
    - EUR/USD: Euro Zone/United States
    - USD/JPY: United States/Japan
    - GBP/USD: United Kingdom/United States
    - USD/CHF: United States/Switzerland
    - USD/CAD: United States/Canada
    - AUD/USD: Australia/United States

Kimberly Amadeo, "Why the Dollar Is the Global Currency," October 25, 2018, https://www.thebalance.com/world-currency-3305931.

56. The London Inter Bank Offered Rate (LIBOR) is the interest rate that banks offer to lend money to one another on a short-term basis in the Eurodollar market, according to the National Association of Insurance Commissioners, https://www.naic.org/capital_markets_archive/buzz_180522.pdf.
57. "Singapore Proposes Changes to Key Financial Benchmark: Sibor," Reuters, December 4, 2017, https://www.reuters.com/article/singapore-moneymarkets-sibor/singapore-proposes-changes-to-key-financial-benchmark-sibor-idUSL8N1O415N.
58. "Financial Institutions Move Closer to Realizing a Blockchain Solution for Syndicated Loans," Ipro, PR Newswire, March 30, 2017, https://www.prnewswire.com/news-releases/financial-institutions-move-closer-to-realizing-a-blockchain-solution-for-syndicated-loans-300431763.html.
59. This answer has been adapted from the main website of Credit Suisse, a provider of syndicated loans: https://www.credit-suisse.com/ch/en/unternehmen/unternehmen-unternehmer/kmugrossunternehmen/finanzierung/corporate-finance/structured-finance.html.
60. See the "Form of Entity" chapter in *Guide to Going Global,* DLA Piper, 2018, https://www.dlapiperintelligence.com/goingglobal/corporate/.
61. One study of syndicated loans found 17 facilities with insurance company dual holders, 105 facilities with finance company dual holders, 47 facilities with hedge fund and private equity fund dual holders, 215 facilities with mutual fund dual holders, and 23 facilities with other types of nonbank institutional dual holders. See Jongha Lim, Bernadette A. Minton, and Michael S. Weisbach, "Syndicated Loan Spreads and the Composition of the Syndicate," *Journal of Financial Economics,* vol. 111, no. 1, pp. 45–69. For the version submitted to the US Securities

and Exchange Commission, see https://www.sec.gov/divisions/riskfin/seminar/weisbach100412.pdf.

62. Bank of International Settlements Annual Report, 2017–2018, p. 10, https://www.bis.org/about/areport/areport2018.pdf.
63. "China Rescue Loops in Top State Bank to Aid Private Firms," Bloomberg, October 18, 2018, https://www.bloomberg.com/news/articles/2018-10-18/icbc-offers-debt-swaps-to-private-sector-firms-as-defaults-jump.
64. http://lexicon.ft.com/Term?term=debt-for-equity-swap.
65. Regulation (EU) No 575/2013 of the European Parliament and of the Council of June 26, 2013, on prudential requirements for credit institutions and investment firms and amending Regulation (EU) No 648/2012.
66. "The EBA believes that the proposed measure would be more effective as a backstop if it would be applied to the entire group of connected companies, which includes other entities that are in a control and/or economic dependency relationships among themselves and that are connected because they constitute a single risk. Regardless of its residence, the default of a client that is a parent entity could lead to the default of all other connected clients because indeed they constitute a single risk. If the parent entity is not resident in France, the bank's exposure to the GCC would not have been limited at 5% of eligible capital, as intended by the proposed measure, although the single risk is the same as with a parent entity that is resident in France." Opinion of the European Banking Authority on Measures in Accordance with Article 458 Regulation (EI), No. 575/2013. https://www.eba.europa.eu/documents/10180/2137845/EBA+Opinion+on+measures+in+accordance+with+Article+458+%28EBA-Op-2018-02%29.pdf.
67. See "Alien Taxation: Certa in Essential Concepts," Internal Revenue Service, https://www.irs.gov/individuals/international-taxpayers/alien-taxation-certain-essential-concepts, accessed November 6, 2018.

68. List of Tax Treaties (current as of October 2015), https://www.irs.gov/pub/irs-utl/Tax_Treaty_Table_3.pdf.
69. For a discussion of this issue in relation to current US tax law, see Reuven S. Avi-Yonah and Brett Wells, "The Beat and Treaty Overrides: A Brief Response to Rosenbloom and Shaheen," University of Michigan Law Scholarship Repository, August 16, 2018, https://repository.law.umich.edu/cgi/viewcontent.cgi?article=1268&context=law_econ_current.
70. David Morgan, "U.S. Tax Cuts Prompt Rethink by Some 'Inverted' Companies," Reuters, August 3, 2018, https://www.reuters.com/article/us-usa-tax-inversions/u-s-tax-cuts-prompt-rethink-by-some-inverted-companies-idUSKBN1KO2HH.
71. "Overview of Entity Classification Regulations," Internal Revenue Service, most recently. For more details, see https://www.irs.gov/pub/int_practice_units/ore_c_19_02_01.pdf.
72. Treas. Reg. 301.7701-5(a).
73. Treas. Reg. 301.7701-2(b)(8).
74. https://www.law.cornell.edu/uscode/text/26/269B.
75. https://www.law.cornell.edu/uscode/text/26/1504.
76. "Benefits of a Section 338 Election to a US Buyer of CFC Stock," McDermott, Will, and Emory, November 15, 2018, https://www.lexology.com/library/detail.aspx?g=0bf36582-867d-41e5-bed0-c5436086c64f.
77. Jerred Blanchard, "The Tax Cuts and Jobs Act: Insights and Planning Tips from Corporate/Business Portions of New Tax Law," Baker & McKenzie, LLP, *Lexis Practice Advisor Journal,* Spring 2018, https://www.lexisnexis.com/lexis-practice-advisor/the-journal/b/lpa/archive/2018/02/28/the-tax-cuts-and-jobs-act-insights-and-planning-tips-from-corporate-business-portions-of-new-tax-law.aspx. See also Jane G. Gravelle and Donald J. Marples, "Issues in International Corporate Taxation: The 2017 Revision," May 1, 2018, (P.L. 115-97), https://fas.org/sgp/crs/misc/R45186.pdf.
78. Subpart F income is defined as including insurance income and

foreign base company income. Foreign base company income includes foreign personal holding company income (e.g., dividends, interest, rents, royalties), foreign base company sales income, and foreign base company services income. Subpart F was enacted in 1962 to ensure that US authorities could tax overseas income.

79. A controlled foreign corporation (CFC) is any foreign corporation of which more than 50 percent of the vote or value is owned by US shareholders that own at least 10 percent.
80. The increase is by the greater of (1) the CFC's "accumulated post-1986 deferred foreign income" determined as of November 2, 2017, without regard to distributions, or (2) such income determined as of December 31, 2017. Blanchard, op. cit., note 77.
81. Internal Revenue Service, https://www.irs.gov/pub/int_practice_units/DPLCUV_2_01.PDF. This discussion, written before the new tax laws, has a cautionary statement that is still true today: Subpart F, therefore, does not purport to tax the CFC. Rather, its rules apply only to a US person who owns, directly or indirectly, 10 percent or more of the voting stock of a foreign corporation that is controlled by US shareholders. The provisions of Subpart F are exceedingly intricate and contain numerous general rules, special rules, definitions, exceptions, exclusions, and limitations. One type of entity through which foreign operations may be conducted is a foreign corporation. A major tax advantage of using a foreign corporation to conduct foreign operations is income tax deferral: generally, US tax on the income of a foreign corporation is deferred until the income is distributed as a dividend or otherwise repatriated by the foreign corporation to its US shareholders.
82. https://tax.thomsonreuters.com/news/irs-issues-guidance-on-tax-acts-deemed-repatriation-rules/.
83. See Kyle Pomerleau, "A Hybrid Approach: The Treatment of Foreign Profits under the Tax Cuts and Jobs Act," https://taxfoundation.org/treatment-foreign-profits-tax-cuts-jobs-act/.

84. A domestic corporation is allowed a deduction in an amount equal to 37.5 percent of its FDII, resulting in an effective tax rate on FDII of 13.125 percent. The deductible percentage of FDII declines to 21.875 percent in tax years beginning in 2026 and beyond, resulting in an effective tax rate on FDII of 16.406 percent. Blanchard, op. cit, note 77.
85. Pomerleau, op. cit., note 83.
86. "What Foreign Taxes Qualify for the Foreign Tax Credit?," Internal Revenue Service, https://www.irs.gov/individuals/international-taxpayers/what-foreign-taxes-qualify-for-the-foreign-tax-credit, accessed November 6, 2018.
87. https://www.law.cornell.edu/cfr/text/26/1.368-2.
88. As the relevant statute states, "If the properties are transferred for cash and deferred payment obligations of the transferee evidenced by short-term notes, the transaction is a sale and not an exchange in which gain or loss is not recognized." https://www.law.cornell.edu/cfr/text/26/1.368-2.

Landmark M&A Legal Cases

The M&A field is rich with opportunity, but it also carries considerable legal risk. Any merger transaction can be second-guessed by plaintiffs. Indeed, most M&A transactions announced by public companies attract lawsuits.[1]

Although all of the nearly 200 sovereign nations in the world have court systems worthy of note, this section will focus on a single country, the United States, which according to Thomson Reuter's annual league tables is home to the highest number of M&A deals every year (more than 12,000 in 2018, the highest of any nation), and which commands a significant percentage of cross-border deals (40 percent in 2018).

This section highlights significant cases from the US Supreme Court as well as federal and state courts, especially Delaware's three courts of note: the Chancery Court (for equity cases based in common law); the Superior Court (Delaware's trial court of general jurisdiction that does not hear the equitable claims filed in Chancery); and the Delaware Supreme Court. Delaware is of special interest because it hosts a dominant percentage of large US public companies.

Organized by topic, each section contains both landmark cases and new cases. Landmark cases are reprinted (with any necessary updates) from the previous edition of this book.[2] For the more recent Delaware cases (2008–2018), thanks go to Francis G. X. Pileggi, partner and vice chair of the Litigation Group at Eckert Seamans Cherin & Mellott, LLC.[3]

Taken together, the landmark and recent cases make an important point. While the fundamental concepts of justice and jurisprudence never change, their judicial interpretation does evolve over time as new situations are seen through new perspectives.[4]

I. Cases Alleging Impropriety in Purchasing (or Disclosing an Offer to Purchase) a Company or Controlling Shares

C&J Energy Services, Inc., v. City of Miami General Employees' and Sanitation Employees' Retirement Trust, 107 A.3d 1049 (Del. 2014). Revlon *and its progeny do not set out a specific route that a board must* *follow when fulfilling its fiduciary duties, and an independent board is entitled to use its business judgment to decide to enter into a strategic transaction that promises great benefit, even when it creates certain risks.*[5]

In this case, the City of Miami General Employees and Sanitation Employees Retirement Trust brought a class action on behalf of itself and other stockholders in C&J Energy Services, Inc., to enjoin a merger between C&J and a division of its competitor, Nabors Industries Ltd. The proposed transaction is itself unusual in that C&J, a US corporation, will acquire a subsidiary of Nabors, which is domiciled in Bermuda, but Nabors will retain a majority of the equity in the surviving company. To obtain more favorable tax rates, the surviving entity, C&J Energy Services, Ltd. ("New C&J"), will be based in Bermuda, and thus subject to lower corporate tax rates than C&J currently pays.

To temper Nabors' majority voting control of the surviving company, C&J negotiated for certain protections, including a bye-law guaranteeing that all stockholders would share pro rata in any future sale of New C&J, which can only be repealed by a unanimous stockholder vote. C&J also bargained for a "fiduciary out" if a superior proposal was to emerge during a lengthy passive market check, an unusual request for the buyer in a change of control transaction. And during that market check, a potential competing bidder faced only modest deal protection barriers.

Although the Court of Chancery found that the C&J board harbored no conflict of interest and was fully informed about its own company's value, the court determined there was a "plausible" violation of the board's *Revlon* duties because the board did not affirmatively shop the company either before or after signing. But the court found that because the board exercised its judgment in good faith, tested the transaction through a viable passive market check, and gave its stockholders a fully informed, uncoerced opportunity to vote to accept the deal, the court could not conclude that the board likely violated its *Revlon* duties. Although *Revlon* prohibits boards from taking "actions inconsistent with achieving the highest immediate value reasonably attainable," it "does not require a board to set aside its own view of what is best for the corporation's stockholders and run an auction whenever the board approves a change of control transaction."

In re Cornerstone Therapeutics Inc. S'holder Litig., C.A. No. 564, 2014 (Del. May 14, 2015). *The Delaware Supreme Court, reversing the Chancery Court's decision, approved dismissal for disinterested directors, even though the entire fairness standard may have applied to the transaction.*

The Delaware Supreme Court held that "plaintiffs must plead a non-exculpated claim for breach of fiduciary duty against an independent director protected by an exculpatory charter provision, or that director will be entitled to be dismissed from the suit . . . regardless of the underlying standard of review for the transaction."

Corwin v. KKR Fin. Holdings LLC, 125 A.3d 304, 312 (Del. 2015).[6] *If a merger that does not involve controlling interests has been approved by a fully informed vote of the disinterested stockholders, the standard for reviewing the board's conduct will be the business judgment rule.*

KKR & Co. L.P. engaged in a stock-for-stock merger with KKR Financial Holdings LLC, a specialty finance company whose primary function was to provide financing for KKR & Co.'s leveraged buyouts. The merger was approved by a majority of Financial Holdings' stockholders other than KKR & Co. and its affiliates. Soon thereafter, several Financial Holdings stockholders commenced an action challenging the merger, claiming that KKR & Co. was a controlling stockholder of Financial Holdings and that the KKR & Co. directors breached their fiduciary duties in approving the transaction. The Chancery Court reviewed the merger under the business judgment rule and dismissed the action.

The Delaware Supreme Court upheld the Chancery Court's decision, affirming the power of a disinterested stockholder majority and the reluctance of Delaware courts to second-guess the stockholder majority's determination of what is in their best interest. The Delaware Supreme Court clarified that once a merger closes, as long as it has been approved by a fully informed vote of the disinterested stockholders, the standard for reviewing the board's conduct will be the business judgment rule unless the transaction is subject to the entire fairness standard (as can be the case in a transaction with a controlling stockholder). The Court stated that business judgment rule protection would also apply in this scenario even if the *Revlon* enhanced scrutiny standard applied to the merger.

Delaware Open MRI Radiology Associates, P.A. v. Kessler, C.A. 2006 LEXIS 84 (Del. Ch. Apr. 26, 2006). *Court of Chancery finds remedy for breach of fiduciary duty identical to appraisal award.*

This case was described by then Delaware vice chancellor Leo Strine as "another progeny of one of our law's hybrid varietals: the combined appraisal and entire fairness action." The court was tasked with determining whether the share price in a squeeze-out merger was fair, and, if not, what the extent of the underpayment to the minority shareholders was. The court found that the merger price was unfair and, finding no difference between the award the petitioners/plaintiffs would receive in appraisal or in equity, the court awarded an amount equivalent to petitioners' pro rata share of the company's appraisal value on the date of the merger.

Ernst & Ernst v. Hochfelder, 425 U.S. 185, 208 (1975). *Mere negligence does not imply manipulation.*

Hochfelder was a customer of First Securities Company. The president of the company, Nay, convinced Hochfelder to invest funds in escrow accounts that would yield a high rate of return. Nay asked Hochfelder to write out checks in Nay's name. When Nay committed suicide, Hochfelder learned that there were no escrow accounts—not even phony ones. Nay's suicide note itself described First Securities as bankrupt and the escrow accounts as "spurious."

Hochfelder filed suit in district court for damages against Ernst & Ernst under Section 10(b) of the Securities Exchange Act of 1934, charging that Ernst & Ernst had aided and abetted Nay by failing to conduct proper audits. The district court dismissed the case on the grounds that Ernst & Ernst's accounting procedures conformed to those in general use. The US Court of Appeals reversed this decision, holding Ernst & Ernst liable for a breach of fiduciary duty of inquiry and disclosure under common law and statutory law.

The US Supreme Court disagreed. It held that mere negligence was not a "manipulative device," and therefore not a violation of Section 10(b) and good faith was indeed a valid defense. Furthermore, the Court held that a private right of action is not possible under Section 10(b) or Rule 10b-5, unless there is an intent to deceive, manipulate, or defraud (scienter).

Escott v. BarChris Construction Co., 283 F. Supp. 643 (S.D.N.Y. 1968). *It is not reasonable to rely on management for key data. Data must be double-checked through an independent investigation. Even outside directors must ask for reasonable assurances that facts are correct.*

When BarChris Construction Company, a bowling alley builder, went bankrupt, bondholders accused its directors and officers of violating Section 11 of the Securities Act of 1933, which forbids material misstatements and omissions in a registration statement. They sued the auditors, the underwriters, and all those who had signed the statement—namely, the company's directors, including five officers and the company's controller.

The court found the auditing firm liable for not following generally accepted accounting principles. It also found the underwriter liable for failing to prevent the material misstatements. The court asked, "Is it sufficient to ask questions, to obtain answers which, if true, would be thought satisfactory, and let it go at that, without seeking to ascertain from the records whether the answers, in fact, are true and accurate?" Its answer: "The Purpose of Section 11 is to protect investors. To that end, the underwriters are made responsible for the truth of the prospectus. If they may escape that responsibility by taking at face value representations made to them by management, then the underwriters among those liable under Section 11 affords the investors no additional protection."

Citing Section 11, the court found that there were misstatements and omissions in both the expert and nonexpert portions of the registration statement. It held the inside directors and financial officers responsible for the expert portions, declaring, "There is nothing to show that they made any investigation of anything which they may not have known about or understood. They have not proved their due diligence defenses." Furthermore, the court held the outside directors liable for the nonexpert portions. Directors showed different degrees of diligence, none high enough. One director, Coleman, who had been an investor banker for the company earlier, had checked with the company's lenders and Dun & Bradstreet, read extensive documents, and interviewed the underwriter. Once he became a director, though, he began to rely on others, including a junior associate from the company's outside law firm. "When it came to verification," said the court, "he relied upon his counsel to do it for him. Since counsel failed to do it, Coleman is bound by that failure."

Feit v. Leasco Data Processing Corp., 332 F. Supp. 544 (E.D.N.Y. 1971). *Directors must conduct an adequate investigation of an acquisition candidate.*

In 1968, Leasco Data Processing Equipment Corporation began negotiations to acquire Reliance Insurance Company. Leasco was particularly attracted to Reliance's "surplus surplus," the portion of surplus beyond what is required by law to maintain the integrity of an insurance operation. Because insurance companies at that time were not permitted to engage in noninsurance business, the surplus surplus (as a highly liquid asset) had to be separated from the insurance operation. Leasco intended to form a parent holding company and to transfer the surplus surplus to it.

After some initial disagreements between the two managements, Leasco obtained 90 percent of Reliance in a tender offer. None of the various prospectuses (a supplement was issued each time the tender exchange period was extended) made any mention of the Reliance surplus surplus, an amount estimated by experts to have been between \$100 and \$125 million. Feit, a Reliance stockholder, brought a lawsuit to recover damages. The lawsuit centered on (1) the materiality of the surplus surplus question to the Leasco prospectus sent to holders of Reliance stock, and (2) the accountability of Leasco's directors for the decision to include no mention of the surplus surplus in the prospectuses.

The defendants contended that they were unable to get a good estimate of Reliance's surplus surplus because of poor relations with Reliance's management. They further argued that, in any case, an estimate of the surplus surplus in the prospectuses would only have made Reliance shareholders more eager to tender, since Leasco was known to be aggressive in employing liquid assets. Finally, they asserted, this kind of information could have violated SEC standards for prospectuses and turned this one into a "selling document."

The court rendered a decision in favor of the plaintiff Feit, according him monetary damages. Relying on the due diligence portions of *Escott v. BarChris* (1968), the court held that the director defendants "failed to fulfill their duty of reasonable investigation . . . and had no reasonable grounds to believe that an omission of an estimate of surplus surplus was not materially misleading." This case showed, said one expert, that officers and inside directors "are highly unlikely ever to sustain a due diligence defense."

Flood v. Synutra International, Inc., Del. Supr., No. 101, 2018 (Oct. 9, 2018). *The issue presented to the Delaware Supreme Court in* Flood v. Synutra International, Inc., *was whether it was proper for the Court of Chancery to apply the* MFW *standard by: "(i) allowing for the application of the business judgment rule if the controlling stockholder conditions its bid on both of the key procedural protections at the beginning stages of the process of considering a going private proposal and before any economic negotiations commence; and (ii) requiring the Court of Chancery to apply traditional principles of due care and to hold that no litigable question of due care exists if the complaint fails to allege that an independent special committee acted with gross negligence."*

The "*MFW* standard" was announced by the Delaware Supreme Court in *Kahn v. M&F Worldwide Corp.*, 88 A.3d 635 (Del. 2014), which was highlighted on these pages. That standard allowed for the deferential business judgment review that would be applied to a merger "proposed by controlling stockholder conditioned before the start of negotiations on 'both the approval of an independent, adequately-empowered Special Committee that fulfils its duty of care; and the uncoerced, informed vote of the majority of the minority stockholders.'"

The high court concluded, in its majority opinion, that the interpretation of the *MFW* standard based on the foregoing principles was correct.

In re Hansen Medical, Inc. Stockholders Litigation, C.A. No. 12316-VCMR (Del. Ch. June 18, 2018).[7] *This case, which arose from a squeeze-out merger, provides a useful reiteration of the reasons why the entire fairness standard will apply to a transaction between a controller and a controlled corporation.*

The court addressed claims by a purported class of minority stockholders who alleged that a group that controlled more than 50 percent of the acquired company used their control to negotiate a beneficial deal for themselves at the expense of the minority stockholders.

The case addressed a number of important topics, including the two ways in which a person or a group of persons will be considered "controllers" for purposes of determining the applicable standard of review, the duty of disclosure, materiality of facts and/or omissions, and prerequisites for satisfying a claim for "aiding and abetting a breach of fiduciary duty."

In the end, the court denied the motion to dismiss filed by the controller and the director defendants, because at the earliest stage of the case, and applying the entire fairness standard, the complaint stated a viable claim against them. Moreover, those claims were not barred by the exculpatory clause in the charter.

Kahn v. M&F Worldwide Corp., Del. Supr., No. 334, 2013 (March 14, 2014). *In controller buyouts, the business judgment standard of review will be applied if and only if several conditions (outlined in the decision) apply.*

The Delaware Supreme Court affirmed the Court of Chancery's decision granting summary judgment to the defendants under the business judgment standard of review (and not the entire fairness standard) where the controlling stockholder, MacAndrews & Forbes,[8] conditioned its offer upon the MFW Board agreeing, *ab initio*, to two procedural protections: approval both by a special committee and by a majority of the minority stockholders.

The Supreme Court noted that "[f]or the combination of an effective committee process and majority-of-the-minority vote to qualify (jointly) for business judgment review, each of these protections must be effective singly to warrant a burden shift." The Supreme Court reviewed the record and found that the defendants "have successfully established a record of independent committee effectiveness and process that warranted a grant of summary judgment entitling them to a burden shift prior to trial." The Supreme Court also found that the majority-of-the-minority vote was "fully informed and not coerced. That is, the Defendants also established a pretrial majority-of-the-minority vote record that constitutes an independent and alternative basis for shifting the burden of persuasion to the Plaintiffs."

The court stated: "To summarize our holding, in controller buyouts, the business judgment standard of review will be applied if and only if: (i) the controller conditions the procession of the transaction on the approval of both a Special Committee and a majority of the minority stockholders; (ii) the Special Committee is independent; (iii) the Special Committee is empowered to freely select its own advisors and to say no definitively; (iv) the Special Committee meets its duty of care in negotiating a fair price; (v) the vote of the minority is informed; and (vi) there is no coercion of the minority."

Koppers Co. v. American Express Co., 689 F. Supp. 1371 (W.D. Pa. 1988). *Companies do not have a duty to disclose all information, merely all* material *information.*

Koppers Co., Inc., brought an action against American Express, Shearson Lehman Brothers, and others seeking to enjoin the parties' hostile tender offer based upon Kopper's allegations that the tender offer violated federal securities laws (more specifically, certain disclosure requirements). American Express and the other defendants requested a preliminary injunction ordering Koppers to correct allegedly misleading statements regarding the tender offer.

The US District Court in the Western District of Pennsylvania went to great lengths in the opinion to state that the case was difficult, the facts were intricate and complicated, and the law was unclear. The court stated that it will not hesitate to enjoin a tender offer until compliance with securities laws can be determined. Citing the purpose and intent of Congress in enacting the various securities laws and regulations, the Court also concluded that "it is more prudent to err on the side of disclosure than obfuscation."

But the court also noted that the Williams Act (of 1968, regarding tender offers) does not require that a tender offer disclose all information that it possesses about itself or the target company. Rather, it is only required to disclose those material objective factual matters that a reasonable stockholder would consider important in deciding whether to tender shares.

Laven v. Flanagan, 695 F. Supp. 800 (D.N.J. 1989). *Outside directors have a "lesser obligation to conduct a painstaking investigation than an inside director with intimate knowledge of the corporation."*

Plaintiffs alleged that directors had approved a flawed registration statement without enough diligence. The court, however, found that the directors had made a reasonable effort to verify the facts alleged in the statement. This case is one of several cases finding that "what constitutes a reasonable investigation is measured largely by the common practices in the industry: i.e., one looks at the standards that have evolved among lawyers, accountants, and investment bankers generally in doing due diligence." The directors' activities in this case, for example, showed more diligence than the passive and total reliance on company management that defeated the due diligence defense in the landmark case of *Escott v. BarChris Construction Corp.*

Morrison v. Berry, No. 445, 2017 (Del. July 9, 2018). *The Delaware Supreme Court declines to apply the business judgment rule to protect directors who presided over a yes vote by shareholders in a go-private deal, saying that the vote may not have been fully informed, and further, that "[o]mitted information is material if there is a substantial likelihood that a reasonable stockholder would have considered the omitted information important when deciding whether to tender her shares or seek appraisal."*

In March 2016, soon after The Fresh Market (the "Company") announced plans to go private, the Company publicly filed certain required disclosures under the federal securities laws. Given that the transaction involved a tender offer, the required disclosures included a Solicitation/Recommendation Statement on Schedule 14D-9 (together with amendments, the "14D-9"), which articulated the Board's reasons for recommending that stockholders accept the tender offer—from an entity controlled by private equity firm Apollo Global Management LLC ("Apollo"). The 14D-9 incorporated certain required schedules by reference.

After reading these disclosures, as the tender offer was still pending, stockholder-plaintiff Elizabeth Morrison suspected the Company's directors had breached their fiduciary duties in the course of the sale process, and she sought Company books and records pursuant to Section 220 of the Delaware General Corporation Law. The Company denied her request, and the tender offer closed as scheduled. Litigation over the Section 220 demand ensued, and Plaintiff obtained several key documents, such as board minutes and a crucial email from Ray Berry's counsel to the Company's lawyers.

Plaintiff then filed this action, including a breach of fiduciary duty claim against all 10 of the Company's directors, including Ray Berry, and a claim for aiding and abetting the breach against Ray Berry's son, Brett Berry, who did not serve on the Board. The thrust of Plaintiff's breach of fiduciary duty claim was that Ray and Brett Berry teamed up with Apollo to buy The Fresh Market at a discount by deceiving the Board and inducing the directors to put the Company up for sale through a process that "allowed the Berrys and Apollo to maintain an improper bidding advantage" and "predictably emerge[] as the sole bidder for Fresh Market" at a price below fair value.

Plaintiff also alleged the Board and the stockholders were misled into believing that Ray Berry would openmindedly consider partnering with any private equity firm willing to outbid Apollo, but, instead, "[t]he reality of the situation was that Ray Berry (a) had already formed the belief that Apollo was uniquely well situated to buy Fresh Market; (b) had already entered into an undisclosed agreement with Apollo; and (c) was incentivized not to create price competition for Apollo." In moving to dismiss, Defendants argued that *Corwin v. KKR Fin. Holdings LLC,* 125 A.3d 304, 312 (Del. 2015), applied.

The Court of Chancery stated that this matter "presents an exemplary case of the utility of th[e] ratification doctrine, as set forth in *Corwin* . . ." The Delaware Supreme Court disagreed, finding defendants did not show, under *Corwin,* that the vote was fully informed. Thus, "the business judgment rule is not invoked." The Supreme Court reversed the Court of Chancery's decision and remanded for further proceedings, finding that "[o]mitted information is material if there is a substantial likelihood that a reasonable stockholder would have considered the omitted information important when deciding whether to tender her shares or seek appraisal."

Omnicare Inc. v. NCS Healthcare, 818 A.2d 914 (Del. 2003). *Deal protection mechanisms that fully lock a merger and contain no fiduciary out are unenforceable and a breach of fiduciary duty.*

NCS Healthcare and Genesis Health Ventures had sought to protect their proposed merger through a lockup of the majority stockholders under a voting agreement, coupled with a merger agreement requirement that a stockholder vote be held even if the board withdrew its recommendation because of a superior offering. Subsequent to signing, Omnicare emerged with a superior proposal. In light of this new proposal, the NCS board of directors withdrew its prior recommendation in favor of the Genesis transaction. Nevertheless, under the terms of the "force the vote" provision, NCS proceeded with the stockholders meeting and submitted the Genesis merger to its stockholders for their consideration. Since the lockup agreements committed more than a majority of the outstanding NCS shares to vote in favor of the Genesis merger and neither the merger agreement nor the lockup agreements contained fiduciary out clauses, stockholder approval of the Genesis merger was virtually assured. Omnicare subsequently instituted a lawsuit to enjoin the consummation of the Genesis merger.

The Delaware Supreme Court held that the absence of a fiduciary out provision in the merger agreement made the deal protection measures (i.e., the force the vote provision coupled with the stockholder voting agreements that represented a majority of the votes on the merger) both preclusive and coercive, a violation of the *Unocal* test.

Smith v. Van Gorkom, 488 A.2d 858 (Del. 1985). *The protections of the business judgment rule are available only when directors show a certain level of due care.*

Shareholders brought a class action against the board of directors of Trans-Union Corporation alleging that the board was grossly negligent in its duty of care to the shareholders for recommending that the shareholders approve a merger agreement at $55 per share. Although the price per share was well above current market values, shareholders alleged that it was inadequate. The Delaware Court of Chancery granted the directors summary judgment, and the shareholders appealed. The Delaware Supreme Court indicated that it would closely scrutinize the process by which the board's decision was made.

Historically, courts would not substitute their judgment for that of a corporate board; however, this case eroded that principle and the court embarked down a road of increasing judicial scrutiny of business decisions. The court struck down the long-accepted practice of affording corporate directors the presumption that, in making business decisions, the directors acted on an informed basis, in good faith, and in the best interests of the company and shareholders. The court held that the determination of whether the business judgment of a board of directors is informed turns on whether directors have informed themselves, prior to making business decisions, of all material information reasonably available to them. The court went on to say that, under the business judgment rule, there is no protection for directors who have made uninformed or unadvised judgments.

Software Toolworks Sec. Lit., 50 F.3d 615 (9 Cir. 1994). *Keeping records of due diligence investigations can support a due diligence defense.*

The court stated that suspicious facts or transactions require inquiry, and offered a list of red flags that should raise suspicion in a reasonable person. The court awarded a summary judgment to the underwriter after the underwriter provided extensive records showing its due diligence investigations.[9] William F. Alderman and John Kanberg of Orrick, Herrington, & Sutcliffe, San Francisco, were friends of the court in this case, representing the Securities Industry Association.

In re Trulia, 129 A.:1d 88,1, 899 (Del. Ch. 2016). *Following this forceful court rejection of a disclosure-only settlement, the number of cases alleging only disclosure violations in Delaware and other state courts decreased. As a result of this case, the overall percentage of mergers targeted in state court litigation dropped while the level of mergers targeted in federal courts rose.*

The Delaware Chancery Court rejected a proposed settlement arising out of a stockholder class action challenging Zillow Inc.'s acquisition of Trulia Inc. on the basis of disclosure issues alone, saying that it will be ''increasingly vigilant'' in scrutinizing disclosure-only settlements. This landmark case effectively barred disclosure-only settlement following disputed M&A transactions. As a result of this case, the percentage of mergers targeted in litigation dropped dramatically.[10] The Trulia court found that, because the supplemental disclosures obtained by the plaintiffs in the settlement were not material, they "provided no meaningful benefit to stockholders." Delaware courts would no longer countenance merger litigation settlements that did not achieve meaningful benefits for shareholders. The court specifically rejected the proposed disclosure-only settlement in that case, which provided for additional nonmaterial disclosures, a broad release, and a fee award to plaintiffs' counsel.

TSC Industries, Inc. v. Northway, Inc., 426 U.S. 438 (1976). *Information is material to investors if it alters the total mix of information available to them as they make a decision.*

Northway was a TSC shareholder who brought a lawsuit against both TSC and National, alleging that the proxy statement was incomplete and materially misleading and therefore violated Section14(a) of the Securities Exchange Act of 1934 and related rules. Northway claimed that the proxy statement was misleading because National did not fully disclose the degree of control it had over TSC, and misrepresented the value of the merger to TSC shareholders. The court ruled in favor of the plaintiff, finding that the omitted information, as part of a mix of information, was material to their decision to sell their shares.

In re Xura, Inc. Stockholder Litigation, C.A. No. 12695-VCS (Del. Ch. Dec. 10, 2018). *Just because shareholders approve a transaction does not mean that the transaction cannot be challenged. A fiduciary defendant pointing to a shareholder vote must demonstrate that stockholders possessed all material information before casting their votes.*[11]

In this case, the court allowed a complaint against an allegedly self-interested CEO to proceed. This case began as an appraisal case but became a breach of fiduciary duty case. The plaintiff, Obsidian Management LLC, was a former stockholder of Xura, Inc. When an affiliate of Siris Capital Group, LLC, acquired Xura via merger, Obsidian dissented and sought appraisal. According to Obsidian, in the discovery that followed the filing of its petition for appraisal in this Court, Obsidian uncovered evidence that Xura's former CEO, Philippe Tartavull, breached his fiduciary duties to Xura stockholders in the sale process leading up to the merger. It initiated this breach of fiduciary duty and aiding and abetting action individually, on its own behalf, against Tartavull and Siris, respectively, soon after.

The appraisal and fiduciary duty actions were consolidated and the appraisal action was stayed pending final adjudication of the breach of fiduciary duty and aiding and abetting claims. Defendants Tartavull and Siris, moved to dismiss those claims. The defendants based their defense on the so-called Corwin doctrine, which says that, unless a transaction has to meet an entire fairness standard (which applies to transactions involving controlling shareholders), a vote by fully informed shareholders to approve a merger can be protected under the business judgment rule. But the court found that the shareholders may not have been fully informed, and allowed this part of the pleading to proceed.

II. Cases Alleging Impropriety in the Valuation and/or Sale of a Business, Assets, or Controlling Shares

Abraham v. Emerson Radio Corp., 2006 WL 1879205 (Del. Ch. July 5, 2006). *Court of Chancery clarifies right to buy control.*

This decision makes it clear that a controlling stockholder may sell control without fear of liability for the actions of the buyer after the transaction closes, with few exceptions. While it has long been the rule that a stockholder may deal with its shares as it sees fit, case law recognized that a controlling stockholder has a fiduciary duty to its company and the minority owners by virtue of the controller's ability to control what the company does. How that duty applied in the sale of control context is the question addressed in this case.

Andaloro v. PFPC Worldwide, 2005 WL 2045640 (Del. Ch. Aug. 19, 2005). *In appraisal action, Court of Chancery employs discounted cash flow and comparable companies' methods to value shares purchased by 98 percent owner in cash-out merger.*

This was a consolidated appraisal and equitable fiduciary duty action (the court did not address the fiduciary claim in this opinion). It arose out of a merger in which PFPC Worldwide, Inc. (PFPC), was acquired by its parent PFPC Holding Corp. (Holding), which held over 98 percent of PFPC's stock before the merger. (The merger was also approved by PFPC's ultimate parent and Holding's immediate parent, PNC Financial Services Group, Inc. [PNC].) The merger resulted in the elimination of the minority shareholders' position in PFPC for $34.26 per share.

Basic v. Levinson, 485 U.S. 224 (1988). *Untruthful denial of merger talks violates 10b-5.*

The plaintiff was a group of Basic, Inc., shareholders who sold stock in Basic, Inc., prior to formal announcement of a merger that caused Basic stock to rise. Basic spokespersons had denied that the merger was under consideration. The stockholders brought an action under Rule 10b-5 alleging material misrepresentation.

The question before the court was whether the public statements denying merger talks constituted material misrepresentation. The US Supreme Court ruled that it is not proper to deny that a company is engaged in merger talks when, in fact, it is so engaged. In handing down its ruling, the US Supreme Court rejected the "bright line" test for materiality offered in an earlier Sixth Circuit Appeals Court decision. Materiality must be decided on a case-by-case basis, opined the high court.

In this instance, negotiations were material—even though the talks had not yet resulted in any agreement on the price and structure of the transaction. The Supreme Court said that the appropriate response to an inquiry about undisclosed merger talks is either "no comment" or disclosure that the talks are taking place. Note: This case was reinforced by the later lower court ruling in *Levinson v. Basic, Inc.,* 871 F.2d 562 (1989).

Calpine Corporation v. The Bank of New York, 2005 WL 3454729 (Del. Ch. Nov. 22, 2005). *Corporation's use of sale proceeds violates language in indenture agreements.*

The plaintiff, an energy company, attempted to use proceeds from the sale of certain assets to fund a series of purchases of natural gas for burning in its power plants. The plaintiff's noteholders objected to those purchases because the relevant indenture agreements only allowed sale proceeds to be used for certain purposes. In response to the noteholders' objection, the indenture trustees refused to authorize release of any additional monies to the plaintiff for those purchases. The plaintiff subsequently sued the indenture trustees, seeking declaration that the corporation's past and proposed use of proceeds was permissible.

In re CompuCom Systems, Inc. Stockholders Litig., No. Civ. A. 499, 2005 (WL 2481325). *Evidence of board diligence prompts the court to dismiss plaintiff allegations of fiduciary duty breaches.*

In this case, former minority shareholders alleged that the defendants, CompuCom directors, had "improperly agreed to sell the company for an inadequate price in order to satisfy the majority shareholder's pressing need for cash." Touching briefly on the duty of loyalty (by saying the board appeared to be independent of the majority shareholder), plaintiffs centered on the duty of care. The Delaware Court of Chancery dismissed the plaintiffs' claims on several grounds:

- The board appointed a special committee to examine possible sale transactions.
- The special committee spent over 18 months soliciting bids for the company.
- The special committee hired outside legal counsel and financial advisors that supplied a fairness opinion.
- The plaintiffs ultimately received the same price for their shares.
- The final merger agreement did not contain "any strong lock-ups or other deal protection measures that would unduly impede a bidder willing to pay a higher price from coming forward."

Understanding the CompuCom decision can help selling companies form a good checklist for exercising due care in the sale of a company.

Credit Managers Ass'n of Southern Cal. v. Federal Co., 629 F. Supp. 175 (C.D. Cal. 1985.). *Just because a company sold is undercapitalized does not mean that the conveyance of the company is fraudulent.*

In 1980, Crescent Food Co., a cheese importation and distribution entity wholly owned by Federal Company, entered into a management-led leveraged buyout. The stock purchase price was over $1.4 million. Crescent received an additional loan from new management of $189,000, as well as approximately $10 million from General Electric Credit Corp. Crescent's debt service increased significantly because of the buyout. Finding itself with insufficient cash to continue operations, Crescent eventually shut down and executed an assignment of its assets for the benefit of creditors. The plaintiff brought action against Federal, alleging that the buyout was a fraudulent conveyance.

The question before the court was whether or not the transaction was a fraudulent conveyance. The US District Court in California held that the law does not require that companies be sufficiently well capitalized to withstand any and all setbacks to their business; it requires only that the companies not be left with unreasonably small capital at the time of conveyance.

Crescent/Mach I Partnership v. Turner, 2005 WL 3618279 (Del. Ch. Dec. 23, 2005). *Court of Chancery grants partial summary judgment with respect to claims that former controlling stockholder extracted excess compensation from acquirer in exchange for supporting merger.*

Former stockholders who were cashed out in connection with a merger sued the corporation's former controlling stockholder and the acquirer for breach of fiduciary duty and aiding and abetting breach of fiduciary duty, respectively. The plaintiffs complained of numerous side deals, allegedly negotiated by the controlling stockholder. The plaintiffs also complained that the controlling stockholder breached his fiduciary duty by supplying growth projections that he knew to be unduly pessimistic and inconsistent with management's view. The defendants moved for summary judgment, which the court granted in part and denied in part.

Dell, Inc. v. Magnetar Glob. Event Driven Master Fund Ltd., No. 565, 2016 (Del. Dec. 14, 2017). *When expert testimonies conflict, deal price should take on "heavy, if not dispositive weight" in calculating deal value, said the court in this landmark valuation case.*

In this unanimous decision, the Supreme Court of Delaware reversed in significant part the decision in the Court of Chancery, which "erred in not assigning any mathematical weight to the deal price" when determining the fair value.[12] In the Supreme Court's view, this "deserved heavy, if not dispositive, weight," compared to the alternative of the results when a "law-trained judge" relies on the valuation theories of "divergent partisan expert testimony."

This case arose when, after a majority of shareholders had already voted to approve the Dell buyout, a number of shareholders exercised their appraisal rights. The Court noted that Delaware's appraisal statute, 8 Del. C. § 262, allows stockholders who demand appraisal rights to receive "fair value" for their shares as of the merger date instead of the amount of money they would have received under the transaction. But the appraisal statute, said the Court, required the Court of Chancery "take into account all relevant factors" when assessing the value of the shares.

The Court of Chancery relied exclusively on its own DCF analysis, which resulted in a fair value of $17.62 per share. The Vice Chancellor concluded that the market, being short-term oriented, and the sale process, involving financial bidders, failed to reflect the company's long-intrinsic value. The Supreme Court turned this argument on its head, finding that the lack of strategic bidders suggested that the deal price was not too low, because if the price had been below market, this would have attracted strategic bidders. The Supreme Court held that the bidding process was fair and that the market pricing was accurate, rejecting claims to the contrary. The Supreme Court concluded that while the Court of Chancery has wide discretion in valuation, the deal price and market price should be carefully considered as indicators of value.

Edelman v. Fruehof Corp., 798 F.2d 882 (6th Cir. 1986). *The court rebuked directors for approving a management buyout without considering other possible buyers.*

In February 1986, the Edelman Group began acquiring Fruehauf stock on the open market. Edelman attempted a friendly acquisition, which Fruehauf's board of directors rejected. Subsequently, members of Fruehauf's management negotiated a two-tier leveraged buyout along with Merrill Lynch. A special committee of Fruehauf's outside directors approved the management-led buyout. Edelman sought a preliminary injunction restraining Fruehauf from completing the buyout.

The question before the court was whether the outside directors breached their fiduciary duty to the company. The Sixth Circuit Appeals Court held that Fruehauf's board of directors, in using corporate funds to finance the buyer, did not act in good faith to negotiate the best deal for shareholders and thus breached their fiduciary duty to the shareholders. Moreover, the court stated that once it becomes apparent that a takeover target will be acquired by new owners, it becomes the duty of the directors to see that the shareholders obtain the best possible price.

In re Emerging Communications, Inc. S'holders Litig., 2004 WL 1305745 (Del. Ch. 2004). *A breach of fiduciary duty in approving a merger does not automatically create a presumption of bad faith or disloyalty; it will be considered mere negligence unless plaintiffs can prove otherwise.*

In this case, the court found that nine directors had breached their fiduciary duties to minority shareholders by approving a particular merger. Nevertheless, the court found that four of the directors were shielded from liability by the company's exculpation provision (in its indemnification agreement with directors and officers). This was because the plaintiffs had failed to present "a prima facie case of bad faith or disloyalty that [those] directors would be called upon to negate or disprove." In other words, as one expert put it in a comprehensive article on the duty of good faith, "a breach of fiduciary duty will not automatically create a presumption of bad faith or disloyalty that the defendant must disprove. Rather, the court will presume that the breach was exclusively the product of a lack of due care until the plaintiffs produce evidence to the contrary."

In re: Family Dollar Stores, Inc. Stockholder Litigation, C.A. No. 9985-CB (Del. Ch. Dec. 19, 2014). *This opinion is useful for its discussion of the enhanced scrutiny standard of review for breach of fiduciary duty claims under the* Revlon *standard.*

This opinion by the Delaware Court of Chancery found that the *Revlon* standard was triggered by sale of control in connection with a merger between Family Dollar Stores, Inc., and Dollar Tree, Inc. The stockholders of Family Tree sought a preliminary injunction to enjoin a vote on the merger because an offer had been made by a third company, Dollar General, Inc., which the stockholders argued was not taken seriously by the board of Family Dollar Stores.

The Chancellor found that the *Revlon* standard applied to the sale of control based on the fact that 75 percent of the consideration was to be paid in cash and 25 percent to be paid in the common stock of the acquiring company, Dollar Tree.

The motion for preliminary injunction was denied because the Chancellor found that the stockholders failed to demonstrate a reasonable probability of success on the claims, and neither demonstrated the existence of irreparable harm nor that the balance of the equities favored the relief they sought.

In connection with the *Revlon* analysis, the court addressed the role that the motivation of the board plays. For example, the court must look at the possibility that personal interests short of pure self-dealing had influenced the board to lock a bid or to steer a deal to one bidder rather than another. The court must consider whether the board was motivated to act for a proper end before determining whether the means used were a reasonable way to advance the end.

The court quickly dispensed with the argument that the board abdicated its responsibility by allowing the CEO to conduct much of the negotiations during the sale process with minimal supervision. Instead, the court noted that the board created an advisory committee that oversaw and was actively engaged in the sale process and received regular updates from the CEO. The board was engaged in making important decisions with the full understanding of the options and the rationale for the decisions. Moreover, the plaintiffs did not identify any material information that was kept from the board.

Interestingly, the court cited a decision of the Delaware Supreme Court issued a few hours before the instant opinion was issued, on the same day, which also addressed *Revlon* standards. The court quoted the Supreme Court opinion in *C&J Energy Services, Inc. v. City of Miami General Employees and Sanitation Employees Retirement Trust*, highlighted previously in this chapter, for the following statement of the *Revlon* principle: "Under *Revlon*, a board of directors may, as the Board did here, 'pursue the transaction it reasonably views as most valuable to stockholders, so long as the transaction is subject to an effective market check under circumstances in which any bidder interested in paying more has a reasonable opportunity to do so.'"

The Chancellor also rejected the claims that the members of the board breached their fiduciary duty by failing to disclose in the Proxy several items of information that the plaintiffs claim were material. The court concluded that those disclosure claims were without merit because they were either "speculation, self-flagellation, or immaterial minutiae." The court's conclusion was based on settled Delaware law that: "When directors solicit stockholder action, they must disclose fully and fairly all material information within the board's control. Information is material "if there is a substantial likelihood that a reasonable shareholder would consider it important in deciding how to vote."

Subsequently the court, in a separate letter opinion in January 2015, denied a motion for interlocutory appeal.

Gantler v. Stephens, 965 A.2d 695 (Del. 2009). *Just because stockholders approve a decision does not mean the board's decision-making process is exempt from a review for fairness.*

The plaintiffs in this breach of fiduciary duty action, who were shareholders of First Niles Financial, Inc. ("First Niles" or the "Company"), appealed the dismissal of their complaint by the Court of Chancery. The complaint alleged that the defendants, who were officers and directors of First Niles, violated their fiduciary duties by rejecting a valuable opportunity to sell the company, deciding instead to reclassify the company's shares in order to benefit themselves, and by disseminating a materially misleading proxy statement to induce shareholder approval. Shareholders voted in favor of the transaction. The court concluded, however, that the complaint included allegations sufficient to overcome the business judgment presumption, and to state substantive fiduciary duty and disclosure claims. The court reversed the Court of Chancery's judgment of dismissal and remanded the case for further proceedings.[13]

Hanson Trust PLC v. SCM Corp., 774 F.2d 47 (2d Cir. 1985). *The court denied the protections of the business judgment rules to directors who approved a lockup option.*

Hanson Trust PLC tendered a $60-per-share offer for any and all shares of SCM Corp. The offer was followed by a counteroffer by the SCM board and their white knight, Merrill Lynch Capital Markets. Hanson then increased its offer to $72 each, contingent upon SCM's agreement not to enter into a lockup agreement. The SCM Merrill counteroffer was revised to $74 along with a lockup option for an SCM crown jewel. Hanson terminated its offer as a direct result of the lockup option. (A lockup option is an agreement that says the option holder, Company A, will acquire all or part of Company B, and that Company A will realize an economic gain if another company buys company B or a specified part of Company B.)

The question before the court was whether SCM's board of directors could be protected under the business judgment rule when they approved of the lockup option. The business judgment rule is a judicial doctrine under which reasonable decisions by directors are insulated from second-guessing by the courts. The Second Circuit US Court of Appeals denied protection under the business judgment rule on the grounds of SCM directors' "paucity of information" and the swiftness of their decision making, which strongly suggested a breach of the duty of care.

In re Healthco International, 208 B.R. 288, 300 (Bankr. D. Mass. 1997). *Director-shareholders who show due care in approving a buyout are not negligent if they exercised due care.*

In the spring of 1990, Healthco was involved in a struggle for corporate control with Gemini Partners L.P. In June 1990, a minority shareholder of Healthco, alleging that the price of Healthco's stock was undervalued, began a proxy contest to remove the incumbent board. In September 1990, Healthco entered into a merger agreement with HMD Acquisition (an acquisition vehicle of Hicks Muse) subject to several conditions including shareholder approval, realization of projected earnings, and the securing of financing. In January 1991, Healthco issued a proxy statement projecting unspecified losses, causing Gemini Partners L.P. to withdraw its bid, leaving HMD as the sole bidder. HMD acquired Healthco for $15 per share—$4.25 per share less than Gemini's highest offer.

In March 1991, the new Healthco board, which included directors who were Healthco stockholders, experienced operating problems. Shareholders brought suit against Healthco, alleging material misstatement in the proxy statement. The question before that court was whether or not the projections of unspecified losses constituted fraud under Rule 10b-5 of the US federal securities laws. Finding in favor of the defendants, the District Court held that "optimistic, vague projections of future success which prove to be ill-founded" do not by themselves trigger Rule 10b-5 liability. This liability is triggered when such overly optimistic projections "imply certainty" or rely on "statements of facts which prove to be erroneous."

In June 1993, Healthco filed for relief under Chapter 11 of the US Bankruptcy Code. Then, in September of that year, the case was converted to Chapter 7 and the company was liquidated, causing severe losses to the company's creditors.

In June 1995, the bankruptcy trustee for the creditors began legal action (independent of the previous securities law suit) in US bankruptcy court against virtually all the participants in the company—65 defendants in all, including the company's directors, who were accused of violating their duty of loyalty. The plaintiffs alleged that the directors' ownership of stock in Healthco rendered them "interested" in its sale. The directors, citing legal precedent and documenting their decision-making process, argued that they had fulfilled their duties of loyalty and care. They asked the bankruptcy court for a summary judgment dismissal, but the court refused, holding that the directors were indeed "interested" parties by law.

Two years later, the case came to trial again in US District Court in Worcester, Massachusetts, where the Court declined to adopt the Bankruptcy Court's ruling, and ordered a jury trial. The directors repeated their defense, this time bringing in an expert witness on behalf of the directors, Dr. Robert Stobaugh, Emeritus Professor at Harvard Business School. He testified Healthco directors had met generally accepted practice with respect to both their duty of loyalty and their duty of care. After a seven-week trial, the jury returned a verdict in favor of all the defendants on all of the claims in the bankruptcy case.

Humana v. Forsyth, 525 U.S. 299 (1999). *The Racketeer Influenced and Corrupt Organizations Act may be extended to cover a failure to conduct full due diligence.*

Shareholders sued Humana, a hospital system, and several hospitals that Humana had sold to Columbia-HCA Healthcare Corp. in 1993.

Apparently, in conducting its due diligence study of the Humana-owned hospitals, Columbia had not discovered that some of the hospitals had failed to pass on an insurance discount they were getting for certain customers. A class-action suit against Humana and against the acquired hospitals (now owned by Columbia-HCA) alleged that the absence of the discount was an attempt to defraud the customers. The plaintiffs sued Humana and Columbia under a federal law called the Racketeer Influenced and Corrupt Organizations Act (RICO), a criminal law that exacts triple damages from defendants who are found guilty.

The RICO case went all the way to the Supreme Court, which had to decide whether the plaintiffs had standing to sue under this federal law. A trial court had said no, because the federal law allows more severe penalties than the state law. But the Appeals Court in San Francisco reversed the decision, saying that it did not matter. The Supreme Court upheld this view. Justice Ruth Bader Ginsburg, writing for the court, said, "RICO's

private right of action and treble-damages provision appears to complement Nevada's statutory and common law claims for relief."

In re LNR Property Corp. Shareholders Litigation, 2005 WL 3418631 (Del. Ch. Nov. 4, 2005, *rev'd* Dec. 14, 2005). *Entire fairness applied to third-party merger transaction where controlling shareholder acquired minority stake in resulting company.*

Former shareholders filed fiduciary class action in connection with a cash-out merger, naming the corporation and former directors as defendants. The complaint alleged that the corporation's controlling shareholder negotiated to sell the company to a third-party investment firm in an all-cash deal. The complaint further alleged that, as part of the transaction, the controlling shareholder and other members of company management agreed to invest approximately $184 million to acquire a 25 percent equity stake in the surviving entity. Defendants moved to dismiss for failure to state a claim.

Minnesota Invco of RSA #7 v. Midwest Wireless Holdings, 2006 WL 1596675 (Del. Ch. June 7, 2006). *Court of Chancery upholds drag along rights.*

In this case, the Court of Chancery was required to interpret complex agreements between the members of a Delaware limited liability company. The court held that the defendant holding company had the right to "drag along" holders of a minority interest in an operating subsidiary of the holding company in connection with the sale of the holding company.

Oliver v. Boston University, 2006 WL 1064169 (Del. Ch. Apr. 14, 2006). *Court of Chancery awards $4.8 million, plus interest, to minority shareholders for damages suffered from director defendants' breach of the fiduciary duty of loyalty.*

Defendant Boston University (BU) was the controlling shareholder of Seragen, a financially troubled biotechnology company. Plaintiffs, a group of former minority stockholders of Seragen's common stock, challenged certain transactions before Seragen was merged and the process by which the merger proceeds were divvied up. The plaintiffs contended that the BU defendants breached their fiduciary duties to Seragen's common shareholders by approving various financial transactions, which were not fair to the common shareholder as a matter of price and process. The Court of Chancery awarded damages in excess of $4.8 million plus interest for breaches of the fiduciary duty of loyalty.

Paramount Communications v. Time Inc., 517 A.2d 1140 (Del. 1990). *Directors, not shareholders, manage a firm, and may take actions against the wishes of a majority of shareholders if the actions are in the best interests of the firm, as directors understand that interest.*

In July 1989, the Delaware Chancery Court ruled that Time Inc. should be allowed to proceed with its planned $14 billion acquisition of Warner Communications, Inc., despite protest from would-be hostile acquirer Paramount, alleging violation of various securities laws. In a landmark 79-page decision affirmed later by the Delaware Supreme Court, Chancellor William T. Allen declared that "corporation law does not operate on the theory that directors, in exercising their powers to manage the firm, are obligated to follow the wishes of a majority of shares. In fact, directors, not shareholders, are charged with the duty to manage the firm."

This decision was widely considered to be an affirmation of the so-called business judgment rule, a judicial doctrine that protects decisions of directors, in their exercise of discretion based on informed judgment, from second-guessing by plaintiffs and judges. On the other hand, several legal commentators noted at the time of the decision that it did not necessarily cover instances of a sale or change of control, as in the classic case of *Revlon.*

Sure enough, in a 1994 case involving Paramount and QVC, the court drew this change-of-control distinction, denying the protections of the business judgment rule to Paramount directors because the transaction they were considering did involve a change of control. (See *Paramount Communications, Inc. v. QVC Network Inc.,* next.)

Paramount Communications, Inc. v. QVC Network Inc., 637 A.2d 34 (Del. 1994) *aff'ing* 635 A.2d 1245 (Del. Ch. 1993). *Directors must seek the best price in a change of control, but not all transactions involve such a change.*

On September 12, 1993, the board of Paramount Communications Inc. announced a proposed merger with Viacom Inc. Viacom was offering $69.14 per share in cash for controlling interests, with the remainder of the purchase price to be paid in stock. On September 27, Paramount directors rebuffed a comparably structured $80-per-share bid from QVC Network Inc., saying they would not talk unless QVC could show evidence of financing. On November 15, Paramount directors refused a revised $90-per-share offer on the grounds that it was too conditional.

Meanwhile, Paramount and Viacom continued to plan their merger. As Viacom's offer rose to the $85-per-share level, Paramount granted Viacom an option to buy Paramount stock and promised to pay a termination fee in the event Paramount rejected Viacom for bidder. Paramount also made plans to redeem a shareholder rights ("poison pill") plan.

QVC sued Paramount and Viacom in the Chancery Court of Delaware, seeking to prevent these actions. The court upheld the termination fee, which it found a "fair liquidated amount to cover Viacom's expenses," but it handed QVC a victory on the other two points. The Chancery Court decision was upheld by the Delaware Supreme Court in a December 9 order, followed by a formal opinion on February 4, 1994.

In its opinion, the Delaware Supreme Court, concurring with the Chancery Court, stated repeatedly that directors in a "sale or change of control" must seek to obtain "the best value reasonably available to the stockholders." In cases that do not involve a sale or change of control, however, the court recognized "the prerogative of a board of directors to resist a third party's acquisition proposal or offer." (The *Paramount* decision spurred Paramount directors to set forth bidding rules in a contest to be decided by shareholders by a certain date. Viacom offered shareholders $105 per share, with certain protections against loss in share value. QVC offered $107 per share, but without such protections. The market chose Viacom, and the rest is history.)

In re PLX Technology Inc. Shareholders Litigation, Consl. C.A. No. 9880-VCL (Del. Ch. Oct. 16, 2018). *Although the* Revlon *doctrine requires boards to obtain the "best transaction" for stockholders, this "is not always a sale; it may mean remaining independent and not engaging in a transaction at all."*

In this case, the plaintiffs made several allegations against the directors, including an allegation of damages. The court rejected the damages claim and found for the defendant, stating that "[t]he fiduciary duties of directors have context-specific manifestations. When directors consider selling the corporation, their fiduciary duties obligate them 'to seek the transaction offering the best value reasonably available to stockholders,' citing *Paramount Communications, Inc. v. QVC Network, Inc.* (Del. 1994). The best transaction reasonably available is not always a sale; it may mean remaining independent and not engaging in a transaction at all.

Revlon v. MacAndrews & Forbes Holdings, 506 A. 2d 173 (Del. Supr. 1985). *Directors have a duty to seek the best offer once a company is known to be for sale.*

In June 1985, Pantry Pride approached Revlon to propose a friendly acquisition. Revlon declined the offer. In August 1985, Revlon's board recommended that shareholders reject the offer. Revlon then initiated certain defensive tactics. It sought other bidders. Pantry Pride raised its bid again. Revlon negotiated a deal with Forstmann Little, which included a lockup provision and relief from Cumulative Convertible Exchangeable Preferred Stock. Revlon also provided Forstmann additional financial information that it did not provide to Pantry Pride.

Eventually, an increased bid from Pantry Pride prompted an increased bid from Forstmann Little. The new bid was conditioned upon, among other things, the receipt by Forstmann Little of a lockup option to purchase two Revlon divisions at a price substantially lower than the lowest estimate of value established by Revlon's investment banker. It included a "no shop" provision that prevented Revlon from considering bids from any third party. The board immediately accepted the Forstmann Little offer even though Pantry Pride had increased its bid.

The questions before the court were (1) whether the lockup agreements were permitted under Delaware law and (2) whether the Revlon board acted prudently. The Delaware Supreme Court held the following:

- Lockups and related agreements are permitted under Delaware law where their adoption is untainted by director interest or other breaches of fiduciary duties.

- Actions taken by directors in this case did not meet that standard.
- Concern for various corporate constituencies is proper when addressing a takeover threat.
- Proper concern for multiple constituencies is limited by the requirement that there be some rationally related benefits accruing to the stockholders.
- There were no such benefits in this case.
- When sale of a company becomes inevitable, the duty of a board of directors changes from preservation of the corporate entity to maximization of the company's value at a sale for the stockholders' benefit. This final point has come to be called the *Revlon* Doctrine.

Treadway Companies, Inc. v. Care Corp., 638 F.2d 357 (2d Cir. 1980). *Directors have certain duties to stockholders in tender offers.*

In 1978, Care Corp. started acquiring shares of stock in Treadway Co., leading Treadway to believe that Care was mounting a hostile takeover. In response to this action, Treadway put certain officers of Care on its board. Then, without fully informing the Care representatives, the Treadway board sought other merger candidates and struck a deal with Fair Lanes. Care filed an action alleging violations of Section 13(d) of the 1934 Securities Exchange Act, breach of fiduciary duties, and misuse of confidential information.

The question before the US District Court for the Southern District of New York was whether the directors had acted improperly in their actions arising out of a struggle for control of their company. The District Court entered a judgment in favor of Care Corp., two of its directors, and Daniel Cowin, an investment banker who was a director of, and financial consultant to, Treadway during the relevant period. The US Court of Appeals for the Second Circuit held that a director does not breach his or her fiduciary duty merely by supporting an effort or promoting a change of management. Moreover, a director does not owe his or her fiduciary duty directly to shareholders with respect to shares of stock they own and has no obligation to afford other shareholders an opportunity to participate in sale of stock.

Unocal v. Mesa Petroleum Co., 493 A.2d 946 (Del. 1985). *Takeover defense must be reasonable in relation to the threat posed.*

In this case, the Delaware Supreme Court had to rule on whether the Unocal board could protect itself against a hostile bidder, Mesa (owned by T. Boone Pickens), which had made a $72-a-share hostile takeover bid, by excluding Mesa from a buyback portion. The court approved this antitakeover measure.

The impact of that controversial decision has been to give management greater power in fighting hostile takeover bids and to discourage raiders from launching "hostile two-tier takeover bids." This tactic involved an offer of cash for 51 percent of a company's shares and high-yield securities known as junk bonds for the remainder.

The court said that since Pickens's two-tier bid for Unocal was coercive and inadequate, and because his past activities "justify a reasonable inference" that his principal objective was greenmail, the company had the right to exclude him from the buyback. Pickens subsequently dropped his bid for Unocal.

Out of this decision came the "enhanced scrutiny" test, to be applied to a target board's decision-making process when a takeover is occurring, to determine if the business judgment rule will apply to their decisions.

There are two parts to the test. The first test is reasonableness. The target board must demonstrate that it had reasonable grounds for believing that a danger to corporate policy and effectiveness existed. If this test is passed, then the court moves to the second part of the test: proportionality. The target board must demonstrate that its response was reasonable in relation to the threat posed. If both parts of the enhanced scrutiny test are satisfied, then the court will use the business judgment rule to evaluate the target board's decisions.

Weinberger v. UOP, Inc., 457 A.2d 701 (Del. 1983).[14] *Withholding a valuation study can cause a shareholder vote on a cash-out merger to be uninformed, giving shareholders the right to sue for breach of fiduciary duty.*

The plaintiff, William Weinberger, brought this action to challenge the shareholder vote for a cash-out merger between Defendant, UOP, Inc., and the Defendant majority shareholder, The Signal Companies, Inc. Plaintiff asserted that Signal defendants breached their fiduciary duty to the minority shareholders by withholding relevant information and not disclosing conflicts of interest. The Chancery Court held in favor of the defendants.

The Supreme Court of Delaware reversed the Chancery ruling, holding that the shareholder vote was not an informed vote and that Signal defendants had indeed breached their duty as a majority shareholder to the minority shareholders. Therefore, the minority shareholders were entitled to a greater value (to be determined by weighing all relevant factors such as a valuation study referenced as the "Arledge-Chitiea" study). The evidence indicated a lack of fair dealing by the majority, such as withholding the Arledge-Chitiea report from the UOP board and the shareholders. The only information the outside directors of UOP had at their disposal was a hurried fairness opinion by an arguably interested party. The board members that served with Signal and UOP breached their duty as UOP directors as well, said the court, by not providing the Arledge-Chitiea study. They were not exempt from their duties because the entities are a parent and a subsidiary.

III. Cases Involving M&A Agreements or Other Contracts

Akorn, Inc. v. Fresenius Kabi AG, C.A. No. 2018-0300-JTL (Del. Ch. Oct. 1, 2018). *In this post-trial memorandum opinion, the court found in favor of the buyer in this case brought by a seller alleging breach of contract, finding that inaccuracies of statements made by the seller could reasonably result in a material adverse effect.*

On April 24, 2017, in a signed merger agreement, Fresenius Kabi AG agreed to acquire Akorn, Inc. In agreement, Akorn made representations about its compliance with applicable regulatory requirements and committed to use commercially reasonable efforts to operate in the ordinary course of business between signing and closing. Both Fresenius and Akorn committed to use their reasonable best efforts to complete the merger, and Fresenius committed to take all actions necessary to secure antitrust approval. The parties agreed to a contractually defined "outside date" for closing, conditioned on Akorn's representations having been true and correct both at signing and at closing, except where the failure to be true and correct would not reasonably be expected to have a contractually defined "Material Adverse Effect" (MAE). If this condition was not met and could not be cured by the outside date, then Fresenius could terminate the merger agreement, unless Fresenius were in material breach of its own obligations under the merger agreement.

Furthermore, Fresenius's obligation to close was conditioned on Akorn having complied in all material respects with its obligations under the merger agreement, but here, too, Fresenius could not exercise the termination right if Fresenius was in material breach of its own obligations under the merger agreement.

Finally, Fresenius's obligation to close was conditioned on Akorn not having suffered an MAE. The failure of this condition did not give Fresenius a right to terminate, but once the outside date passed, either Fresenius or Akorn could terminate, as long as the terminating party's own breach of the Merger Agreement had not prevented closing before the outside date.

This post-trial decision ruled in favor of Fresenius and against Akorn for three reasons: first, Akorn's representations regarding its compliance with regulatory requirements were not true and correct, and the magnitude of the inaccuracies would reasonably be expected to result in an MAE; second, Akorn materially breached its obligation to continue operating in the ordinary course of business between signing and closing; third, Akorn had suffered an MAE.

ATS v. Bachmann, C.A. No. 2374-N (Del. Ch. October 11, 2006). *Delaware's Court of Chancery interprets common merger clause.*

Delaware corporations frequently ask the Court of Chancery to decide if a proposed course of action is appropriate, particularly when the board of directors' fiduciary duties are implicated. In this decision the Court focused primarily on when the Court may provide that guidance and when the matter is not ripe for judicial action. The Court has rejected becoming involved in hypothetical issues not framed by a real-world transaction, but more of a "what if" set of questions. Here, the Court accepted one question for its review and rejected others, thereby illustrating how it will deal with those situations.

The opinion is also interesting in its interpretation of a fairly common clause found in merger agreements that might have been held to operate much like a "no talk" provision. The Court held that as the directors do have a fiduciary duty to consider alternatives to a merger and that in light of the negotiations that had led to this particular clause, the agreement did not bar the board from considering a competing merger offer. Given the wording of the clause in question, this conclusion was not free from doubt and provides guidance to drafters of such merger agreements.

Electro Optical Industries v. White, 90 Cal. Rptr. 2d 680 (1999). *An employer may prohibit an employee from accepting employment with a competitor if the new employment will "inevitably" lead the employee to rely on the competitor's trade secrets, said the judicial panel in this case. But the panel did not find such inevitability here.*

The plaintiff, Electrical Optical Industries (EOI), supplied infrared testing devices to the military and to defense contractors. A key employee—Stephen White—abruptly left after 15 years to join Santa Barbara Infrared, Inc. (SBIR), one of EOI's direct competitors. EOI asked the trial court for a preliminary injunction precluding White from participating in sales or development of infrared testing devices at SBIR. EOI argued that White knew trade secrets and, if permitted to work for SBIR, would inevitably use them. The trial court denied preliminary injunction and EOI appealed.

In an Appeals Court decision rendered December 3, 1999, a three-panel judge adopted the doctrine of "inevitable disclosure," but said that instances must be decided on the basis of fact, and that the facts in this case favored the defendant. The court acknowledged that White possessed knowledge of certain EIO information. Some of the information was technical—namely, existing and future product designs, production methods, materials and process, and the status of patent applications. The court agreed that this information was a trade secret, but it stated that (a) White lacked the training to pass on the information, and (b) SBIR did not need the information. Some of the information was nontechnical, such as customer lists, sales prices, production costs, marketing plans, and sales strategies. But the court said these did not constitute trade secrets. As for customer preferences and specifications, the court said that this information was not a trade secret or, if it were, it would belong to the customer.

ev3, Inc. v. Lesh, C.A. No. 515, 2013 (Del. Sept. 30, 2014, revised April 20, 2015).[15] *In a conflict between a letter of intent and an acquisition agreement, only the latter is dispositive.*

This case was an appeal from a jury verdict finding that ev3, Inc., the buyer of Appriva Medical, Inc., breached its contractual obligations to Appriva's former shareholders, who gave up their shares in the merger. The merger agreement between ev3 and Appriva provided for the bulk of the payments to the Appriva shareholders to be contingent upon the timely accomplishment of certain milestones toward the approval and marketability of a medical device that Appriva was developing. After it became clear that the milestones were not going to be achieved, the former Appriva shareholders sued based on not only the language of the agreement but also the letter of intent, which contained language about funding.[16] In its decision, the Delaware Supreme Court found that the Superior Court had erred in allowing the plaintiffs to cite the letter of intent, and to deny the defendants the ability to refuse the claims, arguing that whether or not the letter of intent survived for some purposes, any provisions that conflicted with the relevant section of the acquisition agreement were "without force and effect."

Facchina v. Malley, 2006 WL 2328228 (Del. Ch. Aug. 1, 2006). *Court of Chancery affirms application of Delaware law to LLC.*

A California corporation merged with a Delaware corporation, and the California corporation ceased to exist. Stockholders of the California corporation wanted to enforce an agreement signed prior to the merger. The Court of Chancery affirmed that Delaware law applies to the internal affairs of any Delaware LLC. In this case, the LLC was the result of a merger of a California corporation into a Delaware LLC. The California entity had a stockholders' agreement that the defendants wanted to enforce. The court rejected their arguments because the California entity had ceased to exist in the merger.

Frontier Oil Corporation v. Holly Corporation, 2005 WL 1039027 (Del. Ch. April 29, 2005). *Court of Chancery finds that substantial litigation expenses are not a sufficient material adverse effect to rescind a contract.*

Frontier Oil Corporation and Holly Corporation are petroleum refiners that sought to merge. In conducting its due diligence review of Frontier, Holly discovered that activist Erin Brockovich was planning to bring a toxic tort suit claiming that an oil rig that had been operating for decades on the campus of Beverly Hills High School caused the students to suffer from a disproportionately high incidence of cancer. This raised concerns for Holly because a subsidiary of Frontier had previously operated the Beverly Hills drilling facility. Although the terms of the merger agreement were modified to address the situation, including broadening the representation to apply to litigation that would reasonably be expected to have a material adverse effect (MAE) on Frontier, the court found that substantial litigation costs were not an MAE and therefore the contract could not be rescinded.

Horizon Personal Communications v. Sprint Corp., 2006 WL 2337592 (Del. Ch. Aug. 4, 2006). *In a postmerger setting, Court of Chancery expands duty to act in good faith.*

Prior to its 2005 merger with Nextel, Sprint had made certain promises to affiliates. In this case the Court of Chancery examined the contract between the parties, determined what is required to act in good faith, and awarded an injunction to preclude a breach of that duty. In doing so, the court's analysis provided a road map for how to honor contracts made prior to a merger.

In re IBP Inc. Shareholders Litigation, 789 A.2d 14 (Del. Ch. 2001). *The party seeking to terminate an agreement on account of the fact that the other party had suffered a material adverse event (MAE) has the burden of proving that the MAE had occurred. Also, a broad MAE clause protects an acquirer only from "unknown events" that "substantially threaten" the target's earnings ability in a "durationally-significant manner."*

IBP Inc. and Tyson Foods Inc. entered into a merger agreement whereby Tyson agreed to acquire IBP in a cash-out merger. In conducting its due diligence of IBP, Tyson learned of several potential issues with

IBP's business going forward. These potential issues included that IBP was likely heading into a downturn in its beef business, and that there might be significant accounting issues at one of IBP's subsidiaries. Tyson nonetheless proceeded to sign the agreement to acquire IBP. After signing the agreement, for a variety of reasons, Tyson sought to terminate the agreement. IBP resisted these attempts.

Because Tyson was aware of the subsidiary's accounting problems and the cyclical nature of the livestock industry, these risks could not qualify as "unknown risks" for the purposes of establishing whether IBP had suffered an MAE. Additionally, the short-term drop in IBP's earnings did not "substantially threaten" its overall earnings potential and thus did not constitute an MAE. In addition, the court granted IBP the remedy of specific performance, ordering Tyson's acquisition of IBP to go forward.

Mehiel v. Solo Cup Co., No. 06C-01-169 2010 WL 4513389 *6 (Del. Super. Ct. Oct. 14, 2010). *After a chain of litigation, an arbitrator accepted the buyer's position that a certain asset was long-term and excludable from working capital, thus leading to a reduction in purchase price.*

In 2005,[17] the Delaware Chancery Court enforced a *provision* in a merger agreement permitting arbitration of disputed representation-and-warranty and working-capital claims.

In 2007,[18] the Delaware Superior Court considered the fact that the merger agreement provided for a postclosing adjustment based on changes to working capital between the time the parties entered into the agreement and the closing, and further provided that any disagreements regarding the closing adjustment must be presented to an arbitrator. The seller had filed litigation challenging the arbitrator's ruling on this matter. Without addressing the merits of the argument, the Court concluded that the seller's argument had been presented to and resolved by the arbitrator; therefore, the seller was barred from attempting to litigate that issue in court, and had to submit to arbitration.

Finally, in the 2010 case, the Delaware Superior court noted that the parties' merger agreement provided for postclosing adjustment based on changes to working capital. The parties disputed a $5.6 million facility, which had been treated as an asset for sale and included in the working capital by the seller, rather than treated as a long-term asset and excluded from working capital. The arbitrator accepted the buyer's position that it should have been treated as a long-term asset and excluded from working capital. This resulted in a $5.6 million decrease in purchase price.

Texaco v. Pennzoil Co., 729 S.W.2d 768 (Tex. App. 1987), *cert. denied,* 485 U.S. 994, (1988). *A handshake M&A deal can be legally binding.*

In December 1983, Pennzoil announced a tender offer for 16 million shares of Getty Oil common stock at $100 per share. Subsequently, Pennzoil met with Getty Oil representatives to discuss the tender offer and possible sale of Getty Oil to Pennzoil. Then, over a period of several days, the following occurred:

- On January 2, 1984, as a result of the meetings, Pennzoil and Getty Oil representatives signed a memorandum of agreement for the sale of Getty Oil to Pennzoil, subject to approval by the board of directors of Getty Oil.
- On January 3, Pennzoil revised its offer to $110 per share, plus a $3 stub. Getty Oil's board of directors rejected the offer but made a counterproposal for a $5 stub. Pennzoil agreed and a memorandum of agreement was executed.
- On January 4, both parties issued a press release.
- On January 5, Texaco contacted Getty Oil representatives to inquire about a possible sale to Texaco for $125 per share.
- On January 6, Getty Oil's board of directors voted to withdraw its Pennzoil offer and accept Texaco's offer. Texaco purchased Getty Oil stock and Pennzoil brought an action for tortious interference.

The question before the court was whether Pennzoil and Getty Oil had a binding agreement absent a definitive purchase agreement. On approval, the Court of Appeals for Texas, citing the language in the prospective stock buyer's draft and the term "agreement in principle" in the press release, found that there was a binding agreement.

In re Toys "R" Us Shareholder Litigation, 877 A.2d 975 (Del. Ch. June 24, 2005). *Court of Chancery denies motion for temporary injunction where breakup fee is alleged to be too high.*

The Court of Chancery considered a motion to enjoin a vote of the stockholders of Toys "R" Us, Inc., to consider approving a merger with an acquisition vehicle formed by a group led by Kohlberg Kravis Roberts & Co. Pursuant to the terms of the merger agreement, the Toys "R" Us stockholders would receive $26.75 per share for their shares. The $26.75-per-share merger consideration constituted a 123 percent premium over the price of TRU stock when merger negotiations began in January 2004. Plaintiffs charged the board did not act reasonably in pursuit of the highest attainable value. The Court of Chancery denied the motion to enjoin a stockholder vote on the proposed merger, saying stockholders could stop the merger by voting if they thought it was unfair.

W.L. Gore & Associates, Inc. v. Wu, C.A. No. 263-N (Del. Ch. September 15, 2006). *Court of Chancery grants 10-year injunction in trade secret case.*

The extent to which a court will enjoin the violation of a confidentiality agreement covering trade secrets is often questioned. In this decision, the Court of Chancery issued an injunction that for ten years barred the defendant from working in a business that might permit him to use the trade secrets he had stolen from his employer. In part, the remedy was based on the useful life of the stolen materials.

IV. Cases Alleging Violation of Antitrust Laws

Ford Motor Co. v. United States, 405 U.S. 562 (1972). *The Supreme Court rules that Ford's attempt to buy a key supplier violated antitrust laws.*

The Court condemned Ford's attempted acquisition of Autolite, a spark plug manufacturer, and emphasized the heightened barriers that the merger would pose to other companies that attempted to enter the market. The Court also emphasized that Ford's argument that the acquisition had made Autolite a more effective competitor was irrelevant.

FTC v. Phoebe Putney Health System, Inc., 133 S. Ct. 1003 (2013). *Although federal antitrust laws do not prevent states from imposing market restraint, states are not immune from legal challenge.*

The Hospital Authority of Albany-Dougherty County in Georgia (Authority) owned Phoebe Putney Memorial Hospital (Memorial), one of two hospitals in the county. The Authority formed two private nonprofit corporations to manage Memorial: Phoebe Putney Health System, Inc. (PPHS), and Phoebe Putney Memorial Hospital, Inc. (PPMH). After the Authority decided to purchase the second hospital in the county and lease it to a subsidiary of PPHS, the FTC issued an administrative complaint alleging that the transaction would substantially reduce competition in the market for acute care hospital services, in violation of Section 5 of the Federal Trade Commission Act and Section 7 of the Clayton Act.

The US Supreme Court, reversing a lower court decision, held in favor of the FTC. Citing precedent, the high court held that although federal antitrust laws do not prevent states from imposing market restraints "as an act of government," nonetheless "state action immunity is disfavored." Referring to "the antitrust laws' values of free enterprise and economic competition," the high court said that state law can prevail only when "it is clear that the challenged anticompetitive conduct is undertaken pursuant to the 'State's own' regulatory scheme," which must be "clearly articulated and affirmatively expressed." The high court did not find such a policy in Georgia and therefore reversed the lower court decision.

Olin Corporation v. Federal Trade Commission, 986 F.2d 1295 (9 Cir. 1993). *The Federal Trade Commission has the right to order divestitures.*

In 1985, Olin Corporation entered into an agreement with FMC Corporation to purchase FMC's swimming pool chemicals business. Since the late 1970s, Olin had been experiencing considerable difficulties in the manufacture of certain swimming pool sanitizing chemicals. The FMC assets that Olin was purchasing included the manufacturing plant for sanitizers.

The FTC challenged the acquisition on the grounds that it would violate federal antitrust laws. The FTC ordered Olin to divest itself of the assets it had acquired from FMC. An administrative law judge agreed with the Commission and concluded that the acquisition would likely result in a substantial lessening of competition in the sanitizers' marketplace. Olin appealed the FTC's divestiture order.

The issue before the Court of Appeals for the Ninth Circuit was whether the FTC had the right to order Olin to divest itself of assets acquired through a merger and whether the acquisition would likely result in substantial lessening of competition. The Court of Appeals affirmed the FTC's ruling that Olin's acquisition of the assets would result in a substantial lessening of competition in the relevant markets. As such, the deal would violate Section 7 of the Clayton Act, 15 U.S.C. 18, and Section 5 of the Federal Trade Commission Act (FTC Act), 15 U.S.C. 45. The court went on to state that the FTC acted within its proper authority in ordering Olin to divest itself of the assets.

Texaco Inc. v. Dagher et al. and ***Shell Oil Co. v. Dagher et al.,*** Docket Nos. 04-805 and 04-814. Reversed: The Ninth Circuit. Argued: January 10, 2006. Decided: February 28, 2006. *Pricing decisions of a legitimate joint venture do not fall within the narrow category of activity that is per se unlawful under Section One of the Sherman Act.*

Is it *per se* illegal under Section 1 of the Sherman Act for a lawful, economically integrated joint venture to set the prices at which the joint venture sells its products? No. *Per se* liability is reserved for only those agreements that are "so plainly anticompetitive that no elaborate study of the industry is needed to establish their illegality." Price-fixing agreements between two or more competitors, otherwise known as horizontal price-fixing agreements, fall into the category of arrangements that are *per se* unlawful. These cases do not present such an agreement, however, because Texaco and Shell Oil did not compete with one another in the relevant market—namely, the sale of gasoline to service stations in the western United States—but instead participated in that market jointly through their investments in Equilon [the joint venture]. In other words, the pricing policy challenged here amounts to little more than price setting by a single entity—albeit within the context of a joint venture—and not a pricing agreement between competing entities with respect to their competing products.

United States v. AT&T Inc., Civil Case No. 17-2511 (RJL) (D.D.C. June 12, 2018). *The US Supreme Court finds that the government failed to show that the merger of defendants AT&T and Time Warner is likely to "substantially . . . lessen competition" in violation of antitrust law.*

On November 20, 2017, the US Department of Justice's Antitrust Division brought this lawsuit, on behalf of the United States of America, to block the merger of AT&T Inc. and Time Warner Inc. as a violation of Section 7 of the Clayton Act, 15 U.S.C. 18. The government claimed, in essence, that permitting AT&T to acquire Time Warner would likely substantially lessen competition in the video programming and distribution market nationwide by enabling AT&T to use Time Warner's "must have" television content to either raise its rivals' video programming costs or, by way of a "blackout," drive those same rivals' customers to its subsidiary, DirecTV. Thus, according to the government, consumers nationwide would be harmed by increased prices for access to Turner networks, notwithstanding the government's concession that this vertical merger would result in hundreds of millions of dollars in annual cost savings to customers and notwithstanding the fact that (unlike in "horizontal" mergers) no competitor will be eliminated by the merger's proposed vertical integration. The court denied the government's request to enjoin the proposed merger.[19] The court found that the government "failed to show that the merger of defendants AT&T and Time Warner is likely to 'substantially . . . lessen competition' in violation of Section 7 of the Clayton Act, 15 U.S.C. § 18."

United States v. Philadelphia National Bank et al., 374 U.S. 321 (1963). *A merger may be rejected on competitiveness grounds, even if it gives economic benefits.*

In November 1960, the Philadelphia National Bank and the Girard Trust Corn Exchange Bank were the second- and third-largest commercial banks in the city of Philadelphia. The boards of directors for the two banks approved a merger of Girard into Philadelphia. The US Department of Justice enjoined the merger, alleging that the consolidation violated the Sherman Anti-Trust Act and the Clayton Act. The US District Court for the Eastern District of Pennsylvania ruled in favor of the banks, and the United States appealed. The question before the Supreme Court was whether a merger that created anticompetitiveness and a monopoly violated the Clayton Act.

The Supreme Court, speaking through Justice William J. Brennan, Jr., rejected the banks' arguments on the basis of the social good. A merger that substantially lessens competition is not saved from violation of the Clayton Act because, on some ultimate reckoning of social or economic debits and credits, it may be deemed beneficial. The court also stated that growth by internal expansion is socially preferable to growth by acquisition.

V. Cases Alleging Violations of Environmental, Health, Safety, and Labor Laws in an M&A Context

Accardi v. Control Data, 658 F. Supp. 881 (S.D.N.Y. 1987), *rev'd and rem'd,* 836 F.2d 126 (2d Cir. 1987). *An acquirer has the right, under certain circumstances, to discontinue benefits to acquired employees.*

The plaintiffs were former employees of International Business Machines (IBM) who worked for the BTSI division. In accord with the Employee Retirement Income Security Act of 1974 (ERISA), they received certain benefits. When IBM sold BTSI to Control Data Corporation (CDC), they entered into a "benefits agreement" under which CDC agreed to continue making benefits payments to the former employees of the division. On June 30, 1985, CDC sold BTSI to Automatic Data Processing (ADP), and the benefits payments stopped. The former BTSI employees requested continuation of their benefits.

The question before the court was whether the plaintiffs were entitled to continued overall benefits under the IBM/CDC benefits agreement, and whether the denial of the plaintiff's request for continued benefits was arbitrary and capricious. The US Court of Appeals of the Second Circuit, affirming a decision by the US District Court in the Southern District of New York, stated that the plaintiffs were no longer eligible employees according to the terms of the benefits agreement. The court ruled that denial of continued benefits was not arbitrary and capricious.

Adcock v. Firestone Tire & Rubber Co., 616 F. Supp. 409 (D.C. Tenn. 1985), *aff'd in part and vacated in part,* 822 F.2d 623 (6th Cir. 1987). *A* *termination pay plan for employees ("tin parachute") may be enforceable following a merger.*

The plaintiffs were nonunion salaried employees of Bridgestone Tire and Rubber Co. On January 1, 1983, Firestone Tire & Rubber Co. sold its Lavergne plant to Bridgestone for $55 million. The 75-page sales agreement included an "employee termination pay plan" stating that Firestone would not terminate the employment of any employee prior to the sale. It also stated that if Bridgestone reduced its workforce, any employee who lost his or her job would receive termination pay. At the time of the suit, Bridgestone had not reduced its workforce, so the plaintiffs remained employed. Nonetheless, they sought to receive termination pay.

The question before the court was whether the termination pay plan was arbitrary and capricious. The US Court of Appeals in the Sixth Circuit, affirming the District Court of Tennessee's interpretation of the federal common law, stated that Bridgestone's application of the termination pay plan was consistent with a fair reading of the plan, and that Firestone's interpretation and application of the termination pay plan was not arbitrary and capricious.

Blau v. Del Monte Corp., 748 F.2d 1348 (9th Cir. 1984). *An employer that denies benefit plans to employees fired following a merger may be found liable for breach of contract under common law.*

In 1966, Del Monte Corp. purchased Granny Good, which became a wholly owned subsidiary of Del Monte. The employees of Granny Good became eligible for coverage under various Del Monte pension and benefit plans. In December 1980, Del Monte sold Granny Good to a group of investors. The new owners kept all but four employees. The four severed employees sued Del Monte for their severance benefits.

The question before the court was whether the denial of the severance benefits violated ERISA and whether the denial was arbitrary and capricious. The Ninth Circuit Court of Appeals held that the actions by Del Monte were arbitrary and capricious, and that ERISA preempted state common-law theories of breach of contract.

Blessit v. Retirement Plan for Employees of Dixie Engine Co., 817 F.2d 1528 (11th Cir. 1987), *rec'd in part and rem'd,* 836 F.2d 1571 (11th Cir.

1988) *vacated* 848 F.2d 1164 (11th Cir. 1988). *An employer under certain conditions has a right to reduce benefits to reflect fewer years of service following postacquisition termination.*

The plaintiffs were employees of Dixie Engine Co. when it established an ERISA plan in 1972. Dixie Engine Co. was sold in 1982 and the ERISA plan was terminated. Employees brought action against their employer for violation of ERISA, claiming that upon termination of a defined benefits plan they were entitled to receive the full, unreduced pension benefits they would have received had they continued to work until normal retirement age.

The question before the court was whether ERISA requires the defined benefits plan to pay an employee the full, unreduced benefits the employee would have received had he or she continued to work until normal retirement age. The US Court of Appeals in the Eleventh Circuit held that when a plan terminates, ERISA does not require that employees receive full benefits, only the benefits provided for under the plan (that is, the benefits calculated on the basis of their actual years of service as of the termination date).

Certainteed Corp. v. Celotex Corp., 2005 WL 217032 (Del. Ch. Jan. 24, 2005). *Court of Chancery holds that claims accrue upon receipt of inquiry notice of wrongful act.*

The plaintiff entered into an asset purchase agreement (APA) with the defendant. The defendant had assumed indemnification obligations relating to the assets sold. After the sale, the plaintiff experienced various losses that it believed fell to the defendant to cover. This suit then ensued. The plaintiff brought a breach of contract action against defendant sellers under their asset purchase agreement for indemnification of losses and other related claims. The court dismissed some on account of late disclosures and the lateness of the complaint itself. However, it did accept environmental remediation-work claims as well as a products liability claim involving third-party indemnification based on the plaintiff's injuries incurred as a result of the defendant's sale of defective materials prior to the APA.

Fall River Dyeing and Finish Corp. v. NLRB, 482 U.S. 27 (1987). *An acquirer does not have to bargain with a union unless the union is certified and continues to represent a majority of employees.*

In 1952, Sterlingwale began operating a textile dyeing plant; the plant continued to run for the next 30 years. For nearly its entire existence, the production and maintenance personnel of Sterlingwale were members of a union. Sterlingwale, along with the entire textile dyeing industry, began to suffer adverse economic conditions in late 1979. In February 1982, Sterlingwale laid off its employees and made an assignment for the benefit of its creditors.

In the fall of 1982, a former officer of Sterlingwale, together with the president of a creditor, formed an entity that purchased the assets of Sterlingwale from the auctioneer. Over time, the entity employed many former employees of Sterlingwale. The union requested that the entity recognize it as the bargaining agent for the employees, and the entity refused. The union then filed unfair labor practice charges with the National Labor Relations Board.

The question before the court was whether a successor employer is obligated to bargain with a union representing its predecessor's employees. The US Supreme Court held that the successor employer's obligation to bargain with the union representing its predecessor's employees is contingent not only upon certification of the union but also on whether a majority of its employees were employed by its predecessor.

Halliburton Co. Benefits Committee v. Graves, 463 F.3d 360 (5th Cir. 2006). *A merger agreement constituted an amendment of the target's welfare plan under ERISA, and therefore the merger agreement's no-third-party-beneficiaries clause did not apply.*

Halliburton acquired Dresser Industries in 1998 via a forward triangular merger. Dresser's retiree medical benefits were superior to Halliburton's at the time of the merger. In order to preserve Dresser's superior benefits, the merger agreement provided that Dresser's nominees to the combined companies' board would maintain such benefits for Dresser employees for three years following the transaction. The parties included a standard no-third-parties-beneficiaries clause, meaning that the clause did not create rights for any party other than the two constituent corporations (e.g., employees and retirees).

Halliburton sought a declaratory judgment in 2003 in the US Federal Court in the Southern District of Texas to affirm its right to reduce

Dresser retirees' benefits to those of Halliburton's. The district court held that the Halliburton-Dresser merger agreement constituted an amendment to Dresser's welfare plan under ERISA. Because of this amendment, the no-third-party-beneficiaries rule did not apply. The constituent corporations had placed specific time limits on the benefits that active Dresser employees were to receive, but did not impose such limitations on retirees' medical benefits. Accordingly, the court concluded that the provision of the merger agreement that allowed Halliburton to change retiree medical benefits only if the company made similar changes to medical benefits for current employees was a revision to the retiree medical program plan documents that restricted Halliburton's otherwise unfettered right to make changes to the Dresser retiree medical program. The 5th Circuit Court of Appeals upheld the lower court's decision.

B.E. Tilley v. Mead Corp., 927 F.2d 756 (4th Cir. 1991). *There is an important distinction between contingent liabilities and accrued benefits in the termination of a pension plan.*

The plaintiffs were employees of Lynchburg Foundry Company prior to its buyout by Mead Corporation. The employees then fell under the Mead retirement plan, which provided for early retirement benefits commencing at age 55. Subsequently, Mead sold off the foundry and terminated the plan. The plaintiffs received a sum of money equal to their portion of the present value of the plan reduced by 5 percent for each year the participant was under the age of 65. Plaintiffs sued Mead in Virginia state court alleging that Mead's failure to pay the present value of the unreduced early retirement benefits violated ERISA. Mead removed the case to the Federal District Court for the Western District of Virginia, where the court granted Mead summary disposition, holding that the plaintiffs were not entitled to the unreduced early retirement benefits. The Court of Appeals for the Fourth Circuit reversed the District Court, and the Supreme Court reversed and remanded to the Court of Appeals.

The Court of Appeals held that, under the terms of ERISA, unreduced early retirement benefits that employees would have been eligible for upon reaching age 62 were "contingent liabilities" that had to be satisfied prior to reversion of the plan's surplus assets to the employer upon termination of the plan. They were not "accrued benefits" that employees had a vested right to receive in full upon plan termination.

Yolton et al. v. El Paso Tennessee Pipeline Co., 435 F.3d 571 (6th Cir. 2006, cert. denied U.S. (U.S. Nov. 6, 2006) (No. 06-201); ***Yolton v. El Paso Tennessee Pipeline Co.,*** 668 F. Supp. 2d 1023 (E.D. Mich. 2009). *Retiree benefits under a collective bargaining agreement may live on after a merger, even if they have been promised for a lifetime and thus exceed an agreed-upon cap.*

In this case, the Sixth Circuit ruled that retirees and surviving spouses of Case (which had become a subsidiary of El Paso Tennessee Pipeline Co., eventually named CNH America, LLC) were entitled to lifetime healthcare coverage pursuant to contracts negotiated between their employer and their union, the United Auto Workers (UAW). The court recognized that there is no statutory right to lifetime healthcare benefits, but also found that life and health insurance benefits carry with them an inference that the parties intended them to continue for life. El Paso appealed to the US Supreme Court, citing an agreed-upon cap on benefits, but the court declined to review this case. In a subsequent case in 2009, the court found that CNH remained contractually liable for above-cap costs of the retirees' vested health insurance benefits.

VI. Cases Dealing with Jurisdiction or Right to Sue Following a Merger

Berger v. Intelident Solutions, 2006 WL 1132079 (Del. Apr. 26, 2006). *Delaware Supreme Court reverses* forum non conveniens *dismissal.*

Plaintiff, a minority shareholder in a Florida corporation, filed a breach of fiduciary duty action in connection with a freeze-out merger. The sole defendants were a Nevada limited partnership, which was the ultimate controlling entity of the Florida corporation, and a Delaware corporation formed to serve as an intermediate holding company in connection with the merger. Defendants moved to dismiss based on *forum non conveniens,* arguing that forcing them to litigate in Delaware would impose an overwhelming hardship. The Court of Chancery granted that motion, finding that the dispute would be more appropriately litigated in Florida and that Defendants had met the exacting standard applied in assessing *forum non conveniens* motions.

Chicago Bridge & Iron Co. v. Westinghouse Electric Co. LLC, 2017 WL 2774563 (Del. June 28, 2017).[20] *If two parties agree to a limited scope for postclosing adjustments, their agreement stands even if one party presents reasons for expanding beyond that scope.*

In this case, the court agreed on a time limit for presenting materials to an auditor in the course of a merger. This case involved the purchase by Westinghouse Electric Company of a subsidiary of the Chicago Bridge & Iron Company. Westinghouse designs nuclear power plants and Chicago Bridge builds them. They had done business together for many years prior to the closing on the purchase of Chicago Bridge's subsidiary by Westinghouse. One of the reasons for the purchase was that two nuclear plants that Chicago Bridge had been building were beset by cost overruns and delays, and Chicago Bridge wanted to limit its future exposure. The deal terms included some unusual provisions such as a bar to post-closing liability for certain representations by Chicago Bridge. The intent of the deal was to transfer future liabilities on the construction of the two nuclear power plants to Westinghouse.

The deal terms provided for post-closing adjustments to determine net working capital, as well as earnout provisions. Any disputes regarding net working capital were to be presented to an independent auditor for a binding and non-appealable decision.

The net working capital adjustment was intended to address changes from the date of the signing of the agreement until the date of closing. Westinghouse wanted the independent auditor to make determinations on time periods and claims that exceeded that limited scope. Chicago Bridge sought an injunction to prevent Westinghouse from presenting those issues to the independent auditor. The Court of Chancery ruled in favor of Westinghouse. The Supreme Court in this decision reversed the opinion of the Court of Chancery and ruled in favor of Chicago Bridge.

Examen, Inc. v. VantagePoint Venture Partners 1996, 873 A.2d 318 (Del. Ch. 2005). *Court of Chancery applies internal affairs doctrine to stockholder vote on merger.*

The plaintiff, a Delaware corporation, sought a judicial declaration that Delaware law governed a stockholder vote on a pending merger because if the vote was governed by Delaware law, common stockholders and preferred stockholders would vote on the merger as a single class. The defendant, a large venture capital firm owning 83 percent of the corporation's preferred stock, argued that California law controlled because if California law were to apply in determining the voting rights of the Delaware corporation's stockholders in connection with the proposed merger, the preferred stockholders would have the right to vote as a separate class, effectively giving the defendant a veto over the merger. The court granted the plaintiff's motion for judgment on the pleadings, finding that Delaware law applied because this case was governed by the internal affairs doctrine.

Gollust v. Mendell, 498 U.S. 1023 (1991). *Under 16b, an ex-stockholder of a company has standing to sue as long as it owns a security traded by the defendant.*

Mendell filed a 16b (insider trading) complaint against a collection of limited partnerships, general partnerships, individual partners, and corporations alleging that these entities, acting as one, were liable for 16b violations with regard to trading activities of Viacom stock. Six months after the complaint was filed, Viacom was acquired by another company and Mendell exchanged his Viacom stock for the new stock. The question before the court was whether a 16b action can be pursued by any party other than an issuer or holder of a security.

The US Supreme Court held that it was not necessary for a plaintiff to continue to hold stock of the issuer in order to maintain a 16b action where the plaintiff has a financial stake in the parent corporation of the issuer. However, the Court also stated that the plaintiff who seeks to recover insider profits must own a security of the issuer whose stock is traded by the 16b defendant.

Neuberger Berman Real Estate Income Fund, Inc. v. Lola Brown Trust No. 1B, Civil No. AMD 04-3056 (D. Md. Oct. 22, 2004). *The Investment Company Act of 1940 does not preclude a closed-ended investment company from adopting a poison pill.*

Investment trusts affiliated with Stewart Horesji began to accumulate shares in the Neuberger Berman Real Estate Income Fund (the Fund), a close-ended investment fund incorporated in Maryland. The Horesji group filed a Schedule 13D stating that the trusts had acquired 10.05 percent and intended to buy over 50 percent, intended to replace the directors, and intended to replace the Fund's adviser with Horesji affiliates. The Horesji trusts started a tender offer for 1,825,000 shares, enough to bring the group's ownership up to 50.01 percent. After a committee of independent directors of the Fund concluded the tender offer was not in the best interests of stockholders, the board adopted a rights plan ("poison pill") with an 11 percent threshold.

The Horesji trusts brought suit, alleging that the poison pill violated section 18(d) of the Investment Company Act of 1940 (ICA). Under this section, the only warrants that a registered management company is permitted to issue are warrants that expire not later than 120 days after issuance and that are issued ratably to all shareholders.

The rights issued by the Fund expire on the 120th day after execution of the rights agreement. The Horesji trusts argued that the rights weren't issued ratably to all shareholders, because shareholders owning above 11 percent would end up being treated differently from other shareholders. The court rejected this argument, noting that courts have consistently found that poison pills do not violate state statutes containing antidiscrimination provisions similar to those in section 18(d). The court noted that the rights were issued proportionately to a class of shareholders, with one right being attached to each share. For similar reasons, the court rejected the Horesji trusts' argument that the rights plan violated section 18(i) of the ICA, which requires that each share have equal voting rights. The poison pill did not change the fact that all shares were granted equal voting rights. According to the court, the triggering of the pill has nothing to do with the voting rights of the shares themselves.

OSI Systems, Inc. v. Instrumentarium Corp., 2006 WL 656993 (Del. Ch. Mar. 14, 2006). *Court of Chancery finds violation of GAAP claim subject to arbitration because claim was actually a breach of warranty and representation.*

In this case, plaintiff buyer and defendant seller in the sale of a business argued over the type of contractual arbitration that should be used to solve a disagreement over the form of arbitration each preferred. The Court of Chancery granted the seller's motion on the pleadings because the buyer's claims were for breaches of representations and warranties, which fell under the indemnity provisions of the contract and the form of arbitration set forth in those provisions must be used by buyer.

VantagePoint Venture Partners 1996 v. Examen, Inc., 871 A.2d 1108 (Del. 2005). *The Delaware Supreme Court affirms the Court of Chancery's denial of a request for permanent injunction against a shareholder seeking to challenge merger after merger is consummated.*

This case arose out of an earlier dispute in which VantagePoint Venture Partners (VantagePoint), an investor holding the majority of a series of preferred stock in Examen, Inc. (Examen), a Delaware corporation, sought to veto a merger between Examen and a Delaware subsidiary of Reed Elsevier Inc. VantagePoint argued for a determination that under California law the holders of the series of preferred stock issued by Examen had a right to a class vote in the merger. The Court of Chancery held that California law did not apply and that all of the stockholders were permitted to vote on the proposed merger. On appeal, the Delaware Supreme Court affirmed the Chancery Court's decision. The high court found that because this was an internal matter, the "internal affairs doctrine" should apply, and noted further that "the United States Supreme Court has recognized the constitutional imperatives of the internal affairs doctrine."

Virginia Bankshares, Inc. v. Sandberg, 501 U.S. 1083 (1991). *Even if a shareholder does not vote for a merger, the shareholder may sue over any material misstatements made about the transaction.*

This case occurred as part of a proposed "freeze-out" merger, in which First American Bank of Virginia (Bank) would be merged into petitioner Virginia Bankshares, Inc. (VBI), a wholly owned subsidiary of petitioner First American Bankshares, Inc. (FABI). The Bank's executive committee and board approved a price of $42 a share for the minority stockholders, who would lose their interests in the Bank after the merger. Virginia law required only that the merger proposal be submitted to a vote at a shareholders' meeting, preceded by a circulation of an informational statement to the shareholders. Nonetheless, Bank directors solicited proxies for voting on the proposal.

This solicitation urged the proposal's adoption and stated that the plan had been approved because of its opportunity for the minority shareholders to receive a high value for their stock. Respondent Sandberg did not give her proxy and filed suit in District Court after the merger was approved. She sought damages from petitioners for, among other reasons, soliciting proxies by means of materially false or misleading statements in violation of 14(a) of the Securities Exchange Act of 1934 and the SEC's Rule 14a-9.

Among other things, Ms. Sandberg alleged that the directors believed they had no alternative but to recommend the merger if they wished to remain on the board. At trial, she obtained a jury instruction, based on language in *Mills v. Electric Auto-Lite Co.,* 396 U.S. 375 (1970), that she could prevail without showing her own reliance on the alleged misstatements, so long as they were material and the proxy solicitation was an "essential link" in the merger process. She was awarded an amount equal to the difference between the offered price and her stock's true value. The remaining respondents prevailed in a separate action raising similar claims.

The Court of Appeals affirmed, holding that certain statements in the proxy solicitation, including the one regarding the stock's value, were materially misleading, and that respondents could maintain the action even though their votes had not been needed to effectuate the merger.

VII. ADDITIONAL CASES

Cases Involving Takeover Defense

First Citizens Bancshares, Inc. v. KS Bancorp, Inc., No. 18 CVS 2022, 2018 WL 1457547 (N.C. Super. Ct. Mar. 21, 2018). *A bank's poison pill fails to pass court muster, leading to an out-of-court settlement with plaintiff shareholders.*

First Citizens Bancshares, Inc., the plaintiff, moved to enjoin a shareholder rights plan implemented by KS Bancorp, Inc. ("KS Bancorp"), the defendant, arguing that KS Bancorp's plan violated North Carolina law by discriminating against only certain shares of stock within a larger class of shares. The court held, among other findings, that First Citizens would suffer irreparable harm if KS Bancorp were permitted to use "an illegal device" to dilute First Citizen's ownership stake, impairing other shareholders' opportunity to sell their shares to First Citizens at a favorable price. The court granted the plaintiff's motion for preliminary injunction and immediately enjoined and prohibited the defendants from taking any action under the shareholder rights plan or from adopting "any similar 'poison pill' plans while this litigation is pending." On May 16, 2018, KS Bancorp announced that it had reached a settlement with First Citizens Bancshares resolving all litigation claims.[21]

Moran v. Household Int'l, 500 A.2d 1346, 1357 (Del. 1985). *In this Delaware Supreme Court decision, the directors of Household received the benefit of the business judgment rule in their adoption of the Rights Plan.*

They had the statutory authority to do so under Delaware law. The court held that the Directors adopted the plan in the "good faith belief that it was necessary to protect Household from coercive acquisition techniques." The court found that the Household board was informed on plan details, and Household demonstrated that the Plan was reasonable in relation to the threat posed.

The court stated, "While we conclude for present purposes that the Household Directors are protected by the business judgment rule, that does not end the matter. The ultimate response to an actual takeover bid must be judged by the Directors' actions at that time, and nothing we say here relieves them of their basic fundamental duties to the corporation and its stockholders."

Cases Involving M&A Advisors, Lenders, or Insurers

Barker Capital LLC v. Rebus LLC, 2006 WL 246572 (Del. Super. Ct. Jan. 12, 2006). *Superior Court finds that plaintiff was entitled to advisory fee pursuant to contract.*

The plaintiff, Barker Capital LLC (Barker), a Delaware LLC, sued Rebus LLC (Rebus), also a Delaware LLC, Mark A. Fox (Fox), and Twinlab Corporation (Twinlab), a Delaware corporation, alleging breach of contract, *quantum meruit,* tortious interference with contract, and unjust enrichment. Rebus and Barker entered into an Engagement Agreement, pursuant to which Barker would act as Rebus's nonexclusive financial advisor to identify and consummate a transaction to purchase two medical newsletters. Under the terms of the Engagement Agreement, Barker was entitled to an Advisory Fee in the amount of 2.5 percent of the transaction's value. Both sides moved for summary judgment. The court found that Barker was entitled to 2.5 percent of a $12 million loan associated with the deal, but was not entitled to a percentage of a $35 million loan connected with the deal. The court also found against the plaintiff on the *quantum meruit* claim because the plaintiff had been made whole when the court ruled in his favor on the breach of contract claim. Turning to the tortious interference claim, which was only alleged against Fox, the court found that it did not have the subject matter jurisdiction to pierce the corporate veil.

In re Cox Communications Inc. Shareholders Litigation, 879 A.2d 604 (Del. Ch. June 6, 2005). *Court of Chancery slashes fees to plaintiffs' counsel where complaint was filed on negotiable merger proposal.*

Vice Chancellor Strine ruled on a fee request in a case arising out of a proposal by the Cox Family to take Cox Communications private. The Family proposed a merger on fully negotiable terms with an opening bid of $32. The proposal was immediately followed by a flurry of class action lawsuits, as well as the formation of a special committee to review and evaluate the terms of the offer. The Family tentatively agreed with a special committee of independent directors to a price of $34.75 per share subject to approval by a majority of the minority stockholders and conditioned on settlement of the outstanding lawsuits, a final fairness opinion, and agreement on the terms of a final merger agreement.

Counsel for the plaintiffs eventually agreed that the $34.75 price accepted by the special committee was fair, accepted the other terms of the transaction, and agreed to settle their claims. After settlement, the Cox family agreed not to oppose a request by plaintiffs' counsel for payment of attorneys' fees of up to $4.95 million. Certain Cox stockholders, however, did object to the fee request, and the Court of Chancery heard their objections. The Court slashed a $4.95 million fee request to an award of $1.275 million and advised the plaintiff's bar to consider that award "generous."

Delaware Ins. Guar. Ass'n v. Christiana Care Health Services, 2006 WL 196382 (Del. Jan. 24, 2006). *Delaware Supreme Court reverses Superior Court and finds that defendant became an "insured" for purposes of 18 Del. C. § 4211(2)(a) by operation of law after named insured merged into defendant.*

The Delaware Insurance Guaranty Association (DIGA) sought reimbursement from Christiana Care Health Services (CCHS) pursuant to one of the Delaware Insurance Guaranty Association Act's provisions for claims paid on behalf of an insolvent insurer. In this case the insolvent insurer had insured a corporation that merged into CCHS. The Superior Court granted CCHS's motion for summary judgment, finding that CCHS was not an "insured" under the insurance policy. Reversing the lower court, the Delaware Supreme Court found that a court must consider the purpose and intent of 18 Del. C. Section 4211 when determining if a company is an "insured." A court may not rely on terms in an insurance policy that are inconsistent with the purpose and intent of Section 4211. The Supreme Court found that CCHS became an insured after the named insured merged into the defendant, and CCHS is obligated to reimburse DIGA pursuant to Section 4211.

K.M.C. Co., Inc., v. Irving Trust Co., 757 F. 2d 752 (6th Cir. 1985). *Every contract, including a loan, implies good faith, and when a lender refuses to advance more funds without giving notice, this refusal may violate that faith.*

In 1979, K.M.C. entered into a financing agreement with Irving Trust Co., whereby Irving Trust would provide K.M.C. with a line of credit to a maximum amount of $3.0 million in exchange for Irving Trust's holding a security interest in K.M.C.'s assets. The line of credit was increased a year later to $3.5 million. In March 1982, without notice to K.M.C., Irving Trust refused to advance $800,000, which would have placed the loan value at just under $3.5 million. K.M.C. suffered a collapse and sued Irving for breach of the financing agreement.

The question before the court was whether Irving had breached its contract with K.M.C. The Sixth Circuit Court of Appeals affirmed the decision and stated that there is "implied in every contract an obligation of good faith." The court further stated that unless Irving's decision to refuse to advance funds without prior notice was made in good faith and in the reasonable exercise of its discretion , the good-faith obligation imposed on Irving a duty to give notice.

RBC Capital Markets, LLC, v. Jervis, No. 140 (Del. 2015). *A financial advisor may be held liable for aiding and abetting a board's breach of its fiduciary duty if the advisor knows that the board is breaching its fiduciary duty and participates in the breach.*

Upholding the lower court's decision in *In re: Rural/Metro Corp. S'holders Litig.*, C.A. No. 6350-VCL (Del. Ch. Mar. 7, 2014), the court found that a financial advisor may be liable for aiding and abetting a board's breach of its fiduciary duty if the advisor knows that the board is breaching its fiduciary duty and participates in the breach. The case focused on the role of RBC bank, which was held liable for aiding and abetting a breach of fiduciary duty on the part of the board of directors of the company when they sold it to Warburg Pincus. (The Rural Metro director defendants had already settled in 2013; prior to litigation, director liability had not been determined.) Counsel for the defense pointed out that there was no breach of fiduciary duty in this matter, so the advisor should not be held liable for abetting it. Giving some credence to this view, the court said that "our narrow ruling premised on these unusual facts effects no shifts in the *Revlon* landscape, affirming that (as stated in an amicus brief from the National Association of Corporate Directors), "directors must be able to consider freely the exploration of strategic alternatives (including a sale), without such discussions triggering *Revlon*'s duty to maximize short-term value."

Varjabedian v. Emulex, No. 16-55088, 2018 WL 1882905 (9th Cir. Apr. 20, 2018). *In a lower court decision appealed to and dismissed by the US Supreme Court (April 23, 2019), a judicial panel affirms in part and reverses in part the district court's dismissal of a putative securities class action complaint arising from a corporate merger.*

Reversing in part, and disagreeing with five other circuits, the panel concluded that claims under Section 14(e) of the Securities Exchange Act of 1934, regarding unlawful tender offer practices, require only a showing of negligence, not a showing of scienter. In other words, this decision said that even if an error in a prospectus was not intentional, it can still lead to a finding of liability under Section 14(e).

The panel affirmed the district court's conclusion that Section 14(d)(4) of the Exchange Act does not create a private right of action for shareholders confronted with a tender offer. It also affirmed the court's dismissal of the complaint as to one defendant because it was not a proper defendant.

Because the plaintiff's Section 14(e) claim survived, his claim under another section of the Exchange Act (Section 20(a), regarding insider trading) also remained. The panel remanded for the district court to reconsider defendants' motion to dismiss under a negligence standard.

Cases Alleging Violation of Tax Law

Indopco, Inc. v. C.I.R., 503 U.S. 79 (1992). *Expenses incurred in a specific friendly acquisition may be capital expenditures that created a benefit, not ordinary business expenses, and so may not be tax-deductible.*

In 1977, Indopco, formerly named National Starch and Chemical Corporation, and Unilever United States, Inc., entered into a "reverse subsidiary cash merger" specifically designed to be a tax-free transaction for National Starch's largest shareholders.

In its 1978 federal income tax return, National Starch claimed a deduction for the approximately $2.3 million in investment banking fees it paid to Morgan Stanley & Co. as ordinary and necessary expenses under Section 162(a) of the IRC. The IRS disallowed the deduction, and National Starch sought a redetermination including the $490,000 legal fees it paid its attorney as well. The question before the court was whether National Starch could deduct its expenses as ordinary and necessary business expenses.

The US Tax Court and the Third Circuit Court of Appeals denied the deduction, saying that the expenses did not "create or enhance . . . a separate or distinct additional asset." The US Supreme Court granted *certiorari* and held that investment banking, legal, and other costs incurred by the target corporation were not deductible as ordinary and necessary business expenses, but instead should be capitalized as long-term benefits to the corporation.

Newark Morning Ledger Co. v. United States, 507 U.S. 546 (1993). *An asset is depreciable if it can be valued, and if the value declines over time.*

In 1976, the Herald company purchased substantially all of the outstanding shares of Booth Newspapers, Inc. The Herald company, which was succeeded by the Newark Morning Ledger, claimed depreciation in the amount of $67.8 million, which represented the depreciable value of the future income stream from the newspaper's current subscribers.

The question before the court was whether an intangible asset such as a subscriber list can be depreciated. The Federal District Court for the District of New Jersey entered a judgment in favor of Newark Morning Ledger Co. and the Court of Appeals for the Third District reversed. The US Supreme Court reversed the Court of Appeals, stating that an asset is depreciable if it is capable of being valued and if the asset's value diminishes over time. The court concluded that if a taxpayer can prove that a particular asset can be valued, and that the asset has a limited useful life, the taxpayer may depreciate the asset's value over its useful life regardless of how much the asset appears to reflect the expectancy of continued patronage.

Cases Involving Patent Claims

Helsinn Healthcare S.A. v. Teva Pharmaceuticals USA, Inc., et al., No. 17-1229, 586 U.S. __, slip op. (Jan. 22, 2019). *An inventor's sale of an invention to a third party who is obligated to keep the invention confidential can qualify as prior art.*

While Helsinn Healthcare S.A., maker of a palonosetron-based treatment for chemotherapy-induced nausea and vomiting was developing its palonosetron product, it entered into two agreements with another company granting that company the right to distribute, promote, market, and sell a 0.25 mg dose of palonosetron in the United States. The agreements required that the company keep confidential any proprietary information received under the agreements. Nearly two years later, in January 2003, Helsinn filed a provisional patent application covering a 0.25 mg dose of palonosetron. Over the next 10 years, Helsinn filed four patent applications that claimed priority to the January 2003 date. Helsinn filed its fourth patent application in 2013. That patent (the '219 patent) covered a fixed dose of 0.25 mg of palonosetron in a 5 ml solution and was covered by the Leahy-Smith America Invents Act (AIA). In 2011, respondents Teva Pharmaceutical Industries, Ltd., and Teva Pharmaceuticals USA, Inc. (collectively Teva), sought approval to market a generic 0.25 mg palonosetron product. Helsinn sued Teva for infringing its patents, including the '219 patent. Teva countered that the '219 patent was invalid under the "on sale" provision of the AIA—which precludes a person from obtaining a patent on an invention that was "in public use, on sale, or otherwise available to the public before the effective filing date of the claimed invention," 35 U.S.C. §102(a)(1)—because the 0.25 mg dose was "on sale" more than one year before Helsinn filed the provisional patent application in 2003. The District Court held that the AIA's "on sale" provision did not apply because the public disclosure of the agreements did not disclose the 0.25 mg dose. The Federal Circuit reversed, holding that the sale was publicly disclosed, regardless of whether the details of the invention were publicly disclosed in the terms of the sale agreements. The US Supreme Court affirmed that decision, holding that a commercial sale to a third party who is required to keep the invention confidential may place the invention "on sale" under §102(a).

Cases Involving Insolvent Companies

Big Lot Stores v. Bain Capital Fund VII, 2006 WL 846121 (Del. Ch. Mar. 28, 2006). *The Court of Chancery dismisses the complaint because a creditor erroneously asserted derivative claims as direct in the hope of escaping bankruptcy court jurisdiction.*

In 2000, in a sponsored management buyout, a corporation sold a subsidiary business that operated a chain of toy stores (KB Toys) in exchange for $257.1 million in cash and a $45 million note due in 2010. In 2002, the new owners refinanced the business and distributed approximately $120 million to the buyout sponsor, affiliates, two officers and directors of the subsidiary that invested in the buyout, and others. In 2004, KB Toys filed for Chapter 11 bankruptcy. Plaintiff Big Lots, Inc., an unsecured creditor and holder of the $45 million note, brought this action asserting direct claims of breach of fiduciary duties, fraud, and civil conspiracy. The plaintiff sought recovery for the amount due on the note and restitution for alleged unjust enrichment. The Court of Chancery dismissed the complaint namely because the claims were derivative in nature, not direct, and thus belong to the bankruptcy estate.

Credit Lyonnais Bank Nederland, N.V. v. Pathe Communications Corp., 1991 WL 277613 (Del. Ch. Dec. 30, 1991). *In a change of control, directors have a fiduciary duty to the enterprise, which has numerous stakeholders, not only shareholders.*

This case involved the leveraged buyout of MGM-Pathe Communications Co., which became distressed. The court found that "At least where a corporation is operating in the vicinity of insolvency, the board of directors is not merely the agent of the residual risk bearers [i.e., shareholders] but owes its duty to the corporate enterprise." In such instances, the board has an "obligation to the community interest that sustained the corporation, to exercise judgment in an informed, good faith effort to maximize the corporation's long-term wealth creating capacity." In *Credit Lyonnais,* the court explained that directors have a fiduciary duty to the enterprise, which has numerous stakeholders whose interests must be protected to maintain the business.[22]

Flowserve Corp. v. Burns Int'l Servs. Corp., 2006 WL 739886 (D. Del. Mar. 22, 2006). *District Court enjoins plaintiff from initiating third-party proceedings against defendants and from pursuing global settlement strategy in pending asbestos cases.*

The plaintiff filed a complaint seeking a declaratory judgment of its right to indemnification in asbestos litigation under the terms of a stock purchase agreement executed by its predecessor-in-interest, which had acquired a subsidiary of Borg-Warner Corp. (BWC). Defendant Burns International Services Corp. (Burns), which had purchased BWC's insurance assets at a liquidation sale, filed a counterclaim alleging that its indemnification obligations to the plaintiff only arose out of a later letter agreement, and that once BWC's insurance was exhausted, the plaintiff had to pay the costs of defending and resolving the asbestos claims. During the pendency of the instant case, the plaintiff informed Burns that (1) it had terminated the counsel chosen by Burns to defend the asbestos claims; (2) it was choosing its own counsel; and (3) it was directing its new counsel to file third-party complaints against defendants and to pursue global settlements in the underlying asbestos cases (together, the "threatened actions"). Burns then sought a temporary restraining order and preliminary injunction to enjoin the plaintiffs from taking the threatened actions.

Merit Management Group, L.P. v. FTI Consulting, Inc., No. 16-784, 583 U.S. (2018). *The safe harbor for transfers involving financial institutions does not protect allegedly fraudulent transfers in which financial institutions served as mere conduits.*

The US Bankruptcy Code, in 11 U.S.C. §548(a), allows trustees to set aside and recover certain transfers for the benefit of the bankruptcy estate, including certain fraudulent transfers "of an interest of the debtor in property." It also sets out a number of limits on the exercise of these avoiding powers, including a securities safe harbor, which provides that the trustee may not avoid a transfer that is a "settlement payment" made by or to (or for the benefit of) a financial institution, or that is a transfer made by or to (or for the benefit of) a financial institution "in connection with a securities contract."

In this case, Valley View Downs, LP, and Bedford Downs Management Corp. entered into an agreement under which Valley View, if it got the last harness-racing license in Pennsylvania, would purchase all of Bedford Downs's stock for $55 million. Valley View was granted the license and arranged for the Cayman Islands branch of Credit Suisse to wire $55 million to third-party escrow agent Citizens Bank of Pennsylvania. The Bedford Downs shareholders, including petitioner Merit Management Group, LP, deposited their stock certificates into escrow. Citizens Bank disbursed the $55 million over two installments according to the agreement, of which petitioner Merit received $16.5 million. Although Valley View secured the harness-racing license, it was unable to achieve its goal of opening a racetrack casino. Valley View and its parent company, Centaur, LLC, filed for Chapter 11 bankruptcy. Respondent FTI Consulting, Inc., was appointed to serve as trustee of the Centaur litigation trust.

FTI then sought to avoid the transfer from Valley View to Merit for the sale of Bedford Downs's Syllabus stock, arguing that it was constructively fraudulent under of the US Bankruptcy Code. Merit, however, contended that a safe harbor in the code (the §546(e) safe harbor) barred

FTI from avoiding the transfer because it was a settlement payment allegedly made by, to, or for the benefit of financial institutions, Credit Suisse and Citizens Bank. The District Court agreed with Merit, but the Seventh Circuit reversed, holding that the safe harbor language did not protect transfers in which financial institutions served as mere conduits. The US Supreme Court agreed with the Seventh Circuit, finding that safe harbor did not apply, because the financial institutions involved were mere conduits of the transaction.

Trenwick Am. Litig. Trust v. Billett, 931 A.2d 438 (Del. 2007). *The Delaware Supreme Court affirms the Delaware Court of Chancery's rejection of a "deepening insolvency" theory in case involving a postmerger bankruptcy.*

The Delaware courts have struggled for the last 15 years over the scope of the duties of directors to creditors when their company is in the vicinity of insolvency. In two landmark decisions, the first in 2004, and just recently in this case, the Court of Chancery sought to define the limits of that duty. Indeed, in this decision, involving a company that became insolvent after a merger, the Court rejected the very idea that there is a duty to avoid taking risks that may have the effect of deepening the insolvency of a Delaware corporation, at least in most circumstances. In a brief opinion referring to the Chancery Court decision, the Delaware Supreme Court affirmed.

Cases Involving International Transactions

Blechner v. Daimler-Benz AG, 2006 WL 167835 (D. Del. Jan. 24, 2005). *District Court dismisses potential securities fraud class action involving only foreign parties.*

The plaintiffs, on behalf of themselves and other foreign shareholders who invested in securities of DaimlerChrysler AG, filed a class action complaint alleging securities fraud in connection with the merger of Chrysler Corporation and Daimler-Benz AG. The defendants moved to dismiss the complaint.

The court rejected the plaintiffs' argument that the complaint alleged sufficient conduct occurring in the United States to warrant the exercise of extraterritorial jurisdiction, and on those grounds dismissed the case. Specifically, the court held that because the conduct complained of took place primarily outside of the United States and because the plaintiff investors were foreign investors who had no connection to the United States, did not surrender any shares on an American market, and did not suffer any effects from the alleged fraud in the United States, the exercise of extraterritorial jurisdiction was inappropriate.

Madison Real Estate Immobbilien-Anlagegesellschaft Beschrankt Haftende KG v. GENO One Financial Place, 2006 WL 456779 (Del. Ch. Feb. 22, 2006). *Court of Chancery denies motion for expedited preliminary injunction hearing for lack of "colorable claim" demonstrating imminent irreparable harm.*

The plaintiff is a German entity organized under that country's laws, as is the second named German limited liability defendant. The latter party is also a general partner in the first defendant entity. The plaintiff was one of two bidders that made an unregulated tender offer for a part of the first-named defendant's Delaware limited partnership interest. The plaintiff filed a motion in the Court of Chancery for expedited injunction proceedings, seeking to enjoin the defendant's general partner.

The Wharf (Holdings) Ltd. et al. v. United International Holdings, Inc., et al., Certiorari to the United States Court of Appeals for the Tenth Circuit No. 00-347. Argued March 21, 2001–Decided May 21, 2001. *Stock options are considered a security for the purpose of interpreting liability under Rule 10(b)5.*

The Wharf (Holdings) Limited verbally promised United International Holdings, Inc., an option to buy 10 percent of the stock in Wharf's Hong Kong cable system if United rendered certain services, but internal Wharf documents suggested that Wharf never intended to carry out its promise. United fulfilled its obligation, but Wharf refused to permit it to exercise the option. United sued in Federal District Court, claiming that Wharf's conduct violated, *inter alia,* Section 10(b) of the Securities Exchange Act of 1934, which prohibits using "any manipulative or deceptive device or contrivance in connection with the purchase or sale of any security." A jury found for United, and the Tenth Circuit affirmed. The court held that Wharf's secret intent not to honor the option it sold United violates Section 10(b) of the Securities Exchange Act of 1934. The Court assumed that the "security" at issue was not the cable system stock, but the option to purchase that stock.

NOTES

1. "Shareholders of public target companies challenged 73 percent of merger and acquisition (M&A) deals valued over $100 million in 2017," according to a Cornerstone Research report released in July 2018. The study noted, "While the majority of M&A deals continue to be the subject of shareholder lawsuits, in recent years the rate of M&A litigation has declined from the 2011–2014 peaks of more than 90 percent. http://securities.stanford.edu/research-reports/1996-2017/Shareholder-Litigation-Involving-Acquisitions-of-Public-Companies-2017.pdf.
2. For cases from 2005 and 2006, credit goes to the law firm of Morris, James, Hitchens & Williams LLP, Wilmington, Delaware www.delawarebusinesslitigation.com.
3. https://www.delawarelitigation.com/author/francispileggi/. See, for example, his summaries for *In re: Family Dollar Stores, Inc. Stockholder Litigation, Flood v. Synutra, In re Hansen Medical, Inc. Stockholders Litigation,* and *Morrison v. Berry.*
4. An excellent overview of recent M&A legal cases can be found in Gail Weinstein, et al., "The Most Important Developments in M&A Law in 2017," January 11, 2018, https://corpgov.law

.harvard.edu/2018/01/11/the-most-important-developments-in-ma-law-in-2017/. For a recent overview of the history of Delaware law (including several M&A cases), see James D. Cox and Randall S. Thomas, "Delaware's Retreat: Exploring Developing Fissures and Tectonic Shifts in Delaware Corporate Law," 42 Del. J. Corp. L. 323 (2018). This article identifies four Delaware cases as landmarks (*Revlon, Inc. v. MacAndrews & Forbes Holding, Inc., Weinberger v. UOP, Inc., Unocal Corp. v. Mesa Petroleum Co.,* and *Blasius Industries, Inc. v. Atlas Corporation*) and traces what happened to them as precedents in subsequent years. Three of the cases (all except *Blasius*) are considered to be landmark legal cases. https://papers.ssrn.com/sol3/papers.cfm?abstract_id=3127687.

5. This summary is based on the case itself, at https://courts.delaware.gov/opinions/download.aspx?ID=216540. *C&J Energy Services, Inc., v. City of Miami General Employees' and Sanitation Employees' Retirement Trust,* 107 A.3d 1049 (Del. 2014). For an excellent discussion of this case, see "Annual Survey of Judicial Developments Pertaining to Mergers and Acquisitions," *Business Law,* vol. 76, issue 12 (2016): 589–631.
6. This summary is based on one provided by Cadwalader, Wickersham, and Taft, LLP, entitled "Fully Informed Vote of Disinterested Stockholders Results in Business Judgment Rule Protection in Post-Closing Review of Merger," October 15, 2015, https://www.cadwalader.com/uploads/cfmemos/92a25ad0f644b2ac8c3447cde3f19af1.pdf.
7. This case summary is based on the writings of Francis G. X. Pileggi, partner and vice chair of the Litigation Group at Eckert Seamans Cherin & Mellott, LLC, who has granted the authors permission to summarize cases using the language of his Delaware Litigation blog, https://www.delawarelitigation.com/author/francispileggi/.
8. It is interesting to note that MacAndrews and Forbes was the defendant in the classic case *Revlon v. MacAndrews & Forbes* (1986).

9. Similar cases exonerating underwriters include: *Weinberger v. Jackson* [1990–91], Fed. Sec. L. Repp. (CCH) par. 95, 693 at 98, 255 (D.D. Cal. 1990); *In re Worlds of Wonder Sec. Litig.,* 814 F. Supp. 850 (N.D. Cal. 1993), *affd. in part, rev'd in part,* 35 F.3d 1407 (9th Cir. 1994), *cert. denied,* 116 S. Ct. 185 (1995); *Phillips v. Kidder, Peabody & Co.,* 933 F. Supp. 303 (S.D.N.Y. 1996); *In re International Rectifier Sec. Litig.* [1997], Fed. Sec. L. Rep. (CCH) par. 99, 469 at 97, 135 (C.D. Cal. Mar. 31, 1997); and *Picard Chemical Inc. Profit Sharing Plan v. Perrigo Co.,* 1998, U.S. Dist. LEXIS 11783 (W.D. Mich. June 15, 1998). The citations in this list were provided by William F. Alderman and John Kanberg, Orrick, Herrington, and Sutcliffe LLP, San Francisco, who served as counsel to the defendants in Software Toolworks (writing a friend-of-the-court brief for the Securities Industry Association), as well as *Worlds of Wonder.*
10. See note 1 re the impact of the *Trulia* case.
11. https://courts.delaware.gov/Opinions/Download.aspx?id=282270.
12. For further analysis, see *Dell, Inc. v. Magnetar Glob. Event Driven Master Fund Ltd.,* No. 565, 2016 (Del. Dec. 14, 2017) (Valihura, J.), a blog from the Potter Anderson law firm. http://www.potteranderson.com/delawarecase-Dell-v-Magnetar-December-14-2017.html. See also "Reconsidering Appraisal Rights for Long-Term Value Realization," by Gary Lutin, Chairman, The Shareholder Forum, December 21, 2017, http://www.shareholderforum.com/access/Program/20171221_report.htm.
13. This summary is based on the language of the case itself. For further insights, see Francis Pileggi, "Delaware Supreme Court Issues Major Ruling on Shareholder Ratification Doctrine and Duties of Corporate Officers," January 28, 2009, https://www.delawarelitigation.com/2009/01/articles/delaware-supreme-court-updates/delaware-supreme-court-issues-major-ruling-on-shareholder-ratification-doctrine-and-duties-of-corporate-officers/.

14. The authors acknowledge insights from Casebriefs.com for this particular case.
15. For previous cases involving these parties, see *Appriva Shareholder Litigation Co., LLC, et al. v. EV3, Inc.,* 2007 WL3208783 (Nov. 1, 2007); *Appriva S'holder Litig. Co. v. EV3, Inc.*, 937 A.2d 1275 (Del. 2007); and *Lesh v. ev3, Inc.,* 2013 WL 6040418 (Del. Super. Aug. 29, 2013).
16. The letter of intent stated that ev3 "will commit to funding based on the projections prepared by its management to ensure that there is sufficient capital to achieve the performance milestones (the "Funding Provision")," but the acquisition agreement only said that the acquirer would fund and pursue the regulatory milestones in its "sole discretion, to be exercised in good faith." The court ruled that this provision in the merger agreement "overrode" any "provision to the contrary."
17. *Mehiel v. Solo Cup Co.,* 2005 WL 3074723 (Del. Ch. Nov. 3, 2005).
18. *Mehiel v. Solo Cup Co.*, 2007 WL 901637, *1 (Del. Super. 2007).
19. Following this decision, AT&T and Time Warner proceeded with their merger, while the FTC, on July 12, 2018, appealed the decision.
20. This description is excerpted verbatim with permission from Francis G. X. Pileggi's blog post "Supreme Court Dismisses Post-Closing Adjustment Claim," June 28, 2017. The full post contains further analysis. https://www.delawarelitigation.com/2017/06/articles/delaware-supreme-court-updates/supreme-court-dismisses-post-closing-adjustment-claim/.
21. "KS Bancorp, Inc. Announces Resolution of Outstanding Litigation with First Citizens BancShares, Inc.," press release, May 16, 2018.
22. Ever since this case, creditors have argued that directors should owe them a fiduciary duty to take their interests into account when the creditors are the residual interest holders

in a corporation that is insolvent or nearly so. A series of recent decisions have limited those creditor arguments. The 2007 recent case *of North American Catholic Educational Programming Foundation, Inc. v. Gheewalla,* 2007 Del. LEXIS 227 (Del. May 18, 2007), further limited creditor claims by holding that creditors may not bring a direct claim for breach of fiduciary duty based on the theory that the entity is in the vicinity of insolvency. For clearly insolvent companies, only creditors whose claims are beyond fair dispute may claim the directors owe them a duty. The Delaware Supreme Court, affirming the Delaware Chancery decision, stated, "The creditors of a Delaware corporation that is either insolvent or in the zone of insolvency have no right, as a matter of law, to assert direct claims for breach of fiduciary duty against its directors. . . . Consequently, the final judgment of the Court of Chancery is affirmed."

INDEX

Page numbers followed by n *indicate notes.*

ABOUT THE AUTHOR

Alexandra (Alex) Reed Lajoux, PhD, MBA, is founding principal of Capital Expert Services, LLC, a diversity-minded company connecting law firms and other professional services firms with business specialists for short-term assignments as expert witnesses or consulting experts. She serves the National Association of Corporate Directors (NACD) as chief knowledge officer emeritus.

During her time at NACD, Dr. Lajoux served as editor in chief of NACD's founding flagship publication *Director's Monthly* for more than 15 years, and also served as one of several leaders in developing the world's largest library of director-centric thought leadership publications.

In addition, Dr. Lajoux has conceptualized and authored or coauthored all the books in the McGraw-Hill Art of M&A series, covering strategy, valuation, financing, structuring, due diligence, and integration, as well as financially distressed M&A and bank M&A. She served as the project manager for the first edition of *The Art of M&A* by her father, Stanley Foster Reed, with the law firm Lane & Edson, P.C, in 1988, and has provided all editions since then, including this fifth edition. She is grateful to McGraw-Hill Education and its predecessor companies for guiding and supporting this book and the series.

Her articles have appeared in *Capital Insights*, *Financier Worldwide, NACD Directorship*, and *Risk & Compliance*. She has been a speaker or panelist at events hosted by a variety of business organizations including the Association for Corporate Growth, the National Association of Corporate Directors, and the US Chamber Center for Capital Markets Competitiveness. She serves as a series editor for Walter De Gruyter GMBH.

Dr. Lajoux serves on the advisory boards of *Campaigns & Elections* magazine and the Caux Round Table for Moral Capitalism, and is an emeritus member of the Board of M&A Standards. She is an associate member of the American Bar Association and a past member of IEEE and the Recording Academy, sponsor of the Grammy Awards in music. She is a Life Member of the NACD, as well as the Association of Princeton Graduate Alumni, where she served as a trustee. At Loyola University (Maryland), she is a member of the Jenkins Society, in support of education. She maintains an active membership in Toastmasters International.

Prior to joining NACD, Dr. Lajoux was the President of Alexis & Company, providing freelance research and writing to a variety of clients, including all the major audit firms. In that capacity she was a regular contributor to numerous periodicals, including *Northeast International Business* magazine, *IR Update*, and *Trustee*. Before joining the business world, she taught language and literature and served as an assistant professor at the State University of New York and as a graduate assistant at Princeton University. In addition to her native English, she speaks French, German, and Spanish.

A nearly lifelong resident of Virginia, she now lives with her husband, Bernard Lajoux, in Fernandina Beach, Florida, where she is active in what may be America's best small town.